ABSTRACT OF BRITISH HISTORICAL STATISTICS

BY

B. R. MITCHELL

WITH THE COLLABORATION OF

PHYLLIS DEANE

CAMBRIDGE

AT THE UNIVERSITY PRESS

1962

PUBLISHED BY
THE SYNDICS OF THE CAMBRIDGE UNIVERSITY PRESS
Bentley House, 200 Euston Road, London, N.W.1
American Branch: 32 East 57th Street, New York 22, N.Y.
West African Office: P.O. Box 33, Ibadan, Nigeria

©

CAMBRIDGE UNIVERSITY PRESS
1962

Printed in Great Britain at the Villafield Press ,Bishopbriggs, Glasgow

CONTENTS

PREFACE

At the outset of the inquiry into the long-term economic growth of the United Kingdom which Dr W. A. Cole and I began at the Department of Applied Economics in 1954, it was recognised that a volume of historical economic statistics would constitute a useful by-product. It would reduce the number of basic series which we should feel obliged to reprint in the economic growth monograph: and it would make generally and conveniently accessible various important long-run series which are at present scattered through many volumes of official papers or a variety of second-hand sources. As the inquiry progressed it became evident that the need for authentic transcriptions from first hand sources and for detailed and specific data on the character of the records concerned was greater than we had supposed. The only published sources of eighteenth-century foreign trade statistics, for example, contain a bewildering variety of copying errors and have never been adequately annotated by the transcribers. The only way of obtaining a reliable and intelligible series for our own use was to go back to the original manuscript records. Even then the character of the records (and some of their arithmetical errors) became apparent only after we had analysed the statistics and begun to process them for our own purposes.

It was apparent, however, that it would not be sufficient merely to reprint the statistics we had gathered in connection with the economic growth inquiry. For one thing it was likely to prove an expensive publication and for that reason, whatever its deficiencies, was likely to discourage imitation for some time to come. This is not the sort of book which it ought to be necessary to publish more than once in a generation. For another thing, the statistics by themselves, divorced from their contexts, are liable to prove useless to just that non-specialist audience of economists and historians who would be most grateful to by-pass the labour of identifying original sources and extracting comparable series. There was an evident need for an adequate text explaining the origins and coverage of the statistics selected for publication and indicating appropriate sources of further comment or detail. This then became another project and we are grateful to the Committee on Economic Growth of the Social Science Research Council for making the additional grant which made this new project possible.

The work of extracting or checking the figures, of searching for missing links, of compiling comparable series and of writing the introductory texts has fallen largely on Dr Brian Mitchell. We have been enormously fortunate, however, in our advisers. Many people have been interested in this project and most of them have been interested to the extent of giving time and serious thought to it. The form of this *Abstract*, the coverage and the principles of policy were worked out with the aid of an advisory committee of Cambridge economists and historians which included K. E. Berrill, D. M. Joslin, Peter Mathias, A. R. Prest, and R. C. O. Matthews. The table of contents, draft texts and bibliography circulated to a wide audience. Each of the sections—text and tables—was sent at an early stage to at least one expert in the relevant field of statistics. In the end of course the errors, misconceptions and deficiencies which remain are our responsibility, but we sought and obtained advice from a large number of individuals whose constructive interest and enthusiasm were such that it is a pleasure to acknowledge our debt to them. They include, besides the members of our advisory committee and Professor E. A. G. Robinson to whom we turned continually for advice and inspiration, the following:

DOROTHY T. ADLER	K. E. HUNT
PROFESSOR T. S. ASHTON	PROFESSOR A. H. IMLAH
A. D. BAIN	R. C. JARVIS
K. E. BERRILL	D. M. JOSLIN
LORD BEVERIDGE	J. T. KRAUSE
W. M. L. BISPHAM	K. S. LOMAX
H. S. BOOKER	A. MAIZELS
R. H. CAMPBELL	P. MATHIAS
SIR HAROLD CAMPION	R. C. O. MATTHEWS
PROFESSOR J. D. CHAMBERS	D. L. MUNBY
PROFESSOR S. G. CHECKLAND	H. C. B. MYNORS
D. C. COLEMAN	PROFESSOR A. T. PEACOCK
OLIVE COLEMAN	PROFESSOR E. H. PHELPS BROWN
W. A. COLE	A. R. PREST
C. H. FEINSTEIN	MISS M. E. RAYNER
G. E. FUSSELL	R. ROBSON
C. O. GEORGE	G. ROUTH
PROFESSOR D. V. GLASS	D. A. ROWE
J. GRANT	J. ROWE
J. L. HARRIS	C. T. SAUNDERS
R. M. HARTWELL	PROFESSOR R. S. SAYERS
PROFESSOR H. HEATON	D. C. SHAW
E. J. HOBSBAWM	E. M. SIGSWORTH
B. HOPKIN	A. J. TAYLOR

Finally we are glad to acknowledge the support for this publication of the Economic History Society and the Royal Economic Society and the courtesy of the following authors and publishers in permitting the publication of copyright or unpublished material:

Professor T. S. Ashton
Lord Beveridge
W. A. Cole
C. H. Feinstein
Mrs. Selma Goldsmith
Professor A. T. Peacock
Professor P. Rousseaux

The editors of the following journals:

The Economic History Review
The Economic Journal
Journal of the Royal Statistical Society
Scottish Journal of Political Economy

The British Iron and Steel Federation
The British Road Federation
The Governor and Company of the Bank of England
The Liverpool Cotton Association
The Ministry of Labour
The National Bureau of Economic Research (New York)
The Registrar General for Scotland
The Trustee Savings Banks Association

The following publishing firms:

Basil Blackwell
Cambridge University Press
The Clarendon Press
Harvard University Press
Longmans, Green and Co. Ltd.
Manchester University Press
Routledge and Kegan Paul Ltd.
John Worrall Ltd.

PHYLLIS DEANE

GENERAL INTRODUCTION

The objective of this *Abstract of British Historical Statistics* is to present within the limits of one volume the major time series for the United Kingdom economy over as long a historical period as possible. The earliest figure is for the year 1199 but for many topics continuous statistical material begins in the eighteenth century, and for most our starting point has been within the nineteenth century. We have restricted ourselves to economic statistics, to the neglect, for example, of social statistics, and we have attempted to cover the whole of the United Kingdom, though for Ireland (and for Scotland in the eighteenth century) the data are not always available in the required form and detail.

In compiling the *Abstract* we have had in mind the needs of economists and historians for data outside their own areas of specialisation and we have accordingly prefaced each section with a commentary on the statistics and concluded with a bibliography. The text is intended to provide the non-specialist with information on the sources, coverage and problems of the series presented and with signposts to other sources of related or more detailed material. The bibliography is limited to works which have a direct bearing on the statistics themselves and may well omit important works of little statistical interest.

What we hope to do, therefore, is to provide the user of historical statistics with informed access to a wide range of economic data without the labour of identifying sources or of transforming many annual sources into comparable time series. To some extent, of course, this has already been done in the annual volumes of the *Statistical Abstract of the United Kingdom*, each of which gives statistics for fifteen years at a time. But the official *Abstract* begins only in 1840; it has varied through time in its coverage; and its successive issues contain many revisions and changes of concept which make the transcription of long series a laborious process. We have adopted the latest revisions, made the series comparable where possible and identified the breaks wherever these were evident. We have also tried to indicate the main problems of interpretation which must confront the users of the statistics, basing our judgments on the published comments of past users, on the experience gained in the course of an inquiry into economic growth for which this *Abstract* is in the nature of a by-product, and on the advice of those experts to whom we submitted our draft texts. Since the snags of a statistical series often emerge only when it has been fully exploited for analytical purposes, and since many of the series reprinted in this volume have been barely used by historians or economists, it will be evident that our notes and comments are at best a tentative and incomplete critique of the statistics to which they relate.

In general we have preferred to use basic data rather than processed versions of these statistics, unless the latter embody much additional information which is not readily accessible. This applies, for example, to the series on national income and its major components, or wage indices, or prices, which may be the end results of substantial projects of research. In cases where there are several competing series of processed statistics, we have tried to cover as long a period as possible with those which seem to us useful and acceptable in that they take account of the most recent research on the subject. In this connection we are glad to acknowledge again our indebtedness to the authors and publishers who have permitted us to reprint processed series and particularly to those authors who have provided us with their results in advance of publication elsewhere.

The statistics selected for presentation have been arranged in sixteen sections. The classification has necessarily been arbitrary in many respects, and some series could easily have been included in several sections. The index should, however, make it possible to locate a particular series fairly quickly. Each of the sections is preceded by a short introduction, discussing briefly the scope of the tables which follow it, and noting the main *general* problems which arise out of their use. More specific problems in their use are dealt with in the notes to the tables themselves.

The Irish statistics raised certain problems both because they were less complete and because changes in administrative relationship between Great Britain and Ireland brought unavoidable breaks into the series. At the time of the Act of Union Ireland accounted for about a third of the population of the United Kingdom, and we have tried to indicate the order of magnitude of the breaks which its inclusion involved. At the time of the secession of the Irish Republic in 1923 Ireland was a less weighty constituent, and we made no attempt to bridge the gap by compiling series for Southern Ireland which then contained less than 7 per cent of the population of the British Isles.

The selection of the year 1938 as the closing date for most of our tables requires a word of explanation. We had hoped originally to bring the series up to date, but the need to keep down the cost of this volume imposed certain restrictions on its size. The fact that most of the series can be continued after 1938 in such easily accessible sources as the *Annual Abstract of Statistics* produced by the Central Statistical Office made this the easiest point at which to economise, and except for a few series this *Abstract* ends before World War II.

The object of the bibliographies which come at the end of each section is threefold: (i) to list systematically the major publications already referred to in the text and tables; (ii) to refer the user of this volume to works in which the statistics we have reproduced are discussed and criticised in some detail; and (iii) to suggest the main sources of additional statistics. We have not repeated all the sources of statistics referred to in the tables, since some of them provide no further information or comment; and we have not attempted to compile an exhaustive list of statistical sources. As a result of following this policy, many valuable historical works which do not contain or comment on statistical series are not included here. Their omission implies no judgment on their general usefulness, but solely on their value as source books of statistics. Readers who want less specialized bibliographies should consult, for example, J. B. Williams, *Guide to the Printed Materials for English Social and Economic History* (New York, 1926).

One series of books, which, though not directly referring to historical statistics in any way, must be mentioned here because of its potential value to users of the bibliographies' is the guides to parliamentary papers by Professor and Mrs Ford. The full list of this series is as follows:

A Breviate of Parliamentary Papers, 1917–1939 (Oxford, 1951),
Hansard's Catalogue and Breviate of Parliamentary Papers, 1696–1834 (Oxford, 1953),
Select List of British Parliamentary Papers, 1833–1899 (Oxford, 1953),
A Guide to Parliamentary Papers (Oxford, 1955).

The bibliographies are divided into sections corresponding to those used for the statistical tables, but to prevent undue repetition, some works which cover a wide field are included in a general section which comes at the end of the book. It has not been possible to include works published later than August 1961.

LIST OF ABBREVIATIONS

The following abbreviations are used throughout the volume:

—	=	nil
...	=	not available
- -	=	less than half of the smallest digit used in the table
Abstract	=	*Statistical Abstract of the United Kingdom*, or *Annual Abstract of Statistics*
A.H.	=	*Agricultural History*
A.H.R.	=	*Agricultural History Review*
E.H.	=	*Economic History* (supplement to *The Economic Journal*)
E.H.R.	=	*The Economic History Review*
E.J.	=	*The Economic Journal*
H.C.J.	=	*House of Commons Journals*
J.E.H.	=	*Journal of Economic History*
J.R.S.S.	=	*Journal of the Royal Statistical Society*. For years before the society received its royal charter the abbreviation *J.S.S.* is used
M.S.E.S.S.	=	*The Manchester School of Economic and Social Studies*
O.E.P.	=	*Oxford Economic Papers*
P.P.	=	*Parliamentary Papers*, 1st series
Porter's Tables	=	*Tables of Revenue, Population, Commerce etc.*, published in sessional papers in 1833 and from 1835 to 1854
R.E.S.	=	*Review of Economic Statistics*
S.P.	=	*Sessional Paper* (followed by the date and volume number)
T.M.S.S.	=	*Transactions of the Manchester Statistical Society*

POPULATION AND VITAL STATISTICS

TABLES

Though the amount and variety of the information collected has grown with practically every census since 1801, the overwhelming significance for British population data of the first census scarcely needs stressing. Estimates for earlier periods are subject to relatively wide margins of error. For Scotland a census was taken by Webster in 1755 and there are Sir John Sinclair's estimates based on the *Statistical Account* he compiled in the 1790's. For England and Wales reputable estimates have been largely based on the (incomplete) returns of baptisms, burials, and marriages which the 1801 census required from the keepers of the parish records, annually for the period 1780–1800 and at decade intervals for the period 1700–80. Later, in 1836, Rickman sent a further circular to parishes where old registers had been preserved, asking for details of baptisms, burials, and marriages for 1570, 1600, 1630, 1670, 1700, and 1750, and for each preceding and following year. It is clear from table 1 that a considerable variety of different results can be obtained when trying to estimate the eighteenth-century population of England and Wales. The three most elaborate estimates, however—those of Farr, Griffith and Brownlee—do not differ very widely so far as the absolute level of population is concerned. Each is, in fact, well within the margin of error of the others. These three estimates have all been subject to criticism;[1] but their methods were more refined than those of the earlier estimators, and the criticisms have been somewhat less damaging. In the more interesting matter of short-period variations and the movements of birth-and-death rates, however, none of the estimates has a sufficiently small margin of error to be helpful.

From the first census of Great Britain in 1801, and from 1821 for Ireland, an increasing flow of information is available, and by 1851 all the population series included in this chapter have been started. But it is proper to draw attention to the possible defects of the censuses. Whilst none is perfect, it seems likely that the first two were alone in omitting a significant proportion of the population. Mr Taylor suggests that this proportion was less than 5 per cent in 1801,[2] whilst Dr Krause thinks it was probably higher, and regards estimated deficiencies of 5 per cent in 1801 and 3 per cent in 1811 as 'moderate'.[3] In these tables, however, the only alterations which have been made to the original census figures are those made retrospectively in later censuses. Tables 2, 4, 5, 6, 7, and 8 are thus derived directly from the censuses—all except the last from the 1951 census. The table of town populations has presented more difficulties than the others, and calls for a word of explanation. The principle of selection was to include all towns with a population of 10,000 or more in 1801, and all of 100,000 or over in 1951 (other than those in Greater London). Since boundary changes were few and their effects cannot be traced exactly before 1851, the populations for earlier years are related so far as possible to the 1851 area. For later years the results of each intercensal growth of area on population are shown, and for certain large towns the effects of such expansions are traced back beyond a single decade. The population of the present areas at earlier censuses than 1931 has not been shown since such a figure would not indicate the true urban populations in the earlier years, and it would not in any event be possible in most cases.

The beginning of civil registration in each of the various parts of the United Kingdom has almost as great an effect on the information available for vital statistics as the 1801 census has for population. In each country the first year of registration produced seriously

---

[1] See for example T. H. Marshall, 'The Population Problem during the Industrial Revolution', in *E.H.R.* vol. I (1929), [reprinted in *Essays in Economic History*, edited by E. M. Carus-Wilson (London, 1954)], and J. T. Krause, 'Changes in English Fertility and Mortality 1781–1850', in *E.H.R.* vol. XI (Aug. 1958).
[2] A. J. Taylor, 'The Taking of the Census, 1801–1951', in the *British Medical Journal*, 7th April 1951.
[3] J. T. Krause, *loc. cit.*, p. 60.

defective figures, and in none was registration virtually complete until well into the 1860's, if not later.[1] Comparisons over time cannot, therefore, be made with a great degree of accuracy until the later part of the century, and comparisons between the kingdoms are, perhaps, equally dangerous.[2] But the civil registration particulars are more complete than the statistics of baptisms, burials, and marriages from the parish registers, which is the only information we have for earlier dates. These statistics, collected at every census before 1851, are shown for all available years to 1840 in table 9.[3] The eighteenth-century figures were collected at the 1801 census, but the returns were not complete. The revised figures published in the 1811 census have therefore been given here. The authorities unfortunately only called for figures of baptisms and burials for every tenth year prior to 1780. A glance at the size of the year-to-year variations after that date is sufficient warning of the dangers of treating the earlier single years as typical of their period. An average of the two years at the beginning and end of each decade is likely to be more useful. Apart from this, and leaving aside the obvious fact that burials were not the equivalent of deaths, and, probably *a fortiori*, that baptisms were not equal to births, these statistics are inadequate because of (i) physical defects in the registers from which they were taken, (ii) Rickman's arbitrary way of adjusting for known gaps in the registers, and (iii) possible errors in transcription by the clergymen who acted as enumerators.

The civil registrations for the various parts of the United Kingdom are shown in table 10–16, together with the birth, death, and marriage rates derived from them and from the estimated mid-year populations shown in table 3. There are in addition certain other rates taken directly from the *Annual Reports* of the Registrars General. Of these tables only 13, 14, and 15 call for special mention here. They have been included in preference to standardised death rates for two reasons. First, no death rate standardised to a single year has been published for the whole period of civil registration; and second, the age-group death rates give additional information, though a single series of rates genuinely comparable over a long period is admittedly lacking. These tables are derived, so far as England and Wales (and Scotland since 1911) are concerned, from the *Annual Reports* of the Registrar Generals. For earlier periods in Scotland, and for Ireland throughout, rates have been computed for the years close to each census by using the published totals of deaths in each age-group together with the age-distribution revealed by the census.

Tables 17–21 give those statistics of migration to and from the United Kingdom which are available. For the years up to 1924 they draw heavily on Ferenczi's and Willcox's *International Migrations*,[4] which contains further information. The general conclusion to be drawn from this book, as also from Professor Brinley Thomas's *Migration and Economic*

---

[1] For a discussion of this question, see D. V. Glass, 'A Note on the Under-Registration in Britain in the Nineteenth Century', in *Population Studies*, vol. v (1951).

[2] So far as Irish infant mortality is concerned this may be true up to 1920. Even allowing for the predominantly rural nature of the country, the figures seem suspiciously low, and the jump to the Northern Ireland figure in 1922 suspiciously high.

[3] County figures are also available in the original sources, but in view of their very probable inaccuracy they have not been included here.

[4] New York, 1929–31, 2 vols.

Growth[1] (where a full discussion of the statistics can be found), is that the early figures, before the 1850's, are not very useful, and that even a century after that the statistics were by no means complete. The two principal deficiencies were the omission of all movements between Britain and the continent of Europe (including the Mediterranean coastlands), and the lack of statistics of migration, as distinct from passenger movements, down to 1912. A further deficiency, of some importance recently, is the lack of any record of movements by air. Apart from these major omissions, the statistics which do exist are far from perfect. The passenger movements from United Kingdom ports shown in table 17 were seriously underestimated in the early years, since it was easy for small sailing ships to evade inspection. Professor Thomas considers that this was significant until the triumph of the large steamship in the 1850's. Moreover, until 1853, there was no distinction between citizens and aliens in the passenger lists, and for ten years after that the larger number recorded as of unknown nationality render the figures virtually useless. According to Leak and Priday, distinction of nationality was imperfect as late as the early 1900's.[2]

Inward movements of passengers from outside Europe, shown in table 18, are available from 1855, but nationality was not distinguished until 1876, and it is only from that date that we can strike a balance of net movements of British passengers. This balance is a rough indicator of net migration, for though the increasing volume of business and pleasure trips was by that time having a serious effect on the aggregate of movements, this type of movements was virtually self-cancelling. Professor Thomas suggests that 'in the first half of the century ending in 1912 the number of British passengers recorded as leaving the United Kingdom is too low and in the second half it is too high. As a measure of aggregate net emigration the total outward balance of passengers is a good approximation for the entire period'.[3] After 1912 statistics of the movement of British emigrants and immigrants are available for countries outside Europe, and the balance is given in table 20. The principal defect of these figures—a defect which is also found in those of passenger movements—is the tendency to exaggerate the numbers bound for British North America, since many whose immediate destination was Canada were ultimately going to the United States.[4]

To complete the picture of British migration, so far as that is possible, table 21 shows the emigration statistics for natives of Ireland during the period when that country was part of the United Kingdom. It indicates the numbers of genuine emigrants who left Irish ports for various destinations, including Great Britain. There is no measure of the proportion coming to Great Britain who were in fact transmigrants.

---

[1] Cambridge, 1954.　　　　[2] *J.R.S.S.* (1933), p. 187.　　　　[3] Brinley Thomas, *op. cit.*, p. 41.
[4] The lack of statistics of migrants travelling by air has become an increasingly significant defect since 1946.

Population and Vital Statistics 1. Estimates of Eighteenth-Century Population—British Isles

NOTES TO PART A

[1] SOURCES: Rickman (1)—*Observations on the Results of the Population Act*, 41 *Geo III*, p. 9 (in *S.P.* 1802, VII); Rickman (2)—1841 Census, *Enumeration Abstract*, preface pp. 36–7; Malthus—T. Malthus, *Essay on Population* (5th edition, London, 1817), vol. II, p. 95; Finlaison—1831 census, *Enumeration Abstract*, p. xlv; Farr—1861 Census, *General Report*, p. 22; Brownlee—J. Brownlee, 'History of the Birth and Death Rates in England and Wales . . .', in *Public Health* (June and July 1916); Griffith—G. Talbot Griffith, *Population Problems in the Age of Malthus* (Cambridge University Press, 1926), p. 18.

[2] Rickman's, Finlaison's and Griffith's estimates are for 1700, 1710, etc., with Rickman and Griffith ending in 1801 and Finlaison in mid-1800. The remaining estimates are for 1701, 1711, etc.

A. England & Wales

(in thousands)

	Rickman (1)	Rickman (2)	Malthus	Finlaison	Farr	Brownlee	Griffith
1700/1	5,475	6,045	...	5,135	6,122	5,826	5,835
1710/1	5,240	...	...	5,066	6,252	5,981	6,013
1720/1	5,565	...	...	5,345	6,253	6,001	6,048
1730/1	5,796	...	...	5,688	6.183	5,947	6,008
1740/1	6,064	...	...	5,830	6,153	5,926	6,013
1750/1	6,467	6,517	...	6,040	6,336	6,140	6,253
1760/1	6,736	...	...	6,480	6,721	6,569	6,665
1770/1	7,428	...	...	7,228	7,153	7,052	7,124
1780/1	7,953	...	7,721	7,815	7,574	7,531	7,581
1785/6	8,016	...	7,998	...	...	...	7,826
1790/1	8,675	...	8,415	8,541	8,256	8,247	8,216
1795/6	9,055	...	8,831	...	...	...	8,656
1800/1	9,168	...	9,287	9,187	9,193	9,156	9,168

NOTE TO PART B

SOURCE: Alexander Webster's census of Scotland, published in J. G. Kyd (editor), *Scottish Population Statistics* (Edinburgh, 1952).

B. Scotland

1755	1,265

NOTE TO PART C

SOURCE: K. H. Connell, *The Population of Ireland*, 1750–1845 (Oxford, the Clarendon Press, 1950), p. 25.

C. Ireland

1687	2,167	1732	3,018	1781	4,048
1712	2,791	1754	3,191	1785	4,019
1718	2,894	1767	3,480	1788	4,389
1725	3,042	1772	3,584	1790	4,591
1726	3,031	1777	3,740	1791	4,753

Population and Vital Statistics 2. United Kingdom Population (by Sex) and Intercensal Increases—1801–1951

NOTES

[1] SOURCES: *Reports* of the census of 1951 (separately for England & Wales, Scotland, Northern Ireland, and the Irish Republic), and of the census of 1911 for Ireland.
[2] The population of Islands in the British Seas has not been included.
[3] In computing the decennial rate of increase the varying lengths of the intercensal periods have been taken into account, and the rates for the periods 1831–41 and 1841–51 have been further corrected by the exclusion of the Army, Navy, and Merchant Service from the population for 1841, and of persons on board vessels from the population for 1851.
[4] Figures for Northern Ireland in 1821–1911 are shown in the current *Annual Abstract of Statistics*.

A. England & Wales

	(thousands) Total Population			(thousands) Increase since previous Census			Decennial Increase per Cent			Females per 1,000 Males
	Persons	Males	Females	Persons	Males	Females	Persons	Males	Females	
1801 Mar. 9/10	8,893	4,255	4,638	...	...	...	...	...	...	1,057 (a)
1811 May 26/27	10,164	4,874	5,291	1,272	619	653	14·00	14·24	13·78	1,054 (a)
1821 May 27/28	12,000	5,850	6,150	1,836	977	859	18·06	20·03	16·23	1,036 (a)
1831 May 29/30	13,897	6,771	7,126	1,897	921	976	15·80	15·73	15·86	1,040 (a)
1841 June 6/7	15,914	7,778	8,137	2,017	1,006	1,011	14·27	14·39	14·15	1,046
1851 Mar. 30/31	17,928	8,781	9,146	2,013	1,004	1,010	12·65	12·68	12·62	1,042
1861 Apr. 7/8	20,066	9,776	10,290	2,139	995	1,144	11·90	11·30	12·47	1,053
1871 Apr. 2/3	22,712	11,059	11,653	2,646	1,283	1,363	13·21	13·14	13·27	1,054
1881 Apr. 3/4	25,974	12,640	13,335	3,262	1,581	1,681	14·36	14·29	14·42	1,055
1891 Apr. 5/6 (b)	29,003	14,060	14,942	3,028	1,420	1,608	11·65	11·23	12·05	1,063
1901 Mar. 31/Apr. 1	32,528	15,729	16,799	3,525	1,668	1,857	12·17	11·88	12·44	1,068
1911 Apr. 2/3	36,070	17,446	18,625	3,543	1,717	1,826	10·89	10·91	10·86	1,068
1921 June 19/20	37,887	18,075	19,811	1,816	630	1,187	4·93	3·53	6·24	1,096
1931 Apr. 26/27	39,952	19,133	20,819	2,066	1,058	1,008	5·53	5·94	5·16	1,088
1951 Apr. 8/9	43,758	21,016	22,742	3,806	1,883	1,923	4·67	4·80	4·52	1,082

B. Scotland

	Persons	Males	Females	Persons	Males	Females	Persons	Males	Females	
1801	1,608	739	869	...	...	...	...	...	...	1,176
1811	1,806	826	980	197	87	110	12·3	11·8	12·7	1,185
1821	2,092	983	1,109	286	156	129	15·8	18·9	13·2	1,129
1831	2,364	1,114	1,250	273	132	141	13·0	13·4	12·7	1,122
1841	2,620	1,242	1,378	256	127	128	10·8	11·4	10·3	1,110
1851	2,889	1,375	1,513	269	134	135	10·2	10·8	9·8	1,100
1861	3,062	1,450	1,612	174	74	99	6·0	5·4	6·6	1,112
1871	3,360	1,603	1,757	298	153	144	9·7	10·6	9·0	1,096
1881	3,736	1,799	1,936	376	196	179	11·2	12·2	10·2	1,076
1891 (b)	4,026	1,943	2,083	290	143	147	7·8	8·0	7·6	1,072
1901	4,472	2,174	2,298	446	231	215	11·1	11·9	10·3	1,057
1911	4,761	2,309	2,452	289	135	154	6·5	6·2	6·7	1,062
1921	4,882	2,348	2,535	122	39	83	2·6	1·7	3·4	1,080
1931	4,843	2,326	2,517	−40	−22	−17	−0·8	−0·9	−0·7	1,083
1951	5,096	2,434	2,662	253	109	145	5·2	4·7	5·7	1,094

See p. 7 for footnotes

C. Ireland (later Northern Ireland and the Irish Republic separately)

	(thousands) Total Population			(thousands) Increase since previous Census			Decennial Increase per Cent			Females per 1,000 Males
	Persons	Males	Females	Persons	Males	Females	Persons	Males	Females	
1821	6,802	3,342	3,460	...	...	...	...	...	...	1,035
1831	7,767	3,795	3,973	966	453	513	14·19	13·55	14·81	1,047
1841	8,175	4,020	4,156	408	225	183	5·25	5·91	4·61	1,034
1851	6,552	3,191	3,362	−1,623	−829	−794	−19·85	−20·62	−19·10	1,053
1861 (c)	5,799	2,837	2,962	−753	−353	−400	−11·50	−11·07	−11·90	1,044
1871	5,412	2,640	2,773	−387	−198	−189	−6·67	−6·96	−6·38	1,050
1881	5,175	2,533	2,642	−238	−106	−131	−4·39	−4·03	−4·73	1,042
1891 (b)	4,705	2,319	2,386	−470	−214	−256	−9·08	−8·46	−9·68	1,029
1901	4,459	2,200	2,259	−246	−119	−127	−5·23	−5·13	−5·32	1,027
1911	4,390	2,192	2,198	−69	−8	−61	−1·54	−0·36	−2·68	1,003
1926 N.I.	1,257	608	648	6	6	φφ	0·5	0·9	0·1	1,066
1926 Irish Rep.	2,972	1,507	1,465	−168	−83	−85	−5·3	−5·2	−5·5	972
1937 N.I.	1,280	623	657	23	15	8	1·8	2·5	1·3	1,054
1936 Irish Rep.	2,968	1,520	1,448	−4	14	−17	−0·1	0·9	−1·2	952
1951 N.I.	1,371	668	703	91	45	47	7·1	7·2	7·1	1,053
1951 Irish Rep.	2,961	1,507	1,454	−8	−14	6	−0·3	−0·9	0·4	965

(*a*) In computing the proportion of females to males, the following estimates of the numbers of men in the Army, Navy, and Merchant Service at home have been adopted:

1801	1811	1821	1831
131,818	145,137	87,740	78,968

(*b*) The figures for this year have been adjusted to counteract a tendency by certain enumerators to confuse males and females in the completion of a new type of enumeration book introduced at this census.

(*c*) In this and subsequent censuses, members of the armed forces at home are included.

7

Estimated Mid-Year Population (by Sex)—
England & Wales, Scotland, and Ireland 1801–1939

NOTES

[1] Sources: England & Wales—*General Tables* of the census of 1951; Scotland—*Annual Report of the Registrar General for Scotland*; Ireland—*Annual Report of the Registrar General for Ireland*, subsequently *Annual Report of the Registrar General for Northern Ireland*.

[2] The sex breakdown for Scotland for 1855–1910 has not been published in the *Annual Report*, but has been supplied to us by courtesy of the Registrar General for Scotland. as have certain corrections to published figures.

(in thousands)

	England & Wales			Scotland			Ireland		
	Persons	Males	Females	Persons	Males	Females	Persons	Males	Females
1801	9,061	4,404	4,657	1,625	752	873	5,216	2,592	2,625
1802	9,130	4,441	4,689	1,644	761	883	5,286	2,625	2,661
1803	9,235	4,494	4,741	1,663	769	894	5,357	2,658	2,698
1804	9,367	4,559	4,808	1,682	778	904	5,428	2,692	2,736
1805	9,513	4,631	4,882	1,702	787	915	5,501	2,727	2,774
1806	9,656	4,700	4,956	1,722	796	926	5,574	2,762	2,812
1807	9,794	4,768	5,026	1,742	805	936	5,649	2,797	2,851
1808	9,924	4,832	5,092	1,762	815	947	5,724	2,833	2,891
1809	10,056	4,895	5,161	1,783	824	959	5,800	2,869	2,931
1810	10,186	4,958	5,228	1,803	834	970	5,878	2,906	2,972
1811	10,322	5,025	5,297	1,824	843	981	5,956	2,943	3,013
1812	10,480	5,103	5,377	1,851	858	993	6,036	2,981	3,055
1813	10,650	5,191	5,459	1,878	872	1,006	6,117	3,019	3,098
1814	10,820	5,280	5,540	1,905	887	1,018	6,198	3,057	3,141
1815	11,004	5,376	5,628	1,933	902	1,031	6,281	3,097	3,185
1816	11,196	5,475	5,721	1,959	916	1,044	6,365	3,136	3,229
1817	11,378	5,568	5,810	1,986	929	1,057	6,450	3,176	3,274
1818	11,555	5,659	5,896	2,014	944	1,070	6,536	3,217	3,319
1819	11,723	5,748	5,975	2,042	959	1,083	6,624	3,258	3,366
1820	11,903	5,843	6,060	2,071	974	1,097	6,712	3,300	3,412
1821	12,106	5,947	6,159	2,100	990	1,110	6,802	3,342	3,460
1822	12,320	6,051	6,269	2,126	1,002	1,123	6,893	3,385	3,508
1823	12,529	6,153	6,376	2,152	1,015	1,137	6,985	3,428	3,557
1824	12,721	6,246	6,475	2,179	1,028	1,151	7,078	3,472	3,606
1825	12,903	6,334	6,569	2,205	1,041	1,164	7,173	3,516	3,656
1826	13,074	6,417	6,657	2,233	1,054	1,179	7,269	3,561	3,707
1827	13,247	6,500	6,747	2,259	1,066	1,193	7,366	3,607	3,759
1828	13,438	6,592	6,846	2,288	1,081	1,207	7,464	3,653	3,811
1829	13,625	6,681	6,944	2,316	1,095	1,221	7,564	3,700	3,864
1830	13,805	6,767	7,038	2,345	1,108	1,236	7,665	3,747	3,918
1831	13,994	6,859	7,135	2,374	1,123	1,251	7,767	3,795	3,973
1832	14,165	6,944	7,221	2,398	1,134	1,263	7,810	3,819	3,991
1833	14,328	7,023	7,305	2,422	1,147	1,276	7,852	3,842	4,010
1834	14,520	7,116	7,404	2,447	1,159	1,288	7,895	3,866	4,028
1835	14,724	7,214	7,510	2,472	1,171	1,301	7,938	3,890	4,047
1836	14,928	7,310	7,618	2,497	1,184	1,314	7,981	3,915	4,066
1837	15,104	7,392	7,712	2,523	1,196	1,326	8,024	3,939	4,085
1838	15,288	7,479	7,809	2,548	1,209	1,339	8,068	3,963	4,104
1839	15,514	7,586	7,928	2,574	1,222	1,353	8,111	3,988	4,123
1840	15,731	7,689	8,042	2,601	1,235	1,366	8,156	4,013	4,143
1841	15,929	7,785	8,144	2,622	1,243	1,379	8,200	4,038	4,162
1842	16,130	7,887	8,243	2,653	1,259	1,394	8,221	4,048	4,173
1843	16,332	7,990	8,342	2,684	1,274	1,409	8,240	4,057	4,183
1844	16,535	8,093	8,442	2,713	1,289	1,424	8,277	4,074	4,202
1845	16,739	8,196	8,543	2,742	1,304	1,438	8,295	4,083	4,212
1846	16,944	8,298	8,646	2,770	1,318	1,452	8,288	4,079	4,209
1847	17,150	8,401	8,749	2,797	1,331	1,466	8,025	3,944	4,081
1848	17,357	8,503	8,854	2,823	1,344	1,479	7,640	3,746	3,893
1849	17,564	8,605	8,959	2,849	1,356	1,492	7,256	3,551	3,705
1850	17,773	8,707	9,066	2,873	1,368	1,505	6,878	3,361	3,517

See p. 10 for footnote

(in thousands)

	England & Wales			Scotland			Ireland		
	Persons	Males	Females	Persons	Males	Females	Persons	Males	Females
1851	17,983	8,809	9,174	2,896	1,379	1,517	6,514	3,181	3,333
1852	18,193	8,910	9,283	2,918	1,389	1,529	6,337	3,095	3,242
1853	18,404	9,011	9,393	2,939	1,399	1,540	6,199	3,031	3,168
1854	18,616	9,111	9,505	2,959	1,408	1,551	6,083	2,977	3,106
1855	18,829	9,212	9,617	2,978	1,417	1,561	6,015	2,946	3,069
1856	19,042	9,311	9,731	2,996	1,424	1,572	5,973	2,926	3,047
1857	19,256	9,410	9,846	3,012	1,431	1,581	5,919	2,898	3,022
1858	19,471	9,509	9,962	3,028	1,437	1,590	5,891	2,882	3,009
1859	19,687	9,607	10,080	3,042	1,443	1,599	5,862	2,866	2,996
1860	19,902	9,704	10,198	3,055	1,448	1,607	5,821	2,845	2,976
1861	20,119	9,801	10,318	3,069	1,454	1,616	5,788	2,832	2,957
1862	20,371	9,923	10,448	3,098	1,468	1,630	5,776	2,827	2,948
1863	20,626	10,047	10,579	3,127	1,483	1,644	5,718	2,800	2,919
1864	20,884	10,172	10,712	3,156	1,498	1,658	5,641	2,762	2,879
1865	21,145	10,299	10,846	3,185	1,513	1,672	5,595	2,741	2,854
1866	21,410	10,427	10,983	3,215	1,528	1,687	5,523	2,701	2,822
1867	21,677	10,557	11,120	3,245	1,544	1,701	5,487	2,681	2,805
1868	21,949	10,689	11,260	3,275	1,559	1,716	5,466	2,669	2,797
1869	22,223	10,822	11,401	3,306	1,575	1,731	5,449	2,660	2,789
1870	22,501	10,956	11,545	3,337	1,591	1,746	5,419	2,642	2,777
1871	22,789	11,093	11,696	3,369	1,608	1,761	5,398	2,631	2,767
1872	23,096	11,242	11,854	3,405	1,626	1,778	5,373	2,616	2,757
1873	23,408	11,394	12,014	3,441	1,645	1,796	5,328	2,590	2,738
1874	23,724	11,548	12,176	3,478	1,664	1,813	5,299	2,576	2,723
1875	24,045	11,704	12,341	3,515	1,684	1,831	5,279	2,569	2,709
1876	24,370	11,862	12,508	3,552	1,703	1,849	5,278	2,572	2,705
1877	24,700	12,023	12,677	3,590	1,723	1,867	5,286	2,579	2,707
1878	25,033	12,185	12,848	3,628	1,743	1,885	5,282	2,580	2,691
1879	25,371	12,350	13,021	3,667	1,763	1,903	5,266	2,575	2,691
1880	25,714	12,517	13,197	3,706	1,784	1,922	5,203	2,543	2,659
1881	26,046	12,673	13,373	3,743	1,803	1,940	5,146	2,519	2,627
1882	26,334	12,808	13,526	3,771	1,817	1,954	5,101	2,497	2,604
1883	26,627	12,945	13,682	3,799	1,831	1,968	5,024	2,462	2,562
1884	26,922	13,083	13,839	3,827	1,845	1,983	4,975	2,440	2,535
1885	27,220	13,222	13,998	3,856	1,859	1,997	4,939	2,424	2,514
1886	27,522	13,363	14,159	3,885	1,873	2,012	4,906	2,410	2,496
1887	27,827	13,505	14,322	3,914	1,888	2,027	4,857	2,387	2,470
1888	28,136	13,649	14,487	3,944	1,902	2,041	4,801	2,361	2,441
1889	28,448	13,795	14,653	3,973	1,917	2,056	4,757	2,341	2,417
1890	28,764	13,942	14,822	4,003	1,932	2,072	4,718	2,323	2,395
1891	29,086	14,093	14,993	4,036	1,948	2,088	4,680	2,306	2,374
1892	29,421	14,252	15,169	4,079	1,970	2,109	4,634	2,282	2,351
1893	29,761	14,414	15,347	4,122	1,992	2,130	4,607	2,268	2,339
1894	30,104	14,577	15,527	4,166	2,015	2,151	4,589	2,260	2,329
1895	30,451	14,742	15,709	4,210	2,038	2,172	4,560	2,247	2,313
1896	30,803	14,909	15,894	4,254	2,061	2,193	4,542	2,239	2,303
1897	31,158	15,078	16,080	4,299	2,084	2,215	4,530	2,234	2,296
1898	31,518	15,249	16,269	4,345	2,108	2,237	4,518	2,230	2,289
1899	31,881	15,421	16,460	4,391	2,131	2,259	4,502	2,222	2,280
1900	32,249	15,596	16,653	4,437	2,156	2,281	4,469	2,205	2,264
1901	32,612	15,769	16,843	4,479	2,177	2,302	4,447	2,196	2,251
1902	32,951	15,934	17,017	4,507	2,190	2,317	4,435	2,194	2,241
1903	33,293	16,099	17,194	4,536	2,203	2,332	4,418	2,189	2,228

See p. 10 for footnote

Population and Vital Statistics 3. *continued*

(in thousands)

	England & Wales			Scotland			Ireland		
	Persons	Males	Females	Persons	Males	Females	Persons	Males	Females
1904	33,639	16,267	17,372	4,564	2,217	2,347	4,408	2,188	2,220
1905	33,989	16,437	17,552	4,593	2,230	2,362	4,399	2,187	2,213
1906	34,342	16,608	17,734	4,621	2,244	2,378	4,398	2,187	2,211
1907	34,699	16,781	17,918	4,650	2,257	2,393	4,388	2,183	2,205
1908	35,059	16,955	18,104	4,680	2,271	2,409	4,385	2,184	2,201
1909	35,424	17,132	18,292	4,709	2,285	2,424	4,387	2,188	2,199
1910	35,792	17,311	18,481	4,739	2,298	2,440	4,385	2,188	2,197
1911	36,136	17,471	18,665	4,751	2,304	2,447	4,381	2,187	2,194
1912	36,327	17,571	18,756	4,741	2,299	2,442	4,368	2,182	2,186
1913	36,574	17,687	18,887	4 728	2,293	2,435	4,346	2,170	2,176
1914	36,967	17,885	19,082	4,747	2,302	2,445	4,334	2,166	2,168
1915	35,284 (a)	16,003 (a)	19,281	4,771	2,308	2,463	4,278	2,111	2,167
1916	34,642 (a)	15,222 (a)	19,420	4,795	2,314	2,481	4,273	2,108	2,165
1917	34,197 (a)	14,661 (a)	19,536	4,810	2,316	2,494	4,273	2,113	2,160
1918	34,024 (a)	14,433 (a)	19,591	4,812	2,309	2,503	4,280	2,119	2,161
1919	35,427 (a)	15,868 (a)	19,559	4,820	2,305	2,515	4,352	2,203	2,149
1920	37,247 (a)	17,582 (a)	19,665	4,864	2,338	2,527	4,361	2,210	2,151
1921	37,932	18,098	19,834	4,882	2,348	2,535	4,354	2,209	2,145

							Northern Ireland		
1922	38,205	18,249	19,956	4,898	2,358	2,540	1,269	619	650
1923	38,449	18,366	20,083	4,888	2,353	2,536	1,259	609	650
1924	38,795	18,571	20,224	4,862	2,329	2,533	1,258	608	650
1925	38,935	18,625	20,310	4,867	2,334	2,533	1,257	608	649
1926	39,114	18,722	20,392	4,864	2,333	2,531	1,254	607	647
1927	39,286	18,802	20,484	4,853	2,327	2,526	1,250	604	646
1928	39,483	18,897	20,586	4,848	2,324	2,523	1,247	602	645
1929	39,600	18,961	20,639	4,832	2,317	2,516	1,240	599	641
1930	39,801	19,072	20,729	4,828	2,316	2,512	1,237	598	639
1931	39,988	19,160	20,828	4,843	2,326	2,517	1,243	601	642
1932	40,201	19,280	20,921	4,883	2,348	2,535	1,251	607	644
1933	40,350	19,357	20,993	4,912	2,364	2,549	1,258	611	647
1934	40,467	19,412	21,055	4,934	2,375	2,559	1,265	616	649
1935	40,645	19,500	21,145	4,953	2,385	2,567	1,271	619	652
1936	40,839	19,591	21,248	4,966	2,392	2,574	1,276	622	654
1937	41,031	19,705	21,326	4,977	2,397	2,580	1,281	624	657
1938	41,215	19,792	21,423	4,993	2,405	2,588	1,286	625	661
1939	41,460	19,920	21,540	5,007	2,412	2,594	1,295	630	665

(a) These figures are for civilians only.

NOTES

[1] SOURCES: *Reports* of the census of 1951 (separately for England & Wales, Scotland, and Northern Ireland), and of the census of 1911 for Ireland.

[2] Partial returns to a question on ages were secured in Great Britain at the census of 1821. The results were as follows (in thousands):

(in thousands)

	England & Wales		Scotland	
	Males	Females	Males	Females
Total Population	5,850	6,150	983	1,109
Number Answering	5,151	5,380	924	1,033
Ages of Those Answering				
0–4	791·6	774·7	138·0	133·7
5–9	693·9	682·5	125·3	121·6
10–14	603·6	569·4	115·2	109·2
15–19	509·6	535·6	95·3	108·3
20–29	755·8	901·5	137·6	182·7
30–39	593·7	649·5	101·1	124·4
40–49	482·3	501·0	82·7	97·0
50–59	342·2	352·2	60·0	73·5
60–69	231·5	249·2	42·3	51·9
70–79	115·0	124·6	20·0	23·3
80–89	29·6	36·3	5·4	6·7
90–99	2·3	3·3	0·6	0·8
100 and over	0·06	0·12	0·04	0·06

A. England & Wales

(in thousands)

PERSONS

	1841 (a)	1851	1861	1871	1881	1891	1901	1911	1921	1931	1951
All Ages	15,914·1	17,927·6	20,066·3	22,712·2	25,974·4	29,002·5	32,527·8	36,070·5	37,886·7	39,952·4	43,757·8
0–4	2,106·3	2,348·1	2,700·7	3,071·2	3,520·7	3,553·4	3,716·7	3,854·3	3,321·8	2,990·3	3,717·8
5–9	1,904·9	2,092·3	2,344·1	2,706·4	3,147·3	3,395·2	3,487·2	3,696·8	3,518·9	3,322·6	3,161·9
10–14	1,732·1	1,913·4	2,105·2	2,424·3	2,800·2	3,223·6	3,341·8	3,499·7	3,659·8	3,207·2	2,811·9
15–19	1,586·8	1,757·2	1,932·6	2,180·4	2,547·3	2,950·9	3,246·1	3,336·6	3,503·0	3,434·6	2,704·5
20–24	1,550·5	1,666·7	1,829·5	2,004·7	2,328·3	2,646·4	3,120·9	3,175·8	3,151·5	3,494·5	2,927·4
25–29	1,282·9	1,470·4	1,569·2	1,780·6	2,048·0	2,350·2	2,824·5	3,079·1	2,960·3	3,357·1	3,279·9
30–34	1,167·0	1,276·1	1,386·8	1,560·0	1,745·5	2,027·5	2,431·4	2,877·2	2,800·9	3,055·3	3,078·5
35–39	884·5	1,088·6	1,224·6	1,341·3	1,541·4	1,781·8	2,145·4	2,613·2	2,745·2	2,803·0	3,323·2
40–44	888·0	968·6	1,134·2	1,229·8	1,399·4	1,547·0	1,850·6	2,232·6	2,601·2	2,663·5	3,365·2
45–49	638·6	799·0	930·8	1,053·0	1,151·4	1,336·8	1,573·2	1,925·6	2,406·2	2,554·0	3,172·2
50–54	634·4	708·8	806·6	944·7	1,022·1	1,160·1	1,329·0	1,602·6	2,014·1	2,381·6	2,824·8
55–59	391·8	526·3	614·0	718·2	806·5	884·2	1,052·6	1,278·4	1,630·7	2,068·4	2,423·0
60–64	439·8	481·3	556·2	622·7	727·7	772·9	890·6	1,020·0	1,282·0	1,657·0	2,142·8
65–69	259·6	327·5	376·5	441·3	502·4	572·0	629·7	806·8	986·1	1,270·7	1,829·4
70–74	224·3	250·1	281·3	324·0	349·9	417·9	446·4	553·6	656·8	870·8	1,427·8
75–79	119·9	146·1	160·7	182·0	202·3	233·3	264·5	310·0	392·5	499·9	923·7
80–84	70·5	73·9	79·7	89·9	95·8	105·6	128·7	144·2	179·9	225·8	446·0
85 and over	32·2	33·2	33·6	37·7	38·2	43·7	48·5	64·0	75·8	96·1	197·8

MALES

	1841 (a)	1851	1861	1871	1881	1891	1901	1911	1921	1931	1951
All Ages	7,777·6	8,781·2	9,776·3	11,058·9	12,639·9	14,060·4	15,728·6	17,445·6	18,075·2	19,133·0	21,015·6
0–4	1,048·4	1,176·9	1,354·9	1,536·4	1,757·6	1,775·1	1,855·3	1,936·0	1,681·5	1,510·2	1,903·7
5–9	953·2	1,050·2	1,173·0	1,350·8	1,568·6	1,693·4	1,738·9	1,847·3	1,766·5	1,677·8	1,616·4
10–14	880·4	964·0	1,059·9	1,220·8	1,402·1	1,610·9	1,671·0	1,747·6	1,837·1	1,620·4	1,428·6
15–19	781·6	873·2	957·9	1,084·7	1,268·3	1,465·2	1,607·5	1,654·9	1,727·8	1,709·6	1,335·3
20–24	723·4	795·5	860·2	951·9	1,112·4	1,247·3	1,472·6	1,502·7	1,448·4	1,699·1	1,427·2
25–29	610·9	699·3	734·3	843·3	981·3	1,111·1	1,328·3	1,455·8	1,340·0	1,629·0	1,625·8
30–34	564·7	617·9	661·7	746·3	840·3	977·9	1,157·7	1,375·9	1,281·3	1,433·3	1,513·9
35–39	435·0	532·7	590·3	640·8	744·9	865·5	1,034·5	1,261·4	1,273·3	1,283·0	1,632·5
40–44	435·6	474·2	551·1	590·1	673·0	745·5	897·5	1,075·1	1,223·1	1,229·3	1,657·9
45–49	313·5	392·9	453·3	506·9	547·5	642·2	760·0	926·1	1,162·2	1,186·6	1,556·4
50–54	307·3	346·1	392·2	455·8	485·8	549·6	636·3	768·2	971·0	1,116·3	1,317·9
55–59	189·7	254·9	299·0	345·9	382·0	413·3	497·5	608·0	781·6	987·4	1,089·3
60–64	209·1	227·2	265·5	294·7	340·6	356·9	410·4	477·2	601·2	778·1	938·8
65–69	120·8	151·6	175·5	205·4	231·5	259·7	282·4	365·9	449·4	578·0	780·6
70–74	104·1	114·7	128·4	149·9	158·3	185·2	195·5	236·9	280·5	376·5	591·2
75–80	55·6	65·0	71·8	82·1	89·8	101·7	113·1	127·5	158·5	204·2	374·5
80–84	31·1	31·7	34·3	38·6	41·2	43·7	52·1	56·4	67·0	83·6	164·8
85 and over	13·2	13·2	13·0	14·5	14·7	16·2	18·0	22·7	24·8	30·6	60·8

FEMALES

	1841 (a)	1851	1861	1871	1881	1891	1901	1911	1921	1931	1951
All Ages	8,136·5	9,146·4	10,290·0	11,653·3	13,334·5	14,942·1	16,799·2	18,624·9	19,811·5	20,819·4	22,742·2
0–4	1,057·9	1,171·2	1,345·8	1,534·8	1,763·1	1,778·3	1,861·4	1,918·3	1,640·3	1,480·1	1,814·1
5–9	951·7	1,042·1	1,171·1	1,355·6	1,578·7	1,701·8	1,748·3	1,849·5	1,752·4	1,644·8	1,545·5
10–14	851·7	949·4	1,045·3	1,203·5	1,398·1	1,612·7	1,670·8	1,752·1	1,822·7	1,586·8	1,383·3
15–19	805·2	884·0	974·7	1,095·7	1,279·0	1,485·7	1,638·6	1,681·7	1,775·2	1,725·0	1,369·2
20–24	827·1	871·2	969·3	1,052·8	1,215·9	1,399·1	1,648·3	1,673·1	1,703·1	1,795·4	1,500·2
25–29	672·0	771·1	834·9	937·3	1,066·7	1,239·1	1,496·2	1,623·3	1,620·3	1,728·1	1,654·1
30–34	602·3	658·2	725·1	813·7	905·2	1,049·6	1,273·7	1,501·3	1,519·6	1,622·0	1,564·6
35–39	449·5	555·9	634·3	700·5	796·5	916·3	1,110·9	1,351·8	1,471·9	1,520·0	1,690·7
40–44	452·4	494·4	583·1	639·7	726·4	801·5	953·1	1,157·5	1,378·1	1,434·2	1,707·3
45–49	325·1	406·1	477·5	546·1	603·9	694·6	813·2	999·5	1,244·0	1,367·4	1,615·8
50–54	327·1	362·7	414·4	488·9	536·3	610·5	692·7	834·4	1,043·1	1,265·3	1,506·9
55–59	202·1	271·4	315·0	372·3	424·5	470·9	555·1	670·4	849·1	1,081·0	1,333·7
60–64	230·7	254·1	290·7	328·0	387·1	416·0	480·2	542·8	680·8	878·9	1,204·0
65–69	138·8	175·9	201·0	235·9	270·9	312·3	347·3	440·9	536·7	692·7	1,048·8
70–74	120·2	135·4	152·9	174·1	191·6	232·7	250·9	316·7	376·3	494·3	836·6
75–79	64·3	81·1	88·9	99·9	112·5	131·6	151·4	182·5	234·0	295·7	549·2
80–84	39·4	42·2	45·4	51·3	54·6	61·9	76·6	87·8	112·9	142·2	281·2
85 and over	19·0	20·0	20·6	23·2	23·5	27·5	30·5	41·3	51·0	65·5	137·0

See p. 14 for footnote

B. Scotland

(in thousands)

PERSONS	1841 (a)	1851	1861	1871	1881	1891	1901	1911	1921	1931	1951
All Ages	2,620·2	2,888·7	3,062·3	3,360·0	3,735·6	4,025·6	4,472·1	4,760·9	4,882·5	4,843·0	5,096·4
0–4	342·8	371·5	417·3	455·6	510·6	502·4	533·0	532·7	472·4	423·3	470·8
5–9	313·5	339·9	363·2	404·8	450·0	477·6	492·7	513·8	477·3	455·7	397·8
10–14	296·9	317·5	322·7	372·1	405·0	452·2	469·3	490·1	490·0	425·8	386·5
15–19	270·2	299·8	307·4	335·6	378·3	418·4	456·0	462·7	478·1	439·3	361·8
20–24	254·5	280·4	280·3	292·4	343·7	363·6	433·3	419·5	428·8	421·6	364·1
25–29	205·9	230·3	232·8	254·8	288·5	312·6	379·0	385·7	376·3	389·0	381·2
30–34	187·9	193·5	202·2	220·3	237·2	270·4	315·2	355·5	337·9	349·5	344·9
35–39	141·8	164·9	174·0	189·3	211·8	237·4	277·9	324·6	324·2	316·2	368·5
40–44	145·9	153·6	162·5	175·7	196·4	205·2	245·4	275·8	308·4	292·2	370·1
45–49	98·4	122·1	135·4	147·4	162·2	182·6	208·8	241·0	290·0	280·6	349·5
50–54	101·3	118·6	124·3	134·7	147·4	162·6	176·5	205·7	244·5	266·5	308·0
55–59	63·0	80·8	94·2	105·0	113·2	124·0	142·8	166·3	200·6	238·0	260·2
60–64	76·5	78·1	94·0	98·4	105·4	113·6	125·6	129·6	161·4	191·8	224·7
65–69	39·2	51·3	57·4	67·5	72·8	79·2	86·8	104·5	123·4	148·8	192·2
70–74	37·4	41·6	43·5	54·4	55·4	60·7	64·1	80·5	83·5	106·2	151·3
75–79	19·9	23·6	26·0	28·8	32·5	35·7	37·3	42·6	49·8	60·2	97·7
80–84	13·8	14·5	15·3	15·9	18·1	18·9	19·9	20·5	24·6	26·5	45·8
85 and over	6·5	6·9	6·9	7·3	7·2	8·6	8·4	9·3	10·6	11·5	19·8
not stated	4·9	—	2·7	—	—	—	—	0·4	0·8	0·2	1·1

MALES	1841 (a)	1851	1861	1871	1881	1891	1901	1911	1921	1931	1951
All Ages	1,241·9	1,375·5	1,449·8	1,603·1	1,799·5	1,942·7	2,173·8	2,308·8	2,347·6	2,325·5	2,434·4
0–4	173·8	189·1	212·0	230·8	258·4	254·8	268·4	268·2	238·6	213·6	241·0
5–9	158·7	172·1	184·3	204·6	227·8	241·7	249·3	257·9	240·2	229·4	202·5
10–14	150·8	162·6	165·1	189·9	205·7	229·2	238·3	246·8	246·6	214·5	195·7
15–19	128·2	145·9	150·4	167·3	189·7	211·0	230·4	233·4	238·8	219·2	173·2
20–24	113·4	128·6	127·5	138·4	166·6	174·1	210·4	201·8	202·9	205·8	172·4
25–29	92·8	104·3	101·2	116·0	137·0	145·1	181·3	182·0	172·5	186·5	187·2
30–34	85·8	88·5	90·7	100·1	112·1	129·0	150·9	170·2	155·0	162·2	166·1
35–39	64·9	75·9	78·5	84·7	98·0	113·7	132·6	157·6	150·1	143·9	177·6
40–44	66·7	70·9	73·8	80·0	90·7	97·3	118·7	133·1	145·8	134·5	180·0
45–49	45·9	56·6	62·4	67·3	73·6	84·7	100·5	115·2	141·9	129·9	168·7
50–54	45·0	53·6	56·4	60·9	66·5	74·0	83·7	98·2	119·3	126·7	141·3
55–59	28·7	36·5	43·0	47·5	50·9	55·6	65·6	79·1	96·5	115·5	115·8
60–64	33·5	33·3	40·6	43·0	45·5	49·6	55·6	59·9	75·9	91·7	97·9
65–69	17·4	22·0	24·5	29·2	31·2	33·7	37·0	46·1	56·8	68·1	83·2
70–74	16·2	17·5	17·8	22·8	22·9	24·8	26·3	32·2	34·8	46·0	65·7
75–79	8·7	9·9	10·7	11·8	13·4	14·2	14·8	16·5	19·4	24·5	41·6
80–84	5·6	5·7	5·9	6·2	7·1	7·1	7·3	7·4	8·7	9·8	17·8
85 and over	2·6	2·6	2·5	2·6	2·5	3·0	2·8	3·0	3·3	3·5	6·4
not stated	3·2	—	2·5	—	—	—	—	0·2	0·4	0·1	0·5

FEMALES	1841 (a)	1851	1861	1871	1881	1891	1901	1911	1921	1931	1951
All Ages	1,378·3	1,513·3	1,612·4	1,756·9	1,936·1	2,082·9	2,298·3	2,452·1	2,534·9	2,517·5	2,662·1
0–4	169·0	182·5	205·3	224·8	252·2	247·6	264·7	264·6	233·8	209·7	229·8
5–9	154·8	167·7	178·9	200·2	222·2	235·9	243·4	255·9	237·2	226·3	195·3
10–14	146·1	154·9	157·6	182·2	199·2	223·0	231·0	243·4	243·4	211·3	190·8
15–19	142·0	154·0	157·0	168·3	188·6	207·4	225·7	229·3	239·3	220·1	188·7
20–24	141·1	151·8	152·8	154·0	177·1	189·5	222·9	217·7	225·9	215·8	191·7
25–29	113·2	126·0	131·6	138·8	151·5	167·5	197·6	203·7	203·9	202·5	194·0
30–34	102·1	105·0	111·5	120·2	125·1	141·4	164·3	185·3	182·9	187·2	178·8
35–39	76·9	89·1	95·5	104·6	113·8	123·7	145·3	167·1	174·0	172·3	190·8
40–44	79·2	82·7	88·6	95·7	105·8	107·9	126·7	142·6	162·5	157·8	190·1
45–49	52·5	65·5	73·0	80·1	88·6	98·0	108·3	125·8	148·0	150·7	180·9
50–54	56·3	65·0	67·9	73·8	80·9	88·6	92·8	107·5	125·2	139·8	166·6
55–59	34·2	44·4	51·3	57·5	62·3	68·4	77·2	87·1	104·1	122·5	144·9
60–64	43·1	44·7	53·4	55·3	59·9	64·0	70·0	69·7	85·4	100·1	126·8
65–69	21·8	29·2	32·9	38·4	41·5	45·5	49·8	58·4	66·5	80·7	108·9
70–74	21·2	24·0	25·7	31·6	32·5	35·9	37·8	48·3	48·7	60·2	85·6
75–79	11·2	13·7	15·3	17·1	19·1	21·5	22·5	26·2	30·4	35·7	56·2
80–84	8·1	8·8	9·4	9·7	11·1	11·8	12·6	13·1	15·9	16·7	28·0
85 and over	3·8	4·3	4·0	4·7	4·7	5·5	5·6	6·3	7·3	8·0	13·4
not stated	1·7	—	0·2	—	—	—	—	0·2	0·4	0·1	0·6

See p. 14 for footnote

C. Ireland

(in thousands)

Ireland — Persons

Persons	1861	1871	1881	1891	1901	1911
All Ages	5,799·0	5,412·4	5,174·8	4,704·8	4,458·8	4,390·2
0–4	693·7	653·3	576·0	470·4	442·7	435·7
5–9	611·2	632·2	621·6	508·8	450·9	437·9
10–14	597·0	629·8	616·4	549·9	459·6	427·1
15–19	672·8	531·6	559·0	549·9	472·8	423·0
20–24	615·1	457·7	477·3	444·5	444·2	376·2
25–34	758·1	732·7	633·8	598·1	656·6	636·0
35–44	595·8	544·0	558·8	488·1	482·8	536·8
45–54	547·5	476·8	443·1	458·6	413·5	394·2
55–64	429·0	424·9	364·1	334·1	351·2	282·5
65–74	184·1	224·8	213·6	191·2	190·9	314·2
75–84	76·5	83·5	93·7	90·2	77·8	110·8
85 and over	14·3	17·3	14·6	19·1	15·8	15·9
not stated	3·8	3·8	3·0	1·8	—	—

Northern Ireland / Irish Republic — Persons

Persons	N.I. 1926	I.R. 1926	N.I. 1937	I.R. 1936	N.I. 1951	I.R. 1951
All Ages	1,256·6	2,972·0	1,279·7	2,968·4	1,370·9	2,960·6
0–4	127·8	287·7	111·9	268·3	137·8	312·2
5–9	116·9	284·6	114·2	269·3	129·2	281·0
10–14	119·7	295·5	120·7	282·8	111·7	260·9
15–19	119·9	286·2	113·7	268·5	108·5	241·2
20–24	109·2	240·2	105·2	254·5	100·9	202·2
25–29	99·0	215·4	101·4	216·8	99·5	198·4
30–35	82·3	183·3	90·8	183·3	91·2	191·6
35–39	76·4	165·8	88·2	192·4	94·1	200·9
40–44	70·0	169·1	75·9	162·9	89·1	180·3
45–49	70·0	168·9	67·6	156·6	80·8	160·9
50–54	65·6	162·7	62·0	152·7	76·3	163·0
55–59	54·4	125·7	58·1	143·4	62·2	128·8
60–64	43·5	105·1	54·2	130·4	54·5	122·0
65–69	39·1	101·2	47·1	113·0	47·4	107·5
70–74	31·6	82·2	35·3	84·2	40·5	100·1
75–79	17·6	46·0	19·9	53·0	27·2	64·5
80–84	8·8	27·4	9·2	23·2	13·7	30·9
85 and over	4·7	14·9	4·2	11·5	6·1	13·3

Ireland — Males

Males	1861	1871	1881	1891	1901	1911
All Ages	2,837·4	2,639·8	2,533·3	2,319·0	2,200·0	2,192·0
0–4	352·2	331·0	292·2	238·9	224·8	220·8
5–9	309·7	319·8	314·5	258·4	228·4	222·1
10–14	306·0	322·4	315·0	280·4	234·2	217·3
15–19	329·4	258·7	274·0	276·3	235·0	214·9
20–24	297·7	214·2	231·8	223·9	217·3	191·3
25–34	367·0	342·8	296·3	286·2	320·9	312·1
35–44	277·3	260·4	262·7	227·0	233·8	273·2
45–54	261·9	224·5	213·6	217·9	194·5	198·1
55–64	204·8	204·7	171·8	163·1	169·2	137·7
65–74	87·2	111·8	106·0	92·5	96·3	144·0
75–84	35·4	39·1	46·8	44·1	38·1	53·0
85 and over	6·4	8·1	6·8	9·4	7·5	8·4
not stated	2·5	2·2	1·8	0·9	—	—

Northern Ireland / Irish Republic — Males and Females

Males and Females	N.I. 1926	I.R. 1926	N.I. 1937	I.R. 1936	N.I. 1951	I.R. 1951
All Ages	608·1	1,506·9	623·3	1,520·5	667·8	1,506·6
0–4	65·0	146·2	57·1	136·4	70·6	160·2
5–9	59·3	144·8	58·1	136·3	66·1	143·5
10–14	60·3	150·8	61·5	143·7	56·9	132·7
15–19	59·4	146·0	56·7	138·1	55·4	125·7
20–24	52·5	124·5	51·0	134·7	48·7	105·4
25–29	45·9	106·6	48·4	113·3	47·9	100·0
30–34	38·0	92·5	43·6	94·1	44·7	96·4
35–39	35·3	87·3	41·6	96·8	45·5	102·3
40–44	32·7	86·1	35·8	83·7	43·0	94·0
45–49	33·5	87·0	31·9	80·5	38·8	82·4
50–54	32·3	85·6	29·4	78·7	36·1	82·9
55–59	26·8	67·1	27·9	75·1	28·9	65·0
60–64	21·3	53·7	26·6	68·1	24·4	61·3
65–69	18·8	51·5	22·8	60·1	21·6	54·1
70–74	13·8	37·5	16·1	40·8	18·3	49·1
75–79	7·5	20·9	8·8	24·6	12·4	31·6
80–84	3·7	12·1	3·9	10·5	6·0	14·6
85 and over	1·9	6·6	1·6	4·9	2·4	5·5

Ireland — Females

Females	1861	1871	1881	1891	1901	1911
All Ages	2,961·6	2,772·6	2,641·6	2,385·8	2,258·7	2,198·2
0–4	341·5	322·3	283·7	231·5	217·9	214·9
5–9	301·5	312·4	307·2	250·4	222·5	215·7
10–14	291·1	307·4	301·4	269·6	225·4	209·8
15–19	343·5	273·0	284·9	273·6	237·8	208·1
20–24	317·4	243·5	245·5	220·6	226·9	184·9
25–34	391·2	389·9	337·5	311·8	335·7	323·9
35–44	318·5	283·6	296·1	261·1	249·0	263·6
45–54	285·6	252·3	229·4	240·7	219·0	196·0
55–64	224·2	220·2	192·3	171·1	182·0	144·8
65–74	96·9	113·0	107·6	98·7	94·6	170·2
75–84	41·0	44·3	46·8	46·1	39·7	57·8
85 and over	7·9	9·2	7·8	9·7	8·2	8·4
not stated	1·4	1·6	1·2	0·9	—	—

Northern Ireland / Irish Republic — (Females)

	N.I. 1926	I.R. 1926	N.I. 1937	I.R. 1936	N.I. 1951	I.R. 1951
All Ages	648·1	1,465·1	656·6	1,448·0	703·1	1,454·0
0–4	62·8	141·5	54·8	131·9	67·2	152·6
5–9	57·6	139·9	56·1	133·0	63·1	137·6
10–14	59·4	144·7	59·2	139·1	54·8	128·2
15–19	60·5	140·1	57·1	130·2	53·1	115·4
20–24	56·7	115·7	54·2	119·8	52·2	96·8
25–29	53·9	108·8	52·8	103·5	51·6	98·1
30–34	44·3	90·8	47·1	89·2	46·6	95·1
35–39	41·1	88·4	46·6	95·6	48·6	98·6
40–44	37·3	83·0	40·0	79·2	46·0	86·3
45–49	36·6	81·9	35·7	76·1	42·0	78·5
50–54	33·3	77·1	32·6	74·1	40·3	80·1
55–59	27·6	58·6	30·2	68·3	33·3	63·8
60–64	22·2	51·5	27·6	62·3	30·1	60·7
65–69	20·3	49·7	24·3	52·9	25·8	53·4
70–74	17·8	44·8	19·2	45·1	22·2	51·0
75–79	10·0	25·0	11·1	28·3	14·8	32·9
80–84	5·1	15·3	5·3	12·8	7·3	16·2
85 and over	2·8	8·3	2·6	6·6	3·7	7·8

(a) Figures for 1841 are only approximate ones.

Population and Vital Statistics 5. Proportions of Each Age-Group (by Sex) according to Marital Condition—England & Wales 1851-1951, and Scotland 1861-1951

NOTES

[1] Sources: *Reports* of the census of 1951 (for England & Wales and Scotland separately).

(per thousand of the appropriate sex in each age-group)

A. England & Wales, Males

		1851	1861	1871	1881	1891	1901	1911	1921	1931	1951
All Ages	S	625	612	613	620	620	608	593	550	518	438
	M	337	351	351	346	345	357	372	414	444	523
	W	38	37	36	34	35	35	35	36	38	39
15–19	S	996	995	995	995	996	997	998	996	997	995
	M	4	5	5	5	4	3	2	4	3	5
	W	—	—	—	—	—	—	—	—	—	—
20–24	S	797	775	767	777	805	826	857	822	861	762
	M	200	223	230	221	193	173	142	177	138	237
	W	3	2	3	2	2	1	1	1	1	1
25–34	S	356	318	316	317	343	359	385	341	352	272
	M	627	667	668	668	645	631	607	649	641	720
	W	17	15	16	15	12	10	8	10	7	8
35–44	S	162	142	137	138	147	158	169	150	125	120
	M	795	821	826	826	818	812	806	827	855	862
	W	43	37	37	36	35	30	25	23	20	18
45–54	S	115	105	97	96	100	110	121	120	108	92
	M	802	821	832	832	827	819	818	831	848	877
	W	83	74	71	72	73	71	61	49	44	31
55–64	S	98	90	89	83	84	89	99	104	102	78
	M	748	761	772	779	771	764	762	782	796	850
	W	154	149	139	138	145	147	139	114	102	72
65–74	S	85	84	82			78	85	91	92	84
	M	626	627	638			630	630	654	673	733
	W	289	289	280			292	285	255	235	183
75–84	S	74	74	71	76	73	66	69	73	72	79
	M	458	438	444	588	590	444	443	468	474	530
	W	468	488	485	336	337	490	488	459	454	391
85 and over	S	76	74	62			62	61	70	56	65
	M	290	272	270			263	258	272	268	311
	W	634	654	668			675	681	658	676	624

B. England & Wales, Females

		1851	1861	1871	1881	1891	1901	1911	1921	1931	1951
All Ages	S	598	587	586	592	596	586	571	535	500	405
	M	330	339	339	333	329	340	356	383	413	487
	W	72	74	75	75	75	74	73	82	87	108
15–19	S	975	970	968	975	981	985	988	982	982	956
	M	25	30	32	25	19	15	12	18	18	44
	W	—	—	—	—	—	—	—	—	—	—
20–24	S	687	664	652	665	701	726	757	726	742	518
	M	308	331	343	331	296	272	242	270	257	480
	W	5	5	5	4	3	2	1	4	1	2
25–34	S	329	305	295	292	326	340	355	337	330	182
	M	643	667	675	682	653	643	632	631	658	798
	W	28	28	30	26	21	17	13	32	12	20
35–44	S	163	159	156	154	164	185	196	192	194	137
	M	757	762	762	765	761	751	753	746	752	821
	W	80	79	82	81	75	64	51	62	54	42
45–54	S	122	119	121	119	124	136	158	164	164	151
	M	716	720	716	711	706	705	709	721	720	759
	W	162	161	163	170	170	159	133	115	116	90
55–64	S	115	109	109	109	110	117	132	153	156	155
	M	589	589	589	581	573	569	584	600	619	624
	W	296	302	302	310	317	314	284	247	225	221
65–74	S	111	105	104⌐			⌐111	121	139	158	156
	M	400	400	393			368	375	393	411	428
	W	489	495	503			521	504	468	431	416
75–84	S	109	102	97	104	108	111	120	132	147	164
	M	211	202	204	326	319	176	177	187	192	222
	W	680	696	699	570	573	713	703	681	661	614
85 and over	S	107	91	91			119	126	130	142	172
	M	81	77	74			59	55	67	61	77
	W	812	832	835⌐			⌐822	819	803	797	751

C. Scotland, Males

		1861	1871	1881	1891	1901	1911	1921	1931	1951
All Ages	S	423	423	432	443	453	445	413	404	307
	M	522	521	513	503	494	500	530	538	635
	W	55	56	55	54	53	55	57	58	58
16–19	S	996	996	996	997	997	997	994	995	995
	M	4	4	4	3	3	3	6	5	5
	W	—	—	—	—	—	—	—	—	—
20–24	S	833	842	848	866	874	884	854	882	800
	M	165	156	150	132	125	115	145	117	199
	W	2	2	2	2	1	1	1	1	1
25–34	S	386	394	400	433	452	475	433	444	335
	M	600	590	584	553	536	515	557	547	658
	W	14	16	16	14	12	10	10	9	7
35–44	S	182	180	179	195	211	229	214	186	159
	M	782	782	783	768	755	739	758	789	823
	W	36	38	38	37	34	32	28	25	18
45–54	S	135	132	127	134	146	160	168	162	130
	M	792	796	800	793	780	769	772	783	833
	W	73	72	73	73	74	71	60	55	37
55–64	S	126	121	112	115	121	128	142	150	118
	M	739	744	750	746	733	729	727	732	792
	W	135	135	138	139	146	143	131	118	90
65–74	S	112	120	109	106	107	114	119	131	130
	M	640	638	635	636	621	607	617	619	648
	W	248	242	256	258	272	279	264	250	222
75–84	S	93	108	108	103	101	101	96	107	116
	M	491	489	468	480	452	443	434	439	457
	W	416	403	424	417	447	456	470	454	427
85 and over	S	81	97	81	89	95	95	82	92	94
	M	338	312	316	305	280	266	263	252	251
	W	581	591	603	606	625	639	655	656	655

D. Scotland, Females

		1861	1871	1881	1891	1901	1911	1921	1931	1951
All Ages	S	426	415	413	425	428	425	408	401	303
	M	444	452	458	452	456	465	477	486	567
	W	130	133	129	123	116	110	115	113	130
16–19	S	973	973	977	984	979	982	974	972	956
	M	27	27	23	16	21	18	26	28	44
	W	—	—	—	—	—	—	—	—	—
20–24	S	741	738	735	764	764	782	754	771	602
	M	255	258	262	233	234	216	242	228	396
	W	4	4	3	3	2	2	4	1	2
25–34	S	392	377	366	402	404	422	405	413	242
	M	577	591	607	578	579	565	565	574	740
	W	31	32	27	20	17	13	30	13	18
35–44	S	237	235	220	224	239	243	243	247	179
	M	668	672	691	700	696	704	694	698	779
	W	95	93	89	76	65	53	63	55	42
45–54	S	201	200	194	187	192	208	207	215	203
	M	610	612	621	638	645	653	672	670	697
	W	189	188	185	175	163	139	121	115	100
55–64	S	205	198	194	186	181	189	204	206	209
	M	461	476	478	497	500	526	542	566	558
	W	334	326	328	317	319	285	254	228	233
65–74	S	211	204	200	195	190	191	199	217	217
	M	295	305	306	316	310	320	342	362	376
	W	494	491	494	489	500	489	459	421	407
75–84	S	210	210	203	199	202	204	194	212	221
	M	148	149	151	160	140	145	147	159	183
	W	642	641	646	641	658	651	659	629	596
85 and over	S	186	194	194	203	207	212	188	203	225
	M	53	61	55	64	40	41	47	52	58
	W	761	745	751	733	753	747	765	745	717

Population and Vital Statistics 6. Population of Conurbations—1801–1951

NOTES

[1] SOURCE: Census of England & Wales for 1951.
[2] The census of Scotland for 1951 contains population figures for the Central Clydeside conurbation for the last three censuses only. Approximate figures can be extracted from the two censuses before that. The results are as follows:

[3] All figures are adjusted to the present area of the conurbation, but for 1911 and preceding years it is not possible to give truly comparable figures; but the errors were small.

Central Clydeside

1901	approx 1,343	1911	approx 1,461	1921 1,638
1931	1,690	1951	1,758	

(in thousands)

	Greater London	South-East Lancashire	West Midlands	West Yorkshire	Merseyside	Tyneside
1801	1,117	...	...	...	...	...
1811	1,327	...	...	...	...	...
1821	1,600	...	...	...	...	...
1831	1,907	...	...	...	...	...
1841	2,239	...	...	...	...	...
1851	2,685	...	...	...	...	...
1861	3,227	...	...	...	...	...
1871	3,890	1,386	969	1,064	690	346
1881	4,770	1,685	1,134	1,269	824	426
1891	5,638	1,894	1,269	1,410	908	551
1901	6,586	2,117	1,483	1,524	1,030	678
1911	7,256	2,328	1,634	1,590	1,157	761
1921	7,488	2,361	1,773	1,614	1,263	816
1931	8,216	2,427	1,933	1,655	1,347	827
1951	8,348	2,423	2,237	1,693	1,382	836

NOTES

[1] SOURCES: *Reports* of the census of 1951 (separately for England & Wales, Scotland, Northern Ireland, and the Irish Republic), and the census of 1911 for Ireland.

[2] The population of Belfast county borough is not shown in any of the counties of Northern Ireland after 1821.
[3] Members of the armed forces serving in Ireland were not included in the population at any census before 1861.

(in thousands)

A. England	1801	1811	1821	1831	1841	1851	1861	1871
Bedfordshire	63	70	84	95	108	124	135	146
Berkshire	111	120	133	147	162	170	176	196
Buckinghamshire	108	118	135	147	156	164	168	176
Cambridgeshire (whole)	89	101	122	144	164	185	176	187
(Isle of Ely								
Cheshire	192	227	270	334	396	456	505	561
Cornwall	192	221	261	301	342	356	369	362
Cumberland	117	134	156	169	178	195	205	220
Derbyshire	162	186	214	237	272	296	339	379
Devonshire	340	383	438	494	533	567	584	601
Dorsetshire	114	125	145	159	175	184	189	196
Durham	149	165	194	239	308	391	509	685
Essex (c)	228	252	289	318	345	369	405	466
Gloucestershire	251	286	336	387	431	459	486	535
Hampshire (whole)	219	246	283	314	355	405	482	544
(Isle of Wight								
Herefordshire	88	94	103	111	113	115	124	125
Hertfordshire	97	111	130	143	157	167	173	192
Huntingdonshire	38	42	49	53	59	64	64	64
Kent (c)	259	306	355	399	448	486	546	631
Lancashire	673	828	1,053	1,337	1,667	2,031	2,429	2,819
Leicestershire	130	150	174	197	216	230	237	269
Lincolnshire (whole)	209	238	283	317	363	407	412	437
(Holland								
(Kesteven								
(Lindsey								
London (c)	1,088	1,259	1,504	1,778	2,073	2,491	2,921	3,336
Middlesex (c)	71	84	99	113	132	141	176	253
Monmouthshire	46	62	76	98	134	157	175	195
Norfolk	273	292	344	390	413	443	435	439
Northamptonshire (whole)	132	141	163	179	199	212	228	244
(Soke of Peterborough								
Northumberland	168	183	213	237	266	304	343	387
Nottinghamshire	140	163	187	225	250	270	294	320
Oxfordshire	112	120	138	154	163	170	171	178
Rutland	16	16	18	19	21	23	22	22
Shropshire	170	185	198	214	226	229	241	248
Somerset	274	303	356	404	436	444	445	463
Staffordshire	243	295	346	409	509	609	747	858
Suffolk (whole)	214	234	272	296	315	337	337	349
(Suffolk East								
(Suffolk West								
Surrey (c)	106	121	139	157	182	197	246	342
Sussex (whole)	159	190	233	273	300	337	364	417
(Sussex East								
(Sussex West								
Warwickshire	207	229	274	337	402	475	562	634
Westmorland	41	46	51	55	56	58	61	65
Wiltshire	184	192	219	237	256	254	249	257
Worcestershire	146	169	194	223	248	277	307	339
Yorkshire (East Riding)	111	133	154	168	194	219	238	265
Yorkshire (North Riding)	158	169	187	191	203	213	242	290
Yorkshire (West Riding)	591	684	833	1,013	1,195	1,366	1,553	1,882
B. Wales								
Anglesey	34	37	45	48	51	57	55	51
Brecknockshire	32	38	44	48	56	61	62	60
Caernarvonshire	42	50	58	67	81	88	96	106
Cardiganshire	43	50	58	65	69	71	72	73
Carmarthenshire	67	77	90	101	106	111	112	116
Denbighshire	60	64	76	83	88	93	101	105
Flintshire	39	46	54	60	67	68	70	76
Glamorganshire	71	85	102	127	171	232	318	398
Merionethshire	30	31	34	35	39	39	47	52
Montgomeryshire	48	52	60	67	70	67	67	68
Pembrokeshire	56	61	74	81	88	94	96	92
Radnorshire	19	20	23	25	25	25	25	25

Continued on p. 21.   *See p. 23 for footnotes*

(in thousands)

C. Scotland

	1801	1811	1821	1831	1841	1851	1861	1871
Aberdeenshire	121	134	155	178	192	212	222	245
Angusshire	99	107	113	140	170	191	204	238
Argyllshire	81	87	97	101	97	89	80	76
Ayrshire	84	104	127	145	164	190	199	201
Banffshire	37	38	44	48	50	54	59	62
Berwickshire	30	31	33	34	34	36	37	36
Buteshire	12	12	14	14	16	17	16	17
Caithness-shire	23	23	29	35	36	39	41	40
Clackmannanshire	11	12	13	15	19	23	21	24
Dumfriesshire	55	63	71	74	73	78	76	75
Dunbartonshire	21	24	27	33	44	45	52	59
East Lothianshire	30	31	35	36	36	36	38	38
Fifeshire	94	101	115	129	140	154	155	161
Inverness-shire	73	78	90	95	98	97	89	88
Kincardineshire	26	27	29	31	33	35	34	35
Kinross-shire	7	7	8	9	9	9	8	7
Kirkcudbrightshire	29	34	39	41	41	43	42	42
Lanarkshire	148	191	244	317	427	530	632	765
Midlothianshire	123	149	192	219	225	259	274	328
Morayshire	28	28	31	34	35	39	43	44
Nairnshire	8	8	9	9	9	10	10	10
Orkney	24	23	27	29	31	31	32	31
Peeblesshire	9	10	10	11	10	11	11	12
Perthshire	126	134	138	142	137	139	134	128
Renfrewshire	79	93	112	133	155	161	178	217
Ross & Cromarty	56	61	69	75	79	83	81	81
Roxburghshire	34	37	41	44	46	52	54	54
Selkirkshire	5	6	7	7	8	10	10	14
Shetland	22	23	26	29	31	31	32	32
Stirlingshire	51	58	65	73	82	86	92	98
Sutherlandshire	23	24	24	26	25	26	25	24
West Lothianshire	18	19	23	23	27	30	39	41
Wigtownshire	23	27	33	36	39	43	42	39

D. Northern Ireland

	1801	1811	1821	1831	1841	1851	1861	1871
Antrim			234	272	291	274	257 (*b*)	246
Armagh			197	220	233	196	190	179
Down			325	352	361	321	299	277
Fermanagh			131	150	157	116	106	93
Londonderry			194	222	222	192	184	174
Tyrone			262	304	313	256	239	216

E. Irish Republic

	1801	1811	1821	1831	1841	1851	1861	1871
Carlow			79	82	86	68	57	52
Cavan			195	228	243	174	154	141
Clare			208	258	286	212	166	148
Cork			730	811	854	649	545	517
Donegal			248	289	296	255	237	218
Dublin			336	380	373	405	410	405
Galway			337	415	440	322	271	248
Kerry			216	263	294	238	201	197
Kildare			99	108	114	96	91	84
Kilkenny			182	194	202	159	125	109
Laoighis (Queen's)			134	146	154	112	91	80
Leitrim			125	142	155	112	105	96
Limerick			277	315	330	262	217	192
Longford			108	113	115	82	72	65
Louth			119	125	128	108	91	84
Mayo			293	366	389	274	255	246
Meath			159	177	184	141	110	96
Monaghan			175	196	200	142	126	115
Offaly (King's)			131	144	147	112	90	76
Roscommon			209	250	254	173	157	141
Sligo			146	172	181	129	125	115
Tipperary			347	403	436	332	249	217
Waterford			157	177	196	164	134	123
Westmeath			129	137	141	111	91	78
Wexford			171	183	202	180	144	133
Wicklow			111	122	126	99	86	79

Continued on p. 22.   *See p. 23 for footnotes*

(in thousands)

A. England

	1881	1891 (a)	1891 (a)	1901	1911	1921	1931	1951
Bedfordshire	149	161	161	172	195	206	221	312
Berkshire	218	239	241	259	281	295	311	403
Buckinghamshire	176	185	187	197	219	236	271	386
Cambridgeshire (whole)	186	189	185	186	199	207	221	256
(Isle of Ely			64	65	71	77	81	89
Cheshire	644	730	755	842	962	1,020	1,088	1,259
Cornwall	331	323	323	322	328	321	318	345
Cumberland	251	267	267	267	266	273	263	285
Derbyshire	462	528	511	596	679	709	750	826
Devonshire	604	632	633	662	700	710	733	798
Dorsetshire	191	195	192	200	221	225	239	291
Durham	867	1,016	1,017	1,187	1,370	1,479	1,486	1,464
Essex (c)	576	785	783	1,084	1,351	1,470	1,755	2,045
Gloucestershire	572	600	656	710	738	760	791	939*
Hampshire (whole)	593	690	694	801	953	1,008	1,103	1,393
(Isle of Wight			79	82	88	95	88	96
Herefordshire	121	116	116	114	114	113	112	127
Hertfordshire	203	220	227	258	311	333	401	610
Huntingdonshire	59	58	55	54	56	55	56	69
Kent (c)	710	807	830	961	1,046	1,142	1,219	1,564
Lancashire	3,454	3,927	3,897	4,373	4,762	4,934	5,040	5,118
Leicestershire	321	373	376	438	477	494	542	631
Lincolnshire (whole)	470	473	474	500	564	602	624	706
(Holland			76	77	83	86	92	102
(Kesteven			103	101	107	108	110	131
(Lindsey			295	321	374	409	422	474
London (c)	3,881	4,266	4,266	4,563	4,541	4,498	4,408	3,353
Middlesex (c)	370	564	543	792	1,126	1,253	1,639	2,269
Monmouthshire	211	252	258	297	395	450	432	425
Norfolk	445	455	468	476	498	501	502	548
Northamptonshire (whole)	273	302	300	336	349	349	361	423
(Soke of Peterborough			35	41	45	47	52	64
Northumberland	434	506	506	603	697	746	757	798
Nottinghamshire	392	446	446	514	604	641	713	841
Oxfordshire	180	185	185	180	190	190	210	276
Rutland	21	21	21	20	20	18	17	21
Shropshire	248	236	237	240	246	243	244	290
Somerset	469	484	428	433	455	462	470	551
Staffordshire	981	1,083	1,053	1,184	1,286	1,356	1,434	1,621
Suffolk (whole)	357	371	362	373	394	400	401	443
(Suffolk East			241	256	277	291	295	322
(Suffolk West			121	118	117	109	106	121
Surrey (c)	439	542	522	654	846	930	1,181	1,602
Sussex (whole)	491	550	548	602	663	728	770	937
(Sussex East			407	451	487	532	547	619
(Sussex West			141	151	176	196	223	319
Warwickshire	737	805	921	1,087	1,250	1,393	1,533	1,862
Westmorland	64	66	66	64	64	66	65	67
Wiltshire	259	265	262	271	286	292	303	387
Worcestershire	380	414	337	360	380	398	420	523
Yorkshire (East Riding)	309	342	342	385	433	461	483	511
Yorkshire (North Riding)	341	360	359	377	419	456	467	525
Yorkshire (West Riding)	2,237	2,507	2,521	2,843	3,131	3,270	3,446	3,586

B. Wales

	1881	1891 (a)	1891 (a)	1901	1911	1921	1931	1951
Anglesey	51	50	50	51	51	52	49	51
Brecknockshire	58	57	51	54	59	61	58	57
Caernarvonshire	119	118	116	123	123	128	121	124
Cardiganshire	70	63	63	61	60	61	55	53
Carmarthenshire	125	131	131	135	160	175	179	172
Denbighshire	112	118	121	134	147	158	158	171
Flintshire	81	77	77	81	93	107	113	145
Glamorganshire	511	687	688	861	1,122	1,254	1,229	1,203
Merionethshire	52	49	49	49	46	45	43	41
Montgomeryshire	66	58	58	55	53	51	48	46
Pembrokeshire	92	89	88	88	90	92	87	91
Radnorshire	24	22	22	23	23	24	21	20

See footnote (a).   See p. 23 for footnotes

C. Scotland
(in thousands)

	1881	1891 (a)	1891 (a)	1901	1911	1921	1931	1951
Aberdeenshire	268	281	283	304	312	301	300	308
Angussshire	266	278	278	284	281	271	270	275
Argyllshire	76	75	74	74	71	77	63	63
Ayrshire	218	226	226	254	268	299	285	321
Banffshire	63	64	61	60	61	57	55	50
Berwickshire	35	32	32	31	30	28	27	25
Buteshire	18	18	18	19	18	34	19	19
Caithness-shire	39	37	37	34	32	28	26	23
Clackmannanshire	26	28	32	32	31	33	32	38
Dumfriesshire	76	74	74	73	73	75	75	86 (b)
Dunbartonshire	75	94	98	114	140	151 (b)	148	164
East Lothianshire	39	37	37	39	43	47	47	52
Fifeshire	172	187	190	219	268	293	276	307
Inverness-shire	90	89	90	90	87	82	82	85
Kincardineshire	34	36	36	41	41	42	41	47
Kinross-shire	7	6	7	7	8	8	7	7
Kirkcudbrightshire	42	40	40	39	38	37	37	31 (b)
Lanarkshire	904	1,046	1,136	1,339	1,447	1,539 (b)	1,586 (b)	1,614
Midlothianshire	389	434	434	489	508	506	526	566
Morayshire	44	43	43	45	43	42	41	48
Nairnshire	10	10	9	9	9	9	8	9
Orkney	32	30	30	29	26	24	22	21
Peeblesshire	14	15	15	15	15	15	15	15
Perthshire	129	126	122	123	124	126	121	128
Renfrewshire	263	291	225	269	315	299 (b)	289 (b)	325
Ross & Cromarty	78	78	79	76	77	71	63	61
Roxburghshire	53 (b)	54	53	49	47	45	46	46
Selkirkshire	26 (b)	27	28	23	25	23	23	22
Shetland	30	29	29	28	28	26	21	19
Stirlingshire	112	126	119	142	161	162	166	188
Sutherlandshire	23	22	22	21	20	18	16	14
West Lothianshire	44	53	53	66	80	84	81	89
Wigtownshire	39	36	36	33	32	31	29	32

D. Northern Ireland

	1881	1891 (a)	1891 (a)	1901	1911	1926	1937	1951
Antrim	238	215	208	196	194	192	197	231
Armagh	163	143	138	125	120	110	109	114
Down	248	224	219	206	204	209	211	241
Fermanagh	85	74	74	65	62	58	55	53
Londonderry	165	152	152	144	141	140	143	156
Tyrone	198	171	171	151	143	133	128	132

E. Irish Republic

	1881	1891 (a)	1891 (a)	1901	1911	1926	1936	1951
Carlow	47	41	42	38	36	34	34	34
Cavan	129	112	112	98	91	82	77	66
Clare	141	124	126	112	104	95	90	81
Cork	496	438	438	405	392	366	356	341
Donegal	206	186	186	174	169	153	142	132
Dublin	419	419	417	448	477	506	587	693
Galway	242 (b)	215	211	193	182	169	168	160
Kerry	201	179	179	166	160	149	140	127
Kildare	76	70	70	64	67	58	58	66
Kilkenny	100	87	89	79	75	71	69	65
Laoighis (Queen's)	73	65	64	57	55	52	50	48
Leitrim	90	79	79	69	64	56	51	41
Limerick	181	159	159	146	143	140	141	141
Longford	61	53	53	47	44	40	38	35
Louth	78	71	71	66	64	63	64	69
Mayo	245 (b)	219	219	199	192	173	161	142
Meath	87	77	77	67	65	63	61	66
Monaghan	103	86	86	75	71	65	61	55
Offaly (King's)	73	66	66	60	57	53	51	53
Roscommon	132	114	119	102	94	84	78	68
Sligo	112	98	94	84	79	71	67	61
Tipperary	200	173	173	160	152	141	138	133
Waterford	113	98	96	87	84	79	78	75
Westmeath	72	65	65	62	60	57	55	54
Wexford	124	112	112	104	102	96	94	90
Wicklow	70	62	64	61	61	58	59	63

(a) The first column headed 1891 relates (for England & Wales) to the Ancient County as altered by the operation of the Counties (Detached Parts) Act of 1844; whilst the second column relates to the Administrative County. For all counties (except London) the figures prior to 1891 relate to the area of the Ancient County in 1891, and figures subsequent to 1891 relate to the area of the Administrative County in 1951. The sole exception is Gloucestershire (marked *), in which case the figures before 1951 have not been adjusted for a boundary change effective on 1st April 1951. The first column headed 1891 relates (for Scotland and for Ireland) to the area in 1891, and the second column to the area in 1901.
(b) Except as indicated in (a), all figures for Scotland and Ireland relate to the counties as constituted at the time of the census concerned. The principal transfers of population resulting from boundary changes were as follows: Between

1871 and 1881—an area transferred from Roxburgh to Selkirk, with a population in 1871 of 5,245; areas transferred from Renfrew to Lanark between 1911 and 1921, with a population in 1911 of about 31,500, and between 1921 and 1931, with a population in 1931 of about 15,000; between 1911 and 1921—an area transferred from Dunbarton to Lanark, with a population in 1921 of 3,825; between 1931 and 1951—an area transferred from Kirkcudbright to Dumfries, with a population in 1931 of 6,175; between 1851 and 1861—an area transferred from Antrim to the city of Belfast, with a population in 1851 of 20,670; between 1871 and 1881—an area transferred from Mayo to Galway, with a population in 1881 of 1,166.
(c) The population of the County of London is for the present area throughout. It has been deducted from the counties previously forming part.

Population and Vital Statistics 8. Population of the Principal Towns of the United Kingdom—1801–1951

NOTES

[1] SOURCES: *Reports* of the censuses of 1851–1951.
[2] Figures for the period 1801–51 (first column) are for the area of the towns in 1851, as nearly as is possible. For the census from 1851 onwards two figures are given—the first as shown in the census for the year concerned (first column), and the second as shown in that census for the area of the town as given at the subsequent census.

(in thousands)

	1801	1811	1821	1831	1841	1851	1851	1861	1861	1871	1871	1881
Aberdeen	27	35	44	57	63	72	72	74	74	88	88	105
Bath	33	38	47	51	53	54	54	53	53	53	53	52
Belfast (figures for 1926 and 1937 instead of 1921 and 1931)	...	...	37	53	70	87	103	122	122	174	174	208
Birkenhead	φφ	φφ	φφ	3	8	24	25	38	38	45	66	84
Birmingham	71	83	102	144	183	233	233	296	296	344	344	401
environs of Birmingham later incorporated (c)	...	...	...	...	19	32	32	55	55	91	91	145
Blackburn	12	15	22	27	37	47	47	63	63	76	85 (a)	101
Blackpool	φφ	1	1	1	2	3	3	4	4	6	...	14
Bolton	18	25	32	42	51	61	61	70	70	83	...	105
Bournemouth	...	...	...	...	...	...	...	...	...	6	...	...
Bradford	13	16	26	44	67	104	104	106	106	146	147	183
Brighton	7	12	24	41	47	66	66	78	78	90	93 (a)	108
Bristol	61	71	85	104	124	137	137	154	154	183	183	207
Cambridge	10	11	14	21	24	28	28	26	26	30	30	35
Cardiff	2	2	4	6	10	18	18	33	33	40	57	83
Carlisle	9	11	14	19	22	26	26	29	29	31	31	36
Chester	15	16	20	21	24	28	28	31	31	35	35	37
Colchester	12	13	14	16	18	19	19	24	24	26	26	28
Coventry	16	18	21	27	31	36	36	41	41	38	38	42
Derby	11	13	17	24	33	41	41	43	43	50	61	81
Dudley	10	14	18	23	31	38	38	45	45	44	44	46
Dundee	26	30	31	45	63	79	79	90	91	119	119	140
Edinburgh (including Leith)	83	103	138	162	166	194	202	203	203	242	244	295
Exeter	17	19	23	28	31	33	33	34	34	35	35	38
Gateshead	9	9	12	15	20	26	26	34	34	49	49	66
Glasgow	77	101	147	202	275	345	357	420	420	522	522	587
environs of Glasgow later incorporated (d)				10	12	18	18	23	23	46	46	86
Greenock	17	19	22	27	36	37	37	43	43	58	58	67
Halifax	12	13	17	22	28	34	34	37	47 (a)	66	66	74
Huddersfield	7	10	13	19	25	31	31	35	61	70	70	82
Hull	30	37	45	52	67	85	85	98	98	122	122	154
Ipswich	11	14	17	20	25	33	33	38	38	43	43	51
King's Lynn	10	10	12	13	16	19	19	16	16	17	17	19
Leeds	53	63	84	123	152	172	172	207	207	259	259	309
Leicester	17	19	26	41	53	61	61	68	68	95	95	122
Liverpool	82	104	138	202	286	376	376	444	444	493	493	553
environs of Liverpool later incorporated (e)				8	13	19	19	28	28	47	47	74
Luton	...	...	3	4	6	11	11	15	15	17	...	24
Macclesfield	11	15	21	30	33	39	39	36	36	35	35	38
Manchester	75	89	126	182	235	303	303	339	339	351	351	341
environs of Manchester later incorporated (f)		7	9	12	17	26	26	43	43	57	57	95
environs of Manchester later incorporated (g)						9	9	17	17	36	36	66

See p. 27 for footnotes

Population and Vital Statistics 8. *continued*

(in thousands)

	1881	1891	1891	1901	1901	1911	1911	1921	1921	1931	1931	1951
Aberdeen	106	125	125	154	154	164	164	159	159	167	170	183
Bath	52	52	52	50	50	51	69	69	69	69	69 (b)	79
Belfast (figures for 1926 and 1937 instead of 1921 and 1931)	208	256	273	349	349	387	387	415	415	438	438	444
Birkenhead	84	100	100	111	111	131	131	146	148	148	152	143
Birmingham	437	478	478	522	523	526	840	919	922	1,003	1,003	1,113
environs of Birmingham later incorporated (c)	...	156	156	238	238	314						
Blackburn	104	120	120	128	129	133	133	127	127	123	123	111
Blackpool	14	24	24	47	47	58	61	100	100	102	106	147
Bolton	105	115	156	168	168	181	181	179	179	177	177	167
Bournemouth	19	38	38	47	47	79	79	92	96	117	117	145
Bradford	194	216	266	280	280	288	288	286	291	298	299	292
Brighton	108	116	116	123	123	131	131	142	147	147	147	156
Bristol	207	222	289	329	339	357	357	377	377	397	404 (b)	443
Cambridge	35	37	37	38	38	40	56	59	59	67	70	82
Cardiff	83	129	129	164	164	182	182	200	220	224	227 (b)	244
Carlisle	37	39	39	45	45	46	52	53	53	57	57	68
Chester	37	37	37	38	38	39	39	41	41	41	46	48
Colchester	28	35	35	38	38	43	43	43	43	49	49	57
Coventry	45	53	59	70	70	106	106	128	148	167	178	258
Derby	81	94	94	106	115	123	123	130	131	142	143	141
Dudley	46	46	46	49	49	51	51	56	56	60	60	63
Dundee	140	154	154	161	161	165	176	168	168	176	177	177
Edinburgh (including Leith)	295	332	342	394	395	401	424	420	420	439	439	467
Exeter	37	37	46	47	47	49	59	60	60	66	68	76
Gateshead	66	86	86	110	112	117	117	125	125	125	125	115
Glasgow	587	658	658	762	776	784	1,000	1,034	1,052	1,088	1,093	1,090
environs of Glasgow later incorporated (d)	86	108	108	142	142	169						
Greenock	67	63	63	68	68	75	75	81	81	79	79	76
Halifax	81	90	98	105	105	102	102	99	99	98	98	98
Huddersfield	87	95	95	95	95	108	108	110	110	113	123	129
Hull	166	200	200	240	240	278	278	287	291	314	314	299
Ipswich	51	57	57	67	67	74	74	79	79	88	88	105
King's Lynn	19	18	18	20	20	20	20	20	20	21	24	26
Leeds	309	368	368	429	429	446	453	458	463	483	483	505
Leicester	137	175	175	212	212	227	227	234	234	239	258	285
Liverpool	553	518	630	685	704	746	753	803	805	856	856	789
environs of Liverpool later incorporated (e)	74	113										
Luton	24	30	30	36	36	50	50	57	60	69	70	110
Macclesfield	38	36	36	35	'35	35	35	34	34	35	36	36
Manchester	462	505	505	544	645	714	714	730	736	766	766	703
environs of Manchester later incorporated (f)												
environs of Manchester later incorporated (g)	...	70	70	101								

See p. 27 for footnotes

(in thousands)

	1801	1811	1821	1831	1841	1851	1851	1861	1861	1871	1871	1881
Middlesbrough	φφ	φφ	φφ	φφ	6	8	8	19	19	40	40 (a)	55
Newcastle-upon-Tyne	33	33	42	54	70	88	88	109	109	128	128	145
Newport (Mon.)	...	...	...	...	10	19	19	23	23	27	27	35
Northampton	7	8	11	15	21	27	27	33	33	41	41	52
Norwich	36	37	50	61	62	68	68	75	75	80	80	88
Nottingham	29	34	40	50	52	57	57	75	75	87	139 (a)	187
Oldham	12	17	22	32	43	53	53	72	72	83	83	111
Oxford	12	13	16	21	24	28	28	28	28	31	31	35
Paisley	25	29	38	46	48	48	48	47	47	48	48	56
Plymouth (including Devonport)	40	51	55	66	70	90	90	113	113	118	118	123
Portsmouth	33	42	47	50	53	72	72	95	95	114	114	128
Preston	12	17	25	34	51	70	70	83	83	85	88 (a)	97
Reading	10	11	13	16	19	21	21	25	25	32	32	42
St. Helens	...	...	...	...	...	15	15	18	32	45	45	57
Salford	14	19	26	41	53	64	85	102	102	125	125	176
Sheffield	46	53	65	92	111	135	135	185	185	240	240	285
Shrewsbury	15	17	20	21	18	20	20	22	22	23	23	26
Southampton	8	10	13	19	28	35	35	47	47	54	54	60
Southend-on-Sea	...	...	...	...	...	...	...	3	3	5	5	8
South Shields	11	15	17	19	23	29	29	35	35	45	45	57
Stockport	17	21	27	36	50	54	54	55	55	53	53	60
Stoke-upon-Trent (h)	...	28	35	35	54	66	66	78	78	101	101	113
Sunderland	24	25	31	39	43	65	64	78	80	98	98	117
Swansea	10	12	15	20	25	31	31	42	41	52	52	66
Tynemouth	13	18	23	23	25	29	29	34	34	39	39	44
Wakefield	11	11	14	16	19	22	23	23	23	28	28	31
Wallasey	1	1	1	3	6	8	8	11	11	15	15	21
Walsall	10	11	12	15	20	26	26	38	38	46	51	59
Warrington	11	13	15	18	21	23	23	26	26	32	32	41
Wigan	11	14	18	21	26	32	32	38	38	39	39	48
Wolverhampton	13	15	18	25	36	50	50	61	61	68	68	76
Worcester	11	14	17	19	27	28	28	31	31	33	33	34
Yarmouth	17	20	21	25	28	31	31	35	35	42	42	46
York	17	19	22	26	29	36	36	40	40	44	44	50

See p. 27 for footnotes

(in thousands)

	1881	1891	1891	1901	1901	1911	1911	1921	1921	1931	1931	1951
Middlesbrough	55	76	76	91	91	105	120	131	131	138	139	147
Newcastle-upon-Tyne	145	186	186	215	247	267	267	275	275	283	286	292
Newport (Mon.)	38	55	55	67	67	84	84	92	92	89	98	106
Northampton	52	61	75	87	87	90	90	91	91	92	97	104
Norwich	88	101	101	112	114	121	121	121	121	126	...	121
Nottingham	187	214	214	240	240	260	260	263	263	269	276	306
Oldham	111	131	131	137	137	147	147	145	145	140	...	121
Oxford	41	46	46	49	49	53	53	57	67	81	81	99
Paisley	56	66	66	79	79	84	84	85	85	86	88	94
Plymouth (including Devonport)	123	139	145	178	178	194	207	210	210	208	202 (b)	208
Portsmouth	128	159	159	188	189	231	234	247	247	249	252	234
Preston	97	108	108	113	113	117	117	117	117	119	120	119
Reading	49	60	60	72	81	88	88	92	92	97	97	114
St. Helens	57	71	72	84	84	97	97	103	103	107	107	110
Salford	176	198	198	221	221	231	231	234	234	223	223	178
Sheffield	285	324	324	381	409	455	465	491	512	512	518	513
Shrewsbury	26	27	27	28	28	29	29	31	31	32	37	45
Southampton	60	65	82	105	105	119	145	161	161	176	176	178
Southend-on-Sea	8	12	13	29	29	63	72	106	106	120	130	152
South Shields	57	78	78	97	101	109	109	117	119	113	113 (b)	107
Stockport	60	70	70	79	93	109	120	123	123	125	126	142
Stoke-upon-Trent (h)	125	145	193	215	215	235	235	240	268	277	277	275
Sunderland	117	131	132	146	146	151	151	159	182	186	186 (b)	182
Swansea	76	91	91	95	95	115	144	158	158	165	165	161
Tynemouth	44	47	47	51	51	59	59	64	64	65	66	67
Wakefield	31	33	39	41	48	52	52	53	53	59	59 (b)	60
Wallasey	21	33	33	54	54	79	79	91	95	98	98	101
Walsall	59	72	72	86	86	92	92	97	98	103	103	115
Warrington	43	53	55	64	64	72	72	77	77	79	82	81
Wigan	48	55	55	61	82	89	89	89	89	85	85	85
Wolverhampton	76	83	83	94	94	95	95	102	121	133	139	163
Worcester	40	43	43	47	47	48	49	49	49	51	52	60
Yarmouth	47	49	49	51	51	56	56	61	61	57	57	51
York	62	67	68	78	78	82	82	84	84	85	94	105

(*a*) These figures are approximate, but are generally accurate to within 0·5 per cent.

(*b*) In the second column for 1931 it was not always possible to take account of boundary changes between 1931 and 1951 because of the destruction of records during the war. Incomplete figures are indicated by this footnote, and seriously defective ones have been omitted.

(*c*) The parishes or townships of Aston, Handsworth, King's Norton, Northfield, and Yardley (except such parts as were already incorporated in Birmingham)—i.e. an area which at the end of the nineteenth century comprised Aston Manor county borough, Erdington, Handsworth, King's Norton, and Northfield urban districts, and Yardley rural district. A part of the area was incorporated in Birmingham between 1881 and 1891, and the remainder between 1911 and 1921.

(*d*) The town of Pollokshaws and the parish of Govan—i.e. the area which at the end of the nineteenth century comprised the burghs of Govan, Partick, and Pollokshaws, and was incorporated in Glasgow between 1911 and 1921. Other areas,

namely Crosshill, Govanhill, Maryhill, Hillhead, and Pollokshields, which were incorporated in Glasgow between 1881 and 1891, were previously classed as suburbs, and are here included with the city throughout.

(*e*) The parishes of West Derby, Toxteth Park, Walton-on-the-Hill, and Wavertree (except such parts as were already incorporated in Liverpool). The whole of this area was incorporated in the city between 1891 and 1901.

(*f*) The parishes of Blackley, Harpurhey, Crumpsall, Bradford, Moston, Newton, Openshaw, and Rusholme, all of which were incorporated in Manchester between 1881 and 1891.

(*g*) The parishes of Moss Side, Gorton, Levenshulme, and Withington (except such parts as were already incorporated in Manchester). A part of this area was incorporated in the city between 1881 and 1891 and the remainder between 1901 and 1911.

(*h*) The townships of Hanley, Longton, Stoke, and Burslem for the period 1811–91. Thereafter the urban districts of Fenton and Tunstall are included.

NOTES

[1] SOURCE: The *Parish Register Abstracts* of the censuses of 1811, 1821, 1831, and 1841.

[2] The figures for 1700–1800 are as printed in the census for 1811, where an adjustment had been made to the figures printed in the census for 1801 by adding to the latter a proportion based on the baptisms, burials, and marriages between 1801 and 1811 in those parishes for which returns were missing in 1801.

(in thousands)

	Baptisms	Burials	Marriages		Baptisms	Burials	Marriages
1700	157	137	...	1792	269	189	75
				1793	264	204	73
1710	144	145	...	1794	257	198	72
				1795	255	210	69
1720	160	166	...	1796	257	191	73
1730	167	183	...	1797	268	191	75
				1798	271	188	79
1740	174	173	...	1799	267	190	78
				1800	255	208	70
1750	186	160	...	1801	237	204	67
1755	...	...	49	1802	274	200	90
1756	...	...	51	1803	294	204	94
1757	...	...	48	1804	295	181	86
1758	...	...	51	1805	292	181	80
1759	...	...	56	1806	292	183	81
1760	193	161	58	1807	300	196	84
1761	...	...	58	1808	296	201	82
1762	...	...	57	1809	300	191	83
1763	...	...	62	1810	299	208	84
1764	...	...	63	1811	305	189	86
1765	...	...	59	1812	302	190	82
1766	...	...	57	1813	314	186	84
1767	...	...	55	1814	319	206	93
1768	...	...	58	1815	345	197	100
1769	...	...	62	1816	330	206	92
1770	213	180	63	1817	332	199	88
1771	...	...	61	1818	331	214	93
1772	...	...	60	1819	333	214	96
1773	...	...	60	1820	344	208	97
1774	...	...	61	1821	355	212	101
1775	...	...	62	1822	373	220	99
1776	...	...	65	1823	370	237	102
1777	...	...	65	1824	371	244	105
1778	...	...	63	1825	375	255	110
1779	...	...	64	1826	380	268	105
1780	228	198	64	1827	374	252	107
1781	231	196	64	1828	392	255	111
1782	225	187	63	1829	380	264	104
1783	221	188	66	1830	382	254	108
1784	230	194	69	1831	389	279	112
1785	245	192	72	1832	388	298	117
1786	243	185	69	1833	400	291	120
1787	245	185	76	1834	406	283	122
1788	251	188	70	1835	405	282	120
1789	251	186	71	1836	405	282	121
				1837	463	337	113
				1838	377	293	113
1790	257	185	71	1839	368	287	117
1791	256	187	73	1840	364	304	116

Population and Vital Statistics 10. Births and Birth Rates—England & Wales 1838–1938, Scotland 1855–1938, Ireland 1864–1921, and Northern Ireland 1922–38

NOTES

[1] SOURCES: *Annual Report of the Registrar General for England & Wales, for Scotland, for Ireland,* and *for Northern Ireland.* (In recent years the volume for England & Wales has been called *The Registrar General's Statistical Review of England and Wales.*)

[2] In each of the kingdoms, the first year shown is a serious understatement, owing to deficiencies in registration. In no case was registration virtually complete until well into the 1860's.

A. England & Wales, 1838–1938

| | Numbers of Births in thousands | | | | Births | |
	Males	Females	Total	Legitimate	per 1,000 Population	per 1,000 Women Aged 15–44
1838	...	...	464	...	30·3	...
1839	252	240	493	...	31·8	...
1840	257	245	502	...	32·0	...
1841	263	249	512	...	32·2	134
1842	265	253	518	483	32·1	134
1843	271	257	527	...	32·3	135
1844	277	263	541	...	32·7	137
1845	278	265	544	505	32·5	137
1846	293	279	573	534	33·8	142
1847	276	264	540	504	31·5	133
1848	288	275	563	526	32·5	137
1849	295	283	578	539	32·9	139
1850	303	291	593	553	33·4	141
1851	315	301	616	574	34·3	145
1852	319	305	624	582	34·3	145
1853	314	299	612	573	33·3	141
1854	324	310	634	594	34·1	145
1855	324	311	635	594	33·8	143
1856	336	322	657	615	34·5	147
1857	340	323	663	620	34·4	146
1858	335	320	655	612	33·7	143
1859	353	337	690	645	35·0	149
1860	350	334	684	640	34·3	146·5
1861	356	340	696	652	34·6	147·4
1862	364	349	713	667	35·0	149·4
1863	372	355	727	680	35·3	150·7
1864	378	363	740	693	35·4	151·7
1865	381	367	748	701	35·4	151·7
1866	385	369	754	708	35·2	151·4
1867	392	376	768	723	35·4	152·6
1868	400	386	787	741	35·8	154·8
1869	395	379	773	729	34·8	150·5
1870	404	388	793	748	35·2	152·9
1871	406	392	797	753	35·0	152·1
1872	421	405	826	781	35·6	155·4
1873	423	407	830	787	35·4	153·9
1874	435	419	855	812	36·0	156·5
1875	434	416	851	810	35·4	153·6
1876	452	436	888	846	36·3	156·7
1877	452	436	888	846	36·0	156·1
1878	455	437	892	850	35·6	154·8
1879	448	432	880	838	34·7	150·7
1880	449	433	882	839	34·2	149·1
1881	450	433	884	841	33·9	147·6
1882	453	436	889	846	33·8	146·2

	Numbers of Births in thousands				Births	
	Males	Females	Total	Legitimate	per 1,000 Population	per 1,000 Women Aged 15–44
1883	453	438	891	848	33·5	144·4
1884	463	444	907	864	33·6	144·9
1885	456	438	894	851	32·9	140·8
1886	460	443	904	861	32·8	140·4
1887	452	435	886	844	31·9	135·7
1888	447	433	880	839	31·2	132·9
1889	451	435	886	845	31·1	132·0
1890	442	428	870	832	30·2	127·9
1891	466	448	914	875	31·4	132·6
1892	457	441	898	860	30·4	128·2
1893	466	449	915	876	30·7	128·2
1894	453	437	890	852	29·6	121·2
1895	469	453	922	883	30·3	124·9
1896	466	450	915	877	29·6	121·9
1897	469	452	922	883	29·6	120·9
1898	469	454	923	885	29·3	119·1
1899	473	455	929	892	29·1	118·0
1900	471	455	927	890	28·7	115·9
1901	474	456	930	894	28·5	114·5
1902	479	461	941	904	28·5	114·6
1903	482	466	948	911	28·5	114·3
1904	481	464	945	908	28·0	112·7
1905	472	456	929	892	27·3	109·7
1906	477	458	935	898	27·2	109·2
1907	468	450	918	882	26·5	106·2
1908	478	462	940	903	26·7	107·6
1909	466	448	914	877	25·8	103·6
1910	457	440	897	860	25·1	100·7
1911	449	432	881	844	24·3	98·0
1912	445	428	873	835	23·9	96·6
1913	449	433	882	844	24·1	97·1
1914	447	432	879	842	23·8	96·2
1915	415	399	815	778	21·9	88·8
1916	402	383	786	748	20·9	85·2
1917	341	327	668	631	17·8	72·1
1918	339	324	663	621	17·7	71·1
1919	356	336	692	651	18·5	73·9
1920	471	467	958	943	25·5	101·7
1921	435	414	849	810	22·4	89·7
1922	399	381	780	746	20·4	82·1
1923	387	371	758	727	19·7	79·4
1924	373	357	730	700	18·8	75·8
1925	363	347	711	682	18·3	73·5
1926	354	340	695	665	17·8	71·9
1927	334	320	654	625	16·6	67·5
1928	337	323	660	631	16·7	67·9
1929	329	315	644	614	16·3	65·8
1930	331	317	649	619	16·3	66·2
1931	324	309	632	604	15·8	64·4
1932	314	300	614	587	15·3	62·6
1933	297	284	580	555	14·4	59·4
1934	307	291	598	572	14·8	61·5
1935	308	291	599	574	14·7	61·0
1936	311	295	605	580	14·8	61·2
1937	314	297	611	585	14·9	61·4
1938	318	303	621	595	15·1	62·4

	Numbers of Births in thousands				Births	
	Males	Females	Total	Legitimate	per 1,000 Population	per 1,000 Women Aged 15–44
B. Scotland, 1855–1938						
1855	47·8	49·6	93·3	86·0	31·3	129·6
1856	52·2	45·5	101·8	93·1	34·0	140·8
1857	53·2	50·3	103·4	94·2	34·3	142·5
1858	53·7	50·3	104·0	94·7	34·4	142·8
1859	54·6	51·9	106·5	96·8	35·0	145·6
1860	54·4	51·2	105·6	95·9	35·6	143·8
1861	54·6	52·4	107·0	97·1	34·9	145·2
1862	55·3	51·8	107·1	96·7	34·6	144·4
1863	56·2	53·1	109·3	98·4	35·0	146·5
1864	57·4	55·0	112·3	101·1	35·6	149·6
1865	58·2	54·9	113·1	101·8	35·5	149·8
1866	58·4	55·3	113·7	102·0	35·4	149·7
1867	58·5	55·5	114·0	102·9	35·1	149·3
1868	59·2	56·3	115·5	104·2	35·3	150·3
1869	58·3	55·0	113·4	102·3	34·3	146·8
1870	59·0	56·4	115·4	104·4	34·6	149·8
1871	60·0	56·1	116·1	105·1	34·5	148·6
1872	61·3	57·5	118·8	107·8	34·9	150·5
1873	61·5	58·2	119·7	108·8	34·8	150·1
1874	63·6	60·1	123·7	113·7	35·6	153·5
1875	63·4	60·1	123·6	112·8	35·2	151·9
1876	64·8	61·7	126·5	115·5	35·6	153·9
1877	65·1	61·7	126·8	116·3	35·3	152·8
1878	65·2	61·6	126·8	116·1	34·9	151·3
1879	64·3	61·4	125·7	115·0	34·3	148·5
1880	63·8	60·8	124·6	114·0	33·6	145·9
1881	64·7	61·5	126·2	115·7	33·7	146·4
1882	64·5	61·7	126·2	115·6	33·5	145·2
1883	63·9	60·6	124·5	114·3	32·8	141·9
1884	66·4	62·8	129·2	118·7	33·7	146·1
1885	64·5	61·6	126·1	115·4	32·7	141·3
1886	65·9	62·0	127·9	117·4	32·9	142·2
1887	63·8	60·6	124·4	114·0	31·8	137·1
1888	63·1	60·1	123·3	113·3	31·3	134·8
1889	63·3	59·5	122·8	113·0	30·9	133·1
1890	62·2	59·3	121·5	112·3	30·4	130·7
1891	64·8	61·2	126·0	116·3	31·2	134·4
1892	64·4	60·7	125·0	115·8	30·7	131·3
1893	65·0	62·1	127·1	117·6	30·8	131·5
1894	63·9	60·5	124·4	115·3	29·9	126·6
1895	64·8	61·7	126·5	117·3	30·0	127·1
1896	66·2	63·0	129·2	119·8	30·4	127·9
1897	65·8	63·1	128·9	119·8	30·0	125·8
1898	66·8	64·0	130·9	122·0	30·1	126·0
1899	66·8	64·0	130·7	122·2	29·8	124·1
1900	67·1	64·3	131·4	122·9	29·6	123·0
1901	67·8	64·4	132·2	123·7	29·5	122·1
1902	67·4	64·8	132·3	124·0	29·3	120·6
1903	68·1	65·4	133·5	125·2	29·4	120·6
1904	67·8	64·8	132·6	123·6	29·1	118·6
1905	66·8	64·7	131·4	122·3	28·6	116·4
1906	67·5	64·5	132·0	122·7	28·6	115·8
1907	65·9	62·9	128·8	120·0	27·7	111·9
1908	66·8	64·5	131·4	122·3	28·1	113·0
1909	65·7	62·9	128·7	119·3	27·3	112·7
1910	63·1	60·9	124·1	115·0	26·2	108·0
1911	62·3	59·6	121·9	112·7	25·6	106·6
1912	62·9	59·9	122·8	113·8	25·9	107·6
1913	61·5	59·1	120·5	112·0	25·5	105·9
1914	63·0	61·0	123·9	115·1	26·1	108·5

	Numbers of Births in thousands				Births	
	Males	Females	Total	Legitimate	per 1,000 Population	per 1,000 Women Aged 15–44
1915	58·4	55·8	114·2	106·3	23·9	99·1
1916	56·5	53·5	109·9	102·1	22·8	94·7
1917	50·0	47·4	97·4	90·1	20·1	83·4
1918	50·4	48·2	98·6	90·7	20·2	83·8
1919	54·8	51·5	106·3	98·8	21·7	90·2
1920	69·7	66·8	136·5	126·3	28·1	115·3
1921	63·1	60·1	123·2	114·4	25·2	103·7
1922	58·8	56·3	115·1	107·2	23·5	96·7
1923	57·3	54·6	111·9	104·4	22·9	94·4
1924	54·9	52·0	106·9	99·8	22·0	90·8
1925	53·4	50·7	104·1	97·3	21·4	88·5
1926	52·4	50·1	102·4	95·4	21·1	87·6
1927	49·3	47·4	96·7	89·7	19·9	83·1
1928	49·6	47·2	96·8	89·7	20·0	83·4
1929	47·8	45·1	92·9	85·7	19·2	80·0
1930	48·1	46·5	94·5	87·6	19·6	81·6
1931	47·0	45·2	92·2	85·6	19·0	79·8
1932	46·6	44·4	91·0	84·5	18·6	78·4
1933	44·8	41·8	86·5	80·6	17·6	74·5
1934	45·4	43·4	88·8	82·7	18·0	76·5
1935	45·0	43·0	87·9	82·2	17·8	74·9
1936	45·3	43·6	88·9	83·2	17·9	75·1
1937	45·0	42·8	87·8	82·4	17·6	73·7
1938	45·4	43·2	88·6	83·2	17·7	74·0

C. Ireland, 1864–1921

	Males	Females	Total	Legitimate	per 1,000 Population	per 1,000 Women Aged 15–44
1864	70·1	66·3	136·4	131·2	24·2	103·6
1865	74·4	70·6	145·0	139·6	25·9	111·7
1866	75·1	71·0	146·1	141·2	26·5	114·1
1867	74·3	70·1	144·4	139·7	26·3	114·4
1868	75·2	70·9	146·1	141·5	26·7	117·4
1869	74·9	70·7	145·7	141·5	26·7	118·8
1870	76·9	73·1	149·8	145·8	27·7	124·0
1871	77·3	74·0	151·4	147·2	28·1	127·2
1872	76·9	72·4	149·3	145·5	27·8	125·8
1873	74·2	70·1	144·4	140·9	27·1	121·9
1874	72·5	68·8	141·3	138·0	26·6	119·5
1875	71·1	67·2	138·3	135·2	26·1	117·2
1876	72·2	68·3	140·5	137·2	26·4	119·4
1877	71·7	68·0	139·7	136·3	26·2	118·9
1878	68·5	65·6	134·1	131·0	25·1	114·4
1879	69·9	65·5	135·3	132·0	25·2	115·7
1880	66·0	62·1	128·1	124·9	24·7	109·8
1881	64·8	61·1	125·8	122·6	24·5	108·1
1882	63·0	59·6	122·6	119·4	24·0	106·2
1883	60·7	57·5	118·2	115·1	23·5	103·3
1884	61·2	57·7	118·9	115·7	23·9	104·8
1885	59·4	56·5	116·0	112·7	23·5	103·1
1886	58·9	55·0	113·9	110·9	23·2	102·1
1887	57·8	54·6	112·4	109·2	23·1	101·6
1888	56·2	53·4	109·6	106·4	22·8	100·0
1889	55·2	52·7	107·8	104·8	22·7	99·2
1890	54·3	51·0	105·3	102·4	22·3	97·8
1891	55·5	52·6	108·1	105·2	23·1	101·3
1892	53·6	50·7	104·2	101·6	22·5	97·8
1893	54·3	51·8	106·1	103·3	23·0	99·8
1894	53·9	51·4	105·4	102·5	22·9	99·2
1895	54·7	51·5	106·1	103·2	23·3	100·1
1896	55·3	52·3	107·6	104·8	23·7	101·7
1897	54·7	52·0	106·7	103·9	23·5	101·0
1898	54·3	51·2	105·5	102·6	23·3	100·3

	Numbers of Births in thousands				Births	
	Males	Females	Total	Legitimate	per 1,000 Population	per 1,000 Women Aged 15–44
1899	53·4	50·5	103·9	101·2	23·1	98·7
1900	52·2	49·2	101·5	98·8	22·7	96·6
1901	52·0	49·0	101·0	98·4	22·7	96·2
1902	52·6	49·3	101·9	99·2	23·0	97·7
1903	52·2	49·7	101·8	99·2	23·1	98·3
1904	53·2	50·7	103·8	101·2	23·6	100·9
1905	52·5	50·3	102·8	100·1	23·4	100·6
1906	53·4	50·2	103·5	100·8	23·5	102·0
1907	52·2	49·6	101·7	99·2	23·2	100·9
1908	52·4	49·6	102·0	99·4	23·3	101·9
1909	52·7	50·0	102·8	100·0	23·4	103·4
1910	52·1	49·9	102·0	99·1	23·3	103·3
1911	52·4	49·3	101·8	99·0	23·2	103·8
1912	51·7	49·3	101·0	98·2	23·0	103·5
1913	51·2	48·9	100·1	97·3	22·8	102·9
1914	50·7	48·1	98·8	95·9	22·6	102·0
1915	49·3	46·3	95·6	92·6	22·0	99·1
1916	47·2	44·3	91·4	88·7	20·9	95·2
1917	44·3	42·1	86·4	83·7	19·7	90·3
1918	44·7	42·7	87·3	84·6	19·8	91·6
1919	51·2	48·9	89·3	97·3	20·0	94·1
1920	51·3	48·3	99·5	96·2	22·8	105·3
1921	46·5	44·2	90·7	87·7	20·8	96·4

D. Northern Ireland, 1922–38

1922	15·1	14·4	29·5	28·3	23·3	100·1
1923	15·3	14·8	30·1	28·8	23·9	102·2
1924	14·8	13·7	28·5	27·3	22·7	96·9
1925	14·2	13·5	27·7	26·5	22·0	94·2
1926	14·6	13·6	28·2	26·9	22·5	96·1
1927	13·7	13·0	26·7	25·4	21·3	90·7
1928	13·4	12·5	26·0	24·8	20·8	88·2
1929	13·0	12·4	25·4	24·2	20·4	85·9
1930	13·2	12·7	25·9	24·6	20·8	87·5
1931	13·2	12·5	25·7	24·4	20·5	86·7
1932	12·9	12·2	25·1	23·8	19·9	84·5
1933	12·6	12·0	24·6	23·4	19·6	84·0
1934	13·2	12·2	25·4	24·1	20·1	86·1
1935	12·8	12·0	24·7	23·5	19·5	83·2
1936	13·3	12·6	25·9	24·7	20·3	86·3
1937	13·0	12·4	25·4	24·2	19·8	85·2
1938	13·2	12·5	25·7	24·6	20·0	85·2

Population and Vital Statistics 11. Deaths—England & Wales 1838–1938, Scotland 1855–1938, Ireland 1864–1921, and Northern Ireland 1922–38

NOTES

[1] SOURCE: *Annual Report of the Registrar General* for the various regions in each year.

[2] In each kingdom, the first year shown is a serious understatement, owing to deficiencies in registration. In no case was registration virtually complete until well into the 1860's.

(in thousands)

	England & Wales		Scotland		Ireland	
	Males	Females	Males	Females	Males	Females
1838	175	168	...	...	...	...
1839	173	166	...	...	...	...
1840	182	177	...	...	...	...
1841	174	170	...	...	...	...
1842	177	173	...	...	...	...
1843	176	171	...	...	...	...
1844	181	176	...	...	...	...
1845	178	172	...	...	...	...
1846	198	192	...	...	...	...
1847	212	207	...	...	...	...
1848	202	196	...	...	...	...
1849	222	219	...	...	...	...
1850	186	183	...	...	...	...
1851	201	195	...	...	...	...
1852	207	200	...	...	...	...
1853	215	206	...	...	...	...
1854	222	215	...	...	...	...
1855	217	209	30·6	31·4	...	...
1856	199	192	29·4	29·1	...	...
1857	212	207	30·9	31·0	...	...
1858	227	222	31·7	31·9	...	...
1859	224	217	30·6	31·1	...	...
1860	215	207	33·6	34·6	...	...
1861	222	213	30·9	31·5	...	...
1862	223	214	33·2	34·0	...	...
1863	242	232	35·6	35·9	...	...
1864	254	242	37·0	37·4	46·3	46·8
1865	252	239	35·2	35·7	46·2	46·9
1866	256	244	35·4	36·0	46·1	46·9
1867	243	228	34·4	34·7	46·9	46·6
1868	247	234	34·7	34·8	43·4	42·8
1869	255	240	37·9	38·0	45·0	44·6
1870	266	250	36·9	37·3	45·5	45·0
1871	266	249	36·8	37·9	44·2	44·1
1872	255	237	37·9	37·4	49·0	48·3
1873	255	238	39·0	37·9	49·0	48·6
1874	272	254	40·7	40·0	46·5	45·5
1875	282	264	40·3	41·4	48·9	49·2
1876	265	245	37·4	36·7	46·1	46·2
1877	261	240	37·2	36·8	47·2	46·4
1878	279	261	38·4	38·4	50·1	49·5
1879	271	255	36·3	37·1	52·3	52·8
1880	273	255	38·1	37·1	51·6	51·3
1881	254	238	36·1	36·2	45·1	45·0
1882	266	251	36·3	36·7	43·6	44·9
1883	269	254	38·3	38·6	47·6	48·7
1884	274	257	37·6	37·6	43·4	43·8
1885	268	254	36·9	37·7	45·1	45·6
1886	276	261	36·4	37·2	43·5	43·8
1887	272	259	36·8	37·7	43·9	44·7
1888	263	248	35·0	36·2	42·5	43·4
1889	266	252	36·3	36·9	41·1	41·8
1890	290	272	39·1	39·9	42·1	43·7
1891	302	285	41·1	42·5	42·1	43·9
1892	286	274	37·5	38·1	44·0	46·0

34

(in thousands)

	England & Wales		Scotland		Ireland	
	Males	Females	Males	Females	Males	Females
1893	292	278	39·6	40·1	40·8	42·0
1894	256	243	35·2	36·0	41·4	42·2
1895	291	278	40·7	41·2	41·8	42·6
1896	271	256	35·3	35·4	37·4	38·3
1897	280	261	39·5	39·6	41·6	42·3
1898	284	268	39·3	39·1	40·7	41·7
1899	299	282	39·9	39·7	39·7	40·0
1900	304	284	41·3	41·0	43·0	44·7
1901	286	266	40·2	39·9	39·3	39·8
1902	277	258	39·2	38·8	38·6	39·1
1903	266	248	38·1	37·9	38·3	39·1
1904	283	267	38·9	39·1	39·3	40·2
1905	268	252	37·2	37·3	37·3	37·8
1906	274	257	37·7	37·9	37·1	37·3
1907	269	255	38·2	39·1	38·6	38·7
1908	269	252	38·9	39·0	38·2	38·7
1909	265	253	37·1	37·5	37·1	37·9
1910	249	234	36·0	36·2	37·1	37·8
1911	273	255	35·8	35·9	36·2	36·3
1912	250	237	36·1	36·3	36·0	36·2
1913	262	243	36·5	36·6	37·5	37·2
1914	267	249	36·8	36·8	35·8	35·5
1915	292	270	41·1	40·5	38·1	38·0
1916	265	243	35·6	35·0	36·0	35·4
1917	262	237	35·4	34·1	36·3	36·4
1918	315	297	39·1	39·2	39·2	39·5
1919	258	246	37·5	37·6	39·0	39·6
1920	240	226	34·6	33·5	33·1	33·4
1921	234	224	33·1	33·1	63·8	

					Northern Ireland	
1922	247	240	36·2	36·7	9·5	10·3
1923	227	218	31·7	31·6	9·0	9·7
1924	241	233	35·2	35·2	9·8	10·5
1925	241	232	33·0	32·5	9·6	10·2
1926	232	222	32·0	31·8	9·2	9·7
1927	247	238	33·1	32·7	8·7	9·5
1928	236	225	32·6	32·7	8·7	9·3
1929	270	263	35·4	35·5	9·5	10·4
1930	234	221	32·4	31·8	8·4	8·8
1931	250	242	32·2	32·0	8·8	9·2
1932	246	238	32·7	33·3	8·7	9·1
1933	251	246	32·6	32·3	9·0	9·2
1934	243	234	32·1	31·6	8·7	8·8
1935	243	234	32·8	32·5	9·2	9·4
1936	253	242	33·9	32·9	9·0	9·4
1937	260	250	35·0	34·0	9·4	9·9
1938	247	232	31·8	31·1	8·7	8·9

Population and Vital Statistics 12. Crude Death Rates and Infant Mortality—England & Wales 1838–1938, Scotland 1855–1938, Ireland 1864–1921, and Northern Ireland 1922–38

NOTES

[1] SOURCES: *Annual Report of the Registrar General for England & Wales, for Scotland, for Ireland, and for Northern Ireland.* (In recent years the volume for England and Wales has been called *The Registrar General's Statistical Review of England and Wales*.)

[2] In each kingdom the first year shown is a serious understatement owing to deficiencies in registration. In no case was registration virtually complete until well into the 1860's, and infant mortality for Ireland as a whole may be understated right up to 1920.

	Deaths per 1,000 Persons			Deaths per 1,000 Males			Deaths per 1,000 Females			Deaths of Infants under one year per 1,000 Live Births		
	England & Wales	Scotland	Ireland	England & Wales	Scotland	Ireland	England & Wales	Scotland	Ireland	England & Wales	Scotland	Ireland
1838	22·4	...	...	23·4	...	...	21·5	...	...	...	...	...
1839	21·8	...	...	22·8	...	...	21·0	...	...	151	...	...
1840	22·9	...	...	23·7	...	...	22·0	...	...	154	...	...
1841	21·6	...	...	22·4	...	...	20·8	...	...	145	...	...
1842	21·7	...	...	22·4	...	...	21·0	...	...	152	...	...
1843	21·2	...	...	22·0	...	...	20·5	...	...	150	...	...
1844	21·6	...	...	22·4	...	...	20·8	...	...	148	...	...
1845	20·9	...	...	21·7	...	...	20·1	...	...	142	...	...
1846	23·0	...	...	23·9	...	...	22·2	...	...	164	...	...
1847	24·7	...	...	25·4	...	...	23·8	...	...	164	...	...
1848	23·0	...	...	23·9	...	...	22·2	...	...	153	...	...
1849	25·1	...	...	25·8	...	...	24·5	...	...	160	...	...
1850	20·8	...	...	21·4	...	...	20·1	...	...	162	...	...
1851	22·0	...	...	22·8	...	...	21·2	...	...	153	...	...
1852	22·4	...	...	23·2	...	...	21·6	...	...	158	...	...
1853	22·9	...	...	23·8	...	...	22·0	...	...	159	...	...
1854	23·5	...	...	24·4	...	...	22·7	...	...	157	...	...
1855	22·6	20·8	...	23·5	21·6	...	21·7	20·0	...	153	125	...
1856	20·5	19·5	...	21·4	20·7	...	19·7	18·5	...	143	118	...
1857	21·8	20·6	...	22·6	21·6	...	21·1	19·6	...	156	118	...
1858	23·1	21·0	...	23·9	22·0	...	22·3	20·1	...	151	121	...
1859	22·4	20·3	...	23·3	21·2	...	21·5	19·4	...	153	108	...
1860	21·2	22·3	...	22·1	23·2	...	20·3	21·5	...	148	127	...
1861	21·6	20·3	...	22·7	21·3	...	20·6	19·5	...	153	111	...
1862	21·4	21·7	...	22·4	22·6	...	20·5	20·9	...	142	117	...
1863	23·0	22·9	...	24·1	24·0	...	21·9	21·8	...	149	120	...
1864	23·7	23·6	16·5	24·9	24·7	16·8	22·5	22·6	16·3	153	126	98
1865	23·2	22·3	16·7	24·5	23·3	16·9	22·0	21·4	16·4	160	125	98
1866	23·4	22·2	16·8	24·6	23·1	17·1	22·2	21·3	16·6	160	122	94
1867	21·7	21·3	17·0	23·0	22·3	17·6	20·5	20·4	16·6	153	119	97
1868	21·8	21·2	15·8	23·1	22·2	16·3	20·7	20·3	15·3	155	118	95
1869	22·3	23·0	16·4	23·6	24·0	16·9	21·0	22·0	16·0	156	129	93
1870	22·9	22·2	16·7	24·2	23·2	17·2	21·6	21·4	16·2	160	123	95
1871	22·6	22·2	16·4	23·9	22·9	16·8	21·3	21·5	15·9	158	130	91
1872	21·3	22·3	18·1	22·6	23·3	18·8	19·9	21·0	17·5	150	124	97
1873	21·0	22·4	18·3	22·4	23·7	18·9	19·8	21·1	17·7	149	125	96
1874	22·2	23·2	17·3	23·6	24·4	18·1	20·9	22·1	16·6	151	125	94
1875	22·7	23·3	18·5	24·1	23·9	19·0	21·4	22·6	18·0	158	132	95
1876	20·9	20·9	17·3	22·3	22·0	17·9	19·6	19·9	16·9	146	121	94
1877	20·3	20·6	17·5	21·7	21·6	18·2	18·9	19·7	16·9	136	115	92
1878	21·6	21·2	18·6	22·9	22·0	19·3	20·3	20·4	18·0	152	123	97
1879	20·7	20·0	19·6	22·0	20·6	20·1	19·6	19·5	19·1	135	108	101
1880	20·5	20·5	19·8	21·8	21·3	20·4	19·3	19·6	19·0	153	125	112
1881	18·9	19·3	17·5	20·0	20·0	17·9	17·8	18·7	17·1	130	113	91
1882	19·6	19·4	17·3	20·7	20·0	17·4	18·5	18·8	17·2	141	118	95
1883	19·6	20·2	19·2	20·8	20·9	19·4	18·5	19·6	19·0	137	119	98
1884	19·7	19·6	17·5	20·8	20·3	17·9	18·5	19·0	17·3	147	118	92
1885	19·2	19·3	18·4	20·3	19·8	18·7	18·2	18·9	18·2	138	121	95
1886	19·5	19·0	17·8	20·6	19·4	18·0	18·5	18·5	17·5	149	116	94
1887	19·1	19·0	18·2	20·2	19·4	18·4	18·1	18·6	18·0	145	122	95

See p. 37 for footnote

	Deaths per 1,000 Persons			Deaths per 1,000 Males			Deaths per 1,000 Females			Deaths of Infants under one year per 1,000 Live Births		
	England & Wales	Scot-land	Ire-land	England & Wales	Scot-land	Ire-land	England & Wales	Scot-land	Ire-land	England & Wales	Scot-land	Ire-land
1888	18·1	18·0	17·9	19·2	18·3	18·0	17·0	17·8	17·7	136	113	97
1889	18·2	18·4	17·4	19·3	18·9	17·6	17·2	18·0	17·2	144	121	94
1890	19·5	19·7	18·2	20·8	20·3	18·2	18·3	19·3	18·2	151	131	95
1891	20·2	20·7	18·4	21·5	21·1	18·2	19·0	20·3	18·5	149	128	95
1892	19·0	18·5	19·4	20·0	19·0	19·2	18·0	18·1	19·6	148	117	105
1893	19·2	19·3	18·0	20·3	19·9	17·9	18·1	18·8	18·0	159	136	102
1894	16·6	17·1	18·2	17·6	17·5	18·2	15·6	16·7	18·1	137	117	102
1895	18·7	19·4	18·5	19·7	20·0	18·4	17·7	19·0	18·5	161	133	104
1896	17·1	16·6	16·7	18·1	17·1	16·5	16·1	16·1	16·7	148	115	95
1897	17·4	18·4	18·5	18·6	19·0	18·4	16·2	17·9	18·5	156	138	109
1898	17·5	18·0	18·2	18·6	18·7	18·0	16·5	17·5	18·3	160	134	110
1899	18·2	18·1	17·7	19·4	18·7	17·6	17·2	17·6	17·6	163	131	108
1900	18·2	18·5	19·6	19·5	19·2	19·5	17·1	18·0	19·7	154	128	109
1901	16·9	17·9	17·8	18·1	18·5	17·9	15·8	17·3	17·7	151	129	101
1902	16·3	17·3	17·5	17·4	17·9	17·6	15·2	16·7	17·5	133	113	100
1903	15·5	16·8	17·5	16·5	17·3	17·5	14·4	16·2	17·5	132	118	96
1904	16·3	17·1	18·0	17·4	17·5	18·0	15·3	16·7	18·1	145	123	100
1905	15·3	16·2	17·1	16·3	16·7	17·1	14·4	15·8	17·1	128	116	95
1906	15·5	16·4	16·9	16·5	16·8	17·1	14·5	15·9	16·9	132	115	93
1907	15·1	16·6	17·6	16·0	16·9	17·8	14·2	16·3	17·6	118	110	92
1908	14·8	16·6	17·5	15·8	17·1	17·6	13·9	16·2	17·6	120	121	97
1909	14·6	15·8	17·1	15·5	16·2	17·1	13·8	15·5	17·2	109	108	92
1910	13·5	15·3	17·1	14·4	15·7	17·1	12·7	14·8	17·2	105	108	95
1911	14·6	15·1	16·5	15·6	15·6	16·6	13·7	14·7	16·5	130	112	94
1912	13·3	15·3	16·5	14·2	15·7	16·4	12·6	14·9	16·5	95	105	86
1913	13·8	15·5 ⎤	17·1	14·8	15·9	17·2	12·9	15·0	17·0	108	110	97
1914	14·0	15·5	16·3	15·0	16·0	16·4	13·1	15·1	16·2	105	111	87
1915	15·7 (a)	17·1	17·6	17·7 (a)	17·8	17·8	13·9	16·5	17·3	110	126	92
1916	14·3 (a)	14·7	16·3	16·7 (a)	15·4	16·8	12·4	14·1	16·1	91	97	83
1917	14·2 (a) ⎦	14·4 ⎦	16·6	17·1 (a)	15·2	17·0	12·1	13·7	16·6	96	107	88
1918	17·3 (a)	16·3	17·9	20·1 (a)	17·0	18·0	15·1	15·7	17·9	97	100	86
1919	14·0 (a)	15·6	17·6	15·7 (a)	16·2	17·3	12·5	15·0	17·9	89	102	88
1920	12·4 (a)	14·0	14·8	13·5 (a)	14·8	14·6	12·0	13·3	15·1	80	92	83
1921	12·1	13·6	14·2	12·4	14·1	...	10·9	13·1	...	83	90	...
			Northern Ireland			Northern Ireland			Northern Ireland			Northern Ireland
1922	12·7	14·9	15·4	13·5	15·4	15·1	12·0	14·4	15·7	77	101	77
1923	11·6	12·9	14·7	12·4	13·5	14·6	10·9	12·5	14·8	69	80	77
1924	12·2	14·5	15·9	13·0	15·1	15·8	11·5	13·9	16·0	75	98	85
1925	12·1	13·5	15·7	12·9	14·2	15·7	11·4	12·8	15·7	75	91	86
1926	11·6	13·1	15·0	12·4	13·7	15·1	10·9	12·6	14·9	70	83	85
1927	12·3	13·6	14·6	13·1	14·2	14·4	11·6	13·0	14·7	70	89	78
1928	11·7	13·5	14·4	12·5	14·0	14·4	10·9	13·0	14·4	65	86	78
1929	13·4	14·7	15·9	14·2	15·3	15·7	12·7	14·1	16·1	74	87	86
1930	11·4	13·3	13·8	12·3	14·0	14·0	10·7	12·7	13·6	60	83	68
1931	12·3	13·3	14·4	13·0	13·9	14·6	11·6	12·7	14·3	66	82	73
1932	12·0	13·5	14·1	12·7	13·9	14·2	11·4	13·1	14·1	64	86	83
1933	12·3	13·2	14·3	12·9	13·8	14·5	11·7	12·7	14·1	63	81	80
1934	11·8	12·9	13·9	12·5	13·5	14·2	11·1	12·4	13·5	59	78	70
1935	11·7	13·2	14·6	12·5	13·8	14·8	11·1	12·7	14·4	57	77	86
1936	12·1	13·4	14·4	12·9	14·2	14·5	11·4	12·8	14·4	59	82	77
1937	12·4	13·9	15·1	13·2	14·6	15·1	11·7	13·2	15·0	58	80	78
1938	11·6	12·6	13·7	12·5	13·2	14·0	10·8	12·0	13·5	53	70	75

(a) Based upon civilian deaths and estimated civilian population.

Population and Vital Statistics 13. Death Rates per 1,000 in Different Age-Groups—England & Wales 1838–1938

NOTES
SOURCE: *The Registrar General's Statistical Review of England & Wales.*

A. Males

	0–4	5–9	10–14	15–19	20–24	25–34	35–44	45–54	55–64	65–74	75–84	85 and over
1838	70·7	9·1	5·3	7·4	9·9	10·7	13·4	19·1	33·6	68·0	148·4	316·0
1839	71·8	9·1	5·1	7·2	9·4	9·9	12·6	17·7	31·6	63·4	139·1	291·2
1840	75·4	10·8	5·4	7·5	9·3	9·9	12·7	17·7	31·2	66·2	144·9	312·2
1841	68·4	9·6	5·1	7·2	9·2	9·8	12·2	17·7	31·3	64·5	142·6	303·0
1842	70·4	9·0	5·0	6·9	8·9	9·3	12·0	17·2	30·3	65·7	145·6	300·6
1843	68·8	8·4	4·8	6·7	8·9	9·2	12·2	17·0	30·0	65·5	140·7	293·5
1844	69·7	9·0	4·7	6·5	8·9	9·4	12·3	17·3	30·4	67·1	146·6	320·7
1845	66·5	8·2	4·6	6·6	9·1	9·2	12·1	17·0	29·6	64·7	143·7	308·4
1846	77·4	8·2	5·1	7·3	10·0	10·2	12·8	17·8	31·1	67·4	150·4	328·9
1847	76·0	9·7	5·5	8·0	10·8	11·0	14·5	20·5	36·5	77·1	173·6	364·6
1848	73·8	10·4	5·3	7·3	10·0	10·3	13·1	18·4	32·5	67·8	149·6	310·3
1849	75·0	11·2	6·5	8·0	11·1	12·4	15·9	22·4	36·4	72·4	151·7	304·7
1850	66·8	8·1	4·7	6·2	8·2	8·8	11·7	17·0	29·7	63·1	140·1	289·7
1851	72·9	8·7	4·9	6·8	8·8	9·5	12·4	17·7	30·2	64·1	140·6	288·6
1852	74·8	9·1	5·2	6·9	9·2	9·8	12·4	18·0	30·5	62·9	142·1	293·4
1853	73·0	8·5	5·1	7·2	9·6	10·3	13·2	19·3	32·4	69·1	159·8	328·3
1854	77·3	9·4	5·5	7·3	9·7	10·5	13·6	19·3	31·8	66·5	149·2	296·0
1855	71·5	8·2	5·0	6·7	8·9	9·8	12·8	18·6	32·8	70·7	162·9	349·2
1856	67·2	7·2	4·5	6·4	8·5	9·1	11·8	16·6	29·1	60·8	131·1	284·2
1857	72·2	7·8	4·7	6·4	8·4	9·2	12·0	17·3	29·9	63·3	143·9	306·1
1858	76·5	10·5	5·0	6·8	8·7	9·3	12·3	17·7	30·9	66·2	147·0	323·5
1859	74·7	9·2	4·8	6·4	8·4	9·2	12·3	17·8	30·8	64·2	140·2	298·9
1860	67·3	6·8	4·1	6·1	8·2	9·0	12·4	17·8	31·5	67·3	151·2	314·9
1861	71·8	6·7	4·3	6·4	8·3	9·2	12·3	17·6	30·9	65·4	146·5	315·7
1862	69·8	7·7	4·4	6·2	8·2	9·2	12·4	18·1	31·3	63·3	139·9	296·7
1863	77·8	10·3	5·0	6·4	8·5	9·4	12·8	18·2	31·7	63·9	139·4	309·7
1864	75·8	9·8	4·9	6·5	9·1	10·3	14·3	20·1	35·2	70·3	151·4	334·4
1865	75·0	8·1	4·7	6·4	9·2	10·6	14·2	20·5	34·7	68·6	151·8	325·6
1866	74·9	7·8	4·6	6·5	9·2	10·9	14·7	20·9	34·7	68·9	150·6	323·5
1867	69·3	6·5	4·0	6·0	8·4	10·0	13·6	19·1	33·5	68·3	152·5	332·4
1868	72·8	7·8	4·2	5·9	8·0	9·7	13·2	18·9	31·9	63·8	139·1	282·4
1869	72·5	8·3	4·3	5·7	7·9	9·9	13·5	19·3	33·3	68·4	149·1	308·9
1870	75·0	8·9	4·5	5·9	8·0	10·1	13·8	19·6	33·9	69·6	152·1	320·7
1871	71·7	8·3	4·4	6·4	9·2	11·1	14·4	20·0	33·9	67·5	145·2	312·8
1872	67·6	7·0	4·1	6·0	8·7	10·3	14·0	19·4	32·5	65·5	140·3	292·0
1873	66·4	6·0	3·7	5·3	7·5	9·5	13·6	19·8	34·1	70·9	150·6	324·9
1874	71·8	7·4	3·9	5·3	7·5	9·6	14·3	20·9	35·8	71·4	146·4	322·8
1875	71·9	6·9	3·8	5·6	7·6	9·7	15·0	21·5	37·7	74·7	165·0	363·8
1876	67·6	6·3	3·5	5·3	7·3	9·3	13·8	19·9	34·3	67·2	145·8	302·6
1877	63·9	6·1	3·5	4·9	7·0	9·1	13·7	19·7	34·7	68·2	145·8	324·9
1878	71·2	6·6	3·6	4·9	6·8	8·8	13·6	20·0	35·1	69·5	154·8	353·9
1879	63·3	6·3	3·3	4·7	6·4	8·6	13·3	20·4	36·8	74·0	168·7	365·5
1880	69·2	6·4	3·3	4·5	6·1	7·9	12·5	19·1	33·7	68·1	145·8	310·9
1881	56·6	5·8	3·2	4·5	6·1	8·3	13·0	19·3	34·0	67·7	144·8	293·5
1882	63·5	6·3	3·2	4·6	5·9	8·2	12·6	19·0	33·8	66·2	139·3	287·1
1883	61·0	6·2	3·3	4·7	6·2	8·3	13·0	19·7	35·1	70·1	149·1	302·2
1884	64·9	5·8	3·2	4·5	6·0	8·0	12·7	19·4	33·5	68·3	142·2	290·1
1885	60·6	5·1	2·9	4·3	5·8	8·0	12·6	19·3	34·4	71·3	151·5	316·2
1886	64·5	4·8	2·8	4·3	5·7	7·6	12·1	19·2	34·7	72·8	153·4	339·1
1887	62·5	5·1	2·9	4·2	5·4	7·3	11·9	18·7	35·0	72·1	149·4	310·1

See p. 41 for footnote

	0–4	5–9	10–14	15–19	20–24	25–34	35–44	45–54	55–64	65–74	75–84	85 and over
1888	57·7	4·7	2·7	4·0	5·4	7·1	11·7	19·0	34·4	71·6	144·5	304·7
1889	61·8	4·7	2·6	3·9	5·1	7·0	11·3	18·3	33·4	68·5	138·9	298·6
1890	62·9	5·0	2·8	4·3	5·7	8·0	13·2	21·7	38·6	75·3	153·3	316·5
1891	64·6	4·7	2·6	4·2	5·6	7·9	13·4	22·4	41·0	81·3	167·9	327·1
1892	62·4	4·7	2·6	4·0	5·2	7·1	12·1	19·8	36·6	75·7	154·6	305·4
1893	65·6	5·0	2·8	4·3	5·4	7·3	12·5	19·9	35·6	71·4	142·5	272·8
1894	56·1	4·2	2·3	3·8	5·0	6·5	10·8	17·3	31·4	62·8	127·6	243·6
1895	66·0	4·1	2·5	3·8	5·0	6·6	11·0	18·5	34·9	71·3	154·1	306·1
1896	61·2	4·5	2·3	3·5	4·8	6·2	10·6	17·3	31·6	63·0	128·6	251·9
1897	62·5	3·9	2·4	3·6	4·8	6·4	10·8	17·7	32·9	65·8	141·7	272·1
1898	63·4	3·8	2·2	3·5	4·8	6·3	10·7	17·6	33·2	66·4	140·3	282·6
1899	63·4	4·1	2·3	3·6	5·0	6·7	11·6	19·2	35·5	72·0	150·3	302·1
1900	61·6	4·2	2·3	3·7	5·1	6·7	11·7	19·9	37·1	74·2	153·7	304·3
1901	59·0	4·0	2·3	3·5	4·7	6·2	10·6	18·0	33·5	67·8	139·8	276·5
1902	54·1	3·9	2·2	3·3	4·6	6·2	10·4	17·8	33·3	66·7	138·5	270·0
1903	52·5	3·5	2·0	3·0	4·2	5·8	9·4	16·6	31·6	63·3	132·8	160·3
1904	57·4	3·6	2·1	3·1	4·3	5·7	9·4	16·5	32·3	65·5	139·7	287·6
1905	50·3	3·4	2·1	3·1	4·2	5·6	9·0	16·1	31·5	63·3	137·2	278·2
1906	51·2	3·5	2·0	3·2	4·1	5·5	9·1	16·1	32·4	64·3	137·3	298·5
1907	46·8	3·4	2·0	3·0	4·0	5·5	9·0	16·1	32·3	65·2	138·8	291·7
1908	46·9	3·3	2·0	2·9	4·0	5·3	8·6	15·4	31·4	64·3	138·4	277·2
1909	42·8	3·4	2·0	3·0	3·9	5·2	8·5	15·6	31·1	66·4	142·5	289·9
1910	39·7	3·0	1·9	2·7	3·7	4·7	7·9	14·5	29·4	61·8	131·6	259·7
1911	46·7	3·5	2·1	3·1	3·8	5·0	8·1	14·9	29·6	63·2	140·5	268·0
1912	35·8	3·1	1·8	2·9	3·6	4·8	7·9	14·6	29·4	63·9	137·1	266·7
1913	40·3	3·2	1·9	2·8	3·6	4·8	7·9	14·7	29·9	64·2	138·0	258·1
1914	39·4	3·4	2·1	3·1	3·9	5·1	8·3	14·9	30·0	64·7	135·3	269·5
1915 (a)	42·0	3·9	2·3	3·3	5·8	6·5	8·9	15·4	31·9	70·7	155·2	309·3
1916 (a)	32·4	3·3	2·2	3·4	6·8	7·2	8·6	14·4	29·5	67·9	150·3	296·3
1917 (a)	31·8	3·3	2·2	3·6	7·9	8·5	9·1	14·1	29·2	67·5	149·4	286·5
1918 (a)	38·9	5·5	3·5	6·2	13·8	19·6	12·6	16·4	29·3	65·7	132·1	234·4
1919 (a)	32·8	3·5	2·3	3·6	5·5	8·1	8·6	13·3	27·2	63·5	145·5	277·6
1920 (a)	36·2	3·3	1·9	2·9	3·9	4·7	7·0	12·0	24·5	56·0	124·6	235·2
1921	32·3	2·8	1·8	2·8	3·6	4·2	6·5	11·4	24·4	55·8	128·7	262·8
1922	30·2	2·6	1·7	2·7	3·7	4·4	6·9	12·0	26·0	61·2	143·9	271·3
1923	24·3	2·3	1·6	2·6	3·4	4·0	6·3	11·2	24·1	56·0	130·2	262·0
1924	25·1	2·5	1·7	2·6	3·3	3·9	6·3	11·6	24·5	59·6	140·2	290·0
1925	25·3	2·5	1·5	2·5	3·1	3·7	6·1	11·1	23·3	56·8	132·7	282·0
1926	23·3	2·5	1·5	2·5	3·2	3·6	6·1	11·0	23·6	55·9	131·1	284·3
1927	23·7	2·5	1·6	2·5	3·4	3·8	6·5	11·9	24·9	59·9	139·8	312·2
1928	21·9	2·4	1·7	2·6	3·2	3·6	6·0	11·2	23·6	56·5	128·0	290·9
1929	26·2	2·6	1·7	2·7	3·5	3·9	6·7	12·9	26·3	64·1	151·5	343·6
1930	20·4	2·4	1·6	2·6	3·2	3·5	5·7	11·2	23·4	55·2	126·6	263·5
1931	22·4	2·3	1·5	2·6	3·3	3·5	5·8	11·6	23·9	58·7	138·4	295·9
1932	21·0	2·2	1·5	2·5	3·2	3·3	5·3	10·8	23·4	57·9	138·0	289·7
1933	19·9	2·3	1·5	2·6	3·3	3·5	5·7	11·7	23·8	56·6	139·4	286·3
1934	19·3	2·5	1·5	2·4	3·1	3·2	5·1	10·9	23·4	55·4	129·3	256·4
1935	17·9	2·1	1·4	2·1	2·9	3·1	5·0	10·8	23·3	55·2	131·8	268·9
1936	19·1	2·1	1·3	2·1	2·9	2·9	4·9	10·8	24·2	56·3	137·3	291·8
1937	18·6	2·0	1·2	2·1	2·8	3·0	5·0	11·1	24·9	57·1	138·5	292·3
1938	17·1	1·9	1·3	2·0	2·7	2·8	4·6	10·2	23·1	53·7	130·1	263·6

See p. 41 for footnote

B. Females

	0–4	5–9	10–14	15–19	20–24	25–34	35–44	45–54	55–64	65–74	75–84	85 and over
1838	61·1	8·6	5·8	8·2	9·3	10·6	13·0	16·4	29·3	58·4	131·4	278·4
1839	61·7	9·0	5·7	8·2	9·0	10·1	12·4	15·4	27·0	55·0	124·2	263·4
1840	64·5	10·6	6·0	8·6	8·9	10·4	12·6	15·6	28·1	58·7	134·7	294·3
1841	58·6	9·2	5·4	8·0	8·8	10·1	12·3	15·4	27·3	58·3	133·5	291·3
1842	60·2	8·9	5·3	7·9	8·7	10·0	12·2	15·3	27·4	60·0	130·6	291·4
1843	59·0	8·2	5·0	7·3	8·4	9·7	12·3	14·9	26·9	58·6	130·2	286·0
1844	58·8	8·8	5·2	7·5	8·6	10·0	12·1	15·3	27·7	60·3	134·8	292·3
1845	56·5	7·8	4·9	7·6	8·6	9·8	12·0	14·7	26·6	58·4	130·2	282·9
1846	66·7	8·0	5·5	8·0	9·3	10·4	12·5	15·7	27·8	61·3	137·8	314·6
1847	65·7	9·4	5·9	8·4	9·9	11·7	14·4	18·1	32·3	69·6	159·9	333·0
1848	63·9	9·8	5·7	8·0	9·4	10·8	13·2	16·0	28·6	60·5	136·0	286·1
1849	64·8	10·9	6·6	9·0	10·9	13·4	16·4	20·2	33·6	65·7	140·3	285·3
1850	57·4	8·1	4·9	7·2	8·3	9·8	11·9	14·9	26·3	56·9	126·9	268·2
1851	63·0	8·6	5·3	7·5	8·8	9·9	12·1	15·4	26·8	58·3	128·3	273·6
1852	64·3	8·8	5·4	7·8	8·8	10·2	12·3	15·3	26·6	56·8	132·3	283·8
1853	63·2	8·1	5·4	8·1	9·0	10·6	12·6	16·0	28·3	60·8	141·8	303·2
1854	67·5	9·2	5·6	7·9	9·2	11·0	13·4	16·7	28·3	59·2	134·3	277·8
1855	61·3	8·0	4·9	7·5	8·7	10·0	12·6	15·6	29·1	63·3	149·3	322·4
1856	58·6	7·3	4·5	6·9	8·0	9·3	11·6	14·2	24·9	53·1	121·1	249·4
1857	63·5	7·7	4·6	7·1	8·4	9·5	11·8	14·8	26·7	58·5	132·6	290·5
1858	67·2	10·4	5·3	7·4	8·7	9·8	12·1	14·9	27·0	60·6	139·1	305·4
1859	65·0	9·4	5·2	7·2	8·3	9·8	12·0	15·2	26·3	57·6	130·1	282·9
1860	57·2	6·9	4·4	6·7	7·8	9·5	11·8	15·0	27·5	60·6	136·7	301·3
1861	62·0	6·8	4·4	7·0	8·1	9·5	11·4	14·7	26·9	57·3	131·2	274·6
1862	60·3	7·4	4·6	6·8	7·8	9·4	11·7	14·8	26·9	57·7	128·7	274·9
1863	67·5	9·9	5·2	6·8	8·1	9·7	12·0	14·9	27·1	56·7	129·1	290·2
1864	65·8	9·4	5·1	7·0	8·4	10·3	12·6	16·5	29·8	63·4	141·1	302·3
1865	65·1	7·8	4·6	6·8	8·5	10·2	12·6	16·6	28·8	60·4	138·4	296·7
1866	65·6	7·2	4·5	6·9	8·6	10·5	13·2	16·9	29·3	61·3	139·8	295·7
1867	59·6	6·1	3·9	6·4	7·8	9·5	12·0	15·6	27·5	59·5	139·4	287·3
1868	63·9	7·4	4·1	6·3	7·7	9·4	11·5	14·9	26·4	55·0	125·8	261·5
1869	63·0	7·8	4·3	6·1	7·3	9·3	11·7	15·7	27·6	59·2	135·4	277·1
1870	64·2	8·3	4·5	6·4	7·6	9·5	11·9	15·8	28·8	60·6	140·2	290·3
1871	62·4	7·5	4·5	6·6	8·2	9·7	12·2	15·9	28·5	60·4	133·6	276·4
1872	58·5	6·5	4·0	6·2	7·6	9·3	11·8	15·1	26·6	56·6	124·7	269·0
1873	56·4	5·6	3·6	5·5	6·8	8·6	11·4	15·6	28·3	61·9	135·2	303·5
1874	61·4	7·1	3·9	5·7	7·3	9·2	12·2	15·9	29·2	61·6	134·0	290·0
1875	61·2	6·4	3·8	5·7	7·3	9·3	12·4	17·0	31·1	65·7	148·8	330·3
1876	57·3	5·9	3·6	5·2	6·7	8·3	11·7	15·4	27·9	58·4	128·7	287·0
1877	53·6	5·6	3·6	5·1	6·3	8·2	11·3	15·3	27·7	58·9	129·1	291·6
1878	61·1	6·1	3·6	5·2	6·3	8·0	11·3	15·4	29·2	61·7	140·5	312·7
1879	52·9	5·8	3·4	4·9	6·0	8·0	11·3	16·0	30·7	66·6	150·2	328·7
1880	59·2	6·0	3·3	4·8	5·9	7·6	10·6	14·7	27·5	58·2	129·1	274·9
1881	48·0	5·7	3·2	4·7	6·0	7·9	11·0	14·9	28·0	58·4	126·4	263·8
1882	54·4	6·0	3·3	4·7	5·9	7·9	11·0	15·0	27·6	56·9	124·1	256·0
1883	51·1	5·8	3·4	4·9	6·1	8·1	11·1	15·6	28·8	60·2	134·2	277·0
1884	54·9	5·8	3·4	4·7	5·9	7·8	10·9	15·3	27·5	57·7	126·8	247·4
1885	51·0	5·1	3·1	4·5	5·7	7·7	10·8	15·2	28·7	62·0	133·2	282·8
1886	54·2	4·8	3·1	4·4	5·3	7·2	10·4	15·0	29·1	63·2	136·5	302·1
1887	52·7	5·1	3·0	4·2	5·4	7·0	10·3	15·2	28·8	62·2	131·6	272·1
1888	48·0	4·7	2·9	4·0	5·1	6·9	9·9	14·5	27·9	60·1	130·0	270·1
1889	51·9	4·7	2·8	3·9	4·9	6·5	9·8	14·3	27·4	58·7	126·5	260·3
1890	53·3	5·0	2·9	4·2	5·1	7·1	10·9	15·9	30·7	64·2	136·9	276·6
1891	53·7	4·7	2·9	4·3	5·2	7·1	11·1	17·1	33·4	70·6	148·1	300·7
1892	52·5	4·6	2·7	4·0	4·7	6·7	10·3	15·5	30·4	66·0	140·9	274·4
1893	55·2	5·1	3·0	4·3	5·1	7·0	10·7	15·2	29·2	62·4	128·7	250·0
1894	47·4	4·3	2·6	3·7	4·5	6·0	9·2	13·5	25·1	53·7	113·6	219·6
1895	55·2	4·2	2·6	3·7	4·5	6·1	9·5	14·8	29·6	62·6	140·9	276·2
1896	52·3	4·5	2·4	3·4	4·2	5·7	8·9	13·6	25·8	53·4	113·9	233·4
1897	52·4	4·0	2·4	3·4	4·1	5·6	8·9	13·7	26·2	55·7	121·2	252·6

See p. 41 for footnote

	0–4	5–9	10–14	15–19	20–24	25–34	35–44	45–54	55–64	65–74	75–84	85 and over
1898	53·5	3·9	2·3	3·3	4·1	5·5	8·9	13·9	26·7	57·5	126·0	259·6
1899	53·6	4·2	2·4	3·3	4·1	5·7	9·4	15·0	28·7	62·3	136·3	273·2
1900	51·8	4·2	2·5	3·3	4·2	5·7	9·3	15·3	29·6	63·2	136·8	273·9
1901	49·5	4·1	2·4	3·2	3·8	5·3	8·7	13·8	26·5	56·5	122·6	247·1
1902	45·0	4·2	2·3	3·1	3·9	5·3	8·4	13·4	25·9	55·7	122·1	252·3
1903	43·7	3·6	2·1	2·9	3·5	4·9	7·9	12·8	24·4	52·9	114·7	233·9
1904	48·5	3·6	2·2	3·0	3·5	4·9	7·7	12·8	25·6	55·1	123·2	256·1
1905	42·1	3·5	2·2	2·9	3·6	4·8	7·5	12·5	24·8	53·8	117·2	256·7
1906	43·1	3·7	2·3	2·9	3·5	4·7	7·5	12·4	24·8	52·5	119·6	258·7
1907	39·1	3·5	2·1	2·9	3·4	4·6	7·4	12·4	25·3	55·1	122·6	259·4
1908	39·0	3·4	2·0	2·7	3·4	4·4	6·9	12·1	24·2	52·7	119·4	248·8
1909	35·7	3·5	2·1	2·8	3·3	4·4	6·9	12·1	24·8	55·5	124·2	256·2
1910	33·1	3·1	2·0	2·6	3·1	4·1	6·5	11·1	22·4	49·8	112·3	232·8
1911	39·5	3·4	2·1	2·7	3·3	4·2	6·6	11·4	22·8	50·9	115·1	229·4
1912	29·8	3·1	2·0	2·7	3·2	4·0	6·3	11·1	22·3	51·6	115·1	239·3
1913	33·3	3·2	2·0	2·6	3·2	4·0	6·4	11·3	22·3	50·7	111·4	230·9
1914	32·9	3·4	2·2	2·7	3·2	4·1	6·5	11·5	22·4	51·4	113·8	238·7
1915	34·4	3·8	2·3	3·0	3·4	4·2	6·5	11·7	23·6	56·2	129·8	269·9
1916	26·4	3·2	2·2	3·0	3·4	4·0	6·1	10·6	21·5	52·2	122·6	262·5
1917	26·3	3·2	2·2	3·2	3·4	3·9	5·8	10·1	20·7	49·2	118·9	246·8
1918	34·1	5·9	4·0	6·0	7·9	9·8	8·5	12·3	21·4	48·3	107·5	216·7
1919	26·4	3·6	2·3	3·4	4·3	5·4	6·1	10·1	20·5	48·8	120·4	251·7
1920	28·8	3·2	2·0	2·7	3·3	4·2	5·4	8·9	18·1	42·6	104·9	213·6
1921	25·8	2·7	1·8	2·7	3·2	3·7	5·2	8·8	18·2	43·6	108·9	232·3
1922	24·5	2·5	1·8	2·6	3·2	3·9	5·3	9·3	19·7	48·6	120·9	251·0
1923	19·6	2·2	1·6	2·5	3·0	3·4	4·8	8·5	18·2	44·1	108·5	231·9
1924	20·2	2·4	1·7	2·5	3·1	3·4	4·8	8·6	18·1	46·2	115·8	269·1
1925	20·7	2·3	1·5	2·4	2·9	3·3	4·6	8·2	17·4	43·9	108·0	254·2
1926	18·8	2·3	1·5	2·4	2·9	3·3	4·7	8·3	17·6	42·7	105·4	240·2
1927	18·9	2·2	1·5	2·4	3·0	3·4	4·9	8·8	18·5	45·9	115·2	262·3
1928	17·3	2·2	1·5	2·4	3·0	3·3	4·6	8·2	17·3	42·7	102·6	242·9
1929	21·6	2·3	1·7	2·5	3·1	3·5	4·9	9·1	19·6	49·9	126·7	298·2
1930	16·0	2·2	1·5	2·3	2·8	3·2	4·4	7·9	16·9	40·7	102·2	226·5
1931	17·4	2·0	1·5	2·4	2·9	3·3	4·5	8·3	17·6	44·4	114·4	255·3
1932	16·8	1·9	1·3	2·2	2·8	3·1	4·3	8·0	17·1	43·2	111·4	253·0
1933	15·8	2·1	1·4	2·3	2·9	3·2	4·7	8·4	17·4	43·8	113·5	256·9
1934	15·6	2·4	1·4	2·2	2·6	3·0	4·1	7·7	16·5	41·7	102·8	227·1
1935	14·2	1·9	1·3	2·0	2·6	2·9	4·0	7·5	16·4	41·2	103·4	234·4
1936	14·9	1·9	1·1	1·8	2·5	2·7	3·9	7·6	16·5	42·2	106·2	253·2
1937	14·7	1·8	1·1	1·8	2·5	2·8	4·0	7·7	16·9	42·5	108·2	261·9
1938	13·4	1·8	1·1	1·7	2·3	2·5	3·6	7·0	15·5	38·8	98·1	228·9

(*a*) Based upon civilian deaths and estimated civilian population.

Population and Vital Statistics 14. Death Rates per 1,000 in Different Age-Groups— Scotland 1860–2 to 1938

NOTES

[1] SOURCE: *Annual Report of the Registrar General for Scotland.*
[2] The figures for 1860–2 to 1900–2 are obtained by dividing the appropriate census figure of population in each age-group into the average yearly number of deaths in that age-group in the census year itself and in the year on either side of that.

A. Males

	0–1	1–4	5–9	10–14	15–24	25–34	35–44	45–54	55–64	65–74	75–84	85 & over
1860–2	152·0	37·4	9·1	5·2	8·7	10·3	12·4	17·3	29·6	64·8	166·9	
1870–2	159·5	35·2	9·8	5·4	9·3	11·2	14·0	20·0	32·5	64·1	159·7	
1880–2	149·6	29·5	7·8	4·3	7·1	8·9	12·5	19·4	33·4	63·6	148·1	
1890–2	159·0	27·5	5·7	3·5	6·5	8·3	12·2	20·8	37·2	72·1	165·2	
1900–2	158·4	22·8	4·3	2·8	5·0	7·5	11·7	19·5	38·0	71·6	158·5	
1911	140·9	17·8	3·7	2·3	4·1	5·5	8·4	15·5	30·6	65·2	148·6	
1912	133·6	17·8	3·5	2·3	4·0	5·6	8·7	15·8	32·8	67·0	156·0	
1913	122·8	16·9	3·6	2·4	3·8	5·4	8·5	14·7	29·8	60·5	151·5	
1914	140·9	17·4	3·7	2·5	3·9	5·7	8·6	15·8	33·3	66·5	165·8	
1915	147·0	22·2	4·1	2·7	4·7	5·9	9·3	17·4	37·3	74·0	182·2	
1916	107·8	16·1	3·5	2·3	4·1	5·3	8·0	15·8	34·2	70·3	174·6	
1917	105·7	17·4	3·4	2·2	3·7	4·7	8·0	15·7	34·0	69·7	171·4	
1918	100·3	18·6	4·4	3·3	6·2	9·1	10·1	17·2	33·7	66·7	158·7	
1919	112·8	15·5	3·7	2·3	4·8	7·2	8·9	16·7	36·0	72·5	185·6	
1920	130·0	10·5	2·9	2·1	3·8	4·7	7·8	16·1	34·4	68·0	165·2	
1921	115·0	10·7	2·7	1·9	3·3	4·3	6·8	14·5	32·7	68·6	163·4	311·8
1922	116·8	21·7	2·8	1·8	3·3	4·9	7·0	12·6	28·2	65·3	148·2	279·5
1923	88·6	14·3	2·5	1·7	3·1	4·2	6·2	11·9	26·8	63·5	137·5	274·8
1924	105·8	19·4	2·5	2·0	3·3	4·3	6·7	12·2	28·1	68·1	156·7	311·2
1925	96·9	13·9	2·7	1·7	3·2	4·1	6·7	11·6	28·0	67·3	144·9	310·7
1926	86·3	12·6	2·5	1·8	2·9	4·1	6·1	12·0	27·8	67·3	146·1	322·1
1927	85·8	12·2	2·7	1·8	2·9	4·3	6·6	12·2	28·8	71·9	154·6	333·7
1928	104·3	12·3	2·6	1·8	3·1	4·0	6·7	11·2	24·3	62·1	144·4	300·5
1929	103·0	13·0	2·5	2·0	3·3	4·1	7·7	12·8	26·7	67·9	163·6	330·8
1930	102·1	10·6	2·8	1·9	3·0	3·7	7·0	11·7	24·5	61·7	151·1	314·1
1931	100·5	10·1	2·6	1·7	3·0	3·9	6·3	11·6	24·5	60·4	140·8	293·8
1932	100·4	10·6	2·7	1·6	3·0	3·8	6·6	11·6	24·1	60·1	142·1	273·7
1933	94·1	8·5	2·4	1·7	3·0	4·0	6·4	12·2	24·9	59·8	139·4	290·5
1934	93·5	9·8	2·9	1·6	2·8	3·8	6·1	11·6	24·0	57·3	135·7	275·7
1935	92·3	7·2	2·4	1·7	2·7	3·5	6·1	11·8	24·2	61·0	145·5	314·1
1936	98·6	7·9	2·4	1·5	2·8	3·5	6·1	12·6	24·6	61·2	145·4	318·6
1937	96·2	7·2	2·2	1·5	2·8	3·8	6·3	12·8	25·8	63·0	150·3	351·2
1938	81·6	7·0	1·9	1·4	2·5	3·2	5·6	11·6	23·8	57·0	137·7	319·9

B. Females

	0–1	1–4	5–9	10–14	15–24	25–34	35–44	45–54	55–64	65–74	75–84	85 & over
1860–2	126·4	37·4	8·8	5·2	7·6	9·6	11·5	14·4	24·9	56·6	155·1	
1870–2	130·8	35·3	9·3	5·8	8·5	10·4	12·4	16·1	27·8	54·6	150·3	
1880–2	121·3	28·8	7·3	4·7	7·0	9·2	11·2	14·9	26·9	53·4	136·6	
1890–2	129·6	27·1	6·0	4·0	6·2	8·8	11·6	15·8	30·4	61·8	149·8	
1900–2	126·0	21·5	4·8	3·2	5·1	7·1	10·0	15·6	32·7	60·2	142·8	
1911	112·2	16·8	3·8	2·6	3·9	5·7	8·1	12·4	24·6	52·4	132·0	
1912	106·1	17·1	3·6	2·4	3·9	5·3	8·2	12·6	25·9	53·6	143·2	
1913	107·6	16·5	3·6	2·6	3·8	5·3	8·2	13·1	26·5	54·9	145·9	
1914	112·5	16·4	3·7	2·6	3·6	5·4	8·4	13·2	26·2	53·5	145·7	
1915	117·8	20·6	3·9	2·8	3·9	5·7	8·4	13·4	28·9	57·1	168·2	
1916	86·4	14·8	3·6	2·5	3·8	4·8	7·5	12·1	25·8	50·5	154·6	
1917	83·6	16·1	3·1	2·5	3·7	4·7	7·4	12·0	24·5	48·0	146·1	
1918	76·3	18·2	4·7	3·7	6·4	8·9	9·3	13·9	26·5	48·9	139·6	
1919	84·1	14·8	3·7	2·8	4·4	6·6	7·7	13·4	27·5	54·2	163·4	
1920	96·9	9·7	2·9	2·0	3·5	5·1	7·1	11·5	25·5	47·5	144·5	
1921	85·3	9·8	2·5	1·9	3·4	4·6	6·8	14·5	32·7	68·6	163·4	311·5
1922	89·2	19·9	2·6	2·0	3·4	5·0	7·0	10·8	22·6	52·6	124·5	267·1
1923	67·4	12·9	2·4	1·7	3·0	4·3	5·8	9·6	21·4	49·9	113·1	240·1
1924	79·5	17·1	2·5	1·8	3·1	4·5	6·1	10·8	22·5	54·2	128·8	278·2
1925	70·0	12·8	2·3	1·8	3·0	4·1	5·5	10·0	22·4	51·3	118·6	274·2
1926	64·3	10·9	2·3	1·6	3·0	4·2	5·7	10·1	21·7	51·2	119·0	272·7
1927	66·0	10·5	2·4	1·5	2·7	4·0	5·9	10·6	22·5	54·1	127·3	286·2
1928	79·5	10·9	2·6	1·6	2·9	4·0	5·6	9·7	19·4	49·6	121·1	284·0
1929	78·7	10·8	2·2	1·7	3·1	4·2	6·2	10·8	21·1	55·0	141·3	327·7
1930	78·2	9·6	2·4	1·7	2·8	3·7	5·5	9·4	19·2	48·5	124·9	278·8
1931	74·4	9·5	2·3	1·4	2·9	3·7	5·3	9·2	19·5	47·0	118·6	266·2
1932	80·0	9·7	2·3	1·7	2·9	4·0	5·5	9·4	19·8	47·7	119·7	268·5
1933	73·6	7·4	2·1	1·5	2·8	3·7	5·3	9·1	19·4	47·8	117·9	257·1
1934	73·0	8·3	2·5	1·5	2·8	3·6	5·0	8·9	19·2	45·0	110·9	246·6
1935	69·6	6·4	2·0	1·4	2·7	3·4	5·1	9·0	19·3	47·4	119·9	265·0
1936	75·6	7·3	1·9	1·2	2·6	3·2	4·9	9·2	18·9	47·8	117·4	263·5
1937	73·5	6·6	1·9	1·2	2·7	3·4	4·9	9·1	19·5	50·0	121·2	288·6
1938	65·7	6·2	1·9	1·3	2·5	3·0	4·4	8·3	18·2	45·2	108·6	261·0

Population and Vital Statistics 15. Death Rates per 1,000 in Different Age-Groups— Ireland 1870–2 to 1910–2 and Northern Ireland 1925–7 and 1936–8

NOTES

[1] SOURCES: *Annual Report of the Registrar General for Ireland*, up to 1910–2, and *for Northern Ireland* thereafter.

[2] All figures are obtained by dividing the census population of each age-group into the average yearly number of deaths in the census years and the years on each side of that.

A. Males

	0–4	5–9	10–14	15–19	20–24	25–34	35–44	45–54	55–64	65–74	75–84	85 & over
1870–2	38·0	5·4	3·2	5·4	8·1	9·0	9·9	14·4	25·4	59·0	126·9	258·9
1880–2	40·0	5·3	3·4	5·5	8·0	8·8	10·5	15·7	29·9	63·5	135·8	300·4
1890–2	38·3	4·1	2·9	4·9	7·6	9·3	10·8	15·8	29·9	66·3	143·8	291·2
1900–2	39·4	3·9	2·9	4·8	7·1	9·0	10·6	15·6	29·5	63·1	140·0	317·1
1910–2	34·7	3·2	2·3	4·0	5·8	7·1	8·8	14·1	27·7	48·9	102·5	248·9

N.I.

	0–4	5–9	10–14	15–19	20–24	25–34	35–44	45–54	55–64	65–74	75–84	85 & over
1925–7	29·4	2·6	1·9	3·1	4·4	4·8	6·6	12·8	25·9	56·5	116·9	236·0
1936–8	25·0	2·0	1·5	2·3	3·4	3·8	6·1	12·3	24·1	58·7	125·4	234·8

B. Females

	0–4	5–9	10–14	15–19	20–24	25–34	35–44	45–54	55–64	65–74	75–84	85 & over
1870–2	34·2	5·4	3·7	5·5	6·4	8·1	9·5	12·2	24·1	59·4	126·0	249·1
1880–2	36·1	5·8	4·1	6·1	7·4	8·9	10·3	14·2	28·8	63·8	134·4	281·9
1890–2	34·5	4·7	4·0	6·2	7·4	9·5	10·4	15·2	31·1	70·3	144·0	283·7
1900–2	35·0	4·8	3·9	6·0	6·6	8·6	10·8	14·9	29·6	67·2	142·2	292·6
1910–2	30·2	3·7	3·2	4·7	5·7	7·3	9·2	13·7	27·5	45·7	96·0	236·3

N.I.

	0–4	5–9	10–14	15–19	20–24	25–34	35–44	45–54	55–64	65–74	75–84	85 & over
1925–7	24·3	2·6	2·3	3·8	5·1	6·0	6·8	13·1	25·3	52·7	101·6	193·2
1936–8	21·8	2·1	1·7	2·4	3·5	4·3	5·2	10·7	19·6	52·3	111·1	218·2

Population and Vital Statistics 16. Marriages and Marriage Rates—England & Wales 1838–1938, Scotland 1855–1938, Ireland 1864–1921, and Northern Ireland 1922–38

NOTES

[1] SOURCES: *Annual Report of the Registrar General for England & Wales, for Scotland, for Ireland and for Northern Ireland.* (In recent years the volume for England & Wales has been called *The Registrar General's Statistical Review of England and Wales.*)

[2] Figures for the earlier years in each kingdom may be somewhat lower than they should be owing to deficiencies in registration.

	Thousands of Marriages			Rate per 1,000 of Population		
	England & Wales	Scotland	Ireland	England & Wales	Scotland	Ireland
1838	118	...	...	15·4	...	...
1839	123	...	...	15·9	...	...
1840	123	...	...	15·6	...	...
1841	122	...	...	15·4	...	...
1842	119	...	...	14·7	...	...
1843	124	...	...	15·2	...	...
1844	132	...	...	16·0	...	...
1845	144	...	...	17·2	...	...
1846	146	...	...	17·2	...	...
1847	136	...	...	15·9	...	...
1848	138	...	...	15·9	...	...
1849	142	...	...	16·2	...	...
1850	153	...	...	17·2	...	...
1851	154	...	...	17·2	...	...
1852	159	...	...	17·4	...	...
1853	165	...	...	17·9	...	...
1854	160	...	...	17·2	...	...
1855	152	19·7	...	16·2	13·2	...
1856	159	20·7	...	16·7	13·8	...
1857	159	21·4	...	16·5	14·2	...
1858	156	19·7	...	16·0	13·0	...
1859	168	21·2	...	17·0	13·9	...
1860	170	21·2	...	17·1	13·9	...
1861	164	20·9	...	16·3	13·6	...
1862	164	20·6	...	16·1	13·3	...
1863	174	22·2	...	16·8	14·3	...
1864	180	22·7	27·4	17·6	14·4	9·7
1865	185	23·6	30·8	17·5	14·8	11·0
1866	188	23·7	30·1	17·5	14·7	10·9
1867	179	22·6	29·7	16·5	13·9	10·8
1868	177	21·9	27·7	16·1	13·3	10·1
1869	177	22·1	27·3	15·9	13·4	10·0
1870	182	23·9	28·7	16·1	14·3	10·6
1871	190	24·0	29·0	16·7	14·3	10·7
1872	201	25·6	26·9	17·4	15·1	10·0
1873	206	26·7	25·7	17·6	15·5	9·6
1874	202	26·4	24·5	17·0	15·2	9·2
1875	201	26·0	24·0	16·7	14·8	9·1
1876	202	26·6	26·4	16·5	15·0	9·9
1877	194	25·8	24·7	15·7	14·4	9·3
1878	190	24·4	25·3	15·2	13·4	9·5
1879	182	23·5	23·3	14·4	12·8	8·7
1880	192	24·5	20·4	14·9	13·2	7·8
1881	197	26·0	21·8	15·1	13·9	8·5
1882	204	26·6	22·0	15·5	14·1	8·6
1883	206	26·9	21·4	15·5	14·1	8·5
1884	204	26·1	22·6	15·1	13·6	9·1
1885	198	25·3	21·2	14·5	13·1	8·6
1886	196	24·5	20·6	14·2	12·6	8·4
1887	201	24·9	20·9	14·4	12·7	8·6

	Thousands of Marriages			Rate per 1,000 of Population		
	England & Wales	Scotland	Ireland	England & Wales	Scotland	Ireland
1888	204	25·3	20·1	14·4	12·8	8·4
1889	214	26·3	21·5	15·0	13·3	9·0
1890	223	27·5	21·0	15·5	13·7	8·9
1891	227	28·0	21·5	15·6	13·9	9·2
1892	227	28·7	21·5	15·4	14·1	9·3
1893	219	27·1	21·7	14·7	13·2	9·4
1894	226	27·6	21·6	15·0	13·3	9·4
1895	228	28·4	23·1	15·0	13·5	10·1
1896	243	30·3	23·1	15·7	14·2	10·2
1897	249	31·1	22·9	16·0	14·4	10·1
1898	255	32·1	22·6	16·2	14·8	10·0
1899	262	33·0	22·3	16·5	15·0	9·9
1900	257	32·4	21·3	16·0	14·6	9·5
1901	259	31·4	22·6	15·9	14·0	10·1
1902	262	31·9	22·9	15·9	14·2	10·4
1903	261	32·4	23·0	15·7	14·3	10·4
1904	258	32·3	23·0	15·3	14·1	10·4
1905	261	31·3	23·1	15·3	13·6	10·5
1906	271	33·1	22·7	15·7	14·3	10·3
1907	276	33·3	22·5	15·9	14·3	10·3
1908	265	31·6	22·7	15·1	13·5	10·4
1909	261	30·1	22·7	14·7	12·8	10·3
1910	268	30·9	22·1	15·0	13·0	10·1
1911	275	31·8	23·5	15·2	13·4	10·7
1912	284	32·5	23·3	15·6	13·7	10·6
1913	287	33·8	22·3	15·7	14·2	10·2
1914	294	35·0	23·7	15·9	14·8	10·8
1915	361	36·2	24·2	19·4	15·2	11·1
1916	280	31·4	22·2	14·9	13·1	10·2
1917	259	30·4	21·1	13·8	12·6	9·6
1918	287	34·5	22·6	15·3	14·3	10·3
1919	369	44·1	27·2	19·7	18·3	12·2
1920	380	46·8	26·8	20·2	19·2	12·0
1921	321	39·2	23·2	16·9	16·1	10·4
			Northern Ireland			Northern Ireland
1922	300	34·4	8·1	15·7	14·0	12·6
1923	292	35·2	8·0	15·2	14·4	12·5
1924	296	32·3	7·5	15·3	13·3	11·9
1925	296	32·5	7·7	15·2	13·3	12·2
1926	280	31·2	7·2	14·3	12·8	11·5
1927	308	32·6	7·2	15·7	13·4	11·5
1928	303	32·9	7·3	15·4	13·6	11·7
1929	313	33·0	7·4	15·8	13·6	12·0
1930	315	33·3	7·5	15·8	13·8	12·2
1931	312	32·7	7·4	15·6	13·5	11·9
1932	307	33·2	7·0	15·3	13·6	11·1
1933	318	34·2	7·6	15·8	13·9	12·1
1934	342	36·9	8·2	16·9	15·0	13·0
1935	350	38·0	8·8	17·2	15·3	13·9
1936	355	37·9	9·1	17·4	15·3	14·3
1937	359	38·4	8·6	17·5	15·4	13·5
1938	362	38·7	8·6	17·6	15·5	13·4

Population and Vital Statistics 17. Passengers from United Kingdom Ports to Extra-European Countries—1815–1938

NOTES

SOURCES: 1815–1924—Ferenczi and Willcox, *International Migrations* (2 vols., National Bureau of Economic Research, New York, 1929–31), vol. 1; 1924–38—*Board of Trade Journal*.

(in thousands)

	U.K. Citizens	Aliens	Nationality Unknown	Total		U.K. Citizens	Aliens	Nationality Unknown	Total
1815	...	...	...	2	1861	65	4	23	92
1816	...	...	...	13	1862	98	3	20	121
1817	...	...	...	21	1863	193	8	23	224
1818	...	...	...	28	1864	187	17	5	209
1819	...	...	...	35	1865	175	29	6	210
1820	...	...	...	26	1866	170	27	8	205
1821	...	...	...	18	1867	157	31	8	196
1822	...	...	...	20	1868	138	52	6	196
1823	...	...	...	17	1869	186	66	6	258
1824	...	...	...	14	1870	203	48	6	257
1825	...	...	...	15	1871	193	53	6	252
1826	...	...	...	21	1872	210	79	6	295
1827	...	...	...	28	1873	228	72	10	311
1828	...	...	...	26	1874	197	38	5	241
1829	...	...	...	31	1875	141	31	2	174
1830	...	...	...	57	1876	109	26	3	138
1831	...	...	...	83	1877	95	21	3	120
1832	...	...	...	103	1878	113	32	3	148
1833	...	...	...	63	1879	164	49	3	217
1834	...	...	...	76	1880	228	100	4	332
1835	...	...	...	44	1881	243	144	5	393
1836	...	...	...	75	1882	279	130	4	413
1837	...	...	...	72	1883	320	73	4	397
1838	...	...	...	33	1884	242	58	4	304
1839	...	...	...	62	1885	208	54	3	264
1840	...	...	...	91	1886	233	94	4	331
1841	...	...	...	119	1887	281	109	6	396
1842	...	...	...	128	1888	280	113	5	398
1843	...	...	...	57	1889	254	83	5	343
1844	...	...	...	71	1890	218	95	3	316
1845	...	...	...	94	1891	219	112	4	335
1846	...	...	...	130	1892	210	107	4	321
1847	...	...	...	258	1893	209	95	4	308
1848	...	...	...	248	1894	156	67	4	227
1849	...	...	...	299	1895	185	83	4	272
1850	...	...	...	281	1896	162	76	4	242
1851	...	...	...	336	1897	146	63	4	213
1852	...	...	...	369	1898	141	61	4	205
1853	278	31	20	330	1899	146	90	4	241
1854	267	38	19	323	1900	169	125	5	299
1855	150	11	16	177	1901	172	124	7	303
1856	148	9	19	177	1902	206	174	7	387
1857	181	13	19	213	1903	260	182	8	449
1858	95	5	14	114	1904	271	174	8	454
1859	97	4	19	120	1905	262	188	9	460
1860	96	5	28	128	1906	325	229	3	557

See p. 48 for footnotes

(in thousands)

	U.K. Citizens	Aliens	Nationality Unknown	Total		U.K. Citizens	Aliens	Nationality Unknown	Total
1907	396	239	- -	635	1923 (a)	338	126		463
1908	263	123	—	386	1924	263	108		371
1909	289	186		474	1925	250	105		355
1910	398	221		619	1926	284	116		402
1911	455	169		623	1927	277	137		414
1912	468	189		657	1928	271	127		397
1913	470	232		702	1929	281	119		399
1914	293	158		451	1930	221	107		328
1915	105	22		127	1931	150	63		213
1916	76	17		94	1932 (b)	166	56		222
1917	21	7		28	1933	177	49		226
1918	17	6		23	1934	187	54		240
1919	180	21		202	1935	183	61		245
1920	353	85		438	1936	198	80		278
1921	268	109		378	1937	194	93		287
1922	248	95		344	1938	185	79		264

(a) From 1st April 1923 the figures are exclusive of passengers who departed from ports in southern Ireland.

(b) From 1932 onwards the figures are inclusive of passengers on pleasure cruises.

Population and Vital Statistics 18. Passengers to United Kingdom Ports
from Extra-European Countries—1855–1938

NOTES

[1] Sources: 1855–1924—Ferenczi and Willcox, *International Migrations* (2 vols., National Bureau of Economic Research, New York, 1929–31), vol. 1; 1925–38—*Board of Trade Journal*.

[2] The figures up to 1870 are only approximations.

(in thousands)

	U.K. Citizens	Aliens	Total		U.K. Citizens	Aliens	Total
1855	...	...	23	1898	91	48	139
1858	...	...	24	1899	100	62	162
1859	...	...	20	1900	98	78	176
1860	...	...	24	1901	100	65	165
1861	...	...	32	1902	104	67	171
1862	...	...	...	1903	113	87	200
1863	...	...	18	1904	145	97	242
1864	...	...	26	1905	123	82	205
1865	...	...	34	1906	130	100	230
1866	...	...	31	1907	161	133	294
1867	...	...	37	1908	172	171	343
1868	...	...	...	1909	149	112	261
1869	...	...	36	1910	164	135	299
1870	...	...	42	1911	193	158	350
1871	...	...	45	1912	199	142	341
1872	...	...	42	1913	228	145	373
1873	...	...	75	1914	230	130	360
1874	...	...	118	1915	130	18	147
1875	...	...	94	1916	85	14	99
1876	71	22	94	1917	21	13	34
1877	64	18	82	1918	15	11	26
1878	55	23	78	1919	153	40	194
1879	38	16	54	1920	180	104	284
1880	47	21	68	1921	149	78	228
1881	53	24	77	1922	148	76	224
1882	55	28	83	1923	147	63	211
1883	74	27	101	1924	175	78	253
1884	91	32	123	1925	163	78	241
1885	85	28	114	1926	161	77	237
1886	80	29	109	1927	174	86	260
1887	85	34	119	1928	188	89	277
1888	94	35	129	1929	188	90	278
1889	103	44	147	1930	197	93	290
1890	109	46	156	1931	185	71	256
1891	103	48	151	1932	215	62	277
1892	98	46	144	1933	206	47	253
1893	102	39	141	1934	199	50	249
1894	118	67	186	1935	194	58	252
1895	109	66	176	1936	208	74	282
1896	102	58	160	1937	198	80	278
1897	95	60	155	1938	182	62	244

Population and Vital Statistics 19. Inward and Outward Movements of United Kingdom Citizens between United Kingdom Ports and Extra-European Countries—1853–1914

NOTE

[1] SOURCE: Ferenczi and Willcox, *International Migrations* (2 vols., National Bureau of Economic Research, New York, 1929–31), vol. 1.

A. Outward Movements, 1853–1914 (in thousands)

Year	Total	U.S.A.	British North America	Australasia	British South Africa
1853	278	191	32	55	...
1854	267	154	36	78	...
1855	150	86	16	47	...
1856	148	95	11	41	...
1857	181	106	17	58	...
1858	95	49	7	36	...
1859	97	57	2	29	...
1860	96	68	3	21	...
1861	65	38	4	21	...
1862	98	49	8	39	...
1863	193	131	10	50	...
1864	187	130	11	40	...
1865	175	118	14	37	...
1866	170	132	10	24	...
1867	157	126	12	14	...
1868	138	108	12	12	...
1869	186	147	21	14	...
1870	203	153	27	17	...
1871	193	151	25	12	...
1872	210	162	24	15	...
1873	228	167	29	25	...
1874	197	114	21	53	...
1875	141	81	12	35	...
1876	109	55	9	32	...
1877	95	45	8	30	5
1878	113	55	11	36	4
1879	164	92	18	41	7
1880	228	167	21	24	9
1881	243	176	24	23	13
1882	279	182	40	37	12
1883	320	192	44	71	6
1884	242	155	31	44	4
1885	208	138	20	39	3
1886	233	153	25	43	4
1887	281	202	32	34	5
1888	280	196	35	31	6
1889	254	169	28	28	14
1890	218	152	23	21	10
1891	219	156	22	20	9
1892	210	150	23	16	10
1893	209	149	25	11	13
1894	156	104	17	11	13
1895	185	127	17	11	20
1896	162	99	15	10	25
1897	146	85	16	12	21
1898	141	80	18	11	20
1899	146	92	16	11	14
1900	169	103	18	15	21
1901	172	104	16	15	23
1902	206	108	26	14	43
1903	260	124	60	12	50
1904	271	146	70	14	27
1905	262	122	82	15	26
1906	325	145	115	19	23
1907	396	170	151	25	21
1908	263	97	81	34	20
1909	289	110	86	38	22
1910	398	132	157	46	27
1911	455	122	185	81	31
1912	468	117	186	97	28
1913	470	129	196	78	26
1914	293	93	94	48	21

B. Difference between Outward and Inward Movements, 1876–1914 (Excess Inward +, Outward −)

Year	Total	U.S.A.	British North America	Australasia	British South Africa
1876	− 38	+ - -	− 3	− 30	...
1877	− 31	− 1	− 2	− 26	...
1878	− 58	− 21	− 4	− 32	...
1879	− 126	− 72	− 14	− 36	...
1880	− 181	− 140	− 16	− 18	...
1881	− 190	− 146	− 18	− 17	...
1882	− 225	− 153	− 34	− 30	− 6
1883	− 246	− 145	− 37	− 64	+ - -
1884	− 151	− 94	− 22	− 36	+ 2
1885	− 122	− 80	− 11	− 31	+ 1
1886	− 153	− 100	− 18	− 34	− - -
1887	− 196	− 143	− 25	− 24	− 2
1888	− 186	− 132	− 26	− 21	− 3
1889	− 151	− 97	− 20	− 18	− 9
1890	− 109	− 78	− 13	− 11	− 4
1891	− 115	− 88	− 13	− 10	− 3
1892	− 112	− 87	− 14	− 5	− 4
1893	− 107	− 82	− 16	− 1	− 7
1894	− 38	− 20	− 7	− 2	− 6
1895	− 76	− 55	− 6	− 1	− 12
1896	− 60	− 40	− 6	− 1	− 10
1897	− 51	− 32	− 6	− 5	− 6
1898	− 49	− 30	− 8	− 4	− 6
1899	− 46	− 39	− 8	− 4	+ 6
1900	− 71	− 48	− 8	− 6	− 7
1901	− 72	− 46	− 7	− 7	− 9
1902	− 102	− 52	− 15	− 4	− 28
1903	− 147	− 65	− 46	− 4	− 28
1904	− 127	− 67	− 51	− 5	+ 1
1905	− 139	− 61	− 63	− 7	− 3
1906	− 195	− 86	− 91	− 10	+ 3
1907	− 235	− 100	− 118	− 14	+ 5
1908	− 91	− 31	− 41	− 20	+ 5
1909	− 140	− 56	− 52	− 25	− 2
1910	− 234	− 74	− 116	− 33	− 8
1911	− 262	− 50	− 135	− 66	− 8
1912	− 268	− 46	− 134	− 80	− 4
1913	− 242	− 52	− 128	− 57	− - -
1914	− 63	− 16	− 30	− 26	+ 4

Population and Vital Statistics 20. Balance of Extra-European Migration of United Kingdom Citizens by Main Countries of Last or Future Permanent Residence—1912–56

NOTES

[1] SOURCES: 1912–24—Ferenczi and Willcox, *International Migrations* (2 vols, National Bureau of Economic Research, New York, 1929–31), vol. I; 1925–56—*Board of Trade Journal*.

[2] This table relates only to travel by sea.

(in thousands)

(Excess Inward +, Outward −)

	Total	To or from: British North America	Austral-asia	British South Africa (a)	Other British Empire (b)	U.S.A.
1912 (c)	−267	−132	− 62	− 3	− 3	− 65
1913	−304	−165	− 56	− φφ	− 2	− 78
1914	−110	− 45	− 24	+ 4	+ 1	− 49
1915	+ 15	+ 22	− 2	+ 1	+ 1	− 13
1916	+ 5	+ 10	+ 1	+ 3	+ 1	− 12
1917	+ 2	− 1	+ 1	+ 1	+ 1	− φφ
1918	− 2	+ φφ	− 2	− 1	− φφ	− φφ
1919	− 54	− 45	− 9	+ 1	+ 3	− 3
1920	−199	− 94	− 28	− 8	− 4	− 60
1921	−128	− 47	− 29	− 7	− 2	− 42
1922	−106	− 30	− 41	− 1	+ 3	− 37
1923 (d)	−199	− 76	− 39	− 1	+ 3	− 86
1924	− 91	− 47	− 39	− 1	+ 2	− 6
1925	− 84	− 25	− 37	− 2	+ φφ	− 22
1926	−116	− 39	− 51	− 3	− φφ	− 22
1927	− 98	− 40	− 38	− 2	+ φφ	− 19
1928	− 78	− 39	− 22	− 2	+ φφ	− 16
1929	− 87	− 53	− 11	− 1	+ 2	− 25
1930	− 26	− 15	+ 3	− φφ	+ 4	− 19
1931	+ 37	+ 10	+ 9	+ 1	+ 6	+ 9
1932	+ 49	+ 18	+ 5	+ 4	+ 6	+ 14
1933	+ 33	+ 14	+ 3	+ 2	+ 4	+ 8
1934	+ 21	+ 10	+ 2	+ 1	+ 3	+ 4
1935	+ 16	+ 8	+ 1	− 1	+ 4	+ 3
1936	+ 17	+ 8	+ 2	− 1	+ 5	+ 3
1937	+ 11	+ 6	+ φφ	− 2	+ 3	+ 1
1938	+ 6	+ 4	− 2	− 2	+ 4	+ 1
1946 (e)	−104	− 43	− 8	− 2	− 2	− 46
1947	− 65	− 15	− 12	− 22	+ 1	− 17
1948	− 96	− 27	− 35	− 28	+ 10	− 17
1949	− 85	− 13	− 54	− 9	+ φφ	− 13
1950	− 64	− 6	− 54	− 2	+ 6	− 9
1951	− 83	− 23	− 54	− 5	+ 5	− 10
1952	− 97	− 30	− 53	− 8	+ 4	− 13
1953	− 75	− 34	− 30	− 3	+ 5	− 13
1954	− 53	− 29	− 27	− 2	+ 14	− 11
1955	− 44	− 16	− 32	− 3	+ 15	− 9
1956	− 66	− 34	− 30	− 5	+ 13	− 11

(a) Includes the High Commission territories and Rhodesia (later the whole Central African Federation).
(b) As constituted at the date concerned.
(c) Nine months only.
(d) The figures for the fourth quarter of 1923 and for all later years are exclusive of migrants travelling via ports in southern Ireland.
(e) Figures are not available for 1939–45, and those for 1946 are stated by the Board of Trade to be about 5 per cent deficient.

Population and Vital Statistics 21. Emigration of Natives of Ireland
by Main Countries of Destination—1851–1921

NOTE

SOURCE: Ferenczi and Willcox, *International Migrations* (2 vols, National Bureau of Economic Research, New York, 1929–31), vol. I.

(in thousands)

	Total	To: U.S.A.	Canada	Australasia	Great Britain		Total	To: U.S.A.	Canada	Australasia	Great Britain
1851 (a)	152	...	...	...	...	1887	83	70	4	4	5
1852	190	...	...	...	...	1888	79	67	3	3	6
1853	173	...	...	...	...	1889	70	60	2	3	4
1854	141	...	...	...	...	1890	61	53	2	2	4
1855	92	...	...	...	...	1891	60	52	1	2	4
1856	91	...	...	...	...	1892	51	47	1	1	2
1857	95	...	...	...	...	1893	48	45	1	1	1
1858	64	...	...	...	...	1894	36	33	1	1	2
1859	81	...	...	...	...	1895	49	45	1	1	2
1860	85	...	...	...	...	1896	39	35	1	1	2
1861	64	...	...	...	...	1897	33	29	- -	1	2
1862	70	...	...	...	...	1898	32	28	- -	1	3
1863	117	...	...	...	...	1899	41	35	- -	1	4
1864	114	...	...	...	...	1900	45	38	- -	1	6
1865	101	...	...	...	...	1901	40	32	1	1	6
1866	99	...	...	...	...	1902	40	34	1	1	5
1867	81	...	...	...	...	1903	40	34	1	- -	4
1868	61	...	...	...	...	1904	37	31	2	- -	3
1869	67	...	...	...	...	1905	31	24	2	- -	3
1870	75	...	...	...	...	1906	35	27	3	- -	4
1871	71	...	...	...	...	1907	39	30	4	1	4
1872	78	...	...	...	...	1908	23	17	3	1	3
1873	90	...	...	...	...	1909	29	22	3	1	3
1874	73	...	...	...	...	1910	32	25	4	1	2
1875	51	...	...	...	...	1911	31	22	5	1	2
1876	38	15	1	5	17	1912	29	20	6	1	2
1877	39	12	- -	6	20	1913	31	22	7	1	1
1878	41	15	1	7	19	1914	20	15	3	1	1
1879	47	23	2	6	15	1915	11	7	1	- -	3
1880	96	75	3	4	14	1916	7	4	- -	- -	2
1881	78	61	3	3	11	1917	2	- -	- -	- -	2
1882	89	66	7	5	11	1918	1	- -	- -	- -	1
1883	109	80	11	8	10	1919	3	1	1	- -	1
1884	76	57	4	6	9	1920	16	12	2	- -	1
1885	62	50	2	4	6	1921	14	11	1	- -	- -
1886	63	51	3	4	5						

(a) Eight months only.

REFERENCES

BOOKS

K. H. Connell, *The Population of Ireland, 1750–1845* (Oxford, 1950).

J. D. Chambers, *The Vale of Trent, 1670–1800* (Cambridge, 1957).

L. Ferenczi and W. F. Willcox (editors), *International Migrations* (2 vols., New York, 1929–31).

D. V. Glass, *Population Policies and Movements in Europe* (Oxford, 1940).

G. T. Griffith, *Population Problems in the Age of Malthus* (Cambridge, 1926).

S. C. Johnson, *Emigration from the U.K. to North America* (London, 1913).

J. G. Kyd (editor), *Scottish Population Statistics* (Edinburgh, 1952).

T. Malthus, *Essay on Population* (London, 5th edition 1817).

A. Redford, *Labour Migration in England, 1800–1850* (Manchester, 1926).

B. Thomas, *Migration and Economic Growth* (Cambridge, 1954).

GOVERNMENT PUBLICATIONS

Reports and *Abstracts* of the Census of Great Britain, 1801–51 (in *Sessional Papers*).

Reports and *Tables* of the Census of England and Wales, 1861–1951 (in *Sessional Papers* up to the 1911 census inclusive, and issued as non-parliamentary papers thereafter).

Reports and *Tables* of the Census of Scotland, 1861–1951 (in *Sessional Papers* up to the 1911 census inclusive, and issued as non-parliamentary papers thereafter).

Reports and *Tables* of the Census of Ireland, 1821–1911 (in *Sessional Papers*).

Reports and *Tables* of the Census of Northern Ireland, 1926, 1937, and 1951 (non-parliamentary papers).

Reports and *Tables* of the Census of the Republic of Ireland, 1926, 1936, and 1951 (Irish Official Publications).

Annual Report of the Registrar General, 1838–1920 (non-parliamentary papers 1838–51, but in sessional papers thereafter).

The Registrar General's Statistical Review, 1921–56 (non-parliamentary papers).

Annual Report of the Registrar General for Ireland, 1867–1920 (in *Sessional Papers*).

Annual Report of the Registrar General for Northern Ireland, 1922–56 (non-parliamentary papers).

Annual Report of the Registrar General for Scotland, 1855–1956 (in *Sessional Papers* 1855–1920, but non-parliamentary papers thereafter).

Board of Trade Journal, 1886–1956.

Report of Land and Emigration Commissioners (in *Sessional Papers*, 1842–73).

Report of the Royal Commission on Population (*S.P.* 1948–9, xix).

Interdepartmental Committee on Social and Economic Research, *Guides to Official Sources, no. 2: Census Reports of Great Britain, 1801–1931*.

ARTICLES

Sir William Beveridge, 'The Fall of Fertility among European Races', *Economica* (1925).

J. Brownlee, 'History of the Birth and Death Rates in England and Wales . . .', *Public Health* (1916).

N. H. Carrier and J. R. Jeffery, 'External Migration, 1815–1950: A Study of the Available Statistics', *Studies on Medical and Population Subjects, no. 6* (1953).

K. H. Connell, 'Some Unsettled Problems in English and Irish Population History, 1750–1865,' *Irish Historical Studies* (1951).

D. E. C. Eversley, 'A Study of Population in an Area of Worcestershire from 1660–1850', *Population Studies* (1956–7).

D. V. Glass, 'A Note on the Under-Registration in Britain in the Nineteenth Century', *Population Studies* (1951).

D. V. Glass, 'Gregory King's Estimate of the Population of England and Wales, 1695', *Population Studies* (1950).

D. V. Glass, 'The Population Controversy in Eighteenth Century England', *Population Studies* (1952).

D. V. Glass, 'Gregory King and the Population of England and Wales at the End of the Seventeenth Century', *Eugenics Review* (1946).

E. C. K. Gonner, 'The Population of England in the Eighteenth Century', *J.R.S.S.* (1913).

H. J. Habakkuk, 'English Population in the Eighteenth Century', *E.H.R.* (1953).

T. H. Hollingsworth, 'A Demographic Study of the British Ducal Families', *Population Studies* (1957).

J. H. Johnson, 'The Population of Londonderry during the Great Irish Famine', *E.H.R.* (1957).

P. F. Jones and A. V. Judges, 'London Population in the Late Seventeenth Century', *E.H.R.* (1935).

J. T. Krause, 'Changes in English Fertility and Mortality, 1781–1850', *E.H.R.* (1958).

Capt. Larcom, 'Observations on the Census of Population of Ireland in 1841', *J.S.S.* (1841).

H. Leak and T. Priday, 'Migration from and to the United Kingdom', *J.R.S.S.* (1933).

T. McKeown and R. C. Brown, 'Medical Evidence Related to English Population Changes in the Eighteenth Century', *Population Studies* (1955).

T. H. Marshall, 'The Population Problem during the Industrial Revolution', *E.H.R.* (1929). [Reprinted in E. M. Carus-Wilson (editor), *Essays in Economic History* (London, 1954)].

T. H. Marshall, 'The Population of England and Wales from the Industrial Revolution to the World War', *E.H.R.* (1935). [Also reprinted in E. M. Carus-Wilson (editor), *op. cit.*]

H. A. Shannon, ' Migration and the Growth of London, 1841-91', *E.H.R.* (1934-5).

T. H. C. Stevenson, 'The Fertility of Various Social Classes in England and Wales from the Middle of the Nineteenth Century to 1911', *J.R.S.S.* (1911).

T. A. Welton, 'By-Products of the Census: A Study of the Recent Migration of English People . . .', *T.M.S.S.* (1903–4).

R. Price Williams, 'On the Increase of Population in England and Wales', *J.S.S.* (1880).

THE LABOUR FORCE

TABLES

From the first, the directors of the census in Britain have been interested in the activities by which the inhabitants have earned their living, and each decade has seen an increase in the amount of this kind of information elicited in the census returns. The attempt at the first census is generally recognised to have been a failure, but the still rougher classification of families by agricultural and non-agricultural branches of activity, made in 1811 and repeated in 1821 and 1831, may have been more successful. The 1831 census also provided a more detailed analysis of the occupations of males of 20 years and over. The first full-scale analysis of individuals' occupations was attempted in 1841. Comparison between 1831 and 1841 must be made, therefore, on the basis of the occupations of males over 20 years old. Here such comparison has been confined to the three broad categories of 1811, but a more detailed one can be made in certain occupations, though not very many.

The officials in 1841 were completely surprised by the enormous variety in the designations of occupations returned, and, as inadequate preparations had been made, a precise and accurate classification was not possible. A very general one was published, but it is not comparable with later censuses. Apart from that, the detailed lists were printed with little explanation of the terms used, and with some aggregation under headings which in later censuses were separated and assigned to different categories. An attempt has been made to fit the information elicited in 1841 into the pattern of the 1911 census; but it is clear that the degree of comparability between 1841 and later censuses is, for many occupations, relatively poor.[1]

[1] Cf. Charles Booth, 'Occupations of the People of the United Kingdom, 1801–1881', *J.S.S.* (1886). '. . . owing to the different methods of tabulation as to ages and the imperfections of the returns, the figures for 1841 do not . . . offer a very safe basis of comparison'.

By 1851 the officials were prepared, and the principle of classification then adopted survives, in essentials, to this day, though there have been many trivial and some important changes. These changes have been such as to render exact comparisons impossible over the period as a whole, and it is generally unwise to attempt detailed comparisons even from one census to the next. Broad comparisons can however be made—except across the two major breaks in 1871–81 and 1911–21, and they are possible for a fair number of occupations between the latter two dates.[1] In one or two other cases where comparison in a particular occupation is likely to be especially inaccurate this has been indicated by a vertical line in the table. Throughout the period 1881–1951 comparison of the totals occupied and unoccupied is broadly valid, provided account is taken of changes in the lower age limit of people covered by the returns.[2] Comparison between 1871 (and earlier) and 1881 is vitiated by the inclusion, prior to 1881, of retired people in their former occupations. The effect of this, however, appears to have been relatively small—much less, in fact, than the effects of the Education and Factory Acts. If attention is concentrated on people aged 15 and over, there was actually a slight rise in the total occupied proportion between 1861 and 1881 despite the exclusion of the retired at the later date.[3]

The validity of all occupation statistics can be called in question on the ground of likely errors in the returns by householders. This has long been recognised, but the criticism has been generally discounted. Stevenson, for example, discussed the matter in the introduction to the mortality tables of 1910–12,[4] and concluded that, for groups at any rate, the errors were unlikely to be significant. A similar conclusion was reached in the *General Report* of the 1951 census, on the basis of a sample enquiry: 'In summary it may be said that, while the occupational classification sometimes falls victim to the combined forces of its own specificity and the human capacity for variation in description, the general impression emerges that the level of reliability of occupational assignment at the census justifies the statistical analyses which are based thereon'.[5]

Statistics of the numbers engaged in coal-mining, iron and steel, and the textile industries can be found in chapters IV, V and VIII, where they have been taken from sources other than the censuses. The differences in the composition of the various categories from census to census make industrial comparisons rather difficult, and, prior to 1921, the census data were analysed by occupation—the employment of the individual—rather than by industry—the employment of the firm or employing agency. For most of the nineteenth century the

---

[1] The *General Report* of the 1921 census, p. 86, states that 'the returns of occupation in this census have been tabulated under a scheme differing so much from those in use previously as to preclude any possibility of an exact comparison with previous census results'. But later (p. 87) it lists certain occupations for which comparison is possible—most professions, some occupations dealt with on occupational rather than industrial lines in 1911, and some which are necessarily confined to certain industries.

[2] This assumes that the efficiency of the enumerators in eliciting occupational information was constant at each census.

[3] The rise was from 40·80 per cent to 40·99 per cent. With children under 15 included there was a fall in the proportion occupied from 45·48 per cent to 42·88 per cent.

[4] Supplement to the 75th *Annual Report* of the Registrar General for England and Wales, part IV, pp. iv–vii.

[5] *General Report* of the 1951 census, p. 51.

factory inspectors' reports are the main source of miscellaneous employment data for individual industries. In 1893 the Labour Department of the Board of Trade was set up with the specific duty of collecting and publishing labour statistics: thereafter its *Annual Abstract of Labour Statistics* gradually absorbed the main employment series available in other sources.[1]

With the coming of widespread compulsory insurance for manual workers late in 1920, annual estimates relating to a substantial proportion of the numbers occupied in different industries became possible, though the Ministry's industry classification was not brought into line with the census of population system until 1923. Changes in the scope of the insurance scheme seriously affect the comparability of figures for some industries over the period 1923–47. But this series, shown in table 2, is particularly valuable for year-to-year comparisons, and it does give some idea of long-period changes.

Table 2 is the basis of the percentage figures of unemployment given in table 5. The total numbers unemployed, shown in table 4, are however, more complete, since they are derived from Labour Exchange records, and include both insured and uninsured workers registered for employment.[2] Before 1922 there are no general statistics of unemployment. But certain trade unions which paid unemployment benefit to their members, did make returns to the Labour Department, and these returns cover a wide variety of industries back to 1888. For a few unions in the engineering, shipbuilding and metal group they go back to 1851.

The percentages computed from these returns have been commonly used as a general indicator of unemployment. In view of the small number of workers covered by them this is obviously a hazardous procedure. They consist almost exclusively of skilled male workers, they tend to over-represent industries which are vulnerable to cyclical employment fluctuations, and they ignore completely some of the more stable industries (agriculture, domestic service, and railways for example). The industries covered by the returns change in relative importance over the period: before 1867 the engineering, metal and shipbuilding trades were preponderant, in the 1880's this group accounted for three-fifths of the totals covered, in the 1920's for two-fifths. Nevertheless the official view of the Ministry of Labour in 1926 (by which time it was possible to check the trade union returns against unemployment insurance data) was that for the period 1881–1925 'the general percentages provide a valuable guide to the direction of the changes in unemployment and a rough indication of the comparative state of employment at different periods, although they cannot be relied upon as an absolute measure of the total amount of unemployment in all industries at any particular date'.[3]

---

[1] The first *Abstract of Labour Statistics* dates from 1894. It gave statistics of employment in coal mines from the *Third Abstract*, in iron and steel and factory trades in the *Tenth Abstract* and in railways from the *Sixteenth Abstract*.

[2] They thus exclude salaried workers, and some wage earners (mainly married women) who would normally be regarded as unemployed but who did not register.

[3] In a memorandum submitted to the Balfour *Committee on Industry and Trade* and published in its 'Survey of Industrial Relations' 1926, pp. 218–9. Further discussion of the reliability of this material is given on pp. 244–5 of the Survey.

It is rather surprising that the trade union enquiry and legislation of the 1860's and 1870's did not lead to the establishment of more annual returns on labour matters, but it was not until about two decades later that official series of trade union membership and finances, and of industrial disputes began to be published. Membership figures for all unions established in Britain first appeared in 1892. These are shown in table 6. Complete financial statistics of all trade unions registered as friendly societies (table 8) were not published until 1910, but details of the 100 principal unions (table 7) go back as far as 1892. Earlier information about 18 individual unions, going back in one case to 1850, is given in the first *Statistical Tables and Report on Trade Unions*.[1] Detailed statistics of industrial disputes date from 1888, and only the most important are shown here in table 9. The break caused by the partition of Ireland is much less important in these (as in all other labour series) than might have been expected, because of the smallness of its industrial population.

[1] *S.P.* 1887, LXXXIX.

Labour Force 1. Occupations—Great Britain 1811–1951

NOTES TO PARTS A, B, AND C

[1] Sources: *Census Reports*, 1811–1921.

[2] For parts B and C slight modifications have been made to the census categories of 1911 in order to achieve comparability over a greater period than would otherwise have been possible. The main occupations under each heading (where these are not obvious) and the modifications of the 1911 census categories are detailed below. The major general difference between these parts and part D is that in 1911 and earlier censuses, owners, general labourers, and dealers were so far as possible counted according to the raw material with which they worked. In addition to this major break, there is another of almost as great significance between 1871 and 1881. In the former and earlier censuses, retired persons were included in the occupation which they had formerly followed, if this was stated by them.

Modified 1911 *Categories—Principal Features*

(i) *Public Administration*—includes government messengers and clerks and Post Office Workers, but not telephonists and telegraphists (except for Scotland in 1911 only).

(ii) *Armed Forces*—includes retired officers, but not other-rank pensioners.

(iii) *Professional Occupations, etc.*—includes professional entertainers and sportsmen. Veterinary surgeons have been excluded throughout, as have chemists and druggists.

(iv) *Domestic Offices, etc.*—catering trades and hairdressers are included, but domestic coachmen, grooms and gardeners have been excluded (except as indicated in note 3).

(v) *Transport, etc.*—government telephonists and telegraphists, and domestic coachmen and grooms are included (except as indicated in note 3).

(vi) *Commercial Occupations*—includes clerks and typists (though not railway clerks except in 1841).

(vii) *Agriculture, etc.*—veterinary surgeons and domestic gardeners are included.

(viii) *Metal Manufacture, etc.*—includes those engaged in making musical and surgical instruments, games tackle, toys, etc. All builders of vehicles and ships are included, whether using wood or metal. Gasfitters, plumbers, locksmiths, and their assistants have been excluded.

(ix) *Wood, etc.*—includes French polishers, undertakers, cane and cork workers, carvers and gilders.

(x) *Building, etc.*—includes carpenters, gasfitters, plumbers, locksmiths, and their assistants.

(xi) *Chemicals, etc.*—includes chemists and druggists, and workers in rubber and waterproof goods.

(xii) *Clothing*—hairdressers and wigmakers are excluded. Boot and shoe makers and repairers are in this category.

(xiii) *Food, Drink, and Tobacco*—the catering trades are excluded.

This modified classification has been followed so far as possible in all years from 1841–1921, though changes in each census render exact comparisons usually impossible. A vertical line has been inserted wherever an approximate comparison is inappropriate.

[3] The 1841 census is particularly difficult to splice on to later figures, since there was scarcely any classification of occupations by the compilers. The following are the principal causes of lack of comparability between 1841 and later years:

Public Administration—some who would later have been included under this heading were simply described as messengers and are included under *Transport and Communications*; others, who were also engaged in trade, are included with *All Others Occupied*.

Professional Occupations, etc.—nurses were returned as domestic servants in Scotland in 1841 (and may have been in England also to a fair extent).

Domestic Offices, etc.—many who in later censuses were returned as domestic coachmen, grooms, and gardeners, were simply described as servants in 1841, thus greatly swelling this category so far as males are concerned.

Commercial Occupations—includes railway clerks in 1841, and also, it seems clear, many who were described as clerks in 1841 who would later have been more precisely defined, and attributed to other categories.

Transport, etc.—many domestic coachmen and grooms were not included in 1841, nor were railway clerks. From the very small number of dockers returned in 1841, it must be presumed that many described themselves as general labourers, and so are included in *All Others Occupied*.

[4] The 1841 census describes as unoccupied many who would later have been assigned to an occupation. This is clear from a comparison of the Totals Occupied and Unoccupied in 1841 and 1851. At the later date there appears to have been a decline of over half-a-million men unoccupied and an increase in the women occupied of over a million. Changes of this magnitude are clearly due to differences in the methods and efficiency of enumeration.

[5] The 1911 census reference numbers of occupations used for each heading here are: *Public Administration* 2–9, *Armed Forces* 10–18, *Professional Occupations, etc.* 19–29 and 31–49, *Domestic Offices, etc.* 50–51, 55–65, 396, and 425–432, *Commercial Occupations* 66–77, *Transport, etc.* 78–116, *Agriculture, etc.* 30, 54, and 117–129, *Fishing* 130, *Mining, etc.* 131–154, *Metal Manufacture, etc.* 155–200 and 203–241, *Building, etc.* 84–85, 201–202, and 242–265, *Wood, etc.* 266–282, *Bricks, etc.* 283–290, *Chemicals, etc.* 291–307, 363, and 447, *Skins, etc.* 308–315, *Paper, etc.* 316–334 and 439–441, *Textiles* 335–375, *Clothing* 376–395, 397–399, and 467 (females only), *Food, etc.* 400–424, and 433, *Gas, etc. Supply* 434–436.

[6] The following numbers of children under ten years old were recorded as occupied:

	1851	1861	1871
Males	26,492	22,755	11,592
Females	15,434	13,760	10,244

With these exceptions, and unrecorded numbers in 1841 and 1881 (the latter very small), the figures for the years before 1921 apply to persons over ten years old. Those for 1921 apply to people of at least twelve years old.

[7] So far as possible, those not gainfully employed are included in the heading *Total Unoccupied*. For 1871 and earlier censuses, therefore, persons returned as land proprietors, house proprietors, capitalists, students, wives (of all kinds), farmers' female relatives, Chelsea pensioners, navy pensioners, etc. have been counted as unoccupied.

A. 1811–41

	Number of Families			Males 20 or over	
	1811	1821	1831	1831	1841
Agricultural Occupations	896	979	961	1,243	1,208
Trade, Manufactures, and Handicraft	1,129	1,350	1,435	1,564	2,028
Others	519	612	1,018	1,137	1,422

B. 1841–1921, Males—based on the 1911 Census Categories

	1841	1851	1861	1871	1881	1891	1901	1911	1921
Public Administration	40	64	72	106	109	146	191	271	383
Armed Forces	51	63	118	124	114	134	176	221	236
Professional Occupations and their Subordinate Services	113	162	179	204	254	287	348	413	415
Domestic Offices and Personal Services	255	193	195	230	238	293	341	456	371
Commercial Occupations	94	91	130	212	352	449	597	739	904
Transport and Communications	196	433	579	654	870	1,104	1,409	1,571	1,530
of which: railways	2	29	60	96	157	212	318	370	354
roads	70	139	193	229	315	407	565	600	595
sea, canals and docks	76	153	202	191	205	235	263	292	311
Agriculture, Horticulture and Forestry	1,434	1,788	1,779	1,634	1,517	1,422	1,339	1,436	1,344
Fishing	24	36	39	47	58	53	51	53	51
Mining and Quarrying, and Workers in the Products of Mines and Quarries	218	383	457	517	604	751	931	1,202	1,240
Metal Manufacture, Machines, Implements, Vehicles, Precious Metals, etc.	396	536	747	869	977	1,151	1,485	1,795	2,125
Building and Construction	376	496	593	712	875	899	1,216	1,140	894
Wood, Furniture, Fittings, and Decorations	107	152	171	186	185	206	267	287	511
Bricks, Cement, Pottery, and Glass	48	75	93	97	111	119	152	145	100
Chemicals, Oil, Soap, Resin, etc.	23	42	47	61	72	89	116	155	93
Skins, Leather, Hair, and Feathers	47	55	61	68	73	80	87	90	72
Paper, Printing, Books, and Stationery	44	62	79	94	134	178	212	253	193
Textiles	525	661	612	584	554	593	557	639	409
Clothing	358	418	413	390	379	409	423	432	315
Food, Drink, and Tobacco	268	348	386	448	494	597	701	806	228
Gas, Water, and Electricity Supply	2	7	12	18	24	38	62	86	...
All Others Occupied	474	438	511	972	862	1,009	887	741	2,186
TOTAL OCCUPIED	5,093	6,545	7,266	8,220	8,852	10,010	11,548	12,927	13,656
Total Unoccupied	1,604	1,060	1,061	1,115	1,776	2,028	2,242	2,166	2,003

C. 1841–1921 Females—based on the 1911 Census Categories

	1841	1851	1861	1871	1881	1891	1901	1911	1921
Public Administration	3	3	4	7	9	17	29	50	81
Armed Forces	—	—	—	—	—	—	—	—	- -
Professional Occupations and their Subordinate Services	49	103	126	152	203	264	326	383	441
Domestic Offices and Personal Services	989	1,135	1,407	1,678	1,756	2,036	2,003	2,127	1,845
Commercial Occupations	1	- -	2	5	11	26	76	157	587
Transport and Communications	4	13	11	16	15	20	27	38	72
of which: railways	- -	- -	- -	- -	1	1	2	3	3
roads	1	3	3	3	2	2	1	3	7
sea, canals and docks	- -	3	1	1	1	1	1	1	3
Agriculture, Horticulture, and Forestry	81	229	163	135	116	80	86	117	105
Fishing	- -	1	1	1	3	1	- -	- -	- -
Mining and Quarrying, and Workers in the Products of Mines and Quarries	7	11	6	11	8	7	6	8	9
Metal Manufacture, Machines, Implements, Vehicles, Precious Metals, etc.	14	36	45	46	49	59	84	128	175
Building and Construction	1	1	1	4	2	3	3	5	5
Wood, Furniture, Fittings, and Decorations	5	8	15	26	21	25	30	35	31
Bricks, Cement, Pottery and Glass	10	15	19	25	27	32	37	42	45
Chemicals, Oil, Soap, Resin, etc.	1	4	3	5	9	17	31	46	35
Skins, Leather, Hair, and Feathers	3	5	8	10	16	20	27	32	33
Paper, Printing, Books, and Stationery	6	16	23	31	53	78	111	144	121
Textiles	358	635	676	726	745	795	795	870	701
Clothing	200	491	596	594	667	759	792	825	602
Food, Drink, and Tobacco	42	53	71	78	98	163	216	308	123
Gas, Water, and Electricity Supply	—	—	- -	- -	- -	- -	- -	- -	...
All Others Occupied	41	75	80	106	78	89	75	98	688
TOTAL OCCUPIED	1,815	2,832	3,254	3,650	3,887	4,489	4,751	5,413	5,699
Total Unoccupied	5,369	5,294	5,762	6,429	7,617	8,537	10,229	11,375	11,968

Labour Force 1. *continued*

NOTES TO PART D

[1] SOURCES: *Census Reports*, 1921–51.

[2] The Standard Industrial Classification as used in the 1951 census has been adopted here with one exception, namely the formation of the heading *Public Administration*. The principal features to be noted are:

(i) *Public Administration*—composed of Civil Service and Local Authority Officials and staff (other than clerks and typists in 1931 and 1951, but including them in 1921), and the police force.

(ii) *Armed Forces*—only effectives are counted.

(iii) *Professional and Technical Occupations*—includes veterinary surgeons.

(iv) *Commercial, etc. Occupations*—wholesale and retail dealers are included.

(v) *Metal Manufacture, etc.*—includes plumbers and gasfitters and some categories which in 1911 came under the heading of gas, water and electricity supply.

(vi) *Wood, etc.*—includes carpenters, but not upholsterers or bedding and mattress workers.

(vii) *Building, etc.*—does not include plumbers, gasfitters or carpenters.

(viii) *Treatment of Non-Metalliferous Mining Products other than Coal*—corresponds closely to the 1911 heading bricks, cement, pottery and glass.

(ix) *Coal-gas and Coke, Chemicals, etc.*—includes many who came under the heading gas, water and electricity supply in 1911, and no longer includes workers in rubber or waterproof goods.

(x) *Textile Goods and Clothing*—includes upholsterers and bedding and mattress workers.

(xi) *Administrators, etc.*—higher Civil Service and Local Authority officials are here excluded.

[3] The figures for 1921 relate to persons of twelve years old and over, those for 1931 to 14-year olds and over, and those for 1951 to all aged fifteen and over.

D. 1921–51—based on the 1951 Census Categories

(in thousands)

	Males			Females		
	1921	1931	1951	1921	1931	1951
Public Administration	261	141	214	78	3	21
Armed Forces	221	189	560	- -	—	18
Professional and Technical Occupations	378	490	788	408	443	588
Professional Entertainers and Sportsmen	74	100	90	30	24	23
Personal Service	372	516	512	1,845	2,129	1,610
Commercial Finance and Insurance Occupations (excluding clerical staff)	1,180	1,621	1,357	579	701	856
Clerks, Typists, etc.	581	778	932	492	648	1,409
Transport and Communications	1,591	1,748	1,569	75	82	149
of which: railways	354	303	310	3	2	8
roads	595	761	811	7	8	37
sea, canals and docks	311	303	217	3	2	1
Agriculture, Horticulture and Forestry	1,341	1,282	1,105	107	71	114
Fishing	51	40	26	- -	- -	- -
Mining and Quarrying	1,204	1,083	675	7	4	2
Metal Manufacture, Engineering and Allied Trades	1,888	1,765	2,517	123	147	208
Building and Contracting (including Painting and Decorating)	738	970	1,268	10	17	14
Wood, Cane and Cork (including Furniture)	453	497	492	10	8	15
Treatment of Non-Metalliferous Mining Products other than Coal	69	82	86	36	46	48
Coal, Gas and Coke, Chemicals and Allied Trades	41	52	102	4	5	14
Leather, Leather Goods (including boots and shoes) and Fur	178	178	125	59	66	67
Paper, Books and Printing	155	178	178	97	108	93
Textiles	314	324	220	634	663	413
Textile Goods and Clothing (other than boots and shoes)	155	164	135	544	544	474
Food, Drink, and Tobacco	147	161	175	77	73	97
Administrators and Managers in Extractive or Manufacturing Industries	287	350	347	25	26	30
Warehousemen, Storekeepers, Packers, Bottlers, etc.	243	268	379	141	162	199
All Others Occupied	1,749	1,851	1,794	319	317	497
TOTAL OCCUPIED	13,656	14,790	15,649	5,701	6,265	6,961
Total Unoccupied	2,016	1,552	2,213	11,966	12,055	13,084

Labour Force 2. Estimated Numbers of Insured Employees (by Industry) at July in Each Year—United Kingdom 1923–47

NOTES

[1] SOURCE: *Ministry of Labour Gazette*, though for the years 1923–36 the figures are to be found more conveniently in the 18th–22nd *Abstract of Labour Statistics*.
[2] All figures include unemployed workers attached to particular industries, but the grand total also includes some unemployed not attached to any industry.
[3] Certain classes of employee were excluded from the scope of the insurance scheme in this period. Briefly these consisted of agricultural workers until the establishment of a special scheme in 1936, most non-manual workers, and certain workers under public authorities, railways and public utilities.
[4] The three major changes in the scope of the insurance scheme during this period were in 1928, when people aged 65 or over were excluded, in 1934, when those aged 14 and 15 were included, and in 1940, when women aged 60 and over were excluded and non-manual workers earning from £250 to £420 per year were included. The first two of these breaks are indicated by giving two figures for 1927 and 1935, one on the old basis and the second on the new.

A. Males

(in thousands)

	1923	1924	1925	1926	1927	1927	1928	1929	1930	1931	1932
Agriculture											
Fishing	24	26	27	27	28	27	27	27	27	30	30
Mining	1,337	1,353	1,329	1,323	1,299	1,260	1,211	1,173	1,169	1,146	1,142
Non-Metalliferous Mining Products	40	40	42	44	46	44	44	46	46	47	48
Brick, Tile, Pipe, etc. Making	54	63	70	75	80	75	74	75	77	80	81
Pottery, Earthenware, etc.	36	38	34	35	35	32	33	35	36	35	36
Glass Trades	37	38	37	37	36	35	35	37	37	38	37
Chemicals, etc.	160	161	159	157	159	161	161	164	162	155	160
Metal Manufacture	342	340	327	326	326	314	304	308	309	293	289
Engineering, Shipbuilding and Repairing, and Metal Trades	1,613	1,583	1,576	1,566	1,557	1,506	1,509	1,537	1,563	1,550	1,521
Textile Trades	521	519	519	523	522	499	506	508	507	470	492
Leather and Leather Goods	49	49	48	46	46	45	44	44	43	42	44
Clothing	203	204	205	202	200	193	192	196	193	195	197
Food, Drink, and Tobacco	297	300	300	308	306	296	295	296	300	303	312
Woodworking, etc.	162	166	169	174	180	172	177	182	185	192	195
Paper, Printing, etc.	213	221	220	229	233	224	230	236	243	251	260
Building and Contracting	835	851	900	962	1,008	951	967	1,008	1,008	1,118	1,136
Other Manufactures	81	85	88	92	95	91	96	101	102	98	98
Gas, Water, and Electricity Supply	166	165	171	177	165	157	157	156	160	166	167
Transport and Communications	762	760	769	774	768	743	755	775	787	837	840
Distributive Trades	750	811	885	917	964	939	974	1,015	1,064	1,137	1,202
Commerce, Banking, Finance and Insurance	147	150	148	149	151	150	149	155	158	160	165
Miscellaneous Trades and Services	663	665	692	700	695	663	680	709	756	820	848
TOTAL INSURED	8,493	8,586	8,717	8,844	8,899	8,576	8,622	8,755	8,932	9,187	9,302

	1933	1934	1935	1935	1936	1937	1938	1939	1945	1946	1947
Agriculture						544	540	533	512	562	574
Fishing	31	31	32	32	34	34	33	32	11	20	25
Mining	1,119	1,078	1,034	1,069	1,025	999	990	968	776	792	807
Non-Metalliferous Mining Products	48	49	52	53	54	59	61	61	40	57	65
Brick, Tile, Pipe, etc. Making	83	90	95	101	103	106	107	99	30	55	63
Pottery, Earthenware, etc.	35	35	33	36	36	36	36	34	15	23	28
Glass Trades	39	40	40	42	42	43	43	42	28	37	43
Chemicals, etc.	162	158	157	162	166	174	185	194	233	218	228
Metal Manufacture	284	288	284	291	304	326	325	336	283	296	320
Engineering, Shipbuilding and Repairing, and Metal Trades	1,499	1,507	1,549	1,650	1,722	1,906	1,977	2,064	2,373	2,253	2,441
Textile Trades	485	478	471	499	488	480	459	493	231	292	340
Leather and Leather Goods	46	47	47	50	51	51	48	48	28	36	44
Clothing	199	195	194	211	207	202	204	203	110	135	164
Food, Drink, and Tobacco	321	328	330	347	348	356	356	359	256	304	341
Woodworking, etc.	194	200	200	219	227	230	230	224	128	179	206
Paper, Printing, etc.	262	264	264	283	286	292	292	294	148	211	248
Building and Contracting	1,150	1,188	1,242	1,273	1,329	1,347	1,393	1,417	637	1,036	1,172
Other Manufactures	102	101	102	110	109	107	105	109	86	138	168
Gas, Water, and Electricity Supply	175	186	192	195	204	212	215	214	142	191	218
Transport and Communications	825	833	842	860	877	885	875	863	764	910	978
Distributive Trades	1,236	1,262	1,267	1,427	1,441	1,418	1,422	1,394	635	827	951
Commerce, Banking, Finance and Insurance	168	176	179	184	183	187	186	181	88	136	146
Miscellaneous Trades and Services	883	900	927	960	978	997	1,115	1,152	1,036	1,262	1,387
TOTAL INSURED	9,344	9,435	9,531	10,055	10,243	11,130	11,358	11,428	8,602	10,647	11,100

B. Females

(in thousands)

	1923	1924	1925	1926	1927	1927	1928	1929	1930	1931	1932
Agriculture											
Fishing	1	1	1	1	1	1	1	1	1	1	1
Mining	10	10	11	10	9	9	8	8	8	8	7
Non-Metalliferous Mining Products	1	2	2	2	2	2	2	3	2	3	3
Brick, Tile, Pipe, etc. Making	7	8	8	8	8	8	7	7	7	7	6
Pottery, Earthenware, etc.	36	36	39	38	38	38	38	39	43	43	39
Glass Trades	7	7	8	7	8	7	7	8	8	9	8
Chemicals, etc.	54	53	52	52	54	54	54	54	56	59	56
Metal Manufacture	18	18	19	18	17	17	17	16	17	17	16
Engineering, Shipbuilding and Repairing, and Metal Trades	224	231	248	254	251	250	259	272	289	290	281
Textile Trades	791	808	812	813	806	797	806	807	832	823	776
Leather and Leather Goods	21	21	21	22	23	23	23	24	24	24	24
Clothing	377	375	379	380	384	383	385	386	394	412	408
Food, Drink, and Tobacco	203	211	220	215	217	216	212	217	226	232	223
Woodworking, etc.	30	29	30	30	31	31	31	32	33	34	34
Paper, Printing, etc.	135	140	142	145	146	145	144	151	157	160	158
Building and Contracting	9	9	9	9	9	9	10	10	11	11	11
Other Manufactures	46	48	49	51	50	50	53	56	56	59	56
Gas, Water, and Electricity Supply	7	6	7	7	6	6	7	6	6	8	7
Transport and Communications	30	27	29	28	29	29	30	32	34	35	34
Distributive Trades	504	544	580	597	617	614	640	664	701	738	749
Commerce, Banking, Finance and Insurance	80	76	73	71	72	72	72	74	75	75	78
Miscellaneous Trades and Services	402	418	437	442	453	447	454	474	494	535	530
Total Insured	2,993	3,078	3,175	3,197	3,232	3,208	3,260	3,339	3,474	3,583	3,506

	1933	1934	1935	1935	1936	1937	1938	1939	1945	1946	1947
Agriculture						41	47	50	143	109	96
Fishing	1	1	1	1	1	1	1	1	—	—	—
Mining	7	6	6	7	6	6	6	6	14	13	13
Non-Metalliferous Mining Products	2	2	2	2	2	3	3	3	8	7	7
Brick, Tile, Pipe, etc. Making	6	6	6	7	6	7	7	7	5	6	6
Pottery, Earthenware, etc.	41	40	40	45	45	46	46	45	24	32	36
Glass Trades	9	9	9	10	10	11	11	11	17	17	15
Chemicals, etc.	59	59	58	67	67	71	73	77	196	129	113
Metal Manufacture	16	16	15	17	18	20	20	21	71	56	47
Engineering, Shipbuilding and Repairing, and Metal Trades	279	289	302	346	367	400	402	419	1,109	712	649
Textile Trades	761	740	715	783	779	778	746	732	430	458	480
Leather and Leather Goods	24	25	25	29	30	31	30	31	22	25	27
Clothing	415	418	413	477	486	488	492	500	309	364	387
Food, Drink, and Tobacco	235	226	223	260	266	271	278	283	226	231	231
Woodworking, etc.	33	33	33	39	40	42	44	43	58	50	44
Paper, Printing, etc.	160	157	156	186	189	194	199	201	124	144	155
Building and Contracting	12	12	12	13	14	15	15	16	25	26	24
Other Manufactures	59	59	58	67	65	67	66	69	72	105	113
Gas, Water, and Electricity Supply	8	9	8	8	10	10	12	12	27	22	19
Transport and Communications	34	35	37	39	41	44	42	43	190	142	112
Distributive Trades	756	743	740	831	854	874	908	924	850	873	862
Commerce, Banking, Finance and Insurance	78	81	81	84	87	91	96	99	144	124	127
Miscellaneous Trades and Services	542	557	584	631	657	690	841	877	1,319	1,245	1,248
Total Insured	3,539	3,525	3,527	3,947	4,042	4,205	4,385	4,424	5,398	4,925	4,820

NOTES

[1] SOURCES: *S.P.* 1905, LXXXIV for 1851-1903, and the *Abstract of Labour Statistics* thereafter.
[2] The figures in columns headed A are partly computed from expenditure on unemployment benefit; those in columns headed B are from returns of unemployment at the end of each month.
[3] From 1867 onwards the total of unions making returns included others besides those separately shown here.

	All Unions Making Returns		Engineering, Metal and Shipbuilding Unions		Amalgamated Society of Carpenters and Joiners	Woodworking and Furnishing Unions		Printing and Bookbinding Unions		All Others Making Returns	
	A	B	A	B	B	A	B	A	B	A	B
1851	3·9		3·9								
1852	6·0		6·0								
1853	1·7		1·7								
1854	2·9		2·9								
1855	5·4		5·4								
1856	4·7		4·9					1·6			
1857	6·0		6·1					2·3			
1858	11·9		12·2					2·5			
1859	3·8		3·9					1·4			
1860	1·9		1·9		0·2			2·1			
1861	5·2		5·5		1·8			3·1			
1862	8·4		9·0		1·8			3·5			
1863	6·0		6·7		1·2			3·2			
1864	2·7		3·0		0·4			1·3			
1865	2·1		2·4		0·3			2·0			
1866	3·3		3·9		1·1			1·8			
1867	7·4		9·1		3·0	4·8		2·7		5·9	
1868	7·9		10·0		2·9	5·0		2·5		6·2	
1869	6·7		8·9		3·6	4·5		2·8		0·4	
1870	3·9		4·4		3·7	4·8		3·5		0·2	
1871	1·6		1·3		2·5	3·5		2·0		0·3	
1872	0·9		0·9		1·2	2·4		1·5		0·0	
1873	1·2		1·4		0·9	1·8		1·3		0·3	
1874	1·7		2·3		0·8	2·1		1·6		0·1	
1875	2·4		3·5		0·6	2·0		1·6		0·3	
1876	3·7		5·2		0·7	2·4		2·4		1·3	
1877	4·7		6·3		1·2	3·5		2·6		2·8	
1878	6·8		9·0		3·5	4·4		3·2		3·0	
1879	11·4		15·3		8·2	8·3		4·0		3·3	
1880	5·5		6·7		6·1	3·2		3·2		2·2	
1881	3·5		3·8		5·2	2·7		2·8		1·5	
1882	2·3		2·3		3·5	2·5		2·4		0·9	
1883	2·6		2·7		3·6	2·5		2·2		1·2	
1884	8·1		10·8		4·7	3·0		2·1		1·4	
1885	9·3		12·9		7·1	4·1		2·5		1·8	
1886	10·2		13·5		8·2	4·7		2·6		5·2	
1887	7·6		10·4		6·5	3·6		2·2		1·9	
1888	4·6	4·9	5·5	6·0	5·7	3·6	3·1	2·5	2·4	1·2	3·2
1889	2·1	2·1	2·0	2·3	3·0	2·6	2·4	2·1	2·5	0·9	0·0
1890	2·1	2·1	2·4	2·2	2·2	1·5	2·5	1·9	2·2	0·6	1·6
1891	3·2	3·5	4·4	4·1	1·9	1·7	2·1	2·9	4·0	0·7	1·7
1892	5·8	6·3	8·2	7·7	3·1	2·4	3·8	3·6	4·3	1·3	5·6
1893		7·5		11·4	3·1		4·1		4·1		2·6
1894		6·9		11·2	4·3		4·4		5·7		1·9
1895		5·8		8·2	4·4		3·6		4·9		3·3

Labour Force 3. *continued*

	All Unions Making Returns		Engineering, Metal and Shipbuilding Unions		Amalgamated Society of Carpenters and Joiners	Woodworking and Furnishing Unions		Printing and Bookbinding Unions		All Others Making Returns	
	A	B	A	B	B	A	B	A	B	A	B
1896		3·3		4·2	1·3		2·0		4·3		2·3
1897		3·3		4·8	1·2		2·2		3·9		1·8
1898		2·8		4·0	0·9		2·3		3·7		1·5
1899		2·0		2·4	1·2		2·1		3·9		1·2
1900		2·5		2·6	2·6		2·8		4·2		1·6
1901		3·3		3·8	3·9		3·7		4·5		2·1
1902		4·0		5·5	4·0		4·1		4·6		1·9
1903		4·7		6·6	4·4		4·7		4·4		2·5
1904		6·0		8·4	7·3		6·8		4·7		3·0
1905		5·0		6·6	8·0		5·8		5·1		2·3
1906		3·6		4·1	6·9		4·8		4·5		1·9
1907		3·7		4·9	7·3		4·6		4·4		1·6
1908		7·8		12·5	11·6		8·3		5·5		2·9
1909		7·7		13·0	11·7		7·6		5·6		2·6
1910		4·7		6·8	8·3		5·4		4·9		2·2
1911		3·0		3·4	4·2		3·3		5·1		2·1
1912		3·2		3·6	3·7		3·1		5·2		2·1
1913		2·1		2·2	3·3		2·4		4·0		1·4
1914		3·3		3·3	3·3		4·1		4·5		2·9
1915		1·1		0·6	2·2		2·1		3·1		
1916		0·4		0·3	0·9		1·0		1·3		
1917		0·7		0·2	0·5		0·6		0·6		
1918		0·8		0·2	0·2		0·5		0·3		
1919		2·4		3·2	1·2		1·3		1·6		
1920		2·4		3·2	0·3		1·4		1·6		
1921		14·8		22·1	3·9		9·4		7·3		
1922		15·2		27·0	7·5		7·6		6·6		
1923		11·3		20·6	5·0		5·8		4·7		
1924		8·1		13·8	1·9		4·5		3·3		
1925		10·5		13·5	2·2		4·4		2·8		
1926		12·2		18·2	5·2		8·2		4·3		

NOTES

[1] SOURCES: 1922–36—18th–22nd *Abstract of Labour Statistics*; 1937–56—*Ministry of Labour Gazette*. The latter is the original source for the whole period.

[2] The figures include people temporarily stopped as well as permanently unemployed. The proportion of the latter to the total is not available for every year, but the following are known:

1926	63%	1934	79%	1943	65%	1951	94%
1927	69%	1935	81%	1944	68%	1952	79%
1928	69%	1936	82%	1945	99%	1953	94%
1929	72%			1946	99%	1954	95%
1930	68%	1939	86%	1947	68%	1955	92%
1931	74%	1940	83%	1948	98%	1956	89%
1932	76%	1941	84%	1949	97%		
1933	78%	1942	95%	1950	97%		

(in thousands)

average of twelve monthly figures in each year

1922	1,543	1931	2,630	1940 (b)	963	1949	308
1923	1,275	1932	2,745	1941	350	1950	314
1924	1,130	1933	2,521	1942	123	1951	253
1925	1,226	1934	2,159	1943	82	1952	414
1926	1,385	1935	2,036	1944	75	1953	342
1927	1,088	1936	1,755	1945	137	1954	285
1928	1,217	1937 (a)	1,484	1946	374	1955	232
1929	1,216	1938	1,791	1947	480	1956	257
1930	1,917	1939	1,514	1948	310		

(a) There was a change in the method of accounting in September 1937, which resulted in a fall in numbers recorded of about 50,000. In arriving at this average, the number recorded on the new basis has been used for September. (b) After July 1940, men at Government Training Centres were no longer recorded as unemployed.

Labour Force 5. Percentages of Insured Workers Unemployed by Industry—United Kingdom 1923–39

SOURCE: *Ministry of Labour Gazette.*

NOTE

(Averages of the Percentages in January and July each year, excluding workers under 16)

	1923(a)	1924	1925	1926	1927	1928(b)	1929	1930	1931	1932	1933	1934	1935	1936	1937(c)	1938	1939
Fishing	12·0	14·1	12·5	16·7	13·8	11·6	11·8	13·3	18·0	22·0	22·8	23·2	21·1	22·0	24·2	26·4	24·6
Coalmining	3·0	5·8	11·5	9·5	19·0	23·6	19·0	20·6	28·4	34·5	33·5	29·7	27·2	22·8	16·1	16·7	12·5
Brick, Tile, Pipe, etc. Manufacture	7·6	7·9	6·8	15·2	6·9	12·4	11·5	13·0	18·0	21·5	20·2	13·3	11·9	11·7	8·2	9·1	10·9
Pottery, Earthenware, etc.	13·2	13·3	18·1	38·6	16·6	18·6	17·0	23·7	36·3	36·2	30·9	23·8	22·3	21·8	17·5	20·7	22·0
Chemicals	11·8	9·9	9·1	10·9	7·2	6·1	6·5	10·0	17·6	17·3	15·2	11·3	11·0	9·2	6·8	7·4	6·4
Pig Iron	10·1	14·1	21·5	43·4	16·4	18·7	14·4	20·3	37·7	43·8	41·5	27·7	22·3	16·0	10·7	12·9	17·6
Steel Melting and Iron Puddling, and Iron and Steel Rolling and Forging	21·2	22·0	25·0	40·4	19·4	22·4	20·1	28·2	45·5	47·9	41·5	27·3	23·5	17·4	11·4	19·5	15·1
General Engineering: Engineers' Iron and Steel Founding	20·5	16·9	13·3	15·1	11·8	9·8	9·9	14·2	27·0	29·1	27·4	18·4	13·6	9·6	5·8	7·0	6·6
Electrical Engineering	7·3	5·5	5·6	7·5	5·9	4·8	4·6	6·6	14·1	16·8	16·5	9·6	7·0	4·8	3·1	4·7	4·4
Construction and Repair of Motors, Cycles and Aircraft	9·7	8·9	7·1	8·2	8·1	8·1	7·1	12·1	19·3	22·4	17·6	10·8	9·0	6·9	5·0	7·2	4·4
Shipbuilding and Repairing	43·6	30·3	33·5	39·5	29·7	24·5	25·3	27·6	51·9	62·0	61·7	51·2	44·4	33·3	24·4	21·4	20·9
Stove, Grate, Pipe, etc., and General Ironfounding	17·7	13·2	11·4	14·7	10·0	12·0	10·9	14·7	24·8	28·6	25·0	15·3	14·4	9·8	7·0	12·7	11·9
Electric Cable, Apparatus, Lamps, etc. Manufacture	16·2	7·7	7·2	7·4	7·7	5·6	5·3	7·5	13·9	13·3	14·5	10·0	8·8	7·9	5·0	8·1	6·2
Cotton Textiles	21·6	15·9	8·8	18·3	15·4	12·5	12·9	32·4	43·2	30·6	25·1	23·7	22·3	16·7	10·9	23·9	16·9
Wool Textiles	9·5	8·4	16·9	17·4	11·0	12·0	15·5	23·3	33·8	22·4	17·0	17·8	15·5	10·3	8·8	21·3	11·0
Linen Textiles	19·8	11·8	25·0	28·2	12·2	19·8	15·7	25·2	35·3	29·7	23·1	17·7	24·0	21·4	16·2	40·3	21·5
Hosiery Manufacture	7·9	7·4	9·8	10·3	7·6	5·8	7·1	12·5	20·8	13·5	12·8	10·9	13·7	9·4	8·1	12·6	7·9
Tailoring	6·7	10·4	11·9	11·2	9·2	9·2	10·0	12·3	17·7	17·6	18·2	16·3	15·3	13·8	12·3	15·5	12·6
Dressmaking and Millinery	6·3	8·6	9·0	7·7	6·2	5·9	6·1	6·6	9·7	11·5	11·7	8·9	8·3	8·8	7·5	9·2	9·4
Boots, Shoes, etc. Manufacture	10·6	8·6	11·3	11·5	11·3	13·4	15·5	15·2	22·2	18·0	19·5	21·4	17·1	14·6	12·1	14·3	10·4
Bread, Biscuits, Cakes, etc. Manufacture	9·9	9·8	9·3	8·4	7·2	6·6	7·2	8·7	12·4	12·2	11·8	10·7	10·6	10·3	8·7	8·8	8·3
Drink Industries	6·4	6·8	6·9	6·3	6·3	6·2	6·8	8·7	12·9	14·4	13·1	10·9	10·6	9·6	7·7	8·0	7·4
Sawmilling and Machined Woodwork	11·5	10·6	9·8	11·1	8·4	9·2	10·0	11·9	18·4	22·0	20·0	16·8	15·8	13·6	10·7	11·9	11·2
Furniture Manufacture and Upholstery	7·8	8·2	6·9	7·8	6·5	5·9	6·5	10·0	19·0	21·7	20·6	15·4	13·9	11·6	9·8	13·4	12·8
Printing, Publishing, and Bookbinding	5·6	5·6	5·2	5·4	5·2	4·6	4·6	6·0	9·8	11·0	10·3	9·2	8·7	8·1	6·7	6·9	7·1
Building	12·2	12·5	10·5	12·1	11·1	13·9	14·3	16·2	22·7	30·2	29·0	21·3	19·7	19·8	14·6	16·7	17·6
Gas, Water, and Electricity Supply	7·2	6·3	6·2	6·0	5·4	5·8	6·1	7·0	8·9	10·9	11·0	10·1	10·4	9·7	8·3	8·3	7·7
Railway Service	6·0	6·4	6·5	12·3	6·1	6·5	6·5	6·9	12·1	15·7	16·7	12·3	10·0	8·5	6·5	7·3	8·4
Tramway and Omnibus Service	3·1	3·1	3·6	4·3	3·7	3·1	3·1	3·8	5·0	5·9	6·1	5·6	4·8	4·0	3·3	3·2	3·1
Other Road Transport	17·3	15·8	13·9	16·1	11·8	11·7	11·7	14·8	19·3	22·2	22·6	20·1	18·7	16·1	12·3	12·5	11·9
Docks, Harbours, Canals, etc. Service	27·5	25·8	29·0	29·7	24·5	29·1	30·7	33·4	39·8	33·3	33·3	31·0	31·0	29·3	27·5	25·0	24·1
Distributive Trades	5·9	6·4	6·7	6·7	5·5	5·5	6·2	8·1	11·6	12·6	12·4	11·3	11·3	9·8	8·9	9·2	9·0
National Government Service	11·1	9·8	13·8	12·3	11·7	12·1	10·0	8·2	10·3	12·4	13·3	14·5	13·8	12·9	11·7	12·1	10·0
Local Government Service	6·0	6·9	8·6	9·0	8·2	8·6	9·6	10·7	13·7	18·2	19·6	20·3	20·2	19·7	17·6	17·2	14·6
Hotel, Public House, Club, etc. Service	9·8	11·3	11·4	9·0	7·9	7·6	8·7	6·1	17·5	17·5	16·7	16·7	15·5	15·0	13·9	15·5(d)	15·3
Laundry and Dry-cleaning Service	5·0	5·8	5·8	4·5	4·1	3·8	4·3	6·1	9·8	9·4	9·0	7·7	7·6	6·9	6·0	6·8	7·0
TOTAL INSURED WORKERS OVER 16 (except those in the Agricultural Scheme)	11·6	10·9	11·2	12·7	10·6	11·2	11·0	14·6	21·5	22·5	21·3	17·7	16·4	14·3	11·3	13·3	11·7

(a) The figures for 1923 are for July only.
(b) In the figures for 1928 and later, people over 65 years old are not counted.
(c) The method of counting the unemployed was changed in September 1937, resulting in a reduction in the total recorded of about 50,000. The effect on the percentage is scarcely significant.
(d) Domestic servants in clubs, hospitals, etc. were included for the first time in 1938.

Labour Force 6.   Numbers and Membership of Trade Unions with Headquarters in Great Britain and Northern Ireland—1892–1939

NOTES

[1] SOURCES: 1892–1936—*Abstract of Labour Statistics* (19th and 22nd issues); 1937–9—*Ministry of Labour Gazette*,
[2] Whilst the table relates to unions with headquarters in Great Britain and Northern Ireland, a small number of members in Southern Ireland is included. Because of the substantial revisions made to the earlier figures in the 19th

Abstract of Labour Statistics it is pointless to include statistics for the United Kingdom as constituted before 1922—the numbers given in the 17th and earlier issues are actually considerably *below* those shown here for the smaller area.
[3] The subdivision of the total membership by sexes is partly estimated as some unions cannot make precise returns.

	Total Unions	Total Members (000's)	Male Members (000's)	Female Members (000's)		Total Unions	Total Members (000's)	Male Members (000's)	Female Members (000's)
1892	1,233	1,576	...	...	1916	1,225	4,644	4,018	626
1893	1,279	1,559	...	...	1917	1,241	5,499	4,621	878
1894	1,314	1,530	...	...	1918	1,264	6,533	5,324	1,209
1895	1,340	1,504	...	...	1919	1,360	7,926	6,600	1,326
1896	1,358	1,608	1,466	142	1920	1,379	8,347	7,005	1,342
1897	1,353	1,731	1,583	147	1921	1,269	6,632	5,627	1,005
1898	1,326	1,752	1,608	144	1922	1,226	5,625	4,753	872
1899	1,325	1,911	1,761	150	1923	1,186	5,429	4,607	822
1900	1,323	2,022	1,868	154	1924	1,188	5,544	4,730	814
1901	1,322	2,025	1,873	152	1925	1,170	5,506	4,671	835
1902	1,297	2,013	1,857	156	1926	1,158	5,219	4,407	812
1903	1,285	1,994	1,838	156	1927	1,153	4,919	4,125	794
1904	1,256	1,967	1,802	165	1928	1,136	4,806	4,011	795
1905	1,244	1,997	1,817	180	1929	1,128	4,858	4,055	803
1906	1,282	2,210	1,999	211	1930	1,114	4,841	4,048	793
1907	1,283	2,513	2,263	250	1931	1,101	4,624	3,859	765
1908	1,268	2,485	2,230	255	1932	1,074	4,443	3,698	745
1909	1,260	2,477	2,214	263	1933	1,074	4,389	3,661	728
1910	1,269	2,565	2,287	278	1934	1,056	4,570	3,833	737
1911	1,290	3,139	2,804	335	1935	1,049	4,867	4,106	761
1912	1,252	3,416	3,026	390	1936	1,036	5,295	4,495	800
1913	1,269	4,135	3,702	433	1937	1,032	5,842	4,947	895
1914	1,260	4,145	3,708	437	1938	1,024	6,053	5,127	926
1915	1,229	4,359	3,868	491	1939	1,018	6,274	5,264	1,010

NOTE
[1] SOURCES: 1892–1910—1st to 17th *Abstract of Labour Statistics*, or annual *Report on Trade Unions* (both in sessional papers), whichever provides the latest figure for any year; 1911–32—18th–21st *Abstract of Labour Statistics*.

	Members (in thousands)	Income (in £000)	Expenditure (in £000)				Funds at end of Year (in £000)
			Unemployment Benefit (a)	Dispute Benefit	Provident Benefits	Management and Other Expenses	
1892	903	1,462	325	398	377	333	1,574
1893	909	1,614	458	574	413	380	1,352
1894	924	1,617	447	168	415	396	1,546
1895	907	1,542	417	197	461	302	1,712
1896	988	1,652	261	168	448	335	2,151
1897	1,107	1,968	330	646	480	432	2,221
1898	1,084	1,902	237	328	505	410	2,644
1899	1,164	1,835	187	120	551	395	3,226
1900	1,210	1,950	263	140	587	453	3,733
1901	1,219	2,050	328	210	619	488	4,139
1902	1,217	2,094	433	221	653	500	4,426
1903	1,206	2,109	517	176	695	535	4,612
1904	1,203	2,124	660	118	749	528	4,680
1905	1,220	2,228	529	214	787	549	4,830
1906	1,307	2,364	429	154	820	570	5,222
1907	1,471	2,518	469	138	866	600	5,668
1908	1,451	2,767	1,026	606	929	672	5,201
1909	1,437	2,585	952	156	923	675	5,079
1910	1,472	2,716	702	352	926	662	5,153
1911(b)	2,218	3,386	448	590	994	733	5,669
1912	2,429	3,535	591	1,672	1,054	871	4,828
1913	3,023	4,132	490	373	1,199	1,012	5,675
1914	3,023	4,494	993	588	1,197	1,055	6,146
1915	3,233	4,403	382	91	1,182	1,138	7,546
1916	3,477	4,532	151	113	1,172	1,181	9,248
1917	4,174	5,211	250	132	1,233	1,393	11,200
1918	5,000	6,304	224	231	1,422	1,879	13,351
1919	6,046	8,721	1,081	2,064	1,479	2,605	14,081
1920	6,335	11,583	1,835	2,792	1,646	3,807	14,645
1921	4,922	19,351	14,925	3,131	1,911	3,833	9,452
1922	4,103	13,842	7,701	1,409	1,853	3,226	8,470
1923	3,952	10,293	3,507	676	1,786	2,793	9,378
1924	4,073	9,993	2,927	1,149	1,896	2,836	9,987
1925	4,050	10,831	4,225	265	1,947	2,789	11,081
1926	3,774	12,599	6,181	5,104	2,079	2,744	7,040
1927	3,509	9,066	2,866	156	2,006	2,532	8,172
1928	3,402	8,704	2,898	183	2,023	2,458	8,932
1929	3,440	8,825	2,557	556	2,094	2,483	9,631
1930	3,428	10,023	4,770	243	2,036	2,493	9,758
1931	3,240	12,223	7,157	375	2,119	2,517	9,389
1932	3,074	11,217	5,962	607	2,113	2,396	9,169

(a) Includes travelling and emigration benefits.
(b) The revised figures for 1911 published in the 18th *Abstract of Labour Statistics* differ considerably from those in the 17th *Abstract*—e.g. the number of members is stated to be 608,000 more in the 18th than in the 17th. It therefore seems reasonable to suppose that there is a break in all series between 1910 and 1911.

Labour Force 8. Financial Summary of Registered Trade Unions—Great Britain 1910–39

NOTE

SOURCES: 1910–21—18th *Abstract of Labour Statistics*; 1922–39—*Report of the Chief Registrar of Friendly Societies*, annually.

	Number of Unions	Members (000's)	Income (£000)	Unemployment Benefit (a)	Dispute Benefit	Provident Benefits	from Political Fund	Working Expenses	Other Outgoings	Funds at End of Year (£000)
1910	548	1,982	3,149	677 (b)	530	1,096	—	682		5,871
1911	542	2,321	3,646	478 (b)	603	1,141	—	737		6,294
1912	539	2,547	3,824	630 (b)	1,655	1,172	—	912		5,589
1913	546	3,205	4,516	507	446	1,373	7	1,120		6,471
1914	540	3,199	4,830	881	661	1,371	21	1,179		6,969
1915	539	3,389	4,766	291	91	1,306	38	1,269		8,552
1916	528	3,649	4,932	117	90	1,284	32	1,329		10,472
1917	522	4,361	5,815	267	137	1,348	43	1,582		12,712
1918	527	5,259	7,068	283	295	1,591	133	2,121		14,948
1919	544	6,516	9,560	967	2,132	1,642	113	3,036		15,956
1920	557	6,929	12,872	1,718	3,219	1,756	185	4,275		15,861
1921	524	5,454	21,065	15,150	3,427	2,150	160	4,401		10,815
1922	514	4,506	15,301	8,359	1,428	2,030	267	3,527	714	9,861
1923	490	4,369	11,267	3,733	721	1,989	228	3,072	550	10,752
1924	484	4,458	11,223	3,139	1,188	2,110	215	3,105	795	11,434
1925	488	4,448	11,834	4,527	313	2,160	114	3,076	473	12,556
1926	485	4,148	13,821	6,377	5,617	2,250	108	2,956	621	8,478
1927	487	3,903	10,072	3,131	187	2,231	134	2,783	364	9,710
1928	481	3,765	9,715	3,234	128	2,242	118	2,707	394	10,602
1929	472	3,779	9,682	2,853	398	2,333	178	2,719	429	11,361
1930	474	3,764	11,374	5,350	319	2,269	95	3,134		11,651
1931	469	3,577	13,807	8,340	169	2,343	167	3,175		11,285
1932	464	3,405	12,538	6,941	257	2,320	88	3,024		11,192
1933	458	3,347	10,989	5,017	190	2,329	94	2,526	271	11,760
1934	449	3,513	10,171	3,633	104	2,253	100	2,548	392	12,893
1935	448	3,795	9,434	2,504	232	2,307	168	2,633	311	14,167
1936	441	4,214	8,673	1,882	195	2,430	102	2,808	680	16,032
1937	433	4,695	9,097	1,708	336	2,535	126	3,086	442	18,105
1938	426	4,867	9,581	3,202	148	2,568	117	3,303	535	20,014
1939	424	5,019	9,702	746 (b)	163	2,659	118	3,408	451	22,183

Expenditure (£000) spans the Unemployment Benefit, Dispute Benefit, Provident Benefits, from Political Fund, Working Expenses, and Other Outgoings columns.

(a) Includes travelling and emigration benefits.
(b) Except in these years, money issued as unemployment benefit from government sources is included as well as that direct from trade union funds.

NOTES

[1] Sources: 1888-1936—*Abstract of Labour Statistics*; 1937-8—*Annual Abstract of Statistics, 1935-1946*.
[2] For the years before 1910 there were revisions in each successive *Abstract of Labour Statistics*. The last figure to be published has been used here. The final figure for totals back to 1893 was given in the 21st issue and for the industry groups back to 1910 in the 18th issue.

[3] Totals for Great Britain and Northern Ireland are given back to 1893 in the 21st *Abstract of Labour Statistics*, but are not shown here beyond 1910.
[4] The number of working days recorded as lost includes those lost by workers at the establishments where disputes occurred, though they themselves were not parties to the dispute. It does not include days lost at other establishments.

Number of Disputes beginning in Year

	Total	Building	Mining and Quarrying	Metal, Engineering and Shipbuilding	Textiles	Clothing	Transport
A. U.K. (G.B. and Ireland) 1888-1913							
1888	517	21	139	138	186	7	9
1889	1,211	86	131	339	241	66	184
1890	1,040	113	104	203	241	78	163
1891	906	125	132	164	220	63	61
1892	700	142	109	131	143	48	38
1893 (a)	615	131	127	117	79	65	31
1894	929	162	232	161	178	65	48
1895	745	146	187	160	124	39	27
1896	926	171	171	266	153	48	25
1897	864	193	127	229	108	56	48
1898	711	183	129	152	99	53	22
1899	719	180	109	140	124	37	47
1900	648	146	136	111	96	38	50
1901	642	104	210	103	96	39	20
1902	442	39	168	71	82	23	14
1903	387	44	125	87	55	25	15
1904	355	37	113	75	52	26	10
1905	358	31	106	70	67	29	11
1906	486	19	96	125	124	42	19
1907	601	22	112	134	153	64	29
1908	399	19	145	62	69	32	21
1909	436	15	207	62	56	29	19
1910	531	17	224	97	90	40	19
1911	903	27	179	255	133	46	99
1912	857	58	155	234	136	68	73
1913	1,497	198	192	392	243	75	123
B. U.K. (G.B. and Northern Ireland) 1910-38							
1910	521	17	221	96	89	40	17
1911	872	14	179	253	133	44	91
1912	834	53	154	231	135	66	68
1913	1,459	192	192	391	240	73	115
1914	972	177	176	232	97	50	53
1915	672	63	85	189	67	40	75
1916	532	73	75	105	74	44	44
1917	730	51	148	225	70	55	32
1918	1,165	107	173	420	75	67	48
1919	1,352	134	250	335	65	77	113
1920 (b)	1,607	268	250	340	126	68	150
1921	763	158	173	151	28	29	42
1922	576	77	169	115	21	23	56
1923	628	65	197	103	35	24	61
1924	710	66	204	136	50	31	81
1925	603	58	175	94	59	31	54
1926 (c)	323	43	69	62	33	12	42
1927	308	34	115	69	27	10	16
1928	302	38	100	51	33	9	16
1929	431	40	162	80	58	17	21
1930	422	47	158	76	44	21	22
1931	420	57	155	61	38	21	17
1932	389	29	115	46	105	24	25
1933	357	20	117	68	43	20	30
1934	471	44	150	81	57	25	31
1935	553	46	233	73	64	28	36
1936	818	77	290	148	79	27	66
1937	1,129	98	470	220	84	33	50
1938	875	110	374	138	42	36	49

See p. 72 for footnotes

Number of Working Days lost through Disputes (in thousands)

	Total	Building	Mining and Quarrying	Metal, Engineering and Shipbuilding	Textiles	Clothing	Transport
A. U.K. (G.B. and Ireland) 1888–1913							
1888	...	...	...	...	...	...	...
1889	...	...	...	...	...	...	...
1890	...	...	...	...	...	...	...
1891	6,809	1,577	584	1,536	1,067	601	757
1892	17,382	1,478	5,376	1,865	6,952	692	362
1893 (a)	30,468	469	24,408	701	3,918	185	335
1894	9,529	378	6,639	1,274	748	100	267
1895	5,725	383	1,086	1,369	1,077	1,617	35
1896	3,746	1,060	1,012	863	520	99	23
1897	10,346	353	1,446	7,141	678	301	76
1898	15,289	379	12,876	1,371	274	70	47
1899	2,516	854	504	421	552	42	62
1900	3,153	727	553	349	411	60	304
1901	4,142	575	2,086	602	276	87	38
1902	3,479	116	2,550	420	238	54	10
1903	2,339	114	1,398	481	117	136	27
1904	1,484	346	657	185	122	13	42
1905	2,470	413	1,256	468	126	71	67
1906	3,029	56	922	1,118	763	92	10
1907	2,162	23	569	468	642	278	85
1908	10,834	74	1,351	3,836	5,365	69	52
1909	2,774	19	2,229	180	178	19	95
1910	9,895	35	5,524	3,147	918	59	71
1911	10,320	75	4,101	1,322	1,434	94	2,730
1912	40,915	107	31,594	1,369	3,698	601	2,985
1913	11,631	824	1,656	2,988	2,028	174	1,245
B. U.K. (G.B. and Northern Ireland) 1910–38							
1910	9,867	35	5,524	3,147	913	59	67
1911	10,155	72	4,101	1,265	1,434	88	2,656
1912	40,890	106	31,594	1,357	3,698	601	2,980
1913	11,631	814	1,656	2,985	2,019	173	1,184
1914	9,878	3,184	3,777	1,308	765	79	87
1915	2,953	130	1,657	357	369	28	152
1916	2,446	103	326	305	1,161	156	103
1917	5,647	68	1,183	3,063	710	142	184
1918	5,875	186	1,263	1,499	1,704	298	277
1919	34,969	391	7,713	12,248	8,160	239	4,200
1920 (b)	26,568	789	17,508	3,414	1,443	727	549
1921	85,872	557	72,962	4,420	6,939	81	296
1922	19,850	179	1,387	17,484	68	46	107
1923	10,672	394	1,212	5,997	1,228	28	1,031
1924	8,424	3,145	1,628	1,400	200	45	1,543
1925	7,952	85	3,740	184	3,173	38	73
1926 (c)	162,233	38	146,456	221	188	8	167
1927	1,174	129	695	81	36	199	7
1928	1,388	84	461	60	695	25	11
1929	8,287	28	666	768	6,752	11	13
1930	4,399	46	671	92	3,392	10	25
1931	6,983	145	2,859	99	3,717	16	13
1932	6,488	36	292	48	5,811	32	194
1933	1,072	9	455	112	85	6	272
1934	959	172	373	160	88	36	44
1935	1,955	37	1,385	93	106	44	82
1936	1,829	44	969	206	97	155	86
1937	3,413	39	1,501	778	156	72	748
1938	1,334	115	701	243	84	33	40

(a) The latest *Abstract of Labour Statistics* to show figures for 1892 (the 4th) also published figures for 1893 which differed very much in some respects from later revisions. The main differences were: (i) the 4th issue showed a larger number of disputes in every group of industries; and (ii) the 4th issue showed a larger number of days lost in some groups, but a smaller number in others. By far the most important variation of this latter kind was in textiles, where the 4th *Abstract* gave only 424,000 days lost in 1893 as against 3,918,000 in later revisions. The other major variation is in the building trades, where the 4th *Abstract* gave 813,000 days lost, compared with 469,000 in later issues. A further break between 1892 and 1893 is caused by the omission from 1893 onwards of stoppages involving less than ten workers, or lasting less than one day, except when the number of working days lost exceeded one hundred.

(b) Owing to changes in the standard industrial classification in 1920, figures before and after that date are not exactly comparable with each other, though for all practical purposes this break can be ignored for the groups shown here.

(c) The General Strike is included in the totals but not in the industry group figures.

REFERENCES

BOOKS

G. D. H. Cole, *A Short History of the British Working Class Movement, 1789–1947* (London, 1948).
D. C. Coleman, *The British Paper Industry, 1495–1860* (Oxford, 1958).
H. S. Jevons, *The British Coal Trade* (London, 1915).
A. H. H. Jenkin, *The Cornish Miner* (London, 1927).
K. G. J. C. Knowles, *Strikes* (Oxford, 1952).
Ivy Pinchbeck, *Women Workers in the Industrial Revolution, 1750–1850* (London, 1930).
S. Pollard, *A History of Labour in Sheffield* (Liverpool, 1959).
R. Robson, *The Cotton Industry in Britain* (London, 1955).
W. F. Spackman, *An Analysis of the Occupations of the People . . .* (London, 1847).
S. and B. Webb, *The History of Trade Unionism* (London, 2nd edition 1920).

GOVERNMENT PUBLICATIONS

Reports and *Abstracts* of the Census of Great Britain, 1801–51 (in *Sessional Papers*).
Reports and *Tables* of the Census of England & Wales, 1861–1951 (in *Sessional Papers* up to the 1911 census inclusive, and issued as non-parliamentary papers thereafter).
Reports and *Tables* of the Census of Scotland, 1861–1951 (in *Sessional Papers* up to the 1911 census inclusive, and issued as non-parliamentary papers thereafter).
Reports and *Tables* of the Census of Ireland, 1841–1911 (in *Sessional Papers*).
Reports and *Tables* of the Census of Northern Ireland, 1926, 1937, and 1951 (non-parliamentary papers).
Reports and *Tables* of the Census of the Republic of Ireland, 1926, 1936, and 1951 (Irish Official Publications).
Reports of the Select Committee on Artisans and Machinery (S.P. 1824, v).
Report of the Select Committee on the Combination Laws (S.P. 1825, IV).
Report of the Registrar of Friendly Societies in Scotland (in *Sessional Papers* 1852–3 to 1875, annually).
Report of the Registrar of Friendly Societies in Ireland (in *Sessional Papers* 1854–75, annually).
Report of the Registrar of Friendly Societies in England (in *Sessional Papers* 1856–75, annually).
Report of the Chief Registrar of Friendly Societies (in *Sessional Papers* 1876–1920, annually, and issued as non-parliamentary papers thereafter).
Report on Trade Unions (in *Sessional Papers* 1887 to 1912–13, annually).
Report on Strikes and Lockouts (in *Sessional Papers* 1889 to 1914–16, annually).
Abstract of Labour Statistics (22 issues in *Sessional Papers* between 1893 and 1936). (See especially the 18th *Abstract* for 1926, covering the period 1910–25.)
Labour Gazette, 1893–1956. (Called *Board of Trade Labour Gazette* from 1905–18, and *Ministry of Labour Gazette* since 1923.)
Report of Departmental Committee on an Eight Hours Day for Miners (S.P. 1907, XIV, and S.P. 1907, XV).
Committee on Industry and Trade, *Survey of Industrial Relations*, (non-parliamentary paper, 1926).

Report of the Royal Commission on the Distribution of the Industrial Population (*S.P.* 1939–40, IV).

Interdepartmental Committee on Social and Economic Research, *Guides to Official Sources no. 1: Labour Statistics*, (revised edition, 1958).

ARTICLES

J. R. Bellerby, 'The Distribution of Manpower in Agriculture and Industry, 1851–1951', *The Farm Economist* (1958).

Sir William Beveridge, 'Some Aspects of Trade Fluctuation', *T.M.S.S.* (1921).

Sir William Beveridge, 'Population and Unemployment', *E.J.* (1923).

Sir William Beveridge, 'An Analysis of Unemployment', *Economica* (1936 and 1937).

Sir William Beveridge, 'Unemployment in the Trade Cycle', *E.J.* (1939).

C. Booth, 'Occupations of the People of the United Kingdom, 1801–1881', *J.S.S.* (1886).

A. L. Bowley, 'The Measurement of Employment: An Experiment', *J.R.S.S.* (1912).

A. L. Bowley, 'Rural Population in England and Wales: A Study of the Changes of Density, Occupations and Ages', *J.R.S.S.* (1914).

D. C. Coleman, 'Labour in the English Economy of the Seventeenth Century', *E.H.R.* (1956).

C. Day, 'The Distribution of Industrial Population in England', *Transactions of the Connecticut Academy of Arts and Sciences* (1927).

E. J. Hobsbawm, 'General Labour Unions in Britain, 1889–1914', *E.H.R.* (1949).

E. J. Hobsbawm, 'The Tramping Artisan', *E.H.R.* (1951).

Leeds Town Council, 'Report upon the Condition of the Town of Leeds and its Inhabitants', *J.S.S.* (1840).

T. A. Welton, 'Forty Years' Industrial Changes in England and Wales', *T.M.S.S.* (1897–8).

AGRICULTURE

TABLES

'The demand for accurate arithmetical information about farming and its net output is of long standing, and the details necessary for administrative purposes were envisaged nearly three hundred years ago'.[1] The necessary centralised government machine, however, did not exist until well into the last century, as was shown by the failure of various official attempts to get crop statistics during the early years of the struggle with Napoleon.[2] Arthur Young's works, it is true, contain a good deal of statistical information; but it is scattered and unsystematic, and not in a form which can be used here.[3] A century before Young, Gregory King had made estimates of agricultural production, which, though no more than guesses, are generally agreed to have been acceptable.[4] Various attempts were made in the two or three decades after Waterloo to get agricultural statistics, mainly about particular areas, but these were not very successful.[5] By the 1850's, however, government interest in the subject was growing. Irish statistical series, collected by the police, had been successfully begun in 1847, and a start was made in Great Britain in 1854. The attempt in England

[1] G. E. Fussell, 'The Collection of Agricultural Statistics in Great Britain: Its Origin and Evolution', *A.H.* vol. 18 (1944).

[2] The results of these attempts are summarised and assessed by W. E. Minchinton, 'Agricultural Returns and the Government during the Napoleonic Wars', *A.H.R.* vol. 1 (1953).

[3] See especially *A Six Weeks' Tour through the Southern Counties of England and Wales* (London, 1768); *A Six Months' Tour through the North of England* (4 vols., London 1770); and *The Farmer's Tour through the East of England* (4 vols., London, 1771). P. G. Craigie, 'Statistics of Agricultural Production', in *J.S.S.* (1883) gives yield statistics from 1770 to his own day, using Young's scattered references, and those of similar writers. More recent and authoritative estimates of wheat production in the eighteenth century are given by G. E. Fussell, 'Population and Wheat Production in the Eighteenth Century', *History Teacher's Miscellany*, vol. VII (1929).

[4] George E. Barnett (ed.), *Two Tracts by Gregory King* (Baltimore, 1936).

[5] Examples can be found in *J.S.S.* (1834, 1835, and 1843).

and Wales failed, however, largely because of the agency used—the boards of guardians. The Scottish attempt, conducted on behalf of the government by the Highland Agricultural Society, was a success; but complaints about its cost led to its discontinuation after 1857.[1]

Nevertheless, James Caird and others persisted in their agitation for the collection of official agricultural statistics, and the first Agricultural Census of Great Britain was taken in 1865. The first continuous and lengthy series begin with the annual acreage and livestock returns in 1867,[2] followed in a few years by the production and yield returns. 'These details are still, with the modifications that experience has shown to be necessary, the backbone of agricultural statistics'.[3]

The acreage and livestock figures, shown here in summary form as tables 1–4, are based on returns from farmers, and the production and yield statistics, tables 5–8 here, on information sent by official crop reporters. Originally the returns in Great Britain were from all farmers, but in 1869 a lower limit of a quarter of an acre was placed on the holdings about which information was required, and this was raised to an acre in 1893. In Ireland there was always a lower limit of one acre. These changes had scarcely any effect,[4] and at first sight it seems as though the tables should be comparable virtually throughout their length. But there are difficulties. In a recent article Dr Coppock wrote: 'It is clear that the figures for the first few years of collection must be treated with the greatest caution. Opposition was still marked, the procedure was unfamiliar to both officials and farmers, and differences of interpretation by farmers were frequent'.[5] This last difficulty probably persisted for rather longer than the other, the most obvious possibilities for changes in interpretation over the years being in rotation grass, permanent pasture, and rough grazing.[6] According to the report of the 1925 census 'the main difficulty in connection with the collection of these annual statistics was in ensuring that all holdings are enumerated. The frequent changes in occupation, especially in recent years, the combination or division of farms, and the withdrawal of land for building or other purposes, make the task of seeing that all the agricultural land in the country is accounted for a very serious one. A proportion of the holdings do, in fact, escape enumeration, especially in the case of the smaller occupations under five acres, though the total area omitted from the returns in this way is a very small proportion of the agricultural area of the country'.[7] The questions of the annual census all relate to the actual position on the farm at a given date in each year, i.e. June 4th.[8]

---

[1] For these Scottish statistics see *S.P.* 1854–5, XLVII; *S.P.* 1856, LIX; *S.P.* 1857 (Secs. 1), XV, and *S.P.* 1857–8, LVI.

[2] The first returns were for 1866, but they were for farms of 5 acres and over, and the livestock returns were taken at the end of the winter, not, as later, in the middle of the summer. For these and other reasons the 1866 returns are not comparable with later ones, and they are omitted here.

[3] G. E. Fussell, *A.H.* vol. 18 (1944).

[4] The estimated reduction in total returned acreage in 1893 was 0·1 per cent.

[5] J. T. Coppock, 'The Statistical Assessment of British Agriculture', *A.H.R.* vol. IV (1956).

[6] Figures for rough grazing are not shown here since they are not available in comparable form for England and Wales and for Scotland.

[7] *S.P.* 1927, XXV—*The Agricultural Output of England and Wales, 1925*, p. 2.

[8] For the first decade the British statistics related to the 25th June, whilst the Irish returns for 1847–57 were compiled in August and September, and for a long time after 1857 at an unspecified date (or dates) in June.

Estimates of the annual production of each crop in Great Britain date from 1884. though in Ireland they were started at the same time as the acreage and livestock returns. They are based on the evidence of crop reporters who are 'for the most part land agents, valuers and others with considerable local experience who estimate the yield per acre of the principal crops parish by parish'.[1] It is possible that their skill has improved through time. Certainly it is likely that year-to-year fluctuations in yields are underestimated as a result of failures of the reporters' judgment. There seems to be a fair amount of evidence that they over-estimate yields in bad harvests and underestimate those in good years. In relation to the livestock returns, it must be remembered that numbers alone do not tell the whole story of animal output. Both cattle and sheep used to be kept to a greater age than has been custom-ary recently, so that a thousand head at the end of the last century represented a smaller annual output than it did in the inter-war years.

In addition to the annual returns, full censuses of agricultural production were taken in 1908 (for Great Britain and Ireland separately), in 1925 (for Scotland, England and Wales, and Northern Ireland), and in 1930–1 (for England and Wales, and Scotland). Official estimates of the quantity and value of United Kingdom agricultural output are now avail-able annually for 1936–7 onwards,[2] and figures of net income for 1938 and 1946 onwards are in the National Income Blue Book.

The quantity statistics of our overseas trade in corn have been included in this section, though the value figures are to be found in Chapter XI. Table 5, dealing with the corn trade of Great Britain during the eighteenth and early nineteenth centuries, links up to some extent with table 6, showing the United Kingdom trade from the end of the eighteenth century. But the link is by no means exact, since British imports from Ireland were sub-stantial. Moreover, the British statistics treat grain and meal or flour separately, whilst the earlier United Kingdom ones take them together. The long overlap between the two sets of figures should help, however, in making comparisons.

---

[1] *S.P.* 1927, xxv—*The Agricultural Output of England and Wales, 1925*, p. 2.

[2] Ministry of Agriculture and Fisheries, Department of Agriculture for Scotland, Ministry of Agriculture Northern Ireland, *Agricultural Statistics United Kingdom Part II: Output and Utilisation of Farm Produce in the Agricultural Years 1939–40 to 1945–46* (London, 1949 and later issues).

Agriculture 1. Acreage of Crops—Great Britain 1867–1939

NOTES
[1] SOURCE: *Agricultural Statistics*.

[2] To maintain comparability, vegetables for human consumption have been included throughout under the appropriate heading.

(in thousands of acres at 25th June 1867–76 and 4th June 1877–1939)

	Wheat	Barley	Oats	Other Corn	Potatoes	Turnips and Swedes	Man-gold	Cabbage Kohl-rabi and Rape	Other Green Crops	Bare Fallow	Rotation Grasses for Hay	Rotation Grasses for Grazing	Permanent Pasture for Hay	Permanent Pasture for Grazing	Small Fruit	Orch-ards	Hops
1867	3,368	2,259	2,750	907	492	2,174	258	134	440	923	3,003		11,136	9,006	...	...	64
1868	3,652	2,151	2,757	873	542	2,165	249	115	333	958	2,920		12,136	8,946	...	...	64
1869	3,688	2,251	2,783	1,035	585	2,172	293	145	401	739(a)	2,637(a)		12,736(a)		...	...	62
1870	3,501	2,372	2,763	912	588	2,211	307	144	361	611	2,069	2,436	3,067	8,997	...	...	61
1871	3,572	2,386	2,716	1,002	628	2,164	361	179	424	543	2,165	2,205	3,490	8,946	...	207	60
1872	3,599	2,316	2,706	953	564	2,084	329	178	476	648	2,300	2,214	3,578	8,997	...	170	62
1873	3,490	2,336	2,676	957	515	2,122	326	175	455	706	2,139	2,228	3,415	9,501	...	148	63
1874	3,630	2,288	2,596	917	520	2,133	323	169	445	660	2,046	2,295	3,279	9,899	...	151	66
1875	3,342	2,510	2,664	935	523	2,143	362	190	454	558	2,109	2,245	3,611	9,702	...	155	69
1876	2,996	2,533	2,798	867	503	2,146	348	179	404	651	2,241	2,299	3,621	9,895	...	157	70
1877	3,169	2,418	2,754	870	512	2,073	358	183	465	616	2,176	2,318	3,759	9,970	...	163	71
1878	3,218	2,470	2,699	781	508	2,032	343	172	443	632	2,308	2,265	3,840	10,071	...	165	72
1879	2,890	2,667	2,657	771	541	2,017	364	168	473	721	4,473		14,167		...	175	68
1880	2,909	2,467	2,797	702	551	2,024	343	162	406	813	4,434		14,427		...	180	67
1881	2,806	2,442	2,901	699	579	2,036	349	143	411	796	4,342		14,646		...	185	65
1882	3,004	2,255	2,834	741	541	2,024	334	150	431	784	4,327		14,822		...	188	66
1883	2,613	2,292	2,975	738	543	2,029	330	146	410	778	4,396		15,065		...	191	68
1884	2,677	2,169	2,915	724	565	2,028	327	147	423	750	4,381		15,291		...	195	69
1885	2,478	2,257	2,940	716	549	2,015	355	153	453	560	2,159	2,495	4,024	11,319	...	198	71
1886	2,286	2,241	3,082	651	554	2,003	349	152	426	553	2,252	2,438	4,418	11,117	...	200	70
1887	2,317	2,085	3,088	656	560	1,972	361	154	421	486	2,325	2,456	4,562	11,109		202	64
1888	2,564	2,086	2,882	656	590	1,944	361	159	419	457	2,292	2,432	4,777	10,969	37	199	58
1889	2,449	2,122	2,889	615	579	1,921	326	147	329	513	2,477	2,401	4,987	10,878	42	200	58
1890	2,386	2,111	2,903	632	530	1,948	331	160	331	508	2,292	2,517	4,779	11,239	46	202	54
1891	2,307	2,113	2,899	606	533	1,919	355	157	337	429	2,130	2,586	4,503	11,931	59	210	56
1892	2,220	2,037	2,998	553	525	1,937	361	151	296	457	2,135	2,537	4,490	11,869	62	209	56
1893	1,898	2,075	3,172	511	528	1,975	347	156	282	515	2,047	2,523	4,270	12,222	65	212	58
1894	1,928	2,096	3,253	578	504	1,957	354	177	311	376	2,122	2,382	4,852	11,613	68	214	60
1895	1,417	2,166	3,296	521	541	1,916	335	153	283	476	2,303	2,426	4,761	11,850	75	218	59
1896	1,694	2,105	3,095	523	564	1,883	338	162	314	432	2,172	2,424	4,638	12,089	76	221	54
1897	1,889	2,036	3,036	496	505	1,833	355	167	331	385	2,286	2,568	4,510	12,003	70	224	51
1898	2,102	1,904	2,918	477	525	1,772	352	166	319	352	2,382	2,530	4,536	12,023	70	226	50
1899	2,001	1,982	2,960	464	548	1,741	374	173	313	339	2,215	2,593	4,339	12,292	72	229	52
1900	1,845	1,990	3,026	474	561	1,689	414	196	320	308	2,202	2,557	4,373	12,356	74	232	51
1901	1,701	1,972	2,996	464	577	1,665	399	180	309	344	2,356	2,500	4,350	12,477	75	235	51

See p. 79 for footnotes

Agriculture 1. *continued*

(in thousands of acres at 25th June 1867–76 and 4th June 1877–1939)

	Wheat	Barley	Oats	Other Corn	Potatoes	Turnips and Swedes	Mangold	Sugar Beet	Cabbage Kohlrabi and Rape	Other Green Crops	Bare Fallow	Rotation Grasses for Hay	Rotation Grasses for Grazing	Permanent Pasture for Hay	Permanent Pasture for Grazing	Small Fruit	Orchards	Hops
1902	1,726	1,909	3,057	491	574	1,609	441	…	193	332	293	2,364	2,468	4,581	12,226	75	237	48
1903	1,582	1,858	3,140	481	564	1,603	402	…	183	313	351	2,412	2,395	4,755	12,180	76	239	48
1904	1,375	1,841	3,253	485	570	1,604	399	…	178	286	433	2,323	2,349	4,765	12,333	78	243	48
1905	1,797	1,714	3,051	492	608	1,589	404	…	179	296	349	2,189	2,288	4,689	12,512	79	244	49
1906	1,756	1,751	3,043	508	566	1,591	431	…	182	312	315	2,192	2,249	4,785	12,460	80	248	47
1907	1,625	1,712	3,123	537	549	1,563	450	…	187	339	261	2,250	2,241	4,937	12,341	82	250	45
1908	1,627	1,667	3,109	512	562	1,551	428	…	173	306	315	2,232	2,189	4,950	12,466	85	250	39
1909	1,823	1,664	2,982	554	575	1,556	456	…	172	324	289	2,036	2,179	4,777	12,675	87	251	33
1910	1,809	1,729	3,021	487	540	1,565	443	…	159	289	354	2,075	2,082	5,005	12,472	84	251	33
1911	1,906	1,598	3,011	526	572	1,563	452	…	157	295	329	2,075	2,045	5,003	12,444	84	251	33
1912	1,926	1,648	3,029	549	613	1,513	488	…	174	329	281	1,979	2,013	5,108	12,227	85	247	35
1913	1,756	1,757	2,913	496(b)	591	1,486	421	…	150	305(b)	396	2,116	1,854	5,227	12,340	84	245	36
1914	1,868	1,699	2,849	529	614	1,476	434	…	152	340	348	1,963	1,900	4,942	12,664	85	245	37
1915	2,247	1,381	3,071	454	608	1,353	416	…	145	322	317	1,928	1,898	4,806	12,773	81	250	35
1916	1,906	1,502	3,075	414	558	1,352	380	…	145	340	430	2,183	1,888	4,985	12,510	80	253	31
1917	1,979	1,619	3,300	409	656	1,387	391	…	126	295	361	2,103	1,884	4,954	12,297	79	261	17
1918	2,636	1,654(c)	4,024(c)	662(c)	803	1,308	404	1	119	293	414	1,836	1,614	4,447	11,449	72	265	16
1919	2,301	1,683	3,675	711	630	1,410	399	φφ	169	339	657	1,895	1,766	4,318	11,464	65	234	17
1920	1,929	1,842	3,304	681	707	1,417	388	3	192	393	573	2,100	1,786	4,547	11,299	65	222	21
1921	2,041	1,606	3,161	616	712	1,306	377	8	170	327	514	2,168	1,858	4,195	11,711	79	…	25
1922	2,032	1,521	3,152	680	719	1,225	425	8	180	374	411	1,959	1,854	4,558	11,545	82	…	26
1923	1,799	1,486	2,946	579	604	1,272	405	17	181	346	443	2,229	1,876	4,510	11,679	71	233(d)	25
1924	1,594	1,466	2,993	618	591	1,238	391	23	179	372	363	2,167	1,895	4,656	11,734	80	241	26
1925	1,548	1,471	2,794	507	635	1,202	360	56	167	313	472	2,125	1,951	4,468	12,081	76	239	26
1926	1,646	1,270	2,804	506	641	1,158	340	129	178	349	424	1,991	1,996	4,525	12,102	77	242	26
1927	1,703	1,166	2,649	474	661	1,093	307	233	172	318	430	1,986	1,971	4,485	12,308	77	250	23
1928	1,454	1,296	2,641	442	633	1,100	300	178	169	298	474	1,969	1,974	4,666	12,262	73	249	24
1929	1,381	1,221	2,743	472	664	1,071	301	231	170	287	331	1,932	1,937	4,864	12,174	73	249	24
1930	1,400	1,127	2,640	493	548	1,044	289	349	180	303	300	2,006	1,917	5,222	11,895	74	248	20
1931	1,247	1,117	2,487	454	575	982	272	234	177	305	364	2,149	1,967	4,943	12,338	70	246	20
1932	1,340	1,029	2,448	426	653	929	231	256	156	278	440	1,935	1,987	4,709	12,707	67	248	17
1933	1,739	811	2,351	422	671	907	239	366	165	283	465	1,653	1,899	4,783	12,671	69	251	17
1934	1,857	957	2,219	416	628	874	248	404	190	288	353	1,683	1,806	5,003	12,386	71	256	18
1935	1,873	868	2,246	410	594	850	253	375	224	304	302	1,785	1,969	4,821	12,353	69	264	18
1936	1,798	891	2,249	407	590	795	248	355	236	304	348	1,736	1,794	4,839	12,531	65	262	18
1937	1,832	904	2,042	332	591	772	209	313	199	230	550	1,878	1,788	4,857	12,479	62	260	18
1938	1,923	984	2,098	386	610	746	217	334	210	253	370	1,571	1,788	4,402	13,007	58	253	18
1939	1,763	1,010	2,135	381	589	705	214	343	215	232	374	1,688	1,838	4,786	12,543	56	256	19

(a) Changes in the official classification of land between 1868 and 1869 affect the comparability of these series.

(b) From 1913 onwards, the Scottish component of the acreage of beans was no longer included wholly with *Other Corn* since beans for fodder were included with *Other Green Crops*.

(c) In 1918 there was a new heading in the *Returns*—mixed corn. This included items previously included with oats and barley.

(d) Prior to 1923 the area of orchards was also shown under the crop grass, or fallow beneath the trees.

Agriculture 2. Acreage of Crops—Ireland 1847–1939

NOTES

[1] SOURCES: 1847–1917—*Agricultural Statistics (Ireland)*, annually; 1918–39—Eire Department of Industry and Commerce: *Agricultural Statistics, 1847–1926* (Dublin, 1928); *Agricultural Statistics, 1927–1933* (Dublin, 1935), and *Statistical Abstract, 1940* (Dublin, 1940), and *Report upon the Agricultural Statistics of Northern Ireland*, annually for 1925–9 and in one volume for 1930–53 (Belfast, 1957).

[2] Before 1857 the returns were obtained during August and September, but from that date they were made in June.

(in thousands of acres)

	Wheat	Barley	Oats	Other Corn (a)	Potatoes	Turnips and Swedes	Mangold (b)	Other Green Crops (c)	Flax	Hay	Pasture
1847	744	333	2,201	36	284	370	14	60	58	1,139	...
1848	...	...	...	...	...	...	...	...	...	...	...
1849	688	352	2,061	74	719	360	19	70	60	1,141	...
1850	605	321	2,143	81	875	347	20	74	91	1,200	...
1851	504	336	2,190	69	869	384	26	95	141	1,246	...
1852	354	290	2,283	49	877	357	31	91	137	1,271	...
1853	327	301	2,158	48	899	399	33	87	175	1,271	9,381
1854	411	253	2,045	34	990	329	21	77	151	1,258	9,501
1855	446	238	2,119	40	982	367	22	73	97	1,315	9,558
1856	529	189	2,037	29	1,105	354	22	78	106	1,303	9,545
1857	560	217	1,981	29	1,147	350	21	87	98	1,370	9,316
1858	547	196	1,981	24	1,160	338	30	90	92	1,424	9,354
1859	464	182	1,983	24	1,200	322	27	87	136	1,437	9,491
1860	466	184	1,966	23	1,172	319	32	85	129	1,595	9,484
1861	401	202	1,999	23	1,134	334	23	81	148	1,546	9,534
1862	356	195	1,978	24	1,018	377	23	79	150	1,553	9,700
1863	260	175	1,954	21	1,023	351	16	87	214	1,561	9,758
1864	276	176	1,815	22	1,040	337	14	85	302	1,610	9,694
1865	267	180	1,745	24	1,066	334	14	87	251	1,678	9,823
1866	299	153	1,700	23	1,050	317	20	94	264	1,601	10,004
1867	261	173	1,661	21	1,002	336	19	76	253	1,658	10,061
1868	285	188	1,702	18	1,035	320	19	83	206	1,692	9,999
1869	280	224	1,685	19	1,042	322	21	84	229	1,671	10,041
1870	260	244	1,650	20	1,044	339	25	91	195	1,774	9,967
1871	244	223	1,636	21	1,058	327	32	94	157	1,829	10,071
1872	225	220	1,625	21	992	347	35	101	122	1,800	10,246
1873	168	231	1,511	21	903	348	38	83	129	1,838	10,414
1874	188	212	1,481	20	892	334	38	89	107	1,907	10,472
1875	159	235	1,502	21	901	333	43	94	101	1,945	10,409
1876	120	221	1,487	21	881	345	49	90	133	1,861	10,507
1877	139	227	1,476	20	873	334	49	98	123	1,925	10,145
1878	154	244	1,413	20	847	330	45	96	112	1,943	10,116
1879	158	255	1,330	19	843	315	51	86	128	1,937	10,211
1880	149	219	1,382	17	821	303	42	82	158	1,910	10,259
1881	154	211	1,393	19	855	295	45	75	147	2,001	10,075
1882	153	188	1,397	19	838	294	36	81	113	1,962	10,110
1883	95	184	1,382	18	806	307	38	79	96	1,932	10,192
1884	68	167	1,348	16	799	304	35	84	89	1,962	10,347
1885	71	180	1,329	16	797	297	37	88	108	2,035	10,251
1886	70	182	1,322	17	800	299	37	85	128	2,094	10,163
1887	67	162	1,315	18	797	300	42	90	130	2,144	10,050
1888	99	171	1,281	20	805	294	46	90	114	2,222	9,905
1889	90	186	1,239	20	787	298	44	91	114	2,188	9,998
1890	92	182	1,221	19	781	295	46	92	97	2,094	10,212
1891	81	178	1,215	18	753	300	52	86	75	2,060	10,299
1892	75	176	1,226	18	740	300	52	83	71	2,143	10,254
1893	55	169	1,248	17	724	303	47	80	67	2,167	10,321
1894	49	165	1,255	15	717	311	52	83	101	2,183	10,214
1895	37	172	1,216	14	710	313	53	75	95	2,194	10,280
1896	38	173	1,194	16	706	308	54	79	72	2,202	10,334

See p. 81 for footnotes

(in thousands of acres)

	Wheat	Barley	Oats	Other Corn (a)	Potatoes	Turnips and Swedes	Man-gold (b)	Other Green Crops (c)	Flax	Hay	Pasture
1897	47	171	1,175	15	677	309	55	75	46	2,176	10,462
1898	53	158	1,165	15	665	307	56	77	34	2,174	10,470
1899	52	170	1,136	15	663	301	63	75	35	2,119	10,575
1900	54	174	1,105	14	654	298	69	78	47	2,166	10,563
1901	43	162	1,099	14	635	290	77	77	55	2,179	10,577
1902	44	168	1,062	12	629	289	77	75	50	2,168	10,635
1903	38	159	1,098	12	620	288	76	76	45	2,224	10,598
1904	31	158	1,079	11	619	286	76	70	44	2,260	10,586
1905	38	155	1,067	12	617	282	73	73	46	2,295	10,598(d)
1906	44	177	1,076	13	616	278	67	72	55	2,330	10,063
1907	38	170	1,075	11	591	275	67	70	60	2,281	9,979
1908	37	155	1,060	10	587	279	72	70	47	2,299	10,037
1909	44	163	1,036	9	580	277	73	71	38	2,279	9,997
1910	48	168	1,074	11	593	275	75	69	46	2,422	9,868
1911	45	158	1,040	11	591	271	78	74	67	2,512	9,847
1912	45	165	1,046	9	595	272	82	73	55	2,487	9,828
1913	34	173	1,049	8	582	277	79	72	59	2,482	9,861
1914	37	172	1,029	9	583	277	82	74	49	2,488	9,928
1915	87	142	1,089	9	594	265	83	68	53	2,496	9,819
1916	76	150	1,072	8	586	263	80	58	91	2,406	9,908
1917	124	177	1,464	9	709	293	93	43	108	2,533	8,784
1918	157	185	1,580	11	702	295	98	51	143	2,470	8,683
1919	70	187	1,442	7	589	273	75	48	96	2,520	...
1920 (e)	50	207	1,332	7	584	276	77	51	121	2,518	...
1921 (e)	43	176	1,254	8	568	266	78	59	38	2,370	...
1922 (e)	41	170	1,213	9	569	248	84	56	32	2,545	...
1923	39	153	1,137	10	554	247	78	60	51	2,488	...
1924	38	159	1,022	11	560	252	86	55	53	2,761	...
1925	26	148	993	10	535	245	80	52	48	2,743	9,810
1926	36	143	968	9	528	240	82	67	37	2,772	9,819
1927	41	122	954	8	518	226	81	67	32	2,651	9,899
1928	36	131	956	7	519	232	86	66	45	2,604	9,864
1929	32	119	980	6	515	230	85	61	40	2,800	9,633
1930	31	118	951	6	483	219	82	53	33	2,774	9,506
1931	24	117	909	5	480	218	85	45	8	2,782	9,488
1932	24	104	918	5	490	214	82	53	6	2,735	9,469
1933	56	119	923	4	480	206	81	53	11	2,692	9,521
1934	102	145	853	3	480	195	84	82	18	2,590	9,580
1935	168	142	887	3	465	185	85	91	33	2,507	9,481
1936	262	133	824	3	466	181	87	94	30	2,466	9,519
1937	224	134	830	3	453	178	87	94	23	2,578	9,545
1938	236	121	866	3	450	169	86	83	25	2,468	9,604
1939	258	77	828	3	432	164	87	70	25	2,497	9,624

(a) Rye, beans and peas.
(b) This generally includes fodder beet, of which the area grown has always been very small.
(c) Including sugar beet.
(d) More careful compilation of returns was demanded from 1906 onwards, and this resulted in some transfers from pasture to mountain and bog land.
(e) The figures for these years are approximations, since the police compiled the returns, not individual farmers.

Agriculture 3. Numbers of Livestock—Great Britain 1867–1939

NOTES

[1] SOURCE: *Agricultural Statistics*.
[2] The changes in the size of the lower limit of holdings making returns, and the level of that limit (referred to in the introduction), are of particular importance for pigs and poultry.

(in thousands at 25th June 1867–76 and 4th June 1877–1939)

	Cattle			Sheep					
	Cows and Heifers	Other Cattle	Total	One Year and Above	Under One Year Old	Total	Pigs	Horses	Poultry
1867	2,038	2,955	4,993	18,449	10,470	28,919	2,967	...	...
1868	2,144	3,280	5,424	19,708	11,004	30,711	2,309	...	...
1869	2,135	3,178	5,313	18,986	10,553	29,538	1,930	...	...
1870	2,162	3,242	5,403	18,410	9,987	28,398	2,171	1,267	...
1871	2,091	3,246	5,338	17,572	9,548	27,120	2,500	1,254	...
1872	2,165	3,460	5,625	17,961	9,961	27,922	2,772	1,258	...
1873	2,238	3,727	5,965	18,778	10,650	29,428	2,500	1,276	...
1874	2,274	3,852	6,125	19,449	10,865	30,314	2,423	1,312	...
1875	2,253	3,760	6,013	18,775	10,393	29,167	2,230	1,340	...
1876	2,226	3,618	5,844	18,258	9,925	28,183	2,294	1,375	...
1877	2,207	3,491	5,698	18,145	10,016	28,161	2,499	1,389	...
1878	2,208	3,530	5,738	18,055	10,351	28,406	2,483	1,413	...
1879	2,255	3,601	5,856	18,172	9,985	28,157	2,092	1,433	...
1880	2,242	3,670	5,912	17,186	9,433	26,619	2,001	1,421	...
1881	2,270	3,641	5,912	16,143	8,438	24,581	2,048	1,425	...
1882	2,267	3,540	5,807	15,574	8,746	24,320	2,510	1,414	...
1883	2,306	3,657	5,963	15,949	9,120	25,068	2,618	1,411	...
1884	2,391	3,878	6,269	16,385	9,683	26,068	2,584	1,414	...
1885	2,530	4,068	6,598	16,538	9,997	26,535	2,403	1,409	...
1886	2,538	4,109	6,647	16,176	9,345	25,521	2,221	1,425	...
1887	2,536	3,905	6,441	16,146	9,813	25,959	2,299	1,428	...
1888	2,450	3,679	6,129	15,727	9,530	25,257	2,404	1,420	...
1889	2,444	3,706	6,140	15,862	9,770	25,632	2,511	1,421	...
1890	2,538	3,971	6,509	16,757	10,516	27,272	2,774	1,433	...
1891	2,657	4,196	6,853	17,787	10,946	28,733	2,889	1,488	...
1892	2,651	4,294	6,945	17,957	10,778	28,735	2,138	1,518	...
				Ewes Kept for Breeding	Other Sheep				
1893	2,555	4,146	6,701	10,129	17,152	27,280	2,114	1,525	...
1894	2,460	3,887	6,347	9,668	16,193	25,862	2,390	1,529	...
1895	2,486	3,869	6,354	9,663	16,129	25,792	2,884	1,545	...
1896	2,512	3,982	6,494	9,926	16,780	26,705	2,879	1,553	...
1897	2,532	3,968	6,500	10,007	16,334	26,340	2,342	1,526	...
1898	2,587	4,035	6,622	10,138	16,605	26,743	2,452	1,517	...
1899	2,671	4,124	6,796	10,461	16,778	27,239	2,624	1,517	...
1900	2,621	4,184	6,805	10,350	16,242	26,592	2,382	1,500	...
1901	2,602	4,162	6,764	10,162	16,215	26,377	2,180	1,511	...
1902	2,556	4,000	6,556	9,999	15,767	25,766	2,300	1,505	...

Agriculture 3. *continued*

(in thousands at 25th June 1867–76 and 4th June 1877–1939)

	Cattle			Sheep					
	Cows and Heifers	Other Cattle	Total	Ewes Kept for Breeding	Other Sheep	Total	Pigs	Horses	Poultry
1903	2,588	4,116	6,705	9,879	15,761	25,640	2,687	1,537	...
1904	2,679	4,180	6,858	9,881	15,326	25,207	2,862	1,560	...
1905	2,707	4,280	6,987	9,936	15,321	25,257	2,425	1,572	...
1906	2,738	4,272	7,011	10,061	15,359	25,420	2,323	1,569	...
1907	2,759	4,153	6,912	10,277	15,838	26,115	2,637	1,556	...
1908	2,764	4,141	6,905	10,569	16,551	27,120	2,823	1,546	...
1909	2,794	4,227	7,021	10,810	16,808	27,618	2,381	1,553	...
1910	2,768	4,270	7,037	10,666	16,437	27,103	2,350	1,545	...
1911	2,825	4,289	7,114	10,443	16,052	26,495	2,822	1,481	...
1912	2,784	4,242	7,026	10,120	14,938	25,058	2,656	1,441/1,611(a)	...
1913	2,695	4,268	6,964	9,613	14,318	23,931	2,234	1,324/1,607	...
1914	2,938	4,155	7,093	9,813	14,472	24,286	2,634	1,296/1,609	...
1915	2,884	4,404	7,288	9,877	14,722	24,598	2,579	1,213/1,487	...
1916	2,870	4,572	7,442	10,066	14,941	25,007	2,314	1,293/1,567	...
1917	2,907	4,530	7,437	9,899	14,144	24,043	2,051	1,324/1,583	...
1918	3,030	4,380	7,410	9,501	13,852	23,353	1,825	1,337/1,586	...
1919	3,009	4,415	7,424	8,590	12,944	21,534	1,936	1,338/1,600	...
1920	2,787	3,925	6,713	7,865	11,879	19,744	2,122	1,312/1,580	...
1921	2,944	3,715	6,660	8,151	12,339	20,490	2,651	1,340/1,601	...
1922	2,974	3,895	6,869	8,301	11,821	20,122	2,450	1,308/1,552	...
1923	3,070	3,946	7,017	8,409	12,213	20,621	2,798	1,253/1,485	...
1924	3,112	3,947	7,059	8,986	12,744	21,729	3,427	1,190/1,426	...
1925	3,164	4,205	7,368	9,453	13,641	23,094	2,799	1,131/1,350	...
1926	3,207	4,244	7,451	9,870	14,192	24,062	2,345	1,307	...
1927	3,251	4,235	7,486	10,201	14,406	24,608	2,888	1,249	49,221
1928	3,183	4,058	7,240	10,112	13,856	23,968	3,167	1,204	49,399
1929	3,166	4,024	7,191	9,998	13,663	23,661	2,509	1,160	52,283
1930	3,128	3,958	7,086	10,136	13,829	23,965	2,454	1,118	58,219
1931	3,244	4,030	7,274	10,678	14,903	25,580	2,945	1,091	63,562
1932	3,337	4,254	7,591	11,077	15,345	26,412	3,350	1,067	69,297
1933	3,439	4,475	7,914	11,154	14,747	25,901	3,236	1,052	73,835
1934	3,491	4,482	7,973	10,663	13,520	24,183	3,526	1,034	73,642
1935	3,548	4,311	7,860	10,466	13,778	24,243	4,074	1,021	70,256
1936	3,571	4,282	7,853	10,548	13,657	24,205	4,040	1,013	70,005
1937	3,563	4,346	7,909	10,606	14,106	24,712	3,883	1,005	63,704
1938	3,576	4,454	8,030	11,917	13,965	25,882	3,822	1,002	64,053
1939	3,615	4,504	8,119	12,050	13,943	25,993	3,767	987	64,137

(a) Where two figures are shown for this and subsequent years, the first is comparable with earlier years and the second with later years. The first is of horses used solely in agriculture (including brood mares and unbroken horses); the second is of all horses on agricultural holdings.

Agriculture 4. Numbers of Livestock—Ireland 1841–1939

NOTES

[1] SOURCES: 1847–1917—*Agricultural Statistics (Ireland)*, annually; 1918–39—Eire Department of Industry and Commerce: *Agricultural Statistics, 1847–1926* (Dublin, 1928), *Agricultural Statistics, 1927–1933* (Dublin, 1935), and *Statistical Abstract, 1940* (Dublin, 1940), and *Report upon the*

Agricultural Statistics of Northern Ireland, annually for 1925–9, and in one volume for 1930–53 (Belfast, 1957).
[2] Before 1857 the returns were obtained during August and September, but from that date they were made in June.

(in thousands)

| | Cattle | | | Sheep | | | Pigs | Horses | | Poultry |
	Cows and Heifers	Other Cattle	Total	One Year and Above	Under One Year Old	Total		for Agricultural Purposes	Total (a)	
1841	...	...	1,863	...	...	2,106	1,413	...	...	8,459
1847	...	...	2,591	1,676	510	2,186	622	...	558	5,691
1848	...	...	...	...	...	...	...	...	...	...
1849	...	...	2,771	1,403	374	1,777	795	...	526	6,328
1850	...	...	2,918	1,393	483	1,876	928	...	527	6,945
1851	...	...	2,967	1,544	578	2,122	1,085	...	522	7,471
1852	...	...	3,095	1,929	685	2,614	1,073	...	525	8,176
1853	...	...	3,383	2,192	951	3,143	1,145	...	540	8,661
				Ewes	Other Sheep					
1854	1,518	1,980	3,498	1,777	1,945	3,722	1,343	388	546	8,630
1855	1,561	2,003	3,564	1,734	1,868	3,602	1,178	393	556	8,367
1856	1,580	2,008	3,588	1,655	2,039	3,694	919	407	573	8,908
1857	1,605	2,016	3,621	1,538	1,914	3,452	1,255	424	600	9,491
1858	1,635	2,032	3,667	1,522	1,973	3,495	1,410	432	611	9,563
1859	1,690	2,126	3,816	1,564	2,029	3,593	1,266	444	629	10,252
1860	1,626	1,980	3,606	1,567	1,975	3,542	1,271	441	620	10,061
1861	1,545	1,927	3,472	1,528	2,028	3,556	1,102	445	614	10,371
1862	1,487	1,768	3,255	1,495	1,962	3,456	1,154	449	603	9,917
1863	1,397	1,747	3,144	1,420	1,888	3,308	1,067	440	580	9,649
1864	1,349	1,913	3,262	1,435	1,932	3,367	1,058	431	562	10,424
1865	1,387	2,111	3,498	1,579	2,115	3,694	1,306	420	548	10,682
1866	1,483	2,263	3,746	1,799	2,475	4,274	1,497	408	536	10,890
1867	1,521	2,187	3,708	2,034	2,802	4,836	1,235	399	524	10,335
1868	1,476	2,171	3,647	2,052	2,849	4,901	870	394	525	10,603
1869	1,506	2,228	3,734	1,938	2,713	4,651	1,082	392	528	10,802
1870	1,529	2,271	3,800	1,807	2,529	4,337	1,461	389	533	11,159
1871	1,546	2,430	3,976	1,752	2,481	4,233	1,621	385	538	11,717
1872	1,552	2,507	4,059	1,742	2,521	4,263	1,389	384	541	11,738
1873	1,528	2,619	4,147	1,822	2,662	4,485	1,044	377	532	11,863
1874	1,491	2,634	4,125	1,818	2,624	4,442	1,099	367	527	12,068
1875	1,530	2,585	4,115	1,750	2,504	4,254	1,252	360	526	12,139
1876	1,533	2,584	4,117	1,639	2,371	4,009	1,425	361	535	13,619
1877	1,523	2,475	3,998	1,629	2,359	3,988	1,469	366	553	13,566
1878	1,484	2,501	3,985	1,654	2,441	4,095	1,269	373	562	13,711
1879	1,465	2,603	4,068	1,625	2,393	4,018	1,072	379	572	13,783
1880	1,398	2,524	3,922	1,440	2,123	3,562	850	378	557	13,430
1881	1,392	2,565	3,957	1,338	1,918	3,256	1,096	375	548	13,972
1882	1,399	2,588	3,987	1,261	1,811	3,072	1,430	372	539	13,999
1883	1,402	2,695	4,097	1,330	1,889	3,219	1,348	368	534	13,382

See p. 86 for footnote

(in thousands)

	Cattle			Sheep				Horses		
	Cows and Heifers	Other Cattle	Total	Ewes	Other Sheep	Total	Pigs	for Agri-cultural Purposes	Total (a)	Poultry
1884	1,357	2,756	4,113	1,333	1,913	3,245	1,307	363	535	12,747
1885	1,417	2,812	4,229	1,421	2,056	3,478	1,269	363	547	13,851
1886	1,419	2,765	4,184	1,386	1,980	3,366	1,263	363	549	13,910
1887	1,394	2,763	4,157	1,382	1,995	3,378	1,408	365	557	14,461
1888	1,385	2,714	4,099	1,485	2,142	3,627	1,398	362	565	14,486
1889	1,364	2,730	4,094	1,542	2,247	3,789	1,381	368	574	14,857
1890	1,401	2,839	4,240	1,752	2,571	4,323	1,570	367	585	15,408
1891	1,442	3,007	4,449	1,922	2,801	4,723	1,368	363	593	15,276
1892	1,451	3,080	4,531	1,970	2,858	4,828	1,113	364	606	15,336
1893	1,441	3,023	4,464	1,822	2,599	4,421	1,152	368	614	16,097
1894	1,447	2,945	4,392	1,686	2,419	4,105	1,389	376	623	16,181
1895	1,434	2,924	4,358	1,603	2,310	3,913	1,338	387	630	16,370
1896	1,430	2,978	4,408	1,656	2,425	4,081	1,405	388	629	17,538
1897	1,435	3,030	4,465	1,703	2,454	4,158	1,327	386	610	17,777
1898	1,431	3,056	4,487	1,746	2,542	4,288	1,254	382	591	17,687
1899	1,444	3,063	4,507	1,785	2,580	4,365	1,363	379	580	18,234
1900	1,458	3,151	4,609	1,798	2,589	4,387	1,269	370	567	18,547
1901	1,482	3,191	4,673	1,692 (b)	2,687 (b)	4,379	1,219	355	565	18,811
1902	1,511	3,271	4,782	1,653	2,563	4,216	1,328	358	580	18,504
1903	1,495	3,169	4,664	1,576	2,369	3,945	1,384	365	596	18,154
1904	1,498	3,179	4,677	1,525	2,303	3,828	1,315	369	605	18,257
1905	1,487	3,158	4,645	1,506	2,243	3,749	1,164	373	609	18,549
1906	1,496	3,143	4,639	1,480	2,235	3,715	1,244	371	604	18,977 (c)
1907	1,561	3,115	4,676	1,522	2,295	3,817	1,317	366	596	24,327
1908	1,587	3,205	4,792	1,635	2,443	4,126	1,218	375	605	24,031
1909	1,549	3,151	4,700	1,638	2,446	4,133	1,149	373	599	24,105
1910	1,558	3,131	4,689	1,581	2,351	3,980	1,200	377	613	24,339
1911	1,566	3,146	4,712	1,523	2,334	3,907	1,415	382	616	25,448
1912	1,599	3,249	4,848	1,515	2,265	3,829	1,324	382	618	25,526
1913	1,606	3,327	4,933	1,412	2,165	3,621	1,060	388	614	25,701
1914	1,639	3,413	5,052	1,408	2,146	3,601	1,306	394	619	26,919
1915	1,593	3,251	4,844	1,432	2,123	3,600	1,205	360	561	26,089
1916	1,611	3,359	4,970	1,504	2,213	3,764	1,290	382	599	26,473
1917	1,592	3,317	4,909	1,511	2,185	3,744	947	390	598	22,245
1918	1,557	3,306	4,863	1,449	2,178	3,627	974	414	619	24,424
1919	1,562	3,467	5,029	1,407	2,061	3,513	978	408	625	...
1920	1,578	3,445	5,023	1,424	2,114	3,586	982	400	624	...
1921	1,631	3,566	5,197	1,138	2,570	3,708	977	425	...	...
1922	1,633	3,523	5,157	1,325	2,242	3,567	1,037	433	...	...
1923	1,657	3,369	5,026	1,388	1,742	3,130	1,482	446	595	23,960
1924	1,636	3,368	5,004	1,462	1,773	3,235	1,127	443	576	23,596
1925	1,514	3,144	4,658	1,440	1,857	3,297	844	428	546	24,012
1926	1,542	3,071	4,613	1,518	2,014	3,532	1,042	418	533	29,283
1927	1,602	3,142	4,744	1,608	2,112	3,720	1,414	408	536	29,481
1928	1,589	3,274	4,863	1,669	2,218	3,887	1,412	408	538	29,694

See p. 86 for footnotes

(in thousands)

| | Cattle | | | | Sheep | | | | Horses | | |
	Cows and Heifers	Other Cattle	Total	Ewes	Other Sheep	Total	Pigs	for Agricultural Purposes	Total (a)	Poultry
1929	1,571	3,266	4,837	1,712	2,317	4,029	1,137	405	540	30,398
1930	1,567	3,144	4,711	1,800	2,419	4,219	1,268	412	552	31,708
1931	1,560	3,150	4,710	1,856	2,513	4,369	1,463	413	552	31,473
1932	1,566	3,174	4,740	1,855	2,398	4,253	1,328	414	550	31,907
1933	1,609	3,262	4,871	1,794	2,361	4,155	1,202	418	544	32,655
1934	1,667	3,188	4,855	1,660	2,032	3,692	1,348	414	530	30,276
1935	1,679	3,239	4,918	1,676	2,184	3,860	1,546	410	519	29,570
1936	1,686	3,208	4,894	1,702	2,195	3,897	1,539	407	522	30,882
1937	1,632	3,053	4,685	1,663	2,166	3,829	1,504	405	528	29,673
1938	1,605	3,183	4,788	1,723	2,367	4,090	1,520	408	540	29,823
1939	1,614	3,196	4,810	1,701	2,242	3,943	1,458	402	542	29,771

(a) This column covers all horses in the country, not solely those on agricultural holdings.
(b) From 1901, only ewes kept for breeding purposes were included under the heading *Ewes*.
(c) From 1907, much better returns were obtained of young birds.

5. Agricultural Production—Great Britain 1884–1939

NOTES
[1] SOURCE: *Agricultural Statistics*.
[2] Since 1906 official estimates have been made of the weight of corn crops, and these statistics are readily available for years from 1910 onwards in the *Abstract*. The extremes and the averages of the conversion factors from bushels to tons for the period 1910–39 are as follows:

	High	Low	Average
Wheat	37·32 (1912)	35·28 (1911)	36·21 bushels per ton
Barley	42·88 (1912)	40·50 (1911)	41·56 bushels per ton
Oats	59·01 (1912)	52·59 (1938)	55·95 bushels per ton

(in thousands of the stated unit)

	Wheat bushels	Barley bushels	Oats bushels	Potatoes tons	Turnips and Swedes tons	Mangold tons	Sugar Beet tons	Rotation Hay tons	Pasture Hay tons	Hops cwt.
1884	80,216	73,913	109,397	3,743	27,073	5,558	—	...	...	...
1885	77,588	79,251	108,365	3,199	20,511	5,470	—	8,731		509
1886	61,468	72,090	116,596	3,168	29,983	7,280	—	3,311	5,763	776
1887	74,323	65,301	107,283	3,565	19,748	5,423	—	3,169	4,724	458
1888	71,940	68,482	107,344	3,059	24,675	6,239	—	3,214	6,738	281
1889	73,203	67,427	113,441	3,588	28,097	6,119	—	4,147	7,284	498
1890	73,354	73,934	120,188	2,812	27,747	6,046	—	3,494	6,378	284
1891	72,127	72,129	112,386	3,053	25,392	6,751	—	3,039	5,289	437
1892	58,561	70,485	116,295	3,049	27,348	6,681	—	2,725	4,290	413
1893	49,247	59,535	112,887	3,476	26,262	4,457	—	1,918	2,681	415
1894	59,173	72,295	135,463	2,789	26,398	6,552	—	3,448	6,942	637
1895	37,176	68,651	122,149	3,593	24,730	5,549	—	3,117	4,559	553
1896	57,053	70,775	114,016	3,562	23,254	5,092	—	2,624	4,060	453
1897	54,941	66,814	116,847	2,608	25,652	6,628	—	3,319	5,635	411
1898	73,029	68,052	118,921	3,283	21,337	6,218	—	4,007	6,632	357

(in thousands of the stated unit)

	Wheat bushels	Barley bushels	Oats bushels	Potatoes tons	Turnips and Swedes tons	Mangold tons	Sugar Beet tons	Rotation Hay tons	Pasture Hay tons	Hops cwt.
1899	65,529	67,716	114,747	3,077	16,061	6,538	—	3,044	4,979	661
1900	52,640	62,315	114,848	2,735	23,960	8,463	—	3,188	5,340	348
1901	52,458	61,108	110,106	3,671	20,414	7,774	—	3,002	3,616	649
1902	56,677	66,495	130,384	3,194	24,169	9,347	—	3,846	6,223	311
1903	47,643	59,474	124,681	2,914	19,927	7,188	—	3,671	6,082	421
1904	36,880	57,193	127,408	3,588	23,036	7,481	—	3,497	5,876	282
1905	58,902	58,110	116,437	3,763	21,841	8,213	—	3,143	5,088	696
1906	59,092	60,553	123,385	3,429	22,628	8,538	—	3,201	5,384	246
1907	55,206	60,370	134,392	2,977	22,086	8,937	—	3,710	6,719	374
1908	52,535	54,720	123,627	3,918	23,768	8,995	—	3,507	6,213	471
1909	61,442	60,939	123,026	3,674	25,124	9,571	—	2,936	5,432	214
1910	54,877	56,472	121,829	3,477	25,695	9,353	—	3,264	6,252	303
1911	62,657	50,989	114,353	3,825	16,397	7,480	—	2,613	4,569	328
1912	55,838	51,239	109,935	3,180	20,279	8,837	—	2,675	6,343	373
1913	55,401	57,949	111,044	3,865	20,125	7,648	—	3,397	6,602	256
1914	61,017	56,775	113,381	4,031	19,762	7,961	—	2,746	5,389	507
1915	70,677	41,248	122,177	3,830	19,340	7,890	—	2,831	4,521	255
1916	56,948	46,625	119,508	3,036	18,882	7,382	—	3,659	6,214	308
1917	59,750	49,921	130,496	4,451	20,217	8,535	—	3,061	5,399	221
1918	87,456	54,056(a)	166,368(a)	5,360	17,532	8,280	...	2,692	4,912	130
1919	66,872	49,904	133,776	3,565	18,305	6,337	...	2,290	3,608	189
1920	55,432	58,464	127,224	4,388	21,885	7,336	...	3,278	5,875	281
1921	72,344	48,384	118,608	3,998	13,740	6,287	65	2,725	3,400	224
1922	63,832	46,432	112,808	5,203	17,788	8,595	55	2,410	4,281	301
1923	57,192	45,608	113,176	3,579	17,440	6,989	104	3,484	5,113	229
1924	51,608	47,840	123,072	3,541	18,290	7,846	180	3,507	5,466	444
1925	50,984	47,504	114,672	4,209	16,013	7,151	431	3,209	4,783	355
1926	49,192	42,256	122,504	3,662	17,876	7,143	1,117	3,071	5,050	332
1927	54,536	39,912	111,776	3,854	14,567	5,468	1,503	2,755	4,424	255
1928	47,528	45,736	117,576	4,545	16,613	5,777	1,370	2,769	4,533	242
1929	47,304	45,544	125,556	4,743	14,909	5,712	2,004	2,429	3,857	359
1930	41,416	35,128	111,832	3,603	13,753	5,463	3,060	2,980	5,843	253
1931	37,128	35,608	104,856	3,154	12,416	4,549	1,667	3,336	5,582	169
1932	42,208	34,616	109,696	4,450	13,322	4,358	2,232	2,836	4,919	188
1933	59,440	28,008	104,696	4,555	10,957	4,168	3,298	2,175	4,406	216
1934	66,576	33,304	97,336	4,464	9,206	4,769	4,095	2,229	4,424	259
1935	62,672	30,160	100,816	3,765	10,301	4,618	3,404	2,482	5,104	248
1936	54,072	30,472	97,192	3,804	11,507	4,756	3,448	2,252	4,976	252
1937	54,432	27,216	89,056	4,048	10,161	3,749	2,583	2,846	5,252	236
1938	70,360	36,984	89,512	4,404	10,605	3,689	2,191	1,913	3,389	258
1939	59,464	36,656	97,448	4,354	9,930	4,050	3,529	2,273	4,783	288

(a) Prior to 1918 mixed corn was included with barley or oats, as appropriate. The break in the series is very small, since the total production of mixed corn in 1918 was under 5 million bushels.

Agriculture 6. Agricultural Production—Ireland 1847–1939

NOTE

SOURCES: 1847–1917—*Agricultural Statistics (Ireland)*, annually; 1918–39—Eire Department of Industry and Commerce: *Agricultural Statistics, 1847–1926* (Dublin, 1928); *Agricultural Statistics, 1927–1933* (Dublin, 1935), and *Statistical Abstract, 1940* (Dublin, 1940), and *Report upon the Agricultural Statistics of Northern Ireland*, annually for 1925–9, and in one volume for 1930–53 (Belfast, 1957).

(in thousands of the stated unit)

	Wheat cwt.	Barley cwt.	Oats cwt.	Potatoes tons	Turnips and Swedes tons	Mangold (a) tons	Hay tons
1847	9,821	5,778	36,977	2,056	5,735	252	2,164
1848	...	...	...	...	...	...	...
1849	7,293	5,881	31,327	4,017	5,796	352	2,282
1850	5,324	5,647	33,002	4,003	5,448	358	2,400
1851	5,040	5,860	34,602	4,443	6,106	468	2,492
1852	3,894	5,253	37,441	4,242	5,676	561	2,669
1853	3,793	5,548	34,096	5,742	6,544	584	2,542
1854	4,850	4,669	35,992	5,061	5,198	361	2,390
1855	5,084	4,118	33,056	6,236	6,092	396	2,630
1856	5,502	2,843	29,740	4,406	4,567	286	2,476
1857	7,000	3,173	24,961	3,509	4,360	299	2,567
1858	7,385	2,977	24,961	4,892	4,365	404	2,701
1859	6,171	2,547	23,003	4,330	3,462	308	2,322
1860	5,359	2,760	24,772	2,741	2,628	290	3,206
1861	3,609	2,506	22,389	1,858	3,393	236	2,810
1862	2,884	2,420	20,373	2,148	3,793	222	2,782
1863	3,510	2,776	25,011	3,446	4,184	185	2,762
1864	3,671	2,793	21,962	4,312	3,468	147	2,607
1865	3,471	2,682	21,464	3,866	3,302	192	3,069
1866	3,379	2,394	20,400	3,069	3,786	250	2,879
1867	3,054	2,715	20,763	3,147	3,910	239	3,070
1868	3,962	3,219	21,275	4,062	3,514	246	2,871
1869	3,332	3,475	19,546	3,372	3,965	264	3,040
1870	3,172	3,778	21,120	4,218	3,941	322	3,387
1871	2,952	3,386	20,777	2,794	4,246	432	3,316
1872	2,565	3,149	18,525	1,806	3,963	432	3,496
1873	1,966	3,671	19,341	2,683	4,430	517	3,306
1874	2,895	4,078	19,994	3,552	4,408	542	3,461
1875	2,321	4,246	22,981	3,513	5,293	717	4,355
1876	2,023 (b)	3,891 (b)	21,415 (b)	4,155	4,541	699	3,458
1877	1,901	3,518	17,847	1,757	3,564	600	4,331
1878	2,308	3,928	19,045	2,527	4,686	685	4,417
1879	1,799	3,268	15,533	1,114	2,058	409	3,599
1880	2,228	3,453	19,558	2,986	4,340	604	3,795
1881	2,297	3,334	19,703	3,434	3,821	602	3,990
1882	2,075	2,758	18,286	1,994	3,392	433	4,115
1883	1,297	2,826	18,851	3,452	4,292	526	3,937
1884	992	2,681	18,109	3,040	3,508	439	3,823
1885	1,097	2,889	18,134	3,176	3,552	500	4,156
1886	1,007	2,776	18,379	2,668	3,974	506	4,429
1887	1,019	2,075	15,149	3,569	2,719	455	3,599
1888	1,367	2,707	17,631	2,523	3,327	590	5,181
1889	1,436	3,249	17,633	2,848	3,910	622	4,854
1890	1,414	3,062	17,796	1,810	4,255	663	4,594
1891	1,401	3,315	18,834	3,037	4,349	807	4,343

See p. 89 for footnotes

(in thousands of the stated unit)

	Wheat cwt.	Barley cwt.	Oats cwt.	Potatoes tons	Turnips and Swedes tons	Mangold (a) tons	Hay tons
1892	1,186	2,881	18,068	2,585	4,071	747	4,501
1893	892	2,773	19,396	3,064	4,848	769	4,483
1894	820	2,815	19,291	1,873	4,279	758	5,309
1895	594	2,847	18,221	3,472	4,491	828	4,562
1896	640	3,147	17,008	2,701	4,783	783	4,731
1897	726	2,589	16,265	1,498	4,134	751	5,088
1898	995	2,982	18,684	2,942	5,163	1,010	5,278
1899	927	3,043	17,896	2,760	4,309	1,066	4,876
1900	901	2,782	17,512	1,842	4,426	1,187	5,214
1901	788	2,918	17,783	3,372	4,884	1,452	4,740
1902	858	3,547	18,734	2,726	4,947	1,463	5,177
1903	630	2,605	16,805	2,363	3,596	1,024	5,202
1904	557	2,348	17,183	2,642	4,997	1,332	5,487
1905	766	3,078	17,358	3,423	4,722	1,280	5,323
1906	818	3,092	17,929	2,661	4,956	1,343	4,927
1907	710	3,001	17,166	2,246	4,096	1,182	5,174
1908	747	3,057	18,240	3,200	5,417	1,579	4,917
1909	940	3,574	19,400	3,203	4,970	1,442	4,576
1910	919	2,934	18,791	2,871	4,624	1,466	5,778
1911	887	3,042	16,916	3,695	5,273	1,735	4,475
1912	838	3,111	19,105	2,547	3,783	1,301	5,006
1913	694	3,430	18,887	3,739	5,189	1,629	5,396
1914	758	3,460	18,082	3,446	4,433	1,562	4,269
1915	1,734	2,522	19,601	3,710	5,091	1,807	5,097
1916	1,514	2,802	17,815	2,433	4,436	1,628	5,325
1917	2,450	3,374	27,046	4,153	4,625	1,834	4,702
1918	3,040	3,580	28,980	3,863	5,303	2,041	4,728
1919	1,320	3,480	24,440	2,747	4,487	1,432	4,810 (c)
1920 (c)	776	3,189	17,831	1,986	4,107	1,246	5,547
1921 (c)	826	2,488	15,086	2,556	3,882	1,510	3,258
1922 (c)	829	2,986	16,300	3,431	3,438	1,330	4,626
1923	762	2,340	14,844	2,363	3,664	1,134	4,421
1924	638	2,509	15,000	2,321	3,147	1,014	5,657
1925	471	2,690	17,188	3,307	4,158	1,336	5,334
1926	740	2,899	18,630	3,001	4,611	1,708	6,330
1927	881	2,738	18,870	3,500	4,187	1,637	5,937
1928	735	2,674	18,276	3,390	4,300	1,622	5,514
1929	714	2,574	19,523	4,131	4,524	1,781	5,900
1930	685	2,404	18,183	3,193	3,929	1,598	5,613
1931	478	2,129	14,936	2,630	3,846	1,552	6,017
1932	505	2,152	18,324	4,141	4,025	1,652	5,626
1933	1,183	2,412	17,744	3,446	3,672	1,587	5,477
1934	2,238	2,965	16,698	3,468	3,311	1,635	5,143
1935	3,782	3,181	17,514	3,464	3,371	1,647	5,143
1936	4,340	2,506	15,519	3,206	3,159	1,624	5,105
1937	3,824	2,403	16,325	3,574	3,218	1,679	5,577
1938	4,083	2,264	16,981	3,172	2,826	1,560	5,418
1939	5,619	1,626	16,193	3,862	2,965	1,710	4,916

(a) This usually includes fodder beet, of which the production was very small.
(b) There is probably a slight break in these series, since before 1876 production has been calculated from the rounded yield and acreage statistics.

(c) The figures for 1920–2, and the figure for hay in 1919, are approximations, the returns being made by the police and not by individual farmers.

Agriculture 7. Yield per Acre of Main Agricultural Products—Great Britain 1884–1939

NOTES

[1] SOURCE: *Agricultural Statistics*.
[2] Since 1906 official estimates have been made of the weight of corn crops, and these statistics are readily available for years from 1910 onwards in the *Abstract*. The extremes and the average of the conversion factors from bushels to hundredweights for the period 1910–39 are as follows:

	High	Low	Average
Wheat	1·87 (1912)	1·76 (1911)	1·81 bushels per cwt.
Barley	2·14 (1912)	2·03 (1911)	2·08 bushels per cwt.
Oats	2·95 (1912)	2·63 (1938)	2·80 bushels per cwt.

	Wheat bushels	Barley bushels	Oats bushels	Potatoes tons	Turnips and Swedes tons	Mangold tons	Sugar Beet tons	Rotation Hay tons	Pasture Hay tons	Hops cwt.
1884	30·0	34·1	37·5	6·6	13·4	17·0	—	...	...	...
1885	31·3	35·1	36·9	5·8	10·2	15·4	—	1·4		7·1
1886	26·9	32·2	37·8	5·7	15·0	20·8	—	1·5	1·3	11·1
1887	32·1	31·3	34·7	6·4	10·0	15·0	—	1·4	1·0	7·2
1888	28·1	32·8	37·2	5·2	12·7	17·3	—	1·4	1·4	4·8
1889	29·9	31·8	39·3	6·2	14·6	18·8	—	1·7	1·5	8·6
1890	30·7	35·0	41·4	5·3	14·3	18·3	—	1·5	1·3	5·3
1891	31·3	34·1	38·8	5·7	13·2	19·0	—	1·4	1·2	7·8
1892	26·4	34·6	38·8	5·8	14·1	18·5	—	1·3	1·0	7·4
1893	26·0	28·7	35·6	6·6	13·3	12·8	—	0·9	0·6	7·2
1894	30·7	34·5	41·6	5·5	13·5	18·5	—	1·6	1·4	10·7
1895	26·2	31·7	37·1	6·6	12·9	16·6	—	1·4	1·0	9·4
1896	33·7	33·6	36·8	6·3	12·4	15·1	—	1·2	0·9	8·4
1897	29·1	32·8	38·5	5·2	14·0	18·7	—	1·5	1·3	8·1
1898	34·7	35·8	40·8	6·3	12·0	17·7	—	1·7	1·5	7·2
1899	32·8	34·2	38·8	5·6	9·2	17·5	—	1·4	1·2	12·8
1900	28·5	31·3	38·0	4·9	14·2	20·4	—	1·5	1·2	6·8
1901	30·8	31·0	36·7	6·4	12·3	19·5	—	1·3	0·8	12·7
1902	32·8	34·8	42·7	5·6	15·0	21·2	—	1·6	1·4	6·5
1903	30·1	32·0	39·7	5·2	12·4	17·9	—	1·5	1·3	8·8
1904	26·8	31·1	39·2	6·3	14·4	18·8	—	1·5	1·2	5·9
1905	32·8	33·9	38·2	6·2	13·7	20·3	—	1·4	1·1	14·2
1906	33·7	34·6	40·6	6·1	14·2	19·8	—	1·5	1·1	5·3
1907	34·0	35·3	43·0	5·4	14·1	19·9	—	1·7	1·4	8·3
1908	32·3	32·8	39·8	7·0	15·3	21·0	—	1·6	1·3	12·1
1909	33·7	36·6	41·3	6·4	16·2	21·0	—	1·4	1·1	6·6
1910	30·3	32·7	40·3	6·4	16·4	21·1	—	1·6	1·3	9·2
1911	32·9	31·9	38·0	6·7	10·5	16·5	—	1·3	0·9	9·9
1912	29·0	31·1	36·3	5·2	13·4	18·1	—	1·4	1·2	10·7
1913	31·5	33·0	38·1	6·5	13·6	18·2	—	1·6	1·3	7·2
1914	32·7	33·4	39·8	6·6	13·4	18·4	—	1·4	1·1	13·8
1915	31·5	29·9	39·8	6·3	14·3	19·0	—	1·5	0·9	7·3
1916	28·8	31·1	38·9	5·4	14·0	19·5	—	1·7	1·3	9·8
1917	30·2	30·8	39·5	6·8	14·6	21·9	—	1·5	1·1	13·0
1918	33·2	32·7 (a)	41·3 (a)	6·7	13·4	20·6	...	1·5	1·1	8·3

See p. 91 for footnote

	Wheat bushels	Barley bushels	Oats bushels	Potatoes tons	Turnips and Swedes tons	Mangold tons	Sugar Beet tons	Rotation Hay tons	Pasture Hay tons	Hops cwt.
1919	29·1	29·6	36·4	5·7	13·0	16·0	...	1·2	0·8	11·3
1920	28·7	31·8	38·6	6·2	15·5	19·0	...	1·6	1·3	13·4
1921	35·4	30·1	37·5	5·6	10·5	16·8	7·8	1·3	0·8	8·9
1922	31·4	30·5	35·9	7·2	14·5	20·3	6·6	1·2	0·9	11·4
1923	31·8	30·7	38·4	5·9	13·8	17·3	6·2	1·6	1·1	9·2
1924	32·4	32·7	41·1	6·0	14·8	20·2	8·0	1·6	1·2	17·1
1925	32·9	32·3	41·0	6·6	13·3	19·9	7·7	1·5	1·1	13·5
1926	29·9	33·3	43·8	5·7	15·4	21·1	8·6	1·5	1·1	13·0
1927	32·0	34·2	42·2	5·8	13·3	17·9	6·5	1·4	1·0	11·1
1928	32·7	35·3	44·5	7·2	15·1	19·3	7·7	1·4	1·0	10·2
1929	34·3	36·5	45·4	7·1	13·9	19·0	8·7	1·3	0·8	15·0
1930	29·6	31·2	42·4	6·6	13·2	18·9	8·8	1·5	1·1	12·6
1931	29·8	31·9	42·2	5·5	12·7	16·8	7·1	1·6	1·1	8·7
1932	31·5	33·6	44·8	6·8	14·4	18·9	8·7	1·5	1·0	11·4
1933	34·2	34·5	44·5	6·8	12·1	17·5	9·0	1·3	0·9	12·8
1934	35·9	34·8	43·9	7·1	10·5	19·3	10·1	1·3	0·9	14·4
1935	33·5	34·7	44·9	6·3	12·2	18·3	9·1	1·4	1·1	13·6
1936	30·1	34·2	43·2	6·5	14·5	19·1	9·7	1·3	1·0	13·7
1937	29·7	30·1	43·6	6·9	13·3	17·9	8·3	1·5	1·1	13·0
1938	36·6	37·6	45·0	7·2	14·3	17·0	6·6	1·2	0·8	13·9
1939	33·7	36·3	45·6	7·4	14·1 (b)	18·9	10·4	1·3	1·0	15·3

(a) This break, caused by the separation of mixed corn from oats and barley, is negligible.

(b) This break, caused by the exclusion of turnips for domestic use, is negligible.

NOTE

SOURCES: 1847–1917—*Agricultural Statistics (Ireland)*, annually; 1918–39—Eire Department of Industry and Commerce: *Agricultural Statistics, 1847–1926* (Dublin, 1928); *Agricultural Statistics, 1927–1933* (Dublin, 1935), and *Statistical Abstract, 1940* (Dublin, 1940), and *Report upon the Agricultural Statistics of Northern Ireland*, annually for 1925–9, and in one volume for 1930–53 (Belfast, 1957).

	Wheat cwt.	Barley cwt.	Oats cwt.	Potatoes tons	Turnips and Swedes tons	Mangold (a) tons	Hay tons
1847	12·2	17·4	16·8	7·2	15·5	18·0	1·9
1848	9·0	...	15·2	3·9	14·3	17·5	2·0
1849	10·6	16·7	15·2	5·6	16·1	18·5	2·0
1850	8·8	17·6	15·4	4·6	15·7	17·9	2·0
1851	10·0	17·4	15·8	5·1	15·9	18·0	2·0
1852	11·0	18·1	16·4	4·8	15·9	18·1	2·1
1853	11·6	18·4	15·8	6·4	16·4	17·7	2·0
1854	11·8	18·4	17·6	5·1	15·8	17·2	1·9
1855	11·4	17·3	15·6	6·4	16·6	18·0	2·0
1856	10·4	15·0	14·6	4·0	12·9	13·0	1·9
1857	12·5	14·6	12·6	3·1	12·5	13·9	1·9
1858	13·5	15·2	12·6	4·2	12·9	13·7	1·9
1859	13·3	14·0	11·6	3·6	10·7	11·4	1·6
1860	11·5	15·0	12·6	2·3	8·3	9·1	2·0
1861	9·0	12·4	11·2	1·6	10·2	10·3	1·8
1862	8·1	12·4	10·3	2·1	10·1	9·6	1·8
1863	13·5	15·9	12·8	3·4	11·9	11·3	1·8
1864	13·3	15·9	12·1	4·1	10·3	10·5	1·6
1865	13·0	14·9	12·3	3·6	9·9	13·3	1·8
1866	11·3	15·7	12·0	2·9	11·9	12·5	1·8
1867	11·7	15·7	12·5	3·1	11·6	12·7	1·9
1868	13·9	17·1	12·5	3·9	11·0	12·9	1·7
1869	11·9	15·5	11·6	3·2	12·3	12·5	1·8
1870	12·2	15·5	12·8	4·0	11·6	12·7	1·9
1871	12·1	15·2	12·7	2·6	13·0	13·5	1·8
1872	11·4	14·3	11·4	1·8	11·4	12·4	1·9
1873	11·7	15·9	12·8	3·0	12·7	13·5	1·8
1874	15·4	19·2	13·5	4·0	13·2	14·1	1·8
1875	14·6	18·1	15·3	3·9	15·9	16·6	2·2
1876	17·0	17·6	14·3	4·7	13·2	14·4	1·9
1877	13·6	15·5	12·1	2·0	10·7	12·3	2·3
1878	15·0	16·1	13·5	3·0	14·2	15·2	2·3
1879	11·4	12·8	11·7	1·3	6·5	8·0	1·9
1880	15·0	15·8	14·2	3·6	14·3	14·6	2·0
1881	14·9	15·8	14·1	4·0	12·9	13·4	2·0
1882	13·6	14·7	13·1	2·4	11·5	11·9	2·1
1883	13·7	15·4	13·6	4·3	14·0	13·9	2·0
1884	14·6	16·1	13·4	3·8	11·5	12·7	1·9
1885	15·4	16·1	13·6	4·0	11·9	13·4	2·0
1886	14·5	15·3	13·9	3·3	13·3	13·5	2·1
1887	15·2	12·8	11·5	4·5	9·1	10·9	1·7
1888	13·8	15·8	13·8	3·1	11·3	12·9	2·3
1889	16·0	17·5	14·2	3·6	13·1	14·1	2·2
1890	15·3	16·8	14·6	2·3	14·4	14·3	2·2
1891	17·3	18·6	15·5	4·0	14·5	15·6	2·1

See p. 93 for footnotes

	Wheat cwt.	Barley cwt.	Oats cwt.	Potatoes tons	Turnips and Swedes tons	Mangold (a) tons	Hay tons
1892	15·7	16·4	14·7	3·5	13·5	14·5	2·1
1893	16·2	16·4	15·5	4·2	16·0	16·3	2·1
1894	16·6	17·1	15·4	2·6	13·7	14·6	2·4
1895	16·3	16·6	15·0	4·9	14·3	15·6	2·1
1896	16·8	18·2	14·2	3·8	15·5	14·4	2·1
1897	15·4	15·1	13·8	2·2	13·4	13·7	2·3
1898	18·8	18·9	16·0	4·4	16·8	18·0	2·4
1899	17·9	17·9	15·8	4·2	14·3	17·0	2·3
1900	16·7	16·0	15·8	2·8	14·9	17·3	2·4
1901	18·3	18·0	16·2	5·3	16·9	18·8	2·2
1902	19·4	21·1	17·3	4·3	17·2	19·0	2·4
1903	16·8	16·4	15·3	3·8	12·5	13·5	2·3
1904	18·1	14·9	15·9	4·3	17·5	17·6	2·4
1905	20·2	19·9	16·3	5·6	16·7	17·6	2·3
1906	18·6	17·5	16·7	4·3	17·8	20·0	2·1
1907	18·6	17·7	16·0	3·8	14·9	17·6	2·3
1908	20·4	19·7	17·2	5·5	19·4	21·9	2·1
1909	21·6	21·9	18·7	5·5	18·0	19·6	2·0
1910	19·3	17·5	17·5	4·8	16·8	19·5	2·4
1911	19·7	19·2	16·3	6·2	19·5	22·2	1·8
1912	18·7	18·8	18·3	4·3	13·9	15·9	2·0
1913	20·4	19·8	18·0	6·4	18·8	20·6	2·2
1914	20·5	20·1	17·6	5·9	16·0	19·2	1·7
1915	20·0	17·8	18·0	6·2	19·2	21·8	2·0
1916	19·8	18·7	16·6	4·2	16·9	20·2	2·2
1917	19·7	19·0	18·5	5·9	15·7	19·7	1·9
1918	19·4	19·4	18·3	5·5	18·0	20·9	1·9
1919	18·9	18·0	16·9	4·7	16·4	19·1	1·9
1920 (b)	15·5	15·4	13·4	3·4	14·9	16·2	2·7
1921 (b)	19·2	14·1	12·0	4·5	14·6	19·4	1·4
1922 (b)	20·2	17·6	13·4	6·0	13·9	15·8	1·8
1923	19·5	15·3	13·1	4·3	14·8	14·5	1·8
1924	16·8	15·8	14·7	4·1	12·5	11·8	2·0
1925	18·1	18·2	17·3	6·2	17·0	16·7	1·9
1926	20·6	19·6	19·2	5·7	19·2	20·8	2·3
1927	21·5	22·4	19·8	6·8	18·5	20·2	2·2
1928	20·4	20·4	19·1	6·5	18·5	18·9	2·1
1929	22·3	21·6	19·9	8·0	19·7	21·0	2·1
1930	22·1	20·4	19·1	6·6	17·9	19·7	2·0
1931	19·9	18·2	16·4	5·5	17·6	18·3	2·2
1932	21·0	20·7	20·0	8·5	18·8	20·1	2·1
1933	21·1	20·3	19·2	7·2	17·8	19·6	2·0
1934	21·9	20·4	19·6	7·2	17·0	19·5	2·0
1935	22·5	22·4	19·7	7·4	18·2	19·4	2·1
1936	16·6	18·8	18·8	6·9	17·5	18·7	2·1
1937	17·1	17·9	19·7	7·9	18·1	19·3	2·2
1938	17·3	18·7	19·6	7·0	16·7	18·1	2·2
1939	21·8	21·1	19·6	8·9	18·1	19·7	2·0

(a) This usually includes fodder beet, the quantities of which were very small.

(b) The figures for these years are approximations based on returns by the police rather than by individual farmers.

Agriculture 9. The Overseas Corn Trade—Great Britain 1697–1842

A. Trade in Wheat and Wheaten Flour, 1697–1842, Distinguishing Imports from Ireland from 1800

(in thousands of quarters)

NOTE
SOURCE: *S.P.* 1843, LIII.

	Imports	Exports		Imports	Exports
1697 (*a*)	- -	15	1742	- -	296
1698 (*b*)	2	7	1743	- -	376
1699	- -	1	1744	- -	234
1700	- -	49	1745	- -	325
1701	- -	98	1746	—	131
1702	—	90	1747	—	270
1703	- -	107	1748	- -	545
1704	- -	90	1749	- -	631
1705	—	96	1750	- -	950
1706	- -	188	1751	- -	663
1707	—	174	1752	—	430
1708	- -	84	1753	—	301
1709	2	72	1754	- -	357
1710	- -	17	1755	—	237
1711	—	81	1756	- -	103
1712	—	149	1757	142	12
1713	—	180	1758	20	9
1714	- -	181	1759	- -	228
1715	—	173	1760	- -	394
1716	—	76	1761	—	442
1717	—	26	1762	- -	295
1718	—	74	1763	- -	430
1719	- -	131	1764	- -	397
1720	—	84	1765	105	167
1721	—	83	1766	11	165
1722	—	179	1767	498	5
1723	—	158	1768	349	7
1724	- -	247	1769	4	50
1725	- -	211	1770	- -	75
1726	—	144	1771	3	10
1727	—	31	1772	25	7
1728	75	4	1773	57	8
1729	40	19	1774	289	16
1730	- -	95	1775	561	91
1731	- -	131	1776	21	211
1732	—	203	1777	233	88
1733	- -	427	1778	106	141
1734	- -	499	1779	5	222
1735	- -	155	1780	4	224
1736	- -	118	1781	160	103
1737	- -	466	1782	81	145
1738	- -	588	1783	584	52
1739	- -	285	1784	217	89
1740	5	54	1785	111	133
1741	8	45	1786	51	205

See p. 95 for footnotes

Agriculture 9. *continued*

(in thousands of quarters)

	Imports	Imports from Ireland	Exports		Imports	Imports from Ireland	Exports
1787	59	...	121	1815	384	190	228
1788	149	...	83	1816	332	122	122
1789	113	...	140	1817	1,090	55	318
1790	223	...	31	1818	1,694	105	59
1791	469	...	71	1819	626	154	45
1792	22	...	300	1820	996	403	95
1793	490	...	77	1821	707	570	200
1794	328	...	155	1822	511	463	160
1795	314	...	19	1823	424	400	146
1796	879	...	25	1824	442	356	62
1797	462	...	55	1825	788	396	39
1798	397	...	60	1826	897	314	20
1799	463	...	39	1827	712	405	57
1800	1,265	1	22	1828	1,410	653	76
1801	1,425	- -	28	1829	2,190	519	75
1802	648	109	149	1830	2,206	530	37
1803	374	61	77	1831	2,868	557	66
1804	461	70	63	1832	1,254	790	290
1805	921	84	78	1833	1,166	844	96
1806	310	102	30	1834	981	780	159
1807	405	45	25	1835	751	662	134
1808	85	43	98	1836	861	599	257
1809	456	67	31	1837	1,109	534	308
1810	1,567	126	76	1838	1,923	543	159
1811	336	147	98	1839	3,111	258	43
1812	291	158	46	1840	2,527	174	87
1813	559	217	...	1841	2,910	219	30
1814	853	225	111	1842	3,111	202	68

(*a*) Year ended Michaelmas.
(*b*) Fifteen months ended 25th December. Subsequent figures are for years ended on that date.

B. Trade in Barley, Oats, and Malt, 1697–1818

(in thousands of quarters)

NOTE

SOURCES: 1697–1764—C. Smith, *Three Tracts on the Corn Trade* (London, 1776); 1770–1800—*S.P.* 1804, VII; 1801–14— S.P. 1814–5, X; 1815—*S.P.* 1816, XIV; 1816–17—*S.P.* 1818 XIV; 1818—*S.P.* 1819, XVI.

Average of:	Barley		Oats		Malt
	Imports	Exports	Imports	Exports	Exports
1697–9	- - (a)	21 (a)	1 (a)	...	37 (a)
1700–4	—	33	- -	...	77
1705–9	- -	21	- -	...	125
1710–14	- -	22	- -	...	170
1715–19	—	24	- -	...	248
1720–4	- -	22	12	...	301
1725–9	6	10	51	...	239
1730–4	1	30	25	...	191
1735–9	—	43	1	...	180
1740–4	3	20	17	...	180
1745–9	- -	97	- -	...	315
1750–4	—	96	11	...	294
1755–9	3	18	12	...	162
1760–4	2	62	71	...	231
1765–9	...	...	...	...	...
1770–4	28	3	218	18	42
1775–9	40	9	329	26	96
1780–4	28	33	166	17	86
1785–9	39	82	408	19	115
1790–4	97	11	787	16	20
1795–9	52	8	592	13	10
1800–4	57	32	566	14	5 (b)
1805–9	28	8	687	20	...
1810–14	56	42 (b)	524	30 (b)	...
1815–18	248 (b)	31 (b)	1,125 (b)	29 (b)	...

(a) The period Michaelmas 1696 to 25th December 1698 has been counted as two years in computing the averages for 1697–9. All other figures are for years ended 25th December.

(b) Average of four years only. The malt statistics end in 1803 and the others in 1818, whilst the export statistics for 1813 were destroyed in the Customs House fire of that year.

C. Imports of Barley, Oats and Oatmeal from Ireland 1800–42

(in thousands of quarters)

NOTE

SOURCE: *S.P.* 1843, LIII.

	Barley and Bear	Oats and Oatmeal		Barley and Bear	Oats and Oatmeal
1800	- -	2	1822	23	569
1801	—	- -	1823	19	1,102
1802	7	341	1824	45	1,225
1803	13	266	1825	154	1,630
1804	3	240	1826	65	1,304
1805	16	203	1827	68	1,343
1806	3	357	1828	84	2,076
1807	23	390	1829	97	1,674
1808	31	580	1830	190	1,471
1809	17	846	1831	185	1,656
1810	8	493	1832	124	2,052
1811	3	276	1833	102	1,763
1812	43	391	1834	218	1,770
1813	64	691	1835	156	1,823
1814	17	564	1836	184	2,132
1815	27	598	1837	187	2,275
1816	62	684	1838	156	2,743
1817	27	611	1839	62	1,905
1818	25	1,069	1840	96	2,038
1819	20	790	1841	76	2,539
1820	87	916	1842	50	2,261
1821	83	1,162			

Agriculture 10. The Overseas Corn Trade—United Kingdom 1792–1938

NOTES

[1] Sources: Part A—*S.P.* 1849, L; Part B—*Annual Statement of Trade*.
[2] The proportion of meal included with barley was negligible, whilst that included with oats was not more than 5 per cent, and usually less.
[3] Conversion factors from bushels to hundredweights are not directly available for the period to 1839. The 1840 ration for barley and oats can probably be used without much concern for earlier years, but the considerable and variable imports of wheaten flour make such a proceeding much less accurate for wheat.

A. Imports and Re-exports, 1792–1840 (in thousands of quarters)

	Wheat and Wheaten Flour		Barley and Barley Meal		Oats and Oatmeal	
	Imports	Re-exports	Imports	Re-exports	Imports	Re-exports
1792	24	29	112	– –	451	10
1793	477	44	142	– –	430	3
1794	340	68	111	1	485	1
1795	299	2	18	—	105	—
1796	879	1	40	—	460	2
1797	421	18	51	– –	274	2
1798	379	21	66	2	411	6
1799	456	6	19	– –	170	5
1800	293	4	131	—	543	– –
1801	1,427	7	114	– –	583	1
1802	542	131	8	1	242	3
1803	314	54	1	– –	255	2
1804	391	32	9	– –	500	4
1805	838	57	28	3	274	—
1806	208	9	2	– –	183	1
1807	364	6	3	– –	426	—
1808	42	16	4	– –	34	1
1809	395	3	13	1	296	– –
1810	1,440	63	18	4	116	1
1811	189	71	40	23	12	2
1812	132	18	40	29	15	5
1813	340	...	20	...	60	...
1814	624	23	29	9	248	1
1815	192	56	2	1	120	– –
1816	210	20	15	– –	75	2
1817	1,064	44	134	4	484	1·
1818	1,594	18	696	– –	987	– –
1819	472	23	373	3	586	2
1820	585	88	29	5	682	4
1821	130	193	14	9	101	14
1822	43	148	19	5	56	15
1823	16	120	– –	5	28	13
1824	83	54	27	3	488	11
1825	385	33	426	4	206	12
1826	577	14	278	5	1,125	9
1827	304	49	208	19	1,741	1
1828	741	74	166	4	165	7
1829	1,663	72	277	10	540	59
1830	1,662	35	139	1	506	26
1831	2,304	63	377	1	623	6
1832	447	288	96	8	29	84
1833	298	94	85	3	23	20
1834	176	159	89	10	175	13
1835	67	132	68	44	113	31
1836	242	255	83	18	131	57
1837	560	308	88	11	419	49
1838	1,372	156	2	20	56	56
1839	2,875	39	579	1	671	40
1840	2,433	84	625	4	546	37

B. Imports of the Main Grains, and Exports and Re-exports of Wheat, 1840–1938

(in thousands of hundredweights)

		Imports				
	Wheat	Wheat Meal and Flour	Barley	Oats	Maize	Exports and Re-exports of Wheat, Wheat Meal and Flour
1840	8,638	1,538	2,234	1,487	100	...
1841	10,442	1,263	945	336	18	95
1842	11,776	1,130	262	828	153	267
1843	4,074	437	640	232	2	273
1844	4,763	981	3,641	824	159	322
1845	3,777	946	1,316	1,624	242	278
1846	6,208	3,190	1,324	2,171	3,025	592
1847	11,511	6,329	2,760	4,691	15,464	1,381
1848	11,184	1,754	3,765	2,659	6,752	46
1849	16,663	3,350	4,932	3,485	9,533	26
1850	16,202	3,819	3,700	3,175	5,473	56
1851	16,519	5,314	2,963	3,296	7,747	304
1852	13,261	3,865	2,234	2,721	6,305	279
1853	21,300	4,622	2,943	2,828	6,619	739
1854	14,869	3,647	1,975	2,791	5,784	633
1855	11,560	1,904	1,247	2,843	5,209	792
1856	17,649	3,970	2,612	3,154	7,619	1,111
1857	14,898	2,178	6,077	4,703	4,932	958
1858	18,381	3,856	5,934	5,105	7,504	94
1859	17,337	3,328	6,171	4,613	5,633	258
1860	25,484	5,086	7,546	6,300	7,936	78
1861	29,956	6,153	5,001	5,114	13,244	2,929
1862	41,034	7,207	6,625	4,427	11,695	142
1863	24,364	5,219	7,384	6,496	12,737	317
1864	23,197	4,512	4,921	5,563	6,286	153
1865	20,963	3,904	7,818	7,714	7,096	116
1866	23,156	4,972	8,434	8,845	14,323	309
1867	34,646	3,593	5,684	9,407	8,540	597
1868	32,640	3,093	7,476	8,113	11,472	509
1869	37,696	5,402	8,054	7,917	17,664	154
1870	30,901	4,804	7,217	10,831	16,757	2,590
1871	39,390	3,978	8,569	10,912	16,820	4,935
1872	42,128	4,388	15,047	11,537	24,533	795
1873	43,863	6,214	9,241	11,908	18,823	2,264
1874	41,528	6,236	11,335	11,388	17,694	1,271
1875	51,877	6,136	11,049	12,436	20,438	211
1876	44,455	5,960	9,773	11,211	39,963	1,325
1877	54,270	7,377	12,960	12,910	30,478	1,184
1878	49,906	7,828	14,157	12,774	41,674	1,652
1879	59,592	10,782	11,546	13,472	36,148	1,330
1880	55,262	10,558	11,705	13,827	37,225	1,845
1881	57,148	11,357	9,806	10,324	33,481	1,422
1882	64,241	13,057	15,540	13,638	18,276	1,598
1883	64,139	16,329	16,461	15,138	31,739	867
1884	47,306	15,095	12,953	12,922	24,780	1,466
1885	61,499	15,833	15,366	13,057	31,527	1,008
1886	47,436	14,690	13,714	13,485	31,012	1,481
1887	55,803	18,063	14,240	14,463	31,167	1,009
1888	57,261	16,910	21,305	18,771	25,370	835
1889	58,552	14,672	17,401	15,991	36,192	857

(in thousands of hundredweights)

Imports

	Wheat	Wheat Meal and Flour	Barley	Oats	Maize	Exports and Re-exports of Wheat, Wheat Meal and Flour
1890	60,474	15,773	16,678	12,727	43,438	852
1891	66,313	16,723	17,466	16,600	26,826	1,049
1892	64,902	22,106	14,277	15,661	35,381	1,321
1893	65,462	20,408	22,845	13,955	32,903	1,156
1894	70,126	19,135	31,241	14,979	35,365	828
1895	81,750	18,368	23,619	15,528	33,944	833
1896	70,026	21,320	22,477	17,587	51,772	1,001
1897	62,740	18,681	18,959	16,117	53,785	907
1898	65,228	21,017	24,457	15,578	57,169	1,471
1899	66,636	22,946	17,189	15,627	62,741	1,820
1900	68,669	21,548	17,055	20,110	54,152	1,408
1901	69,709	22,576	21,873	22,471	51,373	1,523
1902	81,002	19,386	25,211	15,857	44,493	981
1903	88,131	20,601	26,575	16,284	50,099	841
1904	97,783	14,723	27,173	14,098	42,898	1,043
1905	97,623	11,955	21,427	17,095	42,101	1,541
1906	92,967	14,190	19,935	15,287	48,685	1,638
1907	97,168	13,297	19,628	10,485	53,380	2,031
1908	91,131	12,970	18,137	14,269	33,841	2,927
1909	97,854	11,053	21,556	17,836	39,363	1,896
1910	105,223	9,960	18,282	17,495	37,021	2,281
1911	98,068	10,065	24,545	18,273	38,602	2,442
1912	109,573	10,189	20,126	18,300	43,877	2,856
1913	105,878	11,978	22,439	18,163	49,155	2,517
1914	103,927	10,060	16,044	14,157	39,041	2,931
1915	88,668	10,482	12,292	15,640	48,581	2,248
1916	100,070	9,960	15,820	12,504	34,159	1,341
1917	91,435	14,340	9,139	12,622	25,000	810
1918	57,948	26,360	5,025	10,983	14,490	417
1919	71,443	17,711	16,644	6,711	16,861	406
1920	109,328	11,970	12,668	6,102	33,840	447
1921	80,479	15,841	15,813	8,357	36,757	4,629
1922	96,380	13,475	12,703	9,357	37,200	2,677
1923 (*a*)	100,467	11,718	18,129	9,759	34,490	4,878
1924	117,421	11,046	21,656	10,316	37,667	7,598
1925	96,854	9,113	15,779	8,366	27,585	8,826
1926	96,256	10,661	11,570	7,640	31,784	4,797
1927	110,436	10,961	16,419	5,907	41,928	4,829
1928	103,577	8,927	12,975	7,447	33,016	5,317
1929	111,767	9,703	11,986	6,930	34,909	5,389
1930	104,775	11,728	15,208	9,631	34,165	5,408
1931	119,419	10,747	15,423	8,753	53,261	4,861
1932	105,637	8,530	10,178	6,472	52,746	5,963
1933	112,375	9,843	15,985	5,620	51,316	3,780
1934	102,625	9,447	15,476	3,210	61,350	4,006
1935	101,226	7,981	17,097	3,554	59,456	3,314
1936	100,772	8,367	18,294	2,161	73,293	3,202
1937	96,859	8,540	18,176	1,208	71,671	3,369
1938	101,626	7,677	19,876	1,576	57,581	3,448

(*a*) As from 1st April 1923, southern Ireland was treated as foreign territory.

Agriculture 11. Principal Sources of Imports of Wheat—United Kingdom 1828–1938

NOTES

[1] SOURCES: 1828–39—*S.P.* 1842, XL and *S.P.* 1843, LIII; 1840–53—*Abstract*; 1854–1938—*Annual Statement of Trade*.
[2] Figures have not been included for some countries during periods when imports from them were not of much significance.

[3] The main sources of wheat meal and wheaten flour (not shown here) were Canada and the U.S.A., though on some occasions substantial amounts came from Russia and from Australia.

(in thousands of hundredweights)

	Russia	Prussia	Germany	Canada	U.S.A.
1828 (*a*)	80	1,109	...	62	—
1829 (*a*)	1,485	1,565	...	18	4
1830 (*a*)	1,039	2,290	...	261	27
1831 (*a*)	2,055	1,322	...	844	190
1832 (*a*)	402	526	...	398	27
1833 (*a*)	84	389	...	349	—
1834 (*a*)	—	133	...	199	—
1835 (*a*)	—	13	...	62	—
1836 (*a*)	4	442	...	—	—
1837 (*a*)	49	1,392	...	—	—
1838 (*a*)	181	2,435	...	—	4
1839 (*a*)	1,644	3,271	...	—	18
1840	1,162	3,469	...	35	320
1841	432	3,822	...	305	46
1842	1,247	3,197	...	145	70
1843	146	2,851	...	88	—
1844	453	2,387	...	157	10
1845	146	1,836	...	167	101
1846	888	1,560	...	297	742
1847	3,654	2,125	...	385	1,837
1848	2,264	2,262	...	118	339
1849	2,573	2,665	...	45	469
1850	2,766	3,609	...	38	436
1851	3,030	3,017	...	94	877
1852	3,179	1,958	...	150	2,095
1853	4,641	4,960	...	366	3,090
1854	2,196	2,916	...	79	1,810
1855	—	2,323	...	63	1,079
1856	3,291	965	...	485	5,543
1857	3,061	(3,754)(*b*)	5,388	497	2,820
1858	2,653	(2,713)	3,986	437	2,577
1859	3,837	(3,344)	4,256	29	160
1860	5,638	(4,981)	6,543	795	6,497
1861	4,513	(4,454)	6,270	2,381	10,867
1862	5,751	(6,285)	7,588	3,733	16,141

See p. 102 for footnotes

(in thousands of hundredweights)

	Russia	Prussia	Germany	Canada	U.S.A.	Argentine	India	Australia
1863	4,534	(4,410)	5,297	2,094	8,704	...	...	...
1864	5,119	(4,935)	6,364	1,226	7,895	...	...	...
1865	8,094	(5,404)	6,817	307	1,178	...	...	...
1866	8,937	(4,401)	6,261	9	635	...	...	...
1867	14,025	(5,572)	7,103	683	4,188	...	...	...
1868	10,054	(4,585)	6,043	557	5,908	...	...	...
1869	9,158	(4,635)	6,149	2,723	13,182	...	...	...
1870	10,269	...	3,348	2,838	12,372	...	...	...
1871	15,654	...	3,050	3,278	13,386	...	...	...
1872	17,886	...	3,891	1,735	8,720	...	157	501
1873	9,596	...	2,155	3,762	19,796	...	741	1,801
1874	5,726	...	3,063	3,812	23,090	...	1,074	907
1875	10,005	...	5,613	3,622	23,523	...	1,334	1,157
1876	8,781	...	2,324	2,423	19,323	...	3,287	2,606
1877	10,828	...	5,455	2,952	21,387	...	6,105	426
1878	9,022	...	5,118	2,621	29,061	...	1,821	1,454
1879	8,005	...	3,614	4,782	36,042	...	887	2,248
1880	2,880	...	1,599	3,888	36,191	...	3,229	4,246
1881	4,047	...	1,361	2,876	36,083	...	7,335	2,969
1882	9,576	...	3,080	2,689	35,137	...	8,461	2,475
1883	13,347	...	2,871	1,799	26,129	...	11,249	2,684
1884	5,402	...	1,090	1,757	22,641	...	7,981	5,091
1885	11,976	...	1,980	1,745	24,273	...	12,170	5,279
1886	3,721	...	1,317	3,081	24,649	269	11,024	739
1887	5,501	...	1,552	3,969	30,530	1,014	8,512	1,347
1888	21,450	...	3,279	1,090	14,644	1,752	8,166	2,316
1889	21,310	...	2,538	1,171	17,009	38	9,218	1,406
1890	19,389	...	1,101	1,128	17,201	2,810	9,112	3,058
1891	14,553	...	714	3,174	24,195	2,748	13,006	2,086
1892	4,363	...	606	3,875	33,887	3,466	12,495	2,017
1893	10,062	...	362	3,157	32,263	7,846	6,196	2,590
1894	16,776	...	715	2,829	24,658	13,272	5,349	3,877
1895	23,017	...	753	1,845	27,084	11,400	8,803	3,487
1896	17,242	...	1,033	3,618	30,695	4,928	2,113	7
1897	15,050	...	1,333	4,821	34,603	933	573	—
1898	6,233	...	711	5,012	37,855	3,983	9,538	212
1899	2,518	...	466	5,257	34,651	11,369	8,192	3,703
1900	4,478	...	1,828	6,338	32,588	18,524	6	3,788
1901	2,542	...	595	6,692	40,466	8,080	3,342	6,821
1902	6,540	...	...	9,528	43,313	4,315	8,842	4,331

See p. 102 for footnotes

Agriculture 11. *continued*

(in thousands of hundredweights)

	Russia	Canada	U.S.A.	Argentine	India	Australia
1903	17,176	10,802	24,198	14,120	17,058	—
1904	23,530	6,195	7,052	21,440	25,493	10,631
1905	24,703	6,522	6,635	23,236	22,807	10,405
1905 (c)	25,561	6,618	6,539	23,259	22,808	10,405
1906	16,058	11,246	22,554	19,177	12,636	7,865
1907	11,430	13,221	19,946	21,901	18,270	8,328
1908	5,147	15,797	25,769	31,691	2,949	5,518
1909	17,845	16,616	15,504	20,038	14,633	10,402
1910	28,942	16,449	10,949	15,132	17,917	13,748
1911	18,106	14,374	12,939	14,749	20,162	14,641
1912	9,005	21,551	19,974	18,784	25,379	12,193
1913	5,011	21,788	34,068	14,756	18,766	10,183
1914	7,235	31,457	34,220	6,498	10,709	12,122
1915	796	19,725	41,649	12,156	13,957	180
1916	13	21,551	64,544	4,496	5,612	3,730
1917	111	18,408	54,208	6,701	2,745	9,247
1918	—	15,969	24,758	14,389	621	2,014
1919	—	17,865	31,769	6,819	—	14,953
1920	2	10,189	45,422	30,831	20	19,971
1921	—	14,589	36,065	4,186	2,660	20,109
1922	—	22,910	37,262	18,804	488	16,682
1923	151	28,487	31,462	21,026	12,523	4,702
1924	753	38,769	30,321	24,022	9,816	10,871
1925	1,265	29,677	26,509	11,960	7,324	16,306
1926	2,268	35,670	31,183	11,899	2,695	9,186
1927	2,459	32,181	35,619	19,452	5,014	14,839
1928	82	41,005	23,662	24,399	1,546	10,268
1929	—	27,191	22,266	45,378	141	12,897
1930	18,717	26,179	21,036	15,189	3,342	12,733
1931	28,931	27,098	11,242	20,734	482	23,300
1932	3,275	46,853	4,636	20,616	—	24,121
1933	5,754	45,570	5	24,702	—	29,656
1934	2,095	35,703	131	35,081	166	21,658
1935	6,910	36,894	593	22,752	159	17,684
1936	167	57,813	46	957	3,249	23,270
1937	8,123	34,257	3,492	15,472	6,274	22,389
1938	9,543	28,831	15,805	5,811	4,397	30,995

(a) The statistics for 1828–39 were in quarters in the original source. They have been converted into hundredweights using the ratio 1·81 bushels equals one hundredweight. This ratio represents the average of British experience from 1910–39, and whilst it cannot be exactly correct for most years the margin of error cannot be large.

(b) The Prussian figures from 1857 onwards are included in Germany. They have been shown here for as long as they can be separately distinguished, but in brackets.

(c) The first figure for 1905 is comparable with earlier years, and shows imports according to port of origin. The second figure is comparable with later years, and is according to country of consignment.

REFERENCES

BOOKS

L. P. Adams, *Agricultural Depression and Farm Relief in England, 1813–1852* (Westminster, 1932).

D. G. Barnes, *A History of the English Corn Laws* (London, 1930).

J. R. Bellerby, *Agriculture and Industry: Relative Income* (London, 1956).

Sir James Caird, *English Agriculture in 1850–51* (London, 1852).

Lord Ernle, *English Farming Past and Present* (London, 1961 edition).

E. C. K. Gonner, *Common Land and Inclosure* (London, 1912).

W. Marshall, *A Review . . . of the Reports to the Board of Agriculture from the Midland Department of England* (York, 1815).

W. Marshall, *A Review . . . of the Reports to the Board of Agriculture from the Southern and Peninsular Departments of England* (York, 1817).

E. M. O. Ojala, *Agriculture and Economic Progress* (London, 1952).

H. A. Rhee, The Rent of Agricultural Land in England and Wales, 1870–1946.

J. E. T. Rogers, *A History of Agriculture and Prices in England* (7 vols., Oxford, 1866–1902).

R. W. Salaman, *The History and Social Influence of the Potato* (Cambridge, 1949).

C. Smith, *Three Tracts on the Corn Trade* (London, 1766).

A. Young, *A Six Months' Tour through the North of England* (4 vols., London, 1770).

A. Young, *A Six Weeks' Tour through the Southern Counties of England and Wales* (London, 1768).

A. Young, *The Farmer's Tour through the East of England* (4 vols., London, 1771).

A. Young, *A Tour in Ireland* (2 vols., London, 1780).

GOVERNMENT PUBLICATIONS

Report of the Select Committee on Waste Lands, 1795 (*P.P.* IX).

Report of the Select Committee on Returns of Averages (*S.P.* 1820, II).

Returns of Imports, Exports and Prices of Corn (in *Sessional Papers* annually throughout the first half of the nineteenth century, the most valuable summaries being in *S.P.* 1842, XL; *S.P.* 1843, LIII, and *S.P.* 1849, L).

Report of the Royal Commission on Agricultural Depression (especially *S.P.* 1881, XV; *S.P.* 1881, XVI, and *S.P.* 1882, XIV).

Report of the Royal Commission on Agricultural Depression (especially *S.P.* 1896, XVI; *S.P.* 1896, XVII, and *S.P.* 1897, XV).

Agriculture Statistics for England and Wales, 1866–1956 (in *Sessional Papers* annually 1866–1920, and issued as non-parliamentary papers thereafter).

Agricultural Statistics for Scotland, 1866–1956 (in *Sessional Papers* annually 1866–1920, and issued as non-parliamentary papers thereafter).

Scottish Agricultural Statistics, 1854–57 (*S.P.* 1854–5, XLVII; *S.P.* 1856, LXI; *S.P.* 1857 (Sess. 1) XV, and *S.P.* 1857–8, LVI).

Agricultural Statistics for Ireland, 1847–1917 (in *Sessional Papers* annually).

Irish Agricultural Statistics, 1847–1926, Irish Official Publication (Dublin, 1928).

Irish Agricultural Statistics, 1927–1933, Irish Official Publication (Dublin, 1935).

Census of Production (Agriculture) (1907; *S.P.* 1912–13, X; 1925; *S.P.* 1927, XXV and *S.P.* 1928–9, V; 1930–1; *S.P.* 1933–4, XXVI).

Interdepartmental Committee on Social and Economic Research, *Guides to Official Sources, no. 4, Agricultural and Food Statistics* (1958).

ARTICLES

J. R. Bellerby, 'Distribution of Farm Income in the United Kingdom, 1867–1938', *Journal of Proceedings of the Agricultural Economics Society* (February 1953).

J. R. Bellerby, 'Gross and Net Farm Rent in the United Kingdom, 1867–1938', *Journal of the Agricultural Economics Society* (1954).

J. R. Bellerby and A. J. Boreham, 'Farm Occupiers' Capital in the United Kingdom before 1939', *The Farm Economist* (1953).

M. K. Bennett, 'Britain's Wheat Yield for Seven Centuries', *E.H.* (1934).

J. T. Coppock, 'The Statistical Assessment of British Agriculture', *A.H.R.* (1956).

P. G. Craigie, 'Statistics of Agricultural Production', *J.S.S.* (1883).

P. G. Craigie, 'Memorandum on the Methods Employed in the Collection of Annual Agricultural Statistics in Great Britain', *Bulletin of the International Institute of Agriculture* (1900).

L. Drescher, 'The Development of Agricultural Production in Great Britain and Ireland from the Early Nineteenth Century', *M.S.E.S.S.* (1955).

T. W. Fletcher, 'Drescher's Index: A Comment', *M.S.E.S.S.* (1955).

T. W. Fletcher, 'The Great Depression of English Agriculture, 1873–1896', *E.H.R.* (1961).

G. E. Fussell, 'The Collection of Agricultural Statistics in Great Britain: Its Origin and Evolution', *A.H.* (1944).

G. E. Fussell, 'Population and Wheat Production in the Eighteenth Century', *History Teacher's Miscellany* (1929).

G. E. Fussell, 'The Size of English Cattle in the Eighteenth Century', *A.H.* (1929).

G. E. Fussell and M. Compton, 'Agricultural Adjustments after the Napoleonic Wars', *E.H.* (1939).

G. E. Fussell and Constance Goodman, 'Eighteenth Century Estimates of British Sheep and Wool Production', *A.H.* (1930).

G. E. Fussell and Constance Goodman, 'The Eighteenth Century Traffic in Livestock', *E.H.* (1936).

G. E. Fussell and Constance Goodman, 'The Eighteenth Century Traffic in Milk Products', *E.H.* (1937).

J. H. Kirk, 'The Output of British Agriculture during the War', *Journal of Agricultural Economics* (1945).

J. B. Laws and J. H. Gilbert, 'Home Produce, Imports, Consumption and Price of Wheat over Forty Harvest Years, 1852–3 to 1891–2', *Journal of the Royal Agricultural Society of England* (1893).

W. E. Minchinton, 'Agricultural Returns and the Government during the Napoleonic Wars', *A.H.R.* (1953).

R. H. Rew, 'An Inquiry into the Statistics of the Production and Consumption of Milk and Milk Products in Great Britain', *J.R.S.S.* (1892).

S. G. Sturmey, 'Owner-Farming in England and Wales, 1900 to 1950', *M.S.E.S.S.* (1955).

R. J. Thompson, 'An Enquiry into the Rent of Agricultural Land in England and Wales during the Nineteenth Century', *J.R.S.S.* (1907).

COAL

TABLES

The coal industry possesses two attributes which make it especially suitable for relatively extensive treatment—first, it is an old-established industry in Britain, and, moreover, one which concerned government from early days; and second, its product is relatively homogeneous, and consequently comparisons over time are not so bedevilled by differences in definition as in the case of some industries.[1] Official statistics for the coal industry as a whole were not collected until 1854, when *Mineral Statistics* first appeared.[2] But for a long period before that a considerable amount of official material is available about the Northumberland and Durham coalfield, which, at any rate until the end of the eighteenth century, dominated the industry. Estimates of overall output in the first half of the nineteenth century were made by various contemporaries,[3] but, as Clapham pointed out, 'the exact course of the increased consumption of coal, so closely connected at all points with that of iron, is much more difficult to determine, owing to greater uncertainty about the starting point, the obscurities of domestic consumption, and the fact that the definite finishing point falls a few years outside the early railway age'.[4]

Until well into the nineteenth century 'the coal trade' meant the industry of producing coal from the Northumberland and Durham coalfield and shipping it to London. In this trade English government officials had long shown a considerable interest, for, apart from

[1] Some differences have occurred, particularly through the introduction of screening and washing plant—but they represent improvements as opposed to complete alterations of product.

[2] Originally compiled by Robert Hunt and published by the Geological Survey, but subsequently as blue books.

[3] These are shown and discussed in the *Report of the Royal Commission on Coal Supply* (*S.P.* 1871, XVIII), pp. 880 *et seq*.

[4] J. H. Clapham, *An Economic History of Modern Britain*, vol. 1 (Cambridge 1926), pp. 430–1.

the fact that it took place under their noses, it was an important source of revenue, yielding in the 1770's, for example, upwards of £250,000. As a result of this interest there are several statistical series, going back in some cases to the seventeenth century and beyond, connected with shipments from the North-East Coast to London. In the absence of more complete, country-wide figures, these have come to be used as indicators of the overall level of output. Reasonably connected series of shipments from the North-East go back to 1655, and are shown in table 1, whilst table 2 shows the imports into London back to 1700.[1] Both these tables may be regarded as indicators of total British output until the end of the eighteenth century, and as a rough guide for a few decades after that. But with the development of canals, and the increasing use of coal for industrial purposes, Northumberland and Durham gradually lost their absolute dominance in the British coal industry, and for this reason table 1 is not continued beyond 1832. Table 2 has been carried on much longer, but with a different purpose—namely, to show the growth in importance of the railways as carriers of coal.

The official output statistics beginning in 1854 are shown in table 3, together with the estimates of value which were made up to the beginning of the 1939–45 War. As is indicated in the notes to this table the output figures before 1873 are, in some cases at any rate, to be regarded with suspicion. In general, they give a reasonable indication of trend, but are less reliable as evidence of year-to-year fluctuations. The value figures up to 1881 are much less useful. Until 1870 they are based on an assumed constant value per ton, and so merely reflect the output series; and from 1870–81 the methods and carefulness of calculation are doubtful. This table has been continued beyond 1938 since the district figures for the war years are not very accessible elsewhere.

Table 4 needs little or no explanation beyond that given in its notes. It is, perhaps, worth pointing out that, apart from their primary significance, the statistics of numbers employed can be used in conjunction with the output figures to arrive at output per man-year, which may be used (with caution) as a crude indicator of productivity. Unfortunately, the lack of uniform definitions of districts makes this calculation out of the question for some coalfields.

The exports statistics in table 5 suffer from the breaks common to practically all overseas trade statistics. In the case of coal, however, the various series do not overlap in time, so that there is no exact indication of the size of the breaks. Indeed, there is a gap between 1808 and 1816 when not only are there no published statistics, but the definition of 'exports' changed with the exclusion of the Irish trade.

Tables 6 and 7 show the development of various markets for coal over a comparatively recent period. In table 6 the continuous series of comparable statistics from 1913 onwards have been carried back a further forty years at scattered intervals from official sources. These are partly estimates and partly official returns, but it is clear that the officials who gave these figures to the Select Committee and Royal Commission were basing them on

[1] A few earlier figures, back to 1377 and 1580 respectively, can be found in J. U. Nef, *The Rise of the British Coal Industry*, Appendix D (2 vols., London, 1932).

something more than mere guesswork. Table 7, which gives a more detailed picture of the consumption of one of the major users, is based on official figures, but a word of warning is, perhaps, needed, for these figures are notional ones, arrived at by applying a (changing) coefficient to the known output of pig iron.

The final table shows the progress of the mechanisation of the central process of coal-mining—the getting of the coal. The same sources used for this table also give some indication of the spread of mechanical conveying from the coalface.

We had intended to show here statistics of the number of days on which coal was wound,[1] of the number of shifts which wage-earners could have worked,[2] and of absenteeism and output per man-shift.[3] These statistics have, however, been severely criticised in a communication we have received from Mr W. M. L. Bispham.[4] His main conclusions are that the two former series are both overestimates, and that 'there have been so many differences in the bases and methods of calculating absence rates existing side by side and changing over the years that this series cannot be considered an accurate guide to the proportion of men who are absent at any one time, nor to changes in this proportion over time'. The statistics of output per man-shift depend, of course, on knowing the number of shifts which could have been worked.

[1] Published in the *Ministry of Labour Gazette* from 1895 (1894 for a few districts).
[2] Collected by the Department of Mines from 1922, and published in the Ministry of Fuel and Power *Statistical Digest* up to 1954.
[3] Going back to 1913, published in the current Ministry of Power *Statistical Digest*.
[4] Mr Bispham's historical study of miners' attendance is pending publication.

Coal 1. Shipments of Coal from Newcastle and Sunderland—1655–1832

NOTES

[1] Sources: 1655–1709 (except 1691–4) and 1733—J. U. Nef, *The Rise of the British Coal Industry* (2 vols., Routledge, London, 1932), vol. II, appendix D; 1691–4 and (for Newcastle) 1710–66 and 1784–6—F. W. Dendy (editor), *Records of the Company of Hostmen* (Surtees Society Transactions, vol. 105, 1901); 1767–79 (for Newcastle) and 1748–71 and 1800 (for Sunderland)—T. S. Ashton and J. Sykes, *The Coal Industry of the Eighteenth Century* (Manchester University Press, 1929); 1780–93 (for Newcastle) and 1772–99 (for Sunderland)—*Report of the Select Committee on the Coal Trade* (1800), *P.P.* x, appendices; 1794–1832 (for Newcastle)—*Report of the Commissioners on Municipal Corporations, Newcastle-upon-Tyne, S.P.* 1835, xxv; 1801–32 (for Sunderland)—G. R. Porter, *The Progress of the Nation* (London, 1847 edition), p. 278.

[2] The following conversion factors from Newcastle chaldrons to tons are suggested by Nef (*op. cit.* appendix C(i)):

1636–60	1 chaldron = 52 cwt.
1661–86	1 chaldron = $52\frac{1}{2}$ cwt.
after 1686	1 chaldron = 53 cwt.

(in thousands of chaldrons)

	from Newcastle		from Sunderland		from Newcastle and Sunderland	
	coastwise	oversea	coastwise	oversea	oversea	total
1655	147	...	...	...	...	...
1658 (a)	132	6	26	2	8	167
1659 (a)	187	16	43	3	19	250
1660 (a)	167	11	39	11	22	228
1661	167	10	...	1	12	...
1662	194	...	...	...	...	...
1663	179	...	...	...	...	...
1664	198	...	...	...	...	...
1665	124	...	...	...	...	...
1666	84	3	...	- -	3	...
1667	106	4	...	1	4	...
1668	188	...	...	...	...	...
1669	176	...	...	...	...	...
1670	185	...	...	...	...	...
1671	189	...	...	...	...	...
1672	150	...	...	...	...	...
1673	156	...	...	...	...	...
1674	170	14	44	3	17	231
1675	194	...	...	...	...	...
1676	195	10	40	4	15	249
1677	194	15	...	5	19	...
1678	218	12	54	3	15	287
1679	195	...	47	...	...	...
1680	202	16	...	5	21	...
1681	219	...	...	...	...	...
1682	190	...	...	...	...	...
1683	211	...	...	...	...	...
1684	205	...	...	...	...	...
1685	214	21	54	8	29	297
1686	178	...	...	...	...	...
1687	199	...	...	...	...	...
1688	231	...	...	...	...	...
1689	168	...	...	...	...	...
1690	137	...	...	...	...	...
1691	177	...	...	...	...	...
1692	156	...	...	...	...	...
1693	180	...	...	...	...	...
1694	160	...	...	...	...	...
1695	171	...	...	...	...	...
1696	151	...	...	...	...	...

See p. 111 for footnote

(in thousands of chaldrons)

	from Newcastle		from Sunderland		from Newcastle and Sunderland	
	coastwise	oversea	coastwise	oversea	oversea	total
1697	181	...	...	...	...	...
1698	211	...	...	...	...	...
1699	221	...	...	...	...	...
1700	205	...	...	...	...	...
1701	245	...	...	...	...	...
1702	153	...	...	...	...	...
1703	170	...	...	...	...	...
1704	198	...	...	...	...	...
1705	182	...	...	...	...	...
1706	163	...	...	...	...	...
1707	151	...	...	...	...	...
1708	193	...	...	...	...	...
1709	211	...	...	...	...	...
1710	168	...	...	...	...	...
1723	262		...	...	...	...
1724	253		...	...	...	...
1725	266		...	...	...	...
1726	286		...	...	...	...
1727	276		...	...	...	...
1728	247		...	...	...	...
1729	293		...	...	...	...
1730	277		...	...	...	...
1731	311		...	...	...	...
1732	269		...	...	...	...
1733	275	16	104	20	36	414
1734	274		...	...	...	...
1735	282		...	...	...	...
1736	297		...	...	...	...
1737	276		...	...	...	...
1738	271		...	...	...	...
1739	288		...	...	...	...
1740	321		...	...	...	...
1741	263		...	...	...	...
1742	270		...	...	...	...
1743	298		...	...	...	...
1744	273		...	...	...	...
1745	295		...	...	...	...
1746	303		...	...	...	...
1747	259		...	...	...	...
1748	271		147		...	418
1749	299		135		...	434
1750	288		162		...	450
1751	343		129		...	472
1752	308		177		...	485
1753	301		167		...	468

(in thousands of chaldrons)

	from Newcastle		from Sunderland		from Newcastle and Sunderland	
	coastwise	oversea	coastwise	oversea	oversea	total
1754	305		166		...	471
1755	294		174		...	468
1756	311		175		...	486
1757	274		179		...	453
1758	240		187		...	427
1759	302		187		...	489
1760	285		180		...	465
1761	328		170		...	498
1762	294		172		...	466
1763	293		182		...	475
1764	349		205		...	554
1765	349		204		...	553
1766	353		206		...	559
1767	359		196		...	555
1768	...		203		...	...
1769	...		215		...	...
1770	372		213		...	585
1771	...		220		...	...
1772	352		257		...	509
1773	...		241		...	...
1774	...		245		...	...
1775	...		244		...	...
1776	...		262		...	...
1777	...		253		...	...
1778	366		233		...	599
1779	...		215		...	...
1780	366		225		...	591
1781	335		210		...	546
1782	364		212		...	576
1783	413		238		...	652
1784	459		244		...	703
1785	450		266		...	716
1786	429		259		...	688
1787	411		275		...	686
1788	446		279		...	725
1789	490		256	39	...	785
1790	420		236	47	...	704
1791	445		239	54	...	737
1792	499		260	54	...	813
1793	497		248	50	...	795
1794	389	40	240	39	79	708
1795	465	40	283	6	46	789
1796	441	43	247	6	49	737
1797	461	38	267	6	45	773
1798	396	45	264	5	50	710
1799	452	43	284	4	47	783
1800	538	47	322		...	817
1801	452	50	231	4	55	738
1802	494	44	305	31	75	875
1803	505	44	299	10	54	859

Coal 1. *continued*

(in thousands of chaldrons)

	from Newcastle		from Sunderland		from Newcastle and Sunderland	
	coastwise	oversea	coastwise	oversea	oversea	total
1804	580	53	300	4	57	936
1805	553	50	313	6	56	922
1806	588	47	306	3	49	944
1807	530	27	293	4	32	854
1808	619	16	349	2	18	986
1809	539	14	324	1	15	878
1810	632	17	371	2	20	1,022
1811	633	18	331	2	20	984
1812	631	25	339	3	28	998
1813	584	15	347	2	17	948
1814	649	32	373	11	43	1,065
1815	650	42	338	17	59	1,048
1816	678	44	388	16	60	1,126
1817	623	52	364	12	63	1,050
1818	672	48	392	16	64	1,127
1819	640	40	378	15	54	1,074
1820	757	45	416	14	59	1,232
1821	692	48	395	14	62	1,151
1822	655	54	397	16	71	1,123
1823	739	46	497	16	61	1,297
1824	688	49	491	16	65	1,244
1825	687	51	522	16	67	1,276
1826	792	63	549	14	67	1,419
1827	684	65	523	15	80	1,288
1828	725	59	510	23	82	1,317
1829	738	62	565		...	1,365
1830	818	74	524		...	1,416
1831	773	61	474		...	1,308
1832	683	74	452		...	1,211

(*a*) Year ended 24th June. All other figures are for Year ended 25th December.

Coal 2. Coal Imported into London by Sea and Rail—1700-1879

NOTES

[1] SOURCES: 1700–99—T. S. Ashton and J. Sykes, *The Coal Industry of the Eighteenth Century*, appendix E; 1800–79 —returns published in *Sessional Papers* annually.

[2] The figures are quoted as in the sources. One London chaldron equalled 25½ cwt.

(in thousands of tons or thousands of London chaldrons)

	By Sea ooo chaldrons		By Sea ooo chaldrons		By Sea ooo chaldrons
1700	335	1745	471	1786	730
1701	400	1746	487	1787	653
1702	243	1747	469	1788	771
1703	301	1748	450	1789	811
		1749	504	1790	753
1708	361				
		1750	458	1791	822
1710	328	1751	539	1792	850
		1752	508	1793	801
		1753	508	1794	783
1713	346	1754	527	1795	910
1714	414				
1715	388	1755	479	1796	783
1716	412	1756	550	1797	890
1717	440	1757	503	1798	775
		1758	452	1799	880
1718	412	1759	552	1800	1,011
1719	420				
1720	425	1760	499	1801	833
1721	459	1761	505	1802	928
1722	460	1762	530	1803	916
		1763	603	1804	976
1723	458	1764	597	1805 (b)	964
1724	451				
1725	471	1765	588	1806	986
1726	508	1766	639	1807	911
1727	496	1767	599	1808	1,092
		1768	614	1809	974
1728	453	1769	642	1810	1,099
1729	494				
1730	455	1770	613	1811	1,095
1731	475	1771	678	1812	1,065
1732	451	1772	711	1813	1,019
		1773	645	1814	1,118
1733	496	1774	615	1815	1,143
1734	448				
1735	503	1775 (a)	664	1816	1,218
1736	512	1776	690	1817	1,151
1737	476	1777	685	1818	1,204
		1778	640	1819	1,170
1738	491	1779	589	1820	1,321
1739	442				
1740	563	1780	657	1821	1,292
1741	453	1781	651	1822	1,235
1742	457	1782	661	1823	1,434
		1783	695	1824	1,467
		1784	725	1825	1,423
1743	478				
1744	468	1785	733	1826	1,558

See p. 113–14 for footnotes

(in thousands of tons or thousands of London chaldrons)

	By Sea		By Rail
	ooo chaldrons	ooo tons	ooo tons
1827	1,476 or	1,882	—
1828	1,538	1,961	—
1829	1,584	2,019	—
1830	1,631	2,079	—
1831	1,604	2,045	—
1832	1,678	2,139	—
1833		2,010	—
1834		2,079	—
1835		2,299	—
1836		2,398	—
1837		2,627	—
1838		2,581	—
1839		2,625	—
1840		2,567	—
1841		2,909	—
1842		2,723	—
1843		2,629	—
1844		2,491	—
1845		3,403	8
1846		2,954	12
1847		3,280	19
1848		3,418	38
1849		3,339	20
1850		3,553	55
1851		3,237	248
1852		3,330	378
1853		3,373	630
1854		3,400	945
1855		3,017	1,138
1856		3,120	1,246
1857		3,133	1,207
1858		3,266	1,191
1859		3,299	1,191
1860		3,573	1,478
1861		3,567	1,643
1862		3,442	1,513
1863		3,335	1,776
1864		3,117	2,342
1865		3,162	2,733
1866		3,033	2,970
1867		3,016	3,296
1868		2,918	2,979
1869		2,874	3,342
1870		2,994	3,758
1871		2,763	4,449
1872		3,549	4,999
1873		2,666	5,147
1874		2,728	4,690
1875		3,135	5,065
1876		3,272	5,173
1877		3,171	5,416
1878		3,198	5,593
1879		3,509	6,547

(a) For the period 1775–1800 slightly different figures are to be found in other sources. The Ashton and Sykes series has been shown here, since it is the longest. The others are shown overleaf.

(b) From 1805 onwards negligible amounts were also brought to London by canal. The most in any one year was 72,000 tons in 1844; in most years it was much less.

(*a*) *continued*

(in thousands of London chaldrons)

	Customs	Orphans	Metage	City Due	Gillespy	Martindale
1775	...	...	...	640	664	...
1776	...	...	...	703	701	...
1777	...	...	...	693	699	...
1778	...	...	...	669	645	...
1779	...	664	...	639	592	...
1780	657	636	668	624	670	...
1781	660	701	641	646	643	...
1782	676	661	695	622	697	...
1783	662	727	674	690	710	...
1784	720	729	724	732	719	719
1785	740	754	739	712	734	737
1786	750	744	744	763	739	739
1787	740	758	759	738	753	753
1788	797	807	764	785	760	760
1789	786	750	800	773	795	795
1790	745	794	754	794	747	747
1791	805	843	832	794	825	824
1792	877	812	848	853	841	841
1793	818	784	807	801	801	801
1794	790	894	796	823	789	789
1795	879	818	895	830	888	888
1796	836	866	848	853	819	859
1797	851	782	872	828	864	864
1798	795	863	792	856	786	786
1799	872	...	868	839	828	862
1800	1,019	...	...	940	1,005	...

Customs = *Select Committee on the Coal Trade* (1800), *P.P.* x, appendix 45 D—figures 'taken at the Custom House'. Years ended 1st December.

Orphans = *ibid.* appendix 57—figures derived from the yield of the Orphans' Duty of 10d per chaldron. Years ended 5th January in the year following that for which the figures are shown, according to the source, but it seems possible that they were mistakenly given for the year previous to that to which they apply.

Metage = *ibid.* appendix 58—figures derived from the yield of the metage due of 4d per chaldron. Calendar years.

City Due = *Select Committee on the Coal Trade (Port of London) Bill* (S.P. 1837–8, xv)—figures derived from the yield of the city due of 10d per chaldron. Years ended 5th July.

Gillespy = *Epitome of the Coal Trade in the Port of London*, by Thomas Gillespy, printed as appendix 15 to the *Report of the Royal Commission on the Coal Supply (Committee E), S.P.* 1871 XVIII.

Martindale = *Select Committee on the Coal Trade* (1800), *P.P.* x, appendix 19—figures given by John Martindale of the Customs House, Sunderland.

Coal 3. Output of Coal in the United Kingdom and its Main Coalfields, and the Value of Total Output—1854–1945

NOTE

SOURCES: 1854–72—*Mineral Statistics*; 1873–81—*Reports of H.M. Inspectors of Mines*; 1882–1921—*Mineral Statistics*; 1922–38—*Annual Report of the Department of Mines*; 1939–45—Ministry of Fuel and Power, *Statistical Digest*, and its *Supplement*.

(Output in millions of tons and value in £ million)

	North-East (a)	Yorkshire	Midland (b)	Lanca-shire (c)	Stafford-shire (d)	South Wales	Scotland	U.K. Total Output	U.K. Total Value
1854	15·4	7·3	3·9	9·9	7·5	8·5	7·4	64·7	16·2
1855	15·4	7·7	3·8	9·7	7·3	8·6	7·3	64·5	16·1
1856	15·5	9·1	4·3	9·7	7·3	8·9	7·5	66·6	16·7
1857	15·8	8·9	4·8	9·3	7·2	7·1	8·2	65·4	16·3
1858	15·9	8·3	5·1	8·7	6·7	7·5	8·9	65·0	16·3
1859	16·0	8·4	5·4	11·4	6·1	9·6	10·3	72·0	17·2
1860	18·2	9·3	6·2	12·1	7·6	...	10·9	80·0	20·0
1861	19·1	9·4	6·5	13·0	7·3	...	11·1	83·6	20·9
1862	19·4	9·3	6·6	11·4	7·5	10·5	11·1	81·6	20·4
1863	22·2	9·4	6·8	11·7	7·9	11·0	11·1	86·3	21·6
1864	23·3	8·8	6·9	12·4	11·5 (e)	11·0	12·4	92·8	23·2
1865	25·0	9·4	7·5	12·8	12·2	12·0	12·7	98·2	24·5
1866	25·2	9·7	8·0	13·2	12·3	13·8	12·6	101·6	25·4
1867	24·9	9·8	8·2	13·8	12·5	13·7	14·1	104·5	26·1
1868	24·4	9·7	7·7	13·7	12·3	13·2	14·7	103·1	25·8
1869	25·8	10·8	8·6	15·0	12·7	13·5	14·4	107·4	26·9
1870	27·6	10·6	8·5	14·7	13·2	13·7	14·9	110·4	27·6
1871	29·2	12·8	9·3	14·8	14·3	14·0	15·4	117·4	35·2 (f)
1872	28·6	14·6	10·7	18·4	14·6	15·2	15·4	123·5	46·3
1873 (g)	29·7	15·3	11·5	18·4	15·2	16·2	16·9	128·7	47·6
1874	30·6	14·8	12·2	18·7	13·0	16·5	16·8	126·6	45·8
1875	32·3	15·9	12·4	21·0	14·5	14·2	18·6	133·3	46·2
1876	32·3	15·1	12·3	20·6	13·9	17·0	18·7	134·1	46·7
1877	31·4	15·8	12·9	20·9	13·7	16·3	18·3	134·2	47·1
1878	30·2	15·6	13·4	21·0	13·1	17·9	17·8	132·6	46·4
1879	28·8	16·2	14·0	21·5	13·3	17·8	17·5	133·7	46·9
1880	34·9	17·5	14·5	22·2	13·7	21·2	18·3	147·0	62·4
1881	35·6	18·3	15·5	21·9	14·9	21·5	20·8	154·2	65·5
1882	36·3	18·5	15·6	23·0	15·0	22·2	20·5	156·5	44·2 (h)
1883	37·4	19·6	16·6	23·9	15·2	24·1	21·3	163·7	46·1
1884	36·1	19·2	16·1	23·4	14·4	24·8	20·4	160·8	43·4
1885	35·1	18·5	17·0	23·6	14·7	24·3	21·3	159·4	41·1
1886	34·8	19·4	16·8	23·8	13·3	24·8	20·4	157·5	38·1
1887	34·5	20·1	17·2	24·2	13·7	25·4	21·5	162·1	39·1
1888	37·6	20·6	18·1	23·9	14·5	28·2	22·3	169·9	43·0
1889	39·1	22·0	19·7	24·6	14·8	28·1	23·2	176·9	56·2
1890	39·7	22·3	20·5	25·8	14·7	29·4	24·3	181·6	75·0
1891	39·1	22·8	21·6	26·0	15·3	30·0	25·4	185·5	74·1
1892	32·4 (l)	23·2	21·6	26·0	15·0	31·3	27·2	181·8	66·1
1893	39·9	16·0 (l)	16·0 (l)	18·1 (l)	13·9 (l)	30·2	25·5	164·3 (l)	55·8 (l)

See p. 117 *for footnotes*

(Output in millions of tons and value in £ million)

	North-East (a)	Yorkshire	Midland (b)	Lanca-shire (c)	Stafford-shire (d)	South Wales	Scotland	U.K. Total Output	U.K. Total Value
1894	42·1	23·4	21·7	27·1	14·1	33·4	21·6 (*l*)	188·3	62·7
1895	39·8	22·8	21·5	25·6	13·3	33·0	28·8	189·7	57·2
1896	41·8	23·9	22·4	25·5	13·9	34·0	28·3	195·4	57·2
1897	43·6	24·0	23·8	25·7	14·3	35·5	29·1	202·1	59·7
1898	45·3	25·6	25·8	27·5	14·6	26·7 (*l*)	30·2	202·1	64·2
1899	46·1	26·9	27·6	27·6	14·7	39·9	31·1	220·1	83·5
1900	46·3	28·2	28·9	28·7	15·0	39·3	33·1	225·2	121·7
1901	45·2	27·0	28·2	26·8	14·9	39·2	32·8	219·0	102·5
1902	46·4	28·0	29·6	27·6	15·1	41·3	34·1	227·1	93·5
1903	47·9	28·5	29·4	27·7	13·8	42·2	35·0	230·3	88·2
1904	48·4	28·8	29·7	27·1	13·4	43·7	35·5	232·4	83·9
1905	50·1	29·9	31·0	27·1	13·6	43·2	35·8	236·1	82·0
1906	52·1	32·5	33·2	28·4	14·1	47·1	39·2	251·1	91·5
1907	54·0	35·2	37·2	30·0	15·3	50·0	40·1	267·8	120·5
1908	53·9	34·9	35·2	27·9	14·4	50·2	39·2	261·5	116·6
1909	55·3	35·9	35·1	27·3	14·2	50·4	39·8	263·8	106·3
1910	52·6	38·3	35·9	27·2	14·7	46·7	41·3	264·4	108·4
1911	56·4	39·1	36·5	27·4	14·7	50·2	41·7	271·9	110·8
1912	51·3 (*l*)	38·3 (*l*)	35·1 (*l*)	26·3 (*l*)	14·2 (*l*)	50·1 (*l*)	39·5 (*l*)	260·4 (*l*)	117·9 (*l*)
1913	56·4	43·7	38·8	28·1	14·9	56·8	42·5	287·4	145·5
1914	50·0	39·5	39·4	26·2	14·5	53·8	38·8	265·7	132·6
1915	44·8	40·3	36·7	21·7	14·0	50·5	35·6	253·2	157·8
1916	45·0	40·2	37·5	21·7	14·2	52·1	36·1	256·4	200·0
1917	41·1	40·9	38·9	22·1	14·3	48·5	34·2	248·5	207·8
1918	38·3	35·6	34·2	19·9	12·7	46·7	31·9	227·7	238·2
1919	42·0	32·8	33·7	19·9	13·0	47·5	32·5	229·8	314·1
1920	42·0	36·2	33·6	19·0	12·6	46·2	31·5	229·5	396·9
1921	29·8 (*l*)	28·5 (*l*)	24·4 (*l*)	13·1 (*l*)	8·8 (*l*)	30·6 (*l*)	22·5 (*l*)	163·3 (*l*)	213·7 (*l*)
								---------	--------
1922	48·1	42·1	35·5	17·8	12·0	50·3	35·4	249·6 (*i*)	220·0 (*i*)
1923	52·5	46·5	40·2	20·2	14·2	54·3	38·5	276·0	259·7
1924	50·4	46·6	39·3	19·8	14·3	51·1	36·2	267·1	251·7
1925	43·4	45·3	37·5	17·4	13·2	44·6	33·0	243·2	199·0
1926	20·3 (*l*)	21·6 (*l*)	24·4 (*l*)	9·2 (*l*)	8·9 (*l*)	20·3 (*l*)	16·8 (*l*)	126·3 (*l*)	123·4 (*l*)
1927	48·1	45·9	36·4	17·1	13·3	46·3	34·6	251·2	183·5
1928	47·7	43·4	34·5	15·1	11·9	43·3	32·4	237·5	152·5
1929	53·5	46·4	37·5	15·7	12·8	48·2	34·2	257·9	173·2
1930	49·0	44·6	36·9	15·0	12·1	45·1	31·7	243·9	165·7
1931	42·7	40·6	35·3	14·1	11·6	37·1	29·1	219·5	147·7
1932	40·0	38·1	33·4	13·2	11·6	34·9	28·8	208·7	138·4
1933	40·1	37·3	32·5	13·2	11·7	34·4	29·2	207·1	134·6
1934	44·4	39·9	34·3	13·8	12·7	35·2	31·3	220·7	142·1
1935	44·3	40·7	34·6	14·1	13·2	35·0	31·3	222·3	144·5
1936	45·8	42·5	36·7	14·7	13·9	33·9	32·0	228·5	160·1
1937	47·7	45·1	39·6	15·1	13·9	37·8	32·2	240·4	182·7
1938	44·7	42·4	37·8	14·3	13·4	35·3	30·3	227·0	188·8

See p. 117 for footnotes

(Output in millions of tons and value in £ million)

	North-East (a)	Yorkshire	Midland (b)	Lanca-shire (c)	Stafford-shire (d)	South Wales	Scotland	U.K. Total Output	U.K. Total Value
1939	43·5	44·4	40·5	14·3	14·0	35·3	30·5	231·3 (j)	...
1940	38·7	45·2	43·0	13·6	13·6	32·4	29·7	224·3	...
1941	35·4	42·8	42·4	12·2	12·3	27·4	26·6	206·3	...
1942	36·3	41·1	42·8	11·7	11·9	26·7	26·2	204·9	...
1943	35·0	38·9 (k)	41·4 (k)	11·1	11·5	25·1	24·7	198·9 (j)	
		40·3	40·1						
1944	33·4	37·9	38·8	10·8	11·0	22·4	23·4	192·7	...
1945	31·6	36·7	37·1	10·5	10·8	20·5	21·4	182·8	...

(a) Northumberland and Durham.
(b) Derbyshire, Leicestershire, Nottinghamshire, and Warwickshire.
(c) Lancashire and Cheshire.
(d) North and South Staffordshire, and Worcestershire.
(e) It is clear that the Staffordshire figures become progressively more unreliable from 1854–64, at which date there was probably a more comprehensive survey of the output of the very many small mines of the area than had been undertaken since 1854.
(f) The value figures up to 1870 are purely notional, being based on a constant assumption of five shillings per ton as the pitmouth price.
(g) The figures for output in 1854–72 were calculated by the Office of Mining Records on the basis of voluntary returns from a large number of collieries. Those from 1873 onwards were based on compulsory returns to the Inspectors of Mines. Where the two sets of statistics overlap (for the years 1873–9) the compulsory returns have been preferred. The latter are about 1½ million tons higher for Lancashire in 1873–8, and it is clear that for some years before 1873 the output of this

area was underestimated by the Office of Mining Records. Differences are small for other areas. Prior to 1873, estimates were made by some Inspectors, and for the year 1872 these have been preferred to those in *Mineral Statistics* for Lancashire, South Wales and the North-East.
(h) The value figures from 1870–81 are of doubtful value in view of the sudden drop in 1882, in which year adequate methods of obtaining this series were first adopted. (See the preface to *Mineral Statistics*, 1882.)
(i) Output in southern Ireland is excluded after 1921. In 1913 it had amounted to about 90,000 tons valued at £50,000.
(j) Coal mined from quarries is included prior to 1938 in all figures, but thereafter it is not included in the district figures. In 1942–5 it is included in the totals. Opencast coal mined in those years was as follows:

| 1942 | 1,311,000 tons, | 1944 | 8,651,000 tons, |
| 1943 | 4,427,000 tons, | 1945 | 8,118,000 tons. |

(k) In 1943 the boundary between the Yorkshire and Midland districts was redefined. For that date two figures are shown the first on the old basis, the second on the new.
(l) These figures were affected by major strikes.

Coal 4. Numbers Employed in Coal Mines in the United Kingdom and its Main Coalfields—1864–1938

NOTE

SOURCES: 1864–96—*Reports* of H. M. Inspectors of Mines; *Annual Report of the Department of Mines.*
1897–1920—*Mineral Statistics*; 1921–38—

(in thousands)

	Northern (a)	Yorkshire	Midland (b)	North Wales and Lancashire (c)	South Wales	Scotland	Total U.K.
1864	57·5	34·5	26·6	47·8	29·1	39·2	307·5
1865	59·0	35·0	27·1	51·1	29·1	39·5	315·5
1866	61·4	35·5	27·1	55·4	29·2	41·2	320·7
1867	63·3	37·0	27·0	56·8	29·3	50·1	333·1
1868	69·0	37·0	28·0	58·4	29·3	50·2	346·8
1869	69·8	36·0	28·5	58·6	29·0	48·0	345·4
1870	75·1	36·5	28·8	58·5	29·0	47·0	350·9
1871	79·0	38·6	31·1	58·3	38·0	47·0	370·9
1872	84·3	51·1	39·3	62·7	38·4	50·7	418·1
1873 (d)	100·5	57·5	47·0	74·2	45·5	58·6	514·1
1874	104·8	62·5	52·4	79·3	73·3	76·1	538·8
1875	108·6	62·2	52·5	80·9	72·6	71·7	535·8
1876	107·1	61·0	52·4	75·2	57·5	69·9	514·5
1877	104·4	60·6	50·3	72·2	65·3	67·8	494·4
1878	98·3	59·8	49·4	71·2	63·7	66·4	475·3
1879	95·4	60·1	51·0	72·6	66·5	67·0	476·8
1880	100·7	60·5	49·4	72·9	69·2	68·2	484·9
1881	102·2	60·5	50·1	73·9	72·9	69·3	495·5
1882	104·8	61·5	49·9	74·8	74·9	67·9	504·0
1883	105·9	63·2	52·2	76·6	80·7	68·4	514·9
1884	108·9	64·0	53·4	76·3	83·9	69·4	520·4
1885	108·8	63·6	55·2	75·6	85·2	70·0	520·6
1886	108·5	65·7	55·1	76·4	85·1	63·1	520·0
1887	108·5	66·9	55·8	77·3	86·9	71·2	526·3
1888	110·5	67·0	58·0	78·3	91·4	70·5	549·2
1889	115·4	69·9	61·3	81·4	99·4	74·1	581·8
1890	123·9	76·8	66·5	88·8	109·9	81·1	632·4
1891	131·2	82·0	71·6	93·7	116·6	85·1	668·0
1892	131·7	86·6	74·7	96·7	116·7	89·0	683·6
1893	138·5	88·6	76·3	99·3	118·0	90·8	683·0
1894	144·6	91·0	80·1	100·7	124·7	93·8	705·2
1895	143·3	88·7	80·0	99·5	126·1	94·1	700·3
1896	144·9	89·6	79·6	95·3	125·2	88·8	692·7
1897	145·9	89·6	80·3	96·1	126·8	89·0	695·2
1898	147·9	91·2	82·3	94·9	128·8	92·0	706·9
1899	153·3	94·9	85·8	95·4	132·7	95·9	729·0
1900	161·1	100·8	90·4	100·6	147·6	103·8	780·1
1901	164·0	105·3	95·8	106·2	150·4	108·0	806·7
1902	167·9	107·7	99·6	106·7	154·6	109·0	824·8
1903	169·8	109·8	102·2	108·5	159·2	111·1	842·1
1904	174·4	112·0	102·4	106·9	163·0	112·8	847·6
1905	179·0	112·6	103·4	106·6	165·6	114·3	858·4
1906	186·1	115·5	106·6	105·4	174·7	115·7	882·3
1907	195·9	123·9	112·6	109·9	190·3	124·8	940·6
1908	203·7	135·2	116·5	115·5	201·8	132·1	987·8

See p. 119 *for footnotes*

Coal 4. *continued*

(in thousands)

	Northern (a)	Yorkshire	Midland (b)	North Wales and Lanca-shire (c)	South Wales	Scotland	Total U.K.
1909	210·5	141·0	119·4	118·7	205·0	133·6	1,014·0
1910	222·9	146·9	121·2	119·8	213·3	137·9	1,049·4
1911	227·3	148·0	124·3	119·4	220·9	138·4	1,067·2
1912	229·6	152·8	126·0	121·5	225·5	143·3	1,089·1
1913	237·8	161·2	130·6	123·9	233·1	147·5	1,127·9
1914	239·0	164·3	130·6	124·0	234·1	146·2	1,133·7
1915	184·1	140·8	... (e)	105·7	202·7	121·9	953·6
1916	191·3	146·2	... (e)	111·1	214·1	127·1	998·1
1917	195·2	148·7	... (e)	114·0	219·7	130·0	1,021·3
1918	196·2	145·5	... (e)	112·8	218·9	124·5	1,008·9
1919	246·2	166·6	148·2	129·4	257·6	147·0	1,191·3
1920	258·2	173·5	... (e)	136·0	271·5	154·5	1,248·2
1921 (f)	228·7	175·6	149·2	123·5	232·0	133·8	1,131·6
1922	234·2	178·3	151·0	122·5	243·0	134·0	1,148·5 (g)
1923	250·0	187·4	156·7	124·6	252·6	143·3	1,203·3
1924	251·7	195·3	160·2	124·7	250·1	141·8	1,213·7
1925	207·5	192·0	154·8	116·7	217·8	126·0	1,102·4
Mar. 1926 (h)	216·7	193·7	155·3	116·7	217·8	127·5	1,115·6
Dec. 1926 (h)	178·3	177·8	149·1	103·9	156·4	98·9	943·6
1927	192·9	188·7	150·8	106·1	194·1	109·0	1,023·9
1928	187·6	176·2	138·7	96·2	168·3	96·5	939·0
1929	198·1	172·7	138·0	94·5	178·3	100·0	956·7
1930	190·4	171·6	137·4	90·2	172·9	96·6	931·4
1931	167·4	164·3	134·1	86·3	158·2	88·0	867·9
1932	155·4	155·4	129·8	80·9	145·7	82·4	819·3
1933	151·1	144·5	122·2	76·9	142·9	81·6	789·1
1934	158·2	143·4	121·0	72·9	139·8	83·1	788·2
1935	157·7	140·3	117·8	69·4	131·7	83·5	769·5
1936	158·5	140·4	116·9	69·9	126·2	86·6	767·1
1937	167·6	143·2	116·9	70·0	135·9	90·6	791·7
1938	167·8	144·7	118·1	68·1	136·0	90·0	790·9

(a) Northumberland, Durham and Cumberland.
(b) Derbyshire, Leicestershire, Nottinghamshire, and Warwickshire.
(c) Lancashire, Cheshire, Denbighshire, and Flintshire.
(d) The figures for 1864–72 were calculated by the Inspectors of Mines on the basis of voluntary returns from a large number of collieries. After 1873 they were based on compulsory returns. The compulsory returns for 1873 itself were incomplete and were supplemented by estimates.
(e) The figures for Leicestershire and Warwickshire were not given separately for 1915–18 (owing to wartime staff shortage) and for 1920 (owing to the transfer of responsibility to the Department of Mines).

(f) Prior to 1921 the statistics relate to mines under the Coal Mines Act, and thus include a small number of men working minerals other than coal, principally in Scotland, where there were about 6,000. From 1921 only coal mines were covered. Prior to 1925 owners were asked to state the number 'ordinarily employed'. From that date an average of four selected dates in each year was taken. It is not thought that this change made a noticeable difference.
(g) Southern Ireland is excluded from the total after 1921.
(h) The two figures shown for 1926 are for the months immediately before and after the strike.

Coal 5. Coal Exports—England & Wales 1697–1791, Great Britain 1792–1808 and United Kingdom 1816–1938

NOTES

[1] SOURCES: Parts A and B—Elizabeth B. Schumpeter, *English Overseas Trade Statistics, 1697–1808* (Oxford University Press, 1960), tables VIII and IX (converted to tons); Part C—1816–29—S.P. 1830–1, X; 1830–2—*Report of the Royal Commission on the Coal Supply* (*S.P.* 1871, XVIII), appendix 60 to the report of committee E; 1833–70—returns in sessional papers annually; 1871–1918—*Report of the Coal Industry Commission* (*S.P.* 1919, XII), appendix 21; 1919–20—*Mineral Statistics*; 1921–38—*Annual Report of the Department of Mines*.

[2] In converting the original figures to tons, one Newcastle chaldron has been taken to equal 53 cwt. (see table 1, note 2 and one Winton chaldron has been assumed to equal half a Newcastle chaldron, since the valuation rates were respectively 48 shillings and 24 shillings.

[3] In Parts A and B the very small quantities of 'kennel' coal have not been included.

[4] In Parts A and B exports to Ireland are included.

(in thousands of tons)

A. England & Wales, 1697–1791

Year		Year		Year	
1697	37	1729	127	1761	18
1698	66	1730	89	1762	18
1699	56	1731	120	1763	20
1700	68	1732	131	1764	21
1701	75	1733	124	1765	31
1702	55	1734	136	1766	48
1703	46	1735	138	1767	46
1704	50	1736	145	1768	36
1705	...	1737	135	1769	33
1706	47	1738	135	1770	28
1707	57	1739	156	1771	37
1708	60	1740	179	1772	37
1709	69	1741	142	1773	34
1710	64	1742	131	1774	39
1711	67	1743	151	1775	39
1712	...	1744	136	1776	41
1713	81	1745	139	1777	42
1714	103	1746	147	1778	36
1715	98	1747	126	1779	33
1716	100	1748	151	1780	34
1717	87	1749	175	1781	27
1718	95	1750	164	1782	28
1719	103	1751	216	1783	42
1720	92	1752	201	1784	41
1721	104	1753	205	1785	54
1722	105	1754	190	1786	50
1723	107	1755	182	1787	45
1724	165	1756	181	1788	61
1725	100	1757	156	1789	58
1726	122	1758	158	1790	60
1727	132	1759	150	1791	63
1728	99	1760	150		

B. Great Britain, 1792–1808

Year		Year		Year	
1792	667	1798	512	1804	58
1793	689	1799	527	1805	58
1794	605	1800	579	1806	61
1795	514	1801	515	1807	52
1796	590	1802	590	1808	58
1797	513	1803	589		

Coal 5. *continued*

(in thousands of tons)

2. United Kingdom, 1816–1938

Year		Year		Year	
1816	238	1857	6,483	1898	35,058
1817	253	1858	6,292	1899	41,180
1818	272	1859	6,784	1900	44,089
1819	238	1860	7,050	1901	41,877
1820	251	1861	7,561	1902	43,159
1821	263	1862	8,011	1903	44,950
1822	287	1863	8,005	1904	46,256
1823	254	1864	8,537	1905	47,477
1824	282	1865	8,861	1906	55,600
1825	313	1866	9,635	1907	63,601
1826	348	1867	10,053	1908	62,547
1827	369	1868	10,498	1909	63,077
1828	358	1869	10,233	1910	62,085
1829	371	1870	11,162	1911	64,599
1830	504	1871	12,208	1912	64,444
1831	511	1872	12,712	1913	73,400
1832	588	1873	12,078	1914	59,040
1833 (a)	629	1874	13,381	1915	43,535
1834	610	1875	13,979	1916	38,352
1835	729	1876	15,690	1917	34,996
1836	911	1877	14,881	1918	31,753
1837	1,106	1878	14,999	1919	35,250
1838	1,303	1879	15,740	1920	24,932
1839	1,432	1880	17,891	1921	24,661
1840	1,592	1881	18,760	1922	64,198
1841	1,832	1882	19,926	1923	79,459
1842	1,975	1883	21,671	1924	61,651
1843	1,820	1884	22,354	1925	50,817
1844	1,698	1885	22,710	1926	20,596
1845	2,443	1886	22,107	1927	51,149
1846	2,390	1887	23,259	1928	50,051
1847	1,996	1888	25,632	1929	60,267
1848	2,699	1889	27,505	1930	54,874
1849	2,731	1890	28,738	1931	42,750
1850	3,212	1891	29,497	1932	38,899
1851	3,300	1892	29,048	1933	39,068
1852	3,479	1893	27,708	1934	39,660
1853	3,758	1894	31,756	1935	38,714
1854	4,120	1895	31,715	1936	34,519
1855	4,763	1896	32,948	1937	40,338
1856	5,638	1897	35,354	1938	35,856

a) Prior to 1833 the small quantity cf coke exported is included (without conversion to coal equivalent).

Coal 6. Consumption of Coal in the United Kingdom according to Use—1869–1939

NOTE

SOURCES: 1869—*Report of the Select Committee on the Dearness and Scarcity of Coal* (S.P. 1873, x); 1887 and 1903—*Report of the Royal Commission on Coal Resources* (S.P. 1905, XVI); 1913–39—Ministry of Power, *Statistical Digest*, 1956, pp. 92–3, except for iron and steel in 1913, which comes from the *Report of the Coal Conservation Committee* (S.P. 1918, VII).

(in millions of tons)

	Gasworks	Electricity	Railways	Iron and Steel	Coke Ovens	Ships	Mines
1869	6·3 (a)	—	2·0 (a)	32·4 (a)	...	3·3 (a)	6·7 (a)
1887	9·5 (a)	—	6·2 (a)	26·7 (a)	...	...	10·9 (a)
1903	15·0 (a)	3·0 (a)	12·0 (a)	28·0 (a)	...	...	15·0 (a)
1913	17·8	4·9	14·3	36·9	19·7	23·4	18·0
1914	17·5	5·6 (a)	13·9	...	17·1	20·9	18·0 (a)
1915	17·4	5·5 (a)	14·2	...	18·2	15·6	18·0 (a)
1916	17·4	6·0 (a)	14·4	...	20·2	14·7	18·0 (a)
1917	18·8	6·6 (a)	13·6	...	20·5	11·5	18·0 (a)
1918	18·5	7·1 (a)	13·3	...	19·7	9·8	17·0 (a)
1919	17·7	7·7 (a)	13·5	...	17·6	13·3	17·0 (a)
1920	18·6	7·4	14·5	...	18·9	15·6	17·2
1921	16·7	6·3	11·5	...	6·9	12·1	13·7
1922	16·6	6·8	13·3	...	13·3	19·9	16·3
1923 (b)	17·2	7·2	14·0	...	19·8	19·5	16·9
1924	18·1	7·7	14·2	...	18·9	19·2	16·6
1925	17·8	8·1	14·1	...	16·4	17·9	15·4
1926	17·3	8·3	12·1	...	7·1	8·5	7·6 (a)
1927	18·5	9·0	14·3	...	17·4	18·2	14·6
1928	18·3	9·3	13·8	...	17·4	18·1	13·5
1929	18·6	9·8	14·1	...	20·0	18·0	13·7
1930	18·4	9·7	13·6	...	17·2	17·1	13·5
1931	18·1	9·6	13·0	...	12·7	15·9	12·6
1932	17·7	9·8	12·4	...	12·7	15·5	12·0
1933	17·4	10·3	12·4	...	13·1	14·7	11·6
1934	17·9	11·2	12·9	...	16·9	14·9	11·7
1935	18·0	12·2	13·0	...	17·4	13·9	11·6
1936	19·1	13·6	13·5	...	20·1	13·4	11·8
1937	19·4	14·8	13·8	...	21·9	13·1	12·2
1938	19·1	14·9	13·2	...	19·1	11·8	11·9
1939	18·9	15·9	12·9	...	20·4	10·8	12·1

(a) These figures are estimates with a less solid foundation than others.

(b) Irish consumption is excluded after 1922, shipments to southern Ireland being regarded as exports, and those to Northern Ireland being separately recorded.

Coal 7. Coal Used in Pig Iron Manufacture—Great Britain 1867–1927

NOTES

[1] SOURCES: 1867–72—*Report of the Select Committee on the Dearness and Scarcity of Coal* (*S.P.* 1873, x), p. 314; 1873–82—*S.P.* 1884, LXXXV, p. 606; 1883–1920—*Mineral Statistics*; 1921–7—*Annual Report of the Department of Mines.*

[2] These figures are derived from those of pig iron output by applying estimates made annually of the amount of coal required to make a ton of pig iron.

(in thousands of tons)

Year	Coal		Year	Coal	Coke
1867	14,283		1898	17,196	
1868	14,911		1899	19,061	
1869	16,337		1900	18,742	
1870	17,891		1901	16,274	
1871	19,882		1902	17,649	
1872	17,211		1903	18,302	
1873	16,719		1904	17,535	
1874	15,292		1905	19,256	
1875	15,646		1906	20,837	
1876	15,598		1907	21,120	
1877	15,342		1908	18,742	
1878	14,112		1909	19,463	
1879	13,117		1910	20,486	
1880	16,983		1911	19,218	
1881	17,485		1912	17,998	
1882	17,796		1913	21,224	
1883	17,775		1914	18,381	
1884	16,078		1915	2,509	9,747
1885	15,288		1916	2,613	10,301
1886	15,304		1917	2,816	10,962
1887	14,250		1918	2,607	11,287
1888	16,131		1919	2,310	9,384
1889	16,767		1920	2,062	10,036
1890	16,169		1921	651	3,076
1891	15,374		1922	948	5,819
1892	13,860		1923	1,834	8,633
1893	13,806		1924	1,376	8,609
1894	14,885		1925	886	7,466
1895	15,225		1926	282	2,956
1896	17,114		1927	1,093	8,404
1897	17,552				

8. Percentage of Coal Output Cut by Machine—United Kingdom 1900–38

NOTES

[1] SOURCES: 1900–20—*Mineral Statistics*; 1921–38—*Annual Report of the Department of Mines.*

[2] This table relates to both coal-**cutters and mechanical** picks.

Year		Year		Year		Year	
1900	1	1910	6	1920	13	1930	31
1901	1	1911	7	1921	14	1931	35
1902	2	1912	8	1922	15	1932	38
1903	2	1913	8	1923	17	1933	42
1904	2	1914	9	1924	19	1934	47
1905	3	1915	10	1925	20	1935	51
1906	4	1916	10	1926	20	1936	55
1907	5	1917	11	1927	23	1937	57
1908	5	1918	12	1928	26	1938	59
1909	5	1919	12	1929	28		

REFERENCES

BOOKS

T. S. Ashton and J. Sykes, *The Coal Industry of the Eighteenth Century* (Manchester, 1929).
Colliery Year Book, annually since 1922.
F. W. Dendy (editor), *Records of the Company of Hostmen* (Surtees Society No. 105, 1901).
M. Dunn, *A View of the Coal Trade* (Newcastle, 1844).
R. L. Galloway, *Annals of Coalmining and the Coal Trade* (London, 1898).
A. Finlay Gibson, *A Compilation of Statistics (Technological, Commercial and General) of the Coal Mining Industry of the United Kingdom* (London, 1936).
R. Hunt, *British Mining* (London, 1884).
H. S. Jevons, *The British Coal Trade* (London, 1915).
A. H. John, *The Industrial Development of South Wales, 1750–1850* (Cardiff, 1950).
J. H. Jones, G. Cartwright, and P. Guérault, *The Coal-Mining Industry: an International Study in Planning* (London, 1939).
E. D. Lewis, *The Rhondda Valley* (London, 1959).
R. Meade, *The Coal and Iron Industries of the United Kingdom* (London, 1882).
Miners' Federation of Great Britain, *Statistical Report of the Hours Worked at Collieries in every Mining District in Great Britain, except Durham and Cleveland* (London, 1890).
J. H. Morris and L. J. Williams, *The South Wales Coal Industry, 1841–75* (Cardiff, 1958).
J. U. Nef, *The Rise of the British Coal Industry* (2 vols., London, 1932).
A. M. Neuman, *Economic Organisation of the British Coal Industry* (London, 1934).
P.E.P., *Report on the British Coal Industry* (London, 1936).
P. M. Sweezy, *Monopoly and Competition in the English Coal Trade, 1550–1850* (Cambridge, Mass., 1938).

GOVERNMENT PUBLICATIONS

Report of the Select Committee on the Coal Trade (1800), *P.P.* x.
Returns of Coal, Cinders and Culm Shipped Coastwise and Exported (in *Sessional Papers* at intervals from 1810–11 and annually from 1839).
Report of the Select Committee on the Coal Trade (*S.P.* 1830, VIII).
Report of the Select Committee on the Coal Trade (*S.P.* 1836, XI).
Report of the Select Committee on the Coal Trade (Port of London) Bill (*S.P.* 1837–8, XV).
Memoirs of the Geological Survey of Great Britain, vol. II.
Records of the School of Mines, vol. I.
Mineral Statistics, 1854–1920 (printed by the Geological Survey 1854–81, and in *Sessional Papers* thereafter).
Reports of H.M. Inspectors of Mines, 1854–1920 (in *Sessional Papers* annually).
Report of the Select Committee on Coal Mines (*S.P.* 1852, v).
Report of the Royal Commission on Coal Supply (*S.P.* 1871, XVIII).
Report of the Select Committee on the Dearness and Scarcity of Coal (*S.P.* 1873, X).
Return of the Annual Average Price of Best Coal at the Ships' Sides, 1820–1885 (*S.P.* 1886, LX).
Return of the Annual Average Price of Best Coal at the Ships' Sides, 1881–1889 (*S.P.* 1890, LXVII).

Report of the Royal Commission on Mining Royalties (*S.P.* 1890, XXXVI; *S.P.* 1890–1, XLI, and *S.P.* 1893–4, XLI).

Report of the Royal Commission on Coal Resources (*S.P.* 1903, XVI; *S.P.* 1904, XXIII, and *S.P.* 1905, XVI).

Report of the Departmental Committee on an Eight Hours' Day for Miners (*S.P.* 1907, XIV, and *S.P.* 1907, XV).

Report of the Coal Conservation Committee (*S.P.* 1918, VII).

Report of the Coal Industry Commission (*S.P.* 1919, XI, and *S.P.* 1919, XII).

Annual Report of the Department of Mines, 1920–38 (non-parliamentary papers).

Report of the Royal Commission on the Coal Industry (*S.P.* 1926, XIV, with minutes of evidence and appendices issued as non-parliamentary papers).

Ministry of Fuel and Power, *Statistical Digest*, 1944–56 [*S.P.* 1944–5, X, and *S.P.* 1945–6, XXI (with Supplements issued as non-parliamentary papers) and annually as non-parliamentary papers from 1948].

Report of the Technical Advisory Committee on Coal Mining (*S.P.* 1944–5, IV).

ARTICLES

T. Bedford and C. G. Warner, 'A Study of Absenteeism at Certain Scottish Collieries', *Industrial Health Research Board Report*, No. 62 (1931).

R. B. Buzzard, 'Attendance and Absence in Industry: the Nature of the Evidence', *The British Journal of Sociology* (1954).

W. H. B. Court, 'Problems of the British Oil Industry between the Wars', *E.H.R.* (1945).

R. F. George, 'Statistics relating to the Coal Mining Industry', *J.R.S.S.* (1949).

S. Moos, 'The Statistics of Absenteeism in Coal Mining', *M.S.E.S.S.* (1951).

B. McCormick and J. E. Williams, 'The Miners and the Eight-Hour Day, 1863–1913', *E.H.R.* (1959).

A. J. Taylor, 'The Wigan Coalfield, 1851', *Trans. of the Historical Society of Lancashire and Cheshire* (1954).

A. J. Taylor, 'Labour Productivity and Technological Innovation in the British Coal Industry, 1850–1914', *E.H.R.* (1961).

D. A. Thomas, 'The Growth and Direction of our Foreign Trade in Coal during the Last Half Century', *J.R.S.S.* (1903).

R. Price Williams, 'The Coal Question', *J.R.S.S.* (1889).

CHAPTER V

IRON AND STEEL

TABLES

1. Output of Iron Ore in the United Kingdom and its Principal Districts—1854–1938.
2. Output of Pig Iron in Great Britain and its Principal Districts—1720–1938.
3. Output of Pig Iron according to Quality—Great Britain 1891–1938.
4. Output of Puddled Iron—United Kingdom 1881–1938.
5. Output of Steel Ingots and Castings by Process—United Kingdom 1871–1938.
6. Numbers Employed in the Iron and Steel Industries—United Kingdom 1920–38.

7. Imports of Iron Ore—United Kingdom 1855–1938.
8. Iron Imports—England & Wales 1700–91, and Great Britain 1792–1814.
9. Iron and Steel Imports and Re-exports—United Kingdom 1815–1938.
10. Iron and Steel Exports—England & Wales 1697–1791 and Great Britain 1792–1808.
11. Iron and Steel Exports—Great Britain 1805–14, and United Kingdom 1815–1938.

The iron and steel industries have been established in this country for a long time before the industrial revolution. But, in comparison with textiles they were of modest size; and unlike coal, copper or tin, they were widely scattered, and there was no dominant district or overwhelmingly important market to attract the attention of governments on the look-out for easily collected taxes. In consequence there were few statistics, other than those of external trade, until the returns for Hunt's *Mineral Statistics*[1] began in 1854. Indeed, the estimates of pig iron production back to the 1720's, given as part A of table 2, are the only reasonably connected series that we have,[2] and the validity of the earliest of these has been seriously questioned.[3] The two principal output series, therefore—those of ore in table 1 and of pig iron in table 2 part B—begin only in 1854.

The ore series does not, of course, take any account of variations in metal content, which are very considerable between districts, though small over time. As a rough guide

[1] Originally published as part of the records of the Geological Survey, subsequently as blue books.
[2] More scattered statistics, especially relating to forge output, can be found in E. W. Hulme, 'Statistical History of the Iron Trade of England and Wales, 1717–1750' in *Transactions of the Newcomen Society*, vol. IX (1928–9).
[3] By T. S. Ashton, *Iron and Steel in the Industrial Revolution* (Manchester, 1924), p. 235 and E. W. Hulme, *loc. cit.* p. 14. Even more critical is M. W. Flinn in *E.H.R.* vol. XI, no. 1 (Aug. 1958), pp. 144–53. He writes: 'In view of the doubtful validity and inconclusiveness of the available estimates of output for the early eighteenth century, it seems wiser not to attempt to ascertain absolute levels of output, but to concentrate on the dynamics of the industry'.

the following proportions may be used: for hematite (i.e. Cumberland and Lancashire) a half; and for all other sorts a third. More exactly, the former has declined since the 1880's from 55 per cent to 50 per cent, and Jurassic ores (i.e. Cleveland and the East Midlands) from 32 per cent to 27 per cent. Coal measures ore, unimportant by 1938, remained of unchanged metal content.

The next three tables—a breakdown of pig iron output by quality, and steel and puddled iron statistics—did not become part of the returns until much later in the century. This is a pity in the case of puddled iron, since the years of its greatest supremacy, the 1870's, are not covered. Statistics of the number of furnaces, given each year in *Mineral Statistics*, are no more than a very rough guide to the expansion of output up to the 1880's. Clapham reckoned that a maximum for the puddled iron output would be perhaps 1,250,000 tons in 1855 and 1,750,000 in 1865, whilst even in 1872–3 it probably never reached 3,000,000 tons.[1] The most convenient source for these three tables, as indeed for most statistics from about 1870 onwards, is the *Statistical Year Book* of the British Iron and Steel Federation, the issues of the 1920's and 1930's being the most useful from the historical point of view.[2] Occasionally the figures from this source differ somewhat from those published in *Mineral Statistics*. In such cases the former source has usually been used, since it presumably used the latest revisions and published consistently comparable series.

Unlike the coal mines, where the inspectors made estimates of the numbers employed from soon after the middle of the nineteenth century, and official returns from the early 1870's, no attempt was made except in the censuses to find out the number of workers in the iron and steel industries until after the 1914–18 War. At that time we have the start of the insurance statistics, and the B.I.S.F. *Statistical Year Book* began to publish estimates based on returns from a high proportion of works. The latter are presumably more complete, and are shown here, but, as with the insurance statistics, there are unfortunate changes in the basis of collection.

Tables 7–11 cover the statistics of our external trade in iron and steel. The first of these, showing iron ore imports, is taken back only to 1855, for though some ore was brought into the country before then, the amounts were completely insignificant. There is no indication of the metal content of imported ore until about the beginning of the twentieth century, when it was around 50 per cent. Since then it has risen to 58 per cent at the present time.[3] The remaining tables, showing imports and exports of metal, require little additional comment to that given in the notes. In each case the principal constituent items have been given as well as the total trade in iron and steel. From these it is possible to get a good idea of the change in the importance of the various branches of the industries. Statistics of the value of imports and exports have not been given in this section (except

---

[1] J. H. Clapham, *An Economic History of Modern Britain*, vol. II (Cambridge, 1932), p. 52.

[2] The British Iron Trade Federation began systematic publication of iron and steel statistics in 1878. It was followed by the Iron and Steel and Allied Trades Federation of Middlesbrough from 1915 onwards, by the National Federation of Iron and Steel Manufacturers from 1918 and by the British Iron and Steel Federation in 1934.

[3] These proportions were communicated to us by Dr R. Robson of the Iron and Steel Board.

in the case of ore, where value is some guide to metal content), but can be found in the section on trade (Chapter XI). The import and export figures given in the B.I.S.F. publications differ in certain respects from those found in the Trade and Navigation Accounts because of differences in classification.

In the early nineteenth century, the change in the trade records to absorb Ireland in the United Kingdom had virtually no effect on iron imports, since the great majority was intended for further processing, and Ireland had no iron industry. The effect on exports at this period was considerable, but since it can be eliminated in the figures from 1805 onwards, the resulting overlap with Mrs Schumpeter's figures going up to 1808 tells us the exact size of the change. The exclusion of southern Ireland after 1st April 1923 had a proportionately rather larger effect on iron and steel imports and a rather smaller effect on exports than had the nineteenth century political change. But in relation to the total remaining British trade, it was only about 2 per cent in each case. Only for re-exported iron and steel was there any substantial change—the increase in re-exports resulting from the treatment of southern Ireland as foreign was about 10 per cent.

Some statistics of bar iron and pig iron prices from the beginning of the nineteenth century can be found in Chapter XVI.

Iron and Steel 1. Output of Iron Ore in the United Kingdom and its Principal Districts—1854–1938

NOTES

[1] Sources: 1854–1920—*Mineral Statistics*; 1921–38—*Annual Report of the Department of Mines.*

[2] The value of the ore was reckoned at the prices at the mines.

(output in thousands of tons, value in £000)

	U.K.	Cleveland	Lincoln-shire	Leicester-shire, Northants, Rutland and Oxfordshire	Cumber-land and Lancashire	Stafford-shire, Shropshire and Worcester-shire	South Wales	Scotland	Value of U.K. Output
1854	...	...	—	...	580	848 (a)	...	...	...
1855	9,554	865	—	74	538	1,221	1,666	2,400	...
1856	10,483	1,148	—	92	732	2,725 (a)	1,785	2,201	...
1857	9,573	1,414	—	108	926	1,990	1,038	2,500	3,829
1858	8,041	1,367	—	140	787	1,810	752	2,312	2,571
1859	7,880	1,520	2	130	848	1,781	650	2,225	2,508
1860	8,024	1,471	16	96	990	1,685	631	2,150	2,467
1861	7,216	1,243	33	113	991	1,450	546	1,975	2,302
1862	7,562	1,690	50	117	1,093	1,572	472	1,500	2,400
1863	9,089	2,079	70	227	1,350	1,779	420	1,500	3,122
1864	10,065	2,402	75	336	1,555	1,986	468	1,950	3,367
1865	9,910	2,762	125	364	1,504	1,759	388	1,470	3,325
1866	9,665	2,809	176	477	1,524	1,497	369	1,587	3,119
1867	10,021	2,739	192	417	1,558	1,570	501	1,265	3,210
1868	10,169	2,785	201	449	1,695	1,405	713	1,250	3,197
1869	11,509	3,095	221	540	1,833	1,956	715	1,950	3,733
1870	14,371	4,073	217	887	2,093	1,698	560	1,980	4,951
1871	16,335	4,582	218	914	2,234	2,633	970	1,975	7,671
1872	15,584	4,975	256	1,174	2,077	1,412	1,248	1,978	7,775
1873	15,577	5,617	350	1,412	2,206	1,445	944	1,986	7,574
1874	14,845	5,614	463	1,059	2,034	1,478	662	2,120	7,318
1875	15,821	6,122	573	1,086	1,982	1,895	580	2,452	5,975
1876	16,842	6,562	573	1,161	2,263	1,836	554	2,553	6,826
1877	16,693	6,285	509	1,050	2,344	2,161	424	2,622	6,747
1878	15,726	5,606	684	1,189	2,343	2,010	375	2,444	5,610
1879	14,380	4,750	695	1,211	2,204	1,860	353	2,458	4,962
1880	18,026	6,487	1,155	1,550	2,758	1,989	344	2,659	6,586
1881	17,446	6,538	1,022	1,371	2,808	1,959	251	2,601	6,201
1882	18,032	6,326	1,287	1,601	3,135	2,307	205	2,406	5,779
1883	17,383	6,756	1,108	1,585	2,851	2,069	139	2,229	5,122
1884	16,138	6,053	1,349	1,542	2,595	2,100	92	1,885	4,463
1885	15,418	5,932	1,189	1,471	2,438	2,039	63	1,838	3,970
1886	14,110	5,370	1,195	1,387	2,478	1,756	59	1,508	3,514
1887	13,098	4,980	1,306	1,308	2,672	1,051	62	1,322	3,235
1888	14,591	5,396	1,345	1,603	2,690	1,828	42	1,239	3,501
1889	14,546	5,657	1,561	1,840	2,616	1,318	54	1,062	3,848
1890	13,781	5,618	1,052	1,888	2,399	1,283	50	999	3,926
1891	12,778	5,128	1,214	1,689	2,395	1,136	40	748	3,356
1892	11,313	3,411	1,458	1,801	2,200	1,113	47	872	2,971
1893	11,203	4,626	1,039	1,190	2,229	878	37	847	2,828
1894	12,367	5,116	1,554	1,699	2,157	901	36	631	3,191
1895	12,615	5,286	1,544	1,751 (b)	2,013	916	28	825	2,866

See p. 130 for footnotes

(output in thousands of tons, value in £000)

	U.K.	Cleveland	Lincoln-shire	Leicestershire, Northants, Rutland and Oxfordshire	Cumberland and Lancashire	Staffordshire, Shropshire and Worcestershire	South Wales	Scotland	Value of U.K. Output
1896	13,701	5,678	1,577	2,060	2,097	985	27	984	3,150
1897	13,788	5,679	1,765	2,059	2,078	969	29	937	3,218
1898	14,177	5,730	1,848	2,307	2,001	1,150	12	824	3,407
1899	14,461	5,613	2,094	2,669	1,809	1,103	22	844	3,895
1900	14,028	5,494	1,925	2,611	1,733	1,118	20	849	4,224
1901	12,275	5,101	1,494	2,265	1,560	859	17	759	3,222
1902	13,426	5,397	1,844	2,754	1,569	844	20	828	3,288
1903	13,716	5,677	1,903	2,838	1,490	763	21	846	3,230
1904	13,774	5,720	1,953	2,684	1,488	847	19	838	3,126
1905	14,591	5,944	2,151	2,851	1,639	912	18	832	3,482
1906	15,500	6,113	2,358	3,140	1,681	1,028	22	875	4,085
1907	15,732	6,240	2,152	3,499	1,694	1,039	20	799	4,433
1908	15,031	6,081	2,131	3,467	1,450	934	21	704	3,724
1909	14,804	6,191	2,037	3,391	1,558	915	21	697	3,679
1910	15,226	6,160	2,128	3,452	1,743	925	34	648	4,022
1911	15,519	6,050	2,156	3,801	1,712	937	46	689	4,036
1912	13,790	5,158	2,025	3,496	1,568	802	42	570	3,764
1913	15,997	5,941	2,641	3,915	1,767	895	55	592	4,544
1914	14,868	5,574	2,607	3,237	1,631	840	60	538	3,922
1915	14,235	4,746	3,149	3,343	1,656	707	76	375	4,588
1916	13,495	4,316	2,945	3,294	1,608	742	75	365	5,545
1917	14,846	4,822	3,339	3,628	1,569	803	71	444	6,430
1918	14,613	4,568	3,259	3,909	1,516	724	66	452	7,107
1919	12,254	3,718	2,787	3,473	1,213	708	61	309	7,428
1920	12,707	3,718	3,064	3,587	1,257	637	54	279	9,957
1921	3,478	1,004	779	1,078	336	105	21	107	2,205 (c)
1922	6,868	1,170	1,758	2,723	840	170	75	87	2,387 (c)
1923	10,875 (c)	2,080	2,888	4,077	1,190	435	89	100	3,535
1924	11,051 (c)	2,234	2,904	4,268	1,051	423	95	56	3,413
1925	10,143 (c)	2,284	2,498	3,967	952	288	103	39	2,919
1926	4,094	977	1,009	1,455	497	102	36	13	1,247
1927	11,207	2,530	3,196	3,817	1,241	254	128	28	3,240
1928	11,262	2,272	3,218	4,050	1,172	342	183	14	3,074
1929	13,215	2,674	3,783	4,740	1,391	380	213	26	3,646
1930	11,627	2,168	3,358	4,477	1,134	317	141	21	3,091
1931	7,626	1,497	2,362	2,969	709	61	18	8	1,838
1932	7,328	1,083	2,370	3,113	552	138	63	8	1,600
1933	7,462	1,013	2,671	2,944	633	87	107	3	1,608
1934	10,587	1,642	3,590	4,252	813	127	148	11	2,242
1935	10,895	1,640	3,449	4,652	840	151	147	14	2,351
1936	12,701	1,848	4,020	5,549	880	156	230	16	2,838
1937	14,215	2,037	4,386	6,497	857	150	261	22	3,584
1938	11,859	1,514	3,439	5,774	795	127	188	17	3,395

(a) Excluding Shropshire.
(b) The very small output of ore from Rutland and Oxfordshire before 1895 is not included under this heading, since it cannot be separated from the output of Wiltshire and Somerset.

(c) B.I.S.F. *Statistics of the Iron and Steel Industries* gives slightly different figures.

Iron and Steel 2. Output of Pig Iron in Great Britain and its Principal Districts—1720-1938

NOTES

[1] SOURCES: Part A—R. Meade, *The Coal and Iron Industries of the United Kingdom* (London, 1882), pp. 829 *et seq.*, where the original authorities are given, except for the total for 1720, which comes from T. S. Ashton, *Iron and Steel in the Industrial Revolution* (Manchester University Press, 1924), p. 235. The latter's authority is used for the attribution of the first estimates to 1720 instead of 1740, as given in Meade. Part B—1854-1920—*Mineral Statistics*; 1921-38—British Iron and Steel Federation, *Statistical Year Book*, annually.

[2] The B.I.S.F. *Statistical Year Book* during the 1920's gave the estimates shown in Part A, together with the following additional ones of total output:

1818	325,000 tons	1835	1,000,000 tons
1820	368,000 tons	1841	1,500,000 tons
1825	581,367 tons	1842	1,099,138 tons
1827	690,500 tons	1844	1,999,608 tons
1828	703,184 tons	1845	1,512,500 tons
1833	700,000 tons	1850	2,249,000 tons

A. Estimates, 1720-1852—in tons

	Total	Derbyshire	Hampshire	Shropshire	North Staffordshire	South Staffordshire	Sussex	North Wales	Yorkshire	Scotland	Durham and Northumberland	South Wales
1720	25,000(a)	(550)	(1,350)	(2,100)	(1,700)	(1,000)	(1,400)	(400)	(1,400)	...	...	(4,850)
1788	68,300	4,500	...	24,900	4,500	2,400	300	400	5,100	7,000	...	12,500
1796	125,080	9,656	...	32,970	1,959	13,211	173	1,144	10,398	16,086	...	34,101
1806	243,851	9,074	...	54,966	50,002 (N. & S. combined)		...	2,981	27,646	22,840	...	71,107
1823	455,166	14,038	...	57,923	133,590 (N. & S. combined)		...	13,100	27,311	24,500	2,379	182,325
1830	677,417	17,999	...	73,418	211,604 (N. & S. combined)		...	25,000	28,926	37,500	5,327	277,643
1839	1,248,781	34,372	...	80,940	18,200	346,213	...	33,800	52,416	196,560	13,000	453,880
1840	1,396,400	31,000	...	82,750	20,500	407,150	...	26,500	56,000	241,000	...	505,000
1843	1,215,350	25,750	...	76,200	21,750	300,250	...	19,750	42,000	238,550	...	457,350
1847	1,999,608	95,160	...	88,400	65,520	320,320	...	16,120	67,600	539,968	...	706,680
1852	2,701,000	(incl. with Yorkshire)	...	120,000	90,000	725,000	...	30,000	150,000 (incl. Derby)	775,000	145,000	666,000

B. Returns, 1854-1938—in thousands of tons

	Total	Durham and Northumberland	North Yorkshire	West Yorkshire	Cumberland	Lancashire and North Wales	Notts and Derbyshire	Shropshire	North Staffs	South Staffs	Northants	Leicestershire and Lincs	South Wales	Scotland
1854	3,070	174	101	73		53	128	125	104	744	—	—	750	797
1855	3,218	214	85	91		48	117	122	102	754	—	—	840	828
1856	3,586	331	179	96		74	107	110	131	777	—	—	877	881
1857	3,659	348	180	117	31	38	112	117	134	657	12	—	971	918
1858	3,456	310	189	86	26	31	132	101	135	598	10	—	886	926
1859	3,713	402	216	85	50		139	149	144	475	13	—	985	961
1860	3,827	410	249	98	88	130	126	145	147	470	8	—	969	937
1861	3,712	385	235	143	55	156	130	141	188	396	8	—	886	950
1862	3,943	384	283	112	103	171	131	126	184	610	13	—	893	1,080
1863	4,510	509	315	105	106	215	170	136	177	691	15	—	848	1,160
1864	4,768	522	409	102	141	246	175	131	218	629	13	10	938	1,159
1865	4,825	526	486	123	107	257	189	117	206	693	15	11	845	1,163
1866	4,524	349	546	120	136	295	200	121	210	533	19	14	927	994
1867	4,761	509	641	109	110	352	160	124	202	516	25	26	886	1,031
1868	4,970	517	699	100	117	362	159	145	230	532	36	34	894	1,068

See p. 133 for footnotes

Iron and Steel 2. *continued*

(in thousands of tons)

	Total	Durham and Northumberland	North Yorkshire	West Yorkshire	Cumberland	Lancashire and North Wales	Notts and Derbyshire	Shropshire	North Staffs	South Staffs	Northants	Leicestershire and Lincs	South Wales	Scotland
1869	5,446	674	766	106	129	476	188	197	232	570	42	34	801	1,150
1870	5,963	711	917	78	255	466	180	112	303	589	43	32	979	1,206
1871	6,627	793	1,030	115	337	562	270	129	268	726	61	30	1,046	1,169
1872	6,742	799	1,122	149	441	565	283	133	276	673	59	37	1,003	1,090
1873	6,566	844	1,156	152	457	572	296	135	283	673	58	52	818	993
1874	5,991	862	1,158	164	391	541	302	126	274	452	54	67	715	806
1875	6,365	809	1,240	267	486	614	272	121	241	475	81	112	542	1,050
1876	6,556	823	1,201	235	437	586	301	107	214	466	85	125	756	1,103
1877	6,609	734	1,375	229	538	711	328	102	255	428	107	117	711	982
1878	6,381	660	1,358	220	543	639	306	81	232	393	138	125	741	902
1879	5,995	557	1,210	219	532	650	291	61	210	326	165	132	670	932
1880	7,749	750	1,666	307	790	809	367	88	225	385	179	208	890	1,049
1881	8,144	842	1,792	256	925	739	368	79	274	374	190	188	911	1,176
1882	8,587	909	1,804	321	1,001	844	446	80	276	398	192	202	934	1,126
1883	8,529	912	1,867	304	876	836	422	78	268	430	217	237	906	1,129
1884	7,812	779	1,726	248	846	749	438	53	296	357	196	259	851	988
1885	7,415	730	1,748	166	688	736	444	45	269	344	190	235	793	1,004
1886	7,010	701	1,736	137	715	730	346	41	234	294	198	242	667	936
1887	7,560	683	1,841	178	945	793	296	52	260	293	236	252	767	932
1888	7,999	775	1,856	191	854	779	363	61	279	366	237	299	871	1,028
1889	8,323	867	1,915	229	900	830	470	52	276	373	231	336	826	978
1890	7,904	876	1,961	249	833	802	464	43	256	327	225	408	825	737
1891	7,406	862	1,769	228	725	769	471	48	232	350	194	285	761	674
1892	6,709	611	1,334	262	605	639	481	50	241	338	178	263	684	972
1893	6,977	770	1,943	155	713	615	343	40	199	330	144	217	680	793
1894	7,427	886	2,088	225	689	637	377	40	210	333	223	344	709	642
1895	7,703	868	2,058	195	649	581	413	49	194	338	255	349	705	1,049
1896	8,660	1,003	2,209	289	771	729	455	47	236	389	274	361	780	1,114
1897	8,796	1,063	2,135	295	819	760	488	39	243	400	250	363	805	1,137
1898	8,610	1,103	2,095	297	886	792	529	42	268	406	251	382	495	1,063
1899	9,421	1,040	2,211	306	955	811	572	41	283	415	279	409	929	1,171
1900	8,960	973	2,137	291	857	729 (b)	562	39	273	398	248	389	908 (b)	1,157
1901	7,929	961	1,859	247	790	642 (b)	458	41	225	341	206	322	700 (b)	1,136
1902	8,679	987	1,974	284	863	677 (b)	519	41	249	380	247	386	800 (b)	1,272
1903	8,935	1,041	2,067	298	797	689 (b)	547	47	246	397	254	386	876 (b)	1,291
1904	8,694	1,009	2,115	263	696	579	551	{ 287		394	267	377	805	1,351
1905	9,608	1,039	2,447	293	872	649	568	{ 304		430	273	443	912	1,375
1906	10,184	1,072	2,557	336	887	754	640	{ 349		452	290	497	900	1,451
1907	10,114	1,144	2,538	333	857	654	676	{ 356		470	289	482	929	1,389
1908	9,057	931	2,458	282	670	492	638	{ 323		449	296	492	866	1,225
1909	9,532	1,113	2,437	292	723	593	646	335		482	315	475	743	1,377
1910	10,012	1,128	2,551	313	749	640	687	354		495	366	512	788	1,428
1911	9,526	1,107	2,435	284	598	598	666	356		473	386	496	718	1,409
1912	8,751	1,074	2,184	265	548	559	586	350		442	351	450	756	1,186
1913	10,260	1,230	2,639	303	697	667	699	383		467	386	531	889	1,369

Iron and Steel 2. *continued*

(in thousands of tons)

Year	Total	Durham and Northumberland	North Yorkshire	West Yorkshire	Cumberland	Lancashire and North Wales	Notts and Derbyshire	Shropshire	North Staffs	South Staffs	Northants	Leicestershire and Lincs	South Wales	Scotland
1914	8,924	994	2,313	264	564	705	641	339		420	339	472	753	1,126
1915	8,724 (c)	946	2,061	285	623	567	558	345		426	295	533	829	1,109
1916	8,919 (c)	1,033	2,064	293	720	762	499	339		410	285	533	856	1,125
1917	9,338 (c)	1,134	2,096	307	782	788	544	368		433	300	649	779	1,157
1918	9,107 (c)	1,004	1,988	282	797	759	567	372		413	314	639	881	1,091
1919	7,417 (c)	878	1,629	239	591	663	482	335		319	244	535	599	903
1920	8,035	2,639		260	622	719	563	697			283	657	692	903

Notes on the braces: for 1914–1919 North Staffs and Shropshire are combined (values given in the Shropshire column); for 1920 Shropshire, North Staffs and South Staffs are combined (697) and Durham and Northumberland and North Yorkshire are combined (2,639).

Year	Total	North Yorkshire and Durham	West Yorkshire, South Lancashire and North Wales	North-West Coast (Cumberland and Furness)	Derbyshire, Essex, Leicestershire, Northants and Notts	Staffordshire, Shropshire, Worcestershire and Warwickshire	Lincolnshire	South Wales	Scotland
1921	2,616	1,054	219	284	348	194	107	121	289
1922	4,902	1,495	416	560	698	394	383	596	361
1923	7,441	2,127	597	871	1,034	533	702	808	769
1924	7,307	2,247	571	716	1,103	482	657	865	668
1925	6,262	1,905	529	633	1,010	417	549	789	430
1926	2,458	821	167	261	356	167	215	284	189
1927	7,293	2,298	516	879	995	460	714	739	692
1928	6,610	1,940	400	699	1,040	408	721	853	550
1929	7,589	2,349	472	755	1,174	440	865	927	607
1930	6,192	1,861	387	686	1,120	376	754	542	466
1931	3,773	1,137	205	404	979	202	412	280	154
1932	3,574	878	235	346	872	282	463	354	144
1933	4,136	1,063	222	513	750	307	609	451	220
1934	5,969	1,684	388	674	1,104	385	850	492	392
1935	6,424	1,721	398	673	1,441	405	862	513	413
1936	7,721	2,117	460	767	1,699	434	1,023	751	471
1937	8,493	2,429	477	825	1,938	470	1,043	815	497
1938	6,761	1,833	349	722	1,598	317	868	665	409

(a) This figure is regarded as a better estimate than the sum of the district estimates, which is 17,350 tons.

(b) The output of North Wales for these years is included with South Wales and cannot be separately distinguished.

(c) The B.I.S.F.'s *Statistics of the Iron and Steel Industries* gives the following figures for these years

1915	8,794
1916	9,048
1917	9,322
1918	9,086
1919	7,398

Iron and Steel 3. Output of Pig Iron according to Quality—Great Britain
1891–1938

NOTE
SOURCE: British Iron and Steel Federation, *Statistical Year Book*, annually.

(in thousands of tons)

	Hematite	Basic	Foundry	Forge	Blast Furnace Ferro-Alloys	Total (incl. direct castings)
1891	2,992	232	3,990		192	7,406
1892	2,710	262	3,585		152	6,709
1893	3,088	179	3,531		179	6,977
1894	3,165	93	4,011		159	7,427
1895	3,266	278	4,003		156	7,703
1896	3,648	760	4,055		197	8,660
1897	3,651	705	4,212		229	8,796
1898	3,597	780	4,029		204	8,610
1899	4,206	861	4,105		249	9,421
1900	3,865	925	3,866		303	8,960
1901	3,515	795	3,387		232	7,929
1902	3,750	922	3,742		266	8,679
1903	3,698	992	3,940		305	8,935
1904	3,472	1,192	3,815		214	8,694
1905	4,039	1,058	4,232		279	9,608
1906	4,103	1,263	4,447		371	10,184
1907	4,023	1,406	4,352		333	10,114
1908	3,413	1,819	3,576		249	9,057
1909	3,567	1,449	4,214		302	9,532
1910	3,874	1,875	3,939		324	10,012
1911	3,526	1,917	3,813		270	9,526
1912	3,472	1,772	3,252		256	8,751
1913	3,605	2,530	3,802		324	10,260
1914	3,225	2,003	3,370		326	8,924
1915	3,564	2,273	2,598		256	8,794
1916	4,042	2,291	2,318		292	9,048
1917	3,922	2,723	2,379 (a)		298	9,322
1918	3,557	2,987	2,302 (a)		241	9,086
1919	2,782	2,374	1,435 (a)	610	197	7,398
1920	2,942	2,662	1,550	605	244	8,035
1921	842	700	773	240	52	2,616
1922	1,571	1,570	1,202	278	228	4,902
1923	2,431	2,422	1,787	423	285	7,441
1924	2,343	2,445	1,858	376	191	7,307
1925	1,909	2,065	1,704	296	185	6,262
1926	815	759	690	105	46	2,458
1927	2,453	2,359	1,933	277	182	7,293
1928	2,139	2,432	1,570	269	148	6,610
1929	2,348	3,197	1,511	275	179	7,589
1930	1,841	2,408	1,458	283	133	6,192
1931	879	1,436	1,162	175	68	3,773
1932	794	1,550	1,025	134	47	3,574
1933	1,108	1,911	945	101	49	4,136
1934	1,517	2,953	1,295	103	95	5,969
1935	1,466	3,383	1,344	116	111	6,424
1936	1,728	4,343	1,346	147	149	7,721
1937	1,866	4,689	1,607	176	147	8,493
1938	1,484	3,763	1,230	151	130	6,761

(a) Including direct castings, which amounted to 105,000 tons in 1916 and 32,000 tons in 1920.

Iron and Steel 4. Output of Puddled Iron—United Kingdom 1881–1938

NOTE

SOURCE: British Iron and Steel Federation, *Statistical Year Book*, annually.

(in thousands of tons)

Year	Output	Year	Output	Year	Output
1881	2,681	1901	974	1921	218
1882	2,842	1902	998	1922	220
1883	2,731	1903	950	1923	332
1884	2,238	1904	936	1924	309
1885	1,911	1905	939	1925	210
1886	1,617	1906	1,010	1926	111
1887	1,701	1907	975	1927	184
1888	2,031	1908	1,168	1928	160
1889	2,254	1909	1,129	1929	158
1890	1,923	1910	1,119	1930	113
1891	1,734	1911	1,191	1931	62
1892	1,561	1912	1,327	1932	50
1893	1,364	1913	1,207	1933	54
1894	1,339	1914	...	1934	59
1895	1,148	1915	943	1935	55
1896	1,214	1916	960	1936	71
1897	1,238	1917	816	1937	82
1898	1,116	1918	647	1938	54
1899	1,202	1919	540		
1900	1,163	1920	589		

Iron and Steel 5. Output of Steel Ingots and Castings by Process—United Kingdom 1871–1938

NOTE

SOURCE: British Iron and Steel Federation, *Statistical Year Book*, annually. Some additional figures were supplied by the British Iron and Steel Federation.

(in thousands of tons)

	Total	Open Hearth		Bessemer		Electric		Other
		Acid	Basic	Acid	Basic	Ingots	Castings	
1871	329	—		329		—	—	—
1872	410	...		410		—	—	—
1873	573	77		496		—	—	—
1874	630	90		540		—	—	—
1875	708	88		620		—	—	—
1876	828	128		700		—	—	—
1877	887	137		750		—	—	—
1878	982	175		806		—	—	—
1879	1,009	175		834		—	—	—
1880	1,295	251		1,044		—	—	—
1881	1,778	338		1,440		—	—	—
1882	2,109	436		1,673		—	—	—
1883	2,008	455		1,553		—	—	—
1884	1,774	475		1,299		—	—	—
1885	1,887	584		1,304		—	—	—
1886	2,264	694		1,570		—	—	—
1887	3,044	981		2,064		—	—	—
1888	3,304	1,292		2,012		—	—	—
1889	3,571	1,356	72	1,719	422	—	—	—
1890	3,579	1,463	101	1,613	402	—	—	—
1891	3,157	1,415	100	1,306	336	—	—	—
1892	2,920	1,311	108	1,202	299	—	—	—
1893	2,950	1,378	79	1,231	262	—	—	—
1894	3,111	1,470	105	1,140	396	—	—	—
1895	3,260	1,564	160	1,094	442	—	—	—
1896	4,132	2,145	172	1,358	457	—	—	—
1897	4,486	2,394	208	1,374	510	—	—	—
1898	4,566	2,591	216	1,255	504	—	—	—
1899	4,855	2,735	295	1,308	517	—	—	—
1900	4,901	2,863	293	1,254	491	—	—	—
1901	4,904	2,946	351	1,116	491	—	—	—
1902	4,909	2,677	407	1,157	668	—	—	—
1903	5,034	2,613	511	1,317	593	—	—	—
1904	5,027	2,583	662	1,129	652	—	—	—
1905	5,812	3,043	795	1,396	578	—	—	—
1906	6,462	3,379	1,176	1,307	600	—	—	—
1907	6,523	3,385	1,279	1,280	579	—	—	—
1908	5,296	2,579	1,238	906	572	—	—	—
1909	5,882	2,763	1,385	1,111	622	—	—	—
1910	6,374	3,017	1,579	1,138	641	—	—	—

Iron and Steel 5. *continued*

(in thousands of tons)

| | Total | Open Hearth | | Bessemer | | Electric | | Other |
		Acid	Basic	Acid	Basic	Ingots	Castings	
1911	6,462	3,131	1,869	888	573	—	—	—
1912	6,796	3,366	1,908	981	542	—	—	—
1913	7,664	3,811	2,252	1,049	552	—	—	—
1914	7,835	3,681	2,875	797	482	—	—	—
1915	8,550	4,091 (*a*)	2,959 (*a*)	821 (*a*)	480 (*a*)	20	2	177 (*a*)
1916	8,992	4,356 (*a*)	2,979 (*a*)	914 (*a*)	542 (*a*)	43	4	154 (*a*)
1917	9,717	4,545 (*a*)	3,356 (*a*)	916 (*a*)	585 (*a*)	85	14	216 (*a*)
1918	9,539	3,881 (*a*)	3,986 (*a*)	755 (*a*)	551 (*a*)	79	47	241 (*a*)
1919	7,894	2,960 (*a*)	3,935 (*a*)	493 (*a*)	296 (*a*)	47	30	133 (*a*)
1920	9,067	3,380	4,580	587	376	55	34	57
1921	3,703	1,170	2,217	209	54	11	16	28
1922	5,881	1,709	3,626	289	196	21	18	22
1923	8,482	2,568	5,284	387	137	41	23	43
1924	8,201	2,410	5,125	437	109	42	23	55
1925	7,385	2,016	4,750	477	28	40	24	51
1926	3,596	1,055	2,265	174	—	39	22	41
1927	9,097	2,571	5,929	475	—	49	26	48
1928	8,520	2,219	5,669	503	—	50	29	50
1929	9,636	2,451	6,488	559	—	57	30	51
1930	7,326	1,805	5,099	279	—	40	36	66
1931	5,203	1,182	3,785	129	—	28	26	53
1932	5,261	1,123	3,912	125	—	32	23	46
1933	7,024	1,552	5,140	203	—	51	24	54
1934	8,850	1,751	6,678	239	—	66	31	84
1935	9,859	1,858	7,361	199	224	77	29	110
1936	11,785	2,159	8,772	239	324	108	45	138
1937	12,984	2,276	9,673	255	418	155	61	147
1938	10,398	1,721	7,743	164	431	160	63	117

(*a*) Bessemer and Open Hearth castings included in 'Other', ingots only being under their proper heading.

Iron and Steel 6. Numbers Employed in the Iron and Steel Industries—United Kingdom 1920–38

NOTES

[1] SOURCE: British Iron and Steel Federation, *Statistical Year Book*, annually.
[2] Except as indicated in the footnote, these figures relate to all workers employed at blast furnaces, steel furnaces, rolling mills, etc., but do not cover tinplate, galvanised sheet, and wrought iron workers.

At a Day in:			Annual Average	
June	1920	168,492	1920	...
March	1921	121,342	1921	...
June	1922	108,647	1922	114,055
June	1923	137,642	1923	142,922
July	1924	120,982	1924	145,585
July	1925	115,487	1925	131,663
April	1926	130,370	1926	...
July	1927	114,811	1927	129,351
July	1928	108,182	1928	121,706
July	1929	128,440	1929	124,284
July	1930	89,941	1930	...
July	1931	74,534	1931	...
July	1932	76,080	1932	82,026
July	1933	85,302	1933	91,165
July	1934	102,176	1934	113,098
July	1935	110,727	1935	115,596
July	1936	127,301 (a)	1936	139,708 (a)
			1937	155,342
			1938	138,671

a) Workers at coke ovens attached to blast furnaces excluded after 1935.

Iron and Steel 7. Imports of Iron Ore—United Kingdom 1855–1938

NOTES
[1] SOURCE: *Annual Statement of Trade.*   [2] Imports of manganiferous ore are included throughout.

(in thousands of tons and £000)

	Quantity	Value		Quantity	Value
1855	11	...	1897	5,969	4,436
1856	--	...	1898	5,468	4,035
1857	17	13	1899	7,055	5,375
1858	29	22	1900	6,298	5,639
1859	29	22	1901	5,549	4,551
1860	23	15	1902	6,440	4,979
1861	23	19	1903	6,314	4,837
1862	36	28	1904	6,101	4,538
1863	62	46	1905	7,345	5,453
1864	74	57	1906	7,823	6,658
1865	77	72	1907	7,642	7,276
1866	57	49	1908	6,058	4,911
1867	87	69	1909	6,329	4,986
1868	114	95	1910	7,021	6,057
1869	131	102	1911	6,347	5,646
1870	208	166	1912	6,602	6,028
1871	324	343	1913	7,442	7,046
1872	802	1,015	1914	5,705	5,155
1873	968	1,278	1915	6,197	7,177
1874	754	1,021	1916	6,934	11,775
1875	459	584	1917	6,190	12,040
1876	672	796	1918	6,582	13,441
1877	1,141	1,256	1919	5,201	11,271
1878	1,173	1,163	1920	6,500	16,545
1879	1,085	1,050	1921	1,888	3,733
1880	2,633	2,790	1922	3,473	4,284
1881	2,451	2,349	1923	5,860	6,850
1882	3,285	3,063	1924	5,927	6,581
1883	3,191	2,751	1925	4,382	4,774
1884	2,731	2,115	1926	2,088	2,148
1885	2,823	1,957	1927	5,164	5,446
1886	2,878	1,895	1928	4,440	4,656
1887	3,766	2,548	1929	5,689	6,222
1888	3,562	2,470	1930	4,138	4,483
1889	4,031	3,024	1931	2,119	2,083
1890	4,472	3,596	1932	1,795	1,641
1891	3,181	2,453	1933	2,708	2,368
1892	3,781	2,717	1934	4,359	3,680
1893	4,066	2,792	1935	4,547	3,981
1894	4,414	2,979	1936	5,961	5,290
1895	4,450	2,978	1937	7,039	8,078
1896	5,438	3,779	1938	5,167	7,291

NOTES

[1] SOURCES: 1700–1808—Elizabeth B. Schumpeter, *English Overseas Trade Statistics, 1697–1808* (Oxford University Press, 1960), tables XVI and XVII (converted to tons); 1809–14—Returns printed in sessional papers at irregular intervals.
[2] The figures are for years ended on 5th January in the year following that for which they are shown.

[3] Bar iron re-exports for the period 1805–19 were as follows:

1805	2·0	1810	8·3
1806	3·0	1811	4·7
1807	3·3	1812	5·4
1808	3·5	1813	...
1809	4·9	1814	8·8

A. England & Wales, 1700–91 (in thousands of tons)

	Bar Iron	Total Iron		Bar Iron	Total Iron
1700	16·9	17·3	1746	21·9	25·3
1701	17·8	18·1	1747	19·7	23·0
1702	12·6	12·8	1748	26·0	31·0
1703	18·9	19·1	1749	22·7	26·7
1704	16·0	16·2	1750	35·1	40·3
1705	...	...	1751	26·5	31·6
1706	18·1	18·4	1752	24·9	30·1
1707	13·7	14·1	1753	28·8	33·5
1708	17·6	17·9	1754	31·1	36·1
1709	12·8	13·2	1755	29·4	34·9
1710	17·4	17·8	1756	26·2	31·8
1711	14·6	15·1	1757	26·7	32·5
1712	...	...	1758	30·7	38·9
1713	14·1	15·3	1759	33·1	39·3
1714	21·8	22·9	1760	27·7	33·7
1715	17·3	18·2	1761	42·3	47·3
1716	14·9	15·9	1762	32·2	35·5
1717	7·1	7·8	1763	37·6	41·7
1718	17·1	18·5	1764	43·9	48·6
1719	21·1	22·5	1765	51·4	57·0
1720	22·3	23·6	1766	32·4	37·2
1721	15·9	17·0	1767	36·5	42·5
1722	22·6	23·5	1768	44·7	49·8
1723	18·9	19·7	1769	48·6	55·0
1724	20·9	22·5	1770	46·0	53·7
1725	18·2	19·7	1771	46·0	53·8
1726	21·2	22·7	1772	51·9 (a)	57·8 (a)
1727	15·7	17·5	1773	46·5	51·4
1728	21·8	24·3	1774	45·4	50·1
1729	19·3	21·8	1775	41·9	47·1
1730	21·8	25·0	1776	50·2	53·0
1731	24·4	27·9	1777	43·1	45·9
1732	23·3	27·0	1778	31·5	33·9
1733	24·2	28·1	1779	42·1	44·0
1734	24·9	29·0	1780	37·2	39·1
1735	26·3	30·5	1781	51·7	52·1
1736	24·0	27·6	1782	39·9	40·8
1737	29·6	33·2	1783	44·0	45·7
1738	28·3	32·5	1784	48·8	50·6
1739	28·5	32·0	1785	40·4	42·7
1740	23·0	26·4	1786	44·3	47·2
1741	23·1	28·0	1787	42·4	47·0
1742	19·8	23·1	1788	46·9	51·4
1743	15·4	19·4	1789	46·5	51·4
1744	24·1	26·9	1790	43·8	49·9
1745	29·3	32·7	1791	51·6	57·3

(a) The size of the break occasioned by the change in original source can be judged from the following figures from the old source for 1775 and 1780:

	Bar Iron	Total Iron
1775	32·3	37·5
1780	36·4	38·5

B. Great Britain, 1792–1814

	Bar Iron	Total Iron		Bar Iron	Total Iron
1792	57·7	64·2	1804	22·5	23·0
1793	59·0	64·5	1805	27·3	27·8
1794	42·5	46·7	1806	32·1	33·0
1795	49·3	51·0	1807	23·7	24·0
1796	53·2	54·8	1808	21·0	21·1
1797	36·9	37·7	1809	24·5	...
1798	51·9	52·6	1810	20·1	...
1799	48·3	49·4	1811	28·0	...
1800	38·2	38·9	1812	17·4	...
1801	33·4	34·8	1813	...	...
1802	52·9	57·7	1814	21·9	...
1803	43·5	44·7			

Iron and Steel 9. Iron and Steel Imports and Re-exports—
United Kingdom 1815–1938

NOTES

[1] SOURCES: 1815–39—Returns printed in sessional papers annually from 1817; 1840–54—*Abstract*; 1855–1938—*Annual Statement of Trade*.

[2] The figures up to and including 1854 are for years ended on 5th January in the year following that for which they are shown.

(in thousands of tons)

A. Bar Iron, 1815–54

	Imports	Re-exports		Imports	Re-exports		Imports	Re-exports
1815	21·3	13·1	1829	15·1	3·0	1843	12·8	4·0
1816	8·5	8·2	1830	14·9	3·0	1844	24·5	5·9
1817	10·1	3·0	1831	17·4	4·3	1845	33·4	2·6
1818	16·6	3·8	1832	19·2	3·5	1846	34·6	4·1
1819	14·0	3·8	1833	17·9	2·0	1847	33·3	5·1
1820	9·9	3·2	1834	16·2	2·9	1848	23·9	3·4
1821	10·2	3·2	1835	19·8	2·6	1849	29·4	5·0
1822	12·7	3·4	1836	25·0	4·8	1850	34·1	6·0
1823	13·4	2·9	1837	19·3	2·6	1851	40·3	4·8
1824	14·2	3·5	1838	23·0	4·4	1852	33·4	5·8
1825	23·2	6·7	1839	20·8	4·5	1853	44·8	5·5
1826	13·0	2·3	1840	18·9	5·7	1854	41·7	4·3
1827	18·5	3·5	1841	23·8	3·6			
1828	15·1	3·0	1842	18·7	2·2			

	Imports				Re-exports	
	Pig and Puddled Iron	Bar Iron	Part-wrought and Unwrought Steel	Wrought Iron, Steel, and Manufactures	Total Iron and Steel	Bar Iron	Wrought Iron, Steel, and Manufactures
1855	1·8	37·4		—	40	3·2	
1856	1·9	51·9		—	57	6·6	
1857	2·6	50·2	quantities not significant	—	58	6·3	
1858	5·2	25·5		—	35	5·9	
1859	9·8	42·7		1·1	58	9·3	
1860	9·7	54·1		2·4	69	7·6	
1861	8·0	35·5	3·7	3·2	57	6·8	
1862	14·4	49·7	5·1	3·9 (a)	79	14·6	
1863	11·3	46·6	4·0	6·4	70	12·9	
1864	20·1	53·9	7·6	15·9	100	12·9	
1865	11·4	51·5	6·8	21·4	94	9·6	quantities not significant
1866	13·4	64·2	4·5	20·4	92	14·8	
1867	21·6	71·7	8·6	16·0	121	23·1	2·8
1868	21·3	64·7	7·7	16·1	113	21·8	3·8
1869	19·9	68·5	10·8	19·5	121	21·1	5·4
1870	35·9	74·1	8·1	27·9	150	21·3	4·5
1871	55·6	74·3	7·6	22·0	160	20·3	4·9
1872	100·6	82·4	7·5	39·1	230	16·7	8·4
1873	74·8	74·7	9·5	30·7	190	16·3	9·4
1874	56·9	73·5	7·3	52·7	190	24·4	11·8
1875	47·6	89·8	7·5	58·0	203	34·3	12·8
1876	31·4	85·4	9·2	69·5	196	36·1	12·7
1877	44·0	91·8	5·0	84·2	225	42·2	24·5
1878	27·7	102·8	4·6	105·5	241	60·3	22·8
1879	26·3	95·5	5·2	112·3	239	49·0	27·4

See p. 143 for footnotes

(in thousands of tons)

B. Iron and Steel, 1855–1919

	Imports					Re-exports	
	Pig and Puddled Iron	Bar Iron	Part-wrought and Unwrought Steel	Wrought Iron, Steel, and Manufactures	Total Iron and Steel	Bar Iron	Wrought Iron, Steel, and Manufactures
1880	66·9	120·0	5·9	155·4	348	69·4	48·5
1881	55·8	111·5	6·7	175·3	349	62·1	66·0
1882	44·4	139·2	5·9	172·2	362	74·1	68·9
1883	38·9	122·9	4·5	194·0	360	67·4	61·7
1884	37·1	115·5	6·7	185·1	344	62·7	48·5
1885	38·6	122·6	11·2	173·7	346	77·4	47·7
1886	45·2	105·5	12·1	176·9	340	73·5	51·7
1887	38·6	113·0	14·7	198·4	365	85·0	53·5
1888	37·2	113·2	12·1	226·6	389	82·8	52·5
1889	70·3	111·8	10·9	230·4	423	75·4	40·0
1890	61·8	92·9	8·1	222·8	386	65·2	25·3
1891	61·9	77·4	8·4	229·1	377	56·1	27·2
1892	56·5	75·9	6·5	218·4	357	46·5	35·1
1893	35·4	65·8	8·9	216·7	327	28·1	45·6
1894	62·0	63·2	8·6	224·4	358	18·4	34·0
1895	93·1	67·7	10·9	234·4	406	22·8	34·2
1896	106·4	71·1	17·5	264·6	460	16·6	36·7
1897	158·0	68·2	40·0	249·7 (b)	516 (b)	21·5	27·2 (b)
1898	159·5	69·2	40·2	322·4	591	26·5	27·5
1899	171·4	73·2	77·3	323·1	645	18·8	26·9
1900	181·2	80·1	179·3	359·0	800	10·9	24·4
1901	198·5	98·1	182·9	444·1	924	12·4	28·2
1902	226·8	171·9	281·0	451·0	1,131	8·4	24·1
1903	136·6	186·6	274·1	706·5	1,304	8·9	51·3
1904	133·7	104·2	522·7	531·3	1,292	7·0	29·1
1905	129·0	106·0	603·9	517·1	1,356	6·4	19·7
1906	90·9	107·7	486·0	531·1	1,216	6·7	20·8
1907	104·8	80·4	327·2	423·1 (c)	935	6·8	24·8 (c)
1908	68·8	82·9	560·5	407·2	1,119	4·6	17·7
1909	109·9	93·7	550·4	439·4	1,193	2·9	18·3
1910	172·5	96·7	559·0	539·0	1,367	7·4	26·3
1911	175·9	117·1	827·3	641·7	1,762	5·2	45·1
1912	218·1	164·4	873·2	741·0	1,997	2·4	23·5
1913	217·8	200·0	904·7	897·9	2,220	3·5	28·7
1914	223·5	129·9	597·9	666·6	1,618	2·6	20·4
1915	194·4	46·0	458·7	478·2	1,177	1·3	39·5
1916	157·5	44·2	167·0	404·2	773	1·5	40·9
1917	155·2	28·3	65·4	247·1	496	0·3	12·3
1918	129·4	15·1	21·4	171·1	337	0·6	4·4
1919	163·7	32·6	76·0	234·1	506	0·3	15·8

See p. 143 for footnotes

(in thousands of tons)

C. **Iron and Steel, 1910–39**

			Imports		
	Pig Iron and Ferro-Alloys	Steel Blooms, Billets, and Slabs (except Alloys)	Iron and Steel Bars, Rods, Angles, Shapes and Sections (except Alloys)	Total Iron and Steel (*d*)	Total Re-exports of Iron and Steel
1910	172	329	439	1,379	34·2
1911	175	481	623	1,775	50·8
1912	217	564	647	2,012	26·8
1913	217	514	774	2,231	32·7
1914	223	299	591	1,627	29·1
1915	194	428	237	1,182	46·2
1916	159	146	213	776	47·7
1917	155	58	147	497	17·1
1918	129	20	61	337	30·2
1919	163	71	125	509	42·0
1920	230	251 (*e*)	237 (*e*)	1,108	24·9
1921	679	172	341	1,640	15·7
1922	164	171	231	881	4·5
1923	110 (*f*)	418 (*f*)	419 (*f*)	1,322 (*f*)	7·7 (*f*)
1924	308	705	844	2,429	9·1
1925	286	650	1,032	2,720	8·7
1926	492	845	1,395	3,738	13·9
1927	609	926	1,591	4,406	13·2
1928	119	616	1,171	2,897	8·3
1929	153	573	1,120	2,822	8·9
1930	312	566	1,180	2,912	12·0
1931	307	531	1,255	2,844	7·1
1932	153	360	692	1,593	3·4
1933	121	230	327	971	2·0
1934	163	331	502	1,366	2·8
1935	128	262	429	1,152	3·2
1936	311	453	380	1,483	7·0
1937	716	437	500	2,033	7·1
1938	443	317	352	1,342	30·2
1939	427	372	651	1,811	2·8

(*a*) New items included under this heading, making a difference of 500 tons in this year.
(*b*) Cycles and machinery no longer included under this heading.
(*c*) Old rails included under this heading henceforward.
(*d*) The difference between totals here and in Part B results from the inclusion of holloware and the exclusion of old rails.
(*e*) Alloy steels, of which very small quantities were imported, *were* included prior to this date. Also prior to this date, 'Iron Bars, Rods, etc.' included iron ingots and billets.
(*f*) Southern Ireland was treated as foreign from 1st April 1923.

Iron and Steel Exports—England & Wales 1697–1791

and Great Britain 1792–1808

NOTES

[1] Source: Elizabeth B. Schumpeter, *English Overseas Trade Statistics, 1697–1808* (Oxford University Press, 1960), tables VIII and IX (converted to tons where necessary).

[2] The figures are for years ended on 5th January of the years following that for which they are shown.
(3) Exports to Ireland are included throughout.

(in tons)

A. England & Wales, 1697–1791

	Wrought Iron (b)	Total Iron	Total Steel		Wrought Iron (b)	Total Iron	Total Steel
1697	1,459	1,776	20	1745	2,676	4,121	224
1698	1,019	1,844	33	1746	5,500	8,463	831
1699	1,040	1,837	39	1747	4,127	6,369	454
1700	1,085	1,980	19	1748	4,800	7,392	372
1701	1,020	2,177	31	1749	6,477	8,998	481
1702	707	1,263	21	1750	6,126	9,272	436
1703	935	1,676	30	1751	5,952	9,285	544
1704	902	1,567	20	1752	5,455	8,590	532
1705	...	...	...	1753	6,530	9,863	661
1706	703	1,009	25	1754	6,162	8,864	686
1707	893	1,468	24	1755	6,052	8,750	797
1708	865	1,518	31	1756	5,266	7,012	386
1709	876	1,463	19	1757	6,474	8,199	548
1710	967	1,450	34	1758	6,588	8,514	536
1711	977	1,411	80	1759	7,316	8,975	406
1712	...	...	...	1760	8,153	10,779	590
1713	1,359	2,014	50	1761	7,198	8,806	522
1714	1,628	2,399	59	1762	6,788	8,370	610
1715	1,576	2,543	46	1763	7,948	10,328	623
1716	1,358	2,193	19	1764	9,294	12,612	965
1717	1,623	2,806	56	1765	8,532	11,484	1,031
1718	1,292	1,997	34	1766	9,974	14,691	839
1719	1,389	2,386	44	1767	10,568	17,927	1,357
1720	1,283	1,906	26	1768	10,940	16,841	1,403
1721	1,400	2,029	25	1769	10,376	12,194	1,443
1722	1,632	2,726	47	1770	10,918	16,891	1,381
1723	1,575	2,513	52	1771	13,702	21,316	1,675
1724	1,942	3,126	67	1772	13,644(a)	15,761(a)	1,266(a)
1725	2,101	3,063	86	1773	11,643	14,251	1,309
1726	1,828	2,972	50	1774	11,561	13,479	873
1727	1,886	2,834	31	1775	12,243	14,256	1,317
1728	2,168	3,602	26	1776	9,311	10,871	1,001
1729	2,572	3,424	29	1777	8,233	9,644	1,206
1730	2,460	3,694	61	1778	7,565	9,019	2,026
1731	2,323	3,509	76	1779	5,967	7,185	1,300
1732	2,367	3,386	47	1780	7,406	8,997	1,733
1733	2,285	3,300	113	1781	6,458	7,867	728
1734	2,221	3,381	113	1782	8,894	10,477	1,933
1735	2,855	4,014	167	1783	9,512	11,033	870
1736	2,971	4,376	172	1784	11,498	13,165	1,109
1737	2,983	4,677	215	1785	10,543	12,391	1,175
1738	3,278	5,023	151	1786	10,987	14,818	2,414
1739	2,938	4,549	226	1787	12,450	17,783	1,868
1740	3,743	5,851	351	1788	12,201	13,773	2,066
1741	4,361	6,750	269	1789	13,792	16,082	2,337
1742	3,852	5,834	140	1790	15,232	17,884	2,324
1743	3,810	5,701	96	1791	19,655	22,647	2,502
1744	3,238	5,147	341				

See p. 145 *for footnotes*

B. Great Britain, 1792–1808

(in tons)

	Wrought Iron	Iron in Bars or Unwrought	Steel	Total Iron and Steel
1792	23,386	332	3,008	32,156
1793	16,997	180	3,624	25,032
1794	17,248	104	2,883	25,640
1795	16,167	220	2,937	24,019
1796	19,686	408	3,135	28,972
1797	17,672	1,318	2,516	26,530
1798	17,750	1,889	2,007	25,903
1799	23,109	2,676	6,308	38,261
1800	24,372	2,845	4,267	37,846
1801	21,489	3,001	4,769	35,906
1802	23,791	5,459	4,348	41,087
1803	16,948	3,575	4,225	31,414
1804	17,964	6,065	654	30,190
1805	16,397	6,595	498	37,423
1806	20,167	8,124	381	37,306
1807	21,830	10,863	394	42,116
1808	18,902	14,924	492	42,197

(*a*) The size of this break, caused by the change in original source, can be judged by the following figures from the old source for 1775 and 1780:

	Wrought Iron	Total Iron	Total Steel
1775	11,639	13,319	1,305
1780	7,049	8,531	1,733

(*b*) Includes hardware and, presumably, other goods which were not wrought (in the technical sense), but cast.

Iron and Steel 11. Iron and Steel Exports—Great Britain 1805–14, and United Kingdom 1815–1938

NOTES

[1] Sources: 1805–14—*S.P.* 1814–5, x; 1815–18—*S.P.* 1819, xvi; 1819–20—*S.P.* 1821, xviii; 1821–4—*S.P.* 1825, xxi; 1825–8—*S.P.* 1829, xvii; 1829–48—Returns printed in sessional papers annually; 1849–1908—*Abstract*; 1906–39—*Abstract* and *Annual Statement of Trade*.

[2] The figures up to and including 1854 are for years ended on 5th January of the year following that for which they are shown.

A. 1805–1908

(in thousands of tons)

	Pig and Puddled Iron	Iron in Bars or Unwrought and Railroad Iron and Steel	Tin- and Terne-Plates and Sheets	Unwrought Steel	Total Iron and Steel
1805	- -	3	...	...	20
1806	- -	4	...	...	27
1807	- -	5	...	...	24
1808	- -	9	...	...	26
1809	...	...	...	...	...
1810	...	...	...	...	...
1811	...	...	...	...	...
1812	- -	13	...	...	32
1813	...	...	...	...	...
1814	- -	15	...	...	37
1815	- -	25	...	1	49
1816	1	27	...	1	52
1817	4	39	...	1	67
1818	3	48	...	1	79
1819	1	27	...	- -	52
1820	3	42	...	- -	67
1821	4	39	...	1	65
1822	5	39	...	1	70
1823	8	41	...	- -	65
1824	2	30	...	1	59
1825	3	30	...	1	61
1826	7	40	...	- -	76
1827	7	53	...	1	93
1828	8	59	...	1	101
1829	9	63	...	1	108
1830	12	68	...	1	118
1831	12	70	...	1	124
1832	18	81	...	1	148
1833	23	83	...	2	163
1834	22	80	...	2	158
1835	33	108	...	3	199
1836	34	98	...	3	192
1837	44	96	...	2	194
1838	49	142	...	3	257
1839	43	136	...	4	248
1840	50	145	...	3	269
1841	86	189	...	4	360
1842	94	191	...	3	369
1843	155	199	...	3	450
1844	100	250	...	5	459
1845	77	164	...	7	351
1846	159	158	...	8	433
1847	176	228	...	10	550
1848	176	339	...	7	626
1849	162	402	...	8	709
1850	142	469	...	11	783
1851	201	538	...	12	919
1852	240	568	...	16	1,036
1853	334	654	...	20	1,261
1854	293	617	...	21	1,197
1855	292	541	...	17	1,093

(in thousands of tons)

	Pig and Puddled Iron	Railroad Iron and Steel only	Tin- and Terne-Plates and Sheets	Unwrought Steel	Total Iron and Steel
1856	357	462	...	22	1,439 (a)
1857	422	458	60	22	1,593
1858	363	433	54	16	1,404
1859	316	529	61	25	1,526
1860	343	453	60	32	1,503
1861	388	378	36	22	1,359
1862	445	401	50	26	1,557 (b)
1863	466	446	56	29	1,703
1864	466	408	50	27	1,559
1865	548	434	63	24	1,687
1866	501	498	71	34	1,762
1867	566	581	79	33	1,968
1868	553	583	88	31	2,042
1869	711	888	97	34	2,675
1870	753	1,059	100	35	2,826
1871	1,057	981	120	39	3,169
1872	1,331	945	118	45	3,383
1873	1,142	785	121	39	2,958
1874	776	783	123	31	2,488
1875	948	546	138	30	2,458
1876	910	415	133	26	2,224
1877	882	498	153	24	2,346
1878	923	439	155	24	2,297
1879	1,223	464	197	31	2,883
1880	1,632	694	218	69	3,793
1881	1,482	821	243	167	3,820
1882	1,758	933	265	172	4,354
1883	1,564	971	269	73	4,043
1884	1,270	729	289	57	3,497
1885	961	714	298	60	3,131
1886	1,045	740	335	166	3,388
1887	1,126	1,012	354	286	4,143
1888	1,036	1,020	391	153	3,967
1889	1,190	1,090	431	150	4,186
1890	1,145	1,035	422	149	4,001
1891	840	702	448	150	3,240
1892	767	468	395	149	2,739
1893	840	558	379	170	2,857
1894	831	425	354	211	2,650
1895	867	458	366	208	2,836
1896	1,060	748	267	297	3,550
1897	1,201	782	271	300	3,686
1898	1,043	609	251	285	3,244
1899	1,380	591	256	329	3,717
1900	1,428	464	273	308	3,541
1901	839	573	271	214	2,898
1902	1,103	716	312	303	3,576
1903	1,065	723	293	298	3,707
1904	811	689 (c)	360	...	3,426
1905	983	750	355	...	3,870
1906	1,666	656	375	...	4,860
1907	1,944	655 (d)	405	...	5,312
1908	1,297	640	403	...	4,230

(a) Tinplates included for the first time.
(b) Certain manufactures of iron and steel combined (amounting to 6,000 tons in 1862) included for the first time.

(c) Tyres and axles included for the first time. In 1903 they had amounted to 37,000 tons.
(d) Prior to 1907, old rails were regarded as railway iron.

(in thousands of tons)

B. 1906-38

	Pig Iron (incl. Ferro-Alloys)	Railway Material	Tin- and Terne-Plates and Sheets	Other Plates and Sheets	Tubes, Pipes and Fittings	Total Iron and Steel (a)
1906	1,663	656	375	783	295	4,713
1907	1,942	655	405	840	349	5,168
1908	1,294	640	403	661	277	4,115
1909	1,135	774	440	722	281	4,238
1910	1,205	656	483	847	358	4,622
1911	1,203	545	484	887	368	4,552
1912	1,262	651	481	942	399	4,844
1913	1,124	775	494	1,038	400	4,969
1914	781	654	435	767	317	3,910
1915	611	399	369	586	222	3,209
1916	917	127	322	589	170	3,308
1917	734	85	177	288	132	2,338
1918	482	81	223	242	108	1,613
1919	357	218	289	590	148	2,233
1920	580	311	353	784	226	3,251
1921	136	340	226	505	135	1,697
1922	794	477	449	823	162	3,397
1923	893 (b)	493 (b)	551 (b)	1,135 (b)	242 (b)	4,318 (b)
1924	600	370	555	1,128	252	3,851
1925	560	421	511	1,066	286	3,731
1926	313	306	375	941	295	2,988
1927	331	729	472	1,252	383	4,196
1928	455	610	532	1,232	391	4,261
1929	545	487	580	1,228	454	4,380
1930	317	389	508	773	347	3,160
1931	202	206	400	494	204	1,979
1932	128	105	463	556	218	1,887
1933	112	110	453	519	273	1,922
1934	133	190	388	596	339	2,251
1935	157	217	345	651	325	2,369
1936	112	241	370	548	301	2,234
1937	167	241	462	614	376	2,607
1938	101	202	329	357	312	1,960

(a) No longer includes old iron.

(b) Southern Ireland was treated as foreign from 1st April 1923.

REFERENCES

BOOKS

T. S. Ashton, *Iron and Steel in the Industrial Revolution* (Manchester, 1924).

I. Lowthian Bell, *The Iron Trade of the United Kingdom* (London, 1886).

British Iron and Steel Federation, *Statistical Year Book* (London, annually since 1915 under slightly varying titles).

British Iron and Steel Trade Association (*Annual Report*).

D. L. Burn, *The Economic History of Steel Making, 1867–1939* (Cambridge, 1940).

T. H. Burnham and G. O. Hoskins, *Iron and Steel in Britain, 1870–1930* (London, 1943).

R. Hunt, *British Mining* (London, 1884).

A. H. John, *The Economic Development of South Wales, 1750–1850* (Cardiff, 1950).

G. T. Jones, *Increasing Return* (Cambridge, 1933).

R. Meade, *The Coal and Iron Industries of the United Kingdom* (London, 1882).

W. E. Minchinton, *The British Tinplate Industry: a History* (Oxford, 1957).

D. Mushet, *Papers on Iron and Steel* (London, 1840).

H. G. Roepcke, *Movements of the British Iron and Steel Industry, 1720–1951* (Urbana, Illinois Studies in the Social Sciences, vol. 36, 1956).

H. Scrivenor, *A History of the Iron Trade* (London, 1854).

H. R. Schubert, *History of the British Iron and Steel Industry* (London, 1957).

GOVERNMENT PUBLICATIONS

Returns of Iron and Steel Imports and Exports (in *Sessional Papers* irregularly from 1806 and annually from 1831–2).

Memoirs of the Geological Survey, vol. II.

Records of the School of Mines, vol I.

Mineral Statistics, 1854–1920 (printed by the Geological Survey to 1881 and in *Sessional Papers* thereafter).

Annual Report of the Department of Mines, 1921–1938 (non-parliamentary papers).

Committee on Industry and Trade, *Survey of the Metal Industries* (non-parliamentary paper, 1928).

ARTICLES

R. H. Campbell, 'Statistics of the Scottish Pig Iron Trade 1830 to 1865', *Journal of the West of Scotland Iron and Steel Institute* (1956–7).

M. W. Flinn, 'The Growth of the English Iron Industry, 1660–1760', *E.H.R.* (1958).

E. W. Hulme, 'Statistical History of the Iron Trade of England and Wales, 1717–1750', *Transactions of the Newcomen Society* (1928–9).

R. Hunt, 'The Present State of the Mining Industries of the United Kingdom', *J.S.S.* (1856).

R. M. Shone, 'Statistics relating to the U.K. Iron and Steel Industry', *J.R.S.S.* (1950).

J. Strong, 'On the Progress, Extent and Value of the Coal and Iron Trade of the West of Scotland', *J.S.S.* (1855).

TIN, COPPER AND LEAD

TABLES

The tin-mines of Cornwall provide, in table 1, our longest series of statistics, going back, admittedly with large gaps in the thirteenth and fourteenth centuries, as far as 1199. Up to 1837 these statistics relate only to the tin actually coined, and 'can only be regarded as a rough guide to production in view of the time-lag between the actual mining of the tin and its coining', and because some 'tin-stuff and smelted tin were smuggled out of the country without coining'.[1] The significance of British tin-mining becomes, of course, progressively less towards the end of the nineteenth century, but the series have been continued here to 1938.

In comparison with tin, the statistics of copper-mining in the South-West are of recent origin, copper output not being of much significance until the end of the seventeenth century. The earliest figure is for 1726, and even then it was not complete for Cornwall and Devon, which were themselves not the only producing district in Britain. The first point is probably not of much importance until well into the nineteenth century, for it seems clear that by far the greatest proportion of British copper was sold at public ticketings, and for a long period this proportion was fairly constant. When exactly things began to change is not at all certain; but the eventual extent of the change was very considerable. In 1854–56, when Hunt's *Mineral Statistics* enables us to speak with confidence,[2] the proportion of the entire British output which was sold by private contract was not far short of one third.

The South-Western output of copper was not a good guide to national output for the

---

[1] John Rowe, *Cornwall in the Age of the Industrial Revolution* (Liverpool, 1953), p. 327.
[2] The fact that Hunt's sources seem to have been mainly on the smelting side of the industry should help to make his figures more certain on this point.

whole of that period when its statistics are the only ones available. According to Hoffman[1] the South-West produced about 85 per cent of national output at the beginning of the eighteenth century and 80 per cent in 1770. By the 1850's (and almost certainly a good deal earlier) the proportion was virtually back to that level. But the period after 1770 had seen the rise and fall of the easily won Anglesey mines, for which no returns of output were ever published. Various contemporary estimates give a rough picture of their contribution. In

Approx. date	*Output of fine copper in tons*	*Source of estimate*
1778	1,200	R. Hunt, *British Mining* (London, 1884), p. 105.
1784	3,000	*House of Commons Reports* x, p. 671.
1785	2,300	R. Hunt, *loc. cit.*
1787	4,000	Quoted in H. Hamilton, *English Brass and Copper Industries to 1800* (London, 1926), p. 180.
1795	1,900	*House of Commons Reports* x, p. 671.
1798	1,700	*ibid.*
1812	600	A. H. Dodd, *Industrial Revolution in North Wales* (Cardiff, 1933), p. 161.
1823–27	737	J. R. McCulloch, *Statistical Account of the British Empire* (London, 1854), p. 615.

terms of ore the proportion of output derived from Anglesey was much larger, since its metal content was approximately half that of Cornwall.[2]

The statistics of lead output, given in table 3, are simple, in contrast to those of tin and copper, largely because they are not available until Hunt began his *Mineral Statistics*.

There follow three tables showing the imports and exports of these three metals, Parts A of tables 5 and 6 give the exports from England and Wales only, from 1697 to 1791; but they are quite closely comparable with later figures for Great Britain and the United Kingdom. This is so much so in the case of tin that in table 4 the series is continued right through to 1938 in one table. Imports of non-ferrous metals were not very great during this early period, or indeed, until well into the nineteenth century.[3] As they become in the least substantial they are introduced in tables 4, 5, and 6, which also continue the exports statistics, so far as they are available from published sources.

These six tables give all the continuous series of statistics that are available about the three non-ferrous metals which have been historically important in this country. The

[1] W. G. Hoffman, *British Industry* 1700–1950 (English edition, Oxford, 1955), p. 232.

[2] J. Mawe, *Mineralogy of Derbyshire* (London, 1801), p. 168, stated the metal content of Anglesey ore to be $7\frac{1}{2}$ per cent. Hunt (*op. cit.*, p. 828), gives the Anglesey ore output as 64,500 tons in 1784, which represents approximately 5 per cent.

[3] It should be pointed out, however, that in the seventeenth century practically all the copper used in Britain was imported, and that for a short period in the 1730's and early 1740's imports again formed a substantial proportion.

principal gap which they leave is in the statistics of output of finished goods, and these are not available until within the last twenty years, except in the censuses of production. Additional, more detailed information—on county outputs, prices, and the direction of trade, for example—is available in the original sources cited here from the middle of the nineteenth century. There is also similar information on the fourth relatively important metal—zinc. Details about other non-ferrous metals which have sprung into prominence recently is readily available in modern *Abstracts*, *World Non-ferrous Metal Statistics*, the *Metal Bulletin*, etc.

NOTES TO PART A

[1] Sources 1199–1749—G. R. Lewis, *The Stannaries* (Cambridge, Mass., 1908), appendix J; 1750–1837—R. Hunt, *British Mining* (London, 1884), p. 887.
[2] An alternative source for 1750–1837 is 'Statistics of the Tin Mines in Cornwall and of the Consumption of Tin in Great Britain', by J. Carne, in *J.S.S.*, vol. II, p. 261. For the period 1801–11 Carne's figures differ slightly from Hunt's
[3] The figures for the years up to 1749 are for the twelve months ended Michaelmas.

A. Tin Paying Coinage Dues, 1199–1837

(output in tons of 2,240 lb. value in £000)

	Output of White Tin		Output of White Tin		Output of White Tin
1199	483	1549	637	1638	536
1200	432			1639	539
1201	433	1553	866	1640	537
		1554	800	1641	513
1206	325	1555	753	1642	543
		1556	750	1643	363
1209	328			1644	122
		1561	715	1645	316
1211	436			1646	157
1212	537	1563	596	1647	193
		1564	679	1648	4
1214	642	1565	648		
		1566	671	1667	911
1301	329	1567	749		
		1568	522	1669	706
1303	459	1569	747	1670	778
		1570	571	1671	890
1355	266	1571	515	1672	793
		1572	509	1673	956
1379	485	1573	549	1674	635
		1574	530	1675	1,115
1400	854	1575	584	1676	1,122
		1576	642	1677	1,344
1412	757	1577	659	1678	1,308
		1578	573	1679	1,061
1435	469	1579	634	1680	1,161
		1580	734	1681	1,181
1443	453	1581	683	1682	1,364
		1582	673	1683	1,407
1448	566	1583	...	1684	1,212
		1584	651	1685	1,370
1450	487	1585	666	1686	1,543
		1586	656	1687	1,460
1455	429	1587	639	1688	1,400
		1588	665	1689	1,493
1469	540	1589	615	1690	1,268
		1590	632	1691	1,309
1472	586	1591	686	1692	1,233
		1592	708	1693	1,268
1477	476	1593	634	1694	1,197
1478	547	1594	686	1695	1,259
		1595	727	1696	1,195
1489	565	1596	658	1697	1,068
		1597	560	1698	1,258
1495	702	1598	476	1699	1,433
1496	662	1599	541	1700	1,428
		1600	571	1701	1,376
1504	680	1601	644	1702	1,114
		1602	738	1703	1,610
		1603	589	1704	1,490
1517	898	1604	617	1705	1,407
1518	903	1605	593	1706	1,484
		1606	561	1707	1,464
1524	895	1607	550	1708	1,454
		1608	580	1709	1,428
1530	906	1609	557	1710	2,176
		1610	547	1711	1,437
1540	905	1611	587	1712	1,439
		1612	582	1713	1.356
1544	796	1613	610	1714	1,112
1545	866	1614	622	1715	1,189
				1716	1,086
1547	928	1625	751	1717	1,655

(output in tons of 2,240 lb. value in £000)

Year	Output of White Tin		Year	Output of White Tin		Year	Output of White Tin
1718	1,631		1724	1,603		1730	1,546
1719	...		1725	1,663		1731	...
1720	1,477		1726	1,515		1732	1,861
1721	1,145		1727	1,593		1733	1,628
1722	1,396		1728	1,462		1734	1,837
1723	1,379		1729	1,585		1735	1,760

Year	Output of White Tin	Value of White Tin		Year	Output of White Tin	Value of White Tin
1736	1,547	...		1788	3,352	156
1737	1,686	...		1789	3,405	213
1738	1,351	...		1790	3,193	232
1739	1,784	...		1791	3,470	274
1740	1,694	...		1792	3,809	352
1741	1,546	...		1793	3,202	314
1742	1,784	...		1794	3,351	320
1743	1,890	...		1795	3,440	320
1744	1,872	...		1796	3,061	295
1745	1,735	...		1797	3,240	314
1746	1,917	...		1798	2,820	265
1747	1,843	...		1799	2,862	278
1748	2,004	...		1800	2,522	255
1749	1,154	...		1801	2,328	244
1750	2,876	187		1802	2,627	285
1751	2,273	148		1803	2,914	318
1752	2,550	171		1804	2,993	326
1753	2,516	171		1805	2,742	308
1754	2,724	185		1806	2,855	344
1755	2,757	185		1807	2,426	285
1756	2,774	174		1808	2,330	266
1757	2,752	163		1809	2,508	306
1758	2,720	154		1810	2,006	315
1759	2,637	148		1811	2,384	337
1760	2,717	152		1812	2,373	304
1761	2,395	143		1813	2,324	311
1762	2,584	167		1814	2,611	409
1763	2,736	188		1815	2,941	413
1764	2,618	181		1816	3,348	383
1765	2,757	190		1817	4,120	385
1766	3,055	211		1818	4,066	345
1767	2,850	197		1819	3,315	250
1768	2,667	184		1820	2,990	219
1769	2,898	200		1821	3,373	255
1770	2,977	198		1822	3,278	313
1771	2,823	184		1823	4,213	399
1772	3,159	200		1824	5,005	458
1773	2,852	154		1825	4,358	398
1774	2,458	129		1826	4,603	354
1775	2,619	157		1827	5,555	422
1776	2,652	159		1828	4,931	361
1777	2,770	165		1829	4,434	328
1778	2,515	152		1830	4,444	328
1779	2,678	161		1831	4,300	316
1780	2,926	179		1832	4,323	315
1781	2,610	165		1833	4,065	296
1782	2,546	178		1834	3,989	311
1783	2,570	180		1835	4,228	387
1784	2,685	189		1836	4,054	444
1785	2,885	208		1837	4,790	422
1786	3,399	245				
1787	3,204	231				

NOTES TO PART B

[1] SOURCES: 1848–53—R. Hunt, *British Mining* (London, 1884), p. 889; 1854–1920—*Mineral Statistics*; 1921–38— *Annual Report* of the Department of Mines.

B. Output 1848–1938 (output in tons; value in £000)

	Tin Ore		White Tin				Tin Ore		White Tin	
	Output	Value	Output	Value			Output	Value	Output	Value
1848	10,176	...	...	...		1894	12,910	488	8,327	605
1849	10,719	...	...	...		1895	10,612	371	6,648	447
1850	10,383	...	...	...		1896	7,663	260	4,838	308
1851	9,455	...	...	...		1897	7,120	254	4,453	291
1852	9,672	...	...	...		1898	7,380	288	4,648	346
1853	8,866	...	5,763	...		1899	6,392	441	4,013	508
1854	8,747	560	5,974	690		1900	6,800	524	4,268	588
1855	8,952	609	6,000	720		1901	7,288	479	4,560	557
1856	9,350	664	6,177	822		1902	7,560	514	4,392	532
1857	9,708	748	6,582	895		1903	7,382	532	4,282	544
1858	9,959	634	6,920	823		1904	6,742	480	4,132	531
1859	10,180	738	7,100	929		1905	7,201	574	4,468	642
1860	10,462	749	6,695	871		1906	7,153	713	4,522	819
1861	11,640	726	7,450	911		1907	7,080	707	4,407	769
1862	14,127	843	8,476	983		1908	8,008	595	5,052	676
1863	15,157	964	10,006	1,171		1909	8,289	617	5,199	696
1864	15,211	926	10,108	1,082		1910	7,572	656	4,797	738
1865	15,686	867	10,039	971		1911	7,746	838	4,872	932
1866	15,080	732	9,990	885		1912	8,166	1,012	5,254	1,117
1867	13,649	695	8,700	799		1913	8,355	960	5,288	1,081
1868	13,953	770	9,300	901		1914	8,085	662	5,056	801
1869	14,725	1,028	9,760	1,201		1915	8,145	669	4,968	816
1870	15,234	1,002	10,200	1,300		1916	7,892	712	4,697	856
1871	16,272	1,031	10,900	1,499		1917	6,576	784	3,936	935
1872	14,266	1,246	9,560	1,460		1918	6,378	1,116	3,954	1,303
1873	14,885	1,057	9,972	1,330		1919	5,156	679	3,272	842
1874	14,039	788	9,942	1,078		1920	4,858	783	3,065	907
1875	13,995	736	9,614	866		1921	1,078	92	679	112
1876	13,688	601	8,500	676		1922	650	50	370	59
1877	14,142	573	9,500	695		1923	1,760	176	1,021	207
1878	15,045	531	10,106	663		1924	3,547	420	1,986	494
1879	14,665	587	9,532	689		1925	4,032	532	2,339	613
1880	13,738	673	8,918	814		1926	3,878	571	2,327	677
1881	12,898	997	8,615	840		1927	4,321	621	2,593	749
1882	14,045	806	9,158	977		1928	4,844	532	2,761	627
1883	14,469	735	9,307	903		1929	5,640	587	3,271	667
1884	15,117	669	9,574	810		1930	4,146	318	2,488	353
1885	14,376	662	9,331	834		1931	920	59	598	71
1886	14,232	780	9,312	944		1932	2,025	157	1,337	182
1887	14,189	879	9,282	1,049		1933	2,337	272	1,543	300
1888	14,370	895	9,241	1,084		1934	3,224	405	1,999	461
1889	13,809	729	8,912	860		1935	3,535	396	2,050	463
1890	14,911	782	9,602	938		1936	3,558	382	2,099	430
1891	14,488	735	9,353	881		1937	3,367	435	1,987	482
1892	14,357	735	9,270	895		1938	3,172	349	1,999	379
1893	13,689	637	8,837	786						

NOTES

[1] SOURCES: 1726–71 (including decennial averages of value 1726–75)—W. Pryce, *Mineralogia Cornubiensis* (London, 1772), p. XV; 1771–1837—Sir Charles Lemon, 'The Statistics of the Copper Mines of Cornwall', in *J.S.S.*, vol. I, p. 70; 1838–52 (except value)—R. Hunt, *British Mining* (London, 1884), p. 892; 1845–47 (value)—*Memoirs of the Geological Survey*, vol. II, part 2, p. 703; 1848–52 (value)—*Records of the*

School of Mines, vol. I, part IV; 1853–85—*Minera Statistics*.
[2] The quantity and value of copper mined in the United Kingdom was of no significance after 1885, though he mining of ore did not finally cease until 1921, and a little metallic copper was derived from precipitate for some years after that.

(in thousands of tons and £000)

	Copper Ore Sold at Public Ticketings in Cornwall and Devon	Value of Copper Ore Sold Publicly in Cornwall and Devon
1726	5·0	
1727	6·7	
1728	6·8	
1729	6·9	
1730	6·9	
		474
1731	7·0	
1732	7·3	
1733	7·0	
1734	6·0	
1735	5·2	
1736	8·0	
1737	9·0	
1738	10·0	
1739	11·0	
1740	5·0	
		560
1741	5·5	
1742	6·1	
1743	7·0	
1744	7·2	
1745	6·7	
1746	7·0	
1747	4·9	
1748	6·0	
1749	7·2	
1750	9·4	
		731
1751	11·0	
1752	12·1	
1753	13·0	
1754	14·0	
1755	14·2	
1756	16·0	
1757	17·0	
1758	15·0	
1759	16·7	
1760	15·8	
		1,243
1761	17·0	
1762	16·1	
1763	17·9	
1764	21·5	
1765	16·8	

(in thousands of tons and £000)

	Copper Ore Sold at Public Ticketings in Cornwall and Devon	Value of Copper Ore Sold Publicly in Cornwall and Devon	Metallic Copper from Ore Sold Publicly in Cornwall and Devon
1766	21·3	...	...
1767	18·5	...	...
1768	23·7	...	...
1769	26·7	...	...
1770	30·8	...	...
		1,778 {	...
1771	27·9	190	3·3
1772	27·7	190	3·4
1773	27·8	148	3·3
1774	30·3	162	3·6
1775	30·0	192	3·6
1776	29·4	192	3·5
1777	28·2	177	3·4
1778	24·7	141	3·0
1779	31·1	181	3·7
1780	24·4	171	2·9
1781	28·7	179	3·5
1782	28·1	152	3·4
1783	35·8	220	4·3
1784	36·6	209	4·4
1785	37·0	205	4·4
1786	39·9	237	4·8
1787	38·0	191	...
1788	31·5	150	...
1789	33·3	184	...
1790	...	...	...
1791	...	...	...
1792	...	...	...
1793	...	...	...
1794	42·8	321	...
1795	43·6	326	...
1796	43·3	357	5·0
1797	47·9	378	5·2
1798	51·4	423	5·6
1799	51·3	470	4·9
1800	56·0	551	5·2
1801	56·6	476	5·3
1802	53·9	445	5·2
1803	60·6	534	5·6
1804	64·6	508	5·4
1805	78·5	862	6·2
1806	79·3	731	6·9
1807	71·7	609	6·7
1808	67·9	495	6·8
1809	76·2	770	6·8
1810	66·0	570	5·7

Tin, Copper and Lead 2. *continued*

(in thousands of tons and £000)

	Copper Ore Sold at Public Ticketings in Cornwall and Devon	Value of Copper Ore Sold Publicly in Cornwall and Devon	Metallic Copper from Ore Sold Publicly in Cornwall and Devon
1811	66·8	557	6·1
1812	71·5	550	6·7
1813	74·0	594	6·9
1814	74·3	628	6·4
1815	78·5	553	6·5
1816	77·3	448	6·7
1817	76·7	494	6·5
1818	86·2	686	6·8
1819	88·7	624	6·8
1820	91·5	602	7·5
1821	98·4	606	8·5
1822	104·5	663	9·1
1823	95·8	608	7·9
1824	99·7	587	7·8
1825	107·5	726	8·2
1826	117·3	789	9·0
1827	126·7	745	10·3
1828	130·4	756	9·9
1829	124·5	717	9·7
1830	135·7	784	10·9
1831	146·5	818	12·2
1832	139·1	836	12·1
1833	138·3	859	11·2
1834	143·3	888	11·2
1835	150·6	896	12·3
1836	141·0	958	11·6
1837	140·8	909	10·8
1838	145·7	...	11·5
1839	159·6	...	12·5
1840	147·3	...	11·0
1841	147·8	...	10·0
1842	154·2	...	9·9
1843	153·7	...	10·9
1844	152·7	...	11·2
1845	162·6	920	12·9
1846	150·4	796	11·9
1847	148·7	889	12·0
1848	155·6	720	12·9
1849	145·0	764	12·1
1850	150·9	840	11·8
1851	154·3	783	12·2
1852	152·8	976	11·7
1853	180·1	1,155	11·8

Tin, Copper and Lead 2. *continued*

(in thousands of tons and £000)

	Copper Ore Sold at Public Ticketings in Cornwall and Devon			Copper Ore Raised in the U.K.		Metal from U.K. Copper Ore	
	Output	Value	Metallic Content	Output	Value	Output	Value
1854	184·9	1,193	12·0	298·0	1,484	19·9	2,487
1855	195·2	1,264	12·6	320·5	1,640	21·3	3,043
1856	206·2	1,242	13·5	361·3	1,745	24·3	2,984
1857	192·1	1,201	12·2	250·9	1,561	17·4	2,155
1858	183·4	1,058	12·1	226·9	1,337	14·5	1,563
1859	183·5	1,096	12·2	236·8	1,507	15·8	1,735
1860	182·5	1,065	12·2	236·7	1,507	16·0	1,706
1861	...	...	...	231·5	1,365	15·3	1,572
1862	...	...	...	224·2	1,217	14·8	1,493
1863	...	...	...	210·9	1,101	14·2	1,410
1864	...	...	...	214·6	1,156	13·3	1,351
1865	...	...	...	198·3	928	11·9	1,135
1866	...	...	...	180·4	759	11·2	1,019
1867	...	...	...	158·5	700	10·2	832
1868	...	...	...	157·3	642	9·8	762
1869	...	...	...	130·0	520	8·3	644
1870	...	...	...	106·7	438	7·2	551
1871	...	...	...	97·1	387	6·3	475
1872	...	...	...	91·9	444	5·7	583
1873	...	...	...	80·2	343	5·2	503
1874	...	...	...	78·5	336	4·9	443
1875	...	...	...	71·5	333	4·6	413
1876	...	...	...	79·3	317	4·7	391
1877	...	...	...	73·1	262	4·5	340
1878	...	...	...	56·1	201	4·0	271
1879	...	...	...	51·0	177	3·5	223
1880	...	...	...	52·1	191	3·7	253
1881	...	...	...	52·6	190	3·9	264
1882	...	...	...	52·8	207	3·5	253
1883	...	...	...	46·3	146	2·6	181
1884	...	...	...	41·7	109	3·4	203
1885	...	...	...	36·2	80	2·8	135

Tin, Copper and Lead 3. Output and Value of Lead—United Kingdom 1845–1938

NOTES

[1] SOURCES: 1845–47—*Memoirs of the Geological Survey of Great Britain*, vol. II, part II, p. 703; 1848–52—*Records of the School of Mines*, vol. I, part IV; 1853–1921—*Mineral Statistics*; 1922–38—*Annual Report of the Department of Mines*.

[2] The output of the Isle of Man is included throughout. The exclusion of southern Ireland after 1921 does not affect the figures.

(in thousands of tons and £000)

	Lead Ore		Metallic Lead			Lead Ore		Metallic Lead	
	Output	Value	Output	Value		Output	Value	Output	Value
1845	78·3	...	52·7	...	1892	40·0	296	29·5	318
1846	74·6	...	50·2	...	1893	40·8	281	29·7	292
1847	83·7	...	55·7	...	1894	40·6	267	29·7	285
1848	77·9	...	54·9	...	1895	38·4	273	29·0	309
1849	86·8	...	58·7	...	1896	41·1	303	30·8	351
1850	93·0	...	64·5	...	1897	35·3	275	26·6	333
1851	102·0	...	65·1	...	1898	33·0	267	25·4	333
1852	91·2	...	65·0	...	1899	31·0	297	23·6	355
1853	85·1	...	61·0	...	1900	32·0	349	24·4	419
1854	90·6	1,111	64·0	1,498	1901	28·0	224	20·0	255
1855	92·3	1,312	65·5	1,517	1902	24·6	176	17·7	199
1856	102·0	1,432	73·1	1,755	1903	26·6	202	20·0	235
1857	94·4	1,428	67·4	1,524	1904	26·4	206	19·8	240
1858	95·9	1,371	68·3	1,489	1905	27·6	245	20·6	286
1859	91·4	1,257	63·2	1,406	1906	30·8	341	22·3	392
1860	88·7	1,232	63·3	1,413	1907	32·5	419	24·5	480
1861	90·7	1,136	65·6	1,445	1908	29·2	259	21·0	288
1862	95·3	1,194	69·0	1,436	1909	29·7	259	22·5	299
1863	91·3	1,194	68·2	1,419	1910	28·5	232	21·5	283
1864	94·5	1,350	67·1	1,449	1911	23·9	219	18·0	254
1865	90·5	1,153	67·2	1,433	1912	25·4	296	19·2	350
1866	91·1	1,161	67·4	1,382	1913	24·3	294	18·1	342
1867	93·4	1,158	68·4	1,338	1914	26·0	310	19·4	372
1868	95·2	1,151	71·0	1,378	1915	20·7	295	15·5	355
1869	96·9	1,189	73·3	1,397	1916	17·1	339	12·6	389
1870	98·2	1,200	73·4	1,453	1917	15·3	286	11·3	338
1871	94·0	1,156	69·1	1,252	1918	14·8	273	10·9	329
1872	81·6	1,114	60·4	1,208	1919	13·9	256	10·3	290
1873	73·5	1,132	54·2	1,263	1920	15·4	325	11·0	419
1874	76·2	1,024	58·8	1,298	1921	6·8	86	5·2	117
1875	77·7	1,202	57·4	1,290	1922	11·1	151	8·4	200
1876	79·1	1,218	58·7	1,270	1923	12·5	207	9·5	254
1877	80·9	1,124	61·4	1,263	1924	14·3	302	10·9	374
1878	77·4	801	58·0	972	1925	15·6	348	11·8	432
1879	66·9	689	51·6	765	1926	19·1	368	14·5	449
1880	72·2	816	56·9	954	1927	20·4	296	15·5	375
1881	64·7	657	48·6	729	1928	18·8	230	14·1	297
1882	65·0	593	50·3	723	1929	23·3	306	17·7	411
1883	56·5	475	43·4	560	1930	25·4	258	19·3	349
1884	54·5	402	40·1	453	1931	29·5	191	22·4	291
1885	51·3	408	37·7	433	1932	40·6	242	31·3	372
1886	53·4	471	39·5	523	1933	49·1	303	37·7	441
1887	51·6	429	37·9	487	1934	68·1	397	51·1	559
1888	51·3	438	37·6	523	1935	52·9	451	39·2	558
1889	48·5	430	35·6	464	1936	39·1	423	29·0	510
1890	45·7	406	33·6	450	1937	33·4	496	25·1	585
1891	43·9	357	32·2	401	1938	38·1	355	28·3	431

Tin, Copper and Lead 4. Overseas Trade in Tin—England & Wales 1697–1791, Great Britain 1792–1844, and United Kingdom 1845–1938

A. Exports of Tin Blocks, etc.—England & Wales 1697–1791 and Great Britain 1792–1938

NOTES TO PART A

SOURCES: 1697–1808—Elizabeth B. Schumpeter, *English Overseas Trade Statistics, 1697–1708* (Oxford University Press, 1960), tables VIII and IX (converted into tons); 1815–39 —returns in sessional papers annually from 1817; 1840–1920—*Abstract*; 1921–38—*Annual Statement of Trade.*

(in 000 tons)

1697 (a)	0·9	1742	1·5	1787	2·5	1832	1·6
1698	1·3	1743	1·2	1788	2·3	1833	1·2
1699	1·2	1744	1·4	1789	2·2	1834	0·5
1700	1·4	1745	1·5	1790	2·9	1835	0·4
1701	1·3	1746	1·8	1791	1·9	1836	0·6
1702	0·9	1747	1·6	1792	2·9 (c)	1837	0·9
1703	1·0	1748	1·5	1793	2·0	1838	1·3
1704	0·9	1749	1·6	1794	2·3	1839	1·5
1705	...	1750	1·8	1795	2·5	1840	1·8
1706	1·2	1751	1·8	1796	2·8	1841	1·2
1707	0·9	1752	1·9	1797	1·8	1842	3·1
1708	1·4	1753	1·6	1798	2·2	1843	1·8
1709	1·1	1754	1·8	1799	1·7	1844	1·1
1710	3·4	1755	1·7	1800	1·8	1845	0·6
1711	0·5	1756	1·6	1801	1·7	1846	1·2
1712	...	1757	1·6	1802	1·8	1847	1·7
1713	0·7	1758	1·6	1803	1·5	1848	1·8
1714	1·2	1759	1·7	1804	1·9	1849	1·8
1715	1·3	1760	1·9	1805	2·1	1850	1·6
1716	0·7	1761	1·4	1806	1·1	1851	1·0
1717	1·1	1762	1·5	1807	1·6	1852	0·9
1718	1·1	1763	2·2	1808	1·3	1853	1·3
1719	1·8	1764	1·7	1809	...	1854	1·4
1720	1·0	1765	2·1	1810	...	1855 (e)	1·3
1721	1·0	1766	2·0	1811	...	1856	1·9
1722	0·9	1767	2·0	1812	...	1857	2·2
1723	1·3	1768	1·8	1813	...	1858	2·3
1724	1·2	1769	2·0	1814	...	1859	2·8
1725	0·8	1770	1·8	1815	1·2 (d)	1860	2·7
1726	1·3	1771	2·0	1816	1·7	1861	2·8
1727	1·4	1772 (b)	1·3	1817	2·4	1862	4·1
1728	1·2	1773	1·5	1818	1·7	1863	4·4
1729	1·3	1774	2·1	1819	1·4	1864	4·4
1730	1·4	1775	1·7	1820	1·3	1865	5·2
1731	1·2	1776	2·3	1821	1·4	1866	4·3
1732	1·5	1777	2·5	1822	1·8	1867	4·2
1733	1·3	1778	1·3	1823	1·1	1868	4·0
1734	1·4	1779	2·0	1824	1·8	1869	5·1
1735	1·6	1780	2·7	1825	1·6	1870	5·1
1736	1·1	1781	1·7	1826	2·2	1871	5·7
1737	1·5	1782	1·8	1827	2·5	1872	5·7
1738	1·4	1783	1·8	1828	2·1	1873	5·8
1739	1·4	1784	1·7	1829	1·7	1874	7·7
1740	1·4	1785	2·0	1830	1·5	1875	5·2
1741	1·5	1786	2·4	1831	1·1	1876	5·0

See p. 162 for footnotes

Tin, Copper and Lead 4. *continued*

(in 000 tons)

Year		Year		Year		Year	
1877	6·1	1893	6·7	1909	11·2	1924	18·1
1878	6·2	1894	5·9	1910	12·4	1925	25·8
1879	6·2	1895	5·7	1911	11·6	1926	27·4
1880	4·4	1896	6·2	1912	12·0	1927	27·1
1881	4·8	1897	5·0	1913	11·5	1928	23·5
1882	5·5	1898	5·5	1914	13·4	1929	30·4
1883	5·4	1899	4·7	1915	14·2	1930	22·9
1884	5·5	1900	5·6	1916	18·0	1931	12·1
1885	4·7	1901	5·5	1917	19·3	1932	12·8
1886	4·7	1902	6·1	1918	15·2	1933	29·2
1887	4·9	1903	6·2	1919	14·6	1934	16·9
1888	6·0	1904	5·9	1920	13·3	1935	23·0
1889	5·4	1905	7·6	1921	9·9	1936	15·4
1890	5·1	1906	8·5	1922	12·6	1937	14·8
1891	5·2	1907	8·7	1923	20·0 (f)	1938	12·3
1892	5·6	1908	9·3				

(a) Year ended 5th January following henceforth to 1855.
(b) The change in original source from the *Inspector General's Ledgers* to the *States of Navigation and Commerce* makes no discernible break in this series.
(c) The change from English to British statistics almost certainly occasioned no break in this series.

(d) Prior to 1815 Ireland was treated as a foreign country.
(e) Calendar year henceforth.
(f) Southern Ireland was treated as foreign from 1st April 1923.

Tin, Copper and Lead 4. *continued*

B. Imports and Re-exports, United Kingdom, 1845–1938

NOTES TO PART B

SOURCES: 1845–1920—*Abstract*; 1921–38—*Annual Statement of Trade*.

(in ooo tons)

Year	Imports Ore	Imports Blocks, etc.	Re-exports Blocks, etc.	Year	Imports Ore	Imports Blocks, etc.	Re-exports Blocks, etc.
1845 (a)		1·3	0·9	1892	3·5	29·5	16·4
1846		1·0	1·1	1893	3·0	33·6	19·1
1847		1·2	0·6	1894	4·4	39·1	21·5
1848		0·3	0·4	1895	4·7	41·6	20·7
1849		1·8	0·4	1896	4·9	38·4	18·7
1850		1·7	0·2	1897	5·3	26·8	14·8
1851		2·6	0·2	1898	5·6	20·3	15·6
1852		2·4	0·4	1899	6·2	27·2	16·9
1853		2·5	1·1	1900	7·3	33·1	19·8
1854		2·3	0·7	1901	10·5	35·4	20·9
1855 (b)		1·6	0·3	1902	12·1	35·2	23·0
1856		3·5	0·2	1903	12·3	35·5	23·8
1857		2·7	0·4	1904	15·5	39·3	27·2
1858		3·0	0·3	1905	17·8	39·8	29·2
1859		2·7	0·4	1906	20·7	43·6	32·3
1860		2·9	0·5	1907	20·9	43·8	26·8
1861		3·7	1·0	1908	25·0	47·7	32·8
1862		4·4	1·1	1909	24·1	41·7	30·2
1863	negligible	2·7	1·1	1910	26·1	46·3	31·5
1864		4·9	1·4	1911	28·8	45·9	34·0
1865		5·7	2·0	1912	28·7	43·2	32·7
1866		5·5	1·1	1913	34·6	45·7	30·2
1867		5·4	1·3	1914	32·4	41·0	30·8
1868		5·7	1·1	1915	44·7	38·9	23·4
1869		5·4	1·1	1916	33·9	33·6	17·5
1870		4·7	1·1	1917	41·2	27·1	18·1
1871		8·6	2·1	1918	32·3	12·6	4·2
1872		8·3	2·4	1919	35·7	22·9	9·9
1873		7·8	1·4	1920	33·8	28·7	13·6
1874		9·2	2·4	1921	21·6	21·0	15·0
1875		16·8	4·2	1922	38·7	24·7	15·5
1876		15·2	5·3	1923	52·3 (c)	14·2 (c)	8·8 (c)
1877		13·8	3·9	1924	59·3	16·9	11·0
1878		16·6	6·6	1925	64·1	15·9	9·5
1879		16·8	9·0	1926	63·3	13·8	8·8
1880		19·5	8·7	1927	64·3	14·0	4·7
1881		20·3	10·0	1928	81·3	16·4	7·7
1882		24·3	12·4	1929	92·8	14·7	11·9
1883	1·2	26·1	14·2	1930	76·5	11·8	7·5
1884	1·1	26·1	14·7	1931	60·5	12·2	5·3
1885	0·9	25·5	12·1	193⁻	47·2	4·2	2·0
1886	0·7	24·1	14·4	1933	27·4	3·4	0·9
1887	1·4	25·9	12·0	1934	38·6	10·2	2·8
1888	2·4	28·1	18·6	1935	45·2	15·1	6·8
1889	2·0	30·1	17·5	1936	52·0	12·0	6·8
1890	2·7	27·0	14·8	1937	50·9	21·5	13·2
1891	2·3	28·2	14·6	1938	55·5	11·7	4·4

(a) Year ended 5th January following.
(b) Calendar year henceforth.

(c) Southern Ireland was treated as foreign from 1st April 1923.

Tin, Copper and Lead 5. Imports and Exports of Copper and Brass—England & Wales 1697–1791, Great Britain 1792–1811, and United Kingdom 1816–1938

A. Exports from England & Wales in Tons, 1697–1791

NOTES TO PART A

[1] SOURCE: Elizabeth B. Schumpeter, *English Overseas Trade Statistics*, 1697–1808 (Oxford University Press, 1960), tables VIII and IX (converted into tons).

[2] Exports to Ireland are included in this part.

	Unwrought Copper	Wrought Copper	Brass of All Kinds		Unwrought Copper	Wrought Copper	Brass of All Kinds
1697	…	35	37	1745	…	175	451
1698	…	45	85	1746	…	235	582
1699	…	49	81	1747	…	194	592
1700	…	82	87	1748	…	246	707
1701	…	75	62	1749	…	351	855
1702	…	43	54	1750	…	377	1,001
1703	…	50	48	1751	…	361	733
1704	…	35	40	1752	…	354	697
1705	…	…	…	1753	…	568	894
1706	…	33	29	1754	…	408	873
1707	…	22	38	1755	…	394	692
1708	…	16	170	1756	…	452	713
1709	…	32	38	1757	…	462	688
1710	…	51	49	1758	…	405	723
1711	…	46	50	1759	…	383	904
1712	…	…	…	1760	…	591	989
1713	…	85	81	1761	…	804	991
1714	…	107	102	1762	…	1,004	931
1715	…	109	98	1763	…	917	1,176
1716	…	125	98	1764	…	1,091	1,516
1717	…	118	118	1765	…	972	1,379
1718	…	76	103	1766	…	925	1,136
1719	…	76	106	1767	…	1,128	1,567
1720	…	59	99	1768	…	1,086	1,544
1721	…	49	116	1769	…	1,259	1,513
1722	…	62	112	1770	…	1,246	1,601
1723	…	85	122	1771	…	1,200	1,887
1724	…	99	128	1772	—	1,291 (a)	1,844 (a)
1725	…	100	169	1773	—	1,437	1,761
1726	…	87	156	1774	—	1,321	1,559
1727	…	85	154	1775	298	1,616	1,693
1728	…	123	197	1776	191	1,308	1,376
1729	…	130	242	1777	8	963	1,144
1730	…	173	263	1778	3	1,282	1,191
1731	…	148	281	1779	771	1,066	730
1732	…	131	306	1780	630	1,735	611
1733	…	139	265	1781	283	1,074	524
1734	…	107	237	1782	734	3,006	1,525
1735	…	136	306	1783	385	2,344	1,082
1736	…	116	389	1784	362	1,392	1,160
1737	…	186	349	1785	717	1,479	973
1738	…	261	427	1786	658	1,984	1,140
1739	…	164	420	1787	637	1,925	1,101
1740	…	157	345	1788	923	2,849	1,285
1741	…	247	431	1789	446	2,432	1,627
1742	…	286	483	1790	150	3,033	1,953
1743	…	329	601	1791	298	3,036	2,357
1744	…	332	462				

(a) This break is caused by a change in the original source. Its size can be judged by the following figures from the old source for 1775 and 1780:

	Wrought Copper	Brass		Wrought Copper	Brass
1775	1,616	1,629	1780	1,735	614

B. Exports from Great Britain in thousands of tons, 1792–1811

NOTES TO PART B

[1] Sources: 1792–1808—Elizabeth B. Schumpeter, *English Overseas Trade Statistics 1697–1808* (Oxford University Press, 1960), table IX (converted into tons); 1809–11—returns published in sessional papers.

[2] Exports to Ireland are included in this part.

	Unwrought Copper	Wrought and Part-wrought Copper	Brass
1792	2·7	4·1	3·2
1793	0·5	4·4	3·6
1794	0·2	4·5	3·1
1795	0·2	4·1	3·1
1796	2·0	4·4	3·2
1797	1·0	3·7	2·5
1798	0·4	3·9	2·4
1799	0·1	4·9	3·9
1800	—	4·8	4·7
1801	—	4·8	4·1
1802	—	6·3	4·6
1803	—	4·6	3·6
1804	—	2·9	1·3
1805	—	3·0	1·0
1806	—	2·3	0·8
1807	—	3·4	0·6
1808	—	3·0	0·4
1809	—	3·3	...
1810	—	2·8	...
1811	—	2·3	...

C. United Kingdom Imports and Exports in thousands of tons 1816–1938

NOTES TO PART C

[1] Sources: 1816–39—returns in *Sessional Papers* from time to time prior to 1817 and annually thereafter; 1840–1920—*Abstract* (supplemented by annual returns to 1886 and *Mineral Statistics* thereafter); 1921–38—*Annual Statement of Trade*.

[2] Up to and including 1841 most imported ore was smelted in bond and re-exported, the quantities retained being insignificant. In 1842, when import duty was abolished, 16,000 tons were retained, and thenceforward almost all imported ores were retained.

	Imports		Re-exports	Exports		
	Ore (a)	Unwrought and Part-wrought Copper	Unwrought and Part-wrought Copper	Unwrought Copper	Wrought and Part-wrought Copper	Brass
1816 (b)				0·9	4·2	...
1817				1·2	5·4	...
1818				1·0	5·0	...
1819				1·9	2·9	...
1820				2·1	3·1	...
1821	negligible	negligible	negligible	1·7	3·2	...
1822				1·3	4·4	...
1823				1·2	3·9	...
1824				1·0	4·0	...
1825				—	3·6	...
1826				0·1	4·7	...
1827				1·3	5·8	...
1828				1·1	5·1	...
1829	1			2·7	5·3	...
1830	1			3·2	6·2	...

See p. 168 for footnotes

| | | Imports | Re-exports | Exports | | |
	Ore (a)	Unwrought and Part-wrought Copper	Unwrought and Part-wrought Copper	Unwrought Copper	Wrought and Part-wrought Copper	Brass
1831	2			3·7	5·2	...
1832	4			4·6	5·9	...
1833	6			4·0	5·4	...
1834	7			5·3	4·9	...
1835	14			5·9	5·9	...
1836	18	negligible	negligible	3·9	6·1	...
1837	19			6·8	5·5	...
1838	27			7·4	5·6	...
1839	30			6·5	6·9	...
1840	42			8·7	6·5	0·4
1841	49			10·5	5·5	0·3
1842	50			12·4	7·0	0·4
1843	56			8·7	9·1	0·4
1844	60	1·5	1·3	8·7	10·1	0·6
1845	57	0·1	0·3	9·8	8·3	0·6
1846	52	0·6	0·5	7·3	8·4	0·5
1847	41	0·8	0·7	5·8	9·3	0·7
1848	50	1·6	0·3	4·3	9·2	0·7
1849	47	2·6	0·6	7·4	13·1	1·2
1850	46	4·9	0·8	7·7	13·6	1·3
1851	42	5·0	1·3	5·6	11·9	1·0
1852	43	5·2	1·0	5·9	11·0	0·9
1853	50	5·2	1·6	4·8	10·9	0·9
1854	57	3·2	1·8	3·0	10·6	0·9
1855 (c)	67	8·0	1·0	5·1	11·5	0·8
1856	83	3·8	1·3	6·1	15·8	1·0
1857	95	6·4	2·1	7·1	17·0	1·1
1858	97	6·4	2·3	6·7	18·1	1·3
1859	85	10·9	2·4	6·3	16·4	1·3
1860	97	11·8	3·7	7·0	19·1	1·8
1861	95	15·8	3·9	4·4	17·4	1·0
1862	117	13·4	8·7	5·1	22·8	1·9
1863	102	12·2	6·3	12·8	30·3	2·4
1864	93	24·9	9·0	6·0	30·9	2·1
1865	122	21·7	9·3	5·6	26·0	2·2
1866	130	21·0	14·1	6·0	22·5	2·1
1867	103	29·7	14·2	9·6	28·1	2·3
1868	114	35·2	20·9	8·2	30·0	2·1
1869	111	31·5	12·1	12·1	30·5	2·7
1870	107	29·5	14·5	10·7	27·7	2·9
1871	76	32·2	17·3	14·2	25·4	3·5
1872	72	47·7	12·4	14·8	19·6	3·5
1873	79	34·5	20·4	13·0	22·0	4·2
1874	76	37·8	24·3	10·7	24·6	5·2
1875	87	39·7	14·7	11·1	25·6	4·5
1876	103	39·2	17·3	11·9	23·6	4·7
1877	149	40·2	14·2	11·6	28·3	4·6
1878	137	39·6	12·7	17·4	27·0	4·9
1879	134	46·9	17·8	16·8	31·9	4·0
1880	146	36·6	14·9	15·4	33·5	3·8

See p. 168 for footnotes

	Imports		Re-exports	Exports		
		Unwrought and Part-wrought Copper	Unwrought and Part-wrought Copper	Unwrought Copper	Wrought and Part-wrought Copper	Brass
	Ore (a)					
1881	147	32·2	13·8	18·7	32·6	4·7
1882	152	35·2	12·8	12·7	33·8	5·0
1883	164	35·7	11·2	16·9	35·8	4·8
1884	187	39·8	10·8	17·9	40·0	5·3
1885	190	41·9	6·4	18·8	42·0	4·6
1886	152	43·1	8·6	19·0	37·8	4·3
1887	170	29·3	15·4	21·4	36·2	4·5
1888	230	43·7	32·8	25·2	14·4	3·8
1889	251	38·8	14·6	32·5	30·8	5·4
1890	216	49·5	17·0	45·0	31·1	5·3
1891	212	44·2	11·8	35·4	30·2	5·7
1892	226	35·1	11·2	42·3	30·9	5·4
1893	200	42·0	12·8	28·3	31·5	5·8
1894	162	57·1	6·5	19·5	31·2	5·5
1895	191	42·5	8·0	29·5	30·6	5·4
1896	178	61·2	9·7	23·3	26·6	6·0
1897	171	61·1	10·0	20·9	26·0	5·6
1898	165	68·9	13·2	26·7	23·8	5·3
1899	207	59·6	24·1	31·9	18·0	5·7
1900	188	71·1	18·9	18·0	19·4	6·0
1901	193	67·7	23·2	26·6	20·1	5·8
1902	162	90·9	21·5	21·3	27·0	6·3
1903	161	63·6	9·4	23·3	30·9	7·5
1904	146	89·3	7·3	14·5	34·7	8·7
1905	162	70·2	14·3	20·9	31·6	12·3
1906	171	74·3	14·8	19·4	23·0	13·4
1907	176	82·7	17·1	25·2	24·3	11·5
1908	180	120·0	19·6	14·6	34·8	10·2
1909	154	131·7	23·1	12·3	28·2	10·3
1910	167	87·9	31·1	11·9	38·3	12·9
1911	151	99·5	22·3	11·2	39·1	13·0
1912	150	95·0	14·4	13·1	30·0	14·1
1913	133	106·9	19·4	16·8	36·4	13·9
1914	114	150·5	10·8	8·8	31·3	10·5
1915	76	180·4	7·3	7·9	17·7	11·1
1916	78	111·4	7·3	10·7	9·6	11·7
1917	45	142·8	3·1	6·3	3·9	5·0
1918	36	203·9	0·7	4·6	2·7	3·9
1919	31	115·0	7·9	11·1 (d)	22·8 (d)	11·7 (d)
1920	31	111·9	16·9	14·7	25·6	49·2
1921	24	85·6	15·9	10·9	18·5	19·2
1922	33	69·2	9·9	13·6	20·9	26·3
1923	42 (e)	119·0 (e)	8·1 (e)	13·7 (e)	25·8 (e)	27·3 (e)
1924	39	151·5	5·0	5·8	27·0	31·8
1925	37	166·4	7·1	4·4	20·8	26·6

See p. 168 for footnotes

		Imports	Re-exports	Exports		
	Ore (*a*)	Unwrought and Part-wrought Copper	Unwrought and Part-wrought Copper	Unwrought Copper	Wrought and Part-wrought Copper	Brass
1926	35	130·9	7·9	18·4	20·1	22·8
1927	40	148·1	4·6	13·9	22·7	21·8
1928	46	167·3	6·7	7·3	23·0	23·5
1929	39	172·0	6·5	13·4	21·7	21·6
1930	47	173·5	5·3	8·1	19·8	16·6
1931	36	161·7	4·4	5·4	14·0	12·1
1932	33	165·7	3·8	6·2	12·1	16·0
1933	32	161·9	4·2	7·6	15·4	20·3
1934	41	277·7	7·5	11·9	25·0	26·2
1935	31	317·1	29·9	12·7	26·3	22·8
1936	31	309·0	70·3	17·0	19·3	17·7
1937	- -	411·2	98·5	13·1	24·8	21·5
1938	- -	374·0	96·3	10·5	21·9	21·8

(*a*) Includes regulus and precipitate.
(*b*) Year ended 5th January following.
(*c*) Calendar year henceforth.
(*d*) This break was occasioned by changes in the classification of commodities. The difference as regards unwrought copper was negligible. The size of the break in the other two series is indicated by the following extension backwards of the new categories:

	Wrought and Part-wrought Copper	Brass and Alloys of Copper (except Nickel)
1907	16·4	19·4
1913	22·0	23·7
1919	15·3	19·2

(*e*) Southern Ireland was treated as foreign from 1st April 1923.

Tin, Copper and Lead 6. Imports and Exports of Lead—England & Wales 1697–1791, Great Britain 1792–1808, and United Kingdom 1816–1938

A. Exports of Lead and Shot, England & Wales 1697–1791, and Great Britain 1792–1808

NOTES TO PART A

[1] SOURCE: Elizabeth B. Schumpeter, *English Overseas Trade Statistics, 1697–1808* (Oxford University Press, 1960), tables VIII and IX.

[2] There is no break in this series at the change in original source in 1772. The unit of measurement shown previously is the fodder, but this apparently equals the ton.

(in thousands of tons)

Year	Value	Year	Value	Year	Value
1697	8·0	1735	12·7	1772	15·8
1698	13·2	1736	11·8	1773	15·7
1699	11·6	1737	12·0	1774	15·8
1700	11·6	1738	12·1	1775	13·1
1701	12·9	1739	13·8	1776	13·7
1702	9·2	1740	14·5	1777	15·7
1703	11·1	1741	14·0	1778	12·2
1704	10·2	1742	11·8	1779	12·4
1705	...	1743	16·2	1780	15·3
1706	13·0	1744	9·7	1781	11·7
1707	14·7	1745	11·9	1782	14·3
1708	14·1	1746	12·8	1783	11·9
1709	10·6	1747	11·0	1784	15·8
1710	12·9	1748	11·2	1785	15·6
1711	14·1	1749	12·6	1786	18·7
1712	...	1750	14·0	1787	14·6
1713	11·6	1751	13·6	1788	12·4
1714	17·6	1752	10·9	1789	19·0
1715	10·8	1753	15·8	1790	18·4
1716	12·1	1754	13·6	1791	12·9
1717	13·6	1755	12·4	1792	14·2
1718	8·3	1756	14·9	1793	11·0
1719	10·7	1757	13·0	1794	14·1
1720	7·4	1758	12·0	1795	14·2
1721	10·0	1759	12·3	1796	11·5
1722	10·6	1760	12·0	1797	11·7
1723	9·1	1761	10·8	1798	12·2
1724	9·9	1762	13·6	1799	12·8
1725	9·4	1763	14·1	1800	10·7
1726	10·2	1764	17·4	1801	12·4
1727	12·5	1765	17·4	1802	11·8
1728	10·6	1766	17·2	1803	9·9
1729	12·3	1767	15·9	1804	11·2
1730	11·4	1768	19·3	1805	8·4
1731	12·5	1769	18·0	1806	9·4
1732	14·0	1770	17·8	1807	9·2
1733	15·1	1771	13·0	1808	7·7
1734	11·7				

B. Imports and Exports—United Kingdom 1816–1939

NOTES TO PART B

[1] SOURCES: 1816–86—returns printed annually in sessional papers; 1887–1920—*Mineral Statistics*; 1921–39—*Annual Statement of Trade*.

[2] Up to and including 1854 the figures are for years ended on 5th January in the year following that for which they are shown.

(in thousands of tons)

	Imports	Imports	Re-exports Pig and Sheet Lead	Exports Lead and Shot		Imports	Imports	Re-exports Pig and Sheet Lead	Exports Lead and Shot
	Ore	Pig and Sheet Lead				Ore	Pig and Sheet Lead		
1816				17·4	1862	3·1	23·7		34·0
1817				17·7	1863	0·9	28·6		33·6
1818				13·0	1864	3·0	30·6		33·6
1819		negligible	negligible	14·1	1865	5·6	34·9		24·8
1820				18·3	1866	10·2	36·9		27·4
1821				15·6	1867	9·1	45·2		26·7
1822				13·8	1868	11·9	49·5	negligible	41·6
1823				11·0	1869	11·9	52·7		48·4
1824		0·7	0·8	10·8	1870	12·3	58·6		47·8
1825		6·2	3·7	8·6	1871	20·9	64·9		44·5
1826		0·9	1·8	10·2	1872	14·6	69·8		44·3
1827		2·2	2·3	13·3	1873	11·7	62·6		32·0
1828	negligible	2·5	1·8	10·0	1874	15·1	62·0	4·9	36·7
1829		1·5	1·7	6·8	1875	11·9	79·8	3·2	35·4
1830		0·6	0·9	7·4	1876	12·5	80·6	6·8	35·9
1831		1·2	1·2	6·8	1877	12·9	94·5	5·4	42·5
1832		1·1	1·0	12·2	1878	15·4	100·1	2·1	34·4
1833		0·8	0·9	9·0	1879	17·7	102·1	3·7	36·8
1834		1·0	0·9	8·7	1880	14·0	95·0	4·8	33·6
1835		1·3	1·3	11·1	1881	15·2	93·6	5·4	43·0
1836		1·9	0·9	9·8	1882	15·0	87·9	2·6	37·4
1837		1·8	1·5	7·9	1883	20·2	101·7	3·5	39·3
1838		3·4	3·4	7·4	1884	29·8	109·0	3·1	33·6
1839		3·6	3·7	10·5	1885	26·7	108·0	2·9	38·5
1840		1·6	2·5	13·2	1886	34·6	107·9	7·5	42·4
1841		1·2	0·9	12·7	1887	18·0	114·5	6·2	44·3
1842		2·5	1·8	20·2	1888	17·2	132·9	10·5	48·6
1843		2·8	2·4	15·0	1889	14·3	145·2	13·2	52·0
1844		3·1	3·2	15·7	1890	19·2	158·6	15·7	55·6
1845		5·2	3·2	11·5	1891	20·6	169·7	16·0	48·2
1846		7·9	4·7	7·4	1892	18·2	182·8	15·6	58·1
1847		3·9	3·5	9·4	1893	9·9	188·2	18·8	48·9
1848		3·8	3·7	6·1	1894	15·6	161·9	13·8	47·1
1849		7·2	5·2	17·0	1895	31·7	162·9	17·7	41·7
1850		11·9	3·2	21·9	1896	56·3	167·8	12·3	41·2
1851		14·6	4·3	19·5	1897	32·3	167·4	6·9	40·3
1852	negligible	13·3	3·0	20·6	1898	24·2	194·5	16·2	38·1
1853		17·6	1·4	16·2	1899	31·9	198·4	16·7	40·3
1854		11·9		19·6	1900	31·2	195·4	13·2	36·0
1855		7·2		22·2	1901	44·0	218·1	12·9	37·6
1856		10·3		23·1	1902	39·0	231·8	9·3	33·0
1857		12·8		19·3 (a)	1903	16·8	229·3	11·0	35·6
1858		14·1	negligible	17·6	1904	8·6	246·5	20·9	35·0
1859		23·6		18·4	1905	9·4	229·5	18·9	41·5
1860		22·2		22·0	1906	8·7	208·3	13·5	44·9
1861		23·1		17·5	1907	13·4	204·7	13·3	43·4

See p. 171 for footnotes

	Imports		Re-exports	Exports			Imports		Re-exports	Exports
	Ore	Pig and Sheet Lead	Pig and Sheet Lead	Lead and Shot			Ore	Pig and Sheet Lead	Pig and Sheet Lead	Lead and Shot
1908	23·5	237·5	10·2	49·4		1924	8·0	240·1	12·1	17·1
1909	15·5	207·7	7·9	45·7		1925	6·8	275·1	14·6	13·9
1910	18·1	218·9	13·5	46·8		1926	3·3	269·2	7·1	13·3
1911	17·3	213·7	18·0	44·0		1927	2·6	290·2	8·3	12·4
1912	15·7	205·4	11·7	·47·0		1928	4·9	261·7	18·8	12·3
1913	18·5	204·1	13·6	48·4		1929	4·0	297·3	27·3	11·5
1914	28·4	224·9	15·1	35·8		1930	1·3	335·3	41·2	11·4
1915	14·1	256·0	27·8	40·4		1931	1·7	309·7	15·4	9·3
1916	11·4	158·4	5·8	28·4		1932	1·1	265·6	14·1	8·8
1917	8·7	147·1	0·1	9·4		1933	0·4	285·0	5·4	10·8
1918	1·5	207·9	—	4·9		1934	0·3	315·8	4·6	12·1
1919	4·4	217·6	10·8	25·7		1935	0·1	318·9	23·0	12·0
1920	7·5	162·8	27·1	34·1		1936	0·1	358·0	23·6	10·1
1921	1·4	132·6	11·8	16·0		1937	0·6	375·2	37·1	16·9
1922	2·6	181·7	11·6	24·4		1938	0·2	409·5	25·0	17·6
1923	6·1 (b)	205·2 (b)	7·5 (b)	18·4 (b)						

(a) After 1856 exports of shot are no longer included. At that time they amounted to about 2,000 tons per year.

(b) Southern Ireland was treated as foreign from 1st April 1923.

REFERENCES

BOOKS

G. C. Allen, *The Economic Development of Birmingham and the Black Country* (London, 1929).
A. H. Dodd, *The Industrial Revolution in North Wales* (Cardiff, 1933).
H. Hamilton, *The English Brass and Copper Industries to 1800* (London, 1926).
R. Hunt, *British Mining* (London, 1884).
A. K. H. Jenkin, *The Cornish Miner* (London, 1927).
G. R. Lewis, *The Stannaries* (Cambridge, Mass., 1908).
J. Mawe, *Mineralogy of Derbyshire* (London, 1801).
W. Pryce, *Mineralogia Cornubiensis* (London, 1778).
J. Rowe, *Cornwall in the Age of the Industrial Revolution* (Liverpool, 1953).

GOVERNMENT PUBLICATIONS

Returns of Copper, Lead and Tin Imports and Exports (combined annual accounts in *Sessional Papers* from 1826–7 annually. Previously separate accounts had appeared irregularly from 1806).
Memoirs of the Geological Survey, vol. II.
Records of the School of Mines, vol. I.
Mineral Statistics, 1854–1920 (printed by the Geological Survey to 1881 and in *Sessional Papers* thereafter).

ARTICLES

J. Carne, 'Statistics of the Tin Mines in Cornwall and of the Consumption of Tin in Great Britain', *J.S.S.* (1839).
J. S. Gurtney, 'A Treatise on the Statistics of Cornwall,' *Report of the Royal Cornwall Polytechnic Society* (1838).
R. Hunt, 'The Present State of the Mining Industries of the United Kingdom', *J.S.S.* (1856).
Sir Charles Lemon, 'The Statistics of the Copper Mines of Cornwall', *J.S.S.* (1838).

THE TEXTILE INDUSTRIES

TABLES

As Britain's leading industries for so long, it might be expected that the textile trades would be well endowed with historical statistics. This is so, but only to a relative degree. Wool, as the major British manufacturing industry, until it was outstripped by cotton in the early nineteenth century, was the subject of innumerable parliamentary reports and pamphlets during the eighteenth century.[1] At the same time the overseas trade figures for textiles were recorded in considerable detail, and the returns in the sessional papers of the early nineteenth century cover them comparatively fully. Moreover, government regulation of the Yorkshire woollen industry and of the Scottish linen industry gives us two output series for the eighteenth century, which, though admittedly incomplete,[2] are nevertheless useful. Furthermore, in the nineteenth century the factory inspectors were concerned primarily with textile mills for many decades.

But there remain many gaps, of which the main one is, perhaps, the lack of consistent overall output series, such as we have for some of the mineral industries. This is less serious in the cases of cotton and of silk, since virtually the whole of their raw material originates abroad, and the trade statistics given in tables 1, 3, 25, and 26 give a fair indication of their development.[3] It should be noted, however, that imports are not the sole source of waste silk, which, from constituting only about 3 per cent of the raw material in the 1820's, represented over three-quarters by 1900. It should also be noted that the raw material tended to constitute a lower proportion of the weight and value of the final product through time, and hence that input statistics are a biased indicator of output growth.

The tables have been arranged in four groups, dealing respectively with cotton, wool, linen, and silk. But as the same sources are used in most cases for all fibres, they will not be considered separately here. The trade statistics for the eighteenth century,[4] (except those relating to raw cotton imports), are based on the work of the late Mrs E. B. Schumpeter, referred to in the introduction to Chapter XI; whilst those from 1840 onwards come principally from the *Statistical Abstract*. For the period between there is a variety of returns, some annual, some giving figures back into the eighteenth century; there are the annual *Trade and Navigation Accounts*;[5] and there are Porter's *Tables of Revenue, Population and Commerce*.[6] There are many problems in trying to establish comparability during this early nineteenth-century period between the earlier and the later statistics. These problems

---

[1] The contemporary output estimates are discussed in Phyllis Deane, 'The Output of the British Woollen Industry in the Eighteenth Century', *Journal of Economic History*, 1957.

[2] The statistics of cloth milled in the West Riding apply only to woollens, not worsteds, and they do not even cover every variety of the former. Kerseymeres, for example, were exempt. There is an extended discussion of the efficiency with which the stamping acts were carried out, in H. Heaton, *The Yorkshire Woollen and Worsted Industries* (Oxford, 1920), pp. 408–17. Professor Heaton concludes that 'the figures . . . were probably always too low'. Prior to the 1765 Act the broad cloth statistics were more defective than those of narrow cloth. There is evidence that the width of the cloth was liable to vary through time, but the probable extent of this variation remains obscure.

The Scottish linen statistics are incomplete in so far as they omit linen produced for home consumption, not for sale.

[3] The statistics of cotton consumption in table 2 are a refinement in that they take accounts of changes in stocks for most of the period.

[4] It is impossible to summarise the statistics of the volume of exports of cotton or wool goods, except in so far as the official values are an index of volume. These can be found in table 5 of Chapter XI. Detailed statistics of exports of various types of wool and cotton cloth can be found in Elizabeth B. Schumpeter, *English Overseas Trade Statistics, 1697–1808* (Oxford University Press, 1960), tables X, XI, XII, and XIII.

[5] Published as part of the annual *Finance Accounts* in sessional papers up to 1853.

[6] Published in sessional papers in 1833 and annually from 1835.

almost all spring either from the Union with Ireland, or from changes in the system of entering various types of cloth exported.

Ireland was treated as a foreign country in the Customs ledgers until well into the second decade of the nineteenth century, and trade with Ireland continued to be recorded separately until 1826. It is possible, therefore, to continue Mrs Schumpeter's series into the 1820's. This provides an overlap in most cases with the trade statistics for the United Kingdom, which were issued retrospectively in the late 1820's and 1830's for the few years preceding the combination of the British and Irish Customs. In this way, though the problem of comparability is not solved, the size of the break is indicated. And, in fact, it is not very large, except in the case of linen, where, unfortunately, no overlap exists. The difference in that trade can, however, be shown fairly well from the re-export statistics of Irish linen.[1] Statistics of Irish linen exports prior to the Union, nearly all of which came to Great Britain, have not been given here.[2]

The problem of changes in methods of entering cloth is less easily circumvented, though it affects only the exports. In the eighteenth century both cotton and wool goods were entered in a variety of different ways according to the kind of cloth—by number, by weight, by length, or by the piece. As it has proved impossible to combine these into a single unit, eighteenth-century exports of these commodities are shown only at their total official (i.e. constant) values. Prom 1815 onwards, when figures expressed in a single unit of quantity are available, these have been shown. In the case of linen the variety of units used in the ledgers was less, and it has been possible to get a single figure of exports expressed in yards, which is accurate to within 2 or 3 per cent.[3] This is some compensation for the lack of overlap between British and United Kingdom statistics. For silk manufactures the problem of quantities does not arise until 1826, and then it is insoluble. Exports of silk goods were entered by weight prior to 1826 and again from 1840 onwards; but in the intervening period the returns give them in a mixture of pieces, yards, and pounds weight, and Porter's *Tables* give only their declared value.

For statistics of the mechanical equipment of the textile industries in the nineteenth century we have to rely almost entirely on the periodic irregular returns made by the factory inspectors in their *Reports*. These were subjected to some criticism towards the end of that century, notable by Ellison.[4] But if any figure is better than none—which, provided its limitations are known, is surely true—we are better off for the nineteenth century than for the twentieth, except for the cotton industry. In the woollen and worsted industries enough figures of spindles and looms exist, though at irregular and often long intervals, to give a general idea of the changes that took place. But for linen and silk we have less information.

Our statistics of the numbers employed in textiles in the nineteenth century are also largely drawn from the *Reports* of the factory inspectors. So far as they go they are no doubt

[1] See note 2 to table 20.
[2] They can be found in C. Gill, *The Rise of the Irish Linen Industry* (Oxford, 1925), pp. 341-3.
[3] See note 2 to table 19.
[4] T. Ellison, *The Cotton Trade of Great Britain* (London, 1886), p. 325.

reasonably accurate, but since they are for single years at irregular intervals (except for a period in the 1890's), they give a picture of change which is inevitably distorted by the workings of the trade cycle. Moreover, they cover only factory workers, omitting out-workers, who remained important, on Wood's estimate (table 8), until the middle of the century in the cotton industry, and, we may safely say, until much later in wool and linen. For the interwar years there are the annual statistics of insured employees, which are at least as comprehensive as the later returns of the inspectors. These illustrate well the decline of the cotton, wool, and linen industries, but the picture is confused in the case of silk by the inclusion of rayon. Occupation statistics from the decennial censuses, available in some detail from 1841, have not been given here, because of the virtual impossibility of disentangling a comparable series from the differing classifications of successive censuses.

Textiles 1.   Raw Cotton Imports and Re-exports—Great Britain 1697–1819

NOTES

[1] SOURCES: 1697–1780—A. P. Wadsworth and Julia de L. Mann, *The Cotton Trade and Industrial Lancashire, 1600–1780* (Manchester University Press, 1931), pp. 520–1; 1781–1819— E. Baines, *History of the Cotton Manufacture* (London, 1835), p. 347.

[2]   The figure for 1697–8 is for the year ended Michaelmas 1698. Other figures are for the years ended 25th December, or 5th January following.

(in 000 lb.)

	Imports	Re-exports		Imports	Re-exports
1697–8	1,266	404	1738	2,537	169
1699	1,349	60	1739	2,246	82
1700	1,396	313	1740	1,546	82
1701	1,976	208	1741	1,680	109
1702	1,505	125	1742	1,933	169
1703	757	173	1743	1,268	65
1704	1,446	420	1744	2,032	17
1705	...	...	1745	1,635	86
1706	461	95	1746	2,408	33
1707	499	27	1747	2,325	35
1708	2,800	16	1748	5,258	385
1709	907	35	1749	1,837	357
1710	714	51	1750	2,318	64
1711	675	62	1751	2,977	74
1712	...	...	1752	3,496	86
1713	1,798	849	1753	4,278	176
1714	1,755	471	1754	3,181	145
1715	1,762	101	1755	3,820	155
1716	2,161	205	1756	3,089	375
1717	2,034	320	1757	2,706	888
1718	2,082	125	1758	2,225	237
1719	1,489	147	1759	2,552	343
1720	1,968	159	1760	2,359	618
1721	1,513	71	1761	2,996	369
1722	2,103	98	1762	3,519	646
1723	2,144	102	1763	2,707	250
1724	977	76	1764	3,870	223
1725	1,841	103	1765	3,777	78
1726	1,523	115	1766	6,918	65
1727	....	...	1767	3,623	198
1728	1,561	87	1768	4,131	186
1729	1,182	94	1769	4,406	361
1730	1,545	77	1770	3,612	366
1731	1,473	172	1771	2,547	219
1732	1,605	199	1772	5,307	356
1733	1,918	134	1773	2,906	518
1734	1,478	170	1774	5,707	307
1735	2,189	168	1775	6,694	617
1736	2,296	460	1776	6,216	372
1737	1,679	153	1777	7,037	665

(in 000 lb.)

	Imports	Re-exports		Imports	Re-exports
1778	6,569	673	1799	43,379	845
1779	5,861	393	1800	56,011	4,417
1780	6,877	324	1801	56,004	1,861
1781	5,199	97	1802	60,346	3,730
1782	11,828	421	1803	53,812	1,561
1783	9,736	178	1804	61,867	503
1784	11,482	202	1805	59,682	804
1785	18,400	407	1806	58,176	652
1786	19,475	323	1807	74,925	2,177
1787	23,250	1,073	1808	43,606	1,645
1788	20,467	853	1809	92,812	4,351
1789	32,576	298	1810	132,489	8,787
1790	31,448	844	1811	91,577	1,267
1791	28,707	363	1812	63,026	1,741
1792	34,907	1,485	1813	50,966	...
1793	19,041	1,172	1814	60,060	6,282
1794	24,359	1,350	1815	99,306	6,780
1795	26,401	1,194	1816	93,920	7,105
1796	32,126	695	1817	124,913	8,155
1797	23,354	609	1818	177,282	15,159
1798	31,881	601	1819	149,740	16,623

Textiles 2. Raw Cotton Consumption—United Kingdom 1800-1939

NOTE

SOURCES: 1800–10—T. Ellison, *A Handbook of the Cotton Trade* (London, 1858); 1811–65—T. Ellison, *The Cotton Trade of Great Britain* (London, 1886); 1866–1936—Liverpool Cotton Association, *Annual Circular* (using the editions from 1926 to 1937); 1937–39—*Abstract*.

(in million lb.)

Year		Year		Year	
1800	52	1847	441	1894	1,603
1801	54	1848	577	1895	1,664
1802	56	1849	630	1896	1,637
1803	52	1850	588	1897	1,618
1804	61	1851	659	1898	1,761
1805	59	1852	740	1899	1,762
1806	57	1853	761	1900 (c)	1,737
1807	73	1854	776	1901	1,569
1808	42	1855	839	1902	1,633
1809	88	1856	891	1903	1,617
1810	124	1857	826	1904	1,486
1811	89 (a)	1858	906	1905	1,813
1812	73	1859	977	1906	1,855
1813	78	1860	1,084	1907	1,985
1814	74	1861	1,007	1908	1,917
1815	81	1862	452	1909	1,824
1816	89	1863	508	1910	1,632
1817	107	1864	554	1911	1,892
1818	110	1865	723	1912	2,142
1819	109	1866	881	1913	2,178
1820	120	1867	967	1914	2,077
1821	129	1868	992	1915 (c)	1,931
1822	145	1869	939	1916	1,972
1823	154	1870	1,078 (b)	1917	1,800
1824	165	1871	1,207	1918	1,499
1825	167	1872	1,181 (b)	1919	1,526
1826	150	1873	1,245	1920	1,726
1827	197	1874	1,277 (b)	1921	1,066
1828	218	1875	1,229	1922	1,409
1829	219	1876	1,280 (b)	1923	1,362
1830	248	1877	1,230 (b)	1924	1,369
1831	263	1878	1,192 (b)	1925	1,609
1832	277	1879	1,150 (b)	1926	1,509
1833	287	1880	1,361 (b)	1927	1,557
1834	303	1881	1,430 (b)	1928	1,520
1835	318	1882	1,458 (b)	1929	1,498
1836	347	1883	1,526 (b)	1930	1,272
1837	366	1884	1,481 (b)	1931	985
1838	417	1885	1,298	1932	1,257
1839	382	1886	1,450	1933	1,177
1840	459	1887	1,499	1934	1,322
1841	438	1888	1,525	1935	1,262
1842	435	1889	1,564	1936	1,391
1843	518	1890	1,664	1937 (c)	1,431
1844	544	1891	1,666	1938	1,109
1845	607	1892	1,548	1939	1,317
1846	614	1893	1,434		

(a) Figures prior to 1811 are simply exports less re-exports, taking no account of changes in stocks.
(b) Ellison's figures continue up to 1885, and are slightly different from those given here.
(c) Prior to 1900 the figures are for calendar years. From 1900 to 1914 they are for years ended 31st August, and from 1915 to 1936 for years ended 31st July. For 1937–9 they are for periods of 52 weeks corresponding as closely to the calendar year as possible.

Textiles 3. Raw Cotton Imports in Total and from the U.S.A., and Re-exports—United Kingdom 1815-1938

NOTE

SOURCES: 1815–39 (Imports—*S.P.* 1847–8, LVIII; 1820–39 (Re-exports)—*Porter's Tables*; 1840–1920—*Abstract*; 1921–38 —*Annual Statement of Trade.*

(in millions of lb.)

	Total Imports	Imports from U.S.A.	Re-exports		Total Imports	Imports from U.S.A.	Re-exports
1815	101	54	...	1855	892	682	124
1816	95	51	...	1856	1,024	780	147
1817	126	61	...	1857	969	655	132
1818	179	68	...	1858	1,034	833	150
1819	151	62	...	1859	1,226	962	175
1820	152	90	6	1860	1,391	1,116	250
1821	133	93	15	1861	1,257	820	298
1822	143	101	18	1862	524	14	215
1823	191	143	9	1863	670	6	241
1824	149	92	13	1864	893	14	245
1825	228	140	18	1865	978	136	303
1826	178	131	24	1866	1,377	520	389
1827	272	217	18	1867	1,263	528	351
1828	228	152	17	1868	1,328	574	323
1829	223	157	30	1869	1,221	457	273
1830	264	211	9	1870	1,339	716	238
1831	289	219	22	1871	1,778	1,039	362
1832	287	220	18	1872	1,409	626	273
1833	304	238	17	1873	1,528	833	220
1834	327	269	...	1874	1,567	875	259
1835	364	284	...	1875	1,492	841	263
1836	407	290	...	1876	1,488	933	203
1837	407	321	...	1877	1,355	912	169
1838	508	431	...	1878	1,340	1,026	147
1839	389	312	...	1879	1,469	1,082	188
1840	592	488	39	1880	1,629	1,224	225
1841	488	358	38	1881	1,679	1,211	208
1842	532	414	45	1882	1,784	1,155	265
1843	673	575	40	1883	1,734	1,239	247
1844	646	517	47	1884	1,749	1,212	252
1845	722	627	43	1885	1,426	1,051	206
1846	468	402	66	1886	1,715	1,293	198
1847	475	365	75	1887	1,791	1,257	293
1848	713	600	74	1888	1,732	1,349	275
1849	755	635	99	1889	1,937	1,424	278
1850	664	493	102	1890	1,793	1,317	215
1851	757	597	112	1891	1,995	1,618	182
1852	930	766	112	1892	1,775	1,406	233
1853	895	658	149	1893	1,417	1,056	225
1854	887	722	123	1894	1,788	1,393	240

Textiles 3. *continued*

(in millions of lb.)

	Total Imports	Imports from U.S.A.	Re-exports		Total Imports	Imports from U.S.A.	Re-exports
1895	1,757	1,395	203	1917	1,623	1,186	111
1896	1,755	1,394	184	1918	1,489	976	- -
1897	1,724	1,380	225	1919	1,958	1,371	121
1898	2,129	1,805	203	1920	1,949	1,417	256
1899	1,626	1,234	284	1921	1,204	815	157
1900	1,760	1,365	216	1922	1,490	943	88
1901	1,830	1,481	207	1923	1,357 (a)	693 (a)	112 (a)
1902	1,817	1,364	275	1924	1,633	971	144
1903	1,793	1,361	305	1925	1,960	1,254	141
1904	1,955	1,491	254	1926	1,802	1,097	148
1905	2,204	1,734	283	1927	1,637	974	134
1906	2,007	1,488	245	1928	1,570	897	71
1907	2,387	1,756	330	1929	1,609	866	80
1908	2,061	1,589	291	1930	1,276	611	74
1909	2,189	1,640	269	1931	1,154	464	42
1910	1,973	1,470	256	1932	1,326	766	54
1911	2,207	1,682	291	1933	1,487	803	56
1912	2,806	2,165	324	1934	1,353	510	65
1913	2,174	1,585	258	1935	1,376	625	75
1914	1,864	1,284	216	1936	1,658	637	63
1915	2,648	2,022	344	1937	1,800	794	64
1916	2,171	1,647	237	1938	1,324	469	49
				1939	1,434	514	44

(a) Southern Ireland was treated as foreign from 1st April, 1923.

Exports of Cotton Manufactures—United Kingdom 1815–1939

NOTE
SOURCES: 1815–39—*S.P.* 1847–8, LVIII; 1840–1920—*Abstract*; 1921–39—*Annual Statement of Trade.*

	Piece Goods (million yd.)	Thread (million lb.)	Twist & Yarn (million lb.)		Piece Goods (million yd.)	Thread (million lb.)	Twist & Yarn (million lb.)
1815	253	0·2	9	1865	2,014	4·6	104
1816	189	0·2	16	1866	2,576	6·4	139
1817	237	0·3	13	1867	2,832	6·5	169
1818	255	0·3	15	1868	2,977	6·6	174
1819	203	0·3	18	1869	2,866	6·9	170
1820	251	0·4	23	1870	3,267	7·3	186
1821	266	0·5	22	1871	3,417	7·5	194
1822	304	0·6	27	1872	3,538	8·0	212
1823	302	0·6	27	1873	3,484	8·3	215
1824	345	0·6	34	1874	3,607	9·0	221
1825	336	0·7	33	1875	3,562	10·4	216
1826	267	0·8	42	1876	3,669	9·6	233
1827	365	1·3	45	1877	3,838	11·2	228
1828	363	1·3	51	1878	3,619	12·2	251
1829	403	1·1	61	1879	3,725	11·7	236
1830	445	1·2	65	1880	4,496	13·1	216
1831	421	1·5	64	1881	4,777	15·5	255
1832	461	1·7	76	1882	4,349	15·5	238
1833	496	1·9	71	1883	4,539	14·4	265
1834	556	2·3	76	1884	4,417 (*a*)	14·7	271
1835	558	2·3	83	1885	4,375	15·0	246
1836	638	2·2	88	1886	4,850	17·3	254
1837	531	2·2	103	1887	4,904	20·4	251
1838	690	2·5	115	1888	5,038	21·7	256
1839	731	3·0	106	1889	5,001	17·3	252
1840	791	2·8	118	1890	5,125	18·1	258
1841	751	2·8	123	1891	4,912	18·1	245
1842	734	2·5	137	1892	4,873	16·2	233
1843	919	2·8	140	1893	4,652	17·2	207
1844	1,047	3·2	139	1894	5,312	17·1	236
1845	1,092	2·9	135	1895	5,033	23·8	252
1846	1,065	2·8	162	1896	5,218	25·9	246
1847	943	3·5	120	1897	4,792	26·4	253
1848	1,097	3·7	136	1898	5,216	27·1	247
1849	1,338	5·0	150	1899	5,439	30·7	213
1850	1,358	4·4	131	1900	5,032	34·5	158
1851	1,543	4·4	144	1901	5,365	31·1	170
1852	1,524	4·6	145	1902	5,332	32·4	166
1853	1,595	4·9	148	1903	5,157	34·3	151
1854	1,693	4·6	147	1904	5,592	24·3	164
1855	1,938	4·9	165	1905	6,197	23·4	205
1856	2,035	5·4	181	1906	6,261	26·5	207
1857	1,979	4·4	177	1907	6,298	31·7	241
1858	2,324	4·5	200	1908	5,531	27·8	215
1859	2,563	5·4	192	1909	5,722	29·7	215
1860	2,776	6·3	197	1910	6,018	24·4	192
1861	2,563	5·1	178	1911	6,654	23·0	224
1862	1,681	4·6	93	1912	6,913	22·6	244
1863	1,711	4·4	74	1913	7,075	20·7	210
1864	1,752	4·4	76	1914	5,736	19·2	178

See p. 183 for footnotes

	Piece Goods (million yd.)	Thread (million lb.)	Twist & Yarn (million lb.)		Piece Goods (million yd.)	Thread (million lb.)	Twist & Yarn (million lb.)
1915	4,748	20·9	188	1928	3,968	18·5	169
1916	5,254	24·7	172	1929	3,765	18·1	167
1917	4,978	22·3	133	1930	2,491	16·1	137
1918	3,699	17·1	102	1931	1,790	13·6	134
1919	3,524	19·6	163	1932	2,303	15·6	141
1920	... (b)	22·2	147	1933	2,117	15·8	135
1921	3,038	15·0	146	1934	2,060	16·7	130
1922	4,313	17·6	202	1935	2,013	17·2	142
1923	4,324 (c)	17·9 (c)	145 (c)	1936	1,993	16·0	151
1924	4,585	18·1	163	1937	2,023	16·0	159
1925	4,637	18·4	190	1938	1,448	13·5	123
1926	3,923	19·0	169	1939	1,462	14·3	114
1927	4,189	18·2	200				

(a) It was stated that up to 1883 'large quantities of piece goods of mixed materials in which wool predominated were erroneously entered as cotton manufactures'.
(b) Exports of piece goods in 1920 were not recorded in linear yards, only in square yards. At 4,435 million square yards they would have amounted to 4,643 linear yards if the proportion between units had been the same as in 1921.
(c) Southern Ireland was treated as foreign from 1st April, 1923.

Textiles 5. Printed Goods Charged with Duty—England & Wales 1713–1829

NOTES

[1] SOURCE: *Excise Revenue Accounts* in the Customs and Excise Library.

[2] This table covers silks, linens, calicoes and stuffs, but not stained paper.

(in 000 yd.)

1713 (a)	2,028	1753 (b)	4,230	1793	21,142
1714	2,580	1754	4,388	1794	20,502
1715	1,840	1755	4,932	1795	24,054
1716	2,503	1756	4,206	1796	30,058
1717	2,654	1757	4,184	1797	27,205
1718	2,689	1758	5,143	1798	28,294
1719	2,841	1759	5,698	1799	32,178
1720	1,669	1760	6,359	1800	34,134
1721	1,048	1761	6,880	1801	38,727
1722	1,535	1762	5,617	1802	39,496
1723	3,064	1763	5,892	1803	43,344
1724	2,886	1764	6,631	1804	43,667
1725	2,760	1765	6,425	1805	48,342
1726	2,898	1766	7,159	1806	43,543
1727	2,861	1767	7,167	1807	52,907
1728	2,216	1768	7,691	1808	46,963
1729	2,684	1769	9,350	1809	58,068
1730	2,279	1770	8,723	1810	67,539
1731	2,123	1771	8,736	1811	47,271
1732	2,427	1772	9,168	1812	49,969
1733	2,925	1773	7,528	1813	58,553
1734	2,793	1774	8,201	1814	69,759
1735	3,005	1775	8,160	1815	69,790
1736	2,630	1776	8,244	1816	68,744
1737	3,057	1777	9,024	1817	59,490
1738	3,150	1778	8,246	1818	86,003
1739	3,224	1779	7,803	1819	80,374
1740	3,125	1780	8,326	1820	75,516
1741	3,027	1781	10,156	1821	93,335
1742	2,766	1782	9,605	1822	90,386
1743	3,064	1783	10,081	1823	96,044
1744	3,037	1784	11,179	1824	108,580
1745	2,629	1785	14,113	1825	114,636
1746	2,729	1786	13,528	1826 (c)	(56,077)
1747	3,527	1787	15,131	1827 (d)	81,030 (e)
1748	3,220	1788	14,603	1828	117,013
1749	3,997	1789	14,154	1829	103,961
1750	4,417	1790	16,777		
1751	4,224	1791	19,645		
1752	4,208	1792	21,720		

(a) Years ended 24th June henceforth to 1752.
(b) Years ended 5th July. henceforth to 1826.
(c) Half-year ended 5th January.
(d) Years ended 5th January henceforth.

(e) The duty on silks was repealed from 5th April, 1826. In the full year ended 5th January, 1826, 969,000 yards of printed silks had been charged with duty.

Textiles 6. Spindles, Power Looms, and Power Employed in Cotton Factories— United Kingdom 1835–1939

NOTE TO PART A

[1] SOURCE: *Reports of H.M. Inspectors of Factories* published in sessional papers.

[2] It is not always clear whether the figures relate to all machines in place or merely to those in use. The returns for 1870 and 1874 include all machines, but Ellison, in criticising the figures for 1885, suggested that they (and possibly those for 1878 also) related only to machines in use. (*The Cotton Trade of Great Britain* (London, 1886), p. 325. Ellison states quite categorically that 'the figures for 1885 are wrong'.)

A. Spindles, Power Looms, and Power, at intervals 1835–1903, in thousands

| | Spindles | | Power Looms | Horsepower Used | |
	Spinning	Doubling		Steam	Water
1835	...		110	...	...
1838	...		...	46	12
1850	20,977		250	71	11
1856	28,010		299	87	9
1861	30,387		400	281	12
1867	32,000	2,215	379	190	12
1870	33,995	3,724	441	299	8
1874	37,516	4,366	463	...	...
1878	39,528	4,679	515	...	...
1885	40,120	4,228	561	...	...
1890	40,512	3,993	616	...	...
1903	43,905	3,952	684	...	...

B. Spinning Spindles, Great Britain 1906–39, in millions

NOTE TO PART B

SOURCE: *International Cotton Bulletin*, quarterly from September, 1922.

1906 (a)	48·8	1922	56·6	1931	54·2
1907	50·7	1923	56·6	1932	51·9
1908	52·8	1924	56·7	1933	49·0
1909	53·3	1925	57·1	1934	45·9
1910	53·4	1926	57·3	1935	42·7
1911	54·5	1927	...	1936	41·4
1912	55·3	1928	57·1	1937	38·8
1913	55·7	1929	55·9	1938	36·9
1921 (b)	56·1	1930	55·2	1939	35·3

(a) Figures taken at 31st August.

(b) Figures taken at 31st July.

Textiles 7. Spindles and Power Looms in Cotton Factories—Lancashire 1882–1939

NOTES

[1] SOURCE: *The Lancashire Textile Industry, 1959* (J. Worrall Ltd., Oldham).

[2] These figures include waste spinning and doubling spindles.

	Million Spindles	Thousand Looms		Million Spindles	Thousand Looms
1882	38·4	485	1912	58·1	759
1883	...	...	1913	58·5	786
1884	40·5	534	1914	59·3	805
1885	41·3	546	1915	59·9	808
1886–7	41·0	550	1916	59·8	809
1887–8	40·9	583	1917	61·0	808
1889	41·3	597	1918	59·5	788
1890	41·4	607	1919	59·2	791
1891	42·4	611	1920	60·1	798
1892	43·1	616	1921	60·1	790
1893–4	43·0	603	1922	59·8	799
1894–5	43·2	628	1923	59·8	795
1896	42·7	638	1924	59·5	792
1897	42·1	642	1925	59·9	788
1898	41·8	630	1926	60·3	786
1899	42·2	639	1927	60·5	768
1900	42·6	649	1928	60·0	755
1901	43·1	651	1929	59·1	740
1902	44·6	648	1930	57·7	704
1903	44·6	647	1931	57·6	658
1904	45·2	653	1932	55·4	625
1905	46·0	652	1933	53·6	602
1906	48·3	685	1934	49·2	560
1907	52·6	725	1935	47·1	516
1908	55·2	736	1936	44·6	500
1909	57·0	739	1937	43·1	471
1910	57·7	741	1938	40·9	461
1911	58·0	741	1939	39·1	453

Textiles 8. Numbers Employed in the Cotton Industry: Estimates by G. H. Wood—United Kingdom 1806–62

NOTES

[1] SOURCE: *J.R.S.S.* (1910), pp. 598–9.
[2] Wood's estimates are based on T. Ellison, *The Cotton Trade of Great Britain* (London, 1886), E. Baines, *History of the Cotton Manufacture* (London, 1835), and G. R. Porter, *The Progress of the Nation* (London, 2nd edition, 1847), and the returns of H.M. Factory Inspectors, published from time to time in sessional papers.
[3] All increases or decreases between known years were assumed to be uniform and gradual, though allowance was made for the great increase in factories in 1823–5 and 1832–4. Wood says that 'in criticising these numbers it should be borne in mind that they are not intended so much for definite estimates of the numbers employed in the cotton industry as for proportions between factory workers and handloom weavers'.
[4] No account is taken of hand spinners, of winders and warpers for the hand looms, or of those engaged in the finishing trades.

(in thousands)

	Factory Workers	Handloom Weavers		Factory Workers	Handloom Weavers
1806	90	184	1835	220	188
1807	93	188	1836	230	174
1808	95	192	1837	240	160
1809	97	196	1838	250	147
1810	100	200	1839	259	135
1811	102	204	1840	262	123
1812	105	208	1841	264	110
1813	107	212	1842	267	97
1814	110	216	1843	269	85
1815	114	220	1844	271	72
1816	117	224	1845	273	60
1817	121	228	1846	275	57
1818	123	232	1847	277	53
1819	125	236	1848	295	50
1820	126	240	1849	313	47
1821	129	240	1850	331	43
1822	132	240	1851	339	40
1823	135	240	1852	347	37
1824	167	240	1853	355	33
1825	173	240	1854	363	30
1826	175	240	1855	371	27
1827	177	240	1856	379	23
1828	180	240	1857	391	20
1829	182	240	1858	403	17
1830	185	240	1859	415	13
1831	187	240	1860	427	10
1832	196	227	1861	439	7
1833	208	213	1862	452	3
1834	215	200			

Textiles 9. Numbers Employed in the Cotton Industry—United Kingdom 1835–1939

NOTES

[1] SOURCES: Part A—returns by Factory Inspectors, in sessional papers at intervals from 1836; Part B, 1923–36—*Abstract of Labour Statistics*; Part B, 1937–9—*Ministry of Labour Gazette*.

[2] The Inspectors' returns were incomplete owing to the failure of some employers to send information; but it seems clear that the omissions were of little significance, even in the earlier years.

A. Numbers Employed in Factories, by Age and Sex, 1835–1907

(in thousands)

	Children under 13		Children 13–18		All Ages		Grand Total
	Males	Females	Males	Females	Males	Females	
1835	15 (a)	14 (a)	28	38	100	119	219
1838	7 (a)	5 (a)	40	55	113	146	259
1847	11	7	37	57	134	182	316
1850	9	6	37	...	142	189	331
1856	14	10	39	...	157	222	379
1861	22	18	41	...	183	269	452
1867	22	19	34	...	161	240	401
1870	23	20	38	...	178	272	450
1874	34	33	39	...	188	292	480

	Children under 14 Working Half-Time		Persons under 18 Working Full Time				
1878	29	33	35	...	185	297	483
1885	24	26	40	...	196	308	504
1890	23	25	44	...	208	321	529
1895	14	17	42	82	205	334	539
1896	13	16	41	80	204	329	533
1897	12	15	40	80	200	328	527
1898	12	14	39	80	198	328	526
1901	10	11	37	78	194	329	523
1904	8	10	37	72	196	327	523
1907	9	10	46	86	218	359	577

B. Numbers of Insured Employees in the Cotton Industry, 1923–39 (for a date in July each year).

	Males	Females	Total		Males	Females	Total
1923	206	362	568	1931	191	359	550
1924	205	367	572	1932	187	332	518
1925	208	366	573	1933	180	320	500
1926	209	366	575	1934	170	298	467
1927	208	362	570	1935	162	280	442
1927	202 (b)	360 (b)	562 (b)	1936	150	270	421
1928	198	356	554	1937	144	264	409
1929	201	354	555	1938	137	256	393
1930	197	367	564	1939	130	248	378

(a) The numbers of children under 10 years old in 1835 and 1838 were:

	Males	Females
1835	372	331
1838	1,046	686

(b) From 1927 the figures apply only to employees between the ages of 16 and 64 inclusive. Figures on both the old and the new basis are shown for 1927.

Textiles 10.   Broad and Narrow Cloth Milled in the West Riding of Yorkshire—1726–1820

NOTES

[1] SOURCES: 1727–1805—*Report of the Select Committee on the Woollen Manufacture* (*S.P.* 1806, III), p. 25; 1806–20—*S.P.* 1820, XII.
[2] Figures of broad cloth pieces are for years ended 25th March up to and including 1752, and for years ended 5th April thereafter. The narrow cloth pieces statistics are for years ended 20th January up to and including 1752, and for years ended 31st January thereafter. For both cloths in yards the figures are for years ended at the Easter Sessions.
[3] The width as well as the length of cloths was subject to variation. A fair average seems to have been 54 inches for broad and 27 inches for narrow cloths. (The legal minimum for broad cloth was 49½ inches until its abolition in 1765.)

	Broad Cloth		Narrow Cloth			Broad Cloth		Narrow Cloth	
	thousand pieces	thousand yards	thousand pieces	thousand yards		thousand pieces	thousand yards	thousand pieces	thousand yards
1727	29·0				1774	87·2	2,587	88·3	2,134
1728	25·2				1775	95·9	2,841	96·8	2,441
1729	29·6				1776	99·7	2,975	99·6	2,488
1730	31·6				1777	107·8	3,154	95·8	2,602
1731	35·6				1778	132·5	3,796	101·6	2,747
1732	35·5				1779	110·9	3,427	93·1	2,660
1733	34·6				1780	94·6	2,803	87·3	2,571
1734	31·1				1781	102·0	3,099	98·7	2,671
1735	31·7				1782	112·5	4,458	96·7	2,599
1736	38·9				1783	131·1	4,563	108·6	3,292
1737	42·3				1784	138·0	4,094	115·5	3,357
1738	42·4				1785	157·3	4,845	116·0	3,409
1739	43·1		58·8		1786	158·8	4,935	123·0	3,537
1740	41·4		58·6		1787	155·7	4,851	128·1	4,058
1741	46·4		61·2		1788	139·4	4,244	132·1	4,208
1742	45·0		62·8		1789	154·1	4,716	145·5	4,410
1743	45·2		63·5		1790	172·6	5,152	140·4	4,582
1744	54·6		63·1		1791	187·6	5,815	154·4	4,798
1745	50·5		63·4		1792	214·9	6,761	190·5	5,532
1746	56·6		68·8		1793	190·3	6,055	150·7	4,784
1747	62·5		68·4		1794	191·0	6,067	130·4	4,634
1748	60·8		68·1		1795	251·1	7,760	155·1	5,173
1749	60·7		68·9		1796	246·8	7,831	151·6	5,246
1750	60·4		78·1		1797	229·3	7,235	156·7	5,504
1751	61·0		74·0		1798	224·2	7,134	148·6	5,180
1752	60·7		72·4		1799	272·8	8,807	180·2	6,377
1753	55·4		71·6		1800	285·9	9,264	169·3	6,014
1754	56·1		72·4		1801	264·1	8,699	137·2	4,834
1755	57·1		76·3		1802	265·7	8,686	137·1	5,024
1756	33·6		79·3		1803	266·8	8,943	139·6	5,024
1757	55·8		77·1		1804	298·2	9,987	150·0	5,440
1758	60·4		66·4		1805	300·2	10,079	165·8	6,193
1759	51·9		65·5		1806	290·3	9,561	175·3	6,430
1760	49·4		69·6		1807	262·0	8,422	161·8	5,931
1761	48·9		75·5		1808	279·9	9,051	144·6	5,309
1762	48·6		72·9		1809	311·2	9,826	151·9	5,952
1763	48·0		72·1		1810	273·7	8,671	158·3	6,181
1764	54·9		79·5		1811	269·9	8,536	141·8	5,716
1765	54·7		77·4		1812	316·4	9,949	136·9	5,117
1766	72·6 (a)		78·9		1813	369·9	11,703	142·9	5,616
1767	102·4		78·8		1814	338·9	10,656	147·5	6,045
1768	90·0		74·5		1815	330·3	10,394	162·4	6,650
1769	92·5	2,772	87·8	2,144	1816	325·4	10,135	120·9	5,651
1770	93·1	2,717	85·4	2,256	1817	351·1	10,974	132·6	5,234
1771	92·8	2,966	89·9	2,236	1818	324·5	10,246	140·3	5,721
1772	112·4	3,224	95·5	2,378	1819	363·3	8,406	119·7	4,889
1773	120·2	3,636	89·9	2,306	1820	286·7	9,186	129·3	5,226

(*a*) The increase in the number of broad cloths after 1765 is partly explained by more stringent inspection. (See H. Heaton, *The Yorkshire Woollen and Worsted Industries* (Oxford, 1920, pp. 414–416.)

Textiles 11. Estimated Domestic Wool Clip of the United Kingdom—1775–1927

NOTES

[1] SOURCES: 1775 to 1860–4 and 1909–13 to 1927—Committee on Industry and Trade (Balfour Committee); *Survey of Textile Industries*, p. 275; 1865–1908—*S.P.* 1909, CII, quoting Messrs Schwartze's estimates; 1909–11—*Textile Mercury Wool Year Book, 1922*, also quoting Messrs Schwartze's estimates, which were discontinued in 1911.

[2] The annual *Textile Mercury Wool Year Book* in the 1920's and 1930's gives scattered estimates for years after 1927, indicating an apparently continuous decline in the clip to 107 million lb. in 1938.

(in million lb.)

yearly figures or annual averages

1775	80	1870	158	1887	134	1904	132
1776–99	90	1871	152	1888	134	1905	131
1800–19	100	1872	156	1889	133	1906	130
1820–4	110	1873	165	1890	138	1907	131
1825–9	115	1874	167	1891	148	1908	134
1830–4	120	1875	162	1892	153	1909	142
1835–9	120	1876	156	1893	151	1910	143
1840–4	125	1877	152	1894	142	1911	136
1845–9	130	1878	152	1895	135	1909–13	102
1850–4	135	1879	153	1896	136	1919–23	106
1855–9	140	1880	149	1897	139	1924	105
1860–4	145	1881	139	1898	139	1925	110
1865	150	1882	129	1899	140	1926	115
1866	145	1883	128	1900	141	1927	119
1867	163	1884	132	1901	138		
1868	172	1885	136	1902	136		
1869	165	1886	136	1903	133		

12. Raw Wool Imports—England & Wales 1700–80

NOTES

[1] SOURCE: Elizabeth B. Schumpeter, *English Overseas Trade Statistics, 1697–1808* (Oxford University Press, 1960), table XVI.

[2] The equivalent modern weight of a great stone or a bag is uncertain. Indeed, comparison of the figures for 1775 and 1780 in this table and the next suggests that the weight of a bag varied greatly.

	Irish Wool (great stones)	Spanish Wool (bags)		Irish Wool (great stones)	Spanish Wool (bags)
1700	304,160	5,778	1724	113,290	4,220
1701	289,981	8,740	1725	75,621	5,961
1702	303,862	4,605	1726	51,371	6,395
1703	352,343	34	1727	58,179	2,624
1704	333,762	356	1728	49,784	3,700
1705	...	...	1729	38,667	3,755
1706	278,569	4,037	1730	19,824	6,859
1707	247,839	2,970	1731	13,027	4,455
1708	217,395	404	1732	9,734	5,594
1709	224,280	3,626	1733	64,677	4,996
1710	269,799	2,522	1734	88,153	3,815
1711	268,209	7,695	1735	96,713	4,777
1712	...	...	1736	68,013	4,680
1713	157,439	5,712	1737	61,436	4,986
1714	210,586	4,076	1738	55,103	5,356
1715	145,525	3,771	1739	45,131	2,157
1716	207,801	5,984	1740	31,309	2,828
1717	144,390	4,749	1741	39,608	49
1718	144,188	3,606	1742	35,627	7,148
1719	75,369	1,588	1743	20,780	7,630
1720	79,074	4,701	1744	13,518	1,184
1721	139,404	2,766	1745	21,601	4,769
1722	129,582	3,266	1746	71,412	4,395
1723	98,499	4,188	1747	187,661	2,387

	Irish Wool (great stones)	Spanish Wool (bags)		Irish Wool (great stones)	Spanish Wool (bags)
1748	42,837	6,675	1761	1,729	9,742
1749	43,208	3,312	1762	3,675	3,609
1750	45,439	5,269	1763	7,207	10,922
1751	73,037	4,891	1764	13,196	8,598
1752	71,556	4,139	1765	22,264	8,569
1753	15,342	3,653	1766	51,182	7,524
1754	6,622	6,114	1767	49,268	6,674
1755	5,518	5,100	1768	4,389	5,183
1756	4,260	6,656	1769	2,079	9,731
1757	5,975	5,701	1770	678	11,370
1758	4,472	6,422	1771	1,668	8,582
1759	1,880	4,532	1775	258	9,507
1760	5,366	5,655	1780	653	9,576

13. Raw Wool Imports—England & Wales 1772–91, and Great Britain 1792–1824

NOTE

SOURCES: Columns 1 and 2, 1772–1808—Elizabeth B. Schumpeter, *English Overseas Trade Statistics, 1697–1808* (Oxford University Press, 1960), table XVII; Column 1, 1809–20—*S.P.* 1821, XVII; Column 1, 1821–2—*S.P.* 1823, XIII; Column 1, 1823–4—*S.P.* 1825 XXI; Column 3, 1796–1801—*S.P.* 1806, XII; Column 3, 1802–11—*S.P.* 1812, X; Column 3, 1812—*S.P.* 1813–14, XII; Column 3, 1814—*S.P.* 1814–15, X; Column 3, 1815–18—*S.P.* 1819, XVI; Column 3, 1819–24—*S.P.* 1825, XXI.

(in 000 lb.)

	Total	'Spanish'	From Spain, Portugal and Gibraltar		Total	'Spanish'	From Spain, Portugal and Gibraltar
1772	1,571	1,537	...	1799	5,152	5,010	4,106
1773	1,479	1,477	...	1800	8,418	8,131	7,828
1774	2,136	2,058	...	1801	7,387	6,539	6,298
1775	1,487	1,481	...	1802	7,702	6,493	6,167
1776	1,917	1,909	...	1803	6,006	4,702	4,694
1777	2,887	2,852	...	1804	8,151	7,209	7,311
1778	478	453	...	1805	8,542	7,042	7,100
1779	574	520	...	1806	7,334	5,598	5,772
1780	1,813	1,801	...	1807	11,769	10,484	10,595
1781	2,487	2,478	...	1808	2,354	1,982	2,070
1782	997	992	...	1809	6,846	...	5,541
1783	2,637	2,630	...	1810	10,936	...	9,360
1784	1,603	1,603	...	1811	4,740	...	4,582
1785	3,135	3,135	...	1812	7,015	...	6,793
1786	1,557	1,555	...	1813	...	...	...
1787	4,212	4,188	...	1814	15,713	...	9,254
1788	4,195	4,174	...	1815	14,992	...	8,089
1789	2,713	2,694	...	1816	8,118	...	3,477
1790	3,245	3,133	...	1817	14,716	...	7,031
1791	2,776	2,645	...	1818	26,405	...	10,201
1792	4,514	4,351	...	1819	16,190	...	7,352
1793	1,891	1,750	...	1820	10,044	...	3,635
1794	4,486	4,424	...	1821	16,680	...	7,091
1795	4,903	4,764	...	1822	19,333	...	6,121
1796	3,454	3,400	3,413	1823	20,651	...	5,451
1797	4,654	4,603	4,367	1824	23,859	...	5,513
1798	2,398	2,362	2,141				

NOTES

[1] Sources: 1816–39—*S.P.* 1844, XLV and *Porter's Tables*; 1840–1920—*Abstract*; 1921–38—*Annual Statement of Trade.*
[2] This table includes alpaca, vicuna, and llama wool.

[3] At various times sources of supply other than Australasia have been important. These are shown (in million lb.) for the more interesting periods below:

Germany (excluding Prussia)		Germany (excluding Prussia)				Spain, Portugal, and Gibralter				British South Africa			
1816	2·8	1825	28·8	1834	22·6	1843	16·8	1816	3·5	1829	3·8	1860	16·6	1910	104·3
1817	4·8	1826	10·5	1835	23·8	1844	21·8	1817	7·0	1830	2·1	1870	32·8	1922	146·9
1818	8·4	1827	21·2	1836	31·8	1845	18·5	1818	10·2	1831	3·9	1880	51·4	1930	158·2
1819	4·5	1828	22·0	1837	19·7	1846	15·8	1819	7·4	1832	2·8	1890	87·2	1939	84·4
1820	5·1	1829	14·1	1838	27·5	1847	12·7	1820	3·6	1833	4·0	1900	32·2		
1821	8·6	1830	26·1	1839	23·8	1848	14·4	1821	7·1	1834	4·3				
1822	11·1	1831	22·4	1840	21·8	1949	12·9	1822	6·1	1835	2·8				
1823	12·6	1832	19·8	1841	21·0	1850	9·2	1823	5·5	1836	6·4	South America			
1824	15·4	1833	25·4	1842	15·6			1824	5·5	1837	3·4	1860	9·0	1910	69·6
								1825	9·2	1838	2·6	1870	12·7	1922	103·7
								1826	2·2	1839	3·9	1880	10·3	1930	126·5
								1827	4·4	1840	1·9	1890	11·2	1939	141·0
								1828	4·1			1900	35·6		

(in million lb.)

	Imports		Re-exports	Exports (a)
	Total	from Australasia		
1816	7·5	– –	...	...
1817	14·1	—	...	...
1818	24·7	0·1	...	...
1819	16·1	0·1	...	...
1820	9·8	0·1	0·1	...
1821	16·6	0·2	0·3	...
1822	19·1	0·1	0·2	...
1823	19·4	0·5	0·2	...
1824	22·6	0·4	0·4	...
1825	43·8	0·3	0·7	...
1826	16·0	1·1	0·9	0·1
1827	29·1	0·5	0·8	0·3
1828	30·2	1·6	0·9	1·7
1829	21·5	1·8	0·4	1·3
1830	32·3	2·0	0·7	3·0
1831	31·7	2·5	1·0	3·5
1832	28·1	2·4	0·6	4·2
1833	38·0	3·5	0·4	5·0
1834	46·5	3·6	0·8	2·3
1835	42·2	4·2	4·1	4·6
1836	64·2	5·0	0·6	3·9
1837	48·4	7·1	2·8	2·6
1838	52·6	7·8	1·9	5·9
1839	57·4	10·1	0·7	4·6
1840	49·4	9·7	1·0	4·8
1841	56·2	12·4	2·6	8·5
1842	45·9	13·0	3·6	8·6
1843	49·2	17·4	3·0	8·2
1844	65·7	17·6	2·0	8·9
1845	76·8	24·2	2·7	9·1
1846	65·3	21·8	3·0	5·9
1847	62·6	26·1	4·8	5·6
1848	70·9	30·0	6·6	4·0
1849	76·8	35·9	12·5	11·2
1850	74·3	39·0	14·4	12·0

See p. 194 for footnotes

(in million lb.)

	Imports		Re-exports	Exports (a)
	Total	from Australasia		
1851	83·3	41·8	13·7	8·6
1852	93·8	43·2	11·3	13·9
1853	119·4	47·1	11·7	6·7
1854	106·1	47·5	24·5	12·9
1855	99·3	49·1	29·5	16·2
1856	116·2	52·1	26·7	14·4
1857	129·8	49·2	36·5	15·1
1858	126·7	51·1	26·7	13·5
1859	133·3	53·7	29·1	9·1
1860	148·4	59·2	30·8	11·3
1861	147·2	68·5	54·4	15·7
1862	171·9	71·3	48·1	10·2
1863	177·4	77·2	63·9	8·2
1864	206·5	99·0	55·9	7·3
1865	212·2	109·7	82·4	9·1
1866	239·4	113·8	66·6	9·7
1867	283·7	133·1	90·8	8·9
1868	252·7	155·7	105·1	9·5
1869	258·5	158·5	116·6	12·4
1870	263·3	175·1	92·5	9·1
1871	323·0	182·7	134·9	12·0
1872	306·4	173·2	137·5	7·6
1873	318·0	186·7	123·2	7·0
1874	344·5	225·4	144·3	10·1
1875	365·1	238·6	172·1	10·5
1876	390·1	263·9	173·0	9·8
1877	409·9	281·2	187·4	9·5
1878	399·4	276·2	199·3	6·6
1879	417·1	287·8	243·4	15·7
1880	463·5	300·6	237·4	17·2
1881	450·1	329·7	265·6	14·1
1882	489·0	345·8	264·0	13·8
1883	495·9	351·7	277·2	19·4
1884	526·5	381·4	276·9	18·1
1885	505·7	356·1	267·5	23·5
1886	596·5	401·4	312·0	22·2

See p. 194 for footnotes

(in million lb.)

	Imports				
	Total	from Australia	from New Zealand	Re-exports	Exports
1887	577·9	292·5	91·1	319·2	19·6
1888	639·3	343·7	84·2	339·1	23·6
1889	700·9	338·9	92·1	363·6	21·8
1890	633·0	323·1	95·6	340·7	19·5 (*b*)
1891	720·0	372·9	104·8	384·2	16·7
1892	743·0	408·7	104·7	430·8	17·9
1893	677·9	355·3	117·0	346·4	16·1
1894	705·5	377·2	124·8	345·9	13·0
1895	775·4	417·2	124·2	404·9	21·7
1896	718·5	360·0	117·6	334·7	18·0
1897	740·7	363·6	127·7	371·5	40·1
1898	699·6	311·7	135·9	283·3	12·3
1899	668·8	295·9	131·2	292·9	22·6
1900	559·0	250·1	136·2	196·2	24·9
1901	692·4	334·4	139·5	294·2	20·2
1902	643·3	269·2	148·2	285·4	37·2
1903	605·0	223·4	155·1	285·5	36·0
1904	566·7	222·6	133·8	252·3	37·9
1905	620·4	253·7	139·3	277·9	35·3
1906	645·2	253·3	146·8	267·1	29·8
1907	764·3	321·5	158·4	313·5	31·0
1908	723·8	321·1	159·7	326·3	37·8
1909	808·7	312·7	176·5	390·7	62·3
1910	803·3	314·5	189·7	335·2	37·0
1911	799·9	324·0	174·1	304·5	30·8
1912	810·5	285·1	184·2	337·9	47·1
1913	806·4	265·1	181·2	306·8	28·7
1914	717·1	239·2	184·6	295·5	38·5
1915	934·5	426·2	200·0	123·0	32·0
1916	624·8	241·7	157·9	45·4	13·1
1917	628·8	338·2	142·1	30·7	7·0
1918	420·6	204·8	89·3	20·5	2·3
1919	1,046·7	587·6	254·2	169·5	18·5
1920	876·9	508·6	154·2	220·4	22·0
1921	763·1	311·1	148·3	335·0	35·4
1922	1,111·5	457·9	304·7	449·0	61·3
1923	745·6	276·3	181·1	414·5	57·8
1924	767·0	228·8	178·6	361·1	52·3
1925	732·4	225·1	172·5	341·4	53·8
1926	816·6	304·4	184·2	340·6	54·4
1927	828·4	237·6	192·4	347·8	62·0
1928	784·1	222·9	182·3	339·8	48·0
1929	818·7	269·9	194·0	332·6	52·0
1930	786·5	257·0	174·7	290·1	32·7
1931	852·6	290·0	188·4	265·3	35·8
1932	921·9	302·0	201·1	319·5	41·9
1933	956·8	308·7	243·7	352·2	69·4
1934	793·6	255·5	216·5	261·2	54·8
1935	868·4	364·5	172·2	261·1	80·3
1936	917·5	347·8	233·6	266·0	58·5
1937	785·8	301·0	180·5	221·2	45·5
1938	883·8	365·5	198·0	257·0	42·4
1939	904·2	355·1	223·8	197·3	29·0

a) Includes wool from imported skins and foreign wool treated (e.g. carbonised) in the United Kingdom.

(*b*) A very small amount of wool waste had been included under this heading previously.

Textiles 15. Exports of Wool Manufactures—Great Britain 1815–19, and United Kingdom 1820–1938

NOTES

[1] SOURCES: 1815–19—*S.P.* 1821, XVII; 1820–5—*S.P.* 1833, XXXIII, and (for yarn) *S.P.* 1828, XIX; 1826–40—*S.P.* 1844, XLV; 1840–1920—*Abstract*; 1921–38—*Annual Statement of Trade*.

[2] Exports to Ireland have been excluded from the British figures for 1815–19.

[3] It is impossible to bridge completely the break caused by the adoption of a new classification of exports in 1890. Total manufactures including carpets (but excluding blankets which were only recorded by number from 1890) amounted to 233,962,000 yards in 1890, and to 178,175,000 yards in 1909. Thereafter carpets were included with rugs, and recorded by the square yard.

[4] It is impossible to continue the series for *Total Manufactures* after 1919 since several items were thereafter recorded in units other than the square yard.

A. 1815–90

	Woollen and Worsted Yarn (000 lb.)	Wool Goods Entered by the Piece (000 pieces)	Wool Goods Entered by the Yard (000 yd.)	Total Wool Manufacture (including Carpets) (000 yd.)
1815	—	1,483	12,173	...
1816	—	1,285	7,112	...
1817	—	1,400	6,614	...
1818	—	1,626	8,997	...
1819	14	1,231	6,488	...
1820	11	1,293	4,791	...
1821	18	1,610	6,322	...
1822	31	1,706	8,436	...
1823	18	1,656	8,140	...
1824	20	1,857	7,338	...
1825	77	1,743	7,804	...
1826	131	1,619	4,941	...
1827	256	1,852	6,461	...
1828	437	1,821	6,816	...
1829	590	1,773	5,298	...
1830	1,108	1,747	5,562	...
1831	1,592	1,997	5,798	...
1832	2,204	2,297	6,011	...
1833	2,107	2,384	7,456	...
1834	1,862	1,910	6,689	...
1835	2,357	2,390	7,907	...
1836	2,546	2,225	9,100	...
1937	2,514	1,519	5,923	...
1838	3,086	2,052	6,912	...
1839	3,320	2,144	8,171	...
1840	3,797	2,014	8,164	68,675
1841	4,903	...	...	77,962
1842	5,962	...	...	75,285
1843	7,410	...	...	96,314
1844	8,272	...	...	112,367
1845	9,406	...	...	106,832
1846	8,631	...	...	87,949
1847	10,065	...	...	98,953
1848	8,429	...	...	84,792
1849	11,773	...	...	124,035

	Woollen and Worsted Yarn (000 lb.)	Total Wool Manufacture (including Carpets) (000 yd.)
1850	13,794	150,520
1851	14,671	151,231
1852	14,220	165,527
1853	13,965	168,561
1854	15,733	153,325
1855	20,408	133,042
1856	27,340	156,461
1857	24,654	177,132
1958	24,070	166,142
1859	22,849	193,687
1860	27,534	190,371
1861	27,512	164,399
1862	27,821	167,000
1863	32,543	217,167
1864	31,824	241,042
1865	31,671	279,206
1866	27,401	281,878
1867	37,434	249,459
1868	43,654	269,134
1869	38,778	303,017
1870	35,537	292,696
1871	43,726	367,875
1872	39,735	412,541
1873	34,745	345,888
1874	34,981	326,679
1875	31,724	317,537
1876	30,854	282,242
1877	26,973	261,415
1878	31,190	257,877
1879	33,379	251,255
1880	26,464	262,356
1881	29,731	272,875
1882	31,833	265,211
1883	33,489	255,905
1884	39,272	290,275 (*a*)
1885	43,492	268,114
1886	45,650	274,292
1887	40,153	282,629
1888	42,631	265,821
1889	45,360	269,961

See p. 197 *for footnotes*

	Woollen and Worsted Yarn (000 lb.)	Noils (000 lb.)	Tops (000 lb.)	Woollen Tissues (000 yd.)	Worsted Tissues (000 yd.)	Total Wool Manufactures (except carpets and blankets) (000 yd.)
1890	41,083	10,235	9,016	56,486	153,171	223,225
1891	41,439	10,608	6,447	55,914	144,531	212,145
1892	44,820	11,112	9,574	51,189	142,590	203,376
1893	50,101	11,216	11,068	46,610	129,929	185,429
1894	53,016	8,961	11,609	40,922	110,674	160,532
1895	61,071	13,756	14,261	57,657	164,039	233,156
1896	62,239	11,174	18,236	60,247	136,776	209,682
1897	57,075	11,627	25,514	50,117	129,667	190,271
1898	58,807	11,940	24,099	46,308	95,481	152,004
1899	63,700	13,001	29,907	48,954	102,525	162,124
1900	57,148	7,897	28,031	50,503	102,174	164,376
1901	48,498	9,924	27,111	44,879	93,979	148,657
1902	52,725	11,884	40,740	47,140	102,616	158,294
1903	59,804	13,028	42,515	50,732	106,426	165,949
1904	54,378	9,266	37,419	67,121	103,931	180,810
1905	49,600	11,573	35,386	72,288	106,523	188,032
1906	55,328	11,522	38,649	79,957	99,231	187,942
1907	58,099	12,690	35,811	84,881	99,012	192,599
1908	50,912	13,206	34,726	75,660	74,181	156,707
1909	58,261	16,074	40,677	78,699	85,131	171,330
1910	67,894	17,233	42,129	95,274	95,370	199,077
1911	65,375	17,074	37,988	97,717	78,495	183,855
1912	63,026	19,568	44,826	100,530	72,136	180,234
1913	54,716	20,035	43,633	105,884	62,490	176,093
1914	36,666	14,332	36,840	81,997	70,304	159,591
1915	16,564	12,097	16,201	92,331	55,770	154,743
1916	27,980	12,887	22,555	131,762	52,212	199,647
1917	20,970	11,512	14,374	123,547	42,730	176,931
1918	15,183	5,135	15,061	67,383	31,081	102,382
1919	28,677	13,296	14,868	131,129	32,229	167,884

				(000 sq. yd.)		
1920	31,016	10,830	23,770	187,233	77,355	...
1921	29,458	15,564	34,690	76,556	40,814	...
1922	52,615	20,320	41,604	121,591	62,338	...
1923	44,141 (*b*)	20,379 (*b*)	38,995 (*b*)	148,556 (*b*)	62,935 (*b*)	...
1924	53,861	20,758	41,129	164,740	56,843	...
1925	44,728	15,141	32,041	132,174 (*c*)	47,302 (*c*)	...
1926	37,178	13,809	33,622	119,357	42,950	...
1927	51,889	18,821	41,952	130,914	39,980	...
1928	48,951	20,459	34,425	128,339	42,111	...
1929	46,696	17,101	32,737	108,186	47,281	...
1930	37,306	12,837	28,836	79,042	34,712	...
1931	34,927	10,537	27,992	56,331	29,746	...
1932	38,025	12,070	41,754	53,536	28,296	...
1933	43,415	15,047	45,832	61,307	32,893	...
1934	42,904	10,486	41,747	68,940	33,262	...
1935	40,896	16,700	55,930	71,208	38,457	...
1936	37,149	17,646	52,132	78,184	39,800	...
1937	32,323	12,678	40,181	79,875	42,960	...
1938	27,794	11,789	32,461	58,908	31,572	...
1939	26,331	8,630	33,777	59,355	34,079	...

(*a*) It was stated that prior to 1884 'large quantities of piece goods of mixed materials in which wool predominated were erroneously entered as cotton manufactures'.
(*b*) Southern Ireland was treated as foreign from 1st April 1923.

(*c*) Prior to 1925 woollen and worsted tissues included manufactures of pure alpaca, mohair, and cashmere. The size of this break is probably very small, particularly for woollens.

Textiles 16. Spindles, Power Looms, and Power Employed in Wool Factories—

United Kingdom 1835–1954

NOTES

[1] SOURCES: 1835–1904—Returns made by the Factory Inspectors, in sessional papers from 1836; 1918 (first row), Skinner's directory, *The World's Wool, 1930*, quoting the Wool Control Board; 1918 (second row)—Committee on Industry and Trade, *Survey of Textile Industries* (1928), p. 273 for power looms, and the Bradford Chamber of Commerce, *Statistics relating to the Worsted, Woollen and Artificial Silk Trades* for spindles; 1938 and 1943—*Working Party Reports, Wool* (1947), quoting the Board of Trade census and the Wool Control census respectively; 1954—Skinner's *The Wool Trade Directory of the World, 1958–9*, quoting the International Wool Textile Organisation.

[2] This table covers woollen, worsted and shoddy factories.
[3] It is not always clear whether the Inspectors' returns relate to all machines in place or merely to those in use. The 1871 and 1874 returns specifically include all machines, but later returns may not have done. See note 2 to table 7 for Ellison's remarks on the cotton industry figures, which probably apply to wool also. The 1871 returns for wool received particular criticism from Bradford, and 'are, to say the least, strongly suspect'. (Eric M. Sigsworth, *Black Dyke Mills* (Liverpool, 1958), p. 78 note.)

(in thousands)

| | Spindles | | | Horsepower Used | |
	Spinning	Doubling	Power Looms	Steam	Water
1835	...		5	...	...
1838	...		...	17	10
1850	2,471		42	23	10
1856	3,112		53	31	9
1861	3,472		65	53	11
1867	6,456	520	119	85	12
1871	4,486	472	115	103	12
1874	5,449	559	140	...	...
1878	5,518	784	146	...	...
1885	5,375	769	140	...	...
1890	5,605	970	132	...	...
1904	5,625	1,059	105	...	...
1918	8,023		121	...	...
1918 (a)	6,459	1,337	115	...	...
1938	5,493	1,469	78	...	...
1943	5,620	1,423	79	...	...
1954	5,019		60	...	...

(a) The first row of figures for 1918 is for Great Britain and the whole of Ireland, and is comparable with earlier years. The second row is for Great Britain and Northern Ireland so far as power looms are concerned, and compares with later years. The second row of spindle figures for 1918, however, is for Great Britain alone, and does not compare exactly with later years, when Northern Ireland was included.

Textiles 17. Numbers Employed in the Wool Industry—United Kingdom 1835–1939

NOTES

[1] SOURCES: Part A—Returns by the Factory Inspectors, printed in sessional papers from 1836; Part B, 1923–36—*Abstract of Labour Statistics*; Part B, 1937–9—*Ministry of Labour Gazette*.

[2] The Inspectors' returns were incomplete owing to the failure of some employers to send information; but it seems clear that the omissions were of little significance, even in the earlier years.

[3] This table covers woollen, worsted and shoddy factories.

A. Numbers Employed in Factories by Age and Sex

(in thousands)

	Children under 13		Children Aged 13–18		All Ages		Grand Total
	Males	Females	Males	Females	Males	Females	
1835	7 (a)	7 (a)	12	11	32	23	55
1838	5 (a)	5 (a)	14	19	42	45	87
1847	8	7	16	21	59	66	126
1850	8	9	20	...	72	82	154
1856	9	9	18	...	76	91	167
1861	10	10	18	...	81	92	173
1867	15	17	23	...	110	152	262
1870	12	12	24	...	108	130	239
1874	19	19	25	...	125	155	280

	Children under 14 Working Half-Time		Persons under 18 Working Full Time				
1878	15	16	22	...	116	154	270
1885	12	12	24	...	125	158	282
1890	11	12	26	...	132	170	302
1895	7	7	23	37	121	161	282
1896	6	7	23	37	121	163	284
1897	5	6	21	35	111	154	266
1898	4	5	20	34	106	150	256
1901	4	4	19	35	107	153	260
1904	4	4	19	32	109	153	262
1907	4	4	19	34	109	152	261

B. Numbers of Insured Employees in the Wool Industry, 1923–39 (for a date in July each year)

	Males	Females	Total
1923	117	152	269
1924	111	151	262
1925	107	149	256
1926	105	148	254
1927	104	145	249
1927 (b)	96	143	240
1928	98	144	243
1929	96	143	239
1930	96	145	240
1931	96	143	239
1932	96	137	234
1933	96	135	231
1934	95	134	230
1935	93	129	222
1936	94	130	223
1937	93	131	224
1938	90	126	216
1939	91	123	214

(a) The numbers of children under 10 years old in 1835 and 1838 were:

	Males	Females
1835	384	280
1838	1,154	1,018

(b) From 1927 the figures apply only to employees between the ages of 16 and 64 inclusive. Figures on both the old and the new basis are shown for 1927.

Textiles 18. Quantity and Value of Linen Stamped for Sale in Scotland—1728–1822

NOTE

[1] SOURCE: A. J. Warden, *The Linen Trade, Ancient and Modern* (London, 1867), p. 480. Also given in John Horner, *The Linen Trade of Europe during the Spinning Wheel Period* (Belfast, 1920), p. 299.

	Millions of Yards	£000		Millions of Yards	£000
1728	2·2	103	1776	13·6	639
1729	3·2	114	1777	14·8	711
1730	3·8	131	1778	13·3	592
1731	3·9	146	1779	12·9	551
1732	4·4	168	1780	13·4	622
1733	4·7	183	1781	15·2	738
1734	4·9	185	1782	15·3	775
1735	4·9	177	1783	17·1	867
1736	4·5	168	1784	19·1	933
1737	4·7	184	1785	17·3	835
1738	4·7	185	1786	17·5	823
1739	4·8	196	1787	19·4	844
1740	4·6	189	1788	20·5	855
1741	4·9	188	1789	20·0	780
1742	4·4	192	1790	18·1	723
1743	5·1	216	1791	18·7	756
1744	5·5	229	1792	21·1	843
1745	5·5	224	1793	20·7	757
1746	5·5	223	1794	20·5	797
1747	6·7	263	1795	21·4	827
1748	7·4	294	1796	23·1	906
1749	7·4	322	1797	19·5	735
1750	7·6	362	1798	21·3	850
1751	7·9	367	1799	24·5	1,116
1752	8·8	409	1800	24·2	1,048
1753	9·4	445	1801	25·3	1,019
1754	8·9	407	1802	23·8	915
1755	8·1	345	1803	15·9	688
1756	8·5	368	1804	15·2	749
1757	9·8	402	1805	19·4	936
1758	10·6	424	1806	21·5	973
1759	10·8	451	1807	20·8	957
1760	11·7	523	1808	19·4	1,015
1761	12·0	516	1809	22·5	1,172
1762	11·3	475	1810	26·5	1,266
1763	12·4	552	1811	21·5	999
1764	12·8	573	1812	19·0	1,020
1765	12·7	579	1813	19·8	977
1766	13·2	637	1814	26·1	1,254
1767	12·8	634	1815	32·1	1,404
1768	11·8	600	1816	26·1	1,027
1769	13·4	690	1817	28·8	1,093
1770	13·0	634	1818	31·3	1,254
1771	13·5	620	1819	29·3	1,158
1772	13·1	580	1820	26·3	1,039
1773	10·7	463	1821	30·5	1,232
1774	11·4	492	1822	36·3	1,396
1775	12·1	562			

NOTES

[1] SOURCES: 1697–1807—Elizabeth B. Schumpeter, *English Overseas Trade Statistics, 1697–1808* (Oxford University Press, 1960), tables X and XI (converted to yards) with British linens exported with bounty from 1743 to 1764 added from J. Horner, *The Linen Trade of Europe during the Spinning Wheel Period* (Belfast, 1920), pp. 231–232; 1808–9—*S.P.* 1812–3, XIII; 1810–25—Returns printed in *Sessional Papers* annually from 1821 to 1826.

[2] Ireland is treated as a foreign country throughout this table, and re-exports of Irish linen from Great Britain, even though made with bounty, are not included here.

(in thousands of yards)

1697	145	1740	1,523	1783	9,690
1698	285	1741	2,201	1784	8,426
1699	245	1742	2,120	1785	6,397
1700	181	1743	1,690	1786	6,581
1701	141	1744	1,354	1787	9,097
1702	138	1745	1,423	1788	10,029
1703	145	1746	3,031	1789	8,670
1704	147	1747	2,667	1790	7,806
1705	...	1748	2,990	1791	9,045
1706	139	1749	4,068	1792	13,248 (b)
1707	171	1750	4,029	1793	12,083
1708	323	1751	3,868	1794	16,075
1709	348	1752	4,025	1795	12,903
1710	304	1753	5,004	1796	15,616
1711	427	1754	4,802	1797	12,936
1712	...	1755	3,324	1798	18,983
1713	287	1756	4,528	1799	19,466
1714	293	1757	5,982	1800	13,678
1715	363	1758	7,116	1801	17,778
1716	324	1759	8,389	1802	15,706
1717	381	1760	10,494	1803	9,853
1718	576	1761	7,858	1804	13,005
1719	448	1762	7,746	1805	11,392
1720	412	1763	7,605	1806	13,793
1721	497	1764	8,507	1807	13,456
1722	601	1765	7,463	1808	15,858 (c)
1723	451	1766	8,592	1809	20,507
1724	471	1767	8,043	1810	17,926 (d)
1725	672	1768	9,037	1811	12,695
1726	575	1769	7,474	1812	15,275
1727	632	1770	7,618	1813	...
1728	742	1771	10,308	1814	18,752
1729	810	1772	11,619 (a)	1815	17,183
1730	741	1773	8,804	1816	17,541
1731	748	1774	11,318	1817	24,595
1732	707	1775	8,224	1818	28,131
1733	610	1776	6,379	1819	20,591
1734	645	1777	6,639	1820	24,099
1735	955	1778	4,905	1821	28,239
1736	1,040	1779	4,892	1822	33,806
1737	778	1780	7,178	1823	34,716
1738	1,176	1781	3,475	1824	43,978
1739	1,238	1782	5,680	1825	33,765

(a) This break, caused by the change in original source, was not significant.

(b) The inclusion of Scotland in 1792 must have had a considerable bearing on the increase in that and subsequent years.

(c) The figure for 1807 in *S.P.* 1812–13, XIII differs from that derived from Mrs Schumpeter by about 3 per cent. It may therefore be presumed that there is a slight break between 1807 and 1808 when the source is changed.

(d) Prior to 1810 there is no official record of the total yardage of linen exports. Some classes of linen were entered by the yard, others by the ell or by the piece. For this table, these latter entries have been converted to yards on the assumption that each piece was 35 yards long. (This assumption is based on the rates of valuation, which for some types of linen were 35 shillings per piece, *or* 15 pence per ell, *or* one shilling per yard.) For the period 1810–12, when official yardage figures are available as well as the older type of entries, yardage figures based on our assumption differ from the official figures by only 2 or 3 per cent.

NOTES

[1] Sources: 1826–39—Returns printed in *Sessional Papers* annually; 1840–1920—*Abstract*; 1921–39—*Annual Statement of Trade*.

[2] The following table of exports from Great Britain of Irish linen will assist comparison with the previous table:

	(000 yd.)		(000 yd.)		(000 yd.)		(000 yd.)
1814	7,226	1817	9,477	1820	9,422	1823	13,889
1815	9,562	1818	9,385	1821	11,630	1824	15,174
1816	8,801	1819	6,138	1822	12,854	1825	13,801

Exports from Britain to Ireland and from Ireland to foreign parts were not very large, and probably cancelled each other.

	Piece Goods (000 yd.)	Thread (000 lb.)	Yarn (000 lb.)		Piece Goods (000 yd.)	Thread (000 lb.)	Yarn (000 lb.)
1826	37,791	...	...	1871	220,467	2,902	36,236
1827	55,132	...	...	1872	245,019	2,642	31,187
1828	60,287	...	...	1873	208,123	2,302	28,734
1829	57,698	...	...	1874	194,682	2,690	27,155
1830	61,920	...	...	1875	204,573	2,758	27,888
1831	69,234	...	...	1876	162,969	2,638	22,278
1832	49,531	...	110	1877	177,767	2,447	19,216
1833	63,253	...	936	1878	160,802	2,395	18,474
1834	67,834	...	1,533	1879	160,311	2,829	17,429
1835	77,977	...	2,611	1880	164,967	2,878	16,478
1836	82,089	...	4,575	1881	174,011	2,590	18,250
1837	58,426	...	8,373	1882	176,451	2,796	18,156
1838	77,196	...	14,923	1883	162,256	2,253	17,678
1839	85,257	...	16,315	1884	155,317	2,581	19,534
1840	89,373	959	17,734	1885	149,469	2,633	16,600
1841	90,322	1,378	25,220	1886	163,756	2,691	15,892
1842	69,233	1,161	29,491	1887	163,930	2,818	16,381
1843	84,173	1,527	23,358	1888	176,718	2,806	14,711
1844	91,284	2,154	25,971	1889	180,630	2,800	13,945
1845	88,402	1,969	23,289	1890	184,040	2,949	15,313
1846	84,799	1,752	19,484	1891	159,458	2,474	14,860
1847	89,329	1,877	12,689	1892	171,303	2,458	15,461
1848	89,002	1,992	11,722	1893	158,335	2,397	16,259
1849	111,259	2,874	17,264	1894	156,254	2,094	15,540
1850	122,343	3,360	18,221	1895	203,588	2,402	17,046
1851	129,107	2,740	18,841	1896	174,208	2,240	18,462
1852	133,193	3,852	23,929	1897	164,583	2,019	18,366
1853	134,165	4,349	22,894	1898	148,005	1,870	17,355
1854	111,649	3,190	17,697	1899	174,279	2,038	18,152
1855	118,040	3,069	18,177	1900	154,708	1,838	16,347
1856	146,410	4,163	25,118	1901	150,215	1,721	12,971
1857	133,840	3,361	28,848	1902	163,129	1,835	14,370
1858	121,940	3,176	32,047	1903	154,947	1,908	14,090
1859	138,120	2,886	27,290	1904	161,763	1,889	14,751
1860	143,997	3,230	31,211	1905	183,446	2,262	14,694
1861	116,322	2,390	27,981	1906	190,958	2,181	14,978
1862	156,895	3,909	32,559	1907	184,999	2,382	16,442
1863	181,637	4,257	38,452	1908	151,894	2,234	13,706
1864	210,469	3,978	40,177	1909	223,935	2,264	15,533
1865	247,006	3,935	36,797	1910	220,568	2,739	18,549
1866	255,469	3,785	33,608	1911	193,829	2,597	18,012
1867	211,275	2,754	34,002	1912	213,085	2,667	17,685
1868	210,050	2,677	32,779	1913	193,681	2,646	16,307
1869	214,715	2,188	34,566	1914	178,893	2,493	12,445
1870	226,471	2,379	37,239	1915	128,776	3,627	6,418

	Piece Goods (000 yd.)	Thread (000 lb.)	Yarn (000 lb.)		Piece Goods (000 yd.)	Thread (000 lb.)	Yarn (000 lb.)
1916	144,064	4,238	9,585	1928	66,135	2,465	10,186
1917	103,538	3,568	18,144	1929	71,540	2,355	10,101
1918	70,204	936	1,669	1930	61,451	1,968	8,201
1919	76,864	3,217	13,238	1931	65,342	1,718	6,491
	(000 sq. yd.)						
1920	93,045	3,114	6,380	1932	65,890	1,812	6,928
1921	39,962	1,499	4,496	1933	76,860	1,898	10,344
1922	77,436	2,211	7,486	1934	77,597	1,900	9,907
1923	89,666	2,586	7,517	1935	77,163	2,114	9,643
1924	110,786	2,656	10,700	1936	88,728	2,020	10,904
1925	83,694	2,752	8,970	1937	83,115	2,283	10,411
1926	75,283	2,596	7,301	1938	51,790	1,822	8,378
1927	73,911	2,494	11,523	1939	77,414	1,890	7,119

Textiles 21. Spindles, Power Looms, and Power Employed in Flax, Jute, Hemp, and China Grass Factories—United Kingdom 1835–1905

NOTES

[1] SOURCE: *Reports of H.M. Inspectors of Factories*, published in sessional papers.

[2] It is not always clear whether the *Reports* relate to all machines in place or merely to those in use. The returns for 1870 and 1874 include all machines, but later returns may not have done so. See note 2 to table 7 for Ellison's remarks on the cotton industry, which probably applied to linen also.

(in thousands)

	Spindles		Power Looms	Horsepower Used	
	Spinning	Doubling		Steam	Water
1835	...		0·3	...	...
1838	...		...	7	4
1850	965		4	11	3
1856	1,288		8	14	4
1861	1,252		15	32	4
1867	1,679	59	35	42	5
1871	1,620	77	40	52	5
1874	1,712	96	52	...	...
1878	1,499	76	56	...	...
1885	1,447	84	61	...	...
1890	1,445	85	63	...	...
1905	1,321	79	68	...	...

Textiles 22. Numbers Employed in the Flax and Related Industries—

United Kingdom 1835–1939

NOTES

[1] SOURCES: Part A—returns by the Factory Inspectors, printed in *Sessional Papers* from 1836; Part B, 1923–36—*Abstract of Labour Statistics*; 1937–9—*Ministry of Labour Gazette*.

[2] The Inspectors' returns were incomplete owing to the failure of some employers to send information; but it seems clear that the omissions were of little significance, even in the earlier years.

[3] Part A covers flax, hemp, jute, and china grass factories (except for the last in 1904 and 1907); Part B covers only the linen (i.e. flax and soft hemp) industry.

(in thousands)

A. Numbers Employed in Factories by Age and Sex

	Children under 13		Children Aged 13–18		All Ages		Grand Total
	Males	Females	Males	Females	Males	Females	
1835	2·4 (a)	2·9 (a)	3·5	8·5	10	23	33
1838	0·8 (a)	0·7 (a)	5·7	12·4	13	31	42
1847	1·0	1·1	6·8	13·0	18	40	58
1850	0·8	0·8	8	...	21	48	68
1856	0·9	1·0	9	...	23	57	80
1861	1·5	2·2	9	...	27	67	94
1867	1·8	2·9	11	...	40	96	135
1870	2·0	3·6	14	...	44	102	146
1874	5·2	6·3	15	...	52	120	172

	Children under 14 Working Half-Time		Persons under 18 Working Full Time				
1878	5·0	7·0	11	...	45	105	150
1885	6·0	7·8	12	...	50	113	163
1890	5·2	6·4	13	...	52	111	163
1895	4·0	4·7	12	20	51	110	161
1896	4·2	4·8	12	20	52	111	162
1897	4·1	4·8	12	20	50	109	159
1898	3·9	4·6	11	20	49	108	157
1901	3·0	4·1	10	19	46	105	150
1904	1·9	2·7	10	18	45	103	148
1907	1·9	2·7	10	21	46	105	151

B. Numbers of Insured Employees in the Linen Industry, 1923–39

	Males	Females	Total
1923	26	56	82
1924	26	58	83
1925	27	59	87
1926	28	62	90
1927	26	59	85
1927 (b)	25	57	83
1928	25	56	81
1929	25	55	80
1930	25	56	81
1931	24	54	78
1932	23	51	75
1933	23	50	73
1934	23	51	75
1935	23	51	74
1936	23	51	74
1937	23	53	76
1938	22	52	74
1939	21	51	72

(a) The numbers of children under 10 years old in 1835 and 1838 were:

	Males	Females
1835	86	65
1838	117	93

(b) From 1927 the figures apply only to employees between the ages of 16 and 64 inclusive. Figures on both the old and the new basis are shown for 1927.

Textiles 23. Imports and Re-exports of Raw and Thrown Silk—England & Wales 1700–91, and Great Britain 1792–1825

NOTE

SOURCES: 1700–1808 (Imports)—Elizabeth B. Schumpeter, *English Overseas Trade Statistics, 1697–1808* (Oxford University Press, 1960), tables XVI and XVII; 1786–1805 (Re-exports)—S.P. 1806, XIII; 1806–16 (Re-exports) and 1809–16 (Imports)—S.P. 1817, XIV; 1817–25—returns printed in sessional papers in most years.

(in thousands of lb.)

| | Imports | | | Imports | | Re-exports | |
	Raw Silk	Thrown Silk		Raw Silk	Thrown Silk	Raw Silk	Thrown Silk
1700	358	83	1747	406	325	...	...
1701	462	36	1748	373	242	...	...
1702	293	80	1749	357	280	...	...
1703	413	55	1750	233	75	...	...
1704	696	147	1751	355	258	...	...
1705	...	...	1752	396	335	...	...
1706	328	138	1753	508	288	...	...
1707	149	145	1754	357	294	...	...
1708	367	165	1755	399	344	...	...
1790	507	69	1756	331	169	...	...
1710	43	54	1757	549	346	...	...
1711	517	176	1758	279	411	...	...
1712	...	...	1759	491	281	...	...
1713	516	156	1760	371	303	...	...
1714	242	181	1761	548	515	...	...
1715	409	169	1762	307	217	...	...
1716	276	282	1763	446	522	...	...
1717	525	253	1764	488	451	...	...
1718	550	193	1765	502	379	...	...
1719	183	184	1766	556	421	...	...
1720	487	288	1767	584	311	...	...
1721	53	254	1768	567	380	...	...
1722	414	281	1769	698	497	...	...
1723	458	295	1770	535	448	...	...
1724	430	302	1771	591	488	...	...
1725	396	340	1772	587 (a)	436 (a)	...	...
1726	360	294	1773	346	235	...	...
1727	554	292	1774	468	429	...	...
1728	463	266	1775	436	412	...	...
1729	294	226	1776	867	454	...	...
1730	397	267	1777	760	397	...	...
1731	343	242	1778	658	187	...	...
1732	242	269	1779	386	383	...	...
1733	516	287	1780	598	488	...	...
1734	499	305	1781	1,040	443	...	...
1735	381	284	1782	245	332	...	...
1736	369	176	1783	730	495	...	...
1737	347	265	1784	1,115	406	...	...
1738	412	279	1785	730	344	...	...
1739	371	194	1786	473	361	45	25
1740	169	240	1787	771	390	120	13
1741	546	224	1788	812	307	116	47
1742	155	213	1789	843	393	107	23
1743	332	267	1790	745	508	70	20
1744	216	191	1791	977	470	67	22
1745	441	192	1792	932 (b)	437 (b)	35 (b)	11 (b)
1746	204	151	1793	1,020	242	29	3

See p. 206 for footnotes

(in thousands of lb.)

	Imports		Re-exports			Imports		Re-exports	
	Raw Silk	Thrown Silk	Raw Silk	Thrown Silk		Raw Silk	Thrown Silk	Raw Silk	Thrown Silk
1794	683	331	84	24	1810	1,341	451	23	50
1795	731	337	55	27	1811	602	20	29	31
1796	488	399	89	39	1812	1,312	618	40	86
1797	266	402	64	18	1813	...	...	...	...
1798	731	403	43	52	1814	1,634	646	33	61
1799	1,241	468	80	39	1815	1,443	358	94	52
1800	834	335	30	31	1816	946	92	300	52
1801	739	275	34	27	1817	932	274	75	21
1802	560	396	33	36	1818	1,645	457	110	35
1803	804	385	24	19	1819	...	...	...	...
1804	1,032	449	53	74	1820	...	...	...	...
1805	1,190	433	26	69	1821	2,119	339	49	22
1806	803	515	19	52	1822	2,053	493	51	11
1807	778	346	30	59	1823	2,452	360	46	25
1808	328	415	33	22	1824	3,048	335	...	...
1809	698	502	21	48	1825	2,854	770	290	71

(a) This break, caused by a change in the original source, is negligible.
(b) For the period 1786–91 there is no difference between Mrs Schumpeter's figures of English imports and those of British imports given in *S.P.* 1806, XIII. It is probable, therefore, that there is no break at all here.

Textiles 24. Imports and Re-exports of Raw Silk and Silk Yarn—United Kingdom 1814–1938

NOTE

Sources: 1814–30—*Report of the Select Committee on the Silk Trade (S.P. 1831–2, XIX), p. 10; 1831–9—Tables of Revenue, Population, Commerce, etc.; 1840–1920—Abstract* (except for waste silk re-exports, 1851–76, which are only available in the *Trade and Navigation Accounts*; 1921–39—*Annual Statement of Trade.*

(in thousands of lb.)

	Imports		Re-exports			Imports		Re-exports	
	Raw Silk, Knubs and Waste	Thrown and Spun Silk	Raw Silk, Knubs and Waste	Thrown and Spun Silk		Raw Silk, Knubs and Waste	Thrown and Spun Silk	Raw Silk, Knubs and Waste	Thrown and Spun Silk
1814	1,663	646	10	2	1859	12,251	327	2,321	254
1815	1,474	360	75	- -	1860	11,132	224	3,323	427
1816	948	195	269	5	1861	12,029	125	4,191	83
1817	981	248	55	2	1862	13,524	62	5,206	138
1818	1,745	461	80	4	1863	12,798	59	3,975	217
1819	1,555	293	29	3	1864	8,441	73	4,017	334
1820	2,308	334	8	5	1865	11,476	60	3,273	307
1821	2,201	341	8	- -	1866	8,301	67	3,360	72
1822	2,178	503	16	- -	1867	8,429	196	2,420	16
1823	2,512	368	9	5	1868	10,458	327	3,051	58
1824	3,136	342	2	1	1869	8,843	260	3,860	36
1825	3,117	778	129	25	1870	9,820	284	3,111	40
1826	2,488	177	257	22	1871	12,619	177	3,866	41
1827	3,147	464	35	15	1872	11,095	63	3,608	41
1828	4,256	509	23	9	1873	10,008	109	3,103	21
1829	3,595	211	221	33	1874	9,848	115	3,199	22
1830	3,904	414	59	13	1875	8,272	110	2,750	88
1831	3,993	629	26	25	1876	9,339	164	3,537	50
1832	4,048	177	64	29	1877	7,162	114	2,487	18
1833	3,435	229	66	6	1878	7,854	40	2,739	40
1834	4,656	192	207	21	1879	8,172	117	1,939	24
1835	5,159	216	120	17	1880	9,834	204	1,982	8
1836	6,061	397	201	24	1881	8,966	132	1,411	6
1837	5,090	231	367	30	1882	8,336	294	1,693	6
1838	4,404	265	167	31	1883	10,130	292	1,108	6
1839	9,789	225	103	13	1884	12,054	324	1,109	51
1840	4,458	289	147 (a)	13	1885	8,023	230	1,105	76
1841	4,735	231	189 (a)	4	1886	9,850	253	1,609	130
1842	5,388	397	165 (a)	4	1887	9,872	454	912	59
1843	4,964	384	166 (a)	12	1888	12,414	559	1,000	63
1844	5,899	401	228 (a)	22	1889	12,020	608	1,768	31
1845	5,817	512	296 (a)	28	1890	9,872	585	1,515	124
1846	5,303	432	317 (a)	40	1891	11,121	582	877	29
1847	5,286	313	436 (a)	55	1892	6,699	503	992	33
1848	5,518	1,071	291 (a)	44	1893	8,639	345	910	39
1849	6,420	615	473 (a)	133	1894	7,986	398	643	31
1850	6,689	470	557 (a)	75	1895	7,907	460	762	45
1851	6,184	413	550	155	1896	8,745	573	708	74
1852	7,589	426	706	242	1897	7,941	412	648	54
1853	8,608	828	456	253	1898	10,071	424	558	13
1854	9,717	1,022	1,189	525	1899	10,922	378	586	30
1855	7,975	930	2,305	402	1900	8,214	665	861	36
1856	9,399	853	1,502	283	1901	6,726	625	846	49
1857	14,394	641	1,812	239	1902	7,501	803	842	96
1858	8,156	358	2,587	365	1903	8,590	663	1,269	82

See p. 208 for footnotes

(in thousands of lb.)

| | Imports | | Re-exports | | | | Imports | | Re-exports | |
	Raw Silk, Knubs and Waste	Thrown and Spun Silk	Raw Silk, Knubs and Waste	Thrown and Spun Silk			Raw Silk, Knubs and Waste	Thrown and Spun Silk	Raw Silk, Knubs and Waste	Thrown and Spun Silk
1904	9,340	769	1,211	44		1922	5,226	676	144	12
1905	9,230	879	1,703	54		1923	3,497 (b)	687 (b)	165 (b)	13 (b)
1906	8,467	924	455	57		1924	5,242	714	279	18
1907	8,620	938	642	47		1925	4,761	1,299	237	10
1908	8,353	810	314	44		1926	4,152	564	80	14
1909	8,675	831	555	54		1927	3,662	809	238	8
1910	9,736	956	958	55		1928	3,924	810	176	9
1911	10,339	1,086	1,527	61		1929	4,683	774	49	12
1912	9,724	1,213	724	51		1930	3,977	1,034	58	18
1913	8,328	1,054	971	43		1931	3,413	952	81	9
1914	6,875	716	516	34		1932	4,724	472	35	8
1915	8,045	762	215	18		1933	5,548	261	29	3
1916	7,304	819	272	3		1934	7,605	203	454	30
1917	6,347	621	13	1		1935	6,356	204	84	8
1918	7,819	623	532	7		1936	6,824	162	28	6
1919	6,401	533	303	26		1937	7,510	194	69	9
1920	5,787	796	187	12		1938	6,837	126	77	15
1921	1,797	373	169	11		1939	5,414	148	103	9

(a) These figures are of raw silk only. Exports of waste etc. were, however, very small at this period.

(b) Southern Ireland was treated as foreign from 1st April 1923.

Textiles 25. Exports of British Silk Manufactures—England & Wales 1697–1791, and Great Britain 1792–1807, and 1814–23

NOTE

SOURCES: 1697–1807—Elizabeth B. Schumpeter, *English Overseas Trade Statistics, 1697–1808* (Oxford University Press, 1960), tables XI and XIV; 1814–23—returns printed in *Sessional Papers* from time to time.

(in thousands of lb.)

Year		Year		Year	
1697	41	1738	47	1779	61
1698	55	1739	49	1780	95
1699	48	1740	40	1781	86
1700	38	1741	58	1782	60
1701	39	1742	62	1783	105
1702	28	1743	71	1784	146
1703	33	1744	46	1785	78
1704	32	1745	40	1786	78
1705	...	1746	50	1787	88
1706	42	1747	56	1788	82
1707	44	1748	54	1789	80
1708	52	1749	60	1790	98
1709	57	1750	63	1791	120
1710	54	1751	23	1792	121 (b)
1711	46	1752	92	1793	95
1712	...	1753	90	1794	113
1713	44	1754	85	1795	121
1714	52	1755	91	1796	146
1715	58	1756	89	1797	118
1716	47	1757	93	1798	87
1717	62	1758	118	1799	119
1718	71	1759	173	1800	112
1719	40	1760	198	1801	97
1720	41	1761	144	1802	78
1721	38	1762	137	1803	54
1722	43	1763	86	1804	51
1723	44	1764	127	1805	52
1724	49	1765	97	1806	60
1725	86	1766	72	1807	51
1726	50	1767	80		
1727	37	1768	74		
1728	45	1769	53	1814 (c)	242
1729	43	1770	54	1815	269
1730	58	1771	103	1816	205
1731	42	1772	91 (a)	1817	203
1732	47	1773	65	1818	241
1733	45	1774	85	1819	...
1734	36	1775	41	1820	...
1735	45	1776	48	1821	276
1736	47	1777	61	1822	287
1737	46	1778	47	1823	225

(a) There was no break on the change in original source at this time.
(b) There being no silk industry in Scotland, the inclusion of that country at this time makes no break in the series.

(c) The figures for 1697–1807 relate to piece goods only. It is not clear whether those for 1814–23 include sewing silk or not, but it seems probable that there was some difference in definition.

NOTE

SOURCES: 1840–1920—*Abstract*; 1921–38—*Annual Statement of Trade.*

A. Silk Manufactures, in thousands of lb.

1840	622	1848	411	1856	1,164
1841	638	1849	818	1857	1,196
1842	369	1850	1,186	1858	964
1843	398	1851	1,181	1859	1,184
1844	488	1852	1,131	1860	1,307
1845	470	1853	1,377	1861	1,060
1846	470	1854	1,000		
1847	620	1855	835		

B. Silk Broad Piece Goods, in thousand yards

1862	2,603	1882	7,662	1902	9,585
1863	2,828	1883	7,688	1903	9,778
1864	2,771	1884	6,810	1904	10,085
1865	2,873	1885	6,016	1905	11,451
1866	3,067	1886	7,266	1906	13,464
1867	2,377	1887	6,592	1907	13,018
1868	2,926	1888	8,345	1908	8,518
1869	2,900	1889	9,619	1909	10,074
1870	3,854	1890	9,507	1910	11,612
1871	5,160	1891	6,455	1911	11,740
1872	4,417	1892	5,952	1912	11,953
1873	2,984	1893	6,036	1913	11,841
1874	4,025	1894	5,535	1914	10,221
1875	3,655	1895	6,830	1915	9,556
1876	3,944	1896	7,611	1916	10,070
1877	4,356	1897	7,477	1917	7,760
1878	4,819	1898	8,999	1918	6,385
1879	4,724	1899	9,737	1919	8,615
1880	6,219	1900	10,247	1920	8,241
1881	7,051	1901	9,290		

C. Silk Tissues (except ribbons) in thousand square yards

1921	3,224	1927	8,127	1933	2,596
1922	5,142	1928	7,841	1934	2,484
1923	5,001	1929	6,502	1935	3,072
1924	5,308	1930	5,292	1936	2,996
1925	4,728	1931	4,705	1937	3,475
1926	5,240	1932	4,270	1938	2,698
				1939	3,005

27.   Spindles, Power Looms, and Power Employed in Silk Factories— United Kingdom 1835–90

NOTES

[1] SOURCE: *Reports of H.M. Inspectors of Factories*, published in sessional papers.

[2] It is not always clear from the *Reports* whether they relate to all machines or merely those in use. The returns for 1870 and 1874 include all machines, but later ones may not have done so.

(in thousands)

	Spindles		Power Looms	Horsepower Used	
	Spinning	Doubling		Steam	Water
1835	...		2	...	...
1838	...		...	2	1
1850	1,226		6	3	1
1856	1,094		9	4	1
1861	1,339		11	6	1
1867	978	182	15	6	1
1870	940	190	12	8	1
1874	1,115	222	10	...	...
1878	843	176	13	...	...
1885	888	175	12	...	...
1890	847	183	11	...	...

Textiles 28. Numbers Employed in the Silk Industry—United Kingdom 1835–1939

NOTES

[1] SOURCES: Part A—returns by the Factory Inspectors, printed in sessional papers from 1836; Part B, 1923–36—*Abstract of Labour Statistics*; Part B, 1937–9—*Ministry of Labour Gazette*.

[2] The Inspectors' returns were incomplete owing to the failure of some employers to send information; but it seems clear that the omissions were of little significance even in the earlier years.

A. Numbers Employed in Silk Factories by Age and Sex

(in thousands)

	Children under 13		Children Aged 13–18		All Ages		Grand Total
	Males	Females	Males	Females	Males	Females	
1835	3·4 (a)	5·6 (a)	2·6	6·9	10	21	31
1838	3·4 (a)	5·2 (a)	3·2	8·5	11	23	34
1847	3·0	4·8	3·7	9·6	14	31	45
1850	2·4	4·8	3·2	...	13	30	43
1856	2·7	5·4	4·1	...	17	39	56
1861	2·1	4·9	3·2	...	16	37	52
1867	1·3	3·6	2·5	...	12	29	41
1870	2·3	4·7	2·7	...	14	34	48
1874	2·3	4·5	2·4	...	13	32	46

	Children under 14 Working Half-Time		Persons under 18 Working Full Time		All Ages		Grand Total
					Males	Females	
1878	1·4	2·8	2·2	...	12	29	41
1885	1·2	2·0	2·2	...	13	30	43
1890	1·2	1·7	2·5	...	13	28	41
1895	0·5	0·8	2·1	6·1	11	24	36
1896	0·4	0·8	2·0	6·3	11	25	36
1897	0·3	0·8	2·0	6·7	11	26	37
1898	0·3	0·6	1·9	6·2	10	25	35
1901	0·3	0·4	1·7	5·1	9	23	32
1904	0·2	0·5	1·5	4·7	9	21	30
1907	0·3	0·5	1·7	4·8	9	20	29

B. Numbers of Insured Employees in the Silk and Artificial Silk Industries, 1923–39

	All Silk and Artificial Silk			All Silk Manufacture and Artificial Silk Weaving			Artificial Silk Yarn		
	Males	Females	Total	Males	Females	Total	Males	Females	Total
1923	14	23	37	...	...	...	...	...	...
1924	16	26	41	...	...	...	...	...	...
1925	18	28	47	...	...	...	...	...	...
1926	21	30	51	...	...	...	...	...	...
1927	23	32	55	...	...	...	...	...	...
1927 (b)	22	32	54	...	...	...	...	...	...
1928	31	39	70	...	...	...	...	...	...
1929	33	41	74	...	...	...	...	...	...
1930	33	45	78	18	32	49	15	13	29
1931	31	42	73	16	29	45	14	13	27
1932	30	40	70	15	28	44	15	12	26
1933	30	40	70	16	29	45	14	11	25
1934	32	41	73	17	31	48	15	10	25
1935	36	42	78	18	31	49	19	11	29
1936	38	42	80	19	31	50	19	11	30
1937	38	42	81	20	32	52	18	11	29
1938	37	40	77	20	32	52	17	9	26
1939	35	39	74	19	31	50	16	9	24

(a) The numbers of children under 10 years of age in 1835 and 1838 were:

	Males	Females
1835	905	1,353
1838	1,131	1,463

(b) From 1927 the figures apply only to employees between the ages of 16 and 64 inclusive. Figures on both the old and the new basis are shown for 1927.

REFERENCES

BOOKS

Anon. (Sir Joseph Banks), *The Propriety of Allowing a Qualified Exportation of Wool* (London, 1782).

E. Baines, *History of the Cotton Manufacture* (London, 1835).

J. Bischoff, *A Comprehensive History of the Woollen and Worsted Manufacture* (2 vols., London, 1842).

Bradford Chamber of Commerce, *Annual Statistics relating to the Worsted, Woollen and Artificial Silk Trade of the United Kingdom*.

R. Burn, *Statistics of the Cotton Trade* (London, 1847).

Cowper, *A Short Essay on Trade in General* (London, 1741).

W. B. Crump, *The Leeds Woollen Industry, 1780–1820* (Leeds, 1931).

G. W. Daniels, *The Early English Cotton Industry* (Manchester, 1920).

Dundee Trade Report Association, *Statistics of the Linen Trade* (Dundee, 1855).

T. Ellison, *A Handbook of the Cotton Trade* (London, 1858).

T. Ellison, *The Cotton Trade of Great Britain* (London, 1886).

H. Forbes, *The Rise, Progress and Present State of the Worsted, Alpaca, and Mohair Manufactures in England* (London, 1853).

C. Gill, *The Rise of the Irish Linen Industry* (Oxford, 1925).

H. Heaton, *The Yorkshire Woollen and Worsted Industries* (Oxford, 1920).

W. O. Henderson, *The Lancashire Cotton Famine, 1861–65* (Manchester, 1934).

F. Hooper, *Statistics relating to the City of Bradford* (Bradford, 1898).

J. Horner, *The Linen Trade of Europe during the Spinning Wheel Period* (Belfast, 1920).

International Cotton Bulletin, 1922–54, continued as *International Review of the Cotton and Allied Textile Industries*.

J. James, *History of the Worsted Manufacture in England* (London, 1857).

G. T. Jones, *Increasing Return* (Cambridge, 1933).

Liverpool Cotton Association, *Annual Circular*.

J. Luccock, *The Nature and Properties of Wool* (Leeds, 1805).

R. Robson, *The Cotton Industry in Britain* (London, 1957).

J. Smith, *Memoirs of Wool* (2 vols., London, 1757).

E. M. Sigsworth, *Black Dyke Mills* (Liverpool, 1958).

R. Stephenson, *Observations on the Present State of the Linen Trade of Ireland* (Dublin, 1784).

C. Moreau, *Rise and Progress of the Silk Trade* (London, 1826).

A. Ure, *The Cotton Manufacture of Great Britain* (London, 1861).

A. P. Wadsworth and Julia de L. Mann, *The Cotton Trade and Industrial Lancashire, 1600–1780* (Manchester, 1931).

A. J. Warden, *The Linen Trade, Ancient and Modern* (London, 1867).

GOVERNMENT PUBLICATIONS

Report of the Select Committee on the Illicit Exportation of Wool, Live Sheep, Worsted and Yarn (*PP.* xi).

Report of the Select Committee on the Woollen Manufacture (*S.P.* 1806, iii).

Report of the Select Committee on Width and Stamping of Woollen Cloth (*H.C.J.* xxx).

Report of the Select Committee on the Silk Trade (*H.C.J.* xxx and *H.C.J.* xxxiv).

Returns relating to Cotton (in *Sessional Papers* annually from 1802–3, with especially valuable summaries in *S.P.* 1846, xLIV, and *S.P.* 1847–8, LVIII).

Returns relating to Flax, Hemp and Linen (in *Sessional Papers* in most years from 1803–4).

Returns relating to Wool and Wool Manufactures (in *Sessional Papers* in most years from 1806. Especially useful are *S.P.* 1821, xVII; *S.P.* 1825, xXI; *S.P.* 1844, xLV; and *S.P.* 1850, LII).

Returns relating to Silk (in *Sessional Papers* at irregular intervals from 1806).

Report of the Select Committee on the Employment of Children in Manufactories (*S.P.* 1816, III).

Report of the Select Committee on the Laws relating to the Stamping of Woollen Cloth (*S.P.* 1821, vI).

Report of the Select Committee of the House of Lords on the British Wool Trade (*S.P.* 1828, vIII).

Report of the Select Committee on the Silk Trade (*S.P.* 1831–2, xIX).

Reports of H.M. Factory Inspectors (in *Sessional Papers*, 1834–77).

Report of the Chief Factory Inspector (in *Sessional Papers* from 1878).

Returns by Factory Inspectors of Numbers Employed, Machinery, etc. in Factories (in *Sessional Papers* at intervals from 1836 to 1908).

Committee on Industry and Trade, *Survey of the Textile Industries*, (non-parliamentary paper, 1928).

Board of Agriculture and Fisheries, *Production of Wool in Great Britain in 1905 and 1906* (London, 1907).

ARTICLES

E. Baines, 'The Woollen Manufacture of England with Special Reference to the Leeds Clothing District: Paper read before the British Association in 1858, and reprinted in Thomas Baines, *Yorkshire Past and Present*, vol. 1 (1877).

M. Blaug, ' The Productivity of Capital in the Lancashire Cotton Industry during the Nineteenth Century,' *E.H.R.* (1961).

J. H. Clapham, 'The Transference of the Worsted Industry from Norfolk to the West Riding', *E.J.* (1910).

G. W. Daniels, 'Samuel Crompton's Census of the Cotton Industry in 1811', *E.H.* (1930).

Phyllis Deane, 'The Output of the British Woollen Industry in the Eighteenth Century' (1957).

W. Felkin, 'The Lace and Hosiery Trades of Nottingham', *J.S.S.* (1866).

G. P. Fussell and Constance Goodman, 'Eighteenth Century Estimates of British Sheep and Wool Production', *A.H.* (1930).

A. Hamilton, 'On Wool Supply', *J.S.S.* (1870).

H. Heaton, 'Yorkshire Cloth Traders in the United States, 1770–1840', *Thoresby Society* (1941).

F. Merttens, 'The Hours and the Cost of Labour in the Cotton Industry at Home and Abroad', *T.M.S.S.* (1893–4).

J. Spencer, 'The Growth of the Cotton Trade in Great Britain, America and the Continent of Europe during the Half Century Ending in the year 1875', *T.M.S.S.* (1877).

J. Strang, 'The Rise, Progress and Value of the Embroidered Muslin Manufacture of Scotland and Ireland, *J.S.S.* (1857).

J. W. Tumer, 'The Position of the Wool Trade', *Journal of the Agricultural Society of England* (1896).

A. J. Taylor, 'Concentration and Specialisation in the Lancashire Cotton Industry, 1825–1850', *E.H.R.* (1949).

A. C. Wild, 'Statistics of the Cotton Industry', *J.R.S.S.* (1950).

Charles Wilson, ' Cloth Production and International Competition in the Seventeenth Century', *E.H.R.* (1960).

CHAPTER VIII

TRANSPORT

TABLES

British shipping was a matter of close concern to our ancestors, and as a result there are fairly plentiful statistics on the subject. The railways, too, were under parliamentary surveillance from their beginning, and the record of this remains. Continuous and consistent series relating to road transport, however, are of more recent origin. One series only is included in this section, beginning as recently as 1904. This shows the number of motor vehicles and tramcars in use, and is derived from the British Road Federation's useful annual, *British Road Statistics*. Other statistics which may be of interest in this field are those of local authority expenditure on highways and bridges given in Chapter XIV. Even these only go back to 1883.[1] Before that date there are miscellaneous incomplete and scattered collections of statistics which require too much supporting data or are too incomplete in themselves to warrant inclusion in a work of this kind. Details of central government expenditure on roads can be extracted from the detailed finance accounts. There are very occasional returns of expenditure out of highway rates for England and Wales before 1883, and there is a series for the income and expenditure of Turnpike Trusts which begins in 1834 and continues to 1873.[2] Even fewer figures are available for Scotland or Ireland on road expenditure. Mention may also be made here of Jackman's five subdivisions of the period 1700–1830 and his lists of passenger and freight charges for road and canal transport over the period 1750–1830.[3]

Early sources of shipping series are numerous and difficult to interpret without specialised knowledge of the circumstances of collection.[4] From time to time the government

[1] 1893 in the case of Scotland.   [2] See especially *S.P.* 1852–3, XCVII, and *S.P.* 1874, XXV.

[3] W. T. Jackman, *The Development of Transportation in Modern England* (2 vols., Cambridge, 1916) in the Appendices to Volume II.

[4] Some of the early sources are discussed by R. C. Jarvis, 'Sources for the History of Ships and Shipping', in *Journal of Transport History* (1958).

called for lists of merchant ships belonging to various ports. Willan who reproduces figures of coasting vessels belonging to the English ports at each of seven dates in the period 1709–51 comments on the 'suspicious uniformity of some of the figures'.[1] A register of British shipping engaged in the plantation trade was started in 1698,[2] but the figures do not seem to have survived. The port books recorded figures of tonnage of arrivals and departures, and these were returned to the commissioners of customs, but according to Clark the tonnages were 'mere estimates, formed by multiplying the numbers of ships by conventional, standardised, figures of average tonnages for each trade'.[3] Hence, when the port-books overlap with the statutory registry records, the tonnages recorded in these two sources do not agree.

It was not until the Act of 1786 that registration of shipping was statutorily enforced, though *Lloyds' Register*, a voluntary register for marine insurance purposes, goes back (with gaps in the early years) to 1764. Table 1 gives the cumulative total of shipping registered in the United Kingdom from 1787. Table 2 gives the corresponding shipbuilding statistics, though the lack of Irish statistics for most years before 1814, and of printed British statistics for most of the 1800's, necessitates a break in the series. Table 3, showing the materials used in shipbuilding, begins only in 1850 but covers most of the period when this breakdown is of interest.[4]

The principal problem in using the shipping and shipbuilding statistics is caused by the change in the method of reckoning tonnage which came about between 1836 and 1855. Both systems of measurement used during the period covered by these tables were intended to record cargo-carrying capacity. The original system, established by the Tonnage Act of 1773, was based on length and breadth, and thus encouraged the building of deep vessels. In 1836 a new law provided for measurement to be based on cubic capacity, but it was optional. Old ships did not have to be remeasured, and the new Act did not even have to be adopted for new ones. Not until 1855 was the new system made compulsory and rigorously enforced. How great was the change in tonnages recorded as a result of the new system, and when the change came, are two questions which it is not possible to answer with any certainty. G. S. Graham implies in a recent article[5] that the greater part of the change took place in 1855. If this was indeed so, the conclusion to be drawn from the statistics is that the adoption of the new system may have led to a slight increase in the tonnage recorded: but that the only certain thing is that the change was not large. Annual

---

[1] T. S. Willan, *The English Coasting Trade* 1600–1750 (Manchester, 1938), p. 220.
[2] G. N. Clark, *Guide to English Commercial Statistics* 1696–1782 (London, 1938), p. 47.   [3] *Ibid.* p. 51.
[4] J. R. T. Hughes and S. Reiter, 'The First 1,945 British Steamship', in *Journal of the American Statistical Association* (1958) question the commonly accepted view that wood steamers still predominated in the British steamship fleet in the 1850's on the basis of an analysis of steam vessels registered in the U.K. before 1861. However, the return they analyse omits all vessels lost, sold, or scrapped before 1861 and without some measure of the rate at which wooden ships disappeared from the resgiter in the 1840's and 1850's it is impossible to regard their results as conclusive.
[5] G. S. Graham, 'The Ascendancy of the Sailing Ship 1850–85' in *E.H.R.* IX, No. 1 (1956). He writes: '. . . although lengths were somewhat increased after 1836, the same general type of ship continued to be built until the new measurement law came into force in 1855'—i.e. ships of great depth, whose cargo-carrying capacity was understated by the old system.

estimates of the average cost of construction of steamers and of the value of the total British merchant fleet have been published by Dr K. Maywald.[1]

Until the beginning of the present century the question of shipping freight rates received little attention from compilers of statistics, though the firm of Angier Brothers issued yearly reports from 1870.[2] These form part of the material used by L. Isserlis in compiling his index of rates, included here as table 4. Since average rates are not available, that index had to be based on the mean of the highest and lowest for each year. Dr Isserlis admitted the dangers of this method, but believed it gave reasonable results except for years when the rates changed very greatly, such as 1915 and 1920.[3] For a full description of his methods, the reader must consult the original source: Suffice it to say here that it is a chain index, comparing one year with the preceding one, since, as Dr Isserlis says: 'It is clearly impossible to compare directly the freight in 1869 paid to a sailing vessel carrying grain from Odessa to the United Kingdom with a freight in 1936 payable to a modern motor ship for carrying grain from Montreal or New York to Liverpool'. Some comparison of Dr Isserlis's index with post-war freights is made by M. G. Kendall in 'The U.K. Mercantile Marine and its contribution to the Balance of Payments' in the *Journal of the Royal Statistical Society* (Series A, 1950).

For the first quarter of the nineteenth century iron railway construction was limited to small scale localised railroads operated by horse-power or by stationary engines. The opening of the Stockton-Darlington railway in 1825 represented the beginning of the steam railway era. Since all railways that went beyond the bounds of a private estate required an Act of Parliament, the records of these legal proceedings provide records of the railways concerned. There were also company reports issued for the individual railway companies. From these sources a variety of contemporary lists of mileages, capital expenditure, etc. aggregated by years has been compiled,[4] but the aggregates tend to vary according to the source of the data (Bill, Act or company report for example). Similar contemporary lists can be consulted for canals which were also subject to Acts of Parliament.

From 1843 onwards regular returns on the operations of the railways were published by the office of the Commissioner of Railways. The principal series are summarised here in tables 5 and 6, though the *Returns* themselves give very much greater detail. Reference is made to the scattered statistics for the short period before the beginning of the *Returns* in the notes to the table. The *Returns* themselves are reasonably reliable up to 1869 and perfectly so thereafter. Long period comparisons are bedevilled, however, by the changes in the basis of collection of the statistics in 1913, 1928 and 1933.

---

[1] K. Maywald, 'The Construction Costs and the Value of the British Merchant Fleet 1850–1938', *Scottish Journal of Political Economy* (1956).

[2] Collected in E. A. V. Angier, 'Fifty Years Freights 1869–1919' in *Fairplay* (1920), continued in subsequent issues.

[3] L. Isserlis, 'Tramp Shipping Cargoes and Freights 1869–1919' in *J.R.S.S.* (1938).

[4] Lists are given in a number of the contemporary railway histories, some of which are referred to in the Bibliography. See also G. R. Porter, *Progress of the Nation* (London, 1847), pp. 323–32.

Transport 1. Shipping Registered in the United Kingdom 1788–1938

NOTES

[1] SOURCES: 1788–1800—*Navigation Reports* in the Public Record Office; 1801–39 (all ships)—*Finance Accounts* (Trade and Navigation section; 1814–39 (steamships)—G. R. Porter, *The Progress of the Nation* (London, 2nd edition, 1847), p. 319; 1814–39 (sailing ships)—by inference; 1840–1938—*Abstract*.

[2] All tonnage figures are net.

[3] The Isle of Man and the Channel Islands are included in this table.

at 30th September in each year until 1824 and
subsequently at 31st December

	Sailing Ships		Steamships		All Ships	
	Number	000 tons	Number	000 tons	Number	000 tons
1788	...	...	...	...	12,464	1,278
1789	...	...	...	...	12,801	1,308
1790	...	...	...	...	13,557	1,383
1791	...	...	...	...	13,960	1,415
1792	...	...	...	...	14,334	1,437
1793	...	...	...	...	14,440	1,453
1794	...	...	...	...	14,590	1,456
1795	...	...	...	...	14,317	1,426
1796	...	...	...	...	14,458	1,361
1797	...	...	...	...	14,405	1,454
1798	...	...	...	...	14,631	1,494
1799	...	...	...	...	14,883	1,551
1800	...	...	...	...	15,734	1,699
1801	...	...	...	...	16,552	1,797
1802	...	...	...	...	17,207	1,901
1803	...	...	...	...	18,068	1,986
1804	...	...	...	...	18,870	2,077
1805	...	...	...	...	19,027	2,093
1806	...	...	...	...	19,315	2,080
1807	...	...	...	...	19,373	2,097
1808	...	...	...	...	19,580	2,130
1809	...	...	...	...	19,882	2,167
1810	...	...	...	...	20,253	2,211
1811	...	...	...	...	20,478	2,247
1812	...	...	...	...	20,637	2,263
1813	...	...	...	...	20,951	2,349
1814	21,449	2,414	1	- -	21,550	2,414
1815	21,861	2,477	8	1	21,869	2,478
1816	22,014	2,503	12	1	22,026	2,504
1817	21,761	2,420	14	1	21,775	2,421
1818	22,005	2,450	19	2	22,024	2,453
1819	21,973	2,449	24	3	21,997	2,452
1820	21,935	2,436	34	3	21,969	2,439
1821	21,593	2,350	59	6	21,652	2,356
1822	21,153	2,307	85	9	21,238	2,315
1823	20,941	2,293	101	10	21,042	2,303
1824	21,164	2,338	116	12	21,280	2,349
1825	20,442	2,313	153	16	20,595	2,327
1826	20,738	2,387	230	24	20,968	2,411
1827	19,269 (a)	2,154 (a)	255 (a)	27 (a)	19,524 (a)	2,181 (a)
1828	19,372	2,165	274	28	19,646	2,193
1829	18,821	2,170	289	30	19,110	2,200
1830	18,876	2,168	298	30	19,174	2,202
1831	19,126	2,192	324	33	19,450	2,224
1832	19,312	2,226	352	36	19,664	2,262
1833	19,302	2,233	387	39	19,689	2,271
1834	19,545	2,268	430	44	19,975	2,312
1835	19,797	2,307	503	53	20,300	2,360
1836	19,827	2,289	561	60	20,388	2,350
1837	19,912	2,264	624	70	20,536	2,334

See p. 219 for footnotes

	Sailing Ships		Steamships		All Ships	
	Number	ooo tons	Number	ooo tons	Number	ooo tons
1838	20,234	2,346	678	75	20,912	2,421
1839	20,947	2,491	723	80	21,670	2,571
1840	21,883	2,680	771	88	22,654	2,768
1841	22,668	2,839	793	96	23,461	2,935
1842	23,121	2,933	833	108	23,954	3,041
1843	23,040	2,898	858	110	23,898	3,008
1844	23,116	3,931	900	114	24,016	3,044
1845	23,471	3,004	917	119	24,388	3,123
1846	23,808	3,069	963	131	24,771	3,200
1847	24,167	3,167	1,033	141	25,200	3,308
1848	24,520	3,249	1,118	151	25,638	3,401
1849	24,753	3,326	1,149	160	25,902	3,486
1850	24,797	3,397	1,187	168	25,984	3,565
1851	24,816	3,476	1,227	187	26,043	3,662
1852	24,814	3,550	1,272	209	26,086	3,759
1853	25,224	3,780	1,385	250	26,609	4,030
1854	25,335	3,943	1,524	306	26,859	4,249
1855	24,274	3,969	1,674	381	25,948	4,349
1856	24,480	3,980	1,697	387	26,177	4,367
1857	25,273	4,141	1,824	417	27,097	4,559
1858	25,615	4,205	1,926	452	27,541	4,658
1859	25,784	4,226	1,918	437	27,702	4,663
1860	25,663	4,204	2,000	454	27,663	4,659
1861	25,905	4,301	2,133	506	28,038	4,807
1862	26,212	4,396	2,228	538	28,440	4,934
1863	26,339	4,731	2,298	597	28,637	5,328
1864	26,142	4,930	2,490	697	28,632	5,627
1865	26,069	4,937	2,718	823	28,787	5,760
1866	26,140	4,904	2,831	876	28,971	5,779
1867	25,842	4,853	2,931	901	28,773	5,754
1868	25,500	4,878	2,944	902	28,444	5,780
1869	24,187	4,765	2,972	948	27,159	5,714
1870	23,189	4,578	3,178	1,113	26,367	5,691
1871	22,510	4,374	3,382	1,320	25,892	5,694
1872	22,103	4,213	3,673	1,538	25,776	5,751
1873	21,698	4,091	3,863	1,714	25,561	5,805
1874	21,464	4,108	4,033	1,871	25,497	5,979
1875	21,291	4,207	4,170	1,946	25,461	6,153
1876	21,144	4,258	4,335	2,005	25,479	6,263
1877	21,169	4,261	4,564	2,139	25,733	6,400
1878	21,058	4,239	4,826	2,316	25,884	6,555
1879	20,538	4,069	5,027	2,511	25,565	6,580
1880	19,938	3,851	5,247	2,724	25,185	6,575
1881	19,325	3,688	5,505	3,004	24,830	6,692
1882	18,892	3,622	5,814	3,335	24,706	6,957
1883	18,415	3,514	6,260	3,728	24,675	7,242
1884	18,053	3,465	6,601	3,944	24,654	7,409
1885	17,018	3,457	6,644	3,973	23,662	7,430
1886	16,179	3,397	6,653	3,965	22,832	7,362
1887	15,473	3,250	6,663	4,085	22,136	7,335
1888	15,025	3,114	6,871	4,350	21,896	7,464
1889	14,640	3,041	7,139	4,718	21,779	7,759
1890	14,181	2,936	7,410	5,043	21,591	7,979
1891	13,823	2,972	7,720	5,307	21,543	8,279
1892	13,578	3,080	7,950	5,565	21,528	8,645
1893	13,239	3,038	8,088	5,740	21,327	8,778
1894	12,943	2,987	8,263	5,969	21,206	8,956
1895	12,617	2,867	8,386	6,122	21,003	8,989
1896	12,274	2,736	8,522	6,284	20,796	9,020
1897	11,911	2,590	8,590	6,364	2,0501	8,953

	Sailing Ships		Steamships		All Ships	
	Number	000 tons	Number	000 tons	Number	000 tons
1898	11,566	2,388	8,838	6,614	20,404	9,002
1899	11,167	2,247	9,029	6,917	20,196	9,164
1900	10,773	2,096	9,209	7,208	19,982	9,304
1901	10,572	1,991	9,484	7,618	20,056	9,608
1902	10,455	1,951	9,803	8,104	20,258	10,055
1903	10,330	1,869	10,122	8,400	20,452	10,269
1904	10,210	1,803	10,370	8,752	20,580	10,555
1905	10,059	1,671	10,522	9,065	20,581	10,736
1906	9,857	1,555	10,907	9,612	20,764	11,167
1907	9,648	1,461	11,394	10,024	21,042	11,485
1908	9,542	1,403	11,626	10,139	21,168	11,541
1909	9,392	1,301	11,797	10,285	21,189	11,586
1910	9,090	1,113	12,000	10,443	21,090	11,556
1911	8,830	981	12,242	10,718	21,072	11,699
1912	8,510	903	12,382	10,992	20,892	11,895
1913	8,336	847	12,602	11,273	20,938	12,120
1914	8,203	794	12,862 (b)	11,622 (b)	21,065 (b)	12,415 (b)
1915	8,019	779	12,771	11,650	20,790	12,427
1916	7,669	715	12,405	11,037	20,074	11,752
1917	7,186	625	11,534	9,608	18,720	10,232

	Sailing Ships		Steamships		Motor Ships		All Ships	
	Number	000 tons	Number	000 tons	Number	000 tons	Number	000 tons
1918	6,856	604	11,334	9,497			18,190	10,101
1919	6,555	593	11,791	10,335			18,346	10,928
1920	6,309	584	12,307	10,777			18,616	11,361
1921	6,272	610	12,660	10,932			18,932	11,542
1922	6,184	574	12,787	11,223			18,971	11,797
1923	5,962 (c)	551 (c)	10,813 (c)	10,897 (c)	1,624 (c)	263 (c)	18,399 (c)	11,711 (c)
1924	5,842	522	10,690	10,810	1,823	385	18,355	11,716
1925	5,785	520	10,526	10,965	1,965	499	18,276	11,983
1926	5,678	517	10,262	10,760	2,170	629	18,110	11,907
1927	5,609	507	10,032	10,577	2,340	770	17,981	11,853
1928	5,408	496	9,959	10,754	2,681	1,009	18,048	12,259
1929	5,249	480	9,855	10,675	2,940	1,214	18,044	12,369
1930	5,098	468	9,729	10,561	3,237	1,425	18,064	12,454
1931	4,960	462	9,529	10,233	3,483	1,579	17,972	12,274
1932	4,773	472	9,248	9,774	3,650	1,617	17,671	11,863
1933	4,632	466	8,900	9,062	3,863	1,642	17,395	11,170
1934	4,435	432	8,622	8,621	4,168	1,692	17,225	10,745
1935	4,351	414	8,306	8,253	4,494	1,819	17,151	10,486
1936	4,288	419	8,032	8,114	4,888	2,057	17,208	10,590
1937	4,185	415	7,702	7,902	5,294	2,236	17,181	10,533
1938	4,019	402	7,441	7,819	5,789	2,481	17,249	10,702

(a) A new Registry Act in 1827 resulted in the exclusion of many ships that had been lost, but which had been continued on the old register because no evidence of loss had been produced.
(b) The coming into force of a new Registration Act in 1914 caused some increase in the number of steamships recorded.
(c) As from 1923 ships registered in the ports of southern Ireland were no longer included on the United Kingdom register. In the same year motor ships were separately distinguished from steamships.

Transport 2. Ships Built and First Registered in the British Empire and in Great Britain, 1787–1818, and in the United Kingdom, 1814–70; and all Ships Built in the United Kingdom for British Citizens and Companies 1870–1938

NOTES

[1] SOURCES: 1787–1800—*Navigation Reports* in the Public Record Office; 1801–18 (Empire)—*Finance Accounts* (Trade and Navigation section); 1804–5 (G.B.)—*S.P.* 1806, XIII; 1814–18 (G.B.)—*S.P.* 1821, XVII; 1814–38 (all ships)—*S.P.* 1852, XLIX; 1814–26 (sail/steam breakdown)—*S.P.* 1826–7, XVIII; 1827–38 (sail/steam breakdown)—G. R. Porter, *The*

Progress of the Nation (London, 2nd edition, 1847); p. 318; 1840–1938—*Abstract*.
[2] All tonnage figures are net.
[3] The Isle of Man and the Channel Islands are included as part of Great Britain in part A, but they are excluded from the United Kingdom in part B.

A. British Empire and Great Britain, 1787–1818

	All Ships, Britain and Empire		All Ships, Britain Alone	
	Number	000 tons	Number	000 tons
1787	1,427	118·3	943	91·7
1788	1,327	103·3	848	73·5
1789	827	71·1	627	58·0
1790	725	68·7	577	57·1
1791	766	68·9	624	58·8
1792	821	78·1	655	67·0
1793	800	75·1	652	65·6
1794	714	66·0	555	55·6
1795	719	72·2	540	63·2
1796	823	95·0	628	84·9
1797	756	86·2	630	78·3
1798	833	89·3	702	79·9
1799	858	98·0	689	83·7
1800	1,041	134·2	845	115·3
1801	1,065	122·6	918	110·2
1802	1,281	137·5	967	104·8
1803	1,407	135·7		
1804	991	96·0	715	79·9
1805	1,001	89·6	714	71·4
1806	772	69·2		
1807	770	68·0		
1808	568	57·1		
1809	596	61·4		
1810	685	84·9		
1811	870	115·6		
1812	...	...		
1813	...	...	...	...
1814	818	96·0	660	84·1
1815	864	97·9	877	101·0
1816	1,183	128·5	810	82·7
1817	1,274	117·4	656	78·1
1818	1,082	104·4	704	84·7

B. United Kingdom, 1814–1938

	Sailing Ships		Steamships (a)		All Ships	
	Number	000 tons	Number	000 tons	Number	000 tons
1814	701	85·8	5	0·3	706	86·1
1815	904	102·1	9	0·8	913	102·9
1816	843	84·1	8	0·6	851	84·7
1817	751	80·8	7	0·4	758	81·3
1818	746	85·4	6	1·3	752	86·7
1819	773	88·7	4	0·3	777	89·1
1820	611	66·0	8	0·7	619	66·7
1821	563	55·1	22	3·0	585	58·1
1822	537	48·5	27	2·4	564	50·9
1823	575	60·7	19	2·5	594	63·2

See p. 222 for footnotes

	Sailing Ships		Steamships (a)		All Ships	
	Number	000 tons	Number	000 tons	Number	000 tons
1824	782	88·8	17	2·2	799	91·1
1825	951	119·5	24	3·0	975	122·5
1826	1,043	109·7	72	8·6	1,115	118·4
1827	866	89·8	28	3·4	894	93·1
1828	812	86·6	30	2·0	842	88·7
1829	702	74·9	16	1·8	718	76·6
1830	712	73·8	18	1·7	730	75·5
1831	711	81·1	31	2·7	742	83·9
1832	700	87·3	33	2·9	733	90·2
1833	678	86·3	33	2·9	711	89·2
1834	744	95·2	36	5·1	780	100·4
1835	774	105·7	86	10·1	860	116·6
1836	616	77·8	63	8·8	679	86·5
1837	858	119·5	78	11·7	936	131·2
1838	1,005	147·7	84	9·5	1,089	157·3
1839	1,155	175·2	62	6·1	1,217	181·3
1840	1,296	201·1	74	10·2	1,370	211·3
1841	1,063	148·2	48	11·4	1,111	159·6
1842	856	116·2	58	13·7	914	129·9
1843	652	77·0	46	6·1	698	83·1
1844	624	88·9	65	6·1	689	95·0
1845	788	112·3	65	10·9	853	123·2
1846	732	109·4	77	16·0	809	125·4
1847	830	129·7	103	16·2	933	145·8
1848	733	107·2	114	15·3	847	122·6
1849	662	105·5	68	12·5	730	118·0
1850	621	119·1	68	14·6	689	133·7
1851	594	126·9	78	22·7	672	149·6
1852	608	136·7	104	30·7	712	167·5
1853	645	155·0	153	48·2	798	203·2
1854	628	132·7	174	64·3	802	196·9
1855	865	242·2	233	81·0	1,098	323·2
1856	921	187·0	229	57·6	1,150	244·6
1857	1,050	197·6	228	52·9	1,278	250·5
1858	847	154·9	153	53·2	1,000	208·1
1859	789	148·0	150	38·0	939	186·0
1860	818	158·2	198	53·8	1,016	212·0
1861	774	130·0	201	70·9	975	200·8
1862	827	164·1	221	77·3	1,048	241·4
1863	881	253·0	279	108·0	1,160	361·0
1864	867	272·5	374	159·4	1,241	431·9
1865	922	235·6	382	179·6	1,304	415·2
1866	969	207·7	354	133·5	1,323	341·2
1867	879	174·5	279	94·6	1,158	269·1
1868	787	237·7	232	78·5	1,019	316·2
1869	688	230·8	283	123·5	971	354·3
1870	541	117·0	433	225·7	974	342·7
1871	472	56·5	470	297·8	942	354·4
1872	408	55·0	503	338·0	911	393·0
1873	418	88·5	396	282·1	814	370·7
1874	499	187·3	482	333·9	981	521·2
1875	566	241·6	357	178·9	923	420·6
1876	687	236·9	320	123·5	1,007	360·4
1877	703	212·3	389	221·3	1,092	433·7
1878	585	141·2	499	287·1	1,084	428·2
1879	395	59·1	412	297·7	807	356·8
1880	348	57·5	474	346·4	822	403·8
1881	359	92·4	486	408·8	845	501·2

See p. 222 for footnotes

	Sailing Ships		Steamships (a)		All Ships	
	Number	000 tons	Number	000 tons	Number	000 tons
1882	362	145·7	610	521·6	972	667·3
1883	368	146·8	806	621·8	1,174	768·6
1884	431	162·2	570	335·2	1,001	497·4
1885	459	208·4	393	197·0	852	405·4
1886	363	138·4	308	154·6	671	293·0
1887	258	81·3	322	225·4	580	306·7
1888	269	75·7	465	407·4	734	483·1
1889	277	117·5	582	554·0	859	671·5
1890	277	123·2	581	528·8	858	652·0
1891	308	191·9	622	478·7	930	670·6
1892	322	258·7	521	434·1	843	692·8
1893	333	114·9	448	380·4	781	495·3
1894	363	89·2	524	485·5	887	574·6
1895	319	54·2	541	465·5	860	519·6
1896	389	57·5	542	462·5	931	520·0
1897	518	66·7	536	415·5	1,054	482·3
1898	665	41·8	705	654·2	1,370	696·0
1899	570	45·5	675	703·9	1,245	749·4
1900	504	38·6	667	698·3	1,171	736·9
1901	567	55·0	637	720·7	1,204	775·7
1902	650	64·8	645	735·6	1,295	800·4
1903	468	42·3	695	586·8	1,163	629·1
1904	363	33·7	680	701·6	1,043	735·4
1905	286	30·4	713	821·1	999	851·4
1906	334	31·9	819	890·3	1,153	922·2
1907	337	24·3	929	716·5	1,266	740·8
1908	301	26·6	593	386·4	894	413·1
1909	254	26·6	570	484·3	824	510·9
1910	262	20·5	604	580·5	866	601·0
1911	286	26·9	790	887·7	1,076	914·7
1912	289	43·1	721	857·2	1,010	900·3
1913	290	25·2	755	950·0	1,045	975·2
1914	256	26·3	754	812·4	1,010	838·6
1915	149	12·5	373	361·9	522	374·4
1916	114	14·3	365	372·0	479	386·3
1917	58	6·6	339	745·5	397	752·1
1918	11	5·7	309	815·2	320	820·9
1919	186	44·4	571	892·1	757	936·5
1920	270	33·5	543	773·0	813	806·5
1921	205	19·6	427	658·6	632	678·2
1922	150	15·8	289	486·5	439	502·2
1923	269 (b)	26·1 (b)	313 (b)	375·7 (b)	582 (b)	401·8 (b)
1924	238	22·8	476	760·4	714	783·2
1925	324	36·4	438	563·7	762	600·1
1926	183	18·4	280	337·6	463	356·0
1927	205	17·3	481	647·3	686	664·5
1928	170	14·4	550	766·8	720	781·3
1929	171	13·0	611	785·0	782	798·0
1930	232	18·7	544	526·3	776	545·0
1931	104	10·7	283	206·7	387	217·4
1932	92	7·3	191	94·9	283	102·2
1933	111	9·6	284	74·0	395	83·6
1934	188	14·5	421	254·3	609	268·9
1935	266	17·2	480	287·8	746	305·0
1936	298	24·0	608	473·4	906	497·3
1937	203	18·2	564	499·9	767	518·0
1938	147	20·8	454	489·5	601	510·3

(a) Including motor ships throughout.

(b) Ships built in southern Ireland are not included after 1922.

Transport 3. Ships Built and First Registered in the United Kingdom or Built in the United Kingdom for British Citizens or Companies, According to Type and Material—1850–1908

NOTES

[1] SOURCES: 1850–2—*Shipping Returns*; 1853–1908—*Annual Statement of Trade*.
[2] All tonnage figures are net.

[3] Ships built in the Isle of Man and the Channel Islands are not included.

| | Sailing Ships | | | | | | Steamships | | | | | |
| | Wood | | Iron | | Steel | | Wood | | Iron | | Steel | |
	Number	ooo tons	Number	ooo tons	Number	ooo tons	Number	ooo tons	Number	ooo tons	Number	ooo tons
1850	610	117·0	11	2·1			18	3·9	50	10·7		
1851	587	124·9	7	2·0			30	8·9	48	13·8		
1852	605	134·7	3	2·1			45	4·8	59	26·0		
1853	635	146·4	10	8·6			36	3·3	117	44·9		
1854	592	115·8	36	16·9			22	2·1	152	62·2		
1855	818	211·9	47	30·3			38	3·1	195	77·9		
1856	888	175·4	33	11·6			54	2·8	175	54·8		
1857	1,012	184·2	38	13·4			73	3·0	155	49·9		
1858	822	140·4	25	14·5			41	3·6	112	49·5		
1859	755	128·3	34	19·7			44	1·8	106	36·2		
1860	786	144·6	32	13·6			49	2·7	149	51·1		
1861	731	107·2	43	22·7			42	2·5	159	68·4		
1862	758	120·0	69	44·0			40	1·0	181	76·3		
1863	739	146·0	142	107·1			39	2·1	240	105·8		
1864	713	146·8	154	125·7			32	2·4	342	157·0		
1865	806	150·5	116	85·1			38	2·3	344	177·4		
1866	815(a)	112·0(a)	112(a)	69·5(a)			50(a)	3·0(a)	299(a)	129·7(a)		
1867	744	97·2	99	59·0			51	3·2	224	90·8		
1868	596	87·2	162	131·7			39	1·1	188	75·1		
1869	499	71·2	157	138·4			35	2·1	238	118·4		
1870	450	56·1	63	48·8			49	2·5	382	222·9		
1871	435	38·5	30	16·7			51	2·1	416	295·1		
1871	386	39·2	18	15·1			55	2·1	446	335·8		
1873	369	40·4	49	48·1			56	2·5	335	279·1		
1874	382	43·9	116	143·2			78	2·6	393	328·1		
1875	372	41·6	193	198·8			56	1·7	291	175·8		
1876	466	45·2	218	190·7			31	1·1	288	122·3		
1877	532	42·5	174	169·7			29	0·4	355	220·0		
1878	480	37·5	110	103·7			64	1·0	431	285·4		
1879	352	22·1	44(b)	136·8(b)	1(b)	under 50(b)	35	0·7	351(b)	275·9(b)	24(b)	21·0(b)
1880	288	17·8	39	37·3	5	1·8	40	34·8	396	309·8	40	34·8
1881	259	16·5	87	72·4	4	3·1	37	46·3	415	361·5	37	46·3
1882	232	13·4	120	118·5	10	13·9	101	80·3	467	440·2	101	80·3
1883	247 (a)	13·9(a)	96	114·1	23	18·7	54(a)	1·2(a)	613	508·6	137	111·8
1884	297	17·4	107	128·3	23	16·3	57	2·1	369	239·9	139	93·1
1885	265	17·3	154	155·5	32	34·5	51	0·9	182	87·8	159	108·3
1886	227	13·9	93	92·3	39	31·8	29	0·5	122	44·9	155	109·3
1887	179	9·4	44	46·6	34	25·2	18	0·6	76	18·9	227	205·9
1888	176	9·1	55	21·0	38	45·6	24	1·9	91	26·2	350	379·4
1889	191	9·1	24	15·1	62	93·3	23	0·6	113	35·4	445	518·1
1890	182	9·3	25	12·7	70	101·3	32	0·7	125	32·8	424	495·3
1891	167	8·0	25	6·6	116	177·3	22	0·6	181	16·0	419	462·1
1892	156	8·2	28	9·0	138	241·5	23	1·0	88	9·4	410	423·7
1893	184	8·8	50	3·4	99	102·7	35	0·7	85	7·3	328	372·4
1894	178	8·9	46	4·5	139	75·8	20	0·3	87	8·2	417	477·0

See p. 224 for footnotes

	Sailing Ships						Steamships					
	Wood		Iron		Steel		Wood		Iron		Steel	
	Number	000 tons	Number	000 tons	Number	000 tons	Number	000 tons	Number	000 tons	Number	000 tons
1895	180	8·1	46	5·0	93	41·0	37	1·0	79	5·6	425	458·8
1896	209	10·1	51	5·0	129	42·4	21	0·3	89	6·7	432	455·5
1897	256	11·7	90	8·8	172	46·2	56	1·1	65	4·0	415	410·4
1898	297	14·0	113	8·0	255	19·9	21	0·5	93	5·0	591	648·6
1899	273	12·7	75	5·6	222	27·2	31	0·7	71	4·6	573	698·6
1900	250	13·0	52	3·9	202	21·6	75	2·3	84	5·7	508	690·4
1901	259	13·3	66	5·0	242	36·7	98	3·1	24	2·7	515	714·9
1902	289	14·6	49	3·5	312	46·6	80	2·4	38	2·5	527	730·7
1903	262	13·2	6	0·4	200	28·7	89	2·6	15	0·8	591	583·4
1904	240	12·1	5	0·4	118	21·3	63	1·6	2	under 50	615	700·0
1905	180	11·2	20	1·2	86	18·0	41	0·8	2	0·1	670	820·1
1906	171	8·5	8	0·8	155	22·5	119	2·7	3	0·3	697	887·3
1907	195	11·1	3	0·2	139	12·9	210	4·4	2	5·1	717	707·1
1908	152	7·8	8	0·6	141	18·1	120	3·4	—	—	473	383·0

(*a*) From 1866–82 composite ships were separately distinguished. Prior to 1866 they were included in either wood or iron, and after 1882 they were included with wood. The following are the details for 1866–82:

	Sailing Ships		Steamships	
	Number	000 tons	Number	000 tons
1866	42	26·1	5	0·8
1867	36	18·3	4	0·5
1868	29	18·8	5	2·3
1869	32	21·2	10	3·0
1870	28	12·1	2	0·3
1871	7	1·4	3	0·6
1872	4	0·6	2	0·1

	Sailing Ships		Steamships	
	Number	000 tons	Number	000 tons
1873	—	—	5	0·5
1874	1	0·2	11	3·1
1875	1	1·3	10	1·4
1876	3	1·0	1	0·1
1877	—	—	—	—
1878	—	—	4	0·7
1879	3	0·1	2	0·1
1880	21	0·7	5	0·5
1881	9	0·4	4	0·1
1882	—	—	5	0·5

(*b*) Prior to 1878 steel ships were included with iron.

Transport 4.   Index of Tramp Shipping Freights, 1869–1936

NOTE

SOURCE: L. Isserlis, 'Tramp Shipping Cargoes, and Freights' in *J.R.S.S.* (1938).

1869 = 100

Year	Index	Year	Index	Year	Index	Year	Index
1869	100	1886	59	1903	49	1920	374
1870	103	1887	65	1904	49	1921	166
1871	102	1888	76	1905	51	1922	130
1872	103	1889	75	1906	52	1923	123
1873	117	1890	64	1907	54	1924	121
1874	108	1891	63	1908	45	1925	110
1875	99	1892	55	1909	46	1926	133
1876	98	1893	60	1910	50	1927	122
1877	99	1894	58	1911	58	1928	112
1878	91	1895	56	1912	78	1929	115
1879	85	1896	56	1913	68	1930	93
1880	87	1897	56	1914	67	1931	90
1881	87	1898	68	1915	199	1932	88
1882	81	1899	65	1916	365	1933	85
1883	75	1900	76	1917	695	1934	85
1884	64	1901	57	1918	751	1935	88
1885	63	1902	49	1919	490	1936	103

Transport 5. Railway Capital, Mileage, Traffic, and Finances—Great Britain 1838–1938

NOTES

[1] SOURCES: 1838—*S.P.* 1839, x; all other figures—*Railway Returns* and *Abstract*, whichever provides the latest revisions.

[2] United Kingdom figures of paid-up capital and loans and of mileage open are available back to 1843. They were as follows, those for 1848 indicating the proportion between United Kingdom and Great Britain:

	1843	1844	1845	1846	1847	1848
Paid-up Capital and Loans (£ million at 31st December)	65·5	72·4	88·5	126·3	167·3	200·2
Miles of Road Open at 30th June	1,952	2,148	2,441	3,036	3,945	5,127

[3] H. G. Lewin's *Early British Railways* (London, 1925) gives the following figures of mileage open at the end of each year:

1825	26¾	1830	97½	1835	337¾	1840	1,497¾
1826	38	1831	140	1836	403¼	1841	1,775
1827	40¾	1832	166	1837	540¼	1842	1,938¾
1828	44¾	1833	208¼	1838	742½	1843	2,043¾
1829	51	1834	298	1839	969¾	1844	2,235¾

A comparison of these figures with those in note 2 suggests that they apply to the United Kingdom, though this is not stated in the source.

	Paid-up Capital and Loans (*a*) (£ million at 31 Dec.)	Miles of Road Open at 31 Dec.	Millions of Passengers Carried (*b*) (year ended 31 Dec.)	Million Tons of Freight Carried (year ended 31 Dec.)	Train Mileage: Passenger (Million miles, year ended 31 Dec.)	Train Mileage: Goods	Train Mileage: Mixed	Receipts: Passenger Train (£ million, year ended 30 June)	Receipts: Goods Train	Receipts: Total Working	Total Working Expenses (£ million, year ended 31 Dec.)	Net Working Receipts
1838	...	...	5·4	...	...	...	...	...	...	...	...	...
			(year ended 30 June)									
1843	...	...	21·7	...	...	...	...	3·1	1·4	4·5	...	...
1844	...	...	25·2	...	...	...	...	3·4	1·6	5·0	...	...
1845	...	...	30·4	...	...	...	...	3·9	2·2	6·1	...	...
1846	...	...	40·2	...	...	...	...	4·6	2·8	7·5	...	...
1847	...	...	47·9	...	...	...	...	5·0	3·3	8·4	...	...
1848	195·6	4,982	54·4	...	...	...	...	5·6	4·2	9·8	...	...
			(year ended 31 Dec.)					(year ended 31 Dec.)				
1849	224·6	5,538	57·8	...	...	...	...	6·0	5·4	11·4	...	...
1850	234·9	6,084	67·4	...	...	...	...	6·5	6·2	12·7	...	...
1851	241·8	6,266	79·7	...	...	...	...	7·6	6·9	14·4	...	...
1852	256·8	6,628	82·8	...	33·3	24·5	—	7·3	7·7	15·0	...	...
1853	265·2	6,805	95·2	...	34·6	29·7	—	8·0	9·2	17·2	...	...
1854	271·7	7,157	104·3	...	36·0	33·3	—	9·6(*c*)	9·7(*c*)	19·3	8·8	10·5
1855	282·4	7,293	111·4	...	36·9	33·4	—	10·0	10·5	20·5	9·9	10·6
1856	291·6	7,650	121·4	63·7	38·3	35·5	—	10·6	11·4	22·0	10·4	11·6
1857	298·3	8,023	130·6	70·2	41·6	37·6	—	11·1	11·9	23·0	10·8	12·2
1858	307·6	8,354	130·7	71·9	43·7	38·7	—	10·9	11·9	22·8	11·2	11·6
1859	315·2	8,737	140·3	77·3	46·1	42·4	—	11·7	12·8	24·4	...	...
1860	327·5	9,069	153·5	88·4	48·8	48·0	—	12·2	14·2	26·4	12·6	13·8
1861	340·4	9,446	163·0	92·6	49·6	49·5	—	12·4	14·7	27·1	13·6	14·1
1862	361·9	9,953	170·0	91·9	52·8	48·8	—	13·0	14·7	27·7	13·6	14·1
1863	380·7	10,581	192·2	98·8	56·1	53·8	—	13·6	16·1	29·6	14·3	15·4
1864	400·6	10,995	217·4	108·5	61·4	60·6	—	14·7	17·7	32·3	15·3	17·1
1865	429·8	11,451	238·7	112·6	65·8	66·3	—	15·5	18·7	34·0	16·3	17·7
1866	455·3	11,945	261·2	121·8	67·8	67·2	—	16·4	20·1	36·4	17·9	18·5
1867	464·9	12,319	273·7	132·6	69·4	71·4	—	16·8	20·8	37·6	18·9	18·7
1868	...	...	...	...	...	...	...	...	...	...	...	...
1869(*d*)	491·9	(13,170)(*e*)	298·6	...	75·4	74·1	0·2(*f*)	17·6	21·4	40·7	19·8	20·9
1870	502·7	(13,562)(*e*)	322·2	...	80·8	80·0	—	18·1	23·2	42·9	20·6	22·3
1871	525·7	13,388	359·7	166·5	83·8	86·6	—	19·4	25·5	46·6	22·0	24·6

See p. 227 for footnotes

| | Paid-up Capital and Loans (a) (£ million at 31 Dec.) | Miles of Road Open at 31 Dec. | Millions of Passengers Carried (b) (year ended 31 Dec.) | Million Tons of Freight Carried (year ended 31 Dec.) | Train Mileage | | | Receipts | | | Total Working Expenses (£ million, year ended 31 Dec.) | Net Working Receipts (£ million, year ended 31 Dec.) |
					Passenger (Million miles, year ended 31 Dec.)	Goods	Mixed	Passenger Train (£ million, year ended 31 Dec.)	Goods Train	Total Working		
1872	536·4	13,723	406·5	176·2	87·3(g)	92·0(g)	2·2(g)	21·0	28·0	50·8	25·0	25·8
1873	559·1	13,981	439·0	187·8	89·0	96·5	2·3	22·4	30·7	55·2	29·3	25·8
1874	580·1	14,322	461·3	185·4	91·3	97·5	2·2	23·5	30·9	56·7	31·1	25·5
1875	600·0	14,510	490·1	196·2	95·4	102·1	2·5	24·3	32·1	58·6	31·8	26·8
1876	627·5	14,715	517·1	202·4	99·9	103·3	2·8	24·7	32·5	59·4	32·1	27·4
1877	642·8	14,874	532·3	208·3	103·4	104·4	2·0	25·1	32·8	60·2	32·4	27·8
1878	666·6	15,074	547·1	203·2	106·8	102·9	2·2	25·4	32·3	60·1	31·7	28·4
1879	683·9	15,411	546·3	208·6	108·7	104·5	2·1	24·6	32·3	59·2	30·6	28·6
1880	694·6	15,563	596·6	231·7	115·7	112·1	2·1	25·8	34·5	62·8	32·1	30·7
1881	711·3	15,734	608·4	241·4	119·1	115·9	2·2	26·3	35·6	64·5	33·4	31·1
1882	733·9	15,992	636·1	252·4	124·8	119·6	2·1	27·3	36·5	66·6	34·6	31·8
1883	749·5	16,179	664·4	262·4	130·7	124·4	2·1	28·0	37·4	68·2	35·8	32·4
1884	765·7	16,339	675·4	255·5	135·5	122·9	2·6	28·5	36·4	67·7	35·6	32·1
1885	780·3	16,594	678·1	253·6	138·4	122·1	2·1	28·3	35·6	66·8	35·2	31·5
1886	792·4	16,700	706·9	251·0	140·7	121·8	2·2	28·8	35·1	66·8	35·0	31·8
1887	809·5	16,904	714·2	265·2	143·7	124·5	2·2	29·1	36·1	68·1	35·5	32·6
1888	828·2	17,079	722·6	278·0	147·2	128·9	2·2	29·4	37·5	70·0	36·2	33·8
1889	839·6	17,152	754·2	293·3	152·7	134·9	2·2	31·0	39·7	74·0	38·4	35·5
1890	860·2	17,281	796·3	298·8	158·2	139·4	2·3	32·7	40·8	76·8	41·4	35·4
1891	881·6	17,328	823·3	305·9	163·1	144·1	2·4	33·4	41·8	78·7	43·4	35·3
1892	905·9	17,430	841·8	305·3	167·1	144·0	2·5	34·0	41·4	78·9	44·0	34·9
1893	932·6	17,655	849·5	288·1	168·3	137·4	2·6	34·1	39·5	77·4	43·9	33·5
1894	946·2	17,864	886·9	319·8	170·5	144·7	2·6	34·7	41·8	80·9	45·4	35·6
1895	961·8	18,001	903·5	329·5	174·8	145·6	2·7	35·5	42·5	82·4	46·0	36·4
1896	989·8	18,099	953·8	351·8	183·9(h)	152·9(h)	0·4(h)	37·3	44·6	86·6	48·3	38·4
1897	1,050·3	18,265	1,004·5	369·3	192·4	158·7	0·4	38·7	46·2	90·2	51·1	39·1
1898	1,095·1	18,483	1,036·3	373·5	198·9	164·3	0·3	39·9	47·6	92·7	53·9	38·8
1899	1,112·2	18,524	1,079·3	408·4	206·3	172·4	0·4	41·8	50·4	98·0	58·0	40·0
1900	1,136·2	18,680	1,114·6	419·8	209·5	174·8	0·4	43·3	51·8	101·0	62·5	38·5
1901	1,155·3	18,870	1,145·5	410·8	213·2	164·1	0·4	44·6	51·3	102·7	65·1	37·6
1902	1,176·3	18,938	1,160·0	432·0	217·3	164·4	0·4	45·3	52·9	105·4	65·4	40·0
1903	1,192·3	19,165	1,166·6	438·1	221·3	154·3	0·4	45·8	53·3	106·8	66·1	40·7
1904	1,214·5	19,338	1,166·6	444·2	228·7	150·0	0·4	46·2	53·5	107·7	66·6	41·1
1905	1,228·8	19,535	1,170·0	455·4	233·1	149·7	0·4	46·6	54·6	109·4	67·5	41·9
1906	1,242·5	19,700	1,211·1	483·0	242·0	153·8	0·3	47·7	56·5	113·0	70·2	42·8
1907	1,249·5	19,746	1,229·8	509·8	250·3	159·0	0·3	48·7	59·3	117·2	74·0	43·2
1908	1,265·5	19,842	1,249·1	485·6	252·4	151·9	0·3	49·5	56·9	115·6	73·7	41·9
1909	1,269·2	19,889	1,235·5	493·7	251·8	148·5	0·4	49·0	57·5	115·8	72·4	43·5
1910	1,273·2	19,986	1,276·0	507·9	255·1	149·2	0·4	50·5	59·4	119·5	73·8	45·6
1911	1,279·0	20,015	1,295·5	517·0	258·5	151·1	0·5	51·7	61·2	122·7	75·8	46·9
1912	1,289·6	20,038	1,265·2	513·6	247·3	146·5	0·5	52·0	61·9	124·0	78·4	45·6
1913	... (i)	... (i)	1,423·5 (i)	561·5 (i)	... (i)	... (i)	... (i)	54·6 (i)	64·4 (i)	... (i)	... (i)	... (i)
1913	1,282·0	20,266	1,199·3	364·4	260·7	155·4	—	54·5	64·3	119·8	75·7	44·1
1914	...	...	...	...	...	...	...	...	...	...	...	...
1915	...	...	...	...	...	...	...	...	...	...	...	...
1916	...	...	...	...	...	...	...	...	...	...	...	...
1917	...	...	...	...	...	...	...	...	...	...	...	...
1918	...	...	...	...	...	...	...	...	...	...	...	...
1919	1,298·5	20,309	1,522·6	304·9	195·0	139·1	—	104·2	72·1	178·2	164·6	13·5
1920	1,299·3	20,312	1,579·0	318·1	219·0	144·7	—	109·4	126·9	238·9	232·0	7·0

See p. 227 for footnotes

| | Paid-up Capital and Loans (a) (£ million at 31 Dec.) | Miles of Road Open at 31 Dec. | Millions of Passengers Carried (b) (year ended 31 Dec.) | Million Tons of Freight Carried (year ended 31 Dec.) | Train Mileage (Million miles, year ended 31 Dec.) | | | Receipts (£ million, year ended 30 June) | | | Total Working Expenses (£ million, year ended 31 Dec.) | Net Working Receipts |
					Passenger	Goods	Mixed	Passenger Train	Goods Train	Total Working		
1921	1,299·8	20,302	1,229·4	267·9	205·4	109·7	—	105·9	109·6	217·8	226·8	−9·0
1922	1,281·3	20,318	1,194·7	301·6	239·4	131·9	—	101·8	115·6	219·3	174·8	44·5
1923	1,155·5	20,334	1,235·6	343·3	251·7	143·1	—	94·1	109·8	205·8	166·0	39·8
1924	1,161·4	20,349	1,236·2	335·5	254·6	143·8	—	95·1	106·4	203·4	166·9	36·5
1925	1,177·4	20,400	1,232·6	316·0	261·8	141·1	—	94·1	103·7	199·7	165·0	34·6
1926	1,175·5	20,405	1,069·0	215·6	233·6	112·9	—	85·1	85·0	171·9	154·0	17·9
1927	1,191·1	... (k)	1,174·7	321·8	268·9	144·1	—	89·5	109·6	200·8	161·0	39·8
1928	1,110·3(j)	20,271(j)	847·1(j)	306·1(j)	251·3(j)	139·3(j)	—	82·0(j)	103·1(j)	186·9(j)	149·1(j)	37·7(j)
1929	1,112·2	20,271	869·9	329·5	257·1	143·9	—	80·0	106·5	188·2	146·9	41·3
1930	1,119·7	20,265	844·3	304·3	258·4	139·2	—	76·8	99·3	177·7	143·3	34·4
1931	1,119·6	20,269	795·2	268·3	253·7	130·8	—	71·3	90·3	163·1	132·6	30·5
1932	1,124·4	20,248	777·3	249·6	253·8	123·4	—	67·1	81·2	149·6	125·2	24·4
1933	1,126·7	20,233	798·9	251·0	258·2	122·9	—	67·4	80·8	149·6	123·1	26·5
1934	1,126·6	20,216	829·7	270·0	266·6	129·5	—	68·6	85·5	155·6	126·8	28·8
1935	1,127·1	20,152	856·2	270·9	272·9	130·2	—	70·0	86·2	157·7	127·4	30·3
1936	1,127·1	20,121	875·7	280·7	278·9	136·1	—	72·2	90·2	164·0	130·6	33·4
1937	1,127·0	20,080	906·1	297·2	283·4	140·2	—	75·2	94·6	171·4	136·1	35·3
1938	1,126·9	20,007	848·9	264·3	287·4	133·6	—	75·3	87·8	164·7	137·7	27·1

(a) Part of the paid-up capital represented nominal additions. From 1890 the amount so represented is known, and was as follows (in £ million at 31st December):

1890	57·0	1898	183·0	1906	195·0	1913	199·3	1925	54·0	1932	44·6
1891	64·1	1899	184·3	1907	195·7	1919	200·7	1926	49·3	1933	44·6
1892	67·9	1900	186·5	1908	196·1	1920	201·0	1927	49·3	1934	44·6
1893	77·7	1901	187·1	1909	196·5	1921	201·2	1928	44·6	1935	44·6
1894	80·7	1902	189·1	1910	186·9	1922	179·8	1929	44·6	1936	44·6
1895	88·2	1903	190·9	1911	197·9	1923	55·8	1930	44·6	1937	44·6
1896	105·9	1904	193·1	1912	198·2	1924	56·1	1931	44·6	1938	44·6
1897	152·0	1905	194·0	1913	...						

(b) Holders of season tickets are not included.

(c) Prior to 1854 passengers' luggage etc., and mails were counted as goods, whereas subsequently they contributed to passenger train receipts.

(d) Returns were not always made by all companies prior to 1869, though (except in 1868) the defaulters were unimportant. A more serious defect of the statistics before 1869 is that the different companies did not make returns on the same basis. This affects comparison before and after 1869, most particularly so in the case of passengers carried. After 1868 children were treated as units, whereas some companies had reckoned them as half-passengers previously—a practice which had been standard until at least 1850. Also prior to 1869, the receipts and expenses of ancillary businesses were not included in the last three columns.

(e) These figures are of mileage constructed, not mileage open.

(f) This figure related to unclassified trains.

(g) Prior to 1872 mixed trains had been classified as either passenger or goods.

(h) The majority of trains previously classified as mixed were distributed amongst the other two classes from 1896.

(i) Statistics were collected on a new basis in 1913, and in addition the properties of the Manchester Ship Canal Company were no longer included. Comparison with earlier years is made, so far as possible, in the first row of figures for 1913.

(j) Another fresh basis of collecting statistics was adopted in 1927, and in 1933 the properties transferred to the London Passenger Transport Board were excluded. Revised figures for the whole period 1927–38 on the basis used after 1933 are given here. Comparison between 1927 and 1928 can be made by using the following figures, which were collected on the new basis, but which include L.P.T.B. properties:

| | Capital | Miles Open | Millions of Passengers | Million Tons of Freight | Train Mileage | | Receipts | | | Total Working Expenses | Net Working Receipts |
					Coaching	Freight	Passenger Train	Goods Train	Total Working		
1927	1,187·7	20,412	1,174·7	321·8	268·9	144·1	90·3	110·4	202·4	160·6	41·8
1928	1,187·8	20,398	1,195·9	306·1	277·2	139·6	88·9	103·3	194·0	153·5	40·5

(k) No figure of mileage open in 1927 is available which compares exactly with preceding years. Revised figures for 1913–26 were issued on the old basis of collection, but revised figures for 1927 were always on the new basis. The effect of the change of basis seems, however, to have been trivial, and the figure given in footnote (j) can be used.

Transport 6.   Railway Capital, Mileage, Traffic, and Finances—Ireland 1843–1913

NOTES

[1] Sources: *Railway Returns* and *Abstract*, whichever provides the latest revisions.
[2] Irish railway statistics in the inter-war years are extremely confused, and no summaries are available. The Ministry of Transport issued *Railway Returns* for Northern Ireland from 1922–5, and the Irish Free State government issued them for southern Ireland from 1926 onwards.

	Paid-up Capital and Loans (a) (£ million at 31 Dec.)	Miles of Road Open at 31 Dec.	Millions of Passengers Carried (b)	Million Tons of Freight Carried	Train Mileage (million miles)			Receipts (£ million)			Total Working Expenses (£ million)	Net Working Receipts (£ million)
					Passenger	Goods	Mixed	Passenger Train	Goods Train	Total Working		
1843	...	...	2·1(c)	...	...	...	...	0·06(c)	0·01(c)	0·06(c)	...	...
1844	...	...	2·6(c)	...	...	...	...	0·06(c)	0·01(c)	0·07(c)	...	...
1845	...	...	3·4(c)	...	...	...	...	0·10(c)	0·01(c)	0·11(c)	...	...
1846	...	...	3·6(c)	...	...	...	...	0·11(c)	0·02(c)	0·12(c)	...	...
1847	...	...	3·8(c)	...	...	...	...	0·15(c)	0·04(c)	0·18(c)	...	...
1848	8·8	363	3·8(c)	...	...	...	...	0·21(c)	0·07(c)	0·28(c)	...	...
1849	9·8	494	6·1	...	...	...	...	0·29	0·13	0·42	...	...
1850	10·9	537	5·5	...	...	...	...	0·34	0·18	0·51	...	...
1851	11·2	624	5·6	...	...	...	...	0·37	0·20	0·54	...	...
1852	11·9	708	6·2	...	2·4	0·5	—	0·44	0·24	0·68	...	...
1853	13·2	834	7·1	...	2·6	0·7	—	0·54(d)	0·29(d)	0·83	...	...
1854	14·4	897	6·9	...	2·8	0·7	—	0·62	0·26	0·88	...	...
1855	15·2	987	7·2	...	3·0	0·8	—	0·69	0·31	1·0	...	...
1856	16·0	1,057	7·9	1·0	3·2	1·0	—	0·76	0·35	1·1	0·41	0·59
1857	16·9	1,071	8·4	1·1	3·3	1·1	—	0·78	0·36	1·1	0·44	0·71
1858	17·8	1,188	8·4	1·2	3·3	1·2	—	0·78	0·39	1·2	0·46	0·72
1859	19·1	1,265	9·4	1·4	3·6	1·4	—	0·85	0·45	1·3	...	...
1860	20·6	1,364	10·0	1·5	4·1	1·4	—	0·88	0·49	1·4	0·62	0·75
1861	21·9	1,423	10·7	1·7	4·4	1·6	—	0·91	0·54	1·4	0·64	0·81
1862	23·3	1,598	10·4	1·7	4·7	1·7	—	0·88	0·57	1·4	0·70	0·75
1863	23·5	1,741	11·5	1·7	4·9	1·7	—	0·94	0·58	1·5	0·75	0·77
1864	25·1	1,794	11·9	1·8	5·1	2·0	—	0·99	0·59	1·6	0·75	0·83
1865	25·7	1,838	13·2	2·0	5·4	2·0	—	1·1	0·66	1·7	0·81	0·90
1866	26·6	1,909	13·1	2·3	5·6	2·3	—	1·0	0·72	1·8	0·90	0·86
1867	27·4	1,928	14·0	2·5	5·5	2·3	—	1·1	0·77	1·9	0·98	0·89
1868	...	...	...	...	...	...	...	...	...	...	...	...
1869(e)	26·9	(1,975)(f)	13·3	...	5·7	2·2	—	1·2	0·82	2·0	1·0	1·0
1870	27·2	(1,975)(f)	14·3	...	5·8	2·4	—	1·2	0·88	2·1	1·1	1·0
1871	27·0	1,988	15·5	2·9	6·2(g)	2·5(g)	—	1·3	0·97	2·3	1·2	1·1
1872	28·7	2,091	16·3	3·1	5·7	2·7	0·8(g)	1·3	1·1	2·4	1·3	1·1
1873	29·2	2,101	16·3	3·2	5·9	2·8	0·8	1·4	1·1	2·6	1·4	1·2
1874	29·8	2,127	16·5	3·1	5·4	2·5	1·5	1·4	1·1	2·6	1·4	1·1
1875	30·2	2,148	16·9	3·4	5·4	2·5	1·7	1·4	1·2	2·7	1·5	1·2
1876	30·7	2,157	17·4	3·5	6·0	2·8	0·9	1·4	1·3	2·8	1·5	1·3
1877	31·3	2,203	17·3	3·7	6·2	3·0	0·8	1·4	1·3	2·8	1·5	1·3
1878	32·0	2,259	17·9	3·6	6·4	3·1	0·9	1·5	1·3	2·8	1·5	1·3
1879	33·2	2,285	16·4	3·6	6·5	3·1	0·9	1·4	1·2	2·6	1·5	1·1
1880	33·7	2,370	17·3	3·6	6·8	3·3	0·9	1·4	1·2	2·7	1·5	1·2
1881	34·3	2,441	17·6	3·6	7·3	3·6	0·4	1·4	1·2	2·6	1·5	1·2
1882	35·0	2,465	18·7	3·8	7·4	3·5	0·6	1·5	1·3	2·8	1·5	1·3

See p. 229 for footnotes

| | Paid-up Capital and Loans (a) (£ million at 31 Dec.) | Miles of Road Open at 31 Dec. | Millions of Passengers Carried (b) | Million Tons of Freight Carried | Train Mileage | | | Receipts | | | Total Working Expenses (£ million) | Net Working Receipts |
					Passenger	Goods (million miles)	Mixed	Passenger Train	Goods Train (£ million)	Total Working		
1883	35·4	2,502	19·3	4·0	7·5	3·6	0·6	1·5	1·3	2·9	1·6	1·3
1884	35·8	2,525	19·6	3·8	7·6	3·8	0·4	1·5	1·3	2·8	1·6	1·3
1885	35·6	2,575	19·1	3·7	8·0	3·9	0·4	1·5	1·2	2·8	1·6	1·3
1886	36·0	2,632	18·7	3·6	8·1	3·6	0·7	1·5	1·3	2·8	1·5	1·3
1887	36·5	2,674	19·5	3·8	8·1	3·9	0·5	1·5	1·3	2·8	1·5	1·3
1888	36·6	2,733	19·9	3·8	8·3	3·9	0·7	1·5	1·3	2·9	1·5	1·4
1889	37·0	2,791	21·0	4·2	8·4	4·1	0·9	1·6	1·4	3·0	1·7	1·4
1890	37·3	2,792	21·4	4·3	8·5	4·3	0·9	1·7	1·4	3·1	1·8	1·4
1891	37·8	2,863	22·2	4·4	8·6	4·4	0·9	1·7	1·5	3·2	1·7	1·5
1892	38·5	2,895	22·6	4·3	8·8	4·5	0·9	1·7	1·4	3·2	1·7	1·4
1893	38·8	2,991	23·7	4·2	9·1	4·4	1·1	1·7	1·5	3·2	1·8	1·5
1894	39·2	3,044	24·5	4·6	9·3	4·8	1·1	1·8	1·6	3·4	1·8	1·6
1895	39·3	3,173	26·2	4·8	9·4	4·7	1·6	1·8	1·6	3·5	1·9	1·6
1896	39·7	3,178	26·6	4·7	9·8	4·9	1·6	1·9	1·6	3·5	1·9	1·6
1897	39·5	3,168	25·9	5·0	9·8	4·9	1·7	1·9	1·6	3·5	2·0	1·6
1898	39·4	3,176	26·6	5·1	10·1	5·0	1·7	1·9	1·6	3·6	2·1	1·5
1899	40·1	3,176	27·4	5·2	10·4	5·1	1·6	2·0	1·7	3·7	2·1	1·6
1900	39·8	3,183	27·7	5·2	10·5	5·2	1·6	2·0	1·7	3·8	2·3	1·5
1901	40·3	3,208	26·9	5·1	10·8	5·4	1·3	2·0	1·7	3·8	2·4	1·4
1902	40·6	3,214	28·2	5·3	11·0	5·3	1·4	2·1	1·8	4·0	2·4	1·6
1903	43·3	3,270	28·6	5·6	11·1	5·5	1·5	2·1	1·8	4·1	2·5	1·6
1904	43·8	3,296	29·0	5·7	11·3	5·2	1·4	2·1	1·9	4·1	2·6	1·6
1905	43·9	3,312	29·0	5·7	11·3	5·0	1·4	2·1	1·8	4·1	2·5	1·6
1906	44·4	3,363	29·2	5·8	11·6	5·1	1·5	2·2	1·9	4·2	2·5	1·6
1907	44·6	3,362	29·7	6·1	12·2	5·4	1·1	2·2	1·9	4·3	2·6	1·7
1908	45·0	3,363	29·0	6·0	12·1	5·3	1·2	2·2	1·9	4·3	2·7	1·6
1909	45·2	3,391	29·6	6·2	12·0	5·3	1·2	2·2	2·0	4·3	2·7	1·7
1910	45·3	3,401	30·7	6·5	11·8	5·3	1·4	2·3	2·1	4·5	2·7	1·7
1911	45·0	3,402	30·8	6·6	11·7	5·4	1·4	2·3	2·1	4·5	2·8	1·7
1912	45·3	3,403	29·2	6·7	11·4	5·4	1·4	2·3	2·1	4·5	2·8	1·7
1913	...	3,410(h)	31·3(h)	6·7(h)	...(h)	...(h)	...(h)	2·4(h)	2·3(h)	4·9(h)	3·0(h)	1·9(h)

(a) Part of the paid-up capital represented nominal additions. From 1890 the amount is known, and was as follows (in £ million at 31st December):

1890	—	1896	0·48	1902	0·33	1908	0·22
1891	0·06	1897	0·48	1903	0·35	1909	0·22
1892	0·20	1898	0·48	1904	0·35	1910	0·22
1893	0·32	1899	0·49	1905	0·35	1911	0·22
1894	0·32	1900	0·40	1906	0·28	1912	0·22
1895	0·34	1901	0·33	1907	0·22	1913	0·22

(b) Holders of season tickets are not included.
(c) These figures are for years ended 30th June. All others are for calendar years.
(d) Prior to 1854 passengers' luggage etc., and mails were counted as goods, whereas subsequently they contributed to passenger train receipts.
(e) Returns were not always made by all companies prior to 1869, though (except in 1868) the defaulters were unimportant. A more serious defect of the statistics before 1869 is that the different companies did not make returns on the same basis. This affects comparison before and after 1869, most particularly so in the case of passengers carried. After 1868 children were treated as units, whereas some companies had reckoned them as half-passengers previously—a practice which had been standard until at least 1850. Also prior to 1869 the receipts and expenses of ancillary businesses were not included in the last three columns.
(f) These figures are of mileage constructed, not mileage open.
(g) Prior to 1872 mixed trains had been classified as either passenger or goods.
(h) The statistics were collected on a new basis in 1913, though there is probably no significant break in the series for which figures are given here for 1913.

NOTE

SOURCES: British Road Federation, *Basic Road Statistics*, *1958*. Original sources given as: 1904-20 (except trams)—Society of Motor Manufacturers and Traders, *The Motor Industry of Great Britain 1935*; 1921-5 (except trams)—*Return of Motor Taxation*; 1926-38 (including trams from 1933)—*Annual Vehicle Census*; 1904-32 (trams)—*Annual Return of Tramway and Light Railway (Street and Road) Undertakings*.

(in thousands)

March	Private Cars	Motor Cycles	'Buses and Coaches	Taxis	Goods Vehicles	Others (a) (except trams)	Total (except trams)	Tramcars
1904	8	...	5		4	...	...	7
1905	16	...	7		9	...	...	8
1906	23	...	10		12	...	...	9
1907	32	...	12		14	...	...	10
1908	41	...	15		18	...	...	10
1909	48	...	16		22	...	...	11
1910	53	36	24		30	...	144	11
1911	72	48	33		40	...	193	11
1912	88	70	35		53	...	245	12
1913	106	98	39		64	...	306	12
1914	132	124	51		82	...	389	13
1915	139	138	44		85	...	407	...
1916	142	153	51		82	...	428	...
1917	110	119	48		64	...	341	...
1918	78	69	42		41	...	229	...
1919	110	115	44		62	...	331	13
1920	187	288	75		101	...	650	13
Aug. (March for tramcars)								
1921	243	373	83		128	19 (a)	846 (a)	14
1922	315	378	78		151	31	952	14
1923	384	430	86		173	32	1,105	14
1924	474	496	94		203	33	1,300	14
1925	580	572	99		224	35	1,510	14
Sept. (March for tramcars)								
1926	684	637	40	61	257	37	1,715	14
1927	787	681	42	53	283	39	1,886	14
1928	885	713	46	49	306	40	2,039	14
1929	981	731	50	48	330	42	2,182	14
1930	1,056	724	53	48	348	44	2,274	14
1931	1,083	627	49	38	361	43	2,201	13
1932	1,128	600	47	38	370	44	2,227	13
(Sept. for tramcars)								
1933	1,203	563	46	39	387	47	2,285	12
1934	1,308	548	46	39	413	50	2,405	12
1935	1,477	517	47	38	435	56	2,570	11
1936	1,643	506	49	37	459	64	2,758	10
1937	1,798	488	51	35	479	78	2,929	10
1938	1,944	462	53	35	495	96	3,085	9

(a) Includes invalid carriages and exempt vehicles, and agricultural tractors licensed to go on roads. These vehicles, however, were not counted before 1921.

REFERENCES

BOOKS

E. W. Blocksidge, *Hints on the Register Tonnage of Merchant Ships* (Liverpool, 2nd edition 1942).

G. L. Boag, *Manual of Railway Statistics* (London 1911).

British Road Federation, *Basic Road Statistics* (London, annually since 1934 (except during some war years). From 1934–37 the title was *Road Notes in Great Britain*.)

A. K. Cairncross, *Home and Foreign Investment, 1870–1913* (Cambridge, 1953).

E. Cleveland-Stevens, *English Railways: Their Development and their Relation to the State* (London, 1915).

J. Francis, *History of the English Railway, 1820–1845* (2 vols., London, 1851).

W. T. Jackman, *The Development of Transportation in Modern England* (2 vols., Cambridge, 1916).

H. G. Lewin, *Early British Railways* (London, 1925).

A. C. Littleton and B. S. Yamey (editors), *Studies in the History of Accounting*, (London, 1956)—chapter on 'Aspects of Railway Accounting before 1868' by H. Pollins.

C. P. Mossop, *Railway Operating Statistics* (London, 2nd edition, 1923).

D. G. Owen, *Ports of the United Kingdom* (London, 2nd edition, 1948).

J. Priestley, *Historical Account of Navigable Rivers, Canals, Railways, etc.* (London, 1831).

H. M. Ross, *British Railways*, (London, 1904).

H. Scrivenor, *The Railways of the United Kingdom*, (London, 1849).

S. and B. Webb, *English Local Government: The Story of the King's Highway* (London, 1913).

F. Wishaw, *The Railways of Great Britain and Ireland* (London, 1840).

T. S. Willan, *The English Coasting Trade, 1600–1750* (Manchester, 1938).

GOVERNMENT PUBLICATIONS

Trade and Navigation Accounts (in *Sessional Papers* as part of the annual *Finance Accounts* to 1853).

Annual Statement of Trade (in *Sessional Papers* annually from 1853 to 1920, and issued as non-parliamentary papers thereafter).

The County Totals . . . Relative to the Expense and Maintenance of the Highways in England and Wales (S.P. 1818, XVI).

Returns relating to Shipping Registered and Built (in *Sessional Papers* at intervals from 1806, and annually from 1852 to 1921).

Report of the Select Committee on the State of Communication by Railway (S.P. 1839, X).

Report of the Select Committee on Railway Communication (S.P. 1840, XIII).

Report of the Select Committee on Railways (S.P. 1844, XI).

Report of the Officers of the Railway Department (in *Sessional Papers* annually, 1841–5).

Report of the Railway Commissioners (in *Sessional Papers* annually 1846–50 and 1875–81).

Report of the Railway Department (in *Sessional Papers* annually, 1851–74).

Report of the Railway and Canal Commissioners (in *Sessional Papers* from 1882).

Returns of Capital, Traffic, etc. (in *Sessional Papers* twice-yearly 1847–60, annually 1861–1920, and issued as non-parliamentary papers thereafter. (Returns for Southern Ireland were issued annually by the Irish government from 1926.))

Return on Turnpike Trusts, 1834–1850 (S.P. 1852–3, XCVII).

Return of Government Expenditure on Harbours, 1800–1875 (S.P. 1876, LXV).

Returns of Tramway and Light Railway (Street and Road) Undertakings (in *Sessional Papers* annually 1877–1920, and issued as non-parliamentary papers thereafter.

Report of the Royal Commission on Railways (S.P. 1867, XXXVIII).

Report of the Royal Commission on Tonnage (S.P. 1881, XLIX).

Report of the Select Committee on Turnpike Trusts (S.P. 1836, XIX).

Report of the Commissioners on the State of the Roads (S.P. 1840, XXVII).

Report of the Select Committee on Expenditure of County Rates (S.P. 1834, XIV).

Report of Local Government Board Commissioners (in *Sessional Papers* annually 1872–1919).

ARTICLES

E. A. V. Angier, 'Fifty Years Freights, 1869–1919', *Fairplay* (1920 and subsequently).

S. G. Broadbridge, 'The Early Capital Market: The Lancashire & Yorkshire Railway', *E.H.R.* (1955).

C. D. Campbell, 'Cyclical Fluctuations in the Railway Industry', *T.M.S.S.* (1928–9).

R. Davis, 'Merchant Shipping in the Economy of the Late Seventeenth Century', *E.H.R.* (1956).

R. Davis, 'Earnings of Capital in the English Shipping Industry, 1670–1730', *J.E.H.* (1957)

G. S. Graham, 'The Ascendancy of the Sailing Ship, 1850–1885', *E.H.R.* (1956).

J. R. T. Hughes and S. Reiter, 'The First 1,945 British Steamships', *Journal of the American Statistical Association* (1958).

C. W. Hurcomb, 'Official Railway Statistics in Great Britain', *J.R.S.S.* (1925).

L. Isserlis, 'Tramp Shipping Cargoes and Freights', *J.R.S.S.* (1938).

R. C. Jarvis, 'Sources for the History of Ships and Shipping', *Journal of Transport History* (1955).

M. G. Kendall, 'United Kingdom Merchant Shipping Statistics', *J.R.S.S.* (1948).

Lloyd's Register of Shipping complete from 1775–6. Amalgamated with the *New Register Book of Shipping* (1799 onwards) in 1834.

K. Maywald, 'The Construction Costs and the Value of the British Merchant Fleet, 1850–1938', *Scottish Journal of Political Economy* (1956).

F. A. A. Menzler, 'Rail and Road Statistics', *J.R.S.S.* (1950).

S. Pollard, 'British and World Shipbuilding, 1890–1914: A Study in Comparative Costs', *J.E.H.* (1957).

H. Pollins, 'A Note on Railway Constructional Costs', *Economica* (1952).

BUILDING

TABLES

Although it has obviously been one of the most important industries for a long time, building has necessarily been scattered and its organisation has been fragmentary. Until comparatively recent times, therefore, it has escaped official attention, more particularly since by its nature it could not enter into overseas trade. Our first statistical series relating to building is that given in table 1—the output of bricks from 1785 to 1849 according to the excise officials. The general question of the reliability of the excise statistics is discussed in the introduction to the next chapter. This particular series was, of course, the subject of lengthy analysis in Shannon's well-known article.[1] It is enough here to say that it is probably the most reliable of the excise statistics, since the tax was relatively light, and the conditions of manufacture were not conducive to evasion.

Table 2 shows the most important statistics which can be derived from the records of the Inhabited House duty which was imposed in 1851 on *dwelling* houses of £20 annual value and over. The complete lack of information prior to 1875 about houses exempt from duty robs the early part of this table of much of its potential usefulness. Even after that date there are deficiencies, of which two may be singled out for special mention.[2] In the first place, the figures are of net quantities, offsetting much demolition against new building, and it seems probable that demolition was nothing like constant from year to year. Secondly, the value figures for England and Wales were not reassessed annually, and in the reassessment years there was an upward bias, whilst in the other years the tendency was in the opposite direction. The numbers of houses in different categories were also affected by this factor, though not, of course, the total. An earlier series of Inhabited House duty returns is available for 1821–4 (rents of £5 being exempt) and 1825–33 (rents of under £10 exempt). These returns give a detailed distribution by rent groups and distinguish England and Wales from Scotland.[3]

[1] H. A. Shannon, 'Bricks—A Trade Index, 1785–1849', in *Economica*, Vol. I., No. 3 (1934).
[2] There is an extended discussion in J. C. Stamp, *British Incomes and Property* (London, 1916), pp. 107–37.
[3] *S.P.* 1833, XLI.

A rough indication of the increase in the stock of houses over a longer period than the Inhabited House duty statistics is given by the numbers of houses enumerated at the decennial censuses. These are shown in national summary in table 3, but a good deal of regional information is available in the original sources. Two main difficulties in using these statistics are the changes which have taken place in definitions, and the likely omissions of many uninhabited houses.[1] However, according to Miss Bowley 'as far as historical research is concerned with broad trends, the difficulties created by the imperfect definitions and classifications of the earlier censuses are not very important. . . . It was, however, a piece of great good fortune in connection with the assessment of interwar housing problems that the 1911 census contained enough improvements to make its data reasonably useful and capable of comparison with those of the 1921 and 1931 censuses'.[2] It is only since 1919 that statistics of new housing built became available: these were published in the annual reports of the Ministry of Health and the Department of Health for Scotland.

The last two tables give two sets of estimates recently published. The first is Weber's careful estimates of houses built since 1856, which link on to the figures from 1924 in the *Abstract*. The second is Dr Maywald's index of building costs. The provenance of these statistics is best judged by reference to the original sources; but it seems clear that they represent a considerable advance on those previously produced. Weber used hitherto untapped local authority sources in the main, and Dr Maywald's index avoids the extreme rigidity of its principal predecessor—G. T. Jones's.[3] Like the latter, however, it is an index of input costs rather than of selling prices.

One series of statistics, which we have not included, are probably best referred to here, though they do not relate entirely to building. These figures are those of government expenditure on harbours an annual series which exists covering the period 1800–75.[4] The amount of money involved was never very large, but the timing of the expenditure is interesting.

[1] Stamp, *op. cit.* p. 126.

[2] Marion Bowley, 'The Housing Statistics of Great Britain', *J.R.S.S.* 1950.

[3] G. T. Jones, *Increasing Return* (Cambridge, 1933), Part II.

[4] *S.P.* 1876, XIV.

Building 1. Bricks Charged with Duty—England & Wales 1785–1849

NOTE

SOURCE: H. A. Shannon, 'Bricks—A Trade Index, 1785–1849', in *Economica*, vol. I, no. 2 (1934), pp. 300 *et seq.* The original source is an MS. account in the Customs and Excise Library.

(in millions)

Years ended 5th July				Years ended 5th January			
1785	358·8	1801	674·7	1816	673·0	1833	1,011·3
1786	495·7	1802	698·6	1817	701·7	1834	1,152·4
1787	635·8	1803	842·1	1818	952·1	1835	1,349·3
1788	668·2	1804	795·7	1819	1,101·6	1836	1,606·1
1789	590·3	1805	845·5	1820	949·2	1837	1,478·2
1790	711·2	1806	933·2	1821	899·2	1838	1,427·0
1791	749·9	1807	831·3	1822	1,019·5	1839	1,568·7
1792	808·0	1808	841·6	1823	1,244·7	1840	1,677·8
1793	908·9	1809	779·3	1824	1,463·2	1841	1,423·8
1794	787·7	1810	874·4	1825	1,948·8	1842	1,271·9
1795	559·3	1811	950·6	1826	1,350·2	1843	1,158·9
1796	633·0	1812	939·6	1827	1,103·3	1844	1,420·7
1797	517·7	1813	912·0	1828	1,078·8	1845	1,820·7
1798	516·8	1814	758·1	1829	1,109·6	1846	2,039·7
1799	421·3	1815	778·4	1830	1,091·3	1847	2,193·8
1800	543·1			1831	1,125·4	1848	1,461·0
				1832	971·9	1849	1,462·7

Building 2. Inhabited House Duty—Great Britain 1851–1924

NOTES TO BOTH PARTS

[1] SOURCES: 1852–68—*S.P.* 1870, xx; 1869–84—*S.P.* 1884–5, XXII; 1884–1924—*Report of the Commissioners of Inland Revenue*, in sessional papers annually.

[2] Private dwelling houses of under £20 annual value (i.e. exempt) were not separately distinguished from residential shops of like value. The latter are therefore included under the heading *Dwelling Houses Exempt from Duty*.

[3] Exempt farmhouses and farm buildings, and exempt buildings belonging to railways and mines are not included under any heading.

[4] New assessments came into force in the following years: Metropolitan area—1871, 1877, 1882, 1887, 1892, 1897, 1902, 1907, 1912; Rest of England & Wales (including metropolitan area up to 1871)—1852, 1854, 1858, 1862, 1865, 1868, 1871, 1874, 1877, 1880, 1883, 1886, 1889, 1894, 1899, 1904, 1911.

A. Numbers of Houses, 1851–1915 (in thousands)

Years ended 5th April or 31st March	Dwelling Houses Charged with Duty			Dwelling Houses Exempt from Duty			All Premises Charged with Duty			All Premises Exempt from Duty		
	England & Wales	Scotland	Great Britain	England & Wales	Scotland	Great Britain	England & Wales	Scotland	Great Britain	England & Wales	Scotland	Great Britain
1852	251	24	276	...	...	...	434	31	465	...	...	...
1853	253	24	277	...	...	...	436	30	466	...	...	...
1854	257	25	282	...	...	...	441	30	471	...	...	...
1855	266	25	291	...	...	...	454	31	485	...	...	...
1856	270	25	295	...	...	...	458	31	489	...	...	...
1857	274	26	300	...	...	...	464	31	495	...	...	...
1858	281	26	308	...	...	...	474	32	506	...	...	...
1859	290	28	317	...	...	...	486	33	519	...	...	...
1860	299	29	328	...	...	...	498	35	533	...	...	...
1861	307	30	336	...	...	...	509	35	544	...	...	...
1862	316	30	346	...	...	...	520	36	556	...	...	...
1863	332	31	363	...	...	...	540	37	578	...	...	...
1864	343	32	375	...	...	...	556	38	594	...	...	...
1865	357	33	389	...	...	...	576	39	615	...	...	...
1866	378	34	412	...	...	...	608	40	648	...	...	...
1867	390	35	424	...	...	...	623	41	664	...	...	...
1868	415	36	451	...	...	...	658	42	701	...	...	...
1869	435	37	472	...	...	...	687	44	731	...	...	...
1870	448	39	486	...	...	...	708	46	754	...	...	...
1871	481	40	521	...	...	...	749	48	796	...	...	...
1872	486	41	527	...	...	...	757	49	806	...	...	...
1873	494	43	537	...	...	...	767	50	818	...	...	...
1874	513	45	558	...	...	...	797	53	851	...	...	...
1875	523	47	569	3,401	521	3,922	809	56	865	3,667	612	4,280
1876	535	48	583	3,462	533	3,995	824	57	881	3,753	627	4,380
1877	576	52	629	3,487	557	4,045	883	62	945	3,788	656	4,444
1878	596	55	651	3,566	575	4,142	907	66	973	3,827	676	4,503
1879	617	58	675	3,629	589	4,218	932	69	1,002	3,898	701	4,599
1880	653	61	713	3,679	592	4,271	983	72	1,056	3,956	701	4,657
1881	673	61	734	3,732	600	4,332	1,008	73	1,081	4,018	711	4,729
1882	701	62	764	3,768	608	4,376	1,037	74	1,111	4,059	719	4,779
1883	730	64	794	3,836	622	4,458	1,078	76	1,154	4,110	731	4,841
1884	745	64	809	3,896	628	4,524	1,095	76	1,171	4,177	740	4,916
1885	752	65	817	3,952	636	4,589	1,100	77	1,176	4,238	748	4,987
1886	773	66	839	3,979	648	4,627	1,127	78	1,205	4,275	761	5,037
1887	785	67	851	4,029	659	4,688	1,136	78	1,214	4,334	768	5,103
1888	789	68	857	4,089	665	4,753	1,140	79	1,219	4,404	775	5,179
1889	805	69	875	4,144	671	4,815	1,162	81	1,242	4,467	779	5,247
1890	812	70	882	4,213	678	4,891	1,167	82	1,248	4,548	787	5,333
1891	807	71	878	4,264	685	4,950	1,175	83	1,257	4,605	796	5,402
1892	817	73	890	4,333	690	5,023	1,186	84	1,270	4,682	800	5,482
1893	827	74	901	4,378	695	5,073	1,197	85	1,283	4,743	808	5,551
1894	869	77	946	4,370	697	5,066	1,253	89	1,342	4,739	813	5,551
1895	881	79	960	4,422	704	5,126	1,266	91	1,357	4,801	825	5,625
1896	897	82	979	4,491	713	5,204	1,287	94	1,380	4,879	836	5,716

Building 2. *continued*

Years ended 5th April or 31st March	Dwelling Houses Charged with Duty England & Wales	Scotland	Great Britain	Dwelling Houses Exempt from Duty England & Wales	Scotland	Great Britain	All Premises Charged with Duty England & Wales	Scotland	Great Britain	All Premises Exempt from Duty England & Wales	Scotland	Great Britain
1897	927	85	1,012	4,558	725	5,284	1,320	97	1,417	4,957	854	5,811
1898	947	88	1,036	4,627	737	5,364	1,344	100	1,445	5,031	864	5,895
1899	1,024	93	1,117	4,656	740	5,396	1,447	105	1,553	5,067	880	5,947
1900	1,055	97	1,152	4,753	757	5,510	1,480	110	1,590	5,183	900	6,083
1901	1,087	101	1,188	4,843	770	5,613	1,517	114	1,630	5,288	916	6,204
1902	1,128	103	1,231	4,919	784	5,704	1,560	116	1,676	5,375	929	6,304
1903	1,158	107	1,265	4,997	795	5,792	1,593	120	1,712	5,456	941	6,396
1904	1,240	111	1,350	5,034	799	5,834	1,692	124	1,816	5,498	957	6,454
1905	1,267	115	1,382	5,122	813	5,935	1,721	128	1,848	5,601	971	6,571
1906	1,297	117	1,414	5,222	826	6,048	1,746	130	1,876	5,726	987	6,713
1907	1,327	120	1,446	5,294	834	6,128	1,774	132	1,906	5,812	1,000	6,812
1908(a)	(1,345)	(123)	(1,468)	(5,365)	(843)	(6,208)	(1,792)	(135)	(1,927)	(5,894)	(1,013)	(6,907)
1909	1,366	126	1,492	5,440	841	6,281	1,812	138	1,951	5,985	1,010	6,995
1910	1,380	127	1,507	5,522	846	6,368	1,825	139	1,964	6,081	1,015	7,096
1911	1,404	128	1,533	5,528	851	6,379	1,857	141	1,998	6,085	1,027	7,112
1912	1,415	130	1,545	5,607	852	6,459	1,866	143	2,009	6,188	1,028	7,216
1913	1,427	132	1,559	5,652	853	6,506	1,874	144	2,018	6,249	1,031	7,280
1914	1,441	134	1,574	5,698	851	6,549	1,886	146	2,032	6,310	1,031	7,340
1915	1,455	137	1,592	5,751	850	6,601	1,898	149	2,047	6,377	1,031	7,408

(a) The figures for 1908 are estimates. Those originally compiled were incomplete owing to a necessary change in practice following legislation.

B. Value of Houses, 1851–1924 (in £000)

Years ended 5th April or 31st March	Dwelling Houses Charged with Duty England & Wales	Scotland	Great Britain	Dwelling Houses Exempt from Duty England & Wales	Scotland	Great Britain	All Premises Charged with Duty England & Wales	Scotland	Great Britain	All Premises Exempt from Duty England & Wales	Scotland	Great Britain
1852	12,368	1,029	13,397	...	...	...	20,463	1,241	21,703	...	...	...
1853	12,381	1,024	13,405	...	...	...	20,495	1,220	21,715	...	...	...
1854	12,568	1,051	13,619	...	...	...	20,699	1,249	21,948	...	...	...
1855	12,979	1,077	14,055	...	...	...	21,282	1,271	22,553	...	...	...
1856	13,207	1,091	14,297	...	...	...	21,573	1,280	22,852	...	...	...
1857	13,432	1,119	14,551	...	...	...	21,837	1,302	23,140	...	...	...
1858	13,896	1,168	15,064	...	...	...	22,485	1,352	23,836	...	...	...
1859	14,377	1,212	15,588	...	...	...	23,223	1,399	24,622	...	...	...
1860	14,804	1,260	16,064	...	...	...	23,704	1,459	25,162	...	...	...
1861	15,203	1,297	16,499	...	...	...	24,199	1,500	25,698	...	...	...
1862	15,676	1,348	17,024	...	...	...	24,878	1,558	26,436	...	...	...
1863	16,516	1,391	17,907	...	...	...	26,102	1,606	27,708	...	...	...
1864	17,090	1,426	18,516	...	...	...	26,853	1,645	28,498	...	...	...
1865	17,882	1,473	19,355	...	...	...	27,917	1,695	29,612	...	...	...
1866	19,306	1,520	20,826	...	...	...	30,032	1,747	31,779	...	...	...
1867	20,077	1,579	21,655	...	...	...	30,973	1,815	32,788	...	...	...
1868	21,605	1,662	23,267	...	...	...	33,160	1,904	35,064	...	...	...
1869	23,031	1,702	24,733	...	...	...	35,210	1,955	37,165	...	...	...
1870	23,678	1,783	25,461	...	...	...	35,962	2,047	38,009	...	...	...
1871	25,672	1,876	27,549	...	...	...	38,859	2,156	41,015	...	...	...
1872	26,014	1,922	27,936	...	...	...	39,194	2,223	41,417	...	...	...
1873	26,464	1,992	28,456	...	...	...	39,726	2,298	42,024	...	...	...
1874	27,635	2,092	29,727	...	...	...	41,481	2,422	43,903	...	...	...
1875	28,272	2,186	30,458	25,429	3,179	28,608	42,256	2,526	44,782	40,275	6,558	46,834
1876	28,938	2,263	31,201	26,082	3,286	29,368	43,087	2,611	45,698	41,446	6,848	48,293
1877	31,850	2,513	34,363	27,248	3,578	30,826	47,476	2,911	50,387	43,744	7,525	51,229
1878	32,835	2,652	35,487	28,095	3,751	31,846	48,751	3,079	51,830	45,080	7,816	52,896
1879	33,834	2,776	36,610	28,821	3,871	32,692	50,008	3,228	53,236	46,304	8,132	54,436
1880	34,859	2,917	37,776	29,562	3,986	33,558	51,735	3,422	55,157	49,091	8,410	57,511
1881	35,791	2,941	38,732	30,286	4,057	34,345	52,905	3,447	56,351	50,264	8,459	58,723

Building 2. *continued*

Years ended 5th April or 31st March	Dwelling Houses						All Premises					
	Charged with Duty			Exempt from Duty			Charged with Duty			Exempt from Duty		
	England & Wales	Scotland	Great Britain	England & Wales	Scotland	Great Britain	England & Wales	Scotland	Great Britain	England & Wales	Scotland	Great Britain
1882	36,864	2,981	39,845	30,778	4,149	34,927	54,166	3,492	57,658	52,202	8,573	60,775
1883	38,226	3,046	41,271	31,573	4,181	35,755	56,273	3,588	59,861	53,852	8,529	62,383
1884	39,029	3,069	42,098	32,282	4,236	36,520	57,205	3,607	60,812	55,103	8,596	63,698
1885	39,372	3,093	42,465	32,973	4,303	37,276	57,372	3,622	60,994	56,156	8,733	64,889
1886	40,136	3,144	43,280	33,718	4,379	38,097	58,495	3,672	62,167	57,679	8,959	66,638
1887	40,771	3,158	43,929	34,304	4,474	38,779	59,088	3,684	62,773	58,831	9,005	67,836
1888	40,922	3,191	44,113	35,090	4,537	39,827	59,230	3,711	62,941	60,025	9,080	69,105
1889	41,494	3,242	44,736	35,760	4,611	40,371	60,142	3,769	63,911	61,100	9,213	70,313
1890	41,791	3,281	45,072	36,522	4,687	41,209	60,337	3,798	64,135	62,297	9,304	71,601
1891	41,526	3,300	44,825	37,104	4,784	41,888	60,943	3,826	64,769	63,502	9,496	72,999
1892	41,780	3,340	45,120	37,859	4,856	42,715	61,617	3,876	65,493	65,054	9,626	74,680
1893	42,026	3,395	45,422	38,493	4,909	43,402	61,985	3,946	65,931	66,285	9,774	76,059
1894	43,726	3,498	47,224	39,086	5,025	44,111	64,679	4,065	68,744	67,929	10,024	77,953
1895	44,041	3,566	47,606	39,809	5,125	44,934	65,083	4,135	69,218	69,169	10,249	79,419
1896	44,590	3,659	48,249	40,691	5,223	45,914	65,925	4,241	70,166	70,744	10,435	81,179
1897	45,748	3,776	49,524	41,547	5,365	46,912	67,779	4,365	72,144	72,631	10,715	83,346
1898	46,344	3,892	50,236	42,440	5,516	47,955	68,826	4,491	73,317	74,040	11,008	85,048
1899	49,213	4,071	53,284	43,600	5,682	49,282	73,665	4,696	78,361	76,748	11,490	88,238
1900	50,234	4,201	54,435	44,858	5,906	50,764	74,894	4,854	79,749	79,076	11,890	90,966
1901	51,401	4,338	55,739	46,058	6,073	52,131	76,372	5,010	81,381	81,567	12,289	93,856
1902	53,208	4,434	57,642	47,095	6,225	53,320	78,689	5,115	83,804	84,360	12,626	96,986
1903	54,227	4,556	58,783	48,283	6,402	54,684	79,846	5,237	85,084	86,564	12,921	99,486
1904	57,547	4,710	62,257	49,582	6,642	56,224	84,709	5,404	90,113	90,749	13,231	103,981
1905	58,308	4,835	63,143	50,764	6,780	57,544	85,417	5,534	90,951	93,048	13,623	106,671
1906	59,189	4,935	64,124	52,040	6,941	58,981	85,900	5,627	91,527	96,052	13,930	109,982
1907	60,649	5,032	65,682	53,003	7,058	60,061	87,229	5,721	92,950	99,022	14,294	113,316
1908	61,168	5,125	66,293	54,099	7,171	61,270	87,619	5,820	93,439	101,465	14,455	115,920
1909	61,863	5,214	67,078	55,158	7,216	62,375	88,100	5,907	94,007	103,774	14,637	118,412
1910	62,350	5,255	67,605	56,203	7,288	63,491	88,291	5,949	94,240	105,724	14,710	120,434
1911	63,408	5,354	68,761	55,867	7,357	63,224	90,135	6,026	96,161	106,863	14,826	121,689
1912	63,409	5,375	68,784	56,888	7,401	64,289	89,111	6,030	95,141	109,341	14,925	124,266
1913	63,506	5,384	68,890	57,569	7,447	65,016	88,630	6,027	94,657	111,820	15,038	126,858
1914	63,882	5,429	69,311	58,216	7,480	65,696	88,767	6,065	94,833	114,062	15,221	129,283
1915	64,048	5,518	69,567	58,906	7,500	66,405	88,690	6,154	94,844	116,384	15,670	132,054
1916	64,075	5,571	69,646	...	...	...	88,519	6,199	94,718	...	...	...
1917	63,887	5,523	69,410	...	...	...	87,834	6,133	93,968	...	...	...
1918	63,149	5,535	68,684	...	...	...	86,734	6,128	92,862	...	...	...
1919	63,246	5,539	68,785	...	...	...	86,536	6,110	92,645	...	...	...
1920	63,256	5,614	68,870	...	...	...	86,460	6,185	92,645	...	...	...
1921	63,228	5,630	68,858	...	...	...	86,554	6,208	92,762	...	...	...
1922	65,158	5,739	70,897	...	...	...	89,582	6,312	95,894	...	...	...
1923	69,556	5,990	75,546	...	...	...	93,597	6,550	100,147	...	...	...
1924	72,281	6,680	78,961	...	...	...	99,677	7,241	106,918	...	...	...

Building 3. Number of Houses at Censuses—United Kingdom 1851–1951

NOTES
[1] SOURCE: *Abstract*, based on the *Census Reports*.
[2] The definition of the term 'house' has changed slightly from time to time. Details can be found in *Guides to Official Sources*, no. 2 (*Census Reports of Great Britain 1801–1931*). The figures here relate to all houses, whether classed as occupied or unoccupied.

(in thousands)

	England & Wales	Scotland	Ireland	Northern Ireland
1851	3,432	...	1,111	267
1861	3,924	...	1,036	269
1871	4,520	...	993	267
1881	5,218	799	972	273
1891	5,824	869	940	274
1901	6,710	986	932	291
1911	7,550	1,102	931	291
1921	7,979	1,109	...	...
1926	...	...	...	285
1931	9,400	1,197	...	...
1937	...	...	...	322
1951	12,389	1,442	...	346

4. Houses Built—Great Britain 1856–1956

NOTE
SOURCES: 1856–1950—B. Weber, 'A New Index of Residential Construction 1838–1950' in the *Scottish Journal of Political Economy*, vol. II, no. 2 (June 1955); 1950–6—*Abstract*, which is used by Weber for 1924–50. For the methods of estimation for 1856–1923 the original source must be consulted.

(in thousands)

1856	52·6	1882	81·9	1908	100·9	1934	336·7
1857	47·5	1883	81·9	1909	98·8	1935	350·5
1858	50·9	1884	82·4	1910	86·0	1936	365·0
1859	44·6	1885	76·7	1911	67·5	1937	362·2
1860	45·2	1886	75·1	1912	53·4	1938	359·1
1861	45·2	1887	78·7	1913	54·2	1939	255·6
1862	58·1	1888	79·9	1914	48·3	1940	95·1
1863	64·4	1889	79·5	1915	30·8	1941	23·4
1864	60·9	1890	75·8	1916	17·0	1942	12·9
1865	53·6	1891	79·1	1917	...	1943	9·5
1866	55·2	1892	84·0	1918	...	1944	8·1
1867	65·3	1893	85·9	1919	...	1945	13·8
1868	70·4	1894	91·2	1920	29·7	1946	138·5
1869	77·0	1895	89·8	1921	76·1	1947	186·0
1870	85·9	1896	107·1	1922	84·5	1948	245·9
1871	90·4	1897	130·4	1923	66·1	1949	197·7
1872	93·8	1898	157·7	1924	131·2	1950	198·2
1873	81·7	1899	156·2	1925	174·2	1951	194·8
1874	90·9	1900	139·7	1926	222·3	1952	239·9
1875	120·3	1901	139·7	1927	254·9	1953	318·8
1876	130·8	1902	153·8	1928	206·8	1954	347·8
1877	124·1	1903	156·9	1929	212·2	1955	317·4
1878	106·5	1904	136·6	1930	202·4	1956	300·6
1879	86·0	1905	127·4	1931	210·0		
1880	83·1	1906	130·6	1932	218·1		
1881	79·1	1907	121·3	1933	275·2		

Building 5. Index of Building Costs—United Kingdom 1845–1938

NOTES

[1] SOURCE: K. Maywald, 'An Index of Building Costs in the United Kingdom', in *E.H.R.*, vol. VII, no. 2 (Dec. 1954).

[2] Of the two indices presented in Dr Maywald's article, the one shown here is the more complete one, which includes materials used in roofing, installations and painting.

1930 = 100

	Wages	Materials	Total			Wages	Materials	Total
1845	24·7	78·6	51·7		1892	41·6	56·2	48·9
1846	24·7	83·0	53·9		1893	42·2	54·0	48·1
1847	24·7	80·2	52·5		1894	42·4	52·7	47·5
1848	25·0	75·4	50·2		1895	42·5	51·3	46·9
1849	25·2	70·8	48·0		1896	43·0	52·1	47·5
1850	25·2	69·1	47·2		1897	43·7	53·9	48·8
1851	25·2	68·0	46·6		1898	45·0	57·1	51·1
1852	25·2	69·4	47·3		1899	45·9	61·5	53·7
1853	25·2	80·5	52·9		1900	46·4	67·2	56·8
1854	26·1	82·6	54·3		1901	46·6	65·0	55·8
1855	26·1	81·3	53·7		1902	46·6	58·9	52·7
1856	26·1	75·3	50·7		1903	46·5	55·9	51·2
1857	26·1	77·1	51·6		1904	46·5	53·9	50·2
1858	26·1	74·5	50·3		1905	46·5	53·3	49·9
1859	26·9	72·8	49·8		1906	46·5	56·0	51·2
1860	27·4	72·6	50·0		1907	46·5	59·5	53·0
1861	27·4	70·6	49·0		1908	46·6	55·6	51·1
1862	27·4	69·9	48·6		1909	46·5	54·6	50·6
1863	28·2	71·2	49·7		1910	46·5	57·5	52·0
1864	28·2	72·8	50·5		1911	46·6	61·1	53·9
1865	28·4	71·1	49·7		1912	47·2	65·1	56·2
1866	29·8	73·3	51·6		1913	48·6	66·9	57·8
1867	30·8	70·9	50·8		1914	49·9	67·1	58·5
1868	32·0	68·3	50·1		1915	51·7	89·0	70·4
1869	33·6	68·0	50·8		1916	55·5	108·8	82·2
1870	33·9	69·3	51·6		1917	66·3	122·9	94·6
1871	33·9	71·0	52·4		1918	89·7	145·2	117·5
1872	33·9	80·9	57·4		1919	112·8	179·1	146·0
1873	35·5	90·4	63·0		1920	146·8	196·8	171·8
1874	37·2	84·9	61·0		1921	127·6	153·3	140·5
1875	37·4	76·8	57·1		1922	103·4	123·7	113·6
1876	38·1	73·2	55·7		1923	98·8	114·9	106·9
1877	38·1	71·5	54·8		1924	104·3	117·4	110·9
1878	38·1	66·2	52·2		1925	104·7	117·4	111·1
1879	38·1	63·2	50·7		1926	105·2	110·4	107·8
1880	39·7	67·7	53·7		1927	105·4	106·3	105·9
1881	39·8	64·3	52·0		1928	102·8	100·6	101·7
1882	39·7	65·5	52·6		1929	102·6	101·8	102·2
1883	39·5	63·2	51·4		1930	100·0	100·0	100·0
1884	39·5	59·4	49·4		1931	97·7	94·7	96·2
1885	39·4	58·7	49·1		1932	95·0	88·7	91·8
1886	39·5	56·6	48·0		1933	92·4	87·5	90·0
1887	39·5	55·0	47·3		1934	92·5	87·8	90·2
1888	39·5	55·4	47·4		1935	95·0	89·9	92·0
1889	39·6	58·2	48·9		1936	97·9	93·3	95·6
1890	40·4	60·7	50·6		1937	100·2	100·6	100·4
1891	41·0	58·0	49·5		1938	103·3	101·3	102·3

REFERENCES

BOOKS

Marion Bowley, *Housing and the State, 1919–1944* (London, 1945).
A. K. Cairncross, *Home and Foreign Investment, 1870–1913* (Cambridge, 1953).
G. T. Jones, *Increasing Return* (Cambridge, 1933).
J. C. Stamp, *British Incomes and Property* (London, 1916).

GOVERNMENT PUBLICATIONS

Returns of Government Expenditure on Harbours, 1800–1875 (*S.P.* 1876, LIV).
Report of the Royal Commission on the Housing of the Working Classes (*S.P.* 1884–5, XXX, and *S.P.* 1884–5, XXXI).

ARTICLES

I. Bowen, 'Building Output and the Trade Cycle (U.K. 1924–38)', *O.E.P.* (1940).
Marion Bowley, 'The Housing Statistics of Great Britain', *J.R.S.S.* (1950).
A. K. Cairncross and B. Weber, 'Fluctuations in Building in Great Britain, 1785–1849', *E.H.R.* (1956).
E. W. Cooney, 'Capital Exports and Investment in Building in Britain and the U.S.A., 1856–1914', *Economica* (1949).
E. W. Cooney, 'Long Waves in Building in the British Economy of the Nineteenth Century', *E.H.R.* (1960).
K. Maywald, 'An Index of Building Costs in the United Kingdom', *E.H.R.* (1954).
W. Newmarch, 'On the Electoral Statistics of the Counties and Boroughs in England and Wales', *J.S.S.* (1857 and 1859).
R. H. I. Palgrave, 'On the House Accommodation of England and Wales', *J.S.S.* (1869).
H. A. Shannon, 'Bricks—A Trade Index, 1785–1849', *Economica* (1934).
J. C. Spensley, 'Urban Housing Problems', *J.R.S.S.* (1918).
B. Weber, 'A New Index of Residential Construction, 1838–1950', *Scottish Journal of Political Economy* (1955).

MISCELLANEOUS PRODUCTION STATISTICS

TABLES

This chapter covers the eighteenth and nineteenth century excise statistics, numbers of patents granted annually since 1617, Census of Production returns, and indices of production. By far the largest part of the chapter consists of the excise statistics. These spring from the records made by the excise officials of the quantities of the various excisable commodities charged with duty. They were, with the exception of certain allowances for wastage, intended to be records of production; but, of course, there was a premium on evasion, so that they undoubtedly understate the output of all excisable goods. The amount of understatement is, however, indeterminable. It depended on the proportion of tax to price, on the ease of concealment of production, and on the efficiency of the excise officials. We have, however, been able to make some qualitative assessments of the importance of evasion, largely thanks to the kindness of Mrs Selma Goldsmith (Selma E. Fine) in placing at our disposal her unpublished Radcliffe College thesis.

The efficiency of the exciseman seems to have been exceptionally high in the eighteenth century by the standards of the bureaucracy of that day, and this probably accounts for the particular hatred felt for him by the general public.[1] But the contemporary standards were so low that this statement tells us little about the absolute efficiency of the excise.

---

[1] Selma E. Fine, *Production and Excise in England 1643–1825* (unpublished Radcliffe College thesis), p. 142, says, 'The regulation and close inspection of the excise officers was to be seen on all sides and the excise-gauger became an object of scorn and derision'.

From 1708 to 1788 none of the officials received an increase in salary, and 'the temptation to accept bribes in order to eke out their existence was strengthened by the increasing inadequacy of their incomes. . . .'[1] Nevertheless, 'the fall in management costs . . . indicates that, despite the low salaries which must have discouraged the employment of honest and skilful officers, a steady improvement in the organisation and efficiency of the department took place during the eighteenth century'.[2] Writing of the period 1774–92, Dr Binney says, 'The system of check and counter-check must have gone far to ensure that the duties were accurately assessed'.[3] So far as the surveillance of brewing was concerned, efficiency became high in London early in the eighteenth century, but 'as one moved away from the range of the central organisation, so the standards of conscientiousness and the bonds of discipline relaxed. . . .'[4] There seems to be no reason to suppose that what was true of brewing gaugers was not true of the other excisemen. This is of particular importance in the case of soap, which was primarily, though not entirely, a London industry.

The conditions of manufacture prevented much evasion of duty on some of the other excisable goods. This was true of glass,[5] bricks, and, because of the concentration of growing areas, of hops to some extent, though thefts by pickers must have affected this commodity. It may also have been true of printed goods (which are given in table 5 of chapter VII—The Textile Industries), for only small printers with no regular place of business could easily evade duty.[6] It was certainly true of paper, in the sense that papermakers' equipment was too bulky to avoid the exciseman's eye; but in this case evasion took a different form. The variety of rates of duty on the different types of paper encouraged the makers to classify their products in more lowly rated categories than was strictly correct. By following Dr Coleman's methods, however, it is hoped to avoid this defect in the published statistics.[7]

The proportion of tax to price was, for most commodities, relatively high, and in nearly all cases it increased during the eighteenth century. This naturally raised the premium on evasion, but it seems likely that this was counterbalanced by the increasing efficiency of the officials.[8] The only commodity on which the tax was so light that evasion was scarcely worth while was bricks (which are shown in table 1 of chapter IX—The Building Industry).

[1] *ibid*. p. 158. Increases in 1788 did something to alleviate the trouble, and the large increases of 1800 finally cured it.

[2] *ibid*. p. 163.

[3] J. E. D. Binney, *British Public Finance and Administration, 1774–92* (Oxford, 1958), pp. 37–8.

[4] P. Mathias, *The Brewing Industry in England 1700–1830* (Cambridge, 1959), pp. 343–4.

[5] Selma E. Fine, *loc. cit.* p. 203, says, however, that 'in the early years of the tax . . . there was said to have been a good deal of clandestine manufacture. . . . As time progressed the excise regulations were more strictly enforced and the amount of glass which escaped the tax decreased'.

[6] This is implied in A. P. Wadsworth and Julia de L. Mann, *The Cotton Trade and Industrial Lancashire 1600–1780* (Manchester, 1931), pp. 135–44. It is confirmed, but with an important qualification, by Selma E. Fine, *loc. cit.* p. 212, where she writes, 'Not many printing firms escaped the excise, but there is evidence that certain printers were able to defraud the revenue by failing to report the true amount of the material they had printed'.

[7] D. C. Coleman, *The British Paper Industry 1495–1860* (Oxford, 1958), p. 346.

[8] P. Mathias, *op. cit.* p. 370.

The conditions of manufacture were not always a hindrance to tax-evasion, however, and in the cases of candles, starch, and malt, they were virtually an incentive to fraud. These three commodities, together with spirits, seem to have been the ones for which evasion of duty was most common, though it was also appreciable for soap. The processes of manufacture of candles and of starch were both short,[1] and the rates of duty were relatively high. Both series definitely understate the true output, but the degree of understatement for candles appears to have been fairly constant, and, according to Miss Fine 'we can safely use the series for candles as an indication of the movements of the production of that commodity, though the actual output may have been very much larger'.[2] For starch, however, the series does not reflect output accurately, at least for the period 1714–40, when the downward trend is partially explained by an increase in illicit manufacture.[3]

The process of manufacture of malt was not particularly short, but this industry was carried on almost entirely in the countryside, where supervision was difficult, and Mr Mathias notes that 'the reported annual production of malt in the British Isles may underestimate the actual quantities . . . by as much as a quarter, even at the end of the eighteenth century'.[4] English production of spirits was mainly concentrated in London, where close supervision no doubt limited the opportunities for evasion. But in Scotland and Ireland the stills were scattered throughout the country, so that opportunities were generally good. Moreover, the inclination to outwit the exciseman was much stronger in these disaffected regions. We have no means of knowing how successful the people of these parts were in the eighteenth century; but judged by the enormous increase in the quantity charged with duty which accompanied the reduction in rates in 1823, illicit manufacture must have been very large, and can scarcely have been much less than half the total output.[5]

The statistics of patents granted, given in table 13, though not a production series, seem to fit more appropriately into this chapter than anywhere else. The table is divided into two parts by the major break in 1852, when the change in the law resulted in a quadrupling of the numbers, and when the statistics of applications become available. The change effected by the Act of 1883, was however, very nearly as startling. With the exception of these two breaks, the statistics of patents provide a series which permits comparisons over long periods. It must be remembered, however, that the number of patents granted by most of the Stuart monarchs bore more relation to their financial needs than to the progress of invention. In fact it is probably true to say that this series has little significance for economic history until about the middle of the eighteenth century.

---

[1] Selma E. Fine, *loc. cit.* pp. 216–7 and 225.
[2] *ibid.* p. 219.
[3] *ibid.* p. 225.
[4] P. Mathias, *op. cit.* p. 343.
[5] In 1823 the rates were reduced by 2/4¾d per gallon from 5/7½d in Ireland and 6/2d in Scotland, and this reduction was followed by a campaign to suppress illicit distilling which, in Scotland, at least, was almost entirely successful. The increase in the quantity charged with duty is easily apparent in table 5. Taking averages of the years ended 5th January 1819–23 and 1825–9, it rose by 132 per cent in Scotland and 134 per cent in Ireland, compared with 33 per cent in England. If McCulloch (*Dictionary of Commerce* (London, 1847), vol. II, p. 1168) was right in saying that 'consumption . . . was not in any degree increased . . .', then the proportion evading duty before 1823 must have been well over half. Even allowing for some increase in demand resulting from the fall in price of legally distilled spirits, the proportion was evidently very high.

Table 14 summarises the Census of Production returns of 1907, the three inter-war censuses, and the first nation-wide post-war census.[1] The value of gross and of net output is shown by industry-groups and by regions. The census returns, of course, give a very great deal more information than has been selected for reproduction here—more detailed breakdowns by industries, and details of numbers employed and of power used are the major categories omitted here. The principal problem in using the census of production statistics is that of comparability between censuses. To some extent, in particular for the inter-war years, this has been overcome by the compilers of the census themselves, but some problems remain, and these are mentioned in the notes to the table.

The remaining table in this subsection gives two indices of overall industrial production—the Hoffman index and the Lomax index. The former is well known, and has been subjected to much criticism.[2] This criticism seems so cogent in respect of the first century of the index that we have not included here the years before 1801, when the percentage of industrial output covered by statistical series was low. For details of the construction of these indices the reader should consult the original sources.[3]

We considered including in this chapter statistics of bankruptcies back beyond the middle of the eighteenth century. These statistics have been cited by several authorities,[4] some referring to the *Annual Register* or *The Gentleman's Magazine* as their source, but all ultimately supposed to be derived from the *London Gazette*. Unfortunately there are wide differences between the figures quoted in the various sources, and random checks in the original source produced yet more different figures. Three examples will suffice:

[1] This, the 1949 census, is preferred to the 1948 one, which was more complete for Great Britain, because at the later date Northern Ireland was included.

[2] See the reviews by Phyllis Deane in *E.J.*, vol. LXVI (1956), pp. 25–48, and by J. F. Wright in *The Journal of Economic History*, vol. XVI (1956), pp. 356–64; also W. A. Cole, 'The Measurement of Industrial Growth', in *E.H.R.*, vol. XI, no. 2 (1958), pp. 309–15.

[3] The only published criticisms of the Lomax index at present are in the discussion following Mr Lomax's paper, *J.R.S.S.* (1959).

[4] e.g. A. D. Gayer, W. W. Rostow, and Anna J. Schwartz, *The Growth and Fluctuation of the British Economy 1790–1850* (2 vols., Oxford, 1953); T. S. Ashton, *An Economic History of England: The Eighteenth Century* (London, 1955); and W. G. Hoffman, *British Industry 1700–1950* (English edition, Oxford, 1955) have all cited them recently. Older users of these figures include: G. Chalmers, *Estimate of the Comparative Strength of Great Britain* (London, editions of 1794, 1804, and 1812); Sir John Sinclair, *History of the Public Revenues of the British Empire* (London, 1803); J. Bischoff, *Comprehensive History of the Woollen and Worsted Manufactures* . . . (London, 1842); J. R. McCulloch, *Statistical Account of the British Empire* (London, 1854); the *Report of the Select Committee of the House of Lords on the Resumption of Cash Payments* (S.P. 1819, III); and the *Report of the Select Committee on Commercial Distress* (S.P. 1847-8, VIII).

Number of Bankruptcies according to:

	Chalmers	Sinclair	S.P. 1819, III	Ashton	London Gazette (a)
1791	604	583	769	603	614
1792	628	636	934	609	628
1793	1,304	1,802	1,956	1,256	1,290

	Bischoff	McCulloch	Annual Register	London Gazette
1821	1,238	1,773	1,238	1,238 + 175 Scots
1822	1,094	1,592	1,113	1,107 + 160 Scots
1823	1,250	1,381	953	996 + 140 Scots

	S.P. 1847–8, VIII	McCulloch	Annual Register	London Gazette
1842	1,655	1,373	1,923	1,296 + 542 Scots + 91 Irish
1843	1,259	1,169	1,575	1,118 + 407 Scots + 50 Irish
1844	1,099	1,064	1,313	987 + 295 Scots + 31 Irish

(a) These sources are referred to in the previous footnote. In using the *London Gazette* each separate commission (or fiat) of bankruptcy was counted, and no deductions were made for supersessions. It is possible that some of the sources counted the number of individuals mentioned in commissions, though this does not seem such a sensible procedure.

Some of the discrepancies may arise from differences in the dates taken for the end of the year. Professor Ashton, for example, takes 30th September, but the others do not specify any date.[1] Other discrepancies may result from the omission of the Scottish and Irish figures. Yet others may spring simply from misprints. But serious discrepancies there are, whatever the causes, and without further research it does not seem appropriate to select a series derived from secondary sources; and as the labour involved in compiling new series from the *London Gazette* is much greater than the bankruptcy figures appear to merit, no statistics on this subject appear in the tables. Those following the 1861 Act are readily available in the *Reports* of the Bankruptcy Commissioners.[2] Amongst the secondary sources to which reference has been made, some do appear more likely to be reliable than others. Among these we may include Professor Ashton and the *Annual Register*, at any rate from 1837 when Scotland and Ireland are separately distinguished.

[1] Except for the period 1815–19, when the *Annual Register* takes years ended 20th December.
[2] Published annually in sessional papers.

Miscellaneous Production Statistics 1. Malt Charged with Duty—England & Wales 1702–1880, Scotland 1770–1880, and Ireland 1785–1880

NOTE
SOURCES: 1702–1869—*S.P.* 1870, xx; 1870–80—*S.P.* 1884–5, XXII.

(in millions of Imperial bushels)

England & Wales

1702 (*a*)	12·2	1725	27·3	1748	26·4
1703	26·8	1726	27·0	1749	25·0
1704	19·8	1727	25·4	1750	29·3
1705	27·1	1728	21·0	1751	27·0
1706	23·1	1729	23·0	1752	24·3
1707	25·0	1730	28·4	1753 (*b*)	25·2
1708	23·2	1731	25·8	1754	27·3
1709	20·3	1732	27·0	1755	27·9
1710	19·7	1733	29·8	1756	24·1
1711	22·3	1734	27·1	1757	17·6
1712	22·3	1735	25·5	1758	25·0
1713	25·1	1736	23·7	1759	28·1
1714	20·0	1737	24·5	1760	27·8
1715	24·5	1738	26·1	1761	28·9
1716	26·6	1739	26·7	1762	26·0
1717	28·9	1740	22·1	1763	19·6
1718	26·9	1741	20·1	1764	26·3
1719	28·2	1742	25·9	1765	25·6
1720	25·6	1743	26·3	1766	20·8
1721	28·6	1744	31·8	1767	21·9
1722	33·0	1745	24·9	1768	27·1
1723	30·7	1746	24·0	1769	26·5
1724	24·2	1747	24·9		

	England & Wales	Scotland	Ireland	United Kingdom
1770	24·5	1·8	...	...
1771	22·0	1·7	...	...
1772	27·5	1·7	...	...
1773	21·5	1·5	...	...
1774	24·0	1·4	...	...
1775	25·0	1·4	...	...
1776	23·3	1·6	...	...
1777	25·8	1·8	...	...
1778	26·3	1·9	...	...
1779	26·3	2·0	...	...
1780	30·8	2·2	...	...
1781	26·7	1·9	...	...
1782	27·2	2·0	...	...
1783	16·7	1·1	...	...
1784	25·8	1·8	...	...
1785	26·3	1·7	4·4	32·4
1786	22·1	1·6	3·5	27·2
1787	26·4	1·7	3·7	31·8
1788	26·0	1·7	3·9	31·7
1789	23·5	1·6	3·6	28·8

See p. 249 for footnotes

(in millions of Imperial bushels)

	England & Wales	Scotland	Ireland	United Kingdom
1790	22·0	1·5	4·6	28·1
1791	27·1	1·7	4·8	33·6
1792	27·8	2·0	4·7	34·4
1793	23·7	1·7	5·0	30·5
1794	24·8	1·7	4·9	31·4
1795	24·0	1·7	4·7	30·4
1796	27·3	1·2	5·0	33·4
1797	30·0	2·1	4·7	36·7
1798	26·1	1·9	4·4	32·5
1799	30·8	2·4	3·3	36·5
1800	14·1	0·9	0·7	15·6
1801	18·0	0·6	1·0	19·6
1802	29·4	1·7	3·6	34·8
1803	29·6	1·6	3·6	34·7
1804	21·9	1·1	2·8	25·8
1805	21·7	1·1	2·8	25·6
1806	26·7	1·2	2·8	30·7
1807	24·2	1·3	2·4	27·8
1808	21·7	1·0	2·6	25·4
1809	22·1	0·8	3·0	25·9
1810	23·5	0·8	2·5	26·9
1811	26·0	1·0	2·7	29·7
1812	18·1	0·9	2·2	21·2
1813	21·7	0·7	3·0	25·4
1814	25·3	1·3	3·2	29·7
1815	26·2	1·3	2·7	30·2
1816	21·2	1·2	1·9	24·2
1817	20·9	1·1	1·4	23·3
1818	24·6	1·4	1·8	27·8
1819	22·6	1·5	1·7	25·8
1820	23·9	1·2	1·8	26·9
1821	26·1	1·3	1·9	29·4
1822	26·7	1·4	1·8	29·8
1823	24·8	1·6	1·7	28·2
1824	27·6	2·8	2·1	32·5
1825	29·6	3·9	2·7	36·2
1826 (c)	27·3	2·7	2·4	32·5
1827	25·1	2·7	1·8	29·6
1828	30·5	3·9	2·4	36·8
1829	23·4	3·7	2·0	29·2
1830	26·9	4·1	2·0	33·0
1831	33·0	4·2	2·1	39·3
1832	31·7	3·7	2·0	37·4
1833	33·8	4·3	2·0	40·1
1834	34·5	4·5	2·2	41·1
1835	36·1	4·5	2·4	42·9
1836	37·2	4·9	2·3	44·4
1837	33·7	4·6	2·3	40·6
1838	33·8	4·4	2·3	40·5
1839	33·8	4·4	1·7	39·9

See p. 249 *for footnotes*

(in millions of Imperial bushels)

	England & Wales	Scotland	Ireland	United Kingdom
1840	36·7	4·4	1·4	42·5
1841	31·0	4·1	1·2	36·2
1842	30·8	3·8	1·3	35·9
1843	30·9	3·6	1·2	35·7
1844	31·9	3·9	1·4	37·2
1845	30·5	4·4	1·7	36·5
1846	35·7	4·6	1·8	42·1
1847	30·3	3·7	1·4	35·3
1848	31·8	4·0	1·7	37·5
1849	33·2	4·2	1·6	38·9
1850	34·4	4·6	1·7	40·7
1851	34·6	4·1	1·6	40·3
1852	35·5	3·9	1·7	41·1
1853	36·2	4·2	1·6	42·0
1855 (*d*)	30·6	3·2	1·4	35·2
1856	30·7 (*e*)	1·6 (*e*)	1·2 (*e*)	33·5 (*e*)
1857	36·3	1·1	1·7	39·1
1858	38·0	1·3	1·8	41·2
1859	39·1	1·5	2·2	42·8
1860	40·7	1·6	2·2	44·6
1861	33·7	1·6	2·1	37·4
1862	41·3	1·7	2·5	45·6
1863	37·4	1·7	1·9	41·1
1864	43·6	2·0	2·4	47·9
1865	44·0	2·1	2·5	48·5
1866	45·2	2·5	2·5	50·2
1867	46·0	2·5	2·4	50·9
1868	43·6	2·4	2·5	48·5
1869	44·4	2·4	2·8	49·6
1870	45·4	2·4	3·0	50·7
1871	47·1	2·7	3·2	52·9
1872	46·3	2·8	2·9	52·1
1873	51·5	3·0	2·7	57·2
1874	52·9	3·2	3·4	59·4
1875	53·7	2·8	3·2	59·7
1876	52·9	2·8	3·3	59·0
1877	54·2	3·0	3·3	60·5
1878	52·2	2·9	3·1	58·1
1879	51·6	3·1	3·4	58·0
1880	44·9	2·6	2·9	50·3

[*a*] The date for the years' end is not given in the source, but from accounts in the Customs and Excise Library it appears that it was 24th June up to 1752.
[*b*] Years ended 5th July henceforth to 1825. Mr R. C. Jarvis of H.M. Customs and Excise Library points out that our source is defective in not noting this change.

(*c*) Years ended on 5th January of the year following that stated henceforth to 1853.
(*d*) Years ended 31st March henceforth.
(*e*) From August 1855 malt for distillery purposes was not charged with duty. This change had virtually no effect in England & Wales, but was of great importance in Scotland, and moderately important in Ireland.

Miscellaneous Production Statistics 2. Hops Charged with Duty—England 1712–1862

NOTE

SOURCE: *S.P.* 1870, xx.

(in millions of lb.)

Year		Year		Year	
1712 (a)	12·1	1763	19·0	1813	6·4
1713	7·3	1764	21·2	1814	27·4
1714	5·5	1765	4·1	1815	29·3
1715	3·5	1766	17·8	1816	25·9
1716	10·8	1767	28·0	1817	9·7
1717	4·9	1768	6·2	1818	13·9
1718	13·1	1769	27·4	1819	41·6
1719	3·6	1770	3·9	1820	50·5
1720	21·7	1771	24·3	1821	28·9
1721	9·2	1772	8·0	1822	31·8
1722	14·8	1773	24·6	1823	42·5
1723	11·9	1774	11·0	1824	5·4
1724	7·3	1775	33·3	1825	31·2
1725	14·7	1776	10·0	1826 (c)	(5·1)
1726	1·6	1777	30·2	1827	57·2
1727	20·4	1778	10·5	1828	29·4
1728	16·7	1779	38·4	1829	35·9
1729	10·0	1780	12·7	1830	8·0
1730	11·6	1781	27·9	1831	18·5
1731	10·6	1782	25·9	1832	36·5
1732	5·6	1783	3·1	1833	29·0
1733	8·4	1784	15·8	1834	32·7
1734	16·9	1785	19·7	1835	39·6
1735	9·0	1786	23·5	1836	49·1
1736	10·3	1787	20·0	1837	41·9
1737	11·1	1788	8·8	1838	37·3
1738	13·6	1789	30·0	1839	35·8
1739	21·0	1790	21·2	1840	42·9
1740	17·0	1791	22·3	1841	7·1
1741	9·1	1792	18·9	1842	30·5
1742	18·0	1793	33·9	1843	35·4
1743	10·9	1794	5·0	1844	27·9
1744	15·3	1795	42·5	1845	29·3
1745	11·2	1796	17·2	1846	33·0
1746	8·3	1797	15·7	1847	50·7
1747	22·1	1798	32·9	1848	45·1
1748	15·2	1799	11·8	1849	44·3
1749	21·0	1800	15·3	1850	16·7
1750	8·7	1801	15·2	1851	48·5
1751	17·3	1802	50·4	1852	27·0
1752	17·8	1803	3·2	1853	51·1
1753	19·7 (b)	1804	41·3	1854	31·8
1754	21·9	1805	37·1	1855	9·9
1755	27·0	1806	6·9	1856	83·2
1756	19·8	1807	32·0	1857	55·9
1757	11·5	1808	20·9	1858	47·7
1758	16·7	1809	52·6	1859	53·1
1759	17·5	1810	13·4	1860	68·5
1760	10·1	1811	15·3	1861	11·2
1761	28·4	1812	32·8	1862	24·0
1762	19·6				

(a) Years ended 24th June henceforth to 1752. The figure for 1712 is for the period beginning 1st June 1711.
(b) Years ended 5th July henceforth to 1825. Mr R. C. Jarvis of H.M. Customs and Excise Library points out that our source is defective in not noting this change.
(c) Years ended 5th January henceforth. The figure for 1826 is for 6 months only.

Miscellaneous Production Statistics 3.   Beer Charged with Duty—England & Wales
1684–1830, and Scotland 1787–1830

NOTES

[1] SOURCES: 1684–1828—MS. Account in the Customs and Excise Library; 1829–30—S.P. 1830, XXII.
[2] The barrel was reckoned at 36 gallons for strong and small beer and 32 gallons for ale in London. Elsewhere it was 34 gallons for all malt liquor.
[3] Various allowances were made for wastage before 5th January 1826, at which time they amounted to one-twelfth of output. For a full account of these, see P. Mathias, *The Brewing Industry in England, 1700–1830* (Cambridge, 1959).

[4] From 1825 the following small amounts of intermediate beer were charged with duty in England (in thousands of barrels):

Year ended 5 July 1825	10	Year ended 5 Jan. 1828	17
Year ended 5 July 1826	6	Year ended 5 Jan. 1829	63
Year ended 5 Jan. 1826	6	Year ended 5 Jan. 1830	55
Year ended 5 Jan. 1827	8		

A. England & Wales

(in thousands of barrels)

	Strong Beer	Small Beer		Strong Beer	Small Beer		Strong Beer	Small Beer	Table Beer
1684 (a)	4,384	1,934	1717	3,596	2,085	1750	3,736	2,056	...
1685	4,655	2,102	1718	3,716	2,165	1751	3,773	2,060	...
1686	4,780	2,255	1719	3,801	2,256	1752	3,771	1,966	...
1687	5,044	2,435	1720	3,788	2,277	1753 (b)	3,762	1,948	...
1688	4,989	2,544	1721	3,736	2,180	1754	3,733	1,934	...
1789	5,134	2,708	1722	3,795	2,196	1755	3,694	1,915	...
1690	4,691	2,646	1723	3,853	2,252	1756	3,780	1,976	...
1691	4,070	2,375	1724	3,874	2,313	1757	3,497	1,937	...
1692	3,797	2,379	1725	3,797	2,187	1758	3,717	1,877	...
1693	3,529	2,386	1726	3,642	2,205	1759	3,908	1,834	...
1694	3,505	2,466	1727	3,704	2,213	1760	4,137	1,992	...
1695	3,344	2,212	1728	3,443	2,166	1761	4,062	1,973	...
1696	3,680	2,389	1729	3,310	2,044	1762	3,805	1,972	...
1697	3,258	2,162	1730	3,533	2,081	1763	3,759	1,848	...
1698	3,097	2,007	1731	3,645	2,112	1764	3,824	1,796	...
1699	2,973	1,921	1732	3,704	2,184	1765	3,690	1,746	...
1700	3,152	1,971	1733	3,690	2,181	1766	3,682	1,800	...
1701	3,364	2,082	1734	3,679	2,153	1767	3,625	1,745	...
1702	3,721	2,319	1735	3,525	2,104	1768	3,731	1,741	...
1703	3,649	2,278	1736	3,552	2,111	1769	3,791	1,690	...
1704	3,763	2,335	1737	3,613	2,073	1770	3,783	1,702	...
1705	3,807	2,333	1738	3,531	2,015	1771	3,767	1,733	...
1706	3,630	2,214	1739	3,604	2,080	1772	3,791	1,695	...
1707	3,654	2,225	1740	3,515	2,085	1773	3,804	1,717	...
1708	3,566	2,155	1741	3,295	1,985	1774	3,601	1,676	...
1709	3,357	2,066	1742	3,458	2,083	1775	3,863	1,616	...
1710	3,217	1,984	1743	3,469	2,021	1776	3,959	1,677	...
1711	3,154	1,972	1744	3,601	2,042	1777	4,107	1,625	...
1712	3,143	1,926	1745	3,479	1,972	1778	4,130	1,709	...
1713	3,300	1,938	1746	3,416	2,035	1779	4,197	1,798	...
1714	3,415	2,001	1747	3,580	2,009	1780	4,355	1,881	...
1715	3,434	2,035	1748	3,621	2,086	1781	4,343	1,825	...
1716	3,486	2,013	1749	3,707	2,011	1782	4,525	1,908	...

See p. 252 for footnotes

251

(in thousands of barrels)

	Strong Beer	Small Beer	Table Beer		Strong Beer	Small Beer	Table Beer
1783	3,914	1,325	452	1808	5,571	...	1,710
1784	4,336	1,306	468	1809	5,513	...	1,683
1785	4,329	1,244	447	1810	5,753	...	1,636
1786	4,147	1,276	462	1811	5,903	...	1,650
1787	4,426	1,342	486	1812	5,861	...	1,593
1788	4,305	1,335	524	1813	5,383	...	1,456
1789	4,438	1,244	515	1814	5,624	...	1,433
1790	4,526	1,282	546	1815	6,151	...	1,518
1791	4,755	1,347	580	1816	5,982	...	1,515
1792	5,082	1,402	625	1817	5,236	...	1,454
1793	5,168	1,414	620	1818	5,364	...	1,435
1794	5,011	1,447	587	1819	5,629	...	1,460
1795	5,038	1,453	576	1820	5,297	...	1,444
1796	5,504	1,479	566	1821	5,576	...	1,440
1797	5,840	1,519	584	1822	5,713	...	1,492
1798	5,784	1,548	622	1823	6,177	...	1,420
1799	5,774	1,597	611	1824	6,188	...	1,401
1800	4,824	1,361	575	1825	6,501	...	1,486
1801	4,736	1,192	500	1826	6,641	...	1,572
1802	5,346	977	392	1826(d)	7,008	...	1,607
1803	5,583	...	1,661(c)	1827	6,690	...	1,605
1804	5,266	...	1,780	1828	6,395	...	1,532
1805	5,412	...	1,777	1829	6,559	...	1,531
1806	5,444	...	1,772	1830	5,949	...	1,380
1807	5,577	...	1,733				

(a) Years ended 24th June henceforth to 1752.
(b) Years ended 5th July henceforth to 1825.

(c) Small beer merged with table beer.
(d) Years ended 5th January in the year following that shown henceforth.

B. Scotland

	Strong Beer	Small Beer	Table Beer	Twopenny Ale		Strong Beer	Small Beer	Table Beer	Twopenny Ale
1787 (a)	24	108	...	114	1810	127	...	227	...
1788	23	115	...	119	1811	120	...	230	...
1789	34	121	...	116	1812	121	...	222	...
1790	43	136	...	122	1813	116	...	199	...
1791	43	139	...	124	1814	133	...	206	...
1792	47	160	...	145	1815	135	...	222	...
1793	48	172	...	158	1816	127	...	222	...
1794	40	154	...	139	1817	111	...	206	...
1795	40	156	...	139	1818	109	...	192	...
1796	78	178	...	150	1819	124	...	209	...
1797	88	168	...	165	1820	116	...	207	...
1798	77	179	...	171	1821	123	...	206	...
1799	84	184	...	169	1822	125	...	224	...
1800	75	161	...	150	1823	124	...	222	...
1801	73	162	...	102	1824	114	...	229	...
1802	94	95	41	87	1825	124	...	244	...
1803	106	...	249	...	1826	132	...	275	...
1804	93	...	230	...	1826 (b)	134	...	264	...
1805	105	...	221	...	1827	122	...	271	...
1806	119	...	230	...	1828	112	...	241	...
1807	121	...	234	...	1829	119	...	247	...
1808	114	...	234	...	1830	111	...	229	...
1809	118	...	221	...					

[a] Years ended 5th July henceforth to 1826.

(b) Years ended 5th January in the year following that shown henceforth.

Miscellaneous Production Statistics 4. Beer Charged with Duty (or on which Duty was Paid)—United Kingdom 1882–1938

NOTE

SOURCE: *Annual Report of the Commissioners of Inland Revenue.*

(in million of barrels)

1881 (a)	(14·0)	1901	36·4	1921	27·3
1882	27·9	1902	36·0 (b)	1922	24·7
1883	27·1	1903	36·0	1923	18·8 (c)
1884	27·8	1904	35·3	1924	19·5
1885	28·0	1905	34·4	1925	20·7
1886	27·2	1906	34·1	1926	20·8
1887	27·9	1907	34·4	1927	21·5
1888	28·2	1908	34·5	1928	21·2
1889	28·6	1909	33·3	1929	19·4
1890	30·9	1910	32·9	1930	19·7
1891	31·9	1911	33·6	1931	18·5
1892	32·2	1912	35·1	1932	15·9 (d)
1893	32·1	1913	34·8	1933	12·9
1894	32·2	1914	35·9	1934	14·8
1895	31·7	1915	31·6	1935	15·7
1896	33·8	1916	29·9	1936	16·2
1897	34·2	1917	27·2	1937	16·9
1898	35·6	1918	15·8	1938	18·0
1899	36·5	1919	11·8		
1900	37·1	1920	22·1		

(a) Years ended 31st March. The figure for 1881 is for 6 months only.

(b) Prior to 1902 the statistics relate to beer charged with duty in each year, and subsequently they relate to beer on which duty was paid. The difference was seldom as much as 1 per cent.

(c) Southern Ireland excluded after 1922.

(d) Prior to 1932 the figures represent standard barrels—i.e. barrels of 36 gallons at a gravity of 1,055 degrees. From 1932 onwards they represent barrels of 36 gallons irrespective of gravity.

Miscellaneous Production Statistics 5.   British Spirits Charged
with Duty for Consumption—1684–1938

NOTES

[1] SOURCE: *S.P.* 1870, xx, *S.P.* 1884–5, XXII, and subsequent *Annual Reports of the Commissioners of Inland Revenue.*

[2]   This account refers to potable spirits, and relates to the amounts consumed in each kingdom.

(in thousands of gallons)

	England & Wales	Scotland	Ireland	United Kingdom
1684 (a)	527	...	...	...
1685	594	...	...	...
1686	468	...	...	...
1687	516	...	...	...
1688	559	...	...	...
1689	570	...	...	...
1690	544	...	...	...
1691	659	...	...	...
1692	849	...	...	...
1693	948	...	...	...
1694	810	...	...	...
1695	968	...	...	...
1696	1,104	...	...	...
1697	828	...	...	...
1698	846	...	...	...
1699	877	...	...	...
1700	1,233	...	...	...
1701	1,271	...	...	...
1702	1,073	...	...	...
1703	1,146	...	...	...
1704	1,375	...	...	...
1705	1,438	...	...	...
1706	1,675	...	...	...
1707	1,974	...	...	...
1708	1,717	...	...	...
1709	1,738	...	...	...
1710	2,201	...	...	...
1711	2,233	...	...	...
1712	2,067	...	...	...
1713	2,049	...	...	...
1714	1,951	...	...	...
1715	2,266	...	...	...
1716	2,381	...	...	...
1717	2,596	...	...	...
1718	2,418	...	174	...
1719	2,464	...	136	...
1720	2,483	...	131	...
1721	2,793	...	125	...
1722	3,380	...	134	...
1723	3,703	...	133	...

See p. 259 for footnote

Miscellaneous Production Statistics 5. *continued*

(in thousands of gallons)

	England & Wales	Scotland	Ireland	United Kingdom
1724	3,564	146	134	3,843
1725	3,926	221	169	4,316
1726	3,981	275	219	4,474
1727	4,612	252	155	5,019
1728	4,793	191	129	5,113
1729	4,728	186	135	5,048
1730	3,778	209	175	4,161
1731	4,334	213	184	4,731
1732	4,374	227	226	4,827
1733	4,824	237	268	5,330
1734	6,075	204	209	6,488
1735	6,440	225	196	6,861
1736	6,116	524	229	6,869
1737	4,250	538	217	5,095
1738	5,439	412	211	6,062
1739	5,763	411	240	6,414
1740	6,651	261	248	7,160
1741	7,439	352	272	8,063
1742	7,955	404	354	8,712
1743	8,203	360	402	8,966
1744	6,627	591	452	7,671
1745	7,200	598	334	8,133
1746	6,865	512	402	7,779
1747	7,310	522	531	8,364
1748	7,082	569	565	8,217
1749	6,671	575	599	7,844
1750	6,613	776	598	7,987
1751	7,050	849	596	8,495
1752	4,483	839	623	5,946
1754 (*b*)	4,869	731	561	6,161
1755	5,051	653	498	6,202
1756	4,652	674	480	5,806
1757	4,679	459	404	5,542
1758	3,714	105	400	4,218
1759	1,849	68	108	2,025
1760	1,819	55	225	2,100
1761	2,323	75	432	2,830
1762	3,181	59	693	3,933
1763	2,296	48	668	3,013
1764	2,272	51	661	2,985
1765	2,220	54	715	2,989
1766	2,227	54	649	2,931
1767	2,431	54	355	2,840
1768	2,043	70	658	2,771
1769	2,207	83	831	3,121

See p. 259 for footnote

(in thousands of gallons)

	England & Wales	Scotland	Ireland	United Kingdom
1770	2,549	70	801	3,420
1771	2,570	69	734	3,374
1772	2,495	76	759	3,330
1773	2,583	73	960	3,616
1774	2,224	70	1,026	3,320
1775	2,010	72	980	3,063
1776	2,515	72	1,160	3,748
1777	2,519	73	1,115	3,707
1778	2,507	106	1,127	3,740
1779	2,956	144	1,094	4,194
1780	2,639	189	1,229	4,057
1781	2,292	194	1,753	4,239
1782	2,114	196	2,037	4,347
1783	1,942	337	1,738	4,016
1784	1,228	171	1,409	2,808
1785	1,338	239	1,423	3,000
1786	2,743	489	1,814	5,047
1787	3,695	825	1,923	6,443
1788	3,561	...	2,187	...
1789	3,670	...	2,748	...
1790	3,909	...	2,871	...
1791	3,858	...	3,442	...
1792	4,073	...	3,417	...
1793	4,545	...	3,344	...
1794	4,244	...	3,834	...
1795	4,595	...	4,154	...
1796	4,712	...	3,612	...
1797	301	...	3,788	...
1798	2,809	...	4,694	...
1799	3,631	...	4,173	...
1800	4,115	1,670	3,554	9,339
1801	4,353	1,278	1,331	6,961
1802	2,556	296	355	3,207
1803	3,981	1,159	4,715	9,855
1804	5,370	2,022	4,343	11,736
1805	3,691	1,190	3,544	9,124
1806	4,933	1,626	3,686	10,245
1807	4,095	1,812	3,858	9,765
1808	4,747	2,653	5,597	12,998
1809	5,391	2,683	3,575	11,650
1810	4,036	1,315	1,360	6,711
1811	4,788	1,748	4,729	11,264
1812	4,776	1,951	6,378	13,106
1813	5,242	1,688	4,009	10,940
1814	4,292	1,234	3,159	8,685

(in thousands of gallons)

	England & Wales	Scotland	Ireland	United Kingdom
1815	4,957	1,474	5,394	11,825
1816	5,469	1,591	4,324	11,384
1817	4,745	919	3,557	9,222
1818	4,133	1,907	3,587	9,627
1819	5,260	2,067	4,284	11,611
1820	4,147	2,125	3,677	9,948
1821	4,285	1,864	3,300	9,448
1822	4,126	2,385	3,311	9,823
1823	4,694	2,225	2,910	9,830
1824	3,803	2,303	3,590	9,697
1825	4,393	4,350	6,690	15,433
1826	3,684 ·	5,982	9,263	18,928
1827	7,407	3,989	6,835	18,231
1828	6,672	4,752	8,261	19,684
1829	7,760	5,716	9,938	23,414
1830	7,701	5,777	9,212	22,690
1831	7,732	6,008	9,005	22,744
1832	7,434	5,701	8,711	21,845
1833	7,282	5,407	8,658	21,347
1834	7,717	5,989	8,169	21,874
1835	7,644	6,045	9,708	23,398
1836	7,315	6,014	11,381	24,710
1837	7,876	6,621	12,249	26,745
1838	7,134	6,124	11,236	24,494
1839	7,930	6,260	12,296	26,487
1840	8,187	6,189	10,816	25,191
1841	8,278	6,180	7,401	21,859
1842	8,167	5,990	6,485	20,642
1843	7,956	5,595	5,291	18,842
1844	7,724	5,594	5,546	18,864
1845	8,234	5,923	6,451	20,609
1846	9,076	6,441	7,605	23,123
1847	9,180	6,975	7,952	24,107
1848	8,409	6,193	6,037	20,640
1849	8,581	6,548	7,073	22,202
1850	9,054	6,935	6,973	22,962
1851	9,332	7,123	7,408	23,863
1852	9,595	6,831	7,551	23,977
1853	9,821	7,172	8,208	25,201
1854	10,350	6,535	8,136	25,021
1855 (c)	10,852	6,009	8,037	24,898
1856	10,123	5,637	6,509	22,269
1857	11,386	5,368	6,807	23,562
1858	11,634	5,575	6,783	23,993
1859	11,860	5,325	5,418	22,603

See p. 259 *for footnote*

(in thousands of gallons)

	England & Wales	Scotland	Ireland	United Kingdom
1860	12,904	5,581	5,950	24,435
1861	11,198	4,250	4,192	19,640
1862	10,728	4,417	4,190	19,335
1863	10,482	4,511	3,892	18,885
1864	10,721	4,769	3,934	19,423
1865	11,197	5,030	4,157	20,383
1866	11,258	5,203	4,518	20,978
1867	11,591	5,452	5,103	22,146
1868	11,562	4,781	4,677	21,020
1869	11,239	5,027	4,842	21,108
1870	11,592	5,364	5,025	21,981
1871	12,191	5,557	5,213	22,961
1872	13,036	5,802	5,750	24,588
1873	14,856	6,610	6,091	27,556
1874	16,222	6,910	6,177	29,309
1875	16,737	6,990	6,094	29,822
1876	16,749	6,856	6,697	30,303
1877	16,415	7,006	6,381	29,802
1878	17,027	7,142	6,115	30,284
1879	16,518	6,409	6,008	28,935
1880	16,125	6,086	5,075	27,287
1881	17,220	6,394	5,185	28,799
1882	16,950	6,542	5,132	28,624
1883	16,656	6,496	5,377	28,529
1884	16,536	6,708	5,304	28,548
1885	16,323	6,629	5,069	28,021
1886	15,291	6,297	4,755	26,343
1887	14,702	6,122	4,927	25,751
1888	15,139	6,024	4,954	26,117
1889	15,843 (*d*)	5,769 (*d*)	4,224 (*d*)	25,836
1890	16,854	6,264	4,711	27,828
1891	18,459	6,550	4,821	29,830
1892	20,127 (*d*)	6,938 (*d*)	4,405 (*d*)	31,469
1893	19,935	6,446	4,280	30,661
1894	19,765	6,422	4,265	30,452
1895	19,232	6,019	4,040	29,291
1896	20,376	6,490	4,222	31,088
1897	21,297	6,622	4,207	32,126
1898	21,982	6,760	4,157	32,898
1899	23,146	7,079	4,110	34,334
1900	25,623	8,380	4,713	38,717
1901	24,994	7,471	4,238	36,704
1902	22,827	7,115	3,807	33,749
1903	23,357	7,399	4,009	34,765
1904	22,975	7,192	3,936	34,103

See p. 259 for footnote

(in thousands of gallons)

	England & Wales	Scotland	Ireland	United Kingdom
1905	22,661	6,786	3,738	33,158
1906	22,140	6,711	3,636	32,487
1907	22,027	6,852	3,633	32,511
1908	21,916	6,956	3,635	32,507
1909	21,827	6,661	3,563	32,051
1910	14,537	4,559	2,351	21,446
1911	17,485	5,053	2,776	25,314
1912	17,106	5,539	2,729	25,374
1913	16,935	5,709	2,643	25,286
1914	17,891	6,173	2,731	26,795
1915	18,834	6,107	2,871	27,811
1916	19,666	6,108	3,176	28,949
1917	12,849	3,912	2,035	18,796
1918	6,646	2,448	1,230	10,325
1919	8,107	2,445	1,338	11,890
1920	12,548	3,546	1,731	17,826
1921	10,759	3,355	1,350	15,463
1922	10,107	3,068	1,372	14,546
			Northern Ireland	
1923	9,723	2,757	379	12,859
1924	9,942	2,641	314	12,897
1925	9,473	2,532	281	12,287
1926	9,350	2,454	251	12,055
1927	8,398	2,099	215	10,712
1928	9,135	2,314	229	11,678
1929	8,869	2,180	223	11,272
1930	8,303	2,122	205	10,630
1931	8,039	1,958	191	10,189
1932	7,011	1,684	159	8,855
1933	7,187	1,483	152	8,821
1934	7,098	1,342	148	8,588
1935	6,660	1,543	141	8,344
1936	7,184	1,623	163	8,970
1937	7,425	1,692	173	9,289
1938	7,344	1,733	163	9,239

(*a*) Years ended 25th December henceforth to 1754.
(*b*) Years ended 5th January henceforth to 1854.
(*c*) Years ended 31st March henceforth.

(*d*) New systems of accounting for removals from bonded warehouses showed that the previous statistics were somewhat inaccurate in their respective proportions.

NOTES

[1] SOURCE: *S.P.* 1870, XX, *S.P.* 1884–5, XXII, and subsequent *Annual Reports of the Commissioners of Inland Revenue.*

[2] This account relates to all spirits, whether potable or not, produced in the different kingdoms.

(in thousands of gallons)

	England & Wales	Scotland	Ireland	United Kingdom
1850 (a)	5,573	10,847	8,355	24,775
1851	5,913	11,638	8,293	25,845
1852	6,127	10,381	8,036	24,544
1853	6,363	9,942	8,118	24,423
1854	7,309	10,360	8,773	26,442
1855 (b)	6,882	9,862	8,260	25,004
1856	7,922	11,284	8,280	27,485
1857	8,319	12,460	8,911	29,689
1858	8,228	13,350	9,857	31,435
1859	6,784	12,748	7,671	27,203
1860	7,598	13,312	7,406	28,316
1861	7,212	11,212	4,801	23,225
1862	7,853	12,546	4,404	24,803
1863	7,635	13,198	4,138	24,970
1864	7,947	13,712	4,502	26,161
1865	7,806	14,503	5,483	27,792
1866	7,706	13,097	5,747	26,549
1867	7,514	11,806	5,486	24,805
1868	7,008	11,085	5,852	23,944
1869	7,190	12,197	6,011	25,398
1870	7,280	13,799	6,600	27,679
1871	7,576	14,502	8,874	30,952
1872	7,802	13,937	9,616	31,356
1873	8,931	15,836	11,094	35,862
1874	9,804	16,870	10,351	37,025
1875	9,360	16,228	9,674	35,262
1876	9,691	17,589	10,969	38,249
1877	9,599	18,343	11,362	39,305
1878	10,101	18,666	11,303	40,069
1879	9,712	17,394	12,147	39,253
1880	9,694	16,558	11,159	37,412
1881	9,831	16,753	9,721	36,304
1882	10,717	19,216	9,407	39,340
1883	10,041	19,322	9,080	38,443
1884	10,552	20,165	9,642	40,359
1885	10,562	20,611	9,834	41,006
1886	10,359	17,982	10,621	38,962
1887	9,636	17,404	10,627	37,669
1888	9,817	18,160	11,064	39,040
1889	9,017	18,721	11,357	39,096
1890	9,061	20,091	11,818	40,970
1891	10,534	21,101	12,989	44,624
1892	11,543	20,287	14,408	46,239
1893	10,692	20,107	13,616	44,414
1894	10,183	21,472	13,293	44,948

See p. 261 for footnotes

(in thousands of gallons)

	England & Wales	Scotland	Ireland	United Kingdom
1895	9,955	22,236	12,679	44,870
1896	11,000	24,713	13,613	49,325
1897	11,821	28,519	14,283	54,623
1898	12,360	33,745	14,548	60,652
1899	12,914	35,769	14,755	63,438
1900	12,967	31,798	14,481	59,246
1901	12,603	30,196	14,222	57,021
1902	12,439	29,973	12,781	55,192
1903	11,296	26,008	12,441	49,744
1904	11,695	27,111	13,011	51,817
1905	12,157	25,185	11,798	49,140
1906	12,751	23,813	12,651	49,214
1907	13,425	24,840	12,053	50,318
1908	13,328	22,797	11,654	47,778
1909	12,930	24,408	12,192	49,530
1910	10,763	22,309	10,759	43,831
1911	11,422	20,021	9,724	41,167
1912	12,339	23,630	9,748	45,717
1913	12,702	24,115	9,876	46,693
1914	13,900	28,024	9,879	51,802
1915	12,891	26,999	10,249	50,140
1916	11,555	26,741	10,839	49,135
1917	10,445	28,182	13,201	51,828
1918	9,966	14,767	12,408	37,141
1919	3,438	13,200	11,077	27,714
1920	3,929	22,542	13,587	40,058
1921	7,123	29,296	11,129	47,548
1922	5,252	24,588	6,758	36,598

	England & Wales	Scotland	Northern Ireland	United Kingdom
1923	6,565	27,096	2,477	36,137
1924	7,365	27,424	2,534	37,323
1925	8,211	27,436	2,382	38,028
1926	9,758	26,027	1,975	37,759
1927	10,614	16,532	177 (*c*)	27,323
1928	12,392	18,988		31,380
1929	14,278	20,512		34,790
1930	19,762	20,907		40,669
1931	19,592	15,831		35,423
1932	19,141	9,232		28,373
1933	22,178	5,926		28,104
1934	30,364	13,174		43,538
1935	30,683	16,869		47,551
1936	35,340	20,252		55,592
1937	39,898	24,823		64,721
1938	45,878	32,503		78,381

(*a*) Years ended 5th January henceforth to 1854.
(*b*) Years ended 31st March henceforth.

(*c*) Subsequently included with England and Wales.

Miscellaneous Production Statistics 7. Tallow Candles Charged with Duty—England & Wales 1711–1830

NOTES

[1] Sources: 1711–1828—MS. Accounts in the Customs and Excise Library; 1829–30—*Returns Relating to Candles*, in sessional papers.

[2] Figures of the much smaller amounts of wax candles are available but have not been included here.

(in millions of lb.)

Year		Year		Year	
1711 (a)	31·4	1751	37·2	1791	54·4
1712	27·2	1752	37·6	1792	54·9
1713	31·6	1753 (b)	38·6	1793	59·1
1714	29·2	1754	36·9	1794	59·4
1715	30·2	1755	34·9	1795	58·1
1716	30·6	1756	37·8	1796	56·1
1717	30·8	1757	37·1	1797	58·7
1718	31·7	1758	36·3	1798	61·1
1719	33·1	1759	38·2	1799	64·4
1720	32·3	1760	40·3	1800	61·7
1721	33·3	1761	41·4	1801	62·9
1722	34·2	1762	43·2	1802	64·8
1723	36·0	1763	42·7	1803	69·0
1724	35·6	1764	43·3	1804	68·4
1725	35·0	1765	42·3	1805	73·7
1726	35·5	1766	40·2	1806	71·1
1727	36·0	1767	40·1	1807	75·6
1728	33·9	1768	41·8	1808	73·5
1729	32·0	1769	41·8	1809	59·6
1730	31·2	1770	43·2	1810	71·1
1731	32·7	1771	42·7	1811	73·2
1732	33·7	1772	42·1	1812	75·4
1733	34·3	1773	42·2	1813	69·1
1734	36·0	1774	43·0	1814	73·3
1735	37·6	1775	44·1	1815	77·8
1736	38·1	1776	46·3	1816	81·1
1737	36·9	1777	47·3	1817	77·9
1738	37·2	1778	47·9	1818	77·3
1739	37·2	1779	46·8	1819	80·8
1740	34·4	1780	50·5	1820	82·5
1741	29·2	1781	49·8	1821	87·4
1742	29·2	1782	50·8	1822	89·3
1743	30·1	1783	48·4	1823	97·2
1744	32·1	1784	49·6	1824	100·6
1745	32·7	1785	46·1	1825	105·3
1746	33·5	1786	47·9	1826 (c)	(59·3)
1747	34·7	1787	47·7	1827	103·8
1748	35·0	1788	50·5	1828	108·9
1749	34·7	1789	51·5	1829	111·4
1750	35·5	1790	52·0	1830	109·4

(a) Years ended 24th June henceforth to 1752.
(b) Years ended 5th July henceforth to 1825.

(c) Years ended 5th January henceforth. The figure for 1826 is for 6 months only.

NOTES

SOURCES: 1713–1828 (England & Wales)—MS. Account in Customs and Excise Library; all other figures—S.P. 1870, xx. Conversion to tonnage figures has been made by the method described in D. C. Coleman, *The British Paper Industry, 1495–1860* (Oxford, 1958), p. 346. In using this method on the Scottish statistics, it has been assumed that the units in which paper charged *ad valorem* was recorded were pounds sterling, though this is not specifically stated in *S.P.* 1870, xx.

[2]   Figures of pasteboard charged with duty are included throughout.

(in tons)

	England & Wales	Scotland		England & Wales	Scotland		England & Wales	Scotland
1713 (a)	2,583	...	1756	4,706	115	1799	11,599	1,070
1714	2,764	...	1757	4,815	106	1800	12,394	1,189
1715	2,503	...	1758	5,199	125	1801	14,161	1,468
1716	2,634	...	1759	5,234	151	1802	11,575	1,029
1717	2,987	...	1760	5,209	175	1803	14,219	1,354
1718	3,118	...	1761	5,354	213	1804	13,053	1,265
1719	3,027	...	1762	5,329	219	7805	15,126	1,423
1720	2,911	...	1763	5,340	239	1806	14,857	1,490
1721	2,825	...	1764	5,970	281	1807	15,152	1,495
1722	2,726	...	1765	6,084	273	1808	16,213	1,426
1723	2,903	...	1766	6,000	305	1809	15,984	1,498
1724	3,006	...	1767	6,253	306	1810	16,988	1,684
1725	3,038	...	1768	6,339	295	1811	17,228	1,693
1726	3,012	...	1769	6,536	363	1812	17,807	1,681
1727	2,850	...	1770	6,406	374	1813	17,093	1,655
1728	2,867	...	1771	6,286	417	1814	17,513	1,676
1729	2,763	...	1772	6,667	397	1815	18,715	1,820
1730	2,878	...	1773	6,939	411	1816	17,400	1,781
1731	2,815	...	1774	6,684	351	1817	17,173	1,931
1732	2,588	...	1775	6,740	334	1818	19,870	2,018
1733	2,868	...	1776	6,454	311	1819	19,296	1,964
1734	2,967	...	1777	6,770	333	1820	18,913	2,008
1735	2,997	...	1778	6,866	310	1821	20,443	2,274
1736	2,956	...	1779	6,287	285	1822	21,614	2,427
1737	3,034	86	1780	5,943	261	1823	22,005	2,598
1738	3,087	94	1781	6,914	40	1824	23,597	2,681
1739	3,059	86	1782	9,044	305	1825	25,500	3,129
1740	2,989	76	1783	9,223	355	1826	(12,183)(d)	...
1741	3,199	88	1784	8,918	473	1827 (e)	20,362	2,449
1742	3,294	69	1785	9,950	495	1828	24,744	3,146
1743	3,425	72	1786	9,745	384	1829	26,569	3,682
1744	3,509	86	1787	10,976	515	1830	24,464	3,577
1745	3,480	76	1788	10,908	763	1831	25,443	4,238
1746	3,302	62	1789	10,159	869	1832	25,514	4,081
1747	3,496	59	1790	11,086	948	1833	25,839	4,301
1748	3,639	59	1791	10,993	1,122	1834	27,294	4,486
1749	4,024	65	1792	11,183	1,191	1835	28,258	4,674
1750	4,115	84	1793	11,437	1,209	1836	28,973	5,364
1751	4,105	84	1794	11,613	1,309	1837	29,918	5,449
1752	4,493	97	1795	11,133	1,004	1838	32,108	6,152
1753 (b)	4,626	83	1796	12,494	1,301	1839	32,949	7,190
1754	4,610	85	1797	11,548	1,246	1840	34,369	7,677
1755	4,577	111	1798	11,719	1,113	1841	34,277	7,530

See p. 264 for footnotes

(in tons)

	England & Wales	Scotland		England & Wales	Scotland		England & Wales	Scotland
1842	34,059	7,510	1849	40,820	11,072	1856	57,547	16,769
1843	33,738	7,619	1850	44,159	12,028	1857	64,013	18,303
1844	35,329	8,888	1851	47,193	12,768	1858	62,032	18,098
1845	37,594	9,253	1852	50,088	14,162	1859	65,442	19,881
1846	42,440	10,500	1853	51,126	14,542	1860	71,022	20,800
1847	43,550	10,721	1854	59,143	16,573	1861	76,307	21,906
1848	41,451	10,448	1855 (f)	56,511	16,454			

(a) Years ended 24th June henceforth to 1752.
(b) Years ended 5th July henceforth to 1825.
(c) With the improvements in the methods of assessing paper and in the efficiency of collection, it is obvious that a great deal of paper had escaped duty before 1782. Dr Coleman's method of conversion to tonnage statistics reduces the size of the break, since it compensates for evasion by assessment *ad valorem*, but it cannot cover avoidance of duty.
(d) Six months ended 5th January.
(e) Years ended 5th January henceforth to 1854.
(f) Years ended 31st March henceforth.

9. Starch Charged with Duty—England & Wales 1713–1828

NOTE
SOURCE: MS. Account in the Customs and Excise Library.

(in millions of lb.)

1713 (a)	2·7	1742	1·5	1771	2·8	1800	2·9
1714	2·5	1743	1·6	1772	3·5	1801	0·3
1715	2·7	1744	1·6	1773	3·7	1802	2·5
1716	2·5	1745	1·5	1774	5·4	1803	4·9
1717	2·9	1746	1·5	1775	4·9	1804	3·8
1718	2·8	1747	1·7	1776	5·6	1805	3·4
1719	3·1	1748	1·9	1777	4·9	1806	3·7
1720	2·9	1749	2·0	1778	4·7	1807	4·2
1721	2·6	1750	2·3	1779	6·6	1808	4·1
1722	2·7	1751	2·3	1780	6·4	1809	3·1
1723	2·5	1752	2·4	1781	4·9	1810	3·7
1724	2·5	1753 (b)	2·6	1782	6·9	1811	4·0
1725	2·3	1754	2·9	1783	5·4	1812	3·2
1726	2·0	1755	3·3	1784	6·7	1813	1·8
1727	2·4	1756	3·2	1785	6·3	1814	3·9
1728	1·9	1757	2·2	1786	6·6	1815	4·1
1729	1·7	1758	3·4	1787	6·0	1816	2·9
1730	1·8	1759	4·1	1788	6·1	1817	2·4
1731	1·8	1760	3·8	1789	6·4	1818	3·4
1732	2·0	1761	3·5	1790	7·0	1819	4·2
1733	1·9	1762	3·6	1791	7·8	1820	4·4
1734	1·7	1763	3·6	1792	8·5	1821	4·4
1735	1·4	1764	4·0	1793	7·3	1822	5·0
1736	1·4	1765	3·6	1794	7·9	1823	5·9
1737	1·5	1766	3·8	1795	8·6	1824	4·8
1738	1·4	1767	3·6	1796	1·9	1825	5·5
1739	1·4	1768	3·6	1797	3·1	1826 (c)	(3·1)
1740	1·1	1769	4·1	1798	7·3	1827	5·7
1741	0·9	1770	3·9	1799	5·9	1828	6·8

(a) Years ended 24th June henceforth to 1752.
(b) Years ended 5th July henceforth to 1825.

(c) Years ended 5th January henceforth. The figure for 1826 is for 6 months only.

Miscellaneous Production Statistics 10.   Soap Charged with Duty—

England & Wales 1713–1852

NOTE

SOURCES: 1713–1828—MS. Accounts in the Customs and Excise Library; 1829–52—*Returns relating to Soap.*

(in millions of lb.)

Year	Value	Year	Hard	Soft	Year	Hard	Soft
						Hard	Soft
1713 (a)	24·4	1760	29·4		1806	58·7	3·1
1714	24·7	1761	29·3		1807	61·0	3·1
1715	24·6	1762	29·4		1808	64·7	3·6
1716	23·9	1763	29·6		1809	53·6	3·6
1717	24·9	1764	29·9		1810	63·3	4·3
1718	25·1	1765	29·9		1811	61·0	3·3
1719	25·7	1766	30·0		1812	62·0	4·0
1720	26·2	1767	29·5		1813	60·2	3·8
1721	25·4	1768	30·2		1814	61·3	3·9
1722	26·3	1769	30·6		1815	68·7	4·5
1723	27·3	1770	30·8		1816	70·5	4·5
1724	27·8	1771	31·1		1817	64·7	3·8
1725	26·9	1772	30·6		1818	68·0	4·4
1726	27·0	1773	31·7		1819	69·2	4·7
1727	26·7	1774	30·8		1820	74·3	5·3
1728	25·9	1775	31·2		1821	78·9	5·6
1729	24·9	1776	34·8		1822	80·9	5·8
1730	25·0	1777	33·7		1823	88·4	6·5
1731	26·5	1778	33·7		1824	86·6	6·7
1732	26·6	1779	34·2		1825	92·2	7·4
1733	27·7	1780	37·1		1826(c)	(50·1)	(2·8)
1734	26·7	1781	36·8		1827	88·2	5·1
1735	27·5	1782	40·9		1828	94·6	7·3
1736	27·7		Hard	Soft	1829	98·1	7·3
1737	27·7	1783	28·4	2·3	1830	93·3	6·7
1738	27·3	1784	33·0	2·9	1831	107·0	7·5
1739	27·5	1785	33·1	2·8	1832	99·9	7·3
1740	26·2	1786	34·0	2·8	1833	109·1(d)	7·5(d)
1741	24·3	1787	32·0	2·9	1834	126·4	8·3
1742	24·7	1788	34·8	2·7	1835	132·0	7·1
1743	25·3	1789	36·0	2·5	1836	137·8	8·6
1744	26·5	1790	37·3	2·8	1837	135·8	9·7
1745	26·2	1791	38·9	3·0	1838	130·8	8·4
1746	26·5	1792	40·1	2·8	1839	146·8	9·6
1747	27·2	1793	40·4	2·6	1840	144·1	10·0
1748	27·0	1794	44·8	2·5	1841	148·8	8·9
1749	27·6	1795	44·1	2·7	1842	144·7	9·8
1750	28·4	1796	43·5	2·8	1843	144·6	8·1
1751	30·0	1797	43·6	2·6	1844	153·5	10·7
1752	29·8	1798	47·6	2·5	1845	158·9	12·2
1753 (b)	29·8	1799	48·0	2·6	1846	161·4	10·8
1754	29·1	1800	46·9	2·3	1847	156·7	9·5
1755	28·9	1801	45·7	1·9	1848	148·3	8·8
1756	28·5	1802	46·5	2·4	1849	159·2	9·7
1757	28·1	1803	53·2	3·0	1850	164·2	11·1
1758	27·9	1804	51·4	2·6	1851	168·9	12·3
1759	27·9	1805	56·8	3·1	1852	170·8	11·9

(a) Years ended 24th June henceforth to 1752.
(b) Years ended 5th July henceforth to 1825.
(c) Years ended 5th January henceforth. The figures for 1826 are for 6 months only.

(d) Prior to 1833 manufacturers were allowed to deduct 10 per cent before paying duty.

Miscellaneous Production Statistics 11. Hides and Skins Charged with Duty—
England & Wales 1722–1828

NOTES

[1] Sources: 1722–1825—MS. Account in Customs and Excise Library; 1826–8—*Returns relating to Hides and Skins*.
[2] This is not an exhaustive account of all hides and skins charged with duty. The less homogeneous group which was measured in dozens, namely goat skins, horse and cow hides, vellum and parchment, has been omitted.

(Tanned, Tawed, or Dressed in Oil, Measured in millions of lb.)

1722 (a)	29·4	1749	28·7	1776	32·2	1803	39·4
1723	29·0	1750	29·5	1777	33·3	1804	39·2
1724	28·5	1751	28·8	1778	33·6	1805	41·8
1725	29·2	1752	30·4	1779	32·8	1806	44·3
1726	29·8	1753 (b)	30·1	1780	32·7	1807	45·0
1727	29·5	1754	29·1	1781	33·5	1808	44·7
1728	28·5	1755	29·2	1782	34·5	1809	47·3
1729	27·4	1756	30·1	1783	35·1	1810	48·5
1730	28·4	1757	29·5	1784	34·3	1811	48·9
1731	27·8	1758	30·1	1785	35·3	1812	52·1
1732	28·1	1759	31·1	1786	34·9	1813	48·0
1733	28·0	1760	30·2	1787	35·3	1814	48·9
1734	28·4	1761	31·3	1788	35·9	1815	49·4
1735	29·5	1762	32·4	1789	34·1	1816	43·9
1736	31·3	1763	31·7	1790	37·0	1817	43·8
1737	31·3	1764	34·7	1791	37·5	1818	45·5
1738	30·3	1765	32·9	1792	37·4	1819	47·2
1739	30·7	1766	31·6	1793	38·7	1820	45·0
1740	28·1	1767	31·0	1794	39·7	1821	44·6
1741	28·5	1768	30·2	1795	39·0	1822	42·5
1742	27·9	1769	30·9	1796	41·8	1823	51·6
1743	26·7	1770	31·1	1797	38·7	1824	54·9
1744	26·3	1771	32·0	1798	38·7	1825	57·3
1745	25·7	1772	32·9	1799	37·3	1826 (c)	(28·0)
1746	26·7	1773	33·7	1800	38·9	1827	46·3
1747	27·9	1774	33·1	1801	40·0		
1748	27·3	1775	32·8	1802	39·9	1828	48·3

(a) Years ended 24th June henceforth to 1752.
(b) Years ended 5th July henceforth to 1825.

(c) Years ended 5th January henceforth. The figure for 1826 is for 6 months only.

Miscellaneous Production Statistics 12. Glass Charged with Duty—
England & Wales 1747–1845

NOTES

1] SOURCES: 1747–1828—MS. Accounts in the Customs and Excise Library; 1829–45—*Returns relating to Glass*.
2] The term *White Glass* covers all types other than common green bottle glass—namely, flint, plate, crown, German sheet, and broad glass.

(in thousands of tons)

	White Glass	Common Bottles, etc.		White Glass	Common Bottles, etc.
1747 (a)	1·4	9·2	1797	7·9	11·5
1748	2·2	8·6	1798	6·9	8·3
1749	2·5	9·3	1799	7·4	10·0
1750	3·1	11·0	1800	8·2	11·3
1751	3·1	12·8	1801	8·5	12·4
1752	3·4	13·4	1802	9·0	13·1
1753 (b)	3·6	12·2	1803	9·8	14·0
1754	4·1	13·6	1804	8·6	13·0
1755	3·8	13·0	1805	9·9	13·6
1756	3·9	11·6	1806	9·1	13·5
1757	3·9	10·6	1807	9·3	15·7
1758	4·5	9·0	1808	9·1	16·7
1759	4·1	8·3	1809	9·1	16·0
1760	4·6	9·5	1810	9·1	16·5
1761	4·6	10·4	1811	9·3	16·6
1762	5·0	10·7	1812	7·9	15·0
1763	4·9	11·6	1813	6·2	10·7
1764	5·4	13·3	1814	7·0	11·7
1765	5·9	12·9	1815	7·7	13·9
1766	5·9	13·1	1816	6·9	15·4
1767	6·5	12·2	1817	5·9	14·0
1768	6·9	12·1	1818	7·4	15·5
1769	6·6	11·8	1819	8·4	16·7
1770	6·4	11·0	1820	6·7	12·8
1771	6·3	11·2	1821	7·1	11·7
1772	7·0	12·0	1822	7·3	12·4
1773	6·7	11·6	1823	8·3	13·3
1774	6·6	11·5	1824	9·1	15·5
1775	6·7	11·3	1825	10·2	15·9
1776	6·7	11·8	1826 (c)	(7·1)	(8·7)
1777	7·2	12·4	1827	12·3	16·6
1778	6·4	11·3	1828	12·5	16·6
1779	6·6	8·5	1829	10·2	17·1
1780	5·6	6·9	1830	9·1	15·1
1781	5·5	8·3	1831	8·1	13·7
1782	5·7	8·3	1832	8·8	12·2
1783	5·7	8·5	1833	9·0	12·9
1784	5·8	8·5	1834	10·8	13·4
1785	6·2	9·5	1835	11·7	14·1
1786	6·2	9·7	1836	12·6	15·3
1787	6·6	10·4	1837	13·8	17·7
1788	7·3	10·4	1838	13·2	17·5
1789	8·4	10·9	1839	12·7	17·2
1790	8·2	12·3	1840	12·9	18·3
1791	8·1	12·6	1841	13·7	20·4
1792	8·5	12·8	1842	12·6	18·9
1793	8·5	13·6	1843	10·7	14·6
1794	9·1	12·2	1844	11·2	12·7
1795	6·6	11·8	1845	12·3	17·3
1796	7·5	11·8			

a) Years ended 24th June henceforth to 1752.
(b) Years ended 5th July henceforth to 1825.

(c)] Years ended 5th January henceforth. The figures for 1826 are for 6 months only.

Miscellaneous Production Statistics 13.   Patents—England 1617–1852 and United Kingdom 1852–1938

NOTE TO PART A
SOURCE: *Titles of Patents of Inventions* (2 vols., 1854).

A. English Patents Sealed, 1617–1852

1617	(4)	1688	4	1743	7	1798	77
1618	6	1689	1	1744	17	1799	82
1619	5	1690	3	1745	4	1800	96
1620	2	1691	20	1746	4	1801	104
1621	2	1692	25	1747	8	1802	107
1622	3	1693	19	1748	11	1803	73
1623	5	1694	9	1749	13	1804	60
1624	3	1695	8	1750	7	1805	95
1625	2	1696	3	1751	8	1806	99
1626	3	1697	3	1752	7	1807	94
1627	6	1698	7	1753	13	1808	95
1628	3	1699	5	1754	9	1809	101
1629	4	1700	2	1755	12	1810	108
1630	5	1701	1	1756	3	1811	115
1631	2	1702	1	1757	9	1812	118
1632	6	1703	1	1758	14	1813	131
1633	4	1704	4	1759	10	1814	96
1634	12	1705	1	1760	14	1815	102
1635	11	1706	5	1761	9	1816	118
1636	11	1707	2	1762	17	1817	103
1637	15	1708	2	1763	20	1818	132
1638	8	1709	3	1764	18	1819	101
1639	1	1710	—	1765	14	1820	97
1640	3	1711	3	1766	31	1821	109
1641	—	1712	3	1767	23	1822	113
1642	1	1713	2	1768	23	1823	138
1643–59	—	1714	3	1769	36	1824	180
1660	3	1715	4	1770	30	1825	250
1661	4	1716	9	1771	22	1826	141
1662	6	1717	6	1772	29	1827	150
1663	2	1718	6	1773	29	1828	154
1664	4	1719	2	1774	35	1829	130
1665	2	1720	7	1775	20	1830	180
1666	2	1721	8	1776	29	1831	151
1667	5	1722	13	1777	33	1832	147
1668	3	1723	7	1778	30	1833	180
1669	—	1724	14	1779	37	1834	207
1670	2	1725	9	1780	33	1835	231
1671	4	1726	5	1781	34	1836	296
1672	3	1727	7	1782	39	1837	256
1673	4	1728	11	1783	64	1838	394
1674	5	1729	8	1784	46	1839	411
1675	11	1730	12	1785	61	1840	440
1676	4	1731	9	1786	60	1841	440
1677	7	1732	3	1787	55	1842	371
1678	7	1733	5	1788	42	1843	420
1679	3	1734	8	1789	43	1844	450
1680	1	1735	1	1790	68	1845	572
1681	5	1736	5	1791	57	1846	493
1682	8	1737	4	1792	85	1847	493
1683	7	1738	6	1793	43	1848	388
1684	13	1739	3	1794	55	1849	514
1685	5	1740	4	1795	51	1850	513
1686	3	1741	8	1796	75	1851	455
1687	6	1742	6	1797	54	1852 (b)	(470)

(a) From 2nd March only.

(b) To 30th September only.

NOTE TO PART B

[a] SOURCES: 1852–75—*Report of the Commissioners of Patents for Inventions (S.P. 1876, XXVII); 1876–1938—Abstract.*

3. United Kingdom Patents Applied for and Sealed, 1852–1938

	Applications	Sealed		Applications	Sealed
1852 (a)	(1,211)	(914)	1896	30,193	12,473
1853	3,045	2,187	1897	30,952	14,210
1854	2,764	1,878	1898	27,649	14,063
1855	2,958	2,046	1899	25,800	14,160
1856	3,106	2,094	1900	23,924	13,170
1857	3,200	2,028	1901	26,788	13,062
1858	3,007	1,954	1902	28,976	13,764
1859	3,000	1,977	1903	28,832	15,718
1860	3,196	2,063	1904	29,678	15,089
1861	3,276	2,047	1905	27,577	14,786
1862	3,490	2,191	1906	30,030	14,707
1863	3,309	2,094	1907	28,915	16,272
1864	3,260	2,024	1908	28,598	16,284
1865	3,386	2,186	1909	30,603	15,065
1866	3,453	2,124	1910	30,388	16,269
1867	3,723	2,284	1911	29,353	17,164
1868	3,991	2,490	1912	30,089	15,814
1869	3,786	2,407	1913	30,077	16,599
1870	3,405	2,180	1914	24,820	15,036
1871	3,529	2,376	1915	18,191	11,457
1872	3,970	2,771	1916	18,602	8,424
1873	4,294	2,974	1917	19,285	9,347
1874	4,492	3,162	1918	21,839	10,809
1875	4,561	3,112	1919	32,853	12,301
1876	5,069	3,435	1920	36,672	14,191
1877	4,949	3,317	1921	35,132	17,697
1878	5,343	3,509	1922	35,494	17,366
1879	5,338	3,524	1923	32,621	17,073
1880	5,517	3,741	1924	31,370	16,839
1881	5,751	3,950	1925	33,003	17,199
1882	6,241	4,337	1926	33,080	17,333
1883	5,993	3,962	1927	35,469	17,624
1884	17,100 (b)	2,345 (b)	1928	38,556	17,695
1885	16,101	9,308	1929	39,898	18,937
1886	17,176	8,923	1930	39,359	20,765
1887	18,051	9,226	1931	36,117	21,949
1888	19,103	9,309	1932	37,052	21,150
1889	21,008	10,081	1933	36,734	16,568
1890	21,307	10,646	1934	37,409	16,890
1891	22,888	10,643	1935	36,116	17,675
1892	24,169	11,164	1936	35,867	17,819
1893	25,123	11,530	1937	36,266	17,614
1894	25,386	11,699	1938	37,873	19,814
1895	25,062	12,191			

a) October to December.
(*b*) The Act of 1883 greatly increased the numbers of both applications and grants. Under the new Act, the number sealed in each year was given instead of, as previously, the number sealed in respect of applications during the year. This accounts for the low number sealed in 1884, since most of the applications under the new Act were sealed in 1885.

NOTES

[1] SOURCES: *Final Report on the First Census of Production* (1907); *Final Report on the Fourth Census of Production* (1930); *Census of Production for 1951: Summary Tables*; and (for the regional breakdown in 1949 only), *Censuses of Production for 1950, 1949 and 1948: Summary Tables*.

[2] The headings, with the exception of *Public Utilities ... and Government Departments*, correspond to the Standard Industrial Classification. The figures under this single heading collect together the output statistics which cannot be allocated to S.I.C. headings in 1907, 1924, and 1930, namely the output of local authorities; railway companies; tramway and light railway companies; canal, dock and harbour companies; and government departments. Apart from the impossibility of carrying back the statistics for order XVII, the main break caused by the aggregation of the output of these institutions is indicated in footnote (*f*).

[3] The 1907 Census relates to Great Britain and the whole of Ireland. Subsequent censuses relate only to Great Britain and Northern Ireland.

[4] The 1907 census covered all industrial businesses. In the 1930 and later censuses, firms employing ten people or less (five in Northern Ireland) were not included. In the source used here the figures for 1924 were adjusted to the over ten employees basis, except for Northern Ireland.

A. Gross Output (Selling Value)

(in £ million)

	1907	1924	1930	1935	1949
Treatment of Non-metalliferous Mining Products other than Coal	29	71	74(a)	91	272
Chemicals and Allied Trades	90	220	199(b)	206	784
Metal Manufacture	147(c)	280	214(d)	245	1,059
Engineering, Shipbuilding and Electrical Goods	149	285	316(e)	343	1,707
Vehicles	27	118	145(f)	206	899
Metal Goods not elsewhere Specified	46(g)	79	81(d)	105	450
Precision Instruments, Jewellery, etc.	65	44	71	56	151
Textiles	336	762	431	443	1,478
Leather, Leather Goods and Fur	26	47	40	40	118
Clothing	96	178	176	173	527
Food, Drink and Tobacco	283	670	662(b)(h)	665(h)	2,644
Manufactures of Wood and Cork	39	59	69	84	275
Paper and Printing	60	159	175	182	528
Other Manufacturing Industries	15	52	54	56	248
Mining and Quarrying	134	273	187	167	528
Gas, Electricity and Water	51	124	152	181	503
Building and Contracting (Order XVII entire)	…	…	…	295	1,112
Building and Contracting (sub-heading only—i.e. private firms)	88	160	191	(214)	(911)
Public Utilities not included above, and Government Departments	72	161	162	…	…
TOTAL	1,765	3,747	3,371	3,543	13,281
England & Wales	1,491	3,313	2,988	3,206(j)	12,184(j)
Scotland	208	366	325	300(j)	1,231(j)
Ireland	67	67	58	59(j)	253(j)
Northern Ireland	…	…	…	…	…

B. Net Output (Selling Value less Cost of Materials and Work Put Out)

	1907	1924	1930	1935	1949
Treatment of Non-metalliferous Mining Products other than Coal	17	45	46(a)	57	154
Chemicals and Allied Trades	27	73	77(b)	89	261
Metal Manufacture	45(c)	78	69(d)	88	346
Engineering, Shipbuilding and Electrical Goods	72	144	166(e)	192	868
Vehicles	12	55	65(f)	97	382
Metal Goods not elsewhere Specified	21(g)	38	40(d)	53	211
Precision Instruments, Jewellery, etc.	7	16	19	15	62
Textiles	95	221	147	157	484
Leather, Leather Goods and Fur	12	14	12	13	38
Clothing	40	73	77	79	210
Food, Drink and Tobacco	87	172	187(b)	203	461
Manufactures of Wood and Cork	18	27	31	40	116
Paper and Printing	33	93	102	111	262
Other Manufacturing Industries	6	26	27	29	110
Mining and Quarrying	115	226	155	136	422
Gas, Electricity and Water	32	69	94	128	275
Building and Contracting (Order XVII entire)	…	…	…	150	550
Building and Contracting (sub-heading only—i.e. private firms)	43	79	93	(99)	(430)
Public Utilities not included above, and Government Departments	36	96	97	…	…
TOTAL	712	1,548	1,504	1,640	5,212
England & Wales	603	1,363(k)	1,340(k)	1,462(j)	4,748(j)
Scotland	86	161	143	143(j)	480(j)
Ireland	23	24	20	20(j)	…
Northern Ireland	…	…	…	…	81(j)

(a) In 1930 and previously, manufactured fuel cannot be distinguished from coke, etc., and is therefore included in *Chemicals and Allied Trades*.

(b) In 1930 and previously, starch cannot be distinguished from polishes, and is therefore included in *Chemical and Allied Trades* instead of *Food, Drink and Tobacco*.

(c) Manufactures of non-ferrous metals other than copper, brass, gold and silver are included in 1907.

(d) In 1930 and previously the small output of metals in Northern Ireland was all included in *Metal Goods not elsewhere Specified*.

(e) In 1930 and previously includes locomotive manufacture outside railway companies' establishments.

(f) In 1930 and previously does not include locomotive manufacture, or the manufacture of carriages and wagons in railway companies establishments.

(g) In 1907 does not include manufactures of non-ferrous metals other than copper, brass, gold and silver.

(h) Includes the subsidy on home-grown sugar.

(j) Revised figures of the regional breakdown have not been published, and the sum of these figures does not correspond to the revised totals shown.

(k) The estimated excise duty for Northern Ireland is included with England & Wales, but it was not more than £1,100,000 in either year.

NOTES

[1] Sources: Part A—W. G. Hoffman, *British Industry, 1700–1950* (English edition, Oxford, 1955); Part B—K. S. Lomax, 'Production and Productivity Movements in the United Kingdom since 1900', in *J.R.S.S.* (1959).

[2] The Lomax index relates to Great Britain and Northern Ireland throughout.

[3] The weighting periods for the Hoffman index are: 1801–30 (by 1812), 1831–60 (by 1850), 1861–90 (by 1881), and 1891–1913 (by 1907). The percentages of total industrial production covered by the industries used in compiling the index were estimated as follows:

	excluding building %	including building %
1801–30	68	77
1831–60	70	77
1861–90	74	81
1891–1913	68	74

[4] The Lomax index was calculated by interpolation and extrapolation from pivotal years provided by Census of Production or Import Duties Act Enquiry years—namely, 1907, 1912, 1924, 1930, 1933, 1934, 1935, and 1937.

A. The Hoffman Index, 1801–1913 (1913 = 100)

	Total Industrial Production				Total Industrial Production	
	excluding Building	including Building			excluding Building	including Building
1801	5·35	6·64		1839	18·2	19·8
1802	5·65	6·85		1840	17·8	20·4
1803	5·70	7·06		1841	18·1	21·0
1804	5·89	7·27		1842	17·2	21·6
1805	6·02	7·42		1843	18·2	22·2
1806	6·07	7·64		1844	20·5	22·9
1807	6·31	7·80		1845	21·7	23·8
1808	6·00	7·94		1846	21·6	24·4
1809	6·15	8·08		1847	21·0	25·2
1810	6·69	8·22		1848	23·0	26·0
1811	7·03	8·36		1849	23·3	26·9
1812	6·61	8·49		1850	23·3	27·8
1813	6·67	8·63		1851	24·3	28·8
1814	6·78	8·80		1852	25·8	29·9
1815	7·37	8·99		1853	28·0	31·0
1816	7·20	9·24		1854	28·4	32·0
1817	7·87	9·51		1855	27·8	33·0
1818	8·19	9·81		1856	30·6	34·1
1819	7·92	10·13		1857	31·9	35·2
1820	8·13	10·46		1858	29·8	36·3
1821	8·47	10·83		1859	32·6	37·4
1822	8·93	11·25		1860	34·2	38·6
1823	9·41	11·66		1861	33·6	39·7
1824	9·91	12·08		1862	31·6	40·8
1825	10·82	12·50		1863	33·3	42·0
1826	9·88	12·89		1864	34·6	43·4
1827	11·23	13·30		1865	36·9	44·7
1828	11·94	13·71		1866	38·4	46·1
1829	11·55	14·14		1867	37·8	47·5
1830	12·6	14·6		1868	39·9	49·0
1831	12·8	15·1		1869	40·6	50·5
1832	12·7	15·6		1870	43·4	52·0
1833	13·4	16·1		1871	46·1	53·4
1834	14·2	16·7		1872	47·5	54·8
1835	14·7	17·3		1873	49·1	56·2
1836	16·2	17·9		1874	50·1	57·5
1837	15·4	18·5		1875	49·3	58·8
1838	16·8	19·1		1876	49·9	60·0

	Total Industrial Production				Total Industrial Production	
	excluding Building	including Building			excluding Building	including Building
1877	51·2	61·1		1896	70·8	84·6
1878	48·5	62·0		1897	71·3	86·5
1879	46·3	63·0		1898	73·9	88·5
1880	54·2	64·0		1899	77·3	90·2
1881	54·6	64·9		1900	77·1	91·7
1882	58·3	65·9		1901	75·8	93·1
1883	59·8	66·7		1902	77·2	94·4
1884	57·9	67·5		1903	77·2	95·5
1885	56·1	68·4		1904	76·8	96·5
1886	54·9	69·2		1905	82·0	97·6
1887	57·6	70·3		1906	85·1	98·5
1888	61·9	71·6		1907	86·8	99·2
1889	65·9	72·9		1908	82·1	99·7
1890	65·5	74·2		1909	83·4	100·1
1891	65·8	75·6		1910	86·5	100·5
1892	62·9	77·1		1911	89·6	100·8
1893	61·3	78·8		1912	90·9	100·5
1894	65·1	80·6		1913	100·0	100·0
1895	67·3	82·6				

B. The Lomax Index, 1900–38 (1924 = 100)

	Total Industrial Production				Total Industrial Production	
	excluding Building	including Building			excluding Building	including Building
1900	71·1	73·9		1920	92·4	90·3
1901	70·8	73·6		1921	72·0	73·5
1902	72·9	76·4		1922	85·8	85·0
1903	73·2	76·4		1923	92·5	90·0
1904	73·3	75·7		1924	100·0	100·0
1905	76·9	78·3		1925	101·7	103·9
1906	79·1	80·2		1926	93·9	98·4
1907	81·2	81·6		1927	108·9	113·4
1908	78·8	77·1		1928	108·2	110·2
1909	79·2	78·9		1929	113·3	115·8
1910	81·3	80·6		1930	109·0	110·8
1911	84·9	83·0		1931	101·9	103·7
1912	86·4	84·2		1932	102·0	103·2
1913	92·6	90·5		1933	107·7	110·1
1914	87·0	84·8		1934	118·0	121·1
1915	89·9	86·4		1935	127·9	130·3
1916	85·6	81·8		1936	139·1	142·0
1917	80·7	76·4		1937	147·7	150·5
1918	78·2	73·8		1938	144·1	146·4
1919	85·5	81·3				

REFERENCES

BOOKS

T. C. Barker, *Pilkington Brothers and the Glass Industry*, (London, 1960).

D. C. Coleman, *The British Paper Industry, 1495–1860* (Oxford, 1958).

Selma E. Fine, *Production and Excise in England, 1643–1825* (unplublished Radcliffe College thesis).

J. B. Jefferys, *Retail Trading in Britain, 1850–1950* (Cambridge, 1954).

P. Mathias, *The Brewing Industry in England, 1700–1830* (Cambridge, 1959).

L. Rostas, *Comparative Productivity in British and American Industry* (Cambridge, 1948).

J. Vaizey, *The Brewing Industry, 1886–1951* (London, 1960).

GOVERNMENT PUBLICATIONS

Returns relating to British Spirits (in *Sessional Papers* irregularly from 1816 and annually from 1835–83).

Returns relating to Soap (in *Sessional Papers* irregularly from 1816 and annually from 1830–52).

Returns relating to Glass (in *Sessional Papers* irregularly from 1818 and annually from 1834–46).

Returns relating to Hops (in *Sessional Papers* annually from 1821–81).

Report of the Select Committee on Patents for Inventions (S.P. 1829, III).

Reports of the Commissioners of Inquiry into the Excise Establishment and Revenue (*S.P.* 1833, XXI, *S.P.* 1834, XXIV, *S.P.* 1934, XXV, *S.P.* 1835, XXX, *S.P.* 1835, XXXI, *S.P.* 1836, XXVI).

Titles of Patents for Inventions (2 vols. (non-parliamentary), 1854).

Annual Reports of the Commissioners of Inland Revenue (in *Sessional Papers* annually since 1857. Two volumes containing historical summaries—*S.P.* 1870, XX, and *S.P.* 1884–5, XXII—are most valuable).

Report of the Commissioners of Patents for Inventions (S.P. 1876, XXVII).

General Annual Report on Bankruptcy (in *Sessional Papers* annually from 1884–1920, and issued as non-parliamentary papers thereafter).

ARTICLES

B. C. Brown, 'Industrial Production in 1935 and 1948', *L.C.E.S. Bulletin* (Dec. 1954).

A. W. Flux, 'Indices of Productive Activity', *J.R.S.S.* (1927).

H. Leak, 'Statistics of the Census of Production and Distribution', *J.R.S.S.* (1949).

L. Levi, 'Limits of Legislative Interference with the Sale of Fermented Liquors', *J.S.S.* (1872).

K. S. Lomax, 'Production and Productivity Movements in the United Kingdom isnce 1900', *J.R.S.S.* (1959).

A. P. Wadsworth, 'Newspaper Circulations, 1800–1954', *T.M.S.S.* (1954–5).

CHAPTER XI

OVERSEAS TRADE

TABLES

According to Professor Clark, whose systematic study of the early English trade figures is an indispensable guide to this subject: 'The real beginnings of commercial statistics belong to the sixteenth and early seventeenth centuries'.[1] For it was not until the late sixteenth century that the customs figures began to be used to measure the balance of trade and thus to guide policy. In earlier periods the purpose of the statistics was merely fiscal and although medieval figures exist for the chief commodities subject to tax, their extraction from post books and exchequer records presents major problems of scholarship. Research that has been done in these records suggests, however, that they are a more fruitful source of quantitative data than has often been supposed. The export of cloth, for example (which probably accounted for some 90 per cent of England's total exports by the late fifteenth century) can be shown almost annually from 1347 and of wool, which was the leading

[1] G. N. Clark, *Guide to English Commercial Statistics, 1696–1782* (London, 1938), p. x.

commodity at an earlier period, from 1275. We have not attempted to give any of the medieval statistics in this volume since their compilation and presentation is a task for the specialist. Work is now in progress at the London School of Economics on the presentation of the export statistics of wool and cloth to 1575.[1] These will be published (with introduction and commentary on the sources) in tabular and graphic form, port by port and for England as a whole, distinguishing categories of merchants exporting (i.e. natives, aliens and Hanseatics).

Regular and complete central records of English overseas trade date from the establishment of the office of Inspector-General of Imports and Exports in 1696: for Scotland they begin in 1755. The basic source of these statistics for the eighteenth century is the Inspector-General's manuscript ledgers, though aggregates and details have been (often inaccurately) transcribed from these, or from derived parliamentary returns with innumerable secondary sources. So many inaccurate or incomplete published versions of the eighteenth-century trade statistics now exist that the late Mrs E. B. Schumpeter's carefully transcribed series, edited for publication by Professor T. S. Ashton, are a collection of immense importance for students of English trade at this period.[2]

The eighteenth-century trade records have inherent defects, however. A recent historian has referred to them as a 'snare'.[3] One important defect is that most of the rates at which the various commodities were valued by the Customs officials ossified within a few years of the beginning of the Inspector-General's Ledgers in 1696. They did not remain unaltered from the start, as Macpherson[4] and others following him stated, but the changes took place in the early years. This, together with the fact that some goods (especially from Asia) continued to be entered at a declared (i.e. fluctuating) rate, means that the unadjusted figures of official values are a true index neither of value nor of volume. Nevertheless, by applying constant valuation rates to the quantity figures, as Mrs Schumpeter did using the rates of *circa* 1700, the ledgers can be made to supply a good volume index. Except towards the end of the century, when re-exports are exaggerated because some prices, especially those of coffee and tea, fell below the official rates this weighting of the series with the late seventeenth or early eighteenth century prices produces surprisingly little distortion, as is shown by comparing them with an index based on late eighteenth-century prices.[5]

A more serious defect of the trade statistics springs from the importance of smuggling in eighteenth-century Britain. The difficulty of overcoming this defect is increased by the fact that smuggling activity varied at different times. As Dr Cole has shown,[6] there seem

---

[1] By Professor E. Carus-Wilson and Miss Olive Coleman, to be published by Oxford University Press. We are indebted to Miss Coleman for the information in this paragraph.

[2] Elizabeth B. Schumpeter, *English Overseas Trade Statistics 1697–1808* (Oxford University Press, 1960).

[3] G. D. Ramsay, *English Overseas Trade during the Centuries of Emergence* (London, 1957), p. 260.

[4] D. Macpherson, *Annals of Commerce* (4 vols., London, 1805), vol. II, p. 340.

[5] Phyllis Deane and W. A. Cole, *British Economic Growth, 1688–1959* (Cambridge University Press, 1962).

[6] W. A. Cole, 'Trends in Eighteenth Century Smuggling', in *E.H.R.*, vol. x, No. 3 (April 1958). See also the discussion in G. D. Ramsay, *op. cit.* pp. 166–206.

to have been two peaks—in the 1730's and early 1740's, and again during the American War of Independence. But illicit trade was not seriously restricted until Pitt's reforms of the 1780's, and its disappearance had to wait until free trade rendered it superfluous. At its high point during the War of American Independence, Dr Cole estimates that smuggled imports may have been between £2,000,000 and £3,000,000, or up to 25 per cent of the official value of legal imports. This points a very obvious warning that the official figures of imports and re-exports cannot be taken as an exact guide to the volume of trade.[1]

Overall figures of first English and then British trade in the eighteenth century have long been available though it is only recently that a series has been published distinguishing re-exports of foreign and colonial produce from exports of British goods.[2] This series is reproduced here as table 1, together with the statistics of trade with Ireland, collected by Dr Cole but not previously published. The union with Ireland led, eventually, to the unification of the British and Irish Customs, and in consequence to the substitution of United Kingdom for British statistics. These are given in tables 2 and 3. The former shows the official values up to 1853, and, apart from the elimination of the Irish trade, is directly comparable with table 1. It also contains the declared values of exports (which are continued in table 3) together with Professor Imlah's estimates of the values at current prices of imports and re-exports (which also link up, practically without break, with table 3).[3] The increasing artificiality of the official figures in the nineteenth century is well brought out by this table.

Tables 4 and 5 depend heavily on the work of Mrs Schumpeter. Nearly all the figures up to 1808 are taken from her work-sheets, which Professor Ashton kindly allowed us to photograph and use. The later figures, together with the whole of table 6 and the earlier part of table 8, are taken for the most part from the *Trade and Navigation Accounts*.[4] In constructing these tables two main difficulties have been encountered: the provision of links between official and current price values, and between the British and the United Kingdom figures. For this purpose an overlap has been provided for the differing series, together with an indication, where possible, of the exact size of the break caused by the change. The overlap is generally three years, though for the official and current price values of exports, for which it is simple to make it longer, it is fifteen years.

It is, perhaps, unnecessary to stress again the unreality of the official rates of valuation. But the dangers of taking the official statistics as anything other than volume indicators—

---

[1] Exports were influenced to a lesser extent, primarily by illegal exports of raw wool, which continued down to the outbreak of war with France in 1793.

[2] Phyllis Deane and W. A. Cole, *op. cit.*

[3] In the same way, there is no serious break on the change in 1871 from computed real values of imports and re-exports to declared values. Computations of real values were also made for 1805–9 for the Bullion Committee (*S.P.* 1810, III, Appendix pp. 228–9), and for 1840 and 1852 in a Board of Trade report (*S.P.* 1863, LXVI).

[4] Prior to 1854 these were published as a section of the annual *Finance Accounts* in sessional papers. Subsequently they appeared as separate blue books, and, from 1921, as non-parliamentary official papers, entitled the *Annual Statement of Trade*.

and inexact ones at that[1]—are so great that a further warning is justified. This is particularly so in relation to the official value series for the United Kingdom, since by 1826 the rates for most articles bore little relation to their prices, and in the following thirty years the situation became worse. This deterioration was most prominent in export values, as the cost of manufactured articles fell, and these are not given here beyond 1829. In any event, a better volume index has been compiled for the period after 1796 by Professor Imlah and this is shown in table 13, where it is continued up to 1947 from official sources.

Tables 7, 8 and 9 are straightforward, and the main general problems they raise are of continuity or definition of the various commodity groups. These are dealt with in the notes. A full discussion of the problems of valuation, measurement and classification of the trade statistics is given by A. Maizels in 'The Overseas Trade Statistics of the United Kingdom', *J.R.S.S.* (1949). In selecting the groups to be shown, the main principle followed has been to take those which bulked largest in each branch of trade for some considerable part of the period. Some commodities which were important only for a short time (e.g. guano in the mid-nineteenth century) have been omitted, and others (e.g. tobacco and hemp) have been continued, though no longer of major importance, for the sake of comparison with other periods when they were pre-eminent. Still other goods (e.g. silk) have been included, though they were never in the first rank of trade commodities, because of the interest which historians have shown in them.

Tables 10, 11 and 12 show the breakdown of trade on a geographical basis, the first two of these giving the official values up to 1822, and the last the current price values from the earliest date for which they are available. Unfortunately the source of the annual figures in table 10 follows the practice of the eighteenth and early nineteenth centuries in not distinguishing exports from re-exports. The distinction is, however, available for certain years in *British Economic Growth, 1688–1955*,[2] and these are shown as table 11. The constitution of the regions adopted in tables 10 and 11, and in the first part of table 12, is that used in the early nineteenth century by writers such as Cesar Moreau[3] and G. R. Porter.[4] These regions are appropriate to the period for which they are used, but would become less so if their use was continued further into the nineteenth and early twentieth centuries in mind. It should be noted that until 1904 the geographical analysis was given in the trade returns by country of shipment. After 1904 the basis of the analysis was countries of consignment and after 1936 country of origin or consumption.[5]

---

[1] Referring to the first half of the nineteenth century, A. W. Flux wrote, 'The official values appear to give a much better indication of the movements in the volume of trade than one could have expected'. (*Transactions of the Manchester Statistical Society* (1898–9), p. 81). For many purposes the official values provide a good enough guide to volume, and the stress laid on their inexactness here should not be taken to mean that they are useless.

[2] Phyllis Deane and W. A. Cole, *op. cit.*

[3] Cesar Moreau, *State of the Trade of Great Britain with all Parts of the World* (London, 1822).

[4] G. R. Porter, *The Progress of the Nation* (London, 2nd edition, 1847).

[5] Stephen Bourne, *Trade, Population and Food* (London, 1880), pp. 35–6 gives examples of traffic flowing through intermediate ports in the nineteenth century. Much German trade, for example, was routed through Dutch ports and attributed to Holland. For a more recent discussion of this problem see A. Maizels, 'The Overseas Trade Statistics of the United Kingdom', *J.R.S.S.* 1949, pp. 220–1.

Tables 14 and 15 are concerned directly with the terms of trade from the start of our trade statistics. Since the eighteenth century statistics are primarily volume indicators, the terms of trade for that period are gross barter only. Thereafter the nineteenth and first half of the twentieth centuries are covered by the estimates first of Professor Imlah and subsequently of the Board of Trade for the net barter terms of trade. These are given alongside the price indices (or, as Professor Kindleberger more accurately describes them, unit-value indices)[1] on which they are based. Gross barter terms have not been shown after the eighteenth century, but they can easily be estimated from the volume indices in table 13.

Finally, in table 16, we show the main items of Professor Imlah's balance of payments estimates for 1816–1913, and the Board of Trade's estimate for 1907, 1910, 1913, and the inter-war years. In this table we have included bullion and specie movements in the overall balance on current account, which was standard practice prior to 1932. This became inappropriate in the conditions of the 1930's, when most bullion movements were in the nature of a capital rather than a current transaction, but for the sake of continuity it has been followed right through to 1938. It should be particularly noted that the statistics given here do not link up with the post-1945 estimates given in the half years Balance of Payments White Papers.[2] Prior to the Second World War, c.i.f. values of imports were used in estimating the balance of merchandise trade—i.e. payments for shipping were included in visible trade, thus exaggerating both the deficit of the visible balance and the surplus of the invisible balance. Moreover, the estimates of the inter-war years have been severely criticized.[3]

---

[1] C. P. Kindleberger (*The Terms of Trade* (New York, 1956)) has a further series for the terms of trade from 1870–1952.

[2] The figures in the White Papers for their first twelve years have been brought together in H.M. Treasury, *The United Kingdom Balance of Payments 1946–57* (London, 1959).

[3] Cf. *The Banker* (March 1948), where they are described as 'little more than the vaguest haphazard guessing, unworthy of this country and of the technical accomplishments of the men responsible for the task'.

Overseas Trade 1.   Official Values of Overseas Trade—England & Wales 1697–1791, and Great Britain 1772–1804

NOTES

[1] SOURCE: Phyllis Deane and W. A. Cole, *The Course of British Economic Growth* (Cambridge University Press, 1962).
[2]   Prize goods are included throughout, except as indicated in footnote (*c*).

[3]   Bullion and specie are definitely excluded from 1706 onwards, and they have been excluded so far as possible in earlier years.

A. England & Wales 1697–1791

(in £000)

	Total Trade			Trade with Ireland		
	Imports	Domestic Exports	Re-exports	Imports	Domestic Exports	Re-exports
1697	3,344	2,295(*a*)	1,096	...	...	...
1698	4,608	3,582(*a*)	1,608	...	...	...
1699	5,621	3,655(*a*)	1,570	417	131(*a*)	139
1700	5,840	3,731(*a*)	2,081	234	131(*a*)	141
1701	5,796	4,049(*a*)	2,192	285	142(*a*)	164
1702	4,088	3,130(*a*)	1,144	258	106(*a*)	113
1703	4,450	3,888(*a*)	1,622	324	108(*a*)	159
1704	5,329	3,723(*a*)	1,804	321	92(*a*)	125
1705	...	...	...	...	...	...
1706	4,064	4,142(*a*)	1,447	266	95(*a*)	103
1707	4,267	4,173(*a*)	1,602	306	109(*a*)	154
1708	4,699	4,404(*a*)	1,495	275	107(*a*)	145
1709	4,511	4,406	1,507	276	108	144
1710	4,011	4,729	1,566	311	102	184
1711	4,686	4,088	1,875	297	112	149
1712	...	...	...	...	...	...
1713	5,811	4,490	2,402	296	148	159
1714	5,929	5,564	2,440	326	140	257
1715	5,641	5,015	1,908	389	171	249
1716	5,800	4,807	2,243	562	163	182
1717	6,347	5,384	2,613	470	209	221
1718	6,669	4,381	1,980	326	169	165
1719	5,367	4,514	2,321	380	217	171
1720	6,090	4,611	2,300	283	182	147
1721	5,908	4,512	2,689	333	175	196
1722	6,378	5,293	2,972	356	279	210
1723	6,506	4,725	2,671	361	292	262
1724	7,394	5,107	2,494	368	279	190
1725	7,095	5,667	2,814	334	204	271
1726	6,678	5,001	2,692	333	321	249
1727	6,799	4,605	2,670	307	273	163
1728	7,569	4,910	3,797	318	229	247
1729	7,541	4,940	3,299	288	254	264
1730	7,780	5,326	3,223	294	240	293
1731	6,992	5,081	2,782	309	272	347
1732	7,088	5,675	3,196	294	279	336
1733	8,017	5,823	3,015	386	318	277
1734	7,096	5,403	2,897	401	279	348
1735	8,160	5,927	3,402	417	369	400
1736	7,308	6,118	3,585	447	301	419

See p. 281 for footnotes

(in £000)

	Total Trade			Trade with Ireland		
	Imports	Domestic Exports	Re-exports	Imports	Domestic Exports	Re-exports
1737	7,074	6,668	3,414	346	329	402
1738	7,439	6,982	3,214	381	276	420
1739	7,829	5,572	3,272	412	289	385
1740	6,704	5,111	3,086	391	242	387
1741	7,936	5,995	3,575	405	265	434
1742	6,867	6,095	3,480	347	318	457
1743	7,802	6,868	4,442	817	349	511
1744	6,363	5,411	3,780	391	281	454
1745	7,847	5,739	3,333	(1,441)(b)	578	333
1746	6,206	7,201	3,566	533	466	330
1747	7,117	6,744	3,031	541	318	431
1748	8,136	7,317	3,824	464	417	489
1749	7,918	9,081	3,598	568	472	534
1750	7,772	9,474	3,225	613	666	651
1751	7,943	8,775	3,644	664	658	516
1752	7,889	8,226	3,469	564	694	447
1753	8,625	8,732	3,511	561	689	461
1754	8,093	8,318	3,470	610	732	441
1755	8,773	7,915	3,150	643	616	454
1756	8,962	8,632	3,089	828	593	519
1757	9,253	8,584	3,755	687	520	441
1758	8,415	8,763	3,855	1,050	513	414
1759	8,923	10,079	3,869	832	518	413
1760	9,833	10,981	3,714	904	692	358
1761	8,544	10,804	4,069	855	883	593
1762	8,870	9,400	4,351	889	830	699
1763	11,199	9,522	5,146	769	809	831
1764	10,391	11,536	4,725	777	794	840
1765	10,981	10,122	4,451	1,071	800	967
1766	11,513	9,890	4,193	1,154	933	987
1767	12,074	9,492	4,375	1,103	791	1,089
1768	11,879	9,695	5,425	1,226	901	1,348
1769	11,909	8,984	4,454	1,265	998	967
1770	12,217	9,503	4,764	1,214	1,003	1,122
1771	12,822	11,219	5,905	1,381	771	1,213
1772	13,305	10,503	5,656	1,242	893	1,071
1773	11,560	8,976	5,944	1,253	850	1,069
1774	13,098	10,049	5,868	1,447	1,036	1,070
1775	13,550	9,723	5,478	1,550	1,133	1,037
1776	11,703	9,275	4,454	1,517	1,221	958
1777	11,842	8,750	3,903	1,503	1,077	(855)(c)
1778	10,293	7,754	3,797	1,361	796	675
1779	10,660	7,113	5,588	1,384	705	663
1780	10,812	8,033	4,564	1,549	890	1,040
1781	11,919	7,043	3,526	1,434	930	840
1782	(9,533)(d)	8,605	(3,750)(d)	1,349	829	887
1783	12,115	10,096	4,116	1,499	999	1,020
1784	14,119	10,497	3,675	1,523	621	789
1785	14,900	10,315	4,795	1,694	740	1,142
1786	14,610	11,191	4,200	1,905	872	849

See p. 281 for footnotes

(in £000)

	Total Trade			Trade with Ireland		
	Imports	Domestic Exports	Re-exports	Imports	Domestic Exports	Re-exports
1787	16,335	11,310	4,445	1,884	958	1,066
1788	16,551	11,937	4,346	1,862	1,245	852
1789	16,408	12,970	5,201	2,069	1,079	964
1790	17,443	14,057	4,828	2,203	1,114	823
1791	17,688	15,896	5,539	2,102	1,295	907

B. Great Britain, 1772–1804

	Total Trade			Trade with Ireland		
	Imports	Domestic Exports	Re-exports	Imports	Domestic Exports	Re-exports
1772	14,515	10,974	6,746	1,382	981	1,188
1773	12,676	9,418	7,114	1,379	954	1,273
1774	14,300	10,557	6,732	1,602	1,133	1,205
1775	14,817	10,072	6,253	1,688	1,229	1,224
1776	12,449	9,705	5,051	1,654	1,372	1,086
1777	12,644	9,300	4,191	1,653	1,214	(987)(c)
1778	10,976	8,208	4,046	1,482	958	858
1779	11,435	7,648	5,890	1,547	843	802
1780	11,715	8,814	4,785	1,743	1,063	1,152
1781	12,724	7,622	3,710	1,630	1,119	956
1782	(10,342)(d)	9,110	(3,900)(d)	1,498	964	953
1783	13,122	10,710	4,327	1,612	1,156	1,147
1784	15,273	11,274	3,827	1,778	772	862
1785	16,279	10,975	5,143	2,012	890	1,278
1786	15,786	11,830	4,476	2,171	1,023	939
1787	17,804	12,054	4,816	2,222	1,136	1,206
1788	18,027	12,725	4,748	2,185	1,422	1,003
1789	17,821	13,780	5,561	2,405	1,243	1,072
1790	19,131	14,921	5,199	2,574	1,328	937
1791	19,670	16,810	5,922	2,479	1,471	1,000
1792	19,659	18,337	6,568	2,623	1,513	860
1793	19,257	13,892	6,498	2,285	1,055	888
1794	22,289	16,725	10,024	2,750	1,281	1,199
1795	22,737	16,527	10,785	2,637	1,612	1,185
1796	23,187	19,102	11,417	2,765	1,782	1,115
1797	21,014	16,903	12,014	3,114	1,311	1,126
1798	27,858	19,673	13,919	2,736	1,658	1,316
1799	26,837	24,084	11,907	2,771	2,406	1,681
1800	30,571	24,304	18,848	2,313	1,788	1,954
1801	32,796	25,700	16,602	2,360	1,577	1,373
1802	31,442	26,993	19,128	3,134	2,117	1,423
1803	27,992	22,112	11,540	2,888	2,281	1,083
1804	29,201	23,936	13,532	2,747	2,199	1,182

(*a*) In arriving at the export figures for 1697–1708, the original values of woollen goods have not been used, but they have been replaced by figures computed at the 1709 rates of valuation.
(*b*) The figure of imports from Ireland is as given in the Inspector-General's Ledgers. The principal component was exceptionally heavy shipments of linen yarn. But from the Irish export figures given in C. Gill's *The Rise of the Irish Linen Industry* (Oxford, 1925), p. 341, it seems that there must have been an error in the English ledgers.
(*c*) Excluding prize goods.
(*d*) The accounts for this year are defective. These figures are partly based on returns quoted in D. Macpherson, *Annals of Commerce . . .* (4 vols, London, 1805).

Overseas Trade 2. Official Values and Values at Current Prices of Overseas Trade—United Kingdom 1796–1853

NOTE

SOURCES: Computed value of imports and re-exports—A. H. Imlah, *Economic Elements in the Pax Britannica* (Cambridge, Mass., Harvard University Press, 1958), pp. 37–8; declared values of exports and all official values—*S.P.* 1898, LXXXV.

(in £ million)

	Computed or Declared Values			Official Values		
	Imports	Domestic Exports	Re-exports	Imports	Domestic Exports	Re-exports
1796	39·6	30·1(a)	8·5	...	...	...
1797	34·4	27·5(a)	9·3	...	...	...
1798	49·6	32·2(b)	11·3	...	...	...
1799	50·9	36·8(b)	9·4	...	...	...
1800	62·3	37·7(b)	14·7	...	...	...
1801	68·7	40·6(b)	12·9	31·8	24·9	10·4
1802	54·7	45·9(b)	12·9	29·8	25·6	12·8
1803	53·9	36·9(b)	9·1	26·6	20·5	8·1
1804	57·3	38·2(b)	11·0	27·8	22·7	9·0
1805	61·0	38·1	10·0	28·6	23·4	7·7
1806	53·3	40·9	9·2	26·9	25·9	7·8
1807	53·8	37·2	8·3	26·7	23·4	7·7
1808	51·5	37·3	6·5	26·8	24·6	5·8
1809	73·7	47·4	14·3	31·8	33·5	12·8
1810	88·5	48·4	12·5	39·3	34·1	9·5
1811	50·7	32·9	6·7	26·5	22·7	6·2
1812	56·0	41·7	9·1	26·2	29·5	9·7
1813	...	...	...	...	...	...
1814	80·8	45·5	24·8	33·8	34·2	19·4
1815	71·3	51·6	16·8	33·0	42·9	15·7
1816	50·2	41·7	12·6	27·4	35·7	13·5
1817	61·0	41·8	10·1	30·8	40·1	10·3
1818	80·7	46·5	12·3	36·9	42·7	10·9
1819	56·0	35·2	10·2	30·8	33·5	9·9
1820	54·2	36·4	10·4	32·4	38·4	10·6
1821	45·6	36·7	9·5	30·8	40·8	10·6
1822	44·6	37·0	7·8	30·5	44·2	9·2
1823	52·0	35·4	7·2	35·8	43·8	8·6
1824	51·2	38·4	7·5	37·5	48·7	10·2
1825	73·6	38·9	8·2	44·2	47·2	9·2
1826	50·4	31·5	7·3	37·8	41·0	10·1
1827	58·8	37·2	6·8	44·9	52·2	9·8
1828	57·3	36·8	6·5	45·2	52·8	9·9
1829	54·1	35·8	6·6	44·0	56·2	10·6
1830	55·9	38·3	5·6	46·3	61·2	8·5
1831	62·0	37·2	6·7	49·7	60·7	10·7
1832	52·5	36·5	7·3	44·6	65·0	11·0
1833	58·9	39·7	6·9	45·9	70·0	9·8
1834	64·7	41·6	8·0	49·4	73·8	11·6
1835	·68·0	47·4	9·2	49·0	78·4	12·8
1836	84·4	53·3	9·3	57·3	85·2	12·4
1837	70·1	42·1	9·0	54·8	72·5	13·2

See p. 283 for footnotes

(in £ million)

	Computed or Declared Values			Official Values		
	Imports	Domestic Exports	Re-exports	Imports	Domestic Exports	Re-exports
1838	80·1	50·1	9·2	61·3	95·5	12·7
1839	90·8	53·2	10·2	62·0	97·4	12·8
1840	91·2	51·4	10·0	67·5	102·7	13·8
1841	83·9	51·6	9·9	64·4	102·2	14·7
1842	76·4	47·4	8·4	65·3	100·3	13·6
1843	71·0	52·3	7·8	70·2	117·9	14·0
1844	78·9	58·6	8·0	75·4	131·6	14·4
1845	88·4	60·1	9·3	85·3	134·6	16·3
1846	87·3	57·8	9·2	75·9	132·3	16·3
1847	112·1	58·8	11·7	90·9	126·1	20·0
1848	88·2	52·8	8·4	93·5	132·6	18·4
1849	101·4	63·6	12·1	105·9	164·5	25·6
1850	103·0	71·4	12·0	100·5	175·4	21·9
1851	109·5	74·4	12·5	110·5	190·7	23·7
1852	110·0	78·1	13·0	109·3	196·2	23·3
1853	148·5	98·9	16·8	123·1	214·3	27·7

(a) Imlah's estimates based on British and Irish trade.
(b) Declared values of British trade plus Imlah's estimates of the market values of Irish exports. (See Imlah, *op. cit.* p. 20 *et seq.*)

3. Values at Current Prices of Overseas Trade—United Kingdom 1854–1956

NOTES

[1] SOURCE: *Annual Statement of Trade.*
[2] Imports are valued c.i.f., exports and re-exports f.o.b.
[3] The value of bullion, specie, and diamonds is excluded throughout.

(in £ million)

	Imports	Domestic Exports	Re-exports		Imports	Domestic Exports	Re-exports
1854	152·4	97·2	18·6	1878	368·8	192·8	52·6
1855	143·5	95·7	21·0	1879	363·0	191·5	57·3
1856	172·5	115·8	23·4	1880	411·2	223·1	63·4
1857	187·8	122·1	24·1	1881	397·0	234·0	63·1
1858	164·6	116·6	23·2	1882	413·0	241·5	65·2
1859	179·2	130·4	25·3	1883	426·9	239·8	65·6
1860	210·5	135·9	28·6	1884	390·0	233·0	62·9
1861	217·5	125·1	34·5	1885	371·0	213·1	58·4
1862	225·7	124·0	42·2	1886	349·9	212·7	56·2
1863	248·9	146·6	50·3	1887	362·2	221·9	59·3
1864	275·0	160·4	52·2	1888	387·6	234·5	64·0
1865	271·1	165·8	53·0	1889	427·6	248·9	66·7
1866	295·3	188·9	50·0	1890	420·7	263·5	64·7
1867	275·2	181·0	44·8	1891	435·4	247·2	61·9
1868	294·7	179·7	48·1	1892	423·8	227·2(b)	64·4(b)
1869	295·5	190·0	47·1	1893	404·7	218·3	58·9
1870	303·3	199·6	44·5	1894	408·3	216·0	57·8
1871	331·0(a)	223·1	60·5(a)	1895	416·7	226·1	59·7
1872	354·7	256·3	58·3	1896	441·8	240·1	56·2
1873	371·3	255·2	55·8	1897	451·0	234·2	60·0
1874	370·1	239·6	58·1	1898	470·5	233·4	60·7
1875	373·9	223·5	58·1	1899	485·0	264·5(c)	65·0
1876	375·2	200·6	56·1	1900	523·1	291·2	63·2
1877	394·4	198·9	53·5	1901	522·0	280·0	67·8

See p. 284 for footnotes

(in £ million)

	Imports	Domestic Exports	Re-exports		Imports	Domestic Exports	Re-exports
1902	528·4	283·4	65·8	1930	1,044·0	570·8	86·8
1903	542·6	290·8	69·6	1931	861·3	390·6	63·9
1904	551·0	300·7	70·3	1932	701·7	365·0	51·0
1905	565·0	329·8	77·8	1933	675·0	367·9	49·1
1906	607·9	375·6	85·1	1934	731·4	396·0	51·2
1907	645·8	426·0	91·9	1935	756·0	425·8	55·3
1908	593·0	377·1	79·6	1936	847·8	440·6	60·8
1909	624·7	378·2	91·3	1937	1,027·8	521·4	75·1
1910	678·3	430·4	103·8	1938	919·5	470·8	61·5
1911	680·2	454·1	102·8	1939	885·5	439·5	46·0
1912	744·6	487·2	111·7	1940	1,152·1	411·2	26·0
1913	768·7	525·2	109·6	1941	1,145·1	365·4	12·7
1914	696·6	430·7	95·5	1942	1,206·2	391·1	10·6
1915	851·9	384·9	99·1	1943	1,886·1	337·5	13·4
1916	948·5	506·3	97·6	1944	2,362·2	328·3	18·2
1917	1,064·2	527·1	69·7	1945	1,517·9	434·5	51·1
1918	1,316·2	501·4	30·9	1946	1,301·0	914·7	50·3
1919	1,626·2	798·6	164·7	1947	1,794·5	1,138·2	59·8
1920	1,932·6	1,334·5	222·8	1948	2,078·0	1,581·8	64·7
1921	1,085·5	703·4	106·9	1949	2,274·7	1,785·8	58·6
1922	1,003·1	719·5	103·7	1950	2,608·2	2,171·3	84·8
1923	1,096·2(d)	767·3(d)	118·5(d)	1951	3,901·9	2,581·6	127·0
1924	1,277·4	801·0	140·0	1952	3,477·0	2,584·2	143·9
1925	1,320·7	773·4	154·0	1953	3,342·9	2,582·0	105·5
1926	1,241·4	653·0	125·5	1954	3,373·7	2,673·0	100·7
1927	1,218·3	709·1	123·0	1955	3,880·9	2,905·4	118·9
1928	1,195·6	723·6	120·3	1956	3,886·1	3,171·5	146·4
1929	1,220·8	729·3	109·7				

(a) Up to 1870 the values of imports and re-exports were computed by the Board of Trade. All other values were declared by shippers.

(b) From 1892 tobacco manufactured in bond was transferred from re-exports to exports. The effect of this change was very slight.

(c) The value of new ships (with their machinery) sold abroad was included in exports for the first time in 1899, when it came to £9·2 million.

(d) Southern Ireland was treated as foreign from 1st April 1923.

Overseas Trade 4. Official Values of Principal Imports—England & Wales 1700–91, Great Britain 1792–1829, and United Kingdom 1826–56

NOTE

SOURCES: 1700–1807 (except last three columns)—Elizabeth B. Schumpeter, *English Overseas Trade Statistics, 1697–1808* (Oxford University Press, 1960), tables XV and XVII; 1808–56 (including the whole of the last three columns)—*Trade and Navigation Accounts*. Certain figures for 1812 are taken from various returns of specific imports given in *Sessional Papers* from 1818 to 1822.

A. England & Wales 1700–1791

(in £000)

	Corn	Coffee	Sugar	Tea	Wine	Timber(a)	Raw Cotton	Raw Wool	Raw, Thrown and Waste Silk
1700	--	36	668	14	647	119	...	220	377
1701	--	38	599	6	513	97	...	251	388
1702	--	47	358	3	382	95	...	199	334
1703	--	26	565	9	290	113	...	161	316
1704	--	75	436	20	371	130	...	159	682
1705	...	...	...	...	...	...	...	...	...
1706	--	5	459	70	258	111	...	178	423
1707	--	5	533	28	310	140	...	152	204
1708	--	52	521	116	392	125	...	106	543
1709	3	71	546	12	367	100	...	154	494
1710	6	23	697	37	379	95	...	189	213
1711	--	81	505	49	394	66	...	255	640
1712	...	...	...	...	...	...	...	...	...
1713	--	100	700	170	383	138	...	166	621
1714	--	124	708	136	500	121	...	190	410
1715	--	48	854	42	582	138	...	266	534
1716	--	24	939	5	489	97	...	385	556
1717	--	41	1,057	87	537	115	...	278	720
1718	--	72	784	158	587	133	...	133	644
1719	--	64	756	142	501	131	...	63	360
1720	--	38	980	33	464	167	...	109	742
1721	--	55	691	134	619	133	...	117	344
1722	--	133	859	133	615	144	...	119	684
1723	--	121	919	83	544	127	...	108	715
1724	38	130	1,011	132	564	169	...	117	681
1725	1	105	1,182	13	596	170	...	115	708
1726	--	51	928	73	461	140	...	103	633
1727	--	88	897	28	516	138	...	65	782
1728	239	35	1,349	35	729	154	...	75	659
1729	388	75	1,379	143	621	118	...	69	496
1730	64	146	1,446	170	468	133	...	90	610
1731	14	37	1,029	182	583	123	...	66	557
1732	10	86	1,246	156	513	160	...	76	484
1733	--	67	1,393	82	513	147	...	105	729
1734	--	71	956	71	509	150	...	102	747
1735	3	76	1,255	59	586	141	...	126	609
1736	--	72	1,220	65	498	148	...	101	491
1737	--	80	764	166	636	144	...	99	290
1738	--	88	1,200	105	528	135	...	97	645
1739	--	94	1,320	199	446	101	...	58	500
1740	9	81	981	151	358	118	...	53	395
1741	101	93	1,229	127	530	145	...	26	687
1742	1	44	1,014	179	492	157	...	110	356
1743	--	5	1,242	168	203	149	...	107	580
1744	--	52	1,115	75	251	120	...	25	376

See p. 292 for footnotes

(in £000)

	Corn	Coffee	Sugar	Tea	Wine	Timber(a)	Raw Cotton	Raw Wool	Raw, Thrown and Waste Silk
1745	- -	190	1,095	90	397	141	...	73	568
1746	- -	29	1,098	218	304	155	...	98	344
1747	- -	103	1,060	544	361	125	...	140	705
1748	2	81	1,435	376	369	156	...	107	587
1749	- -	66	1,300	239	521	135	...	142	625
1750	1	75	1,270	484	368	171	...	97	276
1751	1	75	1,147	292	353	152	...	109	583
1752	- -	2	1,161	318	330	168	...	94	678
1753	- -	77	1,551	333	451	166	...	55	732
1754	33	79	1,178	352	356	165	...	81	656
1755	1	139	1,636	401	393	191	...	69	699
1756	31	94	1,513	427	288	181	...	86	460
1757	244	406	755	384	345	157	...	80	757
1758	67	246	1,661	166	383	156	...	83	735
1759	1	207	1,814	287	370	178	...	61	728
1760	- -	257	1,799	969	371	147	...	91	626
1761	1	313	2,126	291	346	183	...	138	1,056
1762	13	541	1,996	645	402	158	...	50	691
1763	138	490	2,422	419	405	214	...	142	984
1764	85	150	1,978	678	393	195	...	114	913
1765	198	193	1,652	691	437	245	...	146	862
1766	144	234	2,052	1,018	444	251	...	124	917
1767	987	242	2,103	933	411	197	...	110	779
1768	623	257	2,203	413	450	210	...	67	825
1769	51	283	2,025	703	445	224	...	122	1,088
1770	66	218	2,436	1,093	401	220	...	141	917
1771	126	345	1,977	896	405	271	...	108	1,027
1772(c)	89	457	2,429	1,279	376	277	160	79	927
1773	317	440	1,963	881	402	250	93	86	511
1774	812	411	2,704	385	445	217	178	125	817
1775	1,175	451	2,664	215	438	256	204	86	791
1776	295	363	2,298	337	434	244	194	117	1,123
1777	684	341	1,837	562	455	249	218	163	969
1778	395	272	1,933	340	407	255	187	28	614
1779	256	187	1,983	251	313	238	138	31	697
1780	144	146	1,813	187	502	225	211	110	956
1781	324	98	1,411	1,142	326	221	159	151	1,167
1782	166	201	1,799	403	240	232	357	61	576
1783	1,104	184	2,061	415	333	360	300	160	1,050
1784	476	303	2,451	767	352	242	349	98	1,169
1785	433	304	2,855	1,337	367	226	543	191	869
1786	403	348	2,072	2,144	371	308	568	94	745
1787	366	213	2,474	2,000	523	340	665	254	933
1788	415	225	2,620	1,788	573	331	589	255	866
1789	386	243	2,488	1,779	590	314	917	164	988
1790	770	390	2,402	1,777	656	376	875	193	928
1791	1,133	317	2,304	2,218	736	366	783	163	991

See p. 292 for footnotes

A. England & Wales 1700–1791   (Principal Imports, *continued*)

(in £000)

	Tobacco	Iron	Flax	Hemp	Linen Yarn	Oils, Seeds and Nuts for Expressing Oil, Gums and Tallow(a)	Hides and Skins	Dyewoods and Dyestuffs(a)
1700	315	182	110	71	46	...	...	...
1701	236	185	52	118	94	...	...	...
1702	272	131	47	93	90	...	...	...
1703	148	197	63	150	62	...	...	...
1704	255	164	65	227	59	...	...	...
1705	...	...	...	...	...	...	...	...
1706	145	185	63	35	66	...	...	...
1707	205	142	44	124	99	...	...	...
1708	212	179	59	152	57	...	...	...
1709	252	131	39	146	98	...	...	...
1710	186	177	75	78	68	...	...	...
1711	264	150	55	131	63	...	...	...
1712	...	...	...	...	...	...	...	...
1713	115	144	71	69	125	...	...	...
1714	274	223	76	48	127	...	...	...
1715	167	176	71	168	104	...	...	...
1716	265	157	90	134	140	...	...	...
1717	278	78	77	147	139	...	...	...
1718	299	181	67	124	123	...	...	...
1719	316	218	78	84	219	...	...	...
1720	324	227	65	117	111	...	...	...
1721	350	162	64	119	140	...	...	...
1722	268	228	89	62	124	...	...	...
1723	275	191	66	93	138	...	...	...
1724	250	215	108	123	134	...	...	...
1725	197	187	88	134	107	...	...	...
1726	303	216	104	141	151	...	...	...
1727	406	165	61	139	101	...	...	...
1728	399	223	103	131	97	...	...	...
1729	375	198	92	134	85	...	...	...
1730	329	224	107	155	102	...	...	...
1731	272	251	127	65	120	...	...	...
1732	290	239	128	120	114	...	...	...
1733	376	249	100	172	136	...	...	...
1734	227	255	141	130	156	...	...	...
1735	376	270	100	127	126	...	...	...
1736	355	245	120	128	33	...	...	...
1737	471	302	181	186	111	...	...	...
1738	376	290	152	151	123	...	...	...
1739	438	289	136	202	145	...	...	...
1740	338	235	122	160	118	...	...	...
1741	558	238	133	194	128	...	...	...
1742	408	204	168	195	105	...	...	...
1743	532	160	99	94	131	...	...	...
1744	389	245	91	207	167	...	...	...
1745	385	298	130	203	(1,210)(b)	...	...	...
1746	376	224	110	181	169	...	...	...
1747	481	202	171	206	190	...	...	...
1748	476	267	209	266	142	...	...	...
1749	419	234	148	144	156	...	...	...

See p. 292 for footnotes

(in £000)

	Tobacco	Iron	Flax	Hemp	Linen Yarn	Oils, Seeds and Nuts for Expressing Oil, Gums and Tallow(a)	Hides and Skins	Dyewoods and Dyestuffs(a)
1750	481	359	218	254	182	...	...	...
1751	431	273	178	116	150	...	...	...
1752	537	258	141	252	203	...	...	...
1753	588	297	206	180	197	...	...	...
1754	553	318	209	204	126	...	...	...
1755	461	303	199	354	205	...	...	...
1756	153	271	179	388	174	...	...	...
1757	396	280	161	220	215	...	...	...
1758	413	325	189	176	180	...	...	...
1759	326	342	295	463	223	...	...	...
1760	491	289	128	58	232	...	...	...
1761	442	433	198	243	231	...	...	...
1762	414	329	179	232	326	...	...	...
1763	611	383	275	235	247	...	...	...
1764	512	448	288	293	191	...	...	...
1765	454	523	211	286	75	...	...	...
1766	407	334	225	176	301	...	...	...
1767	367	379	215	130	273	...	...	...
1768	336	456	255	226	315	...	...	...
1769	318	499	241	290	285	...	...	...
1770	395	476	213	307	391	...	...	...
1771	546	472	331	427	339	...	...	...
1772(d)	484	489	245	230	326	...	...	...
1773	543	473	113	291	229	...	...	...
1774	526	503	208	356	307	...	...	...
1775	526	428	296	254	361	...	...	...
1776	69	508	199	268	371	...	...	...
1777	9	438	259	296	423	...	...	...
1778	20	321	216	291	352	...	...	...
1779	43	426	218	441	383	...	...	...
1780	70	361	255	320	450	...	...	...
1781	55	505	179	356	437	...	...	...
1782	45	392	165	427	404	...	...	...
1783	152	433	205	210	389	...	...	...
1784	378	481	197	302	324	...	...	...
1785	323	400	338	259	360	...	...	...
1786	357	439	277	225	404	...	...	...
1787	298	423	289	297	387	...	...	...
1788	368	465	262	455	380	...	...	...
1789	446	463	140	380	380	...	...	...
1790	443	440	254	468	391	...	...	...
1791	362	513	301	281	368	...	...	...

See p. 292 for footnotes

B. Great Britain 1792–1829 (Principal Imports) (in £000)

	Corn	Coffee	Sugar	Tea	Wine	Timber(a)	Raw Cotton	Raw Wool	Raw, Thrown and Waste Silk
1792	777	482	2,721	1,303	863	543	1,129	269	962
1793	1,410	651	2,955	1,589	524	450	632	110	705
1794	1,088	1,396	3,348	2,365	724	413	780	269	661
1795	728	2,214	2,901	2,693	839	477	859	291	712
1796	2,174	2,302	3,057	617	535	690	1,027	207	684
1797	1,175	2,297	2,885	1,624	371	552	768	280	599
1798	1,215	2,748	3,663	4,487	541	431	1,049	144	801
1799	1,108	2,678	4,637	1,508	803	433	1,430	307	1,123
1800	2,673	3,988	4,301	1,510	732	582	1,848	500	739
1801	3,031	4,608	5,436	2,980	932	682	1,629	417	653
1802	1,401	3,169	5,878	2,736	735	527	2,088	423	756
1803	935	1,498	4,356	3,085	914	626	1,871	317	824
1804	1,201	3,513	4,440	2,668	459	627	2,156	460	981
1805	1,835	2,394	4,337	2,854	795	674	2,081	463	1,010
1806	814	3,608	5,205	2,216	854	511	2,034	382	987
1807	1,124	2,821	4,972	1,260	952	714	2,610	666	743
1808(c)	146	4,899	5,128	3,568	1,122	410	1,471	128	246
1809	1,137	4,711	5,451	2,164	1,174	484	3,117	350	947
1810	2,701	5,330	6,558	1,961	1,130	808	4,555	564	1,175
1811	466	3,765	5,346	2,121	499	799	3,148	271	266
1812	379	(2,574)(e)	(5,033)(e)	1,826	839	578	2,131	412	1,288
1813	...	...	...	...	...	...	...	...	...
1814	1,210	6,448	5,493	2,611	766	338	2,031	745	1,478
1815	396	5,340	5,440	2,560	768	602	3,336	655	1,031
1816	406	3,325(f)	5,141	3,623	445(f)	439	3,152(f)	316	596
1817	2,196	3,520	5,189	3,147	680	457	4,158	617	693
1818	3,914	2,804	5,418	2,007	892	565	5,764	1,017	1,249
1819	1,613	2,451	5,568	2,375	576	652	4,869	692	967
1820	1,388	2,974	5,553	3,015	558	591	4,934	375	1,384
1821	273	2,771	5,739	3,073	594	602	4,347	672	1,342
1822	116	2,672	4,977	2,736	676	609	4,735	696	1,535
1823	41	2,755	5,477	2,905	748	672	6,242	679	1,499
1824	456	3,109	5,733	3,168	725	768	4,865	763	1,875
1825	1,128	3,238	5,056	2,935	1,179	979	7,406	1,437	2,366
1826	2,117	2,569	5,603	2,984	786	738	5,727	478	1,272
1827	1,994	2,945	5,328	3,975	868	658	8,964	884	2,080
1828	1,673	2,503	6,312	3,268	1,016	634	7,483	913	2,745
1829	3,500	2,373	6,280	3,054	790	657	7,289	678	1,800

See p. 292 for footnotes

B. Great Britain 1792–1829 (Principal Imports, *continued*)

(in £000)

	Tobacco	Iron	Flax	Hemp	Linen Yarn	Oils, Seeds and Nuts for Expressing Oil, Gums and Tallow(a)	Hides and Skins	Dyewoods and Dyestuffs(a)
1792	424	577	479	522	465	...	...	...
1793	241	589	528	471	438	...	...	...
1794	313	428	682	495	379	...	...	...
1795	216	489	447	486	415	...	...	...
1796	224	526	640	526	404	...	...	...
1797	255	363	410	415	360	...	...	...
1798	389	510	766	551	441	...	...	...
1799	354	480	828	640	525	...	...	...
1800	357	375	795	507	506	...	...	...
1801	423	331	530	636	423	...	...	...
1802	254	531	530	415	418	...	...	...
1803	346	429	575	620	375	...	...	...
1804	217	222	714	618	463	...	...	...
1805	173	268	914	519	540	992	630	1,316
1806	228	317	699	620	501	1,127	499	798
1807	244	233	830	643	325	941	401	1,355
1808(c)	78	205	403	219	35	644	406	1,155
1809	276	240	968	722	234	941	507	673
1810	499	197	945	752	287	1,195	943	1,762
1811	321	273	431	388	12	852	751	1,322
1812	146	171	675	629	12	(907)(e)	272	1,155
1813	...	...	...	...	...	...	...	...
1814	54	214	948	464	273	1,542	576	1,833
1815	416	208	633	620	251	1,272	581	1,413
1816	290	83	435	313	52	1,036(f)	411	1,609(f)
1817	186	99	818	389	127	1,020	305	1,047
1818	419	162	844	561	256	1,516	564	1,945
1819	259	137	795	402	130	1,323	434	1,011
1820	342	96	763	355	111	1,676	454	1,226
1821	214	99	1,013	205	134	1,514	613	1,400
1822	329	124	1,197	509	229	1,720	769	1,261
1823	328	131	1,083	543	317	1,878	935	2,000
1824	201	139	1,456	465	336	1,812	1,161	1,778
1825	372	227	2,079	491	326	2,333	1,212	2,008
1826	242	127	1,347	396	143	1,931	801	1,734
1827	309	180	1,786	463	182	2,417	738	1,693
1828	231	147	1,737	401	162	2,295	1,055	2,460
1829	205	148	1,846	288	166	2,326	1,219	1,811

See p. 292 for footnotes

C. United Kingdom 1826-1856 (Principal Imports)

(in £000)

	Corn	Coffee	Sugar	Tea	Wine	Timber(*a*)	Raw Cotton	Raw Wool
1826	...	...	6,061	2,984	879	1,026	5,823	478
1827	...	...	5,772	3,975	938	823	9,086	884
1828	...	...	6,822	3,268	1,122	836	7,551	913
1829	3,511	2,396	6,808	3,054	894	896	7,344	679
1830	3,280	2,560	6,857	3,190	792	772	8,786	883
1831	4,726	2,669	7,534	3,165	813	875	9,612	930
1832	899	3,131	6,784	3,171	681	898	9,483	803
1833	654	2,110	6,627	3,206	845	870	10,019	1,095
1834	619	2,588	6,650	3,364	1,117	858	10,897	1,292
1835	334	1,762	6,214	4,433	1,044	1,011	12,071	1,138
1836	746	2,100	6,519	4,880	1,078	1,009	13,352	1,792
1837	1,501	2,262	6,286	4,876	926	1,029	13,483	1,323
1838	2,388	2,470	7,040	4,001	980	1,059	16,656	1,420
1839	6,060	2,505	6,618	3,817	1,132	1,190	12,705	1,602
1840	5,156	4,316	5,698	2,802	1,046	1,228(*h*)	19,500	1,332
1841	5,238	2,686	6,845	3,079	872	1,147	15,948	1,486
1842	5,511	2,577	6,738	4,074	827	1,820	17,244	1,206
1843	2,049	2,419	7,139	4,534	769	1,032	22,279	1,289
1844	3,631	2,898	6,929	5,315	973	1,128	21,239	1,797
1845	2,799	3,138	8,762	5,106	953	1,587	23,950	2,062
1846	6,101	3,234	8,150	5,477	868	1,740	15,376	1,775
1847	16,042	3,450	11,742	5,562	890	1,442	15,377	1,656
1848	9,491	3,553	10,185	4,777	852	1,375	23,405	1,813
1849	14,233	3,956	10,521	5,346	893	1,202	24,901	1,996
1850	12,290	3,172	9,787	5,051	1,038	1,265	21,532	1,953
1851	14,178	3,318	12,276	7,147	1,012	1,653(*i*)	24,582	2,204
1852	11,272	3,427	10,448	6,636	749	1,447	30,326	2,463
1853	14,835	3,471	11,043	7,074	1,246	1,801	28,883	3,114
1854	10,139	4,155	13,764	8,579	1,231	1,879	28,657	2,723
1855	8,003	3,996	11,350	8,326	1,012	1,389	28,588	2,533
1856	12,224	3,552	11,297	8,620	1,074	1,706	32,953	3,011

See p. 292 for footnotes

C. **United Kingdom 1826-1856** (Principal Imports, *continued*)

(in £000)

	Raw, Thrown and Waste Silk	Tobacco	Flax	Hemp	Oils, Seeds and Nuts for Expressing Oil, Gums and Tallow(a)	Hides and Skins	Dyewoods and Dyestuffs(a)
1826	1,272	252	1,377	414	2,001	816	1,791
1827	2,080	331	1,827	485	2,522	750	1,730
1828	2,745	243	1,781	425	2,418	1,071	2,590
1829	1,803	226	1,876	302	2,542(g)	1,240	1,850
1830	2,145	283	1,912	394	2,620	1,335	2,113
1831	2,315	330	1,898	449	2,929	1,225	2,284
1832	1,839	197	2,039	501	2,635	944	2,348
1833	1,729	214	2,313	447	2,891	1,290	2,156
1834	1,920	373	1,680	568	3,206	1,903	2,460
1835	2,131	244	1,532	582	2,637	1,534	2,269
1836	2,651	497	3,210	495	3,176	1,566	3,005
1837	2,109	263	2,034	653	3,174	1,439	2,795
1838	2,026	299	3,354	618	3,183	1,495	2,727
1839	2,163	353	2,481	841	3,593	1,666	3,152
1840	2,298	350	2,625	579	3,320	1,487	3,717
1841	2,032	441	2,811	551	3,188	2,135	3,757
1842	2,565	341	2,418	496	3,010	2,102	3,922
1843	2,302	424	2,988	621	3,517	2,279	3,645
1844	2,631	334	3,277	773	3,550	2,194	4,151
1845	2,677	348	2,965	783	3,951	2,560	4,488
1846	2,500	518	2,356	749	3,276	1,961	4,179
1847	2,245	341	2,168	696	3,144	2,154	4,051
1848	3,376	343	3,027	736	4,004	1,963	4,586
1849	3,023	417	3,730	926	4,078	2,355	5,135
1850	2,914	355	3,776	960	4,317	2,187	5,570
1851	2,687	292	2,457	1,143	4,363	2,439	6,215
1852	3,280	312	2,955	940	3,971	2,060	5,850
1853	4,269	382	4,034	1,173	4,531	2,834	4,874
1854	4,734	305	2,773	1,098	3,711	2,296	5,584
1855	3,992	346	2,716	1,245	4,395	2,260	6,257
1856	4,587	425	3,518	1,380	5,218	2,443	6,224

(a) Only the main items of these commodities are included, since the minor ones were not separately distinguished. The heading *Timber* does not include furniture woods.

(b) See footnote (b) to table 1, p. 281.

(c) From 1808 onwards imports of Irish and Manx products into Great Britain are no longer included. The figures of these imports for 1808 can be deduced by subtracting the statistics in the *Trade and Navigation Accounts* from those given by Mrs Schumpeter. These are shown below, together with the imports from Ireland and the Isle of Man in 1814–18, given in the *Trade and Navigation Accounts*.

Main Items of Irish and Manx Produce Imported into Great Britain

	Corn	Wool	Flax	Hides and Skins	Linen Yarn
1808	338	2	76	...	203
1814	716	9	49	21	83
1815	688	34	47	35	75
1816	660	15	67	39	90
1817	481	17	79	68	122
1818	824	42	64	47	83

(d) The break occasioned by the change in basic source in 1772 from the *Inspector-General's Ledgers* to the *States of Navigation and Commerce* is not of much significance for most goods. Mrs Schumpeter collected figures from the former source for 1775 and 1780 for the sake of comparison with the latter. Only in the cases of iron (in 1775) and of coffee (in 1780) are the differences large—namely, 333 in the *Ledgers* as against 428 in the *States etc.* for iron in 1775, and 259 in the *Ledgers* compared with 187 in the *States etc.* for coffee in 1780.

(e) These figures are incomplete to a minor degree because of the non-publication of the accounts of goods imported from Asia—a result of the Customs House fire of 1813.

(f) From 1816 onwards imports of foreign and colonial produce to Great Britain via Ireland are no longer included. The resulting break is extremely slight, and is confined to these commodities.

(g) Tallow is the only item in this column for which Irish statistics are available before 1829.

(h) Some very minor items, previously separately distinguished, cannot be included any longer.

(i) Firewood is included from this date. The resulting break is very slight.

NOTE

SOURCES: 1697–1807 (except Wool Official Value 1697–1771) —Elizabeth B. Schumpeter, *English Overseas Trade Statistics, 1697–1808* (Oxford University Press, 1960), tables VII, IX, X, XI, XII and XIII; 1808–29—*Trade and Navigation Accounts.* Wool Official Values: 1697–1717 and 1725–37—(Sir Joseph Banks), *The Propriety of Allowing a Qualified Exportation of Wool* (London, 1782), p. 83; 1718–24 and 1738–53—J. Smith,

Memoirs of Wool (2 vols, London, 1757), vol. II, pp. 210 and 280; 1754–71—J. Bischoff, *A Comprehensive History of the Woollen and Worsted Manufacture . . .* (2 vols, London, 1842), vol. II, appendix table VI. The value of British linen exported with bounty from 1743 to 1764 was omitted by Mrs Schumpeter, and is added here, the amounts being taken from J. Horner, *The Linen Trade of Europe* (Belfast, 1920), pp. 231–2.

A. England & Wales 1697–1791

(in £000)

	Coal	Iron and Steel	Non-ferrous Metals and Manufactures	Cotton Yarn and Manufactures	Woollen and Worsted Yarn and Manufactures(a) (Official Values)	Woollen and Worsted Yarn and Manufactures(a) (Mrs. Schumpeter's Values)	Linen Yarn and Manufactures	Silk Yarn and Manufactures
1697	33	98	171	11	1,481	1,871	8	72
1698	59	83	274	22	2,455	3,168	14	96
1699	51	91	253	14	2,446	2,908	12	85
1700	62	86	264	28	2,542	2,989	9	69
1701	68	90	263	24	2,697	3,238	7	69
1702	50	54	186	16	2,193	2,617	7	50
1703	41	75	211	6	2,760	3,359	8	57
1704	46	70	189	7	2,740	3,327	7	58
1705	...	...	...	...	2,508	...	...	...
1706	43	51	247	7	2,902	3,503	7	74
1707	52	71	237	13	2,912	3,595	10	78
1708(b)	54	72	279	11	3,257	3,875	16	93
1709	62	71	216	7	3,342	3,916	17	100
1710	58	72	411	6	3,543	4,271	15	96
1711	61	71	222	4	2,933	3,663	21	82
1712	...	...	...	...	3,514	4,181	...	...
1713	73	97	213	10	2,858	3,391	14	77
1714	94	116	321	10	3,650	4,361	16	92
1715	89	119	359	8	3,359	4,053	19	108
1716	90	103	221	8	3,254	3,765	19	83
1717	79	122	275	10	3,706	4,589	20	108
1718	86	96	208	10	2,674	3,262	30	125
1719	93	108	281	9	2,730	3,132	23	71
1720	83	94	192	16	3,059	3,493	21	71
1721	94	100	214	20	2,903	3,427	25	66
1722	95	125	217	27	3,385	3,919	33	75
1723	97	118	235	27	2,921	3,418	24	80
1724	150	142	248	14	3,068	3,570	24	86
1725	91	151	225	14	3,513	4,000	34	164
1726	111	134	255	11	3,038	3,284	29	88
1727	120	136	289	7	2,877	3,250	32	64
1728	90	157	284	15	3,193	3,521	38	79
1729	115	171	327	10	3,199	3,633	45	76
1730	80	172	308	14	3,468	3,840	40	104
1731	109	168	320	12	3,166	3,477	40	75
1732	119	165	343	13	3,567	4,078	39	84
1733	112	164	324	14	3,427	4,440	33	80
1734	123	161	292	9	3,033	3,762	35	64
1735	125	199	356	17	3,713	4,222	51	81
1736	131	208	324	21	4,008	4,468	58	84
1737	122	213	394	18	4,047	4,628	50	81
1738	122	233	356	13	4,159	4,735	69	85
1739	141	211	358	15	3,218	3,835	72	88
1740	162	265	401	14	3,057	3,827	83	70
1741	128	306	454	20	3,670	4,192	117	103

See p. 295 for footnotes

(in £000)

	Coal	Iron and Steel	Non-ferrous Metals and Manufactures	Cotton Yarn and Manufactures	Woollen and Worsted Yarn and Manufactures(a)		Linen Yarn and Manufactures	Silk Yarn and Manufactures
					Official Values	(Mrs. Schumpeter's Values)		
1742	119	271	447	15	3,359	3,793	111	110
1743	137	266	541	9	3,542	3,967	89	125
1744	123	237	415	10	2,763	3,332	72	81
1745	125	195	376	8	2,947	3,503	76	73
1746	133	397	406	8	3,647	4,519	165	89
1747	114	297	398	8	3,554	4,224	150	101
1748	136	338	373	8	3,514	4,471	174	97
1749	158	439	459	9	4,478	5,666	234	110
1750	148	431	489	20	4,320	5,350	225	115
1751	196	428	450	44	4,207	5,282	217	46
1752	182	394	421	73	3,718	4,609	226	166
1753	186	466	489	115	4,223	5,267	273	163
1754	172	422	458	85	3,625	4,605	265	153
1755	165	417	413	65	3,575	4,506	186	171
1756	164	351	441	101	4,934	5,715	256	159
1757	141	426	412	124	4,758	5,660	333	166
1758	143	433	409	116	4,673	5,734	393	208
1759	135	472	431	113	5,352	6,341	446	306
1760	136	539	494	167	5,453	6,445	557	348
1761	171	466	450	151	4,344	5,927	435	254
1762	172	440	496	183	3,905	4,638	425	242
1763	184	515	576	399	3,971	4,908	414	155
1764	197	613	626	200	5,171	6,216	473	224
1765	283	569	624	249	4,475	5,467	413	213
1766	436	656	580	224	4,629	5,669	477	164
1767	421	738	635	273	4,277	5,242	448	189
1768	331	743	656	213	4,359	5,252	498	179
1769	307	664	681	212	3,897	4,705	413	127
1770	261	742	671	199	4,114	5,064	432	132
1771	339	945	679	311	4,960	6,135	559	250
1772(c)	334	875	646	245	4,570	5,552	625	212
1773	315	746	666	181	3,840	4,723	491	153
1774	358	706	674	258	4,438	5,449	632	203
1775	354	742	680	252	4,298	5,144	427	98
1776	376	582	640	289	3,944	4,742	332	103
1777	387	520	602	246	3,772	4,018	371	140
1778	331	511	512	191	3,237	3,918	271	103
1779	292	398	522	303	2,737	3,485	269	131
1780	313	493	670	306	2,614	3,140	354	220
1781	246	409	473	296	2,843	3,314	234	170
1782	255	594	841	405	3,067	3,562	342	128
1783	384	577	694	746	3,560	4,288	554	231
1784	383	671	669	848	3,556	4,635	473	322
1785	497	656	679	826	3,814	4,504	361	209
1786	460	748	792	872	3,578	4,298	373	174
1787	414	811	757	1,025	3,805	4,598	504	211
1788	554	765	855	1,150	4,064	4,864	629	201
1789	528	869	884	1,089	4,280	5,297	573	203
1790	548	955	1,002	1,456	5,093	6,208	544	223
1791	574	1,259	1,048	1,637	5,408	6,085	605	268

See p. 295 for footnotes

B. Great Britain 1792–1829

(in £000)

	Coal	Iron and Steel	Hard-wares and Cutlery	Machinery	Non-ferrous Metals and Manu-factures	Cotton Yarn and Manu-factures	Woollen and Worsted Yarn and Manufactures(a)		Linen Yarn and Manu-factures	Silk Yarn and Manu-factures
							Official Values	(Mrs. Schum-peter's Values)		
1792	590	1,465	...	...	1,271	1,922	5,154(d)	6,472	959	285
1793	605	1,134	...	...	1,183	1,653	3,547	4,482	818	237
1794	535	1,121	...	...	1,206	2,280	4,126	5,153	1,017	284
1795	452	1,044	...	...	1,208	2,309	5,096	6,296	810	316
1796	522	1,277	...	...	1,243	3,061	5,677	7,001	955	373
1797	453	1,152	...	...	1,011	2,464	4,625	6,775	757	296
1798	455	1,145	...	...	1,079	3,622	6,177	7,559	1,103	225
1799	467	1,596	...	...	1,346	5,859	6,435	7,578	1,115	306
1800	510	1,605	...	...	1,414	5,851	6,918	8,099	808	297
1801	465	1,466	...	...	1,349	6,941	7,321	8,463	1,009	280
1802	521	1,610	...	...	1,557	7,667	6,687	7,808	895	232
1803	511	1,197	...	...	1,185	7,143	5,303	6,070	561	155
1804	514	1,102	...	...	874	8,792	5,694	6,533	727	187
1805	509	1,008	...	...	842	9,653	6,006	6,714	657	200
1806	543	1,260	...	...	693	10,482	6,248	7,109	800	218
1807	471	1,394	...	...	818	10,287	5,373	6,050	766	198
1808	527(e)	1,193	...	...	682	13,411(e)	4,854	5,070	874	129
1809	406	1,392	...	...	700	19,732	5,416	...	1,157	190
1810	510	1,578	...	...	717	19,109	5,774	...	1,018	190
1811	524	1,245	...	...	491	12,261	4,376	...	703	137
1812	617	1,446	...	...	737	16,939	5,085	...	840	166
1813	...	...	...	...	...	...	...	...	...	...
1814(f)	675	1,095	355	...	750	17,869	5,629	...	1,543	219
1815	698	1,127	871	...	1,150	22,555	7,480	...	1,619	258
1816(g)	200	938	740	...	1,212	17,564	5,586	...	1,559	162
1817	214	1,065	439	...	1,343	21,259	5,675	...	1,943	153
1818	230	1,288	580	...	1,231	22,589	6,344	...	2,158	168
1819	201	961	443	...	959	18,282	4,602	...	1,547	127
1820	213	1,025	343	...	1,135	22,532	4,364	...	1,935	118
1821	223	1,059	455	...	1,129	23,542	5,501	...	2,303	136
1822	241	1,140	535	116	1,084	26,911	5,944	...	2,595	141
1823	217	1,204	527	158	999	26,545	5,540	...	2,654	140
1824	235	1,125	612	130	1,042	30,156	6,147	...	3,283	160
1825	266	1,107	630	212	822	29,495	5,929	...	2,710	151
1826	298	1,330	563	229	1,033	25,194	5,042	...	2,057	107
1827	314	1,581	714	202	1,399	33,183	5,980	...	2,808	173
1828	302	1,687	711	262	1,196	33,476	5,720	...	3,118	179
1829	313	1,745	766	250	1,286	37,269	5,362	...	2,857	220

(a) The official values of wool manufactures exported before 1709 appear to have been revised in accordance with the rates adopted in that year, and Mrs Schumpeter's valuations are also constant.

(b) Prior to 1708 the small amounts of exports by sea to Scotland are included.

(c) The break in 1772 resulting from the change in basic source from the *Inspectors-General's Ledgers* to the *States of Navigation and Commerce* is insignificant for the items listed here.

(d) Both series of wool manufactures include woollen hats up to 1791. Thereafter the value of woollen hats has been subtracted from the official values series in order to facilitate comparison with later years. If they were included this series for 1792–1807 would read as follows:

1792 5,520	1796 6,011	1800 7,316	1804 5,951
1793 3,807	1797 4,936	1801 7,665	1805 6,237
1794 4,391	1798 6,499	1802 7,054	1806 6,545
1795 5,363	1799 6,871	1803 5,562	1807 5,594

(e) There are presumed to be slight breaks in these series since the figures in the *Trade and Navigation Accounts* differ to some degree from those given by Mrs Schumpeter.

(f) Prior to 1813 the figures relate to British produce exported, thus excluding Irish linens (so described) which went via Britain. After 1813 the statistics relate to British and Irish produce exported from Britain. The extent of the break this change produced cannot be stated, but except in linens it cannot have been significant.

(g) From 1816 onwards British exports to Ireland and the Isle of Man are no longer included. The extent of the break can be gauged from the following figures for 1816 including the Irish and Manx trade:

	Coal	Iron and Steel	Hardwares and Cutlery	Machinery	Non-ferrous Metals and Manufactures	Cotton Yarns and Manufactures	Woollen and Worsted Yarns and Manufactures	Linen Yarns and Manufactures	Silk Yarns and Manufactures
1816	681	1,074	783	...	1,240	17,771	5,862	1,561	196

Overseas Trade 6. Official Values of Principal Re-Exports—Great Britain 1805–29, and United Kingdom 1826–56

NOTE

SOURCE: *Trade and Navigation Accounts.*

A. Great Britain 1805–29

(in £000)

	Coffee	Sugar	Tea	Raw Cotton	Tobacco	Dyewoods and Dyestuffs(a)
1805	2,472	1,060	600	41	195	473
1806	3,027	688	515	26	162	685
1807	3,143	1,539	610	78	176	503
1808	1,848	784	715	60	124	512
1809	5,845	1,713	704	156	202	850
1810	1,455	1,472	569	344	165	876
1811	1,418	1,215	631	48	150	495
1812	4,383	1,570	664	58	218	519
1813	...	...	...	...	...	...
1814	8,072	2,394	1,548	366	212	1,356
1815	6,074	1,984	891	398	256	1,042
1816(b)	4,977	1,255	141	321	220	1,020
1817	3,363	898	122	663	174	596
1818	3,145	770	155	1,124	92	766
1819	2,671	593	124	1,016	361	767
1820	2,755	981	93	371	288	994
1821	2,598	839	91	1,092	329	700
1822	2,217	613	74	1,279	156	605
1823	1,871	728	75	707	197	720
1824	2,464	918	94	904	159	786
1825	1,709	606	68	1,160	55	954
1826	1,988	752	42	1,663	191	1,020
1827	1,841	645	38	1,518	241	862
1828	1,486	928	39	1,401	203	1,155
1829	1,437	744	38	2,216	138	1,102

See p. 297 for footnotes

B. United Kingdom 1826–56

(in £000)

	Coffee	Sugar	Tea	Raw Cotton	Tobacco	Dyewoods and Dyestuffs(a)
1826	1,988	752	42	1,663	194	1,020
1827	1,841	645	38	1,518	247	862
1828	1,486	928	39	1,401	209	1,155
1829	1,439	744	38	2,216	140	1,102
1830	1,255	779	36	718	186	1,104
1831	1,405	1,050	35	1,626	176	1,115
1832	1,608	907	40	1,390	131	1,252
1833	959	914	38	1,255	156	970
1834	953	1,490	177	1,515	248	1,156
1835	834	927	324	2,200	254	1,284
1836	667	695	640	2,708	241	1,267
1837	503	1,115	707	2,853	246	1,152
1838	706	936	387	2,094	232	1,444
1839	797	964	498	2,016	197	1,502
1840	794	573	358	2,617	251	1,928
1841	892	1,058	673	2,643	205	2,006
1842	594	1,004	856	2,928	243	1,732
1843	793	1,434	687	2,474	178	1,560
1844	394	983	725	3,036	166	2,102
1845	1,199	1,932	608	2,740	190	1,769
1846	733	683	530	4,209	270	1,974
1847	835	2,156	708	4,785	241	2,433
1848	1,503	1,116	533	4,725	210	2,625
1849	2,178	1,933	727	6,312	311	3,313
1850	761	1,178	752	6,539	165	2,491
1851	1,420	919	679	7,144	245	3,230
1852	809	1,117	920	7,138	190	2,613
1853	1,665	777	725	9,479	172	2,720
1854	2,036	1,165	1,298	7,870	212	2,947
1855	1,798	687	2,044	7,934	164	3,173
1856	1,725	2,024	858	9,357	197	3,206

(a) Includes only the principal items, which are alone separately listed in the source. These items are fewer in number than those listed as imports.

b) From 1816 onwards re-exports to Ireland and the Isle of Man are no longer included. In that year they were as follows:

	Coffee	Sugar	Tea	Cotton	Tobacco	Dyewoods & Dyestuffs
1816	7	340	406	23	39	30

Overseas Trade 7. Values at Current Prices of Principal Imports— United Kingdom 1854–1938

NOTE

SOURCE: *Annual Statement of Trade.*

A. Computed Value, 1854–70

(in £000,000)

	Grain and Flour(a)	Coffee	Sugar Refined	Sugar Un-refined	Tea	Wine	Meat and Animals (b)	Butter and Margar-ine	Timber (c)	Raw Cotton (d)	Raw Wool(e)	Silk Yarn and Goods	Tobacco
1854	21·8	1·6	0·6	9·6	5·5	3·6	3·3	2·2	11·8	20·2	6·5	3·5	1·3
1855	17·5	1·7	0·7	9·6	5·2	3·1	3·2	2·1	8·5	20·8	6·5	3·1	1·6
1856	23·0	1·5	0·3	11·4	5·2	3·7	3·3	1·8	10·2	26·4	8·7	3·8	2·2
1857	19·4	1·7	0·8	14·7	4·7	4·1	3·5(b)	2·1	9·8(c)	29·3	9·7	3·2	2·2
1858	20·2	1·7	0·8	12·3	5·2	2·0	2·4	1·8	8·0	30·1	9·0	2·6	2·5
1859	18·0	2·0	0·5	11·8	5·8	2·8	2·8	2·1	10·3	34·6	9·9	3·3	1·8
1860	31·7	2·5	0·6	11·8	6·9	4·2	4·0	4·1	11·4	35·8	11·2	3·7	1·8
1861	34·9	2·6	0·4	12·2	6·9	3·9	4·2	4·9	11·9	38·7	10·1	6·1	2·2
1862	37·8	3·3	0·5	10·9	9·2	3·6	5·2	4·9	11·5	31·1	12·2	6·7	2·4
1863	26·0	4·2	0·5	11·5	10·7	4·5	6·2	4·5	12·6	56·3	12·4	6·7	3·0
1864	19·9	3·6	1·7	14·4	9·4	5·0	7·5	5·7	13·1	78·2	16·1	8·0	3·4
1865	20·7	4·6	1·3	11·3	10·0	3·9	8·5	5·9	14·0	66·0	15·5	8·6	3·3
1866	30·1	4·1	1·0	10·8	11·2	4·7	8·1	6·0	12·8	77·5	18·1	9·6	2·6
1867	41·4	4·4	1·3	11·5	10·1	4·8	6·9	5·9	11·1	52·0	16·6	9·5	2·4
1868	39·4	4·9	1·2	13·3	12·4	5·4	5·6	6·3	12·1	55·2	15·5	11·8	2·3
1869	37·4	4·9	1·8	13·5	10·3	5·3	8·9	6·9	12·1	56·8	15·1	12·5	2·3
1870	34·2	4·9	2·7	14·4	10·1	4·8	7·8	6·8	13·3	53·5	16·2	15·8	2·4

B. Declared Value, 1871–1938

	Grain and Flour(a)	Coffee	Sugar Refined	Sugar Un-refined	Tea	Wine	Meat and Animals (b)	Butter and Margar-ine	Timber (c)	Raw Cotton (d)	Raw Wool(e)	Silk Yarn and Goods	Tobacco
1871	42·7	5·4	3·0	15·2	11·6	7·1	10·4	6·9	12·3	55·9	18·4	8·6	3·3
1872	51·2	5·3	3·1	18·0	12·9	7·7	10·7	6·0	14·2	53·4	19·1	9·5	2·7
1873	51·7	7·2	3·8	17·1	11·4	8·3	13·8	7·0	19·1	54·7	20·0	10·3	3·9
1874	51·1	7·1	4·2	15·8	11·5	6·9	13·4	9·1	22·3	50·7	21·7	12·1	4·0
1875	53·1	7·5	4·3	17·2	13·8	6·8	16·4	8·5	15·8	46·3	24·0	12·4	3·0
1876	51·8	6·4	4·1	16·3	12·7	7·0	18·9	9·7	19·6	40·2	24·3	12·0	4·0
1877	63·5	7·8	5·8	21·4	12·5	7·1	17·3	9·5	20·7	35·4	25·3	13·0	3·5
1878	59·1	5·9	4·8	16·0	13·0	6·0	20·5	10·0	14·4	33·5	23·9	12·8	3·7
1879	61·3	7·1	4·1	17·9	11·3	5·4	21·0	10·4	11·2	36·2	24·2	13·0	2·0
1880	62·9	6·9	4·4	18·5	11·6	6·5	26·9	12·1	17·3	42·8	27·2	13·6	2·9
1881	60·9	4·8	4·0	20·3	11·2	5·7	25·1	10·9	15·7	43·8	26·8	11·9	2·6
1882	63·5	5·2	4·0	20·9	11·0	5·5	22·2	11·4	17·9	46·7	25·8	11·5	2·6
1883	67·6	4·9	4·5	20·5	11·5	5·5	28·7	11·8	18·0	45·0	25·7	10·8	2·9
1884	48·1	3·8	4·5	15·2	10·5	5·3	26·1	12·5	15·8	44·5	27·2	11·3	2·7
1885	53·3	3·3	4·8	13·5	10·7	5·1	24·6	11·6	16·0	36·5	21·9	10·5	3·8
1886	43·5	3·3	5·3	10·5	11·3	5·1	21·6	11·1	13·0(c)	38·1	23·2	10·9	3·7
1887	48·3	4·2	5·5	11·0	9·8	5·5	21·2	11·9	12·5	40·2	25·1	10·8	3·4
1888	51·3	3·6	6·0	12·1	10·2	5·4	23·3	12·2	15·2	40·0	26·7	10·9	2·8
1889	51·2	4·3	8·8	13·6	10·0	5·9	29·3	13·9	20·4	45·6	29·3	12·3	3·9
1890	53·5	4·0	8·1	9·9	9·9	5·9	32·3	13·7	17·8	42·8	27·9	11·9	3·5
1891	62·0	3·4	9·4	10·5	10·7	6·0	29·9(b)	15·1	15·6	46·1	28·8	11·7	3·4
1892	58·7	3·9	9·1	10·7	10·0	6·0	32·3	15·7	17·8	37·9	27·6	11·9	3·5
1893	51·2	4·0	10·6	11·5	10 1	5·3	29·3	16·4	16·1	30·7	25·4	12·0	3·5
1894	48·2	3·5	10·8	8·3	9 8	5·0	32·3	16·5	17·8	32·9	25·7	13·1	3·5
1895	49·7	3·8	9·4	8·3	10·2	5·4	33·3	16·8	16·4	30·4	27·0	15·6	3·4

See p. 301 for footnotes

A. Computed Values 1854–70 (Principal Imports, *continued*)

(in £000,000)

	Oils, Oil-seed, Gums, Resins, Tallow etc.(f)	Iron and Steel(g)	Flax(h)	Hemp(i)	Jute	Un-dressed Hides, Skins, and Furs	Dye-woods and Dye-stuffs	Rubber	Non-ferrous Metals and Manu-factures	Paper-making Materials	Petrol-eum	Mach-inery
1854	10·4	0·6	3·4	2·4		2·3	3·8	0·3	1·6	0·3		
1855	12·0	0·6	3·3	1·5	0·4	2·5	3·8	0·3	2·1	0·2		
1856	12·6	0·8	3·7	1·3	0·6	3·6	5·0	0·2	1·7	0·2		
1857	13·8(j)	0·7	3·5	1·3	0·6	5·1(j)	5·5(j)	0·1	2·1(j)	0·3		
1858	12·4	0·3	3·0	1·2	0·6	3·2	4·9	0·1	2·0	0·2		
1859	13·0	0·6	3·8	1·5	0·8	4·2	4·9	0·2	3·0	0·3		
1860	14·9	0·7	3·9	1·2	0·7	4·0	5·5	0·5	2·9	0·3		
1861	13·0	0·6	3·4	1·2	0·7	3·4	5·7	0·4	3·2	0·3		
1862	12·3	0·8	5·2	1·7	0·9	3·6	5·2	0·5	2·9	0·4		
1863	15·0	0·8	4·3	1·9	1·5	3·8	5·3	0·5	3·0	0·6		
1864	14·0	1·0	5·4	1·7	2·2	3·5	5·0	0·5	4·9	0·7		
1865	15·8	1·0	5·4	1·7	1·8	3·4	4·7	0·5	4·3	0·7		
1866	15·8	1·3	4·5	1·7	1·5	4·0	5·5	0·7	4·0	0·8		
1867	14·8	1·3	4·2	1·6	1·4	3·7	5·8	0·7	4·6	0·6		
1868	16·6	1·1	5·2	2·1	1·9	4·2	7·2	1·2	5·1	0·9		
1869	15·8	1·1	4·3	1·9	2·1	4·0	6·4	1·1	4·9	0·9		
1870	17·7	1·3	6·0	2·0	2·3	6·2	6·2	1·6	4·7	1·2		

B. Declared Values 1871–1938

	Oils, Oil-seed, Gums, Resins, Tallow etc.(f)	Iron and Steel(g)	Flax(h)	Hemp(i)	Jute	Un-dressed Hides, Skins, and Furs	Dye-woods and Dye-stuffs	Rubber	Non-ferrous Metals and Manu-factures	Paper-making Materials	Petrol-eum	Mach-inery
1871	18·6(f)	1·8(g)	5·9	2·3	3·7	6·1(k)	7·0	1·7	5·9(l)	1·8	0·6(f)	
1872	17·8	2·9	5·1	2·1	4·0	7·8(k)	6·8	1·8	8·4	1·3	0·4	
1873	17·6	2·7	5·4	2·3	3·6	7·5(k)	6·3	1·7	7·1	1·3	1·0	
1874	16·7	2·9	5·6	2·2	3·6	7·2(k)	6·0	1·3	7·5	1·4	1·0	
1875	18·4	3·2	4·5	2·2	2·6	7·0(k)	5·9	1·6	8·6	1·5	0·8	
1876	18·3	2·9	3·6	1·9	2·8	5·7	6·0	1·5	7·7	1·4	1·4	
1877	18·5	2·8	5·2	2·0	2·9	5·7	5·4	1·5	7·7	1·7	1·8	
1878	16·4	3·0	3·6	1·9	3·2	5·4	5·2	1·3	7·1	1·4	1·2	
1879	15·4	2·8	3·7	1·6	3·3	5·1	5·1	1·6	7·5	1·6	1·4	
1880	16·9	4·0	4·2	1·8	4·0	6·7	5·5	2·4	7·6	2·1	1·3	
1881	16·4	4·1	3·5	2·1	4·0	5·9	5·8	2·3	7·4	2·0	2·0	
1882	17·5	4·2	3·7	2·1	4·3	6·7	6·2	2·8	8·3	2·1	1·7	
1883	18·3	4·4	3·0	2·4	4·5	6·7	6·3	3·7	8·1	2·3	2·2	
1884	16·6	4·1	3·1	2·1	3·6	7·2	6·4	2·3	7·7	2·1	1·7	
1885	15·9	3·9	3·3	2·2	3·2	6·8	5·7	2·0	7·5	2·3	2·3	
1886	13·7	3·5	2·5	1·7	3·0	6·5	5·4	2·2	7·6	2·2	2·1	
1887	13·4	3·6	2·8	2·1	3·7	6·1	5·1	2·7	7·8	2·3	2·1	
1888	14·6	4·0	3·1	2·8	3·9	6·0	5·2	2·6	11·4	2·8	2·6	
1889	15·8	4·4	3·2	3·3	5·4	6·8	5·5	2·6	9·4	2·5	2·6	
1890	14·4	4·5	3·0	2·9	4·9	6·0	5·3	3·3	10·3	2·5	2·4	
1891	15·9	4·4	2·9	3·1	4·2	6·4	4·4	3·4	10·1	2·5	2·7	
1892	15·0	4·0	2·9	2·4	3·9	6·1	4·6	3·0	9·0	2·4	2·4	
1893	15·9	3·8	2·6	2·2	3·7	6·6	4·5	3·3	9·1	2·5	2·5	
1894	16·2	4·0	2·6	2·0	4·6	6·1	4·4	3·3	8·8	2·7	2·5	
1895	15·1	4·4	3·3	2·2	4·4	7·4	4·8	3·8	8·6	2·8	3·4	
1896	15·5	5·7	3·2	1·9	4·2	6·0	4·9	5·0	10·0	2·8	3·7	
1897	14·0	4·5(g)	3·3	1·8	3·9	6·7	4·1	4·6	9·9	3·2	3·3	2·4
1898	14·2	5·0	3·0	2·3	3·8	6·9	3·6	6·2	11·2	3·0	3·7	3·1
1899	15·7	5·6	3·1	2·6	3·7	7·5	3·8	5·9	14·7	3·1	4·6	3·7
1900	18·0	7·3	2·6	3·4	4·1	8·5	3·3	7·0	17·4	3·7	5·6	3·5

See p. 301 for footnotes

(in £000,000)

	Grain and Flour(a)	Coffee	Sugar		Tea	Wine	Meat and Animals (b)	Butter and Margarine	Timber (c)	Raw Cotton (d)	Raw Wool(e)	Silk Yarn and Goods	Tobacco
			Refined	Un-refined									
1896	52·8	3·6	10·0	8·3	10·6	5·9	35·9	17·8	20·3	36·3	25·9	17·1	4·4
1897	53·6	3·6	9·7	6·2	10·4	6·4	39·5	18·4	24·6	32·2	25·3	17·2	4·1
1898	62·9	3·6	10·4	7·1	10·3	6·6	41·0	18·3	22·1	34·1	24·4	16·9	3·9
1899	58·1	3·3	11·2	6·9	10·6	5·6	42·9	19·8	24·2	27·7	24·6	16·4	5·5
1900	58·9	2·5	12·3	6·9	10·7	5·2	46·8	19·9	27·9	41·0	22·7	14·9	4·8
1901	61·2	3·3	12·9	6·4	9·4	4·9	50·4	21·9	24·6	42·0	22·3	13·6	4·7
1902	62·5	2·6	9·7	5·0	8·8	4·9	48·1	23·1	25·2	41·1	20·9	14·1	5·8
1903	66·2	3·1	10·0	5·5	9·6	4·7	50·4	23·1	27·1	44·8	21·5	13·2	4·2
1904	65·2	3·3	10·8	7·5	9·4	3·8	48·7	23·6	23·6	54·7	21·4	13·4	4·5
1905	65·4	2·6	10·9	8·6	9·3	4·1	49·4	24·3	23·3	52·2	24·8	13·1	3·7
1906	63·9	2·0	10·5	6·8	9·9	4·2	52·0	26·2	27·5	55·8	28·4	13·5	4·7
1907	70·8	2·4	11·8	7·3	10·7	4·0	51·9	24·6	27·1	70·5	34·0	13·3	4·2
1908	68·3	2·2	12·2	7·8	10·7	3·5	49·4	26·2	24·3	55·8	29·1	12·3	5·2
1909	79·0	2·1	12·6	9·1	11·6	3·7	47·6	24·7	23·6	60·3	33·1	12·5	5·0
1910	72·6	2·3	13·1	11·4	11·4	4·2	48·9	27·4	26·2	71·7	35·4	13·3	4·6
1911	71·7	2·5	14·4	12·2	13·0	4·2	49·7	27·1	25·9	71·2	34·5	13·2	5·3
1912	83·4	2·5	13·4	11·8	13·1	4·3	49·1	27·9	28·4	80·2	34·4	14·0	6·4
1913	80·9	2·9	12·4	10·7	13·8	4·1	56·7	28·0	33·8	70·6	35·6	14·7	8·0
1914	75·0	3·5	15·6	16·5	14·2	3·6	63·2	28·0	25·3	55·4	32·4	13·1	7·5
1915	103·7	4·9	12·7	19·1	19·6	2·9	86·8	32·8	32·8	64·7	43·2	14·6	8·6
1916	123·0	4·7	12·5	24·9	17·7	3·5	94·1	27·9	40·2	84·7	38·8	13·1	7·4
1917	161·7	1·9	6·4	30·3	14·7	2·4	102·4	26·7	25·6	110·6	51·1	11·4	3·9
1918	140·1	0·7	0·8	33·6	29·0	7·3	173·7	21·3	29·2	150·3	38·7	17·2	18·2
1919	144·0	6·0	19·2	34·7	33·1	18·2	175·4	22·1	72·3	190·2	100·5	22·9	41·7
1920	223·3	4·5	7·7	65·5	27·0	12·8	141·5	30·0	82·1	256·7	90·6	36·9	34·9
1921	130·2	2·4	14·9	20·4	23·1	5·3	132·9	47·6	30·0	73·3	41·9	18·9	22·8
1922	99·9	4·4	11·0	22·4	26·0	5·6	103·3	41·2	37·3	87·3	59·9	20·9	18·6
1923	93·1	2·1	11·6	29·6	33·5	5·7	111·4	48·7	47·7	93·4	47·9	22·5	16·4
1924	116·4	3·3	15·9	28·0	40·4	6·9	106·6	54·4	51·1	121·6	71·9	24·9	17·3
1925	107·1	4·7	13·7	19·5	37·5	7·0	122·4	58·1	46·5	125·8	73·6	22·6	17·0
1926	95·9	3·4	11·2	14·8	38·6	7·3	114·3	53·0	39·3	84·4	63·9	16·7	17·7
1927	107·9	4·8	8·7	18·4	41·6	7·0	103·5	52·3	49·7	67·8	61·0	16·0	19·2
1928	94·7	4·5	3·6	23·4	35·7	5·7	109·3	55·6	42·6	80·8	61·6	14·3	17·5
1929	93·3	3·8	0·7	22·7	37·6	6·2	113·6	57·4	45·8	77·4	61·1	13·0	18·5
1930	70·6	4·8	0·6	16·4	34·1	5·3	111·3	49·3	42·8	45·0	43·5	11·0	15·7
1931	53·9	4·0	0·5	14·3	29·6	5·2	93·7	48·2	29·1	27·2	33·5	8·2	11·4
1932	56·0	3·5	0·3	18·0	25·4	3·7	81·0	41·3	25·6	31·2	32·9	3·7	10·1
1933	53·6	2·9	0·3	15·0	24·9	4·7	77·5	34·4	29·9	36·8	36·1	3·1	11·8
1934	52·8	2·5	0·4	13·3	27·9	5·0	81·5	33·3	39·5	36·1	37·6	3·0	17·0
1935	55·1	1·8	0·4	12·2	25·9	5·5	77·8	39·4	35·5	37·3	36·0	3·0	17·6
1936	67·7	1·6	0·2	14·8	26·4	6·3	78·8	44·5	43·5	45·8	44·6	2·4	18·5
1937	89·3	1·3	0·4	20·0	29·6	6·1	87·1	47·5	61·8	48·7	50·8	2·5	18·0
1938	72·6	1·4	0·3	18·9	30·8	5·3	90·7	51·0	42·9	29·6	41·6	2·0	23·3

See p. 301 for footnotes

(in £000,000)

	Oils, Oil-seed, Gums, Resins, Tallow etc.(f)	Iron and Steel(g)	Flax(h)	Hemp(i)	Jute	Un-dressed Hides, Skins, and Furs	Dye-woods and Dye-stuffs	Rubber	Non-ferrous Metals and Manu-factures	Paper-making Materials	Petrol-eum	Mach-inery
1901	18·1	7·6	3·2	4·1	4·3	8·0	3·7	5·8	15·7	3·5	5·1	4·0
1902	20·0	7·9	3·0	3·9	5·3	8·0	3·8	5·2	16·0	3·4	5·2	4·8
1903	19·2	8·7	3·8	3·5	3·2	7·4	3·6	6·7	15·3	3·4	5·3	4·5
1904	19·5	8·2	3·3	4·1	4·2	6·6	3·7	7·7	18·0	3·6	5·8	4·3
1905	18·2	8·6	3·7	3·8	5·7	8·1	3·5	9·6	18·7	3·8	5·4	4·5
1906	19·8	8·4	3·7	3·7	8·3	10·7	3·6	10·0	23·8	3·9	5·8	5·1
1907	24·6	7·2(g)	4·1	4·2	8·2	10·8	4·1	10·8	24·2	4·4	6·1	5·3
1908	21·9	7·7	3·5	3·0	5·9	9·4	3·9	8·4	21·6	4·6	6·7	4·6
1909	25·0	8·0	3·6	2·7	4·6	11·6	4·1	14·1	21·5	4·5	6·1	4·4
1910	31·9	9·1	3·7	3·1	4·7	12·9	4·1	26·1	21·5	5·0	5·7	4·5
1911	29·4	11·1	3·9	3·3	6·0	11·1	3·9	18·3	24·2	4·8	5·7	5·8
1912	30·1	13·0	5·0	3·8	8·3	13·7	4·0	21·6	27·7	5·6	7·4	6·8
1913	30·7	15·2	4·9	4·3	9·2	15·1	4·4	20·5	29·3	5·8	10·9	7·3
1914	28·6	10·9	4·3	3·5	6·4	12·7	4·0	15·8	27·2	6·0	12·8	6·7
1915	36·4	10·8	6·1	4·8	8·7	14·0	6·6	19·7	39·9	6·2	13·3	8·8
1916	43·6	11·2	7·7	6·8	7·6	13·8	9·9	23·1	35·6	8·1	19·8	8·0
1917	41·9	10·8	12·8	8·7	4·4	18·4	8·1	23·9	41·2	10·4	33·9	8·9
1918	52·5	9·7	5·0	13·4	9·1	29·5	8·4	12·1	44·8	13·2	63·9	10·7
1919	91·4	11·6	3·1	8·9	13·6	29·5	8·3	26·5	33·6	16·5	36·3	15·0(m)
1920	81·9	29·0	8·1	11·5	13·1	32·0	13·9	26·7	39·1	33·3	66·6	20·0
1921	36·4	22·8	3·4	2·7	3·8	10·9	3·5	10·5	18·4	13·8	54·5	10·8
1922	33·9	10·4	3·8	2·8	4·3	14·9	3·8	7·3	18·2	9·6	39·1	8·3(m)
1923	39·2	13·8	3·1	3·2	3·8	16·9	3·4	12·3	25·6	11·5	35·0	9·5
1924	44·2	22·4	5·5	4·3	5·5	21·3	3·8	9·6	32·7	11·6	41·4	10·9
1925	46·6	24·0	4·4	4·7	8·6	21·8	3·1	29·4	38·1	11·1	39·4	12·3
1926	36·3	29·5	3·8	3·5	5·8	19·5	3·0	33·5	37·1	11·9	46·8	12·9
1927	35·5	34·0	3·9	4·1	7·5	23·0	3·5	25·4	32·6	12·8	43·3	16·0
1928	38·8	24·1	3·5	3·5	6·3	26·1	3·7	11·8	33·0	10·2	49·2	16·8
1929	39·2	24·7	4·1	3·5	6·6	20·4	2·9	17·3	37·0	13·2	43·4	19·3
1930	29·4	23·3	3·2	2·7	3·3	16·1	3·2	10·7	29·4	12·1	46·4	18·0
1931	22·0	19·6	2·0	1·9	2·5	11·7	3·1	4·5	21·4	10·0	29·0	15·4
1932	19·2	8·7	2·3	1·3	2·5	12·1	2·5	2·4	14·7	9·8	31·2	10·5
1933	17·7	6·1	2·6	1·5	2·6	14·3	2·5	3·0	15·7	9·3	30·2	8·6
1934	17·4	9·2	3·2	1·8	2·9	14·7	2·9	12·0	22·0	11·1	31·8	11·2
1935	21·6	8·7	4·3	1·9	2·9	14·7	2·8	10·1	28·0	10·8	33·6	13·1
1936	24·5	11·7	4·5	2·6	3·3	19·5	3·1	4·4	33·2	11·9	37·0	18·0(m)
1937	30·2	19·8	4·5	3·2	3·7	25·2	3·3	12·2	55·7	15·9	47·8	24·2
1938	25·4	14·5	4·3	2·1	3·7	18·2	2·8	11·5	40·8	16·0	46·0	21·8

(a) Corresponds to 'Corn' in the eighteenth-century table. It does not include rice, sago, starch, etc.

(b) This does not include horses, poultry, or game. Prior to 1857 it consists only of beef, bacon, ham, pork, and live animals. 'Other meat', included for the first time in 1857, was for some years unimportant. Live pigs were included for the first time in 1891, this break also being negligible.

(c) This includes furniture hardwoods, but not dyewoods. Certain minor items, making a difference of 0·1 in 1857, were not included until that year. Joinery, door frames, etc., which had amounted to 0·3 in 1885, were not included from 1886 onwards.

(d) This includes unmanufactured waste throughout.

(e) This includes woollen rags intended for use as raw material for cloth. It does not include camel or goat hair.

(f) This covers all types of oil (except, from 1871, petroleum), all nuts and seeds used for expressing oil, all types of gum, rosin, tallow and stearine.

(g) Prior to 1871 this includes only bar iron and iron and steel manufactures, though the difference made by the addition of other iron and steel was negligible, being computed at 0·3 in 1870. From 1871 onwards all iron and steel is included under the heading, and for the period 1871–96 machinery is also included. A further, very small break in the series was occasioned by the inclusion of old rails from 1907 onwards.

(h) This includes tow and codilla, whether of hemp or flax.

(i) This covers other fibres used for similar purposes.

(j) Prior to 1857 certain minor items were not shown by value and cannot therefore be included.

(k) A small amount of dressed skins was included in these years.

(l) Various minor metals, amounting to 0·1 in 1871, were included from that year.

(m) There were some minor transfers from this heading in 1919, amounting to less than 0·1 in that year, and some small additions in 1922 and 1935, amounting to 0·1 on each occasion.

Overseas Trade 8. Values at Current Prices of Principal Domestic Exports—Great Britain 1814–29, and—United Kingdom 1826–1938

NOTE
SOURCE: *Annual Statement of Trade.*

(in £000,000)

A. Great Britain 1814–29 (excluding exports to Ireland)

	Coal(a)	Iron and Steel(b)	Hard-wares and Cutlery	Mach-inery	Non-ferrous Metals and Manufac-tures(d)	Cotton Goods(e)	Wool Goods(e)	Linen Goods(e)	Silk Goods(e)	Hats, Haber-dashery, Apparel etc.(j)	Leather Manu-factures(k)	Chemi-cals(l)	Electri-cal Goods	Vehicles and Aircraft(n)	New Ships and Boats
1814	0·1	1·0	0·8	...	1·0	20·0	6·4	1·7	0·5	...	0·5	...	...	...	...
1815	0·1	1·1	2·2	...	1·5	20·6	9·3	1·8	0·6	...	0·6	...	...	...	...
1816	0·1	1·0	1·9	...	1·5	15·6	7·8	1·5	0·5	...	0·5	...	...	...	...
1817	0·1	1·1	1·1	...	1·6	16·0	7·2	1·7	0·4	...	0·5	...	...	...	...
1818	0·1	1·3	1·6	...	1·6	18·8	8·1	2·0	0·5	...	0·5	...	...	...	...
1819	0·1	0·9	1·2	...	1·3	14·7	6·0	1·4	0·4	...	0·5	...	...	...	...
1820	0·1	0·9	0·8	...	1·4	16·5	5·6	1·7	0·4	...	0·4	...	...	...	...
1821	0·1	0·9	1·1	...	1·3	16·1	6·5	2·0	0·4	...	0·4	...	...	...	...
1822	0·1	0·8	1·1	0·1	1·2	17·2	6·5	2·2	0·4	0·9	0·4	...	...	...	...
1823	0·1	0·9	1·1	0·2	1·2	16·3	5·6	2·1	0·4	0·9	0·4	...	...	...	...
1824	0·1	0·9	1·2	0·1	1·2	18·4	6·0	2·4	0·4	1·0	0·4	...	...	...	...
1825	0·1	1·0	1·4	0·2	1·1	18·3	6·2	2·1	0·3	1·2	0·4	...	...	...	...
1826	0·1	1·1	1·2	0·2	1·2	14·0	5·0	1·5	0·2	0·9	0·4	...	...	...	...
1827	0·2	1·2	1·4	0·2	1·5	17·5	5·3	1·9	0·2	1·1	0·4	...	...	...	...
1828	0·1	1·2	1·4	0·3	1·3	17·1	5·1	2·0	0·3	1·1	0·4	...	...	...	...
1829	0·1	1·2	1·4	0·3	1·3	17·4	4·7	1·8	0·3	1·0	0·3	...	...	...	...

B. United Kingdom 1826–1938

	Coal(a)	Iron and Steel(b)	Hard-wares and Cutlery	Mach-inery	Non-ferrous Metals and Manufac-tures(d)	Cotton Goods(e)	Wool Goods(e)	Linen Goods(e)	Silk Goods(e)	Hats, Haber-dashery, Apparel etc.(j)	Leather Manu-factures(k)	Chemi-cals(l)	Electri-cal Goods	Vehicles and Aircraft(n)	New Ships and Boats
1826	...	...	...	...	...	14·1	5·0	1·7	...	...	0·4	...	...	...	...
1827	...	...	...	...	...	17·6	5·3	2·1	...	...	0·4	...	...	...	...
1828	...	...	...	...	...	17·2	5·1	2·2	...	...	0·4	...	...	...	...
1829	0·1	1·2	1·4	0·3	1·3	17·5	4·7	1·9	0·3	1·0	0·4	...	...	...	...
1830	0·2	1·1	1·4	0·2	1·3	19·4	4·9	2·1	0·5	1·0	0·3	...	...	...	...
1831	0·2	1·1	1·6	0·1	1·2	17·3	5·4	2·5	0·6	1·0	0·3	...	...	...	...
1832	0·2	1·2	1·4	0·1	1·4	17·4	5·5	1·8	0·5	0·9	0·3	...	...	...	...
1833	0·2	1·4	1·5	0·1	1·4	18·5	6·5	2·2	0·7	0·9	0·3	...	...	...	...
1834	0·2	1·4	1·5	0·2	1·5	20·5	6·0	2·6	0·6	0·9	0·3	...	...	...	...
1835	0·2	1·6	1·8	0·3	1·7	22·1	7·2	3·2	1·0	1·2	0·4	...	...	...	...

See p. 306 for footnotes

Overseas Trade 8. *continued*

	Coal(a)	Iron and Steel(b)	Hard-wares and Cutlery	Mach-inery	Non-ferrous Metals and Manufac-tures(d)	Cotton Goods(e)	Wool Goods(e)	Linen Goods(e)	Silk Goods(e)	Hats, Haber-dashery, Apparel etc(j)	Leather Manu-factures (k)	Chemi-cals(l)	Electri-cal Goods	Vehicles and Aircraft (n)	New Ships and Boats
1836	0·3	2·3	2·3	0·3	1·7	24·6	8·0	3·6	0·9	1·5	0·4	...	...	...	...
1837	0·4	2·0	1·5	0·5	1·8	20·6	5·0	2·6	0·5	1·1	0·3	...	...	...	...
1838	0·5	2·5	1·5	0·6	1·9	24·1	6·2	3·6	0·8	1·3	0·4	...	...	...	...
1839	0·5	2·7	1·8	0·7	2·0	24·5	6·7	4·2	0·9	1·5	0·5	...	...	...	...
1840	0·6	2·9(b)	1·6	0·6	1·8(d)	24·7	5·8	4·1	0·8	1·4	0·4(k)	0·4	...	...	...
1841	0·7	3·2	1·8	0·6	1·9	23·5	6·3	4·3	0·8	1·3	0·4	0·3	...	...	...
1842	0·7	2·8	1·6	0·6	2·4	21·7	5·8	3·4	0·6	1·3	0·3	0·4	...	...	...
1843	0·7	3·0	1·9	0·7	2·0	23·4	7·5	3·7	0·7	1·4	0·4	0·5	...	...	...
1844	0·7	3·6	2·4	0·8	2·1	25·8	9·2	4·1	0·7	1·6	0·4	0·5	...	...	...
1845	1·0	4·1	2·5	0·9	2·0	26·1	8·8	4·1	0·8	1·7	0·4	0·6	...	...	...
1846	1·0	4·8	2·4	1·1	1·9	25·6	7·2	3·7	0·8	1·8	0·4	0·6	...	...	...
1847	1·0	5·7	2·6	1·3	1·9	25·3	7·9	3·6	1·0	2·0	0·4	0·7	...	...	...
1848	1·1	5·3	2·1	0·8	1·5	22·7	6·5	3·3	0·6	1·6	0·3	0·6	...	...	...
1849	1·1	5·7	2·4	0·7	2·3	26·8	8·4	4·2	1·0	2·1	0·4	0·9	...	...	...
1850	1·3	6·2	2·9	1·0	2·5	28·3	10·0	4·8	1·3	2·5	0·4	1·0	...	...	...
1851	1·3	6·8	3·2	1·2	2·1	30·1	9·9	5·1	1·3	2·9	0·4	1·0	...	...	...
1852	1·4	7·7	3·1	1·3	2·2	29·9	10·2	5·4	1·6	3·5	0·7	1·0	...	...	...
1853	1·6	12·0	4·4	2·0	2·5	32·7	11·6	5·9	2·0	7·2	1·4	1·3	...	...	...
1854	2·1	12·7	4·5	1·9	2·5	31·7	11·7	5·1	1·7	6·2	1·3	1·4(l)	...	...	...
1855	2·4	10·7	3·4	2·2	2·8	34·8	9·7	5·1	1·5	4·1	0·9	1·5(l)	...	...	...
1856	2·8	14·2	4·2	2·7	3·6	38·2	12·4	6·3	3·0	5·7	1·5	1·7	...	...	...
1857	3·3(a)	14·9	4·6	3·9	4·0(d)	39·1	13·5	6·2	2·9	6·3	2·0	1·9(l)	...	...	...
1858	3·1	12·5	3·7	3·6	3·6	43·0	12·5	5·9	2·1	5·6	1·7	1·8	...	...	...
1859	3·3	13·8	4·3	3·7	3·5	48·2	14·9	6·3	2·4	6·7	1·7	2·2	...	...	...
1860	3·4	13·6	4·3	3·8	4·0	52·0	15·7	6·6	2·4	6·5	1·7	2·2	...	...	...
1861	3·7	11·2	3·9	4·2	3·1	46·9	14·4	5·5(i)	2·3	5·9	1·8	1·8(l)	...	...	...
1862	3·8	12·9(b)	3·2(b)	4·1	4·2	36·8	16·8	7·0	2·4	6·5	2·2	2·5	...	...	...
1863	3·8	14·8	3·6	4·4	5·6	47·6	20·4	9·0	2·2	7·6	1·9	2·5	...	...	...
1864	4·2	15·0	3·8	4·8	5·2	54·9	23·8	11·2	2·3	7·8	2·0	2·9	...	...	...
1865	4·5	15·4	4·1	5·2	4·3	57·3	25·3	11·7	2·2	8·2	2·1	3·1	...	...	...

See p. 306 for footnotes

Overseas Trade 8. *continued*

	Coal(a)	Iron and Steel(b)	Hardwares and Cutlery	Machinery	Non-ferrous Metals and Manufactures(d)	Cotton Goods(e)	Wool Goods(e)	Linen Goods(e)	Silk Goods(e)	Hats, Haberdashery, Apparel etc(j)	Leather Manufactures (k)	Chemicals(l)	Electrical Goods	Vehicles and Aircraft (n)	New Ships and Boats
1866	5·2	17·1	4·1	4·8	3·9	74·6	26·4	12·0	1·9	8·8	1·6	3·8	...	...	...
1867	5·5	17·4	3·7	5·0	4·4	70·8	25·9	9·9	1·8	7·1	1·5	4·7	...	...	...
1868	5·4	17·3	3·5	4·7	4·6	67·7	25·8	9·4	2·3	7·3	1·9	4·7	...	...	...
1869	5·2	21·9	4·1	5·1	5·4	67·1	28·2	9·1	2·3	7·5	1·9	4·8	...	...	...
1870	5·6	23·5	4·1	5·3	4·8	71·4	26·7	9·5	2·6	7·5	1·8	5·1	...	...	...
1871	6·2	25·5	4·3	6·0	5·0	72·8	33·3	9·7	3·3	9·3	2·5	6·2	...	...	...
1872	10·4	35·3	5·5	8·2	5·7	80·2	38·5	10·4	4·1	10·6	2·4	7·6	...	...	...
1873	13·2	37·4	5·4	10·0	5·4	77·4	30·7	9·3	3·5	10·9	2·5	7·8	...	...	...
1874	12·0	30·9	4·8	9·8	5·5	74·2	28·4	8·8	3·1	10·3	2·2	8·0	...	...	...
1875	9·7	25·6	4·7	9·1	5·1	71·8	26·8	9·1	2·6	9·2	2·4	7·8	...	...	...
1876	8·9	20·6	3·9	7·2	4·8	67·6	23·0	7·1	2·9	7·7	2·1	7·6	...	...	...
1877	7·8	20·0	3·7	6·7	5·0	69·2	21·0	7·2	2·3	7·7	2·0	7·8	...	...	...
1878	7·3	18·3	3·7	7·5	4·7	65·9	20·6	6·7	2·5	8·2	2·0	7·4	...	...	...
1879	7·2	18·6	3·4	7·3	4·5	64·0	19·6	6·5	2·4	7·6	2·1	7·7	...	...	...
1880	8·4	27·2	3·9	9·3	4·8	75·6	20·6	6·8	2·7	8·1	2·1	8·8	...	...	...
1881	8·8	27·1	4·3	10·0	5·1	80·1	21·4	6·9	3·6	9·0	2·5	9·4	...	...	...
1882	9·6	31·1(b)	4·7	11·9	5·4(d)	75·8	22·2	7·0	3·5	9·7	2·8	9·8	...	...	...
1883	10·6	28·3	4·6	13·4	5·5	76·4	21·6	6·5	3·1	8·7	2·4	10·1	...	...	...
1884	10·9	24·3	4·1	13·1	5·5	72·7(f)	24·0(f)	6·3	2·8	7·9	2·3	10·2	...	...	...
1885	10·6	21·4	3·7	11·1	4·9	67·0	23·2	5·9	2·3	7·6	2·3	9·1	...	...	...
1886	9·8	21·4	3·7	10·1	4·6	68·9	24·1	6·2	2·7	7·1	2·2	8·6	...	...	...
1887	10·2	24·2	3·8	11·1	4·8	71·0	24·6	6·4	2·8	7·4	2·5	9·1	...	...	...
1888	11·3	26·0	4·2	12·9	5·4	72·0	24·0	6·4	3·1	8·2	2·7	9·8	...	...	...
1889	14·8	28·7	4·2	15·3	5·8	70·5	25·7	6·6	3·0	8·6	2·8	10·6	...	...	...
1890	19·0	31·1	4·1	16·4	7·2	74·4	24·5	6·6	2·7	8·4	2·9	12·0	...	...	...
1891	18·9	26·5	3·8	15·8	6·4	71·4	22·4	5·9	2·3	8·4	2·9	12·1	1·7	...	...
1892	16·8	21·4	3·5	13·9	6·3	66·0	22·0	6·1	2·0	7·8	2·5	11·4	1·1	...	...
1893	14·4	20·3	3·3	13·9	5·3	63·8	20·9	5·8	1·9	6·9	2·5	11·4	1·3	0·2	...
1894	17·4	18·5	3·0	14·2	4·2	66·6	18·7	5·4	1·6	6·4	2·3	11·1	1·6	0·2	...
1895	15·4	19·4	3·1	15·2	4·7	63·7	25·1	6·3	1·7	7·0	2·4	11·4	1·1	0·2	...

See p. 306 for footnotes

Overseas Trade 8. *continued*

	Coal(a)	Iron and Steel(b)	Hard-wares and Cutlery	Machinery	Non-ferrous Metals and Manufactures(d)	Cotton Goods(e)	Wool Goods(e)	Linen Goods(e)	Silk Goods(e)	Hats, Haberdashery, Apparel etc.(j)	Leather Manufactures(k)	Chemicals(l)	Electrical Goods	Vehicles and Aircraft (n)	New Ships and Boats
1896	15·2	23·5	3·5	17·0	4·6	69·4	23·9	6·1	1·7	7·9	2·7	11·7	0·3	0·3	…
1897	16·7	24·4	3·5	16·3	4·6	64·0	20·8	5·7	1·6	7·5	2·5	12·0	1·4	0·3	…
1898	18·1	22·4	3·3	18·4	5·0	64·9	18·4	5·3	1·9	7·3	2·3	11·6	1·5	0·2	…
1899	23·1	27·7	3·6	19·7	6·4	67·5	19·7	6·0	2·0	8·3	2·3	12·2	1·9	0·3	9·2
1900	38·6	31·6	3·6	19·6	6·0	69·8	20·2	6·2	2·1	8·0	2·4	13·1	3·3	0·3	8·6
1901	30·3	25·0	3·6	17·8	6·3	73·7	17·7	5·8	1·7	8·3	2·8	12·1(l)	3·7	0·3	9·1
1902	27·6	28·9	3·8	18·8	5·7	72·5	18·8	6·3	1·6	9·3	3·1	12·8	3·5	0·5	5·9
1903	27·3	30·4(b)	4·0	20·1	6·4	73·6	20·1	6·4	1·7	9·5	3·5	13·5	2·5(m)	0·7	4·3
1904	26·9	28·6	3·7	21·1	6·3	83·9	22·2	6·6	1·8	7·2	3·0	13·6	1·6	0·7	4·5
1905	26·1	32·5	3·7	23·3	8·3	92·0	23·8	7·3	2·0	7·3	3·5	14·5	2·4	1·0	5·4
1906	31·5	40·7	4·3	26·8	9·4	99·6	25·9	8·0	2·2	8·2	3·8	15·5	2·4	1·5	8·6
1907	42·1	47·4(b)	4·7	31·7	10·9	110·4	28·2	8·6	2·4	8·6	4·0	17·1	2·5	2·1	10·0
1908	41·6	38·2	4·1	31·0	8·2	95·1	23·8	6·7	1·7	7·7	3·7	16·3	1·9	1·8	10·6
1909	37·1	39·0	3·9	28·1	7·9	93·4	25·7	8·5	1·9	8·4	4·0	16·8	2·2	2·2	5·9
1910	37·8	44·0	4·5	29·3	9·3	105·9	31·6	9·5	2·3	10·6	4·9	18·6	4·1	3·4	8·8
1911	38·4	44·8	4·8	31·0	9·9	120·1	31·8	9·1	2·4	11·5	5·3	20·1(l)	2·8	3·6	5·7
1912	42·6	49·7	5·3	33·2	11·1	122·2	32·0	9·7	2·2	13·0	6·2	21·0	4·3	4·4	7·0
1913	53·7	55·4	5·0	37·0	12·0	127·2	31·8	9·5	2·2	13·3	6·4	22·0	5·4	5·4	11·0
1914	42·2	42·5	4·0	31·4	9·4	103·3	26·6	8·6	1·9	11·1	6·1	19·5	3·0	5·3	6·9
1915	38·8	41·1	2·8	19·2	9·1	85·9	30·5	7·7	1·7	8·7	5·2	22·1	3·2	3·5	1·7
1916	50·7	57·5	3·8	20·2	11·9	118·3	42·8	10·5	2·4	11·1	8·1	27·6	4·1	4·7	1·3
1917	51·3	45·5	2·9	19·5	9·7	145·9	49·7	11·7	2·0	9·4	8·8	23·6	2·9	4·8	1·1
1918	52·4	37·3	2·8	16·1	8·4	180·1	46·3	9·3	2·1	9·6	3·4	22·7	2·4	4·9	1·0
1919	92·3	64·4	5·6	32·7	14·4	241·0	94·2	14·2	3·7	14·1	6·5	29·5	5·7(m)	6·9	2·3
1920	120·3	128·9	10·4	70·5(c)	25·8	401·4(g)	(139·3)(h)	23·9	5·2	30·1	11·0	40·5(l)	11·6	18·8(n)	26·6
1921	46·4	63·6	6·5	84·2	11·7	178·7	51·9	10·3	2·3	12·5	3·8	19·1	13·0	9·8	30·6
1922	77·7	60·9	4·4	58·0	11·5	186·9	57·4	12·5	2·3	13·3	4·2	20·3	7·3	7·1	30·0
1923	109·9	76·2	5·4	48·5	14·5	177·4	60·1	12·6	2·0	15·5	6·0	25·7	10·2	8·0	9·7
1924	78·3	74·5	6·0	47·4	15·7	199·2	64·6	14·7	2·2	18·1	6·9	25·5	10·7	14·4	5·5
1925	54·3	68·2	6·6	52·3	16·8	199·4	57·1	12·5	1·8	16·8	6·4	23·6	11·6	14·1	6·3

See p. 306 for footnotes

Overseas Trade 8. *continued*

	Coal(a)	Iron and Steel(b)	Hardwares and Cutlery	Machinery	Non-ferrous Metals and Manufactures(d)	Cotton Goods(e)	Wool Goods(e)	Linen Goods(e)	Silk Goods(e)	Hats, Haberdashery, Apparel etc.(f)	Leather Manufactures(k)	Chemicals(l)	Electrical Goods	Vehicles and Aircraft(n)	New Ships and Boats
1926	20·5	55·1	6·1	49·1	19·5	154·3	50·2	10·8	2·0	16·5	5·9	21·7	13·4	17·2	4·6
1927	49·2	69·4	5·9	52·8	19·9	148·8	53·5	11·0	2·4	15·5	5·8	23·4	11·9	17·9	4·5
1928	42·7	66·8	6·1	58·4	16·4	145·3	54·1	10·4	2·4	15·6	6·2	25·4	11·6	17·1	15·9
1929	52·9	68·0	6·1	59·6	18·3	135·4	50·5	10·3	2·2	15·5	6·1	26·6	13·2	20·7	15·5
1930	49·2	51·3	4·5	52·0	12·0	87·6	35·5	8·0	1·6	12·3	5·0	23·4	11·9	17·9	20·1
1931	37·6	30·4	3·0	35·1	6·9	56·6	24·0	5·9	1·0	8·8	3·8	18·2	7·4	12·8	10·5
1932	34·3	28·0	3·4	30·3	6·9	62·8	21·7	5·8	1·0	7·5	3·2	18·5	5·8	13·3	3·9
1933	34·1	29·9	3·9	28·4	12·1	58·9	22·8	6·5	0·9	7·3(j)	2·9	18·6	6·7	15·4	2·6
1934	34·6	35·1	4·8	33·8	11·9	59·1	25·9	6·8	1·1	7·5	2·8	19·6	8·0	17·2	1·8
1935	34·6	37·1	5·2	40·9	14·1	60·2	26·0	7·2	1·1	7·7	2·5	21·3	9·5	18·9	3·1
1936	32·3	36·8	5·4	43·2	12·1	61·5	27·4	8·1	1·3	8·9	2·6	21·1	10·0	20·5	3·6
1937	41·9	49·3	6·6	51·7	15·7	68·5	30·7	8·9	1·5	9·2	2·9	24·7	12·5	24·6	4·1
1938	40·7	42·9	5·7	60·7	12·3	49·7	23·6	6·3	1·3	7·7	2·5	22·1	13·4	24·7	8·5

(a) This includes coke and anthracite throughout, and manufactured fuel from 1857, when it amounted to 0·1.

(b) Tinplates were not included under this heading until 1840—an addition of 0·3 in that year. In 1862 manufactures of iron and steel combined were transferred from *Hardwares and Cutlery*—an addition of 0·4 in that year. Other very minor breaks in the series occurred in 1882, when surgical and similar instruments were first included; in 1907, when old rails were included; and in 1926, when needles were added. A more important break took place in 1903, when telegraphic wire was transferred from *Electrical Goods*—a change of 1·0 in that year.

(c) Transformers were included, and agricultural tractors were excluded, from 1920 onwards—a net loss of 0·5 in that year.

(d) This includes tinplates prior to 1840, when they amounted to 0·3. Otherwise the metals covered prior to 1882 were brass, copper, lead, pewter, tin, and zinc. Thereafter all other metals were added—a change of 0·3 in 1882. Ores were at no time included under this heading, but prior to 1910 it did include regulus and precipitate, which were of minor importance in the mid-nineteenth century, but negligible by 1910. A very minor break in the series resulted from the exclusion of lead shot after 1856.

(e) These include yarn.

(f) Prior to 1884 some piece goods of mixed materials in which wool predominated were erroneously entered as cotton goods. The size of the resulting break in the two series is apparently 0·5.

(g) Cotton hosiery and gloves are excluded from 1920 onwards. In 1919 they had amounted to 3·0.

(h) Hosiery and gloves of wool cannot be isolated for the year 1920, and are therefore not included in this figure.

(i) Includes jute goods prior to 1861, when they amounted to 0·2.

(j) This does not include hosiery and gloves of cotton or wool, boots, and shoes. There is a minor break in the series in 1933, when hatters' wares can no longer be excluded. In 1932 they had amounted to 0·2.

(k) Includes unwrought leather prior to 1840. Leather belting was included for the first time in 1906, when it came to 0·5.

(l) Initially this comprises alkali, drugs and chemical products, and painters' colours. The following additions were made before 1867: In 1854 bleaching materials (0·1 in that year); in 1855 coal tar (negligible at that time); in 1857 manures (0·1 in that year); in 1861 naphtha (negligible at that time). In 1867 a new classification was adopted, which greatly raised the figure under this heading. Figures using the old classification for 1867–1870 were as follows: 1867—3·9; 1868—3·9; 1869—4·1; 1870—4·4. Two very minor breaks in the series occurred in 1901 and 1911, caused respectively by the inclusion of saltpetre and the exclusion of photographic plates and paper. A second major change in classification took place in 1920. On the new basis the figure for 1919 was 27·0.

(m) This includes telegraphic wire prior to 1903, when it amounted to 1·0. A very minor break was occasioned by the exclusion of transformers from 1920 onwards.

(n) This covers all mechanically propelled road vehicles and aircraft, included from 1920 onwards agricultural tractors.

306

Overseas Trade 9.   Values at Current Prices of Principal Re-exports— United Kingdom 1854–1938 (a)

NOTE

SOURCE: *Annual Statement of Trade.*

A. Computed Values, 1854–70

(in £ million)

	Coffee	Tea	Raw Cotton(b)	Raw Wool(c)	Oils, Oil-seed, Gums, Resin, Tallow etc.(d)	Dyewoods and Dyestuffs	Hides, Skins and Furs	Non-ferrous Metals and Manu-factures	Rubber	Petroleum
1854	0·8	0·6	2·3	1·5	...	...	...	0·4	...	...
1855	0·7	0·9	2·5	1·9	2·2	2·2	0·8	0·3	- -	...
1856	0·7	0·3	3·3	1·9	1·9	2·1	1·1	0·3	0·1	...
1857	0·5	0·6	3·4	2·8	1·7	2·3	1·3	0·5	- -	...
1858	0·8	0·5	4·0	1·9	2·0	2·3	1·2	0·4	0·1	...
1859	0·9	0·5	4·2	2·1	2·2	2·3	1·3	0·5	0·1	...
1860	1·4	0·7	5·4	2·3	2·4	2·4	1·4	0·6	0·1	...
1861	1·5	0·9	8·6	3·6	2·4	2·8	1·4	0·6	0·1	...
1862	2·0	2·2	13·5	3·3	2·4	2·3	1·5	1·0	0·2	...
1863	2·5	2·0	20·1	4·3	2·1	2·0	1·5	1·0	0·2	...
1864	2·6	2·1	20·9	4·4	2·3	2·2	1·3	1·4	0·2	...
1865	3·3	2·7	18·8	5·9	2·4	2·7	1·3	1·3	0·2	...
1866	3·1	2·4	19·2	5·0	2·1	2·3	1·1	1·5	0·3	...
1867	3·0	2·5	12·4	6·4	2·5	2·9	1·4	1·5	0·2	...
1868	3·7	2·8	11·9	6·4	2·4	3·0	1·4	2·0	0·3	...
1869	3·6	2·5	11·5	6·7	2·5	3·0	1·6	1·3	0·3	...
1870	3·9	2·2	8·1	5·6	2·6	2·3	1·9	1·5	0·5	...

B. Declared Values, 1871–1938

	Coffee	Tea	Raw Cotton(b)	Raw Wool(c)	Oils, Oil-seed, Gums, Resin, Tallow etc.(d)	Dyewoods and Dyestuffs	Hides, Skins and Furs	Non-ferrous Metals and Manu-factures	Rubber	Petroleum
1871	4·7	3·1	11·9	7·6	4·0	3·6	1·9	1·8	0·6	...
1872	4·6	3·3	8·8	9·3	2·9	2·6	2·8	2·0	0·7	...
1873	5·8	2·6	6·5	8·9	2·4	2·5	2·4	2·5	0·6	...
1874	5·2	2·6	6·8	10·2	2·7	2·3	2·5	3·1	0·5	...
1875	5·7	2·6	6·6	12·1	3·2	2·2	2·7	2·3	0·6	...
1876	5·8	2·3	4·5	11·4	2·5	2·1	2·0	2·3	0·6	...
1877	5·3	2·4	4·0	11·9	3·1	1·9	1·9	1·8	0·7	...
1878	4·7	2·6	3·4	12·3	2·2	1·9	1·7	1·6	0·7	...
1879	5·8	2·3	4·3	14·2	2·5	2·1	1·9	2·1	1·0	...
1880	5·3	2·8	5·5	14·5	3·1	2·1	2·3	2·2	1·1	...
1881	4·1	2·5	5·0	15·9	3·4	2·4	2·1	2·3	1·2	...
1882	4·0	2·4	6·3	15·3	3·0	2·6	2·3	2·6	1·5	...
1883	3·4	2·4	5·3	16·0	3·9	2·5	2·7	2·6	1·5	...
1884	3·3	2·5	5·4	15·4	3·4	2·5	2·6	2·4	1·2	...
1885	2·4	2·2	4·5	14·1	3·3	2·2	3·2	1·9	1·0	...
1886	2·6	2·2	4·0	12·1	2·9 -----	1·8	3·4	2·4	1·3	...
1887	2·7	1·7	5·7	13·8	2·7(c)	1·8	2·9	2·7	1·3	- -(c)
1888	3·1	1·8	5·5	13·8	3·1	1·7	2·9	5·3	1·3	- -
1889	2·7	1·7	5·9	15·4	3·5	1·9	3·1	3·2	1·4	- -
1890	2·9	1·7	4·8	14·5	3·4	1·6	2·9	3·4	1·7	- -
1891	2·2	1·6	3·8	15·8	3·3	1·1	2·8	2·8	1·8	0·1
1892	2·4	1·6	4·5	16·8	3·5	1·5	3·4	2·8	1·6	0·1
1893	2·3	1·5	4·6	13·3	3·9	1·2	3·6	2·9	1·6	0·1
1894	2·5	1·4	4·7	13·5	4·4	1·1	3·3	2·4	1·8	0·1
1895	2·1	1·4	3·5	15·2	3·9	1·4	4·1	2·2	2·3	0·1

See p. 308 *for footnotes*

(in £ million)

	Coffee	Tea	Raw Cotton(b)	Raw Wool(c)	Oils, Oil-seed, Gums, Resin, Tallow etc.(d)	Dyewoods and Dyestuffs	Hides, Skins and Furs	Non-ferrous Metals and Manufactures	Rubber	Petroleum
1896	2·0	1·4	3·6	12·3	3·3	1·3	3·2	2·1	2·6	0·1
1897	1·9	1·5	4·3	13·4	3·6	1·1	4·1	1·9	2·8	0·1
1898	2·1	1·5	3·6	10·1	3·7	1·0	4·5	2·4	4·0	- -
1899	2·3	1·4	4·8	10·2	3·8	0·9	4·8	4·5	4·3	0·1
1900	1·5	1·7	4·8	7·5	4·1	0·7	5·2	4·7	3·8	0·1
1901	2·0	1·7	5·0	10·7	4·3	0·8	4·8	4·7	3·6	0·1
1902	1·1	1·8	6·3	10·2	4·7	0·6	4·7	4·3	3·6	0·1
1903	1·7	1·7	7·4	10·4	4·3	0·6	4·1	4·0	4·9	0·2
1904	1·8	1·8	6·8	9·5	4·3	0·5	4·0	4·5	5·0	0·2
1905	2·3	1·8	6·6	11·1	4·4	0·5	5·1	5·7	6·2	0·2
1906	1·8	2·2	6·6	11·3	4·6(c)	0·5	6·5	7·7	6·4	0·2
1907	1·3	2·1	9·5	13·5	5·6	0·5	6·3	6·9	6·0	0·2
1908	1·2	1·9	8·3	12·9	4·6	0·5	5·0	6·0	5·7	0·2
1909	1·5	2·3	7·8	16·0	5·5	0·5	7·0	5·9	9·1	0·1
1910	1·9	2·3	9·8	14·5	7·2	0·5	7·1	7·3	14·9	0·1
1911	2·1	2·4	10·7	13·1	6·1	0·4	6·3	8·4	13·5	0·2
1912	1·6	2·6	10·6	14·4	5·6	0·4	8·3	8·6	16·3	0·2
1913	1·8	2·8	9·1	13·4	5·5	0·5	8·4	8·3	14·8	0·1
1914	2·2	3·3	7·4	13·6	5·5	0·4	6·0	6·3	12·1	0·1
1915	1·9	3·4	9·6	6·8	7·4	1·6	4·8	5·9	16·0	0·4
1916	1·5	3·5	9·8	3·8	5·6	2·7	5·1	5·0	15·1	0·4
1917	0·4	1·0	7·7	3·6	4·5	1·1	3·8	4·8	16·5	0·4
1918	0·1	0·3	- -	2·4	0·7	0·5	2·0	1·7	4·5	0·2
1919	3·9	2·7	11·4	23·4	8·9(c)	1·2	12·3	5·0	14·2	2·0
1920	2·9	3·4	33·7	35·3	10·5	1·3	15·6	8·2	14·1	5·4
1921	2·0	2·0	8·3	19·1	5·1	0·4	7·4	4·6	4·1	1·4
1922	1·1	2·8	5·4	26·4	4·0	0·4	8·7	3·9	4·7	2·3
1923	2·6	5·4	7·3	29·8	3·7	0·2	9·8	3·1	9·9	2·7
1924	1·7	6·9	11·6	31·0	3·6	0·2	13·1	3·8	10·1	2·9
1925	1·6	7·8	11·1	32·0	3·5	0·3	14·3	4·2	22·1	3·0
1926	1·8	7·6	8·5	27·5	2·6	0·2	12·8	3·7	16·3	1·3
1927	1·9	7·7	6·8	27·3	2·4	0·1	14·5	2·5	15·1	1·1
1928	2·2	7·8	4·3	27·1	2·6	0·1	15·3	3·3	12·7	1·3
1929	1·7	7·9	4·6	24·8	2·1	0·1	12·8	4·4	5·4	3·0
1930	2·3	6·8	3·4	16·9	1·5	0·1	9·9	2·8	3·6	2·0
1931	1·9	5·9	1·2	11·0	0·9	0·1	8·4	1·5	1·8	1·2
1932	1·5	4·4	1·6	12·0	0·5	0·1	6·8	1·3	1·4	1·4
1933	1·4	4·3	1·7	13·5	0·4	- -	7·2	0·7	0·9	1·2
1934	0·9	4·6	2·1	12·6	0·5	- -	7·0	1·3	3·2	1·3
1935	0·7	4·5	2·4	11·5	1·2	- -	8·3	4·0	2·9	1·5
1936	0·5	4·8	2·0	13·2	0·7	- -	9·4	6·1	4·9	1·6
1937	0·3	4·6	2·0	14·4	0·7	- -	11·7	13·6	4·4	1·8
1938	0·4	4·0	1·3	12·5	0·5	- -	9·6	9·1	2·7	0·8

(a) Re-exports of raw silk were important up to about 1880, as can be seen from the following figures:

1854 0·8	1859 2·2	1864 4·4	1869 3·6	1874 3·0	1879 1·1
1855 1·5	1860 3·4	1865 4·1	1870 3·4	1875 1·9	1880 0·7
1856 1·4	1861 3·6	1866 2·6	1871 4·0	1876 2·8	1881 0·7
1857 1·9	1862 4·9	1867 2·5	1872 3·9	1877 1·5	1882 0·7
1858 2·1	1863 3·9	1868 3·6	1873 3·7	1878 1·5	1883 0·4

b) This includes unmanufactured waste.

(c) This includes woollen rags intended for use as raw material for cloth.

(d) This covers all types of oil (except petroleum from 1887 onwards), all seeds and nuts used for expressing oil, all types of gum, rosin, tallow, and stearine. A negligible break in the series in 1906 was occasioned by the inclusion of soap stock. From 1919 manufactured oils were excluded—a difference of 0·5 in that year.

Overseas Trade 10. Official Values of Imports and of Exports and Re-exports combined, according to Regional Direction—England & Wales, 1710–58, and Great Britain 1755–1822

NOTES

[1] SOURCE: Cesar Moreau, *State of the Trade of Great Britain with all Parts of the World* (London, 1822).

[2] The source attributes all figures to Great Britain, but a comparison of Moreau's totals with those in tables 1 and 2 indicates that they relate to England & Wales only prior to 1755 (imports) and to 1759 (exports and re-exports).

[3] The heading *Exports* includes re-exports in this table.

[4] *Northern Europe* comprises the ports of Europe as far south as the Franco-Belgian frontier, and *Southern Europe* the remainder plus Turkey and its domains (including Egypt). In determining the regions on the American continent, the frontiers used were those of 1822.

A. England & Wales 1710-58

(in £000)

	Northern Europe		Southern Europe		Asia		Africa		British North America		United States		British West Indies		Foreign W. Indies and South America	
	Imports	Exports	Imports	Exports	Imports	Exports	Imports	Exports	Imports	Exports	Imports	Exports	Imports	Exports	Imports	Exports
1710	1,571	3,475	722	1,776	248	126	14	69	14	13	250	294	781	205	5	34
1711	1,530	3,479	1,258	1,416	637	152	8	64	11	7	325	298	557	222	1	44
1712	1,577	3,514	882	2,207	457	142	11	38	26	12	366	310	649	265	36	69
1713	1,756	3,340	1,536	2,126	953	94	12	112	19	8	303	285	792	358	2	110
1714	1,821	4,119	1,422	2,435	1,046	77	25	63	18	12	396	333	845	333	2	176
1715	1,724	3,317	1,591	1,989	580	37	30	52	11	10	297	451	1,000	302	2	303
1716	1,588	3,243	1,520	2,303	403	106	32	98	23	8	424	402	1,104	413	19	93
1717	1,707	3,682	1,808	2,612	495	83	19	112	20	9	426	540	1,090	340	169	253
1718	1,826	3,094	1,674	1,676	1,333	74	26	93	23	10	457	425	897	347	84	263
1719	1,792	3,347	1,233	2,171	547	88	18	66	15	9	463	393	876	246	29	96
1720	1,604	3,322	1,602	2,372	931	84	25	130	26	14	468	320	1,119	220	6	83
1721	1,578	3,613	1,415	2,240	1,021	128	22	126	29	9	494	332	856	219	4	143
1722	1,780	3,667	1,929	2,216	764	123	34	187	33	14	438	425	1,019	264	11	344
1723	1,670	3,248	1,842	2,245	969	115	30	139	30	13	462	412	1,092	300	23	336
1724	2,237	3,154	1,733	2,563	165	101	47	216	26	14	463	462	1,166	384	167	206
1725	2,125	3,305	1,953	2,858	760	94	68	284	31	22	416	550	1,364	364	25	484
1726	1,957	3,303	1,688	2,597	914	75	36	148	29	16	526	553	1,128	272	47	135
1727	1,815	3,276	1,722	2,397	1,126	98	39	139	49	13	637	503	1,041	249	49	125
1728	2,187	4,499	1,722	2,808	869	116	22	187	51	17	605	518	1,501	333	17	208
1729	2,280	3,514	1,879	2,749	972	138	49	253	57	17	575	423	1,517	380	7	199
1730	2,236	3,388	1,794	2,891	1,060	135	57	261	42	24	573	537	1,572	349	134	393
1731	1,905	3,157	1,722	2,691	825	139	29	206	45	22	651	536	1,312	249	154	124
1732	2,204	3,490	1,568	3,207	981	159	50	204	69	31	519	531	1,316	240	57	346
1733	2,229	3,599	1,875	3,371	1,107	132	58	129	41	34	670	549	1,619	236	12	130
1734	2,210	3,340	1,798	3,052	768	135	69	130	41	23	611	556	1,142	217	33	169
1735	2,290	3,652	1,889	3,373	1,297	186	42	139	40	28	652	669	1,461	263	44	182
1736	2,051	3,837	1,593	3,380	929	261	54	193	42	30	700	559	1,423	295	17	212
1737	2,357	3,487	1,561	3,954	916	378	56	234	55	42	775	682	949	254	9	227
1738	2,118	3,533	1,939	4,186	743	169	62	277	45	38	620	751	1,477	238	5	175
1739	2,256	3,634	1,341	2,815	1,279	217	43	220	60	36	754	696	1,567	246	65	209
1740	2,173	5,166	1,129	2,039	871	282	63	111	55	26	718	813	1,185	343	6	320
1741	2,322	3,736	1,600	2,646	1,130	487	44	133	48	24	912	885	1,403	454	3	417
1742	2,107	3,783	1,107	2,462	1,214	374	35	130	64	43	659	800	1,210	535	4	459
1743	1,945	5,345	1,511	2,367	906	646	26	219	47	39	681	829	1,405	445	3	353
1744	2,010	4,559	956	1,726	744	476	14	95	31	27	668	641	1,157	282	1	222

Overseas Trade 10. *continued*

(in £000)

	Northern Europe		Southern Europe		Asia		Africa		British North America		United States		British West Indies		Foreign W. Indies and South America	
	Imports	Exports	Imports	Exports	Imports	Exports	Imports	Exports	Imports	Exports	Imports	Exports	Imports	Exports	Imports	Exports
1745	1,991	4,213	1,326	1,757	974	293	11	71	40	32	554	535	1,024	280	14	194
1746	1,980	4,890	892	2,061	647	894	25	117	44	41	560	755	1,148	497	2	359
1747	2,210	4,291	1,340	2,361	822	346	2	186	35	56	561	727	941	389	6	345
1748	2,196	4,839	1,332	2,739	1,099	306	18	234	57	43	717	830	1,616	442	5	352
1749	2,010	5,076	1,918	3,665	1,124	557	16	201	52	68	664	1,231	1,481	554	3	185
1750	2,262	4,249	1,315	4,476	1,104	509	29	161	46	63	815	1,313	1,516	547	1	—
1751	2,010	4,262	1,709	3,939	1,097	798	56	215	58	100	836	1,233	1,448	631	1	—
1752	2,041	4,099	1,627	3,630	1,068	628	43	236	50	70	1,004	1,148	1,433	704	4	1
1753	2,261	3,752	1,771	3,845	1,008	788	34	276	49	74	973	1,453	1,903	833	3	—
1754	2,096	3,823	1,575	3,719	1,186	844	22	235	42	70	1,008	1,176	1,467	686	1	—
1755	...	3,904	...	3,123	...	875	...	174	...	65	...	1,113	...	695	...	1
1756	...	4,047	...	3,935	...	489	...	188	...	77	...	1,352	...	733	...	—
1757	...	2,744	...	3,728	...	845	...	154	...	98	...	1,628	...	777	...	1
1758	...	3,679	...	3,050	...	922	...	168	...	119	...	1,713	...	878	...	—
B. Great Britain 1755–1822																
1755	2,267	...	1,606	...	1,247	...	40	...	46	...	940	...	1,869	...	--	...
1756	2,249	...	1,355	...	796	...	39	...	30	...	659	...	1,689	...	4	...
1757	2,392	...	1,349	...	1,112	...	30	...	42	...	611	...	1,910	...	4	...
1758	2,266	...	1,534	...	223	...	44	...	46	...	671	...	1,863	...	1	...
1759	2,413	3,920	1,535	3,797	974	665	24	228	59	139	640	2,345	1,835	935	93	61
1760	2,277	4,347	1,446	3,672	1,786	1,162	39	346	36	179	832	2,713	1,907	1,300	424	120
1761	2,668	5,874	1,741	3,498	841	846	12	325	52	351	895	1,722	2,000	992	491	140
1762	2,249	5,862	1,105	1,603	973	1,067	31	273	70	214	918	1,387	1,809	989	827	460
1763	3,412	5,590	2,036	3,261	1,059	887	18	464	74	226	1,157	1,660	2,349	1,154	1,036	32
1764	2,916	5,903	2,032	4,116	1,183	1,166	86	465	85	354	1,126	2,273	2,528	984	62	7
1765	2,722	4,944	2,156	3,327	1,456	914	52	469	94	345	1,160	1,973	2,302	1,072	85	5
1766	2,445	4,429	2,028	3,318	1,976	784	52	497	105	457	1,048	1,844	2,688	1,195	28	5
1767	3,249	4,151	1,946	2,929	1,981	1,273	56	558	103	281	1,134	1,946	2,851	1,144	34	10
1768	3,021	4,421	1,904	3,511	1,508	1,156	67	612	95	184	1,273	2,198	3,139	1,261	54	12
1769	2,736	4,148	2,222	2,926	1,863	1,205	59	605	105	264	1,073	1,373	2,927	1,370	103	14
1770	2,803	4,288	2,012	3,034	1,942	1,082	68	571	106	374	1,095	1,955	3,342	1,339	112	11
1771	3,278	4,461	2,151	3,529	1,882	1,185	97	703	100	319	1,348	4,201	2,937	1,214	47	6
1772	2,843	4,733	2,046	3,423	2,473	941	92	866	130	354	1,265	3,091	3,405	1,440	92	9
1773	2,358	3,774	1,644	3,361	1,933	846	68	662	123	430	1,374	1,987	2,836	1,336	65	18
1774	3,588	4,981	2,009	3,286	1,387	546	57	847	136	438	1,380	2,599	3,561	1,419	35	14
1775	3,427	5,444	2,148	3,809	1,092	1,041	67	786	136	659	1,953	197	3,628	1,717	59	25
1776	3,076	4,873	2,249	3,398	1,468	726	100	471	119	830	106	56	3,301	1,605	53	20
1777	3,712	4,019	2,103	2,782	1,834	786	63	239	120	1,653	14	59	2,792	1,257	49	3
1778	2,910	4,296	1,429	2,258	1,526	1,200	82	154	132	1,030	18	38	3,011	1,151	53	7
1779	3,671	4,323	667	1,633	716	703	34	159	135	842	24	351	2,831	1,167	16	18

(in £000)

	Northern Europe		Southern Europe		Asia		Africa		British North America		United States		British West Indies		Foreign W. Indies and South America	
	Imports	Exports	Imports	Exports	Imports	Exports	Imports	Exports	Imports	Exports	Imports	Exports	Imports	Exports	Imports	Exports
1780	4,278	4,270	817	922	971	1,116	22	196	120	837	20	829	2,606	1,752	34	127
1781	4,243	3,870	685	840	2,526	595	26	313	119	536	100	855	1,859	1,024	33	31
1782	3,763	4,400	717	1,262	626	1,468	68	352	223	702	38	267	2,506	1,272	100	229
1783	4,704	3,665	1,216	2,050	1,301	701	48	788	150	732	170	1,003	2,892	1,797	29	61
1784	3,753	3,826	1,964	2,433	2,997	731	119	524	180	760	749	3,679	3,405	1,370	136	31
1785	3,567	4,558	2,251	3,009	2,704	1,154	48	587	209	691	894	2,308	4,354	1,236	61	1
1786	3,326	4,258	2,228	2,886	3,157	2,242	118	889	202	791	843	1,603	3,443	1,336	113	45
1787	3,818	4,185	3,031	3,060	3,431	1,551	118	728	243	913	894	2,014	3,783	1,733	71	14
1788	3,703	4,471	2,733	3,655	3,454	1,431	90	735	250	895	1,024	1,886	4,088	1,766	315	28
1789	3,351	5,241	2,956	3,924	3,350	1,957	103	670	237	874	1,050	2,525	3,906	1,764	251	31
1790	4,313	4,913	3,350	3,314	3,150	2,386	72	929	202	841	1,191	3,432	3,891	1,986	229	39
1791	4,591	5,323	3,368	3,971	3,699	2,272	80	856	214	895	1,194	4,225	3,691	2,649	198	56
1792	4,442	6,084	3,977	4,228	2,672	2,438	83	1,368	256	1,120	1,039	4,271	4,183	2,922	280	107
1793	4,944	5,739	1,904	2,039	3,499	2,722	120	385	210	905	904	3,515	4,392	2,695	308	21
1794	4,486	9,649	2,518	2,126	4,458	2,922	49	750	241	971	626	3,860	4,783	3,633	272	54
1795	4,106	10,045	2,566	2,412	5,761	2,383	65	429	315	1,000	1,352	5,254	4,099	2,461	385	206
1796	6,805	8,317	2,072	2,457	3,373	2,377	120	614	204	815	2,081	6,054	3,967	3,223	877	1,041
1797	4,807	9,185	1,277	1,587	3,942	2,288	54	887	213	845	1,176	5,057	4,309	3,144	1,078	665
1798	6,528	10,139	1,303	1,405	7,627	1,146	70	1,291	220	1,054	1,783	5,580	5,419	5,198	1,159	1,264
1799	7,292	7,939	1,842	2,099	4,285	2,436	113	1,622	170	1,092	1,819	7,057	6,162	5,947	1,390	1,048
1800	7,026	14,325	2,403	3,404	4,942	2,860	97	1,099	393	976	2,358	7,886	7,369	4,087	1,497	479
1801	7,235	14,442	2,274	3,545	5,424	2,946	139	1,124	456	1,017	2,707	7,518	8,436	4,386	2,577	589
1802	5,916	15,015	3,242	7,752	5,795	2,930	169	1,161	368	1,351	1,924	5,329	8,531	3,926	1,658	285
1803	5,346	11,372	3,527	3,968	6,349	2,733	94	819	328	1,082	1,914	5,273	6,132	2,380	355	193
1804	6,435	12,716	2,217	3,033	5,215	1,766	164	1,173	378	1,056	1,651	6,398	7,682	4,282	346	312
1805	7,137	13,026	2,872	2,440	6,073	1,669	107	991	294	865	1,767	7,147	6,720	3,832	736	319
1806	5,805	10,533	2,392	2,078	3,755	1,937	116	1,433	330	951	2,000	8,613	8,815	4,734	1,227	1,796
1807	5,154	9,412	2,819	3,278	3,402	1,884	122	798	450	1,061	2,848	7,921	7,980	4,579	1,341	1,326
1808	2,120	4,734	2,091	6,547	3,858	1,933	143	533	827	1,125	836	3,992	8,778	5,929	2,838	4,830
1809	5,660	13,666	3,935	10,055	3,366	1,648	185	706	678	1,748	2,205	5,188	7,703	5,975	5,090	6,382
1810	7,480	11,221	4,996	8,385	4,710	1,717	257	484	885	1,845	2,614	7,813	8,258	4,790	6,961	5,970
1811	2,052	2,358	1,685	12,606	4,106	1,665	189	317	802	1,910	2,309	1,432	8,452	4,123	3,831	3,047
1812	3,213	5,460	2,952	15,528	5,602	1,779	172	444	720	1,419	1,294	4,136	7,487	4,767	2,471	4,115
1813	....	....	....	....	....	....	....	....	323	4,093	23	7	8,497	6,315	6,220	4,302
1814	6,399	22,922	3,443	12,348	6,304	1,698	269	422								
1815	4,986	19,860	3,244	9,071	8,042	2,093	325	393	369	3,099	2,370	11,937	8,527	6,916	3,371	3,786
1816	2,784	18,493	2,068	9,000	8,313	2,205	240	380	493	2,208	2,386	7,800	7,547	4,608	1,974	3,284
1817	4,897	16,988	3,100	9,529	7,688	2,795	348	506	615	1,396	3,057	6,377	8,021	6,762	1,702	4,882
1818	7,875	17,181	4,944	10,141	7,343	3,196	285	479	690	1,795	3,427	8,383	8,347	5,785	2,331	5,552
1819	4,819	16,016	3,175	9,441	7,344	2,422	254	423	751	2,001	2,688	4,302	7,888	4,490	2,017	3,472
1820	4,799	18,982	3,453	10,693	7,568	3,391	174	566	841	1,676	3,651	3,921	8,011	4,353	2,326	4,450
1821	3,966	16,052	3,631	11,264	6,939	4,428	299	684	844	1,396	3,642	6,607	7,978	5,069	2,471	4,927
1822	5,095	15,358	3,824	13,932	6,123	4,101	275	682	781	1,535	4,021	7,368	7,691	4,146	2,108	5,323

Overseas Trade 11. Official Values of Trade with Various Regions—

England & Wales 1700–1 to 1772–3, and Great Britain 1772–3 to 1797–8

NOTES

[1] SOURCE: Phyllis Deane and W. A. Cole, *British Economic Growth, 1688–1955* (Cambridge University Press, 1962).

[2] All figures exclude prize goods. The totals are those given in the ledgers, no allowance being made for changes in the rates of valuation, notably that of woollen goods in 1709. The figures do not, therefore, provide an accurate index of changes in the volume of trade between 1700–1 and 1730–1.

[3] *N.W. Europe* comprises France, the Low Countries, the German states (excluding Prussia) and Belle-Isle. *The North* comprises Denmark and Norway, East Country, Poland, Prussia, Russia and Sweden. *The South* consists of Portugal, Spain, Gibraltar, Italy, Straits, Turkey and Venice (and includes Madeira, the Canaries, and the Turkish dominions). *British Islands* comprise Ireland, the Isle of Man, and the Channel Islands. *The Fisheries* include Greenland and Iceland.

(in £000)

	England & Wales Imports				England & Wales Exports				England & Wales Re-exports			
	1700–1	1730–1	1750–1	1772–3	1700–1	1730–1	1750–1	1772–3	1700–1	1730–1	1750–1	1772–3
N.-W. Europe	1,387	1,424	1,120	1,086	1,941	1,475	2,458	1,461	1,333	1,800	1,790	3,009
The North	541	690	1,084	1,446	241	186	314	290	86	71	90	187
The South	1,650	1,715	1,445	1,769	1,478	2,321	3,562	2,132	233	234	248	459
British Islands	285	325	695	1,303	144	275	695	912	159	345	609	1,102
North America	372	655	877	1,442	256	351	971	2,460	106	208	384	522
West Indies	785	1,586	1,484	3,080	205	374	449	1,168	131	183	140	169
East India(a)	775	943	1,101	2,203	114	116	585	824	11	32	68	69
Africa	24	43	43	80	81	105	89	492	64	128	99	285
The Fisheries	—	56	7	21	—	—	—	—	—	…	—	—
TOTAL	5,819	7,386	7,855	12,432	4,461	5,203	9,125	9,739	2,136	3,002	3,428	5,800

	Great Britain Imports				Great Britain Exports				Great Britain Re-exports			
	1772–3	1780–1	1789–90	1797–8	1772–3	1780–1	1789–90	1797–8	1772–3	1780–1	1789–90	1797–8
N.-W. Europe	1,220	2,172	1,841	2,426	1,539	2,298	2,640	2,063	3,865	1,280	2,664	8,056
The North	1,629	2,092	2,572	3,304	314	364	508	820	206	117	346	914
The South	1,793	748	2,573	1,273	2,143	755	2,229	975	464	123	282	180
British Islands	1,437	1,818	2,563	3,127	1,008	1,162	1,377	1,641	1,262	1,079	1,056	1,286
North America	1,977	219	1,351	1,696	2,649	1,359	3,295	5,700	605	419	468	364
West Indies	3,222	2,322	4,045	5,982	1,226	1,295	1,690	4,612	176	217	202	489
East India(a)	2,203	1,749	3,256	5,785	824	821	2,096	1,640	69	35	77	75
Africa	80	29	87	62	492	165	517	650	285	90	282	437
The Fisheries	27	42	188	248	—	—	—	—	—	—	2	1
TOTAL	13,595	11,189	18,476	23,903	10,196	8,218	14,350	18,288	6,930	3,359	5,380	11,802

(a) i.e. Asia.

Overseas Trade 12. Values at Current Prices of Overseas Trade According to Regions and Principal Countries—

United Kingdom 1805–1938

NOTES TO PART A

[1] SOURCES: Columns 1–9—G. R. Porter, *The Progress of the Nation* (London, 1912, edited by F. W. Hurst), pp. 479–80; columns 10–16 and modifications to columns 6 and 7 for the period 1827–47—*Porter's Tables* (published in sessional papers from 1833) and the first *Abstract*.

[2] *Northern Europe* comprise France, the Low Countries, Scandinavia, Germany, Prussia and Russia. *Southern Europe* consists of Spain, Portugal, Gibraltar, Malta, the Azores, Madeira, the Canary Islands, the Italian states, Turkey, Greece and Austria-Hungary. *Asia* includes Australia and the Pacific settlements. *Germany* comprises Prussia, as well as the other states which were not separately distinguished in contemporary summaries. Prior to 1840 *India* includes Ceylon.

A. Declared Value of Exports 1805–47 (in £000)

	Northern Europe	Southern Europe	Africa	Asia	U.S.A.	British North America	British West Indies	Foreign West Indies	Central and South America	Russia	Germany	Netherlands	Belgium	France	India	Australia and Pacific Settlements
1805	13,626		756	2,905	11,011		7,771	...	...	...	...	...	...	...	...	...
1806	11,364		1,164	2,938	12,389		10,878	...	...	...	...	...	...	...	...	...
1807	9,002		765	3,359	11,847		10,439	...	...	...	...	...	...	...	...	...
1808	9,016		633	3,525	5,242		16,592	...	...	...	...	...	...	...	...	...
1809	15,849		804	2,868	7,259		18,014	...	...	...	...	...	...	...	...	...
1810	15,628		595	2,977	10,921		15,640	...	...	...	...	...	...	...	...	...
1811	12,835		337	2,941	1,841		11,940	...	...	...	...	...	...	...	...	...
1812	...	...	...	...	...	...	...	...	...	...	...	...	...	...	...	...
1813	...	...	...	...	...	...	...	...	...	...	...	...	...	...	...	...
1814	14,114	12,756	372	2,340	8	11,429	1,791		2,683	...	...	...	...	...	...	...
1815	11,972	8,765	334	2,932	13,255	10,688	1,157		2,531	...	...	...	...	...	...	...
1816	11,369	7,284	352	3,071	9,557	7,016	861		2,147	...	...	...	...	...	...	...
1817	11,408	7,685	406	3,725	6,930	7,406	1,280		2,651	...	...	...	...	...	...	...
1818	11,809	7,630	391	3,877	9,451	7,790	1,170		3,996	...	...	...	...	...	...	...
1819	9,895	6,895	316	2,715	4,930	6,861	892		2,376	...	...	...	...	...	...	...
1820	11,290	7,140	393	3,810	3,875	5,757	940		2,921	...	...	...	...	...	...	...
1821	9,044	6,859	482	4,278	6,215	5,462	1,051		2,942	...	...	...	...	...	...	...
1822	8,328	8,274	385	3,985	6,865	4,779	868		3,167	...	...	...	...	...	...	...
1823	8,056	6,801	507	3,941	5,465	5,312	1,074		4,219	...	...	...	...	...	...	...
1824	7,691	8,008	418	3,692	6,090	5,779	1,171		5,573	...	...	...	...	...	...	...
1825	8,548	6,099	402	3,623	7,019	5,847		908	6,426	...	...	...	...	...	...	...
1826	7,823	6,070	296	4,322	4,659	4,601		570	3,195	...	...	...	...	...	...	...
1827	8,533	5,946	671	4,799	7,018	1,397	3,584	907	4,004	1,409	4,829	2,105		447	3,662	340
1828	8,243	5,533	717	4,892	5,810	1,691	3,290	818	5,489	1,319	4,573	2,143		499	...	446
1829	8,346	6,199	829	4,231	4,823	1,582	3,612	970	4,930	1,436	4,663	2,050		491	...	312

Overseas Trade 12. *continued*

	North-ern Europe	South-ern Europe	Africa	Asia	U.S.A.	British North America	British West Indies	Foreign West Indies	Central and South America	Russia	Germany	Nether-lands	Belgium	France	India	Australia and Pacific Settle-ments
1830	8,377	7,234	905	4,455	6,132	1,857	2,839	940	5,189	1,490	4,582	2,022		476	...	316
1831	7,318	6,233	803	4,105	9,054	2,089	2,582	1,040	3,616	1,192	3,836	2,083		603	...	403
1832	9,897	5,687	881	4,235	5,468	2,076	2,440	1,177	4,272	1,587	5,328	2,789		675	...	468
1833	9,314	6,298	937	4,712	7,580	2,092	2,598	959	4,842	1,531	4,500	2,182	886	848	2,579	559
1834	9,506	8,501	993	4,644	6,845	1,671	2,680	1,270	5,178	1,382	4,684	2,470	750	1,117	3,193	716
1835	10,303	8,161	1,146	5,456	10,568	2,158	3,188	1,153	4,887	1,753	4,791	2,648	818	1,454	4,286	699
1836	10,000	9,011	1,468	6,751	12,426	2,732	3,787	1,239	5,955	1,742	4,624	2,510	839	1,591	3,613	836
1837	11,528	7,873	1,440	5,561	4,695	2,141	3,457	1,063	4,313	2,047	5,030	3,040	805	1,643	3,613	922
1838	12,130	10,113	1,848	6,956	7,586	1,922	3,394	1,136	4,727	1,663	5,144	3,549	1,068	2,314	3,876	1,338
1839	12,332	8,466	1,607	7,643	8,839	3,048	3,986	1,285	6,027	1,776	5,422	3,564	882	2,298	4,749	1,703
1840	12,283	9,208	1,615	9,276	5,283	2,848	3,575	1,115	6,202	1,603	5,628	3,416	880	2,378	5,213	2,052
1841	13,160	9,695	1,857	8,167	7,099	2,947	2,504	1,065	5,142	1,607	6,018	3,611	1,066	2,902	4,823	1,337
1842	14,031	9,879	1,733	7,456	3,529	2,334	2,591	854	4,975	1,886	6,579	3,573	1,099	3,194	4,433	959
1843	14,024	10,947	1,714	9,547	5,014	1,751	2,883	973	5,427	1,896	6,651	3,565	985	2,535	5,689	1,307
1844	14,327	11,294	1,616	11,274	7,938	3,044	2,478	1,174	5,440	2,129	6,657	3,132	1,471	2,656	6,919	792
1845	15,092	11,211	1,896	10,974	7,143	3,551	2,794	1,464	5,986	2,153	7,096	3,439	1,479	2,791	5,873	1,244
1846	14,696	11,431	1,803	10,190	6,830	3,308	3,506	1,445	5,578	1,725	7,151	3,576	1,158	2,716	5,773	1,495
1847	13,906	11,703	2,049	9,119	10,974	3,233	2,273	1,510	5,075	1,845	6,840	3,017	1,059	2,554	4,799	1,670

Overseas Trade 12. *continued*

NOTE TO PART B
SOURCE: *Annual Statement of Trade.*

B Computed Values of Imports and Re-exports 1854-70, and Declared Values of Exports 1846-1938 and of Imports and Re-Exports 1871-1938

	North and North-east Europe(a)			Western Europe(b)			Central and South-east Europe(c)			Southern Europe and North Africa(d)			Turkey and the Middle East(e)		
	Imports	Exports	Re-exports	Imports	Exports	Re-exports	Imports	Exports	Re-exports	Imports	Exports	Re-exports	Imports	Exports	Re-exports
1846	...	2·4	...	...	7·5	...	...	8·1	...	...	5·8	...	...	2·5	...
1847	...	2·4	...	...	6·6	...	...	7·6	...	...	4·5	...	...	3·3	...
1848	...	2·5	...	...	4·7	...	...	6·0	...	...	5·6	...	...	3·5	...
1849	...	2·3	...	...	6·9	...	...	7·0	...	...	5·9	...	...	3·4	...
1850	...	2·3	...	...	7·1	...	...	8·4	...	...	5·8	...	...	3·5	...
1851	...	2·2	...	...	6·6	...	...	8·8	...	...	6·5	...	...	3·3	...
1852	...	2·0	...	...	7·9	...	...	8·8	...	...	6·3	...	...	3·6	...
1853	...	2·4	...	...	8·5	...	...	9·0	...	...	6·5	...	...	3·1	...
1854	10·9	1·6	0·6	21·0	9·2	7·5	17·6	9·2	5·8	9·0	6·4	0·9	5·7	4·4	0·4
1855	7·7	1·8	0·7	18·2	12·3	9·3	17·4	10·6	5·8	9·4	7·1	1·2	6·1	8·1	0·6
1856	17·2	3·7	2·6	20·8	13·9	8·8	12·1	13·3	5·1	10·8	8·8	1·8	8·3	6·8	0·4
1857	19·1	5·0	2·3	22·6	14·3	9·8	14·7	14·4	5·2	9·6	8·8	1·5	10·3	5·8	0·2
1858	16·6	4·4	2·7	22·6	12·2	9·5	9·6	14·2	4·3	8·4	9·6	1·4	8·9	7·1	0·5
1859	19·8	5·8	2·9	27·1	11·6	9·8	11·5	12·7	4·5	9·8	8·9	1·6	11·4	6·8	0·5
1860	23·3	5·0	2·9	30·1	13·0	13·4	16·4	14·7	5·7	12·5	11·5	1·5	13·6	7·6	0·3
1861	17·8(h)	4·9(h)	3·5(h)	29·3	17·3	16·0	16·5(h)	14·3(h)	7·1(h)	10·7	13·0	2·2	12·1	6·2	0·2
1862	20·3	4·0	2·3	34·4	17·1	19·9	16·9	13·7	7·8	10·3	11·7	2·7	16·6	6·6	0·5
1863	18·5	4·7	3·4	37·9	17·1	23·9	15·9	14·7	10·2	11·5	14·5	3·3	21·9	11·2	0·4
1864	21·5	5·5	4·3	43·7	17·4	26·5	16·4	16·6	9·7	11·9	13·8	2·6	25·5	13·4	0·5
1865	25·3	5·8	4·5	51·4	20·1	27·1	17·6	18·8	10·4	12·0	12·9	2·6	27·3	13·1	0·4
1866	27·5	6·1	5·0	56·7	23·5	24·7	20·9	16·9	9·5	13·4	12·8	2·8	20·8	15·6	0·3
1867	31·4	6·7	4·5	52·1	24·4	21·0	20·6	21·9	9·6	13·2	11·4	2·4	19·7	14·9	0·4
1868	28·7	7·1	4·1	53·5	24·2	24·4	21·6	24·5	9·8	14·5	11·2	2·2	23·8	13·7	0·4
1869	25·3	9·6	4·4	55·7	26·2	23·4	21·9	25·1	9·5	15·2	12·6	2·5	24·5	15·0	0·5
1870	32·2	11·0	4·6	63·2	27·3	20·9	17·6	22·7	8·1	14·9	12·9	2·3	20·8	15·9	0·5
1871	33·8	10·5	4·9	57·4	38·5	29·8	21·7	29·7	11·6	19·5	14·1	3·0	23·5	13·1	0·5
1872	35·0	12·1	4·6	68·1	40·0	25·7	21·2	33·9	12·1	21·1	15·9	2·6	21·9	15·0	0·6
1873	35·4	16·7	4·9	69·7	41·2	27·8	21·8	29·8	9·9	22·8	17·7	2·8	20·3	14·1	0·5
1874	36·2	16·7	5·1	76·0	36·6	26·7	21·4	27·1	10·8	19·9	16·7	3·3	16·7	11·0	0·5
1875	33·9	14·9	5·5	76·4	34·3	26·9	23·7	25·2	11·2	22·4	16·0	3·4	17·8	9·1	0·6

See p. 327 for footnotes

315

	North and North-east Europe(a)			Western Europe(b)			Central and South-east Europe(c)			Southern Europe and North Africa(d)			Turkey and the Middle East(e)		
	Imports	Exports	Re-exports	Imports	Exports	Re-exports	Imports	Exports	Re-exports	Imports	Exports	Re-exports	Imports	Exports	Re-exports
1876	32·4	12·6	5·1	75·8	33·7	26·8	23·2	21·6	10·1	19·9	16·5	3·2	19·2	8·8	0·5
1877	36·5	10·2	4·6	78·6	29·2	24·3	28·1	20·9	9·7	23·4	15·4	2·8	18·3	8·2	0·5
1878	31·5	10·9	4·8	75·2	29·7	23·0	26·2	21·1	10·2	18·8	13·6	2·8	11·3	10·2	0·7
1879	28·9	11·8	4·7	71·1	29·4	24·5	24·7	20·4	11·4	17·8	12·7	2·9	12·7	9·8	0·6
1880	32·3	13·0	5·4	79·1	30·6	26·0	26·2	18·7	12·4	21·2	13·8	2·7	13·5	10·2	0·6
1881	28·7	11·5	5·2	74·5	32·9	26·0	27·9(i)	19·6(i)	12·2(i)	20·5	15·8	2·6	13·9(i)	10·4(i)	0·7(i)
1882	38·1	11·6	4·7	79·4	34·9	26·2	32·7	20·3	12·5	22·1	15·6	3·2	13·0	9·2	0·8
1883	39·1	11·2	4·5	79·9	35·4	24·6	34·3	21·2	13·7	22·3	16·7	3·1	16·0	10·5	0·9
1884	32·1	11·0	4·4	78·5	35·5	23·9	28·8	20·7	12·6	20·1	16·5	2·9	15·5	9·7	0·9
1885	33·5	9·6	4·0	75·8	31·7	21·1	28·3	18·1	11·1	19·1	14·9	2·4	13·8	10·1	1·0
1886	28·7	9·4	3·6	76·2	28·9	18·6	25·8	17·6	11·2	17·7	14·4	2·4	11·7	9·0	0·8
1887	31·3	9·3	4·5	77·2	28·8	20·0	29·6	17·7	11·9	19·4	16·6	2·3	11·9	8·9	0·7
1888	44·6	10·7	4·8	80·6	30·3	21·9	32·5	17·9	12·1	21·2	14·8	2·3	11·9	8·4	0·6
1889	47·7	12·2	5·7	90·1	31·6	20·5	32·8	20·9	13·3	22·0	17·4	2·6	14·4	9·6	0·7
1890	43·4	13·3	5·5	88·1	34·3	20·4	32·4	21·9	11·7	22·8	19·0	2·3	13·5	11·0	0·7
1891	43·9	12·9	4·9	89·3	33·3	19·3	33·7	21·8	11·6	21·0	17·2	1·9	16·4	11·4	0·7
1892	35·0	12·6	5·6	89·4	30·5	19·3	30·0	20·2	12·5	21·5(j)	15·0(j)	2·1(j)	16·4(j)	9·8(j)	0·6(j)
1893	39·5	13·4	6·1	89·4	29·7	18·8	32·3	20·4	10·8	18·6	13·4	2·1	14·0	9·5	0·5
1894	45·1	14·4	6·8	88·1	29·9	16·7	32·4	20·8	12·0	18·9	14·3	1·8	14·5	11·0	0·5
1895	47·2	14·6	5·8	93·4	28·6	15·0	30·4	23·4	12·7	19·7	13·9	1·9	15·6	9·2	0·4
1896	47·2	15·2	6·5	98·6	30·3	15·0	32·4	25·4	12·3	20·4	13·4	1·9	15·2	9·3	0·4
1897	48·1	16·4	6·5	103·2	30·9	14·7	30·1	24·9	11·1	22·2	13·6	2·1	15·8	11·5	0·6
1898	45·9	19·0	7·6	101·5	31·1	16·3	32·3	25·8	11·5	23·2	13·9	2·3	14·1	11·1	0·7
1899	46·5	23·7	6·8	106·3	34·5	16·4	33·5	29·5	12·7	24·6(k)	17·8(k)	2·7(k)	16·1(k)	10·9(k)	0·5(k)
1900	51·6	24·0	7·4	108·5	41·7	14·0	34·0	31·2	11·3	26·6	20·9	2·3	18·6	11·7	0·5
1901	51·7	20·1	7·7	112·0	33·7	16·4	37·5	27·0	11·5	24·2	19·5	2·2	18·0	14·1	0·5
1902	56·4	19·5	6·9	112·1	32·4	15·5	43·1	26·3	11·0	24·9	19·5	2·2	20·3	12·8	0·4
1903	63·8	20·4	8·7	113·3	33·3	16·6	41·5	26·6	11·8	24·2	19·8	2·3	19·2	12·7	0·4
1904	62·9	19·6	8·5	116·3	32·5	15·6	39·9	28·6	12·2	23·1	20·2	2·6	20·5	16·3	0·4
1905(l) {	64·8	20·8	8·4	119·6	35·9	16·7	39·0	33·4	13·9	23·5	20·2	2·6	20·8	15·2	0·5
{	66·0	20·8	8·4	86·0	35·9	16·7	61·7	33·4	13·9	26·6	20·2	2·5	20·9	15·2	0·5

See p. 327 for footnotes

	North and North-east Europe(a)			Western Europe(b)			Central and South-east Europe(c)			Southern Europe and North Africa(d)			Turkey and the Middle East(e)		
	Imports	Exports	Re-exports	Imports	Exports	Re-exports	Imports	Exports	Re-exports	Imports	Exports	Re-exports	Imports	Exports	Re-exports
1906	65·7	23·0	9·2	89·2	43·6	18·7	66·0	38·2	15·7	30·2	23·6	3·2	23·4	17·7	0·6
1907	69·0	28·2	10·1	88·3	50·3	21·5	68·7	48·8	16·3	32·1	27·9	3·0	28·9	18·6	0·5
1908	66·2	27·9	9·7	82·7	45·5	19·2	65·7	40·6	13·8	27·1	29·0	2·5	23·1	17·3	0·5
1909	73·2	25·8	9·2	87·2	46·6	20·5	69·0	38·6	15·8	27·4	24·6	2·6	25·4	16·2	0·4
1910	81·8	28·6	11·1	91·8	49·4	23·7	72·8	43·9	19·1	28·5	25·7	3·4	26·3	18·4	0·4
1911	82·1	30·2	11·0	91·2	52·7	23·7	79·1	47·9	19·6	29·3	27·8	3·1	27·9	20·9	0·5
1912	83·0	32·2	10·1	101·2	56·1	25·1	80·8	49·6	20·6	31·0	31·9	3·0	33·5	18·9	0·4
1913	86·0	38·5	11·7	104·4	61·8	25·3	90·2(m)	47·6(m)	21·2(m)	30·6(m)	33·8(m)	2·9(m)	27·6(m)	18·7(m)	0·4(m)
1914	75·4	34·7	10·7	88·3	50·4	22·1	54·9	28·6	14·2	31·0	29·6	2·9	22·4(n)	14·8(n)	0·3(n)
1915	77·8	35·0	21·5	71·7	91·4	24·7	0·3	1·4	0·1	40·5	32·0	6·8	24·4	9·7	0·6
1916	78·4	54·3	15·9	65·5	121·7	24·8	0·1	--	--	50·7	42·1	7·0	28·5	12·6	0·7
1917	69·6	67·4	5·9	54·4	139·2	20·8	--	0·7	--	42·6	47·8	7·0	34·3	17·0	0·3
1918	58·2	17·0	0·6	55·9	154·5	14·7	--	--	--	68·0	53·8	5·3	55·2	25·9	0·2
1919	78·8	99·9	17·9	94·3	243·3	81·3	1·5	23·0	9·6	76·9	68·2	10·7	72·2	43·7	1·6
1920	145·5	116·3	16·4	197·0	245·3	76·6	36·3	34·4	31·6	78·2	102·6	12·3	86·1	77·9	2·3
1921	86·7(o)	43·1(o)	7·2(o)	145·3(p)	96·8(p)	32·6(p)	33·1(q)	32·1(q)	26·8(q)	43·9	48·8	4·1	39·4	35·9	0·7
1922	94·1	45·2	5·9	128·4	118·0	35·6	39·0	40·7	18·5	42·2	47·8	3·9	45·5	29·0	0·7
1923(t)	110·0	44·4	8·1	143·0	111·3	36·5	54·5	52·7	19·9	47·0	46·2	4·2	46·4	27·8	0·6
1924	126·5	48·4	13·0	166·6	100·9	36·7	64·5	55·3	31·3	51·2	47·0	4·8	50·8	28·1	0·7
1925	129·9	44·0	18·1	166·6	83·7	41·5	70·1	58·0	29·1	51·1	47·0	4·7	45·3	31·0	0·7
1926	127·7	34·5	12·3	169·1	58·8	34·6	97·9	37·0	22·6	42·8	29·5	3·6	38·7	21·3	0·7
1927	134·1	37·2	10·1	169·5	69·0	33·4	83·1	57·3	29·2	47·9	39·0	3·9	40·1	22·7	0·7
1928	130·9	36·6	5·6	161·8	71·9	35·1	81·0	57·3	28·2	45·5	39·6	3·7	41·6	20·8	0·5
1929	146·6	41·2	6·3	157·1	79·3	33·1	91·6	51·9	24·8	48·0	43·8	3·0	38·1	23·1	0·6
1930	143·4	45·1	5·3	140·0	68·8	26·3	89·8	38·4	18·7	41·6	36·0	2·5	27·5	18·8	0·6
1931	123·1	34·4	3·8	121·3	50·4	17·9	87·7	26·4	14·9	37·5	25·8	1·6	20·5	12·6	0·4
1932	99·7	35·8	3·3	62·7	42·9	15·6	45·9	22·4	11·9	30·9	23·7	1·7	21·2	13·5	0·3
1933	94·7	33·3	3·0	56·1	43·3	14·3	46·8	22·9	11·4	28·2	22·3	1·6	23·5	13·7	0·4
1934	98·5	39·2	6·6	60·9	42·3	13·6	49·2	23·6	10·9	28·9	25·3	2·2	22·9	14·7	0·4
1935	101·3	41·6	9·2	66·2	41·1	14·5	50·1	28·3	9·6	28·3	24·2	2·6	25·9	17·3	0·4
1936	108·5	44·2	12·5	76·3	43·5	15·8	62·2	29·8	9·9	23·6	13·9	1·6	27·6	16·6	0·4
1937	137·1	53·3	19·4	88·8	52·2	17·7	67·5	35·3	10·8	29·2	17·9	2·5	33·8	18·6	0·4
1938	122·4	52·2	13·7	79·4	40·0	15·1	57·6	33·0	9·6	25·0	20·5	1·7	27·9	21·8	0·4

See p. 327 for footnotes

Overseas Trade 12. *continued*

	The Remainder of Africa			Asia			U.S.A.			British North America			The West Indies		
	Imports	Exports	Re-exports	Imports	Exports	Re-exports	Imports	Exports	Re-exports	Imports	Exports	Re-exports	Imports	Exports	Re-exports
1846	...	1·4	...	...	8·7	...	...	6·8	...	...	3·3	...	...	4·0	...
1847	...	1·6	...	...	7·4	...	...	11·0	...	...	3·2	...	...	3·8	...
1848	...	1·6	...	...	7·0	...	...	9·6	...	...	2·0	...	...	2·5	...
1849	...	1·6	...	...	8·8	...	...	12·0	...	...	2·3	...	...	3·6	...
1850	...	2·0	...	...	10·3	...	...	14·9	...	...	3·2	...	...	4·0	...
1851	...	1·9	...	...	10·9	...	...	14·4	...	...	3·8	...	...	4·5	...
1852	...	2·1	...	...	10·6	...	...	16·6	...	...	3·1	...	...	3·9	...
1853	...	2·8	...	...	10·9	...	...	23·7	...	...	4·9	...	...	3·7	...
1854	4·8	2·5	0·4	23·0	12·0	0·6	29·8	21·4	0·9	7·1	6·0	0·3	7·6	3·8	0·2
1855	5·1	2·6	0·4	24·3	13·1	0·5	25·7	17·3	0·7	4·7	2·9	0·2	6·5	3·2(g)	0·2
1856	6·2	3·0	0·4	29·8	15·4	0·6	36·0	21·9	0·7	6·9	4·1	0·3	7·0	3·1	0·3
1857	6·6	4·0	0·5	33·8	16·8	0·7	33·6	19·0	1·1	6·4	4·3	0·3	8·9	4·0	0·3
1858	5·6	3·5	0·4	25·5	22·5	0·8	34·3	14·5	1·3	4·7	3·2	0·3	8·9	3·8	0·2
1859	5·5	3·8	0·4	27·5	28·2	1·2	34·3	22·6	1·9	5·5	3·6	0·4	7·7	3·5	0·3
1860	5·9	4·3	0·4	28·5	26·1	1·0	44·7	21·7	1·2	6·8	3·7	0·3	7·9	3·8	0·3
1861	5·7	4·1	0·5	36·9	24·7	0·8	49·4	9·1	2·0	8·7	3·7	0·5	8·9	3·5	0·3
1862	5·0	4·1	0·5	52·1	20·7	0·9	27·7	14·3	4·8	8·5	4·0	0·8	9·1	4·7	0·4
1863	6·0	3·4	0·5	69·6	27·8	1·2	19·6	15·3	4·4	8·2	4·8	0·7	11·0	5·4	0·5
1864	5·5	4·2	0·5	74·9	28·9	1·2	17·9	16·7	3·5	6·9	5·6	0·7	13·9	6·2	0·5
1865	6·2	3·7	0·4	56·7	29·0	0·9	21·6	21·2	3·9	6·4	4·7	1·0	10·6	5·3	0·3
1866	6·9	3·7	0·4	54·5	34·7	1·1	46·9	28·5	3·3	6·9	6·8	0·9	8·0	5·6	0·4
1867	6·6	4·3	0·4	40·8	36·0	1·5	41·0	21·8	2·3	6·8	5·9	0·9	9·1	5·0	0·3
1868	7·2	4·0	0·4	49·8	35·0	1·5	43·1	21·4	2·4	6·8	4·8	0·7	10·0	5·0	0·5
1869	6·6	3·9	0·4	51·8	32·0	1·5	42·6	24·6	2·2	7·7	5·2	0·8	9·9	3·7	0·4
1870	6·8	4·5	0·5	42·9	35·4	1·5	49·8	28·3	3·0	8·5	6·8	0·8	10·2	6·4	0·5
1871	7·4	4·8	0·5	51·0	33·3	1·8	61·1	34·2	4·5	9·3	8·3	0·9	8·5	6·2	0·6
1872	8·8	6·7	0·7	57·2	34·5	1·9	54·7	40·7	5·2	9·1	10·2	1·1	10·9	7·1	0·7
1873	8·7	7·5	0·8	53·5	35·7	1·6	71·5	33·6	3·1	11·3	8·6	0·8	10·2	6·5	0·7
1874	8·8	7·3	0·9	52·7	39·4	2·0	73·9	28·2	4·0	11·9	9·3	0·9	8·7	5·1	0·7
1875	8·6	7·4	0·9	56·0	41·0	2·1	69·6	21·9	3·2	10·2	9·0	0·6	9·7	6·2	0·6
1876	8·3	6·9	0·8	55·8	37·6	1·9	75·9	16·8	3·4	11·0	7·4	0·7	7·9	4·8	0·8
1877	9·4	7·1	0·9	58·3	42·2	2·1	77·8	16·4	3·5	12·0	7·6	0·6	6·6	5·1	0·7
1878	8·0	7·9	1·0	51·4	37·6	2·2	89·1	14·6	3·0	9·5	6·4	0·6	6·4	4·7	0·9
1879	8·2	8·7	1·0	47·0	36·7	2·6	91·8	20·3	5·2	10·4	5·4	0·7	8·0	4·5	0·9
1880	9·5	9·4	1·0	55·2	48·9	3·0	107·1	30·9	7·1	13·4	7·7	0·8	6·5	4·7	1·2

See p. 327 for footnotes

	The Remainder of Africa			Asia			U.S.A.			British North America			The West Indies		
	Imports	Exports	Re-exports	Imports	Exports	Re-exports	Imports	Exports	Re-exports	Imports	Exports	Re-exports	Imports	Exports	Re-exports
1881	8·8	9·9	1·0	56·0	48·3	2·9	103·2	29·8	7·0	11·3	8·4	0·9	5·5	5·0	0·9
1882	10·0	10·5	1·5	65·1	45·3	2·5	88·4	31·0	7·7	10·4	9·7	1·0	6·1	5·2	1·1
1883	9·6	8·3	0·9	63·6	48·2	2·6	99·3	27·4	9·4	12·3	9·2	1·0	4·6	5·5	1·1
1884	9·3	8·0	0·8	58·0	46·9	2·8	86·3	24·4	8·3	11·0	8·7	1·0	3·8	4·6	1·1
1885	7·3	6·7	0·7	53·1	46·0	2·7	86·5	22·0	9·1	10·3	7·2	1·2	3·7	4·0	1·0
1886	7·3	6·1	0·7	52·9	46·1	2·0	81·6	26·8	10·8	10·4	7·9	1·2	1·9	4·1	1·1
1887	7·5	7·7	0·8	49·4	48·5	2·6	83·0	29·5	10·7	10·6	8·1	1·1	2·1	4·4	1·0
1888	8·1	8·8	0·8	52·7	52·1	2·0	79·8	28·9	12·3	9·3	7·6	1·1	2·7	4·6	1·2
1889	9·0	12·5	1·2	57·7	48·8	2·2	95·5	30·3	13·6	12·2	8·1	1·3	2·4	4·7	1·3
1890	9·4	13·1	1·1	51·6	53·5	2·3	97·3	32·1	14·3	12·4	7·2	1·0	2·1	5·7	1·4
1891	9·6	12·0	1·1	53·3	50·0	2·0	104·4	27·5	13·5	12·6	7·2	1·1	1·8	4·5	1·4
1892	8·7	11·7	1·1	48·7	44·7	1·8	108·2	26·5	14·9	14·6	7·4	1·1	2·1	4·4	1·6
1893	9·1	12·7	1·2	44·7	44·6	1·8	91·8	24·0	11·8	13·3	7·2	1·4	2·0	4·4	1·3
1894	8·5	12·5	1·1	43·9	45·6	1·4	89·6	18·8	12·0	12·9	6·3	1·1	2·3	3·9	1·2
1895	9·0	14·7	1·3	43·5	42·3	1·2	86·5	27·9	16·1	13·4	5·5	1·0	2·1	3·6	1·0
1896	8·9	18·9	1·6	41·8	50·6	1·3	106·3	20·4	11·6	16·4	5·8	0·9	1·9	3·4	0·8
1897	8·9	18·8	1·4	40·0	46·6	1·1	113·0	21·0	16·9	19·5	5·5	1·0	1·6	2·9	0·8
1898	10·4	17·8	1·6	42·9	48·6	1·1	126·1	14·7	13·8	20·8	6·2	1·4	1·4	2·5	0·7
1899	10·6	17·9	1·5	46·1	56·2	1·4	120·1	18·1	16·9	20·7	7·3	1·4	1·6	3·7	1·0
1900	8·4	19·7	1·9	47·0	55·7	1·5	138·8	19·8	17·6	22·2	8·1	1·5	1·8	3·7	1·0
1901	9·5	24·4	2·5	45·8	59·4	1·3	141·0	18·4	19·3	20·4	8·1	1·5	2·0	3·6	1·1
1902	10·2	31·4	2·7	47·0	54·8	1·4	127·0	23·8	19·3	23·6	10·7	1·7	2·3	3·6	0·7
1903	10·9	33·9	2·3	51·1	56·2	1·4	122·1	22·6	19·0	27·3	11·5	1·7	2·0	4·1	0·8
1904	11·3	25·8	2·2	56·5	67·5	1·8	119·2	20·2	19·1	23·1	11·1	1·7	2·2	4·4	1·1
1905	11·3	25·3	2·1	56·5	78·6	2·3	115·6	23·9	23·4	26·2	12·3	1·9	2·2	4·4	1·2
1905	11·8	25·3	2·1	57·2	80·7	2·3	114·7	23·9	23·4	26·2	12·3	1·9	3·4	4·3	1·2
1906	13·0	25·3	2·2	62·4	84·9	1·9	131·1	27·8	25·5	28·7	14·2	1·9	3·8	4·6	1·1
1907	16·7	24·7	2·1	71·7	92·0	1·9	134·3	30·9	27·1	25·8	17·5	2·2	3·6	5·2	1·4
1908	14·2	22·5	2·0	53·8	83·2	2·2	123·9	21·3	21·2	24·8	12·7	2·0	3·8	4·5	1·1
1909	16·9	25·4	2·2	63·8	75·5	1·9	118·4	29·8	29·5	25·5	16·3	2·5	3·8	4·7	1·0
1910	19·7	34·5	2·7	79·5	82·2	2·0	117·6	31·4	30·7	26·2	20·6	3·0	6·3	4·9	1·1

	The Remainder of Africa			Asia			U.S.A.			British North America			The West Indies		
	Imports	Exports	Re-exports	Imports	Exports	Re-exports	Imports	Exports	Re-exports	Imports	Exports	Re-exports	Imports	Exports	Re-exports
1911	19·1	34·5	2·9	83·8	94·7	2·5	122·7	27·5	28·6	25·3	20·3	3·1	3·8	5·5	1·1
1912	20·9	37·3	3·1	97·2	101·8	3·1	134·6	30·1	34·6	27·7	24·3	3·9	5·3	5·7	1·1
1913	22·9	38·6	3·1	92·6	125·7	2·6	141·7	29·3	30·2	31·5	24·7	3·6	6·1	5·1	1·2
1914	23·9(n)	32·5(n)	2·7(n)	93·5	105·2	1·7	138·6	34·0	30·6	32·4	17·9	3·2	7·1	4·4	1·2
1915	33·4	31·3	3·0	130·7	75·4	2·2	237·8	26·2	30·3	42·2	13·6	2·8	12·6	4·1	1·3
1916	38·6	41·1	3·2	151·8	94·9	3·0	291·8	32·7	31·9	60·5	18·5	3·6	18·4	4·7	1·2
1917	39·6	37·2	1·7	148·3	96·7	1·4	376·3	33·2	26·9	85·1	16·6	1·6	24·4	4·6	0·3
1918	47·1	42·0	1·0	157·8	90·3	2·1	515·4	23·3	3·5	125·3	14·7	0·7	31·0	4·1	0·1
1919	74·4	45·9	2·4	230·4	131·2	3·6	541·6	33·9	31·6	117·8	16·5	2·1	29·4	4·8	0·3
1920	80·6	98·7	5·8	238·6	321·1	6·1	563·3	77·1	53·9	97·4	43·7	6·2	41·0	14·9	0·7
1921	48·5	56·7	2·6	101·5	196·3	4·1	274·8	44·0	20·3	63·8	19·8	2·1	13·1	6·5	1·1
1922	42·7	49·0	2·7	100·6	169·7	2·1	221·8	55·5	21·7	56·8	25·7	2·7	15·7	6·2	1·3
1923	46·4	54·8	3·0	130·0	161·5	2·1	210·7	59·7	25·9	55·5	28·2	2·8	16·1	8·4	0·8
1924	52·2	57·7	3·3	142·4	171·7	2·2	241·2	54·0	24·6	67·8	30·0	2·6	21·3	8·4	0·5
1925	60·2	64·2	3·7	160·5	154·7	2·4	245·3	52·1	31·1	72·6	28·9	3·3	22·3	8·2	0·4
1926	53·7	60·2	3·7	137·9	147·2	2·8	228·9	49·1	25·8	65·6	27·4	2·5	13·3	7·0	0·4
1927	56·2	63·9	4·2	142·7	148·3	2·6	200·2	45·4	21·4	57·4	30·0	2·3	16·8	7·8	0·3
1928	60·0	65·8	3·9	127·0	154·7	2·5	188·4	46·7	22·1	59·2	35·5	2·8	22·9	8·2	0·4
1929	59·0	64·3	3·9	135·7	147·3	2·4	196·0	45·6	16·5	48·4	35·9	2·7	18·4	8·2	0·4
1930	45·8	55·7	3·0	106·6	98·6	2·3	153·5	28·7	11·2	40·4	29·9	2·2	17·3	6·9	0·4
1931	29·7	40·4	2·1	79·2	65·2	1·6	104·0	18·2	8·0	34·9	21·0	1·7	13·2	5·5	0·4
1932	35·0	34·9	1·4	68·4	66·5	1·1	83·6	15·1	5·7	45·1	17·1	1·0	18·1	5·9	0·3
1933	33·9	40·1	1·5	69·8	60·1	1·3	75·8	19·1	7·1	48·4	18·1	1·2	19·2	6·0	0·2
1934	32·2	47·1	1·3	89·9	64·3	1·1	82·0	17·6	5·6	52·8	20·5	1·5	20·2	6·4	0·2
1935	37·8	55·6	1·5	86·5	65·1	1·2	87·5	22·9	7·2	58·2	22·3	1·2	22·5	6·6	0·2
1936	44·0	61·0	1·6	94·7	62·7	1·0	93·2	27·6	9·1	77·4	24·4	1·1	27·2	7·1	0·2
1937	59·4	71·1	1·9	122·9	75·4	1·4	114·1	31·4	10·9	92·0	28·7	1·3	33·7	8·5	0·2
1938	46·4	62·4	1·4	108·2	67·4	1·3	118·0	20·5	8·3	81·3	23·5	1·1	31·5	7·9	0·2

See p. 327 for footnotes

	Central and South America			Russia			Germany			Netherlands			Belgium		
	Imports	Exports	Re-exports	Imports	Exports	Re-exports	Imports	Exports	Re-exports	Imports	Exports	Re-exports	Imports	Exports	Re-exports
1846	..	5·6	..	..	1·7	..	..	7·2	..	..	3·6	..	..	1·2	..
1847	..	5·1	..	..	1·8	..	..	6·8	..	..	3·0	..	..	1·1	..
1848	..	5·8	..	..	1·9	..	..	5·3	..	..	2·8	..	..	0·8	..
1849	..	7·2	..	..	1·6	..	..	6·1	..	..	3·5	..	..	1·5	..
1850	..	6·8	..	..	1·5	..	..	7·5	..	..	3·5	..	..	1·1	..
1851	..	8·2	..	..	1·3	..	..	7·7	..	..	3·5	..	..	1·0	..
1852	..	8·5	..	..	1·1	..	..	7·9	..	..	4·1	..	..	1·1	..
1853	..	8·5	..	..	1·2	..	..	8·2	..	..	4·5	..	..	1·4	..
1854	11·3	8·3	0·3	4·3	0·1	..	16·3	8·5	4·6	6·7	4·6	2·3	3·6	1·4	1·9
1855	12·2	9·4(g)	0·4	0·5	—	—	16·3	9·9	5·6	6·5	4·6	2·6	2·5	1·7	2·2
1856	11·5	10·6	0·5	11·6	1·6	1·8	10·5	12·2	4·8	7·4	5·7	2·4	2·9	1·7	2·3
1857	16·0	12·6	0·5	13·4	3·1	1·9	13·5	13·1	4·8	7·2	6·4	2·5	3·4	1·7	2·2
1858	13·8	10·1	0·4	11·9	3·1	2·2	9·0	12·8	4·0	6·3	5·5	2·6	3·1	1·8	2·5
1859	12·1	10·3	0·5	13·5	4·0	2·3	10·5	11·8	4·3	6·7	5·4	2·8	3·5	1·5	2·2
1860	13·0	13·2	0·5	16·2	3·3	2·2	15·4	13·5	5·2	8·3	6·1	3·6	4·1	1·6	2·4
1861	13·8	12·1	0·4	12·8	3·0	2·7	14·1(h)	13·1(h)	6·3(h)	7·7	6·4	4·6	3·8	1·9	3·0
1862	16·2	9·4	0·4	15·1	2·1	1·7	15·1	12·8	7·3	7·9	6·0	4·6	4·9	1·8	2·7
1863	18·6	12·8	0·5	12·4	2·7	2·6	14·4	13·5	9·7	8·7	6·3	6·3	5·2	2·1	3·0
1864	23·1	17·6	0·8	14·7	2·8	3·2	15·2	15·5	9·4	11·7	6·9	7·2	6·4	2·3	3·7
1865	24·8	17·0	0·5	17·4	2·9	3·3	16·6	17·9	10·3	12·4	8·1	6·8	7·4	2·9	4·0
1866	20·9	20·4	0·5	19·6	3·2	3·7	19·1	15·8	9·3	11·8	9·0	5·9	7·9	2·9	3·9
1867	20·4	18·5	0·6	22·3	3·9	3·3	18·9	20·5	9·3	10·8	9·4	5·5	7·6	2·8	4·6
1868	22·4	16·0	0·6	20·1	4·3	3·0	18·2	22·8	9·5	11·4	10·4	6·3	8·3	3·2	5·2
1869	21·5	18·0	0·6	16·7	6·5	3·2	18·4	22·8	9·2	12·7	10·8	6·6	9·4	4·0	4·9
1870	21·6	17·6	0·8	20·6	7·0	3·1	15·4	20·4	7·6	14·3	11·2	6·1	11·2	4·5	4·5
1871	22·5	19·4	1·2	23·7	6·6	3·3	19·3	27·4	11·1	14·0	14·1	8·0	13·6	6·2	6·6
1872	28·3	25·3	1·5	24·3	6·6	2·9	19·2	31·6	11·5	13·1	16·2	8·1	13·2	6·5	6·6
1873	27·7	24·6	1·3	21·2	9·0	2·5	19·9	27·3	9·4	13·3	16·7	7·8	13·1	7·2	7·0
1874	24·5	22·1	1·3	20·9	8·8	3·1	19·9	24·8	10·3	14·5	14·4	6·9	15·0	5·8	6·8
1875	25·1	18·3	1·1	20·7	8·1	3·3	21·8	23·3	10·8	14·8	13·1	7·0	14·8	5·8	8·0
1876	22·8	15·6	1·0	17·6	6·2	2·5	21·1	20·1	9·7	16·6	11·8	6·9	13·8	5·9	7·0
1877	22·7	16·7	1·2	22·1	4·2	2·1	26·3	19·6	9·3	19·9	9·6	6·4	12·9	5·3	6·5
1878	19·5	15·7	1·3	17·8	6·6	2·9	23·6	19·5	9·7	21·5	9·3	5·4	12·4	5·5	5·8
1879	19·6	14·2	0·9	15·9	7·6	3·0	21·6	18·6	11·0	22·0	9·4	6·1	10·7	5·1	6·8
1880	19·4	17·4	1·0	16·0	8·0	3·0	24·4	16·9	12·1	25·9	9·2	6·4	11·3	5·8	7·2

See p. 327 for footnotes

Overseas Trade 12. *continued*

	Central and South America			Russia			Germany			Netherlands			Belgium		
	Imports	Exports	Re-exports	Imports	Exports	Re-exports	Imports	Exports	Re-exports	Imports	Exports	Re-exports	Imports	Exports	Re-exports
1881	18.7	20.1	1.0	14.1	6.2	3.1	23.7	17.4	11.8	23.0	8.9	6.4	11.5	7.1	6.5
1882	21.6	22.0	1.3	21.0	5.8	2.9	25.6	18.5	12.0	25.3	9.4	6.9	14.9	8.1	7.0
1883	19.2	21.3	1.2	21.0	5.0	2.6	27.9	18.8	13.0	25.1	9.5	6.4	16.2	8.3	6.4
1884	17.2	22.2	1.1	16.3	5.0	2.6	23.6	18.7	12.1	25.9	10.2	8.0	15.1	8.5	6.3
1885	15.4	16.8	0.9	17.7	4.2	2.0	23.1	16.4	10.6	25.0	8.9	7.0	15.1	7.8	6.1
1886	13.8	19.0	1.0	13.6	4.4	2.0	21.4	15.7	10.6	25.3	8.2	6.8	14.2	7.2	5.1
1887	16.0	21.8	1.1	16.0	4.2	2.7	24.6	15.7	11.5	25.3	8.2	6.9	14.7	6.9	6.3
1888	17.4	24.3	1.3	26.3	4.8	2.9	26.7	15.8	11.6	26.1	8.5	6.4	15.6	6.8	6.2
1889	15.9	28.9	1.6	27.2	5.3	3.3	27.1	18.5	12.8	26.7	9.7	6.5	17.7	7.2	6.4
1890	17.2	28.4	1.2	23.8	5.8	3.1	26.1	19.3	11.2	25.9	10.1	6.3	17.4	7.6	6.0
1891	16.7	22.8	1.4	24.1	5.4	2.8	27.0	18.8	11.1	27.3	9.5	5.5	17.3	7.4	5.9
1892	17.5	24.1	1.4	15.1	5.4	3.5	25.7	17.6	12.1	28.8	8.8	6.8	17.0	6.9	5.9
1893	18.8	23.0	1.1	18.6	6.4	4.0	26.4	17.7	10.3	28.9	9.2	6.5	16.8	7.1	5.9
1894	18.9	21.3	1.1	23.6	6.9	4.7	26.9	17.8	11.4	27.6	8.8	5.1	17.1	7.6	5.4
1895	21.1	23.8	1.2	24.7	7.0	3.7	27.0	20.6	12.2	28.4	7.4	3.9	17.5	7.3	4.6
1896	21.7	24.2	1.3	22.7	7.2	4.2	27.6	22.2	11.7	29.3	8.3	4.0	19.2	7.8	4.5
1897	17.4	19.3	1.1	22.3	7.5	4.4	26.2	21.6	10.4	29.0	8.9	4.4	20.9	8.2	4.6
1898	21.4	20.2	1.2	19.5	9.2	5.0	28.5	22.5	10.8	28.5	8.6	4.4	21.5	8.8	5.0
1899	23.4	20.9	1.3	18.7	11.7	4.4	30.1	26.0	12.0	30.5	9.4	4.6	22.9	9.8	4.8
1900	28.4	23.8	1.5	22.0	11.0	5.4	31.2	28.0	10.5	31.4	10.9	4.0	23.5	10.8	4.1
1901	26.7	21.3	1.2	21.9	8.7	5.5	32.2	23.6	10.6	32.9	9.1	4.7	24.7	8.2	4.5
1902	29.2	21.5	1.2	25.7	8.6	5.3	33.6	22.9	10.2	34.8	8.4	4.6	26.5	8.4	4.2
1903	35.9	24.3	1.7	30.9	9.1	7.0	34.5	23.6	11.0	35.0	8.7	5.4	27.8	8.8	3.9
1904	41.4	28.3	1.9	31.4	8.2	7.1	33.9	25.1	11.3	34.7	8.2	4.7	27.5	9.1	4.4
1905	46.1	32.7	1.6	33.4	8.2	6.7	35.8	29.7	13.0	35.5	9.7	4.8	27.8	10.1	4.8
{	49.0	32.7	1.6	34.5	8.2	6.7	53.8	29.7	13.0	15.2	9.7	4.7	16.7	8.6	4.7
1906	47.4	43.4	1.7	31.5	8.9	7.1	55.9	33.6	14.8	16.2	11.6	5.2	18.0	10.0	5.1
1907	52.7	47.4	1.9	32.9	11.1	7.9	57.2	41.4	15.4	16.1	13.9	5.0	16.2	10.5	6.4
1908	60.7	39.4	1.7	29.7	12.6	7.9	55.0	33.4	13.0	16.6	11.5	4.2	16.2	9.6	5.2
1909	61.5	41.8	1.7	38.0	11.0	7.4	57.8	32.3	14.9	16.8	11.7	4.5	17.7	10.6	5.9
1910	65.9	52.6	2.0	43.6	12.3	9.0	61.8	37.0	17.9	18.5	12.7	5.2	19.2	10.9	7.0

Overseas Trade 12. *continued*

	Central and South America			Russia			Germany			Netherlands			Belgium		
	Imports	Exports	Re-exports	Imports	Exports	Re-exports	Imports	Exports	Re-exports	Imports	Exports	Re-exports	Imports	Exports	Re-exports
1911	56·6	49·5	2·2	43·2	13·5	8·8	65·3	39·3	18·1	18·7	13·1	4·7	20·8	11·4	7·2
1912	70·3	52·3	2·3	40·5	13·7	8·0	70·0	40·4	19·2	21·4	14·3	5·1	23·6	12·2	7·4
1913	73·7	54·0	2·5	40·3	18·1	9·6	80·4	40·7	19·8	23·6	15·4	5·1	23·4	13·2	7·4
1914	66·2	32·7	1·6	28·1	14·4	7·4	47·0	23·1	13·4	24·3	13·4	7·3	16·1	8·3	5·0
1915	100·1	24·7	1·7	21·4	13·4	11·5	0·2	...	...	23·4	18·0	12·4	1·6	0·2	--
1916	91·8	33·7	1·9	18·3	25·0	9·4	0·1	—	—	22·1	24·1	8·9	1·3	0·3	--
1917	91·6	35·5	1·0	17·9	48·7	4·0	--	—	—	19·9	20·8	4·0	0·3	0·2	--
1918	121·2	44·3	0·4	6·7	0·3	--	--	—	—	7·7	15·0	0·4	0·2	0·1	--
1919	138·7	49·7	1·2	16·4	13·0	4·5	1·0	14·7	8·5	21·7	34·3	26·3	9·2	48·0	17·5
1920	201·9	109·5	2·6	33·5	12·0	4·8	30·3	21·7	29·4	39·3	47·7	14·4	44·9	49·0	19·5
1921	112·2	59·2	1·1	2·7(o)	2·2(o)	1·2(o)	20·5(r)	17·9(r)	22·9(r)	38·8	27·3	9·1	32·9	19·6	9·7
1922	98·2	52·5	1·5	8·1	3·6	0·1	26·5	32·1	17·0	34·1	34·6	6·0	23·6	25·0	10·6
1923	107·0	63·5	1·7	9·3	2·5	2·0	35·0	42·6	18·3	37·1	29·5	5·8	27·5	25·2	10·2
1924	128·2	65·2	1·8	19·8	3·9	7·2	36·9	42·6	28·9	42·7	25·2	7·3	36·4	22·7	10·2
1925	120·9	72·3	1·7	25·3	6·2	13·0	48·4	44·2	27·3	45·6	24·8	6·9	35·6	18·7	10·3
1926	111·5	50·0	1·7	24·1	5·9	8·5	72·6	26·4	20·9	50·3	17·9	4·6	44·9	14·3	8·1
1927	122·7	64·5	1·6	21·1	4·5	6·8	59·9	41·9	27·5	44·5	21·2	4·8	46·5	16·5	8·8
1928	122·6	71·3	1·8	21·6	2·7	2·1	63·7	40·9	26·4	42·9	21·8	4·8	43·4	17·0	10·3
1929	129·3	71·6	1·8	26·5	3·7	2·8	68·8	37·0	23·3	42·4	21·8	5·2	44·0	19·4	9·2
1930	97·4	54·3	1·3	34·2	6·8	2·5	65·5	26·8	17·3	39·5	18·9	4·1	38·0	15·0	6·5
1931	82·7	29·4	0·9	32·3	7·3	1·9	64·2	18·4	13·6	35·2	13·7	3·0	33·2	10·0	4·5
1932	75·3	24·5	0·7	19·6	9·2	1·4	30·5	14·6	10·8	22·0	12·1	2·4	16·0	8·7	4·1
1933	67·9	30·3	0·6	17·5	3·3	1·0	29·8	14·8	9·8	18·6	12·4	2·0	12·9	8·8	4·1
1934	80·1	32·1	0·6	17·3	3·6	3·9	30·6	14·0	8·9	20·9	12·1	2·0	14·6	8·8	4·1
1935	73·8	31·8	0·7	21·8	3·5	6·2	31·8	20·3	7·8	23·1	11·7	2·3	15·5	8·7	4·4
1936	79·7	32·7	0·6	18·9	3·5	9·8	35·3	20·5	7·4	25·1	12·3	2·0	18·6	9·5	4·7
1937	97·9	42·4	0·8	29·1	3·1	16·4	38·8	23·4	8·0	32·0	15·0	2·1	22·7	11·1	5·9
1938	70·7	36·2	0·8	19·5	6·5	10·9	31·9	21·8	6·6	29·3	13·1	1·7	18·6	8·2	4·4

See p. 327 for footnotes

Overseas Trade 12. *continued*

	France			India(f)			Australia			New Zealand			Argentina		
	Imports	Exports	Re-exports	Imports	Exports	Re-exports	Imports	Exports	Re-exports	Imports	Exports	Re-exports	Imports	Exports	Re-exports
1846	...	2·7	...	...	5·8	...	...	1·4	...	...	–	...	...	–	...
1847	...	2·6	...	...	4·8	...	...	1·6	...	...	0·1	...	...	0·2	...
1848	...	1·0	...	...	4·6	...	...	1·4	...	...	0·1	...	...	0·4	...
1849	...	2·0	...	...	6·2	...	...	2·0	...	...	0·1	...	...	1·4	...
1850	...	2·4	...	...	7·2	...	...	2·5	...	...	0·1	...	...	0·8	...
1851	...	2·0	...	...	7·0	...	...	2·6	...	...	0·2	...	...	0·5	...
1852	...	2·7	...	...	6·5	...	...	4·1	...	...	0·1	...	...	0·8	...
1853	...	2·6	...	...	7·3	...	...	14·3	...	...	0·2	...	...	0·6	...
1854	10·4	3·2	3·2	10·7	9·1	0·5	4·3	11·6	1·4	–	0·3	–	1·3	1·3	–
1855	9·1	6·0	4·4	12·7	9·9	0·4	4·5	6·0	0·9	–	0·2	–	1·1	0·7	–
1856	10·4	6·4	4·0	17·3	10·5	0·5	5·6	9·6	1·7	0·1	0·3	0·1	1·0	1·0	–
1857	12·0	6·2	5·1	18·7	11·7	0·5	5·8	11·3	1·5	0·2	0·4	–	1·6	1·3	0·1
1858	13·3	4·9	4·4	15·0	16·8	0·6	5·0	10·0	1·1	0·3	0·5	0·1	1·2	1·0	–
1859	16·9	4·8	4·8	15·2	19·8	0·9	5·5	10·6	1·2	0·3	0·6	0·1	1·6	1·0	–
1860	17·8	5·3	7·5	15·1	17·0	0·7	6·0	9·1	0·8	0·4	0·6	0·1	1·1	1·8	–
1861	17·8	8·9	8·5	22·0	16·4	0·6	6·4	9·8	0·7	0·5	0·9	0·1	1·5	1·4	–
1862	21·7	9·2	12·6	34·1	14·6	0·7	6·5	10·7	0·8	0·6	1·2	0·1	1·1	0·9	–
1863	24·0	8·7	14·6	48·4	20·0	0·8	6·4	10·5	0·9	0·7	2·0	0·2	1·2	1·3	–
1864	25·6	8·2	15·6	52·3	20·0	0·8	8·9	10·0	0·9	1·1	1·9	0·2	1·2	1·8	–
1865	31·6	9·1	16·3	37·4	18·3	0·6	9·0	11·7	0·7	1·3	1·6	0·1	1·0	2·0	–
1866	37·0	11·7	14·9	36·9	20·0	0·7	9·9	11·5	0·8	1·6	2·2	0·2	1·1	2·8	–
1867	33·7	12·1	10·9	25·5	21·8	1·0	11·2	8·1	0·6	1·7	1·5	0·1	0·9	2·8	0·1
1868	33·9	10·7	12·9	30·1	21·3	1·0	11·1	10·4	0·8	1·5	1·7	0·2	1·5	1·9	0·1
1869	33·5	11·4	11·8	33·2	17·6	1·0	10·6	11·6	0·9	1·6	1·9	0·1	1·3	2·3	0·1
1870	37·6	11·6	10·3	25·1	19·3	0·8	11·9	8·4	0·7	2·1	1·5	0·1	1·5	2·3	0·1
1871	29·8	18·2	15·2	30·7	18·1	1·0	12·0	8·7	0·9	2·5	1·4	0·1	2·0	2·5	0·1
1872	41·8	17·3	11·0	33·7	18·5	1·0	13·0	11·8	1·2	2·7	2·3	0·2	1·9	3·9	0·1
1873	43·3	17·3	12·9	29·9	21·4	1·0	14·1	14·2	1·4	3·2	3·4	0·2	2·6	3·7	0·1
1874	46·5	16·4	13·0	31·2	24·1	1·4	15·0	14·7	1·3	3·5	4·4	0·3	1·3	3·1	0·1
1875	46·7	15·4	11·9	30·1	24·2	1·3	17·1	15·6	1·5	3·5	3·9	0·3	1·4	2·4	0·1
1876	45·3	16·1	12·9	30·0	22·4	1·3	18·5	14·5	1·5	3·5	3·2	0·3	1·7	1·5	0·1
1877	45·8	14·2	11·4	31·2	25·3	1·3	18·0	16·0	1·9	3·7	3·3	0·3	1·7	2·1	0·1
1878	41·4	14·8	11·8	27·5	23·3	1·4	16·8	15·3	1·6	4·0	4·3	0·4	1·1	2·3	0·1
1879	38·5	15·0	11·6	24·7	21·4	1·3	17·4	12·7	1·4	4·5	3·6	0·3	0·8	2·1	0·1
1880	42·0	15·6	12·4	30·1	30·5	1·6	20·4	14·0	1·6	5·2	2·9	0·3	0·9	2·5	0·1

See p. 327 for footnote

Overseas Trade 12. *continued*

	France			India(*f*)			Australia			New Zealand			Argentina		
	Imports	Exports	Re-exports	Imports	Exports	Re-exports	Imports	Exports	Re-exports	Imports	Exports	Re-exports	Imports	Exports	Re-exports
1881	40·0	17·0	13·1	32·6	29·2	1·8	21·8	17·6	2·2	5·1	3·7	0·4	0·6	3·3	0·1
1882	39·1	17·4	12·3	39·9	29·1	1·5	20·4	20·1	2·7	4·7	4·3	0·4	1·2	4·2	0·1
1883	38·6	17·6	11·8	38·9	31·9	1·5	20·1	20·2	2·3	5·8	3·9	0·4	0·9	4·9	0·1
1884	37·4	16·7	9·6	34·4	30·6	1·5	22·3	20·1	2·5	6·0	3·7	0·4	1·2	5·8	0·1
1885	35·7	15·0	8·0	31·9	29·3	1·6	18·1	21·2	2·5	5·1	3·9	0·5	1·9	4·7	0·1
1886	36·6	13·6	6·7	32·1	31·4	1·2	16·2	19·1	2·2	4·7	3·3	0·4	1·6	5·2	0·1
1887	37·1	13·7	6·8	30·5	30·7	1·4	17·6	16·7	2·2	5·7	3·1	0·3	2·2	6·2	0·1
1888	38·9	14·9	9·3	30·8	32·6	1·3	19·9	22·5	2·8	5·9	3·0	0·4	2·7	7·7	0·2
1889	45·8	14·7	7·6	36·2	31·0	1·4	20·0	19·7	2·4	6·8	3·2	0·4	2·0	10·7	0·2
1890	44·8	16·6	8·1	32·7	33·6	1·6	21·0	19·7	2·1	8·3	3·3	0·4	4·1	8·4	0·1
1891	44·8	16·4	7·9	32·2	31·2	1·4	23·1	22·1	2·3	8·2	3·4	0·4	3·5	4·2	0·1
1892	43·5	14·7	6·7	30·5	27·9	1·1	22·8	15·8	1·8	7·8	3·5	0·4	4·5	5·7	0·2
1893	43·7	13·4	6·4	26·2	28·8	1·1	21·8	11·8	1·4	8·1	3·3	0·5	4·8	5·5	0·1
1894	43·5	13·5	6·2	27·6	29·3	0·8	23·5	13·0	1·5	8·3	3·0	0·4	6·2	4·5	0·1
1895	47·5	13·9	6·5	26·4	24·8	0·7	25·0	14·2	1·7	8·4	3·1	0·3	9·1	5·4	0·1
1896	50·1	14·2	6·5	25·3	30·1	0·7	21·3	17·9	2·0	8·1	4·0	0·4	9·0	6·6	0·2
1897	53·3	13·8	5·7	24·8	27·4	0·6	20·7	17·3	1·9	8·6	4·0	0·5	5·8	4·8	0·2
1898	51·4	13·7	6·8	27·5	29·7	0·6	19·8	17·1	1·9	9·0	4·0	0·4	7·8	5·6	0·2
1899	53·0	15·3	7·0	27·7	31·3	0·7	23·6	18·0	1·8	9·7	4·5	0·4	10·9	6·2	0·3
1900	53·6	20·0	5·9	27·4	30·1	0·9	23·8	21·6	2·0	11·6	5·5	0·3	13·1	7·1	0·3
1901	51·2	16·5	7·2	27·4	35·0	0·8	24·2	21·4	2·2	10·6	5·6	0·5	12·4	6·8	0·2
1902	50·6	15·6	6·7	28·7	32·7	0·8	19·7	19·5	2·0	10·9	5·7	0·5	14·0	5·9	0·3
1903	49·3	15·8	7·3	32·3	34·5	0·8	17·1	16·1	2·0	13·5	6·4	0·6	19·1	8·0	0·6
1904	51·1	15·3	6·4	36·5	40·6	0·9	23·6	17·3	2·5	12·7	6·3	0·6	23·0	10·8	0·7
1905	53·1	16·1	7·1	36·1	43·0	1·4	27·0	17·0	2·5	13·4	6·4	0·6	25·0	13·0	0·4
⎰ ⎱	46·5	16·0	7·0	36·0	43·0	1·4	27·0	17·0	2·5	13·4	6·4	0·6	25·4	13·0	0·4
1906	47·1	20·3	8·2	37·7	45·2	1·2	29·3	20·2	2·6	15·6	7·4	0·7	23·9	19·4	0·5
1907	46·3	23·3	9·9	43·9	52·0	1·2	33·8	24·1	3·1	17·8	8·7	0·7	26·7	17·8	0·5
1908	41·9	22·2	9·2	29·6	49·4	1·4	29·1	22·9	2·7	14·7	8·8	0·7	36·0	16·4	0·5
1909	44·2	21·4	9·6	35·4	43·6	1·1	32·6	24·0	3·2	17·7	7·4	0·7	32·7	18·7	0·5
1910	44·3	22·5	11·0	42·8	46·0	1·0	38·6	27·7	3·4	20·9	8·7	0·8	29·0	19·1	0·6

See p. 327 for footnote

	France			India(f)			Australia			New Zealand			Argentina		
	Imports	Exports	Re-exports	Imports	Exports	Re-exports	Imports	Exports	Re-exports	Imports	Exports	Re-exports	Imports	Exports	Re-exports
1911	41·6	24·3	11·2	45·4	52·2	1·6	39·1	30·9	3·7	17·9	9·8	0·8	27·3	18·6	0·7
1912	45·5	25·6	11·9	52·1	57·6	2·1	36·1	34·8	3·4	20·3	10·4	0·8	40·8	20·6	0·8
1913	46·4	28·9	11·9	48·4	70·3	1·4	38·1	34·5	3·4	20·3	10·8	1·0	42·5	22·6	0·8
1914	37·8	25·8	9·3	43·3	62·9	0·9	36·9	33·6	3·4	23·0	9·4	1·0	37·2	14·6	0·5
1915	31·4	69·6	11·7	62·2	45·6	1·3	45·2	29·0	2·9	30·4	9·4	0·7	63·9	11·5	0·6
1916	26·6	92·8	14·8	72·4	52·8	1·6	36·2	35·9	3·2	31·6	12·1	0·9	51·6	13·9	0·6
1917	22·9	111·7	16·4	66·8	60·0	0·8	64·3	22·1	1·9	29·1	7·0	0·4	48·4	12·9	0·4
1918	35·0	130·8	13·7	88·5	49·2	0·4	45·4	26·3	1·8	24·5	7·7	0·3	63·0	17·6	0·1
1919	48·5	147·4	36·0	108·2	70·9	1·1	111·4	26·3	1·5	52·7	9·6	0·3	81·7	21·2	0·5
1920	75·8	135·9	39·8	95·7	181·2	2·7	112·3	62·6	5·8	47·5	26·6	1·4	128·0	42·9	0·9
1921	53·0(s)	44·3(s)	12·8(s)	44·3	108·9	2·5	68·1	45·6	2·8	48·7	14·9	0·6	68·4	27·6	0·4
1922	48·5	48·5	17·6	47·7	92·1	1·3	64·8	60·3	5·3	48·5	16·0	0·8	56·6	22·7	0·7
1923	58·5	49·3	19·0	67·0	86·2	1·1	49·0	57·7	4·2	43·0	20·7	1·0	64·9	28·1	0·7
1924	66·6	41·7	17·8	78·9	90·6	1·1	59·0	60·8	5·2	47·0	20·3	1·0	79·0	27·2	0·5
1925	65·0	31·0	23·2	80·1	86·0	1·2	72·6	60·2	3·9	51·3	23·1	1·1	68·9	29·1	0·6
1926	59·2	20·4	20·2	57·6	81·8	1·4	61·0	61·3	2·4	46·8	20·6	0·8	67·5	23·1	0·6
1927	63·4	23·6	18·5	65·8	85·0	1·3	52·7	61·2	2·6	46·5	19·6	0·8	76·5	27·0	0·6
1928	60·6	25·2	18·6	64·5	83·9	1·2	54·4	55·7	2·3	47·3	19·3	0·8	76·8	31·2	0·6
1929	56·5	31·7	17·5	62·8	78·2	1·1	55·6	54·2	2·1	47·7	21·4	0·8	82·4	29·1	0·6
1930	49·3	29·7	14·5	51·0	52·9	1·3	46·4	31·7	1·4	44·9	17·9	0·8	56·7	25·2	0·4
1931	40·9	22·6	9·5	36·7	32·3	0·8	45·7	14·5	0·6	37·8	11·2	0·5	52·7	23·1	0·3
1932	19·1	18·4	8·3	32·3	34·1	0·6	46·0	20·0	0·6	37·0	10·4	0·3	50·9	27·0	0·2
1933	19·1	18·2	7·6	37·4	33·4	0·7	48·6	21·3	0·7	37·2	9·5	0·3	41·7	13·1	0·2
1934	19·2	16·8	6·7	42·1	36·7	0·5	49·9	26·2	0·7	40·4	11·4	0·3	47·0	14·7	0·2
1935	21·6	16·7	6·8	41·2	37·8	0·6	54·3	29·3	0·7	38·1	13·4	0·3	44·0	15·3	0·3
1936	25·6	17·8	8·0	51·9	34·1	0·5	61·4	32·3	0·7	43·6	17·3	0·3	45·1	15·3	0·3
1937	25·6	21·4	8·6	64·7	35·8	0·5	71·7	37·5	0·8	49·9	20·2	0·3	59·8	20·0	0·3
1938	23·6	15·1	8·2	55·9	33·8	0·5	71·8	38·2	0·8	46·9	19·2	0·3	38·5	19·3	0·4

See p. 327 for footnotes

	Eire		
	Imports	Exports	Re-exports
1923	32·7(t)	24·6(t)	6·6(t)
1924	51·1	47·3	11·2
1925	43·4	40·2	11·0
1926	40·9	34·8	10·4
1927	43·2	36·2	9·4
1928	45·1	35·1	9·6
1929	45·1	36·1	10·2
1930	43·0	34·5	9·8

	Eire		
	Imports	Exports	Re-exports
1931	36·5	30·5	8·5
1932	26·5	25·8	6·1
1933	17·8	19·0	4·6
1934	17·2	19·5	5·3
1935	18·8	20·2	4·9
1936	20·4	21·1	4·9
1937	21·1	21·6	5·7
1938	23·0	20·3	5·7

(a) This comprises Russia, Sweden, Norway, Denmark, Iceland, and the Faroe Islands initially, and later creations such as Finland and the Baltic republics.

(b) This comprises the Netherlands, Belgium and France at the start, and Switzerland also when the consignments series begin.

(c) This comprises Prussia, the German states, Austrian territories, and Wallachia Moldavia in the beginning, and later covers states created out of these territories.

(d) This comprises Spain, Portugal, the Italian states, Greece, Morocco, Algeria, Tunis, Tripoli, Gibraltar, Malta and the Ionian Islands initially.

(e) This covers all Turkish territories except Wallachia and Moldavia, Arabia, Aden, and Persia at the start, and later covers states created from them.

(f) Including Burma.

(g) Earlier, British Guiana and British Honduras (exports only in both cases) are included in *West Indies*, but from 1855 they are included in *Central and South America* for all types of trade. The difference in 1855 was about 0·5.

(h) Schleswig-Holstein was transferred to Germany in 1861—a difference in that year of 0·9 imports, 0·1 exports, and 0·1 re-exports.

(i) From 1881 Bulgaria, Montenegro, and Servia were recorded separately from Turkey, and from that date they are included in *Central and South-East Europe*. The difference in 1881 was 0·1 imports, 0·2 exports, and negligible re-exports.

(j) From 1892 Cyprus was recorded separately from Turkey, and from that date is included in *Southern Europe and North Africa*. The difference in 1892 was 0·1 imports, 0·1 exports, and negligible re-exports.

(k) From 1899 Crete was recorded separately from Turkey, and from that date is included in *Southern Europe and North Africa*. The change in 1899 was small.

(l) In 1905 the system of recording overseas trade was changed. Previously goods were entered according to port of destination, and subsequently according to country of consignment. The first row for 1905 uses the earlier, and the second row the later system.

(m) In 1913 all the Balkan states were enlarged and Albania was created at Turkey's expense. There resulted some small but unascertainable transfer to both *Central and South-East Europe* and the *Southern Europe and North Africa*.

(n) In 1914 Sudan was recorded separately from Egypt, and thenceforward it is included in *The Remainder of Africa* instead of *Turkey and the Middle East*. The difference in 1914 was 0·4 imports, 0·4 exports, and negligible re-exports.

(o) From 1921 Poland and Bessarabia are no longer included in *North and North-East Europe* or in *Russia*.

(p) From 1921 Alsace-Lorraine and Luxembourg are included in *Western Europe*.

(q) From 1921 Poland and Bessarabia are included in *Central and South-East Europe*, and Alsace-Lorraine, Luxembourg, and the South Tirol are no longer included there.

(r) From 1921 the South Tirol is included in *Southern Europe and North Africa*.

(s) From 1921 Alsace-Lorraine is included in France.

(t) Southern Ireland was treated as foreign from 1st April 1923.

NOTE TO PART A

SOURCE: A. H. Imlah, *Economic Elements in the Pax Britannica* (Cambridge, Mass., Harvard University Press, 1958), pp. 94–8 and 205–7. The original figures have been rounded.

A. Imlah's Index, 1796–1913. (1880 = 100)

	Total Imports	Re-exports	Net Imports	Exports		Total Imports	Re-exports	Net Imports	Exports
1796	6	9	5	4	1844	20	17	21	23
1797	5	9	4	4	1845	22	19	23	23
1798	7	10	6	4	1846	22	18	22	22
1799	7	9	7	5	1847	27	22	28	22
1800	8	14	7	5	1848	25	20	26	22
1801	8	12	8	5	1849	29	28	29	28
1802	8	15	7	5	1850	28	24	29	32
1803	7	9	7	4	1851	30	25	31	34
1804	8	10	7	5	1852	29	26	30	36
1805	8	9	8	5	1853	35	30	35	41
1806	7	9	7	5	1854	33	32	34	40
1807	7	8	7	5	1855	31	35	30	40
1808	7	6	7	4	1856	36	35	36	48
1809	8	13	7	6	1857	36	33	37	49
1810	10	12	10	6	1858	37	36	37	48
1811	7	7	7	4	1859	39	39	39	52
1812	7	10	6	5	1860	45	43	45	55
1813	...	...	...	...	1861	47	51	46	51
1814	8	19	6	6	1862	48	50	48	48
1815	9	16	7	8	1863	49	54	48	51
1816	10	14	6	7	1864	49	55	48	51
1817	8	10	8	7	1865	52	61	50	55
1818	10	11	10	8	1866	56	60	56	61
1819	9	11	8	6	1867	56	60	55	62
1820	9	11	8	7	1868	60	67	58	66
1821	8	12	8	7	1869	62	66	61	70
1822	8	10	8	8	1870	65	67	64	76
1823	10	10	10	8	1871	75	89	72	85
1824	10	11	10	9	1872	75	82	74	88
1825	13	11	13	8	1873	78	78	79	85
1826	11	12	11	8	1874	80	82	80	84
1827	12	11	13	10	1875	85	87	84	84
1828	13	11	13	10	1876	87	86	88	81
1829	12	12	13	10	1877	90	82	91	84
1830	13	11	14	11	1878	90	85	91	84
1831	14	12	15	11	1879	93	94	93	89
1832	12	14	12	12	1880	100	100	100	100
1833	13	12	13	13	1881	98	103	97	110
1834	14	14	14	13	1882	103	109	102	111
1835	14	16	14	14	1883	109	114	108	114
1836	17	15	17	15	1884	105	115	103	115
1837	16	16	15	13	1885	106	111	105	109
1838	17	16	18	16	1886	107	118	105	114
1839	18	15	19	17	1887	112	120	111	119
1840	19	16	19	18	1888	118	133	115	127
1841	19	18	19	19	1889	128	137	126	132
1842	18	15	18	19	1890	127	132	127	134
1843	18	16	18	21	1891	131	127	132	127

	Total Imports	Re-exports	Net Imports	Exports		Total Imports	Re-exports	Net Imports	Exports
1892	133	139	132	122	1903	177	142	184	154
1893	130	126	130	117	1904	179	141	186	157
1894	140	131	142	122	1905	182	152	188	173
1895	148	139	149	133	1906	187	153	193	186
1896	155	129	160	140	1907	190	161	196	201
1897	159	140	163	138	1908	182	148	189	185
1898	164	139	169	137	1909	189	163	194	193
1899	166	143	170	146(a)	1910	193	166	198	210
1900	166	128	173	140	1911	199	171	204	218
1901	171	141	177	141	1912	214	183	219	230
1902	175	138	182	150	1913	220	183	227	239

(*a*) New ships included from 1900 onwards. In constructing the index the estimated value of new ships in 1880 was added to the recorded export volume of that base year.

NOTE TO PART B

Source: This index has been supplied to the editors by the statistician of the London and Cambridge Economic Service, whose *Bulletin* contains an index of total imports and exports. It is based on statistics of volume appearing in the *Board of Trade Journal*.

B. London and Cambridge Economic Service Index, 1913–47 (1938 = 100)

	Total Imports	Re-exports	Net Imports	Exports		Total Imports	Re-exports	Net Imports	Exports
1913	87	165	81	173	1930	98	126	96	115
					1931	100	120	99	88
1919	77	129	73	95	1932	88	106	86	88
1920	77	148	72	123	1933	88	99	87	89
1921	65	129	60	86	1934	92	90	92	95
1922	74	133	70	119	1935	93	103	92	102
1923	81	141	77	129	1936	99	102	99	104
1924	90	159	86	132	1937	105	106	105	113
1925	93	155	89	130	1938	100	100	100	100
1926	96	135	93	117					
1927	99	141	96	134	1946	67	40	69	99
1928	96	137	93	137	1947	75	45	77	108
1929	101	132	99	141					

Overseas Trade 14. Gross Barter Terms of Trade—England & Wales 1697–1774, and Great Britain 1772–1804

NOTES

[1] SOURCE: Phyllis Deane and W. A. Cole, *British Economic Growth 1688–1955* (Cambridge University Press, 1962). The official values of imports, which were based on first cost in the country of origin, were used by the authors to construct a table of imports c.i.f. The latter, less re-exports f.o.b., was used in compiling this table, together with the official values of exports f.o.b.

[2] Three-yearly moving averages are employed to eliminate random fluctuations caused by the comparatively slow pace of ocean shipping in the eighteenth century.

(Three-yearly Moving Averages)

E. & W.

1698	103	1720	133	1742	150	1764	153	1783	117
1699	102	1721	133	1743	164	1765	149	1784	105
1700	100	1722	133	1744	159	1766	129	1785	100
1701	105	1723	122	1745	178	1767	126	1786	97
1702	117	1724	118	1746	175	1768	123	1787	97
1703	115	1725	119	1747	175	1769	123	1788	100
1704	119	1726	120	1748	170	1770	126	1789	105
1705	129	1727	116	1749	179	1771	127	1790	114
1706	157	1728	112	1750	190	1772	129	1791	123
1707	154	1729	112	1751	183	1773	125	1792	122
1708	147	1730	110	1752	173			1793	121
1709	159	1731	119	1753	166	G.B.		1794	114
1710	158	1732	120	1754	153	1773	125	1795	127
1711	168	1733	123	1755	154	1774	121	1796	137
1712	140	1734	118	1756	137	1775	119	1797	134
1713	148	1735	129	1757	149	1776	113	1798	134
1714	145	1736	140	1758	155	1777	113	1799	137
1715	145	1737	154	1759	168	1778	112	1800	141
1716	140	1738	142	1760	171	1779	116	1801	147
1717	126	1739	133	1761	171	1780	106	1802	140
1718	129	1740	124	1762	166	1781	111	1803	138
1719	121	1741	140	1763	166	1782	112		

NOTE TO PART A

SOURCE: Albert H. Imlah, *Economic Elements in the Pax Britannica* (Cambridge, Mass., Harvard University Press, 1958), pp. 94–8.

A. 1796–1913. 1880 = 100

	Merchandise Price Indices		Net Barter Terms		Merchandise Price Indices		Net Barter Terms
	Exports	Net Retained Imports			Exports	Net Retained Imports	
1796	323·7	175·7	184·2	1843	112·0	99·1	113·0
1797	348·1	174·3	199·7	1844	114·9	99·0	116·1
1798	370·1	178·5	207·3	1845	118·3	98·9	119·6
1799	353·8	180·4	196·1	1846	116·3	101·0	115·1
1800	359·0	203·4	176·5	1847	118·1	105·0	112·5
1801	362·5	214·6	168·9	1848	105·8	86·9	121·7
1802	406·2	177·9	228·3	1849	100·8	87·5	115·2
1803	388·4	185·1	209·8	1850	100·8	90·7	111·1
1804	378·2	188·2	201·0	1851	99·1	90·1	110·0
1805	373·5	195·4	191·1	1852	98·1	93·5	104·9
1806	365·2	183·8	198·7	1853	108·1	107·2	100·8
1807	372·0	180·6	206·0	1854	108·7	114·9	94·6
1808	376·8	199·1	189·3	1855	106·1	118·7	89·4
1809	353·7	236·7	149·4	1856	108·4	118·4	91·6
1810	353·3	222·9	158·5	1857	111·7	128·3	87·1
1811	361·5	180·3	200·5	1858	109·1	111·3	98·0
1812	353·4	211·3	167·2	1859	111·5	113·5	98·2
1813	...	...	...	1860	110·6	116·5	94·9
1814	329·7	254·5	129·5	1861	111·1	113·3	98·1
1815	300·0	217·1	138·2	1862	116·9	110·5	105·8
1816	283·7	185·2	153·2	1863	128·8	120·1	107·2
1817	259·4	186·4	139·2	1864	141·3	134·9	104·7
1818	271·9	191·6	141·9	1865	134·6	125·8	107·0
1819	258·8	158·5	163·3	1866	139·1	126·5	110·0
1820	234·8	150·0	156·5	1867	130·9	121·4	107·8
1821	223·8	136·7	163·7	1868	122·2	121·8	100·3
1822	205·6	132·4	155·3	1869	121·4	117·7	103·1
1823	198·9	133·3	149·2	1870	118·5	115·8	102·3
1824	193·9	125·2	154·9	1871	118·0	107·9	109·4
1825	210·3	143·1	147·0	1872	130·6	115·6	113·0
1826	185·3	117·8	157·3	1873	135·2	115·4	117·2
1827	174·6	119·0	146·7	1874	127·7	112·8	113·2
1828	170·4	113·9	149·6	1875	120·0	107·5	111·6
1829	154·3	109·4	141·0	1876	110·5	104·8	105·4
1830	158·2	107·0	149·8	1877	106·2	107·8	98·5
1831	151·8	109·9	138·1	1878	102·3	99·9	102·4
1832	139·3	108·9	127·9	1879	96·4	94·8	101·7
1833	141·8	115·0	123·3	1880	100·0	100·0	100·0
1834	146·0	117·1	124·7	1881	95·8	99·1	96·7
1835	152·9	124·9	122·4	1882	97·7	98·1	99·6
1836	160·1	128·6	124·5	1883	94·4	95·8	98·5
1837	147·2	114·4	129·6	1884	90·9	91·0	99·9
1838	139·2	116·4	119·6	1885	87·4	85·3	102·5
1839	137·7	122·7	111·8	1886	83·6	80·1	104·4
1840	128·5	122·3	105·1	1887	83·4	78·4	106·4
1841	124·3	113·3	109·7	1888	82·9	81·0	102·3
1842	114·2	108·3	105·4	1889	84·6	82·1	103·0

	Merchandise Price Indices					Merchandise Price Indices		
	Exports	Net Retained Imports	Net Barter Terms			Exports	Net Retained Imports	Net Barter Terms
1890	88·3	80·9	109·1		1902	83·3	73·0	114·1
1891	87·5	81·5	107·4		1903	83·2	74·0	112·4
1892	83·6	78·1	107·0		1904	84·2	74·3	113·3
1893	83·4	76·3	109·3		1905	84·0	74·6	112·6
1894	79·2	71·1	111·4		1906	89·0	77·8	114·4
1895	76·2	68·8	110·8		1907	93·4	81·3	114·9
1896	76·9	69·4	110·8		1908	89·8	78·3	114·7
1897	76·0	69·1	110·0		1909	86·5	79·1	109·4
1898	76·2	69·7	109·3		1910	90·2	83·6	107·9
1899	79·8	71·1	112·2		1911	91·8	81·5	112·6
1900	91·7	76·4	120·0		1912	93·4	83·0	112·5
1901	87·3	73·9	118·1		1913	96·9	83·4	116·2

NOTE TO PART B

SOURCE: *Board of Trade Journal* (4th August 1951).

B. 1913–47. 1938 = 100

	Index Numbers of Average Values		
	Imports	Exports	Net Terms of Trade
1913	97	68	143
1919	233	189	132
1920	277	245	113
1921	185	184	101
1922	148	136	109
1923	145	130	112
1924	150	129	116
1925	151	126	120
1926	138	118	117
1927	132	112	118
1928	133	110	121
1929	130	108	120
1930	114	103	111
1931	92	92	100
1932	86	86	100
1933	83	86	97
1934	87	87	100
1935	89	88	101
1936	93	90	103
1937	107	98	109
1938	100	100	100
1946	211	196	108
1947	258	223	116

NOTES

[1] SOURCES: Part A—A. H. Imlah, *Economic Elements in the Pax Britannica* (Cambridge, Mass., Harvard University Press, 1958), pp. 70–5; Part B—*Board of Trade Journal* (in one of the issues in February in each year from 1923 to 1939).
[2] The various minor breaks in Professor Imlah's series have not been shown here. They are discussed at length in chapter III of his book.
[3] Direct comparison between this table and post-war statistics is inadmissible. Figures for 1938 on the basis now used are as follows:

	Merchandise Trade	Overseas Investment Earnings	All Other Invisible Trade	Bullion and Specie	Overall Balance on Current Account
1938	−302	+175	+57	+74	+4

(Source: *Abstract*, 1935–46.)

A. 1816–1913

(In £000,000. All items are net balances.
+ = excess of receipts, − = excess of payment)

	Merchandise Trade	Overseas Investment Earnings	All other Invisible Trade	Bullion and Specie	Overall Balance on Current Account
1816	+ 4·1	+ 0·6	+ 14·9	− 5·0	+ 14·6
1817	− 9·1	+ 1·5	+ 16·8	− 2·9	+ 6·3
1818	− 21·9	+ 1·9	+ 20·8	+ 3·9	+ 4·7
1819	− 10·6	+ 2·1	+ 14·4	+ 1·4	+ 7·3
1820	− 7·4	+ 2·6	+ 13·4	− 5·4	+ 3·2
1821	+ 0·6	+ 2·8	+ 12·6	− 2·2	+ 13·8
1822	+ 0·2	+ 3·6	+ 12·3	− 2·8	+ 13·3
1823	− 9·4	+ 4·4	+ 13·4	− 2·5	+ 5·9
1824	− 5·3	+ 4·7	+ 13·4	+ 3·5	+ 16·3
1825	− 26·5	+ 5·7	+ 17·8	+ 5·4	+ 2·4
1826	− 11·6	+ 5·4	+ 12·6	− 4·0	+ 2·4
1827	− 14·8	+ 5·0	+ 13·4	− 3·6	0·0
1828	− 14·0	+ 4·5	+ 13·0	+ 0·3	+ 3·8
1829	− 11·7	+ 4·2	+ 12·5	+ 1·1	+ 6·1
1830	− 12·0	+ 3·9	+ 12·2	− 3·5	+ 0·6
1831	− 18·1	+ 3·9	+ 13·1	+ 3·5	+ 2·4
1832	− 8·7	+ 4·3	+ 11·7	− 1·2	+ 6·1
1833	− 12·3	+ 4·8	+ 13·5	− 2·4	+ 3·6
1834	− 15·1	+ 6·1	+ 13·8	+ 2·3	+ 7·1
1835	− 11·4	+ 7·8	+ 15·5	+ 0·8	+ 12·7
1836	− 21·8	+ 8·6	+ 17·2	+ 1·5	+ 5·5
1837	− 19·0	+ 8·4	+ 14·9	− 2·0	+ 2·3
1838	− 20·8	+ 8·1	+ 17·5	0·0	+ 4·5
1839	− 28·4	+ 7·7	+ 19·4	+ 4·4	+ 3·1
1840	− 29·8	+ 7·1	+ 19·5	+ 0·9	− 2·3
1841	− 22·4	+ 6·2	+ 18·3	− 1·0	+ 1·1
1842	− 20·6	+ 6·3	+ 16·6	− 2·9	− 0·6
1843	− 10·9	+ 7·0	+ 16·8	− 3·6	+ 9·3
1844	− 12·3	+ 8·3	+ 17·4	− 3·0	+ 10·4
1845	− 19·0	+ 9·7	+ 19·6	− 1·0	+ 9·3
1846	− 20·3	+ 10·2	+ 19·5	− 1·4	+ 8·0
1847	− 41·6	+ 10·6	+ 24·6	+ 5·3	− 1·1
1848	− 26·9	+ 9·0	+ 19·0	+ 1·0	+ 2·1
1849	− 25·7	+ 8·2	+ 21·4	+ 1·0	+ 3·9
1850	− 19·6	+ 9·4	+ 21·8	− 1·0	+ 10·6
1851	− 22·6	+ 10·4	+ 22·6	− 1·2	+ 9·2
1852	− 18·9	+ 10·9	+ 23·5	− 7·8	+ 7·7
1853	− 32·8	+ 11·8	+ 30·8	− 6·5	+ 3·3
1854	− 36·6	+ 12·6	+ 33·4	− 3·6	+ 5·8
1855	− 25·9	+ 12·9	+ 34·7	− 7·8	+ 13·9
1856	− 32·1	+ 14·9	+ 40·9	− 1·9	+ 21·8
1857	− 40·4	+ 16·2	+ 44·8	+ 6·5	+ 27·1
1858	− 23·8	+ 15·9	+ 40·2	− 9·9	+ 22·4
1859	− 22·6	+ 16·9	+ 43·2	− 1·4	+ 36·1
1860	− 45·5	+ 18·7	+ 48·0	+ 2·5	+ 23·7

(in £000,000. All items are net balances.
+ = excess of receipts, − = excess of payment)

	Merchandise Trade	Overseas Investment Earnings	All other Invisible Trade	Bullion and Specie	Overall Balance on Current Account
1861	− 57·6	+ 19·9	+ 50·0	+ 2·1	+ 14·4
1862	− 58·8	+ 20·7	+ 51·9	− 2·3	+ 11·5
1863	− 51·4	+ 21·3	+ 60·1	− 3·5	+ 26·5
1864	− 61·5	+ 22·9	+ 66·0	− 4·6	+ 22·8
1865	− 51·2	+ 24·1	+ 68·4	− 6·4	+ 34·9
1866	− 55·2	+ 26·4	+ 74·5	− 12·7	+ 33·0
1867	− 48·6	+ 28·2	+ 72·1	− 9·5	+ 42·2
1868	− 65·5	+ 31·1	+ 75·5	− 4·6	+ 36·5
1869	− 57·5	+ 33·1	+ 75·2	− 4·1	+ 46·7
1870	− 57·5	+ 35·3	+ 76·8	− 10·5	+ 44·1
1871	− 46·0	+ 39·5	+ 82·4	− 4·4	+ 71·3
1872	− 36·8	+ 44·3	+ 89·8	+ 0·7	+ 98·0
1873	− 56·3	+ 51·7	+ 90·6	− 4·7	+ 81·3
1874	− 69·1	+ 56·6	+ 90·9	− 7·5	+ 70·9
1875	− 90·5	+ 57·8	+ 89·6	− 5·6	+ 51·3
1876	−117·8	+ 57·5	+ 91·1	− 7·6	+ 23·2
1877	−141·5	+ 55·5	+ 96·5	+ 2·6	+ 13·1
1878	−121·8	+ 55·1	+ 89·1	− 5·7	+ 16·9
1879	−111·8	+ 55·9	+ 88·0	+ 4·4	+ 35·5
1880	−121·1	+ 57·7	+ 96·4	+ 2·6	+ 35·6
1881	− 94·5	+ 59·5	+ 95·0	+ 5·6	+ 65·7
1882	−100·0	+ 62·8	+ 97·5	− 2·6	+ 58·7
1883	−116·9	+ 64·4	+102·1	− 0·8	+ 48·8
1884	− 91·1	+ 66·8	+ 95·0	+ 1·6	+ 72·3
1885	− 98·5	+ 70·3	+ 90·7	− 0·2	+ 62·3
1886	− 79·5	+ 74·0	+ 83·8	+ 0·6	+ 78·9
1887	− 78·5	+ 79·5	+ 87·3	− 0·6	+ 87·7
1888	− 85·9	+ 84·5	+ 92·7	+ 0·6	+ 91·9
1889	−105·0	+ 88·8	+ 99·1	− 2·0	+ 80·9
1890	− 86·3	+ 94·0	+ 99·6	− 8·8	+ 98·5
1891	−122·1	+ 94·3	+ 99·6	− 2·4	+ 69·4
1892	−128·9	+ 94·7	+ 96·7	− 3·4	+ 59·1
1893	−124·6	+ 94·7	+ 85·6	− 3·7	+ 53·0
1894	−131·5	+ 92·6	+ 88·4	− 10·8	+ 38·7
1895	−126·5	+ 93·6	+ 87·8	− 14·9	+ 40·0
1896	−137·9	+ 96·0	+ 92·3	+ 6·4	+ 56·8
1897	−153·9	+ 97·0	+ 94·7	+ 0·8	+ 41·6
1898	−168·9	+101·2	+ 96·8	− 6·2	+ 22·9
1899	−153·7	+103·2	+102·7	− 9·8	+ 42·4
1900	−167·0	+103·6	+109·1	− 7·5	+ 37·9
1901	−173·1	+106·5	+106·7	− 6·2	+ 33·9
1902	−178·4	+109·1	+107·9	− 5·3	+ 33·3
1903	−181·3	+112·2	+113·6	− 0·3	+ 44·8
1904	−179·1	+113·4	+115·5	+ 0·7	+ 51·7
1905	−155·9	+123·5	+120·1	− 6·2	+ 81·5
1906	−146·0	+134·3	+131·0	− 1·8	+117·5
1907	−126·8	+143·8	+142·4	− 5·3	+154·1
1908	−135·6	+151·0	+132·5	+ 6·8	+154·7
1909	−154·2	+158·0	+138·3	− 6·5	+135·6
1910	−142·7	+170·0	+146·7	− 6·7	+167·3
1911	−121·2	+177·3	+146·8	− 6·0	+196·9
1912	−143·8	+186·9	+158·6	− 4·6	+197·1
1913	−131·6	+199·6	+168·2	− 11·9	+224·3

B. 1907–38

(in £000,000. All items are net balances.
+ = excess of receipts, − = excess of payment)

	Merchandise Trade	Overseas Investment Earnings	All other Invisible Trade	Bullion and Specie	Overall Balance on Current Account
1907	−137	+160	+120	− 5	+138
1910	−152	+187	+125	− 7	+153
1913	−146	+210	+129	− 12	+181
1920	−386	+200	+395	+ 43	+252
1922	−183	+175	+150	+ 13	+155
1923	−210	+200	+148	+ 16	+153
1924	−337	+220	+190	+ 12	+ 86
1925	−393	+250	+188	+ 10	+ 54
1926	−463	+250	+199	− 12	− 26
1927	−386	+250	+219	− 3	+ 79
1928	−352	+250	+225	− 7	+117
1929	−382	+250	+233	+ 16	+117
1930	−386	+220	+194	− 5	+ 25
1931	−407	+170	+134	+ 33	− 70
1932	−286	+150	+ 86	− 17	− 67
1933	−258	+160	+103	−201	−196
1934	−284	+170	+117	−142	−139
1935	−275	+185	+108	− 56	− 38
1936	−346	+200	+127	−227	−246
1937	−431	+210	+176	− 99	−144
1938	−388	+200	+122	+ 74	+ 8

REFERENCES

BOOKS

Bank of England, *United Kingdom Overseas Investments, 1938–1948* (London, 1950) (kept up to date annually thereafter in a paper issued with the Bank's annual reprints).

S. Bourne, *Trade, Population and Food* (London, 1880).

A. K. Cairncross, *Home and Foreign Investment, 1870–1913* (Cambridge, 1953).

E. M. Carus-Wilson, *Medieval Merchant Venturers* (London, 1954).

G. N. Clark, *English Commercial Statistics, 1696–1782* (London, 1938).

H. Feis, *Europe, the World's Banker, 1870–1914* (New Haven, 1930).

H. Furber, *John Company at Work* (Cambridge, Mass., 1948).

C. K. Hobson, *The Export of Capital* (London, 1914).

R. W. K. Hinton, *The Eastland Trade and the Common Weal in the Seventeenth Century* (Cambridge, 1959).

E. E. Hoon, *The Organisation of the English Customs System, 1696–1786* (New York, 1938).

A. H. Imlah, *Economic Elements in the Pax Britannica* (Cambridge, Mass., 1958).

L. H. Jenks, *The Migration of British Capital to 1875* (New York, 1927).

A. E. Kahn, *Great Britain in the World Economy* (London and New York, 1946).

C. P. Kindleberger, *The Terms of Trade* (New York, 1956).

J. M. Letiche, *Balance of Payments and Economic Growth* (New York, 1959).

J. R. McCulloch, *A Dictionary of Commercial Navigation* (London, edition of 1882).

D. Macpherson, *A History of the European Commerce with India* (London, 1812).

I. Mintz, *Trade Balance during Business Cycles: U.S. and Britain since 1880* (New York, 1959).

C. Moreau, *State of the Trade of Great Britain with all Parts of the World* (London, 1822).

C. N. Parkinson (editor), *The Trade Winds* (London, 1948).

Eileen Power and M. M. Postan (editors), *Studies in English Trade in the Fifteenth Century* (London, 1933).

G. D. Ramsay, *English Overseas Trade during the Centuries of Emergence* (London, 1957).

F. P. Robinson, *The Trade of the East India Company from 1790–1813* (Cambridge, 1912).

S. B. Saul, *Studies in British Overseas Trade 1870–1914* (Liverpool, 1960).

W. R. Scott, *The Constitution and Finance of English, Scottish and Irish Joint Stock Companies to 1720* (Cambridge, 1912).

Elizabeth B. Schumpeter, *English Overseas Trade Statistics, 1697–1808* (Oxford, 1960).

W. Schlöte, *British Overseas Trade from 1700 to the 1930's* (English edition, Oxford, 1952).

B. E. Supple, *Commercial Crisis and Change in England, 1600–1642* (Cambridge, 1959).

I. Svennilson, *Growth and Stagnation in the European Economy* (E.C.E. Geneva, 1954).

Sir Charles Whitworth, *State of the Trade of Great Britain* (London, 1776).

P. L. Yates, *Forty Years of Foreign Trade* (London, 1959).

GOVERNMENT PUBLICATIONS

Trade and Navigation Accounts (in *Sessional Papers* as part of the annual *Finance Accounts* to 1853, and separately thereafter).

Annual Statement of Trade (in *Sessional Papers* from 1854–1920, and issued as non-parliamentary papers thereafter).

Report of the Select Committee on Frauds and Abuses of the Customs (1733), P.P. I.

Report of the Select Committee on Smuggling (1745), *H.C.J.* xxv.

Report of the Select Committee on Frauds on the Revenue (1783) *P.P.* xi.

Returns of a variety of major articles of commerce in *Sessional Papers* from 1801 onwards, being particularly valuable up to the publication of the *Annual Statement* in 1854.

Report of the Select Committee on the High Price of Gold Bullion (S.P. 1810, iii).

Report of the Commissioners of Customs (in *Sessional Papers* annually from 1857–1909).

Report of the Commissioners of Customs and Excise (in *Sessional Papers* annually since 1910).

Returns relating to Imports and Exports, etc. 1840, 1852, 1860, 1861 and 1862 (S.P. 1863, lxvi).

Customs Tariffs of the U.K., 1800–1897 (S.P. 1898, lxxxv).

Board of Trade Journal, 1887 onwards.

H.M. Treasury, United Kingdom Balance of Payments, 1946–57 (1959).

Memoranda on British Foreign Trade and Industry (S.P. 1903, lxvii, *S.P.* 1905, lxxxiv, and *S.P.* 1909, cii).

National Income and Expenditure (non-parliamentary papers, annually from 1952).

ARTICLES

J. H. Andrews, 'Two Problems in the Interpretation of the Port Books', *E.H.R.* (1956).

S. Bourne, 'The Official Trade and Navigation Statistics', *J.S.S.* (1872).

E. M. Carus-Wilson, 'Trends in the Export of English Wollens in the Fourteenth Century', *E.H.R.* (1950).

W. A. Cole, 'Trends in Eighteenth Century Smuggling', *E.H.R.* (1958).

R. Davis, 'English Foreign Trade, 1660–1700', *E.H.R.* (1954).

F. J. Fisher, 'Commercial Trends and Policy in Sixteenth Century England, *E.H.R.* (1940).

F. J. Fisher, 'London's Export Trade in the Early Seventeenth Century', *E.H.R.* (1956).

A. W. Flux, 'Some Old Trade Records Re-examined: A Study in Price Movements during the Present Century', *J.R.S.S.* (1898).

Lord Kindersley, 'British Foreign Investments', *E.J.* (annually 1929–39).

H. W. Macrosty, 'The Overseas Trade of the U.K., 1924–31', *J.R.S.S.* (1932).

H. W. Macrosty, 'The Overseas Trade of the U.K., 1930–39', *J.R.S.S.* (1940).

A. Maizels, 'The Oversea Trade Statistics of the United Kingdom', *J.R.S.S.* (1949).

D. North and A. Heston, 'The Estimation of Shipping Earnings in Historical Studies of the Balance of Payments', *Canadian Journal of Economics and Political Science* (1960).

G. Paish, 'Great Britain's Capital Investments in Other Lands', *J.R.S.S.* (1909).

G. Paish, 'Great Britain's Capital Investments in Individual Colonial and Foreign Countries', *J.R.S.S.* (1911).

G. Paish, 'The Export of Capital and the Cost of Living', *T.M.S.S.* (1913–4).

P. Ramsey, 'Overseas Trade in the Reign of Henry VII: The Evidence of Customs Accounts', *E.H.R.* (1953).

A. Rive, 'A Short History of Tobacco Smuggling', *E.H.* (1929).

S. B. Saul, 'Britain and World Trade, 1870–1914', *E.H.R.* (1954).

C. T. Saunders, 'Consumption of Raw Materials in the United Kingdom', *J.R.S.S.* (1952).

A. S. Silverman, 'Monthly Index Numbers of British Export and Import Prices, 1880–1913', *R.E.S.* (1930).

L. Stone, 'State Control in Sixteenth Century England', *E.H.R.* (1947).

L. Stone, 'Elizabethan Overseas Trade', *E.H.R.* (1949).

H. Tyszynski, 'World Trade in Manufactured Commodities, 1899–1950', *M.S.E.S.S.* (1951).

CHAPTER XII

WAGES AND THE STANDARD OF LIVING

TABLES

1. Indices of Average Wages—United Kingdom 1790–1938.
2. Indices of Wages of Labourers in London and Lancashire—1700–96.
3. Indices of Average Wages in Certain Industries—United Kingdom 1770–1938.
4. Indices of Average Incomes or Wage-earners by Industry Groups—United Kingdom 1920–38.
5. Cattle and Sheep brought for Sale at Smithfield Market—1732–1854.
6. *Per Capita* Consumption of Coffee, Tea, Sugar, and Tobacco—United Kingdom 1789–1938.
7. Wheat and Potatoes Available *per Capita*—1760–1914.

In travelling backwards from the twentieth century to the nineteenth the student of wages passes from a highway to a thorny path; but in passing to earlier periods he crosses into a morass with but few firm places. In the present century a great deal of information on wages is available; information which has been used, at any rate for the inter-war years, to produce definitive statistics. For the nineteenth century a fair amount of scattered material is available, together with, towards its close, more regular information. Much of this has been organised into a fairly complete statistical picture. But before 1800 even scattered references are scarce—scarcer, indeed, as Thorold Rogers found, for the eighteenth century than for some earlier periods.[1] Such eighteenth-century references as there are in Rogers's work, moreover, are subject to the major criticism that they are not in the main critically examined and qualitatively assessed, and that they are not differentiated by regions.[2] There is now reason to hope that this paucity of early wage statistics will be at least partially remedied when the results of the work of Lord Beveridge's Price and Wage History Research group are finally collated and published.

The importance of regional variations, both in the level and the direction of wage movements, is brought out fully in the only major published work on eighteenth-century wages since Rogers, that of Dr Gilboy.[3] This is itself, however, limited in its scope by the scarcity of information, in particular by the fact that it relates mainly to the building trades and

---

[1] J. E. T. Rogers, *A History of Agriculture and Prices in England* (7 vols., Oxford, 1866–1902).

[2] This applies also to generalisations based on Rogers, such as those in G. Steffen, *Studien zur Geschichte der Englischen Lohnarbeiter* (Stuttgart, 1901), and E. S. Furniss, *The Position of the Labourer in a System of Nationalism* (Cambridge, Mass., 1920).

[3] Elizabeth W. Gilboy, *Wages in Eighteenth Century England* (Cambridge, Mass., 1934), and 'The Cost of Living and Real Wages in Eighteenth Century England', in *The Review of Economic Statistics*, 1936. A general index of wages, based largely on Dr Gilboy's work, can be found in Phyllis Deane and W. A. Cole, *British Economic Growth, 1688–1959*, (Cambridge, 1962).

agriculture, and therefore tells us little about the wages of those in industrial occupations, which were probably more flexible. This limitation should be borne in mind when using the indices of the money and real wages of labourers in London and Lancashire, which, together with Dr Gilboy's cost-of-living index, are shown as table 2. For full details about the construction of these indices the original source must be consulted. Here it is sufficient to say that, though the price index is principally based on institutional prices, we may accept her view that 'crude as our index is, it is based on the most complete, continuous, and homogeneous series now available'.[1]

For the nineteenth century, the study of wages is on firmer ground—increasingly so after 1850. Much of the available material was used by A. L. Bowley and G. H. Wood in their studies published before World War I,[2] and it is doubtful if their general picture would be much changed by filling in the details for the industries which they did not cover. Their overall averages form part of table 1 here, and it also contains the quinquennial index of Miss Deane and Dr Cole,[3] also based on Bowley's and Wood's researches. The individual industry indices constructed by Bowley and Wood are reproduced here as part of table 3.

By the beginning of the 1920's interest in wages was such that there was plentiful material available for the statisticians, and two or three indices were published, notably in the London and Cambridge Economic Service *Bulletin*,[4] a similar one in Bowley's *Wages and Income since 1860*, and by E. C. Ramsbottom of the Ministry of Labour in the *Journal of the Royal Statistical Society*.[5] There is little difference between these indices, though the last is probably based on the most complete information, and it is the one shown here. The general index is the final part of table 1, and some of the component industry series, mainly those industries with which Bowley and Wood dealt, are given in table 3. These indices, however, begin in 1920, thus leaving a gap from 1914 to 1920, which cannot be satisfactorily covered in the type of table shown here. The best way of bridging this gap is by reference to an earlier book by Bowley—*Prices and Wages in the United Kingdom, 1914–1920*.[6] The last table on wages, table 4, presents some of the main results of Agatha Chapman and Rose Knight's *Wages and Salaries in the United Kingdom, 1920–1938*[7] turned into index form.

It is, perhaps, necessary to make a few general comments on the wage indices shown here, for all are subject to certain disadvantages when used, as they often have been, as indicators of the standard of living. Miss Chapman's and Mrs Knight's series is more refined than any of the others, but nevertheless, it relates to employed persons only.

---

[1] E. W. Gilboy, 'The Cost of Living and Real Wages in Eighteenth Century England', *loc. cit.* p. 141.

[2] Contained in articles in the *J.R.S.S.* between 1898 and 1910, and in the *E.J.* for 1898 and 1899. Bowley summarised, refined, and continued some of the series in his *Wages and Income since 1860* (Cambridge, 1937). An earlier version was in his *Wages in the United Kingdom in the Nineteenth Century* (Cambridge, 1900).

[3] *Op. cit.*

[4] Summarised in A. L. Bowley, 'Index Numbers of Wage Rates and Cost of Living', in the *J.R.S.S.* (1952).

[5] Issues of 1935, 1938 and 1939. Indices not published for certain years have been supplied to us by the Ministry of Labour.

[6] Oxford, 1921. [7] Cambridge, 1953.

Wood's series given in Part B of table 1 makes allowance for unemployment—but from the nature of the information available the allowances he made were bound to be rough-and-ready, though reasonably satisfactory for a general index. Dr R. S. Tucker[1] follows Wood and others when he states that 'allowance for unemployment does not affect the picture very much, and especially does not alter the trend'. This may be true in the period with which Wood was concerned;[2] but it certainly did not apply to the inter-war period, nor always before 1850. Of the year 1842, for example, Mr Matthews says: 'The unemployment figures quoted by some members [of Parliament] bear more resemblance to those experienced in the 1930's than to the moderate percentages shown by the trade union records for the years after 1860'.[3]

Aside from unemployment, which is probably not an important factor when long-period comparisons are related to groups of (rather than single) years, there are other points to bear in mind in relating wage indices to living standards. The indices take no account of the effect on welfare of reductions in the hours of work. These reductions are inadequately documented until the late nineteenth century,[4] but they may have varied considerably from time to time, and certainly before the spread of the factory system there was much irregularity of work.[5] Another factor in living standards which does not show up in wage indices is the increase in services provided by the state (especially since 1907), and (since World War II) in employers' contributions to state or private insurance funds. Yet another factor is the change, not completely reflected in prices, in the quality of the goods included in the various cost-of-living indices: an important example of this is housing.

We have not included in this section any statistics of actual wage rates paid. A great many of these figures have survived, but seldom in consistent series, and to attempt comprehensive coverage of them would require a separate volume at the least; and the difficulties of selecting a representative sample are fully described by the makers of the various indices we have shown. Nevertheless, there are occasions when actual wage statistics are required, and it will be useful to point out the major sources for these. Dr Gilboy's book gives the main available published series for the eighteenth century, and Thorold Rogers has several earlier quotations. Of the material for this and earlier periods which has been collected by Lord Beveridge and his colleagues, it is claimed that 'it transcends immeasurably in scale and importance anything available to former students in its field'.[6] For the end of the eighteenth century there is much scattered material in Arthur Young's *Tours*[7]

[1] R. S. Tucker, 'The Wages of London Artisans' in the *Journal of the American Statistical Association* (1936), p. 77.

[2] Probably excepting the years 1858, 1879 and 1886.

[3] R. C. O. Matthews, *A Study in Trade Cycle History* (Cambridge, 1954), p. 164.

[4] Whereafter see the *Abstract of Labour Statistics* and the *Ministry of Labour Gazette*.

[5] See T. S. Ashton, *An Economic History of England: The Eighteenth Century* (London, 1955), pp. 203–6.

[6] Lord Beveridge, 'Wages and Inflation in the Past', in *The Incorporated Statistician* (Oct. 1957). The Exeter building wages from 1339 to 1788 will be of particular interest.

[7] *A Six Weeks' Tour through the Southern Counties of England and Wales* (London, 1768); *A Six Months' Tour through the North of England* (4 vols., London, 1770); *The Farmer's Tour through the East of England* (4 vols., London, 1771); *Tour in England and Wales* (London, 1776); and *A Tour in Ireland* (London, 1780).

and *Annals of Agriculture*,[1] and in Eden's *The State of the Poor*,[2] some of which was collated by Thorold Rogers. The major sources for the nineteenth century are the unpublished collection of wage rates made by G. H. Wood, available on loan from the Ministry of Labour and in the library of the Royal Statistical Society, and the *Returns of Wages Published between 1830 and 1886*,[3] for which Giffen was responsible. This latter collects together the bulk of the material published in the sessional papers of that period, especially in *Porter's Tables* and in the volumes of *Miscellaneous Statistics* issued annually from 1854. From 1886, when the first earnings enquiry was undertaken,[4] onwards, the amount of material increases vastly, the most notable sources being the *Ministry of Labour Gazette*,[5] the *Report on Trade Unions*,[6] and the *Abstract of Labour Statistics*,[7] while part B of the Labour Department's *Report on Standard Time Rates of Wages in the U.K.* in 1900[8] gives a review of wage rates in some occupations over a number of years. This brief survey omits many valuable but specialised sources, mainly in articles in learned journals.[9]

The last three tables in this section contain certain consumption statistics which have been used as indicators of the standard of living. Table 5 shows the numbers of cattle and sheep brought for sale to Smithfield Market, a series which a recent student of the subject, Dr Hobsbawm, thinks 'we can . . . use . . . without too much hesitation',[10] though its deficiencies should be borne in mind. The lack of statistics relating to pig-meat, traditionally the most important to the poorer classes, constitutes a serious gap in our knowledge.[11] Another deficiency, at least as important, is a clear idea of the changes which may have taken place in the size of animals. Mr Fussell discussed this problem for the eighteenth century in articles in *Agricultural History*.[12] He was unable to come to any conclusions about sheep, but for cattle he found that the commonly accepted view of the increase in size during the eighteenth century was greatly exaggerated. 'Some increase in the animal there was', he wrote, but 'the effect of Bakewell's improvements although remarkable, cannot have been approximately universal, and had not been towards increasing size, but towards producing more meat and less bone'. It seems reasonable to suppose that the next stage in improvement, the increase in the size of high-quality beasts, took place during the nineteenth century, but we have no evidence of this. Yet another difficulty in using the

---

[1] Edited by Young, and published from 1784 to 1815.   [2] London, 1797.   [3] *S.P.* 1887, LXXXIX.
[4] Published in *Sessional Papers* from 1889 to 1893–4, with summaries in *S.P.* 1893–4, LXXXIII Pt. II. There were later earnings enquiries in 1906 and 1924.
[5] Its current name. For its earlier designations see the bibliography.
[6] Published in *Sessional Papers* from 1887.   [7] Published in *Sessional Papers* from 1893.
[8] *S.P.* 1900, LXXXII.
[9] Such as those on Scottish agricultural wages by R. Mollond and G. Evans, and by George Houston in the *J.R.S.S.* (1950 and 1955), and those on Sheffield wages and earnings by Sidney Pollard in the *Yorkshire Bulletin of Economic and Social Research* (1954 and 1957).
[10] E. J. Hobsbawm, 'The British Standard of Living 1790–1850', in *E.H.R.*, vol. X, no. 1 (1957), p. 65.
[11] A general account of the diet of different classes in England from the middle ages to modern times can be found in J. C. Drummond and Anne Wilbraham, *The Englishman's Food* (London, 1939), though it contains no serious attempt to estimate exactly how much of his chosen foods the poorer Englishman was able to buy. Contemporary sources of labourers' diet in the late eighteenth century are Eden, *op. cit.* and D. Davies, *The Case of the Labourers in Husbandry* (London, 1795).
[12] G. E. Fussell, 'The Size of English Cattle in the Eighteenth Century' (1929), and (with Constance Goodman), 'Eighteenth Century Estimates of British Sheep and Wool Production' (1930).

Smithfield series is the fact that it can be taken only as an exact indicator of London's meat consumption if the proportion of the London population fed from that market remained constant. This has not yet been established.

Table 6 gives fresh statistics of *per capita* consumption of coffee, sugar, tea, and tobacco, based where possible on the Customs figures of imports entered for home consumption (less quantities over-entered). For the periods when these are not available (for example, when the goods have been duty-free), imports less re-exports have been used. These figures will be found to differ from some previously published.[1] The differences result from minor variations in definition, from small revisions in the Registrar Generals' estimates of population, and from differences in the trade statistics published in early nineteenth-century blue books. In general, the policy pursued here has been to prefer those statistics which were published latest; in particular, to use those in the Customs historical volume of 1898.[2]

The use of these *per capita* consumption statistics as indicators of the standard of living is, of course, fraught with dangers in interpretation. All the commodities for which series exist were imported, and were therefore subject in the early and more controversial period to annual variations arising from wars and the slow irregular pace of ocean shipping.[3] There were secular trends in the consumption of at least three of these commodities at different times—a trend towards tea-drinking, away from beer, in the eighteenth and early nineteenth centuries; a fashionable move against tobacco in early Victorian times; and the well-known decline in the popularity of coffee in the second half of the nineteenth century. One must agree with Dr Hobsbawm that 'sugar is the most sensitive indicator',[4] though that, too, was subject to outside factors, such as the growth of a factory confectionery industry in the late nineteenth century, and the imposition and removal of duties. In general, it would not be unfair to say that the consumption statistics we have are a poor measure of the standard of living, particularly for the period before 1850 for which good indicators are most needed. Only pronounced trends can be clearly interpreted, and there are none of these before the 1840's.[5]

The last table gives Dr Salaman's calculations of the weight of wheat and potatoes available *per capita* from the late eighteenth to the early twentieth centuries. The figures are, of course, estimates based on a number of assumptions, and can only be regarded as rough approximations.

[1] e.g. Those in the *Abstract* for some years, and those given in A. Rive, 'The Consumption of Tobacco since 1600', in *Economic History*, vol. I (1926).   [2] *S.P.* 1898, LXXXV.

[3] This does not seriously affect the *per capita* figures shown here, only the absolute figures in the notes. An exception may be tobacco in the early nineteenth century according to Rive, 'A Short History of Tobacco Smuggling', in *Economic History*, vol. I. For a discussion of the effect of smuggling on the trade statistics, see W. A. Cole, 'Trends in Eighteenth Century Smuggling', in *E.H.R.*, vol. x, no. 3 (1958).

[4] E. J. Hobsbawm, *loc. cit.* p. 57.

[5] Mr A. J. Taylor, in his recent article, 'Progress and Poverty in Britain, 1780–1850: A Reappraisal' (*History*, February 1960), has in part shifted the grounds of the discussion away altogether from these readily available consumption statistics. He writes: 'It was outside the field of necessities, in the narrow sense, that increasing consumption was most evident. . . . If these improvements were purchased in part at the expense of so-called necessities, and specifically of food, this was a matter of the consumer's choice' (pp. 22–3).

Wages and the Standard of Living 1.   Indices of Average Wages—
United Kingdom 1790–1938

NOTES TO PART A

[1] Source: Phyllis Deane and W. A. Cole, *British Economic Growth, 1688–1955* (Cambridge University Press, 1962).
[2] The authors say: 'The index for Great Britain is a weighted average of Wood's general unweighted index of average money wages in towns in the United Kingdom (*E.J.*, 1899) and Bowley's indices of average agricultural earnings in England and Wales, and Scotland respectively (combined according to his weights (*J.R.S.S.*, 1899). No attempt has been made to extract the Irish components from Wood's U.K. index in constructing our G.B. index because they were not sufficiently different or weighty to affect the result. The

index for Ireland is an average of Wood's index of average money wages in Dublin and Bowley's index of average agricultural earnings (allowing for unemployment) in Ireland. The average is again weighted in accordance with our estimates of the proportions employed in agricultural and non-agricultural occupations'.
[3] The authors suggest that the Irish index must 'be treated with considerable reserve', but 'for all its crudeness . . . it offers a more acceptable estimate . . . than any index of British or United Kingdom wages as a whole'.

A.   At Intervals 1790–1860 for Great Britain and Ireland, (1840 = 100)

	Great Britain	Ireland			Great Britain	Ireland
1790	70	107		1824	105	120
1795	82	115		1831	101	114
1800	95	125		1840	100	100
1805	109	139		1845	98	100
1810	124	139		1850	100	100
1816	117	136		1855	117	129
1820	110	122		1860	115	134

NOTES TO PART B

[1] Source: G. H. Wood, 'Real Wages and the Standard of Comfort since 1850', in the *J.R.S.S.* (1909).
[2] Column 1 was continued by A. L. Bowley in *Wages and Income since 1860* (Cambridge, 1937), p. 6, from information supplied by Wood, as follows:

1903	176	1905	175	1907	190	1909	184
1904	176	1906	181	1908	187	1910	187

[3] The index of retail prices was described by Wood as 'experimental' and should not be used for purposes other than that for which it was computed.

B.   Wages and Earnings, 1850–1902, United Kingdom (1850 = 100)

	Average Money Wages		Average Real Wages		
	Not Allowing for Unemployment	Allowing for Unemployment	Not Allowing for Unemployment	Allowing for Unemployment	Average Retail Prices
1850	100	100	100	100	100
1851	100	100	102	102	97
1852	100	98	102	100	97
1853	110	113	105	107	106
1854	114	115	96	97	122
1855	116	114	95	94	126
1856	116	115	96	95	126
1857	112	109	96	94	119
1858	110	101	102	94	109
1859	112	111	104	104	107
1860	114	116	103	105	111
1861	114	112	100	99	114
1862	116	110	105	100	111
1863	117	115	109	107	107
1864	124	126	117	118	106
1865	126	129	117	120	107
1866	132	133	116	117	114
1867	131	126	109	105	121
1868	130	124	110	105	119
1869	130	126	115	111	113
1870	133	133	118	118	113
1871	138	141	121	125	113
1872	146	150	122	126	120
1873	155	159	128	132	122
1874	156	159	133	136	117

	Average Money Wages		Average Real Wages		
	Not Allowing for Unemployment	Allowing for Unemployment	Not Allowing for Unemployment	Allowing for Unemployment	Average Retail Prices
1875	154	156	135	138	113
1876	152	153	137	136	110
1877	151	150	133	132	113
1878	148	143	132	128	110
1879	146	134	137	126	103
1880	147	144	134	132	107
1881	147	147	136	136	105
1882	147	149	135	138	106
1883	149	151	139	142	102
1884	150	144	144	138	100
1885	149	141	148	140	96
1886	148	138	151	142	92
1887	149	143	155	149	89
1888	151	149	157	155	89
1889	156	158	159	161	91
1890	163	166	166	169	91
1891	163	164	164	166	92
1892	162	158	163	159	92
1893	162	156	167	161	89
1894	162	157	170	165	87
1895	162	158	174	170	84
1896	163	164	176	177	83
1897	166	167	176	176	86
1898	167	169	174	176	87
1899	172	174	180	183	86
1900	179	180	183	184	89
1901	179	179	181	181	90
1902	176	175	177	176	91

NOTES TO PART C

[1] SOURCE: A. L. Bowley, *Wages and Income since 1860* (Cambridge University Press, 1937), p. 30.

[2] Bowley heads column 3 'quotient' rather than real wages, 'because of the numerous qualifications with which it must be used'. He suggests the figures should be treated as ±5.

[3] The index is carried back for five years in the period 1860–80, as follows, but the margin of error is much greater:

	Money Wages	Cost of Living	Quotient
1860	58	113	51
1866	66	114	58
1870	66	110	60
1874	80	115	70
1877	77	110	70

[4] In an article in the *J.R.S.S.* (1952), Bowley puts forward the following approximate money wage rate index (converted by us to 1914 = 100):

1915	108	1919	229	1922	210
1916	119	1920	283	1923	187
1917	142	1921	271	1924	192
1918	189				

[5] This cost of living index is discussed in *Wages and Income since 1860*, appendix D. It should not be used for purposes other than those for which it was computed.

C. Wages, United Kingdom (as constituted at each date), 1880–1936, (1914 = 100)

	Money Wages	Cost of Living	Real Wages		Money Wages	Cost of Living	Real Wages
1880	72	105	69	1905	89	92	97
1881	72	103	71	1906	91	93	98
1882	75	102	73	1907	96	95	101
1883	75	102	73	1908	94	93	101
1884	75	97	77	1909	94	94	100
1885	73	91	81	1910	94	96	98
1886	72	89	81	1911	95	97	97
1887	73	88	84	1912	98	100	97
1888	75	88	86	1913	99	102	97
1889	80	89	90	1914	100	100	100

1890	83	89	93					
1891	83	89	92		1924	194	175	111
1892	83	90	92		1925	196	175	112
1893	83	89	94		1926	195	172	113
1894	83	85	98		1927	196	167	117
1895	83	83	100		1928	194	166	117
1896	83	83	100		1929	193	164	118
1897	84	85	98		1930	191	157	122
1898	87	88	99		1931	189	147	129
1899	89	86	104		1932	185	143	129
1900	94	91	103		1933	183	140	131
1901	93	90	102		1934	183	141	130
1902	91	90	101		1935	185	143	130
1903	91	91	99		1936	190	147	129
1904	89	92	97					

NOTE TO PART D

SOURCES: E. C. Ramsbottom, 'The Course of Wage Rates in the United Kingdom, 1921–34', in the *J.R.S.S.* (1935), and similar articles for 1934–7 and for 1938 in *ibid.* (1938) and (1939).

D. Wages, United Kingdom 1920–38, at December in each year. Average of twelve months of 1924 = 100

	Weekly Money Wage Rates	Cost of Living	Weekly Real Wages of Fully-employed Workers
1920	154·8	151·4	102
1921	120·3	109·7	109½
1922	99·2	101·7	97½
1923	97·9	101·1	97
1924	100·8	102·9	98
1925	101·3	100·0	101½
1926	101·7	100·0	101½
1927	99·8	96·0	104
1928	98·9	95·4	103½
1929	98·6	94·9	104
1930	97·9	87·4	112
1931	95·7	84·0	114
1932	94·4	81·1	116½
1933	94·0	81·1	116
1934	94·4	81·7	115½
1935	95·6	84 (a)	114
1936	98·6	86·5(a)	114
1937	103·1	91 (a)	113½
1938	104·3	88·5(a)	118

(a) Taken from the *London and Cambridge Economic Service Bulletin*.

Wages and the Standard of Living 2. Indices of Wages of Labourers in London and Lancashire—1700–1796

NOTES

[1] SOURCE: Elizabeth W. Gilboy, 'The Cost of Living and Real Wages in Eighteenth Century England', *Review of Economic Statistics* (1936).
[2] The years referred to are those *beginning* at Michaelmas.
[3] The cost-of-living index is derived mainly from contract prices, and must be regarded as very rough. It relates principally to London and southern England, but was nevertheless used to estimate Lancashire real wages.
[4] All wage indices relate to the weekly wages of men in full employment.

(1700 = 100)

| | | London Wages | | Lancashire Wages | |
	Cost of Living	Money	Real	Money	Real
1700	100	100	100	100	100
1701	100	99	99	95	95
1702	91	99	109	89	98
1703	99	109	110	89	90
1704	88	114	130	89	101
1705	95	109	115	105	111
1706	86	109	127	105	122
1707	94	109	116	105	112
1708	116	109	94	105	90
1709	135	111	82	89	66
1710	147	109	74	105	71
1711	104	110	106	105	101
1712	98	110	112	105	107
1713	108	110	102	100	93
1714	105	109	104	111	106
1715	100	109	109	111	111
1716	92	109	118	111	121
1717	92	109	118	89	97
1718	92	109	118	111	121
1719	106	109	103	111	105
1720	102	110	108	133	130
1721	91	110	121	123	135
1722	86	110	128	123	143
1723	97	110	113	123	127
1724	99	110	111	123	124
1725	105	110	105	111	106
1726	100	110	110	111	111
1727	106	110	104	133	126
1728	112	105	94	111	99
1729	102	110	108	133	130
1730	89	109	122	133	149
1731	88	114	130	123	140
1732	81	114	141	133	164
1733	89	114	128	133	149
1734	91	114	125	133	146
1735	88	118	134	133	151
1736	93	116	125	133	143
1737	94	118	126	133	141
1738	91	116	127	133	146
1739	109	118	108	133	122
1740	119	116	97	133	112
1741	103	116	113	133	129
1742	98	118	120	133	136
1743	82	115	140	133	162
1744	83	118	142	133	160

346

	Cost of Living	London Wages		Lancashire Wages	
		Money	Real	Money	Real
1745	94	118	126	133	141
1746	92	118	128	128	139
1747	95	118	124	128	135
1748	100	118	118	133	133
1749	98	118	120	133	136
1750	93	120	129	133	143
1751	98	118	120	133	136
1752	94	118	126	133	141
1753	95	118	124	133	140
1754	92	118	128	133	145
1755	98	118	120	133	136
1756	125	118	94	133	106
1757	118	118	100	111	94
1758	108	118	109	111	103
1759	99	118	119	133	134
1760	97	118	122	123	127
1761	99	118	119	123	124
1762	109	118	108	123	113
1763	110	121	110	177	161
1764	115	121	105	156	136
1765	117	121	103	156	133
1766	124	121	98	156	126
1767	123	121	98	156	127
1768	109	121	111	200	183
1769	108	121	112	200	185
1770	118	121	103	200	169
1771	130	121	93	177	136
1772	136	121	89	200	147
1773	131	121	92	200	153
1774	129	121	94	200	155
1775	128	118	92	200	156
1776	120	118	98	200	167
1777	131	118	90	200	153
1778	123	118	96	200	163
1779	117	123	105	200	171
1780	125	123	98	200	160
1781	125	123	98	200	160
1782	144	123	85	211	147
1783	139	123	88	200	144
1784	129	123	95	189	146
1785	132	123	93	205	155
1786	128	123	96	223	174
1787	130	123	95	211	162
1788	127	...	...	228	180
1789	134	...	...	228	170
1790	133	...	...	233	175
1791	131	...	...	223	170
1792	140	...	...	200	143
1793	148	...	...	267	180
1794	168	...	...	233	133
1795	179	...	...	233	130
1796	153	...	...	233	152

NOTES TO PART A

[1] SOURCES: Articles by A. L. Bowley and G. H. Wood (separately and together) in the *J.R.S.S.* 1898 and 1899 for Agriculture (up to 1879), 1899 for Compositors, 1900–1 for Building (up to 1879), 1905–6 for Shipbuilding and Engineering and 1910 for Cotton (up to 1879); A. L. Bowley, *Wages and Income since 1860* for all remaining figures, these being in many cases revisions of the earlier articles. The figures in this book for shipbuilding and engineering simply repeat the series for agriculture. Since there must have been a transcription error, they are not shown here.

[2] In the article on Shipbuilding and Engineering, Bowley and Wood say of possible errors: 'We are making a liberal allowance for these if we affix a ±5 to our earlier index numbers. We may, indeed, depend on them to ±3, or less than a shilling in the average wage' (*J.R.S.S.*, 1906, p. 185). This almost certainly applies to all the figures except the very early Shipbuilding and Engineering ones which are in brackets, and possibly to some of the Agriculture series. What Bowley called the pivot years in the latter—i.e. years for which there is definite information—are printed in bold type. The remaining indices for agriculture are interpolations.

[3] For the West Riding woollen and worsted industries, Bowley produced the following indices 'expressing the average wage of all adults' (*J.R.S.S.*, 1902, p. 125):

1795	80	1860	90	1883	105
1815	115	1866	100	1886	100
1840	75	1874–7	120	1891	100

[4] These index numbers allow for the changing importance of the different occupations within each industry.

[5] The separate index numbers for wages in agriculture continue after 1880 as follows:

	E. & W.	Scot.		E. & W.	Scot.
1880	103	98	1889	98	99
1881	100	94	1890	99	100
1882	97	94	1891	100	100
1883	97	95	1892	102	101
1884	96	96	1893	101	...
1885	94	97	1894	101	...
1886	92	98	1895	100	...
1887	92	98	1896	98	...
1888	97	98			

[6] G. H. Wood ('Real Wages and the Standard of Comfort since 1850', in the *J.R.S.S.*, 1909, p. 93) gives the following index numbers of average wages in three other trades, and a slightly different index for coal-mining, for 1850–1906:

	Coal-mining	Puddling	Gas	Furniture
1850	67	92	70	70
1855	94	124	71	72
1860	76	92	73	76
1866	100	117	76	83
1871	80	108	83	86
1874	108	143	90	97
1877	76	107	93	99
1880	72	113	91	98
1883	77	97	91	98
1886	72	89	91	97
1891	100	100	100	100
1896	87	90	101	101
1900	108	139	104	106
1906	97	108	106	106

A. Indices of Average Earnings in a Normal Week, 1891 = 100

	Agriculture					Cotton		
	England & Wales	Scotland	Compositors	Building	Shipbuilding and Engineering	Factory Workers	All Workers	Coal-mining
1770	...	**18**	...	...	...	...	...	...
1770–88	**51**	...	...	...	...	...	...	...
1777–85	...	...	60	...	...	...	...	...
1786	...	...	62	...	...	...	...	...
1789	52	...	...	...	...	...	...	...
1790	53	**31**	...	...	...	...	...	...
1791	55	31	62	...	...	...	...	...
1792	57	32	62	...	...	...	...	...
1793	59	32	(74)	...	(40)	...	...	...
1794	61	**33**		...	(52)	...	...	...
1795	**67**	35	...			...	...	...
1796	73	37	...			...	...	...
1797	76	38	...	near 44	...	...	...	...
1798	79	39	...		...	...	...	...
1799	81	40	...		...	...	...	...
1800	83	41	...		(56)	...	...	...
1801	85	42	74		...	...	...	...
1802	86	43	74		(56)	...	...	...
1803	87	44	74		...	...	...	...
1804	94	49	...	rising to about 63	...	...	...	...
1805	100	54	79		(65)	...	...	...
1806	105	58	...		...	59	98	...
1807	105	58	...		...	...	87	...
1808	105	58	...		...	...	72	...
1809	105	58	83		...	...	75	...

Wages and the Standard of Living 3. *continued*

	Agriculture		Com-positors	Building	Shipbuilding and Engineering	Cotton		Coal-mining
	England & Wales	Scotland				Factory Workers	All Workers	
1810	105	58				62	76	...
1811	105	58			(71)	62	69	...
1812	105	58				62	76	...
1813	104	55	88			62	79	...
1814	103	53			(72)	62	92	...
1815	102	51				62	73	...
1816	101	51			72	62	61	...
1817	100	49	85			61	55	...
1818	98	48	80	near 63	71	61	53	...
1819	97	47	...		73	61	53	...
1820	95	46	78			61	53	...
1821	88	42	...			60	53	...
1822	77	39			71	60	53	...
1823	77	37				58	52	...
1824	72	37				58	53	...
1825	78	37			71	58	53	...
1826	78	38	78	...	71	58	50	...
1827	78	38				...	50	...
1828	78	38		near 59		...	49	...
1829	78	38			71	...	49	...
1830	76	38				...	45	...
1831	78	38		59		...	44	...
1832	80	39		59		56	45	...
1833	81	39		59		56	45	...
1834	79	38	78	59		...	49	...
1835	76	41		59		...	47	...
1836	77	43	81	60	73	57	48	...
1837	78	46	81	61		...	49	...
1838	80	48	81	62		...	49	...
1839	82	52		63		55	49	...
1840	82	54	83	63	75	55	49	...
1841	82	57		63	75	55	50	...
1842	82	59		63	75	55	50	...
1843	82	62		63	75	54	50	...
1844	77	62	83	63	75	55	51	...
1845	71	61		63	75	58	50	...
1846	77	61		63	75	58	50	...
1847	77	61	83	63	75	...	51	...
1848	72	61		64	74	...	51	...
1849	72	61		64	73	54	51	...
1850	72	61	83	64	73	54	52	...
1851	72	61	83	64	74	55	53	...
1852	72	61	83	64	75	56	54	...
1853	83	69	83	64	77	59	57	...
1854	93	77	83	68	82	58	56	...
1855	96	79	83	70	82	59	57	...
1856	96	79	83	72	82	62	60	...
1857	91	76	83	73	82	62	61	...
1858	84	72	83	73	80	62	61	...

	Agriculture		Com-positors	Building	Shipbuilding and Engineering	Cotton		Coal-mining
	England & Wales	Scotland				Factory Workers	All Workers	
1859	85	72		73	80	64	63	...
1860	89	75		76	79	68	68	...
1861	90	75	83	76	80	68	68	...
1862	90	75		76	81	67	67	...
1863	90	75		76	81	66		...
1864	90	75	83	76	82	66		...
1865	90	75	83	79	84	71		...
1866	90	75	83	83	85	77		...
1867	92	76	84	83	83	77		...
1868	94	77	84	83	83	79		...
1869	95	82	84	83	83	78		...
1870	96	85	85	84	84	81		...
1871	104	88	88	86	85	85		...
1872	113	94	88	88	89	87		...
1873	117	100	88	89	92	89		...
1874	122	106	93	93	94	90		...
1875	117	112	94	98	94	90		...
1876	117	112	95	100	94	92		...
1877	117	112	96	100	95	94		...
1878	114	112	96	98	94	88		...
1879	107	103	96	97	89	84		...
1880	100		96	96	90	87		71
1881	99		96	96	92	90		73
1882	97		96	96	95	90		78
1883	96		96	96	95	91		79
1884	94		96	96	94	91		76
1885	93		96	96	92	90		73
1886	91		96	96	90	89		70
1887	94		96	97	91	90		70
1888	96		96	97	95	94		74
1889	97		96	99	98	95		87
1890	100		98	100	100	96		99
1891	100		100	100	100	100		100
1892	100		100	101	99	101		91
1893	99		101	103	98	101		93
1894	99		101	103	98	101		88
1895	97		101	104	98	101		84
1896	97		101	105	101	102		83
1897	99		101	107	103	102		84
1898	101		101	108	105	103		91
1899	103		101	109	108	104		96
1900	109		...	111	108	107		116
1901	110		...	111	108	108		109
1902	110		...	111	108	107		101
1903	110		...	111	106	107		98
1904	110		...	111	106	108		95
1905	110		...	111	106	110		94
1906	110		...	111	...	115		96
1907	110		...	111	...	...		111

	Agriculture		Com-positors	Building	Cotton		Coal-mining
	England & Wales	Scotland			Factory Workers	All Workers	
1908	110		...	111	...		108
1909	110		...	111	...		103
1910	110		...	111	...		104
1911	112		...	111	...		102
1912	114		...	112	...		108
1913	118		...	114	...		116
1914	122		...	118	...		113

NOTES TO PART B

[1] SOURCE: E. C. Ramsbottom, 'The Course of Wage Rates in the United Kingdom, 1921–34', *J.R.S.S.* (1935), and similar articles for 1934–7 and for 1938, *ibid.* (1938 and 1939). The figures for certain months and years have not been published, and were supplied to us by the Ministry of Labour. [2] The following table will be useful in linking Parts A and B. Its sources is A. L. Bowley, *Wages and Income since 1860* (Cambridge University Press, 1937), p. 17.

Percentage Increase in Weekly Wages, 1924 Compared with 1914.

	Males	Females
Coal-mining	63	—
Iron, Steel, Vehicles, Engineering and Metalwork	87	126
Cotton	92	87
Woollen and Worsted	140	136
Printing	147	—
Wood and Furniture	103	—
Building and Construction	95	—
Agriculture	68	—
Transport	101	—
Public Utilities	105	—
ALL OCCUPATIONS	90·6	112
	94·3	

B. Indices of Weekly Wage Rates, average of 12 months of 1924 = 100

	Agriculture		Coal-Mining	Iron and Steel	Engin-eering (a)	Ship-building and Repair-ing(b)	Cotton	Woollen and Worsted	Printing and Book-binding	Furni-ture	Build-ing	Gas Supply	Rail-way Ser-vice
	E. & W.	Scot.											
1920	160½	142½	187	202½	152	175	162	147½	117	134½	145½	140	127½
1921	158	142½	163½	181½	147	162½	137½	139	118	126½	137	136	125
1922	115	118	95	104	121	118½	109	105	108	106½	105½	111	108
1923	100	100	94	95	100	96½	100	100	101	100	96	100	101½
1924	100	100	100	100	100	100	100	100	100	100	100	100	100
1925	109	99	98½	99	101	106	100	100	101	101	103	103	100½
1926	113	98	98	95	102	106	100	100	101	100½	103	104	100
1927	113	98	94	95	102½	106	100	100	101	100	103	104	100
1928	113	97	88	91½	104	106½	100	100	101	101	101½	104	98
1929	113	95½	87	91½	104	108	98½	100	101	100	101	104	96
1930	113	94	87	92½	104	109½	94	93	101	100	99½	104	98
1931	113	94	84	91	103	110	94	89½	101	99	97	104	95
1932	111	94	84	89	101	108	92	85	101	94½	94½	102	94
1933	109	89	84	90	101	108	86	83	101	92	92½	101	94
1934	110	87	84	91	101	108	86	82	101	92	92	101	94
1935	113	88	84	92	103	109	85½	82	100	92½	92½	102	95
1936	114	90	89	95	105	111	85	84	100	96	96	103	95
1937	118	95	96	104	109½	117	91	89	100	100	99	107	97
1938	123	100	97½	116½	113	124	92	89	100	101	101½	109	99

(a) Includes railway engineering workshops.
(b) This covers time workers only. The available information for pieceworkers is insufficient to provide a basis for index numbers.

Wages and the Standard of Living 4.   Indices of Average Incomes of Wage-earners by Industry Groups—United Kingdom 1920–38

NOTES

[1]   SOURCE: Agatha Chapman and Rose Knight, *Wages and Salaries in the United Kingdom, 1920–1938* (Cambridge University Press, 1953). The indices are constructed from the tables on pp. 18, 22 and 98–103, together with (for Part B) the cost of living index on p. 30.

[2]   United Kingdom here refers to Great Britain and Northern Ireland for the whole period.

[3]   For a full definition of the concept of average income as used here the original source must be consulted. Briefly, it represents the average income per man-year of employment, rather than per person employed, i.e. it is the average income of a man in normal full-time employment, including periods of sickness and recognised holidays, but not periods of unemployment. So far as possible, short-time was treated as partial employment in making the estimates of numbers

employed, whilst overtime was regarded as varying average earnings rather than the level of employment.

[4]   Most of the headings are self-explanatory, but the following seem to require a little elaboration: *Iron and Steel*—covers workers in blast furnaces, smelting and rolling mills, foundries, tube manufacture and tinplate works; *Shipbuilding*—includes ship repairing, but does not cover workers in naval dockyards; *Engineering*—combines mechanical and electrical engineering, other than in ordnance factories; *Printing, etc.*—covers printing, bookbinding and kindred trades, stationery and cardboard box manufacture, and newspaper publication; *Professional Services*—covers wage-earning assistants in the professions, other than those employed by local authorities; *Miscellaneous Services*—comprises wage-earning assistants in entertainment and sport.

A. Index of Average Money Incomes   (1924 = 100)

| | Agriculture and Forestry | Fishing | Mining and Quarrying | Manufacturing | | | | | | | |
				Total	Iron and Steel	Shipbuilding	Engineering	Cotton	Woollen and Worsted	Printing, etc.	Furniture
1920	146	132	159	145	176	175	153	162	142	116	133
1921	154	102	129	137	167	163	147	137	139	118	126
1922	110	91	93	110	106	119	120	109	105	108	106
1923	99	88	94	100	96	97	100	100	100	101	100
1924	100	100	100	100	100	100	100	100	100	100	100
1925	109	98	99	101	100	106	101	100	100	101	100
1926	111	93	83	101	97	106	101	100	100	101	100
1927	111	94	96	101	97	107	102	100	100	101	100
1928	111	98	88	101	95	107	103	100	100	100	100
1929	111	104	88	102	94	108	105	98	99	100	100
1930	112	102	89	100	94	110	105	91	93	100	98
1931	112	97	89	98	94	110	103	92	90	100	97
1932	111	94	90	96	92	109	101	92	85	100	94
1933	109	93	89	96	92	106	101	88	87	100	91
1934	108	99	89	98	95	105	103	89	86	103	91
1935	111	103	89	100	96	103	107	89	91	104	92
1936	115	106	96	101	97	105	109	88	92	104	96
1937	118	109	101	105	105	108	112	94	95	104	99
1938	127	113	106	109	114	115	114	95	95	104	100

B. Index of Average Real Incomes   (1924 = 100)

	Agriculture and Forestry	Fishing	Mining and Quarrying	Total	Iron and Steel	Shipbuilding	Engineering	Cotton	Woollen and Worsted	Printing, etc.	Furniture
1920	103	92	115	102	124	123	108	114	100	82	94
1921	119	79	100	106	129	126	114	106	108	91	98
1922	105	87	89	105	101	114	115	104	100	103	101
1923	100	89	95	100	97	98	101	101	101	102	101
1924	100	100	100	100	100	100	100	100	100	100	100
1925	108	97	98	101	100	105	100	100	100	100	100
1926	113	95	85	103	99	108	103	102	102	103	102
1927	116	98	100	106	101	112	107	104	104	105	104
1928	117	104	93	106	100	113	109	105	105	105	105
1929	119	111	94	109	100	115	112	105	106	107	107
1930	124	113	98	111	104	122	116	101	103	111	109
1931	133	115	106	116	112	130	122	109	107	119	115
1932	135	115	109	117	112	133	123	112	103	122	114
1933	136	117	111	120	115	133	126	110	109	125	114
1934	135	123	111	122	118	130	128	111	107	128	113
1935	135	125	109	122	118	126	131	109	111	127	113
1936	137	126	114	121	116	125	130	105	110	124	114
1937	134	123	114	119	119	123	127	107	108	118	113
1938	142	126	119	122	128	129	128	107	107	117	112

A. Index of Average Money Incomes (*continued*)

(1924 = 100)

	Building and Con- tracting	Gas, Water and Electricity Supply	Transport and Communi- cations	Distri- butive Trades	Insurance, Banking and Finance	Local Govt. Service	Pro- fessional Services	Miscel- laneous Services	Grand Total All Wage- earners
1920	148	129	119	126	146	138	145	144	142
1921	136	123	118	125	140	136	138	138	133
1922	107	107	106	111	108	116	106	107	106
1923	97	99	98	102	96	103	98	99	99
1924	100	100	100	100	100	100	100	100	100
1925	102	102	100	100	100	102	100	101	101
1926	103	102	96	100	99	103	100	101	98
1927	103	103	99	101	101	102	99	99	100
1928	101	103	99	101	99	101	97	98	99
1929	101	101	99	100	98	101	97	98	99
1930	102	100	98	101	97	101	95	96	99
1931	99	97	95	101	97	100	93	93	97
1932	96	94	93	102	95	99	91	92	95
1933	95	94	92	103	92	98	90	90	94
1934	95	95	94	104	94	99	90	91	95
1935	97	96	95	106	95	99	91	91	97
1936	97	97	97	109	96	100	93	94	99
1937	100	97	99	111	101	103	97	94	102
1938	102	102	100	114	102	106	99	100	106

B. Index of Average Real Incomes (*continued*)

(1924 = 100)

1920	104	91	84	88	102	97	102	101	100
1921	106	96	91	97	109	105	107	107	103
1922	102	102	101	106	103	111	102	102	102
1923	98	99	99	103	97	103	98	99	99
1924	100	100	100	100	100	100	100	100	100
1925	102	102	100	99	99	102	100	100	100
1926	105	104	98	102	101	105	102	102	100
1927	107	108	104	105	105	107	104	104	105
1928	107	108	104	106	105	106	103	103	104
1929	108	107	106	107	104	108	104	104	106
1930	113	111	108	111	107	112	106	106	109
1931	118	115	112	120	115	119	110	111	114
1932	117	112	113	124	116	120	111	111	115
1933	118	118	115	129	115	122	112	113	117
1934	118	118	117	129	117	123	111	112	118
1935	118	118	117	130	116	121	111	112	118
1936	116	116	116	130	114	119	110	111	118
1937	113	110	112	126	114	117	110	107	115
1938	114	114	112	128	114	119	111	112	118

Wages and the Standard of Living. 5   Cattle and Sheep Brought for Sale at Smithfield Market 1732–1854

NOTES

[1] SOURCES: 1732–89—*Report on Waste Lands* (1795), pp. 202–3; 1790–1819—S.P. 1822, XXI; 1820–47—Porter's Tables; 1848–54—G. Dodd, *The Food of London* (London, 1856), pp. 240–1.

[2] The *Report on the Waste Lands* gives slightly different figures for the years 1790–4. The only material differences are in the numbers of sheep in 1790–2. which are given (in thousands) as:

| 1790 | 730 | 1791 | 730 | 1792 | 753 |

[3] S.P. 1822, XXI, gives the number of cattle in 1821 as 142 thousand.

[4] For the period 1842–7 Dodd, *op. cit.*, gives slightly different figures from the ones used here.

[5] Earlier estimates of sales at Smithfield were made for 1698 and 1725, as follows (in thousands):

	Cattle	Sheep		Cattle	Sheep
1698	70	540	1725	74	556

The sources are, respectively, Stowe, *Survey* (1754 edition), p. 719, and Maitland, *History of London* (1772 edition), pp. 756–7.

(in thousands)

Year	Cattle	Sheep	Year	Cattle	Sheep	Year	Cattle	Sheep
1732	76	515	1773	90	610	1814	135	871
1733	80	555	1774	90	585	1815	125	963
1734	79	567	1775	94	624	1816	120	969
1735	84	591	1776	98	672	1817	130	1,045
1736	88	587	1777	94	715	1818	138	963
1737	90	607	1778	97	659	1819	135	950
1738	87	589	1779	97	677	1820	133	948
1739	87	569	1780	102	707	1821	129	1,107
1740	85	501	1781	103	743	1822	142	1,340
1741	78	536	1782	101	729	1823	150	1,265
1742	80	503	1783	102	702	1824	164	1,240
1743	76	468	1784	98	616	1825	157	1,130
1744	77	491	1785	99	641	1826	143	1,271
1745	74	564	1786	92	666	1827	138	1,335
1746	72	621	1787	95	669	1828	148	1,288
1747	71	622	1788	93	679	1829	158	1,240
1748	68	610	1789	93	694	1830	160	1,287
1749	73	624	1790	104	750	1831	148	1,189
1750	71	656	1791	101	740	1832	159	1,257
1751	70	632	1792	107	761	1833	152	1,168
1752	74	642	1793	117	728	1834	162	1,237
1753	75	648	1794	109	719	1835	170	1,382
1754	70	631	1795	131	746	1836	164	1,220
1755	74	647	1796	117	759	1837	172	1,329
1756	77	625	1797	108	694	1838	183	1,403
1757	83	575	1798	107	753	1839	181	1,360
1758	84	551	1799	123	834	1840	177	1,372
1759	86	582	1800	125	842	1841	…	…
1760	89	622	1801	135	761	1842	175	1,469
1761	83	666	1802	126	743	1843	175	1,572
1762	103	722	1803	118	787	1844	186	1,609
1763	81	653	1804	113	904	1845	192	1,442
1764	75	556	1805	125	912	1846	200	1,459
1765	82	537	1806	120	859	1847	221	1,438
1766	76	515	1807	134	924	1848	220	1,344
1767	77	574	1808	144	1,015	1849	224	1,514
1768	80	626	1809	138	989	1850	227	1,540
1769	82	643	1810	132	963	1851	241	1,564
1770	87	649	1811	125	966	1852	259	1,565
1771	94	632	1812	134	954	1853	277	1,461
1772	90	610	1813	138	891	1854	263	1,539

NOTES

[1] Sources: Coffee 1789–1839—*S.P.* 1829, xv and *S.P.* 1843, LII; tea 1789–1896—*S.P.* 1898, LXXXV; sugar 1793–1814 —*S.P.* 1847–8, LVIII; sugar 1815–96—*S.P.* 1898, LXXXV; sugar 1897–1901—*Annual Statement of Trade*; tobacco 1790–1870—*S.P.* 1898, LXXXV; all other figures—*Abstract*. The population figures used were the latest estimates in the *Reports of the Registrar General* for the various kingdoms, after 1801, and our own estimates based on extrapolation of later trends, for 1789–1800.

[2] For the years before 1789, for which population estimates are not sufficiently sure to be used to extend this table, the following statistics of quantities entered for home consumption are available:

Tea, in thousands of pounds: (source: *S.P.* 1898, LXXXV)

1740	1,494	1748	3,151	1756	3,813	1764	5,223
1741	1,192	1749	3,335	1757	3,723	1765	5,204
1742	474	1750	2,296	1758	3,521	1766	5,186
1743	711	1751	3,656	1759	3,246	1767	4,921
1744	1,723	1752	2,273	1760	3,861	1768	7,676
1745	2,423	1753	3,253	1761	4,308	1769	9,115
1746	2,496	1754	3,049	1762	4,218	1770	8,634
1747	215	1755	3,437	1763	5,307	1771	6,307

1772	6,722	1777	5,120	1781	4,884	1785	14,801
1773	3,776	1778	4,180	1782	6,202	1786	15,852
1774	6,729	1779	6,342	1783	4,742	1787	15,726
1775	6,156	1780	7,328	1784	10,160	1788	14,765
1776	4,468						

Tobacco, in thousands of pounds: (source: A. Rive, 'The Consumption of Tobacco since 1600', in *Economic History*, vol. I (1926)).

1614–21 (annual average)	140
1628	400
1632–4 (annual average)	600
1699–1709 (annual average)	11,300
1732	5,200 }—much smuggling
1744–6 (annual average)	7,000 }
1770	10,000
1775	27,000—fear of shortage due to political situation.
1775–82 (annual average)	5,000
1786	6,800
1787	6,700
1788	6,900

(in lb.)

	Coffee		Tea	Sugar	Tobacco
	G.B.	U.K.	U.K.	U.K.	U.K.(a)
1789	0·10	...	1·16	...	...
1790	0·10	...	1·14	...	0·75
1791	0·11	...	1·18	...	0·94
1792	0·10	...	1·21	...	0·92
1793	0·11	...	1·18	14·70	0·81
1794	0·10	...	1·25	13·95	1·05
1795	0·10	...	1·42	12·72	1·16
1796	0·04	...	1·34	13·56	1·18
1797	0·06	...	1·23	11·74	1·12
1798	0·07	...	1·45	13·21	1·32
1799	0·07	...	1·46	22·22	1·03
1800	0·08	...	1·48	15·32	1·24
1801	0·07	...	1·49	22·53	1·23
1802	0·08	...	1·58	20·39	1·06
1803	0·08	...	1·53	14·39	1·23
1804	0·10	...	1·34	18·15	1·14
1805	0·11	...	1·45	17·12	1·08
1806	0·10	...	1·31	21·74	1·09
1807	0·10	...	1·39	18·85	1·01
1808	0·09	...	1·45	22·34	1·01
1809	0·78	...	1·19	20·39	0·96
1810	0·44	...	1·37	24·64	1·18
1811	0·53	...	1·24	23·15	1·23
1812	0·66	...	1·34	19·66	1·21
1813	0·70	...	1·36	16·97	1·05
1814	0·50	...	1·29	15·48	0·94
1815	0·47	0·34	1·35	14·71(b)	0·86
1816	0·57	0·40	1·16	16·27	0·95
1817	0·65	0·47	1·24	20·79	0·93(a)
1818	0·59	0·42	1·32	11·83	0·90
1819	0·54	0·38	1·24	17·09	0·81

See p. 358 for footnotes

Wages and the Standard of Living 6. *continued*

	Coffee U.K.	Tea U.K.	Sugar U.K.	Tobacco U.K.(*a*)
1820	0·34	1·22	17·74	0·76
1821	0·36	1·27	18·19	0·75
1822	0·36	1·29	16·71	0·77
1823	0·39	1·25	17·92	0·79
1824	0·38	1·26	18·30	0·77
1825	0·50	1·31	16·44	0·85
1826	0·58	1·29	18·80	0·79
1827	0·68	1·31	17·33	0·82
1828	0·74	1·26	18·73	0·80
1829	0·83	1·25	18·15	0·81
1830	0·95	1·26	19·08	0·81
1831	0·94	1·24	18·92	0·81
1832	0·94	1·29	17·83	0·83
1833	0·92	1·29	17·15	0·84
1834	0·96	1·41	17·70	0·86
1835	0·93	1·46	17·93	0·88
1836	0·98	1·93	15·84	0·88
1837	1·03	1·19	17·68	0·88
1838	0·99	1·25	17·39	0·91
1839	1·02	1·34	16·37	0·88
1840	1·08	1·22	15·20	0·87
1841	1·06	1·37	16·99	0·83
1842	1·06	1·38	16·04	0·83
1843	1·10	1·48	16·55	0·85
1844	1·14	1·50	16·80	0·89
1845	1·23	1·59	19·58	0·94
1846	1·31	1·67	20·95	0·96
1847	1·34	1·66	23·24	0·95
1848	1·33	1·75	24·91	0·98
1849	1·24	1·81	24·20	1·00
1850	1·13	1·86	25·26	1·00
1851	1·19	1·97	26·87	1·02
1852	1·27	1·99	29·27	1·04
1853	1·34	2·14	30·45	1·07
1854	1·35	2·24	33·74	1·10
1855	1·29	2·28	30·38	1·09
1856	1·25	2·26	28·27	1·16
1857	1·22	2·45	29·48	1·16
1858	1·24	2·58	34·51	1·20
1859	1·20	2·67	34·80	1·21
1860	1·23	2·67	34·14	1·22
1861	1·21	2·69	35·49	1·20
1862	1·18	2·69	35·92	1·21
1863	1·11	2·89	35·92	1·13
1864	1·06	2·99	36·74	1·28
1865	1·02	3·27	39·69	1·30
1866	1·02	3·39	41·11	1·34
1867	1·03	3·65	43·06	1·34
1868	0·99	3·48	41·89	1·34

See p. 358 for footnote

(in lb.)

	Coffee U.K.	Tea U.K.	Sugar U.K.	Tobacco U.K.(a)
1869	0·93	3·61	42·44	1·34
1870	0·97	3·76	47·11	1·32
1871	0·97	3·91	46·73	1·35
1872	0·98	4·01	47·32	1·37
1873	0·99	4·10	51·50	1·41
1874	0·96	4·22	53·07	1·43
1875	0·98	4·43	59·35	1·46
1876	0·99	4·49	54·74	1·46
1877	0·96	4·50	60·98	1·49
1878	0·97	4·64	55·14	1·44
1879	0·99	4·68	63·03	1·40
1880	0·92	4·57	60·28	1·42
1881	0·89	4·58	64·44	1·41
1882	0·89	4·69	67·31	1·42
1883	0·89	4·82	68·41	1·43
1884	0·90	4·90	68·60	1·45
1885	0·91	5·06	71·84	1·46
1886	0·87	4·92	64·05	1·44
1887	0·80	5·02	72·00	1·45
1888	0·83	5·03	69·02	1·48
1889	0·76	4·99	74·92	1·51
1890	0·75	5·17	71·09	1·55
1891	0·76	5·35	78·01	1·61
1892	0·74	5·43	75·15	1·64
1893	0·69	5·40	75·49	1·62
1894	0·68	5·51	76·92	1·66
1895	0·70	5·65	85·15	1·66
1896	0·69	5·75	82·19	1·72
1897	0·68	5·79	78·12	1·75
1898	0·68	5·83	82·73	1·82
1899	0·71	5·95	82·07	1·88
1900	0·71	6·07	85·53	1·95
1901	0·76	6·16	91·39	1·89
1902	0·68	6·07	73·86(c)	1·93
1903	0·71	6·04	66·99	1.94
1904	0·68	6·02	78·16	1·96
1905	0·67	6·02	70·41	1·97
1906	0·66	6·22	77·08	1·99
1907	0·67	6·26	78·83	2·04
1908	0·66	6·24	77·19	2·04
1909	0·67	6·36	80·42	1·97
1910	0·65	6·39	78·00	2·00
1911	0·62	6·48	80·27	2·06
1912	0·62	6·50	79·53	2·06
1913	0·62	6·69	83·22	2·10
1914	0·63	6·89	79·87	2·19
1915	0·74	7·15	81·14	2·44
1916	0·66	6·91	68·99	2·35
1917	1·05	6·41	54·73	2·44
1918	1·11	7·21	47·78	2·51

See p. 358 for footnotes

(in lb.)

	Coffee U.K.	Tea U.K.	Sugar U.K.	Tobacco U.K.(a)
1919	0·76	8·70	75·64	3·26
1920	0·72	8·44	52·15	2·99
1921	0·71	8·69	64·92	2·96
1922	0·74	8·67	74·98	2·82
1923(d)	(0·79)	(8·68)	(72·77)(e)	(2·90)
1924	0·78	8·81	78·49	2·87
1925	0·79	8·85	84·50	2·96
1926	0·77	8·91	87·08	3·00
1927	0·80	9·03	84·74	3·04
1928	0·78	9·16	91·39	3·11
1929	0·76	10·16	91·97	3·24
1930	0·77	9·87	92·68	3·31
1931	0·81	9·67	99·02	3·27
1932	0·76	10·53	94·86	3·23
1933	0·70	9·36	92·32	3·22
1934	0·72	9·22	97·42	3·41
1935	0·70	9·42	98·15	3·51
1936	0·72	9·31	101·08	3·72
1937	0·72	9·19	102·11	3·87
1938	0·72	9·09	100·51	4·00

(a) For the period up to 1816 inclusive these statistics are for years ended 5th July. The half-year ended 5th January 1817 is not represented in the table. In that period 8,959,000 pounds were entered for home consumption.
(b) In the Customs historical volume (*S.P.* 1898, LXXXV) it is said of sugar that 'it is impracticable to obtain an accurate view of the consumption of any single year' before 1815. The annual average *per capita* consumption for 1800–14 is put at 16·54 lb. The pre-1815 figures given here, which show an annual average of 18·83 lb. should not, therefore, be used for comparisons with later figures without bearing this difference in mind.
(c) Before 1902 the statistics relate to the combined un-weighted quantities of refined and unrefined sugar, whereas later they represent the equivalent in refined sugar of total consumption. The effect of this change is to lower the *per capita* figure by about 10 per cent.

(d) Southern Ireland was treated as foreign from 1st April 1923. The 1923 figures are not exactly comparable with those for any other years, since they include southern Irish consumption before 1st April but are divided by the population of Great Britain and Northern Ireland only.
(e) Prior to 1923 sugar exported in composite articles was not deducted from imports, and is consequently reckoned as part of home consumption. From 1923 the consumption figures express the estimated equivalent in sugar exceeding 98° polarisation of all sugar refined and unrefined (including sugar in composite articles) entered for home consumption, less sugar re-exported on drawback (including sugar in composite articles). From 25th April 1928 the degree of polarisation was changed to over 99° for Empire sugar—a change which does not affect the *per capita* statistics.

7. Wheat and Potatoes Available *Per Capita*, 1760–1914

NOTES

[1] SOURCE: R. N. Salaman, *The History and Social Influence of the Potato* (Cambridge University Press, 1949), pp. 613–7.

[2] This table relates to availability for either direct consumption by humans, or as animal feeding-stuffs, or for industrial use.

(in lb.)

	U.K. Wheat		England & Wales Potatoes
1760's	1·5		
1770's	1·3	1775	0·25
1780's	1·4		
1790's	1·36	1795	0·40
1800's	1·3		
1810's	1·05	1814	0·47
1820's	0·95		
1830's	0·9	1838	0·62
1840's	0·85		
1850's	0·85	1851	0·70
1860's	1·03	1866	0·80
1870's	1·05	1871	0·90
1880's	1·05	1881	0·64
1890's	1·04	1891	0·65
1900's	1·03	1901	0·58
1910–14	1·05	1911	0·60
		1914	0·53

REFERENCES

BOOKS

L. P. Adams, *Agricultural Depression and Farm Relief in England, 1813–1852* (Westminster, 1932).

W. J. Ashley, *The Bread of our Forefathers* (London, 1928).

J. Barton, *Observations on the . . . Labouring Classes of Society* (London, 1817).

A. L. Bowley, *Wages in the United Kingdom in the Nineteenth Century* (Cambridge, 1900).

A. L. Bowley, *Wages and Income since 1860* (Cambridge, 1937).

Agatha Chapman and Rose Knight, *Wages and Salaries in the United Kingdom, 1920–1938* (Cambridge, 1952).

D. Davies, *The Case of the Labourers in Husbandry* (London, 1795).

G. Dodd, *The Food of London* (London, 1856).

J. C. Drummond and Anne Wilbraham, *The Englishman's Food* (London, 1939).

Sir Frederick M. Eden, *The State of the Poor* (3 vols., London, 1797).

E. S. Furniss, *The Position of the Laborer in a System of Nationalism* (Cambridge, Mass., 1920).

R. Gibson, *Cotton Textile Wages in the United States and Great Britain: A Comparison of Trends, 1860–1945* (New York, 1948).

E. W. Gilboy, *Wages in Eighteenth Century England* (Cambridge, Mass., 1934).

R. Giffen, *Economic Inquiries and Studies* (2 vols., London, 1904).

E. M. Gray, *The Weaver's Wage* (Manchester, 1935).

J. J. Hecht, *The Domestic Servant Class in Eighteenth Century England* (London, 1956).

B. L. Hutchins and A. Harrison, *A History of Factory Legislation* (London, 1903) (Appendix by G. H. Wood on women's wages during the nineteenth century, in the first edition only.)

J. Jewkes and E. M. Gray, *Wages and Labour in the Lancashire Cotton Spinning Industry* (Manchester, 1935).

R. V. Lennard, *Economic Notes on English Agricultural Wages* (London, 1914).

W. Maitland, *History of London* (2 vols., London, 1756).

Ivy Pinchbeck, *Women Workers in the Industrial Revolution, 1750–1850* (London, 1930).

S. Pollard, *A History of Labour in Sheffield* (Liverpool, 1959).

J. W. F. Rowe, *Wages in Practice and Theory* (London, 1928).

J. W. F. Rowe, *Wages in the Coal Industry* (London, 1923).

R. N. Salaman, *The History and Social Influence of the Potato* (Cambridge, 1949).

R. S. Spicer, *British Engineering Wages* (London, 1928).

M. L. Yates, *Wages and Labour Conditions in British Engineering* (London, 1937).

A. Young, *A Six Weeks' Tour through the Southern Counties of England and Wales* (London, 1768).

A. Young, *A Six Months' Tour through the North of England* (4 vols., London, 1770).

A. Young, *The Farmers' Tour through the East of England* (4 vols., London, 1771).

A. Young, *A Tour in Ireland* (2 vols., London, 1780).

GOVERNMENT PUBLICATIONS

Report of the Select Committee on Inadequacy of Wages in the Cotton Trade (S.P. 1808, II).

Report of the Select Committee on Labourers' Wages (S.P. 1824, VI).

Abstract of Returns respecting Labourers' Wages (S.P. 1825, XIX).

Report of the Select Committee on Handloom Weavers (S.P. 1834, X).

Report of the Select Committee on Railway Labourers (S.P. 1846, XIII).

Return relating to Wage Rates, 1830–1886 (S.P. 1887, LXXXIX).

Return of Wages in the Principal Textile Trades (S.P. 1889, LXX).

Return of Wages in the Minor Textile Trades (S.P. 1890, LXVIII).

Return relating to Trades (Hours of Work) (S.P. 1890, LXVIII).

Return of Wages in Mines and Quarries (S.P. 1890–1, LXXVIII).

Report to the Board of Trade on the Relation of Wages in Certain Industries to Cost of Production S.P. 1890–1, LXXVIII).

Return of Wages of Police, Roadmen and Workers in Gas and Water Works (S.P. 1892, LXVIII).

Report on Changes in Rates of Wages and Hours of Labour, and on Standard Piece and Time Rates (in sessional papers irregularly from 1893 to 1914–6).

Labour Gazette, 1893 onwards (called the *Board of Trade Labour Gazette* 1905–18, and the *Ministry of Labour Gazette* since 1923).

Abstract of Labour Statistics (22 issues in sessional papers between 1893 and 1936).

Report of the Royal Commission on Labour (especially S.P. 1892, XXXIV, S.P. 1892, XXXV, S.P. 1892, XXXVI, S.P. 1893–4, XXXII, S.P. 1893–4, XXXIII, S.P. 1893–4, XXXIV, and S.P. 1893–4, XXXIX).

General Report on the Wages of the Manual Labour Class in the United Kingdom (S.P. 1893–4, LXXXIII).

Customs Tariffs of the U.K., 1800–1897 (S.P. 1898, LXXXV).

Report on Money Wages of Indoor Domestic Servants (S.P. 1899, XCII).

Report by Mr Wilson Fox on the Wages and Earnings of Agricultural Labour in the United Kingdom (S.P. 1900, LXXXII. For later statistics see *Abstract of Labour Statistics*.)

Charts Illustrating the Statistics of Trade, Employment, and Condition of Labour in the United Kingdom, prepared for the St Louis Exhibition (S.P. 1904, LXXIX).

Reports of the Earnings and Hours Enquiry (S.P. 1909, LXXX, S.P. 1910, LXXXIV, S.P. 1911, LXXXVIII, and S.P. 1912, CVIII).

Labour Gazette, 1893 onwards (called the *Board of Trade Labour Gazette* 1905–18, and the *Ministry of Labour Gazette* since 1923).

Wages, Earnings and Negotiating Machinery in the Building Industry, 1886–1948 (Ministry of Works Economic Research Section, 1949).

ARTICLES

T. S. Ashton, 'The Standard of Life of the Workers in England, 1790–1830', supplement IX (1949).

Dorothea M. Barton, 'The Course of Women's Wages, *J.R.S.S.* (1919).

Dorothea M. Barton, 'Women's Minimum Wages', *J.R.S.S.* (1921).

Sir William Beveridge, 'Population and Unemployment', *E.J.* (1923).

Sir William Beveridge, 'Wages in the Winchester Manors', *E.H.R.* (1936).

Lord Beveridge, 'Westminster Wages in the Manorial Era', *E.H.R.* (1955).

Lord Beveridge, 'Wages and Inflation in the Past', *The Incorporated Statistician* (1957).

C. Booth, 'Poor Law Statistics as Used in Connection with the Old Age Question', *E.J.* (1899).

A. L. Bowley, 'Index Numbers of Wage Rates and Cost of Living', *J.R.S.S.* (1952).

A. L. Bowley, 'Comparison of the Changes in Wages in France, the U.S. and the U.K. from 1840–1891', *E.J.* (1898).

A. L. Bowley, 'The Statistics of Wages in the United Kingdom during the Nineteenth Century: Agricultural Wages', *J.R.S.S.* (1890–1900).
Building Trades', *J.R.S.S.* (1900).
Printers', *J.R.S.S.* (1900).
Worsted and Woollen Manufacture of the West Riding of Yorkshire', *J.R.S.S.* (1902).
Engineering and Shipbuilding', *J.R.S.S.* (1905–6) (with G. H. Wood).
A. L. Bowley, 'Wages, Earnings and Hours of Work, 1914–1947. United Kingdom', *London and Cambridge Economic Service Special Memorandum*, No. 50.
British Association Committee (E. Cannan and others), 'The Amount and Distribution of Income (other than Wages) Below the Income Tax Exemption Limit in the United Kingdom', *J.R.S.S.* (1910–1).
D. Chadwick, 'The Rate of Wages in Manchester and Salford, and the Manufacturing Districts of Lancashire, 1839–1859', *J.S.S.* (1860).
A. Wilson Fox, 'Agricultural Wages in England and Wales during the Last Fifty Years', *J.R.S.S.* (1903).
G. E. Fussell, 'The Size of English Cattle in the Eighteenth Century', *A.H.* (1929).
G. E. Fussell and Constance Goodman, 'Eighteenth Century Estimates of British Sheep and Wool Production', *A.H.* (1930).
Elizabeth W. Gilboy, 'The Cost of Living and Real Wages in Eighteenth Century England', *R.E.S.* (1936).
E. M. Gray, 'Wage Rates and Earnings in Cotton Weaving', *T.M.S.S.* (1938–9).
R. M. Hartwell, 'Interpretations of the Industrial Revolution in England', *J.E.H.* (1959).
R. M. Hartwell, 'The Rising Standard of Living in England, 1800–1850', *E.H.R.* (1961).
E. J. Hobsbawm, 'The British Standard of Living, 1790–1850', *E.H.R.* (1957).
G. Houston, 'Farm Wages in Central Scotland from 1814–1870', *J.R.S.S.* (1955).
K. G. J. C. Knowles and D. J. Robertson, 'Differences between the Wages of Skilled and Unskilled Workers, 1880–1950', *Bulletin of the Oxford University Institute of Statistics* (1951).
K. G. J. C. Knowles and D. J. Robertson, 'Earnings in Engineering, 1926–1948', *Bulletin of the University of Oxford Institute of Statistics* (1951).
K. G. J. C. Knowles and Monica Verrey, 'Earnings in the Boot and Shoe Industry', *Bulletin of the University of Oxford Institute of Statistics* (1954).
K. G. J. C. Knowles and T. P. Hill, 'The Structure of Engineering Earnings', *Bulletin of the University of Oxford Institute of Statistics* (1954).
W. T. Layton, 'Changes in the Wages of Domestic Servants during Fifty Years', *J.R.S.S.* (1908).
W. A. MacKenzie, 'Changes in the Standard of Living in the U.K., 1860–1914', *Economica* (1921).
Joan G. Marley and H. Campion, 'Changes in Salaries in Great Britain, 1924–39', *J.R.S.S.* (1940).
R. Mollond and G. Evans, 'Scottish Farm Wages from 1870–1900', *J.R.S.S.* (1950).
E. H. Phelps Brown and Sheila V. Hopkins, 'Seven Centuries of the Prices of Consumables, compared with Builders' Wage-rates', *Economica* (1956).
E. H. Phelps Brown and Sheila V. Hopkins, 'Wage-rates and Prices: Evidence for Population Pressure in the Sixteenth Century', *Economica* (1957).
R. Mollond and G. Evans, 'Scottish Farm Wages from 1870–1900', *J.R.S.S.* (1950).
Evelyn Myatt-Price, 'A Tally of Ale', *J.R.S.S.* (1960).
S. Pollard, 'Wages and Earnings in the Sheffield Trades, 1851–1914', *Yorkshire Bulletin* (1954).
S. Pollard, 'Real Earnings in Sheffield, 1851–1914', *Yorkshire Bulletin* (1957).
E. C. Ramsbottom, 'The Course of Wage Rates in the United Kingdom, 1921–1934', *J.R.S.S.* (1935).

E. C. Ramsbottom, 'The Course of Wage Rates in the United Kingdom, 1934–1937', *J.R.S.S.* (1938).

E. C. Ramsbottom, 'The Course of Wage Rates in the United Kingdom, 1938', *J.R.S.S.* (1939).

A. Rive, 'The Consumption of Tobacco since 1600', *E.H.* (1926).

G. Routh, 'Civil Service Pay, 1875–1950', *Economica* (1954).

A. J. Taylor, 'Progress and Poverty in Britain, 1780–1850: A Reappraisal', *History* (1960).

R. S. Tucker, 'The Wages of London Artisans', *Journal of the American Statistical Association'* (1936).

H. A. Turner, 'Trade Unions, Differentials, and the Levelling of Wages', *M.S.E.S.S.* (1952).

S. Webb, 'The Alleged Differences in the Wages Paid to Men and Women for Similar Work', *E.J.* (1891).

G. H. Wood, 'The Course of Average Wages between 1790 and 1860', *E.J.* (1899).

G. H. Wood, 'Real Wages and the Standard of Comfort since 1850', *J.R.S.S.* (1909).

G. H. Wood, 'The Statistics of Wages in the United Kingdom during the Nineteenth Century: The Cotton Industry', *J.R.S.S.* (1910).

CHAPTER XIII

NATIONAL INCOME AND EXPENDITURE

TABLES

1. The Industrial Distribution of the National Income—1688–1955.
2. National Income—United Kingdom 1855–1946.
3. Stamp's 'True Comparative' Series of United Kingdom Taxable Income—1843–1914.
4. Consumers' Expenditure—United Kingdom 1900–56.
5. Estimates of Domestic Fixed Capital Formation—United Kingdom 1856–1914.
6. Estimates of Domestic Fixed Capital Formation—United Kingdom 1920–38.
7. Estimated Stocks of Fixed Capital at First Cost and at Depreciated Values—United Kingdom 1920–38.

Attempts to calculate aggregates indicative of national economic activity as a whole, date from the end of the seventeenth century. For earlier periods the data are scanty and incomplete. There are tax records and manorial surveys, of course, which stretch back to medieval times. But even attempts to assess the incomes of particular social or economic groups at specific points of time yield quantitative results of considerable uncertainty.[1] Moreover it was not until the end of the sixteenth century that contemporaries began to take an interest in statistics of national economic activity considered as a whole. According to Mr Stone 'The first and most extensive compilation of quantitative material was made during a balance of trade scare of the early 1560's when a serious attempt was made to discover the precise nature of English commerce'.[2] The Tudor interest in statistics 'ranged over the whole field of governmental activity. The confused system for public finance was made to yield essential tabular information, the best examples of which are the remarkable estimates of the costs of the two wars from 1539–51, and from 1585–1603. Detailed surveys of English resources in ships and seamen were carried out repeatedly between 1550 and 1583, and provide a wealth of information on these subjects to which there is no parallel until after the Restoration'.[3]

At the end of the seventeenth century, however, an unusual combination of circumstances produced a wealth of economic and statistical data which was more complete than any which had preceded it, and more systematically and informatively analysed by contemporaries than anything which was produced for the next hundred years. The most important factor in this combination was the spirit of the age. It was characteristic of this

[1] See for example H. L. Gray, 'Incomes from land in 1436', *English Historical Review*, vol. XLIX (1934), M. Postan, 'Some Economic Evidence of a Declining Population in the Later Middle Ages', *E.H.R.* (1950); and C. D. Ross and T. B. Pugh, 'Materials for the Study of Baronial Incomes in Fifteenth Century England'; *E.H.R.* (1953).

[2] Lawrence Stone, 'Elizabethan Overseas Trade', *E.H.R.* (1949), p. 34.   [3] *ibid.* pp. 31–2.

period of eager inquiry into scientific questions that writers on political and economic matters should try to comprehend the economic system as a whole, and should try to describe it in quantitative terms. The inventor of 'political arithmetic' was Sir William Petty who produced the first known national income estimate for this country. For him as for later exponents of this method, the key figure in the multiplication table which gave the final aggregates was the population figure and he had very little material on which to formulate a sound estimate.[1] King, who seems to have become interested in political arithmetic in connection with a new tax on births, burials and marriages, imposed at graduated rates for different sections of populations, was more fortunate. He presumably had access to the records of the new tax, which came into operation in 1695 (and provided for the most complete census of population yet attempted) and also to various tax records (hearth tax, excise and house duties, for example) which did not exist or were not returned by the collectors in Petty's time: and of course he had the advantage of being able to use the first systematically compiled returns of overseas trade for the country as a whole. Not until the assessments to Pitt's income tax and the 1801 Census of Population, which became available at the beginning of the nineteenth century, were would-be national income investigators as well supplied with the relevant statistics as Gregory King had been.[2]

It is only within the last fifty years that there has been any attempt to make a continuous historical series of estimates. The first steps in this direction were taken by Bowley and Stamp,[3] who carried back the statistics of major components of the national income well into the nineteenth century. One of the most important of these series, Stamp's 'true comparative' taxable income, is given here as table 3, and others are the basis of the wage indices given in chapter XII. But though Bowley and Stamp made estimates of total national income for particular years, neither produced a connected series for a lengthy period. Nor did Mr Colin Clark in his two pioneer works on national income attempt to go back for consecutive years beyond 1924.[4] It was left to Dr Prest, in 1948, to publish the first long and continuous series of national income estimates.[5] This series, part of which is reproduced here in Part B of table 2, is, in a sense, the basic data on this subject, though,

[1] The first scientific study of the only available vital statistics was Grant's analysis of the London Bills of Mortality for the period 1603–60. See J. Graunt, *Natural and Political Observations on the Bills of Mortality* (1662), included in *The Economic Writings of Sir William Petty*, vol. II, by C. H. Hull (Cambridge, 1899).

[2] For a critical evaluation of contemporary estimates made up to the end of the nineteenth century, see the following articles by Phyllis Deane: 'The Implications of Early National Income Estimates for the Measurement of Long-Term Growth in the United Kingdom', in *Economic Development and Cultural Change*, vol. IV, no. 1 (Nov. 1955); 'The Industrial Revolution and Economic Growth: The Evidence of Early British National Income Estimates', in *ibid.* vol. V, no. 2 (Jan. 1957); 'Contemporary Estimates of the National Income in the First Half of the Nineteenth Century', in *E.H.R.* vol. VIII, no. 3 (April 1956); and 'Contemporary Estimates of the National Income in the Second Half of the Nineteenth Century', in *ibid.* vol. IX, no. 3 (April 1957).

[3] Sir J. C. Stamp, *British Income and Property* (London, 1916); A. L. Bowley, *The Change in the Distribution of the National Income 1880–1913* (London, 1920—reprinted in Bowley and Stamp, *Three Studies in the National Income* (London, 1938); and A. L. Bowley, *Wages and Income since 1860* (Cambridge, 1937).

[4] Colin Clark, *The National Income 1924–1931* (London, 1932), and its expanded and rewritten successor, *National Income and Outlay* (London, 1937).

[5] A. R. Prest, 'National Income of the United Kingdom 1870–1946', *E.J.* vol. LVIII (1948).

of course, Dr Prest drew heavily on the work of his predecessors. Further refinements have been attempted in the last decade, notably those made by Dr Jefferys and Miss Walters,[1] but they have not resulted in any major modification of the Prest series. The most recent, that of Dr Feinstein, extends the Prest series back to 1855. It has been preferred here for the period before 1914 and forms part A of table 2. It must be stressed that, whichever series is used, these estimates are subject to margins of error, which become unpredictably wide as they go back in time.

For 1938 and subsequent post-war years from 1948 there is a consistent series of official estimates, which have been made by the Central Statistical Office. The latest available series of these has been shown here as part C of table 2 for the sake of convenient comparison with the end of the Prest series. The estimates for the years 1939–45 were published in a series of White Papers and have never been fully revised to make them consistent with the concepts which are now current and have been definitely described in a C.S.O. publication, *National Income Statistics: Sources and Methods*.[2]

The *National Income and Expenditure* Blue Books also provide detailed statistics of consumers' expenditure for the recent period, and these are used in table 3. There they are combined with the estimates produced in the series of *Studies in the National Income and Expenditure of the United Kingdom*, produced under the joint asupices of the National Institute of Economic and Social Research and the University of Cambridge Department of Applied Economics.[3] The links between these estimates and the recent blue books have been kindly supplied to us by Mr D. A. Rowe. The Prest and Adams estimates were extended back to 1870 by Jefferys and Walters.[4]

The final tables in this chapter give two sets of estimates of domestic capital formation, broken down by broad categories—Dr Feinstein's for 1855–1914, and others for 1920–38 [5] being prepared at the Cambridge University Department of Applied Economics. The former is an extension and refinement of Professor Cairncross's work.[6] Once again, it must be stressed that these figures are no more than estimates, however carefully they have been made. Dr Feinstein writes of his own series: '. . . even with such improvements as may have been made, no great accuracy is claimed for the present estimates for years so far in the past and concepts for which no adequate basic statistics were kept'.[7] The later series, although based on much more detailed and extensive information than was available for earlier periods, are also subject to wide margins of error.

Statistics of new capital issues on the London money market for the period 1870–1939 can be found in table 12 of Chapter XV.

[1] James B. Jefferys and Dorothy Walters, 'National Income and Expenditure of the United Kingdom, 1870–1952', in *Income and Wealth*, v (Cambridge, 1956).

[2] H.M.S.O., London, 1956.

[3] A. R. Prest and A. A. Adams, *Consumers' Expenditure in the United Kingdom 1900–1919* (Cambridge, 1954); and Richard Stone and D. A. Rowe, *The Measurement of Consumers' Expenditure and Behaviour in the United Kingdom 1920–1938* (2 vols., Cambridge 1954 and forthcoming).   [4] *Op. cit.*

[5] We are grateful to Dr. Feinstein for letting us use his manuscripts in advance of publication.

[6] A. K. Cairncross, *Home and Foreign Investment, 1870–1913* (Cambridge, 1953).

[7] C. H. Feinstein, ' Income and Investment in the United Kingdom, 1856–1914 ', *E.J,* (1961), p. 367.

National Income and Expenditure 1. The Industrial Distribution
of the National Income—1688–1955

NOTES

[1] SOURCE: Phyllis Deane and W. A. Cole, *British Economic Growth, 1688–1955* (Cambridge University Press, 1962).
(2) The 1688 estimates were derived from Gregory King. See Phyllis Deane, 'The Implications of Early National Income Estimates . . .' in *Economic Development and Cultural Change* (1955), for a description of the method of deriving these from King's figures.

[3] The 1955 estimates were derived from the 1958 National Income Blue Book.
[4] The difference between total national income and the branches of economic activity specified here includes government and defence, domestic and personal and professional services, all other services and errors and omissions.

(in £000,000)

	Agriculture, Forestry, Fishing	Mining, Manufacturing, Building	Trade and Transport	Rents of Dwellings	Total Gross National Income
England & Wales					
1688	19·3	9·9	5·6	2·5	48·0(a)
Great Britain					
1801	75·5	54·3	40·5	12·2	232·0
1811	107·5	62·5	50·1	17·2	301·1
1821	76·0	93·0	46·4	17·9	291·0
1831	79·5	117·1	59·0	22·0	340·0
1841	99·9	155·5	83·3	37·0	452·3
1851	106·5	179·5	97·8	42·6	523·3
1861	118·8	243·6	130·7	50·3	668·0
1871	130·4	348·9	201·6	69·4	916·6
1881	109·1	395·9	241·9	89·1	1,051·2
1891	110·8	495·2	289·6	104·0	1,288·2
1901	104·6	660·7	383·0	134·2	1,642·9
1924	168·5	1,655·9	1,234·0	265·2	4,121·1
United Kingdom					
1935	175	1,720	1,367	292	4,516
1955	787	8,101	4,051	534	16,892(b)

(a) The total includes an estimate for domestic service based on but not separately calculated in King's tables.
(b) The 1955 figures are calculated net of capital consumption. No attempt has been made to exclude depreciation from any of the other estimates in this table which may therefore be regarded as gross.

NOTES TO PART A

[1] SOURCE: C. H. Feinstein, 'Income and Investment in the United Kingdom, 1856–1914', *Economic Journal* (June 1961).
[2] For the *per capita* estimates, the Registrar-Generals' population figures (Chapter 1, table 3) were used.

[3] For national income at 1900 prices, A. L. Bowley's cost-of-living index (*Wages and Income since 1860* (Cambridge, 1937), pp. 121–2) was used.

A. Feinstein's Estimates, 1855–1914

	Net National Income at Current Prices		Net National Income at 1900 Prices	
	Total (£ mill.)	per Head (£)	Total (£ mill.)	per Head (£)
1855	636	22·9	508	18·3
1856	665	23·7	531	19·0
1857	645	22·9	502	17·8
1858	635	22·4	545	19·2
1859	656	22·9	553	19·3
1860	694	24·1	559	19·4
1861	727	25·1	591	20·4
1862	741	25·3	597	20·4
1863	759	25·8	600	20·4
1864	795	26·8	629	21·2
1865	822	27·5	662	22·1
1866	846	28·1	675	22·4
1867	840	27·6	670	22·0
1868	836	27·2	673	21·9
1869	867	28·0	711	23·0
1870	936	29·9	774	24·8
1871	1,015	32·2	817	25·9
1872	1,072	33·6	813	25·5
1873	1,149	35·7	857	26·6
1874	1,126	34·6	891	27·4
1875	1,113	33·9	912	27·8
1876	1,099	33·1	909	27·4
1877	1,089	32·4	901	26·8
1878	1,059	31·2	927	27·3
1879	1,032	30·1	930	27·1
1880	1,076	31·1	932	26·9
1881	1,117	32·0	987	28·3
1882	1,160	32·9	1,035	29·4
1883	1,153	32·5	1,029	29·0
1884	1,124	31·5	1,054	29·5
1885	1,115	31·0	1,115	31·0
1886	1,136	31·3	1,162	32·0
1887	1,185	32·4	1,225	33·5
1888	1,259	34·1	1,302	35·3
1889	1,350	36·3	1,380	37·1
1890	1,385	36·9	1,416	37·8
1891	1,373	36·3	1,404	37·1
1892	1,335	35·0	1,350	35·4
1893	1,339	34·8	1,369	35·6
1894	1,418	36·5	1,518	39·1
1895	1,447	36·9	1,587	40·5
1896	1,484	37·5	1,627	41·1
1897	1,538	38·5	1,647	41·2
1898	1,618	40·1	1,673	41·4
1899	1,700	41·7	1,799	44·1
1900	1,750	42·5	1,750	42·5
1901	1,727	41·6	1,746	42·0
1902	1,740	41·5	1,759	42·0
1903	1,717	40·6	1,717	40·6
1904	1,704	40·0	1,685	39·5

	Net National Income at Current Prices		Net National Income at 1900 Prices	
	Total (£ mill.)	per Head (£)	Total (£ mill.)	per Head (£)
1905	1,776	41·3	1,757	40·9
1906	1,874	43·2	1,834	42·3
1907	1,966	45·0	1,883	43·1
1908	1,875	42·5	1,835	41·6
1909	1,907	42·8	1,846	41·5
1910	1,984	44·2	1,881	41·9
1911	2,076	45·9	1,947	43·0
1912	2,181	48·0	1,985	43·7
1913	2,265	49·6	2,021	44·3
1914	2,209	48·0	2,010	43·7

NOTES TO PART B

[1] Source: A. R. Prest, 'National Income of the U.K., 1870–1946', in *E.J.* (1948), pp. 58–9. The figures for 1915–9 are very rough, and are based on A. J. Brown's estimates derived from country bank clearings (*O.E.P.* (1940)). The figures for 1920–38 are derived from J. R. N. Stone, 'Analysis of Market Demand', in the *J.R.S.S.* (1945). For 1938–46 the estimates of the Budget White Paper are used.
[2] For the *per capita* estimates the Registrar-Generals' population figures (Chapter 1, table 3) were used.

[3] For national income at 1900 prices the Ministry of Labour cost-of-living index was used.
[4] The figures for net national income at current prices in the *National Income and Expenditure* blue book (1958) for 1938 and 1948 are as follows:

	Total (£ mill.)	per Head (£)
1938	4,816	101·4
1948	9,507	191·1

B. Prest's Estimates, 1915–46

	Net National Income at Current Prices		Net National Income at 1900 Prices	
	Total (£ mill.)	per Head (£)	Total (£ mill.)	per Head (£)
1915	(2,591)	(56·3)	(1,916)	(41·7)
1916	(3,064)	(66·5)	(1,897)	(41·2)
1917	(3,631)	(78·6)	(1,867)	(40·4)
1918	(4,372)	(94·4)	(1,960)	(42·3)
1919	(5,461)	(117·7)	(2,300)	(49·6)
1920	5,664(a)	129·6(a)	2,079(a)	47·6(a)
1921	4,460	101·4	1,804	41·0
1922	3,856	87·0	1,917	43·3
1923	3,844	86·2	2,011	45·1
1924	3,919	87·3	2,038	45·4
1925	3,980	88·2	2,070	45·9
1926	3,914	86·6	2,071	45·8
1927	4,145	91·3	2,259	49·8
1928	4,154	91·1	2,277	49·9
1929	4,178	91·4	2,319	50·7
1930	3,957	86·2	2,294	50·0
1931	3,666	79·5	2,270	49·2
1932	3,568	77·1	2,271	49·1
1933	3,728	80·2	2,422	52·1
1934	3,881	83·1	2,504	53·6
1935	4,109	87·6	2,616	55·8
1936	4,388	93·2	2,717	57·7
1937	4,616	97·6	2,728	57·7
1938	4,671	98·3	2,725	57·4
1939	5,037	105·4	...	...
1940	5,980	124·8	...	...
1941	6,941	144·3	...	...
1942	7,664	158·3	...	...
1943	8,171	168·5	...	...
1944	8,366	171·8	...	...
1945	8,340	170·2	...	...
1946	7,974	162·1	...	...

(a) Southern Ireland is not included after 1919.

National Income and Expenditure 3. Stamp's 'True Comparative' Series of United Kingdom Taxable Income—1843–1914

NOTE

SOURCE: J. C. Stamp, *British Incomes and Property* (London, P. S. King & Sons, 1916), pp. 318–9.

(in £ million)

	On conditions of 1876–93(a)	On conditions of 1894–1913(b)		On conditions of 1876–93	On conditions of 1894–1913
1843(c)	204·1	186·2	1879	494·5	456·7
1844	201·4	183·6	1880	488·2	449·8
1845	201·3	183·5	1881	494·3	455·6
1846	207·9	189·9	1882	508·1	468·7
1847	209·6	191·6	1883	521·2	481·1
1848	208·5	190·3	1884	535·7	494·1
1849	209·3	190·9	1885	534·3	493·6
1850	208·0	189·4	1886	530·7	489·8
1851	209·1	190·4	1887	528·8	488·0
1852	210·7	192·1	1888	535·7	494·7
1853	213·0	194·2	1889	549·8	508·3
1854	226·4	206·9	1890	573·5	531·2
1855	224·9	205·3	1891	592·6	549·8
1856	226·3	206·5	1892	599·2	556·0
1857	230·9	210·9	1893	601·1	557·6
1858	246·0	224·8	1894	591·7	547·8
1859	247·8	226·5	1895	593·7	551·4
1860	254·1	232·4	1896	609·0	566·7
1861	254·7	232·9	1897	629·0	585·4
1862	267·7	244·5	1898	654·9	610·3
1863	274·8	251·2	1899	686·2	639·6
1864	284·2	260·1	1900	709·6	661·6
1865	307·8	282·4	1901	743·7	694·6
1866	324·7	298·5	1902	764·0	713·9
1867	333·4	306·6	1903	770·2	719·5
1868	336·8	308·7	1904	784·4	731·6
1869	340·2	311·8	1905	791·3	737·9
1870	349·3	320·3	1906	807·8	753·4
1871	376·8	346·1	1907	819·2	763·8
1872	391·8	360·6	1908	855·5	799·3
1873	424·0	391·6	1909	881·5	824·1
1874	452·5	418·6	1910	880·0	822·2
1875	475·4	440·3	1911	897·9	838·3
1876	485·0	449·2	1912	927·5	866·4
1877	495·0	458·0	1913	969·2	907·2
1878	499·0	461·5	1914	1,016·0	951·0

(a) i.e. The income tax exemption limit was £150, and no repairs allowance was made under schedule A.

(b) i.e. The income tax exemption limit was £160, and a repairs allowance was made under schedule A.

(c) Financial years ended in the years stated.

NOTES

[1] SOURCES: This table was kindly supplied by Mr D. A. Rowe, whose original sources were: A. R. Prest and A. A. Adams, *Consumers' Expenditure in the United Kingdom, 1900–19* (Cambridge, 1954) for 1900–19; J. R. F. Stone and D. A. Rowe, *The Measurement of Consumers' Expenditure and Behaviour in the United Kingdon, 1920–1938* (2 vols, Cambridge, 1954 and forthcoming), for 1920–38; Central Statistical Office, *Statistical Digest of the War* (London, 1951), for 1939–45; and *National Income and Expenditure, 1957*, for 1946–55.

[2] The series of total expenditure differs from the concept of consumers' expenditure as usually defined for national income purposes in that it excludes 'income in kind not included elsewhere', largely food and clothing issued to the Forces, and no adjustment has been made for expenditures abroad *less* expenditure by foreign tourists.

[3] Expenditures at constant prices were calculated by revaluing at 1938 prices as many separate components as possible. For 1900–38 this could be done largely commodity by commodity; and for 1939–45 the published figures are available. For 1946–55, however, there are only the figures for a few main subgroups at current and 1948 prices, and it was necessary to assume that

$$\Sigma p_{38} q_i = \Sigma p_{48} q_i : (\Sigma p_{38} q_{38} / \Sigma p_{48} q_{38})$$
$$\simeq \Sigma p_{48} q_i : (\Sigma p_{38} q_i / \Sigma p_{48} q_i)$$

In so far as consumption in these years tended to return to the pre-war pattern, the assumption will not be unreasonable.

A. At Current Market Prices

(in £ million)

	Food(a)	Alcoholic Drink(b)	Tobacco	Rents etc.(c)	Fuel and Light(d)	Clothing (e)	Durable Household Goods(f)	Transport and Communications(g)	Other Goods and Services (h)	Total
1900	531	187	27	177	78	153	58	87	328	1,626
1901	543	185	28	184	74	162	58	90	337	1,661
1902	551	183	29	191	73	153	58	94	338	1,670
1903	568	179	30	196	71	149	56	95	345	1,689
1904	572	173	30	201	71	154	59	96	354	1,710
1905	578	172	31	204	67	157	58	98	364	1,729
1906	588	171	32	208	67	161	58	102	372	1,759
1907	598	171	33	211	77	162	64	103	385	1,804
1908	603	163	33	213	74	168	64	100	385	1,803
1909	616	154	34	221	71	174	61	101	389	1,821
1910	628	163	37	221	71	178	61	109	398	1,866
1911	648	169	38	222	72	195	64	111	407	1,926
1912	679	168	39	225	77	202	67	118	420	1,995
1913	693	175	40	230	79	210	76	124	431	2,058
1914	667	188	42	234	77	173	75	117	433	2,006
1915	834	179	49	237	87	193	82	120	457	2,239
1916	947	207	56	237	105	169	81	121	480	2,403
1917	1,119	201	65	239	115	212	105	132	530	2,718
1918	1,269	232	80	246	134	364	140	154	658	3,277
1919	1,518	391	115	264	160	669	211	251	846	4,425
1920(i)	1,716	450	120	292	179	795	309	265	931	5,057
1921	1,552	409	116	340	172	485	217	247	848	4,386
1922	1,297	356	112	353	160	434	198	254	740	3,904
1923	1,293	332	109	347	150	409	192	252	699	3,783
1924	1,305	337	112	345	162	418	192	267	709	3,847
1925	1,339	338	116	349	160	432	200	286	729	3,949
1926	1,317	323	117	360	146	417	197	286	744	3,907
1927	1,299	320	124	374	168	424	210	289	758	3,966
1928	1,317	310	131	382	154	435	217	295	777	4,018
1929	1,315	311	136	392	164	439	224	293	788	4,062
1930	1,275	301	140	403	164	418	225	288	792	4,006
1931	1,204	282	140	410	163	395	218	266	788	3,866
1932	1,154	264	139	415	158	364	209	265	777	3,745
1933	1,121	258	142	423	159	366	218	273	791	3,751
1934	1,148	262	146	432	163	371	237	290	813	3,862

See p. 372 for footnotes

(in £ million)

	Food(a)	Alcoholic Drink(b)	Tobacco	Rents etc.(c)	Fuel and Light(d)	Clothing (e)	Durable House-hold Goods(f)	Transport and Com-munica-tions(g)	Other Goods and Services (h)	Total
1935	1,179	273	153	447	165	388	249	305	838	3,997
1936	1,212	283	161	462	177	402	260	319	871	4,147
1937	1,276	297	169	475	186	426	277	333	915	4,354
1938	1,301	294	176	488	189	438	264	344	962	4,456
1939	1,386	313	204	510	200	461	226	315	863	4,478
1940	1,440	383	260	519	224	501	218	237	869	4,651
1941	1,502	477	317	515	240	460	205	264	893	4,873
1942	1,553	563	415	509	242	498	184	279	887	5,130
1943	1,487	653	492	511	238	441	151	291	904	5,168
1944	1,580	701	509	516	246	510	138	301	939	5,440
1945	1,635	732	564	534	267	534	189	363	1,045	5,863
1946	1,876	726	602	548	278	638	334	496	1,319	6,817
1947	2,179	750	689	580	298	736	426	550	1,388	7,596
1948	2,345	826	764	604	324	902	479	536	1,434	8,214
1949	2,557	769	753	620	332	1,013	540	581	1,420	8,585
1950	2,829	759	766	641	353	1,063	617	616	1,452	9,096
1951	3,093	794	800	673	388	1,110	701	675	1,530	9,764
1952	3,397	799	821	706	421	1,083	675	771	1,596	10,269
1953	3,704	814	837	758	447	1,092	744	876	1,651	10,923
1954	3,955	823	855	795	485	1,174	832	959	1,718	11,596
1955	4,258	861	880	837	521	1,268	903	1,106	1,780	12,414

B. At 1938 Prices

	Food(a)	Alcoholic Drink(b)	Tobacco	Rents etc.(c)	Fuel and Light(d)	Clothing (e)	Durable House-hold Goods(f)	Transport and Com-munica-tions(g)	Other Goods and Services (h)	Total
1900	879	615	72	283	132	342	122	104	678	3,227
1901	890	610	70	289	132	357	124	107	688	3,267
1902	891	601	72	293	137	339	125	109	690	3,257
1903	908	581	74	298	135	326	120	109	693	3,244
1904	924	567	75	303	136	331	127	108	702	3,273
1905	928	558	76	307	129	325	124	110	712	3,269
1906	944	554	77	311	128	328	125	113	719	3,299
1907	949	556	79	316	138	326	132	115	720	3,331
1908	946	529	79	319	135	338	131	115	728	3,320
1909	957	486	77	323	135	350	124	117	729	3,298
1910	951	484	79	326	138	353	125	124	739	3,319
1911	988	502	83	330	142	378	128	127	744	3,422
1912	984	500	83	334	128	379	132	132	759	3,431
1913	993	519	86	337	140	391	146	141	769	3,522
1914	994	508	89	342	138	336	143	133	763	3,446
1915	969	490	96	343	147	363	136	135	755	3,434
1916	908	435	91	343	146	253	109	134	712	3,131
1917	836	301	92	344	142	236	104	111	673	2,839
1918	829	287	95	346	127	226	109	127	673	2,819
1919	961	428	127	349	136	369	140	179	720	3,409
1920(i)	924	419	118	364	141	383	183	183	761	3,376
1921	955	363	115	365	122	316	150	169	638	3,193
1922	1,001	319	111	368	138	357	175	183	654	3,306
1923	1,057	321	109	371	142	361	188	196	663	3,408
1924	1,074	336	112	374	151	366	189	211	678	3,491

See p. 372 for footnotes

(in £ million)

	Food(a)	Alcoholic Drink(b)	Tobacco	Rents etc.(c)	Fuel and Light(d)	Clothing (e)	Durable Household Goods(f)	Transport and Communica-tions(g)	Other Goods and Services (h)	Total
1925	1,084	338	116	378	153	373	199	229	700	3,570
1926	1,093	323	118	385	133	374	202	232	702	3,562
1927	1,117	321	123	394	165	395	221	242	727	3,705
1928	1,140	310	128	402	159	397	229	250	747	3,762
1929	1,150	310	133	408	166	405	239	256	772	3,839
1930	1,185	300	136	417	165	401	242	257	792	3,895
1931	1,229	273	137	423	164	408	246	244	803	3,927
1932	1,239	238	134	428	160	391	254	247	815	3,906
1933	1,235	250	139	434	163	406	265	261	836	3,989
1934	1,267	262	143	442	167	410	285	282	861	4,119
1935	1,263	273	150	454	173	425	301	303	891	4,231
1936	1,283	283	159	466	181	439	304	322	919	4,356
1937	1,296	296	168	478	187	437	290	336	946	4,434
1938	1,301	294	176	488	189	438	264	344	962	4,456
1939	1,344	299	182	504	199	447	222	314	852	4,363
1940	1,177	281	178	508	203	376	169	211	781	3,884
1941	1,118	296	196	502	205	280	120	221	739	3,677
1942	1,149	277	206	497	199	279	85	239	681	3,612
1943	1,111	281	204	498	187	254	72	249	660	3,516
1944	1,173	289	205	503	193	284	65	258	659	3,629
1945	1,192	316	225	506	197	290	90	305	699	3,820
1946	1,332	299	235	511	208	346	166	354	835	4,286
1947	1,418	302	206	520	219	389	200	388	854	4,496
1948	1,432	287	197	528	224	432	209	375	847	4,531
1949	1,501	276	191	533	223	462	233	398	815	4,632
1950	1,571	282	193	535	234	479	257	404	806	4,761
1951	1,550	290	199	537	247	432	254	414	793	4,716
1952	1,543	287	202	541	244	425	239	430	794	4,705
1953	1,595	290	206	547	248	435	273	471	818	4,883
1954	1,638	294	210	558	260	461	312	500	845	5,078
1955	1,658	305	215	569	271	491	335	546	858	5,248

(a) Includes all food and non-alcoholic beverages. The imputed value of output from backyard poultry, gardens and allotments is excluded. Expenditure on food consumed in hotels and restaurants is valued at retail prices.
(b) Beer, wines, spirits, etc., excluding table waters.
(c) Includes rates and water charges, but excludes occupiers' maintenance costs.
(d) Coal, gas, electricity, etc., excluding rentals.
(e) Excludes expenditure on repairs.

(f) Furniture and furnishings, radio and electrical goods hardware, pottery, and glassware.
(g) All public and private transport (including purchases of vehicles, new and second-hand), and communications services.
(h) Includes other household goods, books, etc., fancy goods, toys and sports goods, drugs and medical appliances, entertainments, domestic service, insurances and other services.
(i) As from 1920 the figures relate to Great Britain and Northern Ireland.

National Income and Expenditure 5. Estimates of Domestic

Fixed Capital Formation—United Kingdom 1856–1914

NOTES

[1] SOURCE: C. H. Feinstein, 'Income and Investment in the United Kingdom, 1856–1914', *Economic Journal* (June 1961), which must be consulted for details of the methods of estimation. The breakdown, which has not been published previously, was kindly made available to us by Dr. Feinstein.

[2] The fact must be stressed that these figures are estimates which inevitably involve a large margin of error. This is especially so of the years before 1870 and of the estimates of depreciation on which the series of net capital formation depend. Revisions to the series are under consideration.

(at current prices (except where otherwise stated) in £ million)

	Gross Residential Building	Gross Mercantile Ship-building	Gross Capital Expenditure by Railways	Loan Expenditure by Local Authorities	Gross Value of 'Machinery' for Domestic Use	Other Gross Fixed Capital Formation (a)	Total Domestic Fixed Capital Formation		Net Domestic Fixed Capital Formation at 1900 Prices
							Gross	Net	
1856	9·3	4·8	9·0	3·0	7·4	10·7	44	28	33
1857	8·5	4·9	8·2	3·0	7·1	10·0	42	27	30
1858	9·0	4·4	8·8	3·0	7·0	10·3	42	28	32
1859	7·8	3·7	8·3	3·5	6·5	9·2	39	25	29
1860	8·0	4·6	9·6	4·0	7·2	9·9	43	27	31
1861	7·9	4·8	14·6	3·5	8·3	10·6	50	33	39
1862	10·1	5·7	17·7	4·0	10·0	13·2	61	41	49
1863	11·5	8·6	17·1	4·0	11·5	15·0	68	46	51
1864	11·1	12·1	21·1	4·5	13·5	16·3	79	54	57
1865	9·7	11·9	25·2	5·5	14·1	16·0	82	56	61
1866	10·4	9·4	30·2	6·5	15·0	17·1	89	61	68
1867	12·1	7·0	15·4	6·0	10·7	15·0	66	45	50
1868	13·0	7·2	7·7	5·5	9·3	14·2	57	39	43
1869	14·5	8·3	4·0	5·0	8·9	14·8	56	38	40
1870	16·5	9·7	13·4	5·5(b)	11·5(c)	17·9(d)	74	51	56
1871	17·7	11·3	16·0	5·9	15·3	19·7	86	59	64
1872	20·2	15·1	16·7	7·3	16·2	22·5	98	68	65
1873	19·4	15·3	14·8(e)	8·8	16·0	22·0	96	68	59
1874	20·9	20·1	18·6	12·5	12·8	24·6	110	80	70
1875	26·1	13·0	17·8	10·8	17·2	28·6(f)	114	83	81
1876	27·8	10·0	17·5	13·4	21·2	31·4	121	88	90
1877	26·1	12·9	17·4	16·1	19·8	28·1	120	87	91
1878	21·4	13·5	14·6	17·0	17·1	24·4	108	75	80
1879	16·9	10·9	14·0	15·4	12·7	21·4	91	65	72
1880	17·3	12·9	12·0	14·8	16·9	20·5	94	67	70
1881	16·1	15·2	14·6	12·8	13·7	18·2	91	63	68
1882	16·9	19·7	15·5	10·7	12·2	20·4	95	64	66
1883	16·6	23·0	16·9	10·9	10·1	21·0	98	64	66
1884	16·1	12·9	16·6	12·8	11·7	18·4	88	57	64
1885	15·0	8·5	13·7	12·4	11·9	17·2	79	49	57
1886	14·4	6·7	8·6	10·8	11·5	14·2	66	39	46
1887	14·9	7·5	9·3	11·6	8·5	12·9	65	39	47
1888	15·3	11·9	9·1	9·2	11·4	15·0	72	43	51
1889	15·7	15·9	11·5	9·0	12·6	17·2	82	48	54
1890	15·6	15·5	14·5	9·5	11·5	19·6	86	50	55

See p. 374 for footnotes

(at current prices (except where otherwise stated) in £ million)

	Gross Residential Building	Gross Mercantile Ship-building	Gross Capital Expenditure by Railways	Loan Expenditure by Local Authorities	Gross Value of 'Machinery' for Domestic Use	Other Gross Fixed Capital Formation (a)	Total Domestic Fixed Capital Formation		Net Domestic Fixed Capital Formation at 1900 Prices
							Gross	Net	
1891	16·2	13·9	15·7	13·1	11·2	21·1	91	52	59
1892	16·8	12·9	17·1	13·3	15·2	22·2	98	58	69
1893	17·0	9·3	12·8	16·7	14·5	20·5	91	56	67
1894	17·9	11·0	12·0	16·4	17·7	21·3	96	61	74
1895	17·5	9·6	11·5	16·2	17·1	21·0	93	62	77
1896	21·2	9·7	12·7	17·5	19·8	24·2	105	72	88
1897	26·6	9·0	17·3	20·3	25·9	31·6	131	91	108
1898	33·9	14·2	20·5	25·2	24·3	37·8	156	111	127
1899	35·4	16·3	19·8	29·1	31·1	40·9	173	125	135
1900	33·6	17·2	21·2	33·4	37·1	48·0	190	141	141
1901	33·1	17·3	19·7	39·5	34·1	47·2	191	142	148
1902	34·6	17·6	19·1	41·2	36·1	47·2	196	146	158
1903	34·4	13·9	17·3	35·9	37·7	53·0	192	141	154
1904	29·5	17·0	19·8	36·4	35·1	47·0	185	134	147
1905	27·5	20·4	16·3	30·7	32·8	45·0	173	123	136
1906	29·0	22·1	15·0	27·3	31·7	39·2	164	113	122
1907	28·0	18·5	15·0	23·6	24·4	40·5	150	100	105
1908	22·5	10·0	8·7	22·1	25·8	30·8	120	77	83
1909	21·9	11·9	8·1	21·9	30·3	27·0	121	75	81
1910	19·7	13·7	5·3	21·3	31·6	32·2	124	81	86
1911	16·1	18·7	5·9	19·9	29·0	30·8	120	78	84
1912	13·3	23·2	7·0	21·2	27·9	36·3	129	84	84
1913	14·0	25·6	10·2	24·1	38·9	44·6	157	105	100
1914	12·5	22·0	7·4	25·3	36·3	47·6	151	101	97

(a) This covers non-residential building, structural work on roads and bridges, electrical engineering, telephones and telegraphs, and miscellaneous fittings and installations.
(b) The figures prior to 1870 are very rough approximations.
(c) The calculations in A. K. Cairncross, *Home and Foreign Investment, 1870–1913* (Cambridge, 1953) were used from 1870 onwards. Prior to that this item was assumed to bear the same relation to the total of the first four columns as it did on average in the period 1870–9.
(d) Since this series is in part proportionate to other series

in which breaks occur at this point, there is an implicit break here also.
(e) There was a change in the original source used for these calculations in 1874.
(f) The Inhabited House Duty statistics from which non-residential building was calculated only begin in 1874–5. For 1856–73 non-residential building was assumed to bear the same proportion to residential building as on the average of 1875–84.

National Income and Expenditure 6. Estimate of Domestic Fixed Capital Formation—United Kingdom 1920–38

NOTE

SOURCE: A study of 'Domestic Capital Formation in the United Kingdom, 1920–38' is being prepared for publication by Dr C. H. Feinstein at the Cambridge University Department of Applied Economics. He has kindly made available these provisional estimates.

(in £ million)

A. By Type of Asset

| | Building and Civil Engineering Works | | | | Plant, Vehicles, Ships, etc. | | | | All Fixed Assets (excluding land) | | | |
| | Gross | | Net | | Gross | | Net | | Gross | | Net | |
	Current Prices	1930 Prices	Current Prices	1930 Prices	Current Prices	1930 Prices	Current Prices	1930 Prices	Current Prices	1930 Prices	Current Prices	1930 Prices
1920	353	206	130	75	240	126	21	17	593	332	151	92
1921	285	201	97	69	226	143	55	29	511	344	152	98
1922	217	191	64	56	212	133	46	18	429	324	110	74
1923	210	195	64	59	166	133	18	16	376	328	82	75
1924	222	200	70	61	169	152	32	30	391	352	102	91
1925	264	240	109	99	177	164	42	36	441	404	151	135
1926	244	226	90	83	151	141	16	14	395	367	106	97
1927	261	247	107	102	167	170	35	39	428	417	142	141
1928	244	239	94	90	201	197	61	61	445	436	155	151
1929	251	246	97	95	191	187	45	46	442	433	142	141
1930	264	264	111	111	175	175	30	30	439	439	141	141
1931	216	223	66	69	172	183	25	29	388	406	91	98
1932	181	196	36	40	140	148	−5	−6	321	344	31	34
1933	203	223	59	64	121	124	−23	−26	324	347	36	38
1934	244	269	98	108	160	172	17	−20	404	441	115	128
1935	266	289	116	124	182	189	28	34	448	478	144	158
1936	293	305	132	138	219	219	57	57	512	524	189	195
1937	337	336	165	166	244	219	52	47	581	555	217	213
1938	339	331	160	159	262	235	65	56	601	566	225	215

National Income and Expenditure 6. *continued*

B. By Industrial Sectors

(in £ million)

Agriculture, Forestry and Fisheries

	Gross		Net	
	Current Prices	1930 Prices	Current Prices	1930 Prices
1920	9	7	−7	−3
1921	9	6	−7	−5
1922	6	5	−7	−7
1923	5	5	−8	−7
1924	4	4	−8	−8
1925	4	4	−8	−8
1926	4	3	−8	−8
1927	3	3	−8	−8
1928	4	3	−7	−7
1929	3	3	−7	−7
1930	4	4	−6	−6
1931	3	3	−6	−7
1932	3	3	−6	−7
1933	2	2	−6	−6
1934	4	4	−5	−6
1935	4	4	−5	−5
1936	5	6	−5	−4
1937	6	7	−4	−4
1938	5	5	−6	−6

Mining and Quarrying

	Gross		Net	
	Current Prices	1930 Prices	Current Prices	1930 Prices
1920	18	10	1	1
1921	11	8	−2	−1
1922	16	14	6	5
1923	18	16	8	7
1924	14	13	3	3
1925	14	13	−3	−3
1926	8	7	−3	−3
1927	9	8	−2	−2
1928	5	5	−5	−5
1929	12	11	2	1
1930	10	10	0	0
1931	8	9	−2	−2
1932	8	6	−5	−5
1933	8	8	−2	−2
1934	9	9	−1	−1
1935	6	6	−1	−1
1936	9	10	−1	−1
1937	10	9	−2	−2
1938	11	10	−1	−1

Gas, Water and Electricity

	Gross		Net	
	Current Prices	1930 Prices	Current Prices	1930 Prices
1920	24	14	−4	−1
1921	35	24	11	7
1922	28	23	8	6
1923	30	26	9	8
1924	38	35	16	15
1925	41	38	18	17
1926	41	39	17	16
1927	48	46	22	21
1928	45	44	18	18
1929	49	46	19	18
1930	52	52	22	22
1931	56	61	26	28
1932	53	58	22	24
1933	47	52	15	17
1934	48	54	15	17
1935	56	61	20	22
1936	63	65	23	24
1937	60	57	15	15
1938	64	60	18	17

Manufacturing

	Gross		Net	
	Current Prices	1930 Prices	Current Prices	1930 Prices
1920	152	79	23	16
1921	117	81	26	18
1922	66	60	−4	−3
1923	57	53	−12	−8
1924	62	55	−8	−8
1925	83	76	14	12
1926	72	67	3	3
1927	69	66	0	1
1928	75	72	7	6
1929	76	73	6	7
1930	68	68	2	2
1931	52	56	−15	−13
1932	50	54	−16	−17
1933	53	55	−13	−15
1934	75	80	−8	9
1935	77	79	7	6
1936	94	91	18	17
1937	126	112	35	32
1938	109	98	16	15

(in £ million)

Transport

	Gross		Net	
	Current Prices	1930 Prices	Current Prices	1930 Prices
1920	117	67	7	3
1921	112	64	12	−1
1922	150	77	38	11
1923	102	75	13	7
1924	95	86	18	16
1925	101	93	25	22
1926	76	70	2	−1
1927	82	89	12	17
1928	100	100	25	24
1929	90	94	12	15
1930	87	87	8	8
1931	79	78	1	1
1932	51	50	−22	−25
1933	35	33	−35	−41
1934	46	51	−20	−20
1935	63	66	−8	−7
1936	86	88	15	15
1937	99	96	22	22
1938	110	104	30	28

Distribution and Miscellaneous Services

	Gross		Net	
	Current Prices	1930 Prices	Current Prices	1930 Prices
1920	86	46	26	14
1921	55	39	9	6
1922	28	25	−9	−8
1923	45	41	8	8
1924	51	45	12	11
1925	39	36	0	0
1926	36	35	−3	−1
1927	39	37	1	1
1928	53	52	14	14
1929	54	51	14	13
1930	58	58	18	18
1931	51	55	10	11
1932	37	40	−4	−3
1933	37	39	−4	−5
1934	49	52	8	8
1935	55	59	13	14
1936	52	52	7	6
1937	58	54	6	6
1938	68	62	15	13

Social and Public Services

	Gross		Net	
	Current Prices	1930 Prices	Current Prices	1930 Prices
1920	14	8	−11	−6
1921	15	10	−6	−5
1922	12	12	−5	−3
1923	13	13	−3	−2
1924	16	14	−1	−1
1925	19	18	2	2
1926	20	18	3	2
1927	20	19	3	3
1928	21	20	4	4
1929	25	25	8	8
1930	34	34	16	16
1931	37	38	19	20
1932	30	33	13	14
1933	24	27	6	8
1934	26	29	8	9
1935	30	32	11	12
1936	38	40	18	19
1937	47	46	25	24
1938	55	52	31	30

Residential Dwellings

	Gross		Net	
	Current Prices	1930 Prices	Current Prices	1930 Prices
1920	173	101	116	68
1921	157	112	109	78
1922	123	108	83	73
1923	106	99	67	63
1924	111	100	70	63
1925	140	126	97	87
1926	138	128	95	88
1927	158	149	114	108
1928	142	140	99	97
1929	133	130	88	86
1930	126	126	81	81
1931	102	106	58	60
1932	92	100	49	53
1933	118	131	75	83
1934	147	162	102	112
1935	157	171	110	120
1936	165	172	114	119
1937	175	174	120	120
1938	178	175	122	119

National Income and Expenditure 7. Estimated Stocks of Capital—
United Kingdom 1920–38 (end of year)

NOTES

SOURCE: A study of 'Domestic Capital Formation in the United Kingdom, 1920–38' is being prepared for publication by Dr C. H. Feinstein at the Cambridge University Department of Applied Economics. He has kindly made available these provisional estimates.

A. By Type of Asset *(continued on p. 378)*

(in £ million)

| | Buildings and Civil Engineering Works | | | | | | Plant, Vehicles, Ships, etc. | | | | | |
| | At First Cost | | | At Depreciated Value | | | At First Cost | | | At Depreciated Value | | |
	Histori-cal Prices	Current Prices	1930 Prices	Histori-cal Prices	Current Prices	1930 Prices	Histori-cal Prices	Current Prices	1930 Prices	Histori-cal Prices	Current Prices	1930 Prices
1920	5,588	18,002	10,555	3,411	10,672	6,254	2,515	6,978	3,443	1,169	2,880	1,415
1921	5,861	15,269	10,729	3,623	8,988	6,323	2,670	5,306	3,468	1,290	2,218	1,444
1922	6,063	12,390	10,890	3,765	7,255	6,379	2,817	5,008	3,503	1,394	2,136	1,462
1923	6,255	11,800	11,054	3,896	6,874	6,438	2,920	4,306	3,532	1,449	1,825	1,479
1924	6,460	12,343	11,221	4,039	7,154	6,499	3,023	3,966	3,585	1,499	1,670	1,508
1925	6,708	12,575	11,431	4,220	7,264	6,598	3,134	3,929	3,650	1,552	1,669	1,544
1926	6,938	12,466	11,628	4,378	7,166	6,681	3,205	3,869	3,686	1,576	1,644	1,558
1927	7,189	12,511	11,839	4,550	7,171	6,783	3,279	3,736	3,734	1,610	1,599	1,597
1928	7,403	12,286	12,040	4,703	7,013	6,873	3,395	3,848	3,816	1,674	1,677	1,658
1929	7,634	12,508	12,247	4,860	7,119	6,968	3,500	4,013	3,888	1,723	1,763	1,704
1930	7,879	12,475	12,475	5,027	7,079	7,079	3,592	3,950	3,950	1,751	1,734	1,734
1931	8,072	12,254	12,655	5,144	6,917	7,148	3,666	3,832	4,002	1,768	1,685	1,763
1932	8,231	11,824	12,808	5,224	6,632	7,188	3,715	3,807	4,024	1,753	1,657	1,757
1933	8,409	11,758	12,985	5,324	6,561	7,252	3,737	3,804	4,018	1,720	1,632	1,731
1934	8,631	11,971	13,212	5,462	6,663	7,360	3,804	3,836	4,067	1,725	1,646	1,751
1935	8,872	12,412	13,453	5,620	6,901	7,484	3,888	4,069	4,129	1,753	1,748	1,785
1936	9,135	13,109	13,703	5,801	7,290	7,622	4,016	4,304	4,232	1,814	1,869	1,842
1937	9,444	14,060	13,981	6,022	7,824	7,788	4,161	4,889	4,329	1,889	2,127	1,889
1938	9,747	14,698	14,245	6,242	8,178	7,947	4,345	4,958	4,450	1,972	2,158	1,945

B. By Industrial Sectors (Fixed Assets only) *(continued on p. 378)*

(in £ million)

| | Agriculture, Forestry and Fisheries(a) | | | | | | Mining and Quarrying | | | | | |
| | At First Cost | | | At Depreciated Value | | | At First Cost | | | At Depreciated Value | | |
	Histori-cal Prices	Current Prices	1930 Prices	Histori-cal Prices	Current Prices	1930 Prices	Histori-cal Prices	Current Prices	1930 Prices	Histori-cal Prices	Current Prices	1930 Prices
1920	395	1,244	745	189	588	349	266	782	426	140	396	217
1930	413	741	741	154	280	280	336	465	465	182	225	225
1938	410	756	738	132	239	233	366	508	478	178	220	207

| | Transport and Communications | | | | | | Distribution and Miscellaneous Services | | | | | |
| | At First Cost | | | At Depreciated Value | | | At First Cost | | | At Depreciated Value | | |
	Histori-cal Prices	Current Prices	1930 Prices	Histori-cal Prices	Current Prices	1930 Prices	Histori-cal Prices	Current Prices	1930 Prices	Histori-cal Prices	Current Prices	1930 Prices
1920	1,921	5,581	3,256	1,034	2,799	1,634	1,151	3,683	2,068	738	2,301	1,309
1930	2,587	3,604	3,604	1,395	1,752	1,752	1,518	2,334	2,334	943	1,371	1,371
1938	2,786	3,914	3,696	1,412	1,811	1,725	1,836	2,727	2,595	1,063	1,486	1,422

A. By Type of Asset   *(continued from p. 377)*

(in £ million)

	All Fixed Assets						Stocks in Trade and Work in Progress		Livestock		Standing Timber	
	At First Cost			At Depreciated Value								
	Histori-cal Prices	Current Prices	1930 Prices	Histori-cal Prices	Current Prices	1930 Prices	Current Prices	1930 Prices	Current Prices	1930 Prices	Current Prices	1930 Prices
1920	8,103	24,980	13,998	4,580	13,552	7,669	2,952	1,111	487	305	140	70
1921	8,531	20,575	14,197	4,913	11,206	7,767	1,849	1,155	456	313	143	71
1922	8,880	17,398	14,393	5,159	9,391	7,841	1,462	1,087	360	313	84	72
1923	9,175	16,106	14,586	5,345	8,699	7,916	1,407	1,035	342	315	86	73
1924	9,483	16,309	14,806	5,536	8,824	8,007	1,463	1,032	347	318	84	74
1925	9,842	16,504	15,081	5,772	8,933	8,142	1,506	1,114	352	320	80	76
1926	10,143	16,335	15,314	5,954	8,810	8,239	1,398	1,128	343	323	78	79
1927	10,458	16,247	15,573	6,160	8,770	8,380	1,378	1,158	318	326	80	80
1928	10,798	16,134	15,856	6,377	8,690	8,531	1,402	1,174	320	319	83	82
1929	11,134	16,521	16,135	6,583	8,882	8,672	1,399	1,211	320	313	86	82
1930	11,471	16,425	16,425	6,778	8,813	8,813	1,302	1,302	314	310	84	84
1931	11,738	16,086	16,657	6,912	8,602	8,911	1,129	1,290	306	321	80	86
1932	11,945	15,631	16,832	6,977	8,289	8,945	1,074	1,272	272	331	76	88
1933	12,146	15,562	17,003	7,044	8,193	8,983	1,013	1,194	243	337	74	89
1934	12,435	15,807	17,279	7,187	8,309	9,111	1,082	1,228	246	334	76	91
1935	12,760	16,481	17,582	7,373	8,649	9,269	1,085	1,232	247	334	80	93
1936	13,151	17,413	17,935	7,615	9,159	9,464	1,144	1,223	256	333	73	95
1937	13,605	18,949	18,310	7,911	9,951	9,677	1,365	1,278	305	333	100	97
1938	14,092	19,656	18,695	8,214	10,336	9,892	1,326	1,353	322	338	94	99

(*a*) The figure of stock in trade at 1930 prices differs from that at current prices because agricultural stocks in the former are valued at the average price for the year, and in the latter at the lower of the average price for the year or the value at the end of the year.

B. By Industrial Sectors   *(continued from p. 377)*

	Gas, Water, and Electricity						Manufacturing					
	At First Cost			At Depreciated Value			At First Cost			At Depreciated Value		
	Histori-cal Prices	Current Prices	1930 Prices	Histori-cal Prices	Current Prices	1930 Prices	Histori-cal Prices	Current Prices	1930 Prices	Histori-cal Prices	Current Prices	1930 Prices
1920	538	1,585	879	302	909	505	1,663	5,212	2,617	871	2,589	1,346
1930	879	1,188	1,188	519	653	653	2,084	2,779	2,779	1,102	1,575	1,575
1938	1,259	1,696	1,582	703	874	817	2,428	3,204	2,938	1,226	1,520	1,409

	Social and Public Services						Residential Dwellings					
	At First Cost			At Depreciated Value			At First Cost			At Depreciated Value		
	Histori-cal Prices	Current Prices	1930 Prices	Histori-cal Prices	Current Prices	1930 Prices	Histori-cal Prices	Current Prices	1930 Prices	Histori-cal Prices	Current Prices	1930 Prices
1920	357	1,167	674	206	661	383	1,815	5,726	3,333	1,099	3,309	1,926
1930	529	816	816	306	407	407	3,125	4,498	4,498	2,180	2,750	2,750
1938	790	1,115	1,061	479	570	543	4,217	5,736	5,607	3,022	3,617	3,536

(*a*) Excludes the value of land, livestock and standing timber.

REFERENCES

BOOKS

D. Baxter, *National Income of the United Kingdom* (London, 1868).

D. Baxter, *Taxation of the United Kingdom* (London, 1869).

D. Baxter, *National Debt* (London, 1871).

H. Beeke, *Observations on the Produce of the Income Tax and its Proportion to the Whole Income of Great Britain* (London, 1800).

B. Bell, *Essays on Agriculture* (Edinburgh, 1802).

A. L. Bowley, *Prices and Wages in the United Kingdom, 1914–1920* (Oxford, 1921).

A. L. Bowley, *Wages and Income since 1860* (Cambridge, 1937).

A. L. Bowley, *Studies in the National Income, 1924–1938* (Cambridge, 1944).

A. L. Bowley and J. C. Stamp, *Three Studies in the National Income* (London, 1938).

H. Campion, *Public and Private Property in Great Britain* (London, 1939).

C. Clark, *The National Income, 1924–1931* (London, 1932).

C. Clark, *National Income and Outlay* (London, 1937).

P. Colquhoun, *Treatise on Indigence* (London, 1806).

P. Colquhoun, *Treatise on the Wealth, Power and Resources of the British Empire* (London, 1815).

G. W. Daniels and H. Campion, *The Distribution of National Capital* (Manchester, 1936).

R. Giffen, *Essays in Finance*, 1st series (London, 1880).

R. Giffen, *Essays in Finance*, 2nd series (London, 1887).

R. Giffen, *The Growth of Capital* (London, 1889).

R. Giffen, *Economic Inquiries and Studies* (2 vols., London, 1904).

L. Levi, *Wages and Earnings of the Working Classes* (London, 1885).

J. Lowe, *The Present State of England* (London, 1822).

M. G. Mulhall, *The Progress of the World* (London, 1880).

M. G. Mulhall, *Balance Sheet of the World, 1870–1880* (London, 1881).

M. G. Mulhall, *Fifty Years of National Progress, 1837–1887* (London, 1887).

J. MacQueen, *Statistics of the British Empire* (London, 1836).

P. Pebrer, *Taxation, Expenditure, Power, Statistics, and Debt of the Whole British Empire* (London, 1833).

A. R. Prest and A. A. Adams, *Consumers' Expenditure in the United Kingdom, 1900–1919* (Cambridge, 1954).

E. A. Radice, *Savings in Great Britain, 1922–35* (London, 1939).

W. R. Smee, *The Income Tax* (London, 1846).

W. F. Spackman, *Statistical Tables of the Agriculture, Shipping, Colonies, Manufacture, Commerce, and Population of the United Kingdom . . . to 1843* (London, 1843?).

W. F. Spackman, *An Analysis of the Occupations of the People . . .* (London, 1847).

J. C. Stamp, *British Incomes and Property* (London, 1915).

J. R. N. Stone and D. Rowe, *The Measurement of Consumers' Expenditure and Behaviour in the United Kingdom, 1920–1938* (vol. 1, Cambridge, 1954).

A. Young, *Political Arithmetic* (2 vols., London, 1774–9).

GOVERNMENT PUBLICATIONS

National Income Statistics, Sources and Methods (1956).
National Income and Expenditure (non-parliamentary paper annually since 1952).
National Income and Expenditure (White Paper, annually since 1941).

ARTICLES

E. J. Buckatzsch, 'The Geographical Distribution of Wealth in England, 1086–1843', *E.H.R.* (1951).

C. Clark, 'Investment in Fixed Capital in Great Britain', *London and Cambridge Economic Service Special Memorandum*, No. 49.

D. J. Coppock, 'The Climacteric of the 1890's: A Critical Note', *M.S.E.S.S.* (1956).

Phyllis Deane, 'The Implications of Early National Income Estimates for the Measurement of Long-Term Growth in the United Kingdom', *Economic Deveolpment and Cultural Change* (1955).

Phyllis Deane, 'The Industrial Revolution and Economic Growth: The Evidence of the Early British National Income Estimates', *Economic Development and Cultural Change* (1957).

Phyllis Deane, 'Contemporary Estimates of National Income in the First Half of the Nineteenth Century', *E.H.R.* (1956).

Phyllis Deane, 'Contemporary Estimates of National Income in the Second Half of the Nineteenth Century', *E.H.R.* (1957).

P. H. Douglas, 'An Estimate of the Growth of Capital in the United Kingdom', *Journal of Economic and Business History* (1929–30).

H. L. Gray, 'Incomes from Land in 1436', *English Historical Review* (1934).

J. B. Jefferys and Dorothy Walters, 'National Income and Expenditure of the United Kingdom', *Income and Wealth*, v (1956).

Kathleen M. Langley, 'An Analysis of the Asset Structure of Estates, 1900–1949', *Bulletin of the University of Oxford Institute of Statistics* (1951).

J. M. Lenfant, 'Investment in the United Kingdom, 1865–1914', *Economica* (1951).

P. Mathias, 'The Social Structure in the Eighteenth Century: A Calculation by Joseph Massie', *E.H.R.* (1957).

P. K. O'Brien, 'British Incomes and Property in the Early Nineteenth Century', *E.H.R.* (1959).

E. H. Phelps-Brown and P. E. Hart, 'The Share of Wages in National Income', *E.J.* (1952).

E. H. Phelps-Brown and S. A. Ozga, 'Economic Growth and the Price Level', *E.J.* (1955).

E. H. Phelps-Brown and S. J. Handfield-Jones, 'The Climacteric of the 1890's', *O.E.P.* (1952).

E. H. Phelps-Brown and B. Weber, 'Accumulation, Productivity and Distribution in the British Economy, 1870–1938', *E.J.* (1953).

M. M. Postan, 'Some Economic Evidence of a Declining Population in the Later Middle Ages', *E.H.R.* (1950).

A. R. Prest, 'National Income of the United Kingdom, 1870–1946', *E.J.* (1948).

P. Redfern, 'Net Investment in Fixed Assets in the United Kingdom, 1938–1953', *J.R.S.S.* (1955).

C. D. Ross and T. B. Pugh, 'Materials for the Study of Baronial Incomes in Fifteenth Century England', *E.H.R.* (1953).

J. R. N. Stone, 'Analysis of Market Demand', *J.R.S.S.* (1945).

J. E. G. Utting, 'National Income and Related Statistics', *J.R.S.S.* (1955).

CHAPTER XIV

PUBLIC FINANCE

TABLES

Men of affairs in this country have no doubt always been concerned about its finances, but until these finances came completely under the control of parliament, no regular and detailed statistics about them were published; nor indeed were they available in overall terms. Before the revolution of 1688 it was common practice to farm out to private contractors the task of collecting the principal taxes. Not until 1674 were the collectors of the excise obliged by their contracts to give full accounts and not until 1679 was a similar stipulation involved in the contract for the farm of the hearth money. As far as contemporaries were concerned published statistics remained deficient until the early nineteenth century. Sir John Sinclair, for example, wrote in 1804 that 'since the reign of Queen Anne the national accounts are far from being distinguished for their regularity and precision; no complete statement has ever been made of the total income and expenditure of the country'.[1] No

[1] Sir John Sinclair, *The History of the Public Revenue of the British Empire* (London, 1804) containing an account of the public income and expenditure from the remotest periods recorded in history to Michaelmas 1802.

balanced annual accounts were made available to parliament or people until 1823. Until then contemporaries had to depend for their information on the parliamentary votes on supplies and ways and means, and similar incomplete statements which appeared in the House of Commons Journals. These were the sources of Whitworth's and other contemporary compilations of public income, wealth and expenditure.[1]

The fact that we now have balanced income-and-expenditure accounts dating from 1688 is due to the twelve years' research in Treasury records carried out by a Chief Clerk of the Exchequer in the middle of last century and published in 1869.[2] Unfortunately the series then published involved a major break, in 1801–2, when the publication of gross accounts was begun. In the historical volume the net accounts end in 1801, and no overlap is provided with the gross accounts beginning in 1802. Reference to the original *Finance Accounts* for this period shows that, in order to maintain long-period comparability, the compilers of the historical volume altered the contents of most categories. As a result an overlap could be provided from these originals only with immense labour—if at all! In this volume, therefore, the break in 1801–2 is left, and one set of tables covers Great Britain in the eighteenth century, and another set the United Kingdom in the nineteenth and twentieth centuries.[3]

The sources of the public finance statistics are given in the notes to the tables, and it is fair to say that these contain practically everything that is available. There is, of course, very much greater detail in the original sources than is given here, and this is increasingly so from the beginning of the nineteenth century onwards. The principle followed in the selection of the items to be shown here has been to include those which were of relative importance at any time during the period, and to show them throughout when available. Items which were of importance for only a short time are, however, usually given in the notes; and the separate listing of the Civil List expenditure has been dropped after the 1801–2 break, since by that time it was relatively small, and on the succession of William IV it became almost negligible.

Three further general points may be made in explanation of tables 1 to 4. First, it should be realised that from 1869 onwards each figure comprises all items under the appropriate heading at the date in question. Thus no account is taken of transfers from, for example, customs to excise or unfunded to funded debt charges, except in so far as the compilers of the historical volume made such transfers effective throughout the period they covered. In making comparisons over long periods especially, therefore, the possibility of such transfers having taken place should be borne in mind. The principal transfers are, of course, well known, and some of the more misleading ones, such as the separation of death

---

[1] Sir Charles Whitworth, *A Collection of the Supplies and Ways and Means from the Revolution to the Present Times* (London, 1763).

[2] *S.P.* 1868–9, xxxv. See Appendix 13 for a full annotation of the accounts written by the compiler, H. S. Chisholm with the advice of the 'most experienced financial officers of the Government'.

[3] See, however, the 'Note on the Public Accounts' by J. E. D. Binney in *British Public Finance and Administration 1774–92* (Oxford, 1958), where he notes that it was not until after 31st March 1857 that 'at last, every item of receipt and every item of expenditure was consolidated into the account submitted to Parliament'.

duties from stamp duties, have been indicated. A second point to note about the income and expenditure tables is that they are concerned with current account transactions—that is they correspond to 'above the line' items in the present-day Finance Statement. This distinction was not made explicitly, however, until the 1890's and it is likely that a few small items of capital expenditure, and of borrowing for such expenditure, are included in the accounts before then. But at that period and earlier they can scarcely have been significant.

The third point concerns the exact nature of the income and expenditure which the tables show, namely the receipts and issues of the Exchequer. These are not quite the same as the actual receipts and expenditure of the various departments, which it would no doubt be preferable to show were they available for as long a period as the Exchequer statistics. Whatever the situation in the eighteenth century, however, it is doubtful if the differences between the two methods of accounting were ever very great in the nineteenth century; and for the period when easy comparison is possible, the differences are only significant in one or two years during and immediately after the upheaval of the 1914–18 war. In fact, between 1901 and 1939, actual revenue differed from Exchequer receipts by more than 1 per cent only in 1920 and 1921, and actual expenditure and Exchequer issues differed by more than 1 per cent only in 1915, 1919, 1920 and 1922.[1] In most years the differences were very much less than 1 per cent. Possibly more interesting than these minor variations between methods of recording the accounts are those between anticipated and realised results—between budgets and financial statements. Whilst there is not sufficient space here to show these, they can be found for an extensive period in the works of Sydney Buxton and Lord Iddesleigh, in the last century, and of Mallet and George in this.[2] These are also informative about the political and parliamentary background to public finance in general in the periods with which they are concerned.

Until towards the end of the nineteenth century much less information is available on local than on central government finance, and what there is for the eighteenth and early nineteenth centuries is mainly scattered, discontinuous, and collected with little regard for uniformity among the various local authorities. Tables 7 and 8 have been included here as the best representatives of local finance in this period. These two series are by far the longest available, and they cover much the largest fields of local taxation, at least until the middle of the nineteenth century. There was, moreover, a greater degree of uniformity in their collection, and they were published in a more readily available form, than any other series. Nevertheless, it is sufficient to draw attention to the remarks of Goschen and of the author of the *Return* of 1839, quoted in the notes to the tables, to show that even these

---

[1] Actual revenue was lower than Exchequer receipts by 7·8 per cent in 1920 and by 2·4 per cent in 1921. Actual expenditure was lower than Exchequer issues by 3·7 per cent in 1915, 13·3 per cent in 1920, and 2·4 per cent in 1922, and higher by 3·9 per cent in 1919.

[2] S. Buxton, *Finance and Politics, An Historical Study, 1783–1885* (2 vols., London, 1888); Lord Iddesleigh, *Twenty Years of Financial Policy* (London, 1862); B. Mallet, *British Budgets, 1887–1913* (London, 1913); B. Mallet and C. O. George, *British Budgets, 1913–1921* (London, 1929); and B. Mallet and C. O. George, *British Budgets, 1921–1933* (London, 1933).

series are far from satisfactory. Additional statistics, not generally going back before the 1830's except for isolated dates, can be found scattered through the early and mid-nineteenth century blue books. The 1843 Report on Local Taxation by the Poor Law Commissioners, which contained a full survey of the existing system of local taxation, summarised as follows the data available for previous years: 'The only distinct rates in respect of which comprehensive information has been obtained are the Church Rates for the years 1827, 1832 and 1838; the Highway Rate for the years 1812, 1813, 1814, 1827 and 1839; the County Rate for the years 1792 to 1841 complete; and the Poor's Rate for the several years 1748, 1749, 1750, 1776, 1783, 1784, 1785, 1803 and continuously from 1813 to 1841'.[1] From the middle of the century there exist municipal borough finance accounts for each town, audited and set out in individual fashion. But the many differences in definition, methods of collection, period covered, and accounting procedure have, in fact, discouraged anyone from attempting to aggregate these latter.

From 1860, official annual Local Taxation Returns were published[2] but their deficiencies were so great, as Goschen pointed out, that they have not been used here. The latter's report in 1869[3] has been taken as the starting point for modern statistics, though it was not until the local Government Board took over publication of the *Returns* in the early 1870's, that the continuous series began; and it was not until twenty years later that Scotland followed suit.[4] For the earliest attempt to bring together statistics of Scottish local authorities see *Report of the Royal Commission on Scottish Municipal Corporations*, 1835. See also Skelton's *Report on Local Taxation in Scotland* (1894). The first Scottish *Local Taxation Returns* were published in 1882 and since statistics for Scotland were collected on a different basis to England and Wales, they have been treated separately in the tables. These tables, 9 to 14, are, with their notes, largely self-explanatory. The sources will yield very much greater detail to those who require it.[5]

The tables shown so far in this section cover, in some detail, the separate expenditures of central and local government. The enormous increase in the total expenditure of public authorities viewed as a whole has recently been the subject of a penetrating study by A. T. Peacock and J. Wiseman,[6] and table 15 showing a brief summary of this total at intervals from the end of the eighteenth century, is taken from their work, which was kindly shown to us before publication.

---

[1] *S.P.* 1843, vol. xx for Report on Local Taxation of the Poor Law Commissioners. The passage given here is quoted in the I.D.S.E.R. *Guides to official Sources No. 3, Local Government Statistics* (H.M.S.O., 1953), p. 4.

[2] In sessional papers.   [3] *S.P.* 1870, vol. iv.

[4] For a more complete guide to, and critique of, practically all the sources of local finance statistics, see *Guides to Official Sources no. 3: Local Government Statistics*. Still more detailed discussions of the mid-nineteenth century statistics are to be found in the contemporary volumes of the *J.S.S.*, particularly those of 1858, 1860, 1871, and 1877.

[5] For a more complete guide to, and critique of, practically all the sources of local finance statistics, see *Guides to Official Sources No. 3; Local Government Statistics, op. cit.* Still more detailed discussions of the mid-nineteenth century statistics are to be found in the contemporary volumes of the *Journal of the Statistical Society*, particularly those of 1858, 1860, 1871, and 1877.

[6] *The Growth of Public Expenditure in the United Kingdom.*

Their book, of course, gives statistics in much greater detail, with various breakdowns of expenditure according to type.

No tax for which much detailed statistical information exists compares for historical interest with the income tax, despite its youth relative to other great sources of revenue, such as customs and excise. Two tables of income tax statistics have, therefore, been selected for inclusion in this section. The first, showing rates and yields, is a relatively straightforward summary of the main national statistics. Much more detail is available on similar lines in the *Reports of the Commissioners of Inland Revenue*, and for the early income tax in Hope-Jones's *Income Tax in the Napoleonic Wars*.[1] Another valuable book in this connection, which also has much useful information on the political and legislative background of the tax, is Dr Shehab's *Progressive Taxation*.[2] The second income tax table, table 17, gives gross assessments under each Schedule, series which have been much used in estimating national income.[3] They contain many traps for the unwary. The main ones are documented in the notes to the tables, but one general word of warning is necessary. Not all income is included in the schedules, and the principles of assessment differ from schedule to schedule. These statistics, therefore, should be used with care, and, for the nineteenth century, J. C. Stamp's comprehensive book, *British Income and Property*[4] provides an indispensable guide to their interpretation.

[1] Cambridge, 1939.
[2] Oxford, 1953.
[3] By many people from the later nineteenth century onwards. The best recent examples are A. R. Prest, in the *E.J.* (1948), and C. H. Feinstein in the *E.J.* (1961).
[4] London, 1916.

Public Finance 1. Net Receipts of the Public Income—Great Britain 1688–1801

NOTES

[1] SOURCE: *S.P.* 1868-9, xxxv.

[2] There are no transfers of component items from heading to heading in this table. Items appropriate to a particular heading at the end of the period were included in that heading throughout.

[3] Gross accounts are available for lotteries, as follows:

	Receipts	Expenditure		Receipts	Expenditure		Receipts	Expenditure		Receipts	Expenditure
						1781	480	481	1792	813	501
						1782	427	482	1793	751	502
						1783	529	406	1794	670	501
						1784	286	481	1795	814	502
						1785	399	361	1796	915	502
1769	770	—	1775	740	601	1786	577	501	1797	499	501
1770	600	602	1776	20	601	1787	731	501	1798	645	501
1771	610	502	1777	495	—	1788	774	501	1799	690	501
1772	760	452	1778	405	501	1789	749	482	1800 (e)	(275)	(—)
1773	40	601	1779	541	482	1790	866	501	1801	790	502
1774	740	—	1780	446	491	1791	781	501			

(in £000 sterling)

	Total Net Income	Principal Constituent Items (a)				
		Customs	Excise	Stamps	Post Office	Land and Assessed Taxes
1688–91(b)	8,613	1,920	2,430	—	163	3,172
1692(c)	4,111	898	1,214	—	57	1,611
1693	3,783	689	905	—	64	1,738
1694	4,004	892	879	45	60	1,914
1695	4,134	899	935	46	64	1,839
1696	4,823	1,028	919	65	76	2,528
1697	3,298	719	1,078	47	59	972
1698	4,578	1,133	1,365	65	63	1,508
1699	5,164	1,472	1,413	95	75	1,578
1700	4,344	1,523	1,030	89	77	1,483
1701	3,769	1,583	986	94	75	991
1702	4,869	1,469	1,396	94	79	1,772
1703	5,561	1,576	1,750	89	66	1,954
1704	5,394	1,554	1,657	94	66	1,914
1705	5,292	1,110	1,807	84	60	2,065
1706	5,284	1,271	1,682	86	61	2,061
1707	5,471	1,366	1,745	87	57	2,034
1708	5,208	1,213	1,682	93	57	1,983
1709	5,206	1,305	1,571	94	56	2,056
1710	5,248	1,338	1,548	98	62	2,074
1711	5,179	1,109	1,673	97	66	2,130
1712	5,748	1,481	1,805	195	92	2,152
1713	5,780	1,428	2,089	107	92	1,884
1714	5,361	1,599	2,056	117	87	1,289
1715	5,547	1,685	2,303	142	95	1,129
1716	5,582	1,504	2,372	130	88	1,368
1717	6,514	1,822	2,355	143	91	1,984
1718	6,090	1,687	2,413	139	95	1,619
1719	6,026	1,644	1,454	136	98	1,589
1720	6,323	1,673	2,478	176	95	1,537

See p. 388 for footnotes

(in £000 sterling)

	Total Net Income	Principal Constituent Items (*a*)				
		Customs	Excise	Stamps	Post Office	Land and Assessed Taxes
1721	5,954	1,446	2,486	140	95	1,573
1722	6,150	1,493	2,676	142	90	1,575
1723	5,993	1,604	2,780	144	93	1,224
1724	5,773	1,624	2,633	151	90	1,207
1725	5,960	1,711	2,741	155	99	1,148
1726	5,518	1,427	2,659	151	95	1,140
1727	6,103	1,648	2,879	157	100	1,287
1728	6,741	1,833	2,626	162	91	1,977
1729	6,294	1,669	2,649	159	100	1,644
1730	6,265	1,601	2,810	154	92	1,558
1731	6,080	1,525	2,786	163	95	1,217
1732	5,803	1,689	2,712	143	90	1,129
1733	5,522	1,521	3,028	127	96	721
1734	5,448	1,560	2,918	138	93	710
1735	5,652	1,479	2,843	137	98	1,070
1736	5,762	1,540	2,837	137	91	1,127
1737	6,077	1,722	2,954	142	97	1,108
1738	5,716	1,370	2,921	138	95	1,145
1739	5,820	1,398	3,025	135	96	1,134
1740	5,745	1,420	2,817	133	89	1,252
1741	6,244	1,435	2,587	131	87	1,983
1742	6,416	1,280	2,815	132	78	2,083
1743	6,567	1,278	2,903	130	97	2,130
1744	6,576	1,141	3,111	135	86	2,079
1745	6,451	1,156	2,921	134	85	2,117
1746	6,249	1,017	2,951	129	64	2,061
1747	6,961	1,328	3,218	132	82	2,174
1748	7,199	1,395	3,410	136	78	2,152
1749	7,494	1,618	3,394	132	96	2,229
1750	7,467	1,537	3,454	136	93	2,212
1751	7,097	1,588	3,468	134	106	1,769
1752(*d*)	6,992	1,635	3,402	135	98	1,685
1753	7,338	1,770	3,582	132	100	1,728
1754	6,827	1,587	3,692	135	100	1,288
1755	6,938	1,782	3,660	137	100	1,236
1756	7,006	1,699	3,649	165	86	1,375
1757	7,969	1,872	3,303	239	74	2,043
1758	7,946	1,918	3,477	277	81	2,139
1759	8,155	1,830	3,615	282	84	2,216
1760	9,207	2,113	4,218	289	87	2,407

See p. 388 for footnote

(in £000 sterling)

	Total Net Income	Principal Constituent Items (a)				
		Customs	Excise	Stamps	Post Office	Land and Assessed Taxes
1761	9,594	2,191	4,671	307	67	2,253
1762	9,459	1,824	4,816	289	99	2,386
1763	9,793	2,283	4,793	299	103	2,288
1764	10,221	2,282	5,027	302	122	2,316
1765	10,928	2,324	4,935	302	165	2,243
1766	10,276	2,514	4,879	308	157	2,225
1767	9,868	2,460	4,521	310	160	2,174
1768	10,131	2,453	4,746	322	165	1,895
1769	11,130	2,675	4,961	320	162	1,814
1770	11,373	2,841	5,139	336	162	1,796
1771	10,987	2,739	4,842	339	154	1,834
1772	11,033	2,457	4,995	336	152	2,092
1773	10,487	2,702	5,141	342	167	1,843
1774	10,613	2,557	4,922	345	161	1,821
1775	11,112	2,756	5,106	350	177	1,756
1776	10,576	2,684	5,383	383	172	1,875
1777	11,105	2,411	5,252	436	152	2,299
1778	11,436	2,348	5,369	442	139	2,497
1779	11,853	2,523	5,625	475	133	2,450
1780	12,524	2,774	6,081	542	136	2,523
1781	13,280	3,019	6,111	626	142	2,635
1782	13,765	2,898	6,420	656	144	2,724
1783	12,677	2,949	5,480	855	166	2,596
1784	13,214	3,026	6,139	991	201	2,460
1785	15,527	4,537	6,142	1,217	304	2,666
1786	15,246	3,783	6,413	1,300	262	2,774
1787	16,453	4,094	7,043	1,196	262	2,909
1788	16,779	3,996	7,257	1,322	330	3,013
1789	16,669	3,647	7,301	1,250	321	3,006
1790	17,014	3,462	7,698	1,324	366	2,993
1791	18,506	4,018	8,433	1,384	338	2,914
1792	18,607	4,100	8,741	1,463	378	3,020
1793	18,131	3,557	8,559	1,452	409	2,952
1794	18,732	4,348	8,387	1,462	471	3,034
1795	19,053	3,419	9,915	1,456	441	2,946
1796	19,391	3,645	9,096	1,785	483	3,021
1797	21,380	3,940	10,303	1,978	558	3,365
1798	26,946	4,741	11,571	2,273	677	4,591
1799	31,783	7,056	11,862	2,447	704	6,446
1800(e)	(9,674)	(2,395)	(3,241)	(763)	...(f)	(1,600)
1801(g)	31,585	6,785	10,594	2,621	...(f)	5,093

(a) The property and income tax, introduced in 1799, was a major constituent of public income at the end of the period, as follows: 1799, 1,671; 1800, (1,020); 1801, 4,513.
(b) 5th November 1688 to 29th September 1691.
(c) Years ended 29th September henceforth to 1751.

(d) Years ended 10th October henceforth to 1799.
(e) Quarter ended 5th January.
(f) The heading *Post Office* does not appear in the accounts for these periods.
(g) Year ended 5th January.

Public Finance 2. Net Public Expenditure—Great Britain 1688–1801

NOTES
[1] SOURCE: *S.P.* 1868–9, xxxv.
[2] There are no transfers of component items from heading to heading in this table. Items appropriate to a particular heading at the end of the period were included in that heading throughout.

(in £000 sterling)

	Total Net Expenditure	Debt Charges				Civil Government		Army	Navy	Ordnance
		Total	Funded	Terminable Annuities	Unfunded	Total	Civil List			
1688–91(a)	11,543	189	—	—	189	1,792	1,730	5,200	3,098	659
1692(b)	4,255	199	—	—	199	662	632	1,900	1,239	254
1693	5,576	222	—	—	222	702	697	2,346	1,925	380
1694	5,602	442	12	111	319	669	662	2,119	2,132	239
1695	6,220	581	107	190	284	774	774	2,559	1,890	417
1696	7,998	651	66	262	323	713	700	1,749	1,922	253
1697	7,915	1,044	127	283	634	871	746	2,646	2,822	521
1698	4,127	1,467	186	469	812	391	375	1,343	877	49
1699	4,691	1,484	243	305	898	913	856	1,018	1,232	44
1700	3,201	1,251	218	331	701	699	683	359	819	73
1701	3,442	1,200	222	304	675	704	688	442	1,046	50
1702	5,010	1,174	256	315	603	523	508	1,102	2,094	117
1703	5,313	1,042	285	307	450	605	590	1,770	1,724	173
1704	5,527	977	260	338	374	656	638	2,107	1,630	157
1705	5,873	1,036	260	435	367	737	725	2,146	1,772	183
1706	6,692	1,078	268	449	350	652	630	2,741	1,949	271
1707	8,747	1,846	322	680	842	1,129	706	3,188	2,297	287
1708	7,742	1,637	315	735	585	784	761	3,183	1,909	229
1709	9,160	2,014	311	1,070	602	777	701	3,969	2,117	282
1710	9,772	1,754	317	733	584	857	840	4,463	2,422	276
1711	15,145(c)	1,813	347	763	612	668	645	4,853(c)	7,476(c)	334(c)
1712	7,864	2,360	709	1,080	485	726	697	2,837	1,776	165
1713	6,362	2,888	943	1,414	531	656	604	1,267	1,457	95
1714	6,185	3,021	834	1,604	583	1,161	1,108	884	1,043	76
1715	6,228	3,276	1,237	1,540	492	734	693	924	1,205	90
1716	7,076	3,027	856	1,689	461	926	874	2,151	792	180
1717	5,885	3,440	1,112	1,870	458	983	901	980	443	39
1718	6,354	2,839	1,383	1,073	375	840	784	1,204	1,350	120
1719	6,152	2,706	1,465	1,003	208	808	698	1,186	1,293	159
1720	6,002	2,769	1,716	943	96	980	880	965	1,181	108
1721	5,873	3,314	2,857	362	88	1,002	890	754	705	99
1722	6,978	3,012	2,544	212	232	1,181	1,101	1,011	1,666	108
1723	5,671	2,919	2,523	267	105	942	847	895	827	89
1724	5,438	2,864	2,461	281	115	968	886	856	630	120
1725	5,516	2,796	2,432	268	86	1,251	1,157	773	601	95
1726	5,543	2,667	2,353	224	88	1,089	825	992	695	100
1727	5,860	2,783	2,448	203	122	939	625	1,191	833	115
1728	6,504	2,335	2,006	208	121	1,051	916	1,378	1,539	201
1729	5,711	2,284	1,998	184	97	1,044	932	1,293	925	164
1730	5,574	2,280	2,001	187	85	935	853	1,203	1,033	123
1731	5,347	2,120	1,850	186	83	918	862	1,353	815	140
1732	4,974	2,217	1,959	182	66	933	867	1,012	700	113
1733	4,595	2,143	1,888	182	73	957	893	791	555	148
1734	6,360	2,052	1,792	182	76	1,060	945	707	2,079	462
1735	5,852	2,174	1,863	186	125	941	856	1,037	1,545	155

See p. 391 for footnotes

(in £ooo sterling)

	Total Net Expenditure	Debt Charges				Civil Government		Army	Navy	Ordnance
		Total	Funded	Terminable Annuities	Un-funded	Total	Civil List			
1736	5,793	2,127	1,829	179	119	949	853	1,185	1,390	142
1737	5,129	2,105	1,808	181	114	930	855	835	933	327
1738	4,725	2,059	1,753	184	122	886	828	846	819	115
1739	5,210	2,047	1,762	181	103	953	876	1,066	988	156
1740	6,161	2,102	1,790	185	128	846	792	1,418	1,607	187
1741	7,388	2,032	1,727	177	128	842	738	1,776	2,419	320
1742	8,533	2,041	1,690	182	170	834	783	2,523	2,795	340
1743	8,979	2,117	1,725	170	181	884	750	2,878	2,736	363
1744	9,398	2,178	1,824	154	191	921	797	3,227	2,709	364
1745	8,920	2,259	1,855	153	169	837	762	2,790	2,688	345
1746	9,804	2,316	1,945	172	189	784	685	3,729	2,396	579
1747	11,453	2,716	2,208	210	282	1,366	1,213	3,679	3,176	516
1748	11,943	2,842	2,306	219	194	997	770	4,172	3,361	571
1749	12,544(c)	2,981	2,449	217	162	1,082	793	2,339	5,606(c)	536(c)
1750	7,185	3,218	2,817	214	186	1,016	813	1,338	1,385	228
1751	6,425	2,978	2,588	212	176	1,068	829	1,383	895	102
1752(d)	7,037	2,944	2,580	215	139	1,108	803	976	1,854	154
1753	5,952	2,762	2,394	212	150	1,068	853	1,140	849	133
1754	6,030	2,823	2,494	211	118	1,043	801	1,071	944	150
1755	7,119	2,731	2,419	211	99	997	785	1,399	1,814	177
1756	9,589	2,761	2,463	207	82	1,292	849	2,396	2,714	426
1757	11,214	2,805	2,525	205	53	1,083	841(e)	3,210	3,595	520
1758	13,200	2,895	2,492	239	151	1,279	840	4,586	3,893	547
1759	15,382	2,947	2,623	240	72	991	809	5,744	4,971	729
1760	17,993	3,372	2,915	237	193	1,152	852	8,249	4,539	682
1761	21,112	3,823	3,247	298	182	1,256	997	9,923	5,256	853
1762	20,040	4,404	3,681	418	225	1,218	942(e)	8,781	4,892	746
1763	17,723(c)	4,666	3,989	474	139	1,056	867(e)	4,067	7,464(c)	470
1764	10,686	4,887	4,230	474	171	1,137	865(e)	2,234	2,150	279
1765	12,017(c)	4,828	4,224	469	134	1,050	806	2,702	3,154(c)	282
1766	10,314	4,686	4,046	472	157	1,069	815(e)	1,815	2,467	276
1767	9,638	5,020	4,274	563	164	1,022	813(e)	1,696	1,657	243
1768	9,146	4,911	4,299	463	130	1,036	807(e)	1,472	1,431	296
1769	9,569	4,803	4,191	466	132	1,498	1,268(f)	1,438	1,527	303
1770	10,524	4,836	4,236	463	136	1,223	898(f)	1,545	2,082	236
1771	10,106	4,611	4,054	458	98	1,057	796	1,514	2,061	361
1772	10,725	4,686	4,466	459	142	1,017	797(e)	1,497	2,738	334
1773	9,977	4,649	4,041	456	150	1,032	803(e)	1,581	1,787	327
1774	9,566	4,612	4,040	450	122	1,095	809(e)	1,532	2,030	298
1775	10,365	4,674	4,010	452	210	1,211	905(e)	1,765	1,765	349
1776	14,045	4,632	3,991	446	192	1,271	811(e)	4,248	2,745	549
1777	15,259	4,709	4,036	455	212	1,769	1,386(e)	4,677	3,531	573
1778	17,940	5,030	4,414	506	181	1,425	1,112(e)	5,464	4,563	957
1779	19,714	5,618	4,543	750	252	1,158	970(e)	7,112	4,271	1,074
1780	22,605	5,995	4,675	964	266	1,251	1,039(e)	7,210	6,329	1,330

See p. 391 for footnotes

(in £ooo sterling)

Principal Constituent Items

	Total Net Expenditure	Debt Charges				Civil Government				
		Total	Funded	Terminable Annuities	Unfunded	Total	Civil List	Army	Navy	Ordnance
1781	25,810	6,917	5,348	1,149	310	1,350	983(e)	8,928	6,589	1,546
1782	29,234	7,364	5,898	1,113	312	1,263	1,005(e)	7,755	10,807	1,564
1783	23,510	8,054	6,447	1,245	275	1,383	1,131(e)	5,332	6,994	1,341
1784	24,245(c)	8,678	6,959	1,323	372	1,324	1,055(e)	3,301	9,447(c)	1,014
1785	25,832(c)	9,229	7,431	1,299	467	1,451	989(e)	2,390	11,851(c)	551
1786	16,978	9,481	7,980	1,295	206	1,513	1,015(e)	1,984	3,127	372
1787	15,484	9,292	7,916	1,021	355	1,513	1,054(e)	1,803	1,991	384
1788	16,338	9,407	7,894	1,267	247	1,522	1,164(e)	2,099	2,262	547
1789	16,018	9,425	7,850	1,265	310	1,664	1,251(e)	1,899	2,073	475
1790	16,798	9,370	7,904	1,277	285	1,703	1,150(e)	2,197	2,482	545
1791	17,996	9,430	7,758	1,344	321	1,886	1,177(e)	2,009	3,400	769
1792	16,953	9,310	7,712	1,294	304	1,565	968(e)	1,829	3,331	417
1793	19,623	9,149	7,661	1,269	219	1,835	1,160(e)	4,829	2,464	844
1794	28,706(c)	9,797	8,016	1,272	452	1,572	1,118(e)	9,209	6,127(c)	1,501
1795	38,996(c)	10,470	8,595	1,351	331	1,751	1,235(e)	14,651	9,626(c)	1,996
1796	42,372(c)	11,602	9,582	1,453	237	2,014	1,272(e)	14,236	11,518(c)	2,500
1797	57,649(c)	13,594	11,609	1,499	246	2,527	1,311(e)	15,327	23,580(c)	2,122
1798	47,422	16,029	13,750	1,517	505	2,178	1,187(e)	14,142	12,793	1,780
1799	47,419	16,856	13,916	1,555	1,158	2,180	1,045(e)	14,289	11,614	1,980
1800(g)	(12,383)	(3,387)	(2,382)	(742)	(44)	(537)	(225)	(4,151)	(3,843)	(465)
1801(h)	50,991	16,749	13,872	1,780	922	2,072	1,039(e)	15,297	14,707	1,663

(a) 5th November 1688 to 29th September 1691.
(b) Years ended 29th September henceforth to 1751.
(c) These figures contain an element of debt funded in these years but contracted previously. The amounts are as follows:

1711	1,133 Army, 6,239 Navy, and 189 Ordnance,					
1749	2,842 Navy, and 230 Ordnance,					
1763	3,484 Navy,					
1765	1,368 Navy,					
1784	6,397 Navy and Ordnance combined—here attributed entirely to Navy,					
1785	9,866 Navy and Ordnance combined—here attributed entirely to Navy,					
1794	1,907 Navy,					
1795	1,491 Navy,					
1796	4,227 Navy,					
1797	11,596 Navy.					

(d) Years ended 10th October henceforth to 1799.
(e) The Civil List was swollen in these years by the addition of certain sums advanced from it for miscellaneous supply services on the understanding that they would be repaid in the following session. The amounts repaid were as follows:

1758	31	1776	7	1789	395
1763	6	1777	48	1790	219
1764	7	1778	85	1791	255
1765	2	1779	71	1792	118
1767	13	1780	124	1793	190
1768	11	1781	96	1794	202
1769	17	1782	97	1795	281
1770	14	1783	103	1796	474
1771	15	1784	145	1797	276
1772	7	1785	69	1798	207
1773	6	1786	123	1799	55
1774	10	1787	30	1800(¼)	—
1775	14	1788	293	1801	77

(f) These figures include grants for Civil List debts—463 in 1769 and 50 in 1770.
(g) Quarter ended 5th January.
(h) Year ended 5th January.

NOTES

[1] SOURCES: 1802–69—*S.P.* 1868–9, XXXV; 1870–1939—*Finance Accounts*, annually.
[2] The figures for Great Britain for the years ended 5th January 1802–17 are as follows:

	Total Gross Income	Customs	Excise	Stamps	Land and Assessed Taxes	Property and Income Tax	Post Office
1802	35·9	8·8	11·6	3·0	4·6	5·8	1·2
1803	37·4	7·7	15·5	3·2	5·3	3·3	1·3
1804	39·1	8·2	18·8	3·4	5·8	0·4	1·2
1805	46·5	9·4	21·5	3·5	6·0	3·7	1·3
1806	51·2	10·1	23·2	4·1	6·3	4·6	1·4
1807	55·7	10·8	24·1	4·3	6·4	6·2	1·5
1808	59·8	10·6	24·7	4·4	7·0	10·2	1·5
1809	62·9	10·3	25·6	4·7	7·6	11·4	1·5
1810	64·1	11·9	23·4	5·3	8·4	12·4	1·6
1811	69·6	12·4	25·8	5·5	7·7	13·5	1·7
1812	67·5	10·9	25·9	5·3	7·4	13·2	1·7
1813	64·7	11·6	23·6	5·3	7·5	13·1	1·8
1814	72·8	11·9	25·3	5·6	7·9	14·3	1·9
1815	74·3	12·6	26·4	5·8	8·0	14·5	2·0
1816	78·6	12·0	26·2	6·1	9·5	14·6	2·1
1817	65·2	10·1	24·2	6·2	7·3	11·8	2·0

[3] The Indian Military Contribution and the Army and Navy Extra Receipts have been excluded throughout this table.

[4] Receipts from taxes assigned to local authorities in lieu of exchequer payments for the period 1890–1907 have been included in this table.

(in £000,000 sterling)

	Total Gross Income	Principal Constituent Items (a)					
		Customs	Excise	Stamps	Land and Assessed Taxes	Property and Income Tax	Post Office
1802(b)	39·1	8·8	11·6	3·2	4·6	5·8	1·3
1803	41·2	7·7	15·5	3·4	5·3	3·3	1·4
1804	42·4	8·2	18·8	3·6	5·8	0·4	1·3
1805	50·2	9·4	21·5	3·9	6·0	3·7	1·4
1806	55·0	10·1	23·2	4·6	6·3	4·6	1·6
1807	60·1	10·8	24·1	4·9	6·4	6·2	1·6
1808	64·8	12·6(c)	26·7(c)	5·0	7·0	10·2	1·6
1809	68·2	12·6	27·6	5·4	7·6	11·4	1·6
1810	69·2	14·6	24·8	6·0	8·4	12·4	1·7
1811	73·0	14·4	27·4	6·2	7·7	13·5	1·9
1812	71·0	13·0	27·9	6·0	7·4	13·2	1·9
1813	70·3	14·0	25·9	6·0	7·5	13·1	2·0
1814	74·7	14·4	27·5	6·3	7·9	14·3	2·1
1815	77·9	14·8	29·5	6·5	8·0	14·5	2·2
1816	79·1	14·3	29·5	6·7	9·5	14·6	2·3
1817	69·2	11·9	26·9	6·8	7·3	11·8	2·2
1818	57·6	13·4	23·2	7·2	8·2	2·3	2·1
1819	59·5	13·9	26·4	7·2	8·2	0·6	2·1
1820	58·1	13·0	26·5	7·0	8·2	0·2	2·1
1821	59·9	11·9	29·6	6·9	8·2	- -	2·1
1822	61·6	12·7	29·9	6·8	8·3	- -	2·0
1823	59·9	13·0	29·1	6·9	7·7	—	2·1
1824	58·5	13·9	27·2	7·1	6·7	—	2·1
1825	59·7	13·5	28·5	7·6	5·3	—	2·2
1826	57·7	18·7	22·6	7·7	5·4	—	2·2
1827	55·2	19·5	20·8	7·0	5·1	—	2·3
1828	54·7	20·1	20·0	7·1	5·1	—	2·2
1829	56·5	19·3	22·2	7·4	5·2	—	2·2
1830	55·3	19·2	21·0	7·4	5·3	—	2·2
1831	54·5	19·4	20·0	7·3	5·4	—	2·2

See p. 395 for footnotes

(in £000,000 sterling)

	Total Gross Income	Principal Constituent Items (a)								
		Customs	Excise	Stamps	Land and Assessed Taxes	Property and Income Tax	Post Office	Tele-graph Service	Tele-phone Service	Death Duties
1832	50·6	18·2	17·5	7·2	5·2	—	2·2	—	—	—
1833	51·1	18·5	17·9	7·2	5·2	—	2·2	—	—	—
1834	50·2	17·8	17·7	7·1	5·2	—	2·2	—	—	—
1835	50·4	20·0	16·1	7·2	4·8	—	2·2	—	—	—
1836	50·0	22·0	14·4	7·2	3·9	—	2·2	—	—	—
1837	52·6	23·1	15·7	7·4	3·9	—	2·3	—	—	—
1838	50·4	22·1	14·6	7·1	3·9	—	2·3	—	—	—
1839	51·3	22·4	14·8	7·2	3·9	—	2·3	—	—	—
1840	51·8	23·2	14·6	7·2	3·9	—	2·4	—	—	—
1841	51·6	23·4	14·9	7·4	4·2	—	1·3	—	—	—
1842	52·2	23·5	14·8	7·3	4·7	—	1·4	—	—	—
1843	51·1	22·6	13·6	7·2	4·5	0·6	1·6	—	—	—
1844	56·7	22·6	14·0	7·1	4·4	5·3	1·6	—	—	—
1845	58·2	24·1	14·4	7·3	4·4	5·3	1·7	—	—	—
1846	57·5	21·8	14·6	7·9	4·4	5·2	1·9	—	—	—
1847	58·2	22·2	15·0	7·7	4·5	5·5	2·0	—	—	—
1848	56·1	21·7	13·9	7·7	4·6	5·6	2·1	—	—	—
1849	57·8	22·6	15·2	6·8	4·5	5·5	2·2	—	—	—
1850	57·1	22·3	15·0	7·0	4·5	5·6	2·2	—	—	—
1851	57·1	22·0	15·3	6·7	4·6	5·5	2·3	—	—	—
1852	56·3	22·2	15·4	6·5	3·8	5·4	2·4	—	—	—
1853	57·3	22·1	15·7	6·9	3·6	5·7	2·4	—	—	—
1854	58·5	22·5	16·3	7·1	3·3	5·7	2·5	—	—	—
1854(d)	(13·5)	(5·1)	(2·6)	(1·8)	(0·2)	(2·7)	(0·7)	—	—	—
1855(e)	62·4	21·6	16·9	7·1	3·2	10·6	2·4	—	—	—
1856	69·7	23·2	17·5	7·1	3·1	15·1	2·8	—	—	—
1857	72·2	23·5	18·3	7·4	3·1	16·1	2·9	—	—	—
1858	66·9	23·1	17·8	7·4	3·2	11·6	2·9	—	—	—
1859	64·3	24·1	17·9	8·0	3·2	6·7	3·2	—	—	—
1860	70·1	24·5	20·4	8·0	3·2	9·6	3·3	—	—	—
1861	69·7	23·3	19·4	8·3	3·1	10·9	3·4	—	—	—
1862	69·0	23·7	18·3	8·6	3·2	10·4	3·5	—	—	—
1863	68·8	24·0	17·2	9·0	3·2	10·6	3·7	—	—	—
1864	68·4	23·2	18·2	9·3	3·2	9·1	3·8	—	—	—
1865	68·7	22·6	19·6	9·5	3·3	8·0	4·1	—	—	—
1866	66·1	21·3	19·8	9·6	3·4	6·4	4·3	—	—	—
1867	67·8	22·3	20·7	9·4	3·5	5·7	4·5	—	—	—
1868	67·8	22·7	20·2	9·5	3·5	6·2	4·6	—	—	—
1869	70·8	22·4	20·5	9·2	3·5	8·6	4·7	—	—	—
1870	73·7	21·5	21·8	4·0(f)	4·5	10·0	4·7	0·1	—	4·7(f)
1871	68·2	20·2	22·8(g)	3·6	2·7(g)	6·4	4·8	0·5	—	4·8
1872	73·1	20·3	23·3	3·9	2·3	9·1	4·7	0·8	—	5·2
1873	74·7	21·0	25·8	4·1	2·3	7·5	4·8	1·0	—	5·1
1874	75·5	20·3	27·2	4·3	2·3	5·7	5·8	1·2	—	5·5
1875	73·6	19·3	27·4	4·2	2·4	4·3	5·7	1·1	—	5·6

See p. 395 for footnotes

(in £000,000 sterling)

	Total Gross Income	Customs	Excise	Stamps	Land and Assessed Taxes	Property and Income Tax	Post Office	Telegraph Service	Telephone Service	Death Duties
					Principal Constituent Items (a)					
1876	75·5	20·0	27·6	4·4	2·5	4·1	6·0	1·2	—	5·8
1877	76·8	19·9	27·7	4·3	2·5	5·3	6·0	1·3	—	5·9
1878	77·7	20·0	27·5	4·2	2·7	5·8	6·2	1·3	—	6·0
1879	81·2	20·3	27·4	4·3	2·7	8·7	6·2	1·3	—	5·6
1880	73·3	19·3	25·3	4·2	2·7	9·2	6·4	1·4	—	6·2
1881	81·9	19·2	25·3	4·4	2·7	10·7	6·7	1·6	—	6·7
1882	84·0	19·3	27·2	4·3	2·7	9·9	7·0	1·6	—	7·1
1883	87·4	19·7	26·9	4·5	2·8	11·9	7·3	1·7	—	7·3
1884	86·2	19·7	27·0	4·2	2·9	10·7	7·7	1·7	—	7·4
1885	88·0	20·3	26·6	4·2	3·0	12·0	7·9	1·8	—	7·7
1886	89·6	19·8	25·5	4·2	2·9	15·2	8·2	1·7	—	7·4
1887	90·8	20·2	25·3	4·4	3·0	15·9	8·5	1·8	—	7·4
1888	89·8	19·6	25·6	4·8	3·0	14·4	8·7	2·0	—	8·2
1889	89·9	20·1	25·6	4·3	3·0	12·7	9·1	2·1	—	8·0
1890	94·6	20·4	27·2	5·0	3·0	12·8	9·5	2·3	—	9·1
1891	96·5	19·7	29·2	6·0	2·6	13·3	9·9	2·4	—	9·9
1892	98·6	19·9	30·2	5·4	2·5	13·8	10·2	2·5	—	11·1
1893	97·7	20·0	30·0	5·5	2·5	13·5	10·4	2·5	—	10·7
1894	98·4	20·0	29·8	5·3	2·5	15·2	10·5	2·5	—	9·9
1895	101·8	20·4	30·7	5·7	2·5	15·6	10·8	2·6	—	10·9
1896	109·4	21·1	31·5	7·4	2·5	16·1	11·4	2·8	—	14·1
1897	112·3	21·5	32·4	7·4	2·4	16·7	11·9	2·9	—	14·0
1898	116·1	22·1	33·3	7·7	2·4	17·3	12·2	3·0	—	15·3
1899	117·9	21·1	34·3	7·6	2·4	18·0	12·7	3·2	—	15·6
1900	129·9	24·1	37·3	8·5	2·5	18·8	13·3	3·4	—	18·5
1901	140·2	26·6	38·4	7·8	2·5	26·9	13·8	3·5	—	17·2
1902	152·7	31·2	36·8	7·8	2·5	34·8	14·3	3·5	—	18·5
1903	161·3	34·7	37·4	8·2	2·6	38·8	14·8	3·6	—	18·1
1904	151·3	34·1	36·9	7·5	2·7	30·8	15·5	3·7	—	17·2
1905	153·2	35·9	36·1	7·7	2·8	31·3	16·1	3·8	—	16·7
1906	153·9	34·6	35·6	8·2	2·7	31·4	16·9	4·1	—	17·3
1907	155·0	33·1	35·7	8·0	2·6	31·6	17·2	4·3	—	19·1
1908	156·5	32·5	35·7	8·0	2·7	32·4	17·9	4·4	—	19·1
1909	151·6	29·2	33·7	7·8	2·6	33·9	17·8	3·0(h)	1·5(h)	18·4
1910	131·7	30·3	31·0	8·1	0·7	13·3	18·2	3·1	1·7	21·8
1911	203·9	33·1	40·0	9·8	4·3	59·1	19·2	3·2	2·0	25·5
1912	185·1	33·6	38·4	9·5	2·9	41·8	19·7	3·1	2·9	25·4
1913	188·8	33·5	38·0	10·1	2·7	41·2	20·3	3·1	5·8	25·2
1914	198·2	33·5	39·6	10·0	2·7	43·9	21·2	3·1	6·5	27·4
1915	226·7	38·7	42·3	7·6	2·6	59·3	20·4	3·0	6·3	28·4
1916	336·8	59·6	61·2	6·8	2·7	111·6	24·1	3·4	6·5	31·0
1917	573·4	70·6	56·4	7·9	2·6	185·9	24·4	3·4	6·4	31·2
1918	707·2	71·3	38·8	8·3	2·6	216·3	25·2	3·5	6·6	31·7
1919	889·0	102·8	59·4	12·4	2·5	255·6	29·4	3·8	6·8	30·3
1920	1,339·6	149·4	133·7	22·6	2·6	316·9	31·0	4·9	8·3	40·9

See p. 395 *for footnotes*

(in £000,000 sterling)

Principal Constituent Items (a)

	Total Gross Income	Customs	Excise	Stamps	Land and Assessed Taxes	Property and Income Tax	Post Office	Telegraph Service	Telephone Service	Death Duties
1921	1,426·0	134·0	199·8(i)	26·6	2·6	338·9	36·1	5·2	8·2	47·7
1922	1,124·9	130·1	194·3	19·6	2·6	337·0	40·0	5·9	10·5	52·2
1923	914·0	123·0	157·3	22·2	2·8	314·8	34·2	5·5	13·6	56·9
1924	837·2	120·0	148·0	21·6	2·5	269·3	32·8	5·6	14·4	57·8
1925	799·4	99·3	135·1	22·9	1·2	273·8	34·9	5·6	15·0	59·5
1926	812·1	103·5	134·6	24·7	0·7	259·4	35·8	5·7	16·0	61·2
1927	805·7	107·5	133·0	24·8	0·7	234·7	35·6	5·9	17·4	67·3
1928	842·8	111·6	139·2	27·0	0·6	250·6	38·3	6·1	18·7	77·3
1929	836·4	119·0	134·0	30·1	0·6	237·6	39·0	6·2	20·1	80·6
1930	815·0	119·9	127·5	25·7	0·7	237·4	40·2	6·3	21·6	79·8
1931	857·8	121·4	124·0	20·7	0·6	256·0	40·3	6·3	22·6	82·6
1932	851·5	136·2	119·9	17·1	0·7	287·4	40·1	6·2	23·3	65·0
1933	827·0	162·2	120·9	19·2	0·6	251·5	39·9	6·3	24·0	77·1
1934	809·4	179·2	107·0	22·7	0·6	228·9	40·6	6·6	25·3	85·3
1935	804·6	185·1	104·6	24·1	0·6	228·9	41·5	7·0	25·6	81·4
1936	844·8	196·6	106·7	25·8	0·6	238·1	42·8	7·1	27·9	87·9
1937	896·6	211·3	109·5	29·1	0·5	257·2	45·4	7·6	30·0	88·0
1938	948·7	221·6	113·7	24·2	...(j)	297·0	47·0	7·8	31·8	89·0
1939	1,006·2	226·3	114·2	21·0	...(j)	335·9	47·3	7·8	33·4	77·4

(a) For short periods other items are of interest or importance, as follows:

Gross Income from Lotteries

1802	1·1	1809	1·1	1816	1·1	1823	0·8
1803	1·1	1810	0·8	1817	1·0	1824	0·6
1804	1·3	1811	1·1	1818	0·8	1825	0·6
1805	1·1	1812	0·9	1819	0·8	1826	1·0
1806	1·3	1813	1·0	1820	0·8	1827	0·3
1807	1·2	1814	0·9	1821	0·8		
1808	1·3	1815	1·1	1822	0·9		

Gross Income from Surtax and Motor Vehicle Duties

	Surtax	Motor Duties		Surtax	Motor Duties
1911	2·9	—	1926	68·5	18·1
1912	3·0	—	1927	65·9	21·4
1913	3·6	—	1928	60·6	24·5
1914	3·3	—	1929	56·2	25·4
1915	10·1	—	1930	56·4	26·8
1916	16·8	—	1931	67·8	27·8
1917	19·1	—	1932	76·7	27·5
1918	23·3	—	1933	60·7	27·9
1919	35·6	—	1934	52·6	30·7
1920	42·2	—	1935	51·2	31·5
1921	55·3	7·1	1936	51·0	30·8
1922	61·7	11·1	1937	53·5	32·7
1923	64·2	12·3	1938	57·1	34·6
1924	60·6	14·7	1939	62·5	35·6
1925	62·7	16·2			

Gross Income from Excess Profits Tax

1917	139·9	1919	285·0	1921	219·2
1918	220·2	1920	290·0	1922	30·5

Gross Income from Corporation Profits Tax

1922	17·6	1924	23·3	1926	11·7
1923	19·0	1925	18·1	1927	4·0

Gross Income from National Defence Contribution (Profits)

1938	1·4	1939	21·9

(b) Years ended 5th January henceforth to 1854.
(c) Prior to 1808 the customs and excise revenues of Ireland cannot be separated. The combined figure has been included in *Total Gross Income*, but not under the headings *Customs* and *Excise*.
(d) Quarter ended 5th April.
(e) Years ended 31st March henceforth.
(f) Death duties were included with *Stamps* prior to 1870. At the same date fee and patent stamps were excluded from the heading *Stamps*—a reduction of about 6 per cent at the time.
(g) From 1871 all assessed taxes except land tax and house duty were replaced by excise licences, their revenue therefore being transferred from *Land and Assessed Taxes* to *Excise*.
(h) Prior to 1909 the telephone service was included with telegraphs.
(i) Prior to 1921 motor licences were included under *Excise*.
(j) In 1938 and 1939 land tax was not separately shown.

Public Finance 4.   Gross Public Expenditure—United Kingdom 1801–1939

NOTES

[1] SOURCES: 1802–69—*S.P.* 1868–9, xxxv; 1870–1939—*Finance Accounts* annually. The cost of the postal packet service in the period 1839–42 is taken from the *Navy Estimates* (see footnote (*f*) p. 400.).

[2] All payments for capital investment, with certain minor exceptions before 1889, have been excluded from this table,

as has all expenditure on debt redemption, other than through the payment of terminable annuities. All costs of collection are included.

[3] Items of expenditure which are of interest or importance only during the period 1909–39 are given in table 4a.

(in £000,000 sterling)

Principal Constituent Items (a)

	Total Gross Expenditure	Debt Charges				Civil Government—Total and Main Constituents						Army and Ordnance	Navy	Costs of Collection	
		Total (b)	Funded	Terminable Annuities	Unfunded	Total	Works and Buildings	Salaries, etc. of Public Departments	Law and Justice (c)	Education, Art and Science	Colonial, Consular, and Foreign			Total	Post Office, Telegraphs, and Telephones
1802(d)	65·5	19·9	16·1	1·9	1·1	5·6	0·09	0·07	0·10	0·06	0·17	20·1	17·3	2·4	0·4
1803	54·8	20·4	17·2	1·9	1·3	6·7	0·10	0·09	0·12	0·08	0·12	13·3	12·0	2·4	0·4
1804	53·0	20·7	17·9	1·9	0·9	5·1	0·13	0·08	0·11	0·08	0·26	15·5	8·1	2·4	0·4
1805	62·8	20·7	18·0	1·9	0·7	5·2	0·13	0·10	0·14	0·07	0·25	22·2	11·9	2·6	0·4
1806	71·4	22·3	18·6	1·9	1·4	5·2	0·22	0·13	0·17	0·10	0·28	25·8	14·3	2·7	0·4
1807	72·9	23·2	19·6	2·0	1·2	4·7	0·24	0·14	0·17	0·10	0·20	24·8	16·3	2·8	0·4
1808	73·3	23·8	19·9	2·0	1·6	5·3	0·39	0·21	0·16	0·12	0·19	24·0	16·9	3·2	0·4
1809	78·0	23·1	20·0	1·6	1·2	4·7	0·31	0·19	0·18	0·12	0·24	27·2	17·6	3·5	0·5
1810	81·5	24·2	20·4	1·6	2·1	5·2	0·21	0·20	0·17	0·11	0·29	28·9	19·4	3·6	0·5
1811	81·6	24·4	20·9	1·7	1·8	5·1	0·26	0·18	0·18	0·14	0·25	28·0	20·0	3·9	0·5
1812	87·3	24·6	21·5	1·6	1·4	5·2	0·24	0·22	0·24	0·20	0·23	33·8	19·6	3·9	0·5
1813	94·8	26·4	22·2	1·7	2·3	5·4	0·29	0·18	0·20	0·26	0·26	36·5	20·8	4·1	0·6
1814	111·1	27·3	23·5	1·8	1·7	5·3	0·36	0·23	0·23	0·13	0·29	49·6	22·5	4·4	0·6
1815	112·9	30·0	25·6	1·9	2·0	5·8	0·45	0·23	0·24	0·15	0·34	49·6	22·8	4·6	0·7
1816	99·5	32·2	26·3	1·9	3·9	6·1	0·41	0·26	0·23	0·15	0·28	39·6	16·8	4·7	0·7
1817	71·3	32·9	28·5	1·9	2·2	5·5	0·38	0·33	0·23	0·19	0·30	18·0	10·2	4·8	0·6
1818	58·7	31·5	27·8	1·9	1·8	5·0	0·30	0·40	0·27	0·08	0·30	11·1	6·6	4·5	0·6
1819	57·6	31·3	27·1	2·0	2·2	6·0	0·32	0·47	0·28	0·12	0·31	9·1	6·6	4·5	0·7
1820	57·5	31·1	28·2	2·0	0·8	5·4	0·16	0·46	0·34	0·09	0·36	10·3	6·4	4·4	0·6
1821	58·4	32·0	28·0	1·8	2·0	5·4	0·26	0·52	0·44	0·08	0·30	10·1	6·6	4·3	0·6
1822	58·4	31·9	28·4	1·8	1·7	5·6	0·21	0·49	0·29	0·07	0·30	10·4	6·3	4·3	0·6
1823	56·5	31·4	28·1	1·8	1·4	5·4	0·17	0·43	0·30	0·08	0·28	8·7	5·2	4·5	0·6
1824	54·3	30·0	26·7	2·2	1·1	5·4	0·24	0·45	0·30	0·08	0·36	8·7	5·6	4·5	0·6
1825	55·5	30·2	26·6	2·5	1·1	6·0	0·28	0·61	0·29	0·17	0·36	9·0	6·2	4·1	0·6
1826	54·1	29·2	25·8	2·5	0·8	5·8	0·39	0·56	0·22	0·11	0·39	9·2	5·8	4·0	0·6
1827	56·1	29·2	25·8	2·6	0·8	6·0	0·52	0·63	0·39	0·14	0·45	10·2	6·5	4·1	0·7
1828	55·9	29·4	26·0	2·6	0·9	6·2	0·39	0·65	0·38	0·09	0·58	9·8	6·4	4·1	0·7
1829	53·5	29·3	25·7	2·6	0·9	5·0	0·42	0·52	0·35	0·12	0·20	9·5	5·7	4·0	0·7
1830	53·7	29·1	25·7	2·6	0·9	5·4	0·69	0·52	0·38	0·10	0·36	9·3	5·9	4·0	0·7
1831	51·9	29·2	25·5	2·9	0·8	4·9	0·40	0·50	0·55	0·08	0·31	8·6	5·3	3·9	0·7
1832	51·5	28·3	24·4	3·3	0·7	5·0	0·73	0·57	0·57	0·04	0·39	8·7	5·7	3·7	0·7
1833	50·6	28·3	24·3	3·3	0·7	4·7	0·27	0·54	0·65	0·05	0·46	8·9	4·9	3·8	0·6
1834	48·8	28·5	24·3	3·5	0·8	4·3	0·23	0·50	0·77	0·06	0·49	7·9	4·4	3·7	0·6
1835	48·9	28·5	24·2	3·7	0·7	4·6	0·22	0·51	0·72	0·11	0·48	7·6	4·5	3·7	0·7
1836	65·2(e)	28·6	23·8	4·0	0·7	4·5	0·24	0·53	0·77	0·08	0·48	7·6	4·1	3·7	0·7
1837	54·0(e)	29·4	24·4	4·2	0·7	4·7	0·25	0·60	0·93	0·19	0·20	7·9	4·2	3·6	0·7
1838	51·1	29·6	24·5	4·2	0·9	5·1	0·30	0·76	1·03	0·18	0·58	8·0	(4·8)(f)	(3·6)(f)	(0·7)(f)
1839	51·7	29·4	24·5	4·2	0·7	5·5	0·24	0·72	1·42	0·20	0·48	8·2	4·4	3·7	0·8
1840	53·4	29·6	24·4	4·3	0·8	5·6	0·25	0·68	1·32	0·17	0·36	8·5	5·3	3·8	0·9
1841	53·2	29·5	24·6	4·2	0·6	5·3	0·25	0·75	1·29	0·27	0·30	8·5	5·4	3·9	1·1

See p. 399 for footnotes

Public Finance 4. *continued*

(in £000,000 sterling)

Principal Constituent Items (a)

	Total Gross Expenditure	Debt Charges — Total (b)	Debt Charges — Funded	Debt Charges — Terminable Annuities	Debt Charges — Unfunded	Civil Government — Total	Works and Buildings	Salaries, etc. of Public Departments	Law and Justice (c)	Education, Art and Science	Colonial, Consular, and Foreign	Army and Ordnance	Navy	Costs of Collection — Total	Costs of Collection — Post Office, Telegraphs, and Telephones
1842	54·3	29·7	24·5	4·1	0·9	5·6	0·24	0·69	1·51	0·29	0·38	8·2	6·2	4·0	1·2
1843	55·1	29·6	24·8	4·1	0·7	5·6	0·28	0·78	1·54	0·27	0·35	8·2	6·2	4·1	1·4
1844	55·4	29·4	24·8	3·9	0·7	6·0	0·26	0·74	1·66	0·25	0·42	7·9	6·2	4·2	1·4
1845	54·8	30·6	26·1	4·0	0·5	5·9	0·32	0·72	1·73	0·25	0·36	8·1	5·4	4·3	1·4
1846	53·7	28·6	24·0	4·0	0·4	5·4	0·38	0·75	1·42	0·29	0·29	8·9	6·3	4·6	1·7
1847	55·4	28·3	23·9	3·9	0·4	6·3	0·39	0·80	1·57	0·33	0·49	9·1	7·3	4·6	1·7
1848	59·1	28·4	24·0	3·9	0·4	8·1	0·61	0·91	1·96	0·30	0·40	10·5	7·5	4·7	1·7
1849	59·0	28·7	24·2	3·8	0·8	7·2	0·51	0·99	2·22	0·36	0·50	9·7	7·3	4·9	2·0
1850	55·5	28·5	24·2	3·7	0·6	6·8	0·48	0·94	2·28	0·37	0·41	8·9	6·2	4·9	2·1
1851	54·7	28·3	24·1	3·7	0·4	6·8	0·50	1·01	2·26	0·45	0·40	9·0	5·7	5·0	2·2
1852	54·0	28·2	24·0	3·8	0·4	6·9	0·50	1·01	2·20	0·46	0·46	8·7	5·0	4·9	2·1
1853	55·3	28·1	23·9	3·8	0·4	6·6	0·68	1·04	1·97	0·48	0·36	9·5	5·8	4·9	2·2
1854	55·8	28·1	23·8	3·8	0·4	7·2	0·78	1·06	2·22	0·56	0·34	9·4 }	(7·8)(h)	(6·2)(h)	(2·7)(h)
1854(g)	(14·0)	(6·6)	(5·8)	(0·6)	(0·2)	(2·1)	(0·15)	(0·25)	(0·17)	(0·17)	(0·17)	(2·2) }			
1855(i)	69·1	28·0	23·3	3·8	0·6	7·7	0·74	1·42	2·39	0·66	0·34	13·8	13·7	4·1	1·9
1856	93·1	28·2	23·4	3·9	0·9	8·7	0·77	1·32	3·04	0·83	0·34	27·8	18·9	5·3	2·4
1857	76·1	28·8	23·8	4·0	1·0	8·4	1·06	1·21	2·71	0·91	0·33	20·8	12·7	5·4	2·4
1858	68·2	28·7	23·8	4·0	1·0	10·1	0·85	1·43	3·07	1·06	0·39	12·9	9·6	5·3	2·7
1859	64·8	28·7	23·7	4·0	1·0	9·1	0·77	1·42	3·29	1·15	0·35	12·5	8·2	5·5	2·9
1860	69·6	28·7	23·9	4·3	0·4	9·7	0·68	1·47	3·44	1·27	0·42	14·1	10·8	5·4	2·9
1861	72·9	26·3	23·9	1·9	0·4	10·7	0·64	1·43	3·19	1·23	0·45	15·0	13·3	5·6	2·9
1862	72·3	26·3	23·9	1·8	0·6	10·8	0·72	1·46	3·40	1·35	0·73	16·5	12·6	5·6	3·0
1863	70·3	26·2	23·8	1·9	0·5	10·9	0·87	1·48	3·53	1·40	0·90	17·3	11·4	5·5	2·9
1864	67·8	26·2	23·8	2·0	0·4	10·8	0·93	1·51	3·50	1·29	0·59	15·4	10·8	5·4	2·9
1865	67·1	26·4	23·6	2·3	0·4	10·2	0·63	1·56	3·39	1·22	0·55	15·0	10·9	5·5	3·0
1866	66·5	26·2	23·5	2·4	0·3	10·3	0·65	1·54	3·66	1·28	0·55	14·4	10·3	5·4	2·9
1867	67·2	26·1	23·4	2·4	0·3	10·5	0·82	1·54	3·55	1·42	0·54	15·1	10·7	5·6	3·1
1868	71·8	26·6	22·9	3·4	0·3	11·2	0·72	1·73	3·87	1·60	0·55	15·9	11·2	5·7	3·1
1869	75·5	26·6	22·5	4·0	0·2	12·0	0·95	1·59	4·65	1·38	0·54	15·5	11·4	6·1	3·5
1870	67·1(j)	27·1	22·4	4·4	0·3	11·0	0·94	1·64	4·25	1·62	0·55	12·1(j)	9·4(j)	6·2	3·6
1871	67·8	26·8	22·3	4·4	0·2	12·0	1·3	1·7	4·6	1·8	0·5	12·1	9·0	6·5	3·9
1872	69·9	26·8	22·2	4·5	0·2	12·2	1·3	1·8	4·7	1·9	0·6	14·7	9·5	6·6	4·0
1873	68·8	26·8	22·1	4·5	0·1	11·8	1·1	1·8	4·5	2·2	0·6	13·8	9·3	7·2	4·6
1874	74·6	26·7	22·0	4·6	0·1	12·7	1·2	1·9	5·0	2·4	0·6	13·5	10·1	7·6	4·9
1875	73·0	27·1	21·8	5·2	0·1	13·6	1·3	2·1	5·2	2·6	0·7	14·0	10·5	7·8	5·1
1876	74·7	27·2	21·6	5·4	0·1	14·8	1·4	2·5	5·5	2·9	0·6	14·2	10·8	7·6	4·9
1877	75·7	27·4	21·6	5·4	0·1	14·9	1·4	2·6	5·5	3·2	0·7	14·5	11·0	7·9	5·2
1878	79·6	27·6	21·6	5·5	0·1	15·6	1·4	2·6	5·7	3·6	0·7	14·3	10·8	7·8	5·1
1879	82·8	28·0	21·5	5·7	0·1	16·6	1·4	2·2	6·3	4·0	0·6	16·9	11·8	8·0	5·2
1880	81·5	28·1	21·5	5·7	0·1	16·9	1·4	2·2	6·5	4·0	0·6	15·0	10·2	8·0	5·2
1881	80·6	29·2	21·5	6·9	0·1	17·4	1·4	2·3	6·5	4·3	0·6	14·7	10·5	8·2	5·4
1882	83·3	29·4	21·4	7·2	0·1	18·0	1·5	2·4	6·7	4·4	0·7	15·7	10·6	8·5	5·7
1883	87·1	29·5	21·4	7·3	0·1	18·9	1·8	2·4	7·1	4·6	0·7	15·1	10·3	8·9	6·1
1884	85·4	29·1	21·3	7·9	0·1	19·0	1·8	2·4	6·8	4·8	0·7	16·1	10·7	9·7	6·9
1885	88·5	29·0	19·2	9·1	0·1	18·7	1·8	2·4	6·8	5·1	0·7	18·6	11·4	9·9	7·1

See p. 399 for footnotes

(in £000,000 sterling)

Principal Constituent Items (a)

	Total Gross Expenditure	Debt Charges				Civil Government—Total and Main Constituents						Army and Ordnance	Navy	Costs of Collection	
		Total (b)	Funded	Terminable Annuities	Un-funded	Total	Works and Buildings	Salaries, etc. of Public Departments	Law and Justice (c)	Education, Art and Science	Colonial, Consular, and Foreign			Total	Post Office, Telegraphs, and Telephones
1886	92.2	23.5	19.0	3.6	0.2	19.2	1.8	2.4	6.7	5.3	0.7	17.0	12.7	10.0	7.3
1887	90.0	28.0	19.0	8.2	0.2	19.3	1.8	2.4	6.7	5.5	0.6	18.4	13.3	10.8	8.1
1888	86.7	25.5	18.4	6.6	0.3	19.7	2.0	2.4	6.8	5.6	0.6	18.2	12.3	10.7	8.0
1889	86.5	25.1	18.6	5.9	0.4	19.4	1.4	2.4	6.8	5.7	0.6	16.0	13.0	11.0	8.3
1890	90.6	24.5	17.0	6.6	0.7	17.1	1.5	2.1	5.2	5.8	0.7	17.4	15.3	11.0	8.3
1891	93.4	23.9	16.2	6.6	1.0	17.6	1.7	2.1	5.0	6.1	0.7	17.8	15.6	11.3	8.7
1892	96.0	23.7	16.1	6.6	0.8	19.0	2.0	2.3	4.9	7.0	0.7	17.6	15.6	12.0	9.3
1893	95.8	23.5	16.2	6.4	0.7	19.3	1.6	1.9	4.3	8.9	0.7	17.5	15.7	12.4	9.8
1894	98.5	23.4	16.3	6.4	0.5	19.7	1.6	2.0	4.2	9.4	0.8	17.9	15.5	12.8	10.1
1895	100.9	23.3	16.4	6.4	0.5	20.4	1.7	2.0	4.1	9.8	0.9	17.9	17.5	12.9	10.3
1896	105.1	22.8	16.3	6.4	0.1	21.2	1.9	2.1	4.2	10.3	1.0	18.5	19.7	13.2	10.5
1897	109.7	23.6	16.3	7.2	0.1	21.4	1.9	2.1	4.1	10.7	0.9	18.3	22.2	13.6	10.8
1898	112.3	23.6	16.2	7.3	0.1	22.9	1.9	2.1	4.2	11.5	1.2	19.3	20.9	14.3	11.6
1899	117.7	23.6	16.2	7.3	0.1	23.4	1.9	2.1	4.2	12.0	1.6	20.0	24.1	15.0	12.2
1900	143.7	23.2	15.4	7.3	0.3	23.9	2.0	2.1	4.2	12.2	1.7	43.6	26.0	15.6	12.8
1901	193.3	19.8	15.3	2.8	0.4	24.9	2.0	2.4	4.2	12.5	2.1	91.5	29.5	16.3	13.5
1902	205.2	21.7	15.3	2.8	0.3	31.9	2.1	2.6	4.3	12.8	8.4	92.3	31.0	17.0	14.0
1903	194.2	27.2	15.2	7.3	0.4	37.6	2.3	2.5	4.3	13.3	13.3(k)	69.4	31.2	17.6	14.6
1904	155.3	25.5	16.6	6.5	2.4	28.3	2.5	2.5	4.3	14.6	2.2	36.7	35.5	18.2	15.1
1905	149.5	24.8	16.1	6.5	2.1	28.8	2.5	2.6	4.3	15.6	2.1	29.2	36.8	18.7	15.6
1906	147.0	24.6	16.1	6.5	1.9	29.8	2.5	2.6	4.3	16.4	2.0	28.9	33.3	19.1	16.0
1907	143.7	22.5	16.0	4.7	1.7	30.6	2.7	2.6	4.3	16.9	1.9	27.8	31.4	19.8	16.6
1908	143.4	21.1	16.0	3.6	1.6	31.9	2.7	2.9	4.4	17.4	2.1	27.1	31.1	20.7	17.5
1909	144.8	21.5	15.8	3.6	1.2	33.8	2.9	2.9	4.5	17.4	1.8	26.8	32.2	21.4	18.1
1910	156.9	20.8	15.7	3.5	1.6	41.4	3.1	3.0	4.6	17.9	1.9	27.2	35.8	22.0	18.7
1911	167.9	20.4	15.6	3.5	1.4	45.9	3.2	3.4	4.8	18.7	2.0	27.4	40.4	23.6	19.7
1912	174.1	20.1	15.4	3.5	1.2	49.2	3.2	4.1	4.9	19.0	2.1	27.6	42.9	24.5	20.5
1913	184.0	19.9	15.2	3.5	1.2	54.6	3.5	4.3	5.0	19.5	2.2	28.1	44.4	27.2	23.0
1914	192.3	19.3	15.0	3.2	1.1	56.8	3.3	4.3	5.0	19.5	1.5	28.3	48.8	29.1	24.6
1915	559.5	21.7	14.8	2.9	1.8	60.0	3.7	4.6	5.3	20.2	1.8	28.9	51.6	30.7	26.1
1916	1,559.2	60.2	13.1	2.9	4.3	57.0	3.4	4.6	5.2	20.7	1.5	--(l)	--(l)	31.3	26.7
1917	2,198.1	127.3	8.3	2.9	8.6	53.9	3.0	4.8	5.0	20.3	1.2	--(l)	--(l)	31.2	26.5
1918	2 696.2	189.9	8.5	2.8	8.5	62.7	2.9	5.4	5.3	25.8	1.3	--(l)	--(l)	30.9	25.7
1919	2,579.3	270.0	8.7	2.6	12.4	69.5	3.4	7.6	7.1	25.6	1.2	--(l)	--(l)	31.9	26.4
1920	1,665.8	332.0	8.8	2.6	12.4	574.5(m)	10.0	15.1	14.6	43.2	2.7	395.0	156.5	57.5	48.1
1921	1,188.1	342.3	8.6	2.6	5.9	477.9	12.4	18.4	20.0	59.3	5.0	181.5	88.4	64.9	53.7
1922	1,070.1	323.2	8.7	2.6	4.1	465.0	11.2	17.1	22.9	65.4	32.5(n)	95.1	80.8	80.2	66.0
1923	812.5	324.0	8.8	3.4	1.9	302.5	6.1	10.8	15.0	49.8	12.3(n)	45.4	56.2	61.2	49.9
1924	748.8	307.3	33.5	0.4	273.4	257.5	5.9	12.1	11.5	47.7	18.1(n)	43.6	52.6	60.6	49.8
1925	750.8	312.2	34.0	0.4	277.7	244.8	6.5	8.9	11.5	48.7	6.8	44.8	55.6	61.3	50.4

See p. 399 for footnotes

(in £000,000 sterling)

Principal Constituent Items (a)

		Debt Charges				Civil Government—Total and Main Constituents						Army and Ord-nance	Navy	Costs of Collection	
	Total Gross Expend-iture	Total (b)	Funded	Termin-able Annui-ties	Un-funded	Total	Works and Build-ings	Salar-ies, etc. of Public Depart-ments	Law and Justice (c)	Educa-tion, Art and Science	Colon-ial, Con-sular, and For-eign			Total	Post Office, Tele-graphs, and Tele-phones
1926	776·1	308·2	34·4	0·4	273·4	263·9	6·9	10·9	12·3	48·6	7·6	44·3	59·7	65·3	54·0
1927	782·4	318·6	36·4	0·4	281·7	260·7	6·4	13·7	12·6	53·2	7·4	43·6	57·6	66·4	54·9
1928	773·6	313·8	43·3	0·4	270·2	253·1	...(o)	...(o)	13·1(o)	53·3(o)	7·7	44·2	58·1	68·5	56·8
1929	760·5	311·5	49·4	0·4	261·7	246·4	...	...	12·6	49·5	5·6	40·5	56·9	68·8	57·2
1930	781·7	307·3	52·5	0·4	254·3	271·7	...	...	12·8	50·1	5·5	40·5	55·8	70·9	58·9
1931	814·2	293·2	50·6	0·4	242·2	333·2	...	...	16·3	55·1	6·0	40·5	52·6	70·9	59·0
1932	818·6	289·5	50·0	0·4	239·0	345·7	...	...	16·5	55·4	5·6	38·5	51·1	69·8	58·0
1933	833·0	282·2	52·0	0·4	229·8	369·2	...	...	15·8	51·6	7·9	35·9	50·0	71·7	59·3
1934	770·5	216·3	118·1	0·4	97·7	368·3	...	...	16·2	51·1	8·4	37·6	53·5	71·4	59·3
1935	784·7	211·7	118·0	0·4	93·2	378·0	...	...	16·7	52·8	8·0	39·7	56·6	74·4	61·8
1936	829·4	211·5	117·8	0·4	93·3	394·5	...		17·7	55·9	8·6	44·6	64·8	79·2	66·1
1937	889·1	210·9	117·8	0·4	92·7	398·6	...		19·2	58·5	9·2	54·8	81·1	85·3	71·9
1938	909·3	216·2	117·6	0·4	98·2	400·4	...		22·7	63·1	8·6	77·9(p)	102·0(p)	86·5	72·9
1939	1,005·7	216·8	117·8	0·4	100·5	435·6	...		28·3	65·3	11·8	121·4(p)	127·3(p)	89·4	75·3

[a] Various items of expenditure which were of importance for relatively short periods only have not been included in the main body of this table. The great majority of these were introduced from 1909 onwards, and are shown in a separate table in note [3], p. 396. Other items were as follows:

Gross Expenditure on Lotteries

1802 0·8	1807 0·5	1812 0·6	1817 0·6	1822 0·7	1827 0·4
1803 1·0	1808 1·1	1813 0·5	1818 0·5	1823 0·6	1828 0·2
1804 0·9	1809 0·5	1814 0·5	1819 0·6	1824 0·6	
1805 0·8	1810 0·6	1815 0·7	1820 0·6	1825 0·4	
1806 0·8	1811 0·6	1816 0·8	1821 0·6	1826 0·7	

Gross Expenditure on Special Expeditions, Votes of Credit, etc. (for dates not shown the amount was nil.)

1802 0·3	1814 2·0	1856 4·2	1871 1·4	1884 1·0
1804 1·3	1815 - -	1858 1·5	1872 0·1	1885 0·6
1805 0·2	1816 - -	1859 0·8	1874 0·8	1886 9·7
1806 1·2	1817 - -	1860 0·9	1875 0·1	1887 0·1
1807 1·0	1823 1·3	1861 3·0	1877 - -	1888 0·1
1808 0·1	1849 1·1	1862 1·3	1878 3·5	1915 357·0
1809 1·9	1852 0·3	1864 0·1	1879 1·5	1916 1,399·7
1810 0·2	1853 0·4	1866 0·8	1880 3·2	1917 1,973·7
1811 0·2	1854 0·3	1868 2·0	1881 0·6	1918 2,402·8
1812 0·2	1854* - -	1869 5·0	1882 1·1	1919 2,198·0
1813 1·5	1855 1·8	1870 1·3	1883 4·4	1920 87·0

* = Quarter ended 5th April.

(b) Debt charges which were regarded as outside the permanent charge of the national debt have been included in this total, but are not shown under the separate items. The only period when they were of much significance was 1915–23 when they were as follows:

1915 2·2	1917 107·5	1919 246·3	1921 325·1	1923 309·8
1916 39·9	1918 170·0	1920 308·3	1922 307·8	

(c) This includes expenditure on courts.
(d) Years ended 5th January henceforth to 1854.

(e) These figures include compensatory payments to colonial slave owners—16·7 in 1836 and 4·1 in 1837.
(f) In the period 1838–60 the postal packet service was paid for out of the navy vote, but in this table its cost has been subtracted from *Navy* and transferred to *Costs of Collection*. In the year 1838, however, it cannot be separated from expenditure on the navy.
(g) Quarter ended 5th April.
(h) These figures are for the 15 months ended 5th April 1854.
(i) Years ended 31st March henceforth.
(j) Prior to 1870 expenditure out of the Indian Military Contribution and the Army and Navy Extra Receipts is included under these headings. Its exclusion in 1870 made a difference of about 10 per cent under the heading Army and Ordnance and 5 per cent under the heading *Navy*.
(k) Includes 8·0 grant-in-aid to Transvaal and the Orange Free State.
(l) During these years all military payments, except purely nominal amounts, were made from votes of credit—see footnote (a).
(m) Many items of expenditure, civilian as well as military, were transferred from votes of credit to *Civil Government* after 1919.
(n) These figures include exceptionally high sums for 'Middle-Eastern services', namely 29·0 in 1922, 11·2 in 1923, and 7·0 in 1924. The normal expenditure on this item was about 4·0.
(o) There was a reorganisation of the system of accounting for civil government expenditure in 1928. The headings *Works and Buildings* and *Salaries etc. of Public Departments* disappeared, the expenditure of the Home Department was included with *Law and Justice* (making an increase of about 5 per cent at that date), and there were minor additions to the heading *Education Art and Science*.
(p) These figures include amounts issued under the Defence Loans Act, which are not, however, included in the total.

Gross Public Expenditure on Selected Items—United Kingdom 1909–1939

NOTE

[1] The notes to table 4 apply to this table.

	Old Age Pensions	Ministry of Pensions	Contributory Pensions	Unemployment Insurance and Labour Exchanges	National Health Insurance and Ministry of Health	Trade and Industry	Unemployment Payments of Various Kinds other than Insurance (a)	Payments to Northern Ireland	Road Fund	Royal Air Force
1909	2·1	—	—	—	—	—	—	—	—	—
1910	8·5	—	—	—	—	—	—	—	—	—
1911	9·8	—	—	—	—	—	—	—	1·4	—
1912	11·7	—	—	—	—	—	—	—	1·7	—
1913	12·2	—	—	0·8	4·0	—	—	—	1·2	—
1914	12·5	—	—	0·9	6·1	—	—	—	1·4	—
1915	12·6	—	—	1·0	6·8	—	—	—	1·5	—
1916	12·7	—	—	0·9	4·8	—	—	—	0·7	—
1917	12·5	—	—	1·1	6·9	—	—	—	—	—
1918	11·9	—	—	1·2	6·3	—	—	—	—	—
1919	11·8	—	—	1·6	7·3	—	—	—	—	- - (b)
				Ministry of Labour						
1920	19·3	99·4 (c)	—	3·3	10·7	—	—	—	—	52·5
1921	25·5	109·3	—	24·6	21·8	—	1·0	—	8·9	22·3
1922	25·3	93·7	—	19·3	26·2	—	3·8	1·1	10·8	13·6
1923	22·5	80·7	—	16·0	19·0	—	3·0	3·3	11·8	9·4
1924	23·2	69·3	—	14·5	19·0	—	2·0	4·0	14·1	9·6
1925	25·8	69·0	—	14·4	21·1	—	2·5	3·8	15·6	14·3
1926	26·2	67·9	—	13·4	23·0	—	1·9	4·9	17·5	15·5
1927	30·3	63·3	—	11·0	21·5	—	6·9	5·8	17·4	15·5
1928	32·5	59·7	4·0	10·7	23·2	9·9 (d)	1·5	5·3	19·7	15·2
1929	34·3	56·1	4·0	11·5	23·7	9·1	1·5	5·1	21·1	16·1
1930	34·9	53·5	4·0	19·5	24·5	10·4	1·8	5·5	21·9	16·8
1931	36·8	52·0	9·0	36·8	22·1	12·6	2·6	6·4	22·9	17·8
1932	37·9	49·6	10·0	47·7	22·1	14·1	3·1	6·3	22·5	17·7
1933	39·7	46·9	11·0	77·9	22·2	9·2	3·5	7·0	22·9	17·1
1934	40·3	44·9	12·0	71·8	21·8	9·3	4·1	6·6	25·5	16·8
1935	41·8	43·2	13·0	65·8	22·6	15·5	7·4	6·8	26·4	17·6
1936	43·2	42·4	14·0	23·0	23·5	17·0	57·9	7·2	25·8	27·5
1937	44·2	41·4	15·0	23·7	25·0	17·8	53·3	8·0	27·4	50·1
1938	45·4	40·2	16·0	23·7	25·7	31·0 (e)	50·2	8·9	—	82·3 (f)
1939	47·9	39·2	17·0	24·2	26·5	48·2 (e)	49·9	9·5	—	133·8 (f)

(a) = Unemployment Grant, Funds for Special Areas, grants for employment schemes, and Road Grants (Unemployed Relief).
(b) = See footnote (l) p. 400.
(c) = Previously spent out of votes of credit.

(d) = New heading resulting from the reorganisation of the system of accounting for civil government expenditure.
(e) = Includes expenditure on roads, which amounted to 15·5 in 1938 and 21·9 in 1939.
(f) = Includes amounts issued under the Defence Loans Act.

Public Finance 5. Nominal Amount of the Unredeemed Capital of the Public Debt of the United Kingdom at the End of Each Financial Year—1691–1939

NOTES

[1] SOURCES: Funded Debt—1691–1785—*S.P.* 1898, LII, 1786–1890—*S.P.* 1890–1, XLVIII, 1891–1939—*Return Relating to the National Debt* published in *Finance Accounts* annually. Unfunded Debt—1691–1835—*S.P.* 1868–9, XXXV, 1836–1939—*Return Relating to the National Debt*. Remaining figures—*Return relating to the National Debt*.

[2] Material prepared by the National Debt Commissioners has been preferred to the alternative source (S.P. 1868–9, XXXV). Differences between the two are slight, and the break in the unfunded series between 1835 and 1836 is inconsiderable. The mistaken attribution of the figures of unfunded debt to the year previous to that to which they actually apply, in S.P. 1868–9, XXXV, Part II, Appendix 12, has been corrected.

[3] All figures of the total national debt result from the addition of the two separate figures of funded and unfunded debt regardless of whether the financial years are the same for both.

[4] From the end of the financial year in 1916, the amount of outstanding external debt is shown in the *Return relating to the National Debt*. It was as follows:

1916	60·6	1924	1,125·8	1932	1,090·8
1917	400·3	1925	1,121·6	1933	1,060·4
1918	1,048·7	1926	1,110·8	1934	1,036·5
1919	1,364·9	1927	1,101·5	1935	1,036·5
1920	1,278·7	1928	1,095·2	1936	1,036·5
1921	1,161·6	1929	1,084·7	1937	1,032·6
1922	1,088·7	1930	1,074·2	1938	1,032·5
1923	1,155·7	1931	1,066·7	1939	1,032·4

(in £000,000 sterling)

	Funded	Un-funded	Total		Funded	Un-funded	Total
1691(b)	—	3·1	3·1	1724	48·6	5·2	53·8
1692	—	3·3	3·3	1725	48·6	4·1	52·7
1693	—	5·9	5·9	1726	49·1	3·8	52·9
1694	0·6	5·5	6·1	1727(b)	48·4	4·5	53·0
1695	1·2	7·2	8·4	1728	48·5	4·2	52·7
1696	1·2	10·4	10·6	1729	48·4	3·7	52·1
1697	3·4	13·3	16·7	1730	47·4	4·0	51·4
1698	5·1	12·2	17·3	1731	47·9	3·7	51·7
1699	4·8	10·6	15·4	1732	46·4	3·7	50·1
1700	4·7	9·4	14·2	1733	46·4	3·6	50·0
1701	4·7	9·4	14·1	1734	45·4	3·7	49·1
1702	4·6	9·6	14·1	1735	45·4	3·9	49·3
1703	4·4	9·1	13·6	1736	46·0	3·7	49·7
1704	4·3	9·2	13·4	1737	45·0	3·6	48·5
1705	4·1	8·9	13·0	1738	44·0	3·5	47·5
1706	4·5	8·5	13·0	1739	43·3	3·7	46·9
1707	4·3	10·2	14·5	1740	43·3	4·2	47·4
1708	4·8	10·5	15·2	1741	43·3	5·4	48·8
1709	7·4	11·7	19·1	1742	45·0	6·4	51·3
1710	7·3	14·1	21·4	1743	47·6	5·9	53·5
1711	11·8	10·6	22·4	1744	50·4	6·7	57·1
1712	25·6	9·4	34·9	1745	52·4	7·7	60·1
1713	26·1	8·6	34·7	1746	56·3	8·5	64·9
1714	27·8	8·4	36·2	1747	61·8	7·6	69·4
1715	29·6	7·8	37·4	1748	68·7	7·4	76·1
1716	29·5	8·4	37·9	1749	71·8	6·0	77·8
1717	31·7	7·6	39·3	1750	72·8	5·2	78·0
1718	34·1	5·6	39·7	1751	72·4	5·7	78·1
1719	37·2	4·4	41·6	1752(b)	71·5	5·5	76·9
1720	49·8	4·1	54·0	1753	71·0	4·1	75·0
1721	50·3	4·6	54·9	1754	70·9	1·3	72·2
1722	48·4	4·3	52·7	1755	71·8	0·7	72·5
1723	49·1	4·4	53·6	1756	73·8	0·8	74·6

See p. 403 for footnotes

(in £000,000 sterling)

	Funded	Un-funded	Total		Funded	Un-funded	Total	Out-standing Investment Borrowing(a)	Aggregate Gross Liabilities of the State
1757	76·8	1·1	77·8	1805	514·2	25·3	539·6	—	...
1758	81·8	1·4	82·1	1806	538·0	26·3	564·4	—	...
1759	89·3	1·9	91·3	1807	556·0	27·1	583·1	—	...
1760	97·6	4·2	101·7	1808	559·2	32·1	591·3	—	...
1761	109·9	4·4	114·2	1809	559·8	39·3	599·0	—	...
1762	121·9	4·7	126·6	1810	567·7	39·7	607·4	—	...
1763	129·1	3·6	132·6	1811	570·8	37·9	609·6	—	...
1764	129·2	5·0	134·2	1812	583·4	42·6	626·0	—	...
1765	130·6	3·0	133·6	1813	607·5	44·8	652·3	—	...
1766	131·2	2·1	133·3	1814	677·5	48·1	725·5	—	...
1767	131·9	1·9	133·9	1815	684·6	60·3	744·9	—	...
1768	130·3	2·3	132·6	1816	733·6	44·7	778·3	—	...
1769	128·6	1·7	130·3	1817	716·3	49·8	766·1	—	...
1770	128·6	2·1	130·6	1818(b)	780·6	62·6	843·3	—	...
1771	127·1	1·8	128·9	1819	795·6	48·7	844·3	—	...
1772	126·4	2·2	128·7	1820	798·5	41·6	840·1	—	...
1773	125·8	3·1	128·9	1821	804·9	33·3	838·3	—	...
1774	125·3	2·4	127·7	1822	798·5	32·7	831·1	—	...
1775	124·3	3·1	127·3	1823	797·4	38·7	836·1	—	...
1776	125·9	5·3	131·2	1824	792·9	35·8	828·6	—	...
1777	130·9	5·7	136·6	1825	782·3	37·9	820·2	—	...
1778	137·1	6·0	143·1	1826	779·3	31·7	811·0	—	...
1779	144·1	9·4	153·4	1827	785·0	25·0	810·0	—	...
1780	156·1	11·2	167·2	1828	778·7	27·6	806·4	—	...
1781	177·4	11·9	190·4	1829	773·6	27·7	801·3	—	...
1782	197·5	16·8	214·3	1830	772·6	25·5	798·2	—	...
1783	212·8	19·0	231·8	1831	758·9	27·3	786·2	—	...
1784	228·7	14·2	242·9	1832	757·0	27·2	784·2	—	...
1785	239·6	5·8	245·5	1833	755·6	27·4	783·0	—	...
1786	239·7	6·4	246·2	1834	753·2	28·1	781·3	—	...
1787(b)	239·2	6·6	245·8	1835	745·3	29·6	774·9	—	...
1788	237·7	7·4	245·1	1836	760·3	30·1(c)	790·4	—	846·1
1789	236·2	8·1	244·3	1837	763·2	27·7	790·9	—	845·5
1790	234·6	9·4	244·0	1838	763·6	25·3	788·9	—	841·9
1791	233·0	10·1	243·2	1839	762·8	25·5	788·2	—	840·4
1792	231·5	10·0	241·6	1840	768·0	20·6	788·7	—	839·0
1793	229·6	13·3	242·9	1841	767·9	22·2	790·2	—	838·8
1794	234·0	15·6	249·6	1842	774·3	19·6	793·9	—	840·8
1795	247·9	19·6	267·4	1843	774·9	18·7	793·5	—	838·7
1796	301·9	8·5	310·4	1844	774·0	20·5	794·5	—	838·3
1797	351·5	7·7	359·2	1845	771·1	18·8	789·9	—	833·8
1798	378·6	12·6	391·2	1846	768·8	18·4	787·2	—	829·8
1799	408·1	18·5	426·6	1847	766·8	18·4	785·2	—	826·1
1800	411·4	...(b)	...(b)	1848	774·7	18·0	792·7	—	831·6
1801(b)	432·3	23·7	456·1	1849	776·5	17·8	794·3	—	831·4
1802	478·1	20·5	498·6	1850	775·7	17·8	793·5	—	828·9
1803	501·0	15·4	516·4	1851	772·0	17·8	789·7	—	823·7
1804	504·3	19·5	523·8	1852	767·9	17·7	785·7	—	818·0

See p. 403 for footnotes

Public Finance 5. *continued*

(in £000,000 sterling)

	Funded	Unfunded	Total	Outstanding Investment Borrowing(a)	Aggregate Gross Liabilities of the State		Funded	Unfunded	Total	Outstanding Investment Borrowing(a)	Aggregate Gross Liabilities of the State
1853	764·5	17·7	782·3	—	813·5	1897	587·7	8·1	595·8	4·0	645·2
1854	758·4	16·0	774·4	—	803·6	1898	585·8	8·1	593·9	3·7	638·8
1855(b)	755·6	24·2	779·7	—	806·7	1899	583·2	8·1	591·3	7·4	635·4
1856	779·4	27·1	806·5	—	833·7	1900	552·6	16·1	568·7	10·0	638·8
1857	784·0	28·0	812·0	—	836·8	1901	551·2	78·1	629·3	14·5	703·9
1858	782·9	25·9	808·9	—	831·2	1902	609·6	75·1	684·7	20·2	765·2
1859	790·5	18·3	808·8	—	828·7	1903	640·1	75·1	715·2	27·6	798·3
1860	789·7	16·3	806·0	—	822·8	1904	637·6	73·6	711·3	31·9	794·5
1861	789·0	16·7	805·7	—	822·0	1905	635·7	71·6	707·3	41·7	796·7
1862	788·2	16·5	804·7	—	821·3	1906	634·0	65·7	699·8	45·8	789·0
1863	787·4	16·5	803·9	—	821·5	1907	631·9	51·7	683·6	49·7	779·2
1864	781·7	13·1	794·8	—	817·2	1908	625·6	44·0	669·6	50·9	762·3
1865	780·2	10·7	790·9	—	812·7	1909	621·8	42·8	664·7	51·4	754·1
1866	773·9	8·2	782·1	—	803·4	1910	614·9	62·5	677·4	49·2	762·5
1867	770·2	8·0	778·1	—	800·9	1911	610·3	40·5	650·8	47·8	733·1
1868	741·8	7·9	749·8	—	797·8	1912	602·2	33·1	635·3	50·1	718·4
1869	741·1	9·9	751·0	—	797·8	1913	593·5	31·5	625·0	54·8	711·3
1870	741·5	6·8	748·3	1·0	793·1	1914	586·7	33·5	620·2	56·4	706·2
1871	732·0	6·1	738·1	0·9	787·3	1915	583·3	493·6	1,076·9	57·0	1,162·0
1872	731·8	5·2	736·9	0·9	784·2	1916	318·5	1,788·5	2,107·0	56·7	2,189·8
1873	727·4	4·8	732·2	0·9	777·5	1917	317·8	3,669·6	3,987·4	52·2	4,063·6
1874	723·5	4·5	728·0	0·9	771·2	1918	317·7	5,532·2	5,849·9	49·2	5,921·1
1875	714·8	5·2	720·0	0·9	767·3	1919	317·6	7,096·7	7,414·3	46·1	7,481·1
1876	713·7	11·4	725·1	0·8	769·4	1920	315·0	7,494·5	7,809·5	46·9	7,875·6
1877	712·6	13·9	726·6	0·8	768·7	1921	314·8	7,241·8	7,556·7	48·7	7,623·1
1878	710·8	20·6	731·4	0·8	770·9	1922	580·6	7,057·5	7,638·1	66·2	7,720·5
1879	709·4	25·9	735·3	0·8	771·8	1923	997·8	6,730·7	7,728·6	70·3	7,812·6
1880	710·5	27·3	737·8	0·7	770·6	1924	980·3	6,647·3	7,627·6	66·5	7,707·5
1881	709·1	22·1	731·2	0·7	765·2	1925	1,022·7	6,562·1	7,584·8	68·0	7,665·9
1882	709·5	18·0	727·5	0·7	759·9	1926	1,073·5	6,472·5	7,546·0	75·1	7,633·7
1883	712·7	14·2	726·9	0·7	753·9	1927	1,219·8	6,322·6	7,542·4	98·1	7,652·7
1884	640·6	14·1	654·7	0·7	745·6	1928	1,350·0	6,165·3	7,515·3	103·2	7,631·0
1885	640·2	14·0	654·2	0·6	739·9	1929	1,478·3	6,009·5	7,487·8	120·5	7,620·9
1886	638·9	17·6	656·5	0·6	742·0	1930	1,456·0	6,000·9	7,456·9	127·2	7,596·2
1887	637·6	17·5	655·2	0·6	736·2	1931	1,425·0	5,976·3	7,401·3	169·6	7,582·9
1888	609·7	17·4	627·1	0·6	704·6	1932	1,467·1	5,955·1	7,422·2	214·0	7,648·0
1889	607·1	16·1	623·2	0·6	697·6	1933	3,376·3	4,255·6	7,631·9	215·9	7,859·7
1890	586·0	32·3	618·2	0·5	689·1	1934	3,374·3	4,435·9	7,810·2	208·1	8,030·4
1891	579·5	36·1	615·6	1·3	683·5	1935	3,368·1	4,420·2	7,788·4	102·0	7,902·4
1892	577·9	35·3	613·3	1·3	677·1	1936	3,366·5	4,417·3	7,783·7	105·8	7,901·6
1893	589·5	20·7	610·3	1·8	671·1	1937	3,364·9	4,420·2	7,785·1	112·6	7,909·9
1894	587·6	21·4	609·1	2·5	667·3	1938	3,364·8	4,648·8	8,013·6	122·8	8,149·0
1895	586·0	17·4	603·4	3·1	659·0	1939	3,364·6	4,785·0	8,149·6	138·0	8,301·1
1896	589·1	10·0	599·1	4·0	652·3						

(a) This relates to loans under Telegraph Acts, Naval Works Act, Barracks Act, Telephone Transfer Acts, etc.
(b) Financial years ended on the following dates: *Great Britain* (*funded debt*) 1691–1751—29th September, 1752–86—10th October, 1787–1817—1st February; *Great Britain* (*except for funded debt*) 1691–1751—29th September, 1752–99 —10th October, 1801–17—5th January; *Ireland* 1691–1726—25th December, 1727–1800—25th March, 1801–17—5th January; *United Kingdom* 1818–54—5th January, 1855–1939 —31st March.
(c) See note 2.

NOTES TO PART A

[1] Source: *S.P.* 1868–9, xxxv.
[2] Items which did not appear in accounts of Exchequer receipts and issues are not included in this part—i.e. conversions are not included, nor are redemptions of debt through the income of the National Debt Commissioners derived other than from the Exchequer direct.

[3] Money raised by simple terminable annuities was as follows:

1693 0·9	1697 - -	1701 —	1705 0·9	1709 0·3
1694 1·4	1698 0·2	1702 —	1706 2·3	1710 2·3
1695 0·2	1699 —	1703 0·1	1707 1·5	1711 3·2
1696 0·1	1700 0·1	1704 1·4	1708 1·9	

A. Great Britain, 1692–1817

(in £000,000 sterling)

	Funded Debt(a)		Unfunded Debt — Total Unfunded		Unfunded Debt — Exchequer Bills	
	Creation	Redemption	Creation	Redemption	Creation	Redemption
1692(b)	—	—	3·1	2·8	—	—
1693	—	—	4·3	3·4	—	—
1694	0·6	—	3·2	3·6	—	—
1695	0·6	—	5·5	3·8	—	—
1696	—	—	5·0	1·7	0·1	0·1
1697	1·2	—	5·4	2·6	2·3	0·4
1698	0·9	0·3	2·2	3·4	0·4	0·8
1699	1·0	0·3	1·9	2·9	—	0·6
1700	- -	0·1	1·0	2·3	—	0·3
1701	—	- -	2·1	2·3	—	0·3
1702	—	- -	3·3	3·1	—	0·1
1703	—	—	3·3	3·7	—	- -
1704	—	—	2·5	3·5	—	- -
1705	—	—	3·3	3·7	—	- -
1706	—	—	3·1	3·7	—	- -
1707	—	0·1	4·6	3·0	1·5	0·1
1708	0·6	0·2	3·2	3·0	0·1	0·2
1709	2·8	0·2	5·7	4·6	2·6	1·7
1710	—	0·3	5·5	3·1	0·5	0·1
1711	9·2	0·1	2·6	4·7	0·1	—
1712	3·1	—	2·5	3·1	0·1	—
1713	0·9	—	2·2	2·8	0·8	—
1714	1·3	—	1·8	2·2	0·6	—
1715	1·5	—	1·5	2·2	—	0·1
1716	0·9	—	2·6	2·1	—	—
1717	2·5	—	1·5	4·4	—	2·0
1718	0·4	—	2·6	2·7	—	—
1719	2·6	1·2	2·1	3·5	—	1·2
1720	0·5	—	3·1	2·8	1·0	0·4
1721	0·3	—	1·8	1·6	—	- -
1722	0·4	—	2·7	3·4	0·9	1·0
1723	- -	0·1	2·9	2·9	1·1	1·1
1724	—	0·1	1·9	1·7	0·1	0·2
1725	—	—	2·0	2·6	0·1	0·8
1726	1·0	0·5	2·8	3·3	1·8	1·6
1727	—	0·6	2·8	2·2	1·5	1·0
1728	1·8	1·7	2·6	2·9	2·0	1·9
1729	1·1	1·2	2·3	2·9	1·7	2·2
1730	0·1	1·2	2·6	2·3	2·1	1·6
1731	0·8	0·3	2·0	2·4	1·5	1·8
1732	0·4	2·0	1·6	1·8	1·3	1·3
1733	—	—	1·2	1·5	0·9	1·1
1734	—	1·0	2·8	1·4	1·7	1·1
1735	—	—	2·0	1·8	1·9	1·5
1736	0·6	—	1·8	1·8	1·0	1·5
1737	—	1·0	1·8	2·0	1·6	1·6
1738	—	1·0	1·9	2·0	1·6	1·4
1739	0·3	1·0	1·9	1·9	1·7	1·7
1740	—	—	2·2	1·9	1·1	1·2
1741	—	—	3·9	2·8	1·6	1·6
1742	1·6	—	3·5	2·6	2·3	1·4
1743	2·3	—	3·3	3·5	2·3	2·1
1744	2·6	—	3·5	3·0	2·9	1·9
1745	1·7	—	3·5	2·9	1·7	2·1
1746	4·0	—	3·5	3·6	1·5	2·7
1747	5·5	—	2·2	3·5	1·7	1·9
1748	6·0	—	2·6	3·4	2·0	2·5
1749	3·6	—	4·4	3·0	3·3	2·0
1750	0·5	—	3·0	3·9	2·5	2·8
1751	2·0	2·4	2·9	2·7	2·4	2·1

See p. 405 *for footnotes*

(in £000,000 sterling)

	Funded Debt(a)		Total Unfunded		Exchequer Bills	
	Creation	Redemption	Creation	Redemption	Creation	Redemption
1752(c)	0·6	0·9	3·4	3·2	2·9	2·6
1753	—	0·4	2·1	3·3	1·6	2·6
1754	—	··	1·9	3·0	1·4	2·4
1755	1·0	—	1·9	2·5	1·4	1·8
1756	1·9	—	2·9	2·0	2·2	1·2
1757	2·4	—	3·9	3·2	2·9	2·1
1758	5·4	··	3·4	3·3	2·4	2·5
1759	6·7	—	3·6	3·1	2·1	2·5
1760	8·0	—	6·4	5·2	4·6	2·5
1761	11·6	—	6·2	5·8	5·0	4·5
1762	11·9	—	4·8	6·6	4·2	5·4
1763	6·9	—	5·7	4·4	5·1	3·9
1764	0·8	—	4·8	5·5	4·8	4·8
1765	1·5	—	4·0	4·4	4·0	4·4
1766	1·4	0·9	4·4	4·5	4·4	4·5
1767	1·6	0·9	3·7	4·4	3·7	4·4
1768	1·8	3·5	5·6	5·0	5·6	5·0
1769	0·1	1·8	4·4	4·7	4·4	4·7
1770	—	—	3·4	4·2	3·4	4·2
1771	—	1·5	4·8	4·0	4·8	4·0
1772	—	0·7	4·6	4·4	4·6	4·4
1773	—	0·7	6·2	4·1	6·2	4·1
1774	—	0·4	3·1	4·0	3·1	4·0
1775	—	0·9	3·5	3·8	3·5	3·8
1776	1·9	0·4	6·0	4·4	6·0	4·4
1777	4·3	—	6·3	6·3	6·3	6·3
1778	6·4	—	5·1	5·5	5·1	5·5
1779	7·2	—	7·2	6·4	7·2	6·4
1780	11·5	—	7·6	7·7	7·6	7·7
1781	12·0	—	7·4	7·1	7·4	7·1
1782	13·1	—	9·6	7·5	9·6	7·5
1783	10·9	—	6·5	5·9	6·5	5·9
1784	12·5	—	5·6	6·8	5·6	6·8
1785	12·1	—	4·5	5·6	4·5	5·6
1786	—	0·3	7·3	6·6	7·3	6·6
1787	—	1·1	9·9	10·2	9·9	10·2
1788	—	1·1	9·5	8·3	9·5	8·3
1789	0·6	1·2	9·4	9·2	9·4	9·2
1790	0·6	1·2	8·3	8·2	8·3	8·2
1791	—	1·3	10·5	9·4	10·5	9·4
1792	—	1·7	8·5	8·9	8·5	8·9
1793	3·9	1·6	8·5	7·1	8·5	7·1
1794	12·9	1·6	10·0	14·3	10·0	12·4
1795	18·8	2·1	13·7	10·7	13·7	9·2
1796	28·6	2·5	7·0	11·8	7·0	7·6
1797	42·8	3·2	10·2	22·9	10·2	9·9
1798	22·8	3·8	14·3	10·9	14·3	10·9
1799	16·3	4·3	27·2	25·0	27·2	25·0
1800(d)	(2·7)	(1·2)	(7·1)	(4·2)	(7·1)	(4·2)
1801(e)	20·5	4·6	26·0	20·7	26·0	20·7
1802	42·1	5·1	23·6	33·4	23·6	27·4
1803	26·1	5·7	16·4	22·4	16·4	22·4
1804	12·0	6·0	18·9	16·2	18·9	16·2
1805	14·2	6·5	18·7	12·3	18·7	12·3
1806	25·3	8·7	27·7	26·1	27·7	26·1
1807	20·1	8·8	30·9	30·3	30·9	30·3
1808	15·5	9·2	34·5	29·6	34·5	29·6
1809	18·2	9·7	45·1	42·6	45·1	38·6
1810	30·6	10·2	36·1	44·1	36·1	36·2
1811	29·9	10·8	37·7	47·0	37·7	38·7
1812	30·8	11·7	41·2	43·8	41·2	36·8
1813	40·4	17·9	45·8	48·2	45·8	42·8
1814	51·1	14·4	54·2	68·3	54·2	52·5
1815	36·6	12·8	52·3	42·4	52·3	42·4
1816	61·8	12·0	44·8	71·8	44·8	60·6
1817	9·3	12·5	46·6	43·5	46·6	43·5

(a) This does not include simple terminable annuities, but many loans had an element of terminable annuity which cannot be separated and is therefore included.
(b) Years ended 29th September henceforth to 1751.

(c) Years ended 10th October henceforth to 1799.
(d) Quarter ended 5th January.
(e) Years ended 5th January henceforth.

NOTES TO PART B

[1] Sources: *Total Public Debt—Return Relating to the National Debt*, published in *Finance Accounts* annually. Those published in 1897, 1916, 1930 and 1940 were used; *Funded Debt* and *Unfunded Debt*—1818–69—*S.P.* 1868–9, xxxv, 1870–1939—*Finance Accounts*.

[2] No attempt is made here to reconcile the figures from the two different sources. Variations between them appear to spring from differences of definition or of timing.

[3] Not all issues applicable to debt redemption were actually applied during the year in which they were issued. But the difference between cash applied and cash applicable is negligible for the years 1930–9, the only period in which easy comparison is possible.

B. United Kingdom, 1818–1939

(in £000,000 sterling)

Total Public Debt

	Creation		Redemption			Funded Debt(a)	
	Total(b)	for Capital Expenditure	Total	from Revenue	via Old Sinking Fund(c)	Creation	Redemption
1818(d)	...	...	...	...	...	--	14·3
1819	...	...	...	...	...	27·2	15·0
1820	...	...	...	...	...	20·2	16·0
1821	...	...	...	...	...	24·4	17·1
1822	...	...	...	...	...	13·9	16·8
1823	...	...	...	...	...	11·4	18·2
1824	...	...	...	...	...	4·6	5·7
1825	...	...	...	...	...	2·4	9·1
1826	...	...	...	...	...	2·3	3·1
1827	...	...	...	...	...	10·0	1·7
1828	...	...	...	...	...	2·2	4·7
1829	...	...	...	...	...	2·0	4·0
1830	...	...	...	...	...	3·0	2·5
1831	...	...	...	...	...	—	4·5
1832	...	...	...	...	...	—	1·2
1833	...	...	...	...	...	—	--
1834	...	...	...	...	...	—	0·8
1835	...	...	...	...	...	—	1·8
1836	17·3	...	3·1	1·8	1·3	16·7	0·5
1837	3·5	...	4·2	1·9	1·6	4·5	0·6
1838	0·2	...	4·0	1·9	2·0	1·5	0·3
1839	0·8	...	2·1	2·0	—	0·6	--
1840	0·6	...	2·3	2·1	—	5·4	--
1841	2·1	...	2·2	2·1	—	0·5	--
1842	2·0	...	2·1	2·0	—	4·5	--
1843	1·7	...	2·1	2·1	—	2·7	--
1844	1·9	...	2·0	2·0	—	--	--
1845	—	...	5·7	2·4	1·6	--	0·3
1846	—	...	6·6	2·1	4·1	—	1·3
1847	—	...	5·8	2·1	3·6	—	1·2
1848	8·0	...	4·3	2·2	1·8	8·0	0·5
1849	1·6	...	2·4	2·2	—	1·6	--
1850	0·4	...	2·2	2·2	--	0·4	--
1851	—	...	4·8	2·5	2·3	—	2·3
1852	—	...	5·4	2·4	3·0	—	3·0
1853	—	...	4·9	2·5	2·4	—	1·9
1854	—	...	11·3	2·5	2·6	1·3	7·1
1854(e)	(0·8)	...	(3·3)	(0·5)	(0·8)	(—)	(2·0)
1855(f)	7·3	...	4·7	2·7	2·0	—	--
1856	25·6	...	2·8	2·8	—	21·6	--
1857	7·5	...	3·3	2·9	—	7·4	--
1858	—	...	5·6	3·1	0·2	—	0·3
1859	—	...	3·3	3·2	--	7·6	--
1860	—	...	6·2	3·6	0·5	—	--
1861	0·7	...	2·1	1·4	0·6	0·2	--
1862	1·0	...	1·5	1·3	—	1·0	--
1863	1·0	...	1·4	1·4	—	1·0	--
1864	0·8	...	5·3	1·4	0·9	0·8	--
1865	0·7	...	6·1	1·6	2·5	0·7	0·9
1866	1·0	...	6·1	1·7	2·6	0·5	1·3
1867	1·3	...	3·4	1·7	1·6	0·5	0·6
1868	1·4	...	4·1	2·2	1·8	0·5	0·9
1869	2·5	...	2·5	2·4	—	0·5	--
1870	6·7	...	6·0	2·5	—	0·2	—
1871	0·4	...	7·4	3·3	4·0	0·2	1·9

See p. 409 for footnotes

B. United Kingdom, 1818–1939

(in £000,000 sterling)

	Unfunded Debt (a)				
	Total Unfunded		Exchequer Bills		Treasury Bills
	Creation	Redemption	Creation	Redemption	Net Increase (+) or Decrease (−)
1818(d)	61·5	50·0	54·8	42·3	—
1819	52·0	65·4	39·4	52·8	—
1820	43·0	44·6	17·1	18·7	—
1821	59·4	73·5	26·2	40·3	—
1822	68·4	69·6	33·1	34·2	—
1823	75·1	71·5	43·6	40·0	—
1824	52·5	54·0	37·5	39·0	—
1825	45·5	42·3	40·8	37·6	—
1826	41·9	48·2	28·7	35·0	—
1827	50·1	56·8	26·2	32·9	—
1828	56·4	53·3	31·2	28·1	—
1829	56·6	56·9	30·5	30·8	—
1830	51·0	53·3	28·5	30·8	—
1831	52·3	49·5	30·5	27·7	—
1832	49·1	49·2	29·2	29·2	—
1833	50·3	49·6	27·1	26·5	—
1834	49·7	49·5	27·9	27·7	—
1835	50·3	48·9	29·2	27·8	—
1836	50·1	49·5	29·1	28·5	—
1837	47·2	49·5	28·3	30·6	—
1838	46·8	49·2	24·6	26·9	—
1839	49·1	48·8	24·4	24·2	—
1840	49·1	53·9	24·6	29·4	—
1841	47·0	45·4	21·9	20·3	—
1842	49·2	51·8	21·5	24·1	—
1843	44·3	46·9	18·5	21·1	—
1844	47·9	46·1	20·1	18·3	—
1845	34·1	35·8	18·8	20·5	—
1846	26·5	26·8	18·4	18·7	—
1847	23·0	23·0	18·3	18·4	—
1848	22·3	22·7	18·0	18·4	—
1849	22·2	22·4	17·8	17·9	—
1850	19·0	19·0	17·7	17·8	—
1851	17·8	17·8	17·7	17·7	—
1852	19·2	19·2	17·7	17·7	—
1853	21·0	21·0	17·7	17·7	—
1854	24·7	26·1	17·5	19·2	—
1854(e)	(11·9)	(11·1)	(7·4)	(7·4)	—
1855(f)	38·4	31·1	17·1	16·0	—
1856	36·7	32·6	22·4	18·4	—
1857	28·7	28·9	21·0	21·2	—
1858	23·1	25·2	20·9	21·0	—
1859	26·5	34·2	20·2	27·8	—
1860	22·5	24·6	13·1	13·2	—
1861	22·0	21·6	13·1	13·2	—
1862	23·9	24·0	12·9	13·1	—
1863	10·1	10·1	—	- -	—
1864	4·2	7·6	—	2·4	—
1865	7·6	10·0	—	2·1	—
1866	8·2	10·7	—	2·6	—
1867	16·2	16·5	5·6	5·8	—
1868	3·9	3·9	—	- -	—
1869	7·4	5·4	—	- -	—
1870	7·7	10·8	—	0·1	—
1871	3·9	4·4	—	0·1	—
1872	10·9	11·9	5·1	5·4	—
1873	—	0·3	—	0·3	—
1874	2·3	2·7	—	0·4	—
1875	6·4	5·0	—	0·2	—
1876	12·2	6·7	—	- -	—
1877	14·4	11·2	4·2	4·2	+ 2·2
1878	22·9	16·2	0·5	0·1	+ 3·6
1879	37·1	31·7	0·7	0·1	− 0·3
1880	35·8	34·2	- -	- -	—
1881	24·2	28·4	- -	- -	—

See p. 409 for footnotes

Public Finance 6. *continued*

(in £000,000 sterling)

Total Public Debt

	Creation		Redemption			Funded Debt(a)	
	Total(b)	for Capital Expenditure	Total	from Revenue	via Old Sinking Fund(c)	Creation	Redemption
1872	1.6	...	5.0	3.1	0.8	0.4	0.7
1873	0.3	...	6.7	3.0	3.2	0.3	3.2
1874	1.6	...	7.8	3.2	4.2	0.5	3.9
1875	1.6	...	5.2	3.6	1.2	0.6	0.8
1876	6.1	...	4.5	4.1	0.3	0.3	0.6
1877	4.4	...	4.8	4.7	—	0.9	0.3
1878	7.8	...	5.6	5.1	0.4	0.8	1.1
1879	6.2	...	5.3	5.1	—	0.7	0.6
1880	4.7	...	5.9	5.3	—	2.0	- -
1881	1.8	...	7.2	6.1	—	6.0	0.4
1882	—	...	7.5	6.4	0.9	—	—
1883	—	...	7.1	6.7	0.4	3.8	0.3
1884	—	...	9.0	6.8	0.1	—	2.6
1885	—	...	7.5	7.0	0.2	—	0.6
1886	3.7	...	1.5	1.3	—	—	0.1
1887	—	...	6.1	5.8	—	—	—
1888	—	...	6.2	5.1	0.8	—	—
1889	1.0	...	7.9	5.2	2.4	—	1.2
1890	—	...	8.3	5.3	0.8	0.5	20.3
1891	4.0	0.9	10.8	6.1	3.2	—	5.5
1892	2.4	—	8.6	6.5	1.8	0.5	0.8
1893	2.1	0.6	8.0	6.6	1.1	—	- -
1894	1.7	0.8	7.2	6.7	- -	—	0.2
1895	0.8	0.8	7.8	6.7	—	—	- -
1896	1.1	1.1	8.4	7.3	0.8	5.0	—
1897	0.7	0.7	8.2	7.4	0.4	—	- -
1898	—	—	8.2	7.7	—	—	- -
1899	3.9	3.9	9.5	7.9	1.1	—	1.1
1900	13.5	3.0	6.6	6.1	0.2	—	1.4
1901	60.1	4.9	1.8	1.6	—	—	- -
1902	66.1	6.3	5.0	1.7	—	56.6	- -
1903	38.0	8.1	6.8	6.5	—	29.9	0.1
1904	7.3	5.3	10.9	7.5	—	—	0.7
1905	10.9	10.9	10.9	8.6	—	—	0.3
1906	5.6	5.6	13.4	10.5	1.4	—	- -
1907	5.6	5.6	15.7	11.5	3.5	—	0.6
1908	5.5	3.0	19.0	13.2	5.3	—	4.1
1909	5.1	2.6	17.0	12.1	4.1	—	1.8
1910	22.3	1.3	6.7	5.9	—	—	5.2
1911	1.0	1.0	30.9	9.1	—	—	2.3
1912	-1.9	4.5	12.3	9.4	2.4	—	5.0
1913	9.9	8.5	16.0	10.4	5.0	—	5.4
1914	7.5	4.4	11.8	10.5	0.2	—	3.9
1915	411.2	3.4	7.2	6.3	0.1	—	2.0
1916	1,354.4	2.6	192.9	5.5	—	—	—
1917	1,646.4	0.7	26.5	5.8	—	—	0.3
1918	2,144.1	0.7	165.0	5.8	—	—	—
1919	1,935.8	0.6	255.6	5.7	—	—	—
1920	921.9	4.8	571.1	9.2	—	—	—
1921	118.2	6.1	377.3	255.7	—	—	—
1922	439.8	22.0	475.8	74.7	—	—	—
1923	232.9	13.3	363.4	130.5	—	—	7.4
1924	90.4	8.5	186.2	93.0	—	—	13.6
1925	112.1	13.1	171.3	49.9	3.7	46.3	13.2
1926	109.4	14.2	157.3	54.7	—	53.7	14.4
1927	105.5	28.9	109.0	64.7	—	27.7	15.1
1928	184.1	13.5	253.6	69.3	—	41.3	23.9
1929	227.6	22.7	265.3	62.2	—	—	26.5
1930	251.2	18.3	272.2	57.9	—	—	26.0
1931	249.1	47.4	259.8	71.5	—	—	25.7
1932	195.7	49.3	176.7	37.5	—	—	25.4
1933	732.0	7.5	549.1	31.9	0.4	—	11.3
1934	227.0	6.5	76.6	22.2	—	—	- -
1935	188.6	7.5	216.0	19.8	31.1	—	0.1
1936	255.6	10.5	265.3	19.2	7.6	—	0.6
1937	209.9	13.5	208.2	19.8	2.9	—	- -
1938	284.5	17.0	47.8	17.3	—	—	—
1939	204.7	22.6	56.2	20.7	—	—	—

See p. 409 for footnotes

(in £000,000 sterling)

| | Total Unfunded | | Exchequer Bills | | Treasury Bills |
| | Unfunded Debt (a) | | | | |
	Creation	Redemption	Creation	Redemption	Net Increase (+) or Decrease (−)
1882	30·3	30·2	5·2	5·2	—
1883	26·0	26·0	11·5	11·5	—
1884	19·0	19·0	—	—	—
1885	23·4	23·4	0·1	0·1	—
1886	37·9	34·3	--	--	+ 3·3
1887	40·6	40·6	5·2	5·2	—
1888	34·1	34·9	—	--	—
1889	36·5	37·9	—	0·6	+ 1·6
1890	52·8	35·8	—	0·2	+ 4·6
1891	54·9	61·5	—	0·4	− 0·7
1892	66·2	67·3	3·6	3·9	− 2·3
1893	57·1	58·7	—	0·3	− 1·1
1894	30·1	35·0	—	--	+ 0·5
1895	27·8	28·6	—	0·1	+ 0·6
1896	9·7	20·9	—	--	− 5·9
1897	11·6	13·5	—	3·1	+ 1·6
1898	9·2	9·2	—	—	—
1899	11·4	11·4	—	—	—
1900	38·2	19·6	—	—	+ 8·0
1901	77·7	49·5	—	—	+ 5·0
1902	40·1	39·8	—	—	—
1903	50·8	50·8	—	—	—
1904	60·6	62·1	—	—	—
1905	65·7	67·8	—	—	—
1906	53·8	59·9	—	—	− 1·9
1907	35·9	49·8	—	—	− 8·5
1908	34·7	42·4	—	—	+ 1·3
1909	41·0	42·1	—	—	+ 2·5
1910	95·9	76·5	—	—	+ 17·0
1911	68·9	91·0	—	—	—
1912	35·3	42·7	—	—	− 6·4
1913	39·3	40·9	—	—	+ 1·4
1914	39·5	37·5	—	—	+ 3·5
1915	532·6	128·0	—	—	+ 64·2
1916	2,127·1	962·8	—	—	+489·7
1917	4,419·3	2,793·4	—	—	−103·1
1918	5,494·2	3,474·8	—	—	+509·7
1919	7,025·4	5,354·3	—	—	− 16·2
1920	6,042·3	5,719·3	—	—	+150·1
1921	5,676·7	5,934·0	—	—	+ 13·5
1922	5,554·6	5,603·5	—	—	−237·6
1923	4,074·7	4,204·9	—	—	−261·2
1924	3,507·6	3,594·7	—	—	− 27·7
1925	3,437·2	3,490·7	—	—	− 12·7
1926	3,318·1	3,367·5	—	—	− 10·8
1927	3,353·1	3,377·0	—	—	+ 34·3
1928	3,396·8	3,464·9	—	—	− 72·2
1929	3,499·3	3,545·5	—	—	+173·4
1930	3,936·9	3,955·0	—	—	−111·4
1931	3,592·4	3,622·6	—	—	− 19·1
1932	3,707·7	3,724·3	—	—	+ 34·6
1933	5,808·0	5,614·2	—	—	+171·5
1934	5,666·9	5,506·7	—	—	+ 23·9
1935	5,251·1	5,269·1	—	—	− 0·5
1936	5,397·5	5,408·4	—	—	− 36·2
1937	5,249·5	5,252·6	—	—	− 88·5
1938	5,947·7	5,718·8	—	—	+154·1
1939	7,651·9	7,508·3	—	—	+ 63·8

(a)   Items which did not appear in the accounts of Exchequer issues and receipts are not included—i.e. conversions are not included, nor are redemptions of debt through the income of the National Debt Commissioners derived other than from the Exchequer direct.
(b) This column contains a net figure for the floating debt. (This accounts for the minus figure in 1912.)

(c) Issues via the Old Sinking Fund were derived from revenue, but not from that of the current year. They represented the surplus of the previous year.
(d) Years ended 5th January henceforth to 1854.
(e) Quarter ended 5th April.
(f) Years ended 31st March henceforth.

Public Finance 7.   Produce of the Poor Rates and Expenditure on the Relief of the Poor—England & Wales 1748–1885

NOTES

[1] SOURCES: 1748–50, 1776, 1783–5, and 1803—*S.P.* 1818, V; 1813–69—*S.P.* 1870, LV; 1870–85—*Poor Rate Returns* in sessional papers annually.

[2] As Goschen pointed out in his Report of 1870, the usefulness of the Poor Rates Receipts series is considerably reduced by the variations in the number of rates levied under the general title 'poor rates' at different periods. Up to and including 1815, Church and By-Highway rates were probably wholly or partially included; and from 1841 onwards Borough and Police rates were definitely included.

[2] Money collected under the title 'poor rates' for Highway Boards is not included in this table.

(in £000)

	Poor Rates Receipts	Expenditure on Relief			Poor Rates Receipts	Expenditure on Relief
1748–50(a)	730	690		1848	7,817	6,181
				1849	7,674	5,793
1776(b)	1,720	1,531		1850	7,270	5,395
				1851	6,779	4,963
1783–5(c)	2,168	2,004		1852	6,552	4,898
1803	5,348	4,268		1853	6,522	4,939
				1854	6,973	5,283
1813	8,647	6,656		1855	7,864	5,890
				1856	8,201	6,004
1814	8,389	6,295		1857	8,139	5,899
1815	7,458	5,419				
1816	6,937	5,725		1858	8,189	5,879
1817	8,128	6,911		1859	8,108	5,559
1818	9,320	7,871		1860	7,716	5,455
				1861	7,922	5,779
1819	8,932	7,517		1862	8,511	6,078
1820	8,720	7,330				
1821	8,412	6,959		1863	9,175	6,527
1822	7,761	6,359		1864	9,448	6,423
1823	6,898	5,773		1865	8,841	6,265
				1866	8,995	6,440
1824	6,837	5,737		1867	9,708	6,960
1825	6,972	5,787				
1826	6,965	5,929		1868	10,440	7,498
1827	7,784	6,441		1869	10,705	7,673
1828	7,715	6,298		1870	10,921	7,644
				1871	10,962	7,887
1829	7,642	6,332		1872	11,442	8,007
1830	8,111	6,829				
1831	8,279	6,799		1873	11,487	7,692
1832	8,623	7,037		1874	11,565	7,665
1833	8,607	6,791		1875	11,682	7,488
				1876	11,270	7,336
1834	8,338	6,317		1877	11,161	7,400
1835	7,374	5,526				
1836	6,355	4,718		1878	11,615	7,689
1837	5,295	4,045		1879	11,916	7,830
1838	5,186	4,124		1880	12,043	8,015
				1881	12,410	8,102
1839	5,614	4,407		1882	13,050	8,232
1840	6,015	4,577				
1841	6,352	4,761		1883	13,225	8,353
1842	6,553	4,911		1884	13,451	8,403
1843	7,086	5,208		1885	13,659	8,492
1844	6,847	4,976				
1845	6,791	5,040				
1846	6,801	4,954				
1847	6,965	5,299				

(a) Average of the three years ended Easter. The returns were incomplete, and Rickman added estimates of the deficiencies in 1818.

(b) Years ended 25th March henceforth.
(c) Average of three years.

NOTES

[1] SOURCES: 1792–1838—*S.P.* 1839, XLIV (*Local Taxation Return*); 1839–71—*Abstract of County Treasurers' Returns*, published in sessional papers annually.

[2] In the *Local Taxation Return* of 1839 the defects of the earlier statistics are pointed out. The introduction says that 'more than one-third of the Treasurers of Counties had no means of affording information of the earliest years concerning which questions were put to them by the Committee of 1825; so that in such an abstract as is now attempted, a defect to that extent is inevitable, and has been supplied by presuming the population of each county in the several years (as nearly as it could be estimated) to represent an equal expenditure in the counties which made no return as was the actual expenditure of the counties which made return'. The percentage increase which had to be added to the returns until, in 1819, they were complete, was as follows:

	Eng-land	Wales		Eng-land	Wales		Eng-land	Wales
1792	44	33	1801	27	33	1810	25	20
1793	45	33	1802	27	43	1811	25	20
1794	45	33	1803	31	38	1812	20	20
1795	45	33	1804	27	25	1813	20	20
1796	43	33	1805	25	25	1814	20	20
1797	38	33	1806	25	25	1815	20	20
1798	33	33	1807	25	33	1816	12	11
1799	31	33	1808	25	25	1817	12	11
1800	31	33	1809	25	25	1818	12	—

[3] The financial years of the different counties did not all end at the same time. The aggregates in this table do not, therefore, represent a genuine figure for any exactly defined period.

(in £000)

	Receipts			Expenditure				
		Principal Constituents				Principal Constituents		
	Total	County and Police Rates	Treasury Grants	Total	Bridges	Gaols and Prisoners (a)	Con-stables and Vagrants	Prosecu-tions
1792	…	218	…	223	33	105	16	8
1793	…	212	…	217	41	92	12	7
1794	…	198	…	210	31	82	11	5
1795	…	217	…	225	43	68	13	7
1796	…	229	…	237	50	71	11	7
1797	…	247	…	275	45	60	11	9
1798	…	269	…	245	41	65	11	10
1799	…	289	…	267	43	76	11	12
1800	…	292	…	288	46	100	17	20
1801	…	326	…	348	52	108	21	24
1802	…	318	…	299	46	93	18	16
1803	…	286	…	273	42	90	15	16
1804	…	299	…	278	42	101	13	16
1805	…	325	…	327	58	121	14	16
1806	…	339	…	332	49	117	14	18
1807	…	367	…	339	52	118	14	17
1808	…	350	…	363	61	126	15	18
1809	…	393	…	411	77	145	15	21
1810	…	436	…	436	89	169	14	22
1811	…	497	…	474	97	168	15	21
1812	…	502	…	500	112	174	18	28
1813	…	548	…	547	122	169	22	33
1814	…	574	…	525	130	194	23	29
1815	…	542	…	573	151	214	30	38
1816	…	558	…	559	114	216	32	44

See p. 413 for footnotes

(in £000)

	Receipts			Expenditure					
		Principal Constituents				Principal Constituents			
	Total	County and Police Rates	Treasury Grants	Total	Bridges	Gaols and Prisoners (a)	Con- stables and Vagrants	Prosecu- tions	Lunacy (b)
1817	...	567	...	590	95	276	45	55	...
1818	...	646	...	658	92	296	53	75	...
1819	...	658	...	664	86	292	57	89	...
1820	...	699	...	679	85	265	61	94	...
1821	...	672	...	653	61	281	59	104	...
1822	...	615	...	595	69	265	27	82	...
1823	...	577	...	579	62	252	19	80	...
1824	...	569	...	599	77	294	16	91	...
1825	...	673	...	664	102	314	17	91	...
1826	...	736	...	743	97	353	22	106	...
1827	...	732	...	762	90	344	27	134	...
1828	...	723	...	721	88	314	27	121	...
1829	...	691	...	714	78	312	30	132	...
1830	...	708	...	727	76	315	33	135	...
1831	...	755	...	773	84	323	42	149	...
1832	...	762	...	799	75	321	43	148	...
1833	...	759	...	745	77	267	36	145	...
1834	...	724	...	692	72	223	28	148	...
1835	...	671	...	649	54	221	23	129	...
1836	...	705	...	639	55	190	22	133	...
1837	...	638	...	652	55	199	22	138	...
1838	...	684	...	700	46	211	25	150	...
1839(c)	...	623	90	737	...	...	...	...	...
						Rural Police			
1840	961	716	101	881	62	290	76	169	9
1841	1,078	832	96	999	64	289	137	174	10
1842	1,078	829	115	1,051	64	317	147	204	11
1843	1,233	886	112	1,111	57	327	160	209	20
1844	1,209	868	102	1,080	59	343	169	187	22
1845	1,213	860	96	1,084	53	335	179	170	23
1846	1,240	835	87	1,093	56	338	188	166	11
1847	1,325	877	148	1,177	57	349	195	179	12
1848	1,585	893	291	1,407	67	430	229	211	15
1849	1,542	865	290	1,382	64	419	226	204	29

See p. 413 for footnotes

(in £000)

	Receipts			Expenditure							
		Principal Constituents				Principal Constituents					
	Total	County and Police Rates	Treasury Grants	Total	Bridges	Gaols and Prisoners (a)	Rural Police	Prosecu-tions	Lunacy (b)	Interest on Debt	Re-payment of Debt
1850	1,574	796	396	1,380	54	381	223	182	185	...	...
1851	1,489	800	275	1,356	59	337	208	190	165	67	...
1852	1,409	810	274	1,252	52	309	219	178	80	109	...
1853	1,479	886	295	1,288	50	333	230	175	94	119	...
1854	1,550	884	298	1,396	58	366	253	185	100	95	...
1855	1,673	992	315	1,483	60	386	258	179	103	104	...
1856	1,701	1,010	292	1,485	56	379	301	142	128	127	...
1857	1,935	1,157	302	1,716	48	378	424	145	191	86	209
1858	2,047	1,222	301	1,841	52	377	563	127	181	94	93
1859	2,038	1,163	291	1,829	48	339	564	105	190	111	93
1860	2,037	1,223	347	1,801	51	336	579	103	175	114	110
1861	2,049	1,234	295	1,860	53	348	590	113	165	109	115
1862	2,044	1,322	294	1,830	55	360	573	131	144	115	121
1863	2,212	1,324	394	1,906	53	372	618	132	160	96	144
1864	2,249	1,305	389	1,959	49	389	620	127	196	115	141
1865	2,251	1,291	418	2,010	52	412	649	126	192	96	157
1866	2,670	1,359	434	2,416	50	447	685	123	209	121	134
1867	2,534	1,449	417	2,279	52	487	709	128	216	97	163
1868	2,545	1,501	488	2,327	53	551	745	132	246	115	169
1869	2,715	1,576	492	2,417	51	515	754	134	310	119	176
1870	2,762	1,556	526	2,412	59	494	760	122	287	121	178
1871	2,537	1,626	400	2,545	53	462	784	114	385	128	238

(a) This covers costs of maintenance of gaols and houses of correction, and of their inmates (including from 1868–71 the costs of reformatories), and the costs of conveying prisoners.
(b) This comprises the costs of maintenance of pauper lunatics, and (from 1850) the costs of lunatic asylums.
(c) Returns for the *Abstract of County Treasurers' Returns* for 1839 were incomplete in that there were none for Buckingham-shire, Lancashire, and Oxfordshire, and there was a lack of uniformity in the treatment of the various items of expenditure. The figures shown for 1839 have been computed by adding estimates for the three missing counties based on their returns for 1840, namely 61 for total expenditure, 55 for receipts from rates, and 11 for receipts from the Treasury.

Public Finance 9.   Receipts of Local Authorities—England & Wales 1868–1939

NOTES

[1] Sources: 1868 (Total Receipts)—*Abstract* (*1889*) (revision of the Goschen Report); 1868 (Rates)—*S.P.* 1893–4, LXXVII; 1868 (Loans)—*S.P.* 1870, LV (the Goschen Report); 1868 (Government Grants)—P. G. Craigie in the *Journal of the Statistical Society* (1877) (revision of the Goschen Report); 1871–9 (Total Receipts)—*Local Taxation Returns* in sessional papers annually; 1871–9 (Rates)—*S.P.* 1893–4,

LXXVII; 1880–1939 (except Water and Gas 1883–5)—*Abstract*; 1883–5 (Water and Gas)—*Local Taxation Returns*, annually.
[2] The financial years of the various authorities did not all end on the same date, though the majority ended on the 25th or the 31st March. The figures are aggregates for the financial years ended in the years shown.

(in £000,000)

Principal Constituent Items

| | | | | | Receipts from Main Trading Services | | | |
	Total Receipts	Loans	Rates	Government Grants, etc.	Water	Gas	Electricity	Transport
1868	30·4	5·5	16·5	0·8	...	...	...	...
1871	30·2	...	...	...	...	...	...	...
1872	31·7	...	17·6	...	...	...	...	...
1873	32·8	...	18·1	...	...	...	...	...
1874	37·4	...	18·9	...	...	...	...	...
1875	43·6	...	19·3	...	...	...	...	...
1876	43·4	...	19·5	...	...	...	...	...
1877	48·1	...	20·1	...	...	...	...	...
1878	51·8	...	21·1	...	...	...	...	...
1879	54·4	...	21·8	...	...	...	...	...
1880(b)	53·0	13·7	22·5	2·7	3·2		...	...
1881	53·9	12·9	22·8	2·7	3·5		...	...
1882	57·5	15·0	23·9	2·9	3·6		...	...
1883	53·8	10·7	24·5	3·3	1·9	3·2	...	...
1884	51·2	7·2	24·9	3·5	2·0	3·4	...	0·1
1885	55·5	10·9	25·7	3·6	2·1	3·3	...	0·1
1886	56·0	11·0	26·2	3·8	2·1	3·3	...	0·1
1887	54·7	8·7	26·6	4·0	2·2	3·4	...	0·1
1888	55·0(c)	8·6(d)	27·2	4·3	2·3	3·5	...	0·1
1889	55·0	7·0	27·4	4·8	2·4	3·7	...	0·1
1890	57·3	7·1	27·7	6·5	2·5	3·9	...	0·1
1891	57·6	6·2	27·8	7·1	2·6	4·2	...	0·1
1892	63·3	10·0	28·5	8·0	2·7	4·3	- -	0·1
1893	67·6	12·1	30·2	8·9	2·7	4·3	- -	0·1
1894	72·6	14·3	32·2	8·8	2·8	4·5	- -	0·2
1895	75·9	15·5	33·9	9·0	2·9	4·8	0·1	0·2
1896	75·5	12·2	35·9	9·2	3·0	4·7	0·2	0·3
1897	79·9	13·3	37·5	9·6	3·2	4·9	0·3	0·3
1898	83·6	14·5	37·6	11·0	3·3	5·1	0·4	0·6
1899	91·9	19·7	38·6	11·8	3·5	5·4	0·6	0·9
1900	100·6	23·4	40·7	12·2	3·7	6·0	0·9	1·6
1901	111·9	29·9	43·0	12·7	3·9	6·9	1·3	1·9
1902	121·6	34·4	46·4	12·5	4·0	7·0	1·7	2·7
1903	129·2	35·3	50·3	12·8	4·2	7·2	1·9	3·8
1904	(133·6)(e)	(31·3)(e)	52·9	15·6	4·3	7·4	2·3	4·8
1905	180·6(f)	67·5(f)	56·0	19·5	7·5(f)	7·1	2·6	5·4
1906	141·2	24·5	58·3	19·9	7·5	7·1	2·9	5·9
1907	141·2	20·4	59·6	21·0	7·5	7·2	3·1	7·1
1908	143·7	21·4	59·6	20·6	7·6	7·6	3·4	7·9
1909	145·5	20·6	61·3	21·4	7·8	7·5	3·5	8·0

See p. 415 for footnotes

(in £000,000)

Principal Constituent Items

	Total Receipts	Loans	Rates	Government Grants, etc.	House Rents	Receipts from Main Trading Services				
						Water	Gas	Electricity	Transport	Harbours, etc.(a)
1910	171·9(g)	42·0(g)	63·3	20·9	...	8·0	7·5	3·7	8·5	...
1911	152·2	18·2	65·2	21·2	0·5	8·0	7·8	4·0	8·9	7·1
1912	157·0	17·8	66·4	22·3	0·5	8·3	8·0	4·4	9·5	7·7
1913	160·8	17·5	68·2	21·9	0·5	8·4	8·6	4·8	9·8	8·1
1914	169·3	20·0	71·3	22·6	0·6	8·7	8·7	5·4	10·3	8·4
1915	175·7	22·4	73·7	23·2	0·6	8·9	8·6	5·7	10·7	8·5
1916	168·5	9·0	75·9	23·4	0·7	9·1	10·1	6·6	11·2	9·3
1917	165·6	5·4	72·9	22·9	0·7	9·3	10·8	8·1	12·1	9·5
1918	176·6	4·1	75·4	26·3	0·8	9·5	12·4	9·5	14·1	9·7
1919	199·2	4·3	84·7	28·9	0·8	9·7	13·9	10·7	16·9	12·3
1920	282·2	24·3	105·6	48·3	0·9	10·7	17·4	13·7	20·4	16·2
1921	457·2	116·1	151·8	63·0	2·3	11·5	21·6	17·9	23·6	18·5
1922	501·8	127·4	170·9	76·7	4·4	12·6	20·3	17·7	23·6	16·2
1923	422·2	61·1	157·3	75·8	6·7	14·9	18·1	18·3	23·4	15·1
1924	396·0	46·5	143·3	78·3	8·0	15·0	17·6	19·0	22·0	13·8
1925	424·4	69·6	142·0	81·7	9·3	15·2	16·7	20·3	22·6	14·4
1926	471·4	99·2	148·6	84·6	11·7	15·8	16·7	21·5	23·5	14·2
1927	515·1	119·4	159·0	87·0	15·3	15·9	20·9	24·5	23·1	13·8
1928	544·0	128·0	166·7	90·1	20·0	16·8	18·7	26·5	25·0	14·2
1929	516·5	92·9	166·5	92·3	23·5	17·3	17·2	27·1	25·8	14·5
1929(h)	516·8	92·9	166·5	89·4	18·9	17·0	17·1	26·7	25·6	13·6
1930	530·2	87·4	156·3	107·8	21·2	17·4	17·0	28·7	26·7	13·9
1931	566·1	100·0	149·9	130·2	22·9	18·1	16·8	30·6	26·7	12·9
1932	556·5	92·6	148·3	126·6	24·7	18·1	16·3	32·6	26·4	12·7
1933	537·1	80·8	146·3	120·5	26·0	18·4	16·3	34·6	25·7	11·7
1934	533·3	62·8	148·6	121·6	26·8	19·0	16·1	37·5	22·3	12·2
1935	539·6	64·8	154·8	125·0	27·5	19·3	16·0	40·6	21·6	12·3
1936	577·2	82·3	164·9(i)	132·9	22·1(i)	20·0	16·7	44·0	22·3	12·6
1937	621·1	101·1	172·8	135·6	22·5	20·6	17·2	48·6	23·1	12·9
1938	659·2	122·7	177·3	136·1	23·4	21·4	18·0	52·5	24·5	13·7
1939	692·3	129·8	191·4	140·2	24·9	21·7	17·7	56·9	25·2	13·6

(a) This covers docks, piers, and similar services.
(b) This is a very slight break resulting from the change in source.
(c) The inclusion of receipts from Pilotage and Light Dues was discontinued, resulting in a fall of about 2 per cent.
(d) From this year loans advanced out of the London County Council Consolidated Loans Fund are included. The break is very small.
(e) These figures do not include loans raised by school boards outside London and the county boroughs, the amount of which was never ascertained, but was probably a little over 1·0.
(f) These unusually large figures result from the formation of the Metropolitan Water Board.
(g) These unusually large figures result from the formation of the Port of London Authority.

(h) The first figure for 1929 is comparable with earlier and the second figure with later years. On the later basis all receipts which were designed for expenditure on capital works were excluded from the individual items and grouped separately. They were as follows (including loans):

1929	104·3	1932	109·8	1935	78·2	1938	141·6
1930	101·6	1933	95·5	1936	95·8	1939	148·4
1931	117·0	1934	86·7	1937	118·0		

No explanation can be offered for the small change in total receipts.
(i) From 1936 rates on local authority houses were excluded both as income and expenditure.

Expenditure of Local Authorities other than out of Loans 1868–1929 and Other than on Capital Works 1929–39—England & Wales

NOTES

[1] SOURCES: 1868 (Total Expenditure)—*S.P.* 1870, LV (the Goschen Report); 1868 (all other items)—P. G. Craigie in the *Journal of the Statistical Society* (1877) (revision of the Goschen Report); 1875 (Education, Poor Relief, and Lunacy) —Craigie, *loc. cit.*; 1872–1902 (all figures)—*Local Taxation Returns*, published annually in sessional papers; 1903–14 (Public Baths, Refuse Disposal, and Fire Service) and 1903–7 (Housing)—*ibid.*; all other figures—*Abstract*.

[2] The financial years of the various authorities did not always end on the same date, though the majority ended on 25th or 31st March. The figures are aggregates for the financial years ended in the years shown.

(Total Expenditure and Main Items in £000,000)

	Total Expend-iture	Educa-tion	Libraries and Museums	Poor Relief (a)	Housing	High-ways and Bridges	Public Lighting	Fire Service	Sewer-age	Refuse Disposal	Police
1868	30·2	- -	...	7·4	...	...	...	...	...	...	...
1870	27·3	...	...	...	...	...	...	...	...	...	...
1871	29·9	...	...	...	...	...	...	...	...	...	...
1872	31·2	...	...	...	...	...	...	...	...	...	...
1873	32·7	...	...	...	...	...	...	...	...	...	...
1874	36·4	...	...	...	...	...	...	...	...	...	...
1875	40·7	2·2	...	6·7	...	...	...	...	...	...	...
1876	43·3	...	...	...	...	...	...	...	...	...	...
1877	48·4	...	...	...	...	...	...	...	...	...	...
1878	49·3	...	...	...	...	...	...	...	...	...	...
1879	52·2	...	...	...	...	...	...	...	...	...	...
1880	50·3	3·3	...	7·0	...	...	...	...	...	...	3·1
1881	52·6	3·2	...	7·1	...	5·7	...	...	...	...	3·1
1882	55·5	3·4	...	7·2	...	6·1	...	...	...	...	3·2
1883(d)	43·5	2·7	...	6·8	...	6·3	...	...	0·6	...	3·3
1884	43·4	2·8	0·13	6·8	0·10	5·7	0·9	0·2	0·8	...	3·4
1885	44·1	3·2	0·14	6·8	0·11	5·6	0·9	0·2	0·9	...	3·5
1886	44·5	3·5	0·14	6·6	0·11	5·8	0·9	0·2	0·8	...	3·5
1887	45·1	3·6	0·14	6·5	0·05	5·7	0·9	0·2	1·0	...	3·8
1888	45·8	3·8	0·17	6·7	0·02	5·8	0·9	0·2	1·0	...	3·8
1889	47·1	3·9	0·18	6·6	0·02	6·1	0·9	0·2	0·9	...	3·9
1890	48·2	4·1	0·19	6·6	0·02	6·3	0·9	0·2	1·0	...	3·9
1891	50·7	4·3	0·22	6·7	0·02	6·4	1·0	0·2	1·1	...	4·1
1892	53·1	4·8	0·27	6·9	0·02	6·9	1·0	0·2	1·1	...	4·5
1893	56·2	5·4	0·29	7·2	0·04	7·4	1·0	0·3	1·2	...	4·7
1894	57·8	5·7	0·31	7·5	0·03	7·7	1·1	0·3	1·4	...	4·8
1895	59·7	6·4	0·32	7·7	0·04	7·4	1·1	0·3	1·3	...	4·6
1896	62·2	6·9	0·34	7·9	0·04	7·7	1·2	0·3	1·4	...	4·7
1897	64·7	7·5	0·37	8·0	0·03	7·9	1·2	0·3	1·4	...	4·8
1898	67·8	7·8	0·38	8·3	0·04	8·2	1·3	0·3	1·6	1·1	4·9
1899	71·2	8·2	0·39	8·6	0·05	8·7	1·3	0·4	1·7	1·4	5·0
1900	76·0	8·8	0·40	8·4	0·05	9·1	1·5	0·4	1·8	1·7	5·1
1901	82·4	9·5	0·42	8·8	0·09	9·6	1·8	0·4	1·9	1·8	5·2
1902	87·4	10·1	0·46	9·3	0·09	12·4	1·9	0·5	1·9	1·9	5·5
1903	92·9	12·9(e)	0·53(e)	10·7(e)	0·10	12·7(e)	2·0(e)	0·5	3·9(e)	2·0	5·8(e)
1904	(98·5)(f)	(15·6)(f)	0·52	11·1	0·12	13·1	2·0	0·5	4·1	2·1	6·0
1905	(107·7)(f)	(21·9)(f)	0·63	11·5	0·12	13·5	2·0	0·5	4·2	2·1	6·1
1906	111·3	23·5	0·72	11·7	0·18	13·6	2·1	0·5	4·4	2·0	6·2
1907	114·1	24·7	0·75	11·6	0·20	13·5	2·2	0·5	4·5	2·1	6·3
1908	**118·7**	25·7	0·73	12·0	0·56(e)	13·5	2·2	0·6	4·6	2·1	6·4

See p. 419 for footnotes

Public Finance 10. *continued*

(Total Expenditure and Main Items in £000,000)

Principal Constituent Items

	Public Baths, etc.	Commons, Parks, etc.	Lunacy (a)	Hospitals	Water Service	Gas Service	Electricity Service	Transport Services	Harbours, etc.(b)	Loan Charges (c)
1868	...	...	0·9	...	...	...	...	...	...	4·6
1870	...	...	...	...	...	...	...	...	...	...
1871	...	...	...	...	...	...	...	...	...	...
1872	...	...	...	...	...	...	...	...	...	...
1873	...	...	...	...	...	...	...	...	...	...
1874	...	...	...	...	...	...	...	...	...	...
1875	...	...	1·4	...	...	...	...	...	...	8·5
1876	...	...	...	...	...	...	...	...	...	...
1877	...	...	...	...	...	...	...	...	...	...
1878	...	...	...	...	...	...	...	...	...	...
1879	...	...	...	...	...	...	...	...	...	...
1880	...	...	1·4	...	...	...	...	...	0·9	...
1881	...	...	1·4	...	...	...	...	...	1·4	10·6
1882	...	...	1·5	...	...	...	...	...	3·8	14·4
1883(d)	...	...	1·3	...	0·8	2·6	...	...	1·1	10·5
1884	0·11	0·14	1·4	0·1	0·9	2·4	...	...	1·2	9·8
1885	0·12	0·15	1·5	0·1	0·8	2·4	...	- -	1·2	9·9
1886	0·12	0·22	1·5	0·1	0·8	2·4	...	- -	1·2	10·0
1887	0·12	0·17	1·4	0·1	0·8	2·5	...	- -	1·1	10·7
1888	0·12	0·19	1·5	0·1	0·9	2·5	...	- -	1·1	10·7
1889	0·13	0·21	1·5	0·2	0·9	2·6	...	- -	1·1	11·2
1890	0·14	0·23	1·5	0·2	0·9	2·8	...	- -	1·2	11·1
1891	0·16	0·27	1·6	0·2	1·0	3·3	...	- -	1·4	11·4
1892	0·17	0·33	1·7	0·2	1·0	3·5	...	- -	1·3	11·4
1893	0·21	0·35	1·8	0·3	1·0	3·5	...	0·1	1·4	11·9
1894	0·21	0·37	1·8	0·5	1·1	3·7	...	0·1	1·4	12·4
1895	0·22	0·40	1·8	0·4	1·1	3·6	...	0·1	1·4	12·7
1896	0·24	0·41	1·9	0·4	1·2	3·6	...	0·1	1·5	13·2
1897	0·25	0·44	2·0	0·4	1·2	3·8	0·2	0·2	1·6	13·8
1898	0·30	0·52	2·1	0·4	1·3	4·0	0·2	0·3	1·6	14·2
1899	0·31	0·51	2·2	0·5	1·4	4·1	0·3	0·7	1·6	14·7
1900	0·33	0·57	2·3	1·0	1·5	4·6	0·6	1·1	1·7	15·7
1901	0·37	0·58	2·5	1·0	1·6	5·7	0·8	1·4	1·9	16·9
1902	0·38	0·63	2·6	1·3	1·7	5·7	1·0	1·8	1·8	18·3
1903	0·39	1·1(e)	3·3(e)	2·0	4·6(e)	6·7(e)	1·9(e)	3·3(e)	3·3(e)	20·3
1904	0·41	1·1	3·4	1·8	4·7	6·7	2·2	4·2	3·5	21·7
1905	0·44	1·1	3·4	1·7	7·4	6·6	2·5	4·9	3·6	24·5
1906	0·48	1·2	3·5	1·7	8·5	6·5	2·7	5·4	3·7	26·7
1907	0·46	1·2	3·6	1·9	8·0	6·5	3·0	6·5	3·9	27·2
1908	0·50	1·2	3·6	2·0	8·1	7·1	3·3	7·0	4·2	28·6
1909	0·51	1·3	3·7	1·9	8·3	7·2	3·3	7·3	4·3	29·3
1910	0·50	1·4	3·8	1·9	8·4	6·9	3·5	7·4	6·8	30·8
1911	0·51	1·4	3·9	1·8	8·6	7·2	3·7	8·0	7·0	31·1
1912	0·54	1·5	4·0	1·9	8·7	7·3	4·2	8·6	7·3	33·0(g)
1913	0·56	1·5	4·2	2·0	9·0	7·8	4·7	9·2(i)	8·4	35·0

See p. 419 for footnotes

(Total Expenditure and Main Items in £000,000)

Principal Constituent Items

	Total Expenditure	Education	Libraries and Museums	Poor Relief (a)	Housing	High-ways and Bridges	Public Lighting	Fire Service	Sewerage	Refuse Disposal	Police
1909	121·9	26·8	0·70	12·3	0·55	13·9	2·2	0·6	4·7	2·1	6·6
1910	125·8	27·5	0·71	12·4	0·58	14·1	2·2	0·6	4·7	2·2	6·7
1911	129·4	28·3	0·72	12·5	0·58	14·6	2·3	0·6	4·8	2·2	6·9
1912	134·1(g)	29·7(h)	0·68	11·9	0·61	15·0	2·3	0·7	4·9	2·3	7·2
1913	140·3	30·6	0·69	12·3	0·64	15·6	2·3	0·7	5·1	2·4	7·5
1914	148·3	31·8	0·70	12·3	0·62	16·5	2·3	0·7	5·2	2·5	7·7
1915	153·3	32·8	0·68	12·9	0·9(h)	17·6(h)	2·3	0·9	5·8(h)	2·6(e)	8·2
1916	154·0	32·6	0·68	13·0	1·0	15·8	1·7	0·9(e)	8·6		8·1
1917	156·1	32·4	0·64	13·0	1·1	14·7	1·1	0·9	8·9		8·0
1918	170·0	37·2	0·69	13·7	1·0	15·1	1·1	1·0	9·6		8·6
1919	193·5	42·6	0·76	14·9	1·1	15·8	1·3	1·1	6·2	4·6	10·3
1920	265·5	56·4	1·0	19·2	1·4	26·4	2·4	1·4	7·3	6·5	17·4
1921	343·2	73·9	1·4	25·3	4·3	39·1	3·5	1·9	8·7	8·3	20·8
1922	365·0	77·8	1·5	34·8	10·2	42·1	3·7	2·0	8·9	7·9	21·3
1923	346·7	74·8	1·5	35·7	14·6	40·2(k)	3·7	1·9	8·1	6·9	18·9
1924	343·3	72·3	1·5	32·5	16·3	41·4	3·6	1·9	8·3	6·5	18·8
1925	354·9	73·9	1·6	31·4	18·1	45·8	3·7	2·0	8·7	6·6	19·1
1926	373·1	75·5	1·7	34·6	21·3	48·8	3·9	2·1	9·0	6·8	20·0
1927	402·2	76·0	1·8	43·7	26·2	49·5	3·9	2·1	9·3	6·9	21·0
1928	402·6	77·0	1·8	34·7	32·2	52·1	4·1	2·2	9·6	6·9	21·1
1929	414·7	81·7	1·9	33·4	36·6	51·4	4·2	2·2	9·8	6·9	21·4
1929(e)	405·9	81·1	1·9	33·4	32·6	47·6	4·2	2·2	9·7	6·9	21·3
1930	423·7	83·7	2·0	33·9	35·1	50·9	4·3	2·3	10·1	7·1	21·7
1931	432·7	86·6	2·2	32·0	38·0	52·4	4·5	2·4	10·5	7·2	22·2
1932	435·0	85·1	2·2	30·4	40·1	51·9	4·6	2·5	10·7	7·3	22·3
1933	430·3	82·6	2·2	32·7	41·8	46·8	4·6	2·4	11·1	7·1	21·5
1934	433·2	83·4	2·3	33·9	42·8	46·3	4·7	2·5	11·4	7·1	21·5
1935	454·8	86·9	2·5	36·2	44·4	47·5	4·9	2·6	11·6	7·2	22·3
1936	470·9	92·2	2·6	37·8	39·8	48·6	5·1	2·7	11·8	7·5	23·9
1937	484·6	95·0	2·8	37·2	40·6	50·1	5·4	2·9	12·0	7·8	24·7
1938	505·6	98·0	3·0	34·3	42·3	49·6	5·6	3·0	12·5	8·3	25·3
1939	532·8	100·4	3·2	35·3	44·9	50·4	5·8	3·1	12·7	8·5	26·1

See p. 419 for footnotes

(Total Expenditure and Main Items in £000,000)

Principal Constituent Items

	Public Baths, etc.	Commons, Parks, etc.	Lunacy (a)	Hospitals	Water Service	Gas Service	Electricity Service	Transport Services	Harbours, etc.(b)	Loan Charges (c)
1914	0·61	1·6	4·3	2·4	9·1	8·5	5·2	10·0	7·8	34·4
1915	0·88	1·7(h)	4·5(h)	2·9	9·4	8·6	5·5	10·5	8·2	35·3
1916	0·92(e)	1·6	4·8	3·8(j)	9·8	9·8	6·6	10·7	8·8	35·9
1917	0·93	1·5	5·0	3·8	10·2	10·8	8·0	11·5	8·9	36·5
1918	1·0	1·5	5·3	4·4	10·4	12·2	9·3	12·9	9·6	36·6
1919	1·1	1·7	5·7	5·4	11·3	13·8	10·7	15·6	11·0	36·5
1920	1·5	2·5	7·3	8·8	13·1	17·2	13·4	20·5	15·3	37·8
1921	2·0	3·5	9·3	13·6(j)	15·6	21·7	17·9	25·2	17·7	41·7
1922	1·8	3·9	9·5	13·6	16·4	20·8	17·4	24·4	16·4	51·5
1923	1·6	3·5	8·9	11·9	15·1	16·8	16·0	22·5	15·3	57·6
1924	1·7	3·8	9·0	11·3	15·4	16·8	17·6	21·7	14·3	59·8
1925	1·7	4·2	9·0	11·6	15·8	17·0	19·1	22·5	14·2	61·5
1926	1·7	4·4	9·4	12·2	17·0	16·7	20·4	23·7	14·2	68·8
1927	1·8	4·5	9·6	13·1	17·3	21·4	25·2	24·1	13·8	74·2
1928	1·8	4·7	9·7	13·2	17·6	17·4	24·1	25·1	15·0	83·4
1929	1·9	5·0	9·9	13·8	18·2	16·8	25·5	26·1	14·5	89·4
1929(l)	1·9	4·8	9·9	12·7	18·1	16·9	26·0	25·8	13·9	89·4
1930	2·0	5·2	10·6	11·5	19·0	16·9	28·6	26·7	13·9	93·2
1931	2·2	5·4	10·8	16·1	19·3	16·7	30·4	27·0	13·4	99·6
1932	2·2	5·5	10·8	19·3	19·3	16·3	32·2	26·9	13·2	102·1
1933	2·4	5·3	11·0	20·2	19·6	16·0	34·2	26·2	12·2	106·7
1934	2·6	5·5	11·4	21·3	20·2	16·1	36·6	22·3	12·5	117·9
1935	2·6	5·7	11·8	22·6	20·5	16·1	40·3	21·8	12·7	109·3
1936	2·7	6·0	12·5	24·4	20·9	16·4	43·3	22·2	13·0	108·6
1937	2·8	6·3	13·2	26·6	21·7	17·1	47·9	23·0	13·2	111·0
1938	3·0	6·9	14·3	30·2	22·5	17·9	52·5	24·2	14·1	114·7
1939	3·1	7·1	15·0	33·3	23·4	18·1	56·9	25·0	13·9	118·1

(a) Expenditure on the maintenance of pauper lunatics is included under *Lunacy*.
(b) This covers docks, piers, and similar services.
(c) Figures under this heading are only included in total expenditure in so far as they are not already included under some other heading.
(d) Prior to 1883 all figures include expenditure out of loans, which was not at that time separately distinguished.
(e) Loan charges attributable to these items are not included with them until these dates.
(f) These figures are incomplete, since the total amounts spent in 1904, and the amounts spent on maintenance in 1905, by school boards outside London and the county boroughs was never ascertained.
(g) There is a very slight break in these series (and a completely negligible one in most other series) as a result of the London County Council substituting actual repayments of debt for payments into their sinking fund in reckoning their loan charges.
(h) Some small, previously unascertainable portion of loan charges is included from these dates.
(i) Prior to 1914 this heading covered tramways and light railways only, but from that year expenditure on motor 'bus and trolley undertakings is included.
(j) Maternity and child welfare and other public health expenditure was included under this heading in two stages, in 1916 and 1921.
(k) From 1923 expenditure on ferries is no longer included, making a difference of a little over 1 per cent.
(l) The first figure for 1929 excludes all expenditure out of loans, and is comparable with earlier years. The second figure excludes all expenditure on capital works, but may include a small amount of current expenditure out of loans, and is comparable with later years.

Public Finance 11. Expenditure of Local Authorities out of Loans 1883–1929, and on Capital Works 1929–39—England & Wales

(in £000,000)

NOTES

[1] Sources: 1883–1903—*Local Taxation Returns*, published annually in sessional papers; 1904–39—*Abstract.*

[2] The financial years of the various authorities did not always end on the same date, though the majority ended on 25th or 31st March. The figures are aggregates of the financial years ended in the years shown.

Principal Constituent Items

	Total Expenditure	Education	Workhouses, etc.	Housing, etc.(a)	Highways and Bridges	Lunatic Asylums	Hospitals, etc.(b)	Sewerage	Water Service	Gas Service	Electricity Service	Transport Services	Harbours, etc.(c)	Commons, Parks, etc.
1883	9·4	...	0·4				...	1·1	1·2	0·4	...	...	1·1	...
1884	8·8	1·2	0·5	0·1	1·8	0·3	−	0·9	1·2	0·5	...	...	0·7	0·1
1885	9·9	1·4	0·6	−	2·6	0·3	−	1·0	1·2	0·6	...	0·1	0·8	0·1
1886	9·4	1·4	0·6	0·1	2·2	0·2	−	1·1	1·1	0·7	...	0·1	0·6	0·1
1887	8·6	1·0	0·4	0·1	1·9	0·3	0·1	1·0	1·1	0·3	...	0·1	0·7	0·2
1888	9·3	0·7	0·3	0·2	1·4	0·2	0·1	0·9	3·3	0·2	...	−	0·6	0·2
1889	7·0	0·7	0·3	0·1	0·9	0·2	0·1	0·9	1·5	0·2	...	−	0·5	0·3
1890	7·1	0·8	0·4	0·1	1·1	0·1	0·1	0·9	1·3	0·2	...	−	0·6	0·4
1891	7·2	0·8	0·3	−	1·2	0·3	0·1	1·1	1·3	0·3	−	−	0·4	0·3
1892	10·6	1·0	0·3	0·1	1·2	0·3	0·1	1·2	1·3	0·5	0·1	−	0·5	0·2
1893	10·6	1·2	0·4	0·3	1·3	0·2	0·1	1·2	1·4	0·5	0·2	0·1	0·5	0·5
1894	14·0	1·6	0·7	0·5	1·4	0·4	0·2	1·5	1·7	0·8	0·4	0·2	0·6	0·5
1895	13·4	2·0	0·8	0·8	1·4	0·3	0·2	1·8	1·8	0·6	0·7	0·1	0·6	0·3
1896	13·4	2·3	0·8	0·5	1·6	0·5	0·2	2·2	1·6	0·5	0·6	0·2	0·7	0·2
1897	13·8	2·4	0·8	0·8	1·4	0·7	0·2	1·9	1·4	0·6	1·1	0·1	0·6	0·2
1898	17·1	2·0	1·2	0·3	2·1	0·8	0·2	2·0	1·9	0·8	0·8	1·7	0·9	0·3
1899	21·5	2·0	1·4	0·5	2·3	1·0	0·3	2·1	2·6	1·3	2·1	1·6	1·5	0·3
1900	24·9	2·1	1·2	0·8	3·2	1·0	0·4	2·0	4·2	1·0	2·8	1·4	1·6	0·5
1901	27·9	2·2	1·4	0·5	4·8	1·0	0·5	2·4	2·8	1·3	3·3	2·9	1·1	0·6
1902	33·9	2·6	1·6	0·8	5·4	1·1	0·9	2·6	3·2	1·9	3·9	4·7	1·3	0·6
1903	36·1	2·5	1·8	...	6·4	1·1	0·9	2·5	4·3	1·0	4·2	4·8	1·5	0·8
1904	(30·7)(d)	(2·1)(d)	1·3	1·0	4·9	0·8	0·6	2·4	3·8	0·7	3·4	4·3	1·8	0·5
1905	(65·5)(d)	(2·4)(d)	1·1	0·7	4·4	1·0	0·7	2·9	37·6(e)	0·8	4·2	4·3	2·0	0·4
1906	25·4	2·4	1·0	0·6	3·1	0·9	0·5	2·8	3·2	0·5	2·4	3·1	1·8	0·3
1907	23·4	2·8	0·8	0·5	2·1	0·8	0·3	2·6	2·8	0·4	1·8	4·2	1·5	0·3
1908	19·4	2·6	0·5	0·3	1·9	0·6	0·1	2·0	2·7	0·5	1·5	2·8	1·5	0·3
1909	18·4	3·0	0·5	0·3	1·9	0·3	0·1	2·0	2·9	0·5	1·3	2·0	1·4	0·3
1910	40·6	2·9	0·4	0·4	1·9	0·3	0·1	2·1	2·6	0·4	1·1	2·3	23·1(f)	0·3
1911	18·2	3·2	0·4	0·2	1·8	0·3	0·1	1·9	2·7	0·4	1·2	1·4	1·9	0·3
1912	17·1	2·7	0·4	0·2	1·7	0·3	0·1	1·8	2·3	0·4	1·4	1·3	1·4	0·4

See p. 421 for footnotes

Public Finance II. *continued*

(in £000,000)

Principal Constituent Items

	Total Expenditure	Education	Workhouses, etc.	Housing, etc.(a)	Highways and Bridges	Lunatic Asylums	Hospitals, etc.(b)	Sewerage	Water Service	Gas Service	Electricity Service	Transport Services	Harbours, etc.(c)	Commons, Parks, etc.
1913	18·3	3·0	0·6	0·4	1·9	0·3	0·1	1·7	2·0	0·5	1·6	1·3	1·3	0·4
1914	21·1	2·9	0·6	0·7	3·2	0·5	0·2	1·9	2·0	0·9	1·9	1·3	1·6	0·5
1915	21·8	2·7	0·6	0·9	3·0	0·6	0·3	1·8	1·8	0·7	2·4	1·4	1·6	0·5
1916	11·6	1·3	0·3	0·6	1·2	0·4	0·3	...	1·2	0·4	1·6	0·7	1·5	0·2
1917	5·8	0·3	0·1	0·5	0·4	0·1	0·1	...	0·6	0·3	1·7	0·2	0·7	– –
1918	3·6	0·1	– –	0·1	0·2	– –	0·1	...	0·4	0·1	1·7	0·1	0·4	– –
1919	4·6	0·1	– –	0·1	0·1	– –	0·1	0·1	0·3	0·2	2·1	0·1	1·0	– –
1920	23·9	0·7	0·1	4·8	1·2	0·1	0·3	0·7	1·9	0·9	3·6	1·4	2·1	0·2
1921	94·5	1·9	0·2	52·2	3·7(g)	0·2	1·2(h)	2·3	4·0	1·9	8·4	2·8	3·6	0·5
1922	128·7	1·8	0·3	81·7	6·2	0·3	1·1	3·5	5·5	2·9	11·5	3·5	2·6	0·9
1923	71·6	0·9	0·4	29·6	9·0	0·2	0·7	4·6	5·4	2·0	9·3	2·5	1·9	1·1
1924	50·0	0·9	0·5	11·3	8·4	0·2	0·6	4·8	5·2	1·2	8·5	2·1	2·0	1·3
1925	70·3	1·4	0·7	24·0	9·9	0·4	0·9	5·0	6·7	1·4	9·7	2·6	2·4	1·4
1926	100·7	3·1	0·9	47·0	10·0	0·4	1·0	5·6	6·5	1·9	11·8	2·6	2·2	1·8
1927	117·4	4·4	1·1	65·3	9·5	0·5	1·2	4·5	5·3	2·8	12·1	2·7	2·0	1·3
1928	120·0	5·7	1·3	66·2	8·4	0·4	0·9	4·2	4·9	2·3	13·1	2·6	3·7	1·2
1929	90·5	6·0	1·2	38·1	8·0	0·3	0·9	3·9	4·6	1·5	14·4	2·4	2·4	1·2
1929(i)	102·8	6·7	1·2	42·9	11·9	0·4	1·0	4·1	4·9	1·6	14·6	2·8	3·0	1·4
1930	108·9	6·0	0·9	42·8	16·2	0·9	1·2	4·5	5·1	1·5	15·3	2·4	1·7	1·7
1931	110·9	7·8	0·8	37·4	18·9	1·1	1·7	6·5	4·9	1·7	14·3	2·6	1·5	2·2
1932	116·8	9·8	0·6	39·6	19·0	1·1	1·5	9·0	5·5	1·4	13·6	2·7	2·0	1·7
1933	84·8	5·7	1·1	28·2	10·2	1·5	1·0	8·3	4·2	1·2	10·9	1·6	1·4	0·8
1934	89·3	3·9	0·6	30·6	8·7	1·4	0·9	5·7	3·7	1·2	11·4	11·1	1·3	0·8
1935	80·7	4·3	0·8	29·3	7·2	1·2	1·2	5·5	4·0	1·2	12·7	1·8	1·0	1·4
1936	96·9	5·8	0·7	37·7	8·3	1·4	1·7	5·3	4·7	1·4	15·3	1·6	0·9	1·9
1937	116·8	7·9	1·0	44·5	9·7	1·8	2·4	5·5	5·8	1·8	17·4	2·3	1·2	2·5
1938	142·1	11·1	1·2	53·7	12·2	2·2	2·6	6·3	6·2	2·2	19·5	4·0	2·2	3·5
1939	150·8	14·8	1·5	55·2	13·5	2·3	3·6	7·5	7·2	1·8	18·3	2·9	3·0	3·0

(a) Includes town and country planning.
(b) Includes public health clinics.
(c) This covers docks, piers and similar services.
(d) These figures are incomplete, since the total spent in 1904, and the amounts spent on maintenance in 1905, by school boards outside London and the county boroughs were never ascertained.
(e) This exceptionally large sum results from the formation of the Metropolitan Water Board.

(f) This exceptionally large sum results from the formation of the Port of London Authority.
(g) From 1921 ferries were no longer included under this heading. The difference was very slight.
(h) From 1921 certain public health items were newly included under this heading. They accounted for 0·3 in 1921.
(i) The first row of figures for 1929 is comparable with earlier years, and covers all expenditure out of loans. The second row is comparable with later years, and covers all capital expenditure.

NOTES

[1] SOURCE: *Abstract*.
[2] The financial years of the various authorities did not always end on the same date, though the majority ended on 25th or 31st March. The figures are aggregates of the financial years ended in the years shown.

(in £000,000)

	Total Receipts	Loans	Rates	Government Grants, etc.	Housing Rents	Principal Trading Services			
						Water	Gas	Electricity	Transport
1880	6·1	1·1	2·6	0·6	...	...	...	...	...
1881	6·1	1·0	2·9	0·5	...	...	...	...	...
1882	6·3	1·1	3·1	0·6	...	...	...	...	...
1883	6·2	0·9	3·1	0·6	...	...	...	...	...
1884	7·3	1·7	3·3	0·6	...	...	...	...	...
1885	7·7	2·1	3·3	0·7	...	...	...	...	...
1886	8·1	2·5	3·4	0·7	...	...	...	...	...
1887	7·5	1·8	3·4	0·7	...	...	...	...	...
1888	7·6(a)	1·8	3·5	0·8	...	...	...	...	...
1889	7·5	1·5	3·5	0·8	...	...	...	...	...
1890	7·5	1·4	3·6	1·0	...	...	...	...	...
1891	8·0	1·8	3·2	1·1	...	0·5(b)	--(b)	...	...
1892	8·5	2·0	3·3(b)	1·3	...	0·5	--	...	...
1893	9·8	1·9	3·3	1·4	...	0·5	1·2	--	...
1894	10·4	2·1	3·4	1·7	...	0·5	1·2	--	--
1895	11·0	2·0	3·4	1·6	...	0·6	1·2	--	0·2
1896	11·1	1·9	3·7	1·6	...	0·6	1·2	--	0·4
1897	12·7	3·1	3·8	1·7	...	0·6	1·3	0·1	0·4
1898	12·5	2·3	3·8	1·8	...	0·7	1·4	0·1	0·4
1899	13·6	3·1	4·0	1·9	...	0·7	1·5	0·1	0·5
1900	15·2	4·1	4·2	2·0	...	0·7	1·6	0·2	0·5
1901	16·5	4·7	4·5	2·0	...	0·7	1·8	0·2	0·6
1902	16·8	4·1	4·9	2·1	...	0·8	1·8	0·3	0·8
1903	16·7	3·5	5·0	2·1	...	0·8	1·8	0·3	0·8
1904	18·2	4·4	5·3	2·3	...	0·9	1·7	0·4	0·9
1905	17·9	3·6	5·5	2·4	...	0·9	1·7	0·4	1·0
1906	18·0	3·3	5·7	2·4	...	1·0	1·8	0·5	1·1
1907	18·4	3·1	5·9	2·6	0·1	1·0	1·8	0·5	1·2
1908	19·5	3·7	6·1	2·6	0·1	1·0	2·1	0·6	1·2
1909	18·5	2·5	6·4	2·6	0·1	1·0	1·9	0·6	1·2
1910	18·8	2·2	6·6	2·8	0·1	1·0	2·0	0·6	1·3
1911	19·5	2·2	6·8	2·9	0·1	1·1	2·0	0·6	1·3
1912	20·0	2·4	7·0	3·0	0·1	1·1	2·1	0·7	1·4
1913	20·7	2·2	7·4	2·9	0·1	1·1	2·3	0·7	1·4
1914	22·3	3·0	7·7	3·0	0·1	1·2	2·4	0·8	1·5
1915	23·1	3·3	8·2	3·1	0·1	1·2	2·4	0·8	1·5
1916	22·2	1·5	8·2	3·0	0·1	1·3	3·0	1·0	1·6
1917	22·4	1·2	8·1	3·2	0·1	1·3	3·1	1·1	1·7
1918	24·3	1·1	8·5	3·5	0·1	1·3	3·5	1·4	1·9
1919	27·1	1·3	9·3	3·9	0·2	1·4	4·1	1·6	2·1
1920	40·6	4·0	13·0	8·0	0·2	1·6	4·8	1·9	2·8
1921	55·0	9·8	18·1	8·3	0·2	1·9	6·0	2·6	3·7
1922	67·0	19·2	18·4	11·0	0·3	2·0	5·5	2·4	3·7
1923	55·6	10·2	17·3	10·3	0·6	2·0	5·1	2·2	3·6
1924	54·5	7·7	17·7	10·9	0·8	2·0	5·1	2·3	3·6
1925	57·5	9·4	18·1	11·4	0·9	2·0	4·7	2·5	3·8
1926	60·9	11·6	18·6	12·1	1·0	2·0	4·6	2·5	3·8
1927	66·4	12·3	20·5	12·8	1·3	2·1	5·6	3·0	3·9
1928	71·0	14·3	21·7	13·4	1·7	2·2	5·4	3·0	4·0
1929	68·1	11·5	21·9	13·3	2·0	2·2	4·7	3·2	4·1
1930	67·8	10·5	19·4	16·1	2·4	2·1	4·6	3·3	4·4
1931	70·3	10·9	19·6(c)	19·7	2·6	0·8(c)	4·4	3·1	4·5
1932	69·3	11·8	18·1	19·7	2·8	0·7	4·2	3·0	4·5
1933	68·4	10·8	18·6	18·8	3·0	0·7	4·2	3·1	4·4
1934	69·8	10·3	19·6	18·3	3·2	0·8	4·2	3·2	4·4
1935	70·1	9·3	20·1	18·9	3·6	0·8	4·2	3·6	4·7
1936	75·0	11·3	20·5	21·0	3·6	0·8	4·2	3·6	4·7
1937	81·2	15·4	21·6	21·3	3·8	0·9	4·5	4·1	4·9
1938	84·4	17·0	21·8	21·4	4·1	0·9	4·7	4·3	5·1
1939	89·0	19·0	22·4	22·0	4·4	0·9	4·6	4·6	5·4

[a] Prior to 1888 receipts from Pilotage and Light Dues are included under this heading. Since these were not recorded separately for the different parts of the United Kingdom it is impossible to indicate the extent of the difference made by their exclusion, but it cannot have been large.

(b) Prior to 1891 receipts from water and gas services were included under the heading *Rates*.
(c) From 1931 water rates, which formed the bulk of the receipts of water services, were included with *Rates* generally.

Public Finance 13. Expenditure of Local Authorities other than out of Loans—

Scotland 1893–1939

NOTES

[1] SOURCE: *Abstract*.
[2] The financial years of the various authorities did not always end on the same date, though the majority ended on 25th or 31st March. The figures are aggregates of the financial years ended in the years shown.

(in £000)

	Total Expenditure	Education	Libraries and Museums	Highways and Bridges	Public Lighting	Police	Sewerage	Refuse Disposal	Commons, Parks, etc.	Lunacy (a)
									Principal Constituent Items	
1893(c)	8,976	1,575	16	674	...	438	...	...	45	101
1894	8,070	1,373	4	663	140	455	...	...	45	11
1895	9,175	1,459	15	669	152	469	...	...	50	18
1896	9,315	1,821(d)	18(d)	760(d)	166(d)	504(d)	158	...	82(d)	87(d)
1897	9,495	1,912	21	784	173	493	152	...	96	77
1898	10,188	1,965	26	855	180	513	158	...	116	77
1899	10,521	2,033	21	821	195	513	166	...	116	87
1900	11,103	2,140	28	865	215	532	182	...	131	104
1901	12,072	2,290	38	894	248	547	188	...	143	113
1902	12,472	2,371	42	959	265	568	199	...	135	113
1903	13,029	2,562	38	991	275	604	223	...	141	125
1904	13,579	2,686	42	1,030	278	620	259	...	145	152
1905	13,972	2,825	47	1,055	299	634	288	...	159	155
1906	14,491	2,921	53	1,069	315	636	298	...	160	162
1907	15,062	3,026	64	1,097	323	652	322	444	168	173
1908	15,758	3,186	70	1,121	342	663	335	455	175	190
1909	16,093	3,351	67	1,179	336	670	355	464	243	168
1910	16,457	3,653	66	1,194	332	677	371	462	183	162
1911	16,872	3,773	70	1,243	325	681	402	458	189	169
1912	17,413	3,910	74	1,305	320	707	405	483	204	163
1913	18,310	4,042	77	1,347	316	717	435	509	238	160
1914	19,054	4,156	82	1,413	311	755	469	535	222	157
1915	19,536	4,244	85	1,484	293	790	481	571	232	448(a)
1916	20,333	4,270	86	1,368	230	773	499	584	217	512
1917	21,042	4,360	86	1,289	162	787	517	614	216	546
1918	22,958	4,879	94	1,362	195	848	518	696	216	543
1919	26,561	5,736	101	1,542	284	1,125	558	821	230	602
1920	36,666	9,483	119	2,600	517	1,920	626	1,062	333	772
1921	45,226	11,272	150	3,468	630	2,104	690	1,331	436	899
1922	47,274	11,488	169	3,942	634	2,329	666	1,266	540	787
1923	45,356	10,577	177	4,214	658	2,091	651	1,123	511	739
1924	46,698	10,550	187	4,691	652	2,131	680	1,124	587	763
1925	48,481	10,954	188	5,342	652	2,195	694	1,115	642	783
1926	50,219	11,356	200	5,711	671	2,299	709	1,158	676	781
1927	56,199	11,921	209	5,943	727	2,416	761	1,152	706	821
1928	53,994	11,932	208	6,072	770	2,351	758	1,176	690	825
1929	54,682	12,135	214	5,907	757	2,379	787	1,190	706	798
1930	56,811	12,566	225	6,282	774	2,403	791	1,214	716	938
1931	57,278	12,947	226	6,619	821	2,449	823	1,242	756	1,309(a)
1932	57,963	12,435	234	7,169	832	2,420	864	1,226	757	1,255
1933	56,505	12,065	225	5,966	797	2,340	863	1,184	708	1,238
1934	57,661	12,024	231	5,494	787	2,349	909	1,201	742	1,208
1935	59,956	12,625	237	5,302	818	2,458	918	1,216	747	1,232
1936	62,610	13,188	245	5,285	853	2,582	957	1,261	783	1,267
1937	64,829	13,566	254	5,559	892	2,625	1,088	1,334	833	1,362
1938	66,309	13,888	258	6,063	970	2,709	1,139	1,396	871	1,490
1939	68,994	14,139	264	6,330	1,003	2,757	1,229	1,423	893	1,553

See p. 424 for footnotes

(in £000)

Principal Constituent Items

	Hospitals, Clinics, etc.	Housing	Poor Relief (a)	Water Service	Gas Service	Electricity Services	Transport Services	Harbours, etc.	Loan Charges (b)
1893(c)	113	...	938	...	...	...	...	721	1,631
1894	...	...	936	...	934	15	...	400	1,790
1895	...	...	970	...	1,057	23	193	430	2,269
1896	132	...	1,027(d)	659	1,254(d)	40(d)	300(d)	894(d)	2,123
1897	148	...	1,069	629	1,253	58	352	883	2,129
1898	163	...	1,100	664	1,302	85	397	939	2,184
1899	185	...	1,105	685	1,423	108	479	950	2,211
1900	205	...	1,109	726	1,619	165	534	925	2,338
1901	241	...	1,155	763	1,897	220	603	963	2,552
1902	264	...	1,184	823	1,759	288	748	961	2,801
1903	244	...	1,234	834	1,751	333	806	1,067	3,046
1904	277	...	1,301	883	1,769	364	864	1,057	3,324
1905	293	...	1,392	928	1,718	410	874	1,031	3,403
1906	278	...	1,406	969	1,750	460	1,070	1,069	3,626
1907	291	138	1,422	987	1,830	516	1,151	1,161	3,852
1908	318	137	1,471	1,036	2,055	562	1,183	1,129	3,898
1909	336	138	1,512	1,047	1,920	564	1,169	1,176	4,046
1910	367	140	1,552	1,047	1,940	570	1,198	1,173	4,178
1911	381	141	1,555	1,073	1,983	617	1,244	1,179	4,160
1912	383	136	1,546	1,108	2,025	658	1,316	1,230	4,251
1913	400	144	1,576	1,148	2,265	716	1,375	1,335	4,367
1914	432	148	1,598	1,191	2,467	775	1,456	1,308	4,506
1915	550(e)	153	1,388(a)	1,243	2,409	781	1,502	1,327	4,421
1916	598	168	1,412	1,245	2,883	1,003	1,577	1,327	4,592
1917	634	192	1,497	1,283	3,141	1,102	1,573	1,323	4,839
1918	687	193	1,538	1,366	3,564	1,446	1,687	1,357	4,636
1919	778	210	1,668	1,472	4,112	1,619	2,054	1,576	4,686
1920	961	269	2,075	1,671	4,672	1,922	2,931	1,961	4,983
1921	1,251	487	2,797	1,906	6,207	2,573	3,572	2,086	5,446
1922	1,259	979	3,775	1,967	5,972	2,367	3,524	1,989	6,289
1923	1,158	1,610	4,516	1,949	4,463	2,172	3,584	2,034	7,404
1924	1,165	1,919	4,370	2,030	4,839	2,362	3,542	1,915	7,698
1925	1,149	2,120	3,965	2,063	4,910	2,518	3,924	2,065	8,097
1926	1,148	2,436	4,352	2,120	4,750	2,526	3,964	1,902	8,588
1927	1,226	2,871	5,621	2,250	6,793	3,108	3,994	1,913	9,295
1928	1,211	3,536	4,888	2,240	4,559	2,847	4,035	2,043	10,012
1929	1,230	4,133	4,565	2,254	4,386	3,146	4,221	2,056	10,853
1930	1,252	4,669	4,672	2,241	4,468	3,299	4,442	1,967	11,404
1931	1,286	5,047	3,868(a)	2,253	4,422	3,119	4,468	1,794	11,848
1932	1,301	5,258	4,317	2,243	4,352	3,040	4,452	1,837	12,242
1933	1,341	5,475	5,080	2,270	4,072	3,106	4,357	1,699	12,599
1934	1,352	6,014	5,919	2,273	4,093	3,179	4,375	1,717	12,907
1935	1,382	6,142	6,896	2,298	4,119	3,466	4,428	1,747	(11,875)(b)
1936	1,408	6,409	7,378	2,322	4,471	3,615	4,632	1,807	12,223
1937	1,440	6,841	7,128	2,416	4,436	4,055	4,829	1,834	12,422
1938	1,561	7,245	5,653	2,438	4,738	4,354	5,060	1,960	12,575
1939	1,960	7,887	5,394	2,479	4,819	4,596	5,447	1,909	13,345

(a) Prior to 1914 the whole cost of pauper lunatics was met out of poor relief. From 1914–30 the cost was halved between *Poor Relief* and *Lunacy*, whilst from 1931 the whole cost came under the latter heading.

(b) Figures under this heading are only included in total expenditure in so far as they are not already included under some other heading. They include small amounts which were paid out of the receipts from new loans, and are therefore also included under the appropriate item in table 14, except in the year 1935, which is therefore placed in brackets.

(c) The figures for 1893 include expenditure out of loans, which cannot be separately distinguished.

(d) Loan charges attributable to the various items are not included with those items until 1896.

(e) From 1915 the cost of tuberculosis treatment was included under this heading. In 1915 it amounted to 180.

Public Finance 14. Expenditure of Local Authorities out of Loans—Scotland 1894–1939

NOTES
[1] SOURCE: *Abstract*.
[2] The financial years of the various authorities did not always end on the same date, though the majority ended on 25th or 31st March. The figures are aggregates of the financial years ended in the year shown.

(in £000)

Financial Year Ended in	Total Expenditure	Principal Constituent Items												
		Education	Highways and Bridges	Sewerage	Commons, Parks, etc.	Lunatic Asylums (a)	Hospitals, Clinics, etc.	Housing	Work-houses, etc.(a)	Water Service	Gas Service	Electricity Service	Transport Services	Harbours, etc.(b)
1894	2,141	294	102	...	100	123	...	...	14	...	98	66	233	254
1895	2,318	323	129	...	73	118	...	...	21	...	95	125	389	194
1896	2,055	355	145	98	87	113	129	...	16	385	57	68	14	301
1897	2,780	356	182	126	114	127	118	...	24	368	273	125	178	291
1898	2,568	283	119	127	81	110	77	...	19	394	124	132	348	375
1899	3,069	275	119	132	58	102	124	...	14	454	270	341	329	366
1900	3,740	347	131	170	25	102	137	...	33	479	276	594	528	394
1901	4,491	376	98	183	155	86	169	...	41	469	383	510	1,100	302
1902	4,187	436	138	282	32	91	138	...	86	505	540	492	469	314
1903	4,092	394	163	501	25	153	149	...	250	563	508	409	222	190
1904	4,467	456	191	403	69	338	117	...	284	1,072	409	309	142	161
1905	3,729	432	166	272	57	132	124	...	184	588	363	381	189	311
1906	3,504	390	180	282	47	166	95	...	162	488	271	288	142	567
1907	3,308	409	126	321	49	138	95	38	114	367	225	338	170	430
1908	3,498	424	130	361	27	110	61	27	61	410	148	274	875(c)	304
1909	2,821	484	143	324	56	67	56	18	47	403	91	314	236	325
1910	2,426	445	156	349	47	46	55	9	25	375	80	184	143	262
1911	2,248	491	120	188	30	47	52	36	13	356	96	129	107	194
1912	2,352	477	131	116	50	43	42	7	19	456	250	142	40	328
1913	2,250	424	123	106	50	44	42	17	47	432	117	236	109	199
1914	2,997	472	212	139	49	65	90	67	40	294	295	347	102	338
1915	3,326	397	171	117	58	107	167	83	16	358	534	341	121	299
1916	1,855	223	105	58	15	53	142	114	2	242	170	243	107	128
1917	1,297	89	26	19	10	19	109	85	1	189	104	364	16	145
1918	1,064	50	31	14	4	2	96	32	—	157	65	404	4	50
1919	1,506	54	66	19	38	3	64	27	3	213	59	722	8	56
1920	4,425	118	178	43	75	44	127	795	1	396	402	1,406	307	212
1921	10,762	390	397	196	106	26	140	3,929	14	688	1,530	2,207	348	300
1922	16,656	421	811	300	187	24	299	8,928	6	918	1,392	1,735	764	288
1923	13,034	269	787	271	256	33	114	6,001	5	972	653	1,740	1,178	204
1924	8,897	267	979	211	250	25	78	2,785	12	833	412	1,001	1,149	297
1925	10,021	345	959	284	256	44	79	3,785	15	943	455	1,106	727	416
1926	11,791	498	1,116	341	158	112	172	5,227	15	869	484	1,183	365	577
1927	13,296	459	995	351	205	44	193	7,537	24	611	291	1,183	194	455
1928	13,530	546	746	304	126	108	223	8,058	27	560	327	943	250	554
1929	13,145	764	796	322	76	138	231	7,545	21	488	312	974	541	366
1930	11,081	998	1,301	292	131	153(a)	178	5,195	29(a)	498	253	714	412	280
1931	11,292	1,659	1,028	589	161	149	132	4,288	2	739	273	642	651	482
1932	11,797	1,139	1,179	822	104	157	76	5,325	19	928	235	539	249	396
1933	11,455	737	738	593	34	174	79	6,311	50	716	226	511	98	234
1934	11,836	574	545	441	69	218	57	7,696	30	493	193	589	83	214
1935	11,524	661	501	312	91	324	72	7,397	63	396	223	688	222	76
1936	12,193	831	449	540	190	339	132	7,068	52	526	254	796	373	90
1937	14,958	1,057	643	793	150	334	208	7,911	66	832	418	1,474	277	66
1938	18,650	1,231	798	1,051	158	161	188	10,297	118	810	383	1,658	686	68
1939	20,441	1,155	770	1,188	124	204	213	12,003	138	763	625	1,518	412	328

(a) Up to 1930 expenditure on lunatic wards of poorhouses and on parochial asylums is included under *Workhouses etc.*, but from 1931 onwards it comes under the heading *Lunatic Asylums*.

(b) This covers docks, piers, and similar services.

(c) Of this figure, 734 was expenditure incurred in previous years and met out of contingent funds, etc.

Public Finance 15. Total Government Expenditure—United Kingdom, at Intervals 1792–1955

NOTE

SOURCE: A. T. Peacock and J. Wiseman, *The Growth of Public Expenditure in the United Kingdom*, (Princeton, 1961).   The figures for 1792–1880 are based on work by J. Veverka.

(in £ million)

	Current Prices	1900 Prices		Current Prices	1900 Prices		Current Prices	1900 Prices
1792	22	17	1895	157	172	1935	1,117	643
1800	71	123	1900	281	281	1939	1,960	...
1814	39	60	1905	242	242	1940	3,905	...
1822	69	49	1910	272	264	1941	5,338	...
1831	63	48	1913	305	284	1942	5,860	...
1841	63	48	1915	958	...	1943	6,265	...
1850	66	62	1917	1,516	...	1944	6,303	...
1860	88	72	1918	2,427	...	1945	5,779	...
1870	93	74	1920	1,592	565	1950	4,539	1,195
1880	117	103	1925	1,072	525	1955	6,143	1,309
1890	131(a)	133(a)	1930	1,145	602			

(a) There is a slight break here resulting from the change in original source. Veverka's figures for 1890 are 130 and 132 respectively.

NOTES
SOURCES: 1798–1918—*S.P.* 1919, XXIII, Part I (*Report* of the Royal Commission on Income Tax), p. 131; 1919–39—*Report* of the Commissioners of Inland Revenue, in *Sessional Papers* annually.

(in £000,000)

	Net Receipt(a)	Net Produce(b)	Standard Rate in the Pound(c)	Net Produce per Penny of Standard Rate(c)
1798	0·9(d)	—	—	—
1799	3·8(d)	1·9	2/-	0·077
1800	1·2(e)	5·7	2/-	0·237
1801	4·9(f)	5·9	2/-	0·245
1802	5·9	5·3	2/-	0·221
1803	3·2		no income tax in force	
1804	0·4	4·9	1/-	0·405
1805	3·7	3·9	1/-	0·323
1806	4·5	5·0	1/3	0·336
1807	6·2	12·0	2/-	0·499
1808	10·2	11·2	2/-	0·467
1809	11·4	12·7	2/-	0·529
1810	12·4	12·8	2/-	0·535
1811	13·5	13·6	2/-	0·567
1812	13·2	13·6	2/-	0·567
1813	13·1	14·6	2/-	0·608
1814	14·3	14·9	2/-	0·620
1815	14·5	14·3	2/-	0·596
1816	14·6	14·7	2/-	0·614
1817	14·7		no income tax in force	
1843	0·6	5·4	7d	0·772
1844	5·4	5·3	7d	0·751
1845	5·3	5·2	7d	0·749
1846	5·2	5·5	7d	0·785
1847	5·5	5·6	7d	0·799
1848	5·6	5·6	7d	0·795
1849	5·5	5·5	7d	0·791
1850	5·6	5·5	7d	0·782
1851	5·5	5·5	7d	0·787
1852	5·4	5·6	7d	0·799
1853	5·7	5·7	7d	0·810
1854	5·7(g)	6·9(g)	5d or 7d(h)	1·006(g)
1855	10·9(i)	13·7	10d or 1/2(h)	1·000
1856	15·2	15·7	11½d or 1/4(h)	1·003
1857	16·1	16·0	11½d or 1/4(h)	1·024
1858	11·4	7·5	5d or 7d(h)	1·091
1859	6·6	5·5	5d	1·095
1860	9·7	9·9	6½d or 9d(h)	1·120
1861	11·0	11·1	7d or 10d(h)	1·124
1862	10·5	10·5	6d or 9d(h)	1·162

See p. 429 for footnotes

	Net Receipt(*a*)	Net Produce(*b*)	Standard Rate in the Pound(*c*)	Net Produce per Penny of Standard Rate(*c*)
1863	10·5	10·7	6d or 9d(*h*)	1·194
1864	9·1	8·5	7d	1·219
1865	8·0	7·9	6d	1·313
1866	6·3	5·5	4d	1·380
1867	5·6	5·7	4d	1·416
1868	6·2	7·1	5d	1·428
1869	8·6	8·6	6d	1·440
1870	10·1	7·4	5d	1·476
1871	6·3	6·4	4d	1·592
1872	9·3	9·9	6d	1·654
1873	7·4	7·0	4d	1·741
1874	5·6	5·6	3d	1·855
1875	4·3	3·9	2d	1·945
1876	4·0	4·0	2d	1·978
1877	5·3	5·7	3d	1·905
1878	5·8	5·7	3d	1·909
1879	8·9	9·4	5d	1·879
1880	9·2	9·2	5d	1·847
1881	10·8	11·2	6d	1·867
1882	10·0	9·6	5d	1·916
1883	12·2	12·8	6½d	1·963
1884	10·7	10·1	5d	2·017
1885	11·9	12·0	6d	2·002
1886	15·2	15·8	8d	1·980
1887	16·1	15·7	8d	1·965
1888	14·3	13·9	7d	1·993
1889	12·5	12·3	6d	2·046
1890	12·8	12·8	6d	2·142
1891	13·1	13·3	6d	2·216
1892	13·9	13·4	6d	2·238
1893	13·4	13·4	6d	2·240
1894	15·3	15·3	7d	2·191
1895	15·6	15·9	8d	1·982
1896	16·0	16·3	8d	2·033
1897	16·9	16·8	8d	2·099
1898	17·2	17·5	8d	2·188
1899	18·0	18·3	8d	2·284
1900	18·9	18·8	8d	2·354
1901	27·6	29·7	1/-	2·475
1902	35·4	35·4	1/2	2·531

See p. 429 for footnotes

	Net Receipt(a)	Net Produce(b)	Standard Rate in the Pound(c)	Net Produce per Penny of Standard Rate(c)
1903	38·7	38·0	1/3	2·536
1904	30·5	28·2	11d	2·563
1905	31·3	31·0	1/-	2·581
1906	31·3	31·6	1/-	2·633
1907	31·9	32·0	1/-	2·667
1908	31·9	32·4	1/-	2·698
1909	33·7	33·4	1/-	2·784
1910	12·8	37·7	1/2	2·691
1911	60·5	38·3	1/2	2·739
1912	41·3	39·6	1/2	2·831
1913	41·1	41·6	1/2	2·970
1914	43·9	43·5	1/2	3·109
1915	59·4	63·4	1/8	3·170
1916	112·4	118·8	3/-	3·299
1917	186·5	201·6	5/-	3·361
1918	214·9	220·1	5/-	3·668
1919	257·7	303·6	6/-	4·217
1920	317·0	336·6	6/-	4·674
1921	340·7	353·2	6/-	4·906
1922	334·9	346·0	6/-	4·805
1923	314·4(j)	291·2(j)	5/-	4·854(j)
1924	271·4	262·9	4/6	4·868
1925	275·5	273·0	4/6	5·055
1926	258·1	236·0	4/-	4·917
1927	230·1	233·7	4/-	4·868
1928	253·5	227·0	4/-	4·730
1929	237·3	235·6	4/-	4·909
1930	237·9	234·0	4/-	4·875
1931	255·3	247·2	4/6	4·578
1932	288·4	274·6	5/-	4·577
1933	250·6	249·8	5/-	4·163
1934	228·6	239·6	4/6	3·993
1935	229·2	227·6	4/6	4·215
1936	237·4	229·2	4/9	4·245
1937	257·0	260·7	4/9	4·574
1938	297·9	296·0	5/-	4·934
1939	336·1	330·8	5/6	5·013

(a) The amount of tax actually collected in a year, less refunds. The end of the financial year for this purpose varied, and changes from time to time are shown in other footnotes.
(b) The yield of the tax assessed in the year ended 5th April.
(c) In the year ended 5th April.
(d) Years ended 10th October. Net receipt is taken as equal to Exchequer receipt as there is some obscurity in the accounts of these years.

(e) Three months ended 5th January.
(f) Years ended 5th January henceforth to 1854.
(g) Income tax was levied in Ireland for the first time in 1854.
(h) The lower rate applied to income from £100 to £150 and the higher rate on income above £150 per year.
(i) Years ended 31st March henceforth.
(j) Southern Ireland was excluded from the end of the financial year in 1922.

Public Finance 17. Gross Assessments (or Gross Income Reviewed)

for Income Tax by Schedule—1815 and 1843–1939

NOTES

[1] SOURCES: Schedule A, D, and E prior to 1915 and Schedule B prior to 1897—J. C. Stamp, *British Incomes and Property* (London, P. S. King & Sons, 1916); all other figures —*Report of the Commissioners of Inland Revenue*, in sessional papers annually.

[2] For the period 1854–74 life assurance premiums were allowed to be deducted *before* gross assessment. No record was kept, and Stamp therefore added to the official figures in proportion to the life assurance deduction of 1875.

[3] Wear and tear allowances, granted in 1878, have been allowed for by Stamp in earlier years.

[4] Stamp only gives figures for Schedule B for the years following reassessment, intermediate figures changing very little.

[5] In 1866 railways, mines, canals, etc. were transferred from Schedule A to Schedule D. Figures for earlier years have been transferred here to avoid any break.

[6] For the period 1873–93 income from Metropolitan Consolidated stocks and Corporation stocks has been transferred from Schedule C to Schedule D to avoid a break in 1894. The break in 1873 is completely negligible.

(in £000,000)

	A (a)	B (b)	C (c)	D (d)	E (d)
1815(e)	58·6				
1843	86·9	22·7	27·9	71·3	9·7
1844	86·2	22·2	27·3	65·0	11·3
1845	86·2		26·3	65·1	11·1
1846	87·9		25·5	70·3	11·5
1847	88·3	22·5	25·9	70·6	11·7
1848	88·8		26·1	70·2	11·9
1849	91·4		26·4	67·1	12·3
1850	91·7	23·2	26·3	64·9	11·8
1851	91·9		26·4	65·7	11·7
1852	91·4		26·3	69·1	11·5
1853	92·0	22·5	26·8	70·0	11·7
1854(f)	105·9	------	28·3	93·0	14·4
1855(g)	106·9	25·3	27·3	91·3	15·3
1856	108·2		25·8	88·2	17·3
1857	108·7		28·3	89·2	17·7
1858	113·8		29·5	90·8	18·3
1859	114·7	26·6	29·3	90·4	19·0
1860	115·7		29·7	95·4	19·1
1861	116·7		27·5	94·7	19·7
1862	123·2		29·1	99·4	20·3
1863	124·2	27·8	30·7	103·1	21·0
1864	125·4		31·5	112·2	21·0
1865	131·8		32·0	124·1	22·1
1866	133·6	28·6	33·1	134·4	23·7
1867	136·9		33·6	173·1	23·7
1868	143·1		33·7	171·8	24·0
1869	144·9	29·6	34·8	173·1	24·1
1870	146·5		35·7	178·4	26·3
1871	152·3		38·1	189·0	26·9
1872	153·8	30·2	38·6	202·9	27·8
1873	155·6		40·3	228·9	29·5
1874	160·3		41·8	249·9	30·7
1875	162·4	30·8	42·4	266·9	32·5
1876	164·8		41·8	272·0	34·0
1877	174·2		39·6	256·9	30·0
1878	177·1	31·7	39·5	260·6	31·5
1879	180·0		39·0	257·4	32·0
1880	185·4		39·4	249·5	32·8
1881	187·6	31·7	39·2	255·4	33·2
1882	190·5		39·2	267·4	34·7
1883	191·5		39·2	279·2	36·1
1884	193·3	29·9	39·5	291·3	37·7
1885	194·4		39·8	292·5	38·3
1886	195·6		40·9	289·4	39·4
1887	196·7	28·4	42·4	285·9	40·3
1888	197·0		45·1	289·5	41·3
1889	196·6		43·7	301·7	42·8
1890	197·7	26·6	41·5	325·3	45·0
1891	199·3		40·2	351·6	47·7

See p. 431 for footnotes

((in £000,000))

	A (a)	B (b)	C (c)	D (d)	E (e)
1892	201·4		38·2	362·3	49·5
1893	202·8		38·3	360·3	51·6
1894	206·7		38·9	351·8	52·6
1895	208·1	26·3	38·6	336·7	51·0
1896	210·6	— (h)	38·6	351·7	53·3
1897	214·2	18·5	38·5	372·8	56·4
1898	216·5	18·3	38·6	396·2	59·8
1899	223·8	17·6	39·4	412·4	65·3
1900	228·4	17·6	39·4	432·5	70·1
1901	232·8	17·6	41·4	466·2	75·4
1902	238·2	17·6	44·3	487·7	79·2
1903	241·9	17·5	46·1	491·6	82·4
1904	251·8	17·5	44·9	502·4	86·1
1905	255·1	17·5	45·6	504·6	89·4
1906	258·9	17·5	46·9	508·7	93·2
1907	263·7	17·4	46·7	518·7	97·1
1908	266·8	17·4	48·2	543·7	104·0
1909	269·9	17·4	47·5	565·6	109·6
1910	272·1	17·4	49·1	558·6	113·8
1911	275·8	17·4	49·6	583·3	119·7
1912	277·3	17·5	49·5	598·7	127·2
1913	279·5	17·4	50·3	628·6	135·6
1914	282·3	17·5	51·2	670·6	145·6
1915	285·0	17·6	54·0	724·5	157·3
1916	286·2	51·5(h)	71·8	732·3	180·9
1917	287·9	51·5	95·3	792·7(i)	435·3(i)
1918	288·3	51·2	76·6	891·0	659·8
1919	288·7	98·8(h)	80·2	1,039·1	938·9
1920	290·8	99·0	90·5	1,197·4	1,293·1
1921	293·2	99·0	102·5	1,441·3	1,541·1
1922	296·7	99·0(h)	110·4	1,563·4	1,145·4
1923	311·6	51·2	144·1	1,516·6	1,058·6
1923	300·6(j)	43·7(j)	142·6(j)	1,494·5(j)	1,038·3(j)
1924	359·1	49·5	144·6	1,326·7	1,032·8
1925	362·6	49·0	151·9	1,323·5	1,083·4
1926	369·3	49·0	153·6	1,361·9	1,010·6
1927	391·3	49·0	153·4	1,377·7	945·2
1928	404·3	49·0	159·3	1,334·1	1,073·9
1929	414·3	48·5	171·5	1,400·0	1,097·1
1930	422·3	48·0	172·9	1,424·4	1,115·9
1931	431·7	48·0	178·2	1,409·9	1,093·6
1932	481·3	47·9	180·7	1,268·7	1,512·4
1933	493·8	47·9	179·5	1,126·6	1,465·5
1934	500·1	47·9	177·0	1,070·6	1,465·0
1935	509·0	47·6	176·7	1,142·4	1,514·7
1936	523·6	47·6	174·4	1,186·4	1,571·4
1937	554·4	47·3	169·1	1,281·1	1,668·0
1938	573·0	47·3	170·7	1,415·1	1,784·1
1939	586·3	47·2	172·5	1,498·7	1,853·4

(a) Schedule A reviews all property—not merely that belonging to taxpayers—except churches, etc., and property occupied (in the legal sense) by the Crown.
(b) Schedule B reviews all farm income, both liable and exempt. The figures given here are of statutory income, which before 1897 had to be deduced from the assessment statistics (*vide* Stamp, *op. cit.* p. 88).
(c) The Schedule C income given here are net figures since, in Stamp's words, the gross assessment 'is an artificial, or administrative, figure, without any statistical significance' (*op. cit.* p. 165).
(d) Schedules D and E exclude exempt incomes. Prior to 1876 this exemption was not complete, but Stamp made the necessary adjustments to the series shown here.
(e) Years ended 5th January.
(f) The income tax was applied to Ireland for the first time in 1854.

(g) Years ended 31st March.
(h) Prior to 1897 Schedule B income was assessed at one-half of the annual value of a farm in England and Wales and at one-third in Scotland and Ireland. From 1897–1915 the income was deemed to be one-third of the annual value everywhere. From 1916–18 and again from 1923 onwards the income was reckoned at the full annual value, whilst from 1919–22 it was put at twice the annual value.
(i) In 1924 weekly wage earners were transferred from Schedule D to Schedule E. They had been separately recorded from 1917, and here the transfer has been made from that date (in which their assessed income was 205·6) in order to avoid a larger break at the later date.
(j) Southern Ireland was excluded from the end of the financial year in 1922.

REFERENCES

BOOKS

S. Buxton, *Finance and Politics: An Historical Study, 1783–1885* (2 vols. London, 1888).

H. Brittain, *The British Budgetary System* (London, 1959).

M. Abramovitz and V. Eliasberg, *Growth of Public Employment in Great Britain* (Princeton, 1957).

J. E. D. Binney, *British Public Finance and Administration, 1774–1792* (Oxford, 1958).

A. K. Cairncross, *Home and Foreign Investment, 1870–1913* (Cambridge, 1953).

Selma E. Fine, *Production and Excise in England, 1643–1825* (unpublished Radcliffe College thesis).

E. L. Hargreaves, *The National Debt* (London, 1930).

Ursula K. Hicks, *The Finance of British Government, 1920–1936* (Oxford, 1938).

A. Hope-Jones, *Income Tax in the Napoleonic Wars* (Cambridge, 1939).

Lord Iddesleigh, *Twenty Years of Financial Policy* (London, 1862).

A. W. Kirkaldy (editor), *British Finance, 1914–1921* (London, 1921).

B. Mallet, *British Budgets, 1887–1913* (London, 1913).

B. Mallet and C. O. George, *British Budgets, 1913–1921* (London, 1929).

B. Mallet and C. O. George, *British Budgets, 1921–1933* (London, 1933).

E. V. Morgan, *Studies in British Financial Policy, 1914–1925* (London, 1952).

A. T. Peacock and J. Wiseman, *The Growth of Public Expenditure in the United Kingdom*, (Princeton, 1961).

H. Robinson, *The British Post Office* (Princeton, 1948).

F. Shehab, *Progressive Taxation* (Oxford, 1953).

Sir John Sinclair, *History of the Public Revenue of the British Empire* (2 vols., London, 3rd edition, 1803).

J. C. Stamp, *British Incomes and Property* (London, 1915).

J. Sykes, *A Study in English Local Authority Finance* (London, 1937).

G. J. R. S. Vine, *English Municipal Institutions: Their Growth and Development* (London, 1879).

W. R. Ward, *The English Land Tax in the Eighteenth Century* (London, 1953).

Sir Charles Whitworth, *A Collection of the Supplies and Ways and Means from the Revolution to to the Present Times* (London, 1763).

GOVERNMENT PUBLICATIONS

Report of the Select Committee on Frauds and Abuses of the Customs (1733) *P.P.* I.

Report of the Select Committee on Smuggling (1745) (*H.C.J.* xxv).

Report of the Select Committee on Frauds on the Revenue (1783) (*P.P.* xi).

Reports of the Select Committee on Finance (1797–1803) (*P.P.* xii and *P.P.* xiii).

Finance Accounts (in sessional papers annually since 1801).

Report of the Select Committee on Expenditure of County Rates (*S.P.* 1834, xiv).

Local Taxation Returns, 1748–1829 (*S.P.* 1830–1, xi).

Reports of the Royal Commission on Municipal Corporations (*S.P.* 1835, xxiii, *S.P.* 1835, xxvii, and *S.P.* 1835, xxix.

Returns of Expenditure of County Rates, 1792–1838 (*S.P.* 1839, xliv).

Abstracts of the Accounts of the County Treasurers in England and Wales (in *Sessional Papers* annually from 1841 to 1883).

Report from the Commissioners of Enquiry on Customs House Frauds (S.P. 1843, XXIX, and S.P. 1844, XXXI).

Abstracts of Receipts and Expenditure of Certain Boroughs (S.P. 1839, XLI, S.P. 1842, XXVI, and annually in sessional papers from 1844 to 1878-9).

Annual Report of the Poor Law Commissioners (in *Sessional Papers* annually from 1835 to 1847-8).

Annual Report of the Commissioners for Administering the Laws for Relief of the Poor in England (in sessional papers from 1848 to 1871).

Annual Report of the Commissioners of Inland Revenue (in *Sessional Papers* annually since 1857. Two volumes containing historical summaries—S.P. 1870, XX, and S.P. 1884-5, XXII—are especially valuable).

Annual Report of the Commissioners of Customs (in *Sessional Papers* annually from 1857 to 1909).

Annual Report of the Commissioners of Customs and Excise (in *Sessional Papers* annually since 1910).

Local Taxation Returns (in *Sessional Papers* annually from 1862).

Local Taxation Returns (Scotland) (in *Sessional Papers* annually from 1882).

Local Taxation Returns (Ireland) (in *Sessional Papers* annually from 1867-8 to 1921).

Public Income and Expenditure, 1688-1869 (S.P. 1868-9, XXXV).

Report on the Progressive Increase of Local Taxation (S.P. 1870, LV).

Report of Local Government Board Commissioners (in *Sessional Papers* annually 1872-1919).

Report of Local Government Board Commissioners (Scotland) (in *Sessional Papers* annually from 1894-5 to 1920).

Report of the Comptroller General to the National Debt Commissioners on their Proceedings from 1786 to the Present Time (S.P. 1890-1, XLVIII).

Report on Local Taxation in Scotland (S.P. 1894, LXXIV Pt. II).

History of the National Debt, 1694-1786 (S.P. 1898, LII).

Report on Local Taxation (S.P. 1893-4, LXXVII).

Report on Financial Relations between Great Britain and Ireland (S.P. 1895, XXXVI, and S.P. 1896, XXXIII).

Customs Tariff of the U.K. 1800-1897 (S.P. 1898, LXXXV).

Report of the Royal Commission on Local Taxation (S.P. 1899, XXXV, and S.P. 1899, XXXVI).

Report of the Royal Commission on Income Tax (S.P. 1919, XXIII).

Interdepartmental Committee on Social and Economic Research, *Guides to Official Sources, no. 3*: *Local Government Statistics* (1953).

ARTICLES

Marian E. A. Bowley, 'Local Authorities and Housing Subsidies since 1919', *T.M.S.S.* (1941-2) and *M.S.E.S.S.* (1941).

W. Farr, 'Statistics of the Civil Service of England', *J.S.S.* (1849).

J. Fletcher, 'Statistics of the Municipal Institutions of English Towns', *J.S.S.* (1842).

H. H. Flower, 'Municipal Finance and Municipal Enterprise', *J.R.S.S.* (1900).

G. Gibbon, 'The Expenditure and Revenue of Local Authorities', *J.R.S.S.* (1936).

H. Mann, 'Cost and Organisation of the Civil Service', *J.S.S.* (1869).

P. K. O'Brien, 'British Incomes and Property in the Early Nineteenth Century', *E.H.R.* (1959).

R. H. I. Palgrave, 'On the Local Taxation of Great Britain and Ireland', *J.S.S.* (1871).

G. H. Pownall, 'Local Taxation and Government', *T.M.S.S.* (1884-5).

F. W. Purdy, 'Statistics of the English Poor Rate before and since the Passing of the Poor Law Amendment Act', *J.S.S.* (1860).

J. Scott, 'On Local Taxation', *J.S.S.* (1871).

BANKING AND INSURANCE

TABLES

In banking, as in so many other aspects of economic life, regular statistical information begins to be available for the period immediately following the revolution of 1688, despite the fact that in this case the majority of the statistics are not of government origin. Indeed, the only official series is that of coinage at the Mint, which is carried back in Sir John Craig's, *The Mint*[1] to 1273, with gaps, however, prior to 1662. It is from the latter date that the series is shown here, and it is not continued beyond the return to the gold standard in 1821. This excerpt thus covers the period of change from a silver standard to the firm nineteenth-century attachment to gold.

The Bank of England, founded in 1694, was treated as an exclusively private body, so far as the details of its operations were concerned, for well over a century afterwards. At the time of the suspension of specie payments in 1797, in 1810 during the Bullion Committee's discussions, and again at each of the banking enquiries of the succeeding forty years, a good deal of retrospective information about the Bank's position was obtained and published. But such information about the Bank's current position was not required by law until 1833, and not in detail until 1844. As a result, the latter year marks a clear division in any table of the Bank's operations. The longest series before 1844 is that provided by the Bank's half-yearly statements in February and August, which were published back to 1778 by the Select Committee on Commercial Distress in 1847.[2] Sir John Clapham, in his *Bank of England*,[3] carried this series back to 1775 from the Bank's own records, and on the basis of a single annual statement he could push it back to 1720. These sources together provide part A of table 2, which can be filled out in more detail for various short periods from the 1790's onwards from the appendices to the reports of the Bullion Committee,[4]

---

[1] Cambridge, 1953.   [2] *S.P.* 1847–8, VIII.   [3] Cambridge, 1944.   [4] *S.P.* 1810, III.

the Committee on the Bank of England Charter,[1] the Committee on Banks of Issue,[2] and the Committee on Commercial Distress. Part B of table 2 shows the Bank's operations after 1844, according to the return required by the Bank Charter Act of that year. Apart from the column for Bankers' Deposits it is comparable (except for changes in the value of money) throughout. Gold continued to be valued at the old statutory price from 1931–9 in spite of the depreciation of sterling. After 1939 practically the whole of the Bank's gold coin and bullion was transferred to H.M. Treasury.

For the commercial banks the information is less complete. Even so recently as 1946 it was possible to say that 'information currently available about the assets and liabilities of the different banks is, even at the present, neither uniform nor comprehensive'.[3] Still more recently it has been said: 'There have in fact been only three important improvements in British monetary statistics since the war. . . . All three . . . relate to information about the assets against which deposit money is created, rather than about the liabilities which constitute the supply of deposit money itself'.[4] No-one ever seriously suggested that the private banks should publish details of their operations, except as regards note issues. But from quite early in the days of joint stock banking, there was pressure to get information from these banks. The number publishing balance sheets gradually increased, and from 1877 it was large enough for *The Economist* to use them to attempt estimates of total bank deposits. Before 1889 the coverage of these estimates was incomplete for Irish and for English and Welsh banks.[5] It was not until the 1890's, however, that the biggest banks began to publish monthly balance sheets—and even then they were not very useful, since the date to which they related varied from bank to bank, giving wide scope for window-dressing. In a recent article on bank statistics in the late nineteenth century, René P. Higonnet says that 'although it was not possible to construct a new and accurate banking series, one may rely tentatively on the estimates of *The Economist*. . . . They are by far superior to any other set of data'.[6] These estimates, reproduced in table 3, are 'to be distinguished carefully from the totals of the banking supplements' of *The Economist*—that is from the total of the banks which actually reported their figures, totals which continually rose partly because of the increasing proportion of reporting to non-reporting banks. These estimates must, however, be used with caution, particularly because, as Dr Higonnet warns, they appear to change in character over the years. In the beginning additions were made for bank notes (other than those of the Bank of England) and deductions for inter-bank deposits, whilst by the 1890's this was apparently not done.[7]

The Economist's estimates came to an end shortly before the First World War, and

---

[1] *S.P.* 1831–2, VI.   [2] *S.P.* 1840, XV, and *S.P.* 1841 (Session 1), V.

[3] T. Balogh, *Studies in Financial Organisation* (Oxford, 1949), p. 28.

[4] Harry G. Johnson, 'British Monetary Statistics', in *Economica*, Feb. 1959, p. 2.

[5] The balance sheets of all Scottish banks were included from the beginning. Cf. W. Manning Dacey, 'Banking Statistics', *J.R.S.S.* (1956). This source gives a table of deposits, investments, advances and discounts, and cash and money at call, annually for all Scottish banks for the period 1900–54, based on annual balance sheets drawn up on various dates throughout the year.

[6] 'Bank Deposits in the U.K., 1870–1914', in the *Quarterly Journal of Economics*, August 1957, p. 330.

[7] *ibid.* p. 344.

afterwards a better measure is available. For the war period and for a few years afterwards there is much useful statistical material in E. V. Morgan's, *Studies in British Financial Policy, 1914–1925*.[1] Beginning in January 1921, the London clearing banks issued joint monthly statements of the average of their position on a selected day in each week. The annual average of these statements is shown in table 4. A full discussion of the usefulness of these figures is to be found in an article by W. Manning Dacey in the *Journal of the Royal Statistical Society* (Series A, 1956), and H. G. Johnson's article, already referred to, also deals with them. Anyone handling post-1930 figures should also consult Part XII in volume 3 of the *Memoranda of Evidence to the Committee on the Working of the Monetary System*.[2] Suffice it to say here that, until January 1947, the selected day of the week for showing their position differed for all but two of the Big Five banks, and opportunity for window-dressing consequently remained fairly wide.

Whilst the commercial banks have until recently shown great reluctance to publish details of their operations, the aggregate of their clearings has been available for almost a century. The total of London clearings is broadly comparable throughout the period; but the continuity of the provincial series is seriously broken by the inclusion of new centres and by many changes of area, of which only the most important are indicated in table 5.[3]

Attention was first focused on the bank note circulation during the restriction period after 1797, and it returned there with each boom and crisis of the first half of the nineteenth century. Until 1833, however, the Bank of England was the only issuing bank about which exact information was available, even to the parliamentary committees of secrecy. Argument about the country bank issues was conducted, perforce, on the basis of the stamping statistics. These are so seriously defective that it is not surprising that much of the argument seems irrelevant or misdirected. As Dr Pressnell says: 'It is certainly unfortunate that statistics relating to private note issues are so defective, and that no alternative figures exist at present, but the hard facts have to be faced. To yield to the temptation to use faulty statistics because no others are available may lead only to faulty conclusions'.[4] Statistics of note circulation, therefore, cannot be relied on until 1833, and later ones only are shown in table 6.[5]

More detailed statistics on the circulation, and on other aspects of banking in the nineteenth century, can be found in the reports of the various committees already mentioned, and in various contemporary books. Among these, three deserve mention: J. Dun's *British Banking Statistics*,[6] Sir R. H. I. Palgrave's *Abstract of Evidence to the House of Commons Committee of 1875 on Banks of Issue*,[7] and the latter's *Bank Rate and the Money Market, 1844–1900*.[8]

It seems appropriate to include in this section some indication of the growth of small savings in the country. Table 7, showing the total deposits in savings banks each year is

[1] London, 1952.   [2] *S.P.* 1958–9, XVII.
[3] A full discussion can be found in W. Manning Dacey, *loc. cit.* pp. 204–7.
[4] L. S. Pressnell, *Country Banking in the Industrial Revolution* (Oxford, 1956), p. 189.
[5] The Bank of England circulation to 1720 is shown in table 2.   [6] London, 1876.
[7] Printed for private circulation, 1876.   [8] London, 1903.

not, of course, a complete record of such savings. But taken in conjunction with the National Savings Certificates and Defence Bonds statistics available in *Finance Accounts*, it is a fair guide.

The yield on Consols from their inception to the present day, shown in table 8, constitutes probably the longest unbroken statistical series we have, particularly since, as a ratio, it is not affected by changes in the value of money. As a measure of the long-term rate of interest it comes as close as we can get to that theoretical abstraction, which demands a loan of infinite duration without any risk of default. As Professor Hicks says: 'It can hardly be maintained that at all points of this majestic sequence the Yield on Consols does satisfy these exacting conditions'.[1] For some years before 1888 the risk of termination by conversion existed, and the risk of default must have been felt at various times—for example in 1781, 1798, 1917, or 1940. Nevertheless, no better indicator of the long-term rate of interest exists.

Short-term rates of interest are represented here by two tables. Table 9, largely reproduced from Sir John Clapham's *The Bank of England*,[2] shows that date of every change in Bank rate from the beginning of the restriction period in 1797 to 1939. Table 10 gives the average market rate of discount for first-class three months' bills, starting in 1824.

The last two tables in this section leave the banking field and show the value of insured property, as derived from the revenue of Fire Insurance duty and new capital issues in London. The former series was much used in the nineteenth century in estimating national wealth. But, as Dr Maywald points out,[3] its usefulness for this purpose 'depends mainly on the following circumstances: (*a*) the specific conditions of valuation for insurance purposes, (*b*) the insurance-mindedness of the owners of assets, and (*c*) the weight of the uninsurable assets in the total of national wealth'. Comparability over a period depends on these circumstances remaining reasonably stable, and also on stable rates of duty or the possibility of making exact allowance for changes in those rates. It seems probable that none of these conditions was fulfilled until after the Napoleonic Wars. During the long period of three shillings per cent duty, from 1815–65, it is not clear to what degree the circumstances were stable, though they must have been more so than before. The proportion of uninsurable assets (mainly land) must have fallen, and quite possibly there may have been an increase in insurance-mindedness. But any attempt at exact measurement must await a systematic investigation of the subject, and until then these statistics must be used with caution.

The statistics of new capital issues in our final table are taken from *The Economist's* annual 'Commercial History and Review' supplements, since this provides the longest available comparable series. These statistics reflect the nominal amounts of capital offered for sale, not the actual amount of capital forthcoming. There is a breakdown by type of issue in the source, which becomes progressively more detailed up to the end of the last

[1] J. R. Hicks, 'The Future of the Rate of Interest', *T.M.S.S.* (1957–8).
[2] 2 vols., Cambridge, 1944.
[3] K. Maywald, 'Fire Insurance in the Capital Coefficient in Great Britain, 1866–1952', *E.H.R.* vol. IX, No. 1 (August, 1956).

century, when statistics at more frequent intervals also become available. Going backwards from the starting point of this table, in 1870, there are figures for some years in the middle 1860's in the same source, in reprints of 'Spackman's Circular'; but those are not exactly comparable with the series in table 12.

Foreign exchange rates are continuously available from at least the beginning of the eighteenth century, but except during the wars of that century, during the restriction period from 1797–1821, and since 1914, they seem to be of limited interest except to the specialist. And during those interesting periods, monthly or even weekly quotations would be necessary for most purposes. For these reasons, and in view of space limitations, no attempt is made to list the foreign exchange rates here. The most accessible sources of foreign exchange rates are: (a) T. S. Ashton, *An Economic History of England: The Eighteenth Century*,[1] appendix table xv, for the first January quotation of the Hamburg exchange in each year of the century; (b) weekly quotations from 1718–1847 in various sessional papers of the first half of the nineteenth century;[2] (c) twice-weekly quotations in Castaing's *Course of the Exchange* from 1697–1810, followed by Wetenhall's *Stock Exchange List* from 1811–1907; (d) weekly quotations from 1844–1933, followed by daily rates until 1939 in *The Economist*; (e) weekly quotations from 1844–1918, followed by daily rates until 1939 in the *Bankers' Magazine*; and (f) weekly quotations since 1847 in the 'Periodical Returns' in each *Journal of the Statistical Society*. The post-war *Annual Abstracts of Statistics* have contained tables of foreign exchange rates, the 1946 issue taking them back to 1935.

[1] London, 1955.
[2] *S.P.* 1810–1, x; *S.P.* 1819, iii; *S.P.* 1840, iv; *S.P.* 1841 (Session 1), v, and *S.P.* 1847–8, viii.

NOTE

SOURCE: Sir John Craig, *The Mint* (Cambridge University Press, 1953), appendix 1.

(in £ thousand sterling)

	Gold	Silver			Gold	Silver
1662(a)	4·4	243·6		1711	435·7	76·8
1663	31·3	364·4		1712	133·4	5·5
1664	9·6	216·5		1713	613·8	7·2
1665	69·3	75·4		1714	1,379·6	4·9
1666	92·5	32·8		1715	1,826·5	5·1
1666(b)	42·3	34·8		1716	1,110·4	5·1
1667(c)	117·3	53·4		1717	709·6	2·9
1668(d)	222·4	122·7		1718	140·6	7·1
1669	120·7	46·4		1719	689·0	3·4
1670	117·6	132·6		1720	885·9	24·3
1671	194·1	124·2		1721	272·5	7·2
1672	86·9	274·0		1722	594·7	6·1
1673	127·2	304·9		1723	388·1	149·1
1674	87·5	41·2		1724	273·8	3·1
1675	53·9	5·8		1725	58·4	7·7
1676	242·4	314·8		1726	873·0	2·6
1677	243·0	451·7		1727	292·8	2·0
1678	130·2	24·7		1728	539·9	2·6
1679	560·1	253·0		1729	—	6·4
1680	603·8	198·1		1730	91·6	3·5
1681	312·4	92·2		1731	305·8	2·2
1682	186·5	29·6		1732	373·5	2·6
1683	376·7	229·7		1733	833·9	3·6
1684	319·2	53·7		1734	487·1	4·9
1685	564·2	94·8		1735	107·2	3·5
1686	648·3	59·8		1736	330·6	5·3
1687	421·4	250·6		1737	67·3	3·7
1688	589·4	76·2		1738	269·8	—
1689	134·9	96·6		1739	283·9	10·5
1690	51·2	2·0		1740	196·2	—
1691	57·2	3·7		1741	25·2	9·5
1692	120·2	4·2		1742	—	—
1693	54·1	2·0		1743	—	7·4
1694	64·8	9·3		1744	9·8	7·8
1695	753·1	0·2		1745	293·0	1·9
1696	145·5	2,511·9(e)		1746	474·5	136·4
1697	126·5	2,192·2(e)		1747	37·1	4·7
1698	495·1	326·6(e)		1748	338·5	—
1699	148·4	60·4		1749	710·7	—
1700	126·2	14·9		1750	558·6	—
1701	1,249·5	116·2		1751	450·7	8·1
1702	170·2	0·4		1752	572·7	0·1
1703	1·6	2·2		1753	364·9	0·1
1704	—	12·4		1754	—	0·1
1705	4·9	1·3		1755	224·7	0·1
1706	25·1	2·9		1756	493·0	0·1
1707	28·4	3·6(f)		1757	—	16·6
1708	47·2	11·6(f)		1758	651·8	62·6
1709	115·3	78·8(f)		1759	2,429·0	0·1
1710	173·6	2·5		1760	676·2	0·1

See p. 440 for footnotes

(in £ thousand sterling)

	Gold	Silver		Gold	Silver
1761	550·9	- -	1792	1,171·9	0·3
1762	553·7	3·2	1793	2,747·4	—
1763	513·0	2·6	1794	2,558·9	—
1764	883·1	- -	1795	493·4	0·3
1765	538·3	- -	1796	464·7	—
1766	820·7	0·3	1797	2,000·3	—
1767	1,271·8	—	1798	2,967·5	—
1768	844·6	—	1799	450·0	—
1769	626·6	—	1800	189·9	0·1
1770	623·8	0·1	1801	450·2	- -
1771	637·8	—	1802	437·0	0·1
1772	843·9	0·3	1803	596·4	0·1
1773	1,317·6	—	1804	718·4	0·1
1774	4,685·6	—	1805	54·7	0·2
1775	4,901·2	—	1806	405·1	—
1776	5,006·4	0·3	1807	—	0·1
1777	3,681·0	—	1808	371·7	—
1778	350·4	—	1809	298·9	0·1
1779	1,696·1	0·3	1810	316·9	0·1
1780	—	—	1811	312·3	—
1781	876·8	0·1	1812	—	0·1
1782	698·1	—	1813	519·7	0·1
1783	227·1	—	1814	—	0·2
1784	822·1	0·2	1815	—	—
1785	2,488·1	—	1816	—	1,805·3
1786	1,107·4	—	1817	4,275·3	2,436·3
1787	2,849·1	55·5	1818	2,862·4	576·3
1788	3,664·2	—	1819	3·6	1,267·3
1789	1,530·7	—	1820	949·5	847·7
1790	2,660·5	—	1821	9,520·8	433·7
1791	2,456·6	—			

(a) Year ended 29th September henceforth to 1666.
(b) 29th September to 21st December.
(c) Year ended 21st December.

(d) Calendar year henceforth.
(e) Plus Country Mints, 1696–8: 1,800·8.
(f) Plus Edinburgh, 1707–9: 320·4.

NOTES TO PART A

[1] SOURCES: 1720–77 and 1778–97 (Drawing Accounts only)—J. H. Clapham, *The Bank of England* (2 vols, Cambridge University Press, 1944), vol. I, appendix C; 1778–1844 —*S.P.* 1847–8, VIII (appendix to the Report of the Select Committee on the Commercial Distress, part II). The figures from Clapham's book are reproduced by permission of the Governor and Company of the Bank of England.

[2] There is an element of conjecture in the figures of circulation and of bullion for the years 1720–8—*vide* Clapham, *loc. cit.*

[3] The years 1720–64 are represented by accounts drawn up on 31st August, 1766–73 by accounts drawn up on the last day of February, and later years by the means of accounts drawn up on the last days of February and August.

A. 1720–1844, in £000

	Circulation	Drawing Accounts	Rest	Bullion
1720	2,480	1,568	145	1,001
1721	1,925	1,108	133	1,048
1722	2,762	1,198	166	1,246
1723	3,323	791	410	1,658
1724	3,758	1,479	537	1,918
1725	4,470	1,233	283	1,178
1726	2,966	1,703	311	1,763
1727	4,465	2,129	303	2,961
1728	4,281	2,256	281	2,444
1729	4,200	1,919	290	2,324
1730	4,416	1,888	298	2,201
1731	5,250	1,805	295	2,691
1732	4,592	2,459	280	2,537
1733	4,543	2,038	275	3,356
1734	4,573	2,825	278	3,714
1735	4,739	2,917	284	3,736
1736	5,078	2,599	291	3,968
1737	4,415	2,607	309	3,317
1738	4,609	2,549	308	2,980
1739	4,062	2,671	307	4,087
1740	4,444	2,845	308	4,801
1741	4,084	3,203	300	4,075
1742	5,011	2,732	325	3,424
1743	4,250	2,745	352	2,613
1744	4,270	2,868	370	1,732
1745	3,465	2,172	346	808
1746	3,845	1,978	308	2,335
1747	3,652	2,441	279	1,938
1748	3,790	1,683	280	2,179
1749	4,183	1,880	338	2,062
1750	4,318	1,914	358	1,959
1751	5,195	1,933	330	2,970
1752	4,750	2,135	290	2,730
1753	4,420	1,723	262	2,289
1754	4,081	1,675	310	2,829
1755	4,115	2,259	285	3,789
1756	4,516	2,815	259	4,034
1757	5,150	3,052	265	3,727
1758	4,864	2,328	295	2,241
1759	4,800	1,620	363	2,208
1760	4,936	1,913	297	2,628
1761	5,247	1,814	347	2,020
1762	5,887	2,121	484	3,053
1763	5,315	1,550	515	367
1764	6,211	1,504	512	1,873

Banking and Insurance 2. *continued*

	Circulation	Drawing Accounts	Deposits	Rest	Bullion	Securities Total	Government
1765	...	...	...	...	...	...	...
1766	5,846	1,497	...	484	1,871	...	...
1767	5,511	1,568	...	384	818	...	...
1768	5,779	1,797	...	499	1,564	...	...
1769	5,707	1,810	...	437	1,379	...	...
1770	5,237	1,820	...	614	2,873	...	...
1771	6,823	1,716	...	593	2,278	...	...
1772	5,962	1,553	...	666	1,504	...	...
1773	6,037	1,784	...	648	1,192	...	...
1774	...	...	...	...	...	...	...
1775	8,762	2,136	...	872	6,829	...	...
1776	8,626	2,108	...	859	5,141	...	...
1777	8,033	1,858	...	1,001	3,279	...	...
1778	7,099	2,182	4,689	1,206	2,570	10,424	7,219
1779	8,145	2,241	4,780	1,316	3,847	10,393	8,178
1780	7,376	2,306	5,690	1,437	3,880	10,623	7,943
1781	6,701	2,564	5,859	1,659	3,071	11,148	7,625
1782	7,394	2,520	6,445	1,857	2,057	13,639	9,667
1783	6,991	1,911	5,285	1,998	956	13,319	9,791
1784	5,898	1,970	5,086	2,186	1,098	12,072	8,113
1785	6,247	2,250	6,461	2,465	4,114	11,059	6,962
1786	7,883	2,506	6,009	2,618	6,145	10,366	7,412
1787	9,008	2,269	5,767	2,792	5,960	11,606	7,854
1788	9,782	2,399	5,353	2,904	6,321	11,717	8,337
1789	10,465	2,815	5,970	2,832	7,937	11,329	8,956
1790	10,737	2,957	6,211	2,729	8,510	11,168	9,197
1791	11,556	3,264	6,401	2,717	7,962	12,711	10,651
1792	11,157	2,564	5,525	2,718	5,913	13,487	10,327
1793	11,377	3,010	5,895	2,802	4,666	15,407	9,966
1794	10,515	2,776	6,914	2,935	6,879	13,486	9,407
1795	12,440	3,716	7,064	3,029	5,632	16,901	13,208
1796	9,988	2,522	6,179	3,246	2,331	17,083	11,914
1797	10,394	2,644	6,328	3,414	2,588	17,549	10,240
1798	12,638	...	7,225	3,399	6,188	17,075	11,086
1799	13,175	...	7,887	3,205	7,282	16,985	10,482
1800	15,946	...	7,699	3,784	5,647	21,781	13,781
1801	15,385	...	9,440	3,980	4,488	24,317	13,942
1802	16,142	...	8,299	4,118	4,022	24,537	13,864
1803	15,652	...	8,934	4,516	3,685	25,417	11,377
1804	17,116	...	9,196	4,726	4,626	26,413	14,839
1805	17,130	...	13,066	4,776	6,754	28,217	14,151
1806	19,379	...	9,809	4,946	6,101	28,032	14,491
1807	18,315	...	11,809	4,863	6,314	28,673	13,431
1808	17,650	...	12,487	5,112	6,936	28,314	14,553
1809	19,059	...	11,120	5,169	4,071	31,277	15,026
1810	22,907	...	13,037	5,579	3,347	38,176	15,761
1811	23,324	...	11,261	5,816	3,297	37,103	19,543
1812	23,218	...	11,722	6,203	3,041	38,101	21,646
1813	24,020	...	11,214	6,583	2,798	39,019	25,314
1814	26,585	...	13,653	7,082	2,151	45,168	29,306

	Circulation	Deposits	Rest	Bullion	Securities	
					Total	Government
1815	27,255	12,199	7,975	2,723	44,706	25,853
1816	26,886	12,123	7,433	6,102	40,340	22,762
1817	28,471	9,955	5,691	10,675	33,442	26,319
1818	26,987	7,963	4,898	8,209	31,638	27,085
1819	25,190	6,359	3,939	3,890	31,598	23,887
1820	23,892	4,257	3,429	6,561	25,017	20,445
1821	22,090	5,721	3,377	11,552	19,636	15,882
1822	18,065	5,545	3,600	10,578	16,632	13,073
1823	18,812	7,504	3,099	11,521	17,894	12,751
1824	19,935	9,889	2,864	12,799	19,888	14,495
1825	20,076	8,290	2,869	6,207	25,029	18,431
1826	23,516	7,068	3,024	4,607	29,001	19,144
1827	22,319	8,427	2,930	10,311	23,364	19,247
1828	21,669	9,700	2,798	10,423	23,743	20,251
1829	19,709	9,295	2,835	6,815	25,023	19,905
1830	20,758	11,192	2,596	10,161	24,385	20,475
1831	19,069	10,141	2,675	7,328	24,557	18,992
1832	18,016	9,906	2,653	6,445	24,130	18,822
1833	19,500	12,492	2,580	9,697	24,875	19,149
1834	19,046	13,575	2,639	7,529	27,730	18,624
1835	18,110	12,282	2,755	6,231	26,917	17,447
1836	18,130	13,299	2,806	6,581	27,654	15,443
1837	18,487	10,485	2,965	5,381	26,556	13,202
1838	19,266	9,825	2,833	10,036	21,888	13,576
1839	17,958	7,979	2,792	4,618	24,110	13,534
1840	16,773	7,058	2,862	4,342	22,350	14,064
1841	16,971	7,215	2,830	4,630	22,386	14,289
1842	18,543	8,661	2,844	8,103	21,944	14,220
1843	19,812	11,285	3,009	11,722	22,383	16,446
1844	21,317	12,333	3,374	15,764	21,260	14,406

NOTES TO PART B

SOURCES: The weekly returns of the Bank of England published in the *London Gazette* are the original source. The yearly averages shown here are taken from the United States National Monetary Commission's *Statistics for Great Britain, Germany and France* (Washington, 1910), and from the original source from 1910 onwards. *Bankers' Deposits for 1844–77* are taken from R. H. I. Palgrave, *Bank Rate in England, France and Germany, 1844–78* (London, 1880), and from 1920 onwards from the Bank of England's *Statistical Summary. Bankers' Deposits* for 1878–1919 (and the figure mentioned in footnote (c)) have not been previously published, and were kindly made available to us by the Bank of England.

B. 1844–1939, in £ million

(in £ million)

| | Issue Department | | Banking Department | | | | | |
| | | | Deposits | | | Securities | | |
	Circulation (a)	Bullion (b)	Total	Public	Bankers	Government	Other	Reserves of Notes
1844	20·3	13·9	13·6	5·2	1·0	14·4	9·5	7·9
1845	20·7	14·6	15·3	5·7	1·3	13·4	12·2	7·9
1846	20·3	14·2	19·2	6·3	1·6	13·1	16·7	7·9
1847	19·1	9·8	15·1	6·4	1·5	11·6	17·2	4·6
1848	18·1	13·2	15·0	5·2	2·4	12·4	12·0	9·1
1849	18·4	14·3	16·2	6·1	2·1	14·2	10·2	9·9
1850	19·4	15·9	17·6	7·8	1·7	14·3	11·0	10·5
1851	19·5	13·9	16·4	7·1	1·7	13·7	12·6	8·5
1852	21·9	20·1	18·8	6·0	3·2	13·8	11·4	12·2
1853	22·6	17·0	18·2	5·7	2·3	13·3	15·1	8·4
1854	20·7	13·3	14·7	3·6	2·7	11·6	14·7	6·6
1855	19·8	13·5	16·7	5·0	3·1	11·9	15·3	7·8
1856	19·7	10·3	16·0	4·8	3·0	11·7	17·1	5·1
1857	19·5	9·7	17·1	6·4	3·3	10·6	20·4	4·7
1858	20·2	17·1	20·0	5·9	4·6	10·4	16·3	11·2
1859	21·3	17·3	21·7	7·3	4·3	11·1	18·2	10·4
1860	21·3	14·5	20·2	6·6	4·3	9·8	20·5	7·7
1861	20·0	12·2	17·8	5·3	4·2	10·1	18·7	6·7
1862	20·8	15·5	21·7	7·1	5·0	11·2	19·0	9·3
1863	20·7	13·8	21·3	7·3	4·7	11·1	20·2	7·7
1864	20·6	12·8	20·1	6·9	4·9	11·0	20·3	6·8
1865	21·1	13·7	20·7	6·7	5·0	10·5	20·6	7·3
1866	23·2	14·0	22·1	5·3	6·3	11·0	23·0	5·8
1867	23·4	20·2	25·6	6·8	6·7	12·9	18·2	11·6
1868	23·9	19·7	25·1	4·9	6·8	14·1	17·6	10·7
1869	23·5	17·8	23·2	5·1	6·5	14·1	16·8	9·3
1870	23·3	19·9	25·7	7·6	6·6	13·2	18·6	11·6
1871	24·4	22·9	28·4	7·1	8·4	13·7	18·8	13·5
1872	25·5	21·9	28·9	8·9	7·6	13·8	21·5	11·4
1873	25·6	21·9	28·5	9·4	8·6	13·1	21·6	11·2
1874	26·3	21·6	25·1	6·3	8·3	14·2	18·5	10·3
1875	27·3	23·2	26·4	5·2	10·3	13·9	19·2	10·8
1876	27·7	27·9	30·3	6·8	11·9	15·2	17·5	15·1
1877	27·9	24·5	28·4	5·8	9·5	15·4	18·9	11·6
1878	28·1	22·9	28·8	5·6	10·8	15·6	20·4	9·9
1879	29·2	31·3	36·6	6·0	13·8	16·4	20·8	17·1
1880	26·9	26·7	33·0	6·9	11·0	16·1	19·2	14·7
1881	26·3	23·5	31·7	6·5	10·8	15·0	21·1	12·7
1882	26·0	21·0	29·5	5·7	10·7	12·9	23·0	10·8
1883	25·6	21·3	29·8	6·6	10·3	13·4	22·1	11·5

See p. 446 for footnotes

(in £ million)

	Issue Department		Banking Department					
			Deposits			Securities		
	Circulation (a)	Bullion (b)	Total	Public	Bankers	Government	Other	Reserves of Notes
1884	25·4	22·0	31·3	7·3	10·5	13·5	22·6	12·4
1885	24·7	23·0	33·5	6·2	12·8	14·7	21·2	14·1
1886	24·7	19·8	29·2	5·2	11·1	14·4	20·7	10·9
1887	24·4	20·5	29·4	5·4	11·4	14·4	19·6	12·0
1888	24·3	19·4	31·0	6·4	11·1	16·4	19·9	11·4
1889	24·4	20·5	32·5	7·2	11·7	15·8	21·6	12·3
1890	24·6	20·8	33·4	5·8	12·2	14·4	23·4	12·7
1891	25·1	23·4	38·0	6·6	15·3	10·9	29·7	14·6
1892	25·9	24·3	36·2	5·9	15·6	11·9	26·2	14·9
1893	25·9	24·6	36·0	5·7	15·2	11·5	25·6	15·2
1894	25·3	31·9	40·6	7·0	16·9	11·4	21·3	23·4
1895	25·8	36·4	48·2	7·6	17·9	14·1	22·1	27·3
1896	26·5	42·0	59·8	10·4	17·7	14·8	28·3	32·3
1897	27·2	33·2	49·8	10·0	18·1	13·9	28·9	22·8
1898	27·4	31·2	49·7	10·5	19·3	13·0	31·9	20·6
1899	27·9	30·3	49·6	10·0	21·4	13·6	32·8	19·3
1900	29·4	31·7	49·8	9·3	22·7	17·1	29·5	19·8
1901	29·6	33·8	50·4	9·7	23·3	15·7	28·8	22·0
1902	29·4	33·4	52·0	11·0	23·9	16·2	29·7	21·9
1903	28·9	32·3	50·1	8·8	24·4	16·4	28·0	21·7
1904	28·3	32·5	49·8	8·5	23·9	17·0	26·3	22·6
1905	28·8	33·9	54·1	11·8	23·4	16·7	30·1	23·5
1906	28·9	32·5	53·9	10·4	23·7	15·7	32·8	22·1
1907	28·9	33·6	53·7	9·2	25·7	15·2	32·1	23·1
1908	28·9	35·7	53·3	9·2	26·2	14·9	29·6	25·3
1909	29·2	35·9	54·3	10·5	25·7	15·5	30·1	25·2
1910	28·3	35·7	54·8	13·1	24·2	15·5	30·2	25·9
1911	28·6	37·1	55·5	13·1	24·3	14·9	30·5	26·9
1912	28·8	37·4	59·6	17·5	24·2	14·0	35·2	27·1
1913	28·7	36·2	54·9	13·4	24·6	12·7	32·3	25·9
1914	31·6	45·9	99·3	19·6	47·0	15·7	67·6	32·7
1915	33·8	58·7	189·1	85·9	48·0	36·3	126·6	43·4
1916	35·5	55·0	153·4	55·3	33·6	38·8	93·1	38·0
1917	40·2	53·2	178·7	48·7	39·1	62·5	100·5	31·5
1918	54·8	65·6	171·1	35·9	41·4	58·9	100·1	29·2
1919	78·0	84·8	144·7	24·0	52·2	56·0	81·8	24·5
1920	102·8	115·9	145·1	19·1	83·3(c)	59·8	83·0	19·1
1921	107·9	126·6	139·7	16·7	85·9	53·3	84·8	17·7
1922	102·6	126·3	134·4	16·7	80·1	51·9	76·6	21·9
1923	101·9	125·8	125·0	15·4	70·0	47·8	72·2	21·2
1924	102·7	126·4	127·1	14·2	69·9	46·3	76·1	20·8
1925	91·8	145·6	126·9	14·1	71·7	41·1	75·0	26·9
1926	84·5	148·6	123·7	16·0	68·6	39·1	73·6	27·6
1927	80·7	150·1	119·4	16·4	66·4	43·6	59·5	32·9
1928	78·8(d)	162·6	117·4	15·0	65·5	36·0	50·6	47·0

See p. 446 for footnotes

(in £ million)

| | Issue Department | | Banking Department | | | | | |
| | Circulation (a) | Bullion (b) | Deposits | | | Securities | | Reserves of Notes |
			Total	Public	Bankers	Government	Other	
1929	362·3	146·9	114·4	14·5	62·9	55·9	31·1	44·6
1930	358·6	155·1	115·9	14·8	65·5	49·8	26·7	56·5
1931	354·8	139·7	118·3	15·4	64·7	45·5	38·6	51·3
1932	359·5	130·4	131·8	16·3	81·3	64·0	39·0	45·9
1933	371·2	176·6	157·8	17·7	99·9	79·6	25·9	69·1
1934	378·5	191·5	155·6	18·6	100·3	80·9	19·0	73·0
1935	394·7	193·7	150·1	15·3	96·7	87·0	21·5	59·0
1936	431·2	227·5	151·3	16·6	96·2	88·8	26·9	52·8
1937	479·6	321·4	153·9	19·5	97·2	98·4	28·0	44·5
1938	485·6	326·4	160·7	18·2	106·2	103·2	30·6	43·9
1939	507·3	211·5(e)	161·9	21·3	102·5	107·0	31·4	40·6

(a) This does not cover notes held in the Banking Department. Notes set aside against currency notes are excluded from 1919–28.
(b) This includes gold and silver coin as well as bullion.
(c) Prior to 1920 this series covers deposits of London bankers only at the Head Office (but not the branches) of the Bank; thereafter it includes total bankers' deposits. The size of the break is indicated by the Head Office only figure for 1920, which was 73·8.
(d) In determining this figure the last eight weeks of the year have been excluded from consideration, since the Treasury's currency notes were amalgamated with the Bank of England issue in that period.
(e) This figure is for the first eight months of the year only.

NOTES TO PART A

[1] SOURCE: *The Economist* series of home banking statistics, though, following Rene P. Higonnet (*Quarterly Journal of Economics*, August 1957, p. 330), the figure shown for 1877 is that given in *The Economist* for June 1878, since the table for October 1877 has an 'inexplicably poor' coverage.
[2] All Bank of England deposits are included, though it is now possible to exclude bankers' deposits using the figures made available to us by the Bank of England, and shown in table 2.
[3] The first estimate in the series was defined as the sum of deposits in all banks, plus the notes of all banks except the Bank of England, but excluding capital, reserves, acceptances, sums held by bill brokers and interbank deposits. According to Higonnet (*loc. cit.* p. 344) there is evidence that by the 1890's the estimate is merely the sum of deposits.

A. The Economist series, 1877–1910

(in £ million)

1877	550–560	1889	630–640	1901	840–850
1878	500–510	1890	660–670	1902	860–870
1879	520–530	1891	670–690	1903	840–850
1880	490–500	1892	680–690	1904	840–850
1881	530–540	1893	670–680	1905	860–870
1882	550–570	1894	690–710	1906	880–890
1883	560–570	1895	760–770	1907	890–900
1884	560–570	1896	770–780	1908	920–930
1885	550–560	1897	780–790	1909	940–950
1886	560–570	1898	810–820	1910	970–980
1887	570–580	1899	830–840		
1888	600–610	1900	840–850		

NOTES TO PART B

[1] SOURCE: Bank of England *Statistical Summary*, November 1932, p. 12.
[2] This series covers all deposit banks in Great Britain and Ireland whose deposits were predominantly those of residents of the British Isles. Deposits (other than bankers' deposits) at the Bank of England are also included.

B. Bank of England series, 1905–31

1905	861·2	1914	1,226·9	1923	2,370·7
1906	876·9	1915	1,372·7	1924	2,340·7
1907	882·5	1916	1,579·1	1925	2,306·2
1908	906·3	1917	1,824·9	1926	2,351·1
1909	926·0	1918	2,111·5	1927	2,403·7
1910	957·4	1919	2,423·8	1928	2,476·3
1911	989·6	1920	2,560·4	1929	2,437·7
1912	1,023·9	1921	2,589·2	1930	2,519·5
1913	1,074·5	1922	2,419·2	1931	2,362·0

NOTES

[1] SOURCE: *Abstract*.
[2] Until September 1939 the figures were annual averages of weekly returns drawn up on varying days by the different banks. From then until the end of 1946 they were annual average figures for a single day in the second half of each month, each bank choosing a day convenient to itself. Since the beginning of 1947 the monthly figures have been drawn up on a single day for all banks.

(in £ million)

	Total Assets or Liabilities	Deposits	Cash and Balances at Bank of England	Balances at other Banks	Money at Call and Short Notice	Bills Dis- counted	Treasury Deposit Receipts	Invest- ments	Advances to Cus- tomers and other Accounts	Accept- ances, Endorse- ments, etc.
1921	1,997	1,812	211	48	105	363	—	331	833	63
1922	1,953	1,774	206	44	113	340	—	391	750	59
1923	1,874	1,674	197	45	110	275	—	356	761	79
1924	1,887	1,671	195	48	105	244	—	341	808	91
1925	1,888	1,662	196	52	117	226	—	286	856	100
1926	1,888	1,665	195	50	120	216	—	265	892	93
1927	1,942	1,713	198	52	137	218	—	254	928	98
1928	2,069	1,766	196	55	150	237	—	254	948	166
1929	2,139	1,800	194	55	145	229	—	257	991	203
1930	2,073	1,801	192	50	140	264	—	258	963	136
1931	2,010	1,760	182	46	121	256	—	301	919	114
1932	2,006	1,791	187	42	116	308	—	348	844	89
1933	2,182	1,953	212	43	102	354	—	537	758	102
1934	2,121	1,880	212	46	134	230	—	560	753	114
1935	2,235	1,999	215	48	142	266	—	615	769	106
1936	2,370	2,142	221	54	158	313	—	614	839	99
1936(a)	2,456	2,216	228	56	165	320	—	643	865	105
1937	2,542	2,287	235	62	167	281	—	652	954	119
1938	2,536	2,277	241	60	151	280	—	637	976	118
1939	2,513	2,248	244	67	149	255	—	608	991	125
1940	2,765	2,506	268	87	148	370	73	666	955	118
1941	3,216	2,970	311	107	134	231	495	894	858	104
1942	3,512	3,275	345	116	133	234	642	1,069	797	95
1943	3,918	3,677	386	123	152	185	1,002	1,147	747	98
1944	4,396	4,153	437	131	180	171	1,387	1,165	750	99
1945	4,942	4,692	492	141	206	188	1,811	1,156	768	104
1946	5,397	5,097	523	165	300	457	1,492	1,345	888	153
1947	6,032	5,650	473	186	450	723	1,308	1,474	1,107	233
1948	6,311	5,913	486	199	473	744	1,284	1,479	1,319	248
1949	6,387	5,974	496	202	510	914	983	1,505	1,440	259
1950	6,476	6,014	497	203	550	1,298	430	1,505	1,603	307
1951	6,787	6,162	511	232	569	1,228	247	1,624	1,822	468
1952	6,667	6,083	505	226	529	1,062	7	1,983	1,838	427
1953	6,754	6,256	509	232	472	1,219	—	2,163	1,732	336
1954	7,014	6,495	528	256	457	1,206	—	2,321	1,804	349
1955	7,095	6,454	529	269	439	1,130	—	2,149	2,019	462
1956	6,902	6,288	516	275	431	1,270	—	1,978	1,897	432

(a) The District Bank was included from January 1936. The first row for 1936 excludes that bank, and the second includes it.

Banking and Insurance 5. Bank Clearings 1868–1938

NOTE
SOURCE: *Abstract.*

(in £ million)

	London	Provinces	Total		London	Provinces	Total
1868	3,425	...	...	1904	10,564	655	11,219
1869	3,626	...	...	1905	12,288	665	12,953
1870	3,914	...	...	1906	12,711	679	13,390
1871	4,826	...	...	1907	12,730	723	13,453
1872	5,916	...	...	1908	12,120	652	12,772
1873	6,071	...	...	1909	13,525	690(a)	14,215(a)
1874	5,937	...	...	1910	14,659	743	15,402
1875	5,686	...	...	1911	14,614	774	15,388
1876	4,963	...	...	1912	15,962	852(b)	16,814(b)
1877	5,042	...	...	1913	16,436	900	17,336
1878	4,992	...	...	1914	14,665	831	15,496
1879	4,886	...	...	1915	13,408	990	14,398
1880	5,794	...	...	1916	15,275	1,212	16,487
1881	6,357	...	...	1917	19,121	1,438	20,559
1882	6,221	...	...	1918	21,198	1,777	22,975
1883	5,929	...	...	1919	28,415	2,284	30,699
1884	5,799	...	...	1920	39,019	3,134	42,153
1885	5,511	...	...	1921	34,930	1,786	36,716
1886	5,902	...	...	1922	37,161	1,797	38,958
1887	6,077	...	...	1923	36,628	1,801	38,429
1888	6,942	...	...	1924	39,533	1,881	41,414
1889	7,619	...	...	1925	40,437	1,866	42,303
1890	7,801	...	...	1926	39,825	1,628	41,453
1891	6,848	...	...	1927	41,551	1,710	43,261
1892	6,482	...	...	1928	44,204	1,673	45,877
1893	6,478	...	...	1929	44,897	1,599	46,496
1894	6,337	...	...	1930	43,558	1,348	44,906
1895	7,593	386	7,979	1931	36,236	1,200	37,436
1896	7,575	464	8,039	1932	32,112	1,238	33,350
1897	7,491	483	7,974	1933	32,138	1,243	33,381
1898	8,097	508	8,605	1934	35,484	1,295	36,779
1899	9,150	571	9,721	1935	37,560	1,283	38,843
1900	8,960	633	9,593	1936	40,617(c)	1,394	42,011
1901	9,561	606	10,167	1937	42,686	1,472	44,158
1902	10,029	615	10,644	1938	39,611	1,258	40,869
1903	10,120	625	10,745				

(a) The first year in which records were kept at Nottingham.
(b) The first year in which records were kept at Bradford.

(c) The District Bank became a member of the London Clearing House in January 1936.

NOTES

SOURCES: 1833-44—S.P. 1857-8, VIII (Report of the Select Committee on the Commercial Distress); 1845-1909—United States National Monetary Commission's *Statistics for Great Britain, Germany and France* (Washington, 1910); 1910—the *Bankers' Magazine*; 1911-39—*Abstract* (except Bank of England 1938-9—*Bank Returns*; and Irish Banks 1928-39—Bank of England's *Statistical Summary*). The original source for all figures is the returns required under the banking acts of 1833 and 1844-5.

(Notes held by the public to the nearest £ thousand 1833-1927, and to the nearest £ million 1928-39)

	Bank of England	Country Banks	Scottish Banks	Irish Banks(a)
1833(b)	18,456	9,991	3,056	5,334
1834	18,820	10,287	3,117	5,216
1835	18,107	10,700	3,098	5,186
1836	17,827	11,770	3,218	5,500
1837	18,288	10,609	3,074	5,119
1838	18,950	11,425	3,113	5,636
1839	17,677	11,716	3,247	5,848
1840	16,839	10,457	3,251	5,391
1841	16,948	9,728	3,195	5,356
1842	18,440(c)	8,306(c)	2,821(c)	5,114(c)
1843	19,523	7,647	2,732	5,168
1844	21,216(b)	8,175	2,951	5,937
1845	20,674	7,710	3,294	6,949
1846	20,252	7,730	3,405	7,260
1847	19,123	7,360	3,551	6,009
1848	18,086	6,280	3,176	4,829
1849	18,438	6,210	3,134	4,310
1850	19,448	6,330	3,225	4,512
1851	19,468	6,210	3,243	4,463
1852	21,910	6,410	3,404	4,818
1853	22,602	6,840	3,789	5,650
1854	20,688	6,830	4,055	6,296
1855	19,830	6,900	4,105	6,362
1856	19,667	6,790	4,093	6,652
1857	19,467	6,640	4,080	6,822
1858	20,248	5,990	3,926	6,183
1859	21,326	6,430	4,111	6,870
1860	21,252	6,450	4,228	6,840
1861	19,992	6,130	4,197	6,266
1862	20,835	6,120	4,153	5,658
1863	20,664	6,040	4,204	5,405
1864	20,605	5,980	4,262	5,594
1865	21,117	5,790	4,383	5,987
1866	23,159	5,150	4,440	5,884
1867	23,438	5,100	4,566	5,811
1868	23,932	5,050	4,608	6,181
1869	23,483	5,050	4,730	6,608
1870	23,327	4,910	4,933	6,880
1871	24,416	5,050	5,178	7,544
1872	25,492	5,100	5,332	7,674
1873	25,645	5,070	5,636	7,077
1874	26,264	4,980	5,900	6,768
1875	27,346	4,812	6,053	7,064
1876	27,734	4,714	6,099	7,500
1877	27,895	4,565	6,116	7,399

See p. 452 for footnotes

(Notes held by the public to the nearest £ thousand
1833–1927, and to the nearest £ million 1928–39)

	Bank of England	Country Banks	Scottish Banks	Irish Banks(a)	Currency Notes
1878	28,058	4,362	5,841	6,968	—
1879	29,212	3,593	5,523	6,066	—
1880	26,915	3,440	5,538	5,727	—
1881	26,321	3,347	5,545	6,587	—
1882	25,985	3,408	5,682	7,297	—
1883	25,568	3,324	5,872	7,124	—
1884	25,358	3,150	5,860	6,514	—
1885	24,667	2,981	5,711	6,063	—
1886	24,659	2,748	5,687	6,019	—
1887	24,350	2,496	5,644	5,885	—
1888	24,283	2,452	5,744	6,114	—
1889	24,389	2,393	5,944	6,663	—
1890	24,561	2,350	6,296	6,800	—
1891	25,145	2,243	6,440	6,500	—
1892	25,863	2,122	6,471	6,189	—
1893	25,858	2,002	6,486	6,317	—
1894	25,300	1,820	6,566	6,327	—
1895	25,753	1,750	6,962	6,380	—
1896	26,470	1,619	7,174	6,287	—
1897	27,198	1,422	7,323	6,226	—
1898	27,448	1,378	7,497	6,144	—
1899	27,820	1,304	7,850	6,363	—
1900	29,366	1,243	7,946	6,830	—
1901	29,552	1,118	7,889	6,763	—
1902	29,407	877	7,865	6,810	—
1903	28,944	735	7,762	7,272	—
1904	28,313	650	7,497	6,713	—
1905	28,968	595	7,441	6,401	—
1906	28,926	546	7,469	6,470	—
1907	28,911	510	7,370	6,784	—
1908	28,840	435	7,101	6,681	—
1909	29,257	304	7,069	6,882	—
1910	28,300	197	7,074	7,439	—
1911	28,610	171	7,151	7,611	—
1912	28,788	159	7,317	7,410	—
1913	28,723	138	7,565	8,293	—
1914	31,605	440	8,189	9,095	29,291(d)
1915	33,761	110	10,808	13,585	56,189
1916	35,456	127	14,117	17,571	121,276
1917	40,195	145	17,049	20,880	166,233
1918	54,921	172	22,599	27,496	255,877
1919	78,114	174	27,023	30,580	335,138
1920	102,770	170	28,953	26,863	346,350
1921	107,869	24(e)	27,148	20,602	328,784
1922	102,541	—	23,986	18,067	297,862
1923	101,877	—	22,896	17,081	285,766
1924	102,727	—	22,224	16,559	288,068
1925	91,751	—	21,670	15,876	292,065
1926	84,465	—	20,833	15,013	291,866
1927	80,732	—	20,831	14,666	293,925

See p. 452 for footnotes

(Notes held by the public to the nearest £ thousand
1833–1927, and to the nearest £ million 1928–39)

	Bank of England	Scottish Banks	Irish Banks(a)	Currency Notes
1928	78·8(f)	21·2	14·8	293·5(f)
1929	362·3	21·2	16·9	—
1930	358·7	21·4	17·4	—
1931	354·8	21·0	16·6	—
1932	359·5	21·1	16·2	—
1933	371·2	21·1	16·8	—
1934	378·7	21·2	16·8	—
1935	394·7	21·7	17·5	—
1936	431·2	22·4	18·5	—
1937	479·6	23·1	19·5	—
1938	485·6	23·6	20·3	—
1939	507·3	24·7	21·4	—

(a) The note issues of Southern Irish banks continue to be included after 1922. Irish legal tended notes are included from 1928.
(b) Average of last four months only.
(c) For the period up to 1841 the figures are annual averages of the average circulation in the twelve calendar months. For 1842–4 (Bank of England) and 1842–1939 (all others) the figures are annual averages of the average weekly circulation in thirteen four-week periods, as closely corresponding to the calendar year as possible. For 1845–1939 (Bank of England) the figures are averages of the weekly returns—i.e. all the Wednesdays in the year.
(d) Average of third and fourth quarters, in the former of which there were issues for seven weeks only.
(e) Average of first two quarters only.
(f) The first five weeks only of the last quarter are counted here, the period after the amalgamation of Treasury and Bank of England notes being ignored.

NOTES

[1]   Source: H. Oliver Horne, *A History of Savings Banks* (Oxford University Press, 1947), appendix II. These figures are reproduced by permission of the Trustee Savings Banks Association.

[2]   Figures for the Post Office Savings Bank are taken at 31st December, and for Trustee Savings Banks at 20th November.
[3]   The Trustee Savings Bank figures are for cash only, and do not include stock owing to depositors.

(Amount due to depositors in £ million)

		Trustee Savings Banks				Trustee Savings Banks	
	Post Office	Ordinary Departments	Special Investment Departments		Post Office	Ordinary Departments	Special Investment Departments
1817	—	0·2(a)	—	1861	—	41·5	0·2
1818	—	1·7(a)	—	1862	1·7	40·6	0·2
1819	—	2·8(a)	—	1863	3·4	41·0	0·2
1820	—	3·5(a)	—	1864	5·0	39·3	0·2
1821	—	4·7(a)	—	1865	6·5	38·7	0·3
1822	—	6·5(a)	—	1866	8·1	36·4	0·3
1823	—	8·7(a)	—	1867	9·7	36·5	0·3
1824	—	11·7(a)	—	1868	11·7	36·9	0·3
1825	—	13·3(a)	—	1869	13·5	37·6	0·3
1826	—	13·1(a)	—	1870	15·1	38·0	0·3
1827	—	14·2(a)	—	1871	17·0	38·8	0·4
1828	—	15·4(a)	—	1872	19·3	39·7	0·6
1829	—	14·3	—	1873	21·2	40·5	0·7
1830	—	14·6	—	1874	23·2	41·5	0·8
1831	—	14·6	—	1875	25·2	42·4	1·1
1832	—	14·4	—	1876	27·0	43·3	1·3
1833	—	15·3	—	1877	28·7	44·2	1·4
1834	—	16·3	—	1878	30·4	44·3	1·6
1835	—	17·4	—	1879	32·0	43·8	1·8
1836	—	18·8	—	1880	33·7	44·0	2·0
1837	—	19·6	—	1881	36·2	44·1	2·3
1838	—	21·4	—	1882	39·0	44·6	2·6
1839	—	22·4	—	1883	41·8	45·0	2·8
1840	—	23·5	—	1884	44·8	45·8	3·1
1841	—	24·5	—	1885	47·7	46·4	3·3
1842	—	25·3	—	1886	50·9	46·8	3·6
1843	—	27·2	—	1887	54·0	47·3	3·8
1844	—	29·5	—	1888	58·6	46·4	4·0
1845	—	30·7	—	1889	63·0	44·9	4·2
1846	—	31·7	—	1890	67·6	43·6	4·4
1847	—	30·2	0·1	1891	71·6	42·9	4·1
1848	—	28·1	0·1	1892	75·9	42·4	4·3
1849	—	28·5	0·1	1893	80·6	42·2	4·5
1850	—	28·9	- -	1894	89·3	43·5	4·6
1851	—	30·3	- -	1895	97·9	45·3	4·7
1852	—	31·8	- -	1896	108·1	46·7	4·7
1853	—	33·4	- -	1897	115·9	48·5	4·6
1854	—	33·7	- -	1898	123·1	50·0	4·6
1855	—	34·3	- -	1899	130·1	51·4	4·6
1856	—	34·9	0·1	1900	135·5	51·5	4·5
1857	—	35·1	0·1	1901	140·4	52·0	4·5
1858	—	36·2	0·2	1902	144·6	52·5	4·6
1859	—	39·0	0·2	1903	146·1	52·5	4·7
1860	—	41·3	0·2	1904	148·3	52·3	4·9

See p. 454 for footnote

(Amount due to depositors in £ million)

	Post Office	Trustee Savings Banks			Post Office	Trustee Savings Banks	
		Ordinary Departments	Special Investment Departments			Ordinary Departments	Special Investment Departments
1905	152·1	52·7	5·6	1923	273·1	79·6	23·6
1906	156·0	53·0	6·4	1924	280·4	82·3	24·7
1907	157·5	52·2	7·1	1925	285·5	83·4	27·0
1908	160·6	51·7	8·2	1926	283·7	82·0	28·8
1909	164·6	52·2	9·8	1927	284·6	81·4	32·5
1910	168·9	52·3	11·0	1928	288·6	81·7	38·9
1911	176·5	53·0	12·2	1929	285·0	79·3	45·1
1912	182·1	53·8	13·4	1930	290·2	79·1	54·1
1913	187·2	54·3	14·4	1931	289·4	77·9	65·1
1914	190·5	53·9	15·6	1932	305·7	80·0	74·8
1915	186·3	51·4	15·4	1933	326·7	88·8	82·6
1916	196·7	53·8	14·7	1934	354·8	94·8	87·1
1917	203·3	52·4	14·1	1935	390·3	107·6	89·8
1918	234·6	61·0	14·1	1936	432·4	120·3	91·8
1919	266·3	71·9	14·9	1937	470·5	131·3	93·3
1920	266·5	75·1	16·2	1938	509·3	142·4	96·5
1921	264·2	73·1	19·3	1939	551·4	152·3	99·4
1922	268·1	75·8	22·5				

(a) The balance due by the National Debt Commissioners to trustees. In 1829 this was £500,000 greater than the amount owing to depositors—*vide* S.P. 1860, XL.

Banking and Insurance 8. Yield on Consols—1756–1956

NOTES

[1] SOURCES: 1756–1830—T. S. Ashton, 'Some Statistics of the Industrial Revolution' in *Transactions of the Manchester Statistical Society* (1947–8); 1831–51—G. F. Warren and F. A. Pearson, *Gold and Prices* (New York, 1935) p. 403 (which also contains the figures up to 1934); 1852–1956—*Abstract*.

[2] The nominal rate of interest on Consols was 3 per cent from their first issue until 1888. From 1889–1902 it was 2¾ per cent, and from 1903 onwards it has been 2½ per cent.

(per cent)

1756	3·4	1807	4·9	1858	3·1	1909	3·0
1757	3·4	1808	4·6	1859	3·2	1910	3·1
1758	3·2	1809	4·6	1860	3·2	1911	3·2
1759	3·6	1810	4·5	1861	3·3	1912	3·3
1760	3·8	1811	4·7	1862	3·2	1913	3·4
1761	3·9	1812	5·1	1863	3·2	1914	3·3
1762	4·3	1813	4·9	1864	3·3	1915	3·8
1763	3·4	1814	4·9	1865	3·4	1916	4·3
1764	3·6	1815	4·5	1866	3·4	1917	4·6
1765	3·4	1816	5·0	1867	3·2	1918	4·4
1766	3·4	1817	4·1	1868	3·2	1919	4·6
1767	3·4	1818	3·9	1869	3·2	1920	5·3
1768	3·3	1819	4·2	1870	3·2	1921	5·2
1769	3·5	1820	4·4	1871	3·2	1922	4·4
1770	3·6	1821	4·1	1872	3·2	1923	4·3
1771	3·5	1822	3·8	1873	3·2	1924	4·4
1772	3·3	1823	3·8	1874	3·2	1925	4·4
1773	3·5	1824	3·3	1875	3·2	1926	4·6
1774	3·4	1825	3·5	1876	3·2	1927	4·6
1775	3·4	1826	3·8	1877	3·1	1928	4·5
1776	3·5	1827	3·6	1878	3·2	1929	4·6
1777	3·8	1828	3·5	1879	3·1	1930	4·5
1778	4·5	1829	3·3	1880	3·1	1931	4·4
1779	4·9	1830	3·5	1881	3·0	1932	3·7
1780	4·9	1831	3·8	1882	3·0	1933	3·4
1781	5·2	1832	3·6	1883	3·0	1934	3·1
1782	5·3	1833	3·4	1884	3·0	1935	2·9
1783	4·8	1834	3·3	1885	3·0	1936	2·9
1784	5·4	1835	3·3	1886	3·0	1937	3·3
1785	4·8	1836	3·4	1887	3·0	1938	3·4
1786	4·1	1837	3·3	1888	3·0	1939	3·7
1787	4·1	1838	3·2	1889	2·8	1940	3·4
1788	4·0	1839	3·3	1890	2·9	1941	3·1
1789	3·9	1840	3·4	1891	2·9	1942	3·0
1790	3·9	1841	3·4	1892	2·8	1943	3·1
1791	3·6	1842	3·3	1893	2·8	1944	3·1
1792	3·3	1843	3·2	1894	2·7	1945	2·9
1793	4·0	1844	3·0	1895	2·6	1946	2·6
1794	4·4	1845	3·1	1896	2·5	1947	2·8
1795	4·5	1846	3·1	1897	2·5	1948	3·2
1796	4·8	1847	3·4	1898	2·5	1949	3·3
1797	5·9	1848	3·5	1899	2·6	1950	3·5
1798	5·9	1849	3·2	1900	2·8	1951	3·8
1799	5·1	1850	3·1	1901	2·9	1952	4·2
1800	4·7	1851	3·1	1902	2·9	1953	4·1
1801	4·9	1852	3·0	1903	2·8	1954	3·8
1802	4·2	1853	3·1	1904	2·8	1955	4·2
1803	5·0	1854	3·3	1905	2·8	1956	4·7
1804	5·3	1855	3·3	1906	2·8		
1805	5·0	1856	3·2	1907	3·0		
1806	4·9	1857	3·3	1908	2·9		

NOTES

SOURCES: 1797–1914—J. H. Clapham, *The Bank of England* (2 vols, Cambridge University Press, 1944), vol. II, pp. 429–32; 1915–39—*Abstract*. The figures from Clapham's book are reproduced by permission of the Governor and Company of the Bank of England.

1797		5	1856	29 May	5	1862	22 May	3
1822	20 June	4	1856	26 June	$4\frac{1}{2}$	1862	10 July	$2\frac{1}{2}$
1825	13 December	5	1856	1 October	5	1862	24 July	2
1827	5 July	4	1856	6 October	6 or 7(c)	1862	30 October	3
1836	21 July	$4\frac{1}{2}$	1856	13 November	7	1863	15 January	4
1836	1 September	5	1856	4 December	$6\frac{1}{2}$	1863	28 January	5
1838	15 February	4	1856	18 December	6	1863	19 February	4
1839	16 May	5	1857	2 April	$6\frac{1}{2}$	1863	23 April	$3\frac{1}{2}$
1839	20 June	$5\frac{1}{2}$	1857	18 June	6	1863	30 April	3
1839	1 August	6	1857	16 July	$5\frac{1}{2}$	1863	16 May	$3\frac{1}{2}$
1840	23 January	5	1857	8 October	6	1863	21 May	4
1842	7 April	4	1857	12 October	7	1863	2 November	5
1844	5 September	$2\frac{1}{2}$ & 3(a)	1857	19 October	8	1863	5 November	6
1845	13 March	$2\frac{1}{2}$	1857	5 November	9	1863	2 December	7
1845	16 October	3	1857	9 November	10	1863	3 December	8
1845	6 November	$3\frac{1}{2}$	1857	24 December	8	1863	24 December	7
1846	27 August	3	1858	7 January	6	1864	20 January	8
1847	14 January	$3\frac{1}{2}$	1858	14 January	5	1864	11 February	7
1847	21 January	4	1858	28 January	4	1864	25 February	6
1847	8 April	5	1858	4 February	$3\frac{1}{2}$	1864	16 April	7
1847	5 August	$5\frac{1}{2}$	1858	11 February	3	1864	2 May	8
1847	30 September	6(b)	1858	9 December	$2\frac{1}{2}$	1864	5 May	9
1847	25 October	8	1859	28 April	$3\frac{1}{2}$	1864	19 May	8
1847	22 November	7	1859	5 May	$4\frac{1}{2}$	1864	26 May	7
1847	2 December	6	1859	2 June	$3\frac{1}{2}$	1864	16 June	6
1847	23 December	5	1859	9 June	3	1864	25 July	7
1848	27 January	4	1859	14 July	$2\frac{1}{2}$	1864	4 August	8
1848	15 June	$3\frac{1}{2}$	1860	19 January	3	1864	8 September	9
1848	2 November	3	1860	31 January	4	1864	10 November	8
1849	22 November	$2\frac{1}{2}$	1860	29 March	$4\frac{1}{2}$	1864	24 November	7
1850	26 December	3	1860	12 April	5	1864	15 December	6
1852	1 January	$2\frac{1}{2}$	1860	10 May	$4\frac{1}{2}$	1865	12 January	$5\frac{1}{2}$
1852	22 April	2	1860	24 May	4	1865	26 January	5
1853	6 January	$2\frac{1}{2}$	1860	8 November	$4\frac{1}{2}$	1865	2 March	$4\frac{1}{2}$
1853	20 January	3	1860	13 November	5	1865	30 March	4
1853	2 June	$3\frac{1}{2}$	1860	15 November	6	1865	4 May	$4\frac{1}{2}$
1853	1 September	4	1860	29 November	5	1865	25 May	4
1853	15 September	$4\frac{1}{2}$	1860	31 December	6	1865	1 June	$3\frac{1}{2}$
1853	29 September	5	1861	7 January	7	1865	15 June	3
1854	11 May	$5\frac{1}{2}$	1861	14 February	8	1865	27 July	$3\frac{1}{2}$
1854	3 August	5	1861	21 March	7	1865	3 August	4
1855	5 April	$4\frac{1}{2}$	1861	4 April	6	1865	28 September	$4\frac{1}{2}$
1855	3 May	4	1861	11 April	5	1865	2 October	5
1855	14 June	$3\frac{1}{2}$	1861	16 May	6	1865	5 October	6
1855	6 September	4	1861	1 August	5	1865	7 October	7
1855	13 September	$4\frac{1}{2}$	1861	15 August	$4\frac{1}{2}$	1865	23 November	6
1855	27 September	5	1861	29 August	4	1865	28 December	7
1855	4 October	$5\frac{1}{2}$	1861	19 September	$3\frac{1}{2}$	1866	4 January	8
1855	18 October	6 or 7(c)	1861	7 November	3	1866	22 February	7
1856	22 May	6	1862	9 January	$2\frac{1}{2}$	1866	15 March	6

See p. 459 for footnotes

1866	3 May	7
1866	8 May	8
1866	11 May	9
1866	12 May	10
1866	16 August	8
1866	23 August	7
1866	30 August	6
1866	6 September	5
1866	27 September	$4\frac{1}{2}$
1866	8 November	4
1866	20 December	$3\frac{1}{2}$
1867	7 February	3
1867	30 May	$2\frac{1}{2}$
1867	25 July	2
1868	19 November	$2\frac{1}{2}$
1868	3 December	3
1869	1 April	4
1869	6 May	$4\frac{1}{2}$
1869	10 June	4
1869	24 June	$3\frac{1}{2}$
1869	15 July	3
1869	19 August	$2\frac{1}{2}$
1869	4 November	3
1870	21 July	$3\frac{1}{2}$
1870	23 July	4
1870	28 July	5
1870	4 August	6
1870	11 August	$5\frac{1}{2}$
1870	18 August	$4\frac{1}{2}$
1870	25 August	4
1870	1 September	$3\frac{1}{2}$
1870	15 September	3
1870	29 September	$2\frac{1}{2}$
1871	2 March	3
1871	13 April	$2\frac{1}{2}$
1871	13 July	2
1871	21 September	3
1871	28 September	4
1871	7 October	5
1871	16 November	4
1871	30 November	$3\frac{1}{2}$
1871	14 December	3
1872	4 April	$3\frac{1}{2}$
1872	11 April	4
1872	9 May	5
1872	30 May	4
1872	13 June	$3\frac{1}{2}$
1872	20 June	3
1872	18 July	$3\frac{1}{2}$
1872	18 September	4
1872	26 September	$4\frac{1}{2}$
1872	3 October	5
1872	10 October	6
1872	9 November	7
1872	28 November	6

1872	12 December	5
1873	9 January	$4\frac{1}{2}$
1873	23 January	4
1873	30 January	$3\frac{1}{2}$
1873	26 March	4
1873	7 May	$4\frac{1}{2}$
1873	10 May	5
1873	17 May	6
1873	4 June	7
1873	12 June	6
1873	10 July	5
1873	17 July	$4\frac{1}{2}$
1873	24 July	4
1873	31 July	$3\frac{1}{2}$
1873	21 August	3
1873	25 September	4
1873	29 September	5
1873	14 October	6
1873	18 October	7
1873	1 November	8
1873	7 November	9
1873	20 November	8
1873	27 November	6
1873	4 December	5
1873	11 December	$5\frac{1}{2}$
1874	8 January	4
1874	15 January	$3\frac{1}{2}$
1874	30 April	4
1874	28 May	$3\frac{1}{2}$
1874	4 June	3
1874	18 June	$2\frac{1}{2}$
1874	30 July	3
1874	6 August	4
1874	20 August	$3\frac{1}{2}$
1874	27 August	3
1874	15 October	4
1874	16 November	5
1874	30 November	6
1875	7 January	5
1875	14 January	4
1875	28 January	3
1875	18 February	$3\frac{1}{2}$
1875	8 July	3
1875	29 July	$2\frac{1}{2}$
1875	12 August	2
1875	7 October	$2\frac{1}{2}$
1875	14 October	$3\frac{1}{2}$
1875	21 October	4
1875	18 November	3
1875	30 December	4
1876	6 January	5
1876	27 January	4
1876	23 March	$3\frac{1}{2}$
1876	6 April	3
1876	20 April	2

1877	3 May	3
1877	5 July	$2\frac{1}{2}$
1877	12 July	2
1877	28 August	3
1877	4 October	4
1877	11 October	5
1877	29 November	4
1878	10 January	3
1878	31 January	2
1878	28 March	3
1878	30 May	$2\frac{1}{2}$
1878	27 June	3
1878	4 July	$3\frac{1}{2}$
1878	1 August	4
1878	12 August	5
1878	14 October	6
1878	21 November	5
1879	16 January	4
1879	30 January	3
1879	13 March	$2\frac{1}{2}$
1879	10 April	2
1879	6 November	3
1880	17 June	$2\frac{1}{2}$
1880	9 December	3
1881	13 January	$3\frac{1}{2}$
1881	17 February	3
1881	28 April	$2\frac{1}{2}$
1881	18 August	3
1881	25 August	4
1881	6 October	5
1882	30 January	6
1882	23 February	5
1882	9 March	4
1882	23 March	3
1882	17 August	4
1882	14 September	5
1883	25 January	4
1883	15 February	$3\frac{1}{2}$
1883	1 March	3
1883	10 May	4
1883	13 September	$3\frac{1}{2}$
1883	27 September	3
1884	7 February	$3\frac{1}{2}$
1884	13 March	3
1884	3 April	$2\frac{1}{2}$
1884	19 June	2
1884	9 October	3
1884	30 October	4
1884	6 November	5
1885	29 January	4
1885	19 March	$3\frac{1}{2}$
1885	7 May	3
1885	14 May	$2\frac{1}{2}$
1885	28 May	2
1885	12 November	3

1885	17 December	4	1892	21 January	3	1903	18 June	3
1886	21 January	3	1892	7 April	2½	1903	3 September	4
1886	18 February	2	1892	28 April	2	1904	14 April	3½
1886	6 May	3	1892	20 October	3	1904	21 April	3
1886	10 June	2½	1893	26 January	2½	1905	9 March	2½
1886	26 August	3½	1893	4 May	3	1905	7 September	3
1886	21 October	4	1893	11 May	3½	1905	28 September	4
1886	16 December	5	1893	18 May	4	1906	5 April	3½
1887	3 February	4	1893	8 June	3	1906	3 May	4
1887	10 March	3½	1893	15 June	2½	1906	21 June	3½
1887	24 March	3	1893	3 August	3	1906	13 September	4
1887	14 April	2½	1893	10 August	4	1906	11 October	5
1887	28 April	2	1893	24 August	5	1906	19 October	6
1887	4 August	3	1893	14 September	4	1907	17 January	5
1887	1 September	4	1893	21 September	3½	1907	11 April	4½
1888	12 January	3½	1893	5 October	3	1907	25 April	4
1888	19 January	3	1894	1 February	2½	1907	15 August	4½
1888	16 February	2½	1894	22 February	2	1907	31 October	5½
1888	15 March	2	1896	10 September	2½	1907	4 November	6
1888	10 May	3	1896	24 September	3	1907	7 November	7
1888	7 June	2½	1896	22 October	4	1908	2 January	6
1888	9 August	3	1897	21 January	3½	1908	16 January	5
1888	13 September	4	1897	4 February	3	1908	23 January	4
1888	4 October	5	1897	8 April	2½	1908	5 March	3½
1889	10 January	4	1897	15 May	2	1908	19 March	3
1889	24 January	3½	1897	23 September	2½	1908	28 May	2½
1889	31 January	3	1897	14 October	3	1909	14 January	3
1889	18 April	2½	1898	7 April	4	1909	1 April	2½
1889	8 August	3	1898	26 May	3½	1909	7 October	3
1889	29 August	4	1898	2 June	3	1909	14 October	4
1889	26 September	5	1898	30 June	2½	1909	21 October	5
1889	30 December	6	1898	22 September	3	1909	9 December	4½
1890	20 February	5	1898	13 October	4	1910	6 January	4
1890	6 March	4½	1899	19 January	3½	1910	20 January	3½
1890	13 March	4	1899	2 February	3	1910	10 February	3
1890	10 April	3½	1899	13 July	3½	1910	17 March	4
1890	17 April	3	1899	3 October	4½	1910	2 June	3½
1890	26 June	4	1899	5 October	5	1910	9 June	3
1890	31 July	5	1899	30 November	6	1910	29 September	4
1890	21 August	4	1900	11 January	5	1910	20 October	5
1890	25 September	5	1900	18 January	4½	1910	1 December	4½
1890	7 November	6	1900	25 January	4	1911	26 January	4
1890	4 December	5	1900	24 May	3½	1911	16 February	3½
1891	8 January	4	1900	16 June	3	1911	9 March	3
1891	22 January	3½	1900	19 July	4	1911	21 September	4
1891	29 January	3	1901	3 January	5	1912	8 February	3½
1891	16 April	3½	1901	7 February	4½	1912	9 May	3
1891	7 May	4	1901	21 February	4	1912	29 August	4
1891	14 May	5	1901	6 June	3½	1912	17 October	5
1891	4 June	4	1901	13 June	3	1913	17 April	4½
1891	18 June	3	1901	31 October	4	1913	2 October	5
1891	2 July	2½	1902	23 January	3½	1914	8 January	4½
1891	24 September	3	1902	6 February	3	1914	22 January	4
1891	29 October	4	1902	2 October	4	1914	29 January	3
1891	10 December	3½	1903	21 May	3½	1914	30 July	4

1914	31 July	8	1922	17 June	$3\frac{1}{2}$	1930	20 March	$3\frac{1}{2}$
1914	1 August	10	1922	15 July	3	1930	1 May	3
1914	6 August	6(*d*)	1923	7 July	4	1931	14 May	$2\frac{1}{2}$
1914	8 August	5	1925	5 March	5	1931	23 July	$3\frac{1}{2}$
1916	19 July	6	1925	6 August	$4\frac{1}{2}$	1931	30 July	$4\frac{1}{2}$
1917	15 January	$5\frac{1}{2}$	1925	1 October	4	1931	21 September	6
1917	29 April	5	1925	3 December	5	1932	18 February	5
1919	6 November	6	1927	21 April	$4\frac{1}{2}$	1932	10 March	4
1920	15 April	7	1929	7 February	$5\frac{1}{2}$	1932	17 March	$3\frac{1}{2}$
1921	28 April	$6\frac{1}{2}$	1929	26 September	$6\frac{1}{2}$	1932	21 April	3
1921	23 June	6	1929	31 October	6	1932	12 May	$2\frac{1}{2}$
1921	21 July	$5\frac{1}{2}$	1929	21 November	$5\frac{1}{2}$	1932	30 June	2
1921	4 November	5	1929	12 December	5	1939	24 August	4
1922	18 February	$4\frac{1}{2}$	1930	6 February	$4\frac{1}{2}$	1939	28 September	3
1922	22 April	4	1930	6 March	4	1939	26 October	2

(*a*) Bills $2\frac{1}{2}$, Notes 3.
(*b*) One-month bills $5\frac{1}{2}$.
(*c*) 60-day at 6.

(*d*) The Secretary of the Bank of England kindly informed us of a misprint in this place in the source.

NOTES TO PART A

[1]   SOURCE: *S.P.* 1857 (Sess. 2), x, p. 463–4.   [2]   These figures are stated to be annual averages.

A. Overend, Gurney's Rates for First-class Three Months' Bills, 1824–56

1824	3·50	1835	3·71	1846	3·79
1825	3·88	1836	4·25	1847	5·85
1826	4·50	1837	4·44	1848	3·21
1827	3·25	1838	3·00	1849	2·31
1828	3·04	1839	5·13	1850	2·25
1829	3·38	1840	4·98	1851	3·06
1830	2·81	1841	4·90	1852	1·91
1831	3·69	1842	3·33	1853	3·67
1832	3·15	1843	2·17	1854	4·94
1833	2·73	1844	2·13	1855	4·67
1834	3·38	1845	2·96	1856	5·86

NOTES TO PART B

[1]   SOURCES: 1845–1910—T. T. Williams, 'The Rate of Discount and the Price of Consols', *J.R.S.S.* (1912). (Williams gives as his sources: R. H. I. Palgrave, *Bank Rate and the Money Market, 1844–1900* (London, 1903) and *The Economist*); 1911–38—*The Bankers' Magazine* (also available from 1919 in the *Abstract*.)
[2]   The figures for 1845–1910 are means of twelve monthly quotations, on or near the first of each month. Williams (*loc.*

cit. p. 380) notes: 'It follows that the averages so obtained are uncertain to a degree not less than about 1 in 10, for frequently there is a considerable fluctuation in the rate of discount during a month, and this fluctuation bears little correspondence to the day of the month'.
[3]   The figures from 1911–38 are means of the monthly means of, respectively, the highest and the lowest quotations on each day.

B. Rates for Three Months' Bank Bills, 1845–1938

					Max.	Min.
1845	3·00	1877	2·62	1909	2·28	
1846	3·75	1878	3·59	1910	3·16	

1847	5·87	1879	2·14		Max.	Min.
1848	3·25	1880	2·53	1911	2·92	2·89
1849	2·25	1881	3·05	1912	3·64	3·59
1850	2·25	1882	3·55	1913	4·38	4·35
1851	3·00	1883	3·22	1914	2·94	2·87
1852	1·87	1884	2·57	1915	3·70	3·61
1853	3·50	1885	2·40	1916	5·24	5·15
1854	4·87	1886	2·33	1917	4·83	4·74
1855	4·55	1887	2·65	1918	3·58	3·55
1856	5·50	1888	2·53	1919	3·96	3·89
1857	6·65	1889	2·85	1920	6·45	6·36
1858	2·75	1890	3·88	1921	5·24	5·09
1859	2·50	1891	2·77	1922	2·68	2·59
1860	4·00	1892	1·76	1923	2·76	2·67
1861	5·00	1893	2·32	1924	3·50	3·41
1862	2·25	1894	1·18	1925	4·18	4·09
1863	4·25	1895	0·96	1926	4·51	4·44
1864	7·00	1896	1·56	1927	4·29	4·22
1865	5·32	1897	1·92	1928	4·18	4·13
1866	6·41	1898	2·62	1929	5·29	5·24
1867	2·66	1899	3·35	1930	2·59	2·55
1868	2·46	1900	3·70	1931	3·65	3·57
1869	3·37	1901	3·17	1932	1·91	1·80
1870	3·28	1902	2·97	1933	0·72	0·66
1871	2·89	1903	3·38	1934	0·84	0·81
1872	4·08	1904	2·68	1935	0·61	0·56
1873	4·70	1905	2·62	1936	0·62	0·60
1874	3·56	1906	3·97	1937	0·60	0·57
1875	3·14	1907	4·49	1938	0·65	0·62
1876	2·26	1908	2·29			

NOTES

[1] SOURCE: *S.P.* 1870, xx (except for years marked *, which are taken from the Revised Report on Fire Insurance Duties, *S.P.* 1863, xxvi).

[2] The following rates of duty were charged: Great Britain —1/6 from 1782 to the middle of 1797; 2/- from then to mid-1804; 2/6 from mid-1804 to mid-1815; 3/- from then to mid-1865, when for one year there was a reduction to 1/6 for stock-in-trade; from mid-1866 to abolition in 1869, 1/6. Ireland—1/- from 1786 to mid-1812; 2/6 from mid-1812 to mid-1842; thereafter the same rates as in Great Britain.

(Value of Property Insured in £ million)

	England & Wales	Scotland	Ireland		England & Wales	Scotland	Ireland
1783(a)	170·5*	...	...	1827	461·2	30·7	20·2
1784	153·2	2·0	...	1828	446·7	31·4	21·2
1785	136·4	1·8	...	1829	470·8	31·7	22·6
1786	132·6	1·7	...	1830	482·2	33·6	22·8
1787	134·3	1·8	...	1831	478·2	34·4	23·4
1788	135·1	1·9	...	1832	499·1	33·8	23·4
1789	139·9	2·1	...	1833	503·7	34·1	23·5
1790	144·9	2·2	...	1834	503·1	34·1	25·2
1791	150·9	2·5	...	1835	521·2	(33·7)(c)	(26·2)(c)
1792	162·1	2·7	...	1836	545·6	38·1	28·0
1793	177·3	2·9	...	1837	563·4	39·2	(29·6)(c)
1794	176·5	2·7	...	1838	582·2	41·5	32·4
1795	176·7	2·9	...	1839	604·6	43·0	33·5
1796	188·3	3·2	...	1840	625·1	43·6	35·2
1797	181·5	3·2	...	1841	641·4	43·2	36·7
1798	183·8*	...	...	1842	652·7	47·3	37·0
1799	198·6	3·5	...	1843	666·8	48·0	...
1800	211·4*	...	...	1844	670·2	47·8	33·0
1801(b)	204·9	3·6	...	1845	678·6	49·8	33·6
1802	219·6	3·8	...	1846	696·5	51·6	34·8
1803	223·5	3·9	...	1847	709·9	54·8	35·9
1804	238·1	5·4	...	1848	727·0	53·4	36·7
1805	248·2*	...	14·5	1849	726·5	47·1	34·5
1806	256·9	5·8	14·2	1850	738·1	46·8	34·2
1807	273·0	7·8	8·2	1851	752·1	48·1	34·6
1808	281·6	9·1	30·3	1852	768·8	48·9	35·5
1809	303·1	9·6	34·9	1853	787·1	49·7	36·4
1810	324·8	10·7	39·5	1854	816·9	52·1	38·2
1811	347·3	13·1	44·8	1855(d)	851·9	44·7	39·7
1812	358·2	13·8	42·7	1856	866·5	58·5	40·2
1813	362·6	12·5	...	1857	893·9	61·1	42·5
1814	349·9	12·7	21·3	1858	911·4	65·5	44·3
1815	389·2*	13·1	22·3	1859	940·9	68·1	46·1
1816	384·8	...	19·6	1860	956·5	71·6	48·6
1817	382·1	12·8	20·5	1861	983·2	77·9	52·2
1818	385·0	13·4	17·8	1862	1,006·6	86·4	54·8
1819	389·5	13·5	17·5	1863	1,035·4	89·5	55·1
1820	396·8	14·6	18·2	1864	1,068·6	92·7	57·0
1821	391·3	14·8	17·4	1865	1,132·1	98·2	59·4
1822	399·7	14·6	17·6	1866	1,172·9	103·4	64·8
1823	405·2	15·6	17·3	1867	1,228·1	114·1	69·2
1824	401·7	16·6	17·5	1868	1,263·5	124·6	57·3
1825	427·7	18·7	21·2	1869	1,358·0(e)	140·9(e)	12·2(e)
1826	442·2	25·4	19·2				

(a) Year ended 1st August. The figure for 1783 is an estimate based on the revenue paid during the 401 days ended 1st August.

(b) Year ended 5th January.

(c) As from 24th June 1833 insurance of agricultural stock was exempt from duty, but returns of the value of such property continued to be made and are included here. These three bracketed figures are exceptions for which no record of exempt property is available.

(d) Year ended 31st March.

(e) From 25th December 1867 British insurance companies were required to account in Great Britain for insurances effected in Ireland.

Banking and Insurance 12.   New Capital Issues on the London
Money Market 1870–1939

NOTES

[1] SOURCE: *The Economist*'s 'Commercial History and Review' supplements from 1883 annually to 1940.

[2] These figures were at first described as 'capital created and issued' and later as 'new capital applications'. A series of new capital issues excluding borrowing by the British government for purely financial purposes, shares issued to vendors, allotments arising from capitalisation of reserves etc., issues for conversion or redemption of securities previously held in the U.K., sales of already-issued securities, short-dated bills in anticipation of long-term borrowings, and the loans of local authorities which were not specifically limited, was published in the *Board of Trade Journal* annually in the inter-war years. It is as follows:

1919	237·5	1926	253·3	1933	132·9
1920	384·2	1927	314·7	1934	150·2
1921	215·8	1928	362·5	1935	182·8
1922	235·7	1929	253·7	1936	217·2
1923	203·8	1930	236·2	1937	170·9
1924	223·5	1931	88·7	1938	118·1
1925	219·9	1932	113·0	1939	66·3

(in £000,000)

1870	92·3	1894	91·8	1918	1,393·4
1871	149·6(a)	1895	104·7	1919	1,036·1
1872	151·6	1896	152·7	1920	367·6
1873	154·7	1897	157·3	1921	389·0
1874	114·2	1898	150·2	1922	573·7
1875	62·7	1899	133·2	1923	271·4
1876	43·2	1900	165·5	1924	209·3
1877	51·5	1901	159·3	1925	232·2
1878	59·2	1902	153·8	1926	230·8
1879	56·5	1903	108·5	1927	355·2
1880	122·2	1904	123·0	1928	369·1
1881	189·4	1905	167·2	1929	285·2
1882	145·6	1906	120·2	1930	267·8
1883	81·2	1907	123·6	1931	102·1
1884	109·0	1908	192·2	1932	188·9
1885	78·0	1909	182·4	1933	244·8
1886	101·9	1910	267·4	1934	169·1
1887	111·2	1911	191·8	1935	236·1
1888	160·3	1912	210·9	1936	255·7
1889	207·0	1913	196·5	1937	251·6
1890	142·6	1914	512·5	1938	180·1
1891	104·6	1915	685·2	1939	91·7
1892	81·1	1916	585·4		
1893	49·1	1917	1,318·6		

(a) The provenance of this figure is different from the remainder of the series, as it is compiled from totals of home new issues and foreign loans shown in a detailed breakdown in *The Economist*'s 'Commercial History and Review of 1871'.

REFERENCES

BOOKS

T. Balogh, *Studies in Financial Organisation* (Oxford, 1949).

Bankers' Almanac.

Bankers' Magazine.

A. Bloomfield, *Monetary Policy under the International Gold Standard, 1880–1914* (Federal Reserve Bank of New York, 1959).

E. Cannan, *The Paper Pound* (London, 1919).

Castaing, *The Course of the Exchange* (London, 1697–1810, twice weekly).

J. H. Clapham, *The Bank of England* (2 vols., Cambridge, 1944).

E. Coppieters, *English Bank Note Circulation, 1694–1954* (Louvain, 1955).

J. Dun, *British Banking Statistics* (London, 1876).

A. E. Feavearyear, *The Pound Sterling* (Oxford, 1931).

F. W. Fetter, *The Irish Pound* (London, 1955).

T. E. Gregory, *The Westminster Bank through a Century* (London, 1936).

T. E. Gregory (editor), *Select Statutes, Documents and Reports relating to British Banking, 1832–1928* (London, 1929).

R. G. Hawtrey, *A Century of Bank Rate* (London, 1938).

H. O. Horne, *A History of Savings Banks* (Oxford, 1947).

W. T. C. King, *History of the London Discount Market* (London, 1936).

E. V. Morgan, *The Theory and Practice of Central Banking* (Cambridge, 1943).

E. V. Morgan, *Studies in British Financial Policy, 1914–1925* (London, 1952).

R. H. I. Palgrave, *Abstract of Evidence to the House of Commons Committee of 1875 on Banks of Issue* (Printed for private circulation, 1876).

R. H. I. Palgrave, *Bank Rate in England, France and Germany* (London, 1880).

R. H. I. Palgrave, *Bank Rate and the Money Market, 1844–1900* (London, 1903).

L. S. Pressnell, *Country Banking in the Industrial Revolution* (Oxford, 1956).

H. E. Raynes, *A History of British Insurance* (London, 1948).

R. S. Sayers, *Bank of England Operations, 1890–1914* (London, 1936).

United States National Monetary Commission, *Statistics for Great Britain, Germany and France* (Washington, 1910).

G. F. Warren and F. A. Pearson, *Gold and Prices* (New York, 1935).

Wetenhall, *Stock Exchange List* (London, 1811–1907, twice weekly).

GOVERNMENT PUBLICATIONS

Report of the Committee of Secrecy on the Bank of England (*1797*), P.P. XI (reprinted in *S.P.* 1826, III).

Report of the Committee of Secrecy of the House of Lords on the Bank of England (*1797*) (*S.P.* 1810, III).

Report of the Select Committee on the High Price of Gold Bullion (*S.P.* 1810, III).

Report of the Select Committee on the Circulation of Notes under the Value of £5 in Scotland and Ireland (*S.P.* 1826, III).

Report of the Select Committee of the House of Lords on the Circulation of Notes under the Value of £5 in Scotland and Ireland (S.P. 1826–7, VI).

Report of the Committee of Secrecy on the Bank Charter and Banks of Issue (S.P. 1831–2, VI).

Returns relating to Fire Insurance Duty (S.P. 1831–2, XXXIV, and in *Sessional Papers* annually from 1833–70).

Report of the Select Committee on the Commercial Distress (S.P. 1847–8, VIII).

Report of the Select Committee on Banks of Issue (S.P. 1840, IV, and S.P. 1841, V).

Return of the Price of Gold, 1796–1849 (S.P. 1850, LII).

Report on the Post Office Savings Bank, 1862 onwards (in *Sessional Papers* 1862–1920, and issued as non-parliamentary papers thereafter).

Returns from each Savings Bank (in *Sessional Papers* annually from 1885–1920).

Report of the Select Committee on Banks of Issue (S.P. 1875, IX).

Report of the Inspection Committee of Trustee Savings Banks (in *Sessional Papers* annually from 1892–1920, and issued as non-parliamentary papers thereafter).

Report on Financial Relations between Great Britain and Ireland (S.P. 1895, XXXVI, and S.P. 1896, XXXIII).

ARTICLES

W. Manning Dacey, 'Banking Statistics', *J.R.S.S.* (1956).

J. R. Hicks, 'The Future of the Rate of Interest', *T.M.S.S.* (1957–8).

R. P. Higonnet, 'Bank Deposits in the United Kingdom, 1870–1914', *Quarterly Journal of Economics* (1957).

H. G. Johnson, 'Clearing Bank Holdings of Public Debt, 1930–50', *London and Cambridge Economic Service Bulletin* (1951).

H. G. Johnson, 'British Monetary Statistics', *Economica* (1950).

J. Johnston and G. W. Murphy, 'The Growth of Life Assurance in U.K. since 1880', *M.S.E.S.S.* (1957).

K. Maywald, 'Fire Insurance and the Capital Coefficient in Great Britain, 1866–1952', *E.H.R.* (1956).

E. H. Phelps Brown and G. L. S. Shackle, 'Statistics of Monetary Circulation in England and Wales, 1919 to 1937' (*London and Cambridge Economic Service Special Memoranda*, No. 46).

T. R. Porter, 'Sketch of the Progress and Present Extent of Savings Banks in the United Kingdom', *J.S.S.* (1846).

G. T. Williams, 'The Rate of Discount and the Price of Consols', *J.R.S.S.* (1912).

PRICES

TABLES

'The importance to economic and social science of having a comprehensive history of prices and wages hardly needs to be emphasised. Prices and wages are the social phenomena most susceptible of objective statistical record over long periods of time'.[1] Yet prior to the efforts of Lord Beveridge and his colleagues of the Price and Wage History Research group there were few long series of prices known, and, as we saw in Chapter XII, still fewer of wages. However, thanks to Lord Beveridge's group 'the material now available on past wages and prices is incomparably richer than anything hitherto known or imagined'.[2] Most of the lengthy price series which have survived are those paid by institutions, often on contracts rather than in the market place, and these are closer to wholesale than to retail prices. Their rigidity suggests that, for some goods at least, they were partially insulated from ordinary fluctuations,[3] though this view is not universally accepted. They can certainly be used as a measure of general price trends for periods before the nineteenth century, when more varied quotations become available; but the information they give on short-period movements and on retail prices is usually indirect, and possibly unreliable. Nevertheless, Mrs E. B. Schumpeter and Dr Gilboy made a notable attempt to produce a cost-of-living index using the Beveridge group's material,[4] and this is shown in table 1. It is

[1] Sir William Beveridge and others, *Prices and Wages in England*, vol. 1 (London, 1939), p. 1.
[2] Lord Beveridge, 'Wages and Inflation in the Past', in *The Incorporated Statistician* (October 1957).
[3] This is certainly not true of all goods (e.g. corn and coal), and for those goods for which there are long periods of constancy, it may be that, whilst prices remained constant, qualities varied.
[4] This material is deposited in the library of the Institute of Historical Research at London University.

admittedly a crude index, and could probably be improved on from the results of later research, but as a broad guide to secular price trends it is useful.

The next four tables are also indices of general prices, mainly wholesale and import prices. In selecting these four we have tried to cover fully the period from 1790–1938 with the best available indices. For the years to 1850, the Gayer-Rostow-Schwartz series, despite some minor criticisms[1] have replaced their predecessors—Silberling,[2] Jevons[3] and Sauerbeck[4]—and they form table 2 here. The Rousseaux indices also cover the greater part of this period, as well as continuing up to 1913. They are not based on such comprehensive material as the Gayer-Rostow-Schwartz series, but they have been included here (as table 3) partly because Rousseaux presents a breakdown into a number of commodity sub-groups, instead of the domestic/imported breakdown of the former. A similar long-period index for 1786–1924 was constructed by Kondratieff, but the method, which used no weights, was crude. With the Sauerbeck-*Statist* index (table 4), more detailed commodity breakdowns were available than could be made for the earlier periods,[5] though only the main sub-groups are shown here. The principal criticism of this index is that these sub-groups do not contain enough commodities. But it covers a period for which no other detailed series are yet available, and its continuation to 1938 gives a long period for comparison, though the commodities tend to be less representative as time goes on. Table 5 shows the various Board of Trade wholesale price indices, which go back to 1871 and are the best for this period.

When compared with the information available on whosesale prices, what we know about retail prices in history is negligible. Apart from the London bread prices, shown in table 13, there is scarcely a series of any length until the end of the nineteenth century. Such as there are can be found in the record of the Board of Trade's enquiry into wholesale and retail prices of 1903.[6] The first official cost of living index was established at the outset of the First World War and was based on a family budget enquiry made in 1904. The base year for the index was 1914 and the pioneers at the Labour Department were unable to push it back beyond 1892. Even then it was not very satisfactory, since it referred only to prices in London, and the data came mainly from large stores, where movements may not always have been the same as in working-class districts. This index is shown in table 6, together with the fresh index constructed after the First World War. All cost-of-living indices using fixed weights are liable to become out-of-date as expenditure habits change, but the inter-war index suffered particularly in this respect, since its weighting was based

---

[1] For example the 'overweighting of mutton as compared with beef, and of soap and tallow as compared with leather and hides, and of wheat in relation to all other commodities', mentioned in T. S. Ashton, 'Economic Fluctuation 1790–1850', in *E.H.R.* vol. VII, no. 3 (1955), p. 381.

[2] N. J. Silberling, 'British Prices and Business Cycles, 1779–1850', in the *Review of Economic Statistics* (1923), pp. 232–3.

[3] W. S. Jevons, *Investigations in Currency and Finance* (London, 1884), pp. 144–5.

[4] A. Sauerbeck, 'Prices of Commodities and the Precious Metals', in *J.S.S.* (1886). This refers to his index for 1818–50.

[5] This may not be true nowadays if the material available to Gayer, Rostow and Schwartz were used.

[6] *S.P.* 1903, LXVIII.

on 1914 expenditure. It was especially affected by the fall in food prices in the 1930's, and the indicated fall in the cost of living is almost certainly excessive. Other cost-of-living indices compiled by Bowley and Wood in connection with their wage enquiries did go back rather longer than the Labour Department's—Bowley's to 1880, with more specu- lative estimates (linked to Sauerbeck's wholesale index) back to 1846, and Wood's to 1850. These were based to a considerable degree on the same material as the Labour Depart- ment's index, and, before 1892, on more scattered information. As careful estimates by experienced investigators they are valuable guides, though their limitations must be recognised: Bowley himself assessed the margin of error of his index at plus or minus 5.[1] These indices are both shown in Chapter XII, table 1, with the wage indices which they were designed to complement.

The second half of this section consists of the actual prices of six of the most important commodities—wholesale and import or export prices of coal, corn, cotton, iron, and wool, and the London bread prices already mentioned. None of these tables pretends to be exhaustive, and in most cases the sources referred to give a much greater amount of detail than is reproduced here, as well as covering other commodities. Our aim has been to give series which continue for as long as possible for representative varieties of the goods in question. For this reason many sources of scattered prices, or of prices of other com- modities, have not been used. One could multiply examples of these, since scarcely a monograph on industrial or commercial history fails to provide some additional price quotations. However, two major studies of prices, in addition to those used, and two collections of material, do deserve to be singled out. The two works are Thomas Tooke's[2] and Thorold Rogers's.[3] The latter, like Lord Beveridge's group, worked largely in the field of institutional prices, covering a long span up to the eighteenth century. The former tackled a shorter period, but was based mainly on market prices derived from *Prince's Price Current*. A collection of series from this and similar price currents back to 1779 was transcribed by Silberling when he was constructing his index, and is in the care of the Harvard Committee on Economic Research.[4] The originals came from the London Guild- hall Library, the library of the Board of Trade, and the British Museum. More recently, other London price currents for the late seventeenth and early eighteenth centuries have come to light, and photostat copies are available in the Goldsmith Library at London University and the Kress Library of the Harvard Business School.[5]

[1] A. L. Bowley, *Wages and Income since 1860* (Cambridge, 1937), p. 31, and the discussion in appendix D, pp. 114–126.
[2] T. Tooke, *A History of Prices, 1793–1847* (4 vols., London, 1838–48), continued for a further decade by William Newmarch in two more volumes.
[3] J. E. T. Rogers, *A History of Agriculture and Prices in England* (7 vols., Oxford, 1866–1902).
[4] A list of the series available is given in A. D. Gayer, W. W. Rostow, and Anna J. Schwartz, *The Growth and Fluctuation of the British Economy, 1790–1850* (2 vols., Oxford, 1953), vol. I, pp. 475–8.
[5] This information is contained in J. M. Price, 'Notes on Some London Price Currents, 1667–1715', in *E.H.R.* vol. VII, No. 2 (1954). The author discusses the advantages and disadvantages of this type of source.

Prices 1. The Schumpeter-Gilboy Price Incides—1661–1823

NOTES TO PART A

[1] SOURCE: Elizabeth B. Schumpeter, 'English Prices and Public Finance, 1660–1822', *Review of Economic Statistics* (1938).

[2] The indices are based very largely on contract prices paid by institutions.

[3] All figures are for years ended Michaelmas.

Part A. 1697 = 100

	Consumers' Goods(a)	Producers' Goods(b)		Consumers' Goods(a)	Producers' Goods(b)
1661	109	96	1680	93	82
1662	113	105	1681	90	79
1663	111	97	1682	90	80
1664	105	95	1683	88	84
1665	105	101	1684	89	83
1666	101	108	1685	91	75
1667	96	112	1686	92	69
1668	96	102	1687	81	71
1669	92	92	1688	81	70
1670	93	92	1689	80	77
1671	92	97	1690	82	89
1672	89	91	1691	83	97
1673	88	96	1692	82	87
1674	94	92	1693	86	89
1675	101	89	1694	95	88
1676	96	91	1695	95	92
1677	89	87	1696	96	101
1678	90	85	1697	100	100
1679	95	86			

(a) *Viz.* broadcloth, kersey, leather backs, tallow candles, and wheat.

(b) *Viz.* deals ordinary, deals sprutia, duck, timber firr, tarr Stockholm, bricks, copper wrought, hemp, lead, and train oil.

B. 1701 = 100

	Consumers' Goods(a)	Consumers' Goods other than Cereals(b)	Producers' Goods(c)		Consumers' Goods(a)	Consumers' Goods other than Cereals(b)	Producers' Goods(c)
1696	121	112	112	1718	93	94	91
1697	122	115	109	1719	97	99	92
1698	128	119	101	1720	102	96	91
1699	132	124	102	1721	100	100	89
1700	115	107	99	1722	92	96	91
1701	100	100	100	1723	89	91	86
1702	99	99	104	1724	94	89	87
1703	94	102	104	1725	97	93	87
1704	98	95	102	1726	102	97	92
1705	89	88	102	1727	96	92	97
1706	101	100	98	1728	99	92	95
1707	88	90	95	1729	104	94	95
1708	92	89	97	1730	95	91	98
1709	107	94	100	1731	88	86	95
1710	122	104	106	1732	89	90	90
1711	135	131	109	1733	85	87	86
1712	101	98	98	1734	88	87	86
1713	97	95	96	1735	89	84	83
1714	103	95	91	1736	87	81	82
1715	104	99	86	1737	93	89	81
1716	99	96	89	1738	91	85	81
1717	95	97	90	1739	89	85	87

See p. 469 for footnotes

	Consumers' Goods(a)	Consumers' Goods other than Cereals(b)	Producers' Goods(c)		Consumers' Goods(a)	Consumers' Goods other than Cereals(b)	Producers' Goods(c)
1740	100	85	89	1782	116	106	120
1741	108	95	97	1783	129	113	117
1742	99	97	97	1784	126	111	108
1743	94	91	91	1785	120	109	107
1744	84	86	98	1786	119	106	113
1745	85	87	81	1787	117	106	111
1746	93	94	91	1788	121	111	113
1747	90	89	86	1789	117	108	107
1748	94	95	89	1790	124	112	107
1749	96	93	91	1791	121	109	107
1750	95	91	88	1792	122	113	111
1751	90	85	85	1793	129	117	124
1752	93	87	81	1794	136	121	119
1753	90	85	81	1795	147	119	122
1754	90	85	89	1796	154	122	138
1755	92	88	91	1797	148	142	141
1756	92	89	93	1798	148	142	129
1757	109	92	94	1799	160	146	128
1758	106	94	101	1800	212	168	144
1759	100	96	101	1801	228	166	162
1760	98	97	102	1802	174	149	...
1761	94	91	101	1803	156	148	...
1762	94	90	102	1804	161	151	...
1763	100	92	102	1805	187	158	...
1764	102	94	101	1806	184	159	...
1765	106	97	99	1807	186	159	...
1766	107	96	99	1808	204	167	...
1767	109	93	99	1809	212	169	...
1768	108	92	98	1810	207	169	...
1769	99	92	92	1811	206	183	...
1770	100	92	94	1812	237	181	...
1771	107	96	94	1813	243	190	...
1772	117	103	98	1814	209	189	...
1773	119	102	99	1815	191	190	...
1774	116	101	98	1816	172	160	...
1775	113	96	98	1817	189	155	...
1776	114	102	101	1818	194	170	...
1777	108	99	102	1819	192	174	...
1778	117	106	104	1820	162	148	...
1779	111	102	110	1821	139	135	...
1780	110	106	113	1822	125	129	...
1781	115	105	110	1823	128	121	...

(a) Viz. barley, beans, biscuits, break, flour, oats, peas, rye, wheat, beef for salting, butter, cheese, pork, ale, beer, cider, hops, malt, pepper, raisins, sugar, tea, tallow candles, coal, broadcloth, hair, felt hats, kersey, leather backs, Brussels linen, Irish linen, blue yarn stockings.

(b) Viz. all items after wheat in footnote (a).
(c) Viz. bricks, coal, lead, pantiles, plain tiles, hemp (to 1794), leather backs (to 1793), train oil (to 1783), tallow (to 1780), lime (to 1779), glue (to 1778), and copper (to 1776).

Prices 2. Indices of British Commodity Prices 1790–1850, Based on the Gayer, Rostow and Schwartz Monthly Indices

NOTES

[1] SOURCE: Annual average of the monthly figures in A. D. Gayer, W. W. Rostow and A. J. Schwartz, *The Growth and Fluctuation of the British Economy 1790–1850* (2 vols, Oxford, 1953), vol. 1, pp. 468–70.

[2] The composition and weighting of the indices is as follows:

Domestic		Imported			
Wheat	745	Sugar	166	Pepper	3
Oats	497	Cotton	163	Beeswax	2
Mutton	461	Wool	119	Brimstone	2
Beef	239	Tea	111	Cochineal	2
Coal	216	Raw Silk	61	Isinglass	2
Tallow	132	Tobacco	58	Liquorice	2
Butter	116	Timber	38	Logwood	2
Pork	116	Rum	28	Madder	2
Iron Bars	83	Flax	27	Mahogany	2
Iron Pigs	66	Brandy	22	Shumac	2
Leather Butts	41	Port wine	22	Annatto	1
Hard Soap	41	Staves	20	Balsam	1
Hides	38	Indigo	19	Barwood	1
Tinplates	21	Hemp	18	Brazilwood	1
Tin	6	Hides	18	Cinnamon	1
Mottled Soap	4	Coffee	18	Cocoa	1
Starch	3	Thrown Silk	13	Fustic	1
Alum	1	Linseed	11	Geneva Spirits	1
Camphor	1	Olive Oil	5	Ginger	1
Linseed Oil	1	Pearl Ashes	4	Jalap	1
Rape Oil	1	Bristles	4	Castor Oil	1
Vitriol	1	Tar	4	Opium	1
Sal-ammoniac	1	Turpentine	4	Whale Oil	1
Clover Seeds	1	Saltpetre	4	Whale Fins	1
		Barilla	3	Quicksilver	1
		Iron	3	Quinine	1

[3] It may seem surprising that in some years the value of the joint index of domestic and imported commodities lies above the values of both its components. This arises apparently from a method of calculation based upon the use of geometric means, together with the decision to make the arithmetic mean of the monthly values of the years 1821–5 equal 100. If the joint index had been calculated simply on the weighted geometric mean of its components the arithmetic average value for this period would not have been 100. To obtain this result each value of the joint series would have to be multiplied by a constant factor, with the effect that some values of this series would lie outside the average of its components.

Suppose we have two indices, A_t, B_t with an arithmetic mean over n values of 100. Then

$$\frac{1}{n} \Sigma_1^n A_t = \frac{1}{n} \Sigma_1^n B_t = 100.$$

Now if we calculate a joint index $A_t^w B_t^{1-w}$ and take the average over the same years we find that

$$\frac{1}{n} \Sigma_1^n A_t^w B_t^{1-w} = c,$$

where c is not in general equal to 100. Then in order to obtain a base of 100 for this series we must multiply each individual value by $\frac{1}{c}$, giving as the joint index $\frac{1}{c} A_t^w B_t^{1-w}$.

(We are indebted to Mr A. D. Bain for this note.)

(Monthly average of 1821–5 = 100)

	Domestic and Imported Commodities	Domestic Commodities	Imported Commodities		Domestic and Imported Commodities	Domestic Commodities	Imported Commodities
1790	89·3	87·1	87·5	1821	99·7	98·4	101·8
1791	89·7	84·5	94·6	1822	87·9	83·9	100·2
1792	88·1	80·6	99·0	1823	97·6	97·0	99·3
1793	96·6	91·6	100·6	1824	101·9	104·2	95·3
1794	98·5	96·3	95·9	1825	113·0	116·5	103·4
1795	114·9	113·6	109·5	1826	100·0	106·7	83·1
1796	116·1	115·8	108·6	1827	99·3	106·2	82·1
1797	106·2	100·8	114·2	1828	96·4	102·9	80·0
1798	107·9	100·2	123·4	1829	95·8	102·8	78·2
1799	124·6	119·9	129·8	1830	94·5	101·7	76·5
1800	151·0	156·6	122·5	1831	95·3	103·0	76·3
1801	155·7	161·7	127·3	1832	91·5	97·9	75·2
1802	122·2	122·3	113·2	1833	88·6	92·2	79·1
1803	123·6	120·4	125·9	1834	86·5	88·4	85·2
1804	124·3	119·7	132·8	1835	84·5	84·3	85·2
1805	136·2	133·5	138·6	1836	95·2	98·4	87·1
1806	134·5	131·9	137·5	1837	94·3	101·6	76·1
1807	131·2	128·3	137·0	1838	97·8	106·0	78·0
1808	144·5	141·3	152·1	1839	104·3	113·4	82·2
1809	155·0	153·8	157·1	1840	102·5	110·4	83·1
1810	153·4	153·5	151·4	1841	97·7	105·9	77·9
1811	145·4	149·2	133·4	1842	88·8	95·3	72·5
1812	163·7	172·2	141·1	1843	79·7	84·5	67·6
1813	168·9	173·1	155·8	1844	81·1	86·7	67·2
1814	153·7	148·5	167·0	1845	83·3	92·0	62·9
1815	129·9	124·6	144·3	1846	86·0	97·2	60·8
1816	118·6	115·0	128·3	1847	96·8	114·0	61·3
1817	131·9	131·8	130·7	1848	81·8	94·8	54·1
1818	138·7	139·8	133·9	1849	73·9	81·4	56·1
1819	128·1	130·4	120·3	1850	73·5	77·4	63·3
1820	115·4	117·4	108·7				

Prices 3. The Rousseaux Price Indices—1800–1913

NOTES

[1] SOURCE: P. Rousseaux, *Les Mouvements de Fond de l'Economie Anglaise, 1800–1913* (Brussels, 1938).
[2] The overall index is an unweighted average of the indices of total agricultural products and of principal in-dustrial products.
[3] The prices used in constructing these indices are mainly wholesale prices and unit-values of imports.

(Average of 1865 and 1885 = 100)

	Vegetable Products(a)	Animal Products(b)	Total Agricul-tural Products	Principal Indus-trial Products(c)	Overall Index
1800	232	111	188	163	175
1801	247	143	210	166	188
1802	184	112	158	146	152
1803	183	116	160	162	161
1804	185	127	157	160	159
1805	211	111	175	166	170
1806	193	107	162	170	166
1807	183	105	155	167	161
1808	207	120	176	202	189
1809	214	129	184	229	206
1810	222	133	190	196	193
1811	190	135	170	186	178
1812	242	140	207	186	196
1813	250	157	216	189	203
1814	243	150	210	195	202
1815	190	117	164	164	164
1816	185	96	152	136	144
1817	229	111	184	137	161
1818	217	121	182	138	160
1819	187	111	160	134	147
1820	169	100	143	121	132
1821	149	88	127	115	121
1822	138	78	116	116	116
1823	151	80	125	116	120
1824	143	84	122	122	122
1825	171	96	144	121	133
1826	144	93	126	107	117
1827	149	90	128	106	117
1828	137	91	122	102	112
1829	141	87	122	98	110
1830	145	86	124	94	109
1831	146	91	126	97	112
1832	145	89	125	93	109
1833	145	80	121	92	107
1834	141	80	119	104	112
1835	140	79	118	106	112
1836	149	94	129	116	123
1837	147	94	129	107	118
1838	156	93	133	105	119
1839	173	93	143	116	130
1840	170	90	141	115	128
1841	149	97	131	110	121
1842	136	94	122	100	111
1843	127	86	113	96	105
1844	137	87	119	96	108

See p. 473 for footnotes

Prices 3. *continued*

See p. 473 for footnotes

(Average of 1865 and 1885 = 100)

	Vegetable Products(a)	Animal Products(b)	Total Agricultural Products	Principal Industrial Products(c)	Overall Index
1845	141	83	120	99	110
1846	136	84	118	99	109
1847	142	92	125	104	115
1848	113	91	107	92	100
1849	109	86	102	87	95
1850	104	81	98	93	95
1851	99	82	94	89	91
1852	100	80	94	93	94
1853	119	96	113	112	112
1854	131	109	125	126	125
1855	134	111	128	122	125
1856	134	109	128	120	124
1857	138	109	130	124	127
1858	114	99	110	112	111
1859	117	103	113	116	115
1860	129	108	122	117	120
1861	121	107	117	114	115
1862	121	102	116	124	120
1863	120	99	114	128	121
1864	117	99	113	125	119
1865	119	109	116	118	117
1866	126	114	123	118	120
1867	137	106	122	114	118
1868	124	104	118	112	115
1869	116	108	114	100	107
1870	113	107	112	109	110
1871	123	105	119	112	115
1872	124	107	129	127	128
1873	130	110	124	129	127
1874	133	111	127	115	121
1875	126	117	124	110	117
1876	126	115	123	107	115
1877	120	109	117	103	110
1878	113	102	110	92	101
1879	111	97	107	88	98
1880	112	100	109	95	102
1881	108	100	105	92	99
1882	107	106	107	95	101
1883	110	106	109	94	101
1884	102	98	101	89	95
1885	91	91	91	85	88
1886	86	84	86	79	83
1887	83	79	82	79	81
1888	88	81	86	82	84
1889	86	83	85	84	84
1890	91	81	91	83	87
1891	96	82	92	79	86
1892	87	85	87	77	82
1893	85	87	86	78	82
1894	77	80	78	71	74

See p. 473 for footnotes

(Average of 1865 and 1885 = 100)

	Vegetable Products(a)	Animal Products(b)	Total Agricultural Products	Principal Industrial Products(c)	Overall Index
1895	73	75	74	71	72
1896	74	71	72	73	73
1897	79	74	78	71	74
1898	85	74	82	75	78
1899	84	73	81	87	84
1900	90	77	87	95	91
1901	86	78	84	87	86
1902	88	82	87	85	86
1903	87	80	85	86	86
1904	82	75	81	86	83
1905	83	78	82	91	86
1906	84	81	83	103	93
1907	90	87	89	104	97
1908	87	86	87	87	87
1909	89	87	89	93	91
1910	93	94	94	100	97
1911	104	87	101	103	102
1912	103	92	100	108	104
1913	100	95	99	114	106

(a) Viz. up to 1850—wheat, rye, oats, bread, peas, flour, hops, beans, oatmeal, tea, coffee, rice, logwood, olive oil, tobacco, pepper, cinnamon, sugar, and rum; after 1850—wheat, flour, barley, oats, hops, bread, potatoes, linseed oil, oatmeal, cocoa, coffee, tea, rice, lemons, oranges, figs, sago, tobacco, cinnamon, pepper, ginger, rum, linseed, currants, palm oil, olive oil, logwood, raisins, raw sugar, linseed oil cake.

(b) Viz. up to 1850—beef, mutton, pig-meat, butter, tallow, cheese, whale oil, and milk; after 1850—beef, mutton, pig-meat, bacon, butter, native tallow, foreign tallow, cheese whale oil, cod-liver oil.

(c) Viz. up to 1850—coal, pig iron, mercury, tin, lead, copper, hemp, cotton, wool, flax, tar, tobacco, hides, skins, tallow, hair, silk, and building wood; after 1850—coal, pig iron, tin, lead, copper, wool (two quotations), hemp, cotton, linseed oil, palm oil, flax, tar, jute, hides, skins, tobacco, silk, foreign tallow, native tallow, and building wood.

Prices 4. The Sauerbeck-*Statist* Price Indices—1846–1938

NOTES

[1] SOURCE: A. Sauerbeck, 'Prices of Commodities and the Precious Metals', in the *J.S.S.* (1886), continued annually thereafter in the same source by Sauerbeck and subsequently by the editor of *The Statist*.

[2] These indices are based on wholesale prices and unit values of imports.

(Average of 1867–77 = 100)

	Food				Raw Materials				
	Vegetable (a)	Animal (b)	Sugar, Tea and Coffee(c)	Total	Minerals (d)	Textile Fibres(e)	Sundry(f)	Total	Overall Index
1846	106	81	98	95	92	77	86	85	89
1847	129	88	87	105	94	78	86	86	95
1848	92	83	69	84	78	64	77	73	78
1849	79	71	77	76	77	67	75	73	74
1850	74	67	87	75	77	78	80	78	77
1851	73	68	84	74	75	75	79	76	75
1852	80	69	75	75	80	78	84	81	78
1853	100	82	87	91	105	87	101	97	95
1854	120	87	85	101	115	88	109	104	102
1855	120	87	89	101	109	84	109	101	101
1856	109	88	97	99	110	89	109	102	101
1857	105	89	119	102	108	92	119	107	105
1858	87	83	97	88	96	84	102	94	91
1859	85	85	102	89	98	88	107	98	94
1860	99	91	107	98	97	90	111	100	99
1861	102	91	96	97	91	92	109	99	98
1862	98	86	98	94	91	123	106	107	101
1863	87	85	99	89	93	149	101	115	103
1864	79	89	106	88	96	162	98	119	105
1865	84	97	97	91	91	134	97	108	101
1866	95	96	94	95	91	130	99	107	102
1867	115	89	94	101	87	110	100	100	100
1868	113	88	96	100	85	106	102	99	99
1869	91	96	98	94	89	109	100	100	98
1870	88	98	95	93	89	106	99	99	96
1871	94	100	100	98	93	103	105	101	100
1872	101	101	104	102	127	114	108	115	109
1873	106	109	106	107	141	103	106	114	111
1874	105	103	105	104	116	92	96	100	102
1875	93	108	100	100	101	88	92	93	96
1876	92	108	98	99	90	85	95	91	95
1877	100	101	103	101	84	85	94	89	94
1878	95	101	90	96	74	78	88	81	87
1879	87	94	87	90	73	74	85	78	83
1880	89	101	88	94	79	81	89	84	88
1881	84	101	84	91	77	77	86	80	85
1882	84	104	76	89	79	73	85	80	84
1883	82	103	77	89	76	70	84	77	82
1884	71	97	63	79	68	68	81	73	76
1885	68	88	63	74	66	65	76	70	72
1886	65	87	60	72	67	63	69	67	69
1887	64	79	67	70	69	65	67	67	68
1888	67	82	65	72	78	64	67	69	70
1889	65	86	75	75	75	70	68	70	72
1890	65	82	70	73	80	66	69	71	72
1891	75	81	71	77	76	59	69	68	72
1892	65	84	69	73	71	57	67	65	68
1893	59	85	75	72	68	59	68	65	68
1894	55	80	65	66	64	53	64	60	63
1895	54	78	62	64	62	52	65	60	62

See p. 475 for footnotes

Prices 4. *continued*

(Average of 1867–77 = 100)

	Food				Raw Materials				Overall Index
	Vegetable (a)	Animal (b)	Sugar, Tea and Coffee(c)	Total	Minerals (d)	Textile Fibres(e)	Sundry(f)	Total	
1896	53	73	59	62	63	54	63	60	61
1897	60	79	52	65	66	51	62	59	62
1898	67	77	51	68	70	51	63	61	64
1899	60	79	53	65	92	58	65	70	68
1900	62	85	54	69	108	66	71	80	75
1901	62	85	46	67	89	60	71	72	70
1902	63	87	41	67	82	61	71	71	69
1903	62	84	44	66	82	66	69	72	69
1904	63	83	50	68	81	71	67	72	70
1905	63	87	52	69	87	72	68	75	72
1906	62	89	46	69	101	80	74	83	77
1907	69	88	48	72	107	77	78	86	80
1908	70	·89	48	72	89	62	73	74	73
1909	71	89	50	73	86	64	76	75	74
1910	65	96	54	74	89	73	81	81	78
1911	70	90	61	75	93	76	81	83	80
1912	78	96	62	81	110	76	82	88	85
1913	69	99	54	77	111	84	83	91	85
1914	75	100	58	81	99	81	87	88	85
1915	108	126	70	107	126	92	109	108	108
1916	133	152	86	130	158	129	136	140	136
1917	177	192	113	169	172	192	174	179	179
1918	168	207	130	174	192	222	202	206	192
1919	179	213	147	185	220	228	219	222	206
1920	227	263	198	234	295	262	244	264	251
1921	143	218	83	158	181	140	145	153	155
1922	107	184	82	130	142	134	124	132	131
1923	98	162	101	122	155	140	117	134	129
1924	119	158	105	130	158	170	120	146	139
1925	118	162	89	128	154	165	119	143	136
1926	108	150	88	119	154	133	114	131	126
1927	108	138	83	114	141	131	118	129	122
1928	107	142	78	114	123	136	117	124	120
1929	99	146	72	110	126	122	111	119	115
1930	77	142	54	96	112	84 ·	97	97	97
1931	68	119	50	83	100	63	85	82	83
1932	72	105	50	79	99	64	81	81	80
1933	60	106	47	74	107	67	80	83	79
1934	63	108	50	77	109	72	80	85	82
1935	66	107	42	76	112	80	83	90	84
1936	76	109	41	81	118	83	88	94	89
1937	93	117	49	93	142	93	101	110	102
1938	81	111	43	84	136	75	87	96	91

(a) Viz. English wheat, American wheat, flour, barley, oats, maize, potatoes, and rice.
(b) Viz. prime beef, middling beef, prime mutton, middling mutton, pork, bacon, and butter.
(c) Viz. West Indian sugar, beet sugar, Java sugar, and averages of various types of coffee and tea.

(d) Viz. iron, copper, tin, lead, coal in London, and coal for export.
(e) Viz. uplands cotton, Dhollerah cotton, flax, hemp, jute, English wool, merino wool, and silk.
(f) Viz. hides, leather, tallow, palm oil, olive oil, linseed oil, and seeds, petroleum, soda crystals, nitrate of soda, indigo, and timber.

Prices 5. Board of Trade Wholesale Price Indices—1871–1938

NOTES TO PART A

[1] SOURCE: 18th *Abstract of Labour Statistics* (collected from the *Board of Trade Journal* and revised).

[2] These indices are based on market prices and on unit values of imports and exports.

A. 1871–1920. 1900 = 100

| | Coal and Metals(a) | Textile Fibres(b) | Corn, etc.(c) | Food and Drink | | | | Miscellaneous Materials (g) | Total Index |
				Animal Products (d)	Sugar, Tea, Tobacco, etc.(e)	Wine and Foreign Spirits(f)	Total		
1871	68·3	146·4	163·5	110·6	239·2	122·7	144·1	145·1	135·6
1872	102·9	166·5	169·2	111·9	242·1	122·8	147·3	151·5	145·2
1873	128·3	161·9	178·3	119·3	229·7	124·4	153·4	156·8	151·9
1874	104·8	151·1	178·5	120·1	216·2	119·2	152·5	154·5	146·9
1875	84·6	147·3	161·6	127·3	213·4	116·1	148·9	140·3	140·4
1876	72·4	137·9	160·2	127·7	207·9	112·4	148·0	141·1	137·1
1877	67·5	135·2	175·5	125·3	228·2	113·2	154·8	139·3	140·4
1878	62·8	131·4	159·7	121·1	202·6	114·8	144·1	125·1	131·1
1879	58·7	123·0	157·4	114·4	192·0	116·9	138·9	113·8	125·0
1880	64·8	130·0	159·0	116·1	197·1	119·1	140·9	124·4	129·0
1881	61·9	127·6	154·1	116·3	192·9	112·9	138·6	123·0	126·6
1882	62·2	123·4	153·7	122·1	191·3	109·4	141·0	123·7	127·7
1883	60·7	119·1	150·5	123·4	183·6	111·3	139·7	121·6	125·9
1884	57·5	115·2	130·1	114·4	150·4	109·5	123·9	114·5	114·1
1885	54·6	108·9	123·6	104·7	137·6	109·8	115·4	111·4	107·0
1886	52·6	99·9	116·4	100·7	128·9	112·8	109·9	101·7	101·0
1887	53·9	102·7	115·4	96·2	120·8	111·3	106·5	95·3	98·8
1888	56·6	101·2	115·3	104·4	131·4	114·4	110·5	98·0	101·8
1889	62·7	105·1	114·0	101·2	141·2	116·3	110·4	103·1	103·4
1890	74·9	105·4	115·3	99·5	125·3	113·2	108·5	99·4	103·3
1891	70·1	101·4	134·3	99·7	127·2	113·4	116·3	95·0	106·9
1892	65·2	95·6	117·9	99·9	127·8	110·3	109·9	92·5	101·1
1893	59·0	96·4	108·9	103·6	132·8	112·4	108·6	89·3	99·4
1894	60·0	88·6	100·7	99·4	117·8	109·6	101·9	84·5	93·5
1895	56·8	84·3	100·1	96·0	106·7	108·0	98·9	84·9	90·7
1896	55·5	92·9	92·7	90·1	107·8	112·3	93·3	86·5	88·2
1897	56·3	86·8	101·7	92·5	100·8	116·4	97·4	86·9	90·1
1898	61·7	80·0	117·5	89·8	99·9	113·4	102·2	89·7	93·2
1899	72·4	82·9	101·6	94·5	99·6	103·5	98·0	91·3	92·2
1900	100·0	100·0	100·0	100·0	100·0	100·0	100·0	100·0	100·0
1901	82·2	93·3	102·6	99·3	94·7	96·7	100·1	96·3	96·7
1902	76·1	92·3	102·3	104·4	84·4	91·8	101·4	92·5	96·4
1903	74·1	101·7	102·2	102·1	86·4	99·5	100·6	91·7	96·9
1904	70·9	112·9	106·9	98·3	92·5	100·8	101·2	88·3	98·2
1905	71·3	106·7	104·2	97·7	104·8	107·9	101·2	91·1	97·6
1906	78·3	121·1	102·3	102·2	88·7	103·2	101·0	95·6	100·8
1907	86·9	127·4	109·3	104·8	94·2	100·0	105·5	99·7	106·0
1908	78·5	109·8	113·8	103·3	99·0	97·8	107·0	94·8	103·0
1909	73·6	112·4	114·7	105·8	100·4	99·0	108·7	96·5	104·1
1910	76·6	136·2	105·9	111·7	111·7	100·2	109·2	104·3	108·8
1911	74·7	128·9	114·3	109·2	114·1	104·1	111·6	105·5	109·4
1912	84·9	119·6	124·0	116·8	120·4	111·9	119·9	110·1	114·9
1913	92·5	135·0	118·6	119·6	106·8	106·4	117·7	109·4	116·5
1914	86·7	128·8	118·2	122·7	127·0	102·1	120·9	111·3	117·2
1915	116·7	119·8	163·8	145·9	169·8	87·8	154·1	143·8	143·9
1916	165·8	180·1	209·5	175·1	196·7	103·6	189·4	204·0	186·5
1917	182·0	270·4	272·5	228·8	248·6	136·7	246·2	256·3	243·0
1918	204·9	354·4	259·3	263·8	256·9	210·6	260·3	268·6	268·1
1919	280·2	373·3	287·5	273·7	284·4	244·3	279·7	317·8	296·5
1920	419·2	503·7	354·8	306·8	401·6	265·8	334·1	336·6	368·8

(a) Viz. coal (34), pig iron (16), copper (5), lead (1½), tin (1½), and zinc (1½).

(b) Viz. cotton (38), British wool (6), foreign wool (13), silk (9), flax (4), and jute (3).

(c) Viz. British wheat (14), imported wheat (33), British barley (12), imported barley (5), British oats (17), imported oats (4), maize (8), hops (4), rice (1), and potatoes (33).

(d) Viz. English beef (52), English mutton (31), imported bacon and ham (21), milk (29), butter and margarine (12), imported cheese (4), imported eggs (5), and fish (7).

(e) Viz. sugar (2), tobacco (2), tea (8), coffee (1), and cocoa (½).

(f) Viz. wine (5), and foreign spirits (1½).

(g) Viz. cotton seed (2), linseed (5), olive oil (1), palm oil (½). paraffin and paraffin wax (½), petroleum (2), rubber (1½), bricks (3), wood and timber (20), and hides (8).

NOTES TO PART B

[1] SOURCE: *Board of Trade Journal*.
[2] Statistics separating coal from other minerals, and wool from other textiles, were not published for the year 1920. Combined indices for 1920 and 1921 were as follows:

	Coal and Other Minerals	Wool and Other Textiles
1920	251·5	358·9
1921	178·9	171·6

[3] These indices are based on market prices.

B. 1920–34. 1913 = 100

	Food				Metals and Minerals			Textile Materials			Other Articles (f)	Total Index (g)
	Cereals (a)	Meat and Fish(b)	Other Foods(c)	Total	Coal	Iron and Steel	Other(d)	Cotton	Wool	Other(e)		
1920	273·4	262·5	278·9	271·8	...	357·8	...	480·2	...	...	272·9	307·3
1921	194·3	218·5	214·1	209·0	242·9	209·9	131·9	192·3	158·3	193·7	195·6	197·2
1922	151·1	172·1	172·3	165·2	171·7	136·8	116·2	182·2	160·6	173·3	166·0	158·8
1923	139·2	155·7	168·4	154·5	179·3	147·2	114·1	201·9	179·2	159·7	161·9	158·9
1924	160·1	153·6	184·4	166·3	172·4	142·9	120·3	227·8	219·0	165·6	157·6	166·2
1925	163·5	161·7	173·2	166·5	146·0	126·0	121·6	209·8	196·9	171·9	157·4	159·1
1926	150·2	153·8	159·7	154·8	184·6	123·5	120·1	158·3	169·5	147·5	145·0	148·1
1927	152·7	137·5	165·4	152·0	133·6	119·9	111·9	154·7	170·2	138·5	142·5	141·6
1928	149·1	140·9	166·7	152·3	117·9	112·3	107·1	164·2	185·9	137·8	142·3	140·3
1929	137·8	146·2	151·9	145·3	124·5	114·2	116·0	154·4	165·6	131·6	135·5	136·5
1930	109·1	140·2	132·4	126·6	121·4	112·7	95·0	121·2	122·4	101·7	123·8	119·5
1931	89·8	116·0	131·0	111·5	123·1	104·9	78·2	96·8	99·9	80·5	105·6	104·2
1932	96·7	105·7	130·4	110·6	123·3	103·7	80·5	95·8	90·2	79·2	96·2	101·6
1933	90·4	107·1	113·3	103·4	122·3	105·8	84·0	96·2	99·9	74·0	101·4	100·9
1934	93·8	110·1	111·2	104·8	126·0	109·6	81·2	106·9	114·2	69·2	105·2	104·1

(a) Viz. wheat (7), barley (5), oats (2), maize (1), and rice (2).
(b) Viz. beef and veal (6), mutton and lamb (3), pig-meat (5), poultry and eggs (1), and fish (1).
(c) Viz. dairy products (7), fruit and vegetables (5), sugar (2), tea, coffee and cocoa (3), and tobacco (2).
(d) Viz. copper (4), tin (1), lead (1), zinc (1), nickel (1), and petroleum (2).
(e) Viz. silk and artificial silk (2), linen (2), jute (1), and hemp (1).
(f) Viz. paper (2), leather (4), rubber (1), timber (4), bricks (1), stone and slate (2), and glass, china, etc. (1).
(g) The weights are as follows: Total Food—52; Coal—10; Iron and Steel—24; Other Metals and Minerals—10; Cotton —16; Wool—9; Other Textile Materials—6; Other Articles—15.

NOTES TO PART C

[1] SOURCE: *Board of Trade Journal*.
[2] These indices are based on market prices.

C. 1930–8. 1930 = 100

	Food and Tobacco				Industrial Materials and Manufactures								
	Cereals (a)	Meat and Fish(b)	Other Foods (c)	Total	Coal	Iron and Steel	Non-ferrous Metals (d)	Cotton	Wool	Other Textiles (e)	Chemicals and Oils(f)	Miscellaneous (g)	Total Index (h)
1930	100·0	100·0	100·0	100·0	100·0	100·0	100·0	100·0	100·0	100·0	100·0	100·0	100·0
1931	82·0	82·9	97·9	88·5	102·6	92·8	80·9	79·0	81·4	78·6	89·8	86·6	87·8
1932	88·2	75·4	97·3	87·7	103·0	91·5	82·9	78·3	74·6	77·1	90·7	80·3	85·6
1933	83·3	76·9	87·2	82·9	101·5	94·3	87·2	78·7	84·9	73·1	90·3	84·4	85·7
1934	86·4	81·2	86·9	85·0	102·5	98·7	83·9	87·5	95·0	66·4	87·4	88·0	88·1
1935	89·6	80·1	89·9	86·8	102·5	100·5	86·9	86·7	90·0	69·2	91·0	86·3	89·0
1936	99·1	81·1	94·8	91·7	107·6	106·6	93·0	88·8	105·0	72·5	93·5	92·3	94·4
1937	127·0	86·4	98·7	102·2	124·9	129·6	117·4	97·7	127·5	76·3	99·4	110·2	108·7
1938	109·9	85·9	97·5	97·3	123·2	139·1	94·4	83·6	101·4	68·7	94·7	93·2	101·4

(a) Viz. wheat (8), barley (8), oats (1), maize (2), and rice (1).
(b) Viz. beef and veal (6), mutton and lamb (3), pig-meat (6), poultry and eggs (3), and fish (2).
(c) Viz. dairy products (9), fruit and vegetables (7), sugar (4), tea, coffee and cocoa (3), and tobacco (2).
(d) Viz. copper (4), lead (1), tin (1), zinc (1), and nickel and aluminium (1).
(e) Viz. silk and artificial silk (5), linen (2), jute (1), and hemp (1).
(f) Viz. chemicals, drugs, dyes, etc. (6), oils and fats (3,) paints (2), and petroleum (4).
(g) Viz. paper (9), leather (5), rubber (2), timber (8), bricks (2), tiles (1), stone and slate (2), cement (1), sand, lime, etc. (1), glass (1), and china, etc. (1).

Prices 6.   Ministry of Labour Indices of Retail Prices (Cost of Living)—1892–1938

NOTE

SOURCES: Part A—*18th Abstract of Labour Statistics* (1926);   Part B—*Abstract.*

A. Partial Indices 1892–1914, 1900 = 100

	Food	Coal	Clothing		Food	Coal	Clothing
1892	103·9	74·4	101·0	1904	102·4	79·4	102·3
1893	99·3	83·4	100·3	1905	102·8	78·4	103·0
1894	94·9	70·5	99·1	1906	102·0	79·5	104·5
1895	92·1	68·8	97·8	1907	105·0	88·9	106·2
1896	91·7	68·2	98·6	1908	107·5	85·6	107·1
1897	95·5	70·2	98·2	1909	107·6	84·1	108·4
1898	99·5	72·1	97·0	1910	109·4	83·8	110·7
1899	95·4	79·3	96·2	1911	109·4	85·1	112·4
1900	100·0	100·0	100·0	1912	114·5	87·0	115·5
1901	100·4	89·0	100·6	1913	114·8	90·7	115·9
1902	101·0	84·6	99·9	Jan.–July 1914	111·6	92·5	117·4
1903	102·8	80·9	99·7				

B. Indices for Food and All Items, 1915–38, 1914 (July) = 100

	Food	All Items		Food	All Items
1915	131	123	1927	160	167½
1916	160	146	1928	157	166
1917	198½	176	1929	154	164
1918	215	203	1930	145	158
1919	219	215	1931	131	147½
1920	256	249	1932	126	144
1921	229½	226	1933	120	140
1922	176	183	1934	122	141
1923	169	174	1935	125	143
1924	170	175	1936	130	147
1925	171	176	1937	139	154
1926	164	172	1938	141	156

Prices. 7 Prices of Coal Delivered at Westminster School 1585–1830, and at Greenwich Hospital 1716–1828

NOTES

[1] SOURCE: Sir William Beveridge and others, *Prices and Wages in England*, vol. 1 (London, Longmans Green & Co., 1939), pp. 193–6 and 294–5.

[2] The London chaldron weighed between 26 and 27 cwt.

[3] Both institutions ordered coal in summer.

[4] Both series include all duties. Except during the Interregnum, these were small prior to the Great Fire of London. According to Professor Nef (*The Rise of the British Coal Industry* (London, 1932), vol. II, p. 83 note) they came to 8d–10d per (London) chaldron, and according to the Beveridge group (*op. cit.* p. 177) they were about 1/- up to 1645 and 2/- when the records restart. A tax of 3/- per chaldron was in force in the 1670's, imposed for rebuilding the London churches, and this continued for over a century afterwards. In 1694 a national tax of 5/- per chaldron was imposed, and 8/- continued to be the rate of the main duties at London up to 1778. The following changes of rate are recorded in the Greenwich accounts thereafter: (Beveridge group: *op. cit.* p. 269.)

1778	8/- + 5 per cent	1804	11·67/-
1781	8/- + 10 per cent	1806	12·47/-
1786	8·83/-	1809	12·50/-
1797	8·83/- + 5 per cent	1814	9·33/-
1802	9·33/-	1823	6·00/-
1802	9·33/- + 12½ per cent		

Other minor dues included the Richmond shilling (i.e. 6d per London chaldron), metage dues of 4d per chaldron, and various others amounting together at their maximum during the Napoleonic Wars to about 8d per chaldron.

[5] Costs of carriage for the coal delivered at Westminster were around 9d–11d per chaldron in the 1590's. From 1610–42 they rose from about 2/-–2/6 per chaldron, and during the eighteenth century they were about 4/-–5/-. (Beveridge group: *op. cit.* p. 174.) Costs of unloading and porterage for the Greenwich coal were as follows for selected years from 1741 onwards: (Beveridge group: *op. cit.* p. 271.)

1741	4·75/- per chaldron		
1749	5·02/-	,,	,,
1759	5·48/-	,,	,,
1768	5·37/-	,,	,,
1779	6·50/-	,,	,,
1791	5·89/-	,,	,,
1799	7·18/-	,,	,,
1809	8·29/-	,,	,,
1819	8·38/-	,,	,,
1827	8·54/-	,,	,,

[6] There is no indication of the quality of coal delivered at Westminster, but at Greenwich Bucksnook followed by Main Team coal was used up to 1797 (and by the brewery until 1811). From 1798 Wallsend or Hebburn (i.e. what was described in the nineteenth century as 'best') was used mainly.

(in shillings per London chaldron)

	Westminster		Westminster		Westminster		Westminster
1585	15·75	1606	17·19	1627	21·55	1672	61·13
1586	15·69	1607	18·66	1628	18·07	1673	...
1587	15·46	1608	18·64	1629	21·42	1674	27·47
1588	19·45	1609	15·91	1630	22·25	1675	...
1589	17·76	1610	15·83	1631	21·25	1676	26·00
1590	14·75	1611	15·67	1632	20·80	1677	24·36
1591	13·07	1612	16·20	1633	20·78	1678	26·40
1592	12·75	1613	18·50	1634	20·32	1679	22·81
1593	15·25	1614	18·53	1635	21·96	1680	...
1594	13·59	1615	19·25	1636	22·17	1681	...
1595	16·92	1616	19·11	1637	20·34	1682	21·00
1596	15·92	1617	15·61	1638	...	1683	...
1597	14·26	1618	15·50	1639	22·13	1684	...
1598	13·97	1619	16·86	1664	29·32	1685	20·53
1599	...	1620	16·42	1665	...	1686	...
1600	13·83	1621	15·50	1666	47·19	1687	...
1601	14·00	1622	15·50	1667	32·54	1688	...
1602	13·85	1623	...	1668	23·32	1689	...
1603	13·42	1624	...	1669	...		
1604	12·50	1625	...	1670	...		
1605	15·50	1626	19·80	1671	...		

See p. 481 *for footnotes*

(in shillings per London chaldron)

	Westminster	Greenwich		Westminster	Greenwich
1690	...	...	1744	35·00	30·04
1691	36·27	...	1745	34·13	29·45
1692	31·92	...	1746	32·82	28·05
1693	33·08	...	1747	31·06	27·63
1694	28·58	...	1748	32·12	28·61
1695	34·40	...	1749	31·77	27·30
1696	27·35	...	1750	29·90	26·14
1697	27·70	...	1751	31·13	28·18
1698	22·04	...	1752	32·04	27·62
1699	25·00	...	1753	32·10	27·57
1700	24·30	...	1754	34·58	31·38
1701	27·77	...	1755	40·59	34·90
1702	33·21	...	1756	38·24	35·70
1703	34·83	...	1757	38·39	36·10
1704	39·03	...	1758	36·78	35·01
1705	30·38	...	1759	34·37	32·13
1706	...	...	1760	36·39	34·44
1707	27·70	...	1761	37·30	37·00
1708	33·72	...	1762	33·97	31·47
1709	32·58	...	1763	35·93	33·42
1710	30·68	...	1764	36·02	33·36
1711	32·03	...	1765	34·56	31·17
1712	30·53	...	1766	33·05	30·01
1713	31·57	...	1767	33·05	30·79
1714	30·38	...	1768	32·07	30·19
1715	28·95	...	1769	32·54	30·19
1716	29·53	30·63	1770	33·88	32·90
1717	32·03	23·81	1771	36·56	32·89
1718	32·53	29·83	1772	34·55	31·08
1719	32·08	28·54	1773	34·39	31·43
1720	28·03	26·85	1774	36·93	32·53
1721	29·33	26·58	1775	38·93	35·58
1722	28·58	25·71	1776	38·44	36·63
1723	28·08	26·10	1777	38·44	38·32
1724	28·40	26·10	1778	38·93	39·96
1725	31·03	27·19	1779	39·90	40·08
1726	28·63	25·71	1780	39·90	41·58
1727	28·45	26·54	1781	42·83	42·68
1728	30·60	28·74	1782	35·03	35·75
1729	28·47	25·00	1783	34·92	34·21
1730	36·33	28·78	1784	36·98	35·76
1731	29·19	25·86	1785	36·39	34·94
1732	27·98	26·41	1786	36·88	34·80
1733	28·84	26·78	1787	38·52	34·54
1734	29·00	27·30	1788	37·53	35·43
1735	...	27·18	1789	39·00	...
1736	29·50	27·25	1790	38·53	37·23
1737	30·12	28·37	1791	38·52	35·87
1738	30·69	...	1792	41·47	41·20
1739	33·67	31·62	1793	46·47	42·03
1740	30·76	26·49	1794	48·35	41·70
1741	30·98	27·89	1795	35·06	39·83
1742	31·63	26·74	1796	...	39·62
1743	33·88	32·65	1797	48·31	40·37

(in shillings per London chaldron)

	Westminster	Greenwich			Westminster	Greenwich	
		...(a)				...(a)	
1798	58·77	...(a)	50·81(b)	1815	63·94	...(a)	52·32(b)
1799	56·70	...	54·33	1816	59·55	...	49·79
1800	50·42	...	47·76	1817	59·55	...	52·50
1801	51·34	42·70	46·78	1818	59·55	...	50·72
1802	58·67	49·30	52·87	1819	57·46	...	50·14
1803	63·10	...	54·25	1820	60·44	...	49·19
1804	65·20	51·56	54·65	1821	56·26	...	47·84
1805	...	52·90	56·14	1822	58·35	...	49·83
1806	65·20	53·25	57·49	1823	49·60	...	47·25
1807	65·20	...	58·77	1824	49·60	...	46·20
1808	70·41	58·77	65·25	1825	49·60	...	43·36
1809	72·53	58·43	64·60	1826	49·08	...	44·40
1810	...	...	64·11	1827	49·08	...	44·03
1811	68·34	54·37	59·90	1828	48·77	...	38·88
1812	71·12	...	60·54	1829	49·29	...	...
1813	71·26	...	66·32	1830	46·29	...	...
1814	69·17	...	58·73				

(a) This column relates to 'ordinary' coal, and continues the previous Greenwich series.

(b) This column relates to best coal.

Prices 8. Average Prices of Coal in London 1788–1938, and for Export 1831–1938

NOTES TO PART A

[1] SOURCES: 1788-1800—S.P. 1830, VII (*Report of the Select Committee on the Coal Trade*, p. 7); 1805-19—S.P. 1871, XVIII (*Report of the Royal Commission on Coal Supply.* committee E, appendix, p. 208); 1820-80—S.P. 1881, LXXXIII; 1881-9—S.P. 1890, LXVII.
[2] The London chaldron weighed between 26 and 27 cwt.
[3] The main government duty is included in the figures for 1805-19 in the source. It has been added to other figures at the following rates: (See table 7, note 4.)

1788-96	8/10 per chaldron
1797-1800	9/3 ,, ,,
1820-3	9/4 ,, ,,
1824-31	6/- ,, ,,

The duty was abolished after 1831.

A. Annual Average Price of Best Coals at the Ships' Side in London, 1788–1889

	per chaldron s. d.			per ton s. d.			per ton s. d.
1788	39	2¾	1832	20	10	1861	18 5
1790	41	7¼	1833	17	2	1862	16 6
1792	39	7	1834	19	5	1863	17 1
1793	43	10¾	1835	20	10	1864	19 0
1795	50	8½	1836	21	10	1865	19 1
1797	44	5½	1837	22	11	1866	19 0
1799	51	3¾	1838	23	5	1867	19 8
1800	61	6½	1839	22	7	1868	17 7
1805	44	9(a)	1840	22	6	1869	17 8
1806	44	5	1841	21	3	1870	17 5
1807	45	10	1842	20	1	1871	18 2
1808	49	3	1843	19	1	1872	23 10
1809	54	6	1844	21	9	1873	31 3
1810	51	8	1845	18	1	1874	24 8
1811	47	8	1846	16	10	1875	22 9
1812	44	10	1847	19	9	1876	20 2
1813	52	5	1848	17	1	1877	18 5
1814	59	1	1849	16	7	1878	16 10
1815	46	9	1850	16	0	1879	16 11
1816	41	8	1851	15	0	1880	14 11
1817	40	4	1852	15	5	1881	16 5
1818	39	10	1853	20	1	1882	16 2
1819	41	10(a)	1854	22	8	1883	17 5
1820	41	9	1855	20	10	1884	15 9
1821	42	6	1856	17	10	1885	15 9
1822	41	10	1857	17	7	1886	15 1
1823	45	1	1858	17	4	1887	15 2
1824	40	6	1859	17	3	1888	15 3
1825	39	10	1860	19	0	1889	16 8
1826	36	2					
1827	37	4					
1828	37	0					
1829	33	11					
1830	35	2					
1831	32	4					

(*a*) The figures for 1805-19 are inclusive of all duties, not merely the government duty. The minor duties came to 1/2 per chaldron in 1819.

Prices 8. *continued*

NOTE TO PART B
SOURCES: 1831–45—*Porter's Tables*; 1846–1938—A. Sauer-beck, 'Prices of Commodities and the Precious Metals', *J.S.S.* (1886), continued annually thereafter in that journal by Sauerbeck and subsequently by the editor of *The Statist*.

B. Annual Average Price of Best Coal in London and of All Exports, 1831–1938

(per ton)

	Wallsend, Hetton in London s. d.	All Exports f.o.b. shillings		Wallsend, Hetton in London s. d.	All Exports f.o.b. shillings
1831	...	7·82	1874	25 0	17·21
1832	...	7·77	1875	24 0	13·28
1833	...	7·29	1876	21 0	10·93
1834	...	7·18	1877	20 0	10·17
1835	...	6·65	1878	18 0	9·46
1836	...	7·26	1879	18 0	8·77
1837	...	7·75	1880	15 6	8·95
1838	...	7·38	1881	17 0	8·97
1839	...	7·49	1882	17 0	9·14
1840	...	7·18	1883	18 0	9·35
1841	...	7·31	1884	16 6	9·29
1842	...	7·34	1885	16 6	8·95
1843	...	7·40	1886	16 0	8·45
1844	...	7·66	1887	16 0	8·32
1845	...	7·69	1888	16 6	8·41
1846	18 0	7·67	1889	17 6	10·21
1847	20 6	7·80	1890	19 0	12·62
1848	18 0	7·81	1891	19 0	12·16
1849	17 6	7·69	1892	18 6	11·04
1850	17 0	7·66	1893	19 6	9·90
1851	16 0	7·51	1894	16 6	10·50
1852	16 6	7·54	1895	15 0	9·33
1853	22 0	8·16	1896	15 0	8·85
1854	23 6	9·87	1897	15 9	8·98
1855	22 0	9·83	1898	16 9	9·92
1856	18 6	9·61	1899	18 6	10·72
1857	18 6	9·52	1900	23 6	16·75
1858	18 0	9·33	1901	20 0	13·86
1859	18 6	9·33	1902	18 6	12·29
1860	20 6	9·06	1903	16 6	11·70
1861	20 0	9·19	1904	16 3	11·13
1862	18 0	9·05	1905	15 6	10·56
1863	18 0	9·00	1906	16 6	10·90
1864	20 0	9·48	1907	19 9	12·75
1865	20 0	9·69	1908	18 0	12·77
1866	19 6	10·29	1909	17 6	11·30
1867	20 0	10·39	1910	17 3	11·72
1868	18 6	9·92	1911	17 9	11·43
1869	18 6	9·62	1912	21 9	12·70
1870	18 6	9·64	1913	21 6	13·94
1871	19 0	9·80	1914	21 3	13·65
1872	25 6	15·83	1915	30 9(a)	16·96
1873	32 0	20·90			

See p. 484 for footnote

(per ton)

	Best Yorks. House s.	d.	All Exports f.o.b. shillings		Best Yorks. House s.	d.	All Exports f.o.b. shillings
1916	27	6(*a*)	24·64	1928	21	5	15·67
1917	27	6(*a*)	27·16	1929	23	5	16·13
1918	33	7	30·6	1930	24	9	16·64
1919	45	4	46·2	1931	24	8	15·98
1920	32	0	79·8	1932	23	5	16·27
1921	32	3	34·83	1933	22	8	16·08
1922	34	5	24·16	1934	20	3	16·08
1923	32	5	25·13	1935	20	3	16·30
1924	27	6	23·38	1936	23	1	16·98
1925	29	8	20·08	1937	24	6	19·05
1926(*b*)	(30	4)	(18·59)	1938	25	8	21·32
1927	23	1	17·80				

(*a*) Approximate figures only. (*b*) Figures for January to April only.

Prices 9. Wheat Prices at Exeter 1316–1820, at Eton 1594–1820, and at Winchester, 1630–1817

NOTES

[1] SOURCES: Exeter series—Sir William Beveridge, 'A Statistical Crime of the Seventeenth Century', *Journal of Economic and Business History* (1929); Winchester series—Sir William Beveridge and others, *Prices and Wages in England*, vol. 1 (London, Longmans Green & Co., 1939), pp. 81–4; Eton series—not previously published, this series has been very kindly made available to us by Lord Beveridge.

[2] All figures in the original sources were adjusted by the Beveridge group to the Winchester quarter (97 per cent of the Imperial quarter).

(in shillings per Winchester quarter)

	Exeter		Exeter		Exeter		Exeter
1316	15·42	1340	3·81	1364	12·09	1388	3·42
1317	8·11	1341	4·17	1365	7·48	1389	5·50
1318	4·17	1342	3·67	1366	5·80	1390	8·25
1319	5·98	1343	5·42	1367	8·02	1391	6·50
1320	6·00	1344	3·70	1368	8·42	1392	3·50
1321	9·90	1345	4·82	1369	10·12	1393	3·25
1322	8·75	1346	6·96	1370	8·92	1394	3·50
1323	7·35	1347	5·82	1371	8·52	1395	3·80
1324	6·36	1348	4·72	1372	7·42	1396	5·25
1325	4·56	1349	6·92	1373	6·25	1397	4·30
1326	3·87	1350	8·78	1374	10·02	1398	5·03
1327	4·75	1351	9·25	1375	7·75	1399	8·00
1328	6·13	1352	5·59	1376	5·32	1400	6·00
1329	6·42	1353	4·55	1377	3·92	1401	9·07
1330	7·30	1354	6·42	1378	3·75	1402	9·33
1331	8·25	1355	7·92	1379	6·42	1403	6·33
1332	6·39	1356	7·52	1380	6·42	1404	5·86
1333	5·11	1357	7·52	1381	6·42	1405	4·21
1334	4·78	1358	7·47	1382	5·50	1406	5·00
1335	4·60	1359	6·37	1383	6·40	1407	5·20
1336	3·64	1360	6·00	1384	5·00	1408	5·69
1337	2·92	1361	4·92	1385	6·40	1409	7·51
1338	...	1362	8·28	1386	6·00	1410	6·00
1339	...	1363	11·62	1387	3·50	1411	5·20

(in shillings per Winchester quarter)

	Exeter		Exeter		Exeter		Exeter
1412	6·00	1455	5·55	1498	6·10	1541	8·27
1413	4·88	1456	6·55	1499	6·10	1542	7·66
1414	4·66	1457	7·14	1500	9·38	1543	9·65
1415	7·34	1458	7·86	1501	7·39	1544	12·70
1416	8·68	1459	4·70	1502	...	1545	19·10
1417	6·40	1460	7·41	1503	7·98	1546	6·46
1418	8·00	1461	8·14	1504	7·98	1547	6·67
1419	6·00	1462	4·05	1505	5·87	1548	9·33
1420	5·40	1463	4·19	1506	...	1549	15·06
1421	5·40	1464	4·80	1507	7·14	1550	15·79
1422	4·70	1465	...	1508	...	1551	20·20
1423	5·20	1466	6·46	1509	5·02	1552	12·66
1424	6·54	1467	6·96	1510	...	1553	10·03
1425	5·60	1468	6·94	1511	6·70	1554	14·51
1426	4·40	1469	7·96	1512	6·83	1555	24·77
1427	5·16	1470	6·64	1513	6·68	1556	32·41
1428	9·27	1471	7·44	1514	5·57	1557	11·47
1429	5·60	1472	5·20	1515	9·14	1558	...
1430	7·04	1473	5·82	1516	6·06	1559	20·64
1431	5·60	1474	5·12	1517	5·51	1560	22·62
1432	7·14	1475	6·15	1518	5·68	1561	15·50
1433	5·28	1476	5·26	1519	8·54	1562	26·96
1434	5·70	1477	6·78	1520	12·94	1563	20·32
1435	7·20	1478	7·54	1521	10·14	1564	21·84
1436	5·34	1479	5·58	1522	6·40	1565	27·03
1437	9·93	1480	5·46	1523	6·94	1566	12·84
1438	11·77	1481	6·15	1524	5·52	1567	14·06
1439	8·25	1482	8·55	1525	6·46	1568	17·06
1440	4·16	1483	9·00	1526	7·04	1569	18·88
1441	4·80	1484	7·28	1527	10·56	1570	...
1442	4·70	1485	5·84	1528	11·21	1571	17·38
1443	5·02	1486	6·22	1529	...	1572	18·21
1444	4·36	1487	7·67	1530	...	1573	20·47
1445	4·76	1488	6·40	1531	...	1574	21·21
1446	7·70	1489	6·31	1532	10·30	1575	29·16
1447	5·66	1490	8·83	1533	8·43	1576	...
1448	5·94	1491	5·44	1534	6·58	1577	22·40
1449	6·68	1492	4·34	1535	10·87	1578	...
1450	7·80	1493	4·97	1536	8·43	1579	...
1451	8·13	1494	5·42	1537	6·64	1580	...
1452	6·64	1495	4·86	1538	7·56	1581	24·38
1453	4·90	1496	6·07	1539	8·70	1582	21·25
1454	5·12	1497	7·51	1540	7·78	1583	...

	Exeter	Eton (a) College	Winchester (b) College		Exeter	Eton (a) College	Winchester (b) College		Exeter	Eton (a) College	Winchester (b) College
1584	21·21	...	...	1635	33·84	45·62	37·51	1686	30·83	30·06	31·03
1585	32·02	...	...	1636	39·08	44·34	30·94	1687	28·00	24·45	22·74
1586	40·57	...	...	1637	46·52	49·40	44·02	1688	20·50	20·17	18·95
1587	22·32	...	...	1638	40·66	37·76	30·50	1689	24·36	28·47	29·30
1588	19·60	...	...	1639	35·40	33·15	27·37	1690	28·01	26·58	23·40
1589	26·66	...	...	1640	38·32	42·68	32·00	1691	39·65	33·47	37·18
1590	20·88	...	...	1641	40·54	35·42	29·35	1692	43·29	42·67	45·92
1591	17·76	...	...	1642	44·38	...	34·17	1693	43·46	62·51	57·67
1592	22·41	...	...	1643	40·92	...	29·36	1694	24·56	34·36	34·59
1593	28·63	...	...	1644	39·53	33·83	25·02	1695	38·69	56·78	53·98
1594	38·88	32·25	...	1645	45·05	35·42	29·59	1696	57·68	44·33	49·24
1595	32·00	32·25	...	1646	50·65	54·22	48·88	1697	55·29	54·00	56·74
1596	62·94	51·59	...	1647	62·72	64·73	54·82	1698	41·25	55·04	55·55
1597	39·92	48·33	...	1648	44·01	69·25	51·94	1699	36·67	39·49	37·53
1598	19·76	30·06	...	1649	43·36	60·58	52·33	1700	33·40	30·59	32·59
1599	20·55	24·33	...	1650	53·88	60·13	48·26	1701	27·20	25·52	24·87
1600	23·83	32·76	...	1651	52·13	47·29	35·89	1702	24·90	23·76	26·52
1601	24·54	23·33	...	1652	40·89	33·01	28·97	1703	27·97	40·25	38·49
1602	...	27·94	...	1653	30·34	25·00	22·18	1704	...	26·89	26·52
1603	...	25·52	...	1654	26·47	19·64	15·80	1705	25·79	21·75	22·29
1604	...	27·64	...	1655	44·56	34·67	28·56	1706	28·01	20·92	23·03
1605	27·98	26·06	...	1656	44·84	33·54	28·98	1707	32·93	24·70	26·91
1606	25·46	30·59	...	1657	47·78	41·08	41·84	1708	55·27	47·00	48·36
1607	42·61	31·73	...	1658	43·66	59·09	46·80	1709	59·47	74·10	69·52
1608	45·58	49·91	...	1659	45·50	49·40	46·21	1710	38·63	45·92	44·98
1609	28·59	32·48	...	1660	50·78	47·52	43·25	1711	34·12	45·39	40·81
1610	28·80	27·42	...	1661	58·37	67·68	53·33	1712	37·02	30·60	35·26
1611	30·13	33·02	...	1662	42·16	46·73	33·53	1713	45·40	50·76	48·89
1612	...	37·31	...	1663	39·50	45·92	34·52	1714	30·29	30·07	31·11
1613	...	38·37	...	1664	36·76	41·39	31·78	1715	34·35	39·50	43·56
1614	31·46	30·06	...	1665	34·94	35·41	30·73	1716	32·08	37·46	38·07
1615	33·08	32·77	...	1666	30·16	25·76	22·36	1717	29·60	35·41	34·96
1616	...	35·41	...	1667	29·32	30·06	24·00	1718	27·80	27·57	25·04
1617	...	39·49	...	1668	45·07	37·61	33·99	1719	39·12	29·53	31·55
1618	37·31	32·25	...	1669	41·16	33·83	27·25	1720	36·39	31·42	31·55
1619	...	35·92	...	1670	35·17	32·78	32·00	1721	29·36	28·56	25·81
1620	22·57	23·33	...	1671	31·91	33·82	27·45	1722	30·69	27·94	28·77
1621	30·73	33·31	...	1672	34·19	33·03	27·65	1723	29·05	29·00	27·99
1622	43·10	52·11	...	1673	54·79	50·46	49·52	1724	34·57	32·25	36·15
1623	37·13	35·94	...	1674	52·11	52·10	46·36	1725	41·04	43·13	38·07
1624	36·30	41·92	...	1675	30·89	35·95	28·89	1726	30·72	31·03	29·55
1625	27·74	41·92	...	1676	30·77	28·16	28·29	1727	46·78	41·18	44·37
1626	33·44	33·53	...	1677	43·20	41·91	46·39	1728	...	42·08	44·22
1627	33·69	24·48	...	1678	39·44	49·92	45·33	1729	...	32·64	30·22
1628	32·88	27·42	...	1679	31·55	36·25	34·81	1730	...	28·16	26·96
1629	36·53	36·49	...	1680	32·00	36·54	37·50	1731	20·00	23·87	22·74
1630	54·68	58·74	48·15	1681	40·69	36·54	33·03	1732	24·46	22·06	22·94
1631	39·33	41·92	35·42	1682	37·90	37·08	34·19	1733	29·22	24·70	24·68
1632	35·02	46·23	34·91	1683	36·21	30·59	32·37	1734	36·53	33·01	31·10
1633	41·53	46·75	39·75	1684	36·00	40·78	43·21	1735	34·67	34·14	33·19
1634	38·00	43·50	38·62	1685	25·12	29·01	26·21	1736	28·50	32·42	26·91

See p. 487 for footnotes

	Exeter	Eton College (a)	Winchester College (b)		Exeter	Eton College (a)	Winchester College (b)		Exeter	Eton College (a)	Winchester College (b)
1737	27·68	29·83	25·94	1765	40·17	39·04	38·35	1793	51·46	45·98	51·17
1738	28·50	27·94	26·50	1766	50·23	46·29	51·60	1794	60·97	57·98	63·08
1739	40·84	34·73	36·39	1767	46·73	52·96	51·46	1795	80·67	85·16	99·83
1740	50·74	48·73	50·20	1768	40·50	41·30	40·72	1796	56·42	54·96	57·25
1741	29·34	28·16	26·64	1769	38·85	35·30	35·00	1797	58·36	56·78	64·75
1742	24·11	22·74	20·92	1770	44·85	44·71	43·37	1798	60·47	51·34	56·83
1743	22·00	19·49	18·13	1771	45·83	49·17	49·79	1799	99·51	98·45	112·00
1744	22·50	20·16	18·55	1772	49·81	54·37	54·94	1800	119·15	138·32	148·50
1745	28·97	28·77	26·22	1773	46·42	50·76	49·37	1801	64·80	67·04	83·75
1746	33·16	29·38	28·03	1774	50·89	52·56	56·34	1802	59·32	57·38	61·75
1747	29·45	27·64	26·98	1775	41·69	39·04	37·37	1803	55·65	53·76	57·04
1748	29·08	29·83	28·58	1776	44·64	40·26	40·79	1804	82·60	76·10	100·50
1749	29·80	27·80	26·78	1777	49·65	45·92	46·54	1805	82·91	76·10	82·50
1750	31·92	26·96	27·61	1778	36·59	34·06	34·62	1806	82·47	78·52	86·21
1751	37·84	37·76	34·93	1779	35·23	33·46	34·34	1807	71·52	66·22	76·50
1752	36·75	35·20	34·59	1780	48·11	47·52	49·78	1808	86·30	88·79	96·00
1753	31·15	32·70	33·19	1781	49·98	44·33	48·07	1809	106·92	105·10	119·00
1754	28·69	25·52	25·94	1782	52·90	52·80	51·73	1810	110·50	94·22	104·50
1755	36·39	29·23	30·40	1783	46·50	47·89	48·59	1811	119·73	112·34	134·50
1756	51·91	49·17	49·92	1784	44·04	45·54	44·45	1812	119·90	115·97	128·25
1757	36·77	43·52	42·12	1785	45·78	39·87	39·56	1813	81·30	85·77	84·08
1758	30·39	34·67	31·24	1786	42·50	38·30	39·42	1814	71·20	74·29	75·00
1759	29·40	29·17	29·00	1787	45·84	45·54	46·76	1815	73·87	65·23	69·00
1760	34·12	27·41	28·59	1788	50·10	46·90	48·13	1816	111·79	101·47	122·00
1761	27·96	28·39	28·59	1789	54·11	50·98	56·48	1817	95·78	92·41	96·00
1762	29·92	30·36	30·54	1790	48·05	48·95	52·33	1818	78·54	77·92	...
1763	36·79	35·28	37·93	1791	40·35	38·67	42·22	1819	73·69	70·67	...
1764	37·92	42·67	39·12	1792	49·10	48·72	51·85	1820	61·09	62·82	...

(a) Means of twice-yearly quotations, adjusted to middling quality wheat by the Beveridge group by reducing the original figures by 9·4 per cent.

(b) Means of four quotations each year, adjusted to middling quality wheat by the Beveridge group by reducing the original figures by 9·0 per cent.

Prices 10. Average Prices of Corn—United Kingdom 1771–1938

NOTES

[1] Sources: 1771–1839—*S.P.* 1843, LIII; 1840–1938—*Abstract*. The original source is the *London Gazette* (though the quotations there up to 1824 were converted into Imperial quarters).

[2] The prices are based on statutory returns from a large number of towns in the British Isles. Before 1801 Ireland, and after 1922 Southern Ireland, are excluded.

(per Imperial quarter)

(per Imperial quarter)

	Wheat		Barley		Oats				Wheat		Barley		Oats	
	s.	d.	s.	d.	s.	d.			s.	d.	s.	d.	s.	d.
1771	48	7	26	5	17	2		1817	96	11	49	4	32	5
1772	52	3	26	1	16	8		1818	86	3	53	10	32	5
1773	52	7	29	2	17	8		1819	74	6	45	9	28	2
1774	54	3	29	4	18	4		1820	67	10	33	10	24	2
1775	49	10	26	9	17	0		1821	56	1	26	0	19	6
1776	39	4	20	9	15	5		1822	44	7	21	10	18	1
1777	46	11	21	1	16	1		1823	53	4	31	6	22	11
1778	43	3	23	4	15	7		1824	63	11	36	4	24	10
1779	34	8	20	1	14	5		1825	68	6	40	0	25	8
1780	36	9	17	6	13	2		1826	58	8	34	4	26	8
1781	46	0	17	8	14	1		1827	58	6	37	7	28	2
1782	49	3	23	2	15	7		1828	60	5	32	10	22	6
1783	54	3	31	3	20	5		1829	66	3	32	6	22	9
1784	50	4	28	8	18	10		1830	64	3	32	7	24	5
1785	43	1	24	9	17	8		1831	66	4	38	0	25	4
1786	40	0	25	1	18	6		1832	58	8	33	1	20	5
1787	42	5	23	4	17	2		1833	52	11	27	6	18	5
1788	46	4	22	8	16	1		1834	46	2	29	0	20	11
1789	52	9	23	6	16	6		1835	39	4	29	11	22	0
1790	54	9	26	3	19	5		1836	48	6	32	10	23	1
1791	48	7	26	10	18	1		1837	55	10	30	4	23	1
1792	43	0	...		16	9		1838	64	7	31	5	22	5
1793	49	3	31	1	20	6		1839	70	8	39	6	25	11
1794	52	3	31	9	21	3		1840	66	4	36	5	25	8
1795	75	2	37	5	24	5		1841	64	4	32	10	22	5
1796	78	7	35	4	21	10		1842	57	3	27	6	19	3
1797	53	9	27	2	16	3		1843	50	1	29	6	18	4
1798	51	10	29	0	19	5		1844	51	3	33	8	20	7
1799	69	0	36	2	27	6		1845	50	10	31	8	22	6
1800	113	10	59	10	39	4		1846	54	8	32	8	23	8
1801	119	6	68	6	37	0		1847	69	9	44	2	28	8
1802	69	10	33	4	20	4		1848	50	6	31	6	20	6
1803	58	10	25	4	21	6		1849	44	3	27	9	17	6
1804	62	3	31	0	24	3		1850	40	3	23	5	16	5
1805	89	9	44	6	28	4		1851	38	6	24	9	18	7
1806	79	1	38	8	27	7		1852	40	9	28	6	19	1
1807	75	4	39	4	28	4		1853	53	3	33	2	21	0
1808	81	4	43	5	33	4		1854	72	5	36	0	27	11
1809	97	4	47	0	31	5		1855	74	8	34	9	27	5
1810	106	5	48	1	28	7		1856	69	2	41	1	25	2
1811	95	3	42	3	27	7		1857	56	4	42	1	25	0
1812	126	6	66	9	44	6		1858	44	2	34	8	24	6
1813	109	9	58	6	38	6		1859	43	9	33	6	23	2
1814	74	4	37	4	25	8		1860	53	3	36	7	24	5
1815	65	7	30	3	23	7		1861	55	4	36	1	23	9
1816	78	6	33	11	27	2		1862	55	5	35	1	22	7

	(per Imperial quarter)					(per Imperial quarter)		
	Wheat	Barley	Oats			Wheat	Barley	Oats
	s. d.	s. d.	s. d.			s. d.	s. d.	s. d.
1863	44 9	33 11	21 2		1901	26 9	25 2	18 5
1864	40 2	29 11	20 1		1902	28 1	25 8	20 2
1865	41 10	29 9	21 10		1903	26 9	22 8	17 2
1866	49 11	37 5	24 7		1904	28 4	22 4	16 4
1867	64 5	40 0	26 0		1905	29 8	24 4	17 4
1868	63 9	43 0	28 1		1906	28 3	24 2	18 4
1869	48 2	39 5	26 0		1907	30 7	25 1	18 10
1870	46 11	34 7	22 10		1908	32 0	25 10	17 10
1871	56 8	36 2	25 2		1909	36 11	26 10	18 11
1872	57 0	37 4	23 2		1910	31 8	23 1	17 4
1873	58 8	40 5	25 5		1911	31 8	27 3	18 10
1874	55 9	44 11	28 10		1912	34 9	30 8	21 6
1875	45 2	38 5	28 8		1913	31 8	27 3	19 1
1876	46 2	35 2	26 3		1914	34 11	27 2	20 11
1877	56 9	39 8	25 11		1915	52 10	37 4	30 2
1878	46 5	40 2	24 4		1916	58 5	53 6	33 5
1879	43 10	34 0	21 9		1917	75 9	64 9	49 10
1880	44 4	33 1	23 1		1918	72 10	59 0	49 4
1881	45 4	31 11	21 9		1919	72 11	75 9	52 5
1882	45 1	31 2	21 10		1920	80 10	89 5	56 10
1883	41 7	31 10	21 5		1921	71 6	52 2	34 2
1884	35 8	30 8	20 3		1922	47 10	40 1	29 1
1885	32 10	30 1	20 7		1923	9 10	9 5	9 7
1886	31 0	26 7	19 0		1924	11 6	13 1	9 9
1887	32 6	25 4	16 3		1925	12 2	11 9	9 9
1888	31 10	27 10	16 9		1926	12 5	10 4	9 0
1889	29 9	25 10	17 9		1927	11 6	11 9	9 0
1890	31 11	28 8	18 7		1928	10 0	11 0	10 5
1891	37 0	28 2	20 0		1929	9 10	9 11	8 10
1892	30 3	26 2	19 10		1930	8 0	7 11	6 2
1893	26 4	25 7	18 9		1931	5 9	7 11	6 3
1894	22 10	24 6	17 1		1932	5 11	7 7	7 0
1895	23 1	21 11	14 6		1933	5 4	7 11	5 7
1896	26 2	22 11	14 9		1934	4 10	8 8	6 3
1897	30 2	23 6	16 11		1935	5 2	7 11	6 8
1898	34 0	27 2	18 5		1936	7 2	8 3	6 4
1899	25 8	25 7	17 0		1937	9 4	10 11	8 7
1900	26 11	24 11	17 7		1938	6 9	10 2	7 7

Prices 11. Raw Cotton Prices—Great Britain 1706–1938

NOTES TO PART A

[1] SOURCE: Thomas Tooke, *A History of Prices* (London, 1838–58), vol. II, pp. 401–2. These prices are stated to be drawn from *Prince's Price Current*.

[2] According to T. Ellison, *The Cotton Trade of Great Britain* (London, 1886), the price range of West Indian cotton in the following periods was:

1771–5	9½ to 14d
1776–80	16d to 25d
1781	19d to 48d

[3] E. Baines, *A History of the Cotton Manufacture* (London, 1835) gives a different series of prices, taken from circulars of Messrs George Holt & Co. of Liverpool, from 1806 for Bowed Georgia and Pernambuco:

	Upland (i.e. Bowed Georgia)	Pernambuco		Upland (i.e. Bowed Georgia)	Pernambuco
1806	15 to 21½	23½ to 29	1814	23 to 37	28¼ to 41
1807	15½ to 19	24½ to 26½	1815	18 to 25½	25½ to 37
1808	15½ to 36	25½ to 42	1816	15 to 21	23 to 30
1809	14 to 34	22½ to 38	1817	16¼ to 23¼	22 to 27¾
1810	14½ to 22½	23 to 29	1818	16½ to 22	22 to 27
1811	12¼ to 16	18 to 23½	1819	10 to 19¾	16 to 23½
1812	13 to 23½	19 to 27½	1820	8 to 13¾	11½ to 18¼
1813	21 to 30	24 to 34			

A. Highest and Lowest Prices in Each Year, West Indies, American and Brazilian, 1782–1820

pence per lb.

	West Indies, Surinam and Berbice	Bowed Georgia	Pernambuco		West Indies, Surinam and Berbice	Bowed Georgia	Pernambuco
1782	20 to 42	—	—	1802	15 to 33	12 to 38	24 to 35
1783	13 to 36	—	—	1803	14 to 27	8 to 15	24 to 29
1784	12 to 25	—	—	1804	12 to 28	10 to 18	21 to 30
1785	14 to 28	—	—	1805	17 to 28	14 to 19	23 to 30
1786	22 to 42	—	—	1806	14 to 26	12 to 15	20 to 24
1787	19 to 34	—	—	1807	14 to 22	10 to 14	21 to 23
1788	14 to 33	—	18 to 31	1808	14 to 33	9 to 30	21 to 33
1789	12 to 22	—	16 to 22	1809	14 to 36	10 to 18	20 to 34
1790	12 to 21	—	19 to 22	1810	17 to 27	10 to 19	21 to 27
1791	13 to 30	—	18 to 31	1811	9 to 21	7 to 14	14 to 22
1792	20 to 30	—	22 to 30	1812	11 to 18	11 to 14	17 to 20
1793	12 to 27	13 to 22	21 to 27	1813	12 to 30	16 to 26	23 to 34
1794	13 to 26	12 to 18	18 to 25	1814	22 to 34	22 to 30	26 to 36
1795	15 to 30	15 to 27	21 to 30	1815	18 to 32	14 to 23	22 to 33
1796	19 to 30	12 to 29	22 to 30	1816	16 to 24	15 to 20	22 to 29
1797	17 to 40	12 to 37	23 to 41	1817	18 to 25	17 to 22	21 to 25
1798	25 to 40	22 to 45	37 to 41	1818	15 to 26	16 to 22	21½ to 26
1799	18 to 55	17 to 60	29 to 52	1819	11 to 23	11 to 19	16½ to 23
1800	20 to 38	16 to 36	33 to 37	1820	8 to 17	8 to 14	12 to 18
1801	21 to 30	17 to 38	32 to 36				

NOTES TO PART B

[1] SOURCES: 1801–1902—*S.P.* 1903, LXVIII; 1903–38—
A. Sauerbeck, 'Prices of Commodities and the Precious
Metals', *J.R.S.S.* (1904) and subsequent issues.
[2] The term 'middling American' is used in *S.P.* 1903,
LXVIII though this is an anachronism for the first half of the

nineteenth century, until the establishment of the Liverpool
Universal Standards. The contemporary designation 'upland'
or 'bowed Georgia' does, however, correspond to the later
'middling American' reasonably closely.

B. Average Prices of Upland or Middling American, 1801–1938

1801	18·00	1836	9·88	1871	8·56	1906	5·95
1802	16·00	1837	7·00	1872	10·56	1907	6·55
1803	12·50	1838	7·00	1873	9·00	1908	5·72
1804	14·00	1839	7·88	1874	8·00	1909	6·33
1805	16·50	1840	6·00	1875	7·38	1910	8·00
1806	18·25	1841	6·25	1876	6·25	1911	7·04
1807	14·50	1842	5·38	1877	6·31	1912	6·45
1808	22·00	1843	4·63	1878	6·13	1913	7·01
1809	20·00	1844	4·88	1879	6·31	1914	6·41
1810	15·25	1845	4·13	1880	6·94	1915	5·87
1811	12·50	1846	4·88	1881	6·44	1916	9·00
1812	16·75	1847	6·13	1882	6·63	1917	16·55
1813	23·00	1848	4·13	1883	5·75	1918	22·30
1814	29·50	1849	5·13	1884	6·00	1919	19·65
1815	20·75	1850	7·00	1885	5·63	1920	23·14
1816	18·25	1851	5·50	1886	5·13	1921	9·40
1817	20·13	1852	5·31	1887	5·50	1922	12·10
1818	20·00	1853	5·75	1888	5·56	1923	15·25
1819	13·50	1854	5·38	1889	5·94	1924	16·26
1820	11·50	1855	5·63	1890	6·00	1925	12·64
1821	9·50	1856	6·31	1891	4·69	1926	9·40
1822	8·25	1857	7·75	1892	4·19	1927	9·54
1823	8·25	1858	6·88	1893	4·63	1928	10·92
1824	8·50	1859	6·75	1894	3·81	1929	10·26
1825	11·63	1860	6·25	1895	3·81	1930	7·49
1826	6·75	1861	8·56	1896	4·32	1931	5·90
1827	6·50	1862	17·25	1897	3·94	1932	5·24
1828	6·38	1863	23·25	1898	3·31	1933	5·54
1829	5·75	1864	27·50	1899	3·56	1934	6·68
1830	6·88	1865	19·00	1900	5·50	1935	6·71
1831	6·00	1866	15·50	1901	4·75	1936	6·70
1832	6·63	1867	10·88	1902	4·88	1937	6·43
1833	8·50	1868	10·50	1903	6·03	1938	4·93
1834	8·63	1869	12·13	1904	6·60		
1835	10·25	1870	9·94	1905	5·09		

Prices 12. Prices of Iron—Great Britain 1801–1938

NOTES TO PART A

[1] SOURCES: Midland Forge Pig Iron—*S.P.* 1833 (evidence of Barclay to the Select Committee on Manufactures); Bar Iron—G. R. Porter, *The Progress of the Nation* (London, 2nd edition, 1847), p. 586.

[2] T. S. Ashton, quoting these pig iron figures, wrote: 'though . . . there was a tendency in times of bad trade for individuals to break away from the associations and to sell at something below official values . . . the figures . . . may be taken as a rough indication of industrial vicissitudes'. (*Iron*

and Steel in the Industrial Revolution (Manchester, 1924), pp. 155–6.)

[3] *The Progress of the Nation* (London, edition of F. W. Hirst, 1912) gives the following prices of merchant bars at Liverpool:

	£	s.	d.
1880	5	15	0
1890	6	0	0
1900	9	10	0

A. Midland Forge Pig Iron and English Merchant Bar Iron, 1801–45

(per ton)

	Midland Forge Pig Iron £ s. d.	English Merchant Bar Iron at Liverpool £ s. d.		Midland Forge Pig Iron £ s. d.	English Merchant Bar Iron at Liverpool £ s. d.
1801	6 15 0	...	1824	5 0 0	8 15 0
1802	6 0 0	...	1825	7 10 0	14 0 0
1803	6 0 0	...	1826	5 0 0	11 0 0
1804	5 16 6	...	1827	4 10 0	10 0 0
1805	6 8 0	...	1828	4 0 0	9 0 0
1806	6 15 0	17 10 0	1829	3 12 6	7 15 0
1807	6 1 3	16 0 0	1830	3 8 9	6 12 6
1808	6 5 0	15 0 0	1831	...	6 5 0
1809	6 5 0	15 10 0	1832	...	6 5 0
1810	6 6 0	14 10 0	1833	...	6 5 0
1811	6 5 0	15 0 0	1834	...	7 15 0
1812	5 10 0	14 0 0	1835	...	6 10 0
1813	5 2 6	13 0 0	1836	...	10 10 0
1814	6 0 0	13 0 0	1837	...	10 10 0
1815	5 0 0	13 5 0	1838	...	9 15 0
1816	3 15 0	11 10 0	1839	...	10 5 0
1817	4 5 0	8 15 0	1840	...	9 0 0
1818	5 10 0	13 0 0	1841	...	8 0 0
1819	6 2 6	12 10 0	1842	...	6 10 0
1820	4 10 0	11 0 0	1843	...	5 5 0
1821	4 0 0	9 0 0	1844	...	4 15 0
1822	3 15 0	8 0 0	1845	...	6 10 0
1823	4 0 0	8 10 0			

NOTES TO PART B

[1] Sources: Scottish Pig Iron and Common Bars—A. Sauerbeck, 'Prices of Commodities and the Precious Metals', in the *J.S.S.* (1886) continued annually thereafter in the same source by Sauerbeck and subsequently by the editor of *The Statist*; Cleveland Pig Iron—*S.P.* 1903, LXVIII up to 1902, and British Iron and Steel Federation, *Statistics of the Iron and Steel Industries* (any annual issue during the 1930's) for later figures.

[2] R. Meade, *The Coal and Iron Industries of the United Kingdom* (London, 1882), p. 741, gives prices of Scottish pig iron back to 1830 differing from Sauerbeck's for the overlap period. They are as follows:

	s.	d.		s.	d.		s.	d.
1830	100	0	1834	85	0	1838	80	0
1831	90	0	1835	90	0	1839	90	0
1832	90	0	1836	135	0	1840	75	0
1833	80	0	1837	90	0	1841	60	0

	s.	d.		s.	d.		s.	d.
1842	50	0	1849	46	1	1856	70	9
1843	56	0	1850	44	5	1857	69	2
1844	54	9	1851	40	3	1858	54	5
1845	...		1852	45	4	1859	51	11
1846	...		1853	61	6	1860	53	9
1847	...		1854	79	9	1861	49	3
1848	44	5	1855	79	9	1862	53	0

[3] G. R. Porter, *The Progress of the Nation* (London, 2nd edition, 1847), p. 586, also gives a different series of Scottish pig iron prices for part of this period, as follows:

	s.	d.		s.	d.		s.	d.
1835	82	6	1838	90	0	1841	67	6
1836	133	0	1839	90	0	1842	50	0
1837	92	0	1840	78	0	1843 (Jan.)	55	0

(The figure for 1843 is given as 45/- in the 1847 edition, but was subsequently corrected.)

B. Scottish and Cleveland Pig Iron and Common Bar Iron, 1846–1938

	Scottish Pig Iron	Cleveland No. 3 Pig Iron	Common Bars		Scottish Pig Iron	Cleveland No. 3 Pig Iron	Common Bars
	s. d.	s. d.	£ s. d.		s. d.	s. d.	£ s. d.
1846	67 3	...	9 10 0	1880	54 6	41 7	6 15 0
1847	65 4	...	9 15 0	1881	49 1	38 4	5 15 0
1848	40 4	...	7 0 0	1882	49 4	42 8	6 5 0
1849	45 6	...	6 5 0	1883	46 9	39 11	5 15 0
1850	44 2	...	5 17 6	1884	42 1	36 5	5 2 6
1851	39 9	...	5 10 0	1885	41 10	33 7	4 17 6
1852	45 1	...	6 5 0	1886	39 11	30 9	4 12 6
1853	62 3	...	9 5 0	1887	42 3	33 0	4 12 6
1854	79 8	...	10 0 0	1888	39 11	32 6	4 17 6
1855	70 9	...	8 10 0	1889	47 9	38 3	6 5 0
1856	72 6	...	8 17 6	1890	49 7	47 8	6 7 6
1857	69 2	...	8 5 0	1891	47 2	40 5	5 12 6
1858	54 4	...	7 0 0	1892	41 10	38 5	5 10 0
1859	51 9	...	6 15 0	1893	42 4	34 6	5 0 0
1860	53 6	...	6 10 0	1894	42 8	35 3	4 17 6
1861	49 3	...	6 0 0	1895	44 5	35 3	4 17 6
1862	53 0	...	6 5 0	1896	46 10	37 6	5 0 0
1863	55 9	...	7 0 0	1897	45 4	40 0	5 5 0
1864	57 3	...	8 5 0	1898	47 2	40 11	5 10 0
1865	54 9	48 1	7 15 0	1899	63 9	53 0	7 5 0
1866	60 6	49 8	7 5 0	1900	69 4	68 1	9 0 0
1867	53 6	44 11	6 15 0	1901	53 9	47 2	6 10 0
1868	52 9	42 11	6 7 6	1902	54 6	46 10	6 2 6
1869	53 3	43 10	6 15 0	1903	52 3	46 7	6 5 0
1870	54 4	46 11	7 7 6	1904	51 5	42 10	6 2 6
1871	58 11	47 2	7 12 6	1905	53 6	46 6	6 10 0
1872	101 10	65 4	11 0 0	1906	58 9	51 4	7 5 0
1873	117 3	98 5	12 10 0	1907	63 6	55 10	7 10 0
1874	87 6	70 1	10 5 0	1908	56 1	50 2	6 15 0
1875	65 9	53 4	8 7 6	1909	55 1	48 7	6 10 0
1876	58 6	46 7	7 5 0	1910	56 1	50 6	6 10 0
1877	54 4	42 0	6 15 0	1911	53 5	48 4	6 7 6
1878	48 5	38 10	5 12 6	1912	64 2	53 3	7 7 6
1879	47 0	34 11	5 15 0	1913	65 6	60 0	7 15 0

	Scottish Pig Iron	Cleveland No. 3 Pig Iron	Common Bars		Scottish Pig Iron	Cleveland No. 3 Pig Iron	Common Bars
	s. d.	s. d.	£ s. d.		s. d.	s. d.	£ s. d.
1914	57 1	51 2	7 0 0	1927	80 5	71 2	11 5 0
1915	71 2	60 8	10 10 0	1928	69 9	63 1	9 18 9
1916	90 0	82 10	13 15 0	1929	74 0	65 5	9 15 0
1917	95 7	97 3	13 15 0	1930	76 0	63 11	9 19 4½
1918	101 0	113 8	14 0 0	1931	71 0	54 5	10 1 10½
1919	143 1	145 0	19 6 8	1932	68 2	52 2	10 0 0
1920	214 11	206 0	28 6 8	1933	66 0	51 2	9 13 9
1921	168 6	141 11	19 2 6	1934	69 6	55 10	9 10 7½
1922	99 10	86 4	11 4 0	1935	70 6	58 10	9 12 6
1923	108 0	99 11	11 17 6	1936	78 6	61 9	10 3 9
1924	96 8	90 1	12 10 0	1937	104 6	72 9(a)	12 6 9
1925	83 4	73 0	11 17 6	1938	118 0	...	13 5 0
1926	87 2	80 7	11 10 0				

(*a*) Average of first three quarters only.

Prices 13.   Raw Wool Prices—Great Britain 1706–1938

NOTE TO PART A

Sources: Anon. (Sir Joseph Banks), *The Propriety of Allowing a Qualified Exportation of Wool* (London, 1782), pp. 83–4.

A. Lincoln Long, per tod of 28 lb., 1706–81

	s. d.		s. d.		s. d.		s. d.
1706	17 6	1728	18 0	1746	17 0	1764	20 0
1707	16 6	1729	18 0	1747	17 3	1765	21 0
		1730	19 0	1748	18 6	1766	21 6
1712	15 0	1731	19 0	1749	19 0	1767	20 0
1713	...	1732	19 0	1750	18 6	1768	16 0
1714	18 0	1733	18 6	1751	18 6	1769	15 3
1715	...	1734	16 0	1752	20 0	1770	14 0
1716	...	1735	14 0	1753	15 0	1771	15 0
1717	23 0	1736	14 0	1754	14 6	1772	15 6
1718	27 0	1737	14 0	1755	14 0	1773	15 6
1719	21 0	1738	13 6	1756	15 6	1774	17 6
1720	21 6	1739	13 0	1757	18 0	1775	18 6
1721	20 0	1740	14 0	1758	20 0	1776	18 6
1722	20 0	1741	14 0	1759	20 0	1777	18 3
1723	17 6	1742	15 0	1760	18 6	1778	17 0
1724	16 0	1743	19 6	1761	18 0	1779	18 6
1725	16 0	1744	21 0	1762	17 0	1780	19 6
1726	15 9	1745	16 6	1763	20 0	1781	20 0
1727	16 0						

NOTES TO PART B

[1] SOURCES: Southdown and Kent Long—*S.P.* 1828, VIII (*Committee of the House of Lords on the State of the Wool Trade*, evidence of T. Legg) for 1759–91; *ibid.* (evidence of W. Nottidge) for 1792–1827; and J. R. McCulloch, *Dictionary of Commerce* (1882 edition), p. 1,541 for 1828–45. Lincoln Half-Hogg—*S.P.* 1903, LXVIII (quoting tables printed by the *Bradford Daily Observer*).

[2] For the period 1759–91 a single price is quoted for each year. This series continues to 1827, but for the period 1792–1827 a series giving two quotations for each year for Southdown wool has been preferred.

[3] After 1845 prices of Southdown wool are quoted in McCulloch, *op. cit.* and in *The Economist* price current, but in a slightly different form.

[4] The Lincoln Half-Hogg series links directly on to that given in Part C.

B. Southdown, Kent Long and Lincoln Half-Hogg, pence per lb., 1759–1845

	South-down	Kent Long		South-down	Kent Long	Lincoln Half-Hogg
1759	$8\frac{1}{2}$	$7\frac{1}{2}$	1803	$18\frac{3}{4}$	$13\frac{1}{2}$	...
1760	$8\frac{1}{2}$	$7\frac{1}{2}$	1804	21	15	...
1761	$6\frac{1}{2}$	6	1805	$23\frac{1}{2}$	16	...
1762	$6\frac{1}{2}$	6	1806	$21\frac{1}{2}$	$14\frac{1}{2}$	...
1763	8	7	1807	$21\frac{1}{2}$	14	...
1764	8	8	1808	20	12	...
1765	$7\frac{1}{2}$	7	1809	$27\frac{1}{2}$	15	...
1766	8	8	1810	30	16	...
1767	9	$7\frac{1}{2}$	1811	19	13	...
1768	7	$6\frac{1}{2}$	1812	$18\frac{3}{4}$	$13\frac{1}{2}$	...
1769	7	$6\frac{1}{2}$	1813	21	15	...
1770	$7\frac{1}{2}$	7	1814	$25\frac{1}{4}$	21	19
1771	8	$7\frac{1}{2}$	1815	$23\frac{1}{2}$	22	22
1772	7	$6\frac{1}{2}$	1816	$16\frac{1}{2}$	15	16
1773	7	7	1817	$19\frac{1}{2}$	15	15
1774	8	7	1818	26	24	22
1775	9	8	1819	$20\frac{1}{2}$	15	$16\frac{1}{2}$
1776	$8\frac{1}{2}$	8	1820	$16\frac{1}{2}$	16	$16\frac{1}{2}$
1777	8	$7\frac{1}{2}$	1821	$14\frac{1}{4}$	13	14
1778	$6\frac{1}{2}$	$5\frac{1}{2}$	1822	14	11	12
1779	6	6	1823	$14\frac{3}{4}$	12	$11\frac{1}{4}$
1780	$7\frac{1}{2}$	$6\frac{1}{2}$	1824	$12\frac{1}{2}$	13	12
1781	$7\frac{1}{2}$	5	1825	16	16	$17\frac{1}{2}$
1782	8	$5\frac{1}{2}$	1826	10	11	13
1783	8	$6\frac{1}{2}$	1827	9	$10\frac{1}{2}$	$11\frac{1}{2}$
1784	$8\frac{1}{2}$	7	1828	8	12	11
1785	9	7	1829	6	9	10
1786	9	$7\frac{1}{2}$	1830	10	$10\frac{1}{2}$	9
1787	11	$9\frac{1}{2}$	1831	13	$10\frac{1}{2}$	12
1788	12	9	1832	12	$12\frac{1}{2}$	13
1789	12	$8\frac{1}{2}$	1833	17	$10\frac{1}{2}$	14
1790	$12\frac{1}{2}$	$9\frac{1}{2}$	1834	19	$19\frac{1}{2}$	$15\frac{1}{2}$
1791	$11\frac{1}{2}$	9	1835	18	18	$15\frac{1}{2}$
1792	15	$11\frac{1}{2}$	1836	20	$20\frac{1}{2}$	16
1793	$11\frac{1}{2}$	$9\frac{1}{2}$	1837	15	15	$13\frac{1}{2}$
1794	$12\frac{1}{2}$	$9\frac{1}{2}$	1838	16	17	14
1795	15	10	1839	16	17	17
1796	16	$9\frac{1}{2}$	1840	15	$14\frac{1}{2}$	14
1797	$15\frac{1}{4}$	$9\frac{1}{2}$	1841	12	11	$12\frac{1}{2}$
1798	$14\frac{1}{2}$	$9\frac{1}{2}$	1842	$11\frac{1}{2}$	10	11
1799	19	12	1843	$11\frac{1}{4}$	11	10
1800	17	$12\frac{1}{2}$	1844	14	14	11
1801	18	$12\frac{1}{2}$	1845	16	15	13
1802	$18\frac{1}{2}$	14				

NOTE TO PART C

SOURCES: Lincoln and Port Philip—A. Sauerbeck, 'Prices of Commodities and the Precious Metals', in the *J.S.S.* (1886), continued annually thereafter in the same source by Sauerbeck and subsequently by the editor of *The Statist*; Import Value—*Annual Statement of Trade*.

C. Lincoln Half-Hogg, Port Philip Merino and Average Import Values, pence per lb. 1846–1938

	Lincoln Half-Hogg	Port Philip Merino Average Fleece	Average Import Value		Lincoln Half-Hogg	Port Philip Merino Average Fleece	Average Import Value
1846	13	18	...	1893	$10\frac{1}{4}$	$12\frac{3}{4}$	8·7
1847	12	16	...	1894	$10\frac{5}{8}$	$11\frac{3}{4}$	8·5
1848	11	13	...	1895	12	12	8·1
1849	10	16	...	1896	$11\frac{1}{2}$	13	8·4
1850	11	17	...	1897	$9\frac{5}{8}$	$12\frac{1}{4}$	8·0
1851	$12\frac{1}{2}$	17	...	1898	$8\frac{3}{4}$	$13\frac{1}{4}$	8·1
1852	$13\frac{5}{8}$	$19\frac{1}{2}$	...	1899	$8\frac{1}{4}$	$17\frac{1}{4}$	8·6
1853	16	20	...	1900	$7\frac{7}{8}$	$15\frac{3}{4}$	9·5
1854	$15\frac{1}{2}$	18	...	1901	$6\frac{7}{8}$	13	7·5
1855	13	$19\frac{1}{2}$	15·8	1902	$6\frac{1}{4}$	15	7·5
1856	16	23	17·9	1903	$7\frac{1}{4}$	16	8·3
1857	$20\frac{1}{2}$	23	17·9	1904	$10\frac{5}{8}$	16	8·7
1858	$15\frac{5}{8}$	$22\frac{1}{2}$	17·0	1905	$12\frac{3}{8}$	$17\frac{1}{4}$	9·3
1859	$18\frac{5}{8}$	$23\frac{1}{2}$	17·7	1906	$13\frac{3}{8}$	18	10·2
1860	$20\frac{1}{8}$	24	17·8	1907	$12\frac{1}{4}$	18	10·3
1861	$19\frac{1}{2}$	22	15·8	1908	$8\frac{1}{2}$	$15\frac{3}{4}$	9·3
1862	$20\frac{1}{2}$	22	16·4	1909	9	$17\frac{3}{4}$	9·5
1863	$22\frac{3}{8}$	22	16·1	1910	$9\frac{7}{8}$	$18\frac{1}{4}$	10·2
1864	$27\frac{3}{8}$	23	18·0	1911	10	$17\frac{1}{4}$	10·0
1865	$25\frac{3}{4}$	$22\frac{1}{2}$	16·9	1912	$10\frac{1}{2}$	$17\frac{1}{2}$	9·9
1866	$23\frac{1}{2}$	$23\frac{1}{2}$	17·6	1913	$12\frac{3}{8}$	18	10·3
1867	$18\frac{7}{8}$	$21\frac{1}{2}$	16·6	1914	$12\frac{5}{8}$	$18\frac{1}{2}$	10·5
1868	$17\frac{1}{2}$	20	14·4	1915	$17\frac{3}{8}$	$21\frac{3}{8}$	10·9
1869	$18\frac{1}{8}$	17	13·6	1916	20	$32\frac{3}{4}$	14·6
1870	$16\frac{3}{4}$	17	14·4	1917	$20\frac{7}{8}$	$46\frac{1}{2}$	19·1
1871	$21\frac{3}{8}$	21	13·3	1918	$18\frac{3}{4}$	$47\frac{1}{4}$	21·1
1872	$25\frac{5}{8}$	26	14·5	1919	$22\frac{5}{8}$	67	22·3
1873	$24\frac{1}{2}$	25	14·7	1920	22	$79\frac{7}{8}$	24·1(a)
1874	$20\frac{3}{4}$	$23\frac{1}{2}$	14·7	1921	$8\frac{3}{5}$	$31\frac{7}{8}$	13·1
1875	$19\frac{3}{4}$	22	15·4	1922	$9\frac{3}{4}$	39	12·8
1876	$17\frac{3}{4}$	$20\frac{1}{4}$	14·5	1923	12	$43\frac{11}{16}$	15·2
1877	$16\frac{1}{4}$	$20\frac{1}{4}$	14·4	1924	$18\frac{7}{8}$	$53\frac{7}{16}$	22·1
1878	15	20	13·9	1925	$17\frac{1}{8}$	$41\frac{1}{16}$	23·7
1879	$12\frac{1}{2}$	$18\frac{3}{4}$	13·6	1926	15	$36\frac{1}{2}$	18·5
1880	$15\frac{5}{8}$	$21\frac{1}{2}$	13·7	1927	$15\frac{11}{12}$	$38\frac{1}{16}$	17·5
1881	$12\frac{3}{8}$	$19\frac{1}{2}$	13·9	1928	$17\frac{29}{32}$	37	18·6
1882	$11\frac{1}{4}$	$19\frac{3}{4}$	12·3	1929	$16\frac{1}{16}$	$35\frac{3}{8}$	17·6
1883	10	19	12·1	1930	$10\frac{3}{4}$	$18\frac{9}{32}$	13·0
1884	10	$18\frac{1}{4}$	12·1	1931	$8\frac{1}{2}$	$14\frac{7}{10}$	9·3
1885	$9\frac{7}{8}$	$16\frac{1}{2}$	10·0	1932	$5\frac{25}{32}$	15	8·5
1886	10	$15\frac{1}{2}$	9·1	1933	$5\frac{29}{32}$	$19\frac{9}{10}$	9·0
1887	$10\frac{1}{2}$	$15\frac{3}{4}$	10·1	1934	7	$21\frac{1}{4}$	11·3
1888	$10\frac{5}{8}$	$15\frac{3}{4}$	9·8	1935	$7\frac{11}{32}$	$20\frac{1}{10}$	9·9
1889	11	$17\frac{1}{2}$	9·8	1936	$10\frac{5}{12}$	$24\frac{7}{10}$	11·5
1890	11	16	10·3	1937	$16\frac{9}{10}$	$26\frac{9}{10}$	15·2
1891	$9\frac{3}{4}$	$14\frac{3}{4}$	9·3	1938	$11\frac{9}{10}$	$18\frac{3}{5}$	11·2
1892	$8\frac{3}{4}$	13	8·7				

(a) Prior to 1920 the value of wool imports includes noils.

Prices 14.   Average Price of Bread in London—1545–1925

NOTES

[1] SOURCES: 1545–1757—material collected by Lord Beveridge's Price and Wage History Research Group, not previously published. This was kindly made available to us by Lord Beveridge; 1758–1800—*S.P.* 1903, LXVIII (based on assize price of a quartern loaf of 4 lb. 5½ oz.); 1801–1903—*S.P.* 1904, LXXIX (based on various sources detailed in this volume); 1904–25—18th *Abstract of Labour Statistics*.

[2]   The table relates to wheaten or household bread.

(in pence per 4 lb.)

1545(a)	1·8	1592	2·6	1639	4·6	1686	5·2
1546	1·0	1593	2·9	1640	5·8	1687	4·5
1547	1·0	1594	4·7	1641	5·1	1688	4·4
1548	1·3	1595	...	1642	5·3	1689	5·3
1549	2·2	1596	6·5	1643	5·1	1690	5·0
1550	...	1597	5·6	1644	4·8	1691	6·4
1551	2·4	1598	3·7	1645	5·3	1692	7·8
1552	1·8	1599	4·3	1646	6·8	1693	8·5
1553	2·0	1600	4·0	1647	9·0	1694	5·6
1554	2·3	1601	3·3	1648	8·6	1695	7·1
1555	3·2	1602	3·4	1649	9·0	1696	7·1
1556	2·7	1603	3·6	1650	7·4	1697	8·0
1557	1·3	1604	3·9	1651	6·4	1698	7·3
1558	1·6	1605	3·4	1652	4·8	1699	5·7
1559	2·4	1606	3·9	1653	3·9	1700	4·8
1560	2·7	1607	5·4	1654	3·9	1701	4·3
1561	2·2	1608	5·1	1655	5·6	1702	4·4
1562	3·8	1609	4·0	1656	5·7	1703	5·7
1563	2·0	1610	4·2	1657	7·5	1704	4·7
1564	2·1	1611	5·3	1658	7·3	1705	4·1
1565	2·6	1612	4·8	1659	7·4	1706	4·1
1566	2·0	1613	5·3	1660	7·5	1707	4·7
1567	1·9	1614	4·5	1661	9·7	1708	7·0
1568	2·2	1615	4·8	1662	6·1	1709	8·7
1569	1·9	1616	...	1663	6·0	1710	6·2
1570	2·0	1617	5·3	1664	5·7	1711	5·9
1571	2·4	1618	4·0	1665	5·0	1712	5·4
1572	2·8	1619	3·5	1666	4·2	1713	6·3
1573	3·8	1620	3·9	1667	4·6	1714	4·9
1574	2·6	1621	5·3	1668	5·9	1715	5·5
1575	2·4	1622	5·8	1669	5·4	1716	5·4
1576	2·9	1623	5·4	1670	5·4	1717	4·7
1577	2·6	1624	6·0	1671	5·4	1718	4·1
1578	2·2	1625	5·3	1672	5·6	1719	4·6
1579	2·2	1626	4·2	1673	7·6	1720	4·8
1580	2·4	1627	3·6	1674	7·4	1721	4·5
1581	...	1628	4·5	1675	5·4	1722	4·7
1582	2·4	1629	6·0	1676	5·1	1723	4·8
1583	2·3	1630	7·0	1677	6·9	1724	5·4
1584	2·3	1631	5·5	1678	7·5	1725	6·0
1585	...	1632	6·1	1679	5·9	1726	5·1
1586	4·8	1633	...	1680	6·2	1727	6·5
1587	2·2	1634	5·8	1681	5·6	1728	6·2
1588	...	1635	6·1	1682	5·8	1729	4·6
1589	2·9	1636	5·4	1683	5·6	1730	4·5
1590	...	1637	6·2	1684	6·6	1731	4·0
1591	2·2	1638	5·0	1685	4·8	1732	4·1

See p. 498 for footnote

(in pence per 4 lb.)

1733	4·7	1782	7·0	1831	10·0	1880	6·98
1734	5·1	1783	7·0	1832	10·0	1881	7·04
1735	5·2	1784	6·9	1833	8·5	1882	7·38
1736	5·3	1785	6·1	1834	8·0	1883	7·00
1737	4·8	1786	5·5	1835	7·0	1884	6·78
1738	5·0	1787	5·7	1836	8·0	1885	6·23
1739	6·2	1788	6·4	1837	8·5	1886	6·25
1740	6·4	1789	7·0	1838	10·0	1887	5·63
1741	4·7	1790	7·0	1839	10·0	1888	5·69
1742	4·1	1791	6·3	1840	10·0	1889	6·02
1743	3·9	1792	5·9	1841	9·0	1890	6·00
1744	4·0	1793	6·8	1842	9·5	1891	6·21
1745	4·9	1794	7·0	1843	7·5	1892	6·23
1746	4·9	1795	9·6	1844	8·5	1893	5·75
1747	4·8	1796	9·7	1845	7·5	1894	5·48
1748	5·0	1797	7·6	1846	8·5	1895	5·08
1749	4·9	1798	7·7	1847	11·5	1896	5·09
1750	4·9	1799	9·6	1848	7·5	1897	5·50
1751	5·4	1800	15·3	1849	7·0	1898	6·02
					----(e)		
1752	5·6	1801	15·5	1850	6·75	1899	5·09
1753	5·0	1802	9·5	1851	6·75	1900	5·23
1754	4·5	1803	8·7	1852	6·75	1901	5·00
1755	5·0	1804	9·7	1853	8·33	1902	5·28
1756	7·2	1805	13·1	1854	10·50	1903	5·59
							------(e)
1757	6·1	1806	11·7	1855	10·75	1904	5·5
1758(b)	5·2	1807	10·8	1856	10·75	1905	5·5
1759(c)	4·7	1808	11·6	1857	9·00	1906	5·5
1760	4·7	1809	13·7	1858	7·50	1907	5·4
1761	4·1	1810	14·7	1859	7·50	1908	5·8
1762	4·9	1811	14·0	1860	8·75	1909	6·1
1763	5·1	1812	17·0	1861	9·00	1910	5·9
1764	5·8	1813	15·7	1862	8·50	1911	5·5
1765	6·7	1814	11·4	1863	7·50	1912	5·8
1766	6·0	1815(d)	10·4	1864	7·00	1913	5·8
			------(e)				
1767	7·3	1816	…(f)	1865	7·50	1914	5·8

1768	7·1	1817	…(f)	1866	8·75	1915	8·0
1769	5·7	1818	…(f)	1867	10·25	1916	9·0
1770	5·8	1819	…(f)	1868	9·25	1917	10·6

1771	6·5	1820	10·1(e)	1869	7·75	1918	8·9
1772	7·3	1821	9·5	1870	8·00	1919	9·1
1773	7·3	1822	9·5	1871	9·00	1920	11·6
1774	7·0	1823	10·3	1872	9·75	1921	12·4
1775	6·9	1824	10·5	1873	8·00	1922	9·2
1776	5·8	1825	10·5	1874	7·25	1923	8·5
					------(e)		
1777	6·6	1826	9·5	1875	6·83	1924	8·7
1778	6·5	1827	9·5	1876	7·15	1925	9·9
1779	5·5	1828	9·5	1877	8·13		
1780	5·7	1829	10·5	1878	7·50		
1781	7·0	1830	10·5	1879	7·13		

(a) Harvest years (September–August) **beginning** in the year shown.
(b) 10th October to 31st December.
(c) Calendar years.
(d) 1st January to 11th March henceforth.
(e) These minor breaks, resulting from changes in original source, are probably negligible.

(f) Prices paid by Charterhouse for the harvest years are given in Sir William Beveridge and others, *Prices and Wages in England*, vol. 1 (London, Longmans Green & Co., 1939), p. 207, and are as follows (translated into pence per 4 lb.):

1814	12·0	1816	16·8	1818	11·6	1820	10·2
1815	11·5	1817	13·3	1819	11·5		

REFERENCES

BOOKS

A. L. Bowley, *Prices and Wages in the United Kingdom, 1914–1920* (Oxford, 1921).
A. L. Bowley, *Wages and Income since 1860* (Cambridge, 1937).
Lord Beveridge, and others, *Prices and Wages in England*, vol. 1 (London, 1939).
N. S. B. Gras, *The Evolution of the English Corn Market* (Cambridge, Mass., 1915).
W. S. Jevons, *Investigations in Currency and Finance* (London, 1884).
J. E. T. Rogers, *A History of Agriculture and Prices in England* (7 vols., Oxford, 1866–1902).
P. Rousseaux, *Les Mouvements de Fond de l'Economie Anglaise, 1800–1913* (Louvain, 1938).
T. Tooke and W. Newmarch, *A History of Prices, 1793–1856* (6 vols., London, 1838–57).
G. F. Warren and F. A. Pearson, *Gold and Prices* (New York, 1935).

GOVERNMENT PUBLICATIONS

Report of the Select Committee on the High Price of Provisions (1764) (*H.C.J.* XXIX).
Report of the Select Committee on Prices and Forestalling (1766–8) (*H.C.J.* XXX).
Report of the Select Committee on the Assize of Bread (1767) (*H.C.J.* XXXI).
Report of the Select Committee on the Assize of Bread (1772) (*P.P.* III).
Report of the Select Committee on the Coal Trade (1800) (*P.P.* X).
An Account of the Official . . . and . . . Current Value of the Imports and Exports of Great Britain . . . 1801–3 (S.P. 1804, VIII).
Return of the Price of the Quartern Loaf, 1758–1814 (S.P. 1814–15, X).
Report of the Select Committee on the Coal Trade (S.P. 1830, VIII).
Report of the Select Committee on the Coal Trade (S.P. 1836, XI).
Report of the Select Committee on the Coal Trade (Port of London) Bill (S.P. 1837–8, XV).
Report of the Select Committee on the Dearness and Scarcity of Coal (S.P. 1873, X).
Returns of the Annual Average Price of Best Coals at the Ships' Side in London, 1820–1885 (S.P. 1886, LX).
Abstract of Labour Statistics (22 issues in *Sessional Papers* between 1893 and 1936).
Board of Trade Journal (from 1887 onwards).
Labour Gazette (from 1893 onwards (called *Board of Trade Labour Gazette* 1905–18, and the *Ministry of Labour Gazette* since 1923)).
Report on Wholesale and Retail Prices in the United Kingdom (S.P. 1903, LXVIII).

ARTICLES

Sir William Beveridge, 'British Exports and the Barometer', *E.J.* (1920).
Sir William Beveridge, 'Wheat Prices and Rainfall in Western Europe', *J.R.S.S.* (1922).
Sir William Beveridge, 'The Yield and Price of Corn in the Middle Ages', *E.H.* (1927).
Sir William Beveridge, 'A Statistical Crime of the Seventeenth Century', *Journal of Economic and Business History* (1929).

Lord Beveridge, 'Manorial Accounts of the Priory of Canterbury', *Bulletin of the Institute of Historical Research* (1951).

G. N. Driver, 'Wool Prices', *J.S.S.* (1938).

D. L. Farmer, 'Some Grain Price Movements in Thirteenth Century England', *E.H.R.* (1957).

Elizabeth W. Gilboy, 'The Cost of Living and Real Wages in Eighteenth Century England', *R.E.S.* (1936).

Alderman Nield, 'An Account of the Prices of Printed Cloth and Upland Cotton', *J.S.S.* (1861).

J. M. Price, 'Notes on Some London Price Currents 1667–1715', *E.H.R.* (1954).

A. Sauerbeck, 'Prices of Commodities and the Precious Metals', *J.S.S.* (1886 and annually thereafter).

Elizabeth B. Schumpeter, 'English Prices and Public Finance, 1660–1822', *R.E.S.* (1938).

N. J. Silberling, 'British Prices and Business Cycles, 1779–1850', *R.E.S.* (1923).

A. S. Silverman, 'Monthly Index Numbers of British Export and Import Prices, 1880–1913', *R.E.S.* (1930).

H. W. Singer, 'The Inflexibility of the Price System', *T.M.S.S.* (1938–9).

K. C. Smith and G. F. Horne, 'An Index Number of Securities, 1867–1914', *London and Cambridge Economic Service Special Memorandum*, no. 37.

R. J. Thomson, 'Wool Prices in Great Britain', *Journal of the Royal Agricultural Society of England* (1902).

G. H. Wood, 'Real Wages and the Standard of Comfort since 1850', *J.R.S.S.* (1909).

GENERAL BIBLIOGRAPHY

BOOKS

A. Anderson, *An Historical and Chronological Deduction of the Origin of Commerce* (4 vols., London, 2nd edition 1789).

T. S. Ashton, *An Economic History of England: The Eighteenth Century* (London, 1955).

T. S. Ashton, *Economic Fluctuations in England, 1700–1800* (Oxford, 1959).

W. Ashworth, *An Economic History of England, 1870–1939* (London, 1960).

T. H. Baker, *Records of the Seasons, Prices of Agricultural Produce, and Phenomena Observed in the British Isles* (London, 1883).

D. L. Burn (editor), *The Structure of British Industry* (2 vols., Cambridge, 1958).

G. Chalmers, *Estimate of the Comparative Strength of Great Britain* (London, 1794).

G. Chalmers, *Caledonia* (4 vols., London, 1807–26).

J. D. Chambers, *The Vale of Trent, 1670–1800* (Cambridge, 1957).

J. H. Clapham, *An Economic History of Modern Britain* (3 vols., Cambridge, 1926–38).

C. Fenn, *A Compendium of the English and Foreign Funds and the Principal Joint Stock Companies* (London, 1837).

H. D. Fong, *Triumph of Factory System in England* (Tientsin, 1930).

F. Grouzet, *L'Economie Britannique et Le Blocus Continental (1806–1813)* (2 vols., Paris, 1958).

Phyllis Deane and W. A. Cole, *British Economic Growth, 1688–1955* (Cambridge, 1962).

A. D. Gayer, W. W. Rostow and Anna J. Schwartz, *The Growth and Fluctuation of the British Economy, 1790–1850* (2 vols., Oxford, 1953).

R. Giffen, *Statistics, 1898–1900* (London, 1913).

H. Hamilton, *The Industrial Revolution in Scotland* (Oxford, 1932).

W. G. Hoffmann, *British Industry, 1700–1950* (English edition, Oxford, 1955).

J. R. T. Hughes, *Fluctuations in Trade, Industry and Finance* (Oxford, 1960).

K. S. Isles and N. Cuthbert, *An Economic Survey of Northern Ireland* (Belfast, 1957).

M. G. Kendall (editor), *The Sources and Nature of the Statistics of the United Kingdom* (2 vols. (to date), London, 1952–7).

Gregory King (edited by George E. Barnett), *Two Tracts by Gregory King* (Baltimore, 1936).

G. F. R. Kolb, *The Condition of Nations Social and Political* (English edition, London, 1880).

J. Lord, *Capital and Steam Power, 1750–1800* (London, 1923).

J. R. McCulloch, *Statistical Account of the British Empire* (London, 1854).

J. MacGregor, *Commercial Statistics* (5 vols., London, 1844–50).

D. Macpherson, *Annals of Commerce, Manufactures, Fisheries and Navigation* (4 vols., London, 1805).

P. Mantoux, *The Industrial Revolution in the Eighteenth Century* (London, 2nd edition 1928).

J. Marshall, *Digest of All Accounts . . .* (London, 1834).

R. C. O. Matthews, *A Study in Trade Cycle History* (Cambridge, 1954).

M. G. Mulhall, *Dictionary of Statistics* (London, 1898).

W. Page, *Commerce and Industry, Statistical Tables* (London, 1919).

Braithwaite Poole, *Statistics of British Commerce* (London, 1852).

G. R. Porter, *The Progress of the Nation* (London, 2nd edition 1847, and F. W. Hirst's edition, 1912).

L. S. Pressnell (editor), *Studies in the Industrial Revolution* (London, 1960).
A. Rees, *The Cyclopaedia* (London, 1819).
S. Salt, *Statistics and Calculations* (London, 1845).
Elizabeth B. Schumpeter, *English Overseas Trade Statistics, 1697–1808* (Oxford, 1960).
Sir John Sinclair, *General Report of the Agricultural State and Political Circumstances of Scotland*.
Sir John Sinclair (editor), *The Statistical Account of Scotland* (21 vols., Edinburgh, 1791–9).
A. Ure, *A Dictionary of Arts, Manufactures and Mines* (London, 1839).
A. J. Youngson, *The British Economy, 1920–1957* (London, 1960).

GOVERNMENT PUBLICATIONS

Tables of Revenue, Population, Commerce, etc. (known as Porter's Tables) (in *Sessional Papers* in 1833 and annually from 1835–54).
Miscellaneous Statistics (in sessional papers annually from 1855–82).
Statistical Abstract of the United Kingdom (in *Sessional Papers* annually from 1854 to 1939–40).
Annual Abstract of Statistics (issued annually as a non-parliamentary paper since 1946).
Memorandum on the Comparative Statistics of Population, Industry, and Commerce in the United Kingdom and some Leading Foreign Countries (S.P. 1902, XCVIII).
Memorandum on British and Foreign Trade and Industry (S.P. 1903, LXVII, S.P. 1905, LXXXIV, and S.P. 1909, CII).
Statistical Digest of the War (1951).
Irish *Statistical Abstract* (Irish Official Publication (Dublin, annually from 1931)).
Report of the Royal Commission on Depression of Trade and Industry (S.P. 1886, XXI, S.P. 1886, XXII, and S.P. 1886, XXIII).
Committee on Industry and Trade, *Survey of Overseas Markets* (non-parliamentary paper, 1925).
Report of the Select Committee on Manufacture (S.P. 1833, VI).
Board of Trade Working Party Reports, issued 1946–8, on Pottery, Cotton, Boots and Shoes, Hosiery, Furniture, Jewellery and Silverware, Linoleum, Heavy Clothing, Wool, Lace, Light Clothing, Cutlery, Rubber-proofed Clothing, Hand-blown Domestic Glassware, Carpets, China Clay, and Jute.

ARTICLES

T. S. Ashton, 'Some Statistics of the Industrial Revolution', *T.M.S.S.* (1947–8) (also *M.S.E.S.S.* (1948)).
T. S. Ashton, 'Economic Fluctuation, 1790–1850', *E.H.R.* (1955).
Sir William Beveridge, 'The Trade Cycle in Great Britain before 1850', *O.E.P.* (1940).
W. A. Cole, 'The Measurement of Industrial Growth', *E.H.R.* (1958).
T. W. Grimshaw, 'A Statistical Survey of Ireland', *Journal of the Statistical Society of Ireland* (1888).
J. G. Kyd, 'The Proposed Third Statistical Account of Scotland', *J.R.S.S.* (1947).
R. C. O. Matthews, 'The Trade Cycle in Britain, 1790–1850', *O.E.P.* (1954).

INDEX